# Fundamentals of Abnormal Psychology

**Richard M. Suinn** *is professor and head of the department of psychology at Colorado State University. He received his Ph.D. in clinical psychology from Stanford University in 1959. He is the author of many books and articles including* Psychology in Sports: Methods and Applications. *In addition to his teaching, research, and writing activities, Dr. Suinn has served as team psychologist for several U.S. Olympic ski and track-and-field squads.*

# Fundamentals of Abnormal Psychology

**Richard M. Suinn**
Professor and Head
Department of Psychology
Colorado State University

**Nelson-Hall**
**Chicago**

Text and photograph credits appear on page 616.

LIBRARY OF CONGRESS CATALOGING IN PUBLICATION DATA

Suinn, Richard M.
Fundamentals of abnormal psychology.

Bibliography: p.
Includes index.
1. Psychology, Pathological. I. Title.
RC454.S868 1984 616.89 84-1997
ISBN 0-8304-1071-6



Manufactured in the United States of America.

10 9 8 7 6 5 4 3 2 1

The paper in this book is pH neutral (acid-free).

*To my partner in life over five and twenty.*

# CONTENTS

# PREFACE

As I write the preface for this book, I find myself wondering why all the effort? Writing my first book on abnormal psychology was a response to a book editor who pursued me for five years. Eventually I concluded that I did have something different to offer students: a book that recognized cultural, biological, familial, physiological factors along with the traditional psychological factors in explaining abnormality. I also wanted to offer a balanced, empirical approach instead of one that represented only a single point of view or theory that didn't represent the state of the art. The second edition of this book wasn't too massive a task since there were only minor modifications. However, the current book required extensive changes, so much so that it is rightfully a new book, rather than a revision. The American Psychiatric Association adopted DSM–III, (*Diagnostic and Statistical Manual,* 3rd Edition), a changed classification system, that added new terminology and new disorders, while dropping some prior disorders. Those readers who enjoyed the first or second editions of my prior text will still see some of these roots in the current text. Cultural, biological, and psychological factors are still presented, although made more concise in order to get more quickly to the "meat" of the abnormal disorders themselves. There is still reliance on a comprehensive approach, but different theories are discussed in greater detail as well. In addition to a whole lot of new content and updated research, this new book also offers:

- A presentation of DSM–III disorders—the modern classification system—including some intriguing new disorders—such as Münchausen's syndrome, the impulse disorders, or *folie à deux*.
- Case histories from my files or those of others to give a firsthand account of the disorders; illustrative quotations placed within the narrative to amplify definitions.
- Focus sections to expand the reader's awareness of related, interesting topics, such as the supernatural, pornography and sexual crimes, the experiences of hostages and astronauts, hypnosis, the personality of Hitler and other war criminals, and the role of imagery in cancer treatment—as they help us to further understand abnormal behaviors.
- Pedagogical aids to facilitate learning—questions to guide readings, table outlines at the start of each chapter to establish familiarity with the various disorders and their characteristics, chapter summaries to provide a total picture, evaluational summaries where appropriate, and a carefully developed student workbook and instructor's manual.
- Chapters that are consistently organized into a format that permits ready understanding—generally starting with a *case history*, followed by a table of the *types* of disorders, descriptions of *symptoms* and *definitions, examples* of the disorders as one would encounter them, statements of the *dynamics* or *causes*, discussion of *treatments* that appear supported by research evidence, and finally, an *evaluation* and chapter *summary.*
- A balanced approach, with equal attention paid to the various theories in the forefront, along with up-to-date research evidence to provide the empirical foundations.
- A comprehensive coverage, rather than a minimal coverage, of information to give a total picture of what is known today about each pathology.
- A student's workbook uniquely designed by an educational specialist, relying upon valuable techniques to promote learning; and an instructor's manual that, for once, is truly an aid to the classroom instructor.

Many of the new features in this book appear in response to a national survey which asked what faculty and students wanted in a text. Also considered were answers to questions like the following: What topics should be included or expanded on in a text? What style of writing best reaches students? What do you see as your needs in a book? Even the decision to use DSM–III was based on a consideration of what best fits current needs. DSM–III, despite controversy, is still *the* accepted classification system in the United States. It has been field tested and has the advantage of a descriptive-behavioral approach. Terms that come from theory rather than data are avoided. Any responsible book must adopt DSM–III as its foundation.

So here is my new text on abnormal psychology. To those of you who have written and rewritten term papers, monographs, articles, or books, I need not say much more about the process itself. To those of you who have not been exposed to such excruciating effort, I can only say that the end product is clearly more rewarding than the exercise. Not unlike a marathon, the activity was at times stimulating, tiring, a test of determination, a philosophical encounter, agonizing, and at other times fun. There are now two sources for evaluating its success: my own subjective reaction, and yours. As always, this book is written for my students, who continue to be a source of inspiration, but also to faculty, whose insights and advice helped make this book possible.

R.M.S.
Ft. Collins, Colorado, 1984

# ACKNOWLEDGMENTS

Taking an author's writing and making it come alive in the form of a book takes the efforts of many talented professionals in the publishing business. Steve and V. Peter Ferrara, as publishers, committed their full support to the Psychology series. Ron Warncke, director of College Publishing, delivered all he promised and added encouragement besides. To Dick Epler goes credit for overseeing the diverse demands of the project. Claudia von Hendricks, designer, is the special person who combined creative talent with organizational vision and the discipline of a marathoner. Bonnie Miller tackled the difficult task of photo-finding; Steve Worchel of manuscript evaluation; and Jim Wicke of marketing the news that the book was available.

A final product also means the efforts of a great many others, including Sandi Schroeder, Kristen Westman, Pamela Teisler, and Dorothy Anderson. What an amazing sight it was to see each completing responsibilities for specific domains.

And, of course, there is Joanne Moran, my own staff member who can match the birth of the new book to the birth of her daughter Lisa. Joanne's efforts in bringing up both across the years deserve special recognition.

The exceptional work that led to the instructor's manual and the student workbook is that of Dr. Geraldine Markel of the University of Michigan. The extremely useful test item file and film resource file is due to Susan Raynis of Colorado State University.

The success of the transformation from written manuscript to published book thus owes much to all of the above, who have my gratitude.

# PART 1

## Perspectives on Abnormal Psychology



*The chapters that follow provide a general foundation for understanding psychopathology. In Chapter 1, we shall cover the various facts often heard in conversations about abnormal behaviors as people seek explanations. Some of these are accurate, and some are misconceptions. This chapter will help you to distinguish among these. It also traces the various definitions of abnormality, including those which rely on statistics, those which come from group consensus, and those from the courtroom, as well as our own working definition of both abnormal and normal behaviors. Since the scientific method is used in studying pathology, we will introduce this topic as well as the modern classification system of mental disorders which forms the basis for Part 2 of this text. In Chapter 2, the historical background is described. The progress of a science is inevitably rooted in its past, and it is surprising how many contemporary trends can be traced to early thinkers. Since science is really made up of people, this chapter will focus on such persons, their ideas, contributions, and personalities.*

*Chapters 3 to 5 will cover current views on possible origins of disorders. However, as you will see, these chapters avoid conclusive or dogmatic statements about the causation of mental disorders. Instead, each chapter reviews suspected origins, and as such really presents the "psychological hypotheses, the biological hypotheses, and the social hypotheses" of mental disorders. Thus, these chapters will take you on the scientific search for origins, a search which is still underway and which challenges the best scientific minds and methods. Among the psychological hypotheses are those major theories coming from psychoanalytic, behavioristic, and humanistic viewpoints. Among the biological hypotheses are those which seek answers from heredity, from toxic factors, and from imbalances within our own glands or nervous systems. Finally, among the social hypotheses are included studies of our environment as represented by our society, our daily surroundings, and our family environment.*

# CHAPTER 1

## Introduction to the Abnormal Personality

- **Are mental disorders inherited?**
- **Is there any truth to the following statement, How ill you are depends on how you define mental disorder; abnormality is really all a matter of definition?**
- **If you wish to plead insanity in a court trial, what should you or your attorney be prepared to show?**
- **What are the basic types of mental disorders that are recognized today?**
- **How can you tell if someone is normal?**
- **Is abnormality always characterized by irrationality?**
- **What various scientific approaches are used to study abnormality?**
- **What does the following statement mean, The correlational approach only identifies association, not causality?**
- **Is it possible to recover from a mental disturbance by simply moving to another geographic location or culture? By taking a pill? By hiring a smart lawyer?**

Abnormal behavior has always been with us, yet the ability to identify and sensitively understand it is still a challenge. Throughout much of history, mental disorders have been viewed with suspicion, superstition, and horror. Fortunately, much of the superstitious fear has been eased by modern science; yet we still have trouble agreeing on common explanations and definitions for mental disorders.

## COMMON QUESTIONS AND MISCONCEPTIONS

In order to begin our study of abnormal behavior with as clear an understanding as possible, we will open this chapter with a review of some common misconceptions and questions. In addition, some basic definitions are included in Focus 1–1.

1. *Are people who have mental disorders strange, violent, or irrational?*

Only people with severe disturbances show violent or irrational behaviors—and they also have frequent periods of highly normal behavior. Two much more likely measures of abnormal behavior are *inappropriateness* and *intensity.*

Inappropriate behavior is unsuited to the circumstances. For instance, a person may have a *phobia*—an excessive, irrational fear of something such as dogs. He or she may be rational in every other sense and may even be able to talk logically about the phobia. Yet that person may not be able to shake the fear—even where it is highly inappropriate, such as when seeing a wiggly puppy.

A second quality that marks abnormal behavior may be its intensity. Many of us sometimes act in ways that others might judge abnormal. Freud himself wrote about the abnormal behavior shown by normal people, in a treatise called *The Psychopathology of Everyday Life* (1938). Thus, a bank teller may compulsively count and recount money several times, as part of the daily process of handling large sums of money. Similarly, children (and even some adults at times) may experience nighttime fears that seem irrational in broad daylight. The intensity of such behaviors—how much recounting becomes necessary, or the degree to which fears interfere with daily behavior patterns—marks the difference between abnormal and normal behaviors.

2. *Will a person with a minor form of mental disorder invariably become worse until a severe disorder is present?*

Among the common types of mental disorders are those known as *neuroses* and those called *psychoses.* The neuroses are relatively minor disorders, which are difficult for the person to handle but not severe enough to involve major life disruptions. An example would be the obsessive-compulsive disorder, in which persons feel compelled, for example, to wash their hands over and over again. Such persons can still function socially, on jobs, and on intellectual tasks despite their disturbance. The psychoses, in contrast, involve very severe emotional disruptions, including personality breakdown. The breakdown may appear in serious irrationality, or highly inappropriate or bizarre behaviors, or even in strange experiences, such as hallucinations.

To date, there is no evidence that a person suffering from a mild disorder will become progressively worse until a psychosis develops. Of course, there are exceptions that involve certain physical types of deterioration. For example, continued alcohol abuse can lead to greater impairment until actual organic damage occurs; and a certain type of psychoses eventually occurs if syphilis is untreated.

3. *Is mental disorder incurable? Even if the symptoms diminish, will the person ever be the same again?*

The incidence of recovery varies with the nature of the disorder, but recovery from both neuroses and the major nonorganic psychoses is common. Of course, only limited recovery or rehabilitation is possible where there are metabolic changes, genetic damage, or cerebral injuries. Even in most of these instances, drugs and physical therapy can provide temporary relief while the person participates in other treatment.

4. *Is it true that people with mental disorders can help themselves become normal if they just exercise their willpower? (And conversely, is it true that mentally disturbed persons are actually helpless to recover unless somebody does something for them?)*

These two fallacies represent opposite ends of the

# FOCUS 1–1

## Abnormality: Common Terms and Definitions

**Abnormal Behaviors** As defined in this book, the term refers to specific behaviors that characterize mental disorders. These include discomfort, lack of predictability, loss of control, and rigidity. Also included may be loss of esteem, bizarre behaviors, distorted perceptions, and inappropriate or maladaptive behaviors.

**Mental Disorder** A general term in the DSM-III *(Diagnostic and Statistical Manual,* 3rd Edition) system that refers to all of the categories of abnormal behavior. It also refers more generally to the existence of abnormality.

**Mental Illness** An earlier term once used interchangeably with mental disorder, psychopathology, and abnormality. Since the term *illness* connotes physical illness or disease, many have argued for limiting this term to organic diseases. Pathology associated with psychological factors would instead be referred to as *disorders*—for example, *mental disorders.*

**Psychopathology** A term which refers to the study of mental disorders or abnormal behaviors. However, it is sometimes used synonymously with the term *mental disorder.*

same misconception about what is needed for recovery. The first assumes that a person will recover through personal efforts; the second sees the client as a passive recipient of treatment.

Neither viewpoint is correct. As for the first question, even though people seeking treatment may want to be rid of energy-consuming fears or tensions, these feelings are often triggered by forces they can neither identify nor control. Thus, motivation alone is not a cure. As for the second question, there is no such thing as a passive cure—a quick, simple solution whereby the burden will magically vanish. All therapies, even drug and shock therapies, require some participation on the part of the person undergoing treatment.

5. *If a person needs professional help, should it be someone with special training?*

A variety of persons have been trained specifically to be therapists for mentally disturbed people. Among these are psychiatrists, psychoanalysts, clinical psychologists, social workers, and psychiatric nurses. The list in Focus 1–2 provides an overview of these specialists, their training, and the kind of help they can provide.

6. *Are all mental disorders inherited? Are persons born crazy, and do they transmit the disorder to their offspring?*

Only a few mental disorders have been definitely proven to be genetically transmitted. *Amaurotic familial idiocy* (also known as Tay-Sachs disease) and *phenylketonuria* (PKU) are both types of mental retardation that are transmitted genetically. The first is a central nervous system disease that results from a recessive gene; the second, a type of retardation caused by lack of an enzyme. *Huntington's chorea* is also genetically linked; it is a form of neurological deterioration first traced by an American country doctor, after whom it is named. There is a strong movement, based on research, to view schizophrenia and bipolar disorder (once known as manic-depressive psychosis) as inherited; however, the evidence is still controversial. To date, none of the less severe disorders have been considered inherited.

7. *Are all mentally disturbed persons mentally retarded?*

Mental disturbance does not mean a loss of intellectual capacities, with the exception of disorders that involve neurological deterioration. However, mental disorders tend to drain energies and resources, so that in an extreme case a person may be so out of touch with reality as to appear intellectually incompetent. In this sense, a person's anxieties or conflicts may mask or even block the ability to function efficiently. This is why depressed persons sometimes score low on intelligence tests—an effect not of subnormal capacity, but only of their inability to muster enough interest to perform well. Scores often improve once the depression lifts and the individual regains interest in tasks.

8. *Does abnormality go hand in hand with creativity or genius?*

There is little reason to believe that either the creative or the intelligent person is more susceptible to mental disorder. In fact, evidence gathered systematically over 40 years demonstrates that intellectually gifted people tend to have relatively high resistance to mental disorder (Terman & Oden, 1959). Other intensive studies (Institute for Personality Assessment and Research at Berkeley, 1961; Barron, 1963) suggest that creative people may have greater resources for maintaining psychological health than do most people.

9. *Should abnormal persons be treated differently? Should they be pampered or humored?*

Some severely disturbed persons are likely to be hypersensitive and may misinterpret or misperceive the actions and motives of others. Nevertheless, even a person with a severe disturbance will appreciate being treated normally, without fear, and without kid gloves. Like anyone else, such persons will be more likely to feel anxious if others appear tense in their presence or to withdraw if others seem to withdraw from them.

These questions are only a sampling of the many suppositions and myths that surround abnormality. The short answers here, of course, only begin to scratch the surface. Indeed, this entire book can only start to tell the story of what we know and of what we don't know. This opening chapter will explore three questions basic to the study of abnormal behavior:

**1.** What constitutes *abnormality* and *normality?*
**2.** How can abnormal behaviors be classified in a way that is meaningful for diagnosis and treatment?
**3.** How do scientists study abnormality?

## FOCUS 1–2:
### Helping Professionals

**Clinical Psychologists** Professionals with a Ph.D. in psychology and an internship in a psychiatric facility. They are trained in psychotherapeutic techniques rather than drug medications.

**Psychiatric nurses** Nurses with R.N. status, and sometimes also an M.A. or Ph.D. Psychiatric nurses have had special training to deal with psychiatric patients. They aid the psychiatrist in medical treatment or supervision.

**Psychiatrists** Physicians who specialize in emotional disturbances, just as some physicians specialize in surgery or pediatrics. They have undergone special residency training in a psychiatric facility and are licensed to prescribe drug treatment and also to offer psychotherapy.

**Psychoanalysts** Professionals, normally with an M.D. (sometimes a Ph.D.), with specialized training in Freudian-related theories and techniques. All psychoanalysts must themselves be analyzed during training. Psychoanalysts are unlike psychiatrists in that analysts tend to prefer psychological treatment methods (such as dream analysis and free association) to drug or other somatic treatment.

**Social workers** Professionals with a master's degree in social work, sometimes a B.A. or Ph.D., with special training in social or mental health settings. The activities of social workers are diverse, ranging from psychotherapy, to work with the courts on cases of child abuse, to providing financial arrangements for medical bills.

*Psychological tests such as the block design test are a tool of the* ***clinical psychologist****. Skills employed include psychotherapy.*

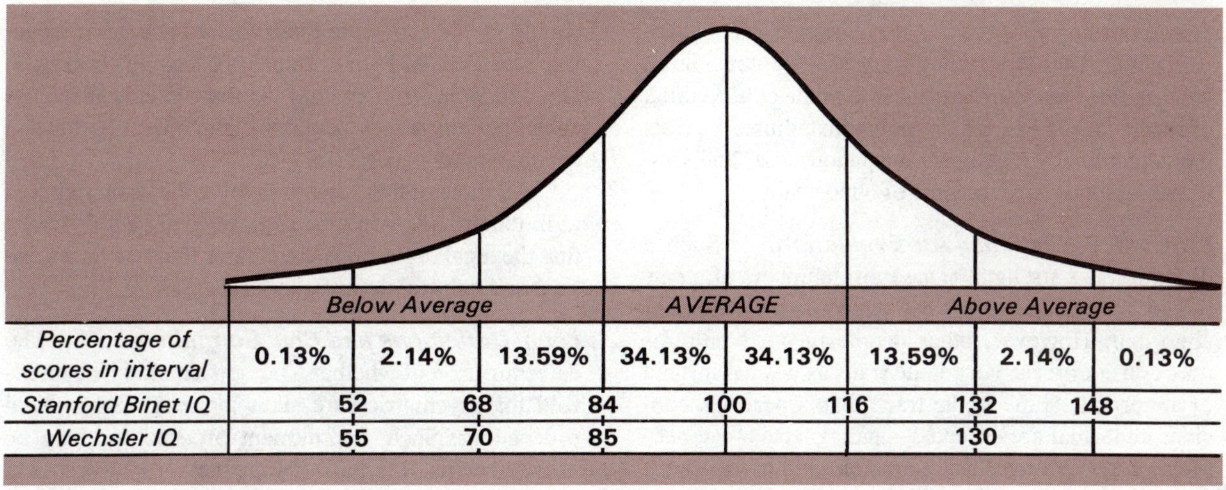


**FIGURE 1-1**

## WHAT IS ABNORMAL BEHAVIOR?

The problem of defining abnormal behavior has not been a simple one. Attempts to provide suitable definitions have included a *statistical* definition, a *cultural* definition, and a *legal* definition.

### Statistical Definitions of Abnormality

The *statistical* definition depends on a mathematical model shown by the normal distribution curve. This curve represents the frequency with which a certain characteristic appears among a large group of people. The curve is typically said to be bell shaped, with a bulge at the middle and tapering off at the extremes. Most people, for example, are between five and six feet in height with fewer and fewer people either shorter or taller than this average height. There are people who do fall at these extremes and who may therefore be considered as statistically deviant or abnormal. By the statistical definition, therefore, any person who is average is normal, and anyone who deviates from the average is abnormal. It is possible to speak of those who are abnormally tall, abnormally small, as well as those with abnormal blood pressure readings or body temperatures.

***Statistical Definitions: An Evaluation.*** While statistical data provide one measure for defining normality, they may not be reliable in every case. The main difficulty is illustrated when we use statistics to measure intelligence. Normal curves can be calculated for intelligence scores (see Figure 1–1). Most people have average intellectual ability, as reflected in IQ test scores of about 100. Relatively fewer people achieve scores far below 100. It makes some sense to consider the low scorers abnormal, for any mental deficiencies they show may interfere with their ability to lead independent lives. However, by the statistical model, the intellectually gifted would also be considered abnormal, since they also deviate from the average. Yet, members of this group are clearly able to lead normal lives.

In addition, the statistical definition suffers from the fact that high incidence of a trait is not necessarily an index of health. Cancer and heart disease afflict great numbers in our society; many smoke cigarettes or gamble their last earnings on poor bets. Yet, none of these conditions would be accepted as normal or healthy simply by virtue of frequency.

### Cultural Definitions of Abnormality

A second definition is the cultural definition of abnormality. In a sense, this definition is also statistical, since it depends partly on numbers of people. But, where the statistical definition involves the number of people who *possess* the trait, the cultural definition involves the trait *accepted* by the greatest number of people. According to the cultural definition, a trait that appears with high frequency may still be considered abnormal if the majority of people in the culture think of it that way. Thus, in our American culture, we treat hallucinations, exaggerated suspiciousness, and irrational violence as symptoms of abnormality.

***Cultural Definitions: An Evaluation.*** Such a definition has strength, since most members of a particular society agree on what behaviors they consider abnormal. However, other people in other cultures may consider these very same traits as normal instead of abnormal. Some of the traits that Americans consider abnormal are accepted—and expected—by people of other cultures. Hallucinations and trance states were normal among the Plains Indians who looked forward to such experiences as part of the transition to adulthood. The natives of Dobu, Africa, were—by our standards—filled with suspicion, as they questioned the motives of strangers. And the tribe of Malays, once called Amuco, were so noted for the frenzied attacks by their warriors that they are remembered in the English language by the term, *to run amok.* In their perception, however, violent rampages were normal.

Even in our own society, rapid social change has meant that some behaviors considered abnormal a few decades ago are now far more acceptable. This is evident in attitudes toward drugs, in the new morality of sexual behaviors, and in many other areas of life. The women's liberation movement, for instance, challenges the stereotypes of what were once considered to be adjusted behaviors for men and women (Broverman et al., 1970). In all, it is questionable whether members within a society can properly provide any universal definition of abnormality.

### Legal Definitions of Abnormality

A third way to define abnormality is through the law. Legal definitions of insanity have evolved out of necessity in response to legal proceedings that involve immediate, critical decisions (Cohen & Mariano, 1983). Thus, these definitions center on somewhat different issues than statistical or cultural definitions. The first issue is that of *civil commitment:* where we must decide if a person should be committed to psychiatric care in an institution. The second is the issue of *criminal responsibility:* where we must decide if a criminal should not be subject to punishment because of insanity. A related issue in criminal proceedings is *competency to stand trial:* where we must decide if the accused person is too mentally disturbed to be able to participate in a court trial.

All three of these issues involve the basic rights of individuals so it would be reassuring to be able to say that the legal definitions are clearer than are the statistical and cultural definitions.

***Legal Definitions and Civil Commitment.*** The determination of whether a person should be hospitalized for psychiatric care takes place through a legal proceeding. Such commitment proceedings may be initiated either voluntarily by the person who wishes to be hospitalized, or by someone else—most often a family member. Once a petition is presented to the court, a hearing is called before a board that usually includes a physician (who in some states need not be a psychiatrist). Testimony is given in a relatively informal atmosphere, and the judge then concludes whether the person is, without reasonable doubt, dangerous to self or others.

The decision about civil commitment is not a decision about criminality, only a determination of whether a person may be dangerous if not institutionalized. In cases where one person petitions to have another person committed, some serious questions may arise. Individuals who are involuntarily committed to a hospital lose many freedoms, against their wishes. What rights do they retain? Some important dimensions of this issue are highlighted in Focus 1–3.

***Legal Definitions and Criminal Responsibility.*** Another area in which it is necessary to have a legal determination of insanity would be in cases where a crime is a central issue. A hypothetical case can illustrate some of the dynamics involved: A retarded boy (the term *retarded* is defined as having an IQ below 70) is brought to trial for shooting a neighbor with his father's gun. The defense attorney could successfully argue that the child was only imitating other children's cops-and-robbers play; that because of his condition, he was unable to differentiate between a real gun and a toy, and thus the killing had no meaning. In all likelihood, such a case would be judged in favor of the defendant because of the absence of criminal intent.

# FOCUS 1–3:
## Individual Rights in an Institution

At one point in American history, patients in psychiatric hospitals had no rights at all. Individuals had little to say about whether they should be hospitalized or about the treatment they received. With a number of far-reaching court decisions and legal revisions in various states, however, some progress has been made toward protecting the rights of these individuals (Ziegenfuss, 1983). Here is a brief highlighting of some of these changes:

- *Civil Commitment.* In some states, civil commitment hearings require that the individual be represented by an attorney and apprised of his or her rights.
- *Informed Consent for Treatment.* Once individuals have been committed to an institution, they still have the right to refuse treatment (Lichtenstein, 1980). Given that certain therapies—for instance, psychosurgery, described in Chapter 21—are irreversible, this becomes a very important right to maintain. Not only do patients have the right to refuse treatment, they also have the right to a clear explanation of what the treatment entails, before they undergo it. The benefits and risks, as well as the exact nature of the treatment, must be explained in language the patient can understand.
- *Standards of Treatment.* Patients also have the right to receive certain standards of treatment, according to the landmark decision of *Wyatt* v. *Stickney* (1972). This case began as a class-action suit where patients protested the firing of employees of a mental institution because of budget cutbacks. The American Psychological Association entered the case as a "friend of the court" to offer expert comment; the resulting ruling stated that involuntarily committed mental patients had the constitutional right to proper treatment, including adequate numbers of staff with qualifications to provide care.
- *Limitations for Criminal Commitment.* In 1972, the U.S. Supreme Court ruled that individuals cannot be committed to a hospital indefinitely, even though they have committed a crime and have been judged incompetent to stand trial. The case on which this judgment was based involved a man named Jackson, who was severely retarded, deaf, mute, and unable to read or write. Jackson was accused of two robberies for a total of $10. When the Indiana court judged him incompetent to stand trial and he was sent to a psychiatric hospital, the U.S. Supreme Court was asked to review the case on the grounds that commitment was equivalent to a life sentence for the crime. The U.S. Supreme Court agreed, ruling that it is not legal to hospitalize a person indefinitely, and that the defendant should be set free if no reasonable time limit could be set.

An actual case took place more than a century ago in Britain, yet it has had a profound impact on American legal interpretations through most of this century. In this case, a man named Daniel M'Naughten shot and killed Sir Robert Peel's secretary. M'Naughten was actually trying to assassinate Peel, the Prime Minister of Great Britain and founder of the English police force that carries his nickname (''bobbies''). The jury found him not guilty by reason of insanity. The famous M'Naughten rule (1843) provided a legal definition of an insane person as one who suffers ''such a defect of reason . . . as not to know the nature and quality of the act he was doing or if he did know it that he did not know he was doing what was wrong.'' M'Naughten, incidentally, was sent to a mental institution where he eventually died after 22 years of incarceration.

A second court case that influenced legal definitions of mental disorder occurred in Ohio in 1834 and was subsequently upheld in 1887 (*Parsons* v. *State*). This case defined the irresistible impulse, where a defendant is deemed to be innocent if that person was driven to commit a crime by an impulse that could not be resisted. The irresistible impulse and knowledge of the definitions of right and wrong were both applied in the trial of John W. Hinckley, Jr., the attempted assassin of President Ronald Reagan. This case and its outcome are discussed in Focus 1–4 for your reaction.

Still a third significant court case was *Durham* v. *United States* (1954) in which the judge concluded that it was best to leave definitions of mental disorder to psychiatric experts. He disregarded any arguments as to the need to know right from wrong (the M'Naughten definition) or to be free from irresistible impulse (the Ohio ruling), concluding instead that the ''accused is not criminally responsible if his unlawful act was the product of mental disease or mental defect.''

***Legal Definitions and the Competency to Stand Trial.*** A third issue in legal definitions of insanity is the question of whether a defendant is capable of standing trial. Even if the accused person were legally sane at the time of the crime, he or she might be too mentally disturbed to participate in a court trial. If this can be proven, the defendant is typically hospitalized for treatment until competency is restored.

A question that should be addressed here is that of *who* determines incompetency and on what grounds. The determination is usually made by the judge, based on expert testimony of a psychiatrist. But according to T. S. Szasz (1965), this expert testimony is not always made as carefully as it should be. He cites the case of a Mr. Perroni, who spent over seven years hospitalized after being judged incompetent to stand trial for shooting at some men. The judgment had been based on the report of a psychiatrist, who had assessed Perroni's incompetence on the grounds that the top button of his shirt was open (an indication of slovenliness) and because Perroni had refused to answer some of the psychiatrist's questions.

***Legal Definitions: An Evaluation.*** In all the areas discussed earlier, the legal system has been called in to provide a definition of insanity. Yet, the judgments provided by the courts have not always been satisfactory. Psychiatrists themselves have rejected the M'Naughten rule and irresistible impulse definitions —the former because it focused entirely on the defendant's ability to know right from wrong, the latter because it failed to recognize symptoms of mental disorder that go beyond impulse control, such as hallucinations. In the case of Sirhan Sirhan, for example, who assassinated Senator Robert F. Kennedy, Sirhan was judged not to be impulsive but was still considered mentally disturbed according to other psychiatric criteria (see Chapter 17).

On the whole, it is felt that the courts have been too judgment oriented in trying to set up tests of a person's mental state based on courtroom criteria. Mental disorder should be diagnosed by psychiatric specialists according to psychiatric criteria, not legal rules. Another problem in legally defining mental disorder is the real differences between a psychiatric examination aimed at helping a client and a courtroom examination involving criminal proceedings. In the courtroom, the aim is to determine competency to stand trial or criminal responsibility for an act. Our court system is an adversarial one, with the defense lawyer obligated to defend the client while the prosecuting attorney seeks to demonstrate guilt. In this atmosphere, a psychiatric expert's testimony may be subjected to cross-examination intended to win the case, rather than to truly assess mental competency. It is no wonder that definitions of mental disorder arrived at for courtroom purposes have been considered unsatisfactory for psychiatric purposes.

Another way of approaching the question of what

# FOCUS 1–4:
## By Reason of Insanity

*The Crime*

On March 30, 1981, John W. Hinckley, Jr., impatiently stood in front of the curving wall leading to the VIP entrance of the Washington Hilton. President Ronald Reagan soon appeared, waving cheerily to an AP reporter and surrounded by the usual contingent of security service agents, reinforced by police officers. Dropping to a crouch, Hinckley raised his .22 calibre Röhm RG–14 revolver, and with a trained two-handed grip, fired on the president. In an instant, Hinckley emptied his revolver: Press Secretary James Brady, Policeman Thomas Delahanty, and Secret Service Agent Timothy McCarthy all fell injured. One bullet entered the president's left side, hit a rib, and punctured the left lung, and finally came to a stop only three inches from his heart. During the instant of the threat, President Reagan froze and went pale "like . . . a person who has seen death reflected in his eyes" (Mathews, 1981, p. 32).

*The Trial*

In June 1982, John Hinckley, Jr., stood trial on the plea of not guilty by reason of insanity. During his defense, Hinckley's background was characterized as that of mental instability. Foremost in the evidence was the motive for the attempted assassination: Hinckley's unrevealed love for a young starlet, Jodie Foster, whom he had seen in the role of a teenage prostitute in a 1976 movie. Prior to his assassination attempt, Hinckley wrote a letter to Miss Foster declaring, "There is a definite possibility that I will be killed in my attempt to get Reagan. [I am performing] this historical deed to gain your respect and love. . . . I just cannot wait any longer to impress you" (Hinckley, 1981, p. 35).

*Reaching the Verdict*

The jury had to face the decision of whether Hinckley was legally sane at the time of the crime, using the criteria of whether or not Hinckley could tell right from wrong and whether or not he had control over his behavior. In addition, the laws within the District of Columbia also demanded that the jury be able to conclude "without any reasonable doubt" that Hinckley was sane. In other words, the burden was on the *prosecution* to prove that Hinckley was *sane.* If there was any doubt whatsoever, then the jury had to find him not guilty.

Psychiatrists for the defense testified their belief that John Hinckley, Jr., was in fact mentally disturbed. One witness cited the "internal rage" and "internal frenzy" and the increasing retreat into a fantasy life that beset Hinckley and caused him to believe that "He had a sense of losing control" (Gest, 1982, p. 12).

The prosecution, on the other hand, brought out their expert psychiatric witnesses. Based upon examinations of Hinckley, one prosecution psychiatrist testified that "John was never so disturbed or distraught that he was unaware of what he was doing or why he was doing it" (Gest, 1982, p. 12).

Many were certain that the trial was a formality, and that Hinckley would quickly be found guilty and sentenced for punishment. Consider that Hinckley was apprehended on the spot, eyewitnesses saw him pull the trigger, and that Hinckley showed premeditation in a letter which stated his intent to kill the president.

*The Results*

The jury found John W. Hinckley, Jr., not guilty by reason of insanity. This finding so startled the judge that he began sentencing Hinckley, only to stop when he realized that commitment to a hospital and not sentencing to prison was the automatic step. The decision has caused great controversy, and steps have been initiated by President Reagan to have the insanity defense examined. The defense under which Hinckley was tried comes from the Model Penal Code designed by the American Law Institute. It requires examination of the case in terms of the ability of the defendant to know right from wrong and to have been in control of his actions at the time of the crime. The Reagan administration favors abolishing the insanity defense. Instead, a person could be found guilty of a crime if this individual's capacities were sufficiently intact that criminal intent could be demonstrated, no matter what the person's mental state or level of control. This *mens rea* approach has already been adopted by two states.

While the debate rages over the best legal definitions (Bonnie, 1983), John Hinckley has been

*Was John Hinckley, Jr., sane when he attempted to assassinate President Ronald Reagan?* ***Legal definitions*** *of insanity are often controversial.*

committed to St. Elizabeths Hospital in Washington, D.C., not far from the White House. As the brainchild of Dorothea Dix, the famed reformer (see Chapter 2), St. Elizabeths has had a lengthy history as a hospital for persons with mental disorders. In addition to noncourt-referred patients, the hospital also has special quarters for the criminally insane. A maximum-security ward with high walls and television monitoring houses 200 such cases. Yet, unlike other persons, John Hinckley lives in a private room and not a dormitory. Under local laws, Hinckley might have been evaluated for release within 50 days of the verdict and every 6 months thereafter. However, his family and attorneys are clear about deferring such requests until Hinckley is completely recovered.

*The Controversy*

Those who disputed the jury decision did so with intense emotions. One report described the "outrage [that] swept Washington and the nation: how could anyone—even a deeply disturbed sociopathic loner like Hinckley—be found *not guilty* of a carefully planned and meticulously photographed attempt on the president's life" (Morgenthau, 1982, p. 30)? Treasury Secretary Donald Regan declared, "I'm outraged, when a person stalks a leading citizen of this country, shoots him, three of the people surrounding him and then goes off scot-free, that's absolutely atrocious" (Gest, 1982, p. 12).

Later, Hinckley himself offered his own view: "The American people are angry with me, my parents' money and my fame. . . . They are jealous . . . and can't stand the thought of my innocence. The 12 people who sat on my jury deserve the Congressional Medal of Honor. . . . They saw all the evidence . . . concluded that I was mentally ill on March 30, 1981. . . . The public outrage over the verdict is disturbing to me because it truly demonstrates the vindictive nature of many Americans" (Hinckley, 1982, p. 30).

*What Do You Think?*

An attempted assassination of a presidential figure brings dramatic attention when insanity is used as a defense. In American history, two attempted assassins have escaped prosecution through successful insanity pleas. In 1835, Richard Lawrence, a house painter who believed himself to be King Richard III, attempted to shoot President Andrew Jackson. Lawrence's pistols misfired and he was taken into custody and tried. John Schrank, a saloon keeper, believed that the ghost of President McKinley instructed him to kill Theodore Roosevelt. Schrank made his attempt in Milwaukee in 1912 as Roosevelt was heading for a campaign speech (Beach, 1981). Is there justification in the insanity defense? Does it matter how important the intended victim is or should the law be the same for all? Has Hinckley "escaped just punishment" and caused the jury to make a mockery of the law?

Keep in mind that under the current system, law and psychiatry or psychology do not really mix well. Expert psychiatric witnesses are limited to testimony that may relate to the *legal* criteria of *insanity,* but not necessarily to modern psychiatric criteria of mental disorders. For instance, many persons suffering from a mental disorder may not show inability to tell right from wrong or an irresistible impulse, and still be severely disturbed—as we shall see in later chapters. In addition, the decision whether or not the defendant is legally insane is made by a jury of nonprofessionals, rather than by psychiatrists or psychologists. Finally, the court system is an adversarial one that pits one side against another side, and one set of witnesses against another set of expert witnesses. Such an atmosphere is not conducive to sound judgments and is even less so when the case provokes national attention.

As a juror, how would you have voted on John W. Hinckley, Jr.?

constitutes abnormality is to examine what normal behavior is.

## WHAT IS NORMAL BEHAVIOR?

Although statistical, cultural, and legal approaches provide much of our basis for understanding abnormality, a complete picture must include a description of the normal personality for comparison. Being normal, or being adjusted, involves far more than the absence of abnormal traits.

### Ability to Act Instrumentally

One correlate of adjustment is the ability to act instrumentally, directing behaviors toward solutions of problems or stresses. An adjusted person seeks to diminish stresses that can build into emotional blockades, developing positive measures to strengthen means for overcoming tensions and fears. When goals are meaningful and valuable, that individual attempts to reach them in spite of tensions.

### Efficiency

An adjusted person utilizes energies with relatively little wasted effort. The individual is realistic enough to realize when obstacles are insurmountable and goals are out of reach and can redirect energies toward more realistic goals. Energy resources seem more available since less energy is consumed by anxiety, emotional conflict, and costly defensive behaviors.

### Appropriateness

Adjusted individuals demonstrate thoughts, feelings, and actions that are appropriate to the social context. They experience fear, worry, anger, or distress; but these are all responses to real circumstances, and they diminish when those circumstances change. The overt expression of such responses is also kept under control: even if a student has every right to feel anger toward a friend, she will express her anger in socially acceptable ways. She will not deny her feelings of anger, however, and for this reason will be spontaneous in her expressions.

Not only are behaviors appropriate to the setting, they are also appropriate for the person's age and maturity level. A normal child may exhibit a low frustration tolerance and weep readily, but a normal adult must endure much more and react with greater composure and maturity.

### Flexibility: Ability to Change

Another correlate of normality is adaptability or flexibility. When individuals are faced with conflict and frustration, they seek new ways of solving problems instead of persisting in unsuccessful efforts. A willingness to learn, to change, and to engage the new is also a part of flexibility. New experiences provide new outlooks and the opportunity to acquire additional skills in meeting life's demands.

### Effectiveness in Interpersonal Relations

The bulk of human life is composed of interactions with other people, and adjusted individuals participate fully. They relate well, with neither excessive dependence nor extreme withdrawal. There is a fine line between being emancipated enough to avoid being directed by what others say or do and having the sensitivity to accept others and respond to their reasonable demands and needs. Part of being adjusted is the ability to stay within those boundaries. Also, adjusted individuals can enjoy the presence of others, while at the same time recognizing their own needs for solitude.

### Self-esteem and Security

The well-adjusted person possesses a sense of self-esteem and security. This is founded on a realistic appraisal of personal weaknesses and strengths, on what he or she is and can become, on what is expected by others, and what is self-determined. Such individuals can either accept things the way they are, or, if they perceive their lot as unacceptable, they can both initiate and control a process of change.

These indicators provide but one measure of normality or adjustment. They represent this author's interpretation; other psychologists offer descriptions that may differ in some minor respects.[1] For instance, Kenneth E. Appel (1957), a past president of the American Psychiatric Association, considered the

1 Further discussions may be found in *The Counseling Psychology*, 1973, **4**(2) devoted to "The Healthy Personality."

***Age-appropriateness** of behaviors is one index of normal. Playing with dolls may be appropriate for a child but not for an older person.*

sound person as having the ability "to meet and handle problems; to make choices and decisions; to find satisfaction in accepting tasks; to do jobs without avoiding them and without pushing them onto others; to carry on without undue dependency on others; to live effectively and satisfactorily with others without crippling complications; to contribute one's share in life; to enjoy life and to be able to love and be loved (p. 363)."

## A WORKING DEFINITION OF ABNORMALITY

As we review the various definitions of abnormality and normality, we start to understand the complexity involved in simply agreeing on what is abnormal and what is normal. As a normal reader, in fact, you may have tried to weigh your own characteristics against the criteria for normality and begun to have some doubts about your own sanity. But keep in mind that any conclusion about a person's mental health must take into account many criteria. For instance, we will see in our later discussion of the new psychiatric classification system (called DSM-III) that it is important to evaluate what types of life stresses may be occurring and how severe they are. Furthermore, a person who lacks some attributes of adjustment is not necessarily maladjusted. No one is completely efficient, effective, or self-confident all of the time. Some theorists even take the extreme point of view that nobody is really mentally disturbed (see the accompanying discussion in Focus 1–5). For the purposes of developing a working definition of abnormality, the following criteria should be considered:

***Discomfort.*** More often than not, the person with a psychological disorder experiences discomfort. The person may feel this as misery, anxiety, depression, loss of esteem, or other negative emotions. Another sign of the discomfort may be in physical ways—such as elevated blood pressure, continuous fatigue, or other bodily symptoms.

***Lack of Predictability.*** One way in which this is seen is in fluctuations in mood. The person feels on top of the world one moment, then plunges into despair or rage the next moment. Unpredictability might show in behaviors we consider bizarre, such as talking out loud to oneself or to a person who doesn't exist. This unpredictable aspect, along with the peculiarity of the behaviors, helps to distinguish between abnormal behaviors and culturally meaningful behaviors. This may be one way of resolving the problems of a purely cultural definition of pathology.

***Maladaptiveness of Behaviors.*** The behaviors of abnormal persons do not appear to be adaptive, directed toward achieving well-being, or actualizing. Instead they are self-defeating, inappropriate, and tend to produce further discomfort for oneself or others. In contrast to the picture of the adjusted person described earlier, the abnormal person is inefficient and ineffective.

***Loss of Control.*** A maladjusted person seems neither to be in control nor to feel in control. Fluctuations in mood may be one example of this, as emotions seem to come and go with a life of their own. It may also be that the individual drifts into circumstances that precipitate such moods, instead of making real choices to avoid unhealthy circumstances. In some cases, bizarre behaviors are adopted in an attempt to reestablish control, as in the obsessive-compulsive disorder where extreme rituals are used.

***Rigidity of Response.*** This is the opposite dimension of the flexibility that characterizes the normal person. Rigidity may be present because the person's discomfort is so all-consuming that the individual devotes all energies to reducing anxious feelings. It may occur because the person is so focused on internal distortions or self-needs as to be unable to perceive that the environmental circumstances have altered. Instead, the maladjusted individual is rigid and is unable to respond to the environment, unable to learn from experience.

These criteria are offered more to provide a context for understanding terms which are often used interchangeably—terms such as *abnormal, psychopathology, mental disorder,* and occasionally *mental illness.*[2] Some may disagree with our criteria for using these terms. For example, the existentialist R. D. Laing contends that all behaviors are adaptive, even psychotic behaviors, as the Focus discussion notes. However, most writers agree with our approach. In addition, as we begin to discuss the specific forms of mental disorder themselves in the coming chapters, the special characteristics associated with each disorder will help to further define each pathology.

## THE CLASSIFICATION OF ABNORMAL BEHAVIOR

Once a working definition of *abnormality* has been agreed on, it is meaningful to make another determination: that of what distinguishes one particular mental disorder from another.

*Symptoms* are subjective or objective characteristics that can be considered signs of illness. The classification of symptoms of abnormality into orderly groups has been a task of great concern to *psychopathologists,* professionals who study the causes and characteristics of abnormal behavior. The goal of these professionals has been to provide a useful classification for identifying different types of disorders, and to suggest a variety of cues regarding possible causes and treatment. As useful as such a classification scheme would be, however, a completely satisfactory system has not yet been developed despite numerous attempts.

### The Controversy over Classifications

Classification schemes are generally considered necessary in science. For instance, in zoology and botany, animals and plants can be grouped according to shared characteristics with only a very few exceptions.

The medical model also uses a classification system of diseases with success. Certain clusters of symptoms can be identified as signs of an underlying disease. Since we know that symptoms of the same disease will run a particular course, both causation and treatment can usually be readily identified.

Although this approach has worked well in physical illnesses, it has been the subject of controversy when it is applied to mental disorders. One reason for this is that the assumptions underlying the medical model often go unquestioned (Price, 1978). For example, we might assume that abnormal conditions such as certain headaches are the result of a disease process, even though organic etiology has not been proven. Such an assumption can be misleading, for if other factors are ignored—for instance, a high-stress situation at work—the treatment will likely be restricted to the assumed physical causes.

Another problem is also in the interpretations by the observers of behaviors. This difficulty involves confusing the behaviors themselves with the disease. For years, homosexual behavior was considered as an illness, but recently homosexuality has been separated into behaviors that may be indicative of pathologies and those that do not represent pathology.

A third danger of classifying psychological disorders is that of making judgments based on the label, rather than attending to the individual as a person. As you will see, the field of psychopathology is not as precise as is physical medicine (Blashfield & Draguns, 1976). Not all persons with the same mental disorder will share in all of the same symptoms. It can be misleading to expect to see the exact symptoms, based on the label given a patient.

Rosenhan (1973) conducted a daring study that illustrates the problem of basing judgments on labels

2 The term *mental illness* sometimes connotes that mental disorders have the same characteristics as physical diseases. To avoid this inference, we will limit the use of that term to historical discussions, where that implication was intended or to instances where organic disease is involved.

## FOCUS 1–5:
### Mental Disorder: Is It a Myth?

In defining abnormality, it is often difficult to draw the line between those behaviors that are normal and those that are symptoms of abnormality. Indeed, some scholars even challenge the basic premise that there is such a thing as mental disorder.

Psychiatrist Thomas S. Szasz (1965) uses the term *problems in living* for what we call "mental disorder." He reminds us that over the course of history, abnormal behavior patterns have gone under different names and have been attributed to different causes. For instance, problems in living were once thought to be caused by demon possession (see Chapter 2). Then later, our cultural conceptions changed to attribute the cause of mental disorder to disease origins.

Szasz believes that the concept of *illness* has outlived its usefulness. By retaining this *myth of mental illness,* he feels we divert attention from the real problems (such as social conflicts), and absolve the individuals who show symptoms of illnesses from the real goals of being personally responsible for change. As Szasz (1960) writes, "Our adversaries are not demons, witches, fate, or mental illness. We have no enemy whom we can fight, exorcise, or dispel by 'cure.' What we do have are problems in living—whether these be biological, economic, political, or sociopsychological" (p. 118).

Offering his own existential orientation, R. D. Laing (1960, 1972; Laing & Esterson, 1964) contends that a psychotic experience is defined as abnormal only because society defines it that way. A belief should not be dismissed as an irrational delusion: it contains an existential truth to the person, even if most other people don't share the same perception. Diagnostic labels are only a means for society to reject and isolate those persons whose experiences are not accepted and as a method for shifting blame. In this, Laing accuses psychiatric classifications of being a "conspiratorial model of illness," relying on the psychiatrist, as society's agent of control, to force the patient into a career or role of being ill and then banishing the rejected person to a hospital until he or she learns to see things society's way.

*The question of whether homosexuality is* abnormal *has aroused a great deal of controversy. DSM-III classes only ego-dystonic homosexuality as a disorder.*

rather than individuals. He and seven friends had themselves committed to different hospitals by feigning the psychotic symptoms of hallucinating an "empty, hollow, thudding" sound. Other than this one symptom, the volunteers simply were themselves. And once admitted, they no longer reported the disturbance but instead informed the staff that the symptoms had disappeared and they now felt normal. The question of whether or not the patients' sanity would be detected was then put to the test, and the answer was no—at least not by the professional staff (some other patients accused them of deception, though). The medical staff's response instead was to prescribe over 2,100 tranquilizers for the pseudopatients. What appeared to have happened was that once the diagnosis was made, later interpretations of normal behaviors were governed by the diagnostic label, rather than vice versa.

In all, it is important to remember that classifications, or diagnostic labels, are mainly a means for shorthand communications. In this function, they *are* useful: if we all agree about what clusters of behaviors go under the term *depression*, for instance, then we can use that label, instead of having to list each and every symptom.

In addition, the classification system and the descriptions of disorders can only represent statements of the *dominant* symptom patterns. To the degree that each human being is unique, such patterns may vary from the common pattern. An individual may show a majority, or only some, of the symptoms and still be classified within one type of disorder; the individual need not exhibit all of the symptoms. Occasionally, some symptoms are exhibited during one examination period, and others during another session. In addition, a single individual may show symptoms suggestive of multiple affliction: for instance, a person may be both psychotic and mentally retarded.

For all of these reasons, as various disorders are explored throughout this book, we will discuss their possible causes or correlates under the heading Dynamics rather than the more specific origins title used for Chapters 3 through 5. It is the variability or dynamic nature of causes that we want to stress, rather than the implication that symptoms can be clearly attributed to the same factors in every case.

## DSM-III

The current classification scheme of the American Psychiatric Association is known as *DSM-III* (the *Diagnostic and Statistical Manual*, 3d edition—to be distinguished from DSM-I and DSM-II, released in 1952 and 1968 respectively). This scheme shares some of the difficulties inherent in any system that seeks to classify mental disorders, and it has been criticized specifically for a few reasons. For instance, the American Psychological Association (1980) expressed concern that DSM-III "perpetuates the use of traditional psychiatric terms such as . . . 'schizophrenia' rather than employing more behavioral descriptions" (p. 10). (Readers will find one example of a behavioral classification in Chapter 3 in Focus on a Behavioral System for Classifying Disorders.) This national organization of psychologists also felt that DSM-III went too far in including behaviors such as cigarette smoking as a mental disorder. And finally, the psychological association viewed the coverage of children's disorders as not adequately representative of developmental difficulties. However, inasmuch as DSM-III is a distinct improvement over prior classification systems, the American Psychological Association offered its qualified endorsement.

For all its shortcomings, DSM-III represents considerable progress over previous classification schemes (Nathan, 1983). The DSM-I classification was not compatible with the system used by the World Health Organization, so it had to be revised thoroughly; and its successor, DSM-II, fell under criticism because it relied too heavily on the disease entity notion, that is, the idea that mental illnesses are analogous to physical diseases (Sarason & Ganzer, 1968).

DSM-III has been introduced in the hopes of improving on DSM-II in several ways (American Psychiatric Association, 1980, 1983). First, the new system is more specific about what symptoms define a disorder, in order to promote more uniformity in diagnoses by different clinicians. Certain concepts have been clarified, such as DSM-II's term *neurosis*. Previously, neurosis was a catchall for several low-severity disorders (such as anxiety disorder, phobia, and obsessive-compulsive and hysterical disorders); and it sometimes implied a cause of these disorders. DSM-III attempts to limit the term to mean disorders of minor severity and tries to avoid even listing the disorders under the title *neurosis*. The new classification does, however, acknowledge that these milder disorders do exist, and that the term *neurotic disorders* would include the *anxiety disorders*, the *somatoform disorders*, the *dissociative disorders*, the *psychosexual disorders*, and some of the *affective disorders* (see Table 1–1).

Second, the new system leaves open the question of *how* a disorder developed, describing only *what* the disorder looks like. In other words, it accepts that the causes of mental disorders have not yet been pinpointed. This acknowledges that some phobias, or irrational fears, may derive from prolonging of separation anxiety, for example, while others may be explained by avoidance learning, and still others may be viewed as unconscious derivatives of other conflicts.

Third, the DSM-III classification involves using multiple axes to recognize that a single person may show several disorders with differing characteristics. The axes are no more than subcategories for listing relevant characteristics, but they provide clinicians with a vehicle that permits them to be more descriptive of behaviors without implying theories of causation.

The three major axes together list the person's primary problems; for instance, "heroin dependence, with antisocial personality disorder, and diabetes." The first axis or term lists the person's maladaptive disorder, such as heroin dependence or schizophrenia; the second axis identifies the person's long-standing personality characteristics, such as antisocial or compulsive; and the third axis states any medical or physical conditions also present, for instance diabetes or epilepsy. A fourth axis is used to state specific psychosocial stressors which may be involved, as well as to rate the overall severity of the stress. A fifth axis is used to further describe the client in terms of the level of personal or occupational functioning over the past year. Table 1.2 illustrates examples of three hypothetical clients.

DSM-III also improves on the DSM-II scheme in some other ways. It includes some new types of disorders (for example, agoraphobia or fear of open spaces); these have not been included in previous categorizations. The new categories are asterisked in Table 1–1. DSM-III has also changed the names of some disorders, in an effort to be more descriptive and precise. For instance, *bipolar disorder* now describes what was once known as manic-depressive disorder; and *psychological factors affecting physical condition* replaces psychophysiologic disorders. Finally, DSM-III has refined some of the criteria for making a diagnosis. Thus, it recognizes that homosexuality per se is not necessarily pathological, and that drug *use* need not always be considered drug *abuse*.

A variety of other classification schemes have been offered,[3] but none have yet reached the wide adoption of the American Psychiatric Association model. Thus far, DSM-III has differentiated reasonably well among the mental disorders, covering the types of conditions afflicting American patients fairly comprehensively and providing significant clues for treatment.

This classification scheme, with some modification, will form the basis for this book. In general, the following are the text's more notable differences from

3 See, for instance, Bandura, 1968; Cattell, 1957; Eysenck, 1952; Staats & Staats, 1963; Thorne, 1953; and Wittman & Sheldon, 1948.

**TABLE 1–1**

**DSM-III Classification of Disorders**

I. *Anxiety Disorders.* These are problems in which anxiety is either prominent in the clinical picture or is experienced if the person tries to resist giving in to the symptoms. Among the anxiety disorders are:

Generalized anxiety disorder
Panic disorder
Phobic disorder
Obsessive-compulsive disorder
Post-traumatic disorder

II. *Adjustment Disorders.* These are problems in which the maladaptive behaviors are related to identifiable stressors in one's life. The stressors are noncatastrophic ones, but the person's failure to cope is displayed in certain symptoms. Among the adjustment disorders are:

Adjustment disorder with depressed mood
Adjustment disorder with anxious mood
Adjustment disorder with disturbance of conduct
Adjustment disorder with withdrawal

III. *Dissociative Disorders.* These are problems where there is a sudden, temporary alteration in consciousness, identity, or motor behavior. Memory may be lost, a new identity assumed, or new behaviors appear. Among the dissociative disorders are:

Psychogenic amnesia
Psychogenic fugue
Multiple personality
Depersonalization disorder*

IV. *Psychological Factors Affecting Physical Conditions (Psychophysiologic Disorders).* These are problems with physical symptoms or structural changes in the body due to emotional disturbances. Among these psychophysiologic disorders are:

Peptic ulcers
Asthma
Essential hypertension
Coronary artery disease
Cancer

V. *Somatoform Disorders.* These are problems in which there are physical symptoms but where there is no evidence of organic factors and where structural changes cannot be confirmed. Among the somatoform disorders are:

Somatization disorder*
Conversion disorder
Psychogenic pain disorder*
Hypochondriasis

VI. *Factitious Disorders.** These are problems in which a patient simulates a physical or psychological illness or structural change. Frequent visits to different hospitals can eventually lead to structural alterations from surgery, self-inflicted damage, or other voluntary activities. Among the factitious disorders are:

Factitious disorder with psychological symptoms
Factitious disorder with physical symptoms

**TABLE 1–1 (Continued)**

**DSM-III Classification of Disorders**

VII. *Disorders of Impulse Control.** These are problems in which the person seems unable to retain control over impulses. The individual acts on the impulse in ways which may be damaging to the person or to others. Among the disorders of impulse control are:

Pathological gambling
Kleptomania
Pyromania
Explosive disorder

VIII. *Psychosexual Disorders.* These are problems relating to sexual behaviors, sexual identity, or sexual arousal and functioning. Among the psychosexual disorders are:

Gender identity disorders
Paraphilias
Psychosexual dysfunctions
Ego-dystonic homosexuality

IX. *Substance Abuse Disorders.* These are problems involving the abuse of substances such as alcohol or drugs. Among the substance abuse disorders are:

Alcohol abuse
Drug abuse
Caffeine intoxication*
Tobacco dependence*

X. *Personality Disorders.* These are problems considered to be deeply ingrained, inflexible, maladaptive behavioral patterns. Impairment of personality development rather than severe emotional stress is the apparent cause. Among the personality disorders are:

Dependent personality
Passive-aggressive personality
Narcissistic personality
Paranoid personality
Schizoid personality
Hysterical personality
Antisocial personality

XI. *Affective Disorders.* These are problems in which there are disturbances in mood. The mood may be prolonged depression or prolonged elation, or there may be a cyclic alteration of these moods. Among the affective disorders are:

Bipolar disorder
Major depression

XII. *Paranoid Disorders.* These are problems in which the dominant symptom is the presence of delusions of persecution. Other than this thought disturbance, the person seems to be functioning appropriately. Among the paranoid disorders are:

Paranoia
*Folie à deux**

**TABLE 1–1 (Continued)**

**DSM-III Classification of Disorders**

XIII. *Schizophrenic Disorders.* These are problems in which there is disintegration of personality, withdrawal from reality, emotional inappropriateness, and bizarreness in behavior. Among the schizophrenic disorders are:

- Disorganized type schizophrenia
- Catatonic schizophrenia
- Paranoid schizophrenia
- Schizo-affective schizophrenia

XIV. *Organic Disorders.* These are problems caused by impairment of brain functioning. Among the organic disorders are:

Organic mental disorders—dementia, senile<br>—dementia, presenile

Organic brain syndrome—amnestic syndrome<br>—delusional syndrome<br>—hallucinosis<br>—affective syndrome<br>—personality syndrome

XV. *Mental Retardation.* These are problems involving a significant deficit in intellectual functioning or development. Among the types of mental retardation are those resulting from:

- Infections
- Traumas
- Metabolic or nutritional disorders
- Prenatal influence

XVI. *Disorders of Infancy, Childhood, or Adolescence.* These are problems occurring in infancy, childhood, or adolescence. Among the types are:

- Attentional deficit disorders
- Anxiety disorders
- Eating disorders
- Stereotyped movement disorders
- Physical disorders
- Pervasive developmental disorders

* Disorders that were not included in the DSM-II classification scheme.

**TABLE 1–2**

**An Example of the Use of DSM-III's Axes for Descriptions of Different Patients**

| | *Example: Patient A* | *Example: Patient B* | *Example: Patient C* |
|---|---|---|---|
| *Axis I* [a] | Heroin dependence | Bipolar depression | Schizophrenia paranoia |
| *Axis II* [b] | Antisocial personality disorder | Dependent personality disorder | None |
| *Axis III* [c] | Diabetes | Epilepsy | None |
| *Axis IV* [d] | Moderate | None | Minimal |
| *Axis V* [e] | Good | Poor | Excellent |

[a]Describes the patient's primary disorder.
[b]Lists any long-standing personality characteristics.
[c]Lists any physical disorders.
[d]Lists the severity of psychosocial stressors.
[e]Lists the patient's highest level of adaptive functioning.

DSM-III. The text will keep the more familiar term *psychophysiologic disorder* instead of the awkward DSM-III term *psychological factors affecting physical condition.* The term *neurosis* will also be kept to connote disorders of lesser severity. In omitting the term *neurosis,* DSM-III noted that such an omission caused "great concern to many clinicians" (p.9) who found it of descriptive value. The text will also only emphasize certain disorders and avoid going into details on some lesser DSM-III disorders such as tobacco dependence and caffeine intoxication. And finally, the chapter on mental retardation will not use DSM-III; instead it uses the more complete classification system accepted by the American Association on Mental Deficiency. The major groups of disorders will be discussed in detail, chapter by chapter, in Part 2 of this book.

## SCIENTIFIC METHODS AND THE STUDY OF HUMAN BEHAVIOR

In the previous discussions, it is clear that abnormal behavior is difficult to define and classify. When we shift from defining *what* constitutes a particular disorder to asking *how* it was caused, it becomes even clearer that mysteries still exist. In Chapters 3, 4, and 5 of this text, you will see that the origins of very few mental disorders have been pinpointed. Genetics, social and cultural factors, family environment, physiological conditions, and psychological variables may all impact on a person's feelings and behaviors; and cause-and-effect relationships must somehow be drawn out of massive piles of findings, many conflicting. It is from these challenges that the scientific approach emerges.

We call on science and its methods in many everyday issues: What kinds of cloud formations signify that it will rain on the afternoon of a picnic? What has caused a lawn to look brown and mottled instead of healthy and green? What type of breakfast should you eat before taking a major exam in school? To answer such questions, we rely on hypotheses drawn from systematic observations.

The same basic rules apply in efforts to diagnose and explain psychological disorders. Specifically, four main approaches are used in the scientific study of abnormality: (1) the case study approach, (2) the correlational approach, (3) the normative or sampling approach, and (4) the controlled experiment approach.

### The Case Study Approach

A *case study* is an intensive study of a single individual and all the variables that seem to be associated with his or her condition. This scientific method was especially important to early pioneers in psychiatry, such as Sigmund Freud, who developed their creative insights through careful attention to individual clients (see Chapter 3). It has also been a rich source of information in studies, such as the well-known examination of a multiple personality, *The Three Faces of Eve*

(Thigpen & Cleckley, 1957), described in greater detail in Chapter 8. This study's in-depth reporting of details, including quotations and changes in the client's mannerisms, has had an important impact on the field of abnormal psychology.

A hypothetical problem illustrates how the case study works. Suppose you wanted to test the hypothesis that *depression*, an emotional state characterized by sadness and gloom, is caused by being overweight. To use this approach, you would study a single person who is depressed, obtaining historical and biographical data: What was your mood like before you became overweight? Were you ever depressed when you were slimmer? Have you ever not been depressed since you gained weight? Is it possible to actually date the onset of your depression to your change in weight? What other things in your life seemed to relate to being depressed? Answering these questions would provide a good deal of information about your subject's condition.

The case study approach has certain advantages, for its comprehensiveness certainly provides the opportunity to discover many facets of a disorder. Yet, the approach also has some important limitations. A major disadvantage is the possibility that the information is unreliable or so unique to the person being studied that it cannot be generalized to other persons. Freud based his thoughts about neurosis in women on the incestual experiences of his clients' early lives; then he discovered that these events were fantasies that had never actually occurred. In our hypothetical study of obesity and depression, the subject might have had some unusual experiences that make his or her situation atypical. Thus, conclusions drawn from a single case can only be tentatively extended to others.

### The Correlational Approach

In the correlational approach, the variable under study is matched against the presence of a second variable that is assumed to be related in the effort to demonstrate an association between the two. In our example, we would measure people's levels of depression and also their weights. If a correlation existed, then we might find that the most depressed persons are also the most overweight, while the least depressed persons show the least weight problems (see Figure 1–2).

Correlational studies add a little more reliability to the study of abnormality than does the case study, since more cases are being evaluated. Such studies are also somewhat more precise, since the observations need to be quantified in some way (to give higher and lower scores) in order to calculate a correlation.

One major caution in correlational studies is that two variables may show an association, but only because they are both influenced by a third variable that the scientist has completely overlooked. Thus, levels of depression and weight might show a high correlation because both are end results of repressed aggression. It is possible that persons who repress anger express their hostility by eating more and hence become overweight. These same persons might become depressed, not because they are overweight, but because they are now turning their anger inward towards themselves. For this reason, it is often stated that a correlation does not prove *causality*, only a relationship. However, such a relationship can still be important to point to directions for further study.

### The Normative or Sampling Approach

In this approach, a *sample* (representative group) of persons showing a particular trait is carefully studied to learn about that trait. Thus, you would (if you could)

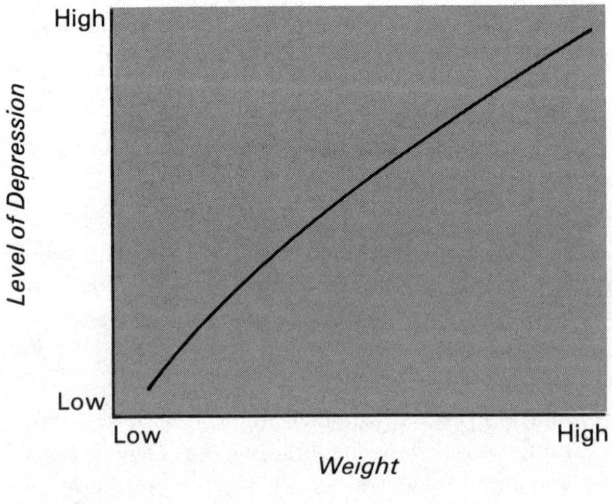


**FIGURE 1–2** Correlation between Depression and Weight.

take all of the overweight persons that existed in the community, if you judged your community to have a reasonably typical population. You might then determine what percent of these folks showed signs of depression. You would probably feel you had gone a long way to confirming your initial hypothesis if you found that 80 percent reported being depressed. Ideally, you would also study a control group of persons who were *not* overweight and examine their level of depression. If you discovered that none of these people were depressed, then your hypothesis that depression is tied to being overweight would indeed seem sound. On the other hand, if you determined that 80 percent of normal-weight persons also reported depression, you might hasten to reexamine your belief.

The sampling approach tends to be useful when it is convenient to categorize persons to be studied. For instance, are there differences in pathology among persons of different socioeconomic levels, or of different ethnic origins, or of different sexes? As you will see later in Chapter 17, studies are underway to follow children identified as *high risk* (that is, from schizophrenic parents) to see what happens to them when compared with nonrisk children in their later personal and school adjustment. This type of sampling study could be highly revealing.

### The Controlled Experiment Approach

In the fourth approach, a researcher actually conducts an experiment, controlling what happens to the subjects and observing what happens when specific variables are changed.

Returning to our example, you might start by selecting persons whose weights were normal and who were not depressed. You could then divide these people into three groups: OW, UW, and N. You would put the OW group on a special diet and a low-exercise program, virtually insuring that each person would soon become overweight. The UW group would be placed on a different program that would lead them to become underweight. The third group, N, would remain at a normal weight. Throughout this experiment, the levels of depression of each group would be monitored. If the OW group showed an increase in depression from their preprogram levels and were also more depressed than either the UW or N groups, then you might conclude that being overweight was a significant factor in depression. You could also reverse the study and bring the subjects back to their normal weights, and once again measure the level of depression. If this led to a reversal of depression as well, then this would add even stronger evidence. This last technique is appropriately known as a *reversal experimental design.*

Unlike the correlational method, the controlled experiment design permits inferences about causality. Although the controlled experiment has this advantage, however, it is not always feasible to achieve. For example, would you be willing to volunteer to be in the OW group if you suspected that you might become depressed as a result? Such situations become far more complicated in real life, where ethical issues often arise. A new therapy may seem to be promising, for instance, but requires testing on individuals who actually have the disorder. Can we deny these patients a drug therapy of known effectiveness in order to evaluate an experimental drug?

The role of science in the study of abnormal psychology cannot be overemphasized. Systematic observations often lead to insights which lead to theories which prompt experiments, which provide the basis for answers. This book will call attention to the findings that shed light on what we know about the origins of different disorders and the preferred treatments. At the same time, evaluations will be offered that give you a feeling for what the state of our science may be, what controversies exist, or what limitations in progress must be accepted. The difference between theories and actual findings will be pointed out throughout our discussions. In many ways, you will therefore not only be reading about psychopathology, but also about science in application.

## SUMMARY

Abnormal behaviors are defined differently by the statistical, cultural, and legal definitions. Statistically, anything that does not match behaviors which are the commonest in a society are defined as abnormal. Cultural definitions are those which are agreed to by consensus by members of the same society, regardless of how frequently the behaviors actually appear. In legal definitions, the ability to know right from wrong, or the ability to control an impulse have been used as definitions. A more suitable approach is to list behaviors or symptoms which appear to impair functioning. The attempts of the American Psychiatric Association in formulating a diagnostic classification system is a move towards defining what clusters of behaviors constitute mental disorders. The system currently accepted, DSM-III, has the advantage of having been field tested, with changes that reflect the best that we have learned from use of two previous systems (DSM-I, and DSM-II). This DSM-III classification forms the basis for the organization and content of this text.

It is possible to shed light on abnormality by looking at normal behaviors. Some definitions of normality have been offered; normal behaviors might be considered as those which are effective, efficient, appropriate, flexible, in persons who are interpersonally secure, able to learn from experience, and interpersonally effective.

The study of abnormality also hinges on the use of research to collect information. Several research designs are used, each with its own advantages in serving science. These include the case study approaches, correlational approaches, normative or sampling approaches, and controlled experiment approaches.

## KEY TERMS

**Bipolar psychosis**
**Case study**
**Controlled experimental design**
**Correlational design**
**Irresistible impulse**
**Neurosis**
**Normal curve**
**Normative study**
**Obsessive-compulsive disorder**
**Phobia**
**Psychophysiologic disorders**
**Psychosis**
**Reversal experimental design**
**Schizophrenia**

# CHAPTER 2

## The Abnormal Personality: A History of Interpretations

- Early humans may well have had severe headaches connected with mental disorders. On what evidence can we draw inferences about the presence of mental disturbances in prehistoric humans?
- "He heard a voice calling, and saw a flaming bush which spoke to him about the need to feel pride . . . after which he fell to the ground." According to biblical sources, would such a report be a sign of good or evil in a person?
- How does the belief in possession by demons explain early attitudes about mental disorders?
- What are the common themes involving explanations of mental disturbances through history?
- Does the diseased body show up in the diseased mind? What does the organic theory of mental disorder entail?
- Is there any truth to the idea that bumps on your head can reflect your personality?
- How were hypnosis, the guillotine, Benjamin Franklin, and magnetism brought together in the history of science?
- What was the influence of hysteria, "the floating uterus," on progress in definitions of mental disorder?
- How would a modern hospital compare to a hospital for mental patients when Dorothea Dix first began her crusade?

There is little doubt that even in the Stone Age, over a hundred thousand years ago, people experienced psychological disorders.

Does this statement seem extreme? After all, how can we know what was in people's minds several millennia before humans could write about their experiences—or perhaps even before they had the mental capacity to think as we do? Certainly, there is a danger of projecting our own ideas and feelings in any archaeological conjectures about early humans, but the guesswork involved here is highly educated. We have cross-cultural evidence, for instance, from modern aboriginal tribes that suggests the kinds of stresses and psychological reactions that exist in cultures without developed societies.

The physical clues of mental disorders in ancient times are even more striking. Stone-Age skull remains provide evidence of a primitive form of surgery known as ***trephining***. The technique involved chipping through the skull with crude cutting implements to make a circular hole. We know that the procedure was intended as a surgery rather than a way of doing away with an unpopular member of the group: regrowth of bone around some trephines, or holes, shows that some people lived for several years after the operation. It seems likely that the hope was to release whatever evil existed within the sick person through the gap in the skull, possibly by relieving pressure on the brain.

The mental disorders that were treated by trephining probably took different forms than many of the disorders we will study in this book, due both to the earlier stage of human evolution and to the different culture and lifestyle stresses experienced by early humans. Yet, despite these differences, it seems reasonable to conclude that mental illness has always been with us, from the Stone Age on up to the present. It has been perceived differently in different periods and cultures throughout history, however; and as a result, people have attempted to deal with mental disorders in different ways.

The story of these various perceptions and treatments is a fascinating one—not only because of the often bizarre nature of some of the theories and cures of the past, but also because even centuries ago, we can recognize some of the origins of modern interpretations and treatments. That story, extending up to the close of the 19th century, is the subject of this chapter. Chapters 3, 4, and 5 will carry the story up to the present as they discuss psychiatry and the explanations of abnormality that have developed in this century.

## PRIMITIVE POSSESSION AND DEMONOLOGY

Although our understanding of prehistoric humans' perceptions of mental disorder has to be pieced together from archeological and cross-cultural clues, we know more about the views of several ancient cultures (Alexander & Selesnick, 1966). Among the early Chinese, Egyptian and Hebrew cultures, explanations for mental disorder took more distinctive shape in the form of *demonology:* the belief that events are controlled by spirits external to humans. This belief was the logical extension of an important development within these cultures: the emergence of a *theology,* or a belief in gods or supernatural spirits. Just as the people of these cultures turned to a belief in spirits or gods to lend meaning to their physical world, so did they refer to evil spirits, demons, and *possession* (the presence of an evil spirit within a person) as a way of explaining sickness. Thus, a daughter of a Pharaoh was said to have been possessed by an evil spirit and cured by a benign one. In China in the *Suen hwo* period (1119–26 A.D.), women of the Imperial harem were known to become suddenly mad on the appearance of apparitions. One apparition was known as *lai,* a specter without head or eyes, with shiny hair covering hands and feet, and moving with thundering noise. Some historians report the possible connection between the dreaded *lai* and later generations' reports of abominable snowmen (Veith, 1975). Biblical sources are full of references to madness attributed to satanic control. In Deuteronomy (6:5) it is said: "The Lord will smite thee with madness." In fact, Saul was described as suffering from depression and suicidal feelings as punishment; the Lord sending these ailments to Saul through an evil spirit (I Samuel 31:4).

The lot of the "possessed" person was usually not a happy one. In most instances, he or she was either stoned or banished to do penance—treatments that have surfaced and resurfaced at several points in the

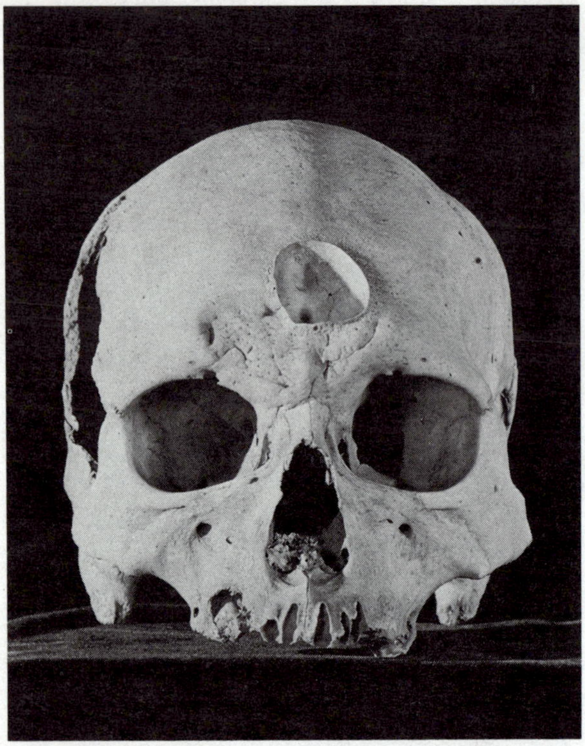

*Archaeological evidence of* ***trephining****, a primitive form of treatment of illness, is illustrated. Holes are made in the skull apparently to permit the evil spirits or demons to leave.*

course of history, as you will see. Occasionally, however, what now seem to be symptoms of abnormality received just the opposite response from society. Prophets, for instance, were often sought after with awe because of their special ability to predict events. The Wise Men are said to have started on their journey to Bethlehem on the belief that the star predicted an important event on earth. Similarly, religious conversions were common after unusual psychological experiences, such as visions or changes in mood. Paul, a persecutor of Christians, was stopped by a vision of light and was converted to Christianity (Acts 9:3). Moses began his deep commitment to become a leader of the Jews following guidance from the Lord appearing in a burning bush (Exodus 3:1). Abraham actually prepared to sacrificially kill his son as a result of hearing the voice of God telling him to do so (Genesis 22:3).

## EARLY INSIGHTS OF THE GREEKS AND ROMANS

The belief in gods and spirit possession provided strong threads in the development of ancient Greek civilization. In early Greece, as in many other ancient cultures, madness was attributed to divine power and influence. Hercules was mad, it is said, because Lyssa, the goddess of night and madness, so decided. The daughters of Proteus, the king of Argos, ran into the forest mooing and acting like cows because of the wrath of the gods. Mythological beliefs and medicine were indistinguishable. And as in other ancient cultures, paradoxes in beliefs existed, such that some mentally disturbed persons were sought after as oracles and soothsayers while others were stoned, feared, and hated. Socrates probably suffered from a form of mental disorder, possibly a hallucination or even paralysis. It has been written that, "From early youth . . . it frequently happened to Socrates . . . that he was restrained . . . by compulsions from within. . . . a voice [he attributed] to a god or a spirit . . ." (Gomperz, 1901, p. 87). In addition, he was described as having remained motionless in the open from early dawn on one day through that night and finally moving again the next dawn. Rather than being diagnosed as possibly mentally disturbed, Socrates' voices were considered as a "prophetic gift" from the gods, and his paralytic state was interpreted as a confirmation of his "powers of concentration" that enabled him to focus all his energies on his thoughts, ignoring his surroundings or the passage of time (p. 47).

### Hippocrates and the Physical Bases for Disorder

The Golden Age of Greece also brought a great surge in the development of both science and philosophy, and with the development of science and medicine came a new understanding of psychological disorders.

The man to whom much of this achievement is attributed was Hippocrates (circa 460 –377 B.C.). This remarkable Greek, known primarily as the father of medicine, may well have also been the father of psychiatry. As a person who believed in the value of keen, systematic observation, it was inevitable that he recorded the first diagnostic description of *melancholia* (severe depression) and spearheaded the study of the causes of mental disorder.

Hippocrates was also the first to explain abnormality in terms of physical causes. In an era when most people believed in divine causation, Hippocrates recognized that psychological symptoms could have physical origins. Injuries, infections, and physiological changes could all affect a person's psychological state. For example, Hippocrates (*Corpus Hippocraticum)* described mental confusion from high fevers (possibly malaria) or from certain liquids (possibly alcohol). In addition, Hippocrates noted that a person's lifestyle could also be a factor in his or her mental well-being. In a famous treatise (*Regimen*), he promoted the value of exercise, careful dieting, and proper hygiene, to protect one's physical health—a threefold lifestyle prescription similar to modern health principles.

In these ways, Hippocrates' ideas seem strikingly modern and represent an important change in people's perceptions of mental disorder. The search for physiological roots of mental disorder is still very much alive today (see Chapter 4), and there are many drug-based treatments that are based on this theory of causation.

Hippocrates was an original thinker groping in the darkness surrounded by mysticism, biases, and lack of systematic knowledge. Thus, despite his own genius, he was subject to misconceptions of his own. One of the foundations of his theory of physiological causation was the belief that the four principal elements of the universe were represented in the human body. Thus, yellow bile was derived from earth; black bile from water; blood from fire; and mucus from air. Mental disorder, according to Hippocrates, was the result of an imbalance of the body's fluids—for example, an excess of black bile would lead to melancholia. This theory no longer finds much support today. Furthermore, some other of Hippocrates' explanations might also raise an eyebrow or two. For instance, we may agree with his general theory that environmental stress can cause emotional disorders. However, we would argue with his conclusion that a fair-skinned woman had conceived a dark-skinned child because of deep emotional stress at her first sight of an Ethiopian tribe.

### Plato and the Soul and Aristotle and the Body

Two other Greek thinkers we remember today also contributed to ancient understanding of mental disorders. Plato lived at roughly the same time as Hippocrates (circa 427–347 B.C.). His psychology, as illustrated in *The Republic,* was in a sense regressive, for it accepted the importance of the divine. The rational soul was seen as divine; the irrational soul as mortal, the source of all impulses and feelings and the cause of madness. Mental disorders, and in effect all human emotions, were relegated to a lower level of humanity. In a more positive direction, Plato did call attention to psychological phenomena such as dreams as being the expression of unexpressed desires (Alexander & Selesnick, 1966). In this way, he anticipated the later work of Freud, who not only believed that the unconscious influenced dreams, but also devised a method for interpreting these unconscious symbols. Despite Plato's judgment that emotions were inferior, he also insisted that the mentally disturbed deserved care rather than punishment. This provided the foundation for later development of special temples for the mentally disturbed. For example, such a temple was built in Alexandria, dedicated to the god Saturn and used as an asylum for treatment through rest, exercise, and music.

Aristotle (384–322 B.C.) did not dichotomize human behaviors as clearly as did Plato. Rather than dividing psychological reactions into healthy and unhealthy or divine and mortal, he saw behavior as a succession of interrelated events. An unhealthy reaction could well serve as a necessary first stage of productive functioning. Thus, for example, the poet Marascos was able to write brilliantly only when suffering from *mania*, a highly excitable, impulsive condition (Isensee, 1845). Aristotle shared Hippocrates' view that psychological disorders have an organic or physical basis (*De Anima*). Because the mind, in Aristotle's view, was impregnable to illness, the body was the only agent through which abnormal mental states could be derived. This organic viewpoint is reflected in the modern-day search for physiological causes and cures for mental disorder, as described in Chapter 4.

### Roman Conceptions of Mental Illness

Although the Age of Rome is well remembered for its military accomplishments, this era contributed relatively little to the science of medicine. Superstition and mysticism returned. (One citizen's epileptic seizure, for instance, was treated as a bad omen, such that a special citizens' meeting was called to discuss it.) Treatment of mental disorders consisted mainly of "harsh, corrective measures," such as the application of chains for restraint. Hunger, punishment, and fear were all used in the attempt to bring the insane to their senses. The theory was that the mentally disturbed had to be taught to attend, so that "he could learn and remember what he was doing" (Celcus, 1935, p. 303).

The Roman world did make some contributions to the understanding of mental disorders, however. What Hippocrates was to Greek medicine, Galen (130–200) was to Rome. Seven centuries separated these two men who were so much alike in temperament: both were vehement in their attacks and outspoken in their beliefs. Galen was an eclectic, a person who neither preached nor denounced a single theory. Instead he selected, collected, and coordinated the best of all accumulated knowledge. He is best known for his idea that an affected part of the body need not be the part where the disease resides (*De locis affectis*, Galen, 1976). The principle of *consensus* states that a symptom can develop in "sympathy" to the actual locus of the disease. This point of view leads directly to the modern-day treatment caution: "Be sure to treat the illness and not the symptom." This is especially true in cases of hysteria or conversion disorder, where it is obvious that the symptom, such as blindness, does not originate in the retina itself. Overall, Galen contributed little that was original to medical thought or practice. However, he did much to synthesize views concerning the brain as the center of the soul, the relationship between mental disorders and the soul, and the role of the environment as it affects the mind.

## THE DARK AGES AND THE RETURN OF DEMONOLOGY

After the death of Galen in 200 A.D., there were few medical advances. By the fall of the Roman Empire in the fifth century, a dark era of superstition and medical ignorance returned to blanket Europe. The Dark Ages extended to the Renaissance in the 15th century, and the historical context of this period is especially relevant to our story.

The most striking aspect of this era was the supremacy of the church. The earlier Greek and Roman advances in science and medicine went contrary to the church's belief that the world was controlled by divine powers: thus, these teachings were banned as pagan. The treatment of mental disorder reflected this change. It became the domain of the priest more than the physician. Indeed, holy chants and invocations were as crucial to the doctor's set of cures as were medicinal preparations.

### Demonology

To explain the causes of mental disorders, priests and physicians alike looked again to demonology. As in the early cultures of the Egyptians, Chinese, and Hebrews described previously, mental disorder was believed to be caused by possession. The devil and his cohorts were thought to take control of individuals, in some cases against their will, and sometimes by invitation, as a result of a voluntary pact. In the latter case, the possessed person was called a *witch.* Often, groups of people could be simultaneously possessed as is discussed in Focus 2–1.

One case is told of a valet living in France named William who had been "tormented and possessed by the Devil" for 14 years. While others prayed on his behalf, he poured strange objects from his mouth, including a girl's wig, feathers, pieces of clothing (Weyer, 1967, p. 80). On being questioned, William claimed his sickness was caused by a woman who had breathed on his face, cursing him with this evil. Later, he confessed that the objects did not really come from his stomach but had been secreted in his mouth, from which he pretended to vomit them. Even then, William proclaimed that the devil had possessed him to lie and had even given him the various objects to place in his mouth.

Because mental disturbances were attributed to

## FOCUS 2–1:
### Medieval "Mass Madness"

During the Dark Ages, from about 1200 to 1400, mass madness became common. As the Black Death (bubonic plague) raged across Europe killing millions, beliefs in demonology and witchcraft spread. Panic often affected large groups. One religious sect took to wearing long white robes with red crosses on the front and back and going from town to town. These *flagellants* as they were called stopped in marketplaces, formed a circle, stripped themselves to the waist, and whipped themselves. This self-mutilation was held twice during the day and once at night, as atonement for the sins that led to God's sending the plague (Russell, 1972).

Another mass outbreak involved *tarantism* or dance frenzy. First, people would dance and whirl about frenetically, presumably because they had been bitten by a tarantula spider. However, observers would themselves become "infected" and large masses of people would fill the streets, dancing themselves to exhaustion.

The belief in *lycanthropy* also had a recurrence, whereby persons believed themselves to be wolves. This affliction traces back as early as Nebuchadnezzar (605–562 B.C.), the king who rebuilt Babylon and who believed himself suffering from lycanthropy. As late as the 16th century, as prominent a physician as Jean Fernel (1497–1558) of France considered lycanthropy as a legitimate medical entity.

*A modern-day Italian* ***flagellant*** *is bloodied from a crown of thorns and other self-inflicted punishment.*

the devil, it seemed only fitting that diagnoses would become directed toward identifying evidence of the devil's influence. For instance, *anesthesias*—patches of insensitivity on the skin—were seen as marks of collaboration with the devil, who was thought to have touched the person on the affected area. Such signs, known as *stigmata diaboli,* were later deliberately sought during the Inquisition, as sharp implements were used to poke a suspect until an insensitive area was found.[1] Detailed descriptions of the types of devils responsible for troubling the soul in different ways were developed to serve as reference for diagnoses and treatments. One such encyclopedia work, *Demonology,* is attributed to a monk named Psellus (circa 1020–1105). He seems to have been particularly well suited to the task, since he himself was plagued by hallucinations.

The Inquisition, which began in 1484, served to formalize the hold of religious emotionalism over medical thought. Pope Innocent VIII charged the clergy with the task of finding and destroying all witches, who were thought to be responsible for all the social ills, storms and droughts, and plagues that beset Europe.

*During the Inquisition, sharp or heated instruments were used by* ***inquisitors*** *to force confessions. Women were often suspected of being witches.*

### The *Malleus Maleficarium*

A text known as *Malleus Maleficarium* (The Witches' Hammer) was born out of the zealous fervor of the Inquisitors. It was a religious document that once and for all replaced scientific analysis as the basis for fact (Summers, 1928). *Malleus* proclaimed that witches and devils did exist and that they were responsible for the inhuman symptoms that appeared in humans. The text also provided a listing of symptoms (such as the *stigmata diaboli*) by which witches could be recognized; and it prescribed treatments for people found to be witches. In addition to not being sensitive to pain in some parts of the body, a person was judged a witch if satanic objects (such as a defiled cross) were found in the home, if the person lived in a locale where an unnatural event occurred (such as cows not giving milk), or if the person gave birth to a deformed infant (proving that copulation with a demon had happened). In fact, a person might be suspect even though the witness making the accusation harbored a grudge, as long as this was not "mortal hatred." Women were particularly singled out as subject to becoming witches, since "they are feebler both in mind and body . . . have slippery tongues . . . are weak . . . and vindicate themselves by witchcraft. . . . are more credulous [and easy to corrupt, and more tempted by] 'carnal lust' " (Summers, 1928, pp. 43–44). All of these traits are derived from the fact that women came from the inferior rib of Adam and have evermore been imperfect. At least one set of historians, however, suggest that this sexism derived from increasing promiscuity among church members—underground connecting passages between monasteries and nunneries were said to confirm this (Alexander & Selesnick, 1966). To regain control, the church initiated an antisexuality movement, blaming women for tempting the men.

With the emphasis on identifying sin and pronouncing punishment, the *Malleus* completely shifted the interpretation of disturbed behaviors from being signs of illness to being signs of deviltry. This book,

1 These same signs were recognized by Jean-Martin Charcot to be symptoms of hysteria, as readers will see in the discussion of 19th-century developments.

therefore, marked the end of all prior gain in psychiatric medicine. The simple phrase, "This is contrary to true faith," proclaimed the diagnosis; and confirmation that a disordered individual actually was a witch was often obtained by cruel tortures, all with the approval of the church.

In cases where a person seemed to be possessed against his will, the complicated ritual of *exorcism* was prescribed to cast out the demons who inhabited the hapless victim. The following was an often used exorcism:

> Let him first make a good confession. . . . Then let a diligent search be made in all corners and in the beds and mattresses . . . [for] instruments of witchcraft. . . . The bodies of animals bewitched to death are at once to be burned . . . and he should change his house and dwelling. . . . And let him who is to be exorcised hold in his hand a Holy Candle . . . and begin the Litany at "Our help is in the name of the Lord" . . . and recite the Psalm "Haste thee, O God, to deliver me"; and let him continue the Litany for the Sick, saying at the Invocation of the Saints, "Pray for him and be favourable; deliver him, O Lord." . . . Also let the Gospel St. John, "In the beginning was the Word," be written and hung around the sick man's neck. . . ." (Summers, 1928, p. 184)

If this exorcism failed, many others were available, including shouting insults. Being proud, Satan might de part if the insults wounded his pride (Deutsch, 1949). Of course, if exorcism and insults did not work, then treatment might involve burning at the stake. This was considered valid on the reasoning that one destroyed Satan by destroying his host. From such a point of view, we can clearly see that the Dark Ages had little room for scientific improvement in the treatment of mental disorder.

## THE RENAISSANCE: THEORIES OF THE MIND EMERGE

The seeds of a revolution that would come bursting through were quietly planted while the darkness still enveloped science. From Johann Weyer came a calm, reasoned attack that would eventually remove the authority of the *Malleus*. And from certain philosophers would come theories about the mind.

### The End of the *Malleus*

Even at the height of the *Malleus*, historical events would lead to intellect eventually conquering the Inquisition. Possibly the greatest contributor to this effort was a German physician named Johann Weyer (1515–88). Unlike many of his vituperous medical predecessors, Weyer was a tranquil, composed, sedate man, unshaken by the swirls and struggles of ignorance that surrounded him. Weyer was the first physician to "specialize" in mental disorder; so in this sense he was truly the first psychiatrist. Well versed in the Bible, he slowly and methodically removed the aura of authority from the *Malleus Maleficarium*, repeatedly referring to the Bible itself to refute the Inquisitors' document (*De Praestigiis Daemonum*, 1563). According to Weyer (1886), persons who "imagine[d] themselves to be animals" (p. 303) were ill rather than sinful. Furthermore, he argued that God would want his people to use their God-given talents to discover the cause of such illness, instead of simply condemning such unfortunate patients.

From our modern vantage point, we credit Weyer with breaking the church's grip on medical psychology—an accomplishment that permitted the renewal of interest in mental disorder as sickness rather than possession. Unfortunately, Weyer was ahead of his time, and his ideas did not immediately gain favor. It was, ironically, his very area of specialization that was used against him. As personal physician to Duke William, Weyer had full responsibility for the duke's health when a cerebral hemorrhage struck. When Duke William developed the mental symptoms associated with a stroke, Weyer's enemies were quick to seize the opportunity to conclude that the physician was a sorcerer. Weyer's ideas were not forgotten, however, and they gradually gained support from other corners.

### Philosophy and Theories of the Mind

The Renaissance was a time of rebirth of philosophy as well as science. The theories of the mind that began appearing during this period were to become a necessary background for those who eventually wished to understand the normal mind, while the progress in medical thinking was to provide a foundation for those who would treat the abnormal mind.

The French philosopher and mathematician René Descartes (1596–1650) offered the view that mind and body interacted with and influenced each other. This idea was developed to the point that he even located the anatomical site of the interaction in the pineal gland, at the base of the cerebrum (Descartes, 1649). Although we no longer accept this literal anatomical link between the mind and body, the mind-reacts-to-body/body-reacts-to-mind idea is still reflected in modern psychosomatic medicine.

In England, somewhat later, two other philosophers, John Locke (1632–1704) and Bishop Berkeley (1685–1753) expressed another view that is highly relevant in our understanding of abnormal psychology today. These two thinkers spearheaded the view that physical reality may well be less significant for understanding the human than reality *as experienced* by man (Berkeley, 1709; Locke, 1700). Viewed in the context of abnormal behavior, a hallucination is often more real an influence on a psychotic's behavior than the real-life surroundings. Indeed, as we will see in Chapter 12, therapists such as R. D. Laing (1964) argue that the disturbed actions of a psychotic are really quite meaningful to the patient, and the therapist should make every effort to understand the meanings.

## THE EIGHTEENTH CENTURY: NOSOLOGIES, REFORMS, AND HYPNOSIS

If people's ways of thinking about mental disorder began to change in the 17th century, this transformation gained momentum in the 18th century. Three developments of this period comprise a seemingly unconnected mixture of activities; yet all had an important impact on the diagnosis and treatment of mental disorders. The first of these was the 18th-century passion for classification systems or *nosologies;* the second, the emerging spirit of hospital reform; and the third, the arrival of Anton Mesmer's spectacular new therapy, now known as hypnosis.

### Diagnosis and Classification Systems

The desire to classify things into orderly categories pervaded the 18th century. This was the time when Carl Linnaeus was offering his systematic classification of plants and animals (such as *homo sapiens*); Johann Scheuchzer was grouping 1,500 fossils into categories; Guyton de Morveau and Antoine Lavoisier were working on the nomenclature for chemistry; and William Smith was successfully describing the various successions of geologic formations.

This practice also extended into the study of the mind, and it was reflected in the development of various schemes for classifying mental disorders. The German, Georg Stahl (1660–1734) was an opinionated and often morose man who was the first to divide mental disorders into those of organic or physiological origin, and those of functional or psychological origin. Others added their schemes until a proliferation of diagnostic systems developed; one earnest physician wrote three volumes with 326 pages devoted to identifying various forms of mental illness.

Others added their own unique principles for diagnosis and classification. Franz Gall (1758–1828) developed a procedure known as *phrenology,* whereby diagnoses were made according to the presence and shape of bumps on the cranium. Examples can be found in Focus 2–2. Johann Lavater (1775) put forth a similar system for diagnosis. According to his science of *physiognomy,* certain facial features and expressions belied mental characteristics. A person who looked like a fox would be said to also be sly and intelligent like a fox.

Certainly, progress in psychiatry was hindered rather than helped by this overabundance of highly inventive but confusing productivity. Even if it was misdirected, however, the activity did reflect the return of medical interest in the clinical observation of mental disturbance. As such, it was a basic element in the beginnings of psychiatry as a specialized branch of medicine.

### Hospitals and Hospital Reforms

Until the end of the 18th century, there were few special treatment centers for people with mental disorders. For most of these individuals, hospitalization or imprisonment were still all they could hope for, and hospitals were often indistinguishable from prisons.

The infamous Bedlam hospital (actually St. Mary of Bethlehem in London) and La Bicêtre in Paris were both dismal places where the insane were kept in darkness, with neither nourishment nor attention for their basic needs. Patients were known to live in their own excrement. Guards considered the inmates as exhibits rather than human equals, and they supplemented their income by charging a fee to those who wished to be entertained by the sight of a madman's antics. For a time, this was the progress that was made from the Dark Ages: the mentally ill finally escaped burning at the stake, only to fall into the dungeons of despair and isolation.

The 18th century saw a rebirth of humanitarianism, however, and conditions began to slowly (and unevenly) improve. The most dramatic hospital reform was initiated by Philippe Pinel. In the fall of 1793, he took over La Bicêtre and proceeded to follow his conviction that the insane needed only "fresh air and . . . their liberty." He carried his plea to the revolutionary government, only to be met with suspicion and doubt regarding his political motives in seeking such reforms.

No permission was granted, yet neither was Pinel expressly forbidden to reform La Bicêtre, provided he accepted full individual responsibility for the consequences. And so, Pinel released a small group of inmates from their chains. Among these were an English officer, who had not seen the sun in 40 years of internment, and a French soldier, who was feared to be insanely violent. In changing the prison atmosphere, Pinel also provided more nourishing food, better ventilation, and kinder treatment.

The effect was remarkable, for the inmates responded dramatically to the more humane conditions. For instance, a priest who for 12 years had believed himself to be Christ was helped to recover in ten months (Zilboorg & Henry, 1941). The most heartwarming story of all, however, concerns the former French soldier, who Pinel had employed as a personal manservant. He was ultimately to save Pinel's life when the physician was chased by a lynch mob.

In 1795, two years after Pinel reformed conditions at La Bicêtre, he was given charge of La Salpêtrière hospital—the companion hospital to the Bicêtre, housing women. Pinel accomplished the same reforms and with similar results. In other parts of the world, such gains were evident in St. Luke's Hospital in England, Pennsylvania Hospital in Philadelphia, the Hospital for the Insane in Moscow, and the Narrenthurm in Vienna (Alexander & Selesnick, 1966).

### Mesmerism Arrives

At the close of the 18th century, two years after the American Revolution, a unique new form of therapy appeared. Anton Mesmer (1734–1815), an Austrian physician, developed a dramatic method for curing mental disorders by bringing people to a hypnotically induced crisis of sudden convulsions, fits of crying, or clairvoyance. Mesmer can only be described as a significant public spectacle: he possessed a turbulent, relentless, electrifying will to exaggerate; to proclaim his belief to both commoner and court; and to demonstrate that his cures were unquestionable, his theory unassailable, and his power unequalled. Yet, he was often successful in living up to his boasting. He was able to restore sight to one patient; and he repeatedly induced crises in groups of patients at a time. And to show that there was no trickery involved, he performed his mesmerism in public.

Mesmer's technique centered on a *baquet* or tub filled with magnetized water, from which protruded magnetic rods (or wands) and mirrors. To conduct his seancelike procedure, he would assemble his patients into a human chain around the contraption of metal and glass. In a darkened room, they heard a flowing explanation that illnesses were caused by the body's imbalance of magnetic fluid from the universe; they were told that they could be cured by restoring the proper balance. To do this, Mesmer would then touch his patients with one or more of the magnetic wands.

As can be imagined, Mesmer's technique caused quite an uproar. When the medical world was finally forced to look his way, it was with a suspicious eye. An investigatory committee was appointed, consisting of Benjamin Franklin; Antoine Lavoisier, the renowned chemist; Jean Bailly, one-time mayor of Paris and an esteemed scientist; and Joseph Guillotin, who is best remembered for his invention of a "humanitarian" execution device. What the committee saw was a volatile,

# FOCUS 2–2:
## Phrenology and Mental Disorders

Phrenologists, under the leadership of Franz Joseph Gall, postulated that mental disorders were caused by physical disorder. Since mental disorders were a condition of the mind, and since the brain was the organ of the mind, then they logically concluded that the brain was the location of mental disturbances. The disease of the brain could be traced either to diseases in other bodily organs, such as the liver, which then affected the brain; or to diseases in the brain itself caused by violations of the "natural laws of man," such as insufficient exercise, excessive use of tobacco, masturbation, or overexposure to religious fervors (Davies, 1955).

Phrenologists believed that they could diagnose the nature of the brain disease by examining the shape of the skull. They made many visits to insane asylums in order to further confirm their beliefs since psychopathology was merely the exaggeration of different functions of the brain. We will summarize a few anatomical locations of the brain, the normal function or human characteristic which phrenologists described for each location, and the abnormal traits which they believed were associated with these same locations.

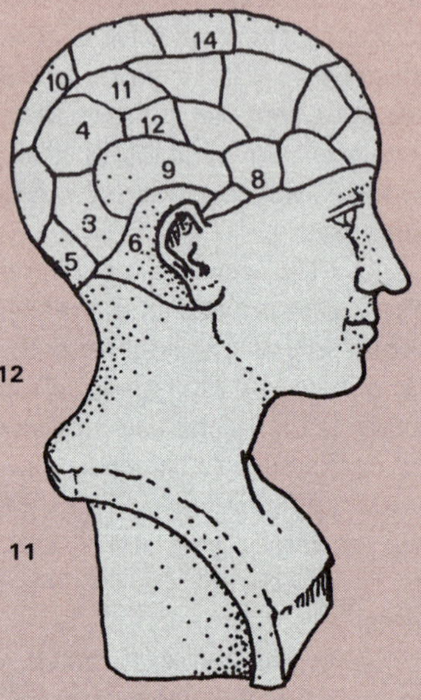


**FIGURE 2–1**

- *Inhabitiveness.* Located about the center of the back of the head. In normal level, enables attachment to living in one place and is necessary in the thoughts of historians. In pathology, an excess of inhabitiveness leads to separation anxiety as well as fear of new ideas and traveling away from home; a deficiency involves the inability to form roots.
- *Attachment.* Located at each side of inhabitiveness. In normal level, enables development of friendly feelings. In pathology, an excess causes feelings to become indiscriminately directed and can include misdirected sexuality towards inanimate objects as in DSM-III's classification, paraphilia; a deficiency involves isolation from people as in adjustment disorder with withdrawal.
- *Combativeness.* Located an inch and a half behind the ears. In normal level, enables person to be resolute and undaunted. (Cowards rub themselves behind their ears to try to excite courage.) In pathology, excess involves quick tempers and aggressiveness as in DSM-III's explosive disorder; a deficiency involves fearfulness and cowardice.
- *Destructiveness.* Located immediately above and backwards from combativeness. A normal level enables the ability to criticize and to judge. In

***Phrenologists** mapped the bumps on a person's head with instruments like this one.*

pathology, an excess involves cruelty and murder; a deficiency involves timidity. Cats are said to enjoy being scratched behind the ears in this area of destructiveness.

- *Acquisitiveness.* Located at each side of the head an inch above the ears. A normal level involves prudence in providing against want. In pathology, an excess involves addiction to stealing or to gambling for gain; a deficiency involves lack of ambition. This area is large in foxes, cats, magpies, and poets.
- *Secretiveness.* Located at each side of the head, just behind acquisitiveness. In normal level, involves mental control over confidences. In pathology, an excess involves unwillingness to share or the severe suspiciousness of paranoia; a deficiency involves a lack of discretion.
- *Self-esteem.* Located at the middle of the upper back of the head, over inhabitiveness. In normal level, it involves self-confidence. In pathology, an excess involves egotism and inflated pride; a deficiency involves self-deprecation and apathy as in DSM-III's classification, major depression.
- *Lobe of Approbation.* Located immediately above attachment and next to self-esteem. In normal level involves attention to the feelings of others. In pathology, an excess involves either high deference or the need for attention; deficiency involves insensitivity to others.
- *Veneration.* Located on the very top of the head somewhat forward of the middle. In normal level, involves the worship of God and display of obedience. In pathology, an excess involves superstitions and ritualistic behaviors; a deficiency involves civil disobedience to authority.
- *Conscientiousness.* Located about an inch to the rear of veneration and about an inch downward on each side. In normal level, enables the sense of duty and knowledge of right and wrong. In pathology, an excess involves obsessiveness or reliance on ritualistic behaviors as in DSM-III's obsessive-compulsive disorder; a deficiency involves lack of care for laws and rules (Miles, 1835).

The classification of brain functions used by the phrenologists did show awareness of differing aspects of human personality and behavior. However, the scientific foundation for such theorizing was sadly lacking.

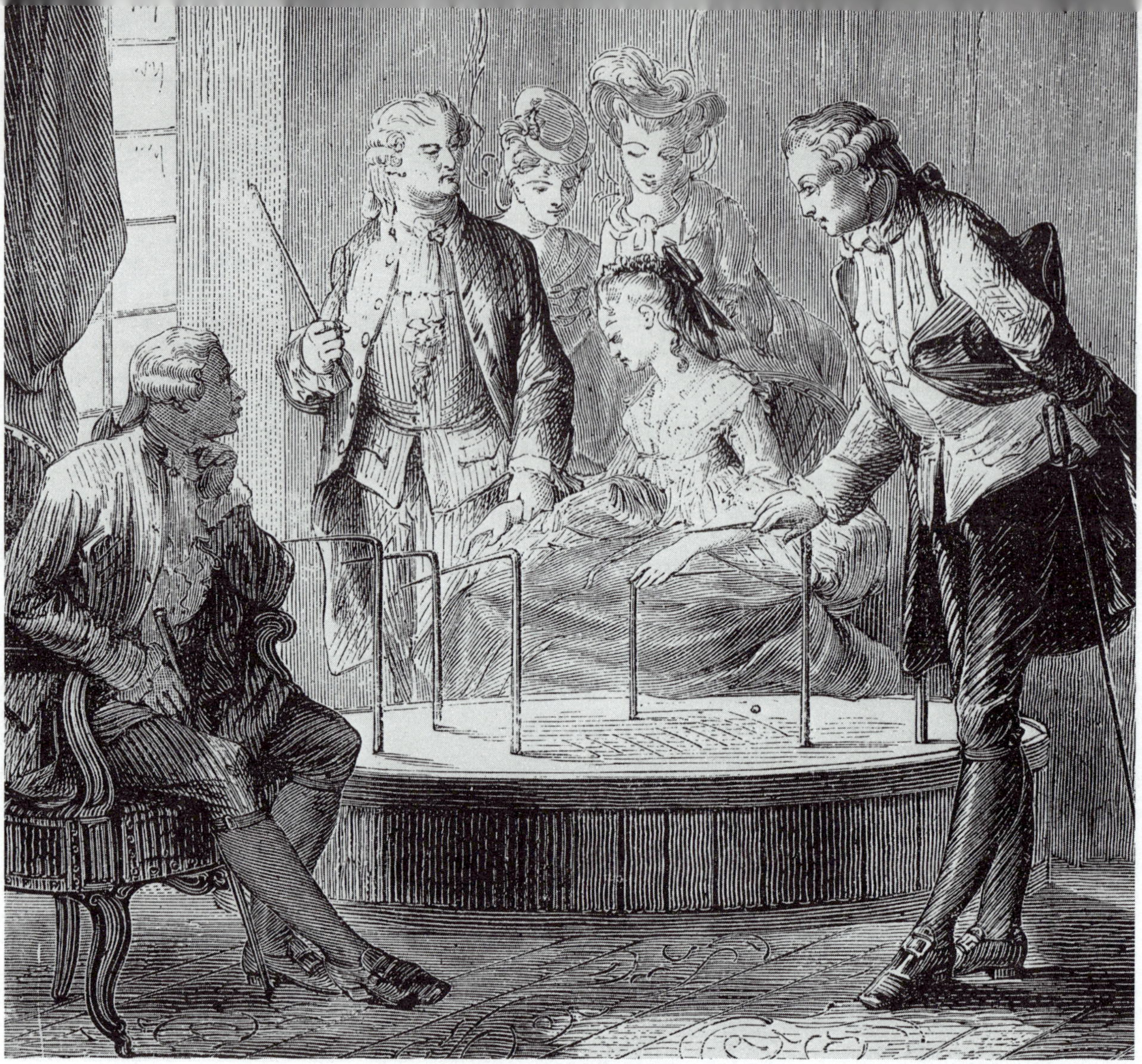

***Mesmer** attends to a woman who is experiencing a "crisis," a fainting spell considered to be a part of the animal magnetism cure.*

egotistical, aggressive man with an ambition for fame and fortune. They condemned the man as a charlatan, proclaiming that "imagination without magnetism produces convulsions . . . [but] magnetism without imagination produces nothing" (Bailly, 1784).

Despite this rebuttal, however, mesmerism continued to hold Europe spellbound for 40 years because of its dramatic appeal and the seemingly miraculous cures. It eventually even became a source of one of the basic insights in modern psychiatry.

## THE NINETEENTH CENTURY: BEGINNINGS OF MODERN PSYCHIATRY

The foundations laid by the 18th-century classifications, hospital reforms, and hypnotic techniques became the basis for much of our modern understanding and treatment of abnormality. We'll look first at the eventual outcome of Anton Mesmer's famous procedure.

### Hypnosis and Hysteria

Despite Mesmer's flamboyance, there was some undeniable truth behind his successes. The idea that symptoms of hysteria could be cured by hypnotic suggestion was a fascinating one. James Braid (1795–1860), a surgeon who was not well informed about psychological theory, had the insight to realize that the effectiveness of mesmerism was *not* in the magnetic powers of man or machine. He dispelled the charlatanism surrounding mesmerism by explaining the trances as a form of fatigue from prolonged concentration. He then related the trance states to sleeping states and renamed mesmerism by the new term *hypnosis* (*hypnos* being Greek for sleep). From this new scientific explanation, psychiatry set out to examine mesmerism for its real value. Two professionally competitive psychological service clinics, one in Nancy, France, and the other at La Salpêtrière hospital in Paris, began to examine the phenomenon of hysteria and hypnosis.

***The Nancy School.*** A French country doctor, Ambrose Auguste Liébeault (1823–1904) is considered to be the founder of the Nancy School. He was a new type of physician—unassuming, concerned not with explaining hypnosis, but with the careful improvement on the method to increase its effectiveness as a tool. Liébeault's clinic performed a service function, treating those who could not afford special care. His school and clinic emphasized trying out treatments to see what worked best, and a humanitarian concern for patients. Along with Braid, Liébeault has often been viewed as the founder of psychotherapy.

What Liébeault and the Nancy School are best remembered for, however, is their contribution to the understanding of hysteria. This disorder had been explained in various ways throughout history, as we have seen. The Greeks and Romans thought it resulted from a wandering uterus; medieval priests and physicians considered it evidence of possession and concluded that symptoms such as anesthesias were signs of the devil.

Liébeault, however, took Mesmer's amazing cures into account as he treated patients with hysteria (Liébeault, 1866), and he was soon joined by another Nancy physician, Hippolyte-Marie Bernheim in 1886. They concluded that hysteria and hypnotism were closely related, that hysteria was *self-induced hypnosis* or autosuggestion. In this way, the Nancy School differed from its nearest rival, the Salpêtrière School.

***The Salpêtrière School.*** At the same time that Liébeault and Bernheim were concluding that hysteria was psychologically based, a great Parisian neurologist named Jean-Martin Charcot reached just the opposite conclusion. Charcot (1882), the director of the Salpêtrière School in Paris, was firmly convinced that hysteria was caused by actual physical damage to the nervous system, which caused symptoms such as hysterical anesthesias or paralysis. He even believed that hypnotic phenomena were symptomatic of organic abnormality. Although Charcot thus disagreed vehemently with Liébeault, he was eventually persuaded to accept Liébeault's psychological-causation explanation when confronted with careful analyses of nearly 10,000 real hypnotic cases who failed to show organic damage.

### Kraepelin, Classification, and Disease Entity Theory

While the French were making headway in understanding and treating hysteria, Emil Kraepelin in Germany was establishing the guidelines for classifying psychoses (disorders of greater severity than hysteria).

Kraepelin described mental disorders in the same way that people had been viewing physical illnesses for years. According to his *disease entity theory,* mental illness exists as a separate and distinct disease, and all the rules that apply to physical diseases also apply to mental diseases. There are separate clusters of symptoms (known as *syndromes*) that characterize and distinguish one mental disease from another, just as the symptoms of mumps differentiate it from meningitis. And as with measles or mumps, once a mental disorder begins its course, it follows a rigid, predictable and unvarying sequence such that a prognosis can be made even during the early stages of the disorder. Detailed descriptions of *dementia praecox* (now known as schizophrenia) and manic-depressive psychoses were presented by Kraepelin as the two major psychoses. Kraepelin's treatises had a profound effect particularly on American psychiatry. The impact of his disease entity views and his clinical descriptions of the major psychoses can be felt to the present day in much of psychiatric thought.

### Hospital Reform in the United States

American hospital reform in the 19th century owed much to two pioneers, Dr. Benjamin Rush (1745–1813) and Dorothea Dix. Rush is often recognized as the father of American psychiatry and the American equivalent of Pinel in terms of hospital reform; Dix (1802–1887) played a primary role in founding a hospital system for care for the mentally disturbed.

***Rush and Moral Theory.*** Rush's reforms represented changing professional attitudes toward the mentally disturbed and the growing trend toward humanitarianism. Part of this trend was the use of *moral therapy* in hospitals. Derived from the approach of Pinel, moral therapy was based on the view that patients are simply normal persons experiencing abnormal psychological and social stresses. Treatment, therefore, was aimed at providing them with a peaceful environment, in which they were encouraged to unburden themselves in friendly discussions, to live quietly, and to engage in useful work (Rees, 1957). The results of this approach were striking at a time when very little was known about therapy. In hospitals where moral therapy was the only treatment provided, about 70 percent of those hospitalized for a year or less improved or were cured.

As was typical of the other psychiatric pioneers, however, Rush himself could not let go entirely of some of the misdirected beliefs of his time. He remained a firm user of bloodletting techniques, for instance, and even invented two diabolic curative devices: the gyrator, designed to increase cerebral circulation by spinning the patient, and the tranquilizing chair, which restrained the patient comfortably by leather straps and a wooden helmet not unlike a modern electric chair.

***Dix and the State Hospital Systems.*** American hospital conditions received a major thrust forward as a result of a truly remarkable woman, Dorothea Dix. As a schoolteacher, she volunteered to replace a nervous divinity student as the teacher for inmates in a prison. She was horrified to discover that the mentally disturbed were not only put in prisons along with criminals, but were also often chained, neglected, and abused. In fact, when she asked why heat was not provided, she was told that the insane were insensitive to heat or cold. She began collecting information and eventually visited and described 500 poorhouses, 300 county jails, and 18 penitentiaries, traveling over 30,000 miles. Through her combination

*A scene from a twentieth century mental hospital illustrates the conditions that provoked modern* ***reform*** *movements.*

of unique political skills and careful objectivity in her documentation, Dix had a primary role in the founding of 32 mental hospitals. Her greatest ambition was to convince the Congress to set aside 5 million acres as a perpetual trust, with the income to be used for the care of the mentally disturbed. Although Congress approved the bill that would have accomplished this dream, President Franklin Pierce vetoed it.

Benjamin Rush and Dorothea Dix—as well as other thinkers of their time—are overshadowed by the revolutionary insights of a physician who worked in the next century, Sigmund Freud. His contributions to our understanding of abnormality, as well as the various directions taken by the field of psychology in the 20th century, will be the subject of Chapter 3.

## SUMMARY

There is little doubt that psychological disorders have always been a part of human experience. Evidence from ancient cultures and even artifacts from the Stone Age support this assumption. Disorders have been interpreted in a number of ways throughout history, however, and in historical interpretations we can see a number of common themes.

The beliefs in organic causes of pathology is one such theme. Hippocrates in ancient Greece explained sickness as coming from imbalances in bodily humors; for example, that excess black bile created depression. This viewpoint was later seen in the statements by Jean-Martin Charcot in the 19th century, as he originally taught that hysteria was traceable to actual physical damage in the nervous system. Finally, we can see the same concept being the foundation for Emil Kraepelin's disease entity theory, that is, that mental illness followed the same type of course as physical illnesses. As Chapter 4 will show, this organic viewpoint still serves as the foundation for modern ideas about mental disorders.

Another common theme is the search for psychological explanations of pathology. Plato's analysis of dreams anticipated Freud's later analysis, as the two theorists looked at dreams as expressions of unconscious desires. By the 17th century, the idea that psychological factors were as important as physical reality reached a high point with John Locke and Bishop Berkeley; this was followed in the 18th century by the startling work of Anton Mesmer, which forced scientists to consider psychological causes of human behavior. In fact, Ambrose Liébeault interpreted hysteria to be psychologically induced through a form of self-hypnosis. As we'll see in Chapter 3, psychological origins of pathology are very much in the forefront of modern thinking about mental disorder.

A third theme across history is the gradual evolution of attitudes toward the mentally disturbed. Ancient societies sometimes viewed disturbed persons as possessed by an evil demon, while other times accepted disturbed behaviors as good omens. During the Dark Ages, catastrophes were interpreted as caused by Satan and his cohorts, witches. What would now be recognized as symptoms of hysteria were then considered as signs of possession by the devil. Naturally, treatment was unknown and was therefore replaced by judgment; and if a person were found guilty of being a witch, then burning at the stake was the likely consequence.

Johann Weyer, in the 17th century, helped break this negative outlook and promoted a more humanistic approach. Towards the latter part of the 18th century, Philippe Pinel spearheaded a revolutionary approach that literally released the mentally disturbed from chains and emphasized their treatment as human beings. By the 19th century, modern hospital reforms were evident in the work of Benjamin Rush and Dorothea Dix. The mentally disturbed had finally become elevated from the level of inferior beings guilty of dastardly sins to that of being persons deserving proper treatment and care. Issues relating to this humanistic orientation towards therapy are still seen in modern theories of therapy (see Chapters 3 and 22).

Finally, as we take an overview of the history of mental disorders, the gradual evolution towards a scientific approach can be seen. In ancient cultures, magic, mythology, and religion were often mixed into explanations about mental disorders. Even the otherwise enlightened Greeks viewed the mind as equivalent to the soul and thereby allowed their beliefs about religion and divinity to become involved. Hippocrates did provide descriptive information on some mental disorders, based on systematic observation; the Dark

Ages, however, brought a regression to beliefs in demons and devils. By the 18th century, persons such as Georg Stahl began devising systems for classifying mental disorders, while Franz Gall and Johann Lavater were offering ideas on how to diagnose human characteristics. Public debates between Liébeault and Charcot on the cause of hysteria stimulated the physicians to obtain scientific evidence to support their different opinions. And ultimately, Kraepelin's arguments that mental illness followed the same rules as physical illnesses permitted the study of mental disorders to become an acceptable branch of the esteemed science of medicine. The emphasis on scientific methodology and objectivity has continued to influence psychopathology.

## KEY TERMS

**Anesthesias**
**Baquet**
**Consensus**
**Conversion disorder**
**Dementia praecox**
**Demonology**
**Disease entity theory**
**Exorcism**
**Flagellant**
**Hypnosis**
**Hysteria**
**Lycanthropy**
**Mania**
**Melancholia**
**Mesmerism**
**Phrenology**
**Physiognomy**
**Possession**
***Stigmata diaboli***
**Syndrome**
**Tarantism**
**Trephining**

# CHAPTER 3

## Origins of Pathology: The Psychological Factors

- **What are the contributions and differences between Freudian, behavioristic, and humanistic views?**
- **How do the differences in Freudian, behavioristic, and humanistic theories affect the types of therapy they offer?**
- **How can mental disorders be experimentally created in animals?**
- **How might our sensory experiences cause hallucinations and other psychotic symptoms?**
- **What are the details of the extremely important case of the infant Albert and Dr. John B. Watson?**
- **What is our current knowledge about dreams and dreaming in relation to mental health?**
- **What arguments would we state if we were to support the contention that mental disorders are caused by psychological factors?**
- **If you were to pick a type of therapy you liked the best—psychoanalytic, behavioral, or humanistic—which orientation would you choose and why?**
- **Who is correct: Freud, who said, "You are your own worst enemy," or Pavlov, who said, "Blame those around you," or Rogers, who said, "You are your own best friend"?**

## Case History 3–1:

### FRAULEIN ELISABETH AND THE POWER OF THE SUBCONSCIOUS

Elisabeth was referred to Dr. Sigmund Freud as a possible hysterical disorder. She was 24 years old and was especially close to her father. Several later events contributed to Elisabeth's stress. Her father died and her mother became ill; her sister's husband took on the care of her mother. As the mother became worse, Elisabeth found herself fighting with her brother-in-law, who she felt was insufficiently concerned about her mother.

Elisabeth's disorder first appeared at a family holiday. She felt sensations of cold; pain radiated from her right leg and she was unable to walk erect. Shortly thereafter, her sister suddenly became ill from heart disease. Elisabeth rushed to her bedside, only to discover that she had died.

On her first visit to Freud, she appeared too cheerful, and seemed indifferent to her problem.[1] This indifference took the form of a lack of response when he pricked her afflicted leg with a pin; however, she responded with "pain" to simple pressure or pinching.

Freud (Breuer & Freud, 1957) diagnosed her case as one of hysteria and decided to use a new technique:

> I would begin by getting the patient to tell me what was known to her and I would carefully note the points at which some train of thought remained obscure. . . . And afterwards I would penetrate into deeper layers of her memories at these points by carrying out an investigation under hypnosis or by the use of some similar technique. (p. 139)

As it happened, Freud was not successful in hypnotizing Elisabeth, but he developed a substitute technique that eventually became *psychoanalysis,* a therapy method involving free association, dream analysis, and the release of unconscious feelings through talking them out.

Through therapy sessions, Freud uncovered the first clue to Elisabeth's symptoms. Elisabeth recalled becoming friendly with a young man, who loved her and persuaded her to meet him at a party. The evening was blissful, but on her return, she found her father in a worsened state. In his initial interpretation, Freud saw Elisabeth as associating her "erotic idea" (her love of her date) with the pain that had occurred when she saw her father; the result was that the love feelings were repressed, while the pain was exhibited as physical pain. The involvement of her legs became somewhat clearer as Freud discovered that the use of her legs had been associated with several traumatic events: she was *standing* by a door when her father was first brought home ill; she *stood* shocked at her sister's death-bed on arriving late; she had *walked* with her brother-in-law after discovering that her sister was ill.

One even more significant connection emerged after long, patient hours of listening (this secret had been hidden so deeply in Elisabeth's unconscious that even she had not been aware of it). Elisabeth recalled that on seeing her sister dead, she had irresistibly thought of her brother-in-law: "Now he is free again and I can be his wife" (p. 156). As Freud wrote, "She succeeded in sparing herself the painful conviction that she loved her sister's husband, by inducing physical pains in herself instead." (p. 157).

On sharing this insight with Elisabeth, Freud received dramatic evidence supporting his suspicions. "She complained at this moment of the most frightful pains and made one last desperate effort to reject the explanation" (p.157). However, Freud encouraged Elisabeth to talk about her repressed feelings until she was completely unburdened. His eventual reward, in his words, "was going to a private ball . . . and I did not allow the opportunity to escape me of seeing my former patient whirl past in a lively dance" (p. 160).

---

1 This indifference is today recognized as a common symptom of hysteria, or conversion disorder, and is known as *la belle indifference* (see Chapter 10).

As the preceding two chapters show, mental disorders have been defined, classified, and explained in many ways. What causes abnormality? There are still many explanations, varying according to the individual disorder and also according to different theories.

## ORIGINS OF PATHOLOGY

There are three primary origins or sources of abnormal behavior. First, disorders may have *psychological* origins: that is, they may derive from mental processes. Second, disorders may be *biologically* derived, relating to factors such as genetics or chemical makeup. And third, they may be caused or exacerbated by *social* conditions—for instance, a stressful family life.

These three explanations of origins of abnormality form the basis for the present chapter and the next two chapters of this text. By presenting them separately here, it is hoped that you will have a clearer sense of perspective as you read about the separate disorders in Chapters 6 to 20. It should be remembered, however, that the separation in these three chapters is an artificial one, for the psychological, biological, and social factors all interact in complex ways.

*The dynamic ideas of* ***Sigmund Freud*** *continue to influence the field of psychopathology today.*

## PSYCHODYNAMIC FACTORS: THE FREUDIAN VIEWPOINT

It is impossible to draw a clear connection between the historical events discussed in Chapter 2 and the current psychological explanations for mental disorders. However, the best place to start is probably with Sigmund Freud (1856–1939), whose insights have profoundly influenced our 20th-century understanding of human psychology. Case History 3-1 at the beginning of this chapter is an illustration of that point. Freud's interpretation of Elisabeth's conversion disorder was built on some of the most important 19th-century insights.

Freud had worked closely with Charcot in Paris and had also become familiar with the Nancy School's work with hysteria and hypnosis. Elisabeth's cathartic experience, followed by the disappearance of the hysterical symptoms, gave evidence of the immense role of the subconscious in human emotions and behaviors. From this case, Freud and physician Joseph Breuer collaborated on a discussion that expounded the first truly psychological explanation for a neurosis (Breuer & Freud, 1957), and Freud went on to explore the subconscious in greater depth.

In this step, Freud broke with the tradition of organic medicine and created his own approach to psychiatry. His *psychodynamic* approach seeks explanations for human conflicts and behaviors in the mental and emotional processes that underlie conscious behavior. His descriptions of the human psyche or mind, its normal development, and its malfunctioning are controversial in many respects. However, they remain among the leading theories that are basic to other psychodynamic approaches today (Fisher & Greenberg, 1977; Kline, 1977). We'll examine some of the key elements of Freudian theory before going on to discuss other psychodynamic approaches such as that of Jung, Adler, and Sullivan. We will then discuss two approaches that contrast with the psychodynamic one: *behaviorism* emphasizes observable events and avoids inferences about the unconscious, while the approach of *humanism* stresses human values and goals.

### Human Motivation

According to Freud, human behaviors are directed by innate psychological motives, or *instincts*. These instincts have several important characteristics:

- Instincts are believed to be quantities of *energy*.
- As energy, instincts exert pressure for release as they increase in intensity.
- The *source* of such energy is traceable to bodily states.
- Such psychic energy is goal-oriented—the ultimate *aim* is to produce effects that reduce the intensity or amount of accumulated energy.

The activities that lead to acquiring the goal, and the goal itself, are known as the *object* of the instinct. Therefore, instincts serve to guide and impel behaviors. They may do this by affecting the senses through a heightened sensitivity to certain environmental cues. Thus, a hungry person will be more likely to notice noises associated with food preparation in the kitchen than will a person who just ate; that person will also be aroused to activity that can obtain food. New instincts may appear as new bodily needs develop. For instance, an infant will be unmoved by sexual cues that some adults might respond to. While these instincts occur in all people, a common goal of humans is to minimize their intensity to reduce tension. Freud grouped the human instincts into two large categories: the *life instincts* (called eros) and the *death instincts* (called thanatos).

***The Life Instincts.*** The life instincts are impulses that are directed toward protecting and preserving the individual and the race. They include thirst, hunger, and other psychological urges which lead to behaviors that maintain life. The sexual instincts also belong in this group. These sexual instincts are not simply erotic or genital in nature: they are more broadly defined as involving pleasurable sensations through the reduction of tensions, particularly around the erogenous zones. As we'll see later in the discussion of developmental stages, Freud theorized that the focus of erogenous sensitivity shifts during the course of development from the mouth, to the anal area, to the genitals.

***The Death Instincts.*** In opposition to the life instincts are the death instincts. The death instinct is but a reflection of a universal principle of life—that all organic processes will return ultimately to an inorganic state. *Anabolism* (life-building, constructive processes) exists side by side with *catabolism* (destructive processes). Of significance is the Freudian belief that aggression is derived from the death instinct and is, therefore, a natural and powerful urge. In essence, aggression toward others is the displacement of the self-destructive instinct toward an external object. Where this is not permitted, and where life instincts are too weak to counterbalance the death instinct, self-destructiveness takes hold, either in the insidious form of masochism (self-punishment) or the form of depression or suicide.

### The Developmental Stages

In Freud's view, people's instincts or motives shift over the normal course of development; and the failure to work out ways of satisfying needs at one stage would create problems or maladjustments at later stages. He divided life into five stages: the oral, the anal, the phallic, the latency, and the genital phase. The specific ages for these stages are approximate, and Freud proposed that overlap could occur from one stage to another.

***The Oral Phase (Ages 0–1).*** In infancy, the primary source of pleasure is obtained through the mouth, by sucking and swallowing, and later, chewing and biting. This latter pair represents the oral-aggressive stage. If a person fails to develop beyond this

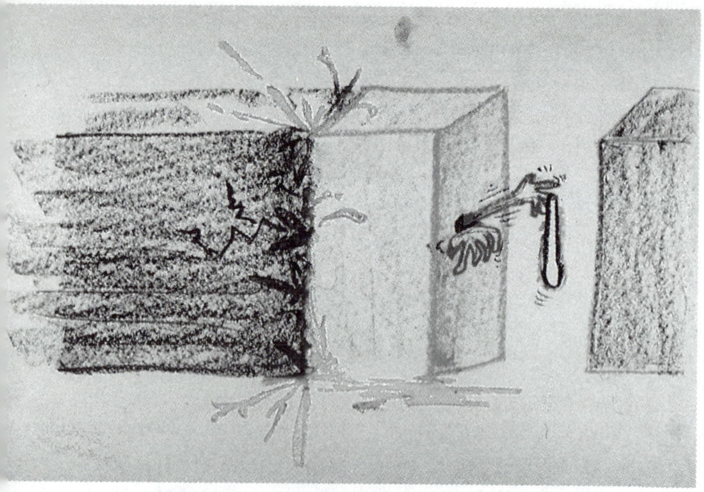

*The sketch shows the patient's powerlessness, as he is crushed between two devastating forces. This is experienced as* ***ego anxiety***.

*Powerful instinctual aggressive* ***id impulses***, *usually controlled by the ego, are displayed by the patient who made this sketch.*

phase, these traits may be prolonged into adulthood, a process called *fixation*. Thus, thumbsucking and other oral acts might carry over into adult life in the form of excessive drinking, eating, or smoking; and oral-aggressiveness might be exhibited as sarcasm or ''biting'' criticism or as verbal argumentativeness.

***The Anal Phase (Ages 2–3).*** The erogenous zones shift in late infancy. Anal stimulation becomes the dominant source of satisfaction as both the retention and the expulsion of waste products become associated with pleasant feelings.

Parents, of course, become increasingly concerned over cleanliness and bowel control during this period, and their efforts along these lines interact with the child's instinctual pleasure-seeking. According to Freud, the way the child resolves this tension leaves a mark on the adult personality. If anal excretion has met with parents' praise, general productivity and creativity will be encouraged. Anal retention during this phase, however, leads to psychological retention, expressed in obstinacy or stinginess; and anal expulsion turns to explosive fury, disorderliness, and wasteful destructiveness or cruelty.

***The Phallic Phase (Ages 3–5).*** For the first time, children direct their emotional drives toward others in their environment. During this phase, the first glimmerings of affection-seeking and vague genital sexuality appear. Children at this age want to possess the total love of their opposite-sex parent; they are envious and hostile toward the other parent, whom they view as a competitor. Freud called this response the *Oedipus complex*, after the mythical Greek hero who killed his father and married his mother. For girls, the term *Electra complex* is used. The guilt that accompanies these hostile, incestuous feelings becomes associated with a fear of retaliation, which Freud saw as being manifested in different but parallel ways in girls and boys.

In young boys, the child's guilt may lead to fantasies of punishment in the form of castration. The result is what Freud calls *castration anxiety*. (One famous case that Freud interpreted as castration anxiety is reported in Focus 3–1. The contrasting behaviorist view is also presented there.) Boys eventually work through these anxieties by repressing their sexual feelings for

## FOCUS 3–1:

### Little Hans' Phobia: Two Interpretations

Nowhere is the comparison between psychoanalysis and behaviorism more dramatic than in the case of Little Hans, a five-year-old phobic child whose case was first analyzed by Sigmund Freud, then reanalyzed, nearly 50 years later, by behaviorists Wolpe and Rachman.

Little Hans showed several symptoms of phobia. He was afraid to go into streets and feared the nighttime. He also had persistent fears that a horse would bite him. Hans' father sought counsel from Freud (Freud actually saw the boy only once during his work on the case). The father reported the fears to have something to do with "sexual overexcitation due to his mother's tenderness" and some problem with his penis. Freud was told that the fear of the night was because "a horse will come"; it was also recalled that the child had been scolded by his mother when he admitted to touching his penis.

Freud recommended that Hans' father tell the boy that the fear of horses was "nonsense," that the boy really wanted to be invited to his mother's bed, and that the fear of horses was associated with his overinterest in the penis. Freud further suggested that Hans be given sexual information about the differences between males and females. These recommendations were followed by a reduction of the phobia. However, after an illness from influenza, Little Hans' phobia returned and worsened. One new fantasy was that he was being given his bath when a plumber came in, took out a "borer," and stuck it into the boy's stomach.

Freud wrote an extensive interpretation of the case, emphasizing how the details supported basic psychoanalytic ideas. In agreement with Little Hans' father, Freud saw the basic issue as an Oedipal conflict that was symbolically represented in the phobia. The boy's sexuality was transformed into anxiety and then into a fear. The horse represented the father, so the phobia of horses really illustrated the boy's fear of the father and the father's retaliation for the boy's fantasized seduction of the mother (present during the bath-plumber fantasy). Hans' eventual complete recovery was explained as resulting from the insights his father gave him in informing the child about the symbolism and the eventual resolution of the Oedipal conflict.

The case of Little Hans has often been cited in support of Freud's psychoanalytic interpretation, but behaviorists Wolpe and Rachman (1960) challenged his evidence and conclusions. They point out that much of the data used by Freud to confirm his theory was secondhand. Further, they imply that the father may have been influenced by Freud not only to report things that fit Freud's beliefs, but to instruct the child about what his actions really meant.

These two behaviorists offer an alternate explanation of Hans' horse phobia. They view the phobia as the result of a conditioned fear—not a symbolic representation of conflict. They cite, from Freud's case files, the reports that Little Hans actually experienced seeing a horse fall in the street; that Little Hans had seen a friend injured enough to bleed when playing with a horse; and finally that Hans had been warned to avoid horses because they bite. Not only the phobia but also its disappearance is interpreted in behaviorist terms, for Wolpe and Rachman see it as extinction rather than Oedipal changes. They suggest that the child was continuously faced with horses in the context of more positive emotions, so that the fear was gradually replaced. In addition, the very frequency of discussions of the fear between father and child permitted the child to experience the fear stimuli again without emotionality, and even perhaps with calm.

The case of Little Hans has provoked much attention, first as a brilliant display of psychoanalytic formulations by Freud, and later as an example to be refuted in favor of an alternate theory. In some ways, neither the Freudian nor the behavioral interpretations receive validation from the case. Instead, the case simply shows how different theorists would approach the same information; Little Hans is, therefore, best viewed as a means for different theorists to illustrate and highlight their particular viewpoints. How fascinating it would have been were Little Hans not only directly treated by Freud, but also directly treated by Wolpe or Rachman; with Freud using psychoanalysis and Wolpe and Rachman using behavior therapy.

*According to Freudian theory, instinctual pleasure is achieved through oral stimulation. This may be the explanation for oral behaviors observed in infants.*

their mothers, and identifying with their fathers. In this way, they acquire masculine sexual traits. The failure to identify, the lack of a satisfactory male model, or the failure to resolve the sexual conflict are all causes of future psychopathology.

Young girls also develop erotic feelings toward their fathers. According to Freud, this occurs mainly through *penis envy,* the girl's recognition that her father possesses an object she lacks—a penis. Penis envy is the female corollary of castration anxiety in Freud's theory, and its successful or unsuccessful resolution affects the girl's future adjustment. Normally, the girl gains vicarious satisfaction by identifying with her mother. The failure to make this adjustment shows up in various traits which Freud considered to be maladjustments. In "masculine protest," for instance, the woman continues to envy the male role but competes with men by entering traditional male occupations. Other signs of unsuccessful resolution may include feelings of inadequacy, sexual confusion, and promiscuity.

***The Latency Phase (Ages 5–12).*** Prior to puberty, a period of quiescence appears, as instinctual drives and sexual concerns become less important for a time. During this period, children's friendships are confined mostly to members of the same sex, and they often express an aversion toward those of the opposite sex. It is as if a phase of consolidation and taking stock occurs. The practice of sex-role behaviors is strengthened, with boys engaging in masculine interests and endeavors and girls participating in feminine role patterns.

***The Genital Phase (Ages 12–Adulthood).*** The adolescent again experiences the stirrings of sexuality. As long as the Oedipal conflict has been properly resolved, children can adjust to these new instincts, which are channeled into true feelings of concern, altruism, and eventually mature genital love. For psychological development to reach this peak, however, each of the earlier steps has to have contributed its share. Failures to develop through and beyond any early phase can block the adjustment of this genital phase. In addition, if adjustments in earlier stages have been weak or borderline, or if earlier impulses have been met with too lavish gratification, the adolescent may *regress,* or return to that earlier stage during stress.

### The Structure of the Psyche

The end product of the normal developmental stages just described is a well-adjusted adult personality. According to Freud, this personality is a composite of three parts that gradually reach an equilibrium in the course of development, but that still often come into conflict with one another. He called these three parts the *id,* the *ego,* and the *superego.*

***The Id.*** The *id* is everything that exists of personality at birth: it includes all psychological processes, including the instincts, in their most primitive form. If one visualizes a hungry newborn infant, all the characteristics of the id can be imagined:

*The Freudian concept of* ***masculine protest*** *hypothesizes that because women are envious of the male role, they actively compete with men. Women's involvement with traditionally male roles may be a form of such a protest.*

- Demands for immediate gratification. The id is characterized by attempts to seek *immediate* release of tension through whatever means available. Freud named this characteristic the *pleasure principle*.
- Ineffective acceptance of unreal substitutes. The id may momentarily be placated by fantasy substitutes, including, for instance, imagining food.
- Irrational, or nonrational, thinking pervades. Thought patterns are not necessarily logical, so that contradictory needs may exist side by side, and magical or superstitious beliefs can occur.

The id is the earliest part of the human personality that exists in the infant, according to the Freudians.

***The Ego.*** As people mature, other psychological processes become more differentiated. Thus, individuals' mental development includes the ability to separate reality from fantasy, to think logically, and to rely on memory of past experiences to determine courses of action. The *ego* is now said to exist. It is characterized by:

- The capacity to delay immediate gratification, or to elect avenues for instinctual satisfaction along socially acceptable lines. This characteristic Freud called the *reality principle*.
- The competence to cope with the realities at hand, instead of being dominated by instinctual demands.
- The ability to differentiate self-identity from the identities of others. The person is aware that others exist, that the universe goes on beyond the self, that crucial events take place outside of subjective experiences.

The ego forms the foundation for perceiving and reacting to reality.

***The Superego.*** As the ego enables the person to become aware of and appraise the presence of others, a third system is stimulated into development. The *superego* is the internal representation of the moral values, code of ethics, and rules for living established by parents and other significant figures. If the ego is concerned with the terms of reality, the superego is more concerned with the attainment of the ideal. If the id is continuously striving after pleasure, the superego is continuously pressing for perfection. If the ego evaluates the environmental situation in order to determine the least dangerous course of action, the superego evaluates the course of action itself to determine its acceptability according to moral standards.

The superego is characterized by:

- An ever-watchful concern for the rightness or wrongness of actions.
- Demands to live up to high standards, without regard for the reasonableness of such expectations.
- Efforts to control instinctual gratification through the powerful tool of raising guilt feelings.

In the normally functioning personality, the id, the ego, and the superego processes all blend in a balanced way. Id mechanisms are associated with stirring a person to activity, ego functions involve alternative choices of courses of action, and superego processes influence selection of choices based on value judgments.

### Anxiety, the Psyche, and the Defense Mechanisms

Anxiety plays a central part in Freud's psychodynamic theory, and this emotion ties in closely to his descriptions of the psyche.

According to Freud, anxiety can derive from three sources. *Reality* or *ego anxiety* derives from the dangers that exist in the real world, such as punishment from parents or others. *Moral* or *superego anxiety* is less concerned with externally based punishment and more oriented toward the threat of internal punishment in the form of guilt feelings produced by the superego, or conscience. *Neurotic* or *id anxiety* stems from a concern that the instincts will become so powerful as to overwhelm the person, forcing actions geared to impulsive gratification. Since these anxieties provoke tension, we seek to get rid of the threat which created the anxieties.

Ordinarily, coping takes the form of realistic problem solving: we reduce ego anxiety by learning to behave in ways that are acceptable to parents or to society in general. We learn to act in ways that are consistent with our moral standards, thus reducing superego cation of needs in order to reduce neurotic or id anxiety.

Another important way to reduce anxiety is through the use of defense mechanisms. Freud identified several of these defense mechanisms, many of which are described in Focus 3–2. According to Freud, defenses are erected for one purpose: to prevent or reduce anxiety. This may be helpful and healthy, as defenses free the person from the debilitating effects of anxiety. Thus, defenses play a role in the normal personality. Throwing darts at a dartboard to vent anger toward a roommate is an example of displacement, for instance; and becoming an actress, according to Freud, may be a way of *sublimating* (that is, productively channeling) exhibitionist tendencies.

### Freud's Theory of Abnormality

Now that we are familiar with Freud's basic ideas about developmental stages, the structure of the psyche, and anxiety and defense mechanisms, we can better understand his theory of abnormal behavior. According to Freud, pathology can develop because of improper development within any of these three aspects of personality concepts.

Developmental stages are important, since fixation at a stage means the person will show the immaturity and problems characteristic of that stage. Further, if a traumatic experience is not properly managed a person may react later in life by regressing to an early developmental stage that was more gratifying. For instance, a child who could not properly resolve the demands of the anal phase might become fixated on the conflicting pleasures of excretion and the parental demands for bowel control. As the person grows to adulthood, these conflicts remain and the person may show the neurotic trait of obsession about actions and decisions, that is, of going over and over little details instead of acting. Freud would interpret such behavior as a reenactment of the person's anxiety about whether to give in to parental wishes to withhold, or to act on one's own impulse to excrete.

Imbalances within the structures of the psyche can also be a source of abnormality. Ordinarily there is a healthy balance among the ego, superego, and id. However, if there is a lack of equilibrium, then one of the systems could become overly dominant. If it is the

# FOCUS 3–2:
## Focus on the Anxiety Defense Mechanisms

According to Freud, people use defense mechanisms in order to reduce tension-producing anxieties. Some of the defense mechanisms postulated by Freud follow.

*Defense.* **Denial**

*Definition.* The conscious refusal to admit to a factual event.

*Example.* Children may cover their eyes and deny that a television monster is still on the screen; or a person may argue, "It can't be true" when told of cancer or the need for surgery.

*Defense.* **Repression**

*Definition.* An unconscious exclusion from consciousness of threatening material.

*Example.* Forgetting the undesirable parts of a prior experience while remembering only the good times; excluding deep feelings or even physical urges, such as sexual arousal, because these are unacceptable.

*Defense.* **Suppression**

*Definition.* A conscious excluding of threatening material.

*Example.* "Counting to ten" to avoid being angry; or repeating over and over again, "I will not get angry. . . . I will not. . . ."

*Defense.* **Rationalization**

*Definition.* Offering a justification for otherwise unacceptable impulses or actions.

*Example.* The fable of the fox who could not reach the grapes and is forced to leave, muttering, "It's a good thing, they were probably sour anyway."

*Defense.* **Reaction formation**

*Definition.* Adopting impulses and actions directly opposite to those we possess but find threatening.

*Example.* The person in conflict about sexual needs, who crusades against pornography or "sex in any guise, shape or form."

*Defense.* **Projection**

*Definition.* Initial repression of a trait, then attributing it to others.

*The defense mechanism called **displacement** involves acting out toward a safer substitute object. This child can be aggressive toward her doll without fear of punishment.*

*Example.* The hostile person who represses the hostility but accuses others of being "out to get me because they hate me."

*Defense.* **Displacement**

*Definition.* Discharging an unacceptable impulse toward a substitute target.

*Example.* An angry employee just scolded by the boss who takes it out on the family through child abuse.

*Defense.* **Sublimation**

*Definition.* Routing an unacceptable impulse into a socially acceptable channel.

*Example.* The aggressive person who becomes a police officer, joins the military, or becomes a surgeon.

Finally, in Freud's theory of abnormality, the presence of defense mechanisms can contribute to pathology. For instance, among the common defenses is *repression*, the banishment of material to the unconscious. Once repression occurs, the repressed information is essentially irretrievable, and henceforth the individual is forced to function without the advantage of the information. Also, repression takes energy that must be continuously activated, otherwise the unwanted material can reappear in slips of the tongue, dreams, or vague feelings of unease. Such continuous commitment of energy can be extremely wearing and fatiguing.

As another example, *displacement*, another defense, can also lead to a neurosis, as in sexual disorders where a person displaces love impulses toward an inanimate object. Freud saw an association between characteristic defenses and several specific pathologies. For example, he saw repression as involved in conversion disorder, as in the case history at the beginning of this chapter. Reaction formation and projection were seen as steps in paranoia related to homosexual impulses: ''I love that person . . . this is unacceptable. . . . I hate that person (reaction formation). . . . No, I don't hate that person; that person hates me (projection).''

*According to Freud,* ***toilet training*** *can have a significant impact on a person's personality, particularly if it was traumatic.*

id, then powerful id impulses may force primitive, thoughtless, impulsive actions that may even be dangerous. The murderer who leaves the message, ''Please stop me before I kill again,'' on his victim's mirror may be expressing a loss of impulse control. An overly rigorous ego may so override the id as to remove all traces of spontaneity, leaving the person incapable of enjoying the normal pleasures in life. And if the superego is too dominant, it becomes a harsh, perfectionistic taskmaster plaguing the person with guilt and inhibitions.

## OTHER PSYCHOANALYTIC THEORISTS

Freud's great insights were to spur stimulating but sometimes heated debate among his followers. Eventually, these disagreements led to several revisions of the basic Freudian tenets, as well as new versions of psychoanalytic theories. Although accepting the basic Freudian psychodynamic approach, these psychoanalysts added concepts of their own. Jung, Adler, and Sullivan are among those who have contributed important new ideas.

### Jung and Analytic Psychology

Carl Jung (1875–1961) had studied with Freud in Vienna. However, he disagreed with Freud regarding the

*Carl Jung, once a student of Freud, started an important school of his own. His approach is known as analytic psychology.*

instincts, the emphasis on early childhood, and aspects of the unconscious. Jung (1953) did not accept Freud's attention to human sexuality as the major emphasis and goal in life. Although life energy is expended for sexual propagation of the species, Jung stated that it also is employed for cultural, creative, and spiritual goals.

***Life Stages.*** Freud's conception of the developmental stages stopped with the genital stage, when individuals reached adulthood. Jung's theory, however, encompasses human development on to later years. In very early life, according to Jung, energies are invested in survival; and during adolescence, such energy is involved in sexual values. The peak of energies and vitality is reached during the early adult years, with career, family, a role in life being important values. In middle age, however, physical vigor and personal goals are replaced by wisdom, and cultural and philosophical issues become more important. In this way, Jung's approach has greater optimism and meaning for older persons than Freud's.

***The Collective Unconscious.*** One of the most fascinating but controversial aspects of Jung's theory is the concept of the collective unconscious. Jung postulated that we all have unconscious memories, not only of the history of the human species, but also of prehuman history. Events that have occurred repeatedly are stored in the *collective unconscious.* It is this unconscious that helps to explain common phenomenon, such as our eerie feelings when isolated in the dark, or the repeated themes of good and evil in folk tales, religions, myths. Jung's writings on this topic have been influential in studies of anthropology, religion, art, and Eastern mysticism.

***Personality Structures.*** Basic to Jung's theory is the premise that several facets of personality exist side by side. First, we are all said to have both masculine and feminine characteristics. In men, the masculine nature (the *animus*) is dominant, while in women, the feminine nature (the *anima*) dominates. Masculine qualities are symbolized by dominance, strength, and power; feminine, by nurturance, sensitivity, and tenderness. We also are said to possess either an extraverted orientation (directed towards the outside world) or an intraversive orientation (directed towards our inner or subjective world).

***Pathology.*** Jung explains pathologies in some ways that involve psychodynamic forces. First, maladjustments may develop as several related conscious and unconscious experiences build a cluster, or *complex,* of emotions, memories, and residual feelings. A person might develop a "power complex," for instance, that consumes all thoughts and interprets all actions in terms of dominance over others. Hitler's actions are interpreted by Jungians as reflecting this lust for power. Another explanation for pathologies is an imbalance of the personality, where one aspect becomes overly dominant and the weaker aspects are suppressed. Thus, an overly strong *animus* in a male can suppress the *anima's* qualities, producing an inability to feel tenderness or care for others. This one-sided animus becomes displayed in symptoms such as extreme competitiveness or even cruelty. Another source of pathology results from certain parts of the unconscious becoming too autonomous through being ignored or suppressed. In a psychosis, there is a collapse into the collective unconscious, as archaic feelings or bizarre symbolic behaviors take over control.

### Adler and Individual Psychology

Alfred Adler (1870–1937) founded the theory of individual psychology. Like Jung, he also broke with Freudian theory, to the extent of being denounced by traditional analysts of the time. He differed with Freud in his attention to social factors and in his concepts of inferiority and the creative self.

***Social Motivation.*** While Freud assumed that individuals are motivated by innate instincts, Adler looked at social motives, saying that people are social beings first. This interest is present at birth and is eventually expressed in group cooperativeness, social relations, and activities directed toward benefiting society. People are not totally without selfish motives, however; and Adler also hypothesized that individuals strive for perfection and *self-actualization,* that is, the development of the self to the fullest.

***The Creative Self.*** In Adler's view, individuals each develop their own unique style as they strive for superiority. Thus, while everyone shares this same goal of actualizing, one person may elect a direction that is intellectual, while another develops interpersonal or physical talents. The creative self is a difficult concept to fully define. It seems not only the guiding force in the search for actualization, but also the filter which gives meaning to life, interprets events, influences attitudes towards the world, and unifies the person. The creative self, the seeking of actualization, and the social altruism proposed by Adler make his theory a precursor of the humanistic approaches discussed later in this chapter.

***Pathology.*** Perhaps the best known of Adler's hypotheses is his suggestion that we are born with a deep sense of inferiority. In the infant's view, everything is larger, better, stronger, and more competent than the self. This perception normally prompts striving, growth, and achievement. However, this does not always occur. One aspect of pathology involves the failure to overcome this early sense of inferiority. Perhaps because of a life of too many failures, the person becomes mired in self-defeat and retreats to childish behaviors, in search for a time in life when a small level of success had occurred. Another aspect of pathology can take just the opposite course. The individual may respond to defeat by increased striving, until the search for success becomes all-consuming. We tend to identify such persons as driven or to view them as selfish or as power hungry.

### Sullivan and the Neo-Freudian School

Harry Stack Sullivan (1892–1949) was the first American psychiatrist to develop a significant theory. His views—as well as those of Erich Fromm and Karen Horney—are representative of the *neo-Freudian* school, which breaks from Freudian theory in its stress on sociological factors and its basic belief in the positive qualities of individuals. While Sullivan wrote only one book (1947), he left a legacy of many lectures and numerous notes. He especially emphasized the interpersonal nature of man, the role of the self, and cognitive variables.

***Interpersonal Psychiatry.*** Sullivan repeatedly argued that individuals do not exist in isolation, but always in an interpersonal context. We manifest who and what we are when we are interacting; and even when alone, we still remember, think about, and imagine the presence of others. People, therefore, become an important part of any individual. Thus, anxiety may originate when we empathically tune in to the display of anxiety in a significant other person.

***Cognitive Concepts.*** Sullivan's analysis of the role of *cognitions,* or thought processes, has had an important influence on our understanding of psychology. First, he observed that thought experiences evolve through a developmental process. In infancy, thoughts or consciousness are simply unconnected experiential moments. Later, a sort of low-level recognition of causality appears, so that the child, for instance, considers two events occurring near each other to have causal associations ("I was bad . . . My mother became hospitalized . . . I caused my mother to become sick because I was bad"). Finally, a higher-order logic appears, enabling the individual to validate his or her thoughts by discussing them with others. Pathology can develop if the more primitive cognitions are held onto and never questioned.

*Personifications* are another example of cognitive processes. These are the stereotypes we form of other persons and of the self. For example, a child may personify the father as authoritarian, mean, and threatening. Later, older men in general may also be personified in this way, with this personification governing relationships.

People also form personifications of their own selves, leading to *self-concepts.* Consistent with his interpersonal emphasis, Sullivan saw self-concepts as formulated through experiences with other people. Thus, if parents respond to children in negative ways, these children will develop a negative self-concept (the personification of "the bad-me"). A positive self-concept (the "good-me") results when people see that others think highly of them. In Sullivan's view, these stereotyped personifications of the self are difficult to change once they are established. A person who learned to think of herself as clumsy as a child, therefore, may always feel awkward.

**Pathology.** Sullivan believed that security from anxiety is a basic human motive. Like Freud, he postulated that we develop security or defense mechanisms to protect ourselves from anxiety; but unlike Freud, Sullivan saw the source of anxiety as contact with other people rather than as subconscious impulses. Early in life, the infant becomes anxious if the parent is anxious, through empathy. Later, the child becomes anxious on sensing disapproval from others. Maladaptive attempts to defend against anxiety can lead to neuroses or psychoses.

The nature of the self-concept is still another possible source of pathology. As mentioned earlier, a person may have adopted a distorted self-image of being clumsy or slow, and may go through life with this self-evaluation. Finally, pathology can also be related to cognitive styles or personifications. In a psychosis, the person loses an adult mode of thought and returns to an earlier, more primitive set of cognitions about causality. Pathological personifications or explanations—such as "I am a prophet" or "I am not successful because authority figures are always mean and unkind to me"—are accepted without being questioned.

## LEARNING FACTORS: THE BEHAVIORISTIC VIEWPOINT

The behavioristic or learning theory offers a very different perspective on both normal and abnormal behaviors. The behaviorist relies on terms and rules of behavior derived from studies of behavior, rather than the psychodynamic forces of subconscious emotions. Behaviorists criticize the psychodynamic interpretation on several counts: its reliance on inner forces that cannot be directly observed; its lack of attention to environmental influences; and its heavy dependence on early childhood experiences to explain current behaviors. One group of behaviorists (Bandura, 1968; Eysenck, 1960; Ferster, 1961; Staats & Staats, 1963; Wolpe, 1958) propose an entirely different scheme for classifying disorders (see Focus 3–3). Four leading behavioristic approaches to pathology will be reviewed here. They include classical conditioning, operant conditioning, social learning, and cognitive behavior modification.

### Classical Conditioning

Ivan Pavlov (1849–1936), the Russian physiologist and Nobel Prize winner, made a discovery that has become a significant part of modern psychology: he saw that learning can take place through a process called *conditioning.*

Pavlov (1897) made his discovery during a series of studies of digestion in dogs. He had been aware that food placed in a dog's mouth would stimulate salivation, but in the course of his experiments, he also observed that the laboratory dogs were salivating before the food reached their mouths. Because these secretions were not connected with direct stimulation of

## FOCUS 3–3:
### A Behavioral System for Classifying Disorders

Albert Bandura, Arthur Staats, and Carolyn Staats have offered a behavioral classification system as an alternative to the classification of DSM-III. Their scheme emphasizes stimulus events and behavioral dispositions as the key to classifying disorders.

Categories of behavioral problems are:

*Behavioral Deficits*

These maladjustments involve the absence of normally expected skills. For example, an *autistic* child (a form of psychosis) may lack the ability to speak, may fail to respond socially to people, and may demonstrate poor emotional responsiveness. In effect, the main difference between the autistic child's behavior and that of normal children is the fact that the normal behavior occurs with less frequency in the disturbed child (Ferster, 1969).

Behavioral deficits occur through a variety of conditions. Since patterns of behavior are acquired through the imitation of social models or through reinforcement, the absence of good models or rewards can lead to behavioral deficits. For instance, the parent may have been too preoccupied to respond to the child or too disinterested in the child to show approval. Of course, a deficit may also derive from organic or physiological sources, for instance in mental retardation.

*Defective Stimulus Control of Behavior*

Abnormality may sometimes appear as unresponsiveness to stimuli in the environment. People with pathological symptoms will often exhibit deviant behavior despite their family's or friends' pleas that they change. An example of a failure to respond to environmental cues would be the person who expresses merriment during a funeral service.

Basically, defective stimulus control involves a failure in *discrimination learning:* that is, the individual doesn't learn to respond one way to one stimulus and another way to a different stimulus. Normally, discrimination is developed if the individual perceives differing consequences for responding to different stimuli. Failure to learn to discriminate may occur if the consequences of behavior do *not* differ when the stimuli differ. If a mother never followed through on her directive to her child, for instance, the child would soon pay her no heed.

*Inappropriate Stimulus Control of Behavior*

This is the inappropriate association between certain stimuli and certain responses. Phobias are a good example. A phobia involves the arousal of intense fear by inappropriate stimuli, such as harmless animals. Behaviorists explain inappropriate stimulus control as a result of classical conditioning. The classic example of this process is Watson and Raynor's experiment with little Albert and a white rat.

*Defective Incentive Systems*

This kind of behavior occurs when rewards that are ordinarily capable of controlling behavior fail to influence an individual. In pathology, praise and recognition do not seem to encourage wanted behavior; conversely, criticism and censure do not discourage it. In its extreme, we have a person who is nonresponsive to the surroundings, for example a withdrawn schizophrenic. The so-called habitual criminal may well be one who not only does not respond to social rewards, but who also reacts adversely to such reinforcers (Cairns, 1961).

Many of our social incentives, such as praise or recognition, acquire their reinforcing value through early association with primary reinforcers. In contrast, defective social incentives result from the absence of such early associations.

*Inappropriate Incentive Systems*

Here, certain inappropriate stimuli acquire reinforcing value. For instance, sexual deviations may involve the responsiveness to unusual cues, such as articles of clothing or animals.

*Aversive Behavioral Repertoires*

These are behaviors, such as aggressive actions, dependency behaviors, and attention-seeking activities, that lead to aversive consequences to others. The way in which aggression becomes part of a person's behavioral repertoire is becoming better known (Goldstein, 1983). Certainly one of the most common reactions to frustration is aggression, and so aggressiveness may be explained as a sign of frustration in some cases. Aggression may also be learned through reinforcement, as when an individual learns that hostile threats cause others to give in. Finally, aggressiveness may have been learned through modeling; for example, through seeing someone else rewarded for violence (Milavsky et al., 1983).

In the behaviorist's view, an inappropriate incentive system develops from the association between a primary reinforcer and a socially uncommon or deviant stimulus. A mother, for example, might always give her child a stuffed animal to hold when she comforts and carries him; this animal will now acquire reinforcing value (becoming a secondary reinforcer). Had she instead provided the child with a shoe or a scarf, the child might develop a positive association with these other items.

*Most fears are* ***learned,*** *sometimes from parents. This child has not yet learned to be afraid of his plaything, a live snake.*

digestive-linked senses, he initially called them "psychical secretions." Pavlov (1904) later discarded these explanations, referring to the phenomenon instead as a *conditioned reflex.*

The procedure used in his laboratory is known today as *classical conditioning:* a neutral cue such as a light (the conditioned stimulus) is paired repeatedly with a cue that is part of a reflex, such as the presentation of food to the mouth (the unconditioned stimulus). With continued pairings, the conditioned stimulus will be able to elicit the same reflex response, such as salivation, even when the unconditioned stimulus is no longer present.

***Watson and the Conditioning of Human Emotions.*** Pavlov's discovery of classical conditioning became basic to the theory of behaviorism founded by John B. Watson (1878–1958). Watson (1919) believed that people could be studied and viewed in the same manner as animals, since observable behavior was the only critical unit for study. Ultimately, he proposed, *all* behavior will be predictable if we know what stimuli are presented.

Watson's famous laboratory study, and his major contribution to psychopathology, applied classical conditioning principles to human emotional responses (Watson & Rayner, 1920). Watson's subject was nine-month-old Albert, a normal young infant. At the beginning of the experiment, Albert was without fears of any type and responded with naive infantile interest when shown a white rat. After some hesitation, Watson assured himself that an experiment in conditioning would be acceptable. For seven trials, Albert was shown the rat but was also severely frightened at the same time by the experimenter's sudden banging on a metal bar. This pairing of the neutral cue (conditioned stimulus) of the animal with the fear-producing sound (unconditioned stimulus) followed the traditional Pavlovian model. The outcome: Albert not only became fearful of the little white rat, he also generalized his fear to a rabbit, a dog, a fur coat, and even a ball of white wool.

This case quite clearly demonstrated that classical conditioning could lead to the development of phobias. It has been cited in support of the belief that many, if not all, phobias are acquired through a paired association between an originally neutral cue (such as the rat) and a fear-producing cue (such as the startling sound). In this way, Watson would outrageously claim, the human learns to fear no differently than Pavlov's dog learned to salivate, and without the complexities theorized by Freud. Several other experiments have also provided insights about the extent to which pathologies can be predictably created in the laboratory (see Focus 3–4).

***Conditioning as Therapy.*** Readers may wonder at the ethics of experiments which create pathology, especially in an otherwise normal infant such as Albert. Albert did not remain with him long enough for

Watson to determine how to eliminate the phobia. However, later experimenters did use behaviorist methods to treat such problems. Mary Cover Jones (1924), with Watson's advice, used conditioning methods to remove an animal phobia in a boy named Peter, who showed a remarkable similarity to Albert in his fear of animals, furs, and cotton wool. In her treatment of this modern case of "Peter and the Rabbit," Jones removed the fear of the rabbit by gradually introducing it when Peter was happily engaged in play with three other children. By the 45th session, the boy's cure of his fear extended to the point where he was actually willing to fondle the animal.

This shift of concern to the problem of *removing* abnormal behavior through conditioning methods was also applied by Mowrer and Mowrer (1938) to *enuresis,* or bedwetting. They attributed this problem to the child's inability to respond to cues of a full bladder when asleep. To teach the child to respond to these cues, they devised an apparatus that awakened the child in response to bladder tension, by setting off a loud bell the moment a little urine was released onto a special pad placed on the mattress. The technique was remarkably successful.

### Operant Learning and Reinforcement Theory

A second behaviorist approach is known as *operant* or *instrumental* learning. This type of learning was first described by Edward Thorndike (1874–1949), and the theory was later refined by Clark Hull (1884–1952). These theorists demonstrated that, in addition to classical conditioning, learning could also take place when rewards or reinforcers occur. According to Thorndike's *law of effect* (1905), behaviors that are followed by satisfaction tend to be strengthened; and those followed by discomfort are weakened.

The full development of this law was reached in the work of Hull, who presented rules of behavioral acquisition and elimination stated in mathematical terms. He perceived, first, that rewards influence the strength of a response. Thus, presenting a strong incentive will cause a person to work harder. Also, Hull noted that the removal of a reinforcer leads to the elimination of a response—as when an employee stops working when paychecks stop coming. Finally, Hull perceived that responses can become attached to stimuli as a result of the presence of reinforcement, thus becoming what we call habits. For instance, a child develops the habit of responding "good morning" to the sight of a parent if this has been rewarded with a pleasant smile or hug.

According to Thorndike and Hull, the principle of reinforcement can be illustrated in much of the learning we do. It is a primary step in our learning how to talk, for instance. As children, we make many sounds. Those which approximate the sounds our parents want to hear are rewarded, by praise, a warm hug, or being given what we want, with the result that children learn the language of their parents.

***Reinforcement Theory and Pathologies.*** There is also evidence that reinforcement can shape the development of pathologies. Masserman (1961) used reinforcement procedures to develop apparent masochistic behavior in laboratory cats. Although cats show an intense dislike of sudden blasts of air, he was able to train these animals to actually administer these air blasts to themselves by rewarding them with food. By this method, animals were also trained to seek electric shock, severe loud noises, and rancid odors, provided that reinforcement always followed the behavior that triggered the painful stimulus. Perhaps this is all akin to the story of the woman who chose to wear extremely tight shoes, two sizes too small, despite the excruciating pain. Her explanation—"I do it because I feel so good when I finally take them off!"

The kinds of laboratory experiments used by Masserman have had valuable implications for learning theorists interested in studying human disorders. If abnormal *symptoms* can be viewed as abnormal *responses,* and if abnormal responses can be viewed as subject to the same principles of learning as other acquired responses, then perhaps this is the key to the origins of psychopathology.

Other learning theorists have expanded on this conception of the origin of abnormality. According to Dollard and Miller (1950), neuroses are learned in the same ways that normal behaviors are acquired. Just as a child learns to say "I'm hungry" and is fed, a soldier may develop an hysterical paralysis because it serves a need (that of removing him from the situation that is producing anxiety). It is not necessary that the person know what is happening; the soldier may be entirely

# FOCUS 3–4:
## Psychological Factors in Mental Pathology: Some Experimental Evidence

To what extent can pathologies be predicted on the basis of an individual's experiences? Some experimental evidence supports the view that psychological factors—such as frustration, conflict, sensory deprivation, and even dream deprivation—can play a predictable role in mental pathology.

### *Frustration and Conflict*

A number of studies have exposed animals to irresolvable conflicts. The result: experimental neurosis.

Possibly the earliest experiment of this type was that conducted by Pavlov through conditioning. He presented a circle during the feeding of a dog, with the result that the animal soon began to salivate at the sight of the circle. The circle is thus considered an *excitatory stimulus.* He also presented a different stimulus, an ellipse, during times when the dog was not fed. The dog learned to inhibit his activity at the sight of this *inhibitory stimulus.* In a classic experiment, Pavlov gradually changed the shape of the ellipse until it was so similar to the shape of the circle that the dog could not tell the difference. The effects were impressive: the dog began to howl, struggle, and rip at its restraining harness with his teeth. It lost its ability to respond correctly even when the ellipse was restored to its original shape. Pavlov concluded that an acute neurotic condition had been duplicated.

### *Conflict and Aversive Stress*

Pavlov produced experimental neurosis through an impossible discrimination task, without other external stress. Later scientists, such as Masserman, produced breakdowns by using aversive stress to create a conflict.

Masserman (1943) trained cats to obtain breaded salmon by pressing a switch. When the cats had become thoroughly accustomed to this procedure, the experimenter added a new element

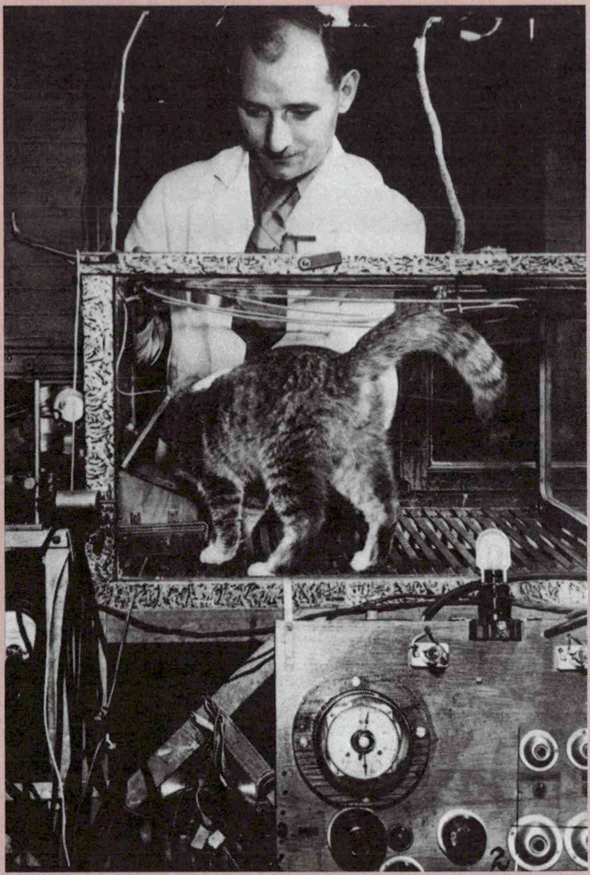

***Experimental neuroses**, involving phobias, psychosomatic ailments, withdrawal, or obsessive-compulsive behaviors, have been produced in cats. Masserman (pictured here) accomplished this by subjecting the animals to an approach-avoidance conflict in the food box.*

that was highly aversive to the cats: a mild blast of compressed air blew across a cat's snout as it began to eat the salmon. After two to seven such experiences, the cats began showing behaviors markedly similar to human neurotic symptoms, including irrational fears of closed spaces, caged mice, and air currents; psychophysiologic illnesses such as asthma and convulsions; peculiar ritualistic behavior, such as circling the food bin three times to the left and head bowing prior to eating; and loss of responsiveness to the environment. These disturbances were apparently the result of the approach-avoidance conflict, whereby the cats were simultaneously attracted (by the food) and repelled (by the air blast).

### *Sensory Deprivations*

Pathological states have also been produced in humans through sensory deprivation. Bexton et al. (1954) quite accidentally became aware of some peculiar effects of sensory deprivation while conducting a military study on the effects of prolonged monotony, such as radar screen watching. Subjects were paid $20 a day for doing nothing other than remaining quiet on a comfortable bed. They wore translucent goggles, gloves, and cuffs to prevent sensory variation. Before long, they became extremely uncomfortable, restless, irritable, and showed impairment in the ability to think on simple problems. Most experienced hallucinationlike types of experiences, ranging from seeing light changes with eyes closed, to seeing a "procession of squirrels with sacks over their shoulders marching 'purposefully' across a snow field" (p. 74).

Similar emotional effects have been subsequently obtained by others. Suinn (1969) observed hallucinationlike reactions in some subjects undergoing brief sensory limitation of one hour's duration. Hebb et al. (1954) stuffed the ears of paid subjects with just enough cotton to make normal hearing difficult. Variable personality changes occurred in these subjects: one reacted with marked irritability to the point of nearly hitting a woman; another developed overwhelming feelings of personal inadequacy.

### *Dream Deprivation*

Even more fascinating studies concern dream deprivation. Dement (1960, 1965, 1974) conducted experiments with humans and cats in which sleeping was permitted but dreaming was prevented. The dream state is identifiable by the occurrence of rapid eye movements (REM)(Aserinsky & Kleitman, 1953). In his experiments, Dement allowed his human subjects to remain asleep as long as they did not have a dream; but he systematically awakened them as soon as he detected a REM state.

Several things happened. One subject became so disturbed after three nights of dream deprivation that he left in a flurry of contrived excuses. Personality changes were apparent in others: anxiety, irritability, and difficulties in concentration all appeared. And marked changes in eating occurred, along with weight gains up to five pounds from increased food intake. Of importance is the fact that none of these results occurred when subjects experienced the same number of interrupted awakenings during the evening provided that awakenings occurred *after* a dream had run its normal course (Dement, 1960).

These studies raise the tantalizing question of the possible relationship between dream deprivation and mental disorders. If personality changes can be contrived in the laboratory after only a few nights of dream deprivation, is it possible that there is a link between some mental disturbances and an inability to dream?

unaware of the relationship between his symptom and need reduction. In fact, evidence on learning indicates that learning without awareness does occur. In many cases of neuroses, the critical reinforcing event is simply the reduction of anxiety or fears from conflict. As long as the reinforcement continues, the neurotic solutions will persist.

***Reinforcement-based Therapy.*** This conception forms the basis for some reinforcement-based therapies. By this approach, the goal of therapy is to set up conditions whereby a patient will learn adaptive or normal behaviors, in place of the maladaptive or pathological behaviors. First, the therapist defines what behaviors are desired. Among hospitalized psychotics, for instance, normal behaviors are defined as showing self-care, being more communicative, and controlling their bizarre symptoms. The second step is the introduction of reinforcers; in many programs in hospitals, the reinforcers are tokens which purchase privileges for the patient. In the third step, the patients are presented with the reinforcers each time the desired normal behaviors are shown. This approach has received great success in retraining psychotic patients who have been living on chronic hospital wards, nearly vegetating for years. In fact, the term *token economy wards* was created to refer specifically to the use of reinforcement therapy approaches (Atthowe, 1973; Krasner & Atthowe, 1968).

### Social Learning

The *social learning approach* of Albert Bandura (1971, 1977) has introduced two additional facets of behaviorist theory: the learning process of modeling, and the concept of self-efficacy.

Although new behaviors can be learned through classical or operant conditioning, Bandura has also confirmed that we learn through watching others. *Modeling* is a process whereby we acquire a new skill by simply observing and then imitating someone else. Reinforcement is not needed, and in many cases, we do not even have to practice the response. In an early series of studies, Bandura and his associates (1963) addressed the question of whether children learn aggressive behaviors from modeling. With the issue of violence on television, these studies carried enormous significance.

In a typical design, Bandura showed one group of nursery-school children an adult model who was aggressive, while another group saw a nonaggressive adult. In some studies, the modeling was live, in others it was filmed; in still others, it was in cartoon form. The aggression model involved unique violent actions, such as pummeling an inflated doll target while sitting on it. After exposure to the models, the children were put into a mildly frustrating situation, where their behavior was observed. The results were shocking. The children who had watched the aggression model not only showed more total aggression in their actions, they also seemed to aggress in the ways used by the models. Such laboratory studies are consistent with other findings that one of the best predictors of assaultive behaviors in children is the display of violent behaviors by their parents (Pfeffer et al., 1983; Lewis et al., 1983).

Bandura has also offered the concept of self-efficacy as a unifying construct to explain behaviors, thoughts, and emotional states. *Self-efficacy* involves our own judgments about how well we think we can function. We form such judgments in several ways: through experiences with previous accomplishments; through watching how others perform; through social influence by others; and through physiological arousal states. To take the example of using a skateboard, you would perceive yourself as capable of riding a skateboard if you had had prior successes with a skateboard, or perhaps roller skates or a surfboard. You also would be more likely to feel capable if you watched someone skateboarding whose characteristics you felt were equal to your own (If she can do it, I can do it); if someone you trusted told you you could succeed; or if you noted through physiological cues that you didn't feel anxious about performing. In Bandura's view, if we believe we can perform a task, we will persist longer in trying, despite obstacles or aversive experiences. If we feel incapable, however, we will be less likely to try as hard, and we might also feel anxious or depressed.

Bandura feels that therapy often works in changing perceived efficacy. For example, a person can overcome a fear by participating in an experience of gradually successfully confronting a feared situation. Each success increases perceived efficacy, which in

*According to Bandura, we can learn through **imitation**. These children adopted the identical aggressive acts that they observed in the adult model.*

turn reduces avoidance behaviors (Bandura et al., 1977).

### Cognitive Behavior Modification

A fourth approach to learning theory that deserves attention involves *cognitive behavior therapy.* Its exponents do not really offer an added form of learning beyond classical conditioning, operant conditioning, or modeling per se, but rather, they call attention to the crucial role of thoughts in behavior change (Beck, 1976; D'Zurilla & Goldfried, 1971; Ellis, 1962; Mahoney, 1974; Meichenbaum, 1977).

The basic tenets of this approach are that maladaptive behaviors develop from maladaptive cognitions, that cognitions develop and are influenced by the same rules as other types of behaviors, and that treatment can be aimed at changing thought patterns. In essence, the belief is that our thoughts influence our behaviors and determine our emotions. Consider the following example:

> You have just received a letter notifying you that your wedding has been cancelled. The letter is signed by your fiance. What are your feelings under each of the following circumstances?
>
> *Thought Pattern A:* "Oh my gosh, it's all off. What's happened? Is _____ mad at me . . . did _____ find someone else? Could it be that _____ really didn't care for me at all? . . . It was all a sham. I'll never find anyone else ever that I could care as much about. How can I continue living, this was the most important thing in the world for me. What a catastrophe!"
>
> *Thought Pattern B:* "Oh my gosh, it's all off. What's happened? What an opportunity, now I can give our relationship more time. We can see one another but not feel pressured into a major commitment until we're completely convinced. I know the date seems so final, any date does. Knowing how _____ feels about me, it took real character to decide to cancel. . . . I am sure lucky that _____ has such strength. . . . This shows _____ really cares about making our relationship work."
>
> *Thought Pattern C:* "Oh my gosh, it's all off. What's happened? This is so unlike _____. And the letter was so short. Something must be wrong, maybe _____ didn't write the letter . . . maybe someone else forced _____ to sign the letter . . . maybe something has happened in the family, some tragedy . . . maybe some accident happened and _____'s keeping it secret so I won't worry."

Now reexamine the feelings or emotions you experienced with each set of thoughts. Were they different? What about your actions? Would the different thought patterns lead you to want to engage in differing actions?

The cognitive behaviorist says that this demonstration is a good representation of what happens in pathology as well. Our thoughts may be unrealistic or inappropriate; yet once they are established, they affect our mood, our emotions, our actions. Within this framework, diagnosis is aimed at understanding the thought structures of the patient: "What is the person saying to himself or herself?" Therapy similarly becomes directed towards altering such cognitions. More will be said about specific cognitive therapy methods in Chapter 21.

## HUMAN POTENTIAL FACTORS: THE HUMANISTIC VIEWPOINT

Abraham Maslow termed the humanistic approach the "third force" in psychology, akin to the other two dominant forces, psychoanalysis and behaviorism. Perhaps more than these two other viewpoints, the humanistic orientation is both a philosophy and a method.

As a philosophy of the individual, humanism contrasts sharply with both psychoanalysis and behaviorism. The psychoanalytic viewpoint considers people as passive victims of inherent conflicts, growing up rapidly in a setting that is less supportive than challenging. Because of the secret power of the unconscious and the defense mechanisms individuals use for self-protection, "Man is his own worst enemy." Behaviorism, on the other hand, redirects attention to scientific laws from the laboratory, substituting the more impersonal influence of observable behavior for the dynamics of internal strife. The humanist finds this impersonality just as unacceptable as the pessimism of Freudian theory: both views limit the individual's freedom to cope with the future. The humanist believes in the individual; in the willful desire of the individual to grow towards positive aims; in the ability of the individual to reach such aims; and in the individual's personal identity as a creature of sensitivity and concern.

### Carl Rogers

Carl Rogers (1957, 1961) is recognized for his statement about self-actualization and his belief in the ability of humans to progress. Self-actualization is the search for maximizing one's inner potential. A healthy state is reached when individuals have gained their optimal level. That optimal level includes the abilities to be open and honest to experiences, to communicate accurately and freely, and to have a subjective reality that is congruent with objective reality. This is the condition of a mature, fully functioning person.

From this frame of reference, Rogers has taken psychotherapy beyond the realm of pathology, extending its use to normally functioning persons who simply want to continue to grow. His therapy has generated interest among executives, clergy, school personnel, and other healthy persons in participating in actualizing experiences. Among the procedures which have found favor are the group methods, such as training or T-groups, sensitivity groups, and marathon groups; institutes for self-study have also attracted devoted followings. These programs will all be discussed later in Chapter 21.

The self-concept plays a central role in the individual's ability to develop fully. Conversely, maladjustment develops where the self-concept does not reflect objective reality experience; where self-regard is so low as to affect performance; or where a person is so afraid or distrustful of accepting experiences as to distort them.

Given the right conditions, however, Rogers asserts that each person is capable of progress towards self-actualization; and therapy is simply a condition for enabling individuals to find themselves. The conditions for successful therapy are not stated in terms of techniques, but rather as qualities of the therapist. These qualities are an ability to experience unconditional positive regard for the client, an ability to experience an empathic understanding, an ability to communicate both, and an ability to be genuine and not artificial towards the client.

### Abraham Maslow

Abraham Maslow, like other humanists, believed in the purposefulness of the individual. He expressed a basic optimism about personal growth, and he believed in self-determinism: in other words, the individual is viewed as possessing control.

Maslow is best known for his statement of man's *hierarchy of needs*. These needs are genetically based; and if anything, they are good or neutral rather than

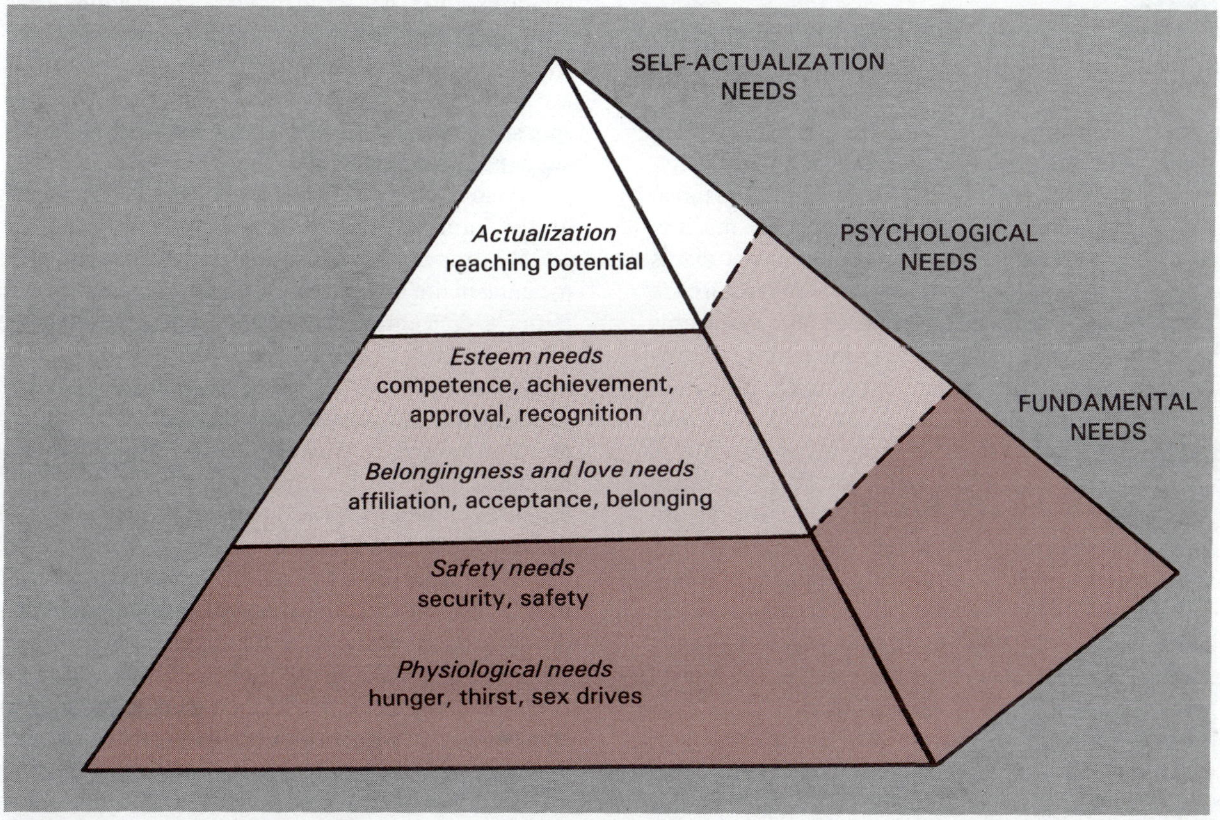


**FIGURE 3–1 Hierarchy of needs**

evil and destructive. Needs are structured along a hierarchy of layers, with the lowest being physiological or biological needs such as for food or warmth; the next layer involves safety needs or the need to receive protection from danger; then come needs for love and association with others; next are the self-esteem needs for worthiness and independence; and finally the self-actualization needs to realize our individual potentials as humans. As one layer of needs is met, then the next layer of needs can be satisfied; if a basic need is not met, then it becomes dominant over the other needs and consumes energies. This listing of needs presents a view of man that accepts the importance of physical needs, denotes the social nature of man, and also adds values which show the potential of man to transcend narrow motives. Maslow distinguishes between basic or *deficiency* needs and *meta-needs* or growth needs. The deficiency needs include needs related to hunger, affection, security, and self-esteem. Growth needs are those involving order, unity, justice, beauty, and goodness.

In Maslow's view, pathology may be influenced by the response to needs. If the deficiency needs are not met, then personal growth needs will suffer inattention. Such failures are shown in signs of alienation, apathy, and cynicism. If we become fearful of satisfying growth needs, then feelings of insecurity and threat will become foremost. The environment has much to do with need satisfactions. In an environment that is stifling, unstable, or demeaning, the effort required to just fulfill basic needs will prevent any efforts towards higher needs. This may happen in the family context, as when domineering parents prevent a person from satisfying the self-esteem needs necessary to become truly independent. The society may also play a role in hindering growth. This happens, for instance, where sex stereotyping prevents a woman from working toward a male-dominated position.

Maslow (1968) has constantly reminded psychologists that the study of all individuals is essential to the understanding of pathology; that if psychology only studies disorders, then what will evolve is a limited psychology. Toward this, he has contributed much in his own research on successful self-actualized persons, such as Lincoln, Beethoven, Schweitzer, Jefferson, Thoreau, Einstein, and Eleanor Roosevelt. He discovered them to be accepting of themselves and of others, spontaneous and open to inner experience, appreciative of deep emotional attachments, democratic and philosophical, realistic and independent.

### Frankl and the Existential View

Finally, one movement very close to humanism deserves mention. It is the *existential* approach, and it stresses the ability of humans to make decisions, to influence their own lives, to be responsible, and to be a significant part of their own world. This point of view considers it artificial to separate the individual from the environment, or to suggest that people are affected only by the environment. Rather, the existentialist claims that the environment is part and parcel of each individual's private existence, and that people can distinctly affect their world. Such beliefs are based on two premises. First, it is more important to examine a person's inner experiences than to presuppose that objective reality governs one's actions. Second, individuals are not simply a product of the past, but they are responsive to personal aspirations, goals, values, hopes, and unrealized potentials.

Among the existentialists who have had an impact on the humanistic movement is Viktor Frankl (b. 1905). Frankl's belief (1963) in the importance of meaning in life is based on his personal encounter with Hitler's concentration camps. Living through the tragic experiences of a Jew incarcerated in prison, he arrived at the insight that finding meaning in life and retaining freedom of choice are crucial. He accepts the idea that the overly scientific, mechanistic attempt to formulate people's behaviors into simple cause-and-effect associations has contributed to a feeling of meaninglessness in life. The valid human becomes lost within the abstractions of drives, or instincts, or past events. We must learn to deal with the here-and-now, deciding on the values which are our own and which we will accept. Given the clarity of values and the commitment to them, we can then gain meaning in our being and can move towards our potential. At this juncture, we will have achieved a measure of freedom and an ability to choose our own direction.

For many therapists, the existential orientation has been expressive of a fundamental attitude toward humanity that is quite compatible with humanism. Individuals are more than the sum of early childhood experiences; they are more than a response conditioned to external surroundings. In reality, each individual has a uniqueness, a need for personal growth, and a self-determinism that transcends simple comprehension.

## SUMMARY

The approach to the psychological study of pathology owes much to certain theories which give it direction. The three major theoretical viewpoints are the Freudian, the behavioral, and the humanistic. The Freudian emphasizes the dynamic interplay of unconscious forces, which are shaped early in life. Anxiety and defense mechanisms, as well as driving motivations, form the basis for pathology. The behaviorists focus on principles of how behaviors are learned or unlearned. Rules such as from classical conditioning and operant conditioning are applied to evaluating pathological behaviors. The unconscious is less important than the reinforcer or the conditioned stimulus. Humanists have reacted to what they see as the pessimism of Freud and the sterility of behaviorism. Instead they emphasize the positive, striving, forward-moving nature of man. Philosophically, they believe in certain innate strengths, which sometimes are blocked.

Experimental studies point out that pathology can be traced to certain experiences. Frustration, such as in unsolvable problems, can cause emotional symptoms. Conflict, such as in being forced to approach an undesirable stimulus, can also create stress. Deprivations of basic needs, such as for stimulation, can prompt unusual symptoms. Dream, or REM-sleep, deprivation has also been shown to be a possible cause of temporary symptoms.

## KEY TERMS

**Anabolism**
**Anal phase**
**Analytic psychology**
**Anima**
**Animus**
**Behaviorism**
**Castration anxiety**
**Catabolism**
**Classical conditioning**
**Cognition**
**Cognitive behavior therapy**
**Collective unconscious**
**Complex**
**Conditioned reflex**
**Creative self**
**Death instinct**
**Defense mechanism**
**Denial**
**Discrimination learning**
**Displacement**
**Drive**
**Ego**
**Ego anxiety**
**Electra complex**
**Enuresis**
**Excitory stimulus**
**Existentialism**
**Extinction**
**Fixation**
**Genital phase**
**Hierarchy of needs**
**Humanism**
**Id**
**Id anxiety**
**Inhibitory stimulus**
**Instinct**
**Latency phase**
**Law of effect**
**Life instinct**
**Modeling**
**Neo-Freudian school**
**Oedipus complex**
**Operant learning**
**Oral phase**
**Penis envy**
**Personification**
**Phallic phase**
**Pleasure principle**
**Projection**
**Psychoanalysis**
**Psychodynamics**
**Rationalization**
**Reaction formation**
**Reality principle**
**Reinforcement**
**Regression**
**Repression**
**Self-actualization**
**Self-efficacy**
**Social learning**
**Sublimation**
**Superego**
**Superego anxiety**
**Suppression**

# CHAPTER 4

## Origins of Pathology: The Biological Factors

- **Can you inherit mental disorders?**
- **How do we go about trying to prove that genetics is involved in mental disorders?**
- **What can we learn about pathology through family pedigrees, or what may be called ''tracing one's roots''?**
- **If you were a marriage counselor, what premarital advice would you give to a person engaged to a cured schizophrenic?**
- **Just how alike are identical twins when it comes to sharing in mental disorders?**
- **Judging from the genetic evidence, is it possible for a person to be ''born to kill''?**
- **How may toxic agents be related to mental disorders?**
- **How do the brain and your glands affect your personality or behaviors?**
- **How have LSD and amphetamines implicated norepinephrine and dopamine in mental disorders?**

# Case History 4–1:

## Heredity and Environment in Schizophrenia: The Case of the Genain Quadruplets

At midnight on April 13, Mrs. Gertrude Genain arrived at the hospital in severe pain. By morning she delivered four infant girls, quadruplets with the same heredity. Reports of what transpired at delivery as stated by Dr. Booth, the obstetrician, and Mrs. Genain disagreed on many counts: According to Mrs. Genain, the obstetrician had been expelled from one medical society for practicing abortion, and she disagreed with what he said about the delivery. Dr. Booth, the obstetrician, said that all infants were immediately placed in incubators, while Mrs. Genain said only one was; Dr. Booth, the nurse, and another physician reported that Mrs. Genain was completely anesthetized during delivery, while Mrs. Genain claimed she was conscious and heard every baby cry.

The early years showed disturbing events in the lives of Nora, Iris, Myra, and Hester,* the quadruplets. Nora experienced crying spells, Myra occasionally sat wordlessly rocking, and Iris and Hester were tied to their beds for a month, on Dr. Booth's advice, to stop their masturbating. During these years, difficulties between Henry Genain, the father, and Gertrude Genain mounted. Henry Genain became abusive to his wife, and drank heavily (Rosenthal, 1963, p.33). He had some seizures and blackouts.

Mrs. Genain showed the strains of an unhealthy marriage, and exhibited questionable behaviors of her own. The advice to tie her two girls' hands nightly was carried out by Mrs. Genain in spite of her earlier distrust of Dr. Booth, and because of her own extreme concerns about sexuality among her girls.

Despite a continuous history of family conflict and abuse, the quadruplets developed into adults without serious signs of pathology. However, at age 22, Nora was hospitalized suffering from severe agitation. She believed that others were talking about her and walking on her and feared she was losing her sight. She was diagnosed as schizophrenic. Within three months, Iris showed her first signs of emotional disturbance, involving vomiting, sleep disturbance, and a belief that people were looking at her. Soon she became agitated and panicky. She was hospitalized with a diagnosis of schizophrenia. At age 23, Hester showed extreme emotionality, kicking out with anger and clicking her tongue. She became confused, apathetic and complained of being paralyzed. Eventually Hester was hospitalized as a schizophrenic.

Meanwhile, Myra began to fear that she would be next, egged on by her father who continued to gleefully warn her that she would soon go crazy too. During her 24th year, Myra recounted an incident of an attempted seduction and assault. Afterward, she vomited, complained of blurred vision, and began to hear the voice of the man who had threatened her. Although she recalls struggling "to keep myself going"(p.149) since everyone else was sick, Myra also was soon hospitalized as a schizophrenic. Eventually, all of the quadruplets were hospitalized and all were diagnosed as schizophrenic disorder, catatonic type.

The case of the Genain quadruplets has been interpreted as an inherited predisposition to mental disorder precipitated by life stressors. In support of the hereditary nature of their disorder, Dr. David Rosenthal, who reported the case, cites these facts: all the girls experienced the same type of schizophrenia (catatonic); they exhibited the same sequence of symptoms (first underactivity, then speaking too little, then speaking too softly, then experiencing sadness, then failing to socialize, and finally being uncooperative); and they showed nearly identical personality traits early in life. Regarding the role of environmental stresses, Rosenthal points out the extreme pathology in the family life and the irrationality of both parents. The quadruplets' father was volatile, subject to rages, openly suspicious and distrustful; and he frightened and deceived his children. The quadruplets' mother was not as openly irrational. Still, her accusation concerning Dr. Booth's expulsion, as well as her complaint that he neglected her during a physical test while he was having intercourse with his nurse, were incredible. At the same time, these accusations were consistent with her general life beliefs—she accused another physician of infidelity, she accused her husband of being a sexual animal, and she embellished substantially on the causes of her four daughters' breakdowns, claiming that three could be traced to attempted rape. Personality analyses described her as a self-sacrificing, overprotective martyr—a pattern sometimes associated with schizophrenia in the offspring (see Chapter 17).

* All names were disguised to provide anonymity. Since the girls were treated at the National Institute of Mental Health (NIMH), their fictitious first names come from these initials. The surname Genain derives from the Greek words meaning "dreadful gene."

One glance,'' the medical scientist will say, ''and the organic nature of humans becomes obvious,'' for we see a body and not the mind, the brain but not the intellect, and the nervous system and not emotions. There is no question that we are made of flesh and blood; basically we are composed of a bony structure of calcium within a sheath of epidermal tissue filled out with muscles and fatty substance and interlaced with a network of nerves and blood vessel canals. Our basic biological needs have the power to influence our thoughts and fantasies—view what happens when appetite turns into hunger and takes over our senses. Our endocrine glands produce biochemical substances that affect our emotional state; for example, when adrenaline is released into the system, the results are subjectively similar to anxiety and fear experiences.

In studying the organic or biological origins of pathology, scientists have proceeded in two directions. One is genetics: To what extent are mental disorders inherited? The second involves toxic factors: Can certain mental disorders result from imbalances of biochemical substances within the body?

## THE BIOLOGICAL FACTORS: GENETICS

Although much is known about the role of genetics in lower animals, the great puzzle regarding its contribution to psychological traits in humans has plagued psychologist and geneticist alike. We know that heredity is the major determinant of certain physical or medical abnormalities; for example, red-green color blindness, hemophilia, and diabetes mellitus. Nevertheless, great controversies have arisen over how genetics influences psychological characteristics such as intelligence. The nature-nurture issue caused scientists to separate into opposing camps depending on their belief in the critical importance of heredity (nature) or of environment (nurture) in intellectual behavior.

In general, the environmental or nurture approach has been received more favorably by psychologists. As we saw in Chapter 3, there has been an impressive demonstration that environmental manipulation and reinforcement can produce behavioral change; and data regarding the formation of experimental neuroses has also been conclusive, within the limits of the laboratory (see Focus 3–4).

Yet events have developed that refocus attention on genetics. New technology now permits scientists to probe into the secrets of heredity; and at the same time, a strong relationship has been discovered between the properties of genetic molecules and certain physiological functions.

To what extent can a mental disorder—or at least a predisposition to mental disorder—be inherited? This chapter will first explore that question, then examine the relationship between the endocrine and nervous systems and mental health, and finally, the role that foreign substances may play.

### Genetics: A Review

It is appropriate to start with a short review of genetics. A rudimentary knowledge of the way traits are inherited provides a basis for understanding how genetics might also be linked to some pathologies. In our review, we will first identify the major building blocks in heredity, then discuss the unique role of genes.

***Fundamentals of Human Heredity.*** Modern genetics shows that the human cells contain elongated, microscopic substances called *chromosomes.* With the exception of the male sperm and the female ovum, each human cell contains 23 pairs of these chromosomes arranged in a spiral. Of these pairs, half represent the chromosomes contributed by the individual's father, while the other half represent those from the mother. Each chromosome is itself composed of thousands of jellylike parts, called *genes.* These genes are living molecules of a protein containing the vital substance known as DNA—*deoxyribonucleic acid*—that is responsible for determining human traits. The total number of genes is yet unknown, but present estimates range from between 40,000 to 80,000 minimum in the 23 pairs of chromosomes.

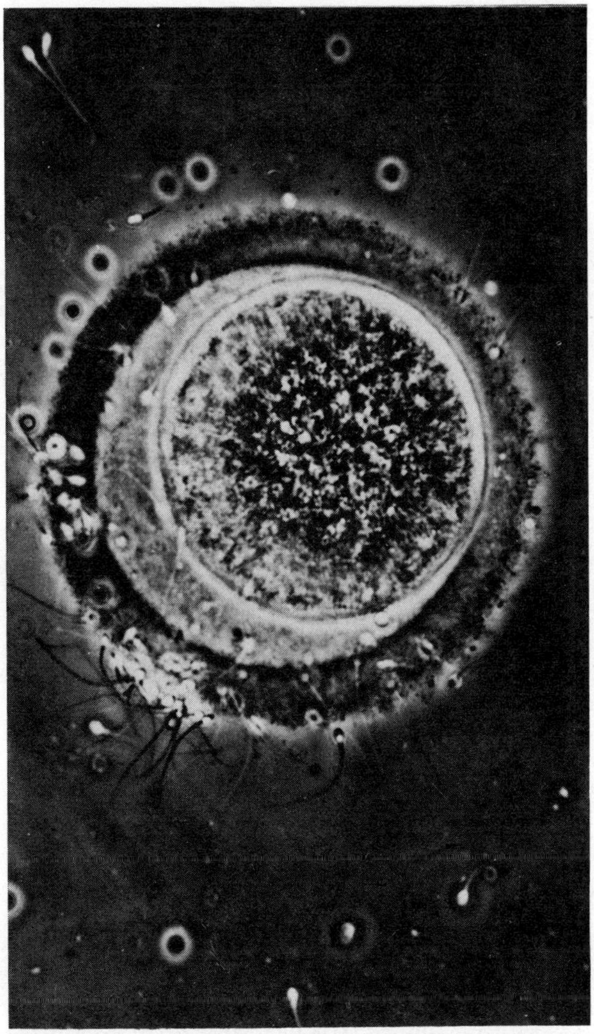

*Of the many* ***sperms*** *surrounding the* ***ovum****, only one penetrates to begin a new life.*

*How Genes Influence Traits.* Physical characteristics are determined by these genes, sometimes by only a single pair, although most traits are multiply determined. Blood type, for example, is determined by the presence or absence of the type A gene, the type B gene, or the type O gene. Every gene in any one chromosome has a corresponding partner in the paired chromosome. When both are the same—for example, if both are type A (written AA)—then the person is said to be *homozygous* for these genes. When there is a mixture—for example, if one gene is type A and the other in the pair is type B (written AB)—the person is said to be *heterozygous*.

*Dominant and Recessive Genes.* What characteristics you will actually show from inheritance are not only determined by what *types* of genes are present but also by the genes' *penetrance*—that is, their power to become expressed. Some genes are *dominant* and are so powerful that they will always show up and will suppress lesser genes in heterozygous pairs. Others are *recessive* in that they will not penetrate, or express themselves, unless they are paired with the same recessive gene, as part (b) of Figure 4–1 shows. Many genes that produce pathological conditions are presumed to be recessive and will not lead to the appearance of the trait unless the person is homozygous for these genes.

*Intermediate Genes and Polygenes.* The inheritance of traits is not always so simple. *Intermediate* genes, which are neither dominant nor recessive, are found in cases where an effect is exhibited to a greater or lesser degree instead of in an all-or-none present-versus-absent manner. Skin color is an illustration. If a dark-complexioned person mates with a light-skinned person, the offspring's skin color will likely be somewhere in between that of the parents.

It is also plausible to assume the existence of *polygenes*. These are genes that must combine in a cumulative effort to control a characteristic. Basically, it is believed that each of these genes individually fails to have sufficient penetrating power to be expressed, but collectively, they are able to exert an influence. For example, the level of your intelligence may be the result of polygenes. The premise is that superior, bright-average, average, dull-normal, and retarded intelligence are reflections of the differing combined effects of polygenes (Gottesman, 1963).

In other cases, the polygenes collectively still fail to lead to the appearance of a trait. However, their

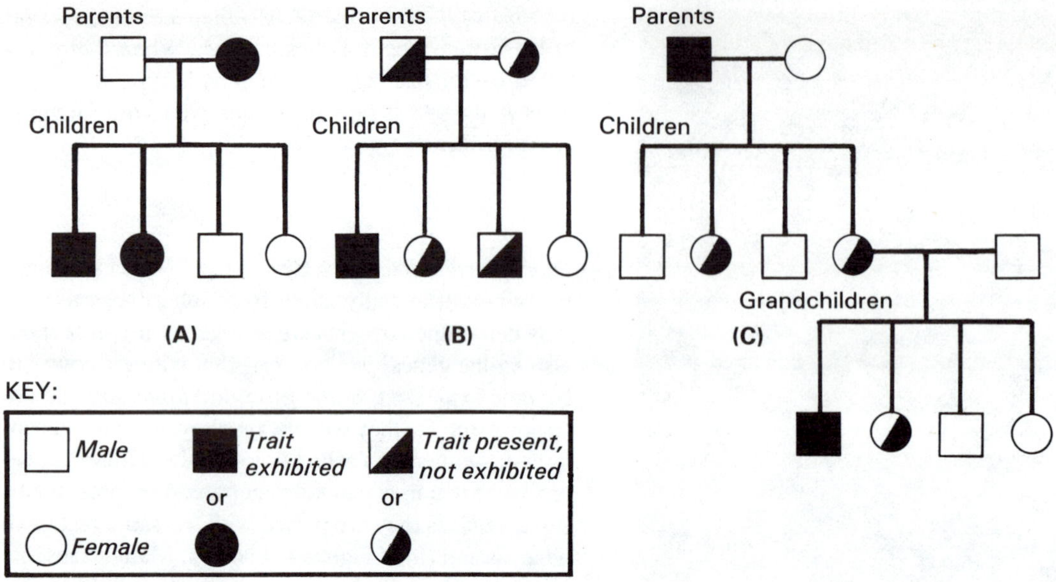


**FIGURE 4–1** Inheritance of dominant, recessive, and sex-linked genes. **(A)** Dominant pedigree (heterozygous parents illustrated): Parent who carries a dominant gene will exhibit the trait, and have one in two children showing the trait. If parent has two dominant genes, all children will show the trait. **(B)** Recessive pedigree (heterozygous parents illustrated): For the trait to show, both parents must carry a recessive gene. On the average, one in four children will have both genes and exhibit the trait; two in four will carry one gene and be carriers but will not exhibit the trait; and one in four will be entirely free of the gene and therefore the trait. **(C)** Sex-linked pedigree: Father with trait passes gene on to all daughters who do not exhibit trait but act as carriers. In the grandchildren, chances are one in two that any grandson will exhibit the trait, and one in two that any granddaughter will be a carrier.

**TABLE 4–1**

**Some Common Dominant and Recessive Human Characteristics**

| *Caused by dominant genes* | *Caused by recessive genes* |
|---|---|
| Dark hair | Blond hair |
| Curly hair | Straight hair |
| Black skin | White skin |
| Normal hair | Baldness |
| Short stature | Tall stature |
| Nearsightedness | Normal vision |
| Double-jointedness | Normal joints |
| Normal color vision | Color blindness |
| Normal blood clotting | Hemophilia |
| Immunity to poison ivy | Susceptibility to poison ivy |
| Blood type A, B, and AB | Blood type O |
| Brown, green, or hazel eyes | Blue or gray eyes |

presence makes the person more susceptible or predisposed to exhibit the trait under the proper triggering circumstances. Schizophrenia, as we'll see later, might be hypothesized to involve the inheritance of a number of faulty genes, which predispose the person to a mental breakdown under the proper conditions of stress.

***Individuals with Identical Genes.*** The union of a sperm and an ovum is called a *zygote.* With fertilization, the zygote first divides into two daughter cells, each of which is a perfect replica of the other. Ordinarily, the two daughter cells remain attached and again divide and subdivide to form millions of cells. Ultimately, these cells differentiate into the nerves, muscles, connective tissue, skin, and so forth, of the embryo.

In some instances, however, the first two daughter cells do not stay attached but actually separate. After separation, the usual process of multiplication and differentiation occurs, but this time two embryos are formed, each with the identical genetic structure—and the result is identical (*monozygotic*) twins: individuals who possess the same genes. Fraternal (*dizygotic*) twins, on the other hand, develop from the fertilization of two separate ova by two separate sperms at the same time. The two zygotes do not share any genes, and the embryos are no more similar to each other than are brothers or sisters who are born at separate times. However, fraternal twins do share the same intrauterine environment while other types of siblings do not. The differences between identical and fraternal twins have led to studies on the relative roles of heredity versus environment in personality. Identical twins share both the same heredity and the same intrauterine environment; fraternal twins share only the same environment. Non-twin siblings have neither the same genes nor the same intrauterine environment.

Monozygotic twins are of great interest in our study of whether or not genetics influences personality, since we are sure of their genetic similarity. Therefore, similarities in mental characteristics can be attributed to genetic factors just as are similarities in physical characteristics. Of course, we are never absolutely certain that other factors can be ruled out, such as family upbringing. Our case is strengthened, however, if identical twins continue to show the same or similar personality traits when reared in separate environments, as will be shown later.

### Evidence of Genetic Influence on Personality

It is not too difficult to visualize how obvious physical traits, such as height or hair color, are genetically traced in humans. The influence of genes on personality is another question, however. As Chapter 3 indicated, many characteristics of behavior seem to be learned. The crucial question, then, is how scientists can go about studying the effect of genes on personality and behavior. To answer that question, we'll look at four research approaches and some of the evidence provided by each. These approaches are animal studies, human family history studies, human studies involving *morbidity risk,* and chromosome studies.

***Animal Studies.*** Animal studies should present ideal conditions for genetic work: the time span between generations is short, and environmental factors are easily controlled. There has been very little sound research, however, into the inheritance of emotional characteristics. Three traits that have been studied most successfully are fearfulness, aggressivity, and tendencies toward alcoholism.

The research of Calvin Hall (1934) presents significant data about the ability to inherit fearfulness, a trait which he traced through several generations of rats. To measure this trait, he confronted his rats with an open-field test: rats are normally threatened at being unprotected in the open. Hall rated his rats according to the degree of panic with which they responded to this situation. Then, selectively mating high-emotionality rats with other high-emotionality rats, and low-emotionality rats with other low-emotionality rats, Hall was able to show the role of genetics on behavior. Whereas the parent generation showed a mean emotionality score of four, the ninth-generation offspring of *fearful* parents showed an average score of ten. The nonemotional strain showed a different result. By the very *first* generation, the offspring showed a decline in fearfulness with a mean score of below 0.5, indicating almost no fearfulness during the open-field test.

Fearfulness is not the only psychological trait that has been studied; the role of genetics and aggression has also been documented. John Paul Scott (1947) studied the possibility that a punishing experience would discourage genetic aggression. His C57 mice (an aggressive strain) were raised in isolation, then exposed to the extreme experience of facing another mouse carefully selected for its highly skilled aggressivity. For 30 minutes per session, the fighting mouse battled and subdued the experimental animals. Hopefully, all aggressive instincts would be literally "beaten out" of the normally aggressive experimental mice. However, genetics proved a more powerful determinant of behavior—Scott found instead that the experimental animals showed *increased* aggressiveness when later paired with a helpless subject. Later research confirms the increase in aggression of animals exposed to single severe defeats, although findings also indicate that aggressiveness does decrease with successive, continuing, severe defeats (Cairns, 1973; Kahn, 1951; Motshagen & Slangen, 1975). Chamove

*Monozygotic twins show similarities in behaviors assumed due to* ***heredity****. The Mahre twins are both highly talented members of the U.S. Olympic Men's Ski Team.*

(1980) has put forth the intriguing hypothesis that the early aggressivity of maternal animals increases the aggression in their offspring. If aggression is a trait that is evolutionarily adaptive, then these offspring as adults may select an animal with a similar level of aggressiveness as a mate. Thus, early nurture may set the foundation for passing on aggression by influencing later mate selection.

Of final interest are those studies of the alcoholic mice. Rodgers and McClearn (1962) were able to identify strains of mice who showed quite distinct preferences for alcohol, as well as strains who were teetotalers in the sense of preferring water. In addition, there seemed to be some relationship between drinking and sleep patterns: the nondrinking strains spent more time sleeping off alcohol when they imbibed it. The drinkers slept for a shorter period, perhaps due to more rapid oxidation of the alcohol from the action of liver enzyme found in their system.

Selective breeding studies with animals certainly suggest that fear, aggressivity, and perhaps even reactions to alcohol may be inherited, at least in animals. However, applying such conclusions to humans requires much more definitive studies (Turkington, 1982). Some progress will be reported next in our review of family history studies.

***Family History Studies.*** Another approach to investigating genetic factors is the *family history method.* Here, the investigator looks backward into the family trees of individuals with certain psychological disorders. Since we cannot systematically mate humans according to predetermined scientific patterns, the next nearest thing is to trace the results of marriages for which there is information on several generations of offspring. The prime examples of this type of evidence are connected with Huntington's chorea, schizophrenia, and defects of intelligence.

Huntington's chorea is a severe neurological disorder involving brain atrophy and increased loss of coordination. It is named after the doctor who first traced it. (His physician-father and physician-grandfather before him had noted the disease symptoms in generation after generation of certain local families.) Sjögren (1935) systematically documented the family tree of one case of Huntington's chorea. During five generations of marriages where all spouses were normal, 2 offspring in the first generation were affected, 7 in the next, 15 in the third, and 2 in the fourth.

Another study (Kallmann, 1946), this one of a family with schizophrenia, showed an inheritance pattern similar to that for Huntington's chorea in that the disorder showed a strikingly high incidence in offspring (see Figure 4–2). Just how directly schizophrenia is linked to genetic makeup is still a matter of conjecture, however, as will be discussed later.

One of the most famous examples of a family history study concerns the Kallikaks, who have often served as an example of what can happen from the transmission of defective genes. This study, made

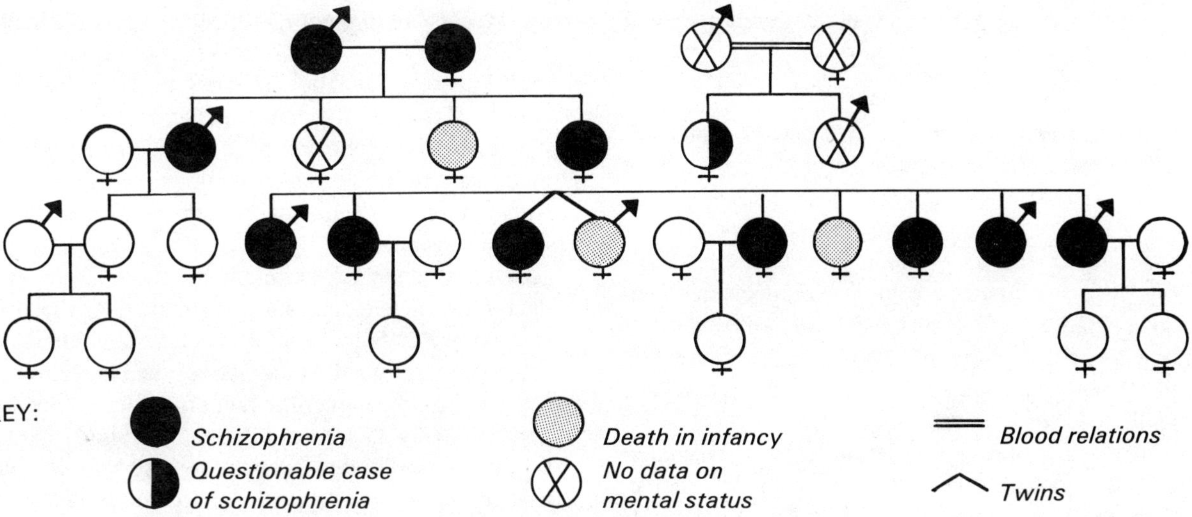


**FIGURE 4–2** Pedigree of a family showing frequent occurrence of schizophrenia.
SOURCE: From "The Genetic Theory of Schizophrenia" F.J. Kallman, 1946, *American Journal of Psychiatry, 103,* pp. 309–322. © 1946, the American Psychiatric Assn.

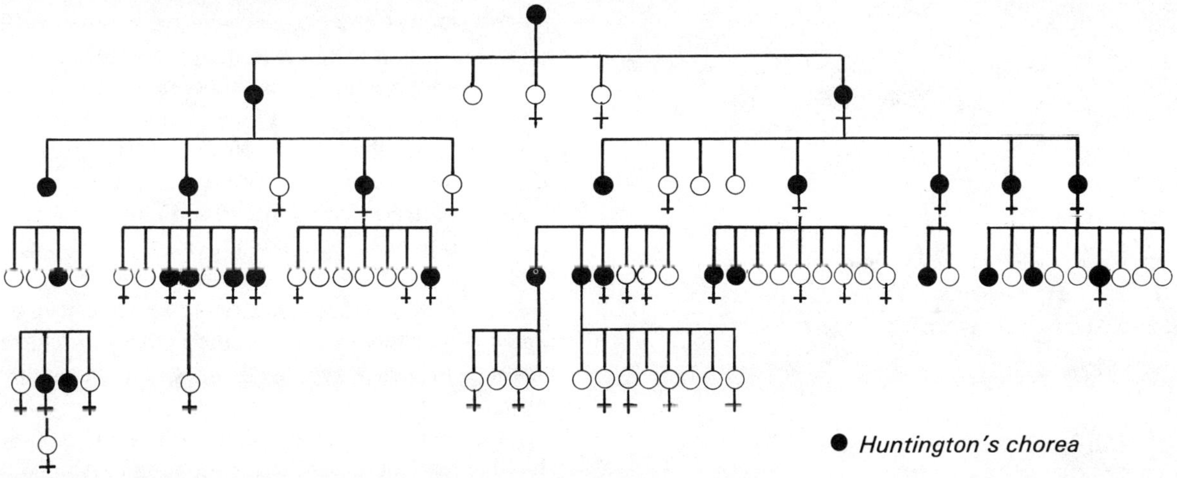


**FIGURE 4–3** Inheritance of Huntington's Chorea in a Family.
SOURCE: Based on "Verebungsmedizinishe Untersuchunger über Huntington's Chorea in einer schweidischen Bauernpopulation" by T. Sjögren, 1936, *Zeitschrift für menschliche Vererbungs-und Konstitutionslehre,* Bd. 19, Berlin:Springer, S. 131–165.

some 60 years ago, traces two genealogical family lines originally fathered by a soldier of the American Revolution, Martin Kallikak, Sr. (Goddard, 1919). During his military career, he started one lineage by impregnating a feebleminded tavern maid. Later, he married an intellectually capable woman of his own social status and thus began a legitimate line of progeny. According to the study, the offspring of Kallikak's feebleminded mate abounded in mental deficiency, immorality, alcoholism, and character defect. The legitimate progeny, in contrast, were normal, self-respecting persons, many of whom achieved distinction.

While this report was for a time hailed as conclusive proof of the strength of heredity over environment, it has subsequently been soundly criticized. There were no controls over the types of environment to which the various offspring were exposed, a problem often characteristic of genetic studies. In addition, psychologists have felt highly dubious about the ge-

genetic transmission of such traits as degeneracy and immorality.

***Morbidity Risk Studies.*** In *morbidity risk studies,* the researcher calculates the chances or risk of varying members of a family being affected (becoming morbid) by the disorder that affects the *proband*—that is, the subject who was originally affected by the disorder. These risk figures are compared against the general population's risk of being affected by the disorder. If the disorder is genetically influenced, then the blood relatives of the patient should show a higher incidence rate than do nonrelatives.

There are three approaches to reporting risk data: the first is to report the incidences of the disorder in offspring of varying parental matings (one parent affected, or both parents affected); the second is to compare incidences among persons of varying degrees of blood relationships (twins, full-siblings, half-siblings, step-siblings); and the third is to examine whether the risk changes when environment is changed (as in the case of adoption). Although some information is available on other disorders, the most exciting data come from studies involving schizophrenia.

*Risk from Parent Matings.* Some striking data come from studies of parents and children. One study by Kallmann (1946) found the risk rate for schizophrenia to be 0.9 percent when both parents were normal; a similar, more recent study reported figures of 10 percent risk for children of one schizophrenic parent and 35–45 percent risk when both parents are schizophrenic (Kringlen, 1978). These figures are slightly lower than those of Kallmann, shown in Figure 4–4, but the proportions are consistent: the chance of a schizophrenic psychosis developing in a child born of two psychotic parents is about four times the risk rate when only one parent is schizophrenic, and 35–45 times that of the general population.

*Risk to Relatives.* Kallmann's research (1946, 1953) is often cited as one of the classic studies relating morbidity risk to the degree of blood relationships with the proband. He obtained information on 1,382 twins, 2,741 full siblings, 134 half-siblings, and 74 step-siblings. In all instances, the patient had been hospitalized for schizophrenia.

According to theory, if this psychosis is affected by heredity, then the risk figures should be increasingly higher as genetic similarity to the proband increases. Thus, the incidence should be highest among identical twins, followed by fraternal twins, full siblings, half-siblings, step-siblings, and finally, lowest for nonrelatives. Kallmann's results confirmed this, as Figure 4–4 indicates.

A few conclusions might be drawn from these data. First, all persons with some blood ties to the original patient-subject showed a higher incidence of schizophrenia than did nonrelatives; and the closer the relationship, the higher the rate of incidence. Second, approximately 85 percent of both full siblings and fraternal twins did *not* develop schizophrenia—even though 10 percent had a schizophrenic brother or sister, and most shared the same family environment. This raises a significant question: If schizophrenia is caused by environmental factors alone, how did these normal siblings escape, and why were fewer of the identical twins able to avoid being affected?

A third, very intriguing point relates to the occurrence of schizophrenia in twins. Among the monozygotic twins who were both affected, 17.6 percent had their breakdowns on *exactly the same day* and 70.5 percent occurred within four years. Finally, among the monozygotic twins who lived together, the incidence figure was 91.5 percent, compared to a risk figure of 77.6 percent among identical twins who had been separated. This supports the hypothesis that genes have a powerful influence even with changes in the environment.

We have been emphasizing the documentation showing how increased risk is found in persons more and more closely related to a proband who is schizophrenic. The fact that more studies have examined risk rates among schizophrenics possibly is due to the greater ease of locating such patients for large-scale studies. Other studies of other disorders have discovered similar results for bipolar disorder as well as a form of schizophrenia occurring in childhood, and two types of psychosis appearing later in life (senile dementia and major depression with melancholia). As summarized in Table 4–2, these disorders appear most frequently in the identical twin of the proband, with less frequency appearing in persons who are not as directly related.

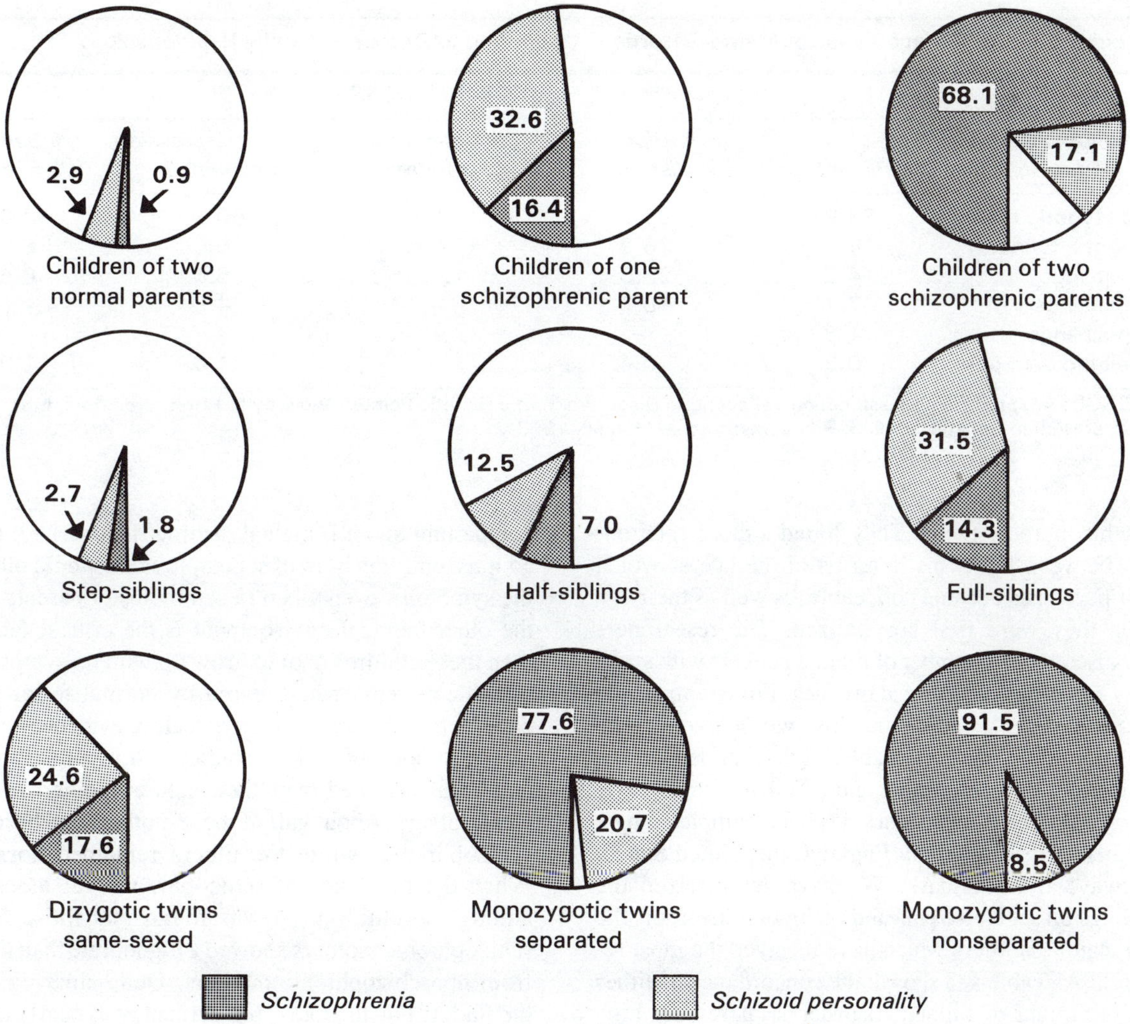


**FIGURE 4–4** The expectancy of schizophrenia and schizoid personality in blood relatives of persons with schizophrenia.

SOURCE: From "The Genetic Theory of Schizophrenia" by F.J. Kallmann, 1946, *American Journal of Psychiatry, 103,* pp. 309–322. © 1946, The American Psychiatric Assn.

*Risk and Similarities in Twins.* Many studies of risk have concentrated on twins alone, focusing on the chances of both being affected by (or *concordant* for) the same disorder. Where a genetic factor is present, concordance rates are naturally expected to be higher for the monozygotic than for the dizygotic twins.

A few studies of concordance have produced notable findings. As our case history reported, there has been an incredible discovery of identical quadruplet girls all concordant for schizophrenia—an occurrence that takes place only once in every 1.5 billion births (Rosenthal, 1963). Intensive psychological study of these girls showed that they had similar personality traits before their disorder, and similar symptoms during the course of their disorder.

In another major study, Gottesman and Shields (1972) began with the files of more than 45,000 patients from the same hospital. They uncovered 57 pairs

**TABLE 4–2**

**Morbidity Risk for Various Types of Mental Disorders, According to Degree of Family Relationship**

| Family relationship | MENTAL ILLNESS % Schizophrenia | % Bipolar disorder | % Childhood schizophrenia | % Major depression, melancholia | % Senile dementia |
|---|---|---|---|---|---|
| Monozygotic twins | 86.2 | 95.7 | 70.6 | 60.9 | 42.8 |
| Dizygotic twins | 14.5 | 26.3 | 17.1 | 6.0 | 8.0 |
| Full-siblings | 14.2 | 23.0 | 12.2 | 6.0 | 6.5 |
| Half-siblings | 7.1 | 16.7 | — | 4.5 | — |
| Step-siblings | 1.8 | — | — | — | — |
| Unrelated gen. pop. | 0.9 | 0.4 | — | 1.0 | 1.0 |

SOURCE: Adapted from Classification of Psychotic Disorders from a Genetic Point of View by L. Hurst. Proc. Sec. Intl. Cong. of Human Genetics, vol. 3, Rome: Instituto G. Mendel, 1963.

of schizophrenic twins. They found a close relationship between the twins in terms of the age at which their psychosis became noticeable, as well as their age when they were first hospitalized. The researchers also discovered a number of related patients with strikingly similar psychological profiles. For example, the test results on a father and his two schizophrenic daughters showed considerable similarities despite age differences between parent and offspring.

Twin concordance work has been completed by a number of researchers in England, the United States, Norway, and Denmark. We have summarized the findings on schizophrenia and on bipolar disorder, the two major disorders which have received the most research. As Table 4–3 shows, the concordance of either schizophrenia or bipolar disorder is extremely high among identical twins, and clearly higher than among fraternal twins. This overall pattern exists even though the exact numbers across all studies do not match exactly. The consistency of the direction of the finding, however, does lend substance to the speculation that genetics may be an important factor in such mental disorders. Still another approach to the question of heredity versus environment involves looking at children who have been adopted, whereby the environment has been changed very early in life. Our next section will discuss the evidence from this area.

*Risk and Adoption.* The fourth type of morbidity risk study examines siblings who have been separated from one another. *Adoption studies* have a simple but compelling logic: if mental disorder is inherited, then adopted children born of schizophrenics should inherit the symptoms even when raised by foster parents. On the other hand, if environment is the critical factor, then these children should grow up with no symptoms of schizophrenia when reared by normal foster parents. A few studies provide revealing evidence.

Heston (1966, 1971) studied foster children who had been separated from their natural mothers at two weeks of age. About half of these mothers had become schizophrenic, while the others remained normal. When the incidence of schizophrenia was assessed among the children, it was found that those from schizophrenic mothers showed a higher rate than those from nonschizophrenic mothers. Quite amazing was the finding that the rate (16.6 percent) was nearly identical with that discovered by Kallmann for children raised by their schizophrenic natural mothers (16.4 percent).

Some other researchers (Rosenthal et al., 1978) reversed the design by picking families where the *child* was schizophrenic, then studying the parents' health. They also studied adoptions, comparing three groups: the biological parents and their schizophrenic child; parents who adopted a child who became schizophrenic; and parents who adopted a child who remained normal. If genetics is a causative factor, then we would expect the true parents of schizophrenic children to show a higher incidence of pathology than the foster parents of either a schizophrenic or a normal child. Indeed, this turned out to be the case.

**TABLE 4–3**

**Concordance for Psychotic Disorders in Twins**

| | *SCHIZOPHRENIA* | | *BIPOLAR DISORDERS* | |
|---|---|---|---|---|
| *Investigator* | *% Identical* | *% Fraternal* | *% Identical* | *% Fraternal* |
| Rosanoff, U.S.A. | 61 | 13 | 70 | 16 |
| Kallmann, U.S.A. | 69 | 11 | 93 | 24 |
| Slater, England | 64 | 17 | 57 | 23.5 |
| Kringlen, Norway | 31 | 7 | 33 | 0 |
| Bertelsen, Harvald, and Hauge, Denmark | 29 | 6 | 58 | 17 |

***Chromosome Studies.*** Besides animal studies, family history studies and morbidity risk studies, a fourth source of information about how genetics relates to pathology is *chromosome studies.* The direct examination of chromosomes has been made more precise through actual photographs (called *karyotypes*) of chromosomes. For some disorders, it is possible to compare karyotypes of affected persons with those of people who do not share the disorder, to determine whether genetic aberrations are present.

Mongolism, or Down's syndrome, is a type of mental retardation characterized by short stature, protruding tongue, Asian-looking eyes, and intellectual deficit. It is discussed in more detail in Chapter 19. Current evidence indicates that affected individuals usually have three chromosomes instead of the normal two in one of the sets (Lejeune et al., 1959). Many believe that this provides conclusive proof that mongolism is genetically caused. However, we return to the question of what correlations prove, as discussed in Chapter 1: Another possibility is that the additional chromosome is instead another symptom of mongolism, rather than being the cause.

Two publicized court cases emphasize another chromosomal aberration and its relationship to pathology. Normally, men carry an XY set of sex chromosomes while women have an XX set; but occasionally, an extra Y chromosome occurs in men (XYY), and there is some evidence that this is linked to behavior. In 1968, a Melbourne jury ruled that a 20-year-old laborer was "legally insane," and acquitted him of a murder charge. The defense argued that an extra Y chromosome was present in the defendant's cells, causing the tendency toward violence that led to the stabbing crime. In the United States, Richard Speck, tall and mentally dull, was convicted of the murder of eight nurses in Chicago in 1966. Speck is also said to have the additional Y chromosome.

**FIGURE 4–5** Illustration of the degrees of blood relationship among various relatives.

SOURCE: From "The Genetic Theory of Schizophrenia" by F.J. Kallmann, 1946, *American Journal of Psychiatry, 103,* pp. 309–322. © 1946, The American Psychiatric Assn.

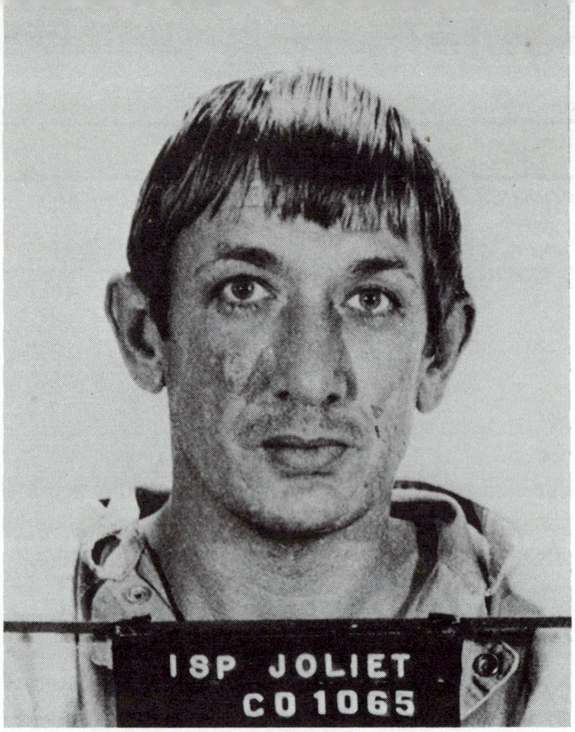


*Richard Speck murdered eight nurses before being captured. In an examination of his chromosomes, he was found to have the unusual **XYY** combination.*

To date, results have shown that a greater proportion of male aggressive patients and prisoners possess extra chromosomes than tend to occur in normal persons (Wiener et al., 1968). The presence of the extra Y chromosome also seems to be associated with tall stature, with the XYY men generally measuring well over six feet. Such evidence is again correlational and suggestive, but much more research is necessary before it can be considered conclusive (Dorns, 1980; Suinn, 1969). An important piece of information yet to be gathered is the frequency with which the XYY appears in prisoners convicted of nonviolent crimes. Basically, we must determine whether the XYY condition *invariably* leads to violence; whether it must be paired with other factors to produce violence; or finally (as is the question with mongolism), whether the XYY condition is a remarkable coincidental occurrence that has little or no influence on violence.

### Genetics: A Cause of Pathology?

The question of what role genetics plays in pathology has been asked and studied by many people for a long time. However, a great deal of mystery still exists. The exact mechanisms whereby disorders are transmitted is still unclear, and several theories are still being examined.

It is likely that genetics is not important for all forms of mental disorders. For instance, certain phobias in some persons are clearly acquired through learned experiences, as we saw in Chapter 3's discussion of conditioning. It is also likely that genetics plays a very important role in a few disorders—including Huntington's chorea and the genetic aberration of Down's syndrome. Personality traits also may turn out to be associated with the extra Y chromosome in males, although this relationship is still uncertain.

A third kind of relationship seems to exist for some other disorders. There is some evidence that inheritance influences schizophrenia and perhaps certain affective disorders, but in concert with environmental factors. A very persuasive explanation of this relationship is Rosenthal's *diathesis-stress theory* (1963). He proposes that schizophrenia is caused by an interaction between heredity and environment. What is inherited is a predisposition to mental disorder, perhaps as a result of polygenes which accumulate to determine differences in symptom severity. Environmental stresses—for instance, a disruptive early home life or a traumatic experience—serve to activate the predisposition, and this leads to the expression of the disorder (Chapters 5 and 17 will explore some family patterns that may well contribute to schizophrenia). In other words, it is possible for a potentially schizophrenic individual to remain symptom-free for years in the absence of appropriate stressors.

Most genetic-oriented scientists favor this diathesis-stress hypothesis in explaining the role of genetics in schizophrenia (Gottesman, 1978; Kety, 1980; Kidd, 1978; Shields, 1978). The degree of this relationship is still controversial, however. Gottesman asserts that genetics contributes 80 percent, while environment contributes only 20 percent to liability to schizophrenia; others support the idea that a relationship exists, but find it less direct than what Gottesman proposes (Abrams & Taylor, 1983).

In all, the concept of interaction between heredity and environment has stimulated much progress in research, redirecting the search for causality away from a simplistic focus on either nature or nurture alone. Certainly, we will have more information in the future, as research continues into the role of genetics.

## THE BIOLOGICAL FACTORS: TOXIC CAUSES

Another way in which biology may influence psychology is through the presence of certain biochemical substances in the body. Our bodies are incredibly complex, delicately balanced pieces of machinery. A single disturbance in the basic physiology of the person, and the effects may appear in intellectual retardation or personality instabilities. Such a close linkage between the psychology and physiology of humans has encouraged many to seek the answers to mental disorders through the study of physiological issues. We will first briefly outline some of the relevant aspects of human physiology in the normal state. Then, with this foundation, we will examine the evidence that some biochemical substances may be related to mental illness.

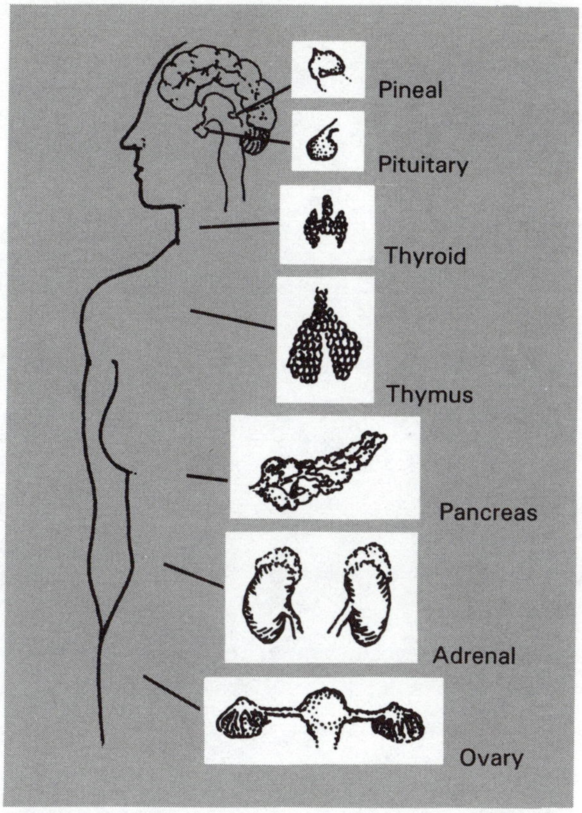


**FIGURE 4–6** Schematic representation of the endocrine system.

### Physiology: A Selective Review

Two body systems in particular which seem to be related to personality and behavior are the endocrine system and the nervous system (Gale & Edwards, 1983).

***The Endocrine System.*** The endocrine system consists of several important glands that are distributed throughout the body: the pituitary gland, in the center of the head; the thyroid and parathyroids in the neck; the adrenals near the kidneys; the pancreas along the stomach; and the gonads (see Figure 4–6).

Each of these glands plays a role in the individual's development or functioning. The *pituitary* is often called the master gland because of its controlling effects on the other glands. Excessive activity produces excess growth, leading to exceptionally tall physical stature. The *thyroids* regulate heat and energy within cells. Thyroid deficiency in infancy leads to *cretinism,* a form of mental retardation marked by dwarfism and lethargy. The *parathyroids* help to maintain the calcium and phosphorous balance in the blood, and can cause nerve irritability leading to muscle twitches if imbalances occur. The *adrenal* glands produce a chemical substance called epinephrine (or adrenaline). Epinephrine helps prepare the organism for emergency situations by elevating blood pressure and heart rate. Epinephrine may also be related to some psychological disorders, as will be seen in our later discussion. The *pancreas* produces digestive secretion and, more important, the hormone insulin that prevents the occurrence of diabetes. The gonads are the human sexual glands responsible for sperms or ova and hormones that influence other sexual characteristics, such as body hair.

***The Nervous System.*** A second body system closely tied to behavior is the nervous system. This system is composed of cells called *neurons,* each having a cell body and fibrous projections called *axons*

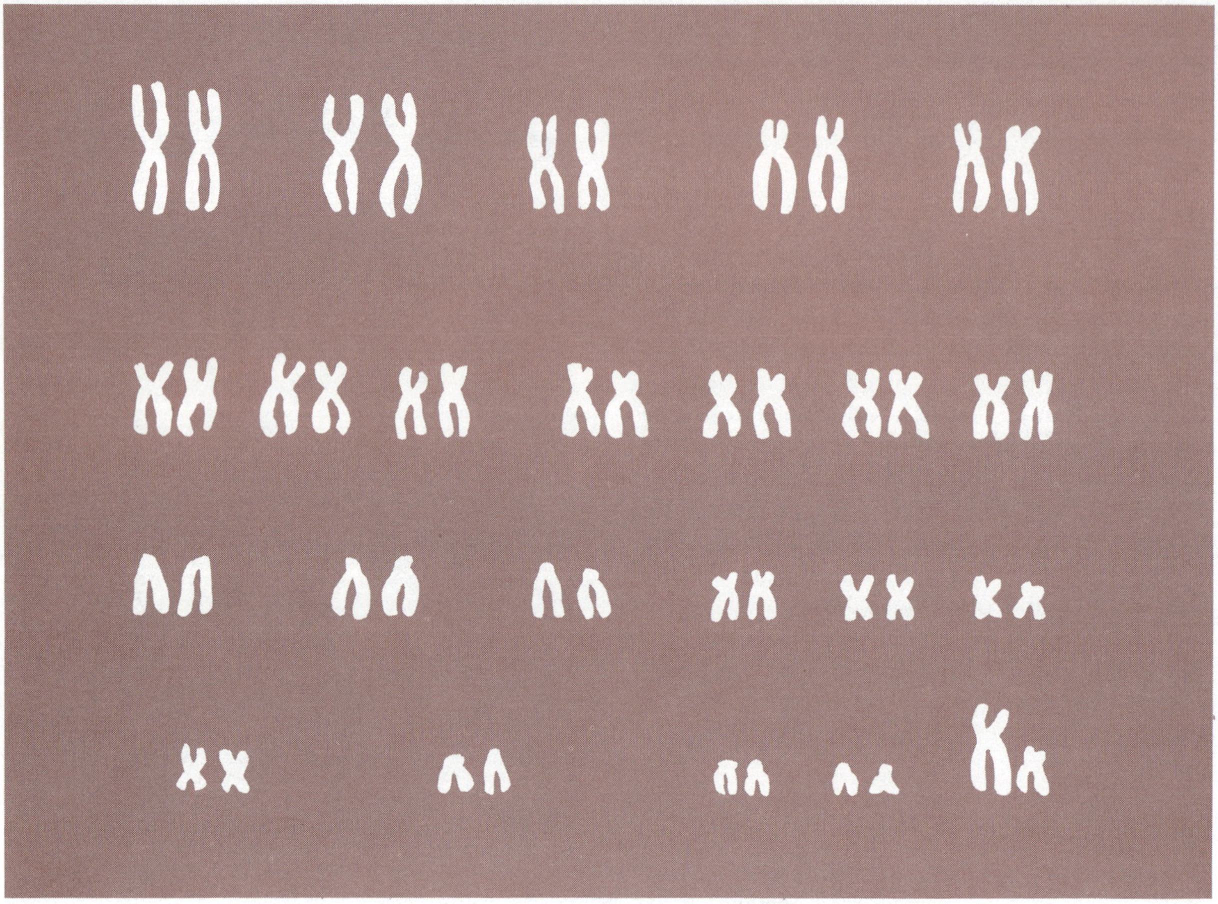

*Normal pairs of* ***chromosomes*** *appear in the photograph above. The photo on the facing page shows the chromosomes of a Mongoloid; one set (21) has three instead of two chromosomes.*

and *dendrites.* Neural impulses are carried away from the cell body by way of the axons while incoming impulses are transmitted through the dendrites, like a well-organized telephone exchange system of wiring. Neurons, interestingly enough, do not actually touch one another. They are separated by a gap called a *synapse.* A chemical called acetylcholine is released at the nerve endings to ferry nerve impulses across the synapse. Other neural transmitters have also been identified in the central nervous system, such as norepinephrine and dopamine. We will later see how these two have roles in affecting mental disorders.

The nervous system can be classified into two major parts: the peripheral nervous system and the central nervous system. The *peripheral nervous system* is composed of the autonomic nervous system and the somatic nervous system; and the *central nervous system* is composed of the brain and the spinal cord.

*The Peripheral Nervous System.* The two parts of the peripheral nervous system act to control many of the unconscious aspects of bodily functioning. The *au-*

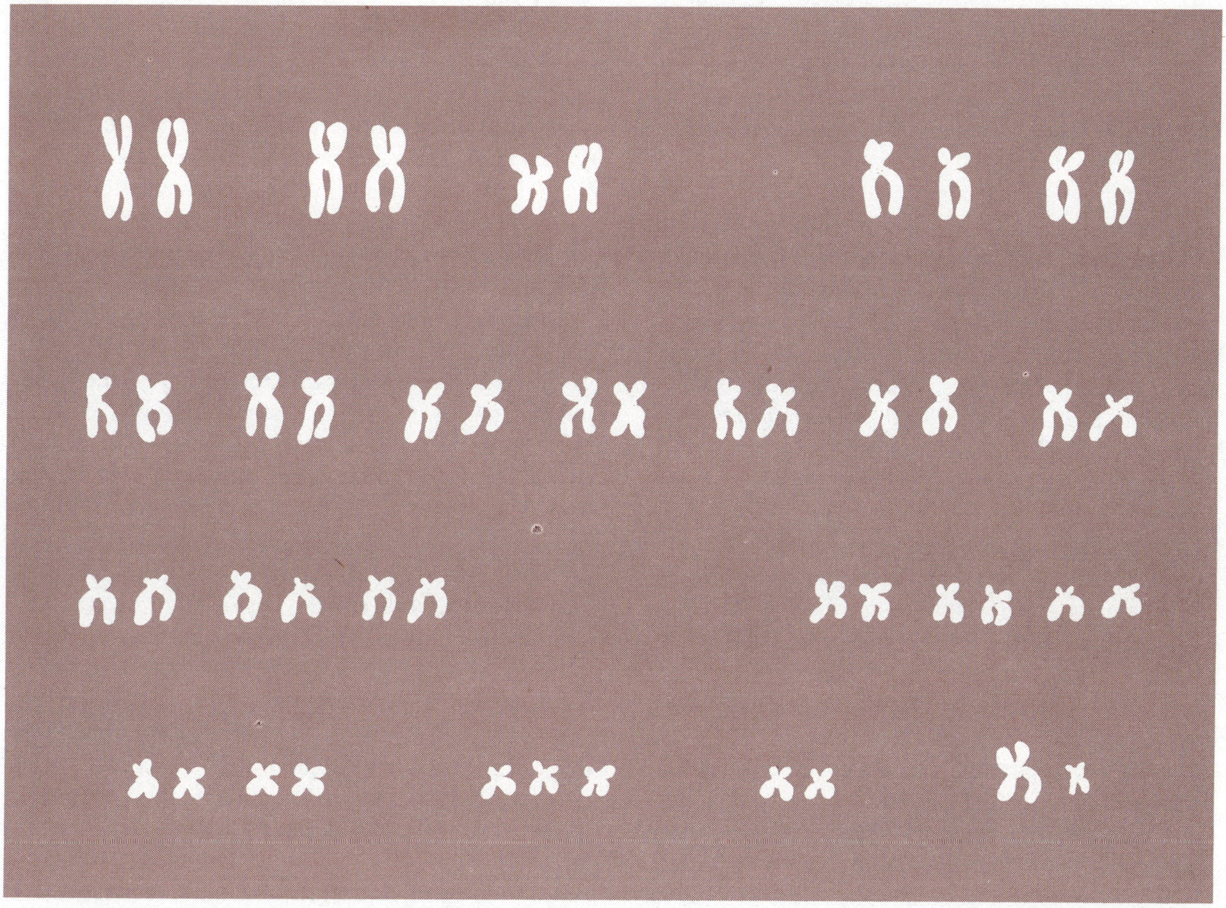

*tonomic nervous system* runs parallel to the spinal cord and reaches into and controls many of the glands and organs of our bodies. The autonomic system is actually made up of the *sympathetic nervous system* and the *parasympathetic nervous system.* These two have reciprocal actions: the sympathetic generally activates an organ or gland, while the parasympathetic inhibits the same organ or gland (see Figure 4–6). The sympathetic system is said to prepare us for danger, fight, or flight, for instance, through activating the adrenal gland. The parasympathetic system governs automatic functions, such as breathing and the pumping of the heart. *The somatic nervous system* includes those nerves which end in muscles, and sensory cells. It is, therefore, responsible for sensory-motor actions.

The exact mechanisms whereby mental disorders are affected by either the peripheral or the somatic nervous systems are not known. It is possible that psychophysiologic disorders, such as high blood pressure and others described in Chapter 9, are the result of autonomic system difficulties. Regarding the somatic nervous system, we might speculate on the types of mental disorders which might involve this system. These might include psychogenic pain, as illustrated in Chapter 10, in that pain sensitivity starts with pain receptors in the skin. Chapter 10 will also discuss in detail the conversion disorders which can involve the inability to experience pain (anesthesias) or the inability to engage in voluntary motor actions.

The endocrine system can produce psychiatric-like symptoms itself; however, these are diagnosed as a medical disorder and not a psychiatric disorder. For instance, an abnormally low level of glucose (hypoglycemia) can precipitate tremors, confusion, hallucinations, or bizarre behaviors. In fact, one study reported that 46 percent of a group of patients examined for psychiatric symptoms actually were suffering from a medical problem, such as hypoglycemia, anemia, or hypothyroidism (Hall et al., 1981).

Stress has a clear sequence of effects on the autonomic nervous system. Stress to the body triggers alarm signals apparently through the hypothalamus which acts as a bridge between the brain and the autonomic system. In one chain of events, the adrenal glands are stimulated and epinephrine is released, causing the heart to speed up so that more blood is available. Other parts of the chain governed by the autonomic system are dilations of the pupils and the suspension of digestive functions. The blood also takes on a greater ability to clot, and blood sugar is increased.

This series of changes has been called the *fight or flight response* to stress, for all of these processes prepare the individual to deal with danger (Cannon, 1963). As one example, if the danger involves being in a fight where a wound is possible, the increased blood sugar and increased circulation make energy available to the muscles to carry on the effort needed in the battle; the enlarged pupils let in more light to improve vision; the blood-clotting change prepares the individual for injury; and the decreased digestive action frees the energies and also anticipates possible wounds to the digestive organs. The fact that the fight-flight response can be triggered by psychological threat is very important. As we will see in Chapters 6 and 7, certain signs of anxiety are correlated with autonomic nervous system action under stress. For instance, one symptom of anxiety is increased heartbeat and respiration, both controlled by the autonomic nervous system.

*The Central Nervous System and Emotions.* The brain is the most fascinating structure of the central nervous system. Focus 4–1 provides an overview of its parts and functions. Three areas of the brain in particular have prominent roles in emotions. These are the *hypothalamus,* the *septal* area, and the *amygdala.*

The hypothalamus has been credited with having major responsibility for release of emotions. Animals whose cortexes have been removed show violent rage reactions as if the hypothalamus went berserk in releasing rage, when not under the restraining control of the cortex (Andy & Jurko, 1977).

While direct electrical stimulation of the hypothalamus precipitates rage, stimulation of the septal area seems to produce a pleasurable emotion instead (Olds, 1956). Destruction of the septal area has resulted in a mixture of fear and rage responses (Phillips & Lieblich, 1972). An interesting contrast is produced by the destruction of the amygdala. This has been shown to cause wild animals to stop biting and scratching and to become abnormally tame, even when pinched or mishandled. Such findings have led some physicians to experiment with isolation of the amygdala or hypothalamus as a way of reducing violence in human patients, on the premise that removing such "rage centers" might eliminate such emotions (Schvarcz, 1977; Cox & Brown, 1977).

### Evidence of Physiological Influences on Mental Disorders

As our brief overview has indicated, human behavior is closely linked to the functioning of both the endocrine system and the nervous system. Quite naturally, much scientific effort has been aimed at seeking the origin of mental disorder in these systems. Chapter 22 will discuss some of the chemical, shock, and surgical treatments for certain disorders; these all are based on different theories linking disorders directly to physiological disruptions.

The remainder of this chapter will look at one major focus in physiological research: the attempt to identify biochemical substances that might bring about changes in the functioning of either the brain or the endocrine system. Two approaches have been pursued: a search for toxic substances foreign to the body and the

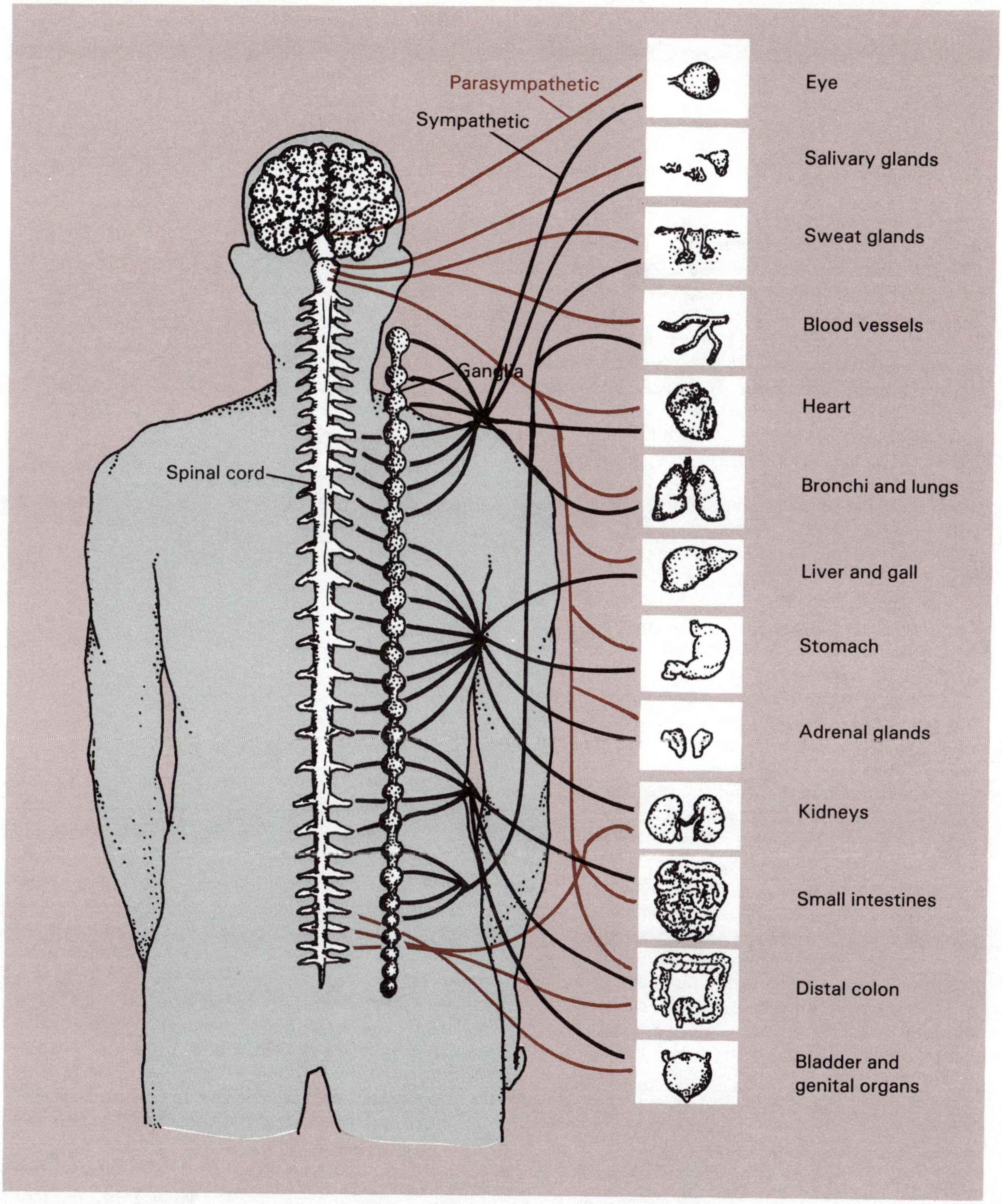


**FIGURE 4–7** Schematic representation of the autonomic nervous system.
SOURCE: Based on *Basic Psychology* by Howard H. Kendler, 1963, New York: Appleton-Century-Crofts.

# FOCUS 4–1:
## Anatomy of the Brain

The brain is composed of several structures that control several critical functions. Viewing it from the top, it forms two distinguishable halves called the *cerebral hemispheres* or the *cerebrum.*

As we look at it from the side (as in Figure 4–8), two large grooves can be seen with one coming down from the top and the other proceeding from the bottom upward diagonally: the top central groove is known as the *fissure of Rolando,* while the lower groove is called the *fissure of Sylvius.* These landmarks will help us as reference points to identify other functional parts of the brain. The four principal lobes separated by the two fissures are the *frontal lobe,* located in front of the fissure of Rolando; the *parietal lobe,* immediately to the rear of the fissure of Rolando; the *temporal lobe,* situated below the fissure of Sylvius; and the *occipital lobe* at the very rear of the brain.

Functionally, the different lobes play distinct roles. The *frontal lobe* appears to control motor behavior and higher mental processes such as reasoning and memory. However, cases have been reported involving surgical removal of large portions of this lobe without significant damage to the patient's intellect (see Chapter 22). In fact, this type of operation has been prescribed as a method for treating certain mental disorders, since it seems to reduce anxieties (Stuss & Benson, 1983). The *parietal lobe* is involved in body sensations and movement receptors. When stimulated, patients report sensations such as, "I suddenly felt a warm feeling" or "I thought my leg was moving." The *temporal lobe* is involved in hearing; stimulation of this area produces buzzing or ringing in the ears. Persons with epilepsy, a convulsive disorder often associated with damage to the brain, sometimes experience an auditory reaction prior to a seizure. The *occipital lobe* is directly connected to vision; destroying this region will lead to complete blindness even though the person's eyes are normal. In some persons suffering from migraine headaches, a warning aura of flashing light occurs; this suggests that the occipital lobe may be involved for those persons.

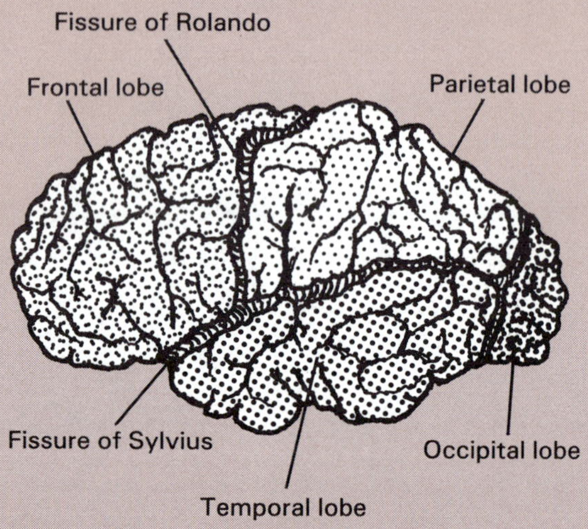


**FIGURE 4–8** The lobes of each cerebral hemisphere.

SOURCE: Based on *Basic Psychology* by Howard H. Kendler, 1963, New York: Appleton-Century-Crofts.

The cerebral hemispheres are covered by a layer called the *cerebral cortex,* meaning literally the "brain's bark." This covering is convoluted, ranging in thickness from one eighth to one fourth of an inch. The cerebral hemispheres and their cortex form the most significant difference between the human brain and brains of other mammals, for in humans, these parts form the largest and most visible part of the brain. Approximately three-fourths of the cortex is believed to be connected with learning, memory, and thinking. Damage to parts of the cortex may, for example, lead to strange disturbances in speech whereby the patient may be able to pronounce a simple word or sentence, but not be able to comprehend its meaning (see Chapter 18).

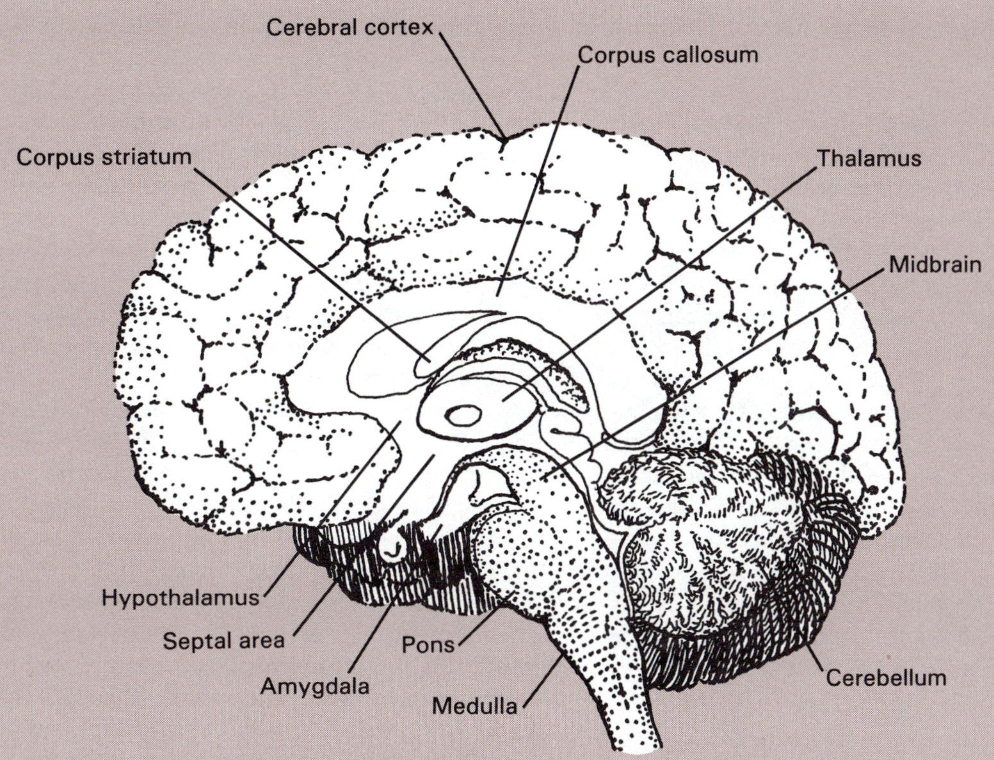


**FIGURE 4–9** Side view of the human brain showing major areas.

So far we have pointed out the major part of the brain's anatomy, but a number of other parts should also be recognized. Figure 4–9 highlights the location of the following: the thalamus and the hypothalamus (forming the forebrain along with the cerebral hemispheres); the midbrain area deeply enfolded in the center; the septal area and the amygdala (which form the 'nosebrain'); and the cerebellum, the pons and the medulla (which comprise the hindbrain). Each serves a function: the *thalamus* acts as a relay center between the cortex and sensory organs; the *midbrain* seems to control visual and auditory reflexes; the *cerebellum* is needed for body posture and coordination; the *medulla* regulates reflex body functions such as breathing; and the *pons* acts as a connecting link between the cerebellum and the cerebrum.

study of substances which are normal to the body but pathological if imbalanced.

***The Search for Foreign Toxic Substances.*** The hypotheses that mental disorders are caused by toxic substances seem at first glance to be a natural line of thought. Such views are predicted by the disease entity orientation: diseases of the body are attributable to invasion by foreign agents such as bacteria; and symptoms reflect the damage caused by the disease-carrying agent. A disorder known as *general paresis* follows this pattern. The foreign agent is a spirochete passed on during intercourse, causing syphilis. The syphilitic infection spreads into the nervous system, and as the cortex becomes damaged, both physical and mental symptoms are seen, such as slurring of speech and loss of memory. If the infection can be halted by destroying the spirochete before it damages nervous tissue, then recovery can be expected. From this example, scientists have conducted similar searches for toxic agents or substances that might act in the same way to cause mental disorders.

*Research into the Toxic Substance Theory.* According to the toxic substance theory, mental disorders are caused by the presence of a substance not normally found in the body. Following this line of pursuit, the first step in research requires the demonstration that the infectious substance taken from a ''diseased'' person will, in fact, show up as potentially harmful. As early as 1903, Berger injected blood taken from acutely ill schizophrenics into his own bloodstream on seven different occasions. For four trials, nothing happened: but on the fifth, he felt vertigo within 15 minutes; within two hours, he experienced increased salivation; within four hours, palpitations and headache; and by evening he felt a severe and aimless depression. Following the seventh injection, he experienced a slight deafness and fainted. Such studies have continued in many forms by other researchers: blood sera have been found a cause of aberrant web-spinning in spiders (Witts, 1956); and the bile from catatonic schizophrenics has led to catatoniclike symptoms in animals—a loss of spontaneous body movements and prolonged suspension of posture (Baruk & Camus, 1949).

Unfortunately, the promise of these works has never become fruitful. It is difficult to know, for example, whether Berger experienced the effects of a toxic factor within the blood, or whether he was simply the victim of his own expectations. In addition, such studies are often complicated by the lack of control of other factors that may be important in explaining apparent differences between the ''body chemistry'' of a person with schizophrenia and that of persons who don't share the disorder. Differences in diet, activity, and general health can all lead to significant differences in body products when affected persons are compared to another population group.

One classic example of misreading a causal relationship is worth note here. At one time, a strange factor was identified in the bloodstream of individuals affected with catatonic schizophrenia; the substance was believed to be responsible for their disorder (De Jong, 1934; Freud & Dingemanse, 1932). The factor was given the name *catatonine,* and one can imagine the excitement that was aroused by its discovery. Further study ultimately led to the correct identification of this factor—to the obvious disappointment and embarrassment of the researchers—for the catatonine was more correctly identified as *nicotine* (Dingemanse & Freud, 1933). The chemical substance that had shown as a toxic factor was related to smoking habits of the patients rather than to mental disease. Perhaps the most telling argument for caution in interpreting reports on toxicity results is the contradictory evidence of later studies. For example, while some researchers have found a lethal effect of psychotic blood serum or urine, other equally competent scientists have not been able to confirm these findings (Goldner & Ricketts, 1942). Neither has there been support for the reported behavioral changes from either bile, urine, blood, or cerebrospinal fluid (Rieder, 1957).

*The Case for Taraxein.* Another effort to find a cause-and-effect relationship between toxic substances and disorders is the still-controversial work of Robert Heath and his associates (1957) at Tulane University School of Medicine. In an effort to find what caused certain human behavioral characteristics, they implanted electrodes deep within the brains of both humans and animals, for periods up to two years (Heath & Mickle, 1960). When they analyzed the resulting electroencephalographic (EEG) data, they saw a rela-

*The photo on the left shows a normal spider web. The web in the second photo was constructed by a spider in a* ***drugged state.***

tionship between EEG abnormalities from the septal region of the brain and psychotic behavior. The research team then began to search for the factor that might account for such abnormalities; a substance was found and given the name *taraxein* (from the Greek *Tarasso,* mind disturbing). When taraxein was given to subjects with no previous disturbances, it was found to lead to abnormal EEG patterns and abnormal behavioral effects, including delusions of persecution, auditory hallucinations, as well as catatonic and *hebephrenic* symptoms (such as silly, regressive behaviors).

The story of taraxein is still incomplete. Taraxein has proved to be a highly unstable substance and its toxic properties are extremely sensitive to temperature and temporal changes. Other scientists have failed to confirm the psychological effects of taraxein administration even when using extracts prepared and supplied directly by Heath (Robins, Smith, & Lower, 1957). Perhaps the best evaluation of the status of taraxein is that supplied by Heath (1955) himself when he wrote, "These studies . . . are provocative but inconclusive" (p. 387).

***The Search for Natural Toxic Substances.*** Another major area of research in the effort to find physiological causes derives from the theory that disorders are caused by imbalances of natural chemical substances—that is, substances that are normally present in the body. One such substance, endorphin, has been very tentatively linked to schizophrenia and affective disorders, as is described in Focus 4–2. Some other exciting research has focused on the chemicals—known as *neurotransmitters*—that carry nerve impulses across the synapse from one neuron to another (Crow, 1983). Two related neurotransmitters, with similar chemical structures, are epinephrine and dopamine. *Epinephrine* is a secretion of the adrenal glands; *dopamine* is an intermediate product from the body's synthesis of norepinephrine. We'll look briefly at the case for each as a cause in mental disorder.

## FOCUS 4–2:
### Endorphins and Mental Disorders

Endorphins are natural substances produced in the pituitary gland and the brain, especially the hypothalamus and amygdala. Researchers have found that they are released in response to chronic pain, and they act as strong pain relievers in the same way that narcotics suppress pain (Hughes, 1975). The discovery of endorphins could be important for understanding drug addiction and pain tolerance (as Chapters 10 and 13 will discuss). Endorphins act like morphine since injections of endorphins lead to the same withdrawal signs upon discontinuance as in drug addiction. Endorphins also cause pain reduction and may thus be involved in pain tolerance differences. Some recent works have also sought possible links between endorphins and schizophrenia and some other affective disorders.

As with the cases of both epinephrine and dopamine, discussed in the text, research into the effects of endorphins has relied on inference. Among the research on endorphins and schizophrenia are findings that implicate either excess or deficiency in endorphin levels with schizophrenia. It has been found that endorphin levels appear to be elevated in schizophrenic patients; also, drugs which might be expected to block endorphin activity seem to reduce psychotic symptoms such as hallucinations in patients (Manchanda & Hirsch, 1982). And finally, when endorphins have been injected in rats, catatonic symptoms have been produced (Davis et al., 1979).

An intriguing fact is that similar findings also link endorphins to manic-depressive symptoms in bipolar disorders. It seems that endorphins decrease as manic activity decreases, while giving endorphin extracts to patients tends to reduce depressive symptoms (Gerner et al., 1980; Lindstrom et al., 1978). It is possible, therefore, that too many endorphins are correlated with manic behavior, while too little might be associated with depressive behaviors.

The story is still inconclusive because of methodological difficulties and inconsistent findings (Berger et al., 1980). However, endorphin research may well be opening a new chapter in the further study of physiological causes of psychopathology.

*The Case for Epinephrine.* Epinephrine (also known as adrenaline) and norepinephrine (noradrenaline) are two hormones found in the adrenal glands and in the brain. Epinephrine is formed from norepinephrine. Their implication in certain severe disorders reads like a detective story. Here is a quick review of the evidence:

The first clues come not from natural substances, but from certain synthetic drugs whose effects are familiar to us. These drugs, called *psychomimetic* drugs, have been known to produce psychoticlike symptoms. Mescaline, for example, produces feelings of depersonalization, depression, or euphoria, as well as auditory hallucinations. It has been discovered that mescaline is structurally quite similar to norepinephrine (see Figure 4–10).

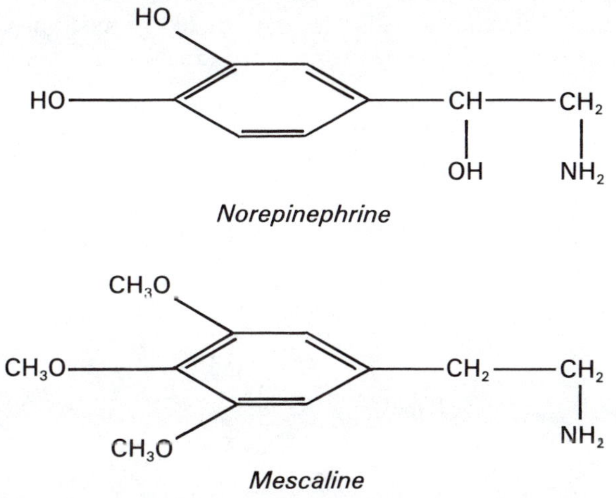


**FIGURE 4–10** Structure of mescaline emphasizing the relationship to norepinephrine.

A second clue relates to other familiar drugs. Certain tranquilizers, such as chlorpromazine and reserpine, are frequently prescribed to block the symptoms of disorders such as schizophrenia (see the discussion of treatments in Chapter 22). These drugs have also been found to block or displace norepinephrine.

A third clue in this detective story comes from experimental evidence. Certain products of epinephrine (such as *adrenochrome,* a substance formed by the oxidation of epinephrine) have been found to trigger schizophrenialike symptoms such as catatonia in pigeons, and also to impair web spinning in spiders (Hoffer & Osmond, 1959).

Added to this evidence are reports that this same epinephrine by-product, adrenochrome, appears in higher concentrations in the blood of humans affected with schizophrenia. Amounts of adrenochrome are also increased after the injection of lysergic acid diethylamide, or LSD, another psychomimetic drug (Hoffer et al., 1960). Epinephrine itself also has long been noted for creating an emotional state subjectively described as ''anxiety,'' restlessness, agitation, or excitability. Other fascinating data have found that low levels of norepinephrine may be associated with depression, and high levels with pathological euphoria; and that drugs known to relieve depression are also known to increase norepinephrine (Bunney et al., 1972).

This cumulative evidence leads some scientists, such as Hoffer and Osmond (1960), to conclude that they have now uncovered the culprit responsible for certain mental disorders. To date, however, there have been many inconsistent results and controversies over this theory. For example, sophisticated analyses have failed to confirm the presence of even traces of adrenochrome in the blood of acute or chronic schizophrenics.

*The Case for Dopamine.* Another neurotransmitter implicated in mental disorder is dopamine, which is formed in the human body as a precursor to norepinephrine. According to the dopamine hypothesis, excess dopamine prompts schizophrenia (Davis, 1978). The hypothesis derives its support from indirect evidence similar to work on epinephrine.

One line of research has been the study of drugs that are effective in treating schizophrenia. One of these drugs, chlorpromazine, was mentioned previously in the discussion of epinephrine. Besides alleviating schizophrenia, chlorpromazine also has side effects resembling Parkinson's disease, a motor-movement disease characterized by finger tremors, awkward gait, and rigid facial muscles. Dopamine in part causes Parkinson's; and comparisons of chlorpromazine and dopamine suggest that the former acts to block the latter. This then becomes the theoretical link between the two disorders of movement and madness

(Paul, 1977). If chlorpromazine reduces schizophrenic symptoms, and if chlorpromazine decreases dopamine, then schizophrenia may be caused by too much dopamine.

Additional evidence relates to the drug, amphetamine, which can produce psychotic conditions similar to paranoid schizophrenia, and which will worsen symptoms when given to schizophrenics. Amphetamines apparently act by increasing dopamine. Thus, once again the dopamine hypothesis seems supportable—for as amphetamines increase schizophrenic symptoms at the same time that they increase dopamine, then high levels of dopamine may well be linked to schizophrenia.

The evidence is intriguing. As with the epinephrine hypothesis, however, much more definitive work is needed. Even with further data, however, as one scientist observed, "A 'one transmitter' theory . . . is probably overly simplistic, as it is now recognized that many complex interrelationships exist between individual neurotransmitters" (Paul, 1977, p. 386). But the search must and will go on.

### Toxic Factors: A Cause of Pathology?

The search for a toxic substance, either a foreign substance or a product of the body's own neurotransmitter system, is an incredibly complex task. Among the neurotransmitters themselves there exist highly involved interrelationships, with similarities in structure and with equivalent involvements with tranquilizers or psychotomimetic drugs. A major concern in the research is always the issue of the elusive third factor—the extraneous uncontrolled variable such as smoking habits, activity level, and even the residuals of therapeutic drugs. Diet differences have always been a problem; in fact, one well-equipped hospital was found with patients with major dietary deficiencies. Finally, it is possible that differences in neurotransmitters or toxic bodies may exist because these substances are not the primary but only the second link in a chain—perhaps a chain that started with genetic vulnerability, environmental stress, or experiential learning.

## SUMMARY

In the search for the possible origins of mental disorders, it rapidly becomes clear that no single factor will explain all disorders, or perhaps even a single disorder. Biological factors have been prime suspects from genetic evidence and evidence on toxic factors. From the genetic direction, data comes from family history studies, morbidity risk studies, and chromosome studies. The morbidity risk research offers the strongest evidence. At least for some disorders, the risk of being affected tends to increase the closer the individual is in blood relationship to an affected person. Children raised apart from their biological parents have a higher risk of being affected by a disorder if these true parents had also shown that disorder.

A different line of biological studies has examined the possible role of toxic substances, either foreign to or native to the human body. Initial search for a unique toxic substance causing mental illness has not proven very rewarding. Current search is for possible natural substances which may be involved, such as epinephrine or dopamine. The case for both of these substances is rather similar. They can be connected to drugs which precipitate psychotic symptoms; they are also associated with the actions of medications which reduce psychoses; and, in some cases, the substances or their derivatives are found during certain psychotic states. In general, the circumstantial evidence is striking, in the sense that a consistent pattern of evidence continues to appear.

Those who are experts in either genetic studies or toxic substance studies tend to believe that these factors are involved in some mental disorders, but only as part of a more complex sequence of events which might include environmental factors. No longer is there major support for the idea that genetics or toxicity will alone account for the mental disorders, other than for some rare and known exceptions (such as the chromosome abnormality in Down's syndrome). As technology continues to develop and researchers' skills reach new levels, more secrets regarding the source of some mental disturbances are gradually being uncovered.

## KEY TERMS

**Adoption studies**
**Adrenal glands**
**Amygdala**
**Autonomic nervous system**
**Axon**
**Central nervous system**
**Cerebral cortex**
**Cerebral hemispheres**
**Cerebellum**
**Chromosome**
**Chromosome studies**
**Concordance**
**Cretinism**
**Dendrite**
**Deoxyribonucleic acid**
**Diathesis-stress theory**
**Dizygotic twins**
**Dopamine**
**Endocrine glands**
**Endorphins**
**Epinephrine**
**Fight or flight response**
**Fissure of Rolando**
**Fissure of Sylvius**
**Frontal lobe**
**Gene**
**General paresis**
**Hebephrenic**
**Heterozygous**
**Homozygous**
**Huntington's chorea**
**Hypothalamus**
**Karyotypes**
**Medulla**
**Midbrain**
**Monozygotic twins**
**Morbidity risk studies**
**Neuron**
**Neurotransmitters**
**Norepinephrine**
**Occipital lobe**
**Pancreas**
**Parasympathetic nervous system**
**Parathyroid glands**
**Parietal lobe**
**Penetrance**
**Peripheral nervous system**
**Pituitary gland**
**Pons**
**Proband**
**Septal area**
**Somatic nervous system**
**Sympathetic nervous system**
**Synapse**
**Taraxein**
**Temporal lobe**
**Thalamus**
**Thyroid**
**Zygote**

# CHAPTER 5

## Origins of Pathology: The Social Factors

- **To what degree is behavior controlled by our society?**
- **In what way might schizophrenia be explained as a reaction against society?**
- **Based on your own socioeconomic class status, can you predict what mental disorder you would be statistically likely to develop?**
- **How may your neighborhood environment affect your mental health?**
- **Based on statistical probability of being hospitalized for a disorder, which sex is the weaker sex?**
- **Is there a price to marriage? How does it differ between women and men?**
- **What should you know about pathology if you must be separated from your child for a length of time?**
- **Are there types of parents or types of family interaction patterns that seem to be associated with the development of a child's disorders?**
- **Based on the discussions in Chapters 4 and 5, how might biological and social factors combine to produce symptoms of schizophrenia in an individual?**

## Case History 5–1:
### Depression in a Child

In the writings of Dr. Melitta Sperling, a renowned psychoanalyst, is a description of a case she treated involving depression. In this case, the child's mother was physically present but psychologically rejecting.

> . . . this little girl had been referred to me for psychiatric investigation at the age of twenty-two months because of attacks of paroxysmal tachycardia [high heart rate], for which no cause could be established . . . the child developed a severe anorexia [unwillingness to eat] and sleep disturbance. She stopped eating and her sleep became fitful and interrupted by nightmares of hallucinatory quality. Her tendency to withdraw . . . became more pronounced and she now spent hours in a crouched position in the corner of her room, fingering her blanket and clicking her tongue. . . . This case was characterized by two of the most conspicuous features found in certain forms of depression in adults, namely severe anorexia and insomnia. In addition, she suffered from motor retardation . . . moodiness, and phobias.
>
> The relationship between mother and child had been very precarious prior to the birth of the baby brother. The traumatic effect of this event was derived mainly from the disturbed mother-child relationship in which the birth of the baby brother meant to the child loss of the mother. . . . Her mother, in actuality, preferred the baby brother because of his sex. She had unconsciously identified her daughter with her own mother and grandmother, both of whom she considered ''weak'' and ''inferior'' and held in contempt. In treatment the mother discovered that she, too, had a ''weak'' female part, and that it was this rejected part of herself which she had denied and projected onto her daughter and which she was so vigorously suppressing now in her child.
>
> In this case the highly ambivalent feelings of the mother toward her child had become even more intense after the birth of the baby boy. The mother was openly triumphant over the fact that she had given birth to a boy, while her grandmother and mother had been unable to bear sons. This gave prestige and value to her life, while the sickly, moody daughter was an unfavorable reflection of herself. . . .
>
> [Treatment for the child involved] play analysis . . . with dolls [where she] worked through her intense repressed oral-sadistic impulses directed toward her mother and the baby brother. . . . In addition to direct psychoanalytic play therapy with the child, treatment included work with the mother. . . . When the child was unresponsive and moody, the mother had found it very difficult to be with her; in fact, she had considered it a relief when the child remained quietly by herself for long periods of time. At my suggestion, and supported through treatment, the mother now spent much time with the little girl, inventing games to stimulate the child's interest and thus prevent her from withdrawing. In the main, this new regime served to provide the child with the essential ''emotional supplies'' from her mother. (Sperling, 1974, pp. 387–89)

Chapters 3 and 4 discussed psychological and biological explanations of abnormality. In direct contrast to these perspectives is the view that the social environment molds human nature—that personality, and abnormality, is a product of the social environment.

There seems no doubt that we are social beings. We choose to live near others and make efforts to increase our means of communicating with others. We establish laws that govern behaviors to facilitate living in a society. And on a more personal level, we rely on one social group in particular—the family—as the immediate resource for many needs.

Certainly, both culture and family are important in the structuring of personality and in our everyday sense of well-being. It seems inevitable that these two factors also play a role in the development of abnormalities. This chapter explores that connection between culture, family, and mental disorders. For some basic definitions of the sociological concepts and processes involved, see Focus 5–1.

*Through recreational activities and heroes, a* ***culture indirectly*** *influences its members. Here, a youngster is not only exercising like the adults, but also becoming a fan of soccer.*

## THE SOCIAL FACTORS: CULTURE

Ample evidence can be found that each society leaves a strong impression on the personalities of its members. Most individuals embody in their personalities the dominant motivations, values, ways of thinking, and traits of their society, to one degree or another. An Asian, for instance, is likely to appreciate different kinds of music than a European; he or she will also probably have different definitions of personal needs such as privacy and independence. Personality characteristics also vary, at least in a broad sense, from one society to another. And at the same time, certain values and lifestyles—and also certain maladjustments—are more prevalent in some groups within the same society than in other groups. In the first half of this chapter, we'll be exploring both cross-cultural and intracultural (within the culture) differences, and the ways in which they may relate to personality disorders. The second part of the chapter examines the family's role in personality development.

### Cross-cultural Comparisons

A great deal of attention has been given to the idea of *national character*—the assumption that temperamental differences exist across cultures, and that people from each country show certain personality traits. During World War II, this idea was given impetus as Western military leaders were concerned with guessing the probable actions of the Japanese, who were noted for their self-discipline, imperturbability, and sense of honor (Benedict, 1946). In this same time period, the Russian was typified as lacking interpersonal trust; having little individual interest in personal planning or self-control; tending to acquiesce to strong authoritarian leadership; and being concerned with receiving loyalty, respect, and sincerity (Inkeles et al., 1958). For readers interested in measuring themselves

## FOCUS 5–1:
### Fundamentals of the Study of Culture

This chapter uses several terms and concepts that are more basic to the field of sociology than to abnormal psychology, for example:

A *society* includes the organized population of people living together and sharing a mutual sense of belonging. In modern times, the term *society* has become nearly synonymous with nation. Each society or nation exposes its members to cultural influences. A *culture* is the socially transmitted mass of attitudes, ideas, values, perceptions, practices, and beliefs of the society.

Culture influences us all, both indirectly and directly. *Indirect influences* derive from cultural themes repeated over and over again—in advertisements, in fictional readings, in visual entertainment, and even in fairy tales that describe good and evil. The family has a major role in the transmission and shaping of cultural values through *socialization,* that is, direct training in behaviors agreeable to the broader society.

The society's set of customs or formal laws are *direct influences:* violating them results in sanctions or punishments. *Stratification,* the assignment of different people to different social levels, also provides control. Each person's social status defines the social contacts that person may have, as well as self-perceptions, interests, motivations, and even behaviors.

Social standards and customs are functional in that they promote stability within the society. One consequence is the subjective commonality among members of the same society, as the members feel identified with one another since they share common customs.

These various characteristics of a society are all related to issues of psychopathology as we shall see in this chapter. If customs impose certain restrictions on behaviors, they are also potential sources of individual conflict and guilt. Social stratification is often associated with environmental conditions which sometimes relate to pathology. Social control, through formalized law, may be a method for protecting the values of the society; however, critics such as Laing suggest that social conformity itself contributes to pathology (see Chapter 1). Societal demands for heterosexual behaviors, for example, may be a source of stress for those with homosexual preferences that might be considered normal in another culture. Overall, the society we live in may contribute in visible and invisible ways to bettering our lives, and also to influencing our adjustment.

against their own national character yardstick, Table 5–1 outlines one sociologist's perception of typical American characteristics and values.

**TABLE 5–1**

**The American National Character**

| *Traits* |
|---|
| • A belief in the "personal success story." |
| • An orientation toward active mastery, and away from passivity. |
| • A wish to alter the status quo. |
| • A personal sense of generosity toward others, almost as a sense of duty. |
| • A concern with moral and ethical justifications for personal actions. |
| • A fear or distaste for hypocrisy. |
| • A strong belief in the right to individual freedom. |
| • A feeling of being uncomfortable when idle. |

SOURCE: Adapted from *American Society: A Sociological Interpretation,* by R. Williams, 1951, New York: Knopf.

Obviously, few Americans are typical in all respects; the same is true of individual Japanese, Russians, or any other nationality. Yet, people of the same society do share many common values, philosophies, perceptions, and assumptions, which are the result of the complex process of socialization. And just as there are cultural differences in values and behaviors, there is also evidence that variations exist in both the perception and expression of abnormal behaviors (Favazza & Oman, 1978; Landis & Brisler, 1983; Tseng & Hsu, 1979).

***Cross-cultural Differences in Abnormality.*** When Europeans first arrived in northeastern Canada, a disorder known as the *windigo psychosis* was common among some native groups. This psychosis was based on a belief in a superhuman, man-eating, fearsome giant (the windigo) who preyed on humans. This grotesque monster, some 20 to 30 feet tall, was believed to have a heart of ice. Persons suffering from windigo psychosis were said to be possessed by the giant spirit and therefore turned into cannibals, often with "hearts of ice."

A different disorder was prevalent among the Eskimos—so prevalent, in fact, that 8 of the 17 women associated with Peary's 1908 expedition were affected by it during one winter season. In this disorder, known as *pibloktoq,* the individual shows sudden fits of shouting, tearing of clothes, and frantic plunges across the snowdrifts, followed by convulsive seizures and finally stuporous sleep or coma (Wallace, 1972).

Among the Chinese and natives of the Celebes and West Borneo, a sadly ludicrous phobia exists called *shook yong* or *karo* (Linton, 1956). Among men, this disorder is marked by an intense fear that they will die unless they can prevent their penis from becoming inverted into their body. The condition in a woman is the fear that her breasts will disappear into her chest, thus causing her death. In both cases, the fear is so intense that members of the family are desperately enlisted to grip and retain the sex organ. Another intense fear involving dying is known as *hwa-byung* (Lin, 1983). Among Koreans, this fear of impending death centers around pains in the stomach. One common belief is that anger has been building in the patient, which leads to an imbalance of yin-yang elements in favor of the fire element, and this leads to the pains in the abdomen.

The fact that these four disorders seem so exotic to most Americans, yet are commonly recognized in their own cultures, is evidence that culture does affect abnormality. Thus, different cultures appear to develop disorders that may be unique only to their society.

Even when a disorder is found to exist across several cultures, there may be differences in their frequency. Epidemiological studies across the world suggest that the incidence of schizophrenia is high in some countries, yet low in others, as Figure 5–1 illustrates. Drug abuse, prevalent in our own society, is rare among the Meo tribe of Laotians who farm opium (Westermeyer, 1974). Suicide rates also vary strikingly from society to society. In Japan, Germany, Denmark, and Switzerland, the incidence is between 18 to 25 per 100,000 as compared to 5 to 10 per 100,000 in Canada, Italy, Norway, and Venezuela (Farberow, 1975; World Health Organization, 1973).

***Cross-cultural Differences in Treatment.*** Cross-cultural differences in the mode of treatment offered the mentally disturbed are also clearly definable (Higginbotham, 1979; Prince, 1980). The Iroquois In-

*Different cultures show unique forms of mental disorders. This photo shows an Eskimo woman during an attack of* ***pibloktoq****, or arctic hysteria.*

dians believed that the dream was used by a spirit to convey its wishes. To prevent being plagued by an unsatiated spirit, compliance to the dream wish was therefore demanded. Thus, a warrior who dreamed of being tortured by his enemies was routinely put through part of the torture cycle.

One interesting study found clear differences in attitudes of doctors regarding treatment of mental disorder (Levine, 1972). Czechoslovakian physicians viewed mental patients more as an inferior class requiring coercive treatment, while British physicians took a more paternalistic, humanistic view. West German physicians felt that such patients were a threat to society and hence should be restricted during and after hospitalization. Different societies also foster different attitudes on care, based on broader cultural beliefs. Thus, the Asian family is more likely to care for a relative at home, because of the strong familial values, and to avoid embarrassment (Sue & Morishima, 1982).

***How Culture Affects Pathology.*** Psychological disorders exist in all cultures. Yet, each society seems to add its own distinctive flavor to the psychodynamics of a disorder (Marsella, 1980). Different cultures produce differences in the expression of mental illness, as well as perceptions and treatments of disorders. Draguns (1980), for instance, notes that schizophrenia, affective disorders, and hysteria are all present in all cultures, although their expression is subject to cultural shaping.

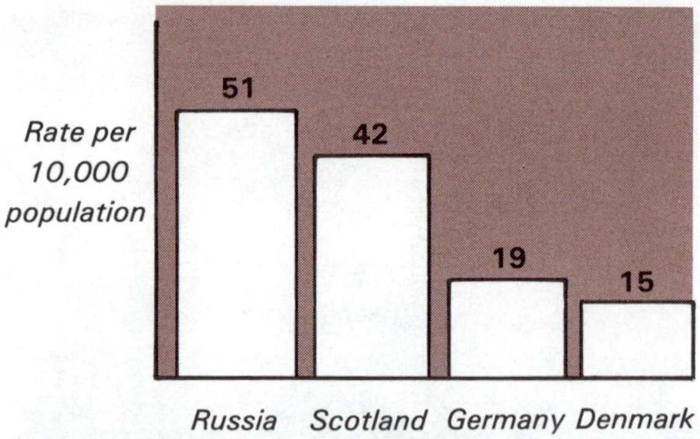


**FIGURE 5–1** Cross-cultural differences in prevalence of schizophrenia: Russia, Scotland, Denmark, and Germany.

SOURCE: Based on "Epidemiology" by B. Cooper, 1978, in J. Wing (Ed.), *Schizophrenia: Towards a New Synthesis,* London: Academic Press.

How does this shaping process occur? Schooler and Caudill (1964) suggest that the symptoms of schizophrenia are the patients' ways of expressing resistance to the major expectations of the culture. They found interesting support for their view. While Japanese normally exhibit a strong degree of personal decorum, Japanese schizophrenics, in contrast, are likely to be physically assaultive. Furthermore, the normally rational American becomes bizarre during schizophrenic episodes, losing control over perceptions and thoughts.

Do mental disorders represent—at least to some extent—a reaction against society? Or is society a source of solutions for mental disorders? Experts continue to provide careful analyses of the inextricable link between the culture that raises us and the person we become (Draguns, 1980; Marsella, 1979). Perhaps the best summary of the influence of culture on personality is that of Spiro (1959):

> It is my guess . . . that each culture creates stresses and strains—some of them universal, some unique—with which the personality must cope; that the cultural heritage provides, to a greater or lesser degree, institutional techniques for their reduction, if not resolution; that the incidence of psychopathology in any society is a function not merely of the strains produced by its culture but also of the institutional means which its cultural heritage provides for the resolution of strain; that those individuals who, for whatever the reasons, cannot resolve the culturally created strains by means of the culturally provided instruments of resolution resolve them in idiosyncratic ways (neuroses and psychoses); and that to the extent that different cultures create different types of strain, idiosyncratic resolution of strain (neuroses and psychoses) will reveal cultural variability. (p. 142)

According to cross-cultural evidence, then, many abnormalities can be seen to reflect the stresses and strains of a culture. But the culture also provides guidance for resolving these pressures as well.

***Evaluation of the Cross-cultural Data.*** It is important to note that such cross-cultural comparisons can only be considered suggestive information. Careful, systematic data are extremely difficult to obtain for a variety of reasons. For one, the accuracy of rates varies with the investigator's ability to obtain the cooperation of individual members of a culture, just as in any scientific survey. Language handicaps present real barriers; and definitions of illness as well as methods of observation may vary for different investigators. Also, estimates obtained from one country or even one region are not always comparable or as reliable as data from other areas. For example, hospital rates may be affected by the artifact of differences in the willingness to keep at home or to hospitalize persons with disorders.

### Intracultural Correlates of Disorder

Just as mental disorders may vary from one culture to another, differences also exist within a culture, varying according to social background or demographic factors. Several large-scale surveys have been conducted over the last several decades in the attempt to determine both the *incidence* (number of new cases of a disorder) and *prevalence* (total number of existing cases) of mental disorders among various population groups in the United States. And several social factors have been identified that might be seen as correlates. These include social stratification, neighborhood, urbanization, religion, ethnic or minority group membership, and marital status.

***Social Stratification.*** In a classic study (1958), Frederick Hollingshead, a sociologist, and August Redlich, a psychiatrist, teamed up to examine socio-

*Different cultures hold different beliefs about the causes and treatment of disorders. Here, the woman* ***caralo*** *is using* ***rituals****, including a cigar, to bring a member of her congregation to a trance state.*

economic groups in New Haven, Connecticut. Five classes were identified, ranging from class I families to class V families. These groupings were based on levels of education and occupations, with class I representing the highest achievement levels.

The results of this study were revealing. They showed that the lower-class members exhibited the highest prevalence and incidence of mental disorders (see Figure 5–2). Moreover, some neuroses appeared to be class related: antisocial and immature reactions were concentrated in classes III and V; phobias, anxiety, and psychophysiologic reactions were clustered among class IV members; and the depressive reactions tended to affect the class I and II persons. In a thumbnail summary, the authors described the class members in the following way: "The class V neurotic behaves badly, the class IV neurotic aches physically, the class III patient defends fearfully, and the class I–II patient is dissatisfied with himself" (p. 240). The incidence of psychosis for the class V members was nearly

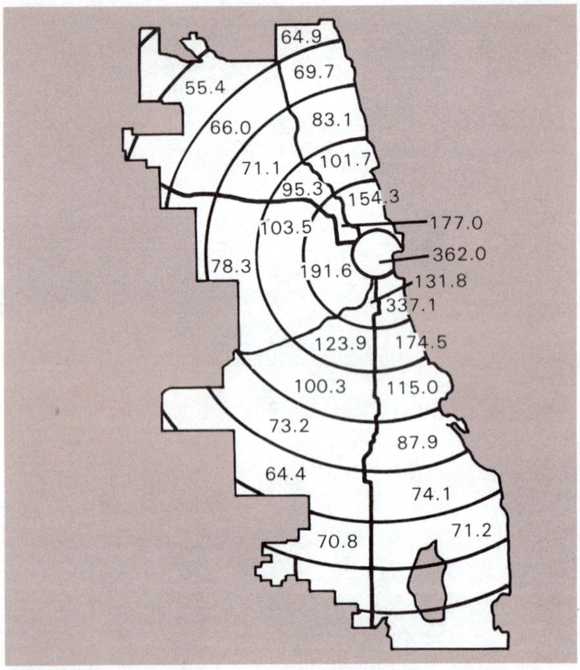


**FIGURE 5–2** A census map of Chicago showing the decrease in mental disorder rates from the center to the edge of the city.

SOURCE: Based on *Mental Disorders in Urban Areas* by R. Faris and H. Dunham, 1939, Chicago: University of Chicago Press.

three times that of classes I and II combined. However, like neuroses, these disorders also seemed class typed, to a degree. Bipolar psychosis was more common among class I and II members, although schizophrenia was found to be a nondiscriminator of class, as it appeared equally as prevalent in all classes.

Another well-known study, the Midtown Manhattan Study (Sree & Fischer, 1980), was also significant. It was an eight-year study of mental health in midtown New York City. As in the Hollingshead and Redlich study, this investigation found disorders more prevalent among the lower socioeconomic groups. Definite impairment in mental health was noted for 33 percent of the persons on the lowest socioeconomic level, as compared with 18 percent of those on the highest level. At the same time, the members of 24 percent of the highest socioeconomic group were symptom free, but only 10 percent of the lowest group could claim to be well.

Support for these general findings has also been obtained in studies of other cultures.[1] In Japan, for example, psychosis rates were greatest in lower-income groups (Japan Ministry of Health and Welfare, 1954); and in Singapore, the business and professional class showed a much lower rate of hospitalization for mental illness than did the unskilled laboring class (Murphy, 1959).

***Neighborhood.*** Another factor related to incidence of mental disorder appears to be the neighborhood a person lives in. A pioneering study of Chicago in the 1930s (Faris & Dunham, 1939) demonstrated that rates of mental disorder decrease from the center of the city to the periphery, in a pattern similar to that for delinquency rates (see Figure 5–3). Mental breakdown was 10 times less common among residents of the outlying residential districts (48 per 100,000), as compared to those living in the center city (499 per 100,000). As in the socioeconomic class studies, types of disorders also varied according to neighborhood. Incidence of bipolar disorders was higher among those who were able to afford the apartments in the higher-priced districts, while paranoid schizophrenia was more prevalent among the rooming-house tenants.

In explaining these differences, the authors linked breakdowns to a chain of events related to living in an inner-city neighborhood: the disorganized community life in such areas promotes social isolation; social isolation encourages extreme seclusiveness; and this break of successful and normal interaction with the society ends in mental disorder. In this sense, social isolation is the result of neighborhood disintegration and, in turn, is the cause of mental disorganization.

This study is relevant to the *downward drift* hypothesis. According to this theory, the inverse relationship that exists between rates of psychosis and living area or socioeconomic level is the result of the disordered person's downward drift—the inability to maintain a previous level of achievement. As a disorder worsens, the person drifts further into the lower-class environment, in a sort of vicious cycle. While intriguing, this hypothesis appears to be refuted by the Hollingshead and Redlich work (and that of others, such as Brown et al., 1975). They demonstrated that

1 For Formosa, see Lin, 1953; and for South America, see Strainbrook, 1952. Other studies producing supportive data include Dohrenwend, 1975; and Noyes et al., 1980.

91 percent of the patients were still in the same class as their parents: only 1.3 percent had drifted down to a lower class than their parents, while 69 percent of class I–II patients originally belonged to class I–II families. In other words, the lower-class patients did not appear to drift downward and, in fact, some of the upper-class patients were upwardly mobile.

***Urbanization.*** For all types of mental illness, the figures for urban residents are clearly higher than those for rural residents around the world (Cooper, 1978). For example, Jaco (1960) has reported that urban areas contribute over two times as many first admissions to mental hospitals as rural regions. Cases of schizophrenia tended to concentrate in the most densely populated centers of each of these regions.

Those who accept these differences point to the stresses involved in urban living, such as the loss of personal relationships, the extreme competitiveness, greater material needs and higher-density living.

The urbanization figures appear on the surface to be convincing. However, critics point to the detailed population studies of Sjögren and Larrson (1954) which failed to confirm the higher urban rates. These critics suggest that even if there are more urban residents in hospitals this may be due to factors not necessarily associated with greater stresses of urban living. For example, higher rates of admission may reflect the greater availability of hospital resources or the greater willingness of families to rely on hospitalization in the cities than in the rural zones.

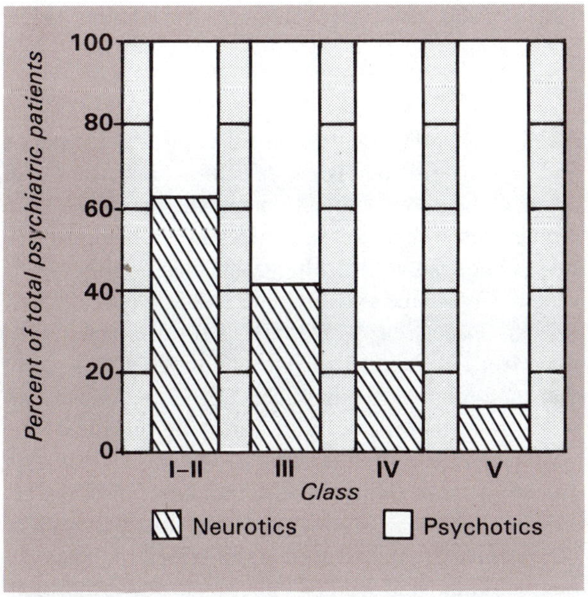


**FIGURE 5-3** Percentage of neurotics and psychotics found in each social class.

SOURCE: Based on *Social Class and Mental Illness* by A. Hollingshead and F. Redlich, 1958, New York: Wiley.

***Religious Affiliation.*** Another factor that seems to relate to incidence of certain types of disorders is religious background. Psychotic disorders appear to be more prevalent among Protestants than among Catholics or Jews (Frumkin & Frumkin, 1957). On the other hand, for the more moderate types of disorders seen in mental health clinics, the number of Jewish patients in treatment was double their proportionate number in the population. Catholics were next, followed by Protestants (Eichler & Lirtzman, 1956). Jews have a relatively low number of persons troubled with alcohol abuse; while Catholics comprised the highest numbers of alcohol abusers (Malzberg, 1936; Snyder, 1955). The Jewish mores against excessive drinking and the Catholic atmosphere of guilt may help to explain these differences. However, with modern changes in religious orientations, these conditions may be changing.

***Ethnic Group.*** Ethnic minority groups comprise about 20 percent of the population of the United States (Seymour et al., 1982). However, the study of ethnic group differences in mental disorders is extremely difficult because of the frequent association between racial background and other factors, such as socioeconomic level, education, and occupational status (Giordano & Giordano, 1976).

Some reports have found higher admissions rates for blacks than for whites (Alers, 1978) while others have found no significant differences (Kramer et al., 1973). In fact, one study (Jaco, 1960), which canvassed the entire state of Texas, found Anglo-Saxon whites to have a higher incidence of psychosis than either nonwhites (blacks, Native Americans, Asians) or Hispanics. On the other hand, when hospital admission rates across the United States are examined, nonwhites show more than twice the totals for whites (U.S. Department of Health, Education & Welfare, 1977).

Furthermore, minorities are more likely to termi-

*Racial **discrimination** in the United States was at a high point when this photo was taken. Discrimination is still considered to be a contributor to stress and pathology among many groups today.*

nate traditional psychotherapy contacts, possibly because of the inappropriateness of such approaches (Levine & Padilla, 1980; Miranda et al., 1976). Asians, Mexican Americans, and Native Americans in California mental hospitals have been noted to be underrepresented in continuing treatment; this has led some to argue that therapists are less accepting, or that minority patients feel misunderstood and hence continuing treatment is either not offered or not received (Martinez, 1982; Mollica, 1983; Sue & Morishima, 1982). Such conclusions, however, must take into account a finding that some white patients also share such feelings of being misunderstood by their therapists. Thus, 4.3 percent of white patients felt that their therapist was prejudiced against them; the comparable figures for black patients was 6.1 percent, and 4.3 percent for Mexican-American patients (Yamamoto et al., 1968).

With increasing public consciousness over minority interests, a variety of claims have been made regarding minority group membership and personality (Newton et al., 1982). In contrast to writings that imply that Asian Americans are models of success and free of worries, surveys have pointed out their depression, isolation, and feelings of powerlessness (Sue & Morishima, 1982; Yoshioka et al., 1978). Fear of success, which could create feelings of conflict, has been said to characterize 67 percent of black men, 64 percent of white women, 29 percent of black women, but only 10 percent of white men (Horner, 1970). This points out the plight of both the black male and the white female in our society.

We can conclude by saying that some of the mental health concerns of minority persons derive from several correlates associated with belonging to a minority group. These correlates include the stresses of racism, status inconsistencies, poverty, urban densities, and conflicts over cultural identity (Albee, 1980; Smith et al., 1978). And finally, for minority-group members who have recently immigrated to the United States, such as Cubans and Indo-Chinese, mental health adjustment is sorely pressured by additional factors. Mental, physical, and social breakdowns can occur from value conflicts, communication barriers, loss of traditional roots, gaps between what is aspired to and what is achievable, and alienation (Guthrie & Tanco, 1980; Smither & Rodriquez-Giegling, 1979; Sue & Chin, 1982).

***Sex.*** Another factor that relates to the incidence and type of disorder is gender. In general, men still seem to be more subject to mental disorders than women, or at least to the degree shown in admission rates to hospitals. Over the years, men have been admitted at twice the rate of women (U.S. Department of Health, Education & Welfare, 1977). Exactly what this means is a matter of interpretation. It may mean that men are more vulnerable. Or, it may mean that women are more successful at staying outside of the hospital in spite of emotional problems, or that men and women are subject to different types of disorders (Blechman, 1983; Brodsky & Hare-Mustin, 1980). If we examine the information more closely, it turns out that both men and women experience about the same incidence of schizophrenia. On the other hand, the most frequent reason for hospitalization of men is alcohol abuse, with schizophrenia the second-ranked reason. For women, schizophrenia accounts for most of the new admissions, with the affective and depressive disorders being the second most frequent diagnosis (U.S. Department of Health, Education & Welfare, 1977).

Regarding women, it has been pointed out that a double standard in mental health definitions seems to exist (Al-Issa, 1982). The characteristics of the normal or healthy adult are similar to those defined for the normal male, but the conception of the healthy female is quite different and includes some less-than-healthy traits. Thus, the woman is supposed to be normal if she is submissive, less independent, less aggressive, and less competitive than the normal male (Broverman et al., 1970). The societal role for women emphasizes responsibility for family care and temporary suppression of personal growth activities until the young reach independence. After a review of common symptoms of mental disorder in women, Phyllis Chesler (1972) poses an intriguing definition of mental illness which stresses the conflicts produced by societal role assignments. She considers that mental illness in women "is either the acting out of the devalued female role or the total or partial rejection of one's sex-role stereotype." Some support for this comes from data which show women who originally accepted the role of child-rearing became depressed when it was no longer necessary (Guttentag et al., 1980; Collier, 1983).

The connection between traditional gender roles and disorders relates also to the question of how employment affects women's sense of well-being. Brown and Harris (1978) found that this factor did relate to depression in women, although not in a consistent fashion. Although employment can be viewed as a potential shelter from depression, since it offers the woman a positive role identity and also broadens her social contacts, they also found that depression can be precipitated by employment. This is likely to happen if a woman's child-rearing obligations prevent her from successfully attending to the demands of the job, or if the job experience generates a sense of failure.

***Marital Status.*** Marital status is another factor found to be associated with mental illness. As with other correlates discussed earlier, several interpretations may be offered in explaining this relationship. At least one study has shown that married persons are less susceptible to mental illness (Wing, 1978). Persons without a mate, whether by choice, by divorce, or by death, tend to show higher rates of illness. As Figure 5–4 shows, the rates for first admissions to hospitals in the United States are markedly higher for single, divorced, and widowed persons than they are for married persons.

There are several explanations for this relationship. The single life, divorce, and widowhood are all states that may provoke certain stresses, such as feelings of alienation, isolation, rejection, and incompetence. The particularly high incidence among divorced persons might also be related to the antagonistic system adopted by courts in handling divorces. It has been suggested that this system encourages attitudes of rejection and condemnation of the previous partner. Another explanation for the relationship between marital status and mental health may simply be a matter of self-selection. If emotional instability prevents achieving a successful married life, then it is reasonable that fewer unstable persons remain married. Poorly adjusted persons may also be less attractive as potential mates, and so they may be less likely to marry in the first place.

With all these explanations and data, it is interesting to note that the evidence isn't entirely clear-cut. On closer inspection, there seem to be differences between women and men in adjustment to married life. Radloff's findings (1975) regarding depression, sex,

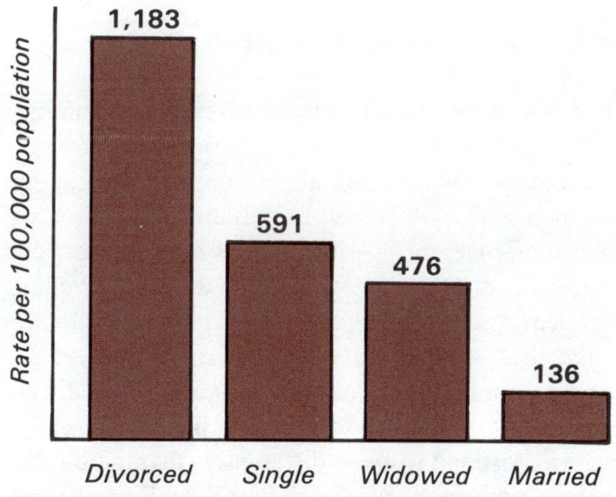


**FIGURE 5–4** Rates for first admissions to U.S. mental hospitals according to marital status.

SOURCE: "Admission Rates by Age, Sex, and Marital Status: State and County Hospitals, 1969," by C. Taube, Statistical Note, 32, Washington D.C.: Dept. of Health, Education, and Welfare, 1970.

and marital status are worth noting here; they are drawn from a major survey of both men and women by the Center for Epidemiologic Studies. Among married, divorced, and separated persons, women were found to be more depressed than men. However, among never-married or widowed persons, men showed more depression than women. Being married seemed to help men, in that married men showed less depression than single men. However, marriage did not serve to protect women, and so we find that married women are as depressed as single women. Radloff did not find support for the sometimes-stated premise that being a housewife makes one more subject to depression, since no substantial differences were found between the women who were housewives and those who were employed. In all, there is some evidence to support the idea that the married state may have certain stabilizing features. Positive interpersonal relationships, a sense of belonging and worth, and reassuring companionship can all certainly contribute to a person's ability to adjust. Specifically regarding women, Brown and Harris (1978) suggest that the presence of a husband or male friend can serve to prevent depression; and Weissman and Paykel (1974) also emphasize the role of the husband in helping relieve a wife's depression.

#### Evaluation of Culture as a Cause

There seems little question that both culture and demographic factors relate to pathology in a variety of ways. At the broad level of cultural environment, we can see that the society we belong to defines the stresses we will experience, the possible ways we will express our problems, and the acceptability of different avenues for releasing or reducing tensions. There is ample evidence that Americans who live in an industrial, densely populated environment will experience different stresses, will learn to perceive them differently, and will respond to them differently, than would the Eskimo, or the native of Celebes or West Borneo mentioned earlier in this chapter.

Within a society, too, factors relating to each individual's immediate background and environment also influence pathology. Socioeconomic and marital status, the type of neighborhood we live in, and other personal and community variables can increase vulnerability.

*Among the **sources of pathology** are poverty, deprivation, and the environment we live in. Studies show the incidence of mental disorders to be highest in the low socioeconomic areas of cities.*

On the other hand, as with evidence on biological factors, much study is still needed in identifying the exact mechanisms whereby culture operates on abnormality and personality. Does commonality in national character exist because the society's rules of behavior control our *actions*, both normal and abnormal? Or is there commonality because of shared *perceptions* and values? Does social class relate to mental disorder because of status conflicts affecting one's esteem, or more indirectly through nutritional or quality-of-life deprivations?

One other point should be remembered in evaluating any cross-cultural or sociological correlates of mental pathology. The point is that, to the extent that such correlates exist, they relate to broad statistical population groups, and not to the individual. Because a person belongs to a particular minority group, lives in an urban environment, or has a particular religious affiliation does not invariably mean that person will be affected by a particular disorder. Far more immediate are the effects of another social environment—a person's family. The remainder of this chapter will ex-

## THE SOCIAL FACTORS: FAMILY

Unlike any other animal, humans experience a period of growth and development that is extraordinarily long. Many animals are born fully developed and independent of their parents, but humans must wait many years before their physical and mental capacities completely mature. Children are highly dependent on their parents through these formative years, and consequently, the parents play a significant role in the personality development of their offspring. Some aspects of the family that we shall examine next include *parental presence*, and *pathology in the family unit.*

### Parental Presence

***Feral Children.*** Perhaps the most extreme illustrations of the importance of the role of parents are the few known cases of what happens when adult humans are absent during infancy or childhood. *Feral children* are children said to have been raised by wild animals. Although not well-documented, cases have been cited of children raised in the wilds without human companionship, such as the "Wild Boy of Aveyron" and the "Wolf Children" of India (Singh & Zingg, 1942). Such children were said to have survived through the aid of wild beasts who adopted them as part of the litter. When finally discovered, the children's behavior typically showed more similarity to their adopted animal brethren than to their human counterparts. They were found to have difficulty in walking erect, in speaking intelligibly, and in acquiring human social skills. In one instance, it was said that the child was able to run faster on all fours than he could walk standing erect.

Such cases are extraordinary in that they combine the absence of normal human socialization with another factor—the presence of a quite different kind of socialization from the adopted animal family. More common are incidents of another deprivation situation: maternal separation. The discussion in Focus 5–2 summarizes a few of the many animal experiments that have explored what happens when nonhuman infants are deprived of maternal and other social contacts. In plore how the family environment relates to adjustment and abnormality. the next several pages, we'll also look at evidence of how the lack of warm family life may affect human children.

***Effects of Maternal Separation.*** More recently, and with more detailed and sounder reporting, the necessity of parental presence has been documented through several studies of *maternal separation.* In contrast to the feral children, the youngsters of this group experienced both human companionship and care and the comforts and medical care of city living. However, they lacked the presence of their own mothers and were either being raised in orphanages or separated temporarily because of illness.

In all such cases the effects attributed to separation have been appalling. Major deviations in personality of such children involve:

- *Affect hunger* (Goldfarb, 1945; Freud & Burlingham, 1944). In some cases, the children developed an insatiable and indiscriminate demand for attention and affection when near others as if to compensate for their deprived life.
- *The affectionless character* (Bowlby, 1944). In a larger number of cases, an avoidance of or indifference to social interaction has been apparent. This is accompanied by a sense of social apathy and a lack of the capacity to form meaningful rela tionships with people.
- *Anaclitic depression or mourning* (Spitz & Wolf, 1946; Robertson & Bowlby, 1952). This deviation, particularly noted in cases of separation, involves a dramatic sequence of behavior. It begins at separation with initial protest and efforts to recapture the lost mother; followed by mourning and despair accompanied by decreased activity level; and it results finally in either complete physical and intellectual deterioration in young children, or, in older children a denial of the need for a mother—to the extent that the child may even refuse to recognize his or her own parent on later reunion.

***Separation Factors Influencing Deviations.*** The maternal deprivation studies just cited leave many significant questions unresolved (Kagan, 1982), and the soundness of such research has been seriously questioned on a few grounds. Among the criti-

# FOCUS 5–2:

## Social Deprivation and Mental Disorders: Experimental Evidence

It is virtually impossible to conduct experiments to test the long-term effects of social deprivation on humans. However, several experiments have explored how isolation and maternal deprivation affect animals. Their findings are relevant to our understanding of how the social environment may relate to disorders.

In one series of experiments, Rowland (1964) raised groups of infant monkeys in total social deprivation. Each monkey was raised in a solid, illuminated cage and never saw any other living creature. Physically, the animals appeared to have developed normally, but psychologically, the monkeys seemed to have been affected. For example, when they were given their first glimpse at the world outside their quarters by the removal of the opaque screen, profound terror gripped the young monkeys. A typical reaction pattern was self-clutching, freezing, and hiding, head covered, in a corner (Akisal & McKinney, 1973). When placed with other monkeys, the deprived ones were totally unresponsive socially as if their capacity for social activity was completely obliterated. When subjected to abusive and even dangerous aggression by others, the deprived monkeys remained passive and vulnerable.

Similar results were obtained by Melzack and Scott (1957), who also tested their animals' ability to respond to stimulation. Six litters of terriers were divided into two groups, one raised in a sensory and socially deprived environment. At maturity the animals were tested. In two tests for pain, being jabbed by a dissecting needle and burned with a match, the deprived dogs accepted the painful stimulus passively, without attempting to move away. They acted as if they were totally oblivious, did not have to be restrained; and in fact, even *approached* the pain-provoking stimulus.

Of final interest in the deprivation-type studies is the work of Harlow (1958) in exploring the *contact-comfort hypothesis:* the idea that intimate physical contact is necessary for an animal to acquire security feelings, particularly security from a mother figure. In the experiments (Harlow & Suomi, 1974), two surrogate-mother monkeys were constructed: one of bare welded wire, the other with the wire sheathed in terry cloth. Infant rhesus monkeys were raised apart from their own mothers, either with a wire or a cloth mother. Testing involved placing the infants in a strange environment with unfamiliar objects. Those monkeys raised without the benefit of the terry cloth mother showed significantly higher emotional reactions than those raised with the security of the cloth mother. However, even the terry cloth-raised monkeys seemed to have suffered some loss by being raised without a real mother. Although they developed seemingly normally, at maturity they were deficient in sexual relations.

cisms has been the lack of initial screening of the children which might have identified other factors responsible, such as their initial emotional stability. In addition, observations have not been standardized, and the studies did not always assess the quality of the mother-child relationship prior to separation.

Despite these objections, however, we can draw some tentative conclusions regarding the relationship between maternal separation and the development of some personality disorders.

First, single or brief (less than three weeks) separation experiences (such as a short hospital stay) occurring in a healthy family are recovered from fairly promptly and completely. However, there is some possibility that a hidden scar remains to make the person more vulnerable to future threats; for example, susceptibility to later depressions. Brief separation leads to overanxious overdependency and clinging following reunion; while prolonged separation leads to detachment and affectionless withdrawal.

Second, prolonged (over four weeks) deprivation experiences have variable effects according to the age of the child. In early infancy, prolonged deprivation followed by reunion can result in dramatic improvements in social and intellectual functioning, although speech appears to be retarded. From about the third month of life, prolonged and severe deprivation (continuing as long as three years) usually leads to severe intellectual and personality deficits that appear irreversible. This age difference seems relevant to the fact that infants appear to first become responsive to people at about three months.

In general, children seem to be less able to sustain separation experiences before five years of age than after. Also, the degree of persistence of the effects of separation seems to vary, with impairments in language, the ability to think in abstractions, and the capacity for meaningful interpersonal attachments being the most resistant to recovery. And finally, many other factors mediate the effects of deprivation or separation: these include the nature and duration of the experience; the quality of parental substitute figures; the quality of mothering received both before and after the separation; and the child's own physical and psychological inner resources for coping with the stress (Lamb, 1982).

***Maternal separation** can be trying for a child. The long-term consequences of separation depend upon many factors, including the age of the child.*

***The Role of Parent-presence.*** Why is the presence of a parent so crucial to normal development? No one yet knows the precise answer. Perhaps the traumatic experience of loss of an adult's presence is too extreme for the young child's immature system to adequately react to. But this does not cxplain the equally drastic effects where some minimal human companionship is provided. Another possible answer relates to social learning. In an adequate family relationship, the infant will respond to and be responded to by the parent. By this process, a reciprocal intimate interpersonal relationship evolves. In severe conditions of deprivation, however, the infant is never stimulated nor rewarded for responding. This loss of socialization, in turn, leads to further isolation, and as the child becomes further out of touch with social reality, it also becomes increasingly vulnerable to a break with psychological reality (Papousek & Papousek, 1983).

## The Pathological Family Unit

While the prior discussions relate to disorders that result from an absence of parents, mental disorders certainly also develop where the family is intact. Since the family's role is so critical in molding personality, establishing behavior patterns, and developing a sense of well-being in the individual, many scientists have been prompted to look to the family itself to find the origins of abnormal behavior (Perlmutter, 1983). We'll look at a few *pathogenic* (literally, the genesis of pathology) family patterns, as well as some parental traits that may be related to the development of one disorder, schizophrenia.

***Two Pathogenic Patterns: The Schismatic or the Skewed Family and the Double-bind.*** In looking for the origins of abnormal behavior, it has become more and more common to examine the workings of the family as a unit, rather than singling out the individual who is affected by the disorder (Haley, 1980; L'Abate, 1983). In this sense, the patient is seen as being no more or less ill than the family unit. In some cases, in fact, the members of a family show the same pathogenic modes of interaction over several generations, so that the same neurosis may be perpetuated from generation to generation. Two such pathogenic patterns that have been noted are the family that is either schismatic or skewed, and the family involved in double-bind communications.

*The Schismatic or Skewed Family.* In one study, researchers looked to the family milieu in the effort to explain disorders shown by individuals (Fleck et al., 1963). The pattern they discovered was a basically distorted family structure, with one or both parents exhibiting serious psychopathology. These families can be classified as either *schismatic*, with the parental hostilities and recriminations dividing the family into opposing factions, or *skewed*, with one spouse passively going along with the aberrant ways and child-rearing practices of the more disturbed parent. In either case, the children are raised in an atmosphere permeated by irrationality, distortions, and lack of adaptive role models with which to identify. Unlike other parent pairs, no ameliorative role is assumed by the more normal parent to compensate for the deficiencies of the disturbed parent.

Fleck (1976) reports one case that illustrates the fragmentation of a skewed family. Although neither parent was ever considered aberrant by community staff, the patient's mother blatantly distorted reality, with the father subservient to his wife's demands, no matter how aberrant. Their disturbed family communication can easily be seen in the following excerpt:

> MOTHER: She [the patient] is not ready to work—I could smash these guys [the doctors].
>
> DAUGHTER: I want to be on my own. I got to be, I want to . . . [move out].
>
> MOTHER: She doesn't know anything about money. She can't handle it. The relatives don't know what's going on. We are broke.
>
> FATHER: I can't keep on handing out money. [Long recital on how dangerous it is to live away from home.]
>
> DAUGHTER: It's some physical thing holding me back.
>
> MOTHER: [Before therapist could speak.] Nothing has worked. It's a virus. I need help and nobody believes me. I wanted to take care of my kids. Why doesn't somebody listen to me? All we get is hurt, and wrong advice (p. 218). . . . If you move out, that day my marriage is over. I can't live with a man who doesn't believe that you are making progress. Who is going to take care of me when I have my nervous breakdown?

As we can see, the patient-daughter is actually striving for independence. Although she is in her 30s, she is dominated into remaining a patient by a mother who blocks her desires to "be on my own" and a father who acquiesces. Under circumstances such as these, it might be argued that growing up free from pathology is difficult indeed.

*The Double-bind.* Another family interaction pattern that may sometimes be associated with pathologies is the *double-bind* communication. In this pattern, the family presents the child with a situation where he or she is faced with messages that are directly contradictory (Bateson et al., 1956; Olson, 1972). For example, a father may condemn the worth of women, including his own wife and daughter, yet tell his daughter he needs her love and respect. For the daughter, this situation represents a tragic dilemma: if she attempts to identify and side with the father, she will be faced with his hostility; yet if she refuses to do so and attempts to join with her mother, she will arouse her father's rejection and again come under pressure. She is condemned if she does and condemned if she does not.

***Can Parental Traits Be Linked to Schizophrenia?*** The schismatic, skewed, and double-bind patterns have been identified as three of several patterns often found in families of schizophrenic patients. However, more specific personality traits of the *schizophrenogenic* (schizophrenia-producing) mother or father have yet to be consistently identified (Hirsch & Leff, 1975), although this question has been the subject of much study. The mothers of schizophrenic patients have been reported as being rejecting by some researchers (Clardy, 1951), but overprotective and more devoted by others (Alanen, 1968); aloof and cold by some (Hill, 1955), yet overinvolved and intrusive by others (Freeman & Grayson, 1955). Fathers have been described as distant, aloof, passive, neglecting, in conflict with their wives, weak and ineffectual, and unable to assume the adaptive-instrumental role (Donnelly, 1960).

It is entirely possible that the search for a single type of cluster of traits which characterize *all* schizophrenogenic mothers or fathers will always be futile, simply because this approach is too narrow. The more conclusive results will continue instead to derive from examining the family pathogenic patterns we previously covered in this chapter.

### Evaluation of the Family as Cause

There seems little doubt that family factors can act as triggering or protective forces. The association between pathology in an individual and pathological conditions in the family continues to be discovered. Correlations, however, neither prove causation, as we have seen several times in this text, nor do they clearly identify the mechanisms of the association. Although we can conclude that a pathological environment is not conducive to normal development, the questions of why and how still remain. Perhaps disturbed behaviors in a parent are directly imitated by the child; perhaps distorted communications between parents lead to confused thinking in the child; perhaps offspring are forced to accept the patient role because of their aberrant parents; or perhaps the trauma and incoherence of disturbed child-rearing practices are intolerable in the vulnerable and immature child (Masson & O'Bryne, 1983).

As a final comment, the findings of the previous two chapters on psychological and biological factors, and this one on social factors, may be viewed as "complementary rather than contradictory." In the context of adoptive research, some scientists suggest that the findings "support *both* a genetic hypothesis *and* a psychosocial hypothesis" (Wynne et al., 1976). As we discussed in Chapter 4, inheritance or early biological damage may be viewed as producing a high-risk person. Social influences, such as disturbed family relations or cultural pressures, may then stress this individual until a breakdown occurs—this being one example of the diathesis-stress concept. In addition to biological causes, vulnerability or risk may be due to environmental reasons, such as peer experiences or life event stresses (Wynne, 1978; Zubin & Spring, 1977). Finally, looking back to Chapter 3's discussions of the growth process, developmental stages must be acknowledged. Stress to a person at-risk occurring at one time in life may be more troublesome than at another time.

## SUMMARY

Cultural, social group, and family influences have been actively studied in the search for the origins of mental disorders. Cross-cultural factors support the belief that the stresses we experience, the ways in which we express our conflicts, and the coping behaviors we use, are all influenced by the society around us. In addition, certain factors within our culture are broadly associated with mental disorder: lower socioeconomic level, single marital status, and perhaps urban living, and minority group status.

Parental and family influences also appear important. Early separation can have an effect, as can being raised by parents who themselves experience disorders. Poor intrafamily communication and pathological family interactions can create emotional symptoms. Among such disturbed patterns are the schismatic or skewed family, and the presence of double-bind communications.

Finally, as a previous section pointed out, it has become clear that the picture of mental disorders is one that includes psychological, biological, and social factors, possibly in different combinations, and possibly in different sequences, in an incredibly complex interaction.

## KEY TERMS

**Affect hunger**
**Affectionless character**
**Anaclitic depression**
**Contact-comfort hypothesis**
**Double-bind hypothesis**
**Downward drift hypothesis**
**Feral children**
***Hwa-byung***
**Incidence**
**Maternal separation**
**National character**
**Pathogenic family pattern**
***Pibloktoq***
**Prevalence**
**Schismatic family**
**Schizophrenogenic**
***Shook yong***
**Skewed family**
**Socialization**
**Stratification**
**Windigo psychosis**

# PART 2

## Types of Mental Disorders, Their Dynamics and Treatment



*The chapters in Part 2 present the substance of psychopathology—descriptions of persons suffering from each of the various mental disorders. Chapters 6 to 20 all follow the same organization for ease of study and comparisons: the disorder and subtypes are defined and the symptoms of each disorder are described along with illustrative quotations or case histories to give you a sense of such symptoms. This is followed by sections on the dynamics or potential origins and the evidence and the various treatment approaches. Finally, we end with an evaluation and a summary.*

*You should be aware that the sections on dynamics and treatment present knowledge as we know it today. For a few disorders there are clearly identified, single causes, and only one acceptable therapy. However, for most of the mental disorders, the origins are still being researched. Also, there is reason to believe that there may be not only multiple origins but also multiple treatments. For these reasons, we will be tracing the dynamics of each disorder relying on those hypotheses about origins which are the most meaningful. Regarding treatment, we will also emphasize those therapies which have the greatest history of success. This is a pragmatic approach. Thus, since certain depressions appear to be particularly responsive to electroshock, shock treatment is discussed in detail for this disorder; on the other hand, since phobic disorders are most responsive to behavior therapy, this mode of treatment is given most attention. For some disorders, one or more forms of psychological therapy—such as psychoanalytic, or humanistic, or behavioristic—may be primary, while for others the medical therapies may be highlighted, such as chemotherapy or electroshock.*

*Overall, the orientation is, therefore, eclectic and comprehensive, rather than narrowly attentive to one theory or method. Such an approach is consistent with the current state of the art; we hope scientific knowledge will continue to advance so that future texts can provide a single, unified point of view that is neither eclectic nor foolishly biased.*

# CHAPTER 6

## The Anxiety Disorders: States of Tension, Anxiety, and Stress

- **Is anxiety bad? What is the function of anxiety in the human?**
- **What contributes to a person's vulnerability to anxiety?**
- **Can you explain the statement that the hallmark of panic is feeling, while the hallmark of a phobia is behaving?**
- **How can a realistic fear be distinguished from a phobia?**
- **Identify the common themes that seem to underlie the diverse fears of agoraphobics and the coping tricks that help them overcome their fears.**
- **Why are obsessive-compulsive behaviors considered to be a type of anxiety disorder?**
- **What is the basic distinction between the post-traumatic stress disorder and the other anxiety disorders?**
- **Is there any substance to the belief that "Everyone has a breaking point"? Can people's breaking points be changed through training, such as the astronauts received?**
- **A tornado has hit the center of a community. What will the effects be, psychologically?**

**TABLE 6–1**

**Anxiety Disorders**

| *Type* | *Major Characteristics* |
|---|---|
| Generalized anxiety disorder | Presence of apprehension and threat so diffuse as to be free floating. |
| Panic disorder | Recurring waves of anxiety so intense as to feel overwhelming. |
| Phobic disorder | Fearfulness attached to specific objects or situations that are harmless. |
| Obsessive-compulsive disorder | The persistence of unwanted thoughts or the compulsion to repeat certain actions. |
| Post-traumatic stress disorder | Stress responses involving events outside the range of normal human experiences, such as disasters. |

# Case History 6–1:
## Generalized Anxiety Disorder

Ethel B. was referred for treatment of a generalized anxiety disorder of five years' duration. She was never completely relaxed and complained of vague feelings of restlessness and a fear that something was "just around the corner." Although she felt she had to go to work to help pay the family bills, she could not bring herself to start anything new for fear that something terrible would happen on the job. She had experienced a few extreme anxiety attacks during which she felt "like I couldn't breathe, like I was sealed up in a transparent envelope. I thought I was going to have a heart attack. I couldn't stop shaking. . . ." After these attacks she often thought of taking her own life as the only way to get rid of the tensions.

The patient was an only child who had been made extremely dependent on her mother. Her father was boisterous, impatient, and intolerant of the daughter's attachment to his wife but unable to provide love himself. He found fault with the patient in virtually all her endeavors and continued to belittle her reliance on her mother. Ethel B.'s marriage was as much motivated by her desire to escape from home as it was by her fondness for her somewhat ineffectual fiance. When her husband was unable to earn an adequate income, Ethel B. was forced to consider seeking employment herself. Soon after, her first wave of anxiety attacks began.

The course of treatment prescribed for her involved exploration of her feelings of inadequacy and her fear of accepting the challenge of employment. Clarifying her perceptions of what to expect in the world of work helped to allay some of her misperceptions and fears. Finally, assertiveness training was initiated to counteract her anxiety.

Anxiety represents the apprehensions, the dreads, the fears, and the worries that haunt the human being. The experience of anxiety may be characterized in many ways: as an existential sense of being in the grips of an "alien power," as a squeezing physical sensation encircling your chest or forehead, or as a shadowy threat that lurks around dark corners awaiting your action. However anxiety is experienced, it can become a dominant force in a person's life.

The *anxiety disorders,* listed in Table 6–1, are those emotional disturbances in which anxiety is a dominant feature, either as the major symptom or as the reason for certain reactions. In the first case, the person is overwhelmed by the presence and awareness of anxiety; in the second, symptomatic actions—such as a compulsive need to keep the shades drawn—reflect the anxiety or reflect attempts to deal with it. The *generalized anxiety disorder* and the *panic disorder* are examples of anxiety disorders where the primary focus is the experience of anxiety itself. In the *post-traumatic stress disorder,* this distress is traceable to dramatic life events. Examples of disorders where anxiety precipitates symptomatic actions to cope with the anxiety are *phobic disorder* and the *obsessive-compulsive* disorder. In the phobic disorder, a person shows avoidance of objects that arouse anxiety; in the obsessive-compulsive disorder, a person engages in thoughts or behaviors to control the anxiety. DSM-III lists several conditions as anxiety disorders; this chapter will discuss the following:

- Generalized anxiety disorder
- Panic disorder
- Phobic disorder
- Obsessive-compulsive disorder
- Post-traumatic stress disorder

## GENERALIZED ANXIETY DISORDER

As the opening case history illustrates, the generalized anxiety disorder can dominate a person's life. The essential features of this condition include persistence over at least one month and being free-floating—that is, it doesn't seem to be linked to a specific cause. The most gripping feature of this disorder is the experience and display of anxiety, which may show up in a variety of symptoms.

### Symptoms of Anxiety

The response patterns that are symptomatic of anxiety may be expressed autonomically, behaviorally, or cognitively (Suinn, 1977a; 1982). These responses may be combined, or they may be independent of one another (Lang, 1971).

The *autonomic* signs of anxiety can be displayed in several forms. Reports include the following: "My hands get cold and clammy . . . ," "There's a lump in my throat . . . ," "My stomach lets me know . . . ," "My heart pounds so loudly in my ears, I think everyone must know. . . ." Such reactions are the result of sympathetic and parasympathetic changes in the autonomic nervous system. In states of anxiety, your heart rate will increase, your respiration will speed up, and your palms will sweat more. Even at rest, persons with anxiety disorders will often show irregular breathing and frequent sighing; they may also have a more rapid pulse, an unstable or elevated blood pressure, and a diminished blood flow to the hands, leading to clamminess (Lader, 1975).

There are also *behavioral* expressions of anxiety: "My hands start to tremble out of control . . . ," "I begin to stutter . . . ," "I get jerky, I lose my motor coordination . . . ," "I feel frozen, I can't move . . . ," "I'm restless . . . I get jumpy." The athlete who is suddenly beset with anxiety may lose his or her motor coordination and may become inhibited and lose the spontaneous flow of motion; thus, problems in accuracy or timing may result. Similarly, an anxious person may show behavior disruptions, becoming jittery, shaky, and easily startled. The muscular tensions associated with prolonged anxiety may lead to complaints of fatigue or muscle aches.

*Cognitive* signs of anxiety include things we say or think to ourselves; "I just know that something is going wrong . . . ," "Others are not going to like me . . . ," "I'm a failure, and I can't cope . . . ," "I shouldn't have done this; I wish I'd done that instead. . . ." Such thoughts involve ruminating over actions to come, worrying about actions already past, or about actions that did not happen but that the person *wishes* had happened. Typically, gloom and doom pervade such thoughts and apprehensions, which may be either general or very specific.

Subjectively, the anxiety state can be terrifying. Most of us have had glimpses of this experience during normal instances of anxiety at one time or another—before a crucial school examination, a critical interview for a job, an athletic competition, or an encounter with the unfamiliar or the unknown. In a generalized anxiety disorder where the condition persists across time, it sometimes leads to side effects such as insomnia, interrupted sleep, and fatigue. Another side effect may be the reliance on tranquilizers, sleeping pills, or alcohol. The dynamics and background of the generalized anxiety disorder are similar to those of another anxiety disorder, the panic disorder. Thus, we will discuss these together in the following section.

## PANIC DISORDER

### Symptoms and Diagnosis

Whereas the generalized anxiety disorder involves a continuous and persisting state, the *panic disorder* involves repeated attacks of high intensity. The attacks are sweeping periods of overwhelming terror and may last from several minutes to several hours, with the recovery from the attack taking as long as a day or more. The diagnosis of panic disorder is used only where at least three attacks have occurred within a three-week period.

Panic attacks are marked by a number of intense symptoms: a momentary disintegration of control, choking or smothering sensations, dizziness, fainting, hot and cold flashes, uncontrollable shaking, chaotic behavior, feelings of unreality, or such outbursts of apprehension as to lead the person to fear insanity or death. The person may feel severe changes in bodily sensations: "I'm going to pieces . . . I feel my body and mind are going to burst apart." The sudden attacks are unpredictable, and this leads to even further difficulty, since the individual cannot prepare for them but must continuously live with the threat of another attack. As a result, he or she may be generally apprehensive in between such spells.

For a panic disorder to be diagnosed, the attacks must be discrete rather than continuous, of high intensity, episodic, and not attributable to either a feared object or to specific events such as life-threatening situations or excessive physical exertion. The tone of a panic state can be grasped in the following report:

> I was riding my bicycle to my first class, stopped outside the building, and suddenly I began to feel that I was going to fall over. My legs were trembling and shaking, and my head felt like it was being pushed to the ground. My whole body seemed to be churning up, like something was driving up from inside of myself, trying to explode. My heart was going so fast I was sure I was having a heart attack. I wanted to hide somewhere before this thing inside of me took over completely and I fell into a quivering puddle. I was petrified, I was afraid, I was terribly scared about something, but I didn't know what. I thought: "I can't hold on any more, I'm slipping, I'm going mad."
>
> I couldn't breathe, I panted extra hard for fear I was going to black out. I couldn't see any more, I was in a dark tunnel. My head was being stretched out of shape. I knew I was going crazy, these sensations don't happen to normal people. But the feelings were even more scary, the dread, like a monstrous blanket, and mixed with the fright that made me want to scream, like I was possessed . . . and then it all lifted . . . I don't want to ever go through that experience again."

### Dynamics of Anxiety and Panic

The response of the body to a threat of danger is normally a useful protective reaction. The individual becomes alert and vigilant, the body physiology alters itself for "fight or flight," readying itself for self-protective responses.

However, in certain pathologies, the normally useful reaction becomes an overreaction, either because no actual threat exists, or because the level of response to an existing threat is exaggerated. Further, the focus begins to center on the anxiety itself, rather than the anxiety acting as a signal for coping. Soon the anxiety acts as a handicap and hindrance rather than a functional state of preparedness (Hamilton, 1976;

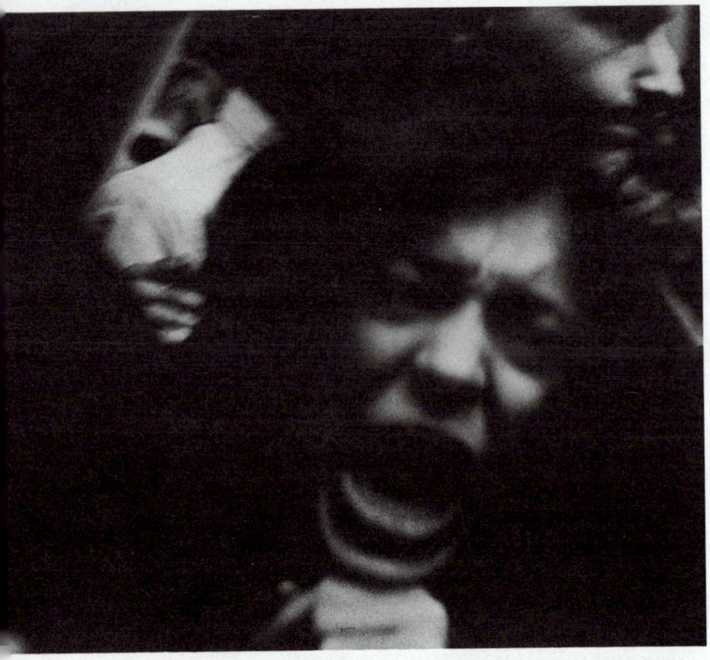

*Generalized **anxiety** disorder involves severe tensions, feelings of threat, loss of control, trembling, and subjective apprehension.*

Sarason, 1972). The persistence of the anxiety leads also to a steady rise, as the individual soon lives in dread of the anxiety itself and its frightening focus. As the person is unable to mobilize defenses against the anxiety, the threat of being overwhelmed by the anxiety itself now becomes an added danger, which further intensifies the anxiety level. What might have once been a *state anxiety* (an anxiety prompted by situational causes) has now become a *trait anxiety* (a pervasive anxiety that is now characteristic of the person rather than the situation) (Spielberger, 1966).

What are the factors that can lead to such pathological anxiety? Among the several possible origins, four important sources of anxiety can be identified and will be discussed next.

***Inadequate Learning of Adaptive Behavior.*** Since anxiety is a signal of danger, it will be triggered whenever people feel they are faced with events they cannot readily manage. Those who have learned adaptive skills will find fewer situations threatening; while those with inadequate, inflexible, or limited psychological capabilities will experience more events as dangerous.

At the core of anxiety is a feeling of utter helplessness in the face of life's demands. The case histories of individuals with generalized anxiety disorder frequently reflect immaturity of development, dependency, insecurity, and poor preparation for coping with life. This is often related to early parental overprotection or indulgence; not only did the individual have limited opportunity to learn adaptive behaviors, but the sense of self-esteem was never well developed. Thus, feelings of anxiety are more threatening to the self-concept than they might otherwise seem (Shaw, 1982).

***Direct Training and Sensitization.*** Childrearing practices can also contribute to anxiety. Overambitious, punitive parents may have expectations that are extremely difficult for a child to meet. Disciplinary techniques that rely on the arousal of guilt make the individual acutely aware of the inadequacy of his or her performance. Thus, even though a person may be competent to deal successfully with the environment, he or she may still be subject to anxiety attacks. This type of individual is driven by a fear of failure, yet expects failure and is spurred on even further by this threat. Should the person's performance be evaluated as competent, that praise is difficult to accept into the self-image.

***Acquisition of Parent's Anxiety.*** A third possible origin of anxiety disorders was pointed out by the famous American psychiatrist, Harry Stack Sullivan. As discussed in Chapter 3, Sullivan noted that parents transmit their feelings of anxiety to their children—even to very young infants. A mother who is tense when she nurses will soon be aware that her infant shows signs of anxiety. It is as if the infant empathizes with the mother. If such interactions continue, the child may experience this state of anxiety later in life without being fully aware of its origin.

Feeling-what-others-feel is not a mystical concept. Much can be communicated from one person to another without any attempt to use words. We have all had experiences during which our own moods were altered by simply being with someone who is deeply saddened over a recent experience. The emotions aroused during the viewing of a movie may continue long after we leave the theatre unless we make a deliberate attempt to shake them off. Some persons are more readily influenced and more deeply affected than others.

***Generalization of Learned Anxiety.*** Finally, anxiety is a response that can be learned in one setting and generalized to another. It may initially appear as the normal warning response to a real threat, perhaps of punishment, rejection, isolation, or helplessness. However, the evidence from learning studies indicates that anxiety responses can also *generalize* or become attached to other cues in the environment without the individual's awareness. Thus, anxiety can be later elicited by the presence of these other or similar cues, and the anxiety attack might simply consist of the generalized cuing of the anxiety pattern. For instance, a student who feels anxious during exams may become anxious just entering a classroom weeks before the exam. Since the person is unaware of what is happening, he or she can identify neither when the attacks will occur nor why they occur.

### Treatment of Anxiety and Panic

Ideally, the best treatment for generalized anxiety or panic is to prevent the conditions that predispose the individual to anxiety. Positive mental health planning can do much to stop pathological anxiety before it starts. Effective parenting practices and the development of sound mental health techniques—such as developing problem-solving skills—are essential. Such prevention is not aimed at removing *all* anxiety, for we've seen that anxiety serves a protective function. Mental health programs should, however, be concerned with promoting those conditions that will prevent the development of pathological states in the first place. Parent-training programs are certainly helpful in this (MacQuiddy & Hamilton, 1983). Additionally, individuals can be helped to deal with developmental tasks in ways that strengthen coping strategies, rather than threatening or weakening existing skills.

Once anxiety states affect an individual, several steps must be taken. The first goal is to alleviate the anxiety; then, treatment aims to eliminate the source of anxiety. Several common treatments are helpful in alleviating the symptoms of anxiety. These include various drug therapies; *hydrotherapy* (relaxation therapy that involves immersing the body in warm water); the reduction of responsibilities and pressures that further aggravate the problem; and the reassurance that the symptoms are not the precursors of serious organic involvement. Tranquilizers are often prescribed as a means of alleviating anxiety, but these also involve the danger of drug dependence or abuse.

Once the symptoms themselves have been alleviated, the next step is to learn to control future threats of anxiety. Two effective treatments are anxiety management training and cognitive therapy.

***Anxiety Management Training.*** A program called *anxiety management training* (Suinn, 1983) has been used in training persons to control anxiety attacks. In this treatment, the individual is taught to recognize the early bodily signs that anxiety is building, then to actively eliminate the anxiety through the use of relaxation techniques.

A typical anxiety management training session (Suinn, 1975) has the patient relaxing, then on instruction deliberately arousing an anxiety experience. Patients may do this by either visualizing the entire sequence of events leading up to an anxiety attack that actually occurred, or by simply reexperiencing the anxiety state itself—the heart palpitations, the tremors, the constricted feelings, the dreadful thoughts. Patients are instructed to attend to these feelings as stimuli, so that they can learn a new way of reacting to them in the future. This new response—an anxiety-coping response such as relaxation—is usually taught to patients by having them imagine a highly relaxing circumstance from their own experience.

Basically, what is happening in anxiety management training relates back to the behavioral techniques discussed in Chapter 3: the patient is being trained to develop a new habit pattern. To the stimulus of anxiety, the person is now responding with a new response of relaxation, instead of remaining helpless. Anxiety management training has been successfully used with generalized anxiety in a number of clinic cases and has even been used with normal persons who need anxiety control for unique situations (for instance, athletes at the Olympic games) (Shoemaker, 1976; Suinn, 1976, 1983).

***Cognitive Controls of Anxiety.*** Anxiety management training helps to control the thoughts associated with anxiety (Hutchings et al., 1978). However, a variety of behavioral therapies are more directly aimed at cognitive control. These treatments are called *cognitive behavior therapies.* In these approaches, the target is not the emotions or autonomic reactions, but rather the thoughts believed to instigate the anxiety conditions (Smith, 1983). Thus, cognitive therapists such as Ellis (1962) and Beck (1976) point out the major role of thoughts in engendering anxiety—thoughts such as "I don't have any job experience. This interview will make or break me, and the interviewer knows I'm not qualified."

Cognitive therapy can aim either at enabling the person to see the irrationality of such thoughts and to successfully refute them or at helping the individual to acquire different thoughts that are more constructive. One approach to changing irrational thoughts is sometimes called *rational restructuring* (Goldfried, 1979). This technique may involve having the individual reevaluate the anxiety-provoking thoughts. For instance, instead of the train of thought described earlier, the individual might consciously think more realistically: "Chances actually are that I will do well in the interview since I was prepared for it. My qualifications are as good as those of most applicants." A second approach involves training patients to use thoughts as part of coping rather than as part of the problem. The Canadian therapist Donald Meichenbaum (1977) uses this in a technique he calls *stress inoculation.* He has clients plan more carefully how to deal with anxiety situations ahead of time, so that they will know what to do if anxiety is aroused. He also has them practice "self-talk" to keep focused on coping (keep calm; take a deep breath; don't panic; remember what you need to do to stay in control).

***Predicting Success.*** It is interesting to note that the pattern of anxiety symptoms shown by an individual may be related to that person's chances for successful treatment.

Not everyone will experience or show anxiety in the same ways. Some persons might say that they feel apprehensive, but will show no signs of physiological activation: their heart rate, for instance, will remain steady; and they may not feel either clammy hands or a lump in the throat. Others may experience heightened physiological arousal, and yet they will act as though they were calm. And finally, some persons may show extreme avoidance behaviors or disrupted behavior, but they will not report any subjective sensations of distress (Lang, 1971; Leitenberg et al., 1971). These different arousal patterns have been tentatively linked to individuals' differing abilities to respond to treatment (Meyer & Reich, 1978). Lang et al. (1974) studied reactions to anxiety-arousing imagery. Some subjects showed sharp increases in heart rate along with subjective reports of anxiety; but others showed no serious changes in their heart rates even though they reported that they felt increased anxiety. Later, following behavioral treatment for anxiety, results showed that those persons who had experienced both subjective and physiological increases in anxiety signs profited from therapy, while the other group did not.

## PHOBIC DISORDER

*Phobias* (from the Greek *phobos,* meaning panic, dread, or fear) have much in common with generalized anxiety and panic disorders. In all three, the state of tension may be experienced autonomically, behaviorally, or cognitively. However, if we examine the role of stimuli, we can arrive at a useful working distinction between these three disorders. The generalized anxiety disorder and panic disorder involve diffuse states where the individual cannot identify which stimuli have precipitated anxiety.

Phobias, on the other hand, are disorders where the cue situation triggering the anxiety reaction is identifiable. These stimuli often fall into a common class of conditions that form the basis for classifying phobias. For instance, common phobias among Americans include a fear of snakes, a fear of injury or illness, a fear of heights, and a fear of either open or closed spaces

## Case History 6–2:
### Phobic Disorder

David R., a freshman at the state university, was first seen because of his interest in the counseling center's test desensitization program.

> I am the perfect subject for you. . . . I can't take tests without freezing. I'm not afraid of anything else in the world. Give me a bear to tackle and I'll do it without blinking, but give me a test and I'm like jelly. I get into the exam after a whole night's unrest, I can't sleep, I'm so worried. Then even the Breakfast of Champions, my cereal, looks puny in the morning, mainly because my stomach is in knots. I want to be anywhere but in the classroom, but I know I can't get out of it. It's not that I haven't studied; I take decent notes, and I remember the right answers as soon as I leave the test room. But in between, when I'm starting the exam, and I'm staring, I'm not thinking, just staring. It's as if a ray gun were turned on my brain, and I'm a solid blank. Then my hands sweat, and the harder I try, the worse I get. This sounds funny, but I'm scared to death.

David has thus far achieved a fair but not outstanding grade point average. He had previously been involved in a confrontation with an instructor whom he accused of having administered an unfair test in that there was not enough time to answer all the questions. It soon became evident that such antagonistic behavior was a displacement of his frustration with himself. He soon realized that the time limit had not been long enough because he had wasted most of his time in attempting to control his anxieties. He had already skipped two other examinations by remaining in bed petrified with his fears of failure.

Behavior therapy was started with this patient. He first made up a hierarchy of circumstances which he felt produced fear responses. He was then instructed in relaxation of muscle groups. Then, while he was relaxing, he was asked to imagine the lowest item on his anxiety hierarchy list (being asked a question of fact by his kid brother). When it was evident that he could tolerate this situation well, the next item on the list was evoked, and so on. Within a month, David reported being able to take midterm examinations with only a modicum of tension. During final examinations, however, the paralyzing fear returned. Further training continued with an emphasis on generalizing the relaxation responses to a wider variety of testing situations. Excellent progress has been noted, and David has recently been notified of his acceptance for graduate admissions.

(Agras et al., 1969). Among Canadians, the most common fears were those of animals, heights, closed spaces, and of people (Costello, 1982).

Another distinction between phobias and generalized anxiety disorder or panic disorder is in the response pattern that predominates. While the hallmark of panic disorder is the sudden autonomic discharge and associated feelings, phobias are characterized more by the avoidance *behaviors* associated with a fear.

Children tend to be more susceptible to phobias than adults are, with the fear of school being a relatively common phobia of childhood (Morris & Kratochwill, 1983). However, phobias are most prevalent in middle adulthood, around 50 years of age, as Figure 6–1 shows.

### Symptoms and Diagnosis

Unlike normal fears, which are based on realistic danger, phobias are irrational and either groundless or greatly exaggerated. Some individuals with phobias will claim that the avoidance behavior is rational, since getting away from the source of fear does serve the direct function of lowering the anxiety. On the other hand, they do not claim that the anxiety is justified, but will acknowledge that it is out of proportion to the actual threat. There are times when a phobic condition does become associated with a realistic fear, as when a person is phobic about being burglarized, then reads about a theft in the neighborhood. In such cases, the resulting fear is said to be *overdetermined* (Goodwin, 1983).

### A Common Phobia: Agoraphobia

One of the most common phobias is *agoraphobia*, a fear of going out into public and open spaces. The term comes from the word *agora*, the marketplace in ancient Greece. Marks (1969) estimated that 60 percent of patients seeking treatment for phobias at a hospital were agoraphobic. In a study of residents of Burlington, Vermont, agoraphobia was identified as the foremost of the severe fears experienced (Agras et al., 1969).

Agoraphobia seems to occur more frequently in women than in men. It tends to first appear between the ages of 18 and 35, and is rare among children. Often, the individuals can recall a stressful event around the time of the onset—a serious illness, being jilted, an unwanted pregnancy, an unhappy marriage, a miscarriage, or even a frightening experience such as an unpleasant scene in the street or in a store. For example, one woman reported, "I was in a crowded street and a car accident occurred right in front of me, with people screaming and blood on the windshield. . . . I haven't been out since." Because of the recall for these stressful life incidents, agoraphobia has sometimes been labeled the "calamity syndrome" (Fensterheim & Baer, 1977). In point of fact, these events do not account for the origins of the phobia, but may only be tangentially related.

***Common Complaints.*** Symptoms of agoraphobia are manifold and highly restrictive. The woman described earlier who refused to return to the street is not unique in her reaction. Individuals affected by this phobia are afraid of going into the streets, crowded shops, or open malls; they may panic in buses, or trains, or airplanes (but not usually automobiles); or they may be afraid of tunnels, churches, or bridges. One survey of "The Open Door," a club for agoraphobics with some 900 members, revealed the most common fears to be riding in underground trains, speaking to audiences, and going to the hairdresser, as well as crowds, open spaces, and streets (Marks & Herst, 1970). Here is a typical case:

> I see the streets aren't as busy, and I tell myself I have to go out for a change, so I leave my house; but a block away I feel weak, the ground starts to shift and wave under me, I want to scream; in my panic I run to the nearest friend's house. . . .

***Claustrophobia** is a form of phobic disorder involving severe apprehension when in closed or confined spaces.*

> I would reserve tickets way ahead of time, to the theatre, a play, a movie, a concert, or just a car show . . . then I'd realize how many people would be there, and my hands would go clammy, and my knees would shake, and my muscles would ache, and my eyes would blur, and I'd start to sweat, and I'd barely catch myself . . . and I wasn't even there and it was so bad already, so I'd give the tickets away.

***Some Coping Tricks for Agoraphobia.*** Various safety valves can often help individuals with agoraphobia to live more normal lives. The agoraphobic may feel more comfortable in the presence of a familiar companion, either human or animal, and can become highly dependent on that association. Props—such as a briefcase to clutch or a shopping basket to grip—may provide "something to hang onto." Outings may be carefully planned so that the agoraphobic will pass by a friend's house, a doctor's office, or a police station, to assure that aid will always be nearby. Somehow, many agoraphobics find it easier to travel when it is dark or in the daytime while wearing dark glasses, or during rain or snowstorms.

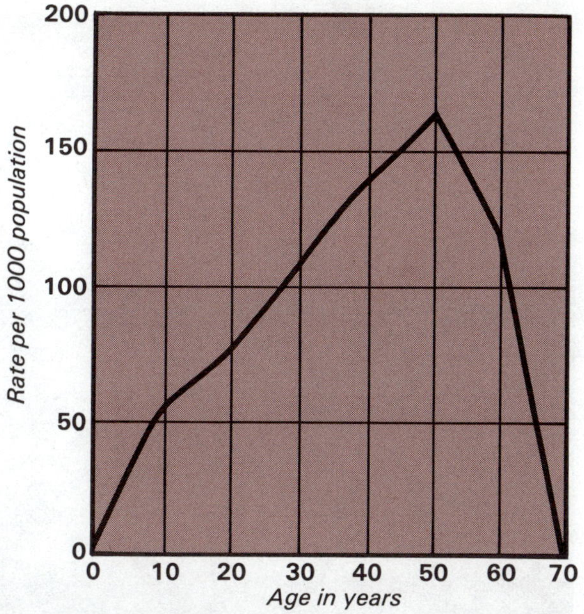


**FIGURE 6–1** Rates of phobias within the general population.

Some coping tricks may themselves interfere with normal life as individuals try to manage their fears. Isaac Marks (1978) cites the case of the woman who "had the urge to rid herself of all clothing when she panicked, could wear only garments which could be closed in front by zippers, and had to carry a pair of scissors and a bottle of beer in her purse when she left home." He also describes "a man with fear of crowds [who] was able at times to face them when he clutched a bottle of ammonia in his hands in case he felt he was about to faint . . . a clergyman [who] felt dizzy as soon as he went into the open, but obtained relief by creeping around hedges and trees or, as a last resort, by putting up his umbrella" (pp.87–88).

Amidst all of these various coping strategies or conditions which relieve the fearfulness is the common theme of safety and self-protection (Hallam, 1978; Marks, 1970).

### Dynamics of Phobias

How do phobias develop? Attempts to understand the dynamics of phobias have examined genetic, biochemical, as well as psychoanalytic and learning variables. We'll look at each.

***Biological Variables.*** To date, there is very little direct evidence that phobias are genetically acquired. There is some evidence that selective breeding can develop animals that are either fearful or fearless, as Chapter 4's discussion of Hall's classic experiment (1934) illustrates, but there have been—understandably—few human studies (Broadhurst & Bignami, 1965). The little evidence on humans includes one report that phobias are more frequent among monozygotic twins than dizygotic twins (Carey, 1977), and reports that heightened autonomic nervous system sensitivity (which may lead to a susceptibility to fearfulness) is influenced genetically (Lacey, 1976).

The role of biochemistry or neurology is as unclear as the role of heredity, again because of the difficulty of obtaining human data. There is speculation, but lack of conclusiveness, about a biochemical substance known as *scotophobin* which is found in animals who have been exposed to fear training (Malin et al., 1976). Brain pathology may also play a role in a few cases. This explanation has been supported by an interesting case of a woman whose fears of men or the dark seemed linked to abnormal discharges from her temporal lobe (Marks, 1969).

While there is still scanty evidence for a relationship between biological factors and phobias, the explanations offered by both the psychoanalytic and learning perspectives have received more support.

***Psychoanalytic Explanations.*** In an application of symbolism and psychoanalytic theory, Freud (1909) explained phobias as a displacement of fear.[1] His famous case of the childhood phobia of "Little Hans" is an example which we cited in Chapter 3. Here, Freud treated a boy's fear of being bitten by a horse. Hans was said to be in the throes of an Oedipal conflict which gave rise to a fear of being punished severely by the father, of being castrated. This fear was repressed and transformed instead into a fear of being bitten (a disguised castration fear).

Such symbolic displacement has been viewed as the source of many other phobias. Agoraphobia, for instance, may be symbolic of a fear of being sexually molested in an open street, a fear that a loved one will die while one is away from home, or a fear of being

1 Freud himself was said to have an inordinate dread of and obsession about dying (Jones, 1957).

tempted into running away. *Claustrophobia* (a fear of closed spaces) and fears of being buried alive might symbolize the fantasy of life within the mother's womb. Fears of the dark may be interpreted as a vestigial fear originating from prehistoric humans' vulnerability to attack by animals, as Jung proposed in his theory of the collective unconscious (see Chapter 3). Such fears may also represent the fear of being isolated, alone, and helpless. It is intriguing to note that being suddenly thrust into total darkness by a power failure forces people to call out to or touch others to reassure themselves that they are not as alone as it seems.

***Agoraphobia*** *is a phobic disorder involving open space. The afflicted person is often unable to travel outside the home and may rely upon coping tricks such as staying near walls.*

***Learning Explanations.*** Phobias can also be acquired through direct learning. In general, this can happen in two ways: through vicarious learning or by a combination of classical conditioning and reinforcement.

A mother who continues to exhibit her own fears towards an object will provide a model for her offspring to imitate, the learning being through what is called *vicarious learning*, or modeling (Bandura, 1965). Hagman (1932), for example, found a significant correlation between the number and types of fears of the parent and child. Further, histories of military men in combat showed that 49 percent experienced significant increases in their fears when they observed another soldier showing panic in battle (Stouffer et al., 1949).

Another form of direct learning is classical conditioning. As we saw in Chapter 3's description of Watson's famous "Little Albert" experiment, a neutral object may acquire fearful qualities if it is associated with a traumatic event. A similar process can be identified in many other phobias, such as a fear of flying some bomber pilots developed after surviving exposure to dangerous flak, or as in the case of agoraphobia, discussed previously, that followed the witnessing of a bloody auto accident.

*Two-factor Theory.* Laboratory experiments have identified a well-documented principle of learning: As an individual reduces anxiety through avoidance or escape from an anxiety-provoking stimulus, the avoidance behavior is reinforced and thereby strengthened. This principle has recently led to the proposal that current classical conditioning explanations of phobias should include a *two-factor theory* of fear acquisition (Mowrer, 1947). In brief, this theory emphasizes two processes in the development of a phobia. *Factor one* is the classical conditioning experience that starts the fear—for instance, flying a bomber plane through heavy attack or witnessing a car accident. *Factor two* comprises the avoidance behaviors of the phobia itself, for as these behaviors reduce the fear, they also reinforce the phobia. The pilot who avoids flying, reduces his fear; but this reduction of fear acts as a reinforcement, which further strengthens the avoidance behaviors characteristic of phobias (Ost & Huydahl, 1981).

*The Question of Preparedness.* At the center of the learning explanations of phobias is an interesting question. Why do phobias seem to focus more on some objects than others? Why should such large numbers of persons be afraid of open spaces, or heights, or snakes; while fewer are afraid of doorknobs, weeds, or pencils? A case is reported of an experiment in which a child was given opera glasses to touch, then a loud whistle was blown simultaneously behind her. Instead of becoming frightened, the child simply looked around casually to see where the noise came from. Yet, when this was repeated as the child was about to touch a caterpillar, the child's reaction was to scream in fear of the caterpillar (Valentine, 1978). Such examples have led to the speculation that the idea of preparedness should be added to theories of fear (Delprato, 1980; Seligman, 1971). What this suggests is that a conditioning or vicarious experience might leave you with a fear if the experience involves some object, but you would be completely unaffected by the same experience involving other objects.

***The Usefulness of Phobias.*** One other dynamic of phobias deserves mention here. That is simply that despite the very real fears associated with phobias, this condition also serves a function.

The phobia has the advantage of permitting individuals to circumscribe their conflicts and anxieties—to limit them to a definable and therefore controllable situation. As such, this is a partial solution that helps to reduce the anxieties, as long as the individual stays clear of the feared object. When away from this object, a person can function fairly adequately and rationally. In addition, a phobia itself may help a person focus attention on the feared object and away from the true source of psychological threat. Of course, secondary gains aid in maintaining the phobia. For instance, the possession of a fear provides a person with a certain degree of control over others, since it forces others to behave protectively and submit to his or her demands.

### Treatment of Phobias

Since the phobic person recognizes the irrationality of the fears, direct suggestions to exercise willpower or simply to convince the person that the fears are unsupported, just do not work. Similarly, suddenly confronting the person with the feared object may trigger such a high level of anxiety that panic may result and the problem becomes worsened. On the other hand, we need to accept that the phobic individual is truly concerned about the symptoms and often sufficiently upset as to be highly motivated to seek treatment. The treatment chosen reflects both the nature of the fear and the orientation of the therapist.

***Psychoanalytic Therapy.*** In general, psychoanalytic theory tends to interpret phobias as involving both repression and projection. The belief is that the individual is really threatened by some internal problems, but that these are repressed and the danger is instead projected on the external world.

In cases where the therapist can identify some symbolic involvement, intensive psychotherapy is aimed at the gradual, systematic uncovering of fundamental repressed conflicts. An example might be the situation in which a person has a social phobia that prevents development of meaningful relationships. Here, the fear may actually be associated with a deficiency in giving or receiving love, and the phobia may serve to protect the individual from having to deal with the issues of intimacy.

***Behavior Therapy.*** Recently, behavior therapy approaches have been highly successful in dealing directly with the immediate tensions of phobias (Berzins & Berzins, 1984). Among the various behavioral methods are desensitization, flooding, modeling, and cognitive behavior therapy. Chapter 21 provides more details on each of these methods, but we'll provide a brief overview here.

*Desensitization.* This technique is based on the principle that if a response which is incompatible to fear is attached to an initially phobia-inducing cue, then this new response will replace the fear response (Wolpe, 1958).

Desensitization generally relies on the anxiety-inhibiting response of muscle relaxation as the means of replacing fear. The basic method involves initiating relaxation, then presenting an aspect of the feared situation which arouses only mild fear (for example, being asked questions by a kid brother as in Case History 6–2). With repeated presentations, the relaxation response soon replaces the fear response. This approach seems to be particularly useful in eliminating the emotional tensions and avoidance behaviors associated with phobias.

***Desensitization** therapy has proven useful for phobias. The student on the left was successfully treated for a snake phobia, while the person on the right was treated for a fear of heights.*

*Flooding Therapy.* *Flooding* uses an approach quite different from that of desensitization. It aims at eliminating a phobia by preventing the person from avoiding the feared stimulus (Hafner, 1983). It is based on the premise that if the person learns that nothing drastic happens when the feared situation actually occurs, the phobia will be extinguished.

Flooding can use either imaginary or real-life situations. In the former, the person is asked to visualize what it is like to be in one of the worst circumstances that prompted fear and to continue to imagine that scene in spite of the fear response. In flooding that involves real-life situations, the person is actually sent into a situation to directly experience it (Sinnott et al., 1981). Thus, a person who is afraid of heights might be required to stand on the open roof of a 20-story building, looking down at the street.

Flooding relates closely to the two-factor theory described earlier. It acts on the second factor, that is, the avoidance behaviors, which maintain the phobia. Flooding has been quite successful in treating agoraphobia, and appears more successful when several treatments occur close in time than when they are spread over a long period of time (Foa et al., 1980a; Marks, 1983).

*Modeling Therapy.* Just as flooding relates closely to the two-factor theory, *modeling therapies* are based on our understanding of the vicarious learning of fears. In this technique, the phobic person is shown movies or videotapes of someone else coping calmly with the feared situation (Rosenthal & Bandura, 1978).

As the individual watches the tape or film, several types of observational learning seem to take place. First, coping and approach behaviors may be learned. For instance, the model's behavior may show how a dog can be approached without startling it and causing it to snap. Also, as the viewer sees that another person is able to approach the feared situation without negative consequences, this may support the feeling that he or she can do the same, too. This is especially relevant where the person perceives the model to be similar to him or herself. Thus, a child with a phobia is far more likely to benefit from modeling therapy if the model is another child. In fact, this procedure has proven to be especially valuable in helping fearful children (Morris & Kratochwill, 1983).

A rather important discovery has been the fact that a model who is coping leads to better fear reduction in observers than a model who is a mastery model. Alan Kazdin (1973) had snake-phobic persons watch two types of models perform: the coping model started off fidgeting and uncertain, but eventually managed to approach the snake without any dire effects; the mastery model seemed always to be in control from the very beginning and easily and confidently approached the snake. A third group had no models to help them. As Figure 6–2 illustrates, the modeling approach was quite helpful in increasing the ability of phobic persons to now approach the once-feared snake; however, the coping model appeared to produce greater improvements. It is as if the phobic subjects perceived the coping model as more nearly like themselves, and hence they could identify with this model's behaviors more than the mastery model's.

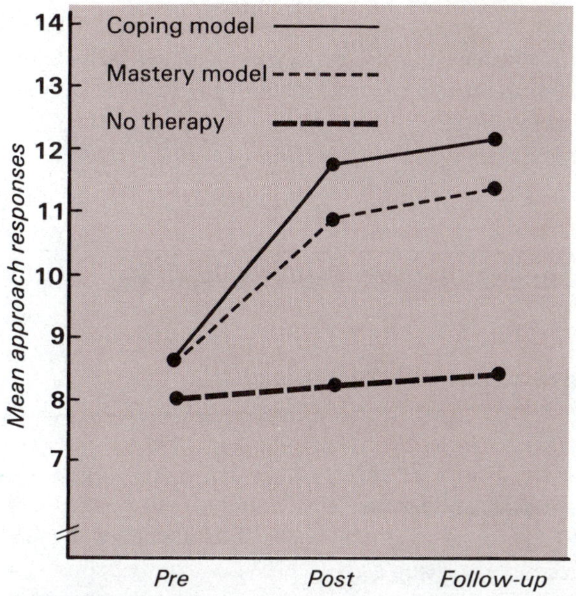


**FIGURE 6–2** Eliminating snake phobia through coping or mastery modeling.

SOURCE: Adapted from "Covert Modeling and the Reduction of Avoidance Behavior" by A. Kazdin, 1973, *Journal of Abnormal Psychology, 81,* p. 90. © 1973 by The American Psychological Assn. Adapted by permission of the author.

*Cognitive Therapy.* Cognitive behavior therapy involves a variety of approaches, including *rational-emotive therapy* (Ellis, 1979) and *systematic rational restructuring* (Goldfried, 1979). In these approaches, the emphasis is placed on more systematically guiding fearful persons to be aware of the false beliefs which make them afraid, to learn how to generate alternative, more realistic thoughts, and to provide guidance in applying these alternatives.

In this framework, it is what persons think, say to themselves, or believe that really prompts the fear response. For example, if you find yourself afraid of speaking in public, you might discover that you have talked yourself into that fear, with thoughts such as "What if I forget my speech?" As in the discussion of the use of rational restructuring for panic and anxiety attacks, restructuring for phobias will involve changing the false assumptions or unrealistic standards underlying these thoughts.

*Doing-It-Yourself.* A number of self-management books have been published which make use of various behavioral approaches to fears (Fensterheim & Baer, 1977; Marks, 1978; Tasto & Skjei, 1979). Useful cautionary advice is offered by Marks before recommending any self-directed activity. He recognizes that there may be conditions under which self-managed desensitization or self-directed cognitive restructuring might *not* be appropriate—for example, when a physical disease might be exacerbated. Other conditions include the need for professional consultation, or cases where the discomfort seems more generalized and ambiguous (for instance, "I just feel miserable all the time" or "I feel frightened about myself and my future"). Self-control approaches are being refined and seem to be of some value when used with caution under such conditions as those previously mentioned (Suinn & Deffenbacher, 1982).

## OBSESSIVE-COMPULSIVE DISORDER

### Symptoms and Diagnosis

A third type of anxiety disorder is the obsessive-compulsive disorder. This disorder really consists of two types of conditions, both of which are characterized by recurring activities over which the individual has no control. *Obsessions* are recurring thoughts that interfere with normal behavior; *compulsions* are recurring actions which the individual is forced to enact. Thus, persons with *obsessive-compulsive disorders* are faced with irresistible thoughts or actions in which they must engage.

***Obsessions.*** Freud (1963) described the obsessive disorder as follows:

> Obsessional neurosis is shown in the patient's being occupied with thoughts in which he is in fact not interested, in his being aware of impulses which appear very strange to him, and in his being led to actions the performance of which give him no enjoyment, but from which it is quite impossible for him to omit. The thoughts (obsessions) may be senseless in themselves, or merely a matter of indifference to the subject; often they are completely silly. . . . He is obliged against his will to brood and speculate as though it were a question of his most important vital problems. (p. 258)

Freud's writings provide an apt description. Obsessive thoughts may center around very serious issues as well as trivial matters. Sometimes the obsessions appear to be so trivial as to be amusing. One complaint to the author was the following:

> A friend of mine is driving me up the wall, before we can go out, he has to make sure he remembers the sizes of his shoelaces . . . he's worried that he'll break one and will look foolish unless he replaces it immediately, and he thinks he can't replace it if he doesn't know the size, but he feels he'll be too embarrassed to take the other one off to measure it in public.

There are countless other examples. A person may not be able to stop wondering whether the lights were turned off and feel forced to get out of bed time and time again to make sure, repeating this well into the night. (Here, the obsession is accompanied by a compulsive behavior.) Or a bank teller may have a recurring belief that he *might* commit a violent crime or break into his own bank and may ruminate over this possibility. Such thoughts will persist for awhile, then vanish, only to reappear during the oddest and most unexpected moments to plague the individual.

***Compulsions.*** Compulsions may involve rather simple acts or more elaborate and complex activities. A ritualistic quality is associated with such behavior. Compulsions may include hand-washing rituals, an inability to walk by a piece of furniture without brushing it, or moving books from shelf to shelf each time the room is entered. These behaviors may be repeated so often as to become physically harmful. For example, one woman washed her hands up to 100 times a day until her skin was raw and bleeding (yet, she would not take a bath or wash her body, such that her body odor became noxious to others).

Other examples are found listed in a book by Judy Reiser (1980), who interviewed over 600 normal persons on the premise that most people have hidden idiosyncrasies they worry about. Among the examples from normally functioning persons so interviewed was the management consultant who reported, "When I wake up in the morning, I count to 100. . . . I always think I counted too quickly and start over. I go through this about five or six times before I actually get up"; and the writer/producer whose fastidiousness includes, "If the toilet paper is hanging off the inside of the roll, I change it so that it's hanging off the outside, otherwise I won't use it. This applies to all bathrooms, public or private."

The prominent characteristic of the obsessions and compulsions is the rigid, uncompromising, inflexible control they exert. Much as the individual may wish to stop, he or she cannot. If a compulsion is involved, it must be carried out with exactitude; not even the minutest modification is tolerated— the act must be perfectly executed.

## Case History 6–3:
### Obsessive-compulsive Disorder

A department store clerk quickly lost her job because of complaints from customers over her slowness in making change and her eccentric behavior. She was obsessed with the number seven. If the number appeared in the cents column, she found herself unable to stop repeating the figure over and over. If the number appeared in the dollars column or in any other circumstance, she felt a strong urge to omit it. She could not take the seventh step on a stairway in stride but always managed to do a little skip. Rather than getting off the elevator on the seventh floor of any building, she preferred the inconvenience of going to a higher or lower floor and walking the rest of the way. She changed her residence several times in order to live in a district where the telephone was given an area code without a seven. When asked about the inconveniences, she commented: "You think it would be easy to stop this thing with numbers altogether; actually it's worse if I don't count. Then I start to feel like something bad is going to happen. And pretty soon I feel this ball inside me, growing like a cancer, a tension that's going to explode . . . and I can't concentrate, until I count my seven's again. Now I'm comfortable again, and I feel safe, really safe."

The patient had been raised by her divorced mother. Throughout her life she heard endless accounts of the cruelties of life and the necessity of being so self-reliant and competent that she would never have to rely on anyone else. Her mother used every waking moment to instruct her daughter by continuously evaluating her performance on trivial as well as important matters. The mother died after an agonizing battle with cancer. She died on the seventh day of July.

### Dynamics of Obsessive-compulsive Disorders

Many explanations of obsessive-compulsive disorders are rooted in Freudian theory, but learning theory also offers explanations. We'll look at both.

***Psychoanalytic Explanations.*** The psychoanalytic viewpoint traces obsessive-compulsive behavior to the anal stage of development (Pollak, 1979). During this phase, bowel training and cleanliness are desired by the parent and impressed on the child. Partly because the child enjoys being messy, and partly out of sheer defiance, the child resists the demands of the parent. The parent relies on punishment and guilt, forcing the child to deny any pleasure-oriented behavior. Reaction formation develops and the child becomes excessively neat and perfectionistic. Later, as an adult, the child may recreate the judgmental attitude of the parent, repeatedly worrying about inadequate behavior. Thus, a compulsion may develop to realign the books as if anticipating the parent to inspect the shelves, or the individual may avoid touching certain objects to avoid becoming soiled.

In some instances, the obsessive-compulsive behavior seems to be a symbolic attempt to reverse the outcome of a childhood scene. The hostility and rage felt by the individual as a child become expressed in vaguely disguised recurring thoughts of death, usually toward someone close (Pollak, 1978). The sudden obsessional thought of "What if I should kill someone?" is more accurately "Why didn't I kill that demanding parent of mine?" The compulsion to crumple up stray pieces of paper might be interpreted as the expression of a wish to crush the parent. The fact that the obsessive-compulsive is disturbed by the obsession reflects the threatening quality of the impulse such that the individual cannot admit to such feelings. The sense of not being in control of these thoughts or actions, which act as though they had a life of their own, suggests the strong influence of repression.

Guilt also plays a prominent role in the dynamics of obsessive-compulsive behavior. Individuals are taught to monitor their own behavior by the instigation of guilt. Individuals with well-developed consciences do not require supervision; they have already internalized the evaluative-supervision role. For the obsessive-compulsive person, this phenomenon has been developed to its extreme. The compulsion to con-

*In the famous scene from* ***Macbeth****, Lady Macbeth illustrates an* ***obsessive-compulsive*** *hand-washing disorder.*

fess to any and all crimes that appear in the newspapers is a clear-cut example of the overly developed conscience. Hand-washing may represent attempts to expiate or atone for an unclean act. Compulsive acts may also serve to neutralize unacceptable impulses by blocking them or ritualizing them (in much the same way as religious rites are used to make unacceptable acts acceptable; for example, prayers proclaiming the righteousness of soldiers prior to combat).

***Learning Explanations.*** Learning principles are also involved in obsessive-compulsive behaviors (Queiroz et al., 1981). Hypercritical, demanding, perfectionistic parents reward similar behaviors in their offspring. In some cases, the obsessive characteristic has been known to appear in the parent and to then be quickly adopted by the child. In addition, the ritualistic behaviors of a compulsive disorder are maintained by another type of reinforcement, anxiety reduction. As was noted earlier, the compulsive person becomes increasingly anxious when prevented from proceeding with the compulsion, but receives temporary relief when allowed to finish such activity. This reduction of anxiety serves to strengthen the compulsive behavior and increases its likelihood of reappearing.

### Treatment of Obsessive-compulsive Disorders

Obsessive-compulsive conditions are among the most difficult neuroses to treat, for a number of reasons. Intellectualizing often occurs during the course of treatment as part of the defensive maneuvers. In addition, the client sincerely fears what will happen if a proven way of reducing anxiety is taken away. Frequently, the client will ask the therapist's advice on what to do and how to live, thereby substituting the obsessions and compulsions derived from the therapist for his or her own.

***Psychodynamic Therapy.*** Psychodynamic therapy is aimed at encouraging the person to deal constructively on the adult level with guilt and repressed feelings. An attempt at reconstructing the emotional reactions felt in early life is sometimes useful. Humanistic-existential therapists encourage clients to realize that they have not lost control, despite the apparent strength of the obsessions or compulsions. To show this, *paradoxical intention* might be used involving deliberately repeating the obsession or compulsion in an exaggerated way, such as washing the hands 50 instead of 5 times. Through this, the client is led to learn that the symptoms can be brought under personal control, and that choice about how to behave is still possible.

***Behavior Therapy.*** Behavior therapy has appeared promising in treating obsessions or compulsions. *Response prevention* is a method which encourages the person to first continue with the ritual, but to then gradually limit the compulsive actions (Foa et al., 1980b; Turner et al., 1979).

An example of this technique is provided by the case of Ann, a 23-year-old woman who feared that a small wart on her ring finger was cancerous. Believing that she would contaminate objects with her cancer germs, she developed the ritual of washing her hands 125 times daily, using three bars of soap a day and refusing to touch dishes or to eat with the affected hand. Ann was required to systematically and gradually eliminate the ritual. For example, she was to reduce hand-washing to one bar of soap per day, but without running water and with a plug in the sink (to reduce the amount of washing possible). Later, Ann reduced the amount of washing and the amount of time spent washing. Her recovery was complete to the extent that she prepared and ate meals without the fears of contamination and no longer felt compelled to wash inappropriately (Marks, 1978).

## POST-TRAUMATIC STRESS DISORDER

The disorders discussed previously may reflect a variety of origins. The *post-traumatic stress disorder,* however, differs from all of these conditions in that it is clearly linked to the occurrence of events outside the normal range of experience. These traumatic experiences go beyond the more common stresses, such as loss of a loved one, marital discord, and so forth. Instead, they include such stressors as natural disasters, accidental disasters (for instance, an airplane crash), or planned disasters such as warfare, as Case History 6–4 illustrates.

### Symptoms and Diagnosis

The post-traumatic stress disorder is characterized by anxiety symptoms that follow catastrophes. These symptoms vary considerably and may include:

- Reexperiencing the trauma through nightmares or reliving the event in a dissociativelike state.
- Constricted ability to feel emotions—often reported as numbness or emotional anaesthesis—or a feeling of being detached or estranged.
- Excessive physiological-autonomic arousal, such as an exaggerated startle response, hyperalertness, an inability to fall asleep, or irritability to sounds.
- Apathy, depression, and loss of initiative.
- Feelings of apprehension, sometimes including the experiencing of tremors.
- Impairment of concentration and memory.
- Impulsive outbursts or behaviors such as aggressivity or sudden changes in lifestyle.

***Types of Reactions.*** Some symptoms appear to be related to the nature of the stress situation. Apathy and depression were so characteristic of concentration camp survivors, for instance, as to lead to the observation that these patients could be immediately identified in the therapist's waiting room (Hocking, 1970). In contrast, escaped prisoners tend to show prominent symptoms of anxiety and tension over their depression. Occasionally, the appearance of a survival guilt pattern is shown by people who have been held hostage by terrorists (Cole, 1980; Keerdoja, 1980; "*Trauma,*" 1979). (See the discussion in Focus 6–1.) Similar symptoms have been shown by survivors of major disasters, such as the Japanese survivors of World War II's nuclear bombing and the survivors of the 1972 flood in Buffalo Creek, West Virginia (Gleser et al., 1981). This survival guilt pattern involves severe self-reproach for having lived when others have died (Frederick, 1981a).

The post-traumatic stress disorder was once referred to as the *gross-stress reaction,* an umbrella term that included two classifications: *combat reactions* of war and *civilian catastrophic reactions.* These terms distinguished between the source of stress (warfare or national disasters) which caused an individual to reach his or her breaking point. These divisions are no longer included in DSM-III's classification. Still, a brief look at the two may be useful in understanding the kinds of stress that may precipitate this disorder.

*Combat Reactions.* Combat reactions develop from the unnatural stresses of warfare (Blank, 1983).

# Case History 6–4:
## Post-traumatic Stress Disorder

Wilbur A. had been drafted from a pleasant, middle-class, protected environment. "I guess I didn't realize how much I was taken care of, or what the real world was like, I mean the seamy side, the cruel side. War was all flags, and patriotism, and uniforms." After basic training, Wilbur was sent on to relieve front-line troops as his first combat experience. After a particularly heavy series of continuous mortar attack, he was found wandering around in a daze, trembling and muttering to himself. He seemed oblivious to the real dangers that still existed around him. Attempts by field hospital physicians to communicate with him met with failure: he did not seem to hear their inquiries. Yet, he was unusually responsive to very slight noises such as the crinkling of a pack of cigarettes. He was transferred to a psychiatric ward because of unpredictable outbursts of aggressive behavior during which he attacked others, destroyed furniture, and ripped his clothing. He was subject to extreme nightmares during which he shouted incoherently and thrashed about in his bed. On awakening, however, he was again mute and apparently amnesic for the evening's dream. The following was reported under hypnosis:

> We were told to hold the line at all costs. The days were bad enough but the nights were worse—you couldn't see anything or anyone. . . . I kept thinking I heard someone creeping up on me. Pretty soon I had to close my eyes and bite my lips to stop from panicking. I wanted to give up, to go home, to hide somewhere. I couldn't take it anymore. And then they started bombarding us. It just went on and on and on. The noise was so loud I thought my head would explode inside. I saw someone tossed into the air like a rag doll . . . and his arm. . . .

After nine months of active hypnotic therapy, the patient was eventually discharged. He was able to return to his prewar occupation as a service station attendant. However, there were a few residual symptoms. His dream life was still troublesome although no longer nightmarish; and he had a noticeable stammer. He was encouraged to continue in outpatient therapy to further root out the effects of the trauma.

World War I, World War II, the Korean War, and the Vietnam conflict are all examples of situations that have tested the psychological strength of vast numbers of soldiers (Roberts et al., 1982). Case History 6–4 provides one example of a combat reaction; other typical examples have been reported to the author.

> Things changed so fast up front, you never knew what was on your left or even behind you, I used to get turned around and think I was surrounded, I was scared all the time.
>
> The constant feeling of being all alone . . . unreal . . . sounds, explosions, vague crying, then dark, and light again . . . everything goes on and on.
>
> I used to be sick all the time or afraid of being sick, from the blood . . . and the smell of blood. . . . I remember over and over again the arm falling in front of me . . . you couldn't afford to make friends, it rips you up too much if they bleed on you, or if you see them crippled for no good reason . . . or worse, if they die next to you.

The world of combat is marked by persistent intolerable suspense, never-ending fatigue, and inescapable turmoil of waiting and wondering and wishing. If tuberculosis accounted for the highest percentage of medical casualties in World War I, the highest percentage of disability discharges in World War II was from psychiatric problems (Bartemeier et al., 1946). In a special study of combat exhaustion in the European Theatre of Operations in 1945, some common stress reactions were noted: the phobic reactions to shellfire; the angry feeling of impotence from being pinned down; and the horror of seeing mutilating wounds in comrades.

*Civilian Reactions.* Civilian reactions derive from the sudden occurrence of disaster which forces the individual to call on every personal resource to avoid being overwhelmed. Explosions, destructive tornadoes,

# FOCUS 6–1:
## Prisoners of War: Helpless or Helping Hostages?

For 444 days until early 1981, 52 American citizens were isolated in captivity in Iran. Information on their physical and mental condition was limited to brief statements released on videotapes or carried by ministers. Overall, the impression was that all were treated well, and in fact, one soldier held hostage confirmed this on a taped statement. However, almost immediately after the hostages set foot once again on American soil, an outpouring of reports disclosed that they had been harassed, tortured, and terrorized.

Coincidentally, at about the same time the hostages were receiving the warm welcome of the nation, Private Robert Garwood was standing before a judge. Stiffly erect, he heard a court-martial verdict of "guilty" for collaborating with the enemy while he was a prisoner of war in Vietnam. Garwood had been charged with being an informant, with cooperating with his captors, and with cooperating on enemy propaganda statements. He was accused by nine other former POWs who withstood the same treatment but resisted collaborating. Garwood's defense attorney called on three psychiatrists, maintaining that Garwood's actions were due to the mental disturbance that was caused by his isolation and torture.

What can we expect the normal human being to tolerate? There is a clear relationship between psychiatric problems and the length of imprisonment, degree of social isolation, and harshness of treatment an individual receives; and treatment of hostages or POWs is certainly harsh (O'Connell, 1976; Hunter, 1976). Brainwashing may be employed; and prisoners may be placed in complete isolation to increase the need for companionship. Food and bodily needs may be threatened, as a means of developing dependency. Torture and the threat of death or disability are offered as the alternative to cooperation. Self-criticism is required as a first step to eliminate self-esteem and resistance. Boredom and apathy are used to increase interest in attending indoctrination meetings.

With this combination of mental and physical stress, perhaps the definition of normal behavior changes. Is it normal to continue to resist until the body collapses mentally and physically; or is it normal to resist inwardly but to outwardly cooperate? If a prisoner (such as Garwood) cooperates while under intense pressure, how does one decide whether this is intentional treason as opposed to irrational action for which a person cannot be held responsible? It is interesting to compare these issues with those raised in Chapter 1, regarding legal use of insanity as a defense in court trials.

fires, floods, nuclear plant accidents, and mine cave-ins have all occurred without warning, resulting in post-traumatic stress disorders among survivors (Malick et al., 1983).

The following report, from the sinking of the *Andrea Doria,* provides a vivid example of the kinds of symptoms that may result:

> On July 25, 1956, at 11:05 P.M., the Swedish liner *Stockholm* smashed into the starboard side of the Italian liner *Andrea Doria* a few miles off Nantucket Island, causing one of the worst disasters in maritime history. . . . During the phase of initial shock the survivors acted as if they had been sedated . . . as though nature provided a sedation mechanism which went into operation automatically . . . the survivors presented themselves for the most part as an amorphous mass of people tending to act passively and complaisantly. They displayed psychomotor retardation, flattening of affect, somnolence, and in some instances, amnesia for data of personal identification. They were nonchalant and easily suggestible . . . [later, there was] . . . an apparently compulsive need to tell the story again and again, with identical detail and emphasis. (Friedman & Linn, 1957)

### Dynamics of Post-traumatic Stress Disorders

How can we explain severe reactions such as those shown by the *Andrea Doria's* survivors? One factor involved is the breakdown of normal coping patterns; another, according to some theorists, is the physiological strain imposed on the organism.

***Coping Mechanisms and Traumatic Stress.*** In everyday life, we gradually learn to adjust to normal conditions. Certain defenses are erected to cope with recurrent internal or external stressors. We acquire specific strengths that let us adapt to our needs in our given surroundings, and we soon learn to expect certain demands and stresses from life.

In a situation of exceptional stress, that world of expectations collapses. The surroundings are drastically altered; the nature, intensity, and duration of the stresses are suddenly changed; and as a result, our usually adequate coping skills are no longer sufficient to serve as defenses. In situations such as these, an individual's sense of efficacy is disturbed so severely that the traumatic effects extend long after the situation itself has ended.

The relationship between a person's inability to cope with the environment and the onset of post-traumatic stress disorder may be seen when we examine persons trained to deal with catastrophic or highly stressful events. Barton (1963) observed that persons with definable disaster roles, such as firefighters or disaster-relief workers, could rely on their knowledge of how to behave to see them through a crisis.

Persons who feel in control or have mastery skills are better able to resist stress (Johnson & Sarason, 1978; Thompson, 1981). Soldiers in Vietnam with decision-making duties tended to resist stress longer than those who had little control (Strange, 1969). American astronauts felt exhilaration rather than anxiety during launching, due to their prior mastery experiences—"Each of them has faced situations in which fear was appropriate and found that he was able to function despite its effects" (Ruff & Korchen, 1964). The discussion in Focus 6–2 illustrates some procedures taken by the NASA program to help prevent the development of traumatic stress.

Some level of adaptation may also be provided by defense mechanisms. A long-time career officer friend of the author, much decorated for bravery, said, "It doesn't ever occur to me that there is any danger to me personally . . . in the spotter plane . . . even when I'm drawing fire . . . you feel invulnerable!" In many cases like this, defenses that involve restructuring perceptions of the environment appear to reduce stress.

***Physiological Components of Post-traumatic Stress.*** The progress of the post-traumatic stress disorder appears to be similar to biological reaction to stress described by Selye (1979). This University of Montreal medical scientist suggested that prolonged stress from trauma, infections, and emotional upheaval can result in a condition he calls the *general adaptation syndrome.*

During the first phase of such excessive stress, the body mobilizes its resources in an alarm-reaction phase, whereby physiological defenses are alerted. Metabolic changes occur including the activation of the adrenal cortex, blood changes, and gastrointestinal alterations. As the stress is prolonged, excessive secretions such as adrenaline may outlast their original fight-or-flight function and may actually cause damage or pathological changes to the brain or other organs.

The second phase of the general adaptation syn-

## FOCUS 6–2:

### Traumatic Stress Prevention: Planning for Space Flights

The astronauts have experienced a minimum of stress reactions even though the conditions of physical and psychological stress have been high. Among the stresses which the astronauts were expected to encounter were confinement, sensory and social isolation in long trips, the threat of unexpected danger, the continuing stress of noise levels, the problems of wake-sleep cycles, and weightlessness.

Plans were made to prevent these situations from becoming unduly stressful. The issue of sensory isolation was quickly and simply handled by the great variety and number of tasks which the astronauts were given prior to takeoff and during flight. If anything, there was the danger of sensory overload rather than deprivation. Explicit contact with other people through voice communication, and implicit communication through physiological sensing apparatuses, such as heart readings, provided a buffer against social isolation. Sleep disturbances did occur in Apollo 8, and these led to minor crew procedure errors. As a result, later missions had all crew members sleep concurrently so as to establish a common sleep pattern. In addition, the day-night cycle of Cape Kennedy was used as the reference point for the wake-sleep pattern.

Intense training in the appropriate behaviors in the event of disaster situations were conducted. For instance, astronauts were trained in what to do if instrument warning signals went on. This reduced the threat of the unknown while providing the astronauts with disaster roles and confidence in their abilities (McLaughlin, 1970).

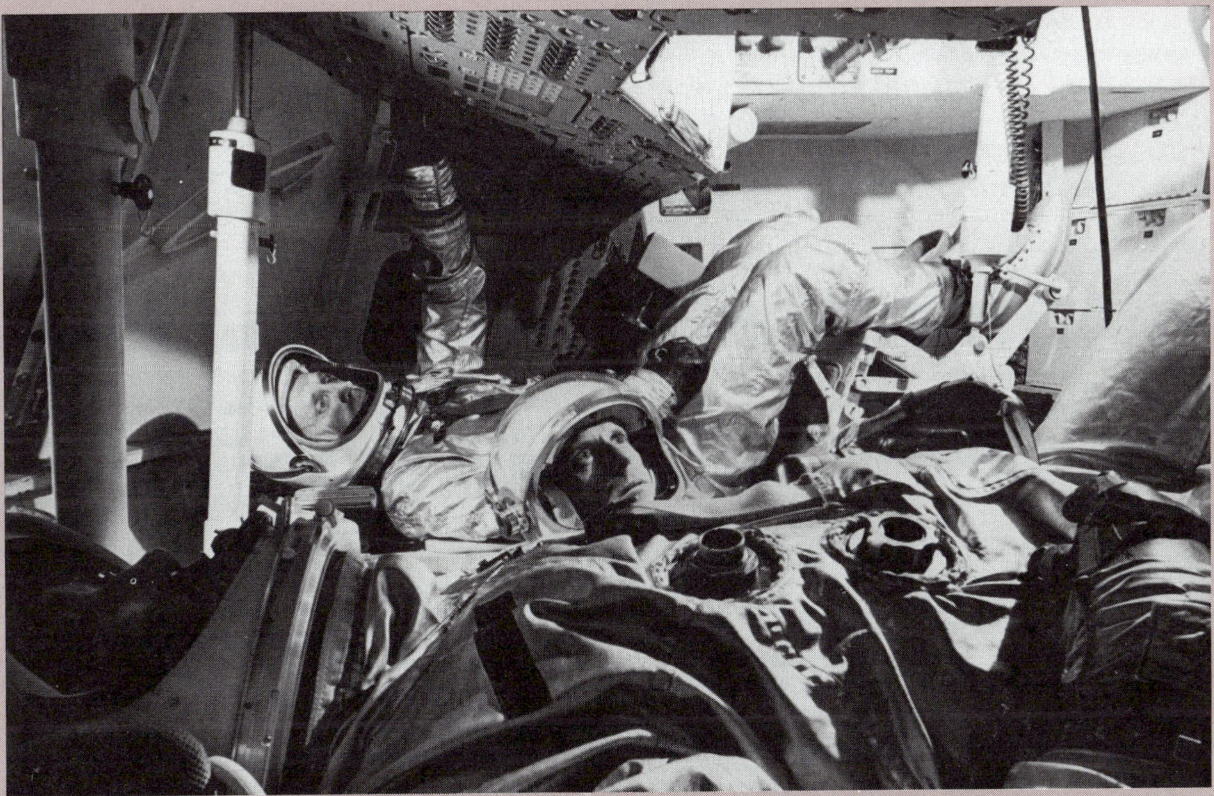

*The astronauts have been trained to **cope** with circumstances that might produce stress in others. The Apollo command module provided sensory variety including different tasks to avoid boredom.*

drome is the stage of resistance, characterized by specific resistance to the particular stress that is occurring and a lack of responsiveness to other stimuli. The stage of exhaustion is the final phase; it results from the organism's exhausting its adaptive resources in dealing with the original stress. The individual is no longer able to resist as defenses are stripped away. Such pathological changes within the body may also develop when relatively mild stress is presented over a long period, forcing the individual to continuously cope with the stressful conditions. In essence, constant exposure to a high-pressure life can be responsible for insidious pathological damage to the body and its normal functioning (Catalano, 1979).

Some early symptoms of the post-traumatic stress disorder are somewhat akin to the alarm-reaction phase. The soldier is tense, alert, and ready to react to danger. The phase of resistance might be equivalent to the symptoms of loss of concentration, where the person is unable to respond. Finally, the phase of exhaustion shows many similarities to symptoms of stress reactions, for instance, irritability, lowering of intellectual efficiency, loss of interest, and outbursts of temper.

Of course, it must be remembered that the symptoms of stress reactions are not due solely to physical strain and exhaustion. The more critical component is the psychological. In this new catastrophic world, the individual now feels incapable, ineffective, and overwhelmed. The surroundings have been transformed from a safe, secure, comfortable situation to a threatening, tension-provoking, disturbing condition; and the most immediate reaction, flight, has been made quite impossible.

### Treatment of Post-traumatic Stress Disorders

The most significant factor in treating post-traumatic stress is early treatment (Frederick, 1981b). If the individual has been left alone long enough to consolidate the symptoms, it is extremely difficult to change (Egendorf, 1978). He or she stops trying to adapt to the stresses, reduces efforts, and begins to live a parasitic life depending on others for care. In the early phase of the illness, treatment is directed toward preventing the patient from seeking refuge in escape. In the combat zone, the soldier is encouraged to remain with his unit in a less strenuous role and with sedatives for sleep at

*Wars create conditions for stress such as **combat reactions**. This soldier under fire may later develop symptoms known as post-traumatic stress disorders.*

night. Reassurance that he has not reached the point of complete breakdown permits the soldier to accept his fear and exhaustion. Another helpful form of treatment is hypnosis. Hypnotic recall is used as a means of preventing the retreat from trauma through repression. A protective reconstruction through hypnosis or even direct conscious recall enables the patient to take an active hand in coping with the traumatic events. Such early handling of traumatic stress leads to an optimistic outlook for recovery. Of course, in cases where the patient was already predisposed to a mental breakdown under any circumstances, long-term treatment is likely.

The prevention of post-traumatic stress disorders has been another focus of concern. Although it is believed that everyone will ultimately reach a breaking point given specific severe stresses over a long duration, nevertheless it may be possible to prevent immediate breakdown and increase tolerance to stress. Disaster control training is available to professionals and volunteers, emphasizing what reactions to expect of various-age victims to prevent symptoms from consolidating (Cohen & Ahearn, 1980; National Institute of Mental Health, 1978).

Military psychologists, learning from previous data, have pointed out certain factors that helped during the Vietnam fighting (Bourne, 1970). For instance, soldiers were rotated out of the Vietnam assignment after one year. It is believed that this clearly designated, short period of exposure to stress enables the combat soldier to remind himself that the stress will end. In addition, the buddy-system of the Korean War, whereby emotional attachments were encouraged, has been modified. Instead, soldiers in Vietnam were given every opportunity to retain emotional independence, keeping their feelings attached to home and family, through opportunities to telephone the United States and a better mail delivery system. This reinforcement of stable home ties helped protect soldiers from the trauma of injury or death of close comrades on the front. An older method, still useful, is the procedure for training a soldier to perceive and react to military stresses as impersonal, routine exercises, devoid of threat. Thus, combat operations are viewed as a series of operational demands to be reacted to with precise, overlearned military behaviors, rather than emergency, emotion-filled stressful situations (Rado, 1943). In some respects this is equivalent to Barton's earlier concept of the value of possessing definable, disaster-related role behaviors.

## EVALUATION

The analysis and treatment of anxiety disorders have received a great deal of attention by psychological theorists and clinicians, possibly because of their prevalence among nonhospitalized patients. The views of Selye about normal human reactions to continued stress have proven a useful model, especially in understanding the post-traumatic stress disorder. Other useful analyses include the distinction among various ways in which anxieties or fears can be acquired, through modeling, through conditioning, or by a sort of default in being more susceptible to threat because of the absence of coping or adaptive skills.

Although psychoanalytic theory continues to seek symbolic bases for anxiety disorders, it is noteworthy that behavioral approaches seem to have accumulated the greatest successes in treatment and research. Cognitive behavior therapy, desensitization, modeling, anxiety management training, and response-prevention have proven of value in altering anxiety states, often within relatively brief treatment programs. In fact, for the phobic disorder, enough evidence exists that behavior therapy is extremely helpful; and that virtually no one should have to suffer from such common fears as snakes, heights, closed spaces, darkness, or flying. If drug treatments can be credited with major contributions to the control of schizophrenia (see Chapter 17), certain behavior therapies can be recognized for their impact on phobic disorders. Post-traumatic stress disorders are also being successfully treated, especially when treatment is begun early. Preventative steps where persons are helped to avoid unusual stress are also critical in avoiding post-traumatic stress disorders.

## SUMMARY

The anxiety disorders represent a diverse set of milder disturbances which all share the component of anxiety in common. For some, such as the generalized anxiety disorder and the panic disorder, the anxiety experience is itself the primary characteristic. These disorders involve respectively the presence of diffuse chronic apprehension or recurring waves of anxiety so intense as to be overwhelming. For other anxiety disorders, the reaction to anxiety is the primary symptom. For example, in the phobic disorder, avoidance behaviors are characteristic as the person attempts to escape from situations associated with anxiety. For the obsessive-compulsive, anxiety is controlled by the person engaging in continual thoughts or ritualistic behaviors to occupy attention or reduce anxiety. The post-traumatic stress disorder appears to be the persistence of psychological reactions to disastrous and traumatic life experiences which are stressful. Treatment is most optimistic for the phobic disorders and, when caught early, the post-traumatic stress disorder. Promising new methods, mainly behavior modification techniques, appear to offer hope for generalized anxiety and obsessive-compulsive disorders through anxiety management training, cognitive behavior therapy, and response prevention.

## KEY TERMS

**Agoraphobia**
**Anxiety disorders**
**Anxiety management training**
**Behavior therapy**
**Civilian catastrophic reaction**
**Claustrophobia**
**Cognitive behavior therapy**
**Combat reactions**
**Desensitization**
**Flooding**
**General adaptation syndrome**
**Generalized anxiety disorder**
**Gross-stress reaction**
**Hydrotherapy**
**Modeling**
**Obsessive-compulsive disorder**
**Panic disorder**
**Paradoxical intention**
**Phobic disorder**
**Post-traumatic stress disorder**
**Psychoanalytic therapy**
**Rational emotive therapy**
**Rational restructuring**
**Response prevention**
**State anxiety**
**Stress inoculation training**
**Trait anxiety**
**Two-factor theory**
**Vicarious learning**

# CHAPTER 7

## Adjustment Disorders: Maladaptive Responses to Stress

- **Both the post-traumatic stress disorder and the adjustment disorders relate to stress; how do these two types of disorders differ?**
- **What are the varieties of conditions that may act as stressors?**
- **Would you still be diagnosed as suffering from an adjustment disorder if you explained that you were grieving over a close friend's death?**
- **What circumstances or conditions would make you more vulnerable to stress than someone else?**
- **Can you tell how much stress you may be currently undergoing?**
- **Why should inheriting money be a source of stress?**
- **Would you choose to live near an airport if you are concerned about the level of stress you are undergoing?**
- **What does 80° + F temperature have to do with rioting?**
- **How can you develop better stress tolerance?**

**TABLE 7–1**

**Adjustment Disorders**

| *Type* | *Major Characteristics* |
|---|---|
| Adjustment disorder with anxious mood | Experiencing anxiety related to stress, where the anxiety persists or is greater than is appropriate |
| Adjustment disorder with depressed mood | Experiencing depression related to a stress, where the depression persists or is greater than is appropriate |
| Adjustment disorder with disturbance of conduct | Reacting to stress through acting-out behaviors, such as vandalism |
| Adjustment disorder with withdrawal | Reacting to stress through withdrawing from the environment |

# Case History 7–1:
## Adjustment Disorder with Anxious Mood

George M. is a 21-year-old college student in preveterinary medicine. His spouse had recently resigned from her job because of the birth of their child. Although proud of his family, George has felt pressures from his multiple roles and varying values. "I should have married later, or delayed the family, or changed my major. . . . I feel like my life is compressed into too short a period. . . . I have to be a father and earn a living, I have to be a successful husband and spend time with my wife, I have to study late into the morning to make it in school. . . ."

It is as though any single demand could be tolerated, but the accumulation leads to being pushed and pulled in contrary directions. To obtain a full-time job would mean giving up schooling and his career desires; but staying in the university means not having enough time to be with his wife or to even have enough energy to listen to her needs; and obviously separation or divorce is out of the question. "I seem constantly irritable, I either ignore my wife or I accuse her of asking too much of me, or I just leave home and go to the library to get away. But I can't study, I can't sleep because I feel I should be studying. Vet school is hard to get into, so I don't even know if I'll qualify and not be wasting my time."

There have been some good moments, but these have been transitory. George took his family on a three-day vacation, a birthday gift from his parents. Being away from school, with expenses reasonably paid, George felt calmer and his wife enjoyed the private moments to themselves. "It was like I was a new man." However, once back in school, George feels that the symptoms of stress returned and have been compounded by academic difficulties. Although he is holding a B average, George feels that it is not sufficient, worries about the possibility of getting even one C (although he has never received one on even a quiz), studies late but inefficiently because of the brooding worry, and now reports his marriage as gradually becoming less satisfying.

The previous chapter discussed those disorders in which a state of anxiety predominates. In the last of these disorders, the post-traumatic stress disorder, the state of anxiety is focused on a tension-producing event, called a *stressor.*

The disorders we discuss in this chapter are also related to stressors. The *adjustment disorders* are conditions that involve maladaptive responses to a variety of stressors. In the sense that they are responses to stress, the adjustment disorders are similar to the post-traumatic stress disorder; but there are several important differences. While the post-traumatic stress disorder involves a traumatic event or catastrophe outside the normal range of human experience, the stressors in the adjustment disorders are typically less-severe life events. In the post-traumatic stress disorder, too, the condition seems mainly a response to extreme trauma, with the trauma in a sense controlling the psychological and physical reaction. In the adjustment disorders, however, there is more interaction between the stressor and the psychological characteristics of the individual. Thus, adjustment disorders are characterized by the presence of a stressor, impairment of social or occupational functioning, and symptoms in excess of normal reaction to the stressor.

## STRESS AND VULNERABILITY TO STRESS

Before going on to discuss the specific adjustment disorders, it is useful to briefly introduce both stress and stressors. *Stress* can be defined as a state of the body caused, as Selye (1974, 1980) puts it, by undue demands being placed on it. These states of tension involve complex patterns of responses, including subjective feelings of apprehension or tension, accompanied by or associated with physiological activation or arousal (Spielberger, 1966).

The response patterns of stress may involve *cognitive sets* (self-perceptions such as, "I am always jumpy, I'm really a tense person"); *autonomic reactions,* such as that reported by the person who says, "I can hear my heart pounding in my ears"; or *physical or behavioral responses,* as in the case of the student who starts to stutter in front of an audience or the athlete who tightens up. These response patterns may not always be present all the time for all people experiencing stress; and as we saw in Chapter 6, there is reason to believe that the autonomic, the behavioral, and the cognitive responses can be independent of one another (Van Dyke et al., 1983). Consider your own reactions when you are stressed; then listen to others describe how they know when they are stressed. You may become aware of what appear to be discrepancies. For example, one person may overtly seem calm and handle a difficult situation smoothly and easily, yet confess later, "You don't know how scared I was." Similarly, another person may show severe motor disruptions, yet deny having felt anxious during the performance. However, for most persons, there is some correlation across these three response patterns, so that subjective apprehension is also associated with autonomic and behavioral signs of stress.

Stress is the body's reaction to certain events or circumstances called *stressors.* A stressor is traditionally considered a threatening or aversive environmental event. Many events or conditions can act as stressors. These may include *single events* (such as a death in the family), *multiple events* (losing a job during a divorce), *recurrent events* (such as seasonal crop crises), *continuous events* (a lingering cancer), *individual events* (such as being a victim of rape), *group problems* (suffering from racial discrimination), *culture-bound events* (such as facing forced retirement), or *environmental events* (noise pollution from air traffic). Any of these stressors may vary in severity, and the severity of the stressor will be likely to affect a person's response (Goldberg & Breznitz, 1982). Thus, any diagnosis of an adjustment disorder takes into account the severity of the stressor, which is assessed on a continuum from mild to harsh.

Although adjustment disorders are closely related to the presence of a stressor, that does not mean that stressors automatically produce adjustment disorders. As we saw in the preceding chapter's discussion of post-traumatic stress disorders, a second factor—individual resources, coping skills, or other personality variables—can clearly affect a person's ability to cope with stress. Personality variables will be discussed in more detail in the dynamics section of this chapter.

A third factor that affects a person's ability to

*Modern living brings with it new and increasing stresses that tax human resilience and ability to adapt. Ever louder and continuous* ***noise levels*** *may have a psychological effect because of the stress they can create.*

withstand stress is the environmental support or resources available (Lieberman, 1983). An elderly man who has no close friends will be more likely to become depressed in response to his wife's death than he would if he had even one or two close friends. Likewise, a young teenager whose family rejects her when she becomes pregnant will be far more likely to develop an adjustment disorder than she would if she received support and reassurance from her family.

In all, then, the likelihood of a person's developing an adjustment disorder seems to be expressed in the following formula:

*Stressor + Environment + Person =*
*Adjustment Disorder*

A slightly different way of expressing this relationship is represented in Figure 7–1.

## SYMPTOMS AND DIAGNOSES

The adjustment disorders are all related to stress. For this reason, they may be short term in nature compared to most other disorders discussed in this text; or, at least, the disorder often becomes less severe or disappears as the stressor is resolved.

Adjustment disorders are classified according to the symptoms that predominate (see Table 7–1). The major disorders include:

- Adjustment disorder with depressed mood
- Adjustment disorder with anxious mood
- Adjustment disorder with disturbance of conduct
- Adjustment disorder with withdrawal

### Adjustment Disorder with Depressed Mood

Symptoms of the adjustment disorder with depressed mood typically include sadness or sorrow, a sense of hopelessness, tearfulness, loss of energy and interest in activities, and insomnia. These symptoms are often linked to a state of bereavement. This relationship, however, is not necessary. A person may show an entirely different response to a death—as when a young person rebels at the unfair death of a friend and becomes angry instead of depressed. And while bereavement is often associated with a depressed mood, such a reaction would be considered an adjustment disorder only if the depression persists or is of a magnitude beyond the normal range. Thus, a clinical judgment must be based not only on the nature and level of the stress, but also on an understanding of what bereavement responses are typical or normal and at what point responses become overreactions.

The adjustment disorder with depressed mood might also be confused with another state, the depression associated with the bipolar disorder discussed in Chapter 16. These two disorders may be distinguished by a few features, however. The depressed adjustment disorder differs both in the severity of personality disorganization that takes place and in the recovery aspects. The depression of the bipolar disorder involves a much more severe personality disruption than can be attributed to the presence of a stressor; the symptoms

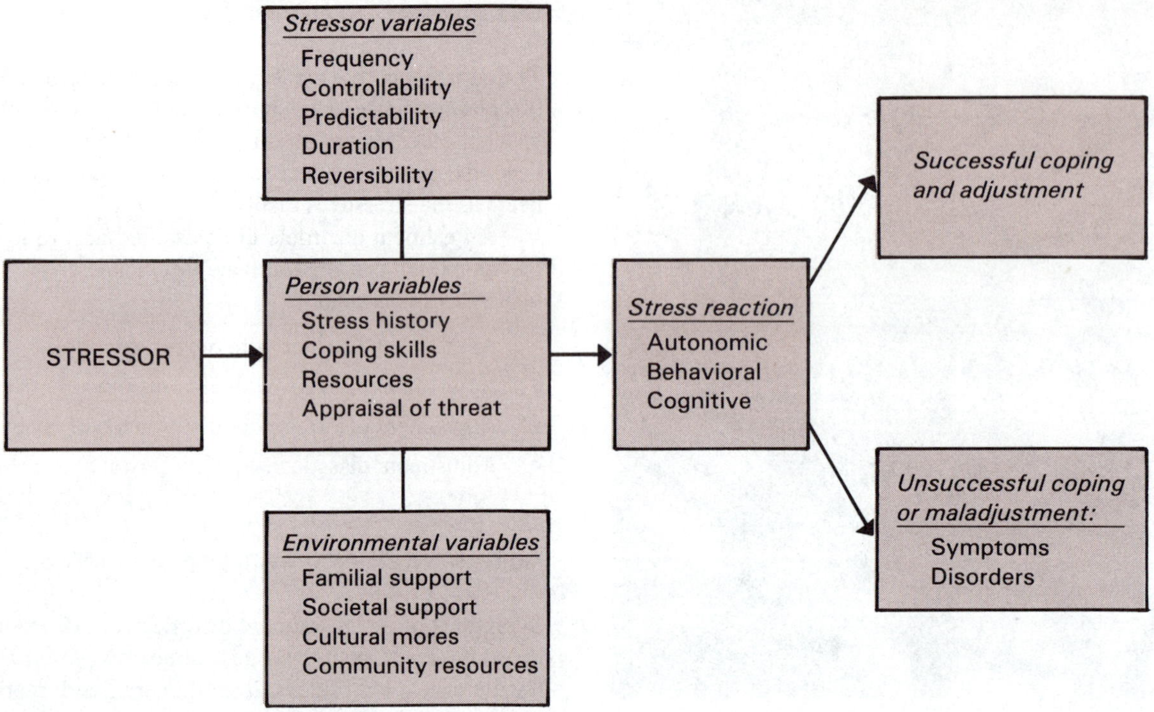


**FIGURE 7–1** A model of stress.

are more intensive and pervasive. Furthermore, the adjustment disorders are all directly related to the presence of a stressor, while the bipolar disorder is not. Thus, a person affected by an adjustment disorder is expected to recover rapidly after termination of the stressor, while recovery from a bipolar depression is less clearly associated with changes in life circumstances.

### Adjustment Disorder With Anxious Mood

The adjustment disorder with anxious mood, as illustrated in the opening case history, seems to more closely reflect tensions precipitated by the stressor. As mentioned earlier, the symptoms of this tension may be expressed in any or all of the systems of the body—autonomic-physiological, behavioral, or cognitive. Thus, symptoms of an adjustment disorder with anxious mood might include increased heart rate, palmar sweating, speech or motor disruptions, an inability to sit still, irritability, and worry or apprehension.

These symptoms tend to abate when the stressor is removed, and they also tend to become aggravated if the stressor recurs. Thus, the farmer who has lasted through one drought may become increasingly anxious as the next growing season draws near; similarly, the young couple may become more at ease as their major hospital bill and mortgage and car payments are consolidated into a more manageable monthly bill. In this sense, there is a chronological relationship between the onset of stress and the onset of symptoms. On the other hand, because the adjustment disorder is a form of maladaptive response to stress, and not a normal reaction, the simple onset or termination of the stressful event does not guarantee an immediate change in symptoms. Remission may be delayed or gradual following the removal of the stressor. Also, as is charac-

*Although grieving is a normal reaction to death, such a response would be considered an* ***adjustment disorder*** *if it were extreme or if it persisted.*

teristic of all the adjustment disorders, the reaction to the stress includes an impairment of functioning beyond that normally expected.

The adjustment disorder with anxious mood shares some symptoms with the *generalized anxiety disorder* discussed in Chapter 6. However, the two disorders differ in two ways. First, the adjustment disorder is clearly associated with a stressful event or circumstance in the life of the individual, while the generalized anxiety disorder is not. Furthermore, the adjustment disorder, unlike the generalized anxiety disorder, does not normally last beyond six months. It is possible for an adjustment disorder to persist longer if the stressor continues to be present. However, this is a relatively infrequent condition.

### Adjustment Disorder with Disturbance of Conduct

In this adjustment disorder, the individual responds to the stressor through acting-out behaviors, or *conduct.* Conduct disturbances may take a number of forms including truancy, vandalism, reckless driving, assaultiveness, excess drinking, or illegal acts.

The nature of the acting-out may be influenced by a range of factors: previous learning, environmental opportunities, the social context, as well as the influence of the stressor. Thus, a youngster experiencing the pressure of school discipline and grades may skip classes on the day of examinations with the encouragement of peers. Vandalism may represent an attempt to strike back at the perceived cause of the stress. It is more likely, however, to be aimed at unguarded property such as cars, billboards, theater seats.

As with the disorder called *antisocial personality* (see Chapter 15), conduct disturbance involves behaviors that violate others' rights, legal statutes, or societal norms of conduct. The two types of disorders differ in that the adjustment disorder is clearly stress linked, while the role of stressors in the antisocial personality disorder is not as clear. Furthermore, the antisocial personality disorder appears to have origins in other factors, such as a failure to develop meaningful affectional or social ties to others, or a long-term shaping of antisocial behaviors by gang membership. Although the youngster or adult showing an antisocial personality disorder may glibly blame environmental stress as the reason for misconduct, removal of such stressors ensures neither the elimination of illegal behaviors nor, necessarily, the display of adequate social functioning. In the adjustment disorder, however, resolution of stress typically brings a return of social or occupational functioning.

### Adjustment Disorder with Withdrawal

Like the adjustment disorder with disturbance of conduct, the adjustment disorder with withdrawal is a *behavioral* symptom of stress. In this way, these two disorders contrast with the disorders with depressed or anxious moods, both of which are manifested as emotional states. The two behavioral adjustment disorders are significantly different, however. Activity seems to characterize the conduct adjustment disorder, while the withdrawal disorder is distinguished by escape from activity. It is as though the conduct disorder involves a desire to strike out at the stressful situation,

## Case History 7–2:
### Adjustment Disorder with Disturbance of Conduct

Coreen B. is a 15-year-old student living in Los Angeles with foster parents—a temporary measure until her actual parents resolve divorce proceedings. The parents are well-known in the community. They have both been active in school parent committees aimed at protecting moral values in education and in censoring books in the school library. Several television and radio interviews have permitted them to publicly express their concerns about declining moral training in the schools.

Although the divorce proceedings have been kept reasonably quiet, many rumors have been circulating in Coreen's school, and her peers have been making fun of her. A major rumor is that the divorce relates to adultery by one parent. In fact, the father is accusing the mother of not having revealed an affair she had during their engagement 17 years ago. Many angry accusations and counteraccusations have made it hard to assess just what is going on, and Coreen has felt confused and embarrassed. She has watched her parents become vengeful and spiteful towards one another in private, while still displaying a public image of sweetness in their crusade for sounder moral values. This has forced her to feel isolated from her parents. "If I can't trust my own parents to be honest with themselves and with others, can I believe what they've said to me?"

As conflict between her parents has increased, Coreen has also been struggling with her own values; two boyfriends—both of whom she likes—have been demanding sexual relation. Although she is no longer a virgin, the sexual battles of her parents have been so traumatic that Coreen feels she must avoid serious sexual contact until her own values are better established. She has never felt able to know fully her own feelings about sexuality since such topics were always considered taboo within the family.

Another source of stress is Coreen's foster family. Her temporary stay with them was at her own request, since she had always liked these friends of her parents. However, her foster parents are now casting innuendoes about what a financial burden she is. In addition, the older son has made sexual passes at Coreen. Since then, she has felt frightened and unhappy with her choice to leave her parents.

Within recent months, Coreen has developed the reputation of being a delinquent. She has cut classes, her grades are falling, and she has been seen drinking heavily. She has been reprimanded twice for minor defacing of school property and has been suspected of damaging the seat of her foster family's car. She has become sullen in school, especially to authorities, but has continued to be cooperative and reasonable to her foster parents.

A school counselor has taken an interest in Coreen. Coreen has slowly developed a sense of trust in him, to the degree that she shared her confusion about her parents and her continuing fears about being molested. She has not admitted to the vandalism of the car and still misses classes, but the truancy seems to be diminishing somewhat. The counselor plans to seek Coreen's transfer to a more accepting home while continuing his sessions, which emphasize reassurance and support. In addition, he intends to recommend that she temporarily discontinue seeing her parents: perhaps more isolation from their problems will help Coreen regain her own stability.

while the withdrawal disorder involves a wish to get away from it all. Symptoms of the withdrawal disorder may include avoidance behaviors, apparent apathy, social disinterest, aloofness, and a restriction of activities to those that seem safe.

The adjustment disorder with withdrawal should be distinguished from the *schizoid personality disorder* discussed in Chapter 15. The major differences are in the importance of stressors in the adjustment disorder and in the fact that the schizoid disorder appears to involve an overlearned, long-term, persistent way of behaving. Thus, in the adjustment disorder, the withdrawal behavior is precipitated by the onset of stressors; whereas the introversive, seclusive, and solitary behaviors of the schizoid personality appear to be independent of the immediate environment.

*Vandalism such as graffiti may be a symptom of an adjustment disorder with* ***disturbance of conduct.***

## DYNAMICS OF THE ADJUSTMENT DISORDERS

In examining the adjustment disorders, we have seen that they all relate closely to the presence and severity of life stressors. These stressors may derive from any of four variables: physiological or biological sources, sociological sources, psychological sources, and living-environmental sources. Another variable that is also important in the development of an adjustment disorder is the personality characteristics of the individual facing the stressor. We will look at each of these factors next.

### Biological Sources

Physiological or biological threats may constitute serious stressors. Infection from bacterial attacks, as well as tissue injury, fatigue, and other threats to life or physical well-being, represent important stressors. In a study of how college students rate various life events (Marx et al., 1975), personal injury or illness was rated 65 on a scale where 100 represented extreme stress.

This is not to say that all physical stress is harmful. You will recall from Chapter 6 that Selye observed that biologically related stressors precipitated a natural defensive reaction. If you are trapped in an accident that threatens you with physical injury or death, your body machinery instantly initiates internal physiological measures. This alarm or arousal reaction prepares you through autonomic nervous system activation, adrenaline discharge, increased heart rate in preparation for wounds, and increased blood flow for brain functioning. Of course, if a resolution to the threat is not achieved quickly, and the danger persists, these physiological defensive reactions may themselves turn into threats. For instance, continued discharge of adrenaline may create nervous tension, until complete exhaustion takes over.

A less dramatic example of physiological or biological sources of stress derives from jet travel. Both animals and humans appear to develop biological clocks which govern normal biological functioning. These clocks, technically referred to as *circadian cycles,* comprise the 24-hour rhythmic fluctuations in sleep, activity level, and body temperature. Abrupt time changes, as happen with jet travel, can adversely affect the timing of our clocks, causing symptoms of stress (Weitzman & Luce, 1970).

### Social Causes

Sociological factors, such as problems of urban living and racial prejudice, can also contribute to stress (Pearlin, 1983). Some of the issues of urban living, including community size, neighborhood disintegration, and socio-economic status, have already been summarized in Chapter 5. A new breed of urban planners is emerging who are attempting to integrate sound principles of architectural and community planning with psychological perspectives. Planned communities for the elderly are designed to reduce stressors by simple steps, such as easing access to recreation or shopping. Psychological security is enhanced by systems aimed at insuring immediate medical warning signals to go off if an elderly resident living alone has a heart attack and cannot reach a telephone.

Minority group membership may subject a person to another source of stress: prejudice. It is estimated that minorities represent about 20 percent of the nation's total population. A U.S. senator from Hawaii, in proposing a minority mental health program, justified this program to the president on the basis that ". . . All indications are that these individuals continue to suffer from the stressors of prejudice and racism. . . . Minorities face specific problems in the alcoholism and drug abuse areas, especially since the problems are compounded by poverty and racism" (Inouye, 1979, p. S4192). Minority professionals assert that being a member of a minority group in a traditionally white environment tends to mean fewer educational opportunities, higher unemployment, poorer housing, and lower-quality services—all factors which in themselves are stressors (Bass et al., 1982; Becerra et al., 1982; Sue & Morishima, 1982). Even when services are available, there is some evidence that minorities may not be offered the same opportunities. For example, Cole & Pilisuk (1976) reported that, although 40 percent of whites seeking help from a crisis clinic received psychotherapy, only 20 percent of blacks did. Although the literature regarding minority mental health is still confusing (partly because rhetoric sometimes gets in the way), the fact does seem to be that minorities experience many serious stressors in major life arenas.

### Psychological Causes

The third type of stressor is psychological. As we saw in Chapter 3, psychological needs include nurturance, achievement, security, self-esteem, structure and meaning in life, and sensory and social stimulation. The denial of any of these needs is one prominent source of stress. Conflicts are also sources of psychological stress, as they present obstacles to satisfying needs. If you are faced with opposing wants that pull in different directions—for instance, if you feel you need to move away from home at the same time that an aging parent requires your care—it may prove difficult to satisfy either need.

Another psychological source of stress can be a life change. The work of both Holmes and Rahe (1967) and Marx et al. (1975) is of special interest here. These scientists developed lists of life events that also involve changes in life the level of stress associated with each of these events is measured according to Life Change Units (LCU). Table 7–2 presents the questionnaire developed by Marx et al. to measure stress associated with life changes, and it indicates how several life changes are rated on a scale from 0 to 100. It is geared to college students' assessments of stress related to life changes. You can use it to assess your own level of life stress.

Looking at life changes as stressors provides an interesting perspective that may put some events in a different light from that which may be customary. Inheriting a considerable amount of money, for instance, or having an outstanding personal achievement may not usually be considered a stressful experience. However, these life events do represent changes, and such changes require adaptation. The stress level for a major change in financial status is rated in LCUs as 33 (mild stress), while the level for outstanding achievement is 40 for college students. High LCU scores have been found to be associated with greater susceptibility to physical illness in college students (Johnson & Sarason, 1979; Marx et al., 1975), a greater number of health visits to physicians or dentists (Suinn, 1978), greater incidence of sudden cardiac death (Rahe & Lind, 1971), and even a greater number of colds, bruises, and minor aches and pains (Holmes & Holmes, 1970). One fascinating Swedish study of identical twins found that it was life stress scores—and not the traditional medical or physical variables such as blood pressures, smoking habits, or cholesterol—that identified the twin with heart disease from the one who was healthy (Liljefors & Rahe, 1970).

### Environmental Causes

A fourth source of stress includes *living-environmental factors*—living conditions such as noise, pollution, heat, and overcrowding (Kaminoff & Proshansky, 1983).

We are exposed more and more to a society of noise. Consider the trail of noise that results from our reliance on jet air travel, our constant building programs, our daily transportation needs, and even creature comforts such as air-conditioning. Although it is not yet conclusive, there is some evidence that exposure to high noise levels is stressful and may relate to mental disorders (Cohen et al., 1977; Kryter, 1970). In a controversial study (Abey-Wickrama et al., 1969), scientists found higher admissions rates to a

**TABLE 7–2**

**L.C.U. Scores for Each of Life Change Events on CSRE**

| *Indicate the number of times during the last 12 months that you:* | *Life change units* |
|---|---|
| 1. Entered college | 50 |
| 2. Married | 77 |
| 3. Trouble with your boss | 38 |
| 4. Held a job while attending school | 43 |
| 5. Experienced the death of a spouse | 87 |
| 6. Major change in sleeping habits | 34 |
| 7. Experienced the death of a close family member | 77 |
| 8. Major change in eating habits | 30 |
| 9. Change in or choice of major field of study | 41 |
| 10. Revision of personal habits | 45 |
| 11. Experienced the death of a close friend | 68 |
| 12. Found guilty of minor violations of the law | 22 |
| 13. Had an outstanding personal achievement | 40 |
| *14. Experienced pregnancy, or *fathered a pregnancy* | 68 |
| 15. Major change in health or behavior of family member | 56 |
| 16. Had sexual difficulties | 58 |
| 17. Had trouble with in-laws | 42 |
| 18. Major change in number of family get-togethers | 26 |
| 19. Major change in financial state | 53 |
| 20. Gained a new family member | 50 |
| 21. Change in residence or living conditions | 42 |
| 22. Major conflict or change in values | 50 |
| 23. Major change in church activities | 36 |
| 24. Marital reconciliation with your mate | 58 |
| 25. Fired from work | 62 |
| 26. Were divorced | 76 |
| 27. Changed to a different line of work | 50 |
| 28. Major change in number of arguments with spouse | 50 |
| 29. Major change in responsibilities at work | 47 |
| †30. Had your *spouse* begin or cease work outside the home | 41 |
| 31. Major change in working hours or conditions | 42 |
| 32. Marital separation from mate | 74 |
| 33. Major change in type and/or amount of recreation | 37 |
| 34. Major change in use of drugs | 52 |
| 35. Took on a mortgage or loan less than $10,000 | 52 |
| 36. Major personal injury or illness | 65 |
| 37. Major change in use of alcohol | 46 |
| 38. Major change in social activities | 43 |
| ‡39. Major change in amount of participation in *school* activities | 38 |
| 40. Major change in amount of independence and responsibility | 49 |
| 41. Took a trip or a vacation | 33 |
| 42. Engaged to be married | 54 |
| 43. Changed to a new school | 50 |
| 44. Changed dating habits | 41 |
| 45. Trouble with school administration | 44 |
| §46. Broke or had broken a marital engagement or a *steady relationship* | 60 |
| 47. Major change in self-concept or self-awareness | 57 |

**Underlined* phrase added; †Wife changed to spouse; ‡Co-curricula changed to school; §*Underlined* phrase added.
SOURCE: From "The Influence of Recent Life Experiences on the Health of College Freshmen" by M. Marx, T. Garrity & F. Bowers, 1975. *Journal of Psychosomatic Research, 19,* pp. 87–98.

*Smog has become an environmental source of human stress. Some studies suggest that there may be an* ***air pollution*** *syndrome involving irritability, insomnia, and depression.*

psychiatric hospital for residents living in high-noise areas around London's Heathrow Airport than for residents who lived in low-noise neighborhoods. (Consider the implications of the finding that discotheque music is only about 10 decibels less than the noise of a jet aircraft on takeoff.)

Other research has investigated the role of noise in aggression and violence. In a typical experiment, a subject is given the opportunity to deliver electric shock to a victim (really a confederate of the experimenter), with the shock level an index of aggression. Subjects are then made angry, exposed to noise, and permitted to decide how great a shock they want to deliver. A series of studies suggest that noise does have an effect, but only if the subject is angry. If angered, the subject would deliver more intense shocks when noise was present, and especially if the noise was unpredictable or uncontrollable (Donnerstein & Wilson, 1976).

Air pollution, including cigarette smoke, has become a recent focus of concern, and there is some indication that it may also be a source of stress. Some experts believe that an air pollution syndrome actually can be identified, involving irritability, insomnia, depression, back pain, headache, fatigue, impaired judgment, burning of the eyes, and gastrointestinal problems (Hart, 1970; LaVerne, 1970). One analysis suggests that breathing the air in New York City is equivalent to smoking 38 cigarettes a day (J. Rotton, personal communication, 1980). One study did find a small correlation between air pollution levels and the appearance in emergency rooms of higher numbers of schizophrenics; however, the researchers are uncertain whether or not pollution is actually causing schizophrenic problems. They also discovered that low barometric pressure was associated with increases in depression, reporting this to be consistent with others who discovered a similar relationship between air pressure and suicide rates (Briere et al., 1983).

Another environmental source of stress is temperature. High temperatures can act as a stressor in many ways—through muscle fatigue, body dehydration, and reduced endurance. There seems to be a relationship between temperature and violence, so there may be some element of truth to the popular belief that a "long, hot summer" is conducive to rioting and violence, as Figure 7–2 indicates.

To the extent that this belief is true, however, it must be mediated by a few factors. First, other variables—such as preexisting social tensions—would first set the stage for rioting or violence. And second, the relationship between temperature and aggression is probably more curvilinear than direct. In other words, up to a point, higher temperatures are associated with higher aggression; however, beyond a certain temperature, aggressiveness instead seems to decline (Baron & Bell, 1976). What is this crucial temperature? One study of 102 cases of group violence between 1967 and 1972 suggests that violence peaked when the temperature was in the mid-80s (Baron & Ransberger, 1978).

Of final interest as a living-environmental stressor is overcrowding. Some evidence suggests that being in a crowded area even for a few hours leads to physiological signs of stress, such as increased blood pressure (Aiello et al., 1975). There is also evidence that crowding may be related to withdrawal behaviors. A variety of studies suggest that the expectation of facing high social density, the actual involvement in a high-density interaction, and the later consequence of being in a high-density interaction all tend to prompt withdrawal behaviors (Baum & Koman, 1976; Joy & Lehmann, 1975). Given that one of the adjustment disorders involves serious withdrawal behaviors, such information on overcrowding is provocative.

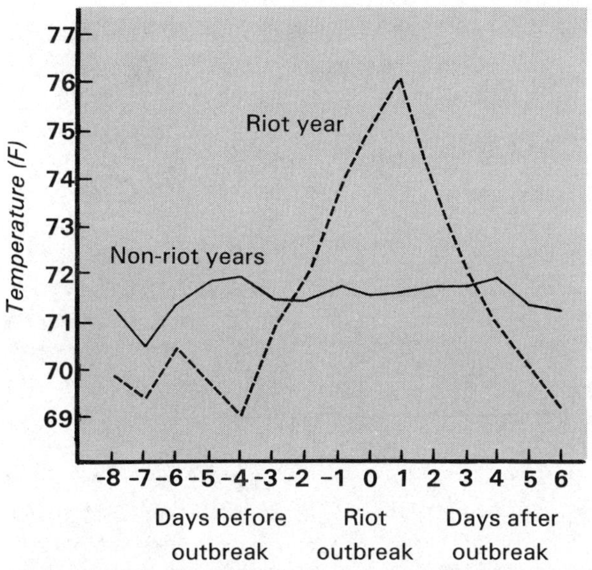


**FIGURE 7–2** The relationship between heat and outbreak of riot.

SOURCE: From "Rioting and Daily Temperature: Analysis of the U.S. Riots in 1967" by R. Goranson and D. King, 1970, unpublished manuscript, York University.

On the other hand, we should be reminded that the relationship between overcrowding and withdrawal is influenced by many factors. Cultural attitudes toward personal space, privacy, and affiliation, for instance, all help to shape a person's tolerance for crowded living or work conditions. Arab or Asian families may traditionally expect several generations to share a home, so that grandparents, parents, grandchildren, and sometimes other relatives live comfortably under the same roof. An American, on the other hand, would perceive such conditions as highly stressful.

This last issue brings up another highly important component in the dynamics of adjustment disorders. That is the individual's own degree of vulnerability to stress.

### Personal Vulnerability

What is it that makes it possible for one person to cope with business pressures, or a chronic illness, or a stressful life change, while another person reacts excessively? The question of why people react differently to life circumstances is really the basic riddle underlying all of psychopathology. Perhaps it is highlighted in the adjustment disorders, where we can observe differences in the ability to adjust to the same stressor. Several variables are relevant in determining a person's vulnerability to an adjustment disorder (Holroyd & Lazarus, 1983).

Recent experiences with other stressors are one factor that may lower a person's resistance to a new stressor. A person recovering from an illness will be less capable of resisting another illness. Similarly, a person will be more vulnerable to tensions or errors in judgment while recovering from jet lag. If a person experiences the death of a loved one shortly after losing a job, the loss of both emotional security and financial security at the same time will make that individual even more vulnerable to adjustment difficulties.

The availability of personal resources is also important in determining how a person adjusts to a stressful situation. For example, while job interviews are often stressful, knowledge of basic social skills may help reduce such tensions and stress. Intelligence and training are also helpful resources: a very bright or comprehensively trained student is better equipped to deal with some problems than is a student who lacks such resources. Age, and the wisdom and experience that come with it, may also make a difference in a person's ability to withstand stressors. Marx et al. (1975) determined that the stress of being fired from a job seemed more serious to a college student than a noncollege adult. In their rating scale, they found that college students rated the stress of job loss at 62; in contrast, other adult subjects rated this stressor at 47 (where 100 represents extreme stress). Perhaps this is because the college student may lack the financial support or environmental resources to afford being without employment.

Since a person's appraisal of the environment may influence the way he or she perceives a threat, failure experience can also play an important role in the development of adjustment disorders (Lazarus et al., 1982; Neufeld, 1982). There is reason to believe that the impact of a stressor may partly be a function of the specific meaning we attach to the situation. Experiences of failure in coping can shape not only our appraisal of our environment, but also our appraisal of our own adequacy in coping. Such failure can contribute to *learned helplessness*, a condition in which a person simply gives up trying to succeed because of repeated

*Cultural attitudes differ regarding population density. In this Chinese commune, sharing space may not be experienced as stressful* ***crowding.***

experiences of loss of control over decisions (Miller & Seligman, 1982). Learned helplessness and lowered self-confidence persist even when control is restored to the individual. In contrast, self-efficacy is enhanced by personal mastery experiences, as well as vicarious experiences with success. As we saw in Chapter 4, seeing someone else succeed who shares our own characteristics can increase our sense of efficacy (Bandura, 1977).

Failures, of course, can affect the status of our needs-satisfactions; and the presence of problematic needs can create difficulties in adjusting to certain stressors. A person who has a heightened need for approval and achievement will probably be more threatened by disapproval from a supervisor than would someone else.

Finally, stress tolerance can influence the level of reactivity to stressors. Developmental age, of course, affects stress tolerance; a young child is less able to cope with even minor stressors than is an adult. The availability of coping skills that can be directly brought to bear to solve problems will enable a person to better tolerate the stressor because he or she can initiate the solutions. On the other hand, excessive defense mechanisms that prevent problem solving will also impair stress tolerance.

## TREATMENT: THE ROLE OF STRESS MANAGEMENT

Since the adjustment disorders are responses to identifiable life events or circumstances, we might expect recovery to follow when such stressors are removed. This is true to some extent; however, the reaction is also a function of both the characteristics of the person and the environmental context. Thus, the recovery may not be immediate.

To the extent that both personal and environmental factors influence reactions to stress, steps that strengthen resources in these areas will improve recovery (Cohen, 1980). In a general way, the various therapeutic approaches discussed in Part 3 of this book speak to methods that are appropriate.

In addition, some stress management techniques might be valuable for reducing or preventing adjustment disorders. We will look briefly at some steps for stress management.

### Recognizing Stress

One of the most important elements in stress management is learning to know when stress is having an effect. Many persons fail to recognize that their reactions are being governed by stressors; hence, they do not take steps to manage the stress. Recall that stress may be experienced in a number of ways—autonomically, behaviorally, or cognitively. There is reason to believe that each person has his or her unique stress profile (Suinn, 1977), with one person responding mainly autonomically, while another reacts most with thought disruptions.

### Recognizing Stressors

A second important element is to identify those events which are common stressors for the individual. A review of the list of life-change events in Table 7–2 may be an illustrative starting point. However, there are probably also special circumstances that are unique to each person. For instance, success might be very important for one person's sense of well-being, while another is stressed when feeling disliked, unwanted, or useless. Some individuals become tense when around people with dominant manners, while others are affected when interacting with dependent persons.

### Identifying Obstacles to Stress Reduction

Once stressors have been identified, it may not be easy to overcome them. The resolving of adjustment disorders must focus on the major obstacles to problem solving—for instance, poor communication may be leading to misunderstanding; or the problem may be one of overload—a tendency to overcommit or accept too much responsibility. Emotional control may also be an obstacle, so that anger or anxiety gets in the way of clear thinking or performance. Finally, anxiety-provoking thoughts can be another obstacle to adjusting to stress.

### Learning Coping Skills

A variety of programs target different objectives in improving coping skills. Communications training aims at showing persons how to listen accurately and also how to reply more accurately. Time-management programs, or programs which focus on the setting of priorities, can also be useful in reducing stress related to overload or overcommitment. Training in anger inoculation (Novaco, 1976) or anxiety management (Suinn, 1983) can aid in anger or anxiety control, as Chapter 21 will discuss in more detail. Cognitive or thought management techniques have also been devised with successful results for coping with self-defeating or anxiety-provoking thoughts, as seen in Chapters 6 and 21.

### Using Environmental Resources

Environmental resources exist that can facilitate stress management, and these should be evaluated. Family members are one important resource; they may be helpful in providing needed reassurances and intimacy. Respected associates and professional counselors may also be valuable in offering an objective perspective on decisions, while peers may provide freedom from pressure and an opportunity for relaxation. Just as it is important to evaluate how friendly relationships can help provide support or objective advice, it is also important to recognize which relationships are troublesome and represent simply another stressor.

### Controlling the Presence of Stressors

To the degree that it is possible, events should be planned so as not to present too many stresses simultaneously. Even during the day, activities can be arranged so that high stress ones take place at different times, to permit recovery time, time to use environmental support persons, and time to prepare for confronting the next stressor.

### Recognizing that Different Stressors May Require Different Coping Skills

Different stressors demand different adjustments. Job hunting requires patience to take the time to make many appointments, and to avoid discouragement. Other stressors may not permit time but require immediate resolution. A decision about an insensitive and irresponsible roommate may have to occur without a delay and be confronted immediately before it becomes unmanageable. Finally, some stressors have no solutions. For these issues, the only solution is to acknowledge that no immediate answers are likely, and one must simply be prepared to accept the stress and attempt to reduce the emotional costs.

## EVALUATION

The adjustment disorders represent a new category in the psychiatric classification system, with some new disorders added. Previously, a classification had been introduced in DSM-II which recognized the interaction between environmental events and personal emotional states or behaviors. Thus, a form of depression known as reactive depression (depression caused by environmental events) was accepted as a type of disorder. The general concept has been expanded into the adjustment disorders, so we now have the adjustment disorder with depression, the adjustment disorder with anxiety, the adjustment disorder with conduct disturbance, and the adjustment disorder with withdrawal. The value of this classification is in providing a category that accepts the relative importance of environmental experiences in an emotional state. The post-traumatic stress disorder acknowledges the source to be environmental catastrophes. The adjustment disorders acknowledges that maladjustive reactions can derive from stresses of lesser severity than catastrophes. This permits us to think a little more broadly about psychopathology in terms of origins. For the adjustment disorders, we discover that the examination of the environment is important, but that the characteristics of the person are also important. Although this seems a natural idea, the dominant theme of past theories of psychopathology often emphasized personal variables, such as internal conflict, emotional deprivation, or traits such as reactivity to guilt. The role of the environment is given more attention in the new DSM-III classification, and this is a positive feature.

## SUMMARY

The adjustment disorders are those characterized by maladaptive responses to stressors which are less severe than major catastrophes. These disorders involve symptoms that are in excess of the normal reaction to similar stressors. The stresses may be a variety of events, ranging from interpersonal experiences (such as death of a loved one), impersonal experiences (such as excessive noise), or goal-related experiences (such as failing in a career). The adjustment disorder derives from a combination of personal vulnerability and the presence of stressful events. The nature of the maladaptive reactions can involve depressed mood, anxious mood, conduct disturbance, or withdrawal, and the various disorders are classified by these moods. In general, a diasthesis-stress model applies to predicting the development of an adjustment disorder; that is, an interaction between personal traits and the presence of a stressor that pressures the person to adapt. Among the personal factors which make an individual vulnerable are recent experience with other stresses, personal resources, level of self-efficacy or felt helplessness, level of need, and stress tolerance. Recovery is expected when the stressor is removed, although personal characteristics will influence the rate of recovery.

## KEY TERMS

**Adjustment disorders**
**Adjustment disorder with anxious mood**
**Adjustment disorder with depressed mood**
**Adjustment disorder with disturbance of conduct**
**Adjustment disorder with withdrawal**
**Autonomic reactions**
**Circadian cycles**
**Cognitive sets**
**Learned helplessness**
**Stress**
**Stress management**
**Stressor**

# CHAPTER 8

## Dissociative States: Disorders of Memory or Identity

- **What normal experiences are examples of dissociative states?**
- **Amnesia may involve a malfunction of memory either as recall or as retention. What is the importance of this crucial distinction?**
- **What is the significance of remembering many trivial childhood experiences, yet failing to remember many important ones?**
- **What role do wars or natural catastrophes have in influencing the incidence of dissociative disorders?**
- **Is this a true statement: "Normal persons tend to remember negative experiences; it is only the pathological person that cannot tolerate such recall"?**
- **How is it possible for persons to be completely amnesic for their identity and past friends and jobs and still manage to survive?**
- **If you were to develop a multiple personality, in all probability what traits would your alternate personality possess?**
- **What do amnesia, fugue, multiple personality, and depersonalization have in common?**
- **Is hypnosis effective in treating the dissociative disorders?**

**TABLE 8–1**

**Dissociative Disorders**

| *Type* | *Major Characteristics* |
|---|---|
| Depersonalization disorder | Having a sense of unreality about one's self, or environment, or things going on |
| Multiple personality | The cyclical appearance of two or more distinct personalities which take over |
| Pschygenic amnesia | Suddenly losing one's memory because of psychological reasons |
| Psychogenic fugue | Leaving one's customary residence/work area, taking on a new identity, with loss of memory for one's previous identity |

SOURCE: Cermak, L. (Ed), Human memory and amnesia, Hillsdale, N.J.: Erlbaum, 1982

# Case History 8–1:
## A Case of Psychogenic Amnesia

Gene P. was a 19-year-old college student. His early life was highly successful by most standards. He was part of a close-knit family that did everything together. He graduated within the top 1 percent of a class of 400, and held high school leadership positions. The long chain of academic successes may have suggested that success came too easily to Gene. None of these factors would have caused problems, however, had life events not turned out as they did.

Gene decided to go away to a large, impersonal university. As a mathematics major, his first term's course load was extremely heavy, demanding much time and late evening study. Gene dated and fell in love with the very first girl he had ever met outside his hometown. She soon expressed her fears that she was pregnant and cried bitterly when Gene called her ''stupid'' in a tense outburst. Gene quickly apologized, and marriage was planned. Gene speaks here:

> It wasn't that easy. I wanted to marry her because I did love her. But I thought about my parents and could just hear my mother asking about her hometown and my father talking about my career, not with disapproval, but with disappointment in me. The more I thought, the more ''disappointed'' seemed to mean ''disapproval'' and the more I knew it would be disapproval of me. We'd always talk things out as a family, and decisions were never made by one person—we shared. But this one wouldn't be; and besides, if they found out about the pregnancy, I wouldn't even be able to convince them that it was only the final reason, not the only reason. Then, with all of this on my mind, I couldn't study, and my grades dropped rapidly. I had nowhere to turn:, I couldn't talk to Shirley [his fiance] because she really was too close to the problem and wouldn't understand me; besides, she wasn't family. . . . And then it hit me: she wasn't family; she was a stranger, really. Then she called me that very night and asked me to come by to see a wedding dress, and I walked out the door to her place.

Gene vanished from campus that night. He was found sitting in a bus depot, identified from his wallet by the police, and admitted into the hospital for amnesia. He failed to recognize his fiance or his parents, who flew out to see him. Approval was obtained for drug-induced hypnosis, and progress is being made, with Gene now recognizing his family but thus far not Shirley.

The *dissociative disorders* include some uniquely fascinating symptoms. The essential characteristics of these disorders is the sudden, transitory change in consciousness or identity and, in some cases, in behavior, such that one of these three may be impaired. Impairment in consciousness will mean that memory is affected, such as in amnesia. Impairment in identity will mean that one's normal identity is replaced by a different one, or that one's feeling of reality or place in reality becomes tenuous and shaky. Impairment in both behavior and consciousness or identity will together produce a condition known as a fugue state, whereby the person leaves one identity and one life for a new one by actually moving somewhere else.

Some of these dissociative symptoms, to a lesser degree, are experiences that many persons might recognize as having occurred in their lives. For example, how often have you had a mild form of amnesia, forgetting someone's name, or even forgetting the negative aspects of your home life or your early education? In stressful circumstances, such as in hearing of the death of a close friend or relative, you may have experienced a temporary feeling of unreality. Or you may have suddenly returned to awareness while driving on a long trip, to realize that you had been functioning quite adequately and competently behind the steering wheel, yet without the slightest ability to recall anything that happened during the last 60 miles. You may even have experienced those sudden conflicts between impulses or ambivalent feelings that led you to wonder if you were actually two people pushing or pulling in different directions. In the pathological versions of such dissociative experiences, several disorders are recognized:

- Psychogenic amnesia
- Psychogenic fugue
- Multiple personality
- Depersonalization disorder

These disorders are identified in Table 8–1; they will be described and discussed in detail in this chapter.

## PSYCHOGENIC AMNESIA

*Psychogenic amnesia* involves the sudden onset of memory loss, whereby the person is unable to remember important personal information. Although amnesia may be caused by organic factors such as alcoholism (see Chapter 13), brain damage or aging (see Chapter 18), the term *psychogenic* is reserved for memory loss due to purely psychological causation (Hirst, 1982).

### Symptoms of Psychogenic Amnesias

Amnesia from organic causes, such as concussion, is not unusual. Psychogenic amnesia, however, is rare—except under highly stressful circumstances such as wars or natural catastrophes (Frederick, 1981).

Psychogenic amnesia is distinguished from other amnesias in that it is a problem of *recall,* not retention. In the case of amnesia from brain degeneration, retention is faulty because information is not properly stored in memory banks to begin with. In the psychogenic amnesias, the information is believed to be available if only the blockage can be removed, as occasionally happens through hypnosis. On recovery, memory returns fully and completely, and the amnesia rarely recurs.

Psychogenic amnesias also show other differences from organically caused amnesias. Typically, but not always, an individual with psychogenic amnesia displays *anterograde amnesia*—that is, loss of memory for events following a disturbing experience. In contrast, amnesia from concussions is usually *retrograde,* involving loss of memory for events preceding a disturbing experience. In amnesia associated with alcohol abuse or degeneration due to aging, it is usually short-term events that are forgotten (Golden et al., 1983). Furthermore, symptoms such as *confabulation* (making up facts to replace the memory that is lost), may be associated with these types of amnesias. Finally, in amnesia that involves actual damage to portions of the brain or where surgery has necessitated removal of parts of the brain, memory for certain events is irretrievably lost.

DSM-III identifies four major types of memory problems that appear in psychogenic amnesias. These are localized amnesia, selective amnesia, continuous amnesia, and generalized amnesia.

***Localized Amnesia.*** The most common form of psychogenic amnesia is *localized amnesia.* This disorder involves memory loss over a set period of time. One case may serve as a representative example:

A 12-year-old boy, Jimmy, was removed from a four-car accident in which his entire family was killed; the boy had been pinned under the dead body of his pet dog for two hours. Jimmy remembers all events up to the accident, including the exact words of his father when the car was skidding, but does not remember anything through three days of hospitalization. Jimmy is suffering from localized amnesia over the period starting with the trauma and extending to his own hospitalization.

***Selective Amnesia.*** A second form of amnesia, *selective amnesia,* involves memory loss for some but not all of the events associated with a set period of time. The case of Maureen provides a typical illustration. Maureen was interviewed following a hostile divorce that had been fought in court and involved many accusations and much publicity. While she remembers some details precisely, her memory of the court activity, in general, is inconsistent:

> *What do you remember?*
>
> I dressed conservatively, with my tailored grey suit, no earrings, no wedding ring. I was asked by my attorney whether I agreed with my husband's accusations, and I cried because I was so mixed up; I was angry and embarrassed, and confused, and I wanted to stand up and shout at him. . . .
>
> *How did you answer your attorney?*
>
> . . . I don't know. . . . I must have said something, because I remember his saying "Thank you" in his soft voice, and I was so relieved, and I looked at the judge and he nodded, and I had to think about walking so I wouldn't fall when I stepped down.

As is typical of cases of selective amnesia, Maureen shows perfect recall for some events during the time in court, but is faulty on other details during the same period.

***Continuous Amnesia.*** A third form of amnesia involves a longer time span than both localized or selective amnesia. *Continuous amnesia* is the loss of memory for events subsequent to a set time and up to and including the present. An example of continuous amnesia is the case of Frank. During World War II, Frank had been found wandering in the woods following a battle and was hospitalized. He had no recall for the events during or after the battle, but "awoke" suddenly aware of being in the hospital. He did not remember his conversation with the field medics, his transfer from the emergency ward to the current convalescent ward, or the Red Cross volunteer he had been seeing for weeks. He could recall boot camp, the trip by troop carrier, and the first sight of enemy land. His last memory was the sight of shells pluming the water as they fell. He does not remember feeling any emotions at all—instead, this memory is only a visual picture of water exploding, as in a still photograph.

***Generalized Amnesia.*** More extensive than any of the other forms of amnesia, *generalized amnesia* involves a loss of all memories of one's life. An illustration of generalized amnesia linked to a traumatic event is the case of Debbie. Nine-year-old Debbie was discovered in a field, suffering from overexposure after

*Rip Van Winkle went to sleep and had no memory of events. In* ***psychogenic amnesia,*** *the individual was awake during an experience, but does not remember it.*

an evening outdoors. She was identified by her parents as their child who had been missing for two days. Medical examination showed signs of forcible rape, along with bruises and burns. The bruises might have been caused by falls; the burns were from a cigarette. Debbie recognized that she was in a hospital, but did not know her own name, her parents, why she was hospitalized, or the location of the hospital. She was unable to say whether anyone looked familiar or whether her clothing "seemed right on her"; and she lacked any emotional response to viewing the field in which she was found. She was fully functional in every other way—for example, she knew the right procedure to board a bus from the shopping center to her home—yet she did not recognize her house as her home.

### Dynamics of Psychogenic Amnesia

What explains the loss of memory common to the various cases described earlier? The answer to this question focuses mostly on amnesia as a means of coping with a threatening experience.

***The Role of Repression.*** Amnesia itself is a dissociative disorder, in that one area of a person's experience is split off or lost so that it becomes inaccessible to consciousness. The defense mechanism of repression, described in Chapter 3, is believed to play a significant role, with dissociation providing the means of banishing emotionally disturbing or painful material to the unconscious.

Some theorists use the psychodynamic explanation to shed light on even common amnesic experiences that seem to be a part of the normal developmental process. Cameron (1963) proposes that repression enables us to establish the "ego-boundaries" that allow normal human development even early in life. He points out how few persons really can remember pre-Oedipal or Oedipal childhood experiences. More particularly, he notes, "All of us do remember much that is trivial and unemotional from our childhood, while we cannot remember the vivid and significant events in which we took part during those same years. This massive amnesia for the events of early childhood seems to be a necessary result of the development of repression through which functional ego boundaries are formed and maintained" (pp. 367–368).

In psychogenic amnesia, the onset may be linked not to normal developmental processes but to a severe emotional disturbance. This may result from a threatening incident in the environment, from an internal conflict of desires or motives, or from externally produced conflicts. Thus, the threat may be the overwhelming stress of remembering a rape or beating or the devastating force of constant emotional pressure from a divorce trial, or the stressful conflict of wanting to courageously attack an enemy yet at the same time fearing for one's own safety. The use of hypnosis, discussed further in the treatment section of this chapter, has demonstrated over and over again the presence of emotional trauma associated with forgotten memories. The case of Karen is an illustration.

Sixteen-year-old Karen is absolutely certain that she neither remembers nor actually saw any events prior to the discovery of her parents' lifeless bodies. Yet, witnesses saw her enter and leave the household during the time of the shots, suggesting that she may have been an eyewitness. Under hypnosis, the following was revealed:

DR. W. (hypnotist): Now that you are comfortable, tell me what you remember during (time and place given).

KAREN: I don't remember a thing, I was not there in the house when it happened. . . . I came back and found them.

DR. W.: All right, now we're going to have you just sit back and watch, as though a movie were being unraveled in front of you, and your eyes are the projector, and the film is in your head. Just describe the movie. . . . You're not involved yourself, but you are seeing what was going on during (time and place). . . . It's all right for you to remember, because you won't be upset, you'll remain comfortable, just describe as though you were describing a movie.

KAREN: There's the door, and beyond it there's noises, like someone weeping, crying . . . and there is Mom on the floor and the rug is different colors, red, and a stream of red, and Dad is weeping over her. . . . It's like slow motion, he has the pistol to his mouth, and there's a "pop," not noisy but it makes you want to cover your ears . . . and a splash and he doesn't look like himself, because he's falling on Mom. . . . They're dying, but I can't do anything. I'm too late!

Although Karen's experience was highly traumatic, less extreme aversive experiences also seem to play a role in memory loss. This relationship has been documented in several laboratory experiences. (You may even wish to try a demonstration on yourself; see Focus 8–1.)

In a typical laboratory experiment, college students were given a series of difficult puzzles to complete (Rosenzweig, 1941). One group was told that the puzzles were intelligence tests, while the other group received neutral instructions. The intelligence test instructions were designed to communicate the idea that failure to complete the various puzzles was an index of personal failure; presumably, this produced a sense of threat to self-esteem. Members of both groups were permitted to finish only half of the series of puzzles. Later, each student was asked to name the puzzles. Only 8 of 30 students under the threat condition remembered a preponderance of the unfinished puzzles.

This finding may not seem noteworthy. However, it reverses another finding so consistent to have been labeled the *Zeigarnik effect:* that individuals have a *better* memory for unfinished tasks than for completed ones (Zeigarnik, 1927). Studies such as the Rosenzweig study, which indicate poor memory for incompleted tasks that imply a sense of failure, offer evidence that memory loss can be very selective. This supports the idea that humans tend to be amnesic for threatening information—even mildly threatening experiences such as those in the laboratory study.

## PSYCHOGENIC FUGUE

The term *fugue* derives from a Latin word meaning wild or confused flight. As a disorder in the DSM-III classification scheme, fugue refers to a sudden fleeing from one's immediate and customary locale and work, with amnesia for the past identity and the assumption of a new identity. Fugues are relatively uncommon; in one survey of admissions to a medical center, Kirshner (1973) found only 7 out of 1,795 cases to involve fugue states.

### Symptoms of Psychogenic Fugue

The fugue state or disorder is considered a more serious version of psychogenic amnesia, since it includes actually taking action to leave an area. Thus, the fleeing is said to involve two types of flight: *psychological flight,* via amnesia; and *physical flight,* via actual departure.

As with amnesia, the actions characteristic of the fugue state are involuntary and unplanned. The individual does not consciously decide to lose his or her memory and pack up and leave for a predetermined location, with a new job and identity already planned. Instead, the fugue is precipitated; the individual is propelled into frantic departure; and then, he or she may sometimes wander aimlessly in the new location before the trauma and confusion end. When the person starts in on a new life, there is no recall for the events of the episode.

The fugue episode and the ensuing change in identity may vary along a continuum of complexity. In some cases, it involves a brief wandering with little social contact and an incomplete identity change. In other instances, as in Case History 8–2, there is a complete identity change, with the establishment of a new residence, a new name, new occupation, and, eventually, new social networks. Interestingly, where a change of identity is adopted, the new person is often viewed as more gregarious and outgoing, and less inhibited than the person left behind.

In those rare cases where the person is later able to describe the onset of the fugue, it is variously described as "like I was going to sleep, then blacked-out," or "I felt faint," or "I began to feel fuzzy inside my body, and in my head, confused," or other reports of dizziness, confusion, depersonalization, blurred vision, headache, or somatic discomfort (Laughlin, 1967).

### Dynamics of Fugue

Fugues are typically explained as a final attempt to resolve an intolerable situation. Calling fugues daytime sleepwalking, Laughlin interprets the fleeing as a symbolic representation of the desire of the ego to flee from punishment and censure by the superego. In ef-

## FOCUS 8–1:
### Repression and Memory Loss: A Demonstration

What role do aversive experiences play in memory loss? To explore this question from your own experience, you may want to try a favorite demonstration of the author.

The exercise involves keeping a log of daily events for one week. Record at least three events at the end of each day, labeling them as either positive or negative, and using a rating system from 1 to 5 to measure the intensity of the emotion you associate with each experience. (Thus, a positive 5 would describe an event you felt extremely good about.)

At the end of the week, put the log away and do not refer to it for five weeks. Then, write down as many of the details of each event as you can recall from memory alone.

Now, classify these events as positive or negative, and count up the number of positive versus negative events you managed to recall. What do you find? (After you complete this five-week experience, read the following discussion.)

#### *Discussion*

You will probably discover that you have remembered more of the positive and forgotten more of the negative events. According to Freud, this is because you have repressed those tension-producing memories. An alternative interpretation would be that negative experiences are not as readily stored in memory, and therefore not easily recalled. Whatever the explanation, the phenomenon does tend to happen for most people.

fect, the emphasis is on guilt and fear of or need for punishment.

Abse (1959) lists examples illustrating how fugue may be interpreted as a flight from an intolerable situation and towards a more gratifying alternative. For example, he reports one case of a military person who returned in his fugue state to a resort town that turned out to be the site of his honeymoon and many annual vacations. In another case, a former priest, dissatisfied with the celibate life, was traced to a city, miles away and across the ocean from his former parish; his last recall was of finding himself strolling along a beach. By the time his past was discovered, this individual had married and had established a new, successful life in business.

An intriguing question may be helpful in explaining the identity change of a fugue state. What does an amnesic person do on regaining consciousness in a strange place, with neither an identity nor a place to stay? A common solution is to invent an identity including a past, while keeping the amnesia a secret in the hope that something will eventually trigger eventual recall. Meanwhile, the victim of the fugue attempts to initiate a normal life without calling attention to any unique memory gaps. Inasmuch as most amnesic states do not involve amnesia for common skills or common daily habits, the individual with a fugue condition is still able to behave normally, even holding a job. In applying for employment or housing, it is a simple matter to create a name, a place of birth, and a previous life history (usually involving a distant town), inasmuch as such facts are seldom verified. As

## Case History 8–2:
### A Case of Psychogenic Fugue

The case of Lawrence M. recently came to light in a newspaper story in a small city. An article, entitled "Man Lives Double Lives," described the discovery of a past life of an otherwise respectable businessman.

Lawrence has lived for 20 years in this city, a suburb of a major industrial metropolis. He owns a computer firm that has grown from two employees to a consulting staff of 10 plus a clerical staff of 8 and a computer staff of 8. Lawrence travels weekly. Here, he tells his story:

> We have grown so successful that the business is no longer local; in fact, my largest account is in Philadelphia. At first, when the reporter contacted me I thought she was going to accuse me of having a mistress in another city when she started to ask me about whether I traveled a lot, and had I ever been to Houston? Then it turns out that this reporter claims she found a woman who identified my photograph as her missing husband. I was sure this was a joke or some attempt to spoil my name or my company. So I laughed it all off as a bad deal.
>
> Then I began thinking, and I started to remember that my past is somewhat hazy. I've worked hard and furiously, initially late into the nights because the business was just getting started and I did just about everything, and recently because of the trips, and I'm often fatigued.
>
> I don't think too much about the past, there's too much today to think and worry about. I have the general childhood memories, you know, like most people have. . . . you sometimes think you remember having seen a place and then you find out you didn't, so you chalk it up to faulty early childhood memories. I'm precise about my work, but somehow I haven't been too bothered about my past. . . . It's there, and that's been enough. I mean, my home, my true home is this house I've lived in for 20 years, and my friends are those I know here who give me a hand when I need it.

Lawrence agreed to meet with Mrs. J. from Houston. The meeting was both dramatic and perplexing. Mrs. J. greeted Lawrence with tears, calling him "Rudy" and identifying him unmistakably as Rudy J., her husband who had disappeared 21 years ago. Lawrence does not recognize either Mrs. J. or the name Rudy and has asked to meet with his attorney. "I'm touched by her, and a little saddened by her joy, but I honestly don't know her. Maybe she is my wife, or maybe I just remind her of someone . . . anyway what about that extra year, she says it was 21 years not 20. Besides, I'm not a bigamist."

life goes on, and the fugue victim becomes more established and successful, not only does the now-distant past become less important, but the individual may even come to believe in his or her own fictionalized history as if it were now fact.

## MULTIPLE PERSONALITY

A third dissociative disorder, *multiple personality,* involves the appearance in an individual of two or more distinct personalities, each personality being a fully integrated and complex unit with its own memories, behavior patterns, interests, likes and dislikes, and needs. Cases of multiple personality are rare. Taylor and Martin (1944) found only 76 cases up to 1944, while Hale (1983) totaled fewer than 300 cases. Chris Sizemore (1982), who was herself a case of multiple personality, believes that there are between 100 and 200 examples of true multiple personalities.

### Multiple Personality: Symptoms and Diagnosis

Multiple personality, one of the most dramatic and spectacular of the mental disorders, has received much publicity and attention. One case, that of Sybil (Schreiber, 1973), illustrates the variety of interests and characters that may coexist in this disorder. Sybil's personalities included eight different characters: the assertive and enthusiastic Peggy Lou; the listless and timid Sybil Ann; the self-assured, sophisticated Victoria; the fearful Peggy Ann; the highly emotional Marcia; the determined Helen; and even two male personalities—Mike and Sid.

Transition from one personality to another is usually abrupt, typically with amnesia for the other personalities. Usually one of the personalities is dominant. The secondary personalities may have full awareness of the primary personality, although the primary personality is usually unaware of the existence of the others.

Unlike fugue states, multiple personality involves the coexistence of different "persons" and identities without physical flight. If the analogue of fugues in normal persons is our occasional impulse "to go somewhere else and leave all these problems behind," then the analogue of multiple personality in normal persons are those occasional situations when we observe a friend under pressure unexpectedly give in to an impulse, and we remark, "You sure weren't yourself today."

***Two Famous Cases.*** Two well-documented reports of multiple personalities have increased our understanding of this disorder. We'll look first at the case of Miss Beauchamp, then at the well-known case of Eve.

*The Case of Miss Beauchamp.* Morton Prince is credited with focusing psychiatric attention on multiple personality at the beginning of this century. Prince, a neurologist whose interests ranged from thought-transference to forensic medicine, introduced the classical case of Christine Beauchamp, a Radcliffe student. In his book, *Dissociation of a Personality* (1908), Prince describes his meeting with three distinct personalities over the six-year course of treatment:

THE SAINT: Miss Beauchamp herself, who was the epitome of selflessness and good works, and who viewed rudeness and white lies as evil sins to be cast out by fasting and prayer.

THE DEVIL, OR SALLY: Childish, impish, self-centered, a fibber, a church-hater, and remorselessly mischievous towards Miss Beauchamp, of whom she is aware. Sally writes notes to Miss Beauchamp criticizing her flaws and dwelling on secret thoughts or desires that the Saint tries to deny she has. She pins these notes to the wall, along with reports of things that others (fictionally) have said about her. Knowing that Miss Beauchamp was deathly afraid of snakes and spiders, the Devil once collected some in a box, addressed the package to Miss Beauchamp and awaited Miss Beauchamp's horrified discovery of the contents.

THE WOMAN: This personality suddenly appeared following an emotional experience. She was formal, distant, amnesic for Dr. Prince, the Saint, or the Devil, and quick-tempered. However, she seemed a direct link to the childhood past.

Continuous conflict occurred among the three personalities, mainly instigated by Sally's hostility.

Knowing that Miss Beauchamp tired easily, Sally would go by car seven miles into the country, walk away to a deserted area, then awaken Miss Beauchamp, who would be forced to hike wearily home. Yet, when Miss Beauchamp turned on the gas in an attempt to commit suicide, it was Sally who saved her by opening the window and turning off the gas.

Prince successfully integrated the best of the personalities, and his book received popular acclaim (Marx, 1970). A successful Broadway play, "The Case of Becky," was eventually based on this case.

*Three Faces of Eve.* Another case that has stirred the interest of both professional and lay audiences is that treated by Thigpen and Cleckley and described in their book, *The Three Faces of Eve* (1957). Eve White, a demure, utterly controlled, "colorless" person, sought therapy because of severe and blinding headaches often followed by blackouts. Then one day, Eve Black made her appearance:

> Eve seemed momentarily dazed. Suddenly her posture began to change. Her body slowly stiffened until she sat rigidly erect. An alien, inexplicable expression then came over her face. This was suddenly erased into utter blankness. The lines of her countenance seemed to shift in a barely visible, slow, rippling transformation. . . . Closing her eyes, she winced as she put her hands to her temples, pressed hard, and twisted them as if to combat sudden pain . . . then the hands lightly dropped. . . . A pair of blue eyes popped open. . . . There was a quick reckless smile. In a bright, unfamiliar voice that sparkled, the woman said, "Hi there, Doc!"
>
> With a soft and surprisingly intimate syllable of laughter, she crossed her legs, carelessly swirling her skirts in the process. She unhurriedly smoothed the hem down over her knees in a manner that was playful and somehow just a little provocative. . . .
>
> "She's been having a real rough time. . . . Would you give me a cigarette, Doc?"
>
> He handed her a cigarette, and then lighting it, said, "Who is 'she'?"
>
> "Why, Eve White, of course. Your long-suffering, saintly, little patient."
>
> "Well, who are *you*?" he asked incredulously.
>
> "Why, I'm Eve Black," she said (giving Mrs. White's maiden name). (pp. 20–22)

Eventually, a third personality, Jane, appeared, following a discussion of a painful early recollection (not dissimilar to the circumstances of the appearance of the Woman in Prince's case). According to Thigpen and Cleckley, Jane was more mature and poised than either Eve White or Eve Black and seemed to be a combination of their assets, but without their weaknesses.

The observed differences among the three personalities were documented even further in several different tests and films. Personality tests demonstrated constriction, anxiety, and obsessive-compulsiveness in Eve White and hysterical features in Eve Black. Handwriting experts insisted that the handwriting samples were from three different persons. EEG differences were found, with Eve Black showing signs of a pattern similar to that in psychopathic personality disturbances. This pattern was not found in either Eve White or Jane. Eve eventually went through a total of 22 personalities, always in sets of three. One set included a 21-year-old, a 46-year-old, and a 58-year-old personality; the first could read with good vision, the second required reading glasses, and the third needed bifocals. Another set experienced different menstrual cycles, leading to menstruation three times a month.

There is an interesting postscript to the well-publicized story of Eve. In 1975, Mrs. Chris Sizemore of Fairfax, Virginia, publicly revealed herself to be Eve, publishing her own memoirs in 1977 (Sizemore & Pittillo, 1977). In her autobiography, *I'm Eve,* she sometimes grieves over the mistaken premature belief that Jane was her final, cured self. Instead, Mrs. Sizemore accuses Jane of being maladaptive and responsible for several attempts at killing herself. Sizemore also reports in detail the occurrence of an eventual 22 personalities, including Bell Lady, Blind Lady, the Virgin, Turtle Lady, Card Lady, the Banana Split Girl, Purple Lady, Strawberry Girl, Retrace Lady, and Andrea de Cosna. More information on her is found in Focus 8–2. All in all, the case of Eve still leaves many questions unanswered. How do psychologists explain multiple personality? The next section will explore some major ideas.

### Dynamics of Multiple Personality

Most analyses of multiple personality emphasize dissociation as the means of gratifying varied, conflicting impulses while avoiding the extreme risk of conflict.

# FOCUS 8–2:

## Multiple Personalities: A Meeting with Eve

In 1982, the author had the truly remarkable and inspiring experience of actually meeting Chris Sizemore, the "three faces of Eve." She was the major speaker at the annual meeting of the American Psychological Association and met later with some members of the Association. Mrs. Sizemore is now a warm, articulate, frequently humorous person, who chats openly, honestly, and unabashedly. She is a wondrous speaker in her soft Southern accent, and she caused many persons in the audience to tearfully thank her for her sharing.

Chris does not attempt to diagnose the cause of her disorder, but tentatively offers, "It was a defense and a unique coping mechanism, which created satellite persons to cope with conflicts that were unbearable." Her earliest recollection of being aware of a coexisting personality involves her mother's accidentally cutting herself. Chris recalls that "I tucked my head under the pillow, while another girl went to get father." Mrs. Sizemore experienced 22 personalities, in sets of three. Each set actually died prior to another set appearing; the personalities are aware of their upcoming disappearance, and some have prepared wills or put aside memorabilia. Chris concludes that in most cases, the new personalities were more adaptive.

Although she was aware of having multiple personalities, she did not initially consider herself as different or in need of help. She changed her view and did seek therapy, however, when one of her personalities attempted to choke her daughter.

She spoke comfortably about her family, attributing much support to her husband: "After all, he supported three wives at a time . . . with three wardrobes . . . he had to go to all the PTA meetings for me . . . bought our daughter her first prom dress since I was in hiding during this period." He was also apparently adaptable, in that "whichever personality appeared was his wife"; some of the personalities did not like him, but this seemed to work out, since "he didn't like them either."

***Chris Sizemore** publicly revealed herself to be Eve of **Three Faces of Eve.***

Her daughter was informed early about her mother's disorder. This child adapted readily through reversing roles, and became protective of her mother. The son did not discover his mother's condition until he was a teenager. On being told he commented, "Is that all? I thought there was something drastically wrong. . . . You looked like you might be dying during some changes." This youngster soon developed his own daily method for adjusting: on arriving home daily from school, his opening greeting was always, "How are you, mom?," meaning which personality are you today?

Although hypnosis is sometimes used with dissociate disorders, Mrs. Sizemore has her own opinion of its value. She is concerned that the hypnosis will precipitate another personality structure and will lead to the client giving up responsibility for her actions. Chris felt she personally made good progress when the therapist encouraged her to accept responsibility for herself. This is especially important, she believes, when a person with a multiple personality disorder commits a crime but tries to deny involvement. (Such criminal cases are complicated, as we have seen in Chapter 1 in our discussion of law and mental disorders.)

During the course of our meeting, Mrs. Sizemore revealed two interesting experiences. First, she believes that she has experienced precognition, that is, the ability to predict a future event. She recalled around age 6 to 8 years dreaming about meeting Jesus, who said, "Your sister has diphtheria, go tell your mother." Chris remembers that this diagnosis was later medically confirmed. She also believes that she can detect another multiple personality, and startled us all with the revelation "There is one here!" As it turned out, she meant that she had passed a woman in the restroom and before any words were exchanged, Chris said, "You're a multiple, aren't you?" The stranger admitted this, expressed her relief that she did not have to initiate the revelation, and the two made arrangements for further discussion. Mrs. Sizemore explains this event as her being able to empathize with the other person's struggle and emotional agony.

A logical question for Mrs. Sizemore is how she can be so confident that her current personality is her final one. With quiet humor, she admitted to having experienced a headache recently (a prior sign of dissociation), and fearfully contacted her therapist . . . only to be reassured by his advice, "So take an aspirin." She feels certain she is completely recovered, since "I waited a year . . . and no one else appeared."

During the meeting, Mrs. Sizemore shared some personal insights which have special meaning, coming from a person who successfully coped with a "wilderness of pain" in her life. She acknowledges the possible influence of the therapists on the appearence of Jane, referring to this personality as representing "everything they wanted" (see page 179 for more elaboration on this topic). She confirms the self-protective function of dissociation in her observation that she resisted progress at one time because of her fear that "I would find out something about myself." However, she credits her recovery to reaching a stage where "I was ready to accept myself, to be as I am." Finally, she is motivated to appear in public in order to convey a message to all: "We need to accept mental illness as we do other illnesses and remove the stigma from it!"

A meeting with Chris Sizemore, the 22nd personality of Eve, was a moving experience. She can trace a life of intense emotional challenges and recurring trials, yet has reached a level of adjustment that makes her impressive as a person. How many others can state, as she did, "Sure I still have problems, after all it's not easy being just one person" (Sizemore, 1982).

Thus, a Sally, an Eve Black, or a Peggy Lou can openly express vivaciousness and even toy with seductiveness—while Miss Beauchamp, Eve White, or Sybil might feel too frightened or inhibited to display such shocking behaviors or desires. (If this concept of coexisting, contradictory personae is difficult to understand, the hypnosis demonstration described in Focus 8–3 may help to shed some light.)

Complete amnesia of each personality for the other apparently enables some continuity to exist among the various lives of the individual. In some ways, this permits the patient to "have her cake and eat it too," not only in terms of permitted gratification but also in the expiation of guilt. Thus, Sally can release the repressed and "sinful" desires that Miss Beauchamp could never admit to, but Sally can also punish not herself but Miss Beauchamp. Furthermore, although punishment can be administered, Miss Beauchamp's amnesia for Sally protects her from the more devastating punishment of being aware of her own secret desires. In a later analysis, published 12 years later, Prince (1920) confirmed that each of Miss Beauchamp's personalities represented separate inner strivings.

Sybil's story also illustrates painful conflict. Her mother's attitude toward being a woman was highly negative, so that when Sybil first menstruated, her mother jabbed Sybil in the abdomen saying, "It's simply awful. The curse of women. It hurts you here, doesn't it?" (p. 118) Sybil's mother was also a cruel woman, abusing Sybil so that she suffered a fractured larynx as well as a dislocated shoulder, among other injuries. Her father, in contrast, was kind. It is no wonder that Sybil not only refused to identify with her mother, but actually developed a later personality that showed her desire to be like her father. Sid, one of Sybil's personalities, was not only a male but also a carpenter . . . just as her father had been.

A second factor that may be important in the development of multiple personality are intense childhood experiences. The therapists in the cases of Sybil, Miss Beauchamp, and Eve, and others, as well, seem to find early experiences that are associated with the appearance or the special characteristics of the various personalities, as though the formation of such personalities began earlier in life.

In the case of Eve White, the therapists discovered that she had been an only child until the birth of twin sisters. Although there would have been good cause for the five-year-old Eve White to experience jealousy, Eve reports no memory of any such feeling. However, Eve Black appeared at this time, with such powerful feelings of resentment that she tormented the twins to the point of even biting them to make them cry! Chris Sizemore recalls another specific trauma in her early childhood when she saw the body of a man killed in a sawmill accident. She vividly remembers seeing the three separated segments of his body; but although it is tempting to view this as the cause of her personalities always being split in threes, Mrs. Sizemore considers this as speculative.

One final, possible factor presents a rather interesting speculation about multiple personality and what we know about it. In his discussion of the case of Miss Beauchamp, McCurdy (1941) suggests that therapists themselves may play a role in influencing multiple personalities. According to McCurdy, a more complete picture of the dynamics of Miss Beauchamp is achieved when her behaviors are seen in the context of Prince's interaction. McCurdy observes that the Saint showed her traits in being submissive to Prince's requests, while the Devil, Sally, first appeared during a period when Miss Beauchamp was experiencing a rebelliousness towards Prince. Given the frequent use of hypnosis, it is difficult to determine those cases when a personality is released through the hypnosis and when the personality is actually created by suggestions or expectations conveyed by hypnosis. However, there are sufficient cases reported where the therapists have been extremely cautious about influencing their patients, as to rule out suggestibility as the only explanation for multiple personalities.

## DEPERSONALIZATION DISORDER

*Depersonalization disorder* involves a disturbance in perception of the self, such that there is a sense of unreality. It tends to occur more frequently in women.

# FOCUS 8–3:

## Divided Consciousness: The Hidden Observer

During a classroom demonstration of hypnosis, Dr. E. R. Hilgard (1977) induced hypnotic deafness in a student. Since another student asked if ''another part'' of the hypnotized subject could still be aware, Hilgard tried the unique suggestion, ''Although you are hypnotically deaf, perhaps there is some part of you that is hearing. . . . If there is . . . [raise] the index finger. . . .'' To everyone's surprise and consternation, the finger rose, and the subject said, ''Please restore my hearing. . . . I felt my finger rise . . . and I want to know what you did'' (p. 186).

In explaining this phenomenon, Hilgard says that consciousness may be divided into an executive and a monitoring function. The executive function makes plans and initiates actions; the monitoring function scans or attends to external events and the executive-directed actions. Dissociative states in hypnosis partly occur when the subject gives up part of the executive function to the hypnotist, who now can direct and control movements (''your hand is rising''). But the monitor state of consciousness can also be ordered to stop scanning. This explains how pain is not experienced even though a painful stimulus is applied. In the hidden observer experience, part of the monitoring is given up, but part is retained and can even function. Hilgard has had subjects consciously report ''0'' level pain while *their hands* wrote down a pain intensity of ''9.'' This approach to describing dissociative experiences is amazingly similar to dissociative states, such as multiple personality. In fact, when asked to describe their ''hidden observers'' hypnotic subjects used phrases such as, ''There's Me 1, Me 2, and Me 3 . . . the Me 1 was also busy floating. Me 2 is watching all of this. . . . The hidden observer is analytical, unemotional, businesslike. . . . I felt like I had two personalities. . . . They're both me. . . . In the experiment they got separated'' (p. 210).

## Symptoms of Depersonalization

Case History 8–3 provides a striking illustration of a depersonalization experience. As it shows, this disorder may bring a distorted state of consciousness. It is as if one could observe one's own actions, but could no longer control them; and at the same time, the external world appears strange or new. There is a discontinuity between the self and the environment, and between the self-as-identity and the physical or bodily self that is acting. Phrases such as "I was beside myself" or "I was a bystander" are accurate portrayals of this state.

Weckowicz (1970) cites five salient characteristics of depersonalization:

- *Feeling of change:* A sudden feeling of strangeness, that the person does not recognize himself or herself anymore.
- *Feeling of unreality:* A feeling that one's body is amorphous, like "cotton fluff" rather than solid, or that the environment is unreal, "houses are cardboard, people are like robots moving through life mechanically."
- *An unpleasant aspect to experiences:* The feelings of change or unreality are evaluated as negative, and the person fears that he or she is going insane.
- *Lack of delusions:* The strangeness and unreality is judged to be perplexing, but it is not accepted as real. Instead, there is an "as if" quality: the person does not believe the body has actually become cotton fluff; only that it feels "as if" it were amorphous.
- *Loss of affect:* A common complaint is the loss of capacity to feel emotions, although in fact the person does experience feelings, mainly of distress.

Some of these symptoms may seem familiar to readers. In fact, many persons apparently have experienced depersonalization at some time or another in their lives. Dixon (1963) surveyed a sample of over 100 college students and concluded that one-third to one-half had depersonalization experiences in their lives.

For such experiences to be diagnosed as a mental disorder, however, would require that they have been repeated several times. The American Psychiatric Association's DSM-III system arbitrarily requires that such episodes last at least 30 minutes, and be repeated at least 6 times within a 6-week period. Of course, if the origins of these episodes are attributable to specific

*In **depersonalization** disorder, an individual has experiences of unreality and of strange feelings.*

factors such as alcohol, sensory deprivation, drug usage, brain tumors, or physical illnesses, then the diagnosis of depersonalization disorder is not considered appropriate. The validity of depersonalization disorder being categorized as a *dissociative* disorder has been questioned to some degree by the American Psychiatric Association, inasmuch as no amnesia occurs. However, it has been retained in DSM-III on the basis that the unreality symptoms constitute a form of identity dysfunction.

## Dynamics of Depersonalization

As a type of dissociative disorder, a common interpretation of the symptoms of depersonalization is their function as defenses against conflict or stress. Thus, the patient's statement can be taken at nearly face-value, that is, "This isn't real"; and not being real, the individual's conflict can therefore be negated. Where the person experiences the separation of the self from the acting self or physical self, such separation permits avoidance of guilt, for, after all, "I" am not responsible for the action. Depersonalization, of course, can be a type of flight from danger, without the actual physical flight shown in fugue, or the blanking out of the

## Case History 8–3:
### A Case of Depersonalization

Harold K. had been a farmer most of his life in a small town in Nebraska:

> Our life was simple but disciplined: Up early, chores, and very little time for people.
>
> Then the war came, and I was drafted, and put in training, and before I knew it on a troop ship where I would not see a neighbor or a new face for a month. I felt like one of a herd of cattle, jammed in with strangers from strange places with different ideas and personalities. We were all a little scared first, then bored, then seasick, then scared again as we neared the island where the enemy was.
>
> There was gunfire, and huge explosions . . . and we were scrambling into the assault boats. But the rush and frenzy and disorganization made everything worse . . . .
>
> It was unreal, like I was watching a bad movie or in a bad dream. In fact, I could not feel any emotions at all . . . just moving like in sleepwalking. Pretty soon I don't even think I was aware of sounds in spite of what must have been tremendous explosions . . . .
>
> Almost like I didn't care, I was watching it all and half-thinking, "These poor bastards must be scared out of their pants." Every so often I'd have an irrelevant thought, or at least it seemed irrelevant, as though it just came on me, such as "I shouldn't be here, the crops are green."
>
> You remember how those newsreels were in black and white and disconnected? You're seeing it, but you're not there. I know there was color, but it seemed more like black and white, like faded . . . in fact, the whole scene seemed faded and distant. Then I would say to myself, "Wait a minute, I'm here, it's real," and I'd pinch myself, but I didn't feel that either.
>
> We landed, and it's a blur . . . running, falling, diving, hiding, sand in the teeth, spitting, screaming I think, and the thought over and over, "This is not real, this is not happening, this is not happening to me." It's all compressed in time, one brief short-circuit of my life.
>
> Then it's all over, and the cigarette and the dark, and it was calm, and I could sit there and feel real again. I wasn't scared like they talk about the shakes hitting you afterwards; maybe I did have the shakes earlier, but when this reality came back, I didn't.

threatening stimuli shown in amnesia. The danger exists and is recognized, but is harmless either because the danger is perceived as unreal, or because one is separated from one's body and hence harm is avoided. Heightened anxiety states may contribute more directly to depersonalization. This may be seen when athletes report being "outside their bodies" during the initial stages of a competitive event. The author, as team psychologist for Olympic athletes, has interviewed many world-class athletes who at some time have observed:

> For a couple seconds, I'm watching myself, as though I'm just along for the ride, at the back of my head, and this body below me is churning along, but I'm not controlling it . . . and then suddenly I snap into place, and I'm in control again; when I move the hand, there's a direct link, and my hand in fact does move.

In some cases, the depersonalization apparently occurs after a danger is over, as a sort of relief or as a means of putting distance between the trying experience and one's life. Thus, an individual might express the feeling, "I can't believe it *really* happened to me."

Finally, some humanistic theorists propose that depersonalization is a sign of a loss of personal direction, and a realization of the artificiality of one's values (Schneider, 1958). The depersonalization is simply a reflection of a loss of genuineness of feelings.

## TREATMENT OF DISSOCIATIVE DISORDERS

The treatment of the dissociative disorders takes two primary directions, depending on the causative factors. If the cause relates to a traumatic experience that is being blocked out, then treatment will attempt to recover the event. Similarly, if the cause is a current stress that the person is attempting to avoid, then therapy will seek to remove the threat. A different approach, the attempt to integrate conflicting needs, would be used if a more complicated conflict has led to defenses such as those in the multiple personality disorders. We will look at both approaches.

*Olympic athletes sometimes experience a mild form of* ***depersonalization****. The athlete feels "outside" his or her body.*

### Removal of Threat

Typically, the less severe dissociative disorders, such as psychogenic amnesia, derive from a recent traumatic incident. In an attempt to avoid the anxiety of confronting the event, the individual instead becomes amnesic.

Hypnosis is one approach to treating amnesia. It is based on the premise that if the memory of the event can be retrieved, then tensions may be released through *abreaction,* the recall of the experiences and the expression of the accompanying emotions. This technique was first used by Freud and Breuer, who were able to cause symptoms of hysteria to disappear through the use of hypnosis.

In treating psychogenic amnesia through hypnosis, drugs such as sodium amytal or sodium pentothal are sometimes used to more easily induce hypnosis. Typically, the amnesic person is placed in a hypnotic trance, then gradually asked to recall the trauma, as in Karen's case described earlier in this chapter.

A major danger of hypnotic recall is the possibility that the individual lacks the psychological strength to tolerate the emotions associated with the memory. Instead, a person might recall part of the event, but be so flooded with traumatic feelings as to once more lapse into amnesia. For this reason, the hypnotist must carefully assess the individual's ability to cope with the memory before forcing recall. In many cases, the hypnotist will instruct the individual to remember the event while "still retaining your current comfort," or the recall may be couched in the form of describing the event—as one describes a movie—instead of reexperiencing it.

In cases where a person's amnesia is a response to current stressors, the removal of these stressors can help recall. For instance, recovering is often spontaneous for amnesia associated with the battlefield, as in the case of Frank (see page 173). The fact that Frank awakened without special treatment rather than remaining in a fugue state was a positive sign that the stresses had reduced sufficiently to permit some recovery. His hospitalization in a safe area, without even battle sounds, enabled him to regain awareness. In some other cases, where the stress can be viewed as limited, sleep has sometimes been used to psychologically remove the person from the stress. Thus, sedatives may be used to enable the person to stop thinking about problems. Sleep might also be valuable in permitting the body to recover physically from exhaustion as a result of the constant wear-and-tear of the stress.

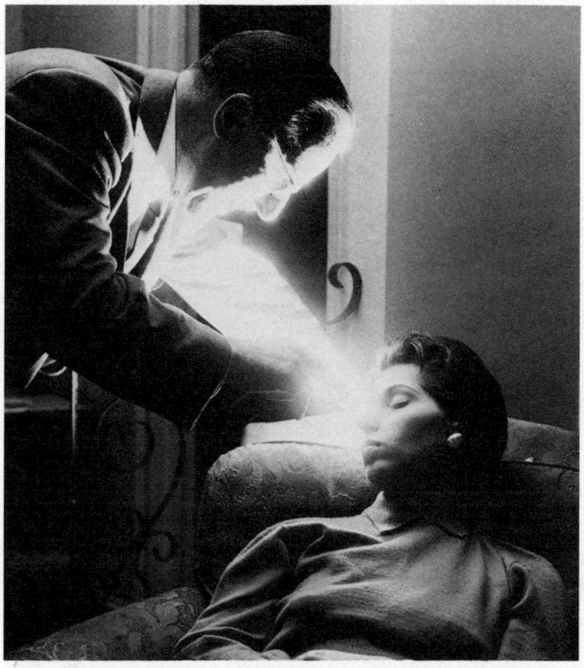

***Hypnotism** has sometimes been successfully used to promote recall or personality integration.*

### Achieving Integration of Needs in Multiple Personality

A more complex set of factors appear to be involved in cases of multiple personality. In fact, such cases are a prime example of psychodynamic origins that may influence a disorder. Multiple personalities seem to be one response to multiple, conflicting needs. In the normal situation, the person will struggle with these conflicts, seeking and trying various alternatives towards a resolution. The resolution may develop through a decision to prioritize, meeting one need while postponing others, or through a decision to completely give up an incompatible desire through a change of goals, or through cognitive restructuring in which a need is reexamined and found less pressing. For the multiple personality, the solution lies in being different persons entirely, with different behaviors and values that can variously gratify differing needs.

From this analysis, it would seem clear that a major step in treating multiple personality is to refocus on the issue of the conflict across needs and on more adaptive styles of coping. Although it might appear that the multiple personality patient has found a better solution than some, it should be recognized that multiple personality patients do suffer. Recall the pain inflicted by Sally on Miss Beauchamp (more factually, the pain she inflicted on herself); the blinding headaches that pursued Eve; and the nervousness that troubled Sybil. Treatment, therefore, aims at achieving a more integrated structure for need-gratification. The therapists who have treated cases of multiple personality have approached their cases with great patience and caution, carefully evaluating the contributions of each new personality and determining whether the final personality was truly a synthesis of adjustment or another index of maladjustment.

## EVALUATION

The dissociative disorders are forms of pathology which seem to be most illustrative of psychodynamic effects of stress and conflicts. In a mild form, amnesia, the loss of memory is selective and permits the person to avoid confronting threatening information or experiences. In the severe form of multiple personality, conflicts are apparently partially released through acting out under different personalities. Other possible explanations can, of course, be offered for these symptoms—for example, that multiple personalities are extreme forms of role playing, or examples of malingering, or cases of high suggestibility. Yet, the conflict-avoidance interpretation still seems the most acceptable. Whether repression, as defined by the Freudian, is at the basis of dissociation is open to question. Nevertheless, some process of self-protection does seem at work in these disorders. Treatment for the milder conditions, such as amnesia, seems to be useful where the therapy aims at removal of the person from the stressors or sources of threat. For the rare, and more severe, cases of multiple personality, traditional psychotherapy has been the preferred mode of treatment.

A final observation should be made: the dissociative disorders do demonstrate the close relationship between pathological symptoms and similar behaviors in normal persons (Cermak, 1982). The amnesic state is not very dissimilar from our forgetting an unpleasant appointment. Multiple personalities that exhibit different traits in one person are not too far from the occasional outbursts which we might display under pressure, that leads a friend to observe, "You sure didn't seem like yourself."

## SUMMARY


The dissociative states are rare disorders, perhaps gathering much interest more because of their dramatic nature than because of their frequency. Among the dissociative disorders are psychogenic amnesia, psychogenic fugue, multiple personality, and the depersonalization disorder. In the psychogenic amnesia, persons forget some details in their lives. Several types of amnesias are recognized: localized amnesia, defined as memory loss for a period of time; selective amnesia, defined as loss for some but not all events over a period of time; continuous amnesia, defined as memory loss for events prior to a set period as well as up to the present; and generalized amnesia, defined as loss of memory for all of one's prior life.

The psychogenic fugue state is a more serious version of psychogenic amnesia. A fugue disorder involves not only loss of memory, but physical flight from an area, as well. The individual usually wanders to a new location and begins a new life with a new identity. In cases of multiple personality, the new identity does not require leaving one's current location. Instead, the individual switches from one personality to a completely new one, showing different personality traits. Several personalities may coexist, each appearing to take over until replaced by a different personality.

Depersonalization is a disorder characterized by a sense of unreality about one's actions and about the surroundings. The individual no longer feels in control, and may even experience an out-of-body sensation. Unlike with amnesiacs, the person is still aware of what is happening and will have no memory loss.

In general, the dynamics of dissociative disorders share the presence of severe stress or emotional trauma that is not resolved. This unresolved stress leads to flight of some sort—loss of memory for the event, leaving the location of the trauma, shifting to a different personality, or simply developing a sense that the experience is "not real." Repression might also be involved in conditions such as amnesia, fugues, and multiple personality. Finally, for the multiple personality disorder, the development of new personalities represents a mechanism for the individual to gratify unacceptable needs.

Treatment of the dissociative disorders begins with the recognition that a threat or stress is a contributing factor. Therefore, psychotherapy aims at reducing the anxiety associated with the threat or trauma. Careful use of hypnosis can sometimes bring about release of such tensions. If the trauma is a current and ongoing one, then sedatives and sleep can help remove physical exhaustion. For the more complicated multiple personality disorder, psychotherapy attempts to bring about an integration of conflicting needs. The source and role of each personality are examined, and a synthesis is sought to bring about a more stable person.


## KEY TERMS

**Abreaction**
**Anterograde amnesia**
**Confabulation**
**Continuous amnesia**
**Depersonalization disorder**
**Dissociative disorders**
**Fugue**
**Generalized amnesia**
**Localized amnesia**
**Multiple personality**
**Psychogenic amnesia**
**Psychogenic fugue**
**Retrograde amnesia**
**Selective amnesia**

# CHAPTER 9

## Psychological Factors Affecting Physical Conditions: Psychophysiologic Disorders

- **Is there truly such a thing as mind over body?**
- **Is an ulcer an automatic sign that one is under undue stress?**
- **How can a person tell if an asthmatic attack is real or psychological?**
- **Are psychophysiologic disorders all in the mind?**
- **The statement "You make my blood boil" implies that anger causes high blood pressure. Is there any truth to this statement?**
- **Why are high-achieving executives more at risk to an early death than lower achievers?**
- **How can control of finger temperature bring relief to migraine headaches?**
- **Can biofeedback help control psychophysiologic disorders?**
- **Can stress be related to the growth of cancer?**

**TABLE 9–1**

**Psychological Factors Affecting Physical Condition**

| *Type* | *Major Characteristics* |
|---|---|
| Asthma | Difficulties in breathing due to spasms in the lungs related to psychological factors. |
| Cancer | Uncontrolled growth of cells, perhaps influenced by psychological factors. |
| Coronary artery disease | Heart disease such as blockage, heart failure, or acute chest pains associated with psychological factors. |
| Essential hypertension | High blood pressure influenced by psychological factors. |
| Migraine headaches | Pain unilaterally along with nausea, diarrhea, sensitivity to light, associated with vascular dilation and psychological factors. |
| Peptic ulcers | Burning sensations from rawness in the stomach wall due to psychological factors. |
| Tension headaches | Pain located bilaterally in the forehead or occipital area; considered to be associated with muscle tension and psychological factors. |

## Case History 9–1:
### Peptic Ulcers

Mark M., aged 30, worked as an electronics engineer in an aerospace firm. His assignment involved the design of a new type of supersonic aircraft being submitted by the firm for contract support by the government in competition with several other companies. Although the responsibilities were enormous, he seemed to delight in the challenge. In fact, the experience of planning was perceived as an important step toward further advancement in the firm. The first sign of gastric difficulty was a burning discomfort after an evening meal. This gnawing sensation disappeared only to return periodically after eating. Physical examination disclosed the presence of a peptic ulcer.

Mark had lived a hard-working, independent life ever since adolescence. As the oldest son in a large family, he was soon ignored as his parents devoted their efforts toward the younger offspring. He obtained his first job while still in high school and began to learn a trade. He stayed in the same occupation on receiving his high school diploma. After an adequate showing on the job, he decided to further his education in order to increase his future earning power. College was difficult, and Mark was pleased when he received his bachelor's degree. From that date forward, he was engaged in a number of transfers from firm to firm in an ever-increasing attempt to reach a higher-level position. He kept an eye out for property investments and lived on a cautious budget which permitted him to buy some land while still having an adequate amount for his family. He had just begun to feel the pressures of a number of major decisions—the purchase of a new home, his oldest son's shift to a better school, his wife's plans to go on an extensive vacation, the sale of his investment property.

Following the diagnosis of his ulcer, a strict diet and an enforced regime of recreation was initiated. Mark retained his assignment but was confronted with the heightened stress it placed on him. He was advised to declare a moratorium on any financial ventures including the sale of the property. Discussions with his wife regarding the family and occupational pressures were begun, and her role in facilitating their relief was examined. The ulcer pains diminished within a few months.

The other chapters of this text discuss disorders that are primarily of the mind. This chapter is different: it deals with physical disorders—such as cancer, heart disease, and asthma—all of which are very real physical illnesses that involve structural changes.

## PSYCHOLOGICAL FACTORS AFFECTING PHYSICAL CONDITIONS

A person with an ulcer *does* have a perforation that requires medical attention. An asthmatic individual *does* experience constriction in the lungs that blocks air intake. And the person with *essential hypertension* (high blood pressure) *does* show measurably higher blood pressure. Why should an abnormal psychology text discuss such illnesses?

Although these disorders are physiological, they can also be influenced by psychological events, as Case History 9–1 illustrates. The DSM-III category, *psychological factors affecting physical condition,* attempts to acknowledge both the organic basis for the physical symptoms and the added involvement of psychological factors (Leigh, 1983).

In this sense, the DSM-III classification reflects an evolution in terminology: DSM-I introduced the term, *psychosomatic* (meaning mind over body), then DSM-II substituted the better term, *psychophysiologic,* and finally DSM-III developed the term, *psychological factors affecting physical conditions,* to refer to the same disorders; yet only the longer, DSM-III terminology adequately describes the physiological base of these disorders and encourages a holistic understanding of them. Because of the unwieldiness of the DSM-III terminology, however, we will use the shorter term *psychophysiologic* in this chapter.

In a sense, nearly all of the bodily illnesses to which humans are subject may be affected by psychological factors. However, DSM-III lists the more common examples of physical disorders with psychological factors. In this chapter, we will look at the following disorders:

- Peptic ulcers
- Asthma
- Essential hypertension
- Coronary artery disease
- Tension headaches
- Migraine headaches
- Cancer

Neurodermatitis (itching of the skin), rheumatoid arthritis, and vomiting are also included in the DSM-III classification, but they will not be discussed here for reasons of space.

### Dynamics of Psychophysiologic Conditions

The psychophysiologic disorders show the intimate relationship between body and mind—the inseparable interaction between personality and conflict on the one hand and the autonomic nervous system on the other. We see this relationship in everyday life, as when a person blushes with shame, when the blood drains from a frightened person's face, or when stress produces "butterflies in the stomach."

Modern physiology recognizes that the *autonomic nervous system* is involved in such reactions. As was discussed in Chapter 4, the autonomic nervous system serves the two functions of preparing the body for emergencies or danger and maintaining the *homeostasis* (equilibrium) of the body under normal conditions. For these functions, the autonomic nervous system is subdivided into the *sympathetic system,* which is significantly involved in emotional behavior, and the *parasympathetic system,* which is primarily concerned with maintaining body functions. As the center of endocrine and autonomic nervous system control, the hypothalamus coordinates and controls the organ behavior and hormone secretions of the body during emotions.

What causes psychophysiologic symptoms such as those outlined in Table 9–1? A popular view links psychophysiologic disorders with the failure to successfully cope with stress. Reiser (1975) shows how this might happen by postulating a three-phase development of psychophysiologic disorders. In *phase one,* a person's behavior patterns, needs, and physiological functioning are constitutionally programmed by genetics, then further shaped by early parent-infant experiences. In *phase two,* the person experiences psychosocial stresses beyond his or her defenses; these stresses precipitate tensions that have physical symptoms—such as headache or tightness in the stomach. In *phase three,* the physical symptoms that first appeared in the previous phase now become well established as an identifiable physical disease. The patient now reacts to the illness experience and incorporates it into the self-image so that it is repeated in future conflicts.

This model provides a useful perspective for understanding how an ulcer might develop. First, an ulcer-prone person might be born with a tendency towards higher-than-normal gastric secretions and be raised in an environment that fosters dependency conflict. Later in life, that person may remain basically healthy until a series of experiences—for instance, job advancement pressures—activate daily stresses. Because of the hyperreactivity of this person's stomach, acids are released in response to the stress, and thus an ulcer develops.

In a similar theory, Pierloot (1979) sees psychophysiologic disorders as involving three components, as outlined in Figure 9-1. The *psychopathological component* is the person's psychological vulnerability to stress. This may be caused by early psychological experiences, such as early conflict or inadequate development of coping skills. Part of this psychopathological component is the personality characteristics that seem to predispose some individuals to vulnerability to certain physical illnesses. The evidence here, while suggestive, is fascinating; and we will refer to it in several discussions of specific illnesses in this chapter.

The second component, the *psychophysiological* component, involves physiological vulnerability—such as heightened autonomic nervous system reactivity—which may be the result of early health experiences. The third, *physiopathological* component, consists of an actual state of physical weakness or pathology. This may have been caused by physical damage from a state of exhaustion, or organ weakness caused by prior physical illness.

The interaction of these components forms the basis for a psychophysiologic disorder, with presence of all three being necessary for the appearance of somatic symptoms instead of other reactions to stress. This pattern seems to hold true, to one degree or another, for all the psychophysiologic disorders designated by DSM-III. The relationship is illustrated by the peptic ulcer, the disorder we shall discuss next.

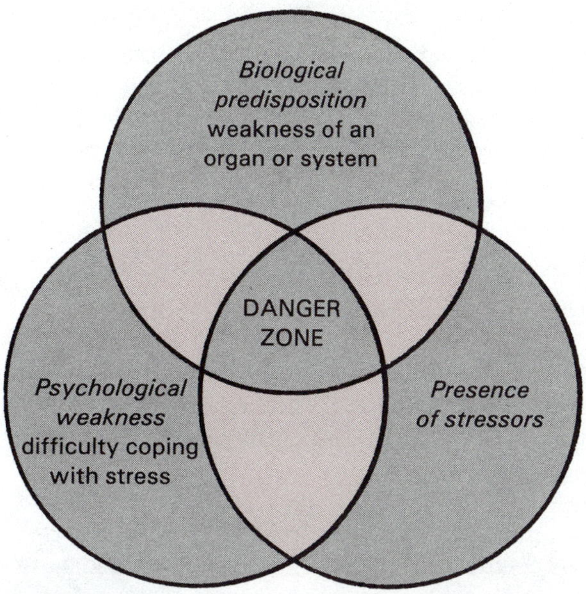


**FIGURE 9-1** Factors in stress-related illness.

SOURCE: Based on "Psychogenesis of Somatic Disorders" by R. Pierloot, 1979, *Psychotherapy and Psychosomatics, 32,* pp. 27-40.

## PEPTIC ULCERS

### Symptoms of Peptic Ulcer

A *peptic ulcer* is a condition involving the gradual sloughing off of a small area of the stomach tissue, leading to a raw lesion or hole in the lining of the stomach. The ulceration is due to an overproduction of *pepsinogen,* a substance that stimulates digestive enzyme production. As a result, gastric secretions fail to cease after food passes into the intestines. These normal gastric secretions include hydrochloric acid, which can lead to inflammation of the stomach wall if not stopped. The ulcer may vary in size from a pinhead to a silver dollar and is usually situated near the outlet of the stomach to the duodenum.

A person first becomes aware of a burning, gnawing pain in the stomach appearing regularly within a few minutes to an hour or two after each meal. In more severe cases, vomiting results, and hemorrhaging may take place to such an extreme that the patient passes black, tarry stools. Loss of blood may then occur so rapidly as to leave the patient weak and in serious danger.

### Dynamics of Ulcers

What factors are involved in the increased gastric activity that leads to ulcers? Three variables seem important. These are emotions, stress, and physical predisposition.

***Anger, Anxiety, and Ulcers.*** Certain research has contributed specifically to our understanding of how emotions may be linked to ulcers. Wolf and Wolff (1943) recorded the relationship between specific emotions and gastric activity in a patient with a fistula (opening) following surgery. Realizing that a unique opportunity was available, these scientists conducted extensive observations. The patient was carefully supervised and his gastric reactions analyzed during various emotional states. The researchers found that panic reactions led to a temporary paling of the mucous membrane of the stomach wall, accompanied by a reduction of gastric secretions. Just the opposite occurred during anger and anxiety. Blood flow increased, as did secretions of hydrochloric acid.

Both these conditions—mucous membrane swelling and increased hydrochloric acidity—heighten the vulnerability of the stomach tissues to injury. This relationship between anger and anxiety, gastric secretions, and stomach injury was also documented in some research by Mittelman and Wolff (1942). These researchers worked together on an experimental study that included both ulcer patients and a control group with no symptoms. Gastric secretions were obtained by means of a nasal catheter. The subjects were studied when relaxed; then again after the experimental arousal of stress. In the normal subjects, hydrochloric acid secretions were found to decrease during relaxed sessions and to increase during emotional sessions. For one peptic ulcer patient, however, the gastric secretions increased to such a high level during a period of intense anger that hemorrhaging was soon detected. It seems conclusive, therefore, that emotions such as anger and anxiety may establish a condition within the stomach that makes the individual vulnerable to ulcers.

***Environmental Stress and Ulcers: "Executive" Monkeys and Rats.*** Another factor that has been offered as a basic cause of ulcers is environmental stress (Wolf et al., 1979). Some initial evidence regarding this relationship was found by Sawrey and Weisz (1956). They created a stressful environment in which rats received a shock whenever they approached their food or water. This situation is known as an *approach-avoidance conflict* (the approach being caused by the need to eat and drink, the avoidance being caused by the pain of the shock). Within two weeks, many of the animals developed ulcers. Since not all animals developed ulcers, however, there must have been more to ulcer proneness than the approach-avoidance conflict.

The research of Brady (1958) provided some fascinating additional information. Brady's studies of executive monkeys looked at environmental stress, but they added a new dimension—responsibility. Brady confined two monkeys in the same apparatus. Each monkey received the same shock at the same time as the other. Both monkeys had identical levers within reach. The only difference was that one monkey could prevent the shock by pushing the lever; the other's lever offered no control over the shock. The executive monkey who controlled the shock developed ulcers so severe that he died; however, the monkey with the dummy lever developed no ulcers.

The Brady study has often been quoted in support of the belief that ulcers are an executive ailment found in persons with high-pressure, responsible jobs. Further support has been some evidence that higher rates of death from ulcers appear in cities with corporate headquarters—possibly reflective of higher job stress (Catalano, 1979). Persuasive as such findings may be, however, later studies have not been as supportive.

Weiss (1977) reanalyzed the possible relationships between stress, decision making, and ulcers in rats. A series of executive rat experiments used circumstances similar to Brady's study: the executive animal could avoid shock by an action (in this case, turn-

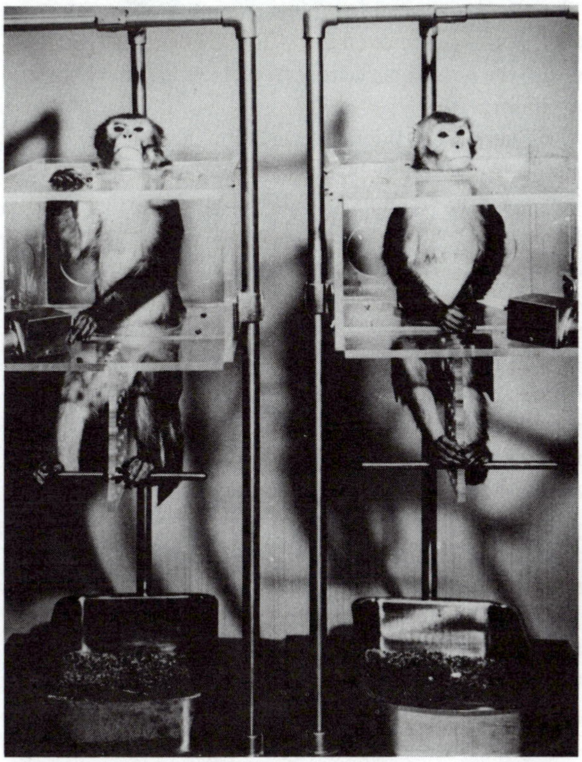

*The "executive" monkey on the left learned that pressing a lever prevented a shock to himself and his companion. The companion monkey on the right lost interest in his dummy lever. Only the executive monkey developed* **ulcers**.

ing a wheel), while the other rat had no control. Unlike Brady's studies, however, Weiss provided two signals: a sound, warning that shock was imminent, and a signal after the executive rat acted, to indicate that the action did prevent shock from occurring. Under these conditions, the executive rat actually showed fewer ulcers than the control rat. This suggests that having control—or at least having the perception of control—can be extremely important protection against stress. As we will see later in this chapter's discussion of hypertension, the perception of control contributes to a major degree to the prevention of certain stress-related physical illnesses.

***Physical Predisposition.*** A third element that seems to be related to the development of ulcers is physical predisposition. This relates to the *diathesis-stress* concept—that an illness is caused by a combination of physical predisposition in the presence of a stress that triggers the illness.

Mirsky and his colleagues (1952) examined the relationship of stress, ulcers, and individual differences to gastric activity. He first reported a relationship between pepsinogen in both blood and urine and peptic ulcers, with peptic ulcer patients showing more pepsinogen than normal persons. The level of pepsinogen in blood is determined early in life, perhaps genetically, and remains constant throughout life. Thus, it is possible that people who are susceptible to ulcers are those whose secretion level is already high.

This interpretation is supported by a later study, in which 120 army inductees were selected out of 2,073 on the basis of their high or low pepsinogen values (Weiner et al., 1957). Before the end of basic training (an assumed stressful circumstance), 9 men developed ulcers. Of these 9, 8 were in the upper 5 percent of the pepsinogen distribution and the remaining man was in the upper 15 percent. In addition, they had been correctly identified by psychological measures as being vulnerable on the basis of dependency conflicts. Thus, the combination of physical predisposition, rigorous physical stress, and psychological traits seems to support the theory of interacting components outlined in Figure 9–1.

## Treatment of Peptic Ulcers

The evidence from the several studies cited earlier supports the conclusion that a combination of factors play a role in ulcers. Accordingly, the treatment of these disorders may follow several strategies, often in combination.

Medical treatment includes a prescribed diet, rest, and the avoidance of alcohol, tobacco, and coffee. In severe cases, surgery may be needed to remove the ulcerated area. Because both stress and certain responses to it are typically factors in ulcers, treatment often includes an attempt to reshape behavioral responses to stress. Patients are helped to identify which environmental circumstances they can already deal with adaptively, which demands they must learn to meet with more healthy behaviors and which situations they must completely avoid (Nemiah, 1971). Since emotional responses to stress may be involved, Brooks and Richardson (1980) developed an emotional skills training program. This was composed of Anxiety Management Training (Suinn, 1977) and training in the control of negative emotions. In a three-year follow-up, 8 of the 9 patients treated in this program remained free of ulcers.

Humanistic-existential therapy takes a slightly different approach. This view sees disorders such as ulcers, hypertension, and tension headaches as warning signals—messages that the person has lost touch with more important personal values and is under pressure from the social environment. Such symptoms are an index that the body is still healthy enough to send out such signals, and that the person should reevaluate priorities and values. Humanistic therapy is therefore aimed at helping the person look at the discrepancies between personal values, goals, satisfactions and those that are actually dominating the individual's life. Humanistic-existential approaches encourage the person to get in touch with personally valid goals and to liberate the true inner self from the demands of the world.

## ASTHMA

### Symptoms of Asthma

Bronchial asthma, like peptic ulcers, is a physical illness. Asthma is characterized by the inability to breathe freely because of muscular spasms and the accumulation of serum in the bronchial tissue (a condition known as *edema*). The movement of air through the lungs is a function of both the elasticity of the bronchial tubes and the amount of obstruction in these tubes. In an asthmatic attack, the muscles of the small bronchials contract, decreasing the amount of air flow. At the same time, the swelling of the lining membranes and the onset of edema both act as obstructions, resulting in a wheezy breathing sound. Mild asthma attacks produce labored breathing, severe attacks bring subjective feeling of suffocation. A sudden onset leaves the patient extremely distressed and fighting for air, the chest heaving with effort and convulsive coughing. The attack may last for a few minutes, or it may continue for hours or even days. In the period between attacks, the person is entirely free of symptoms (Dawson & Simon, 1983).

There is considerable variation in what initiates an attack. Attacks may be highly seasonal, subject to certain specific irritants, or they may be triggered by physical activity. In asthmas which are allergenic, the attacks are clearly associated with the presence of *allergens* (substances such as pollens or foods to which the patient is extremely sensitive). Some asthmatic conditions are due solely to allergen-reactions. The irritating substance may be a pollen such as ragweed or a food such as cereal or eggs. Changing weather conditions, which produce shifts in the pollen count in the atmosphere, can bring on an attack.

Research also indicates that for some persons, their asthmatic attacks are caused entirely by emotional variables. Emotional stresses or continuing conflicts can be responsible for arousing the spasmodic breathing attack (Weiner, 1977). It is toward these latter conditions that the diagnosis of psychophysiological disorder applies.

### Dynamics of Asthma

As in the other psychophysiologic disorders, research into nonmedical causes of asthma has used a variety of approaches. Some of the most intriguing studies explore the relationship of asthma to stress, family conflict patterns, and to certain personality traits.

***Stress and Asthma: Experimental Evidence.*** Experimental findings have linked symptoms of asthma to stress, for both animals and humans. During some studies in which experimental neuroses were created in animals, for instance, symptoms such as labored breathing and recognizable wheezing were produced (Liddell, 1951; Gantt, 1941).

Research has also explored the effects of stress on human subjects. In one remarkably daring study, asthmatic patients were isolated in small chambers locked from the outside and filled with an array of electronic instruments (Stein, 1962). Although the box was allergen-free, one patient showed marked apprehension (an understandable reaction) and went into a severe asthmatic attack. A placebo solution was administered, but it was ineffective: only the correct medication was helpful. The general line of evidence from these various studies supports the belief that emotionally distressing circumstances may well trigger asthma.

***Psychodynamic Explanations.*** Another line of explanation involves psychodynamic theories that suggest specific conflict patterns that may be characteristic of the asthma patient. One frequent explanation points toward an early fear of separation from the mother, which leads to a "cry for help" that is the prototype for the later asthmatic gasps. In this light, the isolation experiment just described becomes even more intriguing, with its simulation of a separation experience.

Other psychodynamic theories interpret the spasmodic intake of breath as a suppressed rage reaction. The person is seen as harboring ambivalent feelings toward the parent, with resentment and rage suppressed for fear of complete rejection by the mother. French and Alexander (1941) extensively examined 10 asthmatic patients and their parents. They noted that all 10 expressed strong feelings of ambivalence toward their mothers, associated with a feeling that they had been deprived of maternal love. This interpretation is relevant to Johnny's story in Case History 9–2. This finding is somewhat controversial, however, since there is some evidence that the mothers are actually overprotective rather than overtly rejecting (Parker & Lipscombe, 1979). Overall, however, a common thread in psychodynamic interpretations appears to center on the ambivalent relationship and interplay between the person and the mother.

***Personality and Asthma Control.*** A series of studies have looked at personality variables from another standpoint: the way in which certain behavior patterns may exacerbate already present asthma conditions. Are there different ways in which asthmatic persons react to their conditions? If so, do such differences affect the asthmatic attacks?

The answer to these questions seems to be yes. Researchers have identified two problematic types of asthma patients: *high panic-fear responders* and *low panic-fear responders* (Jones et al., 1979; Kinsman et al., 1980). The high responders become emotional and anxious about their asthma attacks—a response that prompts more rapid breathing and exacerbates their existing struggles to take in air. Individuals in this group are generally pessimistic about coping with their illness, tending to feel helpless. In contrast, the low responders seem unwilling to give in to the asthma,

## Case History 9–2:
### Asthma

Ten-year-old Johnny R. was hospitalized with severe asthmatic attacks. According to his mother, the first symptoms appeared at age two, becoming progressively worse with time. The mother had little time for the youngster since she worked full time as a clerk in a department store. The father, a traveling sales representative, was away most of the time on the road. The little boy was first cared for by an aunt, then by a baby-sitter, and finally by a practical nurse. He often missed school because of severe attacks which left him too exhausted to attend classes. However, he still managed to do quite well through extensive reading and a strong interest in academic work to the exclusion of all other activity. He always seemed to develop a close relationship with his teachers.

The recent attacks began soon after the mother had considered a transfer of schools. She had explored the possibility of a boarding school and was planning to visit one. Two days before the visit, Johnny came down with bronchial spasms so severe that his usual medication was not effective. He was rushed to the hospital and has been under close supervision since. Although Johnny has not been told yet, his parents are seriously considering admitting him to a special hospital for asthmatic children for intensive tests and treatment. At the same time, they are afraid to do this, since they are wondering for the first time if the asthma is an expression of his feeling unwanted. The mother is consulting with a psychologist, with whom she has shared her emerging guilt feelings.

**TABLE 9–2**

**Hypothesized Psychological Traits of Four Physiologic Disorders**

| | *Asthma* | *Peptic ulcer* | *Essential hypertension* | *Migraine headaches* | *Hives* |
|---|---|---|---|---|---|
| *Emotional conflicts* | Unresolved dependence on mother | Oral dependent, but desirous of independence | Repressed aggression | Anxiety over perfectionism, resentment | Resentment over frustration of needs for nurturance |
| *How the person feels* | Feeling left out | Feeling insecure and driven | Feeling threatened with dangers | Feeling the need to get things done | Feeling beaten and helpless |
| *Other characteristics* | Impulsive, irritable, desirous of being rid of responsibilities | Competitive, dominant, successful | Rigidly principled, hot tempered but controlled | Outwardly calm and composed but very concerned over reaching standards | Low self-esteem |

SOURCES: From *Psychosomatic Medicine: Its Principles and Application,* by F. Alexander, 1950, New York: Norton; "The Place of Personality Traits in Specific Syndromes: Cause or Effect" by J. Bastians, 1965, in J. Wisdon and H. Wolff (Eds.), *The Role of Psychosomatic Disorder in Adult Life,* London: Pergamon; "Relationship of Specific Attitudes and Emotions to Certain Bodily Diseases" by W. Grace and D. Graham, 1952, *Psychosomatic Medicine, 14,* pp. 243–251; "Psychosomatic Medicine" by D. Graham, 1972, in N. Greenfield and R. Steinback (Eds.), *Handbook of Psychophysiology,* New York: Holt, Rinehart & Winston.

refusing to panic and often delaying taking medication for the attack.

Each of these two patterns contributes different types of maladjustment to asthma. The high-response pattern adds panic to the suffering; and the person also fails to learn to use medication effectively. The low responders, on the other hand, often complicate the problem further by waiting too long, and they tend to be hospitalized more often.

### Treatment of Respiratory Disorders

A variety of drugs, including epinephrine hydrochloride [1], aminophylline, and antihistamines, often bring relief from an asthmatic attack. In addition, where allergens are involved, preventive treatment may include both the avoidance of irritants and injections designed to increase the body's tolerance (Yetiv & Bianchine, 1983).

Several other treatments have a psychological rather than medical basis. Deep trance suggestion has been reported successful in inhibiting allergic reactions in persons who are capable of deep hypnosis (DePiano & Salzberg, 1979; Wadden & Anderton, 1982). Behavioral therapy techniques have been used to train persons to increase the flow of air through the bronchial tubes, through relaxation techniques or biofeedback (Hock et al., 1978). The effectiveness of this approach is not yet established: one review concluded that the results are not impressive to date (King, 1980). And finally, psychotherapy is sometimes used to help adult asthmatic patients resolve hostility or resentment that may reflect early family conflicts. Once the individual learns to release the original repressed feelings, he or she is frequently more able to deal with present difficulties with greater insight.

## ESSENTIAL HYPERTENSION

### Symptoms of Hypertension

A third psychophysiologic disorder, hypertension, is characterized by high blood pressure. Normal systolic arterial pressure is about 120 mm. Hg (mercury) and

1 A medication based on the adrenal gland secretion, epinephrine, discussed in Chapter 4.

the diastolic pressure is about 80 mm. Hg. *Systolic pressure* reflects the pressure when the heart has contracted, while *diastolic pressure* measures the level when the heart is relaxed.

Hypertension may occur quite independently of psychological factors. Chronic increase of arterial blood pressure occurs with hardening of the arteries, a disease connected with aging. This hardening is basically a narrowing of the arteries, and since the same volume is being circulated, the result is an increase in pressure. *Essential hypertension* is the term for chronic high blood pressure with no known organic origin, and which is therefore assumed to be psychologically based. All hypertensive ailments pose a potential threat to life. Death from heart failure and other diseases of the heart or arteries lists among the leading causes of mortality in the United States (see Figure 9–2). Cerebral hemorrhage, or stroke, can also be fatal, or may be survived with paralysis as a result.

### Dynamics of Essential Hypertension

***Hypertension and Stress.*** Studies into the causes of essential hypertension focus on the contribution of stress. Additionally, the roles of self-control and of anger have been examined. Finally, physical susceptibility has been examined. Essential hypertension is one of the prime examples of a psychophysiologic response to stress (Krantz et al., 1983). Whereas in other psychophysiologic disorders, the influence of environmental stress may be highly complex, an increase in blood pressure can be demonstrated as a direct correlate of stress. For example, research shows that increased blood pressure is a natural response to stress—both mental stress, as when a person is faced with a math test, and physical stress, such as immersing a hand in very cold water. The increase is a functional response: the body increases blood flow to the muscles to ready itself for possible action (Harrell, 1980). Increased blood pressure also takes place in response to stresses that derive from life events such as the loss of a job, or a transfer to crowded living quarters (Jenkins et al., 1979).

Two variables seem involved in maintaining high blood pressure over some length of time: the chronicity of the stress and the intensity of the stress (Shapiro et al., 1979). *Chronicity* refers to the time over which an individual is subjected to stress. As an example, air traffic controllers are faced with having to be continuously alert and responsible for the lives of innumerable passengers in the planes they monitor. At least one study found a higher rate of hypertension among this occupational group (Cobb & Rose, 1973). *Intensity* refers to the degree of stress experienced. An explosion

## Case History 9–3:
### Essential Hypertension

Anna H., a 45-year-old housewife, was admitted to a clinic for headaches and dizziness. Her blood pressure was found to be extremely high, requiring intensive medical therapy after which it returned to a normal level. She remained healthy and symptom free for six months. At this time her daughter eloped with a boy who was a stranger to the mother, although the father had known him. Anna, who had previously cautioned her daughter over and over again about the necessity of care in choosing a mate, was able to remain outwardly serene in the face of the seemingly impulsive wedding. Within a week of the elopement, however, she experienced a recurrence of hypertension.

Anna had always been a hard-working, extremely neat housekeeper. Dishes were immediately cleaned and stacked after meals, soiled clothing washed and dried. She had strong opinions regarding family discipline, but very seldom did she engage in open arguments with her husband. In fact, she was never known to be cranky or to shout in anger. Her children said that the best sign that she was losing her temper was her "sudden quiet manner." She maintained that arguments never won any battles and that someone had to be reasonable.

Her blood pressure was again brought under control through medication. However, with the encouragement of her husband, Anna also sought stress counseling. She soon learned to identify her angry feelings, to accept them as normal, and to permit herself reasonable expressions.

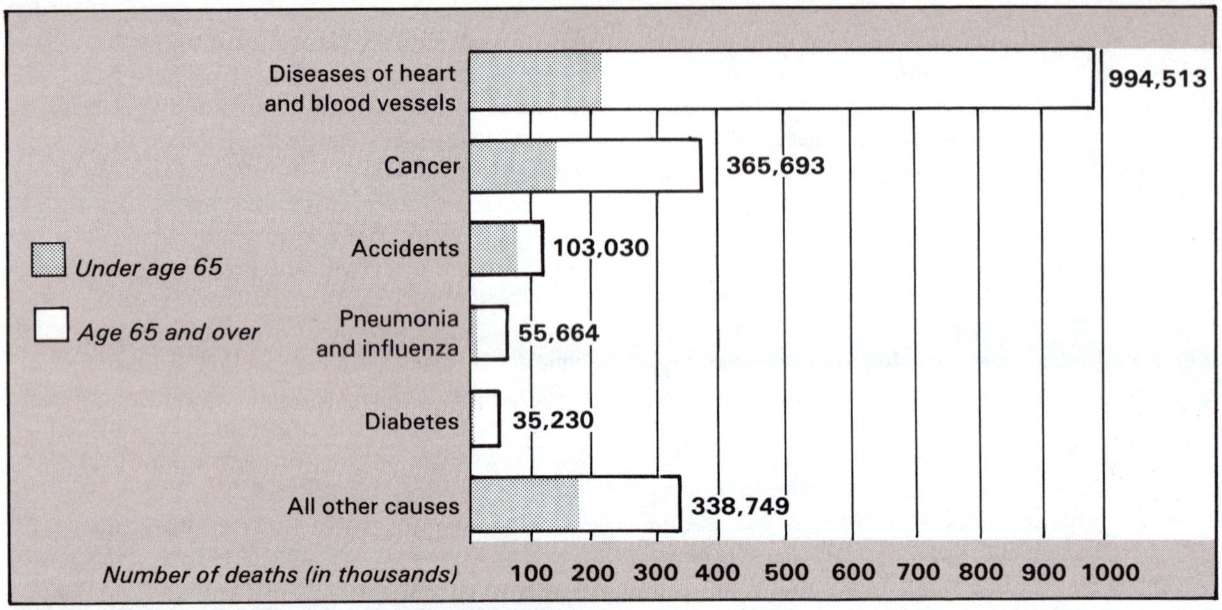


**FIGURE 9–2** Leading causes of death in the United States.

SOURCE: Based on data from the National Center for Health Statistics, U.S. Public Health Service, DHEW, 1978.

called the Texas City disaster presented a briefer but highly intense experience. This disaster, which occurred in 1947, involved the combined explosion of a ship and the Monsanto Chemical Plant, with a force equal to the Bikini atom bomb. Medical data showed that 57 percent of those who survived showed quite abnormal diastolic pressures (over 95 mm. Hg) and that this hypertension was maintained for up to one or two weeks after the incident (Rusking et al., 1948). Another accident of high intensity occurred at the Three Mile Island nuclear power plant in Pennsylvania in 1979. Being threatened by potential radiation, residents within a ten-mile radius of the disaster area also showed heightened blood pressures, as well as other symptoms of anxiety and stress (Davidson et al., in press).

From such findings, we know that stress is highly influential in increasing blood pressure conditions. Another crucial factor is the influence of personality on blood pressure, a topic we will discuss next.

***Locus of Control and Hypertension.*** Cognitive factors, such as expectations about control, seem to interact with stress to increase blood pressure. Julian Rotter's theory (1966) provides a useful perspective. He suggests that some persons are characterized by *internal locus of control* (a belief that events are under personal control) while others hold an *external locus of control* (a belief that events are controlled by outside factors). Other research indicates how this grouping might relate to hypertension in certain situations.

In one study, the control over shock was varied with internal-external loci of control (DeGood, 1975). Persons whose locus of control was internal experienced greatest increases in blood pressure when shock-free intervals were beyond or *external* to their control. Similarly, the external-control persons experienced larger blood pressure increases when the shock was made subject to *internal* control.

Another study adds some additional information to our understanding of the role of perceived control. This study found that blood pressure increased in situations where subjects were led to *perceive* that they had available a coping response, but then found it difficult to use that response (Manuck et al., 1978). Thus, a discrepancy between expectations and actual ability to exert control seems associated with hypertension.

***Hypertension*** *can result from chronically stressful working conditions such as those encountered by air traffic controllers.*

***Anger and Its Suppression.*** In addition to stress and the perception of control, a third variable that may be a factor in hypertension is anger or hostility. A traditional approach to psychophysiologic disorders has been the search for common personality types or conflicts associated with essential hypertension. In this approach, a popular hypothesis has been that anger elevates blood pressure (as in the saying, "You make my blood boil") and that the venting or release of anger seems to reduce blood pressure. This theory has been supported by some research (Diamond, 1982; Shapiro et al., 1979).

Building from this theory, it is tempting to speculate that hypertension is related to suppression of anger. In cases such as Anna's in Case History 9–3, a person suppresses chronic rage, while beneath a calm facade blood pressure rises, physiological changes occur over time, and the eventual result is essential hypertension. This hypothesis has received some indirect support. For example, Joseph Sapira and his colleagues (1971) showed hypertensive subjects a film in which the main actor behaved in a clearly unpleasant manner without cause. In contrast to persons with normal blood pressure, the hypertensive viewers were un-

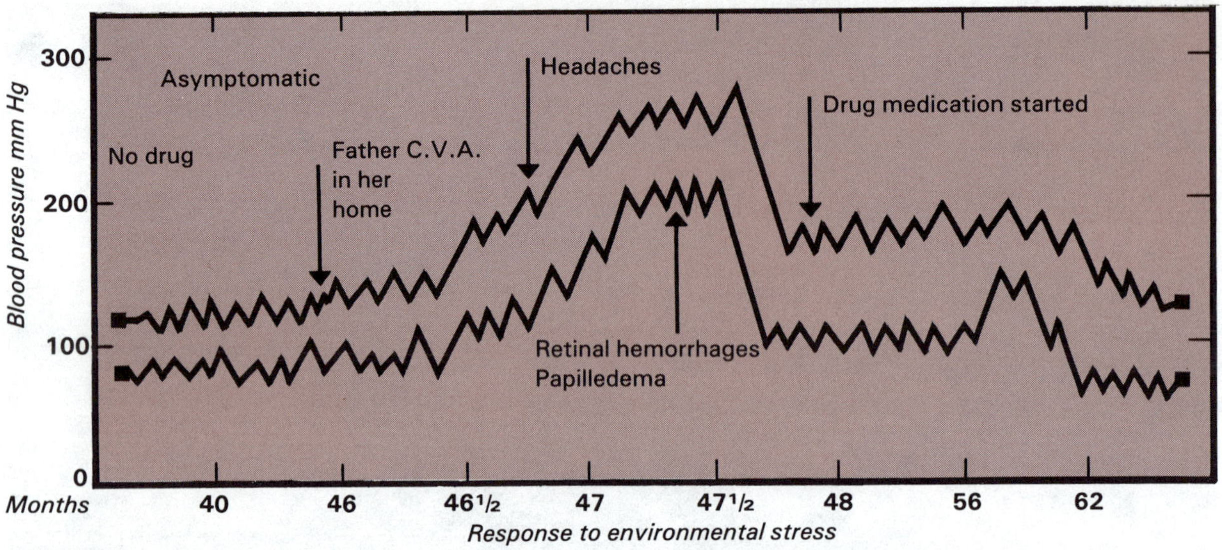


**FIGURE 9–3** Progress of essential hypertension during stress and medication. Patient shows severe recurrence after death of father to whom he was deeply attached.
SOURCE: Based on "Psychodynamic Factors in Hypertension" by L. Mills, 1962, in J. Nodine and J. Moyer (Eds.), *Psychosomatic Medicine,* Philadelphia: Lea & Febiger.

willing to make negative remarks about these behaviors. On the whole, however, findings have been inconclusive and often contradictory (Harrell, 1980), mainly because it is extremely difficult to find an accurate way of measuring suppressed anger. At best, only a cautious conclusion can be drawn—not that suppressed anger invariably underlies hypertension, but that hostility is a factor in hypertension in some individuals and not in others (McClelland, 1979).

***Psychophysiologic Vulnerability.*** A fourth factor in hypertension may be a physiological predisposition (Olson & Elliot, 1983). As in ulcers, this vulnerability may involve higher secretions of certain substances than normal; and that may then cause damage.

In the ulcer patient, as we saw earlier, persons considered to be predisposed were already higher producers of pepsinogen. In hypertensives, several substances associated with sympathetic nervous system overactivity have been examined, including norepinephrine and the enzyme renin, which affect blood vessels and blood pressure. One research study (Chobanian et al., 1978) subjected both hypertensive patients and a control group to a cold stress, by immersing their hands in ice water (about 5° C) for five minutes. The control subjects showed some increases in norepinephrine following this icy experience; but many of the hypertensives showed abnormally high increases. Also interesting was the fact the level of norepinephrine correlated significantly with the level of blood pressure.

### Treatment of Essential Hypertension

At the present, drug medication relies on tranquilizers and sympathetic nervous system inhibitors (Goodfriend, 1983). Corrective and preventive measures include the use of sedatives, weight reduction, and the avoidance of emotionally stressful situations. Unfortunately, a great many patients have waited too long before seeking treatment and the disease has progressed to an advanced state. If hospitalization is required, the patient is encouraged to engage in whatever is most relaxing, such as staying in bed or light recreational activity. In outpatient treatment, the capacity to release frustration and hostility through acceptable routes is necessary.

***Biofeedback.*** A more innovative treatment for hypertension is *biofeedback,* which involves training patients to control their own blood pressure (see Chapter 21). A typical training program uses an automatic device to read and display changes in blood pressure, either visually or through sound. The person is then instructed to find a way of lowering the blood pressure readings. Although results have been promising, a major problem has been the difficulty of reproducing the same results or of obtaining stable, large decreases (Andrasik & Blanchard, 1983).

***Behavior Therapy.*** Behavior therapy is also used to help patients learn to reduce anxiety. Such therapy is based on the assumption that stress and blood pressure are interconnected. In one instance, Bloom and Cantrell (1978) used Anxiety Management Training with a pregnant woman who wanted to avoid drugs that might affect the fetus. They reported success in reducing the woman's blood pressure, and the baby was born without complications. Although it is not an active method for stress management, relaxation training—through techniques such as meditation—can be useful as a means of preventing anxiety. Once again, some reductions in blood pressure have been achieved through this technique (Surwit et al., 1978).

Finally, Patel (1977) and her colleagues appear to have achieved the most consistent and impressive results with hypertension. She has developed a treatment package that combines relaxation, biofeedback, and stress management, achieving decreases in blood pressure by as much as 28 mm. Hg systolic and 16 mm. Hg diastolic.

## CORONARY ARTERY DISEASE

### Diagnosis of Heart Disease

Coronary artery or heart disease is a term used in medicine to describe several disorders: *coronary occlusion* (vascular blockage), *myocardial infarction* (heart failure), and *angina pectoris* (acute chest pains occurring after exercise or emotional stress). Although coronary

*Increased risk of heart disease has been associated with* ***Type A behaviors****. Among the Type A charcteristics are multiple activities and intense drive.*

disease is distinctively a medical illness, psychological factors have been noted, pointing to the fine line that exists between the two realms of influence. Because of an exciting series of studies, certain behavior patterns are recognized to be related to coronary artery disease. Friedman and Rosenman's research breakthrough (1959)—the well-known delineation of the Type A and Type B behavioral styles—is a fascinating example of diligent research into psychological factors that may relate to heart disease.

Drs. Meyer Friedman and Ray Rosenman are two cardiologists who saw many heart attack patients in their practices. The puzzle of why men were more likely to have heart attacks than women seemed unsolvable, until the president of the San Francisco Junior League volunteered the startling explanation, "What is giving our husbands heart attacks? . . . it's stress, the stress they receive in their work, that's what's doing it" (Friedman & Rosenman, 1974, p. 56). This insight prompted the two physicians to then recall another experience involving their waiting room chairs. The upholsterer fixing the seats pointedly

## Case History 9–4:
### Coronary Artery Disease

George S., a 45-year-old data-processing supervisor, is a typical case of heart disease. He is married, smokes an average of 26 cigarettes a day, and earns $42,000 annually. His occupation gives him little opportunity for exercise outside of work other than walking, although his company has made available a program of planned physical activity for its administrative employees during work hours. He drinks a manhattan or two each evening to unwind from the day's work, but then he continues to be occupied as he plans the next day's activities.

At work, he has the utmost respect from his employees and his superiors as a man who gets things done. He keeps intimately in touch with each and every job being processed and is always ready to take on new challenges. He prefers walking to directly meet with people to the delay of putting through a telephone call. Outside of work, he is part of a community volunteer committee surveying food prices and is also a member of the school board. His home is more like an extension of his office as he utilizes evening hours in order to accomplish more. And yet, the predominant tone of his activities is competency—although he seems pressed for time, he is efficient. He has taken on the task of writing an instructional book for data processing in industry, a task which has filled up the last remaining gap in his active schedule.

George recently underwent his annual physical under a new physician's care. Unlike previous cursory examinations, this one was quite extensive and included laboratory workups. He was found to be in good health, although a little overweight. However, the medical history taken by the physician revealed that he had had a brief period of discomfort several months earlier. This was characterized by an uncomfortable tightness in the chest as he climbed a flight of stairs after an unusually heavy luncheon. The chest sensation of pressure soon passed. The examining physician ordered an electrocardiogram, which was found to be abnormal: there was indisputable evidence of a heart attack. George was advised of his condition and placed on a preventive program. His dietary habits were modified; he was encouraged to enroll in the physical activity program at work; and he was cautioned about his behavioral pattern of life.

asked what types of patients they had, "because it's so peculiar that only the front edge of your chair seats are worn out" (p. 55). From such unusual beginnings, Friedman and Rosenman shifted their work to looking for psychological factors causing heart disease.

### Behavioral Patterns and Heart Disease

In their search, Friedman and Rosenman conducted several studies, which were carefully planned and executed to rule out any significant influences related to differences in exercise, calorie or fat intake, alcohol, cigarettes, age, height, or weight. Soon they identified two behavior pattern groups, *"Type A"* and *"Type B,"* and they showed how these patterns are relevant to heart disease. Table 9–3 outlines the characteristics of each group.

The researchers conducted several studies. In the early study of men (Friedman and Rosenman, 1959), Type A subjects were drawn from engineering, paper manufacturing, and aluminum corporations, newspaper organizations, advertising agencies, grocery chains, and independent businesses. Type B men came from two unions (municipal government and professional embalmers) and several accounting firms during relatively quiet business months. As Figure 9–3 shows, 28 percent of Type A men showed clear-cut signs of coronary disease, compared with only 4 percent of Type B men. It is interesting to note that only 4 of the 23 Type A subjects with evidence of the disorder had been even the slightest bit aware that they had a cardiac ailment, although the clinical signs were indisputable. ("Quiet heart attacks" can often occur and go unnoticed, as is illustrated in Case History 9–4.)

**TABLE 9-3**

**Type A and Type B Characteristics**

| *The Type A Personality* | *The Type B Personality* |
|---|---|
| 1. An intense, sustained drive to achieve self-selected but usually poorly defined goals. | 1. Lack of desire to compete. |
| 2. A competitiveness, aggressiveness, and hostility. | 2. Relative absence of drive for advancement and recognition. |
| 3. Persistent desire for recognition and advancement. | 3. Lack of involvement in deadlines. |
| 4. Continuous involvement in multiple and diverse activities. | 4. Lack of propensity to accelerate speech, mental, and physical activities. |
| 5. Impatience about time and the need to set deadlines. | 5. Placidity. |
| 6. Accelerating the rate of execution of many physical and mental functions. | |
| 7. Extraordinary mental and physical alertness. | |

SOURCE: Adapted from *Type A Behavior and Your Heart* by M. Friedman and R. Rosenman, 1974, New York: Alfred A. Knopf.

Rosenman and Friedman (1961) conducted a separate study of women, with similar findings. Here, 125 Type A women included attorneys, physicians, political executives, white-collar workers, unemployed women, and nuns from an ''admittedly forceful'' order of sisters. The 132 type B women consisted of housewives, white-collar workers, and placid nuns from a teaching order. Type A women showed four times the incidence of coronary artery disease as Type B women, as well as a higher cholesterol level and a faster blood-clotting time (see Figure 9–3). In addition, there was a significantly higher incidence of hypertension in Type A women (three to seven times higher).

The researchers conducted another study to explore possible differences in fat ingestion with cholesterol level (Friedman et al., 1964). In this study, they studied Type A and B men in pairs, with each fasting overnight for 13 hours, then eating the same breakfast. Vascular physiology was examined by means of photographs of the blood vessels of the eye, taken through a microscope. The results showed that the Type A and B men were alike in the free flow of blood prior to breakfast; however, four hours later, Type B men showed no change while Type A men showed significant vascular obstruction by ''clumsily transported, irregular masses that caused an intermittence and marked sluggishness of flow.'' It seems evident that Type A is related not only to the onset of coronary disease, but also that the faulty removal of cholesterol and fat, a condition that can be a preliminary to coronary disease.

One other, longer-term study is relevant here; it is known as the Western Collaborative Group Study (Rosenman et al., 1975). Over 3,000 men from 11 industries and scientists from three major cities across two states participated in this eight-year study of the development of coronary disease. In a period of two years, Type A men incurred coronary disease at a rate three times that for Type B, with the younger Type A men (ages 39–49) showing a rate over six times that for Type B men of the same age. This trend was maintained through the more than eight years of follow-up studies. In addition, the behavior pattern diagnostic method was compared with predictions based on purely medical examinations of factors such as cholesterol level. Of the two methods, the behavior pattern method was the more useful in predicting coronary disease.

The researchers also attempted to determine the characteristics which made an individual immune to coronary disease. They discovered that low cholesterol level was associated with high immunity. Type B behavior patterns were also good insurance against coronary disease; however, even the slightest tendency toward some of the Type A traits immediately increased an individual's vulnerability to the disease. The researchers were so impressed by this that they concluded that immunity was a function of low cholesterol and *fully developed* pattern B behaviors.

### Dynamics of the Type A Pattern

Since the early painstaking research of Friedman, Rosenman, and their colleagues, evidence has continued to build in support of the presence of Type A patterns both from laboratory and clinical studies[2]. The exact details that explain the link between the behavioral patterns and heart disease are not yet known, although many researchers are deeply involved in seeking answers (Matthews, 1982; The Review Panel, 1981).

A few leads are notable. Cohen and her associates (1979) suggest that culture may play a role. She confirmed that fewer Japanese-American males than white American males fit the Type A pattern, when the former have retained their Asian cultural values. However, the prevalence of heart disease increased for the Japanese who adopted Western Type A values and rejected their traditional customs.

Another approach, based on the observation that Type A patterns seem to include a motif of achievement, explores factors that might influence this achievement pattern. Matthews (1977) placed Type A boys and their mothers together to work on a series of achievement tasks, observing the parents' aspirations for their sons as they were reflected in the interaction. Although complex, the results seemed to support the idea that Type A mothers seemed more concerned about their children's achievement. In essence, then, a form of achievement training may provide the early setting for Type A behaviors.

Another view in explaining the maintenance of Type A behaviors relies on the concept of stress. Suinn (1976) has suggested that Type A behaviors are repeated as overlearned reactions to stress—patterns that the individual sees as ways of reducing tension. Basically, a vicious cycle is involved; Type A behaviors are strengthened because the high-drive behaviors prove successful in a Westernized environment, but some of these behaviors place the person in high-stress settings such as self-imposed deadlines. In response to the tension rising from the self-imposed stress, the Type A person relies on the overlearned behaviors which worked in the past—that is, more Type A behaviors.

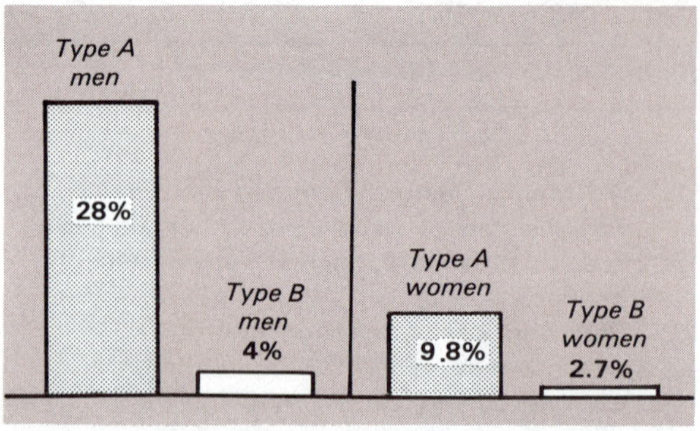


**FIGURE 9-4** Type A behavior and coronary disease: Percentages of coronary disease among men and women.

SOURCES: From "Association of Specific Overt Behavior Pattern with Blood and Cardiovascular Findings" by M. Friedman and R. Rosenman, 1959, *Journal of the American Medical Assn., 169,* p. 1286; and "Association of Specific Behavior Pattern in Women with Blood and Cardiovascular Findings" by R. Rosenman and M. Friedman, 1961, *Circulation, 24,* p. 1173.

Glass (1977) is more specific in his definition of the type of stress to which Type A persons respond. He interprets the behaviors as "a characteristic style of responding to environmental stressors that threaten an individual's sense of control." He has supported his views through a series of studies, placing persons in laboratory experiments with inescapable noise. After being faced with brief exposures to this uncontrollable stress, Type A persons put forth greater efforts to regain some control on later tasks, rather than giving up. It is important to note that stress research confirms links between stress and physiological reactions which could eventually lead to heart disease. For example, Friedman et al. (1958) sampled the cholesterol levels

2 See, for instance, Dembrowski et al., 1978; Gastorf, 1980; Glass, 1977; and VanEgeren, 1979.

of accountants from January to June. Results showed substantially higher levels in April—income tax time, and a period of high work stress for these accountants.

***The Role of Anger.*** In studies examining the individual characteristics of the Type A, time impatience and aggressive competitiveness surfaced as major correlates of heart disease (Matthews, 1982). Further analyses have focused on aggressivity as it involves anger and hostility. Several research findings now point to the association between anger and heart disease risk in Type A persons. Carver and Glass (1978) set up a study where subjects were led to believe that they controlled the delivery of shock to another subject (actually, a confederate). Type A persons were found to deliver more shocks than Type B persons, especially when frustrated. Williams (1982; Williams et al., 1980) discovered that scores on an anger/hostility scale were so predictive of heart disease and other serious illnesses, that he sometimes refers to the scale as a "death scale." In his work, Type A persons scored higher on this scale.

How does anger influence heart disease in a Type A person? Some insights into the complex process were obtained by Glass et al. (1980). Subway train drivers competed on a TV game against a trained confederate (who could not lose). Both Type A and B drivers showed similar increases in blood pressure and epinephrine during the game. However, when the confederate began to harass his opponent with derogatory remarks such as, "My sister can do better than you!" the Type A drivers showed substantially greater physiological reactions. What this suggests is that three interrelating factors may be involved in heart disease. First, being a Type A means that the individual is more susceptible, possibly because of the anger/hostility aspect. Next, the Type A characteristics may not make a difference unless certain situational conditions are present, such as harassment. Finally, the Type A person's reaction to the situational provocation may involve specific physiological reactions that increase risk of heart disease, such as increased blood pressure. Once again we see that environment, personality, and physical factors might all be necessary to explain the appearance of disorders.

### Treatment for Type A Persons

Despite the rather long history of study on the Type A personality, very little data have been collected on useful treatment programs (Suinn, 1982). Suinn and Bloom (1978) have used Anxiety Management Training as a therapy, helping a small group of Type A persons learn different patterns for managing stress. Their program has had some initial success. Roskies and her colleagues (1979) compared two different treatments: behavior therapy for stress and psychotherapy. Following up six months after the treatment was finished, they reported the behavioral treatment to be more helpful.

The success of stress management procedures is consistent with the belief that a key in Type A behaviors is the existence of stressors in life. Such stressors can also be controlled through procedures such as better time management to avoid too many tasks building up at once, delegating responsibilities to others, and learning how to gauge one's limitations (Suinn, 1980).

Rosenman and Friedman (1977) themselves suggest a variety of approaches for changing Type A behaviors. First, they recommend that cognitive restructuring might be important, for instance, to recognize that it is a false belief that one's past success in business has been due to Type A behaviors. Instead, Type A persons need to realize that success can be accomplished without being Type A; moreover, that getting rid of the unessential Type A qualities can even lead to being more efficient as one is less harassed. Type A persons need to recognize that the impulse to speed up every action and to worry about time does not help their careers, and, in fact, may harm their hearts and life span. Finally, these cardiologists suggest that group psychotherapy be considered as an adjunct for dealing with unconscious feelings of anxiety. In their estimation, Type A persons throw themselves into their work partly as a way of avoiding having to think about other personal problems.

As research on treatment progresses, more methods are being examined. Hart (1980) used Anxiety Management Training to help Type A persons control their anger. Lobitz and Brammell (1981) achieved some success by prescribing exercise. Levenkron et al. (personal communication, 1982) provided a broad behavior therapy program involving cognitive restructuring, desensitization, and goal-setting. Of special interest is the Recurrent Coronary Prevention Project (RCPP) (Friedman et al., 1981) which also used a broad behavior therapy program aimed at cognitive, autonomic, and behavior changes with a group of over 1,000 Type A patients. After three years, the RCPP not only achieved reductions in Type A characteristics, but also accomplished significant reduction in recurrence of heart disease among the treated patients. Interestingly enough, the role of anger was again noticed. Those patients who experienced repeated heart attacks also were higher in hostility than those patients without recurrent heart disease.

## TENSION HEADACHES

### Symptoms of Tension Headaches

The experience of a headache is a common one for everyone at some time or another. However, the experience of a *tension* or *muscular contraction headache* is one not easily forgotten. It is characterized by feelings of pressure; a dull, throbbing pain in the head; and tightness in the occipital section at the back of the skull. Sufferers have reported these headaches as lasting for weeks, sometimes as continuous nonstop pain, at other times as pain that starts on awakening and leaves only with sleep. In a study of over 1,000 cases, results point to women as more likely to be afflicted, with the first onset coming sometime after age 20 (Friedman et al., 1954). In some cases, the headache includes a tenderness to the scalp if pressed. Unlike migraines, which will be discussed next, there are no sensory experiences such as flashes of light which precede the headache. Nausea and vomiting are rare.

### Dynamics of Tension Headaches

At one time, it was believed that headaches with psychological origins were symbolic—that humans were paying for having pride in "using their heads" (Wolff, 1963). The modern view is that tension headaches trace to prolonged strains of the muscles of the neck, shoulders, and head. These strains may start two hours before the headache is finally precipitated. Individuals may differ in the exact muscle groups involved, with the forehead muscles often a prime area of tightness.

Just what stresses precipitate these tensions are not yet known. Nor do we understand why some persons show tension headaches rather than other symptoms, such as back pains, that could just as well result from prolonged muscle tensing. The author (Suinn & Vattano, 1980) did discover that a group of severe sufferers reported great variability in their sources of stress, ranging from fretting about the frantic quality of holiday homecoming, to more personal identity-career matters. These persons were a diverse group, representing all socioeconomic levels and a range of ages and vocations, from a young foreign student to a woman executive. It is interesting to note that the years of constant headache pain brought with them a sense of isolation: "When you complain daily about constant pain, pretty soon even your loving relatives fail to understand."

### Treatment of Tension Headaches

Beyond the use of medication as pain-killers and tranquilizers, behavior therapy has been extremely important. Since the headache seems to involve muscle tension, then relaxation training has been provided either through training exercises or biofeedback (Gray et al., 1980). Since the buildup of tension is cumulative, most patients are instructed in frequent and regular application of relaxation to block this process. A cognitive approach to stress control has also been offered (Bakal, 1982; Holroyd & Andrasik, 1978). Here, patients are taught to see the role of their thoughts and their headaches. Training involves directing the individual's attention to questions such as: What am I thinking of that makes me feel stressed? Does this really make sense to believe this? Remember to stay calm, examine the facts, avoid seeing life as a catastrophe. This approach shows some promise although the relaxation methods still seem to be prescribed more frequently.

## MIGRAINE HEADACHES

### Symptoms of Migraine Headaches

If tension headaches are notable for the agony of the days and weeks they can go on, *migraine headaches* are notorious for their severe and unusual symptoms such as those in Case History 9-5. Migraine attacks are often preceded by sensory experiences, known as an *aura,* that involve sudden flashes of light, extreme sensitivity to anything but complete darkness, blurred vision or depth perception, double vision, or tingling. Other bodily symptoms can include nausea, vomiting, vertigo, diarrhea, or mood changes. At the same time, there is a pounding, throbbing headache on one side or at the front of the head. Internally, it appears that the blood vessels have first constricted and then dilated.

Migraine is often found to have a family history, and it may show up early in life as associated with a history of car or motion sickness. On the whole, women seem to suffer more from migraines than men; although one report found no real differences between men and women (DeLozier & Gagnon, 1975). The migraine victim tends to experience between one and four attacks per month, with each attack lasting for as long as 24 hours (Adams et al., 1980).

***Dynamics of Migraine Headaches.*** The dilation or widening of cranial and cerebral blood vessels is generally accepted as being related to headache pain, while constriction is probably related to the preheadache phase of migraines. A number of biological and biochemical factors contribute to migraines; however, our interest centers on the psychological factors that can influence migraines. The experiencing of certain emotions and tensions—including anger, anxiety, frustration, criticism, increased responsibility, and even the stress of planning vacation—seems capable of precipitating migraine headaches (Harrison, 1975).

***Personality and Migraine.*** As might be expected, a number of studies have attempted to identify a "migraine personality"; the composite profile describes a "tense, driving, obsessional perfectionist, with an inflexible personality, who maintains a store of bottled-up resentments which can neither be expressed

## Case History 9–5:
### Migraine Headache

Mrs. Margaret W. has suffered from migraines nearly all her adult life. She can always tell when they are coming on, since she feels a little strange: "My eyes blur, I feel like I'm going into a hypnotic trance, the surroundings kind of get hazy." The migraine itself is an agonizing experience for her: "I feel sick to my stomach, like vomiting, but my head is so painful that I can't stay upright to even go to the bathroom. I shut off all the lights, curl up tightly in bed to try to stop the pain, and it's awful because I'm cold and warm and sick and my head feels like it wants to come off and I can't sleep to get rid of the pain."

Mrs. W. has a history of car sickness. She becomes nauseated if she isn't careful about how she rides in cars or planes. She cannot sit in the rear or in seats that face backwards. She cannot sit close to the smell of oil or gas. She cannot read while riding. She must keep her head rigidly upright and facing forward. Although the car sickness has improved, her migraines have not.

The migraines come at unpredictable times. Sometimes they appear before an important social event, preventing her from participating in something she had looked forward to. Sometimes they come during periods of inactivity, such as vacations. She has medication which can reduce her headaches if she takes it in time, but she does not always have it with her. Biofeedback training has just been started, and she reports: "I feel better in my life, more relaxed, but I can't tell about the headaches yet . . . it's too early, but I'm hoping."

nor resolved'' (Henryk-Gutt & Rees, 1973). Some support seems to have been found for this cluster, mainly through psychiatric interview material, although other studies argue that the data is still far from conclusive (Adams et al., 1980; Harrison, 1975).

Experts now suggest that future study be directed not simply at exploring whether or not such a personality cluster exists, but rather at identifying specific behavior reactions to specific conditions (Bakal, 1975). This approach would be similar to that reported in our earlier discussion of the possible relation of expectations of control and hypertension and loss of control in Type A persons. It may be, for example, that migraine-prone persons experience a blood vessel constriction when faced with certain environmental demands—for instance, having to work with precision under unpredictable conditions (Dalessio, 1972).

### Treatment of Migraines

For the migraine sufferer, relief is possible through medications: a commonly used drug is ergotamine. Unfortunately, medication only succeeds in controlling the pain and aborting the headache; therefore, the person is dependent for life on the medication. Also, there may be side effects to medications (Medina & Diamond, 1977). For this reason, other solutions are often sought.

***Psychotherapy.*** Psychotherapy is sometimes used to resolve attitudes or conflicts that may underlie some migraine conditions. This treatment is usually directed at resentment or hostility considered part of a ''migraine personality'' and at modifying driving perfectionistic needs. In one case report, rather dramatic decreases in the intensity of migraine attacks were achieved once the woman understood her resentments (Lambley, 1976). Patients are also led to reevaluate their belief that ''I simply must get this done now; the quicker I take care of it the better I'll feel.''

***Biofeedback.*** Another approach that is receiving more and more attention is temperature biofeedback training (Jessup, 1982). The principle behind this approach relates to the changes in blood flow that seem to be associated with migraines. Sargent et al. (1973) reasoned that increased blood flow to the fingers could produce relief because it brings decreased blood flow to the cranial regions. Since finger blood flow is reflected by increases in temperature, clients are taught to increase their finger temperature. This is actually very easily learned with thermal biofeedback equipment. The equipment uses a simple heat sensor taped to a finger which registers body temperature at that place. In a quiet setting, the patient is given instructions such as: ''Concentrate on increasing your temperature; when you're successful you'll see the temperature dials change.'' Through this type of method, Sargent was able to obtain improvement in about 81 percent of migraine patients. Since relaxing is another way of increasing peripheral temperature, other clinicians have taught migraine sufferers relaxation techniques with success (Blanchard et al., 1978). Because there have been some discrepancies in obtaining consistent results, current evaluations of biofeedback are optimistic but cautious: there is much promise, but not yet perfect results (Bild & Adams, 1980).

## CANCER

One illness, cancer, may not seem to belong in a text such as this; few of us would presume that cancer has anything to do with psychopathology. Certainly, one reason for its inclusion might be to review the known effects of cancer on a person's emotional state, and information is available on this interesting topic (Meyerowitz, 1980). Such information reflects the field called *somatopsychology*, the study of people's reactions to their illnesses or disabilities. For example, certain psychological stages such as depression are typically experienced by persons as they react to physical disability or chronic illness (Gordon et al., 1980; Suinn, 1967). Such reactions are generally expected and normal, if they are not exaggerated or prolonged. There are expected somatopsychological emotional reactions to a disease such as cancer, too; but it is the reverse process that is relevant to us. In the final few pages of this chapter, we will explore the ways in which psychological experiences may lead to or affect cancer.

***Biofeedback** methods may involve temperature feedback or muscle feedback using a sound or a visual display. Temperature feedback has been used successfully in treating migraine headaches.*

## Psychological Influences on Cancer

How does one go about examining the role of psychological factors in cancer? In some ways, the history of cancer studies is representative of the typical history of most psychophysiologic medical studies. Some speculative hypotheses have looked at purely psychological explanations, some have attempted to uncover a "cancer personality," and some analyses have focused on the possible interactions between stress, physiological responses, and disease (Jenkins, 1983).

***Psychological Theories.*** A simplistic search for purely psychological explanations can be seen in the idea that a person develops cancer as the worse of two evils. The proposition is that cancer and psychoses form two extremes of reactions to psychic problems, and the cancer victim is one whose "body has chosen" to express the problem through physical rather than psychological breakdown (Bahnson & Bahnson, 1964). No firm support has been found for this hypothesis; and there is certainly no reason to believe that mental disorder leads to a decrease in cancer (Fox, 1978).

***The "Cancer Personality."*** As we have seen in this chapter, research has at various times attempted to define certain personality types associated with physical illnesses. In the same way, some researchers have been drawn toward the search for a cluster of personality traits that might predict cancer-proneness (Dattore et al., 1980).

An interesting combination of findings offers some circumstantial evidence. Some have reported cancer patients to be nonaggressive (LeShan, 1966) or nonassertive (Abse et al., 1974), as well as yielding and compliant (Fox, 1978). These findings seem to form a pattern, when we consider other evidence that patients whose cancer progressed more slowly were judged as hostile persons (Stavraky et al., 1968). Could personality be involved in the ability to fight off the disease? We'll return to that point later.

***Early Experiences and Family Relationships.*** Another interesting connection is pointed out by LeShan (LeShan & Worthington, 1956), Kissen (1969), and Bahnson (1969). These researchers have each suggested that the early life history of cancer patients includes events that disrupt their ability to relate to others. These life events lead to a belief that forming meaningful relationships will only bring pain and despair; thus, the end product is an inability to express emotions and a more compliant approach to life. One set of reports by Thomas and her associates (1979) provides some credibility to a small portion of these ideas.

Originally studying hypertension and heart disease, Thomas collected personality information on all medical students who had graduated from Johns Hopkins from 1948 to 1964. Now aged 40–59, these physicians had been examined annually for hypertension, heart disease, mental disorder (including suicide), and cancer. Thomas found differences among persons with different diseases in their ability to relate to their parents. Those with cancer reported being distant from their fathers, while those with coronary disease were closest. Of special interest is the finding that this dimension separated those with malignant tumors from those with benign tumors or more minor cancer (such as skin cancer).

These findings are certainly far from conclusive. One issue is the fact that although these persons *perceived* their early relationships to be distant, this does not prove that this was true. However, this is one of the few studies available in which the initial personality information was collected long before the individuals developed cancer. A major problem of many studies is that patients who already have cancer are studied and extrapolations are made to their precancer life or characteristics—a very risky business, since we know that the very experience of suffering from cancer can well affect one's personality, adjustment, behaviors, and outlook on life (Cullen et al., 1976).

***Stress and the Breakdown of Immune Systems.*** Another focal point for psychological cancer research has been the possible role of stress. This approach has received some support. A number of animal studies have associated stress with increased risk of cancer (Sklar & Anisman, 1981). The same research line has been pursued in a study of human lung cancer patients (Horne & Picard, 1979). This survey found that 68 percent of these patients had recently experienced stress through loss of a job, or a death, as compared to 33 percent of nonpatients.

One of the most fascinating theories connects stress with disease via the body's immune system. It is known, for example, that certain parrots can coexist with a dormant virus for long periods without signs of illness. Once they are subjected to stress, as through crowded living conditions, however, these birds succumb to the virus (Meyer, 1942). This concept might be extended to humans: perhaps some forms of cancer exist in a dormant form in humans, but are suppressed unless there is a breakdown in the immune system (Glade et al., 1976). Some research supports the explanation that the presence of stress impairs immunity, perhaps by disrupting the physiological endocrine system (Becker, 1979). This is an application of Selye's analysis of stress discussed in Chapter 6, for it relates closely to his idea that body resistance is lowered in the stage of exhaustion, making a person much more vulnerable to disease.

The logical extension of this idea brings up another question: Does a person's ability to cope with stress affect the development of cancer? We mentioned earlier that one study found hostile cancer patients to have a slower progress in their cancer; other qualities have also been tentatively linked to resistance. One study (Achterberg et al., 1977) looked at patients who significantly outlived their predicted life expectancy, observing that they were nonconforming, flexible, self-sufficient, and unrelenting in the face of stress. Perhaps such qualities, represented in the persistent attitude of active coping, prevent cancer, either through preserving the body's immune system or through regulating the growth of cancerous cells. This idea has formed the basis for a controversial therapy, described in Focus 9-1.

In the final analysis, the studies linking psychological factors to cancer are intriguing. However, few would claim they have reached the level of scientific support to be conclusive. At present, they are excellent signposts, and they point the way for future research that may eventually make a major breakthrough in understanding this feared disease.

## EVALUATION

In some ways, the study of psychological factors affecting physical conditions is one of the oldest areas of research and speculation; yet it still provides one of the most exciting challenges. Even if we did discover an unvarying relationship—for instance, between one personality trait and one disease—many more questions would still cry for answers. Cancer is an example. Stress and cancer seem to be associated; but how? There are several possible answers. In one view, cancer is seen as a physical-symbolic expression of emotional conflict. According to a second theory, cancer is dormant, but does not emerge unless stress reduces our immunity to a cancer virus. A third answer is that the normal growth of cells is regulated by physiological-hormone balance, which is upset by stress and leads to uncontrollable, cancerous growth. And a fourth theory, while it sees cancer as caused by nonpsychological sources, argues that certain coping behaviors may provide controls that can slow down but not prevent cancer. Basically, the same type of questions will need exploring in all psychophysiologic

## FOCUS 9–1: Cancer

### Can an All-in-the-Mind Therapy Work?

According to one theory, cancer may be related to the breakdown of the body's natural immune system. This breakdown could in turn be related to a person's ability or inability to cope with stress.

At the Cancer Counseling and Research Center in Fort Worth, Texas, O. Carl Simonton, Stephanie Matthews-Simonton, and their colleagues carry this premise through into recommendations for treatment. These researchers have observed that patients who lived longer than expected before dying from cancer seemed to share certain characteristics. They were nonconforming, self-sufficient, and unwilling to give up (Achterberg et al., 1977). The Center therefore supplements the traditional medical therapies of radiation, chemotherapy, and surgery with psychological training.

Training at the Cancer Center aims at removing negative emotions and increasing a positive sense of being in control. It offers specific psychological techniques to fight the cancer and control the emotions. Relaxation exercises are used to reduce anxiety and any fears associated with having cancer. Individuals are instructed in the view that cancer patients' beliefs have been known to influence the course of cancer. The Simontons work with the patients to change their belief that the cancer is incurable or out of their personal control. They aid the patient in comprehending that negative emotions and beliefs can undermine the body's efforts towards recovery. Instead, they encourage patients to accept the more positive outlook that health and recovery are possible.

In addition to the instruction in relaxation and positive thinking, patients are taught to use imagery in self-treatment. They visualize their white blood cells vigorously and successfully attacking and consuming the cancerous cells. This technique gives the patients a renewed hope that help is possible; thus, it is consistent with the goal of continuing to cope rather than give in. Simonton and his coworkers have reported some remarkable and dramatic successes with patients who were originally considered to be incurable. Some of these cases have actually shown remissions; others have shown a slowing down of the disease rate; and still others have reported reductions in pain. Of 159 advanced cases who had been given one year to live, 96 eventually died, but after surviving for nearly two years. Of 63 patients who still lived, 19 percent showed a remission in their cancers and 22 percent showed no signs of pathology (Simonton et al., 1978).

Most scientists are still skeptical that psychological methods can have value in cancer treatment beyond helping the person to adjust to being ill. Holland, chief of psychiatry at Sloan-Kettering Institute, refers to the Simonton method as a "cruel hoax" (Scarf, 1980). Critics of the Simonton approach argue that false hopes are being raised, that patients are made to feel guilty for not possessing the right attitude, and that any gains are due to placebo effects—that is, they are due to the patients' expectations rather than any active ingredient in the therapy. In this regard, though, it is interesting to note that some researchers speculate that placebo effects on pain tolerance may have some physical basis, in that the placebo may precipitate the release of endorphins, natural pain killing substances in the body (see Chapter 10). Obviously, much work and cautious research is needed on the entire topic of psychological factors in cancer causation and cancer therapy. Until then, the mystery will continue.

studies, whether they be of cancer, hypertension, or asthma.

Some progress is apparent if we look at the promising directions of research. There is recognition that psychological factors can influence physical states, which in turn may relate to physical disease. The *diathesis-stress* concept seems useful; it is illustrated in the study of ulcers among army inductees, as well as studies of stress and cancer in animals. The specific form of stress and the specific behavioral reactions may be more important than the presence of a "hypertension personality," "migraine personality," or "coronary-prone personality." Current ideas suggest that such characteristics are often better understood in the context of what is happening to the person. Also, a modern view is that behavioral traits do not necessarily appear in all persons who are clustered together at all times. For some Type A persons, the anger aspect of Type A behaviors might be most predictive of heart disease, while the time-urgency, deadline-anxiety aspect may be more important for another Type A person (Jenkins et al., 1978). Finally, a highly promising direction is the approach which attempts to identify the nature of the stress which influences the disease process. For the coronary-prone individual, the stress may well relate to loss of mastery or control, while for migraines the stress may involve environmental demands for precision work.

Regarding treatment, the most hopeful progress in the use of psychological, rather than drug, treatments relates to the relaxation, biofeedback, and stress training programs. Such approaches have had some success in increasing air flow in asthma; in keeping blood pressure lowered in hypertension; in preventing migraine headaches; and in reducing the severity of tension headaches. Exciting vistas still lie ahead—so much so that a new field, *behavioral medicine,* has developed, combining professionals from medicine, psychology (especially behavior modification), nursing, social work, and other helping professions (Daitzman, 1983).

## SUMMARY

This chapter summarizes the physical conditions affected by psychological factors. Such psychological stresses can be found involved in peptic ulcers, asthma, tension headaches, migraine headaches, hypertension, coronary artery disease, and even cancer. In these disorders, there is basically an organic illness which is further influenced by psychological factors which play a primary role in the physical symptoms. Thus, psychological pressures can cause increased stomach acidity and ulcers in persons who are susceptible. Persons with internal locus of control orientations may become more reactive with higher blood pressure increases, where the stress is perceived as being external to their control. Asthma sufferers may be less able to adapt to medication regimes if they are high panic-fear responders. Increased emotionality may be a trigger in the onset of migraine headaches.

Thus far, there has not been firm support for the belief that a specific type of personality is subject to developing specific psychophysiologic disorders. However, among the psychological factors that have been explored have been stress, emotional responses such as anger, internal conflict over the inability to predict or control stressors, and lifestyle. Lifestyle seems particularly implicated in heart disease, among those whose lifestyles are called the Type A pattern. This pattern involves high drive, impatience and hostility, and tensions over time or mastery. The study of psychological factors in cancer has taken several directions, including the possible reduction of the body's immunity because of stress experiences.

Treatment for the psychophysiologic disorders aims first at the physical condition itself: diet restrictions for ulcers, epinephrine for asthma attacks, ergotamine for migraine headaches. Additionally, surprising success has been achieved through behavior therapies which aim at control of the physical symptoms rather than any underlying conflicts—symptoms such as the amount of air flowing to the lungs for the asthmatic, the level of blood pressure for the hypertensive, or the degree of muscle tension for the person with tension headache.

Traditional psychotherapies continue to be used, with some value, to deal with conflicts presumed to be the source of certain physical symptoms. For example, psychotherapy is used to cope with anger or resentment that may be related to some asthma or migraine conditions.

## KEY TERMS

**Anxiety management training**
**Approach-avoidance conflict**
**Aura**
**Biofeedback**
**Coronary artery disease**
**Diathesis-stress theory**
**Essential hypertension**
**Homeostasis**
**Humanistic-existential therapy**
**Locus of control**
**Migraine headache**
**Pepsinogen**
**Peptic ulcer**
**Psychophysiologic disorders**
**Somatopsychology**
**Tension headache**

# CHAPTER 10

## Somatoform Disorders: When the Mind Worries about the Body

- **A common statement is, "It's all in your mind!" How seriously can our mind affect our body's health?**
- **Multiple physical complaints, such as headaches, nausea, and stomach pains, can appear in a variety of mental disorders. How are these disorders distinguished from one another?**
- **A controversy has developed over Briquet's syndrome and conversion disorder. What is this controversy and how is its resolution important for science?**
- **What is the origin of the disorder that causes some persons to become unable to see yet not be blind or unable to walk but not be paralyzed?**
- **How does *management* versus *treatment* of a patient differ?**
- **Some of the somatoform patients worry a lot about their physical health, while others seem indifferent to the presence of disabling illness. Which types of mental disorders are characterized by concern? Which by lack of concern?**
- **What steps do our bodies go through for us to experience pain?**
- **Without hypnosis, is it possible for a patient experiencing pain to behave as though the pain were nonexistent?**
- **Is a person who for health reasons exercises routinely, takes vitamins daily, is careful about diet, and has medical and dental examinations annually a hypochondriac?**

**TABLE 10–1**

**Somatoform Disorders**

| *Type* | *Major Characteristics* |
|---|---|
| Conversion disorder | Medical symptoms that inexactly mimic true disease states, where the patient ordinarily seems indifferent to the symptoms. |
| Hypochondriasis | Preoccupation with and exaggerated concern about health; these patients seem to be fearful that they have a disease, while the somatization patients know the disease exists and are seeking treatment. |
| Psychogenic pain disorder | Reports and concerns over pain not traceable to physical cause. |
| Somatization disorder | Recurring complaints about multiple physical symptoms, such as headaches, back pain, and fainting. |

# Case History 10–1:
## Conversion Disorder

Sam B., a college student, was involved in a minor traffic accident on his way home from classes. Although he was slightly bruised, medical examination showed no serious physical involvement, and the patient was discharged from the hospital. "I woke up the next morning and couldn't feel my legs, they were numb. . . . I supposed they had gone to sleep on me, but then I tried to move them, and my legs wouldn't move. . . . I couldn't walk anymore." Sam was returned by ambulance to the hospital for extensive neurological and X-ray examinations with negative results. Throughout, he seemed bemused by the procedures, intrigued by the machinery, and taken by the nurses. The diagnosis: conversion disorder.

When Sam was interviewed by a psychologist, the following facts came to light. Just prior to the accident, he had another of many arguments with his family over his education. He wanted to get a job in order to make some money. His parents, both from immigrant backgrounds, had forced him to continue his schooling in spite of constant bickering. He was on an allowance on the condition that he remain in school. Money had always been a problem, since the patient tended to squander it on social activities, girl friends, and his motorbike:

> I was on my bike going home and thinking about the exams coming up the next day. I had the bad luck of having three exams on the same day, and it's tough getting up for them all, you know how it is with teachers, they give you a bundle of stuff to read at the last moment. . . . Anyway, I had to really ace the finals because things hadn't gone so good on the quizzes I took . . . the way grades were determined, if I didn't get three As on these three finals, I could wind up with two Fs and one D.
>
> So I guess I was distracted going home, I knew there was no way I could cram, I tried that before and look at what it got me. My big worry was the draft, I could be called up if I lost my student deferment. . . . They already took some of my friends.

The accident itself came as a surprise since Sam had always been reasonably cautious on his motorbike. Yet, he had been driving in a carefree and even reckless fashion when the accident occurred. When he was first released from the hospital, he felt "kinda lucky that I wasn't killed, but kinda sorry I wasn't scraped up more than I was." The impression was that a disabling injury would have been painful but useful.

The *somatoform disorders* are those disorders in which physical symptoms are prominent, but there is no evidence of organic causation so that psychological factors are considered important (see Table 10–1). Unlike the psychophysiologic reactions discussed in Chapter 9, the physical complaints of the somatoform patients cannot be confirmed by medical laboratory procedures, although the complaint persists. Thus, a somatoform patient may complain of various pains or may show a disability such as blindness, but careful medical and laboratory examination fails to find any physical cause. Yet, as is illustrated in the cases in Focus 10–1, the strength of these psychological factors on the body may be no less than remarkable.

Somatoform patients are convinced their illness is medical; hence, they spend a great deal of time in physicians' offices or hospitals seeking medical solutions. As medical examinations fail to provide sensible organic explanations, however, the patients are referred for psychological or psychiatric examination—and this usually leads them to feel misunderstood and mistreated. The major types of somatoform disorders include:

- Conversion disorder
- Somatization disorder
- Psychogenic pain disorder
- Hypochondriasis

Each of these will be discussed in the following sections.

## CONVERSION DISORDER

In the *conversion disorder,* there is a loss or disability of some physical functioning. There may be a loss of sensations or of sight; a dysfunction of coordination or speech; or loss of use of a limb or other part of the body, as happened to Sam in Case History 10–1. Among the mental disorders, the conversion disorder is known as "the great imitator" because the disabilities are often similar to those of organic illnesses.

### Symptoms of Conversion Disorder

The physical symptoms of conversion disorder are as diverse as the different varieties of real physical illnesses. Major symptoms can be grouped according to the type of disability or dysfunction they represent. The first group, *sensory disabilities,* may include *anaesthesias* (the diminution of sensation); *paresthesias* (the disturbance of sensation, as in "tingling" or "pins-and-needles" sensations); and *perceptual impairments* (such as blindness, blurred vision, and deafness). A second group of dysfunctions, *motor disabilities,* may include *epilepsy* (seizures and convulsions); *astasia-abasia* (inability to stand and walk, although movements are possible when sitting or lying); and *aphonia* (the loss of voice leading to whispering). A third group of conversion disorders are *visceral disturbances,* such as vomiting, diarrhea or constipation, hiccoughing, and *pseudocyesis* (false pregnancy).

Of course, other symptoms and entire disease patterns may be duplicated by the patient suffering from the conversion disorder. There may be a *hypersensitivity* to light or sound, so that even normal amounts produce painful reactions. *Hemiplegia* may show, that is, the paralysis of an entire side of the body; or the symptoms of a heart attack might occur.

***Differentiating Organic and Conversion Disorders.*** The similarities between conversion disorder and organic illnesses often make it difficult to tell whether an illness has a true physical base, or whether it is entirely *functional* (that is, due to psychological factors). To complicate matters, *somatic compliance* may be involved—an already weak organ or part of the body may become the focal point for the conversion symptoms—so that a physician may find some physical disturbance, but not enough to warrant the complaint. There are certain signs, however, that may help the psychologist or psychiatrist to distinguish conversion-based symptoms from organically caused ones.

*The Lack of Conclusive Medical Evidence.* Frequently, the pattern of symptoms is based on the patient's limited knowledge of anatomical, neurological, or physical conditions. Thus, the conversion epileptic does not become completely unconscious and resists having his or her eyes opened. The classic glove and stocking anesthesias were once common examples of anatomical errors exhibited by patients with conversion disorder in their symptoms (see Figure 10–1). These anesthesias affected only the areas that such gar-

## FOCUS 10–1:
### Mind-Body Mysteries

*Date: 1223*

Francis of Assisi was a gentle person who loved nature, possessed a passionate desire to serve others, and was blessed with humility. During prayer one day, Francis heard Christ speaking to him; this formed the ultimate inspiration for his founding of the Franciscan Order.

Within a year after the rules of his order were formally approved by Pope Honorarius III, Francis of Assisi was afflicted with a strange malady: his hands, feet, and sides developed bloody wounds. These intensely painful wounds are known as *stigmata* and are believed to represent the nail and spear wounds suffered by Christ on the cross (although some writings depict the crucifixion as using ropes instead of nails) (Kaufmann, 1976). In writing about the stigmata, Smart (1976) observes: "In mystical experience physical events (such as controlled breathing) . . . are a prelude to, and a preparation for, physical occurrences. In the case of stigmata, intense meditation on the crucifixion of Christ has been the prelude to the occurrence of a physical reproduction of Christ's wounds." Francis is said to have suffered from these stigmata until his death two years later.

*Date: 1954*

A male patient suffering from advanced cancer of the lymph nodes is seen for chemotherapy. The drug krebiozen is used, and in only one treatment, the cancer disappears. The drug is new, but there is optimism that it may be powerful enough to cure cancer. However, it is later revealed that the drug has been shown to be ineffective. Shortly after the patient hears this sad news, his cancer reappears.

Fortunately, the patient's physician is a concerned doctor and reassures the patient that the report was untrue. Furthermore, the doctor tells his patient that a double-strength dosage of krebiozen will be even more effective and administers this through an injection. The cancer again disappears, even though the double-strength krebiozen was really only water. Once again, however, the patient discovers that both the Federal Drug Administration and the American Medical Association declare krebiozen to be ineffective. This time the patient is unsalvageable: within a few days, he dies. (Klopfer, 1954)

*Date: 1977*

Mrs. W. is taken into surgery for removal of her thyroid. She has been trained in autohypnosis, with a particular emphasis on learning anesthesia to produce insensibility of the neck. The surgery proceeds for 70 minutes, and although no drug anesthesia is ever administered, Mrs. W. experiences no pain. In fact she reports, "I could feel only pressure and tugging at my throat. The scalpel felt like a feather being drawn across my neck" (Kroger, 1977, p. 219). Immediately after surgery, she was able to sit up without discomfort, to talk, and to eat and drink. Although she spent five days in the hospital, she was never confined to bed, but amazed the hospital personnel with her recovery.

*Date: 1978*

In a review of modern and historical practices of voodoo, Haskins (1978) cites the case of a 22-year-old woman from Baltimore. This woman frantically rushed into the emergency room of a hospital seeking help. Her story was that she was born on Friday the 13th, near the Okefenokee Swamp, and had been delivered by a midwife. This midwife was actually a practitioner of voodoo and cursed every child born on this unlucky day. The midwife had promised that none of three children would live: the first would not live to be 16 (she died in a car accident at age 15), the second was not to see 21 (she was shot in a night club on the eve of her 21st birthday), and the third—the woman in question—would never live to 23. Although dubious, the hospital staff admitted the woman for observation. She was found the next morning by a nurse—dead. Medical records show that the cause of death was listed as unknown.

How does one properly comprehend these various examples of life experiences? Clearly, there are events which seem to show the close interrelationship of mind and body. We know that our mental condition can affect our physical state with respect to our feelings and emotions. But how does one understand the appearance of stigmata, or the appearance and disappearance of a cancer, or a seeming invulnerability to pain, or death? Both blindness and anesthesia have been known to occur in conversion disorders. In turn, it is possible to create "blindness" and anesthesia in a normally functioning person through hypnosis. Is it possible that the spiritual state of meditation of Francis of Assisi, the belief of the cancer patient when reading about krebiozen, and the voodoo expectation of death are all cases of autohypnosis similar to that achieved by Mrs. W.? But even were this the case, do we advance scientific understanding any further when we also have to admit that not much is known about why hypnosis works? It may be more fruitful to avoid relying upon hypnosis as a *causative* explanation and to keep cases of hypnosis as simply another example of the fact that mental processes can have profound and dramatic influences on bodily states.

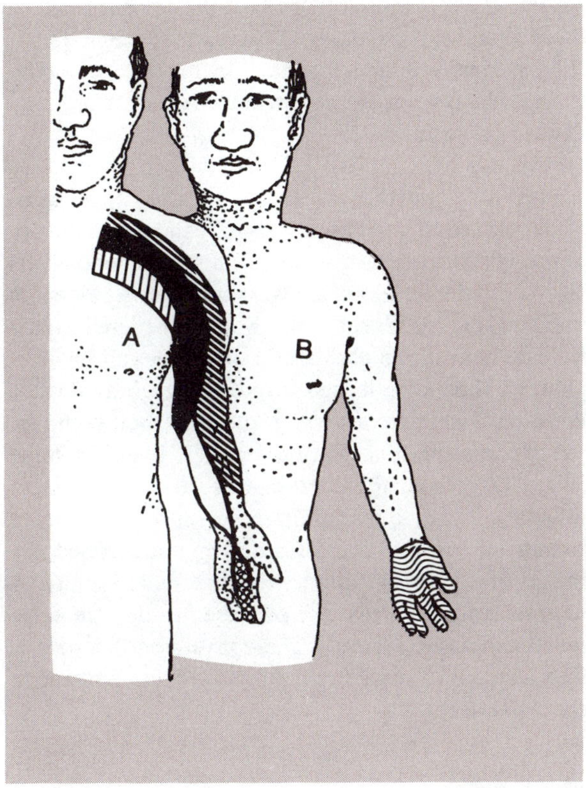


**FIGURE 10–1** A person with a conversion symptom of "glove anesthesia" **(B)**, fails to realize that nerves serve differing sections of the hand and arm **(A)**.

ments would normally cover, the patients forgetting or not knowing that the nerves of the human body do not innervate simply the fashionably covered portions of the body. More difficult to diagnose are cases where the individual is well informed about anatomy or neurology.

*Survival Reflexes.* In some instances, survival reflexes are maintained. For example, conversion patients with convulsions will not fall in dangerous surroundings; nor will they bite their tongues during seizures. Although one would expect the patient to be particularly in danger because of this disability, the patient with a conversion disorder does not tend to be injured. In fact, as will be seen under the discussion of the dynamics, the conversion disorder is a self-protective mechanism.

*La Belle Indifference.* Occasionally, the patient with a conversion disorder has been noted for being peculiarly blasé or unconcerned by the physical disability, no matter how serious it may be. This lack of appropriate emotion has been labeled *la belle indifference*. It is one of the features that sometimes distinguishes the conversion disorder from the hypochondriac, discussed later in this chapter. Also, the person with the conversion disorder *has* a disability, while the hypochondriac *worries* about having a disability.

It is possible, however, for a patient with a conversion disorder to become quite involved in the disability rather than show complacency. Unlike the traditional conversion patient, this individual will actually seek medical (nonpsychiatric) treatment. The more typical conversion patient, however, tolerates medical diagnostic procedures and gives the impression of submitting to examination because others think it necessary.

*Disappearance of Symptoms When Unconscious.* The symptoms frequently disappear when the patient is asleep or under hypnosis. It is as if the involved portion of the body is released from its chore of representing the basic conflict. A paraplegic man, for example, was first suspected of suffering from this condition when his wife reported, "I felt great pity for him, waited on him because he was paralyzed, then last night he tossed and turned and used his arms and legs in his dreams." On the other hand, it is quite difficult to trick these persons out of their symptoms when they are conscious. Moreover, the symptoms are real and not faked. A person with anesthesia does, in fact, possess a diminished ability to respond to pain or pressure sensations. A pain in the neck or in the back is often accompanied by muscle rigidity. Patients with conversion disorders will agree to surgery if informed that such intervention is needed. No malingerer would submit to such treatment.

### Dynamics of Conversion Disorder

Historically, the conversion disorder was called *hysteria,* a condition that was at one time believed to be caused by a wandering uterus. Conversion disorders have since been explained in many other ways.

***Psychoanalytic Explanations.*** Freud presented the belief that the conversion symptoms involved emotionally charged conflicts or traumas that were repressed, then converted (thus, the term *conversion*) into physical symptoms that served as outlets. The conflicts were said to involve genital-sexual wishes that had remained unresolved (Jones, 1980). Freud's patient Dora (Freud, 1905), for instance, who developed coughing attacks, was perceived as unconsciously trying to identify with Mrs. K. who had a cough. This identification served to satisfy Dora's wish to be the wife of Mr. K. Many psychoanalysts accept this broad viewpoint today, attempting to understand the symbolism involved in conversion symptoms. Thus, cases that involve simulated pregnancy are interpreted as wish fulfillment and perhaps a carryover from the Oedipal conflict.

Symbolic expression of conflict does appear to lend some understanding of conversion symptoms. Conversion blindness may result from intense guilt feelings over a visual act ("If thy eye sins, pluck it out"); an inability to speak may be punishment for cursing; a paralyzed hand can never be used again in a hostile or criminal act. In some situations, the conversion symptoms present an enactment of the traumatic event, as in the soldier whose paralysis continued from the battlefield: "I was petrified with all the shells falling, and the noise, it was like I was rooted to the spot . . . and then it struck me, I really was rooted, because I couldn't move my legs at all."

*Self-protection.* The conversion disorder is basically a self-protective mechanism. In its most straightforward form, the symptoms help to remove tensions and agony. The front-line platoon leader who becomes blind is freed from the sight of his men being brutally torn into shreds by shrapnel. The young immigrant mother becomes deaf and is spared from hearing the pathetic cries of hunger and pain from her infant. The frightened youth loses his ability to stand and walk and is able to postpone plans for the wedding which he is not ready for. The tense student develops intestinal pain and a distended stomach just prior to final examinations which will determine the difference between promotion or dismissal from school. The long-suffering spouse exhibits an ache in the neck as the only means for safely paying tribute to a nagging mate who has been a constant "pain-in-the-neck." In all of these situations, the patient is protected from a dreadful experience or mental conflict by the onset of a condition which permits a momentary release from psychological pain.

*Conflicts.* Ambivalence, or the approach-avoidance conflict, is often a significant part of the dynamics of conversion disorders. This aspect of conversion symptom development was particularly evident in incidents during World War I. Soldiers ordered to participate in crude, nightmarish, over-the-wall bayonet charges often experienced severe approach-avoidance conflicts wishing to achieve respect for their courage, yet at the same time fearing for their lives. In some cases, of course, the conflict was of the avoidance-avoidance type—a fear of death versus a fear of being branded a coward. Conversion symptoms provided a means of psychologically leaving the field in safety. A man who does not advance because his legs are paralyzed cannot be blamed. The conversion disorder is thus a means of resolving conflicts without damage to the self-esteem.

## Treatment of Conversion Disorder

Therapists have noted some tendency for patients with a conversion disorder to be suggestible and dependent. For these reasons, it is often possible to rid patients of their current symptoms by persuasion or by suggestive methods of treatment by an authority or expert. So-called miracle cures or faith-healing—dramatic recoveries when patients undergo experiences in which they believe —can be explained in this way. Unfortunately, such cures are not permanent. A new and more severe symptom can soon develop to replace the symptoms now given up. Of course, this new ailment can in turn be chased away by suggestion, but again at the risk of establishing a new and more serious illness. Such a transfer of symptoms is appropriately called symptom chasing.

Individuals with a conversion disorder respond differently to treatment, and behaviorist Joseph Wolpe (1958) offers a distinction that may well be the most relevant way of determining the appropriate therapy. In his theorizing, he defines two conversion types:

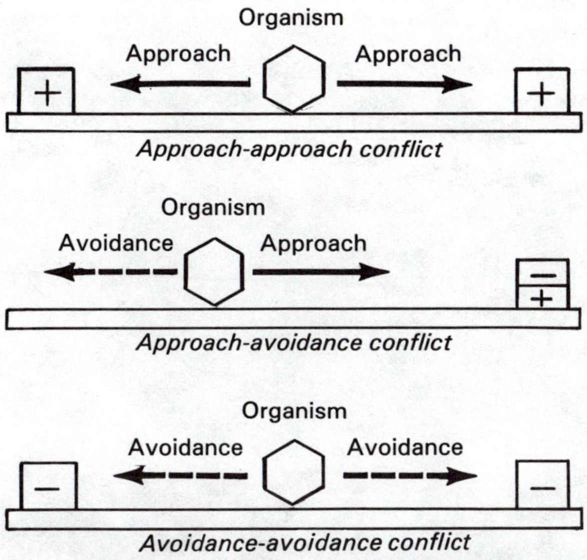


**FIGURE 10–2** Types of conflict situations schematically represented. In approach-approach, the person is pulled by two equally desirable choices; in approach-avoidance, the person is both attracted and repelled; in avoidance-avoidance, both choices are equally distasteful.

those with high anxiety and those with very low anxiety. The low-anxiety patients responded well to psychoanalytic treatments, such as *abreaction* (talking out problems) or hypnosis; the high-anxiety patients were best treated by behavior therapy.

***Free Association and Abreaction.*** Breuer and Freud (1895) based their treatment of conversion disorder on the premise that hidden or repressed conflict is the source of this disorder. They first used abreaction, then free association (a technique devised by Freud,[1] as discussed in Case History 3–1) as techniques for recovering and then releasing repressed anxiety. Psychoanalytic treatment continues to be oriented toward removing the core trauma or conflict that has been converted into the physical symptoms. Prognosis has been generally considered favorable, provided that the patient's somatic symptoms are not wrenched away before he or she can develop more suitable adjustment skills. Hypnotic techniques may also be used to gain access to the traumatic past.

***Behavior Therapy.*** The use of behaviorist techniques for treating conversion symptoms is becoming more widespread. For example, Malmo et al. (1952) paired electric shock with a tone to successfully treat a 19-year-old girl with hysterical deafness. Brady and Lind (1961) used operant conditioning to restore sight to a conversion patient two years after the onset of blindness. The therapists relied on monetary reward for reinforcement as well as the more personal effects of social approval. The task required the patient to press a small lever. A light was turned on at irregular intervals and the patient was rewarded whenever he pressed the lever following the presentation of the light. He soon learned to respond to the light stimulus, first as a vague visual sensation and later as a distinct visual image.

While both psychoanalytic treatments and behavior therapy have had successes with conversion disorders, it is somewhat puzzling to find that such diverse therapies should show similar effects. Psychoanalysis is based on the belief that the conversion symptoms are due to deeply ingrained conflicts which must be recognized by the person before recovery can occur. Behavior therapy, in contrast, treats the symptoms, generally ignoring the psychoanalytic explanations. We will continue to see this phenomenon in other disorders, and the best advice seems to be to rely on the treatment approach that appears to have the best record of recoveries. In the case of conversion disorder, although both approaches appear to have equal successes, it may be that Wolpe's distinction (1958) regarding high and low anxiety will prove the most useful.

## SOMATIZATION DISORDER

A second type of somatoform disorder, called the *somatization disorder*, or *Briquet's syndrome*, has been the topic of some controversy among experts. Some suggest that it is synonymous with conversion disorder

1 Freud used free association while Breuer relied on hypnosis. It is said that this choice was made because Freud found himself to be an unsuccessful hypnotist and had, therefore, found an alternative treatment method.

and that its separate classification only adds confusion. Others argue that it is different enough to deserve separate attention. This controversy represents a basic issue of contention in classifying pathologies, as is discussed in Focus 10–2.

### Symptoms of Somatization Disorder

Briquet's syndrome is listed as a distinct somatoform disorder within the DSM-III classification system. It is diagnosed from the following information:

1. The client has a history of repeated medical complaints, often dramatic or complicated.
2. The complaints are *polysymptomatic*. That is, there are a variety of symptoms, such as headaches, back pain, fainting spells, weight or eating problems, and breathing difficulties.
3. The symptoms are severe enough to have led to medication or visits to a physician or to have interfered with the patient's life in a significant way.

The multiple symptoms of Briquet's syndrome help to distinguish it from conversion disorders. These complaints span differing anatomical-physiological systems, without any logical connections. Thus, the patient may have complaints involving the urinary system, the respiratory system, the cardiovascular system, the sensory system, as well as appetite complaints, depression, nervousness, or fatigue.

It is believed that the somatization disorder is essentially an illness of young adults, primarily women. Symptoms typically interfere with the patient's life prior to age 35, with the peak complaints occurring in the 20s, followed by a gradual decline (Guze et al., 1972). One writer describes the signs of Briquet's syndrome by saying that this is a patient "who has multiple (often vague) complaints, who bears the badge of doctor shopping (a paper bag containing a potpourri of pills), who appears to cling to ill health no matter how expert the treatment or who, with one symptom successfully treated, triumphantly returns with two more" (Morrison, 1978, p. 483).

This description seems especially apt when one reviews the common complaints heard, "I have headaches . . . am fatigued and tired all the time . . . have palpitations . . . faint a lot . . . am nauseated . . . vomit . . . have abdominal pains . . . trouble with my bowels . . . am allergic . . . have menstrual problems. . . ." Anxiety and depression may appear, including suicidal thoughts. Because of the persistent appointments for medical treatment, the somatization patient may have acquired many drug prescriptions and become addicted, thereby further compounding the patient's problems.

***Psychoanalysis** was one of the earliest psychological treatments used by Freud with conversion disorder patients. The couch was a means for encouraging free associations.*

***A Diagnostic Checklist.*** In the past few decades, diagnosis of somatization disorder has become easier, as standard patient interview procedures have been improved. A checklist was developed in the

## FOCUS 10–2:

### Classifying Disorders: Where Do You Draw the Line?

Should Briquet's syndrome, or somatization disorder, be considered as a separate disorder, or should it be classified as synonymous with conversion disorder? This question highlights a recurring problem in the classification of psychopathology: how or where does one draw the line between similar disorders?

According to one school of thought, there is no reason to classify Briquet's syndrome separately from conversion disorder. Dr. Ian Munro (1977), editor of the medical journal *Lancet,* wrote a critical editorial against the separate classification of somatization disorder on the grounds we know too little about its causation. According to this perspective, disorders belong in the same classification if they share common characteristics, such as causation. A new category should be created only if different causes are found for these disorders.

The opposite point of view states that disorders should be classified on the basis of their diagnoses—instead of waiting for research to discover causation. This argument cites the Washington University checklist-screening procedure (see Table 10–2) which provides a means for consistently identifying Briquet's syndrome. Since we can isolate a homogeneous population of patients, why shouldn't we give this disorder a separate diagnosis? In this view, then, the discovery of causation is perhaps the *last* step in differentiating disorders (Guze, 1967).

Which point of view is right? Actually, both, as can be seen in an analogy. Suppose you wanted to study why students fail in college. One way of doing this would be to start from a hypothesis: you might theorize that poor study habits or high test anxiety are the causes of failure. To test this theory of causation, you could study both students with poor study skills and those with high anxiety. If your research supported your hypothesis, you would then have isolated two academic failure disorders: a study skills deficit disorder and a test anxiety disorder. This separate classification would be useful in that it points toward separate types of treatment.

Alternatively, you might decide to study student failures from just the opposite approach. Instead of beginning with a set of preconceived assumptions, you could simply analyze what you find as you systematically observe diagnostic characteristics of students who are failing. This tactic would provide you with a wealth of data from which you could extrapolate certain shared characteristics common to failing students. For instance, they might have in common the fact that they were all from towns with populations less than 8,000, and all had only one science and one reading class in high school. From this, we might hypothesize that failure in college was associated with poor preparation in high school. This second approach may yield quite different results from the first (although not always)—but it is equally valid as a scientific method. In fact, this type of approach is actually used in *epidemiology,* a branch of medicine that attempts to identify unknown causes of epidemics by looking for commonalities.

At this stage, the DSM-III classification of Briquet's syndrome as a separate disorder is more justified by the second approach than the first. As we shall see in more detail, persons suffering from Briquet's syndrome do apparently share many characteristics that distinguish them from persons with other disorders. Although we do not as yet know whether Briquet's syndrome has a common etiology or a common treatment, we at least know that it has certain common symptoms.

1960s and early 1970s by medical diagnosticians at Washington University (Woodruff et al., 1971). This enabled the identification of Briquet's syndrome based on surveying the patients' breadth of complaints. The checklist involves 10 special symptom groups; and Briquet's syndrome is suspected if the patient in question admits to a history of 25 symptoms from nine of the groups. In a refinement of this checklist in 1977, the Washington University clinicians have proposed a briefer screening interview, covering about 14 physical symptoms in a special sequence. A sample from this sequenced checklist is shown in Table 10–2.

**TABLE 10–2**

**Sample Interview Questions Used for Somatization Disorder**

"Did you ever have a problem with vomiting?"
"Did you ever have difficulty walking?"
"Did you ever have back pain?"
"Have you ever had difficulty with your breathing?"
"Do you remember a time when you lost your appetite?"
"Have you ever lost your voice so that you could not speak above a whisper for at least half an hour?"

SOURCE: From "Evaluation of a Screening Interview for Briquet's Syndrome (Hysteria) by the Study of Medically Ill Women" by M. Reveley, R. Woodruff, L. Robins, M. Taibleson, T. Reich & S. Helzer, 1977, *Archives of General Psychiatry, 34,* pp. 145–149. © 1977, American Med. Assn.

***Comparisons with Other Patients.*** Briquet's syndrome patients have been compared with other patients and found to show a greater concern over somatic complaints and higher self-ratings on socially desirable virtues than conversion disorder patients (Slavney & McHugh, 1978). In addition, when compared with patients having organically diagnosed physical illnesses, those with Briquet's syndrome were found much more likely to admit to every one of the 14 physical symptoms, except in the area of sexual indifference. It has also been interesting to note that Briquet's syndrome patients with depression seem to respond very differently to electroconvulsive shock therapy (EST) than other patients suffering from depression. Nursing records have shown that EST diminished neither the number nor intensity of complaints of Briquet's patients. In one case, in fact, the treatment led to the development of a new symptom, unexplained blackout spells (Bigg & Guze, 1972).

Briquet's syndrome shares some similarity to hypochondriasis (discussed later in this chapter) and Münchausen's syndrome (discussed in Chapter 11). Although the hypochondriac also seems to "cling to ill health," this type of patient differs from Briquet's in being more focused on worries about being ill, while Briquet's patients are more concerned with doing something about their illness. The hypochondriac is essentially fearful and seeking a diagnosis, the Briquet's patient seems to accept being ill and is seeking a treatment.

### Dynamics of Somatization Disorder

Very little information is available on either the dynamics or the treatment of Briquet's syndrome. Until the work on the diagnostic checklist, Briquet's syndrome was considered another name for conversion disorder and hence not studied. As diagnosticians have now seen that differences do exist, studies will no doubt begin to provide information on differences in etiology and treatment. Some hypotheses are beginning to be examined. Kaminsky and Slavney (1976) suggest that the most important fact is that somatization patients *complain* of many more symptoms. They feel that these complaints are simply ways of expressing a more general complaint of being unloved and misunderstood. The individual suffering from Briquet's syndrome is a chronically unhappy person, who seeks attention through expressions of dissatisfactions to others, including physicians.

Additional speculations about the dynamics of somatization disorder include the belief that the entire interpersonal environment is under stress. Marital and family relations are considered strained, perhaps due to the person's negativism and frequent drug and alcohol-abuse problems common to Briquet's syndrome. These self-defeating behaviors apparently have received some gains, partly because they enable the person to display the subjective dissatisfactions and also to achieve some sympathy. Suicide threats and attempts are common, although very few attempts are successful. Once again, it seems that the person suffering from somatization disorder is pronouncing an intense unhappiness with life. With such conditions contributing to the development and maintenance of somatization disorder, successful treatment becomes a complex issue.

### Treating Somatization Disorder

Effective treatment techniques for somatization disorder have not yet been discovered. However, Morrison (1978) suggests certain procedures that can help in the *management* of the somatization patient. Among his commonsense recommendations are that the care of such patients be limited to only one professional to prevent "doctor shopping"; that the professional avoid "fruitless confrontation with the patient as to whether symptoms are real or imaginary" (p. 485); and that a great deal of patience be adopted since the course will be long and exhausting. He also advises withdrawing the various medications that may be in the patient's possession, not by terminating all of them, but by limiting them to the ones that are really needed.

In all of these recommendations, a main direction is the gradual shift of emphasis from relieving, diagnosing, or curing the physical symptoms, to an attitude that the symptoms may not improve, but are likely to continue to bother the patient. Further, Morrison suggests that the patient may need to learn to ignore the

> symptoms about which she can do nothing [and] . . . focus attention on factors she can change: the way she deals with her alcoholic husband, the rearing of her hyperactive children or her own drinking problem. By degrees she will learn to seek attention for talking, and recognize that she does not need somatic symptoms as a ticket of admission to the doctor's office. (p. 486)

Morrison uses a learning theory analysis that suggests that the previous attentiveness of family members or physicians have reinforced the somatic complaints of the patient. Hence, both the therapist and the family need to more systematically encourage the development of self-control. He also assumes that reducing stress and conflict will lead to the reduction of symptomatic complaining behaviors.

## PSYCHOGENIC PAIN

A third somatoform disorder, *psychogenic pain,* involves the subjective experience of pain that cannot be explained by organic causation, nor can it be attributed to another mental disorder.

Pain normally serves as a type of danger detection system, an alarm that goes off to signal damage, or threat of damage, to tissues. Thus, pain might signal a wound, the presence of an infection, a reaction to toxicity, or the threat of a burn that would destroy skin tissue. In a psychogenic pain disorder, the alarm seems to go off without actual threat or danger or with only minimal cause. It is as though a warning is being cried out in anticipation of a nonexistent danger.

### Symptoms of Psychogenic Pain

Psychogenic pain can be described in a variety of ways. It may be localized in different places for different patients: the lower part of the back, the joints, and the abdomen are frequent centers of pain. It may be reported as intermittent or as constantly present. It may feel either sharp or dull and throbbing. It may also be either vague and diffuse or pinpointed in a particular locale. The pain may mimic a known medical ailment, such as the chest pains associated with a heart attack, or it may resemble no known medical disease. Pain itself is not measurable directly; hence, the diagnostician must rely on the patient to provide information to evaluate the pain.

Ultimately, in psychogenic pain, the evaluation centers not so much on pain but on the person who has been termed the "pain patient." The pain patient "says he hurts. He describes the pain experience. He grimaces, holds a painful body part, asks for analgesics or stops an activity to rest because of his pain" (Fordyce et al., 1973, p. 399). Sternbach (1974) further describes the pain patient as follows:

> His pain is insistent enough, but now he notices all the other bodily feelings that previously went unnoticed; the

> twinges, itches, tinglings, and aches. Noticing and paying attention to them magnifies them, and soon they are more frequent and more noticeable, and soon the patient begins to answer more doctors' questions affirmatively, and then even volunteers the information about these sensations as new symptoms which bother him. . . . As time goes on, and the patient feels more wretched and desperate, he begins to cast about for some magical cure. He hears about cases similar to his who were treated successfully, or he reads something about a new clinic or treatment technique, and soon he is seeking out a hypnotist, an acupuncturist, or an evangelical preacher. Their treatments may help for a while, but then the pain returns, and the patient returns to his doctor asking for stronger analgesics or surgical relief. (p. 10)

***Comparison with Other Somatoform Diagnoses.*** Psychogenic pain shares some features with other somatoform disorders, but one characteristic that differentiates this disorder is its clear focus on pain. Somatization patients complain about a variety of symptoms and ill health, but the pain related to these symptoms rarely dominates the picture. Conversion patients tend to report disabilities or dysfunctions that attempt to replicate a specific medical syndrome; but once again, pain reporting tends not to be a part of the overall pattern. Instead of reporting, "I can't walk because I hurt when I try to move," the conversion patient is more likely to say, "I can't walk because my legs won't move." Finally, in hypochondriasis, the patient is more worried about the illness than about the pain or severity of suffering. Whereas the minor twinges or tinglings initially go unnoticed by the pain patient (but may become magnified as part of the overall wretched condition), these minor symptoms capture the attention of the hypochondriac at the very start, forming the core of the worries and concerns.

## Dynamics of Psychogenic Pain

Why do some people suffer extreme pain from sources that do not trouble others? The question is a fascinating one, and several explanations have been suggested. Some of these center on psychological causation; others suggest that physiology may play at least some role; still others focus on interpersonal needs. A model of pain responses provides a good overview for understanding how these factors may be involved.

***A Model of Pain Responses.*** A useful analysis of pain has been offered by Fordyce (1979) in a model that has four stages: nociperception, perception, suffering, and pain behavior (see Figure 10–3). *Nociperception* describes the reaction of pain receptors at the tissue level when stimulated by a threat such as a hot flame to the fingertips (Urban, 1982). The second stage, *perception,* involves the interpretation of this tissue response by the brain—that is, the registering of the sensations. The third stage, *suffering,* involves the emotional reaction to the pain perception, that is, the subjective experience of suffering. Finally, the suffering precipitates certain *pain behaviors,* such as a groan of pain and hand withdrawal.

According to Fordyce's model, pain patients may differ from others in either the perception stage or in the pain behavior stage. In the first case, they may perceive milder stimulation as more painful; that is, the perception of the tissue response may be exaggerated. In the second, these patients may show more pain behaviors, such as grimaces, groans, or complaints of hurting, than other persons.

What factors could contribute to either heightened perception of pain or increased pain behaviors? There seem to be three types of factors at play: physiological makeup, psychological forces, and social or interpersonal factors.

***Physiological Dynamics of Heightened Pain.*** Although psychogenic pain is recognized to be primarily psychological in origin, two physiological theories may be helpful in understanding at least some of the reasons why people respond so differently to pain. The first of these explanations is known as the gate-control theory and the second as a biochemical theory about the role of endorphins. In the model of pain response just described, physiological differences would cause or influence responses at the second level perception.

*The Gate-control Theory.* According to the gate-control theory, there is a mechanism in the spinal cord that acts as a gate, controlling the neural transmission from the periphery of the skin to the spinal cord (Melzack, 1973). The theory further proposes that cer-

## Case History 10–2:
### A Case of Chronic Pain

The following case is from the files of Dr. Wilbert Fordyce, a scientist who has done considerable work with pain patients.

> Mrs. Y is a 37-year-old white female high school graduate with a teenage son. Her husband is a school administrator. Since 1948, approximately one year after marriage, she has had virtually constant low-back pain, and has been decreasingly able to carry out normal homemaking activities. At time of admission to the hospital, she complained of a continuous pain which increased with any activity. She reported her maximum continuous period without an interval of reclining rest as approximately 20 minutes. Her husband reported that she was active in the home an average of less than two hours daily. The remainder of her time was spent reclining—either reading, watching television, or sleeping. During Mrs. Y's 18-year history of back pain, she had undergone four major surgical procedures, including removal of a herniated disc and a lumbosacral spine fusion. At the time of admission, Mrs. Y was taking four or five habit-forming analgesic tablets por day when she experienced pain.
>
> Medication was placed on a time rather than a pain contingency regime, utilizing a color- and taste-masking vehicle. The time interval initially was within her observed tolerance but was gradually extended. She was allowed to rest in occupational therapy only after the completion of a progressively increasing production schedule; a walking program was instituted, a diary of daily activities begun, and her husband attended weekly training sessions. She was seen daily for 10–15 minutes by a psychologist to construct graphs from her records in order to document and to reinforce daily progress.
>
> At the end of seven weeks' hospitalization (on the behavior modification program), Mrs. Y was walking just under a mile in both morning and afternoon sessions. . . . She had reached a walking speed approximately twice that of normal. By the thirteenth day of admission, Mrs. Y was working voluntarily during the full period of available occupational therapy time, slightly under two hours daily. Forty days after admission, the narcotic content of Mrs. Y's medication was deleted completely. . . . The family has acquired a second car and she has become independently mobile in the community. (Fordyce et al., 1968, pp. 183–85)

tain large-diameter nerve fibers on the periphery close the gate, thereby decreasing the perception of pain, while other fibers open the gate, thereby increasing pain.

There is some experimental evidence for this concept. The application of a mild electrical current to the skin will temporarily reduce pain in chronic pain sufferers and raise the pain threshold for normal persons (Satran & Goldstein, 1973). Acupuncture may also be explained by this model. In obstetrics, having a husband press his fist over the sacrum of his wife during a delivery contraction is said to alleviate pain, equivalent to 50–100 mg. of Demerol, a common pain killer (Pace, 1977). If you exert pressure with a round object on the palm of your hand, this could act to "close the gate" and reduce the sensations of a pin prick inside this circle. Even though these experimental data support the gate-control theory, other research has failed to demonstrate support. Hence, the theory remains a theory that has promoted much interest but is not fully accepted.

*Endorphins and Pain.* A second physiological explanation of pain tolerance relates to a modern biochemical discovery discussed earlier in Focus 4–2. As we saw there, a group of substances called endorphins have been found at the base of the brain, in the pituitary gland. Interestingly, these naturally produced chemicals seem to affect the transmission and moderation of brain activity and signals. Although it is not exactly clear how they work, they are believed to play an important role in our reactions to pain, perhaps as a natu-

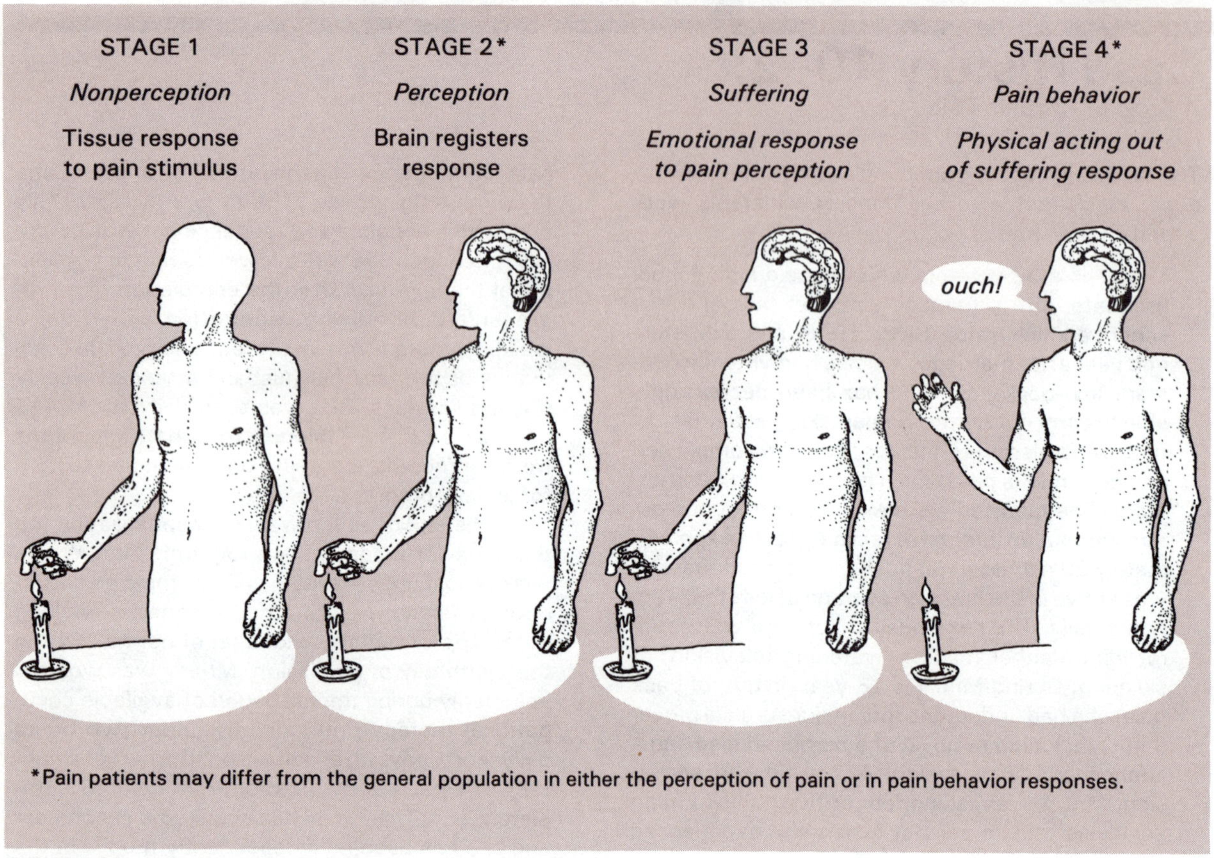


**FIGURE 10–3** Stages of pain response.

ral narcotic or pain killer. (The name "endorphin" literally means morphine within.) It is now hypothesized that persons with deficiencies in endorphin production might be more sensitive to pain than other persons and therefore react more to the same pain stimulus. As we will later see in Chapter 13, endorphins have also been thought to be involved in drug abuse. Once again, the hypothesis is that deficient endorphin production prompts greater sensitivity to pain—a condition that may lead some individuals to seek narcotics (such as morphine itself) as a pain killer.

***Psychological Factors in Heightened Pain.*** Another explanation for the differences in pain perception relates more directly to psychological factors. Such factors are involved in both the perception stage and the behavior stage of pain.

A variety of explanations focus on different psychological factors. One theory is that pain is sought out by individuals who have excessive guilt reactions, with pain serving as punishment to relieve the guilt (Engel, 1959). Research suggests that there may be characteristic differences between those patients who are more sensitive to pain and those who have a higher pain threshold. We'll look at some of these factors, as well as the relationship between stress and pain.

*Personality and Pain Response.* One study of personality and pain response looked at women with advanced cancer (Bond & Pearson, 1969). It identified two groups: those with pain and those without pain.

EKM-Nepenthe/Robert V. Eckert, Jr.

EKM-Nepenthe/John Maher

## *How can you tell if someone is normal?*

EKM-Nepenthe/Robert V. Eckert, Jr.

EKM-Nepenthe/Jill Cannefax

EKM-Nepenthe/Robert V. Eckert, Jr.

EKM-Nepenthe/Rick Grosse

EKM-Nepenthe/M. Button

***To what degree is behavior controlled by our society?***

***Is abnormality characterized by irrationality?***

EKM-Nepenthe/Robert V. Eckert, Jr.

EKM-Nepenthe/Gary Bloomfield

EKM-Nepenthe/LeJeune

EKM-Nepenthe/Tim Jewett

EKM-Nepenthe

EKM-Nepenthe/Tim Jewett

EKM-Nepenthe/Robert V. Eckert, Jr.

*The Dutch painter, Vincent Van Gogh, suffered from extreme shifts in mood, ranging from profound depression to heightened enthusiasm. It has been conjectured that his paintings mirrored his mental deterioration. How might the shift in feeling and style of these self-portraits reflect changes in the artist's mental state?*

Stedelijk Museum–Amsterdam / Art Reference Bureau

Courtauld Institute Galleries/Art Reference Bureau

Bulloz/Art Reference Bureau

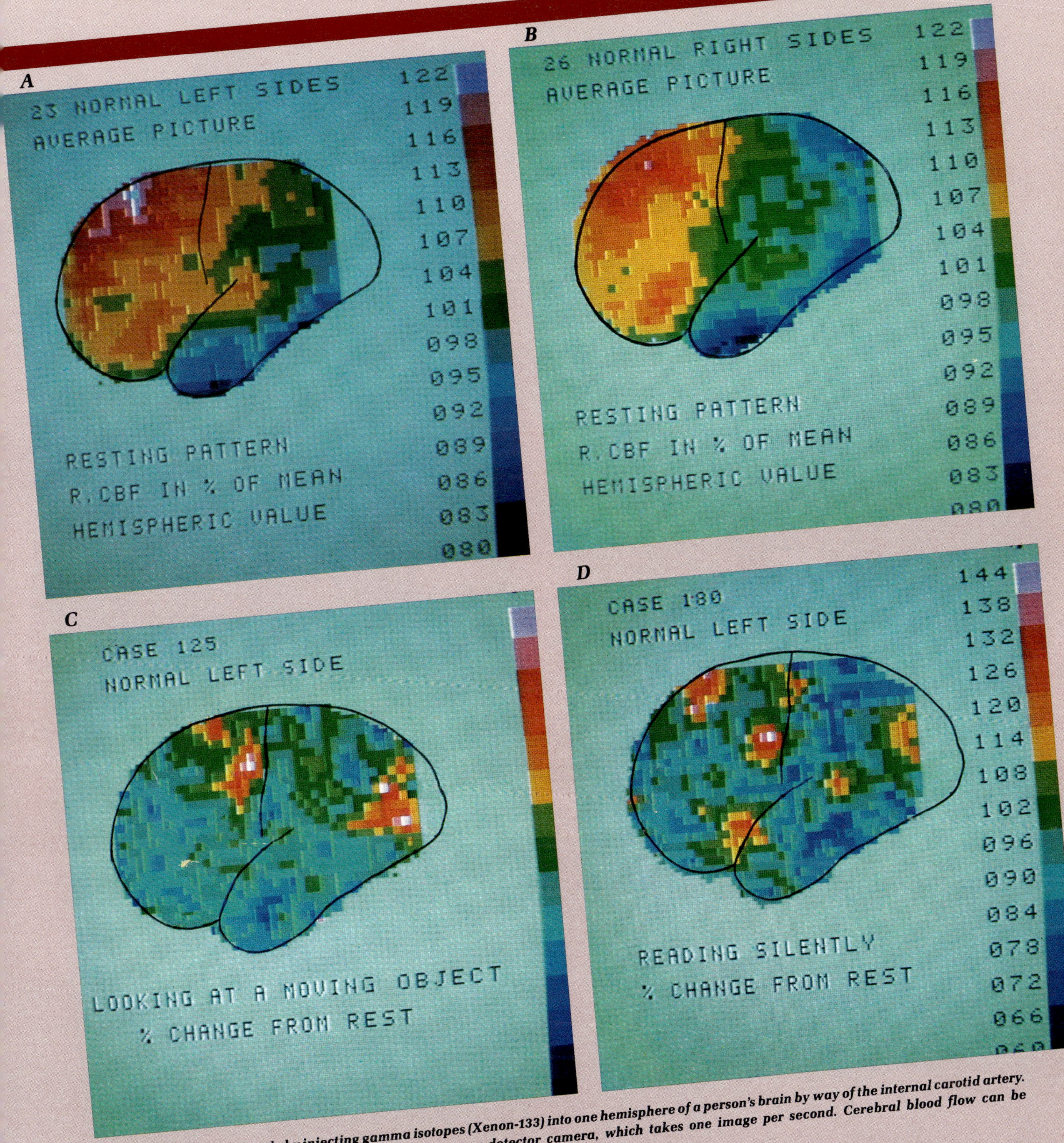


*These images were made by injecting gamma isotopes (Xenon-133) into one hemisphere of a person's brain by way of the internal carotid artery. The brain is observed with an ultrarapid 254 gamma-detector camera, which takes one image per second. Cerebral blood flow can be calculated visually in all 254 brain regions simultaneously.*

*Images A and B show blood flow for the left and right side when the subject is at rest.*

*Image C shows blood flow when the subject is looking at a moving object. Cerebral blood flow is augmented in the visual association area (right posterior), in the frontal eye field (central sulcus), and just above and a little anterior to the frontal eye field in the premotor cortex, which includes the supplementary motor area involved when one moves one's eyes.*

*Image D shows blood flow activity when the subject reads silently. Activity in the same three areas is seen, but in addition, augmented blood flow is apparent in the lower part, below and anterior to the frontal eye field. This is Broca's area of language, activated because the visual message is now linguistic. A very small area in the temporal lobe, called Wernickes language area, also shows increased blood flow. This area is between the frontal eye field and the visual area.*

*credit: N. A. Lassen, MD, Bispebjerg Hospital, Copenhagen, Denmark.*

EKM-Nepenthe/Robert V. Eckert, Jr.

EKM-Nepenthe/Robert V. Eckert, Jr.

EKM-Nepenthe/Robert Ginn

***Are there types of parents or types of family interaction patterns that seem to be associated with the development of a child's disorders?***

***Can you inherit mental disorders?***

EKM-Nepenthe/Robert V. Eckert, Jr.

EKM-Nepenthe/John Maher

EKM-Nepenthe/Tim Jewett

***How might your neighborhood environment affect your mental health?***

EKM-Nepenthe/Robert V. Eckert, Jr.

EKM-Nepenthe/Rick Grosse

EKM-Nepenthe/Robert V. Eckert, Jr.

***Can a retarded person hope to make it in a normal environment?***

EKM-Nepenthe/Tim Jewett

EKM-Nepenthe/Robert V. Eckert, Jr.

***We all have ups and downs in our moods. What causes these highs and lows?***

EKM-Nepenthe/Robert V. Eckert, Jr.

***"My grandparent is getting on in years, and I think I'm seeing signs of depression. What should I look for?"***

EKM-Nepenthe/Robert V. Eckert, Jr.

EKM-Nepenthe/Robert V. Eckert, Jr.

EKM-Nepenthe/Robert V. Eckert, Jr.

EKM-Nepenthe/Robert V. Eckert, Jr.

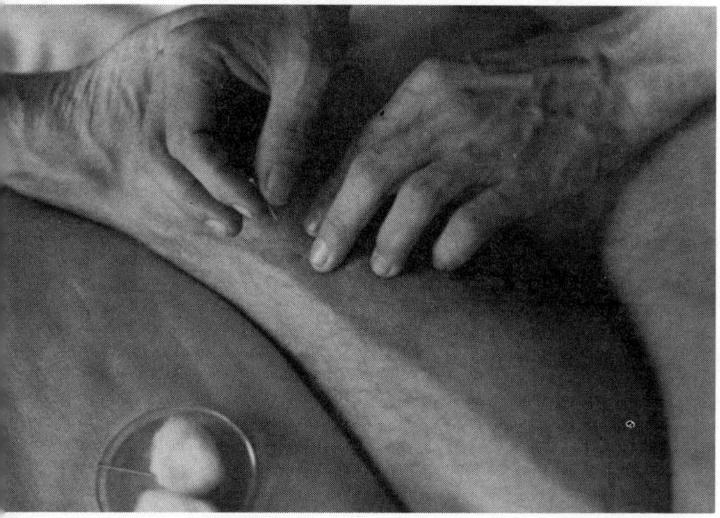

***Acupuncture*** *eliminates pain apparently by stimulating neural gateways.*

They discovered that those with pain showed higher neuroticism scores on a personality test. These cancer patients with pain were in turn subdivided into those who required pain medication versus those who managed without analgesics. The finding showed that those who required medication scored higher on extraversion. These scientists conclude that the neuroticism scores are an index of sensitivity to pain (Fordyce's *perception* stage) while the extraversion score may reflect a willingness to communicate pain or to complain (the *pain behavior* stage).

*General Stress and Pain Response.* It is also possible that sensitivity to pain may be influenced by the general level of stress a person is experiencing. Cases of low-back pain, back spasms, or neck pain have all been reported associated with emotional tension (Stein & Fruchter, 1983; Trief & Yuan, 1983). There is also evidence that the person who feels life to be hopeless, meaningless, or dreary, whose work is unrewarding or boring, and who lives a life of isolation or alienation from others, may be more likely to become a pain patient. Pain seems to become a substitute for the negative emotion of depression, thus transforming an emotional condition into a physical one (Timmermans & Sternbach, 1974).

***Pain Behavior as a Learned Response.*** In examining pain behavior itself, other possible dynamics of psychogenic pain become evident. In one sense, pain behavior might be considered as responses that a person might exhibit if they lead to some gain. For instance, a dependent person may discover that complaining about pain leads to being cared for; this encourages further pain behaviors—that is, further complaints about hurting.

Perceiving psychogenic pain in this way, we can see that the pain behavior acts as a signal which causes other people to respond. The nurse administers to the pain-signaling patient; the parent nurtures the pain-signaling child; the spouse consoles the pain-signaling mate; the employer gives special consideration to the pain-signaling employee. In a case of psychogenic pain, the pain-signaling soon occurs even without pain perception. The gain need not be sympathy or being cared for; in some cases the gain is the gratification of some other need.

In explaining this concept, Szasz (1968) suggests that pain has general communication features, communicating a cry for help for example, but also acting as an attack or retribution or complaint or resentment. Expanding on this idea, Szasz further proposed that pain patients might eventually adopt behavioral patterns towards physicians which he termed *painsmanship*. This view of pain sees a cycle of response and reinforcement, in which the patient is always one step ahead of the doctor. The conception of pain as a learned response provides a clue to one possible approach to treatment: behavior therapy. As we saw in this section, however, the disorder involves other dynamics besides learning. We'll look at other treatments, in addition to behavior therapy, in the following discussion.

### Treatment of Psychogenic Pain

The treatment of pain can aim either at removing the need for pain or at reducing the need for pain behaviors. If the need for pain is based on guilt feelings, depression, or alienation, or if it is a method for the patient to communicate resentment or retribution, then psychotherapy aims at resolving such problems (Pinsky, 1978). If stress is a major factor, then the patient is helped to develop self-control over the emotional tensions and pain experiences (Merskey, 1980; Thompson, 1982). Caution is always used to avoid counterproductive confrontations. That is, the therapist avoids asking whether the pain is real or imaginary.

***The Family's Role in Therapy.*** In some cases where the patient is a child, the role of the parents may be crucial in creating not only the need for pain, but in having the pain centered in the child. There is some evidence in cases of youths who have psychogenic pain that their parents have assigned them the role of being sick, leading these children to perceive themselves as frail, vulnerable, weak, or special and needing extra care and protection. Often, this attribution is a mechanism the parents are using to avoid their own marital or emotional problems—in order to focus instead on the child. In such cases, therapy is aimed at carefully enlisting the parents to work together to encourage gains in their child's health by showing how they can help the child develop a sense of mastery to replace the vulnerability in the self-concept. The parents' own problems may be expected to flare up and threaten a return of the child's illness, but family therapy can prevent this relapse (Liebman et al., 1976).

***Behavioral Treatments for Pain.*** Where the pain behavior is a learned response, a program based on behavioral principles can modify such behaviors (Sanders, 1982; Swanson et al., 1979; Wernick et al., 1981). The behavior modification programs used by Fordyce et al. (1973) are of special interest here. These programs centered on pain behaviors rather than perceptions of pain. They defined three pain behaviors: asking for medication for pain relief, emitting complaints that lead to attention or help from others, and avoidance of exercise or physical activity "because of pain." The subjects who participated in these programs included many patients from the University of Washington's treatment facilities; they had long-standing back pain (as long as 18 years) that had led to many hospitalizations and surgical operations.

The principles underlying the behavioral treatment are interesting. Regarding medication, the observation was that a patient hurts, complains about the pain, and is rewarded by medicine which reduces the pain, which then strengthens the complaining behavior further. To stop this cycle, medication was made *noncontingent* rather than complaint-contingent. That is, the patient was now given medication at fixed-time intervals whether the need was expressed or not.

A second underlying principle recognized that patients who complained about pain were usually rewarded with rest. To counteract this pattern, the program provided rest as a reward for activity, rather than for pain behavior. A baseline was first established to determine how much exercise or occupational therapy the person could tolerate. The client was then given a quota of such activities well under the tolerance limits, with rest and attentiveness from staff acting as reinforcers for success. Since pain behaviors also are rewarded by the attention of professional staff, by offers of help, or by expressions of sympathy or concern, all staff were instructed to be as socially nonresponsive to pain behaviors as seemed appropriate.

Within about seven weeks of the new program, these patients who had experienced literally years of incapacitation for pain showed remarkable improvements. Gains were shown in a significant decrease in the medication taken; an increase in activities undertaken; and a reduction of times patients stopped activities because of pain or fatigue. In a follow-up after discharge, many patients reported that their level of pain continued to be reduced, so that it no longer interfered with their lives as substantially as it might have previously. Behavioral treatment of psychogenic pain promises to make psychogenic pain one of the most treatable of the somatoform disorders.

## HYPOCHONDRIASIS

A fourth somatoform disorder, *hypochondriasis,* is a condition characterized by a preoccupation and exaggerated concern with physical health. An example is an electrical engineer who used up his sick leave rapidly with many visits to different physicians for such concerns:

I'd get up in the morning and notice how bloodshot my eyes were and how coated my tongue was becoming . . . plus I have not felt all that well for years. I used to feel vigorous, but now I feel fatigued. . . . I take my temperature and plot it daily. I also eat cautiously. . . . I do my job even though it sometimes costs me physically; I pay for it later when I feel run down, or I notice my breathing isn't right, or my stomach doesn't digest the foods easily any more. . . .

It's amazing how much you can learn from scientific magazines or articles on science, like even the newspaper. . . . There's new drugs, new diets, exercise programs, breathing programs for better health, special things you can send for. . . . I try to keep up with the latest, since my health really is fragile. . . . No, I don't jog or run and I'm careful about exercising, my system can't be taxed too heavily, otherwise I discover that my heart might skip beats or my lungs don't carry enough oxygen to my brain.

## Symptoms of Hypochondriasis

The preceding quote illustrates the most notable symptom of hypochondriasis: a preoccupation with the body and its functions. This preoccupation typically usurps all other interests. As in both Case History 10–3 and the example just cited, the individual is attentive to virtually every breath taken, to every beat of the heart, and every twitch of the muscle. This concern is so overriding that the hypochondriac will often consult the nearest physician for healthy conditions. Among the multiple complaints of the hypochondriac are insomnia, variable aches and pains, gastrointestinal difficulties, pressures in the head, poor memory, and inability to concentrate.

Health, or the lack of health, is a serious business for hypochondriacs. Jokes about their physical condition are taken seriously, as are any comments such as "you look pale" or "take it easy!"—even when these comments are made in jest. Thus, for many drug and health product firms, hypochondriacs represent big business: these individuals are especially susceptible to promises of relief, particularly when the illness is portrayed in vivid detail. Such advertisements not only attract the person to another source of medication in which to become engrossed, but also feed into the individual's extreme interest in signs of disease. When health food fads or diets are undertaken, they are discussed in great detail with the emphasis on the consequences of not following the routine. As in the case study, many hypochondriacs become virtual walking encyclopedias of health information, mostly information of possible detriments to health. Such individuals may give the impression of being comfortable only when they can worry about their bodies, and they seem anxious if they are prevented from such concerns.

## Dynamics of Hypochondriasis

It should be emphasized that the suffering and fears of the hypochondriac are real and not faked. The person's energies are bound up in the many aches and pains, permitting little time to enjoy life and people. The hypochondriac is continuously being prevented from new or pleasant endeavors because of somatic fragility. Thus, the world becomes constricted. However, it is this very constriction which gives us the first clue into the dynamics of the illness.

***Social Barriers and Secondary Gains.*** Frequently, the hypochondriac is a person with low self-esteem, who is fearful of close interpersonal relations, and who has had repeated experiences of disappointment, friction, and unhappiness. Living in a constricted world of disease, medication, and trips to the doctor may be a more tolerable existence than facing the challenges of interpersonal relationships. Endless discussions of one's somatic symptoms also act as a sort of social barrier: when the main topic of conversation is ill health, it is nearly impossible to become intimately acquainted with others.

Despite this self-erected barrier, there is a certain element of ambivalence present in hypochondriasis. The individual is fearful of interpersonal closeness, yet is pleased when someone else expresses sympathy and interest. This indirect advantage of a disorder is referred to as *secondary gain.* Sympathy, the satisfaction of dependency needs, and the removal of responsibility are all types of secondary gains which can accrue and help to maintain symptoms.

## Case History 10–3:
### A Case of Hypochondriasis

Jeff N., a middle-aged man with an eighth-grade education, worked as a clerk in a drugstore. The first to try out every new product on the market, he soon became known as the pharmacist's best customer. Although he was exhorted not to take pills indiscriminately, Jeff argued that he did so only when he felt they might help, which was often. "There's nothing wrong if you're careful and knowledgeable. . . . I know more about pills and vitamins than the druggists do. . . ." He spent long hours compulsively describing his health and was always pleased when the druggist would refer him to a doctor in sheer exasperation. The patient preferred to see qualified physicians for his complaints, but he was increasingly more willing to visit known quacks since "the real docs don't know everything there is to know. I tell them about my irregular heartbeat and my poor digestion and my slow reflexes, but they're stumped. These problems have to mean something, and I'm not getting any better, I just don't feel up to par. . . ." A year ago he stopped eating a certain type of fish after hearing rumors that cancer had been found in one fish.

Jeff continues to live an isolated life with a few close friends who can tolerate hearing about his many complaints. Some find him amusing for his widespread knowledge of the latest medical discoveries—which as often as not turn out to be Jeff's parroting from popular magazine articles. He has remained single because of a fear that his ill health would not permit him to be a good provider. A brief attempt at self-improvement ended in dismal failure when he found he could not concentrate on studies because of "pains in the chest and a feeling of pressure in the head." He will talk about psychiatry as "maybe" helping other people who are "tetched in the head" but denies that he personally has any emotional problems. He attributes the inability of medical experts to find any organic base for his symptoms to their "backward techniques." He will occasionally confide that his illness is probably such a rare and special disease that it eludes modern medicine's advances.

***Anxiety.*** Another dimension involved in hypochondriasis is anxiety, even beyond the anxieties about illness and health. In fact, the hypochondriac's physical concerns are probably the displaced expression of psychological anxiety. Tensions are transposed and given a tangible focus. This explains the inability of hypochondriacs to receive a complete cure for their physical problems. The drug may treat the physical symptom, but it fails to remove the underlying anxiety and conflicts. In fact, although hypochondriacs will "shop doctors" and move from physician to physician or from quack to quack, they will invariably avoid attempting psychiatric treatment. As far as they are concerned, the ailment is a medical disease, and not a psychiatric one. And as long as they can occupy their attention with the intricate details about body functions, dosages of medication, foods to avoid, and diets to keep, they can avoid admitting their disappointments with themselves and their surroundings.

### Treatment of Hypochondriasis

The successful treatment of hypochondriasis is extremely difficult, for several reasons. In the first place, such patients will avoid psychiatric referrals, since it represents to them an admission that the disorder may not be physical. Second, the hypochondriac has received some reinforcement for pill-taking and for visits to medical physicians in that just taking such action reduces some of the anxiety—hence some of the symptoms. Third, the secondary gains that accompany physical suffering also prevent the development of insight. As other persons offer help and sympathy, these further reduce the hypochondriac's interest in seeking the causes of the symptoms.

Tranquilizers provide some symptomatic relief, but care must be taken to avoid the misconception that the pill is a miracle cure-all. Such medications typically do reduce physical symptoms on a short-run basis, but the changes are not stable. Extensive psychotherapy is necessary for any permanent resolutions. Great care is needed to avoid antagonizing the patient by confrontation. Many will be helped on realizing that emotions play a significant role in affecting bodily conditions and are reassured to know that psychiatric consultations do not mean an admission of insanity or that it is "all in the head."

## EVALUATION

The somatoform disorders vary in the extent to which they are recognized and accepted by diagnosticians. The conversion disorders can be traced to early psychiatric history (see Chapter 2) and hypochondriasis has long been recognized as a legitimate classification. However, recognition of the somatization disorder and psychogenic pain disorder have been recent occurrences. As we saw, somatization disorder as a classification distinct from conversion disorder is still controversial; some diagnosticians still prefer to view it as a subtype of conversion disorder, while others believe there is sufficient evidence to keep it separate. Although psychogenic pain has only recently been recognized as a separate category, there is good reason for its inclusion since it identifies patients whose complaints are related to psychological rather than organic factors.

It is somewhat discouraging to notice that conversion disorder is still in most ways a mystery. From the speculations in early history that it is caused by a wandering uterus, we moved to speculations that it is caused by repressed sexual conflicts, then on to current speculations that the conflicts have broader sources. Even assuming that conflict leads to self-protective actions, we still don't really know much about the exact mechanism whereby the human being can control bodily functions to the extent of causing anaesthesia or blindness or paralysis. For that matter, the mechanisms involved in pain perception and pain tolerance are also unclear. If there are gates which control pain signals, exactly how does pressure or electrical stimulation open or close these gates? If acupuncture can cause anesthesia, what new questions are raised by the fact that the points used by the acupuncturist correspond to Eastern theories and do not match a Western physician's conception of human anatomy?

Behavioral explanations provide some understanding of somatoform disorders in the idea of secondary gain and behavioral patterns. Certainly, hypochondriacs, pain patients, and some conversion patients are being reinforced for their aches and pains. Similarly, the physical complaints of the somatization person may be no more than a general reflection of an overall behavioral characteristic of life dissatisfaction and complaints. It is encouraging to note that behavioral therapy has had some success with conversion disorders and psychogenic pain patients. On the other hand, as we pointed out earlier, the fact that psychoanalytic treatment and behavioral therapy have both had successes with similar patients raises an interesting question. The theories have totally different ideas about what is causing the problem, and hence approach treatment in different ways. So how can both techniques have similar success, for instance, in helping conversion disorder? All in all, the somatoform disorders form a cluster of disorders which can be easily characterized, but not as easily understood.

## SUMMARY

The somatoform patients are the physical-illness worriers. Their conditions include somatization disorder, conversion disorder, psychogenic pain disorder, and hypochondriasis. They all have in common the patient's complaint about a physical symptom, but they lack confirming medical evidence of a true organic basis. Conversion patients experience physical symptoms that mimic real disease processes, but inexactly. Somatization patients have multiple physical symptoms which lead to a history of seeking medical attention. In psychogenic pain, chronic pain is noticed that is resistant to normal treatment. The hypochondriacal patient seems more worried about the possibility that a small discomfort is a sign of a major disease. Conversion disorders are often understood as attempts to resolve conflicts such as approach-avoidance problems. Psychogenic pain may derive its origins in attempts to reduce guilt; there is some evidence that the reporting of pain and the seeking of help for pain could be learned behaviors. Hypochondriacs seem to have channeled their many anxieties as persons into specific anxieties about health. There is some reason to believe that these patients are uncomfortable in interpersonal relations, and are better able to manage social contacts by focusing on their illness rather than on more meaningful issues.

A variety of therapeutic approaches have been used with the somatoform disorders. Psychotherapeutic techniques with somatization and hypochondriacal disorders aim at shifting the focus away from the physical complaints and more towards managing life's anxieties. Behavior therapy has been successful in chronic pain patients and in some cases of conversion disorders.

## KEY TERMS

**Abreaction**
**Briquet's syndrome**
**Conversion disorder**
**Endorphins**
**Epidemiology**
**Free association**
**Gate-control theory**
**Hypochondriasis**
**Hysteria**
***La belle indifference***
**Nociperception**
**Polysymptomatic**
**Psychogenic pain**
**Secondary gain**
**Somatization disorder**
**Somatoform disorders**

# CHAPTER 11

## Factitious Disorders: When Faking Approaches Fact

- **What is the nature of the faking in factitious disorders?**
- **Conversion disorders in particular share many characteristics with factitious disorders. The individual, for instance, may undergo extensive hospitalization and examinations with great patience. How do the two disorders differ?**
- **What does the term *vorbeigehen* (to go past something) have to do with Ganser's Syndrome? Which is an example: "The first president of the United States was Martha Washington" or "The first president was George Washington"?**
- **In what way is the real Baron von Münchausen's reputation appropriate for describing individuals with factitious disorder with physical symptoms?**
- **Why would hospitals create the "Münchausen lists" as a means of looking out for persons with this disorder?**
- **How can impersonators and public impostors who often catch the public's fancy help us understand the Münchausen's patient?**
- **It can be quite easy to confuse the symptoms of a person suffering from a factitious disorder with one suffering from a somatoform disorder. What signs can you use to tell them apart?**
- **Both the Ganser's and the Münchausen's syndromes involve the display of rather bizarre symptoms: How would you differentiate one type of patient from the other?**
- **A common trap facing the therapist of a factitious disorder is the message, "If you don't let me talk about my symptoms, then you really don't care for me." How does a therapist avoid this trap?**

**TABLE 11–1**

**Factitious Disorders**

| *Type* | *Major Characteristics* |
|---|---|
| Ganser's syndrome | Voluntary simulating of psychological disturbances. |
| Münchausen's syndrome | Voluntary simulating of physical symptoms, to the degree of accepting surgery. |

## Case History 11–1:
### Münchausen's Syndrome

A most interesting patient . . . claimed to be a Moroccan oceanographic physicist, with Jacques Cousteau. An intellectual 48-year-old black man speaking with an impressive French accent, on his way to an oceanographic symposium at Duke University, he came to the Wilmington (Delaware) Medical Center emergency room and was admitted with a history of calf pain and sudden onset of pleuritic chest pain, dyspnea, and hemoptysis. He gave the fantastic story of having sustained abdominal gunshot wounds in the Indochina War necessitating extensive surgery, including left nephrectomy, splenectomy, right hemicolectomy, and a 50 percent small-bowel resection. He gave a pertinent history of having had an acute myocardial infarction. . . . Results of physical examination were remarkable for median sternotomy, left flank, and multiple abdominal incisions as well as numerous cutdown scars. . . .

As suspicions were raised, he attempted to call his "personal physician in Casablanca" for advice and finally left after five days without notifying anyone. Calls to (other) hospitals revealed hospitalization for "hemorrhagic cystitis" and for "chest pain, etiology unknown, and personality disorder," respectively. Other cards identified him as "Major F., an SAC Fighter Pilot and former POW." A Veterans Administration patient data card . . . gave his address as the Department of Physics, California Polytechnic Institute.

He was seen the same day he left the Wilmington Medical Center in a local physician's office claiming a history of narcolepsy and requesting 12 dextroamphetamine tablets. The next day he was admitted to the Wilmington V.A. Hospital with chest pain. . . . he next attempted to gain admission to nearby Chester-Crozier Hospital . . . had, prior to our experience, been at Cooper Hospital in Camden, N.J. . . . had been described in a (medical) journal from Poudre Valley Memorial Hospital, Fort Collins, CO, where he was treated for a genitourinary pain . . . as "Major F., an SAC pilot and counterintelligence agent." Confirming letters uncovered his notoriety at Kansas University Medical Center . . . at Missouri V.A. Hospital, and later in Lawrence, KS. (Heym et al., 1977, p. 1248)

The *factitious disorders* are those mental disorders in which a patient simulates an illness, either psychological or physical. The term *factitious* means manufactured, not genuine, fictitious.

Symptoms of illness are presented as real complaints to a physician, often along with an involved tale, as in Case History 11–1. The individual's complaints carry sufficient mix of reality and fantasy as to be convincing to the admitting official, yet somewhat perplexing when the patient is carefully examined. The symptoms can lead to decisions for rather drastic treatment, such as surgery, to which the patient submits. Yet, the symptoms are believed to be under the patient's voluntary control—even to the degree that the patient may deliberately induce symptoms by taking hallucinogens, for instance, or deliberately infecting a physical wound.

The factitious disorders may at first be confused with the somatoform disorders discussed in Chapter 10: both involve a complex interplay between mind and body. However, the disorders differ in a number of ways, as follows:

- The somatization disorder tends to be characterized by multiple vague complaints involving many organs but without supporting laboratory evidence. In contrast, the person with factitious disorder has complaints and may even be involved in self-mutilating actions to simulate an illness, leading to evidence such as fever.
- The conversion disorder tends to be an imitation of a physical disease with *la belle indifference* sometimes present. Symptoms are not under voluntary control. The factitious patient's symptoms, however, are considered under voluntary control and are offered with great flair and a seeking of the "patient role."
- Hypochondriasis tends more to be a preoccupation with illness, but it is seldom associated with an actual disabling symptom. In contrast, the individual with a factitious disorder may actually experience incapacitation that in some cases is self-inflicted.

The factitious disorder appears to be under voluntary control in the sense that the symptoms are not recognized by experts as an unconscious derivative. Rather, there is a voluntary production of symptoms, where the only apparent goal is to assume the role of a patient. The patient enters many hospitals and develops a lengthy history of self-admissions. Sometimes in an incompetent fashion, other times in a highly ingenious fashion, the patient reproduces symptoms and seeks treatment. There does not seem to be any obvious secondary gain to the patient, as there would be in *malingering,* where a person consciously fakes an illness for gain (such as to win a court decision). Instead, the opposite seems to be true on the surface—so that many patients go through extensive inconvenience and even pain because of their symptoms. Two major types of factitious disorders are recognized and will be discussed in this chapter:

- Factitious disorder with psychological symptoms
- Factitious disorder with physical illness

## FACTITIOUS DISORDER WITH PSYCHOLOGICAL SYMPTOMS (GANSER'S SYNDROME)

### Symptoms and Diagnosis

This disorder, once referred to as *Ganser's syndrome,* was named after Dr. S. J. Ganser (1898) who first described the symptoms in three prisoners. The disorder is characterized today by the presence of mental symptoms that correspond to a lay person's imperfect conception of mental disorder. The person may claim a variety of types of memory losses, hallucinations, dissociative symptoms, or suicidal thoughts. Bizarre behaviors such as eating by putting a spoonful of food in the ear or trimming an imaginary rosebush in one's room, may be shown. The diagnostic picture may become confusing, as persons with Ganser's syndrome may agree to having many more symptoms simply on being asked by the examiner. Later, they may become negativistic, uncooperative, truculent, and resistant. An example of the facetious tone, which can be highly frustrating to those trying to provide help, is reported in an interview by Whitlock (1967):

On questioning he responded as follows:

Q: "What is your name?"
A: "It may be the same as yours."
Q: "How old are you?"
A: "How should I know that?"

Later, he gave his correct age, but gave the year of his birth as 1922 instead of 1933. When this inaccuracy was commented on, he replied in an offhand manner, "Well, it's nearabouts." . . . Asked on what street he lived, he replied, "It may be the street we have been trying to find tonight." He was then asked to state the colour of his (blue) pyjamas and he replied that it might be red. The colour of a red chair he gave as brown, but later correctly as red. (p. 23)

***Vorbeigehen Answers.*** The preceding quotation illustrates a feature often believed associated with Ganser's syndrome. This symptom, known as *vorbeigehen* (literally to go past something) involves the patient giving a related, but not quite exact answer to a question, and just barely "missing the point." Answers are not right, but still reflect that the patient understands the question and is giving an answer related to the question.

It is almost as if the examiner and patient are engaged in a game of sorts. The examiner begins to ask questions which are almost silly in their simplicity, while the patient offers an even sillier answer, and both parties continue to participate in a serious manner. For example, to the question, "Who is the president of the United States?" one patient answered, "Mrs. Jimmy Carter." When asked to give the name of an object (a spoon) being held up, another patient replied, "Why its name might be George if spoons are males or Georgette if spoons are females!" Simple questions involving numbers often elicit this symptom of *vorbeigehen,* as seen in the patient who says that "Dogs have five legs" or that "4 + 3 = 5." Although the ludicrous answers often cause the diagnostician to suspect that the patient is deliberately being ridiculous, the evidence is that these patients are serious and simply displaying their symptoms as they believe them to exist.

***Simulation of Symptoms.*** The chronic simulation of psychological complaints also characterizes the factitious disorders. In turn, since the complaints persist, they interfere with everyday functioning, and with proper determination of treatment, if the examiner does not know about the individual's past history. An unsuspecting examiner, in fact, may quickly diagnose a severe pathology. This is especially likely in cases in which the person has artificially produced or exacerbated the symptoms. For example, hallucinogens may be used to produce an altered state of consciousness, caffeine to produce irritability and restlessness, barbiturates to produce lethargy and loss of attentiveness, or alcohol to produce loss of inhibition or frenzy. Some patients may even take several different drugs simultaneously to precipitate especially bizarre symptoms just before reporting in to a clinic.

***Diversity of Symptoms.*** Despite the simulation apparent in *vorbeigehen* and in the self-administration of drugs, individuals consider their variety of symptoms to prove their need for help. As examples of the creative diversity of symptoms, cases have been reported where patients fell asleep during the examination; could not give the answer "Saturday" verbally but could do it in writing; lighted a cigarette, then put the match in the mouth to "smoke"; or appeared generally confused and disoriented at the correct door of a clinic.

Despite these seemingly artificial symptoms, there is a genuine disorder behind the manufactured symptoms—just as in Münchausen's syndrome, discussed next. Because the dynamics of these two disorders are similar, we'll discuss them together, later on in this chapter.

## FACTITIOUS DISORDER WITH PHYSICAL SYMPTOMS (MÜNCHAUSEN'S SYNDROME)

Factitious disorder is currently also known as *Münchausen's syndrome,* so named by Dr. Richard Asher in 1951 after the legendary Baron Hieronymus von Münchausen, who wandered from city to city during the 18th century telling tall tales. The Baron was immortalized as a hoax by another teller of tales, Rudolph Raspe, who wrote what was purported to be a log of Münchausen's adventures, some excerpts of which appear in Focus 11-1.

## FOCUS 11–1:
### von Münchausen's Fabulous Adventures

In the 18th century, a book appeared documenting the travels of Baron von Münchausen. Among his famous adventures described were his fighting for the Russian czar against the Turks, being captured and made a slave in care of the Sultan's bees, traveling by ship to Ceylon as a representative of the states of Holland, sailing on an English man-of-war to America, going to the Nile as a French ambassador, single-handedly saving the English from the Spanish militia's siege on Gibraltar, slaying thousands of polar bears in the Arctic Circle with only a knife, capturing a shark off the East Indies, and offering the first detailed description of the moon and its inhabitants. We might compare the Baron's adventures with the account of a modern Münchausen in Case History 11–1.

The psychiatric syndrome, new in the DSM-III classification, is named after Baron von Münchausen because of the fantastic tales attributed to the Baron, which also characterize patients with this disorder. The following excerpts from the Baron's *Singular Travels, Campaigns, and Adventures of Baron Münchausen* (Raspe, 1971) will give you some of the flavor of these tales.

> When I was going home, a terrible bear came up to me in great speed, with open mouth, ready to fall on me. All my pockets were searched in an instant for powder and ball, but in vain—I found nothing but two spare flints; one I flung with all my might into the monster's open jaws, down his throat. . . . I level[ed] the second at him also. . . . It flew in, met the first flint in the stomach, struck fire, and the bear blew up with a terrible explosion. (pp. 18, 20)
>
> On another occasion I wished to jump across a lake. When I was in the middle of the jump, I found it was much larger than I had imagined at first. So I at once turned back in the middle of my leap and returned to the bank I had just left to take a stronger spring. The second time, however, I again took off badly . . . [and] should . . . have come to an untimely end, had I not, by the force of my own unaided arm, lifted myself up by my pigtail, together with my horse, whom I gripped tightly with my knees. (p. 36)
>
> [About the moon]: On the eighteenth day . . . a hurricane seized our vessel, whirled it to a height of nearly 1,000 leagues above the sea and kept it there for some time. At last a fair wind filled our sails and carried us along at a great rate . . . [and] we discovered a great land in the sky. . . . I need hardly tell you that the glittering island on which we had landed was the moon. We saw there beings of gigantic stature riding on griffins, each of which had three heads. . . . The inhabitants of the moon use these birds, instead of horses, for riding and driving.
>
> When we arrived we found the king of the country at war with the sun. He offered me an officer's commission—an honor, however, which I begged his majesty forgive me for declining.
>
> Everything there is of extraordinary size. . . . The weapons in common use among the inhabitants of the moon are sticks of horseradish, which they handle as we do javelins, and which kill all who are struck by them. . . . Enormous mushrooms serve them for shields. . . .
>
> I know, gentlemen, that all this must appear very strange to you; but I beg anybody who doubts my veracity to go to the moon, and there see for himself, and he will find that I have stuck more closely to the truth than any previous traveller has done. (pp. 112, 118)

In some ways, Rudolph Raspe, the creator of the tales of Baron von Münchausen, was "an untrustworthy rascal" similar to the Baron. Although a member of the elite Royal Academy for scientists in Germany, he fell into debt and embezzled funds through his position as councilor, professor of antiquity, and keeper of the collection of coins for Frederick II. He fled Germany, arrived in England and published his tales of Baron von Münchausen in order to earn a living. Although patients suffering from Münchausen's syndrome engage in actions which lead to injury (and the Baron obviously always came away unscathed), their flair for dramatic storytelling is very reminiscent of the Baron.

### Symptoms of Münchausen's Syndrome

Münchausen's syndrome represents one of the more colorful psychological disorders and at the same time one of the most irritating to clinicians who must interact with such patients. As with factitious illness with physical symptoms, Münchausen's syndrome patients show:

- Fraudulent but dramatic symptoms reported in a way that blends reality with fiction.
- The seeking of medical help and treatment for the symptoms which are perceived as real.
- A voluntary control over symptoms, including self-inflicted causation or exacerbation of symptoms.
- Initial cooperativeness with hospital personnel followed by truculence and evasiveness.
- Acceptance of severely painful or drastic treatment for the "illness."
- Continued drifting from clinic to clinic and hospital to hospital for further care.

The syndrome may also display itself as a form of child abuse. Cases have been reported of mothers who gave false information about their children, tampered with their urine specimens or dipped the child's thermometer in hot water to raise the temperature, or actually gave the child large quantities of salt to induce vomiting. These parents were otherwise loving, and in one case, the child was a much-wanted baby (Vaisrub, 1978).

***Hospital Hoboes.*** As with Baron von Münchausen, Münchausen's syndrome patients are well traveled, going from hospital to hospital in the way that Münchausen went from tavern to tavern to share his tales. The wandering characteristic of Münchausen patients is so common as to give rise to the terms *hospital hoboes* and *hospital addiction.* Some hospitals use "Münchausen lists" to aid physicians in keeping a watchful eye for these patients, who cause bewilderment, frustration, irritation, anger, and finally contempt among medical professionals. Recently, the Danish Medical Association listed a man who had been admitted 20 times to emergency wards and 27 times to hospitals (Danish Medical Association, 1983).

A sense of exasperation on the part of medical professionals is understandable, for the patients' demeanor, once admitted, may be enough to make them less than welcome. They are often truculent or hostile, using abusive language, complaining about being neglected, making fun of other patients, and even accusing hospital staff of stealing from them. To add insult to injury, they may re-admit themselves several times to the same hospital in the hope of being assigned to a physician that does not know them.

***A Typical Case.*** In a typical pattern, a patient suffering from an acute illness suddenly appears at a hospital. The complaints are often (but not always) supported by laboratory or physical evidence. For instance, there may actually be a high temperature where fever is the complaint. There may also be physical evidence that lends credence to the medical history reported by the patient. Thus, the complaint of agonizing pains following "battlefield surgery after I threw myself in front of the machine gun to save my commander" may be supported by actual abdominal scars.

The medical history offered by the patient is usually dramatic fantasy that has some ring of reality. The patient's life story—like the Baron's—is also fanciful and fascinating, with reports of being a priest on the way to a foreign monastery or of being an ex-opera singer helping in the French underground.

The author recalls examining a patient who claimed to be a former dramatic actress, being followed by a wealthy man who was seducing her, but whom she resisted only because her "womb was hemorrhaging." Asher (1951) in his original report cited the following illustrative cases:

- Thomas Beeches, who variously said that he was suffering from "bursting open of an old torpedo wound" or that he had been shot down over Mannheim while in the R.A.F. after which he needed "eight abdominal operations and three short-circuits." (p. 340)
- Margaret Coke, who complained at various hospitals of "abdominal pain and vomiting," "inability to urinate," and "intestinal blockage." She was found collapsed on the street twice, the second time on the very day that she had signed herself out of another hospital. Her abdomen was a mass of scars, which she claimed came from a "horse doctor" in Houston, Texas [she was now in England]. She was eventually identified not only as Margaret Coke, but also as Elsie Silverbo-

rough and Elsie Packoma, all names she used in obtaining admission to different hospitals. She was believed to be a life-long resident of London, and a prostitute. (p. 340)

- Elsie De Coverley—alias Joan Morris, Joan Summer, Elsie Layton, Joan Lark, Joan Malkin, Jean Hops, and Elsie Shackleton—had been admitted to 18 hospitals with various complaints and various occupations to go along with her various names. She underwent several surgical operations as physicians attempted to diagnose her condition, and on one occasion discharged herself three days after surgery, not returning to have her stitches removed. On another occasion, when she was told that she was not to have an operation, she pulled out her stomach tube and walked out of the hospital. In one instance, she discharged herself after a few hours when she found she was recognized by a surgeon. (pp. 340–41)

## DYNAMICS OF THE FACTITIOUS DISORDERS

On the surface, behaviors such as those just described for Münchausen patients and those that typify Ganser's syndrome patients defy comprehension. The whole pattern of symptoms—the simulated illness, the scarring and surgery, the lengthy examinations, the involved life histories, and the hostile behaviors in hospital—appear to be senseless. Why would anyone wish to run the risk of exposure and embarrassment and even seek out treatment that will involve hospitalization and even surgery? And why, after seeking admission, would individuals typically behave in a hostile manner?

While there is no all-encompassing answer, a number of explanations throw some light on several aspects of this mixture of behaviors. We'll look at some of the most persuasive of these.

### Role Playing: The "Compulsive Actor"?

One explanation emphasizes the "patient role" which seems to be part of the goal of the factitious disorder. This view provides an interesting insight. The patient may be seen as being caught up in a "blurred play where real life and acting are indistinguishable. . . . What appears to the casual observer to be the play slips beyond the control of the patient. True, he knows when he is 'acting' (unlike the hysteric), but even with this knowledge he *cannot stop acting*" (Spiro, 1968, p. 574).

The patient with factitious disorder is compared to the compulsive gambler, the pathological liar, the drug addict, the alcoholic, who all seem to have lost control over what were originally willful acts. Compulsive gamblers, for instance, consciously know the odds against winning, and act as though their betting is rationally controlled, yet the fact that the compulsive gambler is incapable of stopping proves that control has really been lost. The alcohol abuser will continue to emphasize, "I can stop anytime," yet it is clear that this is not the case. In a similar style, it may be that the person suffering from a factitious disorder began by impersonating a patient seeking help, only to discover that he has truly become one.

Recent cases of the "professional imposter" have some of the dramatics of Münchausen's syndrome, wherein an individual seems compelled to impersonate famous persons, such as baseball players in an all-star game. Such imposters seem to enjoy the challenge of beating the system or may have other less clear motives, such as in Focus 11–2.

### Challenge to Authority

Another explanation of the factitious disorder behaviors helps in understanding the initial deception and later hostility that is often characteristic. In some ways, the factitious disorder may provide a means of attacking the system, either the hospital system generally or the authority and knowledge of physicians specifically.

It has been noted that patients with Münchausen's syndrome often show a history of early deprivation, similar to that of imposters (Spiro, 1968). Perhaps, then, the challenge of authority can be viewed as revenge against the frustrating parent who is held responsible for the deprivation. Or perhaps the revenge motive does not trace to displaced aggression at all, but is instead an expression of a direct grudge against doc-

## FOCUS 11–2:
### A Man with 34 Lives

Persons with factitious disorders appear driven by psychological motives to adopt extreme roles with pathological consequences. The conscious adoption of different roles and different identities can also be found among persons whose motives may not be a result of pathology, but whose actions are often still as mysterious.

In 1981 Peter DeWitt Connaught began seeing a young woman he met through the "In Search of" singles column in the *Washingtonian* magazine. His sudden departure for London and his failure to prove that he had really left for England raised the woman's suspicions. A private detective uncovered the strange information that the post office address on Connaught's business card was the address for a warehouse rented to a Paul A. Crafton; however the telephone number on this card rang at a condominium in Baltimore belonging to an Arthur Holland . . . yet this telephone was attached to a remote switching device which transferred the calls to a Rockville condominium purchased by . . . Paul A. Crafton. At this stage the detective wondered about whether he had inadvertently discovered an undercover CIA agent.

Peter Connaught was not a CIA agent but simply a man with many identities. Peter Connaught was also Paul Crafton and Arthur Holland and Jonathan David North and Peter Pearse and John Byron Hext. Also, he was John Michael Ashworth and R. W. Bates and Dr. Alfred Hoge Budge, Jr. and sufficient enough other persons to total 34 different lives. In essence, all of these persons actually were aliases used by Paul Arthur Crafton throughout 30 years of being an imposter.

Crafton's career covered an incredible variety of jobs. As Crafton, he invented a new method for drilling tunnels and held two full-time jobs simultaneously, as an associate professor at George Washington University and as a physical scientist for the Naval Research Lab. He also held teaching positions at four other colleges at this time but under different names; for instance, at the University of Delaware as Jonathan David North, Rutgers University as Peter Pearse, and Shippensburg State College as John Byron Hext. The daring arrogance of Crafton was shown by the unbelievable fact that there really exist a Peter Pearse and a John Byron Hext. Pearse, interestingly enough, is a professor, but in forestry at the University of British Columbia, and Hext is also a professor, at Macquarie University in Australia. In fact, nine of the identities assumed by Crafton were those of real people. An equally fascinating fact is that the information obtained by the private detective had been revealed to the dean of a university employing Crafton, but ultimately this information was ignored and no further inquiries made.

Crafton's unusual life finally came to an end as a result of one job too many. Criminal charges were filed in connection with his employment as Peter Pearse, teaching economics at Millersville State College after leaving Rutgers. He has also been charged with theft by deception and tampering with public records and forgery related to his position at Shippensburg State College under the name of John Byron Hext.

What motivated this person with an obviously brilliant mind to assume so many identities and take so many risks? One speculation was that the jobs were essential to pay for expensive operations for his cerebral palsied daughter. But no one seems to really know. In the event that Crafton's unique life does turn out to be explained as due to a psychological disorder, it is interesting to speculate on how his case relates to those disorders or origins we have discussed in various chapters in this book. Is he similar to the persons with factitious disorders who are compelled to play out certain roles to unconsciously gain superiority over others? How similar would his actions be to the dissociative disorders which involve living new and complete lives with amnesia for prior lives, such as the fugue state? Or are his multiple lives similar to the cases of multiple personality? Or possibly Crafton is really demonstrating a type of antisocial personality disorder whereby his actions are perceived as outside of the law? Whether Paul A. Crafton's 34 lives were prompted by psychopathological origins or more simply by the need for money to meet hospital bills for a daughter he cared for, his case study highlights the complexities of normal and abnormal human life.

tors and hospitals (Asher, 1951). Such a grudge would certainly be satisfied each time the patient successfully carried through a deception.

The eventual relationship which the patient establishes with hospital personnel can be described as a kind of sado-masochistic relationship, not in a sexual sense, but in the sense of a symbiotic hostility. The patient continues to court danger, either of being discovered and incurring the anger of professional personnel who have been duped, or of undergoing surgery, or electroshock treatment or lobotomy for mental symptoms, or the various discomforts of laboratory tests, and long examinations. The eventual truculence and hostile outbursts of the patient will certainly try the patience of even the most considerate staff member. It is almost as if the patient is trying to precipitate a return of hostility or punishment from others. Thus, unlike somatoform patients who seem gratified when receiving the care and attentiveness of others for their ''diseases,'' the factitious disorder patient seems prepared to subvert and sabotage the care givers.

### Search for Mastery

Another facet of the factitious disorder is the patient's search for mastery (Grinker, 1961). One way of explaining factitious behaviors may be that an earlier childhood trauma relating to hospitalization or illness is being symbolically repeated. As an adult, the patient is reexposed to the uncertainty, fear, and pain associated with illness, but now, he or she is able to make demands rather than being under the control of the hospital. The patient fabricates symptoms as a way of entering the hospital routine and ritual, but this initial action is secondary to the desire to test how helpful or knowledgeable the personnel really are. Since the patient now has voluntary control over the symptoms, he or she may not feel in any danger. Furthermore, the patient can simply walk out of the hospital at will, thereby showing not only mastery over the hospital system but also over the illness itself. This theory is difficult to confirm since there have been few reports on the actual early life histories of persons with factitious disorders.

### Attention Seeking

Throughout the pattern of factitious symptoms, there still remains some element of attention seeking. This sets the factitious disorder apart from the somatoform disorders discussed in Chapter 10. While the conversion patient or the hypochondriac simply shows a symptom, the factitious patient shows off a symptom. There is a display, a dramatizing, an exhibiting of oneself. The patient is not content to be seen for an illness, but has to unroll a drama at the same time. It is insufficient to be suffering from dizziness, or confusion, or thoughts that ramble, or an hallucination, or convulsions, or fainting spells, or hemorrhaging. The factitious patient must also explain that the illness derived from an early war experience or embellish it with other heroic overtones.

## TREATMENT OF THE FACTITIOUS DISORDERS

Effective methods of treating the factitious disorders are not yet known. This is primarily because of two factors. The first of these, as we have seen in this chapter, is the speed with which factitious disorder patients usually discharge themselves. Few cases have been diagnosed quickly enough to be studied, let alone treated. The second factor is the hostile relationship such patients usually develop with hospital staff. After hearing ''wolf'' cried too often, therapists may come to view the patient as not only untrustworthy, but also unworthy. Mental symptoms may have been found to be caused by the patients having taken drugs; a high temperature was once traced to a patient's deliberately rubbing her own and her parrot's feces into her wound to cause an infection.[1] Such situations are highly frustrating to the hospital staff who may be tempted to throw the patients out, and to consider such symptoms as faked. However, the patients are in fact ill—not simply with the induced mental disorder or the infection, but also with the factitious disorder itself. While a malingerer fakes an illness for a very specific gain, persons with factitious disorder cause an illness without clear gains; they are almost compelled to fabricate.

1 This happened in the case of the ''Fraudulent Feculent Fever in a Female Fabulist'' reported by Raff et al. (1975).

The first step of treatment involves recognizing symptoms of factitious disorders quickly, so that the patients may be transferred to a psychiatric ward. This will prevent the hostile interchanges with frustrated staff and will also offer some stability to the environment housing the patients. Within this element of stability, professionals can then work with the patients with greater continuity.

In the author's experience, factitious patients will test the limits of therapists' abilities to remain objective. Such patients will wish to talk about their symptoms, focusing on the dramatic explanations and accusing the therapist of being uncaring if a tolerant listening ear is not always provided. In fact, the interaction strongly suggests that patients have lost control over one impulse—the impulse to tell their stories—but at the same time want to be very much *in* control of their listeners by demanding that the conversation remain centered on their symptoms. In one case, a factitious disorder patient accused the author of proving his insensitivity and "revealing his true indifference" when he attempted to refocus the interaction away from the symptoms. Yet, treatment must eventually aim at encouraging the patient to deal with the need to fabricate, rather than the fabrication itself.

A second step towards this end combines firmness with understanding. The therapist must continuously demonstrate an interest and concern for the patient, but avoid the trap of using the patient's definition—"you are caring if you let me talk about my symptoms; you are uncaring if you won't permit me to go on." The therapist must aim at two goals; developing a trusting relationship, and communicating an interest in *all* aspects of the patient, not simply the dramatized symptoms. It is indeed possible that achieving this step may represent passing a major test. In one sense factitious patients may be testing those around them: "If you let me control you by centering on my symptoms or causing you to become hostile, then you are not good enough to offer me therapy." This testing could prove once again to the patient that hospital personnel are incompetent and disinterested.

If this hypothesis is correct, then the chances for relapse into symptom complaints would be expected to occur whenever patients become distrustful. Therefore, work with such patients would be a slow process, gradually unravelling a more complete picture of their true histories and the important contributing factors. As such factors are revealed, the therapy will gradually be directed towards enabling patients to achieve alternative ways of resolving problems.

Some speculations about what these factors were might be included in the prior discussion of dynamics, including the possibility of early deprivation, of aggressive impulses, of the need for attention, and the need for mastery. To our list of treatments, we would add the importance of learning impulse control, through learning to resist the compulsion to manipulate all discussions, but instead to devoting energies to other personal topics beyond symptoms. The therapist can be of help by allowing the patients to describe their symptoms only if they also spend equal time on topics the therapist suggests.

## EVALUATION

The factitious disorders classification is a new addition to the American Psychiatric Association's diagnostic system, although there have been prior references to the disorders at various times in the literature. Judging from the consistency of case histories, there seems little doubt that persons with the types of characteristics attributed to the factitious disorders do exist. It is a wonder that more have not been described in psychiatric writings. For the Ganser's syndrome, it is probable that many individual cases have not received special attention because the bizarre symptoms are easily mistaken for other psychiatric problems. For persons with Münchausen's syndrome, their hostility and truculence may cause hospital staff to feel relieved when the patient leaves; hence, prolonged efforts to study and understand such patients may not have been attempted—who would want to take the energy and abuse necessary to do so?

Because of the limited experience with either disorder, we still do not fully understand how they develop. The most promising theories hold either that these patients are locked into the patient role and are unable to stop acting the role or that the behaviors are displays of vengefulness against authority. Still, it is difficult to comprehend how such factors can become powerful enough to lead patients to submit themselves to the discomforts, complications, indignities, and actual damage that can result from hospitalization. It is seemingly a characteristic that psychopathological disorders tend to seem incomprehensible. Yet, how many times have we become victims of our own resentments and risk "cutting off our noses to spite our faces" or waver on the brink of self-disaster just to prove a point? And isn't this analogous to factitious disorders?

Inasmuch as the factitious disorders have been generally ignored as subjects for study or diagnosis, almost nothing is known about the most suitable methods for treatment. The possible presence of a real mental or physical symptom associated with a source such as drugs or a real infection must always be investigated. Psychotherapy to develop alternate ways of resolving anger or resentments needs to be examined if future research confirms that such issues form the relevant basis for the symptomatology.

## SUMMARY

The factitious disorders are ones in which physical or psychological complaints are fabricated. The symptoms are under voluntary control to the degree that some are actually self-inflicted. Where psychological symptoms are the major complaint, the disorder is known as Ganser's syndrome. A major feature seems to be a circumstantial aspect to answers, where questions are answered but not quite accurately or directly. Symptoms are offered seriously and the patient seems quite intent on receiving treatment.

The factitious disorder with physical symptoms, or Münchausen's syndrome, is characterized by fraudulent physical symptoms that are often accompanied by fanciful tales. Both types of patients are likely to become hostile and truculent with medical staff sometime during this hospitalization.

A prime explanation for the appearance of these disorders is the patient role which seems important to the patients. They seem intent on receiving the attention and acceptance afforded those considered patients. Another explanation suggests that the disorders are means for obtaining revenge against perceived deprivations. Finally, it has been hypothesized that the symptoms may be an exaggerated way of compensating for fears of being out of control from illnesses and an attempt to gain mastery. Because these disorders are rare and little is known about them, data about treatment methods has yet to be developed.

## KEY TERMS

**Factitious disorders**
**Ganser's syndrome**
**Malingering**
**Münchausen's syndrome**
***Vorbeigehen***

# CHAPTER 12

## Disorders of Impulse Control: When Desires Get Out of Control

- **What features do the disorders pathological gambling, kleptomania, and pyromania have in common?**
- **How do kleptomaniacs explain their stealing?**
- **Why is there a "desire to be caught" in the kleptomaniac?**
- **In what ways is the compulsive gambler self-deceptive?**
- **Who is the "snitch" and what is a "booster"?**
- **Are all fire-watchers pyromaniacs?**
- **What is the role of sexuality in fire-setting?**
- **How can a single episode of "spree killing" be explained?**
- **Can your brain make you into a killer without your choosing to kill?**

**TABLE 12–1**

**Disorders of Impulse Control**

| *Type* | *Major Characteristics* |
|---|---|
| Explosive disorder | Loss of control over aggressive behaviors leading to destruction of property or assault on people. |
| Kleptomania | The compulsion to steal for reasons other than inability to afford the objects stolen. |
| Pathological gambling | The compulsion to continue gambling activities for reasons other than profit. |
| Pyromania | The compulsion to set fires. |

# Case History 12–1:
## A Pathological Gambler

Dave G. is a traveler, not because his job demands it but because being on the move enables him to satisfy his need to be where the action is. Some traveling is connected with the seasonal sports, some is from the allure of the ''big game'' that is somehow known to the card players, and some is just to keep ahead of creditors.

Dave is now 32, has been married and divorced and still speaks with some regret about his former wife and child. But his favorite talk is about different occasions when he has won; sometimes it is about the excitement of a win that waited on the last turn of the card, sometimes it is about the last minute gamble after he had lost all his earnings and borrowed a stake, inevitably it is about the emotional concentration and the stimulation of gambling. There is an undertone of reminiscence about his family, but there is an overt excitement when he recalls the last game or talks about a future game.

Dave had been an engineer, and his enjoyment of figures first led him into minor card games with friends. These weekly events proved eventually insufficient and he soon canvassed the city to play with strangers nightly. Dave takes pride in his understanding of probability and odds and views his approach as a ''scientific statistical solution'' to betting. Although he is deeply in debt, he is still convinced that his system will work; the failure of it thus far being because he has not yet found all the different variables at work in the different sporting events. He speaks freely of what he will do ''when I come into the money'' as he is certain he will. Dave is no longer an engineer since he has lost two jobs due to absenteeism, later discovered to be due to late-evening poker games, after which he was too wrung out to go to work. Dave will bet on anything and for any amount and seems to need to have a bet on in order to attain any interest in the activity. His divorce was amicable, although Dave spent all of his earnings and his wife's savings as well through gambling. He finds employment however he can, doing whatever he can, just as long as he can find a game.

For most of the hours of the day, I am a normal person . . . but then there are those times when my impulses drive me and it's like a demon has possession of me.''

This chapter is about those persons who experience uncontrolled desires and temptations—desires and temptations which instead control them.

## SYMPTOMS OF IMPULSE CONTROL DISORDERS

The names of these disorders are familiar to you: the pathological or compulsive gambler, the kleptomaniac, the pyromaniac, the explosively violent person (see Table 12–1). These addictions share the characteristic of the compelling drive of other impulse problems such as the substance addictions and the paraphilias discussed in the next two chapters. The difference is in the nature of the impulse. For the substance addictions, it is the need for drugs or alcohol; for paraphilias such as fetishism or voyeurism, the impulse is sexual in nature; while for the impulse disorders in this chapter, the controlling drive is the need to gamble, steal, set fires or to release aggressive feelings.

### The Norm of Self-control

A society survives by establishing certain restrictions on impulsive actions. We agree to regulations about how fast to drive, how emotionally expressive we can be in a restaurant, and even implicitly on what hours of the night we can disturb the sleep of friends with telephone calls or visits. Most importantly, once we agree to guidelines for regulation, we also agree to the norm of self-regulation. We value self-control to the extent that being out of control is one of the few events that can arouse a person's concern about mental health. Each of us must believe that we are in control of our own needs, thoughts, and at least actions. Recall that demon possession was an early explanation of pathology or of ''not being in the right mind.''

Although the disorders of impulse control vary according to the nature of the characteristic behavior, they share a lack of control as a common feature. Common symptoms or characteristics of these four disorders include:

- A failure to resist acting on an impulse.
- An action that is harmful to the individual or others.
- An increased sense of tension prior to the action.
- An experience of release or gratification at the time of the action.
- Guilt or regret or self-reproach may or may not be associated with the action.

### Impulse Disorders versus Similar Behaviors

The behaviors that characterize at least three of the impulse control disorders are similar to the actions of some people who do not share this pathology. If one judges from the money spent in gambling—nearly 50 percent of adults spend over $21 billion in gambling activities (Bureau of the Census, 1980)—then gambling is a frequent condition for many of us. Theft occurs so often as to be among the major serious crimes in the United States, with one robbery happening every 72 seconds. And aggravated assault occurs once every 70 seconds.

These frequently occurring behaviors are certainly similar to those of the impulse control disorders; but the difference lies in the stimulus or motivation. For such actions (including fire-setting) to be considered a form of impulse control disorder, there must be present the irresistible, repetitive single impulse as the basic force. Thus, many people gamble, but not with the single-minded driven quality of the compulsive gambler. Robberies occur, but they are more often motivated by other forces such as material gain, poverty, peer group pressure, or antisocial striking out. Violent aggressiveness may occur, but again, this may be a consequence of criminal influence or subcultural norms. For the impulse control disorders, the impulse is not so easily explained. Instead, it is emphatically present as the prime issue. Among the impulse disorders to be considered in this chapter are:

- Pathological gambling
- Kleptomania
- Pyromania
- Explosive disorder

## THE PATHOLOGICAL GAMBLER

*Gambling* involves staking something of value on an uncertain outcome. Most people who gamble are able to maintain complete personal control over the amount of money or property they risk. In placing a wager on a football season, for instance, they can bet a large amount on the first game, then lower their bet, change their choice of teams, stop betting on football, or even stop gambling entirely. Gambling may be motivated by the hope of increasing one's earnings, the excitement of taking a risk, the enjoyment of being in a fantasy world where money is less important than the game, or the challenge of being in a competitive exchange.

### Symptoms of Compulsive Gambling

A revealing perspective is provided by a researcher who spent four years gambling, then intimately interviewed the compulsive gamblers he had befriended or met (Martinez, 1976).

In a description of the states that envelop the compulsive gambler, Martinez identified five symptomatic moods:

- *The risk-taking mood:* knowing that the risks are high (experts say that less than one person in 5,000 ends up a winner in gambling) but feeling stimulated by the challenge.
- *The here-and-now mood:* the person is so immersed in the immediacy of the action that every other activity not involving gambling is a downer in contrast.
- *The fantasy mood:* luxuriating in the grandiose fantasy of a life where the game is most important. Gambling takes place *with* money, instead of *for* money.
- *The euphoric mood:* the peak experience of positive rapture.
- *The mood of mysticism:* gambling takes on a ritualistic meaning.

Although not all of these moods are always present, Martinez argues that at one time or another, the compulsive gambler is likely to experience the gamut of such moods. Further, as the pathology increases, denial and self-deception appear: "I deserve a little fun once in a while" or "I can stop anytime I want to."

### Consequences of Compulsive Gambling

While the description just cited offers an idea of what this disorder is like from the gambler's perspective, it is also important to note the consequences of the addiction, both to the gambler and others. The intense preoccupation with gambling action leads to personal, social, familial, and vocational consequences. The gambler may lose his or her job as a result of inattentiveness to work details, lack of interest in work quality, or even absenteeism in order to stay a little longer in a card game, as happened in Case History 12–1. In maintaining the illusion that money is not important, the gambler fails to keep up with bookkeeping and soon may default on debts. Taking from joint accounts, selling the family car, borrowing from illegal sources, fraud, forgery, embezzlement, all become possible and probable. Among some irrational actions taken by compulsive gamblers have been: "Conning a boss into a loan by telling him your wife has had a miscarriage when she hasn't. . . . Betting $200,000 on a single football Sunday, all on credit, because you had access to . . . embezzlement . . .[and] Locking yourself in the bathroom at 3 A.M. to listen to 40 basketball scores you had tape-recorded from earlier radio broadcasts—'to make sure I heard it right, who won' " (Cady, 1975, p. 187). Separation, divorce, family disruption, unemployment, and criminal arrests are all sad side effects of a loss of control and pathological gambling. The professional quarterback for the Baltimore Colts, Art Schlicter, turned to the FBI for help. As a compulsive gambler, he received threats from bookies over his $750,000 worth of debts (Looney, 1983).

### Dynamics of Pathological Gambling

It is not easy to explain how a person can jeopardize a job, life savings, even family life over a voluntary act such as gambling. What is the source of the impulse? Several theories have been offered, ranging from Freudian interpretations to behavioral explanations. We'll look at these in the next few paragraphs.

***Psychoanalytic Explanations.*** The psychoanalytic explanation of compulsive gambling brings together two famous figures: Sigmund Freud and Fyodor Dostoevski. A pathological gambler, the Russian novelist lost everything in a gambling spree, implored his wife's forgiveness, reproved himself for his impulsiveness . . . but then begged her for more money. Freud's analysis of the famous author provides an excellent illustration of psychoanalytic interpretation.

Dostoevski wrote of getting a kick from losing. Freud (1961) interpreted this as a need to be punished—a masochism that was rooted in a strong feminism combined with a hatred for his father. This Oedipal sexual conflict plays an important role in the Freudian view of gambling. Early childhood sexual actions or fantasies once produced guilt, and they are now compulsively repeated in adult actions that produce guilt. The "vice of masturbation" during childhood is now repeated as the vice of gambling, where the hands once again engage in "playing" in ways that are punishable.

Other psychoanalytic interpretations may not focus entirely on sexual conflict. One theory, for instance, emphasizes submerged hostile impulses or omniscience, as sometimes seen in the gambler's belief in "winning the big one" (Lindner, 1950). Another common theme is the interplay between guilt and the pleasure principle. Risk-taking may provide a stimulating blend of pleasure and painful tension. If the gambler wins, a sense of guilt makes it virtually impossible to quit while ahead. When he or she is behind, however, there is an equally powerful unconscious desire to lose more and be punished—and this also blocks quitting (Bolen & Boyd, 1968).

***Research on Personality Traits.*** In contrast to Freudian theory, some more recent research shows other origins of gambling. Several studies have looked for common personality traits in compulsive gamblers. Some have found the traits of rebelliousness and unconventionality, along with a need for stimulation and excitement (Zuckerman et al., 1980). One study observed Gamblers Anonymous members for two years, testing and interviewing 55 pathological gamblers who were trying to stop (Livingston, 1974). Results showed that these gamblers were narcissistic and had a need for recognition and adulation, held an intensely competitive view of the world, and tended to equate money with achieving recognition, as well as with being shrewd, intelligent, and successful. Although the compulsive gambler is uncomfortable when in debt, he or she easily slips into fantasies about winning everything back, thus quickly dispersing any discomfort.

***Unpredictable Reinforcement.*** Finally, one behavioral analysis offers another perspective that seems to explain at least the persistence of gambling (Knapp, 1976). This analysis looks to reinforcement as the sustaining force, and it lays the blame not on the actual amount of rewards or wins in one's gambling history, but on the pattern or schedule of such reinforcement. In B. F. Skinner's views (1953), persistence develops when a reinforcement is delivered in an unpredictable, variable sequence, as in a slot machine: "The pathological gambler exemplifies the results. Like the pigeon with its five responses per second [that it emits] for many hours, he is the victim of an unpredictable contingency of reinforcement. The long-term net gain or loss is almost irrelevant in accounting for the effectiveness of this schedule." In fact, Skinner disclaims any motivation related to a "desire to master, to dominate, to win"; he also denies that illness interpretations of compulsive gambling have any basis. In his view, the only acceptable explanation is based on reinforcement history. Although Skinner's approach does help to explain why gambling activities are sustained,

*People readily spend money on* ***slot machines*** *because of the reinforcement or payoff schedule. This may be one of the reasons compulsive gamblers are unable to stop gambling.*

it fails to explain what maintains a gambler in the early stages, before the effects of the reinforcement schedule take hold.

### Treating Pathological Gambling

As can be seen, pathological gambling involves complex factors that are often difficult to sort out. One approach that has had some limited success is that used by the organization, Gamblers Anonymous, which was founded by two addicted gamblers in 1957 and is modeled after Alcoholics Anonymous. Gamblers Anonymous asserts that compulsive gamblers can never be cured, only helped to stop gambling behaviors. In group meetings, the gamblers confess their defect, see their errors reflected in the confessions of others, and accept support from other members towards gaining control. The effectiveness of Gamblers Anonymous is open to question. Some evaluative data estimate that only 20 percent of those who inquire about Gamblers Anonymous meetings actually make it to one meeting, about 2 in 5 attend more than one meeting, and 1 in 10 is successful in terminating gambling behaviors (Moody, 1964; Strine, 1971).

Another approach sees gambling as a symptom of family problems. Boyd and Bolen (1970) treated both male gamblers and their spouses on the theory that the marital context played an important role. At the start, the ''patients'' were seen as the husband-gamblers, with the problem being the gambling. As time progressed and the gambling decreased, however, the wives became depressed and suddenly aware that the gambling was really a symptom of more general marital discord. The wives became aware of their role as martyrs and the roles they played in fostering the gambling. Although intriguing, these findings must be viewed with caution since the participants were unique in having sought therapy to keep their marriages together. Interestingly, one speculation is that gambling, although a problem, may also provide a means for keeping a marriage intact through meeting the neurotic needs of *both* spouses (Hirsch, 1974).

## KLEPTOMANIA

Even more so than gambling, shoplifting represents a broad social problem in our country. Amateur shoplifting, or snitching, accounts for formidable losses, ranking as the fourth highest type of criminal theft. Known cases of shoplifting number about 700,000 a year and amount to about $42 million of actual loss (Bureau of the Census, 1980). Most shoplifting tends to occur on Thursdays, Fridays, and Saturdays, between 3:00 and 6:00 P.M., and it usually amounts to petty theft. One study showed the average value of merchandise stolen to be about $3.75 (Cameron, 1974).

To determine how common shoplifting is, one researcher instructed members of his staff to follow the first person who entered a store on their left, regardless of age, sex, race, or any characteristic at all. They were to remain with that customer, watching his or her activities in the store. Of 169 customers thus randomly selected, 20 stole something and 3 more changed their actions when they realized someone was watching.

There are a number of different types of shoplifters, including the amateur shoplifter, the professional thief (or booster), and the thief who steals for basic needs or for serious debts, drug addiction, and so forth. Among the amateur shoplifters are those who may steal once on the spur of the moment, but never again. The typical shoplifter is a woman, aged 18 to 30, married, often with enough money in her purse to have paid for the purchase without stealing. Among what are called amateur shoplifters is a small group that interests us: the *kleptomaniac* who seems to steal for pathological reasons. These persons who steal uncontrollably compose about 1 percent of all shoplifters (Curtis, 1971).

As with the other impulse disorders, kleptomania involves a failure to inhibit an action, in this case stealing. Compulsive stealing is impulsive, not preplanned, and in fact it does not seem to make any sense. The monetary value of the action is irrelevant, as is the item stolen. Cases are reported of a drug salesman stealing from a counter the very product that he distributed; or of an unmarried woman taking a child's garment; or of an elderly person walking off with cereal that the person does not even like. While other shoplifters confine their thievery to department stores or retail businesses, the kleptomaniac will steal from almost anywhere, including clotheslines. When caught, the individual experiences fright, humiliation, and bewilderment; nevertheless, the stealing may recur without any further thought of consequences.

### Dynamics of Kleptomania

A number of possible factors may contribute to compulsive stealing, ranging from hostile wishes to sexual

## Case History 12–2:
### Kleptomania

Sharon D. is the wife of a successful surgeon. She has been in court and was released to her husband:

> I don't know why I've been stealing, it's like something comes over me when I'm in the store and looking for something else, and I see a small thing like perfume or a pair of gloves, and I have this tense feeling. I try to resist and dawdle around, but then the tension says "I must" and before I know it, I take it.
>
> It really is so easy anyway. No one watches very well, and I'm always surprised at how many times I've not been caught. Sometimes it's silly things. I don't smoke, but I took three cigarette lighters and five ashtrays, and even a pack of cigarettes. I even caught myself thinking about not paying my lunch bill. But after I take something and leave the store, I feel somehow mixed, like I'm secretly pleased about it and yet I'm sure I'm going to get caught and I sometimes fantasize about what my husband will say or think in front of the judge and all his friends.

Sharon, on her way home, usually throws away the goods she has stolen when they are unusual and might raise questions. Other things which have some daily use she simply stores with the rest of the same items that she may have purchased on a previous day. She vividly recalls an early childhood experience of being refused attention from her father, then sitting on the steps and feeling sorry for herself, thinking, "Just you wait, I'm going to steal a wallet, get caught, and when you come to the jail you'll find out I took it to give to you for a present, because I cared, and you didn't, and now it's too late."

Her fantasy was never acted out and Sharon's life had been uneventful, including her marriage. However, her husband's professional success eventually meant she was now seeing less and less of him during the evenings. She says she has filled her time with a book club, volunteer work, and a hobby of collecting stamps of medical themes. The compulsive stealing developed suddenly not long after the stamp collecting began. Her reaction after her first theft was shock and embarrassment "I'm not a criminal, how could I do that?" After that, however, she no longer considered the urge pathological, although she did worry about the embarrassment if she were ever caught.

dynamics. The individual may be expressing a hostile challenge of all authority by stealing, or a more specific defiance of early parental morality. In some cases, the stealing involves a need for punishment for guilt feelings of a sense of unworthiness. Once caught, the kleptomaniac will at least feel the punishment of public humiliation, and perhaps even of material punishment. Perhaps the feeling of tension associated with the moments prior to stealing reflects this awareness of the possibility of being caught, while the feeling of release on completion of stealing shows the relief that punishment did not occur.

Psychoanalytic views hold that the excitement and tension associated with the stealing is in reality a sexual excitement, and that the relief is equivalent to that of sexual release. Psychoanalysts also report that sexual frustration is common among compulsive stealers, as illustrated by the woman in Case History 12-2, whose shoplifting began soon after her sexual life with her husband became unsatisfactory.

### Treating Kleptomania

Treatments for kleptomania may take several approaches. Of these, the psychodynamic and behavior therapies are predictably different from one another, but each approach has had some success. We'll look at both.

***Psychodynamic Therapy.*** Traditional psychodynamic treatment aims at what is believed to be the underlying source of the pathological stealing symptom. In the cases reported by Meyers (1970), therapy is aimed at helping the patients recognize the role of sexuality in the impulse to steal. In some cases, this increased awareness and acceptance of such needs is helpful. In cases where the stealing reflects a need for attention from the spouse, marital counseling has proven useful. Where the stealing is a form of retaliation or of defiance against conventionality or authority, then it is believed that longer therapeutic work is needed as such issues are worked through.

***Behavior Therapy.*** Various forms of behavior therapy have also been attempted. An aversive technique was prescribed for a woman who stole several times a day ''as far back as she could remember.'' Any time the impulse to steal appeared, she was told to hold her breath until she experienced mild pain—a method that led to the disappearance of stealing within six weeks.

Basing his treatment on the premise that the anxiety precipitates the stealing, Wolpe (1973) successfully treated a person using desensitization, a behavioral method of reducing anxiety discussed in Chapter 6. The client stole because of two aspects: her tension at having to spend over six dollars for anything; and her tension if she missed an opportunity to acquire something without cost. Desensitization removed both types of anxieties, bringing a corresponding elimination of the kleptomania. Wetzel (1966) used social rewards to reduce stealing in a child. Finally, a combination of aversive training and extinction was used by Kraft (1970), who first required the client to always send payment to the store for the stolen goods, and then to return to the store and practice resisting stealing.

## PYROMANIA

A third impulse control disorder, *pyromania,* exaggerates a fascination people have always had for fire. Its values and dangers are reported in Greek mythology, where Prometheus gave humans fire stolen from Olympus and was forever chained to a mountain in punishment. Our own slang alludes to both the attraction and danger of fire: ''Be careful not to get burned'' is a common expression of warning.

Arson, the setting of fires, is a highly dangerous crime, causing not only property damage but risk to lives. It is done for profit, as intimidation, as social protest (''burn, baby, burn''), as vandalism, to hide a crime, or even as part of a cultural or religious ritual. Some fire-setting is associated with emotional factors—as when an angry employee burns down a workplace in the ''heat of anger'' after being fired, or when a person with severe paranoid tendencies sets a fire because of an imagined slight. These various motivations are different from the impulse that spurs pyromania. It is the compulsive fire-setter, the pyromaniac, to whom we now turn our attention.

### The Uncontrollable Impulse in Pyromania

As in the other impulse control disorders, *pyromania* is characterized by the failure to resist an impulse, in this case to set fires. Pyromania shares the same driven quality as is found in kleptomania and pathological gambling; in fact, at one time these disorders were considered versions of obsessive-compulsive behavioral disorders. Unlike kleptomania or pathological gambling, however, the pyromaniac may need to have considerable materials on hand in order to set a fire, so acting on this impulse requires some advance preparation.

As with all of the impulse disorders, pyromania is characterized by an increase in tension prior to fire-setting. This builds into an impulse that demands action, then there is an intense sensation of release during the act. This sense of satisfaction, release, or even pleasure may result from setting fires or simply from watching fires set by others or by accident. The pyromaniac may set off false alarms because of a fascination with the fire-fighting equipment and may be recognized by firemen as a person who is a regular watcher at fires. There is a variable reaction following the fire-setting. The pyromaniac may or may not derive satisfaction from seeing the destructive aspects of the fire. Some individuals may actually experience remorse, while others, such as Harold in Case History 12–3, have no sense of guilt. This may be true even when massive destruction of property or death result from the fire.

***Pyromania** involves intense pleasure from deliberately setting fires.*

### Dynamics of Pyromania

Many interpretations of pyromania have focused on the tension-reducing or pleasurable sensations of starting a fire. A major psychoanalytic interpretation compares the experience with sexual excitement (Watkins, 1983). Indeed, some pyromaniacs report either sexual fantasies or a return of potency following the setting of a fire (pyromania seems more common among males than females). One young man who had set over 30 fires in four years used words that are easily descriptive of sexuality: "All the excitement, the smoke, the firemen working, it made me proud, glad, very glad that I was the one who did it. It gives me a sort of sex feeling, the female, the fire, and the color. Every time I set a fire it makes me excited. . . . I just couldn't control myself" (Macdonald, 1977, p. 191).

Fenichel (1943), a renowned analyst, suggests that children show a similar sexual excitement related to fires, with a mixed component of sensual pleasure in the warmth as well as the sadistic urge to watch the fire consume and destroy. The symbolic sexual aspect of fire hoses spouting water is often compared either to ejaculation or to childish fascination with urination.

## Case History 12–3:
### Pyromania

Harold P. is in intensive psychotherapy with a prison psychologist. He has been sentenced for setting fires and has accounted for 300 fires over a five-year span. The fires differ in location and circumstances, nearly all being set with whatever materials were readily available. Some were set after Harold felt a need at home, then rounded up a can of gasoline, and set fire to the first vacant building he found.

Harold does not understand his compulsion but similarly does not seem much concerned about it:

> I enjoy seeing the flames. Especially the spectacular ones that roar and get caught up in the wind and race through the rooms, and you can see people's faces tinged with the red haze. The smoke isn't so much fun and you have to be careful not to breathe it or you'll choke. But it's exciting, seeing the firemen unraveling their hoses and running all over, and the noise of more engines coming, and the crackle. It's better than watching television or an explosion. Sometimes I look at the crowd, some people in their nightgowns and bathrobes, and I pick out a good-looking gal, and I wonder if she's enjoying the sights too. But mostly I lose myself in the flames.
>
> No, I don't think there's anything wrong with me. I've always had a fascination with fire. I used to hide in the yard and light matches, great fun when you have enough and you can set off an entire matchbook, the old wooden matches and matchboxes were fun too. I thought about being a fireman, about putting out those fires, dreaming about being a hero, drenching the fire before it got me. But I figured I'd have more freedom if I wasn't a fireman. I still have dreams, about a huge fire walking towards me, and then I wake up and I have this itch to set one and watch it. I don't know about the damage, but I'm sure everybody has insurance, and the owner collects anyway and can build himself a better place than that old place, so there's no harm.

Harold is otherwise unspectacular. He is unprepossessing, a careful and meticulous bookkeeper, viewed as a friendly neighbor. He is single, but he has not been viewed as socially isolated and, in fact, has had some casual girl friends. His arrest came as a shock to those that knew him as a person or employee. In therapy he is lucid, cooperative, and nondefensive; yet very little progress has been made towards even an admission that his enjoyment of fires is unusual.

Sexual inadequacy feelings are viewed as an underlying aspect as the pyromaniac watches the unsuccessful attempts of the fire hoses to achieve success, reminiscent of similar feelings of inadequacy as the child first examines and evaluates his penis. At the same time, there is a suggestion of power and compensation from the fire-setting for the pyromaniac. It is the fire that the fire hoses cannot overcome, and the pyromaniac controls the fire. Thus, the pyromaniac may fantasize that he has the power; that he is in control and can "set the world on fire" if he so desires.

Another element of fire-setting that has received attention is its passive-aggressive quality (Blanco, 1972). The destructive aspect of fires, and fire-setting, may represent the unconscious aggressivity of the fire-setter who is unable to directly express hostility. Rather, the arson is the result of "an impulse that made me do it." One study of fire-setting in children discovered many aggressive fantasies about burning some family member (Yarnell, 1940). Often apparent in these children were the presence of some sexual conflicts, as well as the presence of other passive conduct disturbances such as truancy, running away from home, and stealing.

### Treating Pyromania

To the extent that fire-setting impulses may have several origins, treatment first aims at discovering the underlying motives. The factor of sexuality tends to be emphasized, and feelings of sexual inadequacy are explored in therapy. These feelings may respond either to psychotherapy aimed at returning self-esteem or to referral for sexual therapy.

Sexual motivations are not always involved, however, nor may they be the only factors involved. Thus, a competent therapist will examine the case history with an open mind. Therapists recognize the importance of passive-aggressiveness, for instance, and any current focal points for such emotions may be confronted and examined. Is there a good reason to be angered? If so, what alternative steps can be taken to resolve the conflict? Feelings of ambivalence or powerlessness are also considered, for they may contribute to fire-setting behaviors.

The approaches just described are directed toward underlying conflicts or motivations; other treatments are based either on the behaviors themselves or on the cognitive processes that may be involved. It is conceivable that new programs of *impulse control training* may have some value for pyromania and the other impulse disorders, although it has not yet been systematically applied to pyromania. Impulse-control training starts with the premise that people can learn to inhibit behaviors. As applied to hyperactive children with attention deficits (see Chapter 20), such children are made aware of steps they can take to control their impulses and attend more carefully to tasks. For example, children may be taught to use self-instruction by talking to themselves to counteract impulses. In a way, the extinction program described earlier for treating kleptomania could have involved some impulse-control training, when the patient was instructed to return to the store and practice inhibiting shoplifting.

Other treatments have relied more heavily on reinforcement. Mahoney and Mahoney (1973) used a *token economy system* to reinforce a child for reduced fire-setting behaviors. Here, the child earned a token for each occurrence of the desired behavior of resisting fire-setting; these tokens could later be traded in for a reward. Another creative behavior modification approach was used with a seven-year-old child; it has been called "fable mod" (Stawar, 1976). Using real reinforcers such as pieces of candy, the boy was encouraged to retell a story involving a "boy who found some matches," with rewards being given for correct repetition. The story centered around a boy who finds matches, but immediately turns them in to an adult and is then (in the story) praised for this action. As a follow-up treatment, the boy's mother was instructed to put matches in the home and to reward her son for turning them in. This treatment provides an interesting variation on other behavior techniques discussed here, for it aims not at the undesirable behavior itself, but at the necessary prerequisite of having matches in order to set a fire. It proved to be successful.

Other behavior approaches have also been used. Some have combined reinforcement and aversive behavior therapy, for instance, in the treatment of a 17-year-old boy who had set four fires, one of which destroyed his home and nearly killed his own family. He admitted that "voices in his head" commanded him to set the fires. The boy was shown color slides with himself at various stages of fire setting: as long as the slide was shown, the boy received an electrical shock; when the boy removed the slide, the shock ceased and instead a pleasant slide appeared. Treatment was conducted by the parents. Following treatment, the fire-setting stopped, as did the auditory hallucinations and the boy's social, school, recreational, and work accomplishments all improved (Denholtz, 1972).

## EXPLOSIVE DISORDER

A fourth disorder of impulse control, the *explosive disorder,* is characterized by the *loss* of control over aggressive impulses that results in serious destruction of property or in assault. As Case History 12–4 illustrates, the magnitude of the violence has no relation to the actual intensity of the stressor that precipitates it.

The explosive disorder shares many features with the other impulse disorders. There is a suggestion that this disorder involves a buildup of tension, which is then released in response to even minimal cues when it reaches an intolerable point. After the violent outburst, the individual will have periods of calm, without signs of unusual impulsivity or aggression. He or she tends to experience a genuine regret and self-reproach, but disclaims being in control of such impulses.

*The* ***explosive personality*** *may suddenly show violent outbursts of aggression, during which the person may destroy property or engage others in fights.*

Two types of explosive disorders are recognized: the *intermittent explosive disorder* and the *isolated explosive disorder*. They differ purely on the basis of frequency. The intermittent explosive disorder seems to be a repetitive pattern of episodes of loss of control, while the isolated explosive disorder involves only one discrete episode involving a single catastrophic violent act. An example of the latter would be a person who suddenly begins shooting at others in a real fit of rage, then commits suicide. Although this example is reminiscent of Mark, described in Case History 12–4, his case would actually be considered an intermittent explosive disorder because of the recurrence of violent episodes.

### Dynamics of the Explosive Disorder

Because the behaviors are so violent, explosive disorders seem to be in the news more than the other impulse disorders. The sudden killing spree by Charles Whitman mentioned in Focus 12–1 captures more attention than the sad consequences of compulsive gambling.

The behaviors themselves are difficult to predict, because they seem to be triggered by so many events. The intensity of the outbursts and the individual's inability to control them distinguish the explosive disorder from normal aggressive reactions to frustration. A

## Case History 12–4:
### Explosive Disorder

A number of "spree killings" have been reported over the years; Mark F. is an example. He was a telephone repairman in a small community, where he lived in a trailer court with his wife. Although he enjoyed spending Friday evenings at the local bar with his friends, he would invariably be brought home early and under protest. After a few drinks, he would become unruly, irritable, and easily angered. Once, while drinking alone, he discovered that another car had blocked his easy exit from the parking lot. In a rage, he grabbed a wrench and proceeded to break all the windows in the offending car.

As an adolescent, Mark was raised in a tough neighborhood, but quickly became the leader of a small gang and was respected for his physical strength. Mark's own parents were never legally married; his father occasionally boxed and used his skill to punish and discipline the children. The raising of the children was left to the mother—unless they were in trouble with the law. When this occurred, the father would severely beat them to teach them a lesson.

On a recent summer weekend, police were called to the trailer court because of shootings. They found Mark barricaded and shooting randomly at anyone in sight. Neighbors feared that Mark had killed his family; however, it soon became known that Mark's wife had left him the week before. A drinking companion filled in the information that Mark had been in his irritable mood the evening before, and seemed high strung and restless. The shooting began in the early morning hours. Mark shot a barking dog, and as the neighbors turned on their lights to see what was going on, he proceeded to shoot at their windows. He had already injured two neighbors when the police were called. A SWAT (special weapons squad) team was called in, and they tried unsuccessfully to talk him out. Tear gas was eventually used, but Mark was found already dead of self-inflicted gunshot wounds.

number of clues that help in understanding the explosive disorder will be discussed next.

***Physiological Factors.*** Some evidence points toward the involvement of physiological factors in explosive disorders (Simmel et al., 1983).

Such evidence is inferred when explosive symptoms are found correlated with signs of organic involvement. For instance, hypersensitivity to sensory input is sometimes reported to be similar to epilepsy, in that loud noises or bright or flickering lights may trigger the explosive outburst. A background of hyperactivity as a child is often found, a behavioral symptom sometimes viewed as organically caused.

Still another level of organic involvement is suggested by animal studies, which have found that the hypothalamus may play a role in rage behaviors (see Chapter 4). In one study, stimulation of the hypothalamus prompted two entirely different types of aggression in cats (Flynn et al., 1970). In the "quiet biting attack," the cat showed the normal quiet stalking and pouncing. In the "affective attack," however, the cat hissed, salivated profusely, leaped to its feet when stimulated, and savagely bit a rat victim, tearing at it with its claws. Other animal studies have shown that normally non-mouse-killing rats can be stimulated to kill through the injection into the hypothalamus of cholinergic agents (Smith et al., 1970).

More research is certainly needed to evaluate how closely the hypothalamus is associated with violence. Obviously, research into human behavior cannot attempt to test the same relationships as these animal studies have explored; and even in the studies of cats and rats, the exact brain mechanisms that control rage are highly complex and not completely understood. Other areas of the brain such as the septal area and the hippocampus have also been implicated in various studies (Gorenstein, 1982; Gorenstein & Newman, 1980).

***Childhood Experiences and Environmental Factors.*** Equally impressive information comes from studies of aggression in children. Here, early experiences seem to play a role (Chamore, 1980). Kagan and Moss (1962) discovered that parental restrictiveness toward a child aged three to ten appeared to lead to the development of aggression when the child became an adult. That is, children with severely punitive mothers grew up to be adults whose anger was easily aroused and expressed. Similarly, maternal hostility during this same age period was associated with rage reactions in later childhood.

In another series of studies, Bandura has pointed out the potency of modeling as a factor. As will be recalled from Chapter 3, children were shown to exhibit more aggressive actions after they had seen such aggression demonstrated by others (Hayes et al., 1980). Finally, given the influence of environmental factors such as noise and heat on aggression (see Chapter 7), it is conceivable that the explosive disorder may be a complex product of organic disturbance, early aggressive training, and environmental triggers.

## Treatment of the Explosive Disorders

As might be guessed with such a complicated phenomenon, little is known about the appropriate treatment. Although no medication has been found directly pertinent to aggression, sedatives may be tried to temporarily quiet an especially prolonged episode, simply for purposes of control. Delgado (1969) has suggested the use of direct brain stimulation to create inhibitory reactions. In severe instances, psychosurgery has been examined, but usually because of the presence of other serious symptoms or in a search for the presence of brain tumors.

An interesting behavioral approach has proved useful for some persons experiencing chronic anger (Novaco, 1979). This approach stresses the importance of self-regulation. Cognitive techniques are used to help the client prepare before an anger-provoking event and also to maintain control both during and after the event. Clients rehearse an easy-does-it attitude, reminding themselves to retain emotional control, using relaxation techniques at the first signs of aggravation. The practice of self-reinforcement for success—treating one's self to a reward—is an important element of this approach. It is possible that some aspects of this program may have relevance for the explosive disorder. Another preventive measure is simply the el-

# FOCUS 12–1:
## Aggression and Violence: "It Could Never Happen to Me"

One afternoon in the summer of 1966, Charles Whitman stood on the top of a tower commanding a view of the University of Texas campus, and with icy marksmanship shot 38 people, killing 14. The evening before, he had written:" I don't really understand myself these days. . . . I have been a victim of many unusual and irrational thoughts. . . . I felt overcome by overwhelming violent impulses. . . . After my death I wish that an autopsy would be performed on me to see if there is any visible physical disorder." Whitman was killed by police officers that afternoon: A postmortem was performed and a highly malignant tumor was found in his brain (Sweet et al., 1969).

Could anyone become a victim to explosive aggressive impulses? Our immediate reaction is "no, never me . . . unless I had a tumor in my head too." In fact, a number of experiments raise some doubts about just how resistant normal persons may be to aggressive impulses.

***Doing What You're Told.*** One very dramatic study (Milgram, 1963) asked the question of just how far people will go to obey instructions. Subjects were led to believe that the study was about the role of punishment in learning. They were told to act as teachers and to administer a higher and higher electrical shock

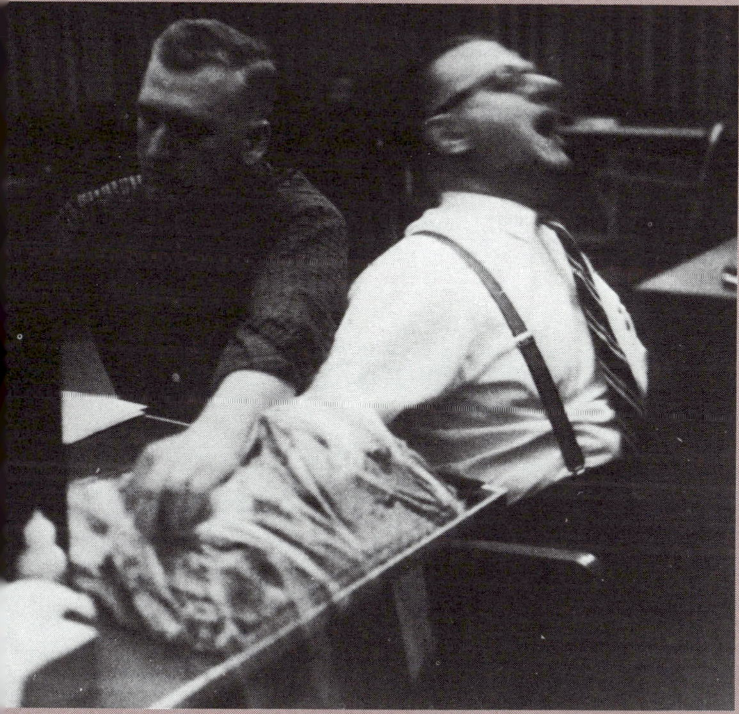

***Eichmann*** *(right) blamed his war crimes on "following orders." Psychologist* ***Stanley Milgram*** *proved that normals were also willing to administer shocks powerful enough to be considered sadistic (left).*

each time the learner performed poorly on a task. The shock-control apparatus had switches to deliver shocks from 15 volts to 450 volts. Subjects were themselves given a taste of how a 45-volt shock felt, and the switch for 450 volts was labeled "Danger: Severe Shock."

As the study progressed, the learner continued to perform poorly, and subjects were commanded by the experimenter to deliver higher shocks. The learner could be heard to cry out in pain which increased with the voltage, until the 300-volt shock was given. At this point, he screamed that his heart would not take it, then he failed to respond on the remaining trials. (In actuality, the learner was a confederate of the researcher and felt no shock at all.) Despite these reactions, Milgram found that 62 percent of the subjects obeyed the experimenter's command to administer the 450-volt shock. Most did so under protest, but they still obeyed.

Were these subjects uniquely sadistic, abnormal persons? Personality tests did not support this, and results were the same for paid volunteer Yale students, high school students, unskilled workers, and even doctoral graduates.

***Give Me Opportunity and Give Me Cause.*** A second study was based on the theory that opportunity and cause were both associated with our susceptibility to show aggression (Berkowitz, 1965). Thus, frustration creates the readiness of anger, while external events may present the cue that actually elicits aggression.

The experiment tested this theory by altering three sets of variables to see how subjects reacted. First, early in the experiment, subjects met with a confederate of the researcher who was introduced as either a speech major (nonbelligerent image) or as a physical education major and boxer (belligerent image). Second, the confederate either angered the subjects or he treated them neutrally. And third, after this experience, subjects were shown one of two films: either a neutral film on English canal boats or a violent prize-fight scene.

Subjects were then given the opportunity to administer a shock to the confederate. In general, nonangered subjects were less aggressive in the sense of their willingness to use the shock. However, the angered subjects administered more *and* longer shocks, especially after viewing the violent film. And more aggression was displayed when the confederate was perceived as a boxer than a speech major.

In all, aggression seems to exist within all of us under the right circumstances. If we have cause, we may show aggression. Whether the cause be someone else's behavior, our belief that they "deserve punishment," or our own obedience to authority, such "special circumstances" can sometimes cause us to break our own rules or ethics and act aggressively.

ement of avoidance. If known precipitants can be identified as setting the stage for loss of control (such as drinking alcohol or the presence of loud music), then the individual can take extra measures to avoid such irritants.

## EVALUATION

The disorders of impulse control bring together those problems long recognized by the lay public as signs of pathology, such as pyromania and kleptomania. Although the problems of pathological gambling, pyromania, and kleptomania have all been analyzed by psychoanalytic theorists, with a common emphasis on sexual symbolism, actual research has been lacking.

In the one area with some research, pathological gambling, there has not been support for psychoanalytic theory. Instead, other origins have emerged, including the need for excitement and recognition by others. Once a person develops gambling behaviors, it is possible that the unpredictable, intermittent pattern of actual reinforcement becomes a major influence in *maintaining* the pathological gambling. This sporadic reinforcement prevents easy extinction.

Much more research has been published regarding the explosive disorder. Although the research has been indirect, rather than directly focused on persons with this disorder, it has important implications. Studies on aggression suggest that the aggressive behaviors may themselves be the result of early training, modeling, and the presence of environmental triggers. The role of brain activity in inhibiting or releasing aggressive outbursts also seems a highly relevant factor. Future research could uncover the mechanisms, but it is anticipated that such discoveries will take time given the complexity of the problem.

Treatment of pathological gambling still needs careful study. The hoped-for success of Gamblers Anonymous has yet to be confirmed. A few case reports with behavior therapy or psychotherapy are available on kleptomania and pyromania, but controlled group studies are yet to be reported. Finally, given the lack of clarity of the origins of the explosive disorder, it comes as no surprise that suitable treatment approaches have yet to be defined.

## SUMMARY

The impulse disorders are those which involve an inability of the individual to be in control of behaviors which become excessive. The pathological gambler cannot control the need to bet, the kleptomaniac is compelled to steal, the pyromaniac sets fires and the explosive disorder patients lack control over violent behaviors. It is not simply the frequency of occurrence of such behaviors that mark them as pathological. Instead, it is the driven quality that seems to compel the actions. The person suffering from the impulse disorders appears out of control and is unable to prevent the behaviors from taking place. For most, there is an increased sense of tension prior to the action and an experience of release when the action occurs. Feelings of guilt or self-reproach may or may not be a consequence. The impulse disorders differ from similar behaviors in other persons in that such actions are related to identifiable gains; for instance, a normal person may steal because of poverty, while a kleptomaniac often does not need the item stolen.

Freudian or psychoanalytic approaches provide some hypotheses about the origins of various impulse disorders. For example, pathological gambling is said to represent a desire for punishment due to long-term guilt feelings. Freudians also consider compulsive gambling a symbolic repetition of earlier unacceptable sexual behavior involving the hands, such as masturbation. In kleptomania, the psychoanalytic view is that the stealing induces a type of sexual excitement and release, possibly associated with sexual frustrations in life. This same interpretation is also applied to understanding pyromania, except that the fire-setting is viewed as a means of regaining potency.

Nonpsychoanalytic interpretations of the impulse disorders have examined the personality characteristics or the physiological basis for these disorders. In pathological gambling, research has suggested that the individuals need recognition, require excitement and stimulation in their lives, or are controlled by fantasies about winning. Among those suffering from pyromania, the fire-setting may reflect a means for a passive-aggressive person to release hostility indirectly through the fires. Regarding the explosive personality, some indirect evidence suggests a possible organic origin, possibly related to the hypothalamus.

Treatment for the various impulsive disorders has varied in accord with what origins have been hypothesized. Therapies using psychoanalytic explanations have centered on resolving the underlying conflicts, such as the sense of sexual frustration or inadequacy. An organization, Gamblers Anonymous, provides peer support from other former gamblers in a way similar to Alcoholics Anonymous. Where the gambling is viewed as a symptom of difficulties in a marriage, then marital counseling appears to be valuable. Various types of behavior therapies have been used, including aversive training to inhibit undesirable behaviors and reinforcements to strengthen socially desired behaviors. Finally, although little is known about the explosive disorder, a self-control training program, used originally for anger-control, may eventually prove useful for this impulse disorder.

## KEY TERMS

**Aversive training**
**Disorders of impulse control**
**Explosive disorder**
**Impulse-control training**
**Kleptomania**
**Pathological gambling**
**Psychosurgery**
**Pyromania**
**Token economy system**

# CHAPTER 13

## Substance Abuse Disorders: The Consequences of Alcohol or Drug Abuse

- **"Am I abnormal if I use marijuana occasionally?"**
- **What is the significance of being able to tell when your blood alcohol level is about 0.06 percent?**
- **Alcoholics often feel that they are really only social drinkers. How can one tell the difference?**
- **If your roommate is a regular "Jekyll-and-Hyde" after a few drinks, what might you suspect?**
- **Since pathological intoxication and delirium tremens are considered acute disorders, while Korsakoff's is not, what are the implications for handling patients?**
- **What causes a person to be alcoholic?**
- **Discuss the controversy over the controlled drinking approach and Alcoholics Anonymous.**
- **If use of a drug involves no physical dependence or tolerance, is it considered nonaddicting?**
- **There is much discussion about the legalization of marijuana. What are the pros and cons of the drug?**

**TABLE 13–1**

**Substance Use Disorders**

| *Type* | *Major Characteristics* |
|---|---|
| Alcohol abuse | Inability to control the intake of alcohol. |
| Alcohol dependence | Symptoms of tolerance or withdrawal. |
| Drug abuse | Inability to control the use of drug substances. |
| Drug dependence | Symptoms of increased tolerance or of withdrawal. |
| Substance-induced organic mental disorders*: | |
| Alcohol amnestic disorder | Loss of memory and making up of "memories" related to alcoholism. |
| Alcohol hallucinosis | Auditory hallucinations related to alcoholism. |
| Alcohol idiosyncratic intoxication | Temporary confusion, emotional outbursts, or hallucinations related to alcoholism. |
| Alcohol withdrawal delirium | Tremors, hallucinations, fright following withdrawal from alcohol. |

*Although these are classified under DSM-III under the organic mental disorders (see Chapter 18), they are discussed in this chapter since the etiology relates to alcohol use.

## Case History 13–1:
### Alcohol Dependence

Joan G. was a 42-year-old woman committed to the hospital following an episode of drinking and drunken driving. She had attended a party during which she consumed the equivalent of a bottle of wine. On the way to the party, she had stopped at an inn and fortified herself with two quick beers. The evening's affair ended at midnight, after which she headed for home in her car. "I felt a little down in the dumps, and so I took a handful of some tranquilizers I keep in my purse." She proceeded to drive into the back end of a moving bus and was arrested while she sat in her car giggling.

The patient had been married and divorced twice. Her first husband introduced her to social drinking through cocktail parties which he attended as part of his business. She found herself spending more and more time avoiding the other guests in order to remain situated near the kitchen where the glasses were being filled. Soon she began experimenting with a variety of ways of mixing liquor, serving it only to herself. Her housework suffered as she spent more and more of each day in sampling, sipping, then gulping alcohol.

Her current hospitalization is her second. She was previously treated for *delirium tremens* during which she hallucinated imaginary mice. "I was in tears. . . . they climbed all over my body, ripped at my clothes. . . . I couldn't stop them, even when I turned a hose on myself." She screamed incessantly, remained in this condition for five days, then went into a deep sleep. She awakened with complete amnesia and was subsequently discharged.

Currently, she is being treated with a combination of psychotherapy and aversion therapy. She has shown some minimal insight into her maladaptive use of alcohol and hopes for the day when she can abstain completely. However, she still exhibits a tendency to see psychotherapy as a magical arrangement which will effect a cure without her intensive involvement. The therapist feels that her prognosis for recovery is actually poor.

In our society today, drugs have become a part of everyday life. Take a quick inventory of the musts in your own home or apartment: a medicine cabinet containing aspirin and perhaps other drugs; a living room with ashtrays and matches; a refrigerator stocked with beer and wine (there may also be hard liquor in a cabinet); and certainly, the kitchen contains either coffee or tea, or both.

Despite the 10 million persons who have stopped smoking since 1966, there are still some 51 million persons over the age of 17 who smoke, with nearly 1.5 million teenagers being added yearly. Figures on the use of alcohol vary. However, it is estimated that about 93 million Americans drink alcohol to some extent—or nearly 71 percent of the total adult population. And surveys suggest that 34 million Americans have smoked marijuana at least once, with 12 million current users. The use of drugs becomes an issue in psychopathology when the use becomes abuse or dependence. The *substance use disorders* are the subject of this chapter, with major reference to alcohol and drug abuse (as listed in Table 13–1).

## CLASSIFYING SUBSTANCE USE DISORDERS

The substance use disorders are those disorders involving behavioral changes caused by taking substances that affect the central nervous system. The classification excludes medical use of drugs or certain recreational uses where pathological behavior changes are absent, such as in social drinking.

DSM-III has divided *substance use disorders* into two major headings: substance abuse and substance dependence. Substance abuse includes those disorders in which there is a pattern of pathological use of the drug, impairment of either social or occupational function due to substance abuse, and a duration of the disturbance for at least one month. *Substance dependence* includes those disorders in which there is tolerance or withdrawal. *Tolerance* involves the need for higher amounts of a substance to achieve the same effects. *Withdrawal* involves the appearance of certain physical symptoms, such as nausea or craving, on discontinuing use of the substance. In the pages that follow, we will look at the two major substance use disorders, alcohol abuse and drug abuse.[1]

## ALCOHOL ABUSE

Alcohol abuse stands fourth among leading health problems in the United States, outranked only by heart disease, cancer, and other forms of mental disorder. Many famous persons have been problem drinkers, including William Sidney Porter (O. Henry), Jack London, Douglas Fairbanks, Sr., and John and Diana Barrymore. Noah (Genesis 9:21) may have been the first heavy drinker recorded in history. Sinclair Lewis drank a quart of brandy per day and, toward the end of his career, he avoided friends and wandered aimlessly. F. Scott Fitzgerald was known to his intimate friends as F. ''Scotch'' Fitzgerald.

In the overview provided in the next few pages, we will look more closely first at the *substance use disorder* involving alcohol abuse and dependence; then at the *organic mental disorders* that are related to alcohol abuse.

### Symptoms of Alcohol Abuse and Dependence

*Alcohol abuse* is diagnosed by several symptoms. These include the need for daily use of alcohol; the inability to reduce or discontinue drinking despite attempts at abstinence; the occurrence of binges (intoxication for two days or more); blackouts or amnesia during intoxication; impairment of social or occupational functioning; having the above symptoms last for at least one month. *Alcohol dependence,* in turn, is diagnosed when a person shows signs of moving a step beyond the alcohol abuse behaviors. The signs of dependency include both increased tolerance and the effects of withdrawal, so that cessation of drinking causes physical distress (Skinner & Allen, 1982).

1 Although tobacco smoking has been found to cause dependence and is listed as a substance use disorder by DSM-III, it is outside our interest and will not be discussed in this book.

**TABLE 13–2**

**Amount of Alcohol and Degree of Intoxication***

| *Amount of whiskey ingested* | *Percentage of alcohol in blood* | *Stage of intoxication* | *Clinical effects* |
|---|---|---|---|
| 2.5 oz. or less | 0.05 or less | Subclinical | Appears normal. |
| 2.5 to 4.5 oz. | 0.05 to 0.09 | Subclinical | Appears normal; minor changes can be detected by special tests. |
| 4.5 to 10.5 oz. | 0.09 to 0.21 | Stimulation | Seems less inhibited; more emotional; coordination is impaired. |
| 9.0 to 15.0 oz. | 0.18 to 0.30 | Confusion | Disturbed sensation; lowered sense of pain; unstable walk; slurred speech. |
| 13.5 to 19.5 oz. | 0.27 to 0.39 | Stupor | Marked lack of response to stimuli; nearing paralysis. |
| 18.0 to 24.0 oz. | 0.36 to 0.48 | Coma | Unconsciousness; respiratory depression; temperature below normal; anesthesia; disturbance of circulation; possible death. |

*Based on formula of Dr. H. Heise: x/0.02 no. of oz. of 86 proof liquor taken by 165 pd. man, where x = blood alcohol percent. Overlapping figures are used since differing individuals with differing physical and mental conditions will vary in their reactions.
SOURCES: Adapted from *Aspects of Alcoholism,* 2nd ed., vol. 1, by Roche Laboratories, 1963, Philadelphia: Lippincott; and *Report of the Committee for Intoxication* by C. Muehlberger, 1938, Chicago: Natl. Safety Council.

Alcohol abuse is illustrated by the insurance salesman who says, "Sure I drink a little, it helps me relax and I enjoy life a little more, after all, I work hard for what little I get . . . . Some people take aspirins. I find that a small taste of good bourbon makes me sharper and a more alert businessman anyway . . . . The real problem is that everyone passed the rumor that I'm a drunk just because of one party . . . ." But his wife says, "He drinks all the time, alone, with others, in the morning, at lunch . . . . His best friend won't ask him out . . . . I wish he could stop like he says, but he can't . . . . He just thinks he can . . . . His business is down because he drinks and not the reverse." Joan, whom we described in Case History 13–1, provides an illustration of alcohol dependence.

***Four Phases.*** A number of researchers have attempted to describe a pattern of development by which alcohol use becomes alcohol abuse. In very general terms, the alcohol abuser seems to go through several phases on the way to becoming alcohol dependent. One early study characterizes these stages as the *prealcoholic symptomatic phase,* the *prodromal phase,* the *crucial phase,* and the *chronic phase* (Jellinek, 1946).

In the *prealcoholic symptomatic phase,* the individual begins to establish a drinking pattern. More and more reasons for celebrating are found. A routine is established: the eye-opener in the morning, the martini before lunch, the quick one before going home, the one to relax after a hard day's work, and the nightcap before turning in.

The *prodromal phase* is initiated by the occurrence of periods of amnesia or a "pulling of the blanks," during which time the individual remains conscious and carries out activities, but without any later recall. In addition, the person is becoming aware of being different from friends or acquaintances. However, the individual will still deny having a problem. He or she slyly gulps the first drink in order to have another while friends are still fixing their first. In a subtle fashion, the entire attitude toward drinking has changed from being a part of an everyday routine to a consuming need.

In the *crucial phase,* the person becomes somewhat alarmed at his or her dependence and strives for control. Temporary abstinence may be possible, but this lasts for shorter and shorter periods. Alcohol has become more and more crucial—to the extent that nutritional needs are neglected and the person is concerned only about protecting the supply of liquor.

The *chronic phase* is ushered in by drinking and prolonged intoxication during the day, the so-called benders. The individual lives only to drink. All else in life—family, occupation, friends, appearance, health, self-esteem, honor, and social or ethical obligations—becomes secondary. There is no longer any attempt to offer a defense or excuse for drinking—the ultimate result may be death or organic mental disorder.

Current evidence indicates that not all problem drinkers pass through these phases, and that they may overlap (Pattison et al., 1977). Although they do not represent inexorable progressions expected of all alcohol abusers, the phases do provide a means of helping to understand the various experiences involved in alcohol abuse and developing dependency.

## Alcohol-induced Organic Disorders

We have been discussing the substance use disorder of alcohol abuse and dependence. The presence of these disorders can also cause an organic disorder. In this event, a person would be diagnosed as possessing both a *substance use disorder* and an *organic mental disorder*. Four major types of organic mental disorders related to alcohol are: alcohol idiosyncratic intoxication, alcohol withdrawal delirium (delirium tremens), alcohol amnestic disorder (Korsakoff's psychosis), and alcohol hallucinosis. These organic mental disorders derived from substance abuse will be described in the next sections.

***Alcohol Idiosyncratic Intoxication.*** This condition is a form of *acute* reaction in that the symptoms have a sudden onset, are short in duration, and are considered reversible. Its primary symptoms are rigidity of the pupils, the sudden onset of mental confusion, and emotional change. Even moderate amounts of alcohol produce a transitory state far beyond the condition of simple intoxication. The person may become confused, disoriented, and excitable. Hallucinations, sensory distortions and illusions, and brief delusions may dramatically and suddenly appear. Emotions—ranging from severe anxiety to deep depression to extreme rage—could lead to suicidal or homicidal actions. Criminal acts of violence, including murder, rape, arson, burglary, and manslaughter are sometimes attributed to this disorder.

Different factors may be relevant in explaining each individual case. It may be that the alcohol simply acts as a precipitating factor in a person who is already typically impulsive and emotional. Since pathological intoxication also occurs among epileptics (persons with brain disorders involving convulsions), there is a possibility that this acute reaction to alcohol is a form of epilepsy. The symptoms of alcohol idiosyncratic intoxication last from a few minutes to a day or more. The confusion and excitement or emotional change are usually followed by a prolonged sleep, after which the individual remembers nothing of the episode.

***Delirium Tremens.*** *Delirium tremens,* or alcohol withdrawal delirium, is an acute reaction that appears in chronic alcoholics (usually individuals who have been alcoholics for 5 to 15 years). The condition most often occurs after a severe or prolonged period of heavy drinking. Because it takes place after the person has stopped drinking, the DTs are considered withdrawal reactions. A lack of food and sleep also seems to be associated with the condition.

Symptoms include pupil dilation; tremors of the fingers, lips, face, and even tongue; and a rapid, irregular, and weak pulse rate. As is common in all states of delirium, the person may misidentify people, lose sense of time and place, and may show marked interference of attention.

The DTs are often characterized by vivid illusions and hallucinations. Visual hallucinations may involve frightening or fantastic animals that threaten and horrify. Intense tactile hallucinations may make the person feel that gruesome, fast-moving animals, such as ants, spiders, or mice, are crawling on them or are under their skin.

The emotional state most often associated with delirium tremens is understandable—apprehension, terror, and irritability. The mood is associated with the illusions and hallucinations that appear. Thus if the telephone wire turns into a threatening snake, the individual may cringe, cower in fear, or desperately cry out for his or her life.

Part of these experiences may be a product of the person's extreme suggestibility, another characteristic of delirium tremens. This suggestibility can be seen in the ease which some patients can be prompted to respond to a suggestion. For example, an individual may take an imaginary string, under instructions, and wind it into a ball. Or the person may actually begin to read from a blank sheet of paper when asked.

Delirium tremens normally terminates in two to three days. During hospitalization, the person is kept in bed and placed on a soft diet rich in vitamins, carbohydrates, and dextrose. Often, the individual awakens in a lucid and oriented state after a deep, prolonged sleep—although brief periods of delirium may occur at night during convalescence. Occasionally, the delirium tremens merges into Korsakoff's psychosis.

***Alcohol Amnestic Disorder (Korsakoff's Psychosis).*** This alcohol-related organic disorder was first described in 1887 by the Russian psychiatrist Sergei Korsakoff, who associated it with polyneuritis, a nerve inflammation, although the two do not always appear together.

Typical symptoms of Korsakoff's psychosis are disorientation of time and place, irreversible anterograde amnesia (loss of memory for events that have just occurred), and a marked tendency to *confabulate,* or fabricate answers to fill in the past. Unlike the previously described organic disorders, the person with Korsakoff's psychosis seems clear instead of confused, and may readily identify friends and relatives. On further examination, however, it becomes evident that the person remembers little beyond immediate observation or recent memory. In some cases, even memory for long-past events may become lost. Yet, the individual is jocular and willingly answers questions about the past, calling on fictitious memories to conceal the amnesia.

There is evidence that Korsakoff's psychosis results from poor nutrition, especially vitamin B deficiency, rather than from alcoholic intoxication. The chronic problem drinker is particularly prone to such deficiencies because of poor dietary habits. However, recent research has also shown that even with good nutrition, long-term alcohol use can still cause brain damage (U.S. Department of Health, Education & Welfare, 1980).

The treatment of Korsakoff's psychosis centers on dietary prescriptions. Foods rich in vitamin B complex are liberally provided to correct the vitamin deficiency. Within six to eight weeks, the person usually returns to normal mental and physical functioning. In some cases, the improvement takes place with no return of memory, and with intellectual damage.

***Alcohol Hallucinosis.*** A fourth alcohol-related organic disorder, *alcohol hallucinosis,* takes its name from the primary symptom involved, auditory hallucinations. The individual typically suffers no loss of memory, and remains oriented for place, time, and person. Yet he or she is more and more disturbed by sounds or voices.

These voices may start off mildly reproachful, but eventually become increasingly accusatory, threatening, or humiliating, arousing fearfulness and terror. They may accuse the person of sexual crimes, or plot punishments in great detail, such as, "When he's least suspecting, we'll sharpen our knives and cut him up and burn the remains." Sounds of a rhythmical, mechanical nature can accompany the voices, such as the sound of knives being sharpened or the measured fall of footsteps approaching. Although the auditory hallucinations are most common, olfactory and visual hallucinations may also occur.

There may also be delusions that are consistent with the hallucinatory content, so that the person begins to believe what he or she hears. The individual may run panic-stricken for help, turn to attack an imaginary foe, or finally succumb to despair and attempt suicide. The hallucinosis may persist anywhere from a few days to a month. If excessive drinking continues, recurrence of the symptoms is probable.

Despite the association between alcohol and hallucinosis, it is currently unclear whether the disorder is directly attributable to alcohol or whether alcohol simply releases the symptoms of an existing disorder. In some cases, the alcohol may be a precipitating factor disclosing a hidden schizophrenic reaction. Other conditions—such as prolonged physical illness, drugs, or exhaustion—might just as well have triggered the same reaction.

### Dynamics of Alcoholism

In exploring the dynamics of alcohol abuse or dependence, probably the most salient point to remember is that all alcohol abusers are not alike. Lemere (1953) reviewed the evidence and concluded that the only characteristic that all alcoholics share is that they drink too much. Consequently, there are probably multiple causations for alcohol abuse. Among the most important approaches to understanding alcohol abuse are the psychoanalytic explanations, psychological explanations based on personality, sociocultural explanations, and genetic and physiological explanations.

**Psychoanalytic Viewpoint.** According to the *psychoanalytic* viewpoint, alcohol abuse derives from a developmental fixation at the early oral stage. This fixation predisposes the individual to be dependent and also to be intolerant of frustration or pain (see Chapter 3). This fixation leads to the reliance on oral behaviors such as drinking, eating, and smoking. As an infant, the problem drinker found that hunger, anxiety, and loneliness were all eliminated by an almost magical fluid, milk. As an adult, the alcohol abuser again searches for a similar liquid that is able to accomplish the same feats (Menninger, 1938). Alcohol comes the closest. In a sense, alcoholic intoxication is an attempt at self-cure of tensions and conflicts.

Psychoanalytic interpretation also views the individual as having hostile feelings that cannot be directly expressed because of another trait, extreme dependency on others (Zirich, 1981). Alcohol meets both needs: it provides a release for the hostility, but also provides a built-in excuse (it was the alcohol acting, not me). It also acts as a form of self-punishment for this release of hostility. The self-destructive effects of alcohol have often been emphasized as providing a form of atonement for the guilt caused by aggression, as a form of slow suicide. Although the results differ considerably for different samples, suicide attempts and actual suicide completions do appear to be higher among alcohol abusers (Ellermann, 1948).

**Psychological Explanations.** A second approach in explaining alcohol abuse examines common childhood and personality characteristics. A national study by Cahalan et al. (1969) and work by others (Brown, 1980; Puskash & Guereski, 1980) suggest that alcohol abusers describe themselves as having more problems and being more unhappy than non-problem drinkers. They appear insecure, anxious, guilt-ridden, emotionally unstable, and low in self-esteem. As children, they had experienced more tensions and had developed fewer ways of handling life's difficulties than most. As adults, the heavy drinkers tended to be aggressive, engaging in self-destructive, attention-seeking behaviors. They also tended to resent authority, lacking both feelings for others and self-control (Sher & Levenson, 1982). Interestingly enough, both abstainers and heavy drinkers showed evidence of personality maladjustment, in contrast to the moderate drinkers.

*Tension Reduction or Pleasure Production?* Still another psychological hypothesis suggests that alcohol is used to reduce anxiety and social tensions. There is some support for this theory. For instance, alcohol abusers have been found to have a low frustration tolerance, a low capacity for coping with any tensions, and a tendency to sidestep or make concessions in order to avoid unpleasantness or decisions. There are also reports that drinking may reduce anxiety and depression (Farber et al., 1980; Sher & Levenson, 1982). Although the tension-reduction hypothesis is persuasive, other reports have revealed inconsistencies. For example, there is some evidence that alcohol in higher doses may actually heighten negative emotional states, and that it may not reduce anxiety (Keane & Lisman, 1980; Steer et al., 1983).

A substitute hypothesis is that alcohol is initially used because of the pleasant feelings it generates, rather than the negative feelings it reduces (Malatesta et al., 1981). There is now information that confirms that alcohol does provide positive feelings such as elation and sociability, and that the individual experiences a warm glow. In all, then, it would seem that drinking may have some tension-reducing features results, although for some alcohol users anxiety and depression may remain untouched or even worsen.

*Limits of Psychological Research.* Despite mounting research on the psychological traits of alcohol abusers, one serious drawback limits the significance of the data. Nearly all studies have been based on analyses of chronic problem drinkers: persons who are already either hospitalized or receiving other treatment for their condition. It is difficult to determine whether the traits discovered are cause or effect. Chronic exposure to alcohol may itself lead to personality changes, creating new conflicts and perhaps even hiding a person's real prealcoholic traits. From the vantage point of hindsight, research reveals traits such as low self-esteem, guilt feelings and anxiety, a low frustration tolerance, and an inability to face conflicts. The key question is whether such traits are the results of problem drinking, or whether they are factors that led to the drinking problem in the first place.

***Sociocultural Explanations.*** Another way of explaining alcoholism looks not so much at the individual, but at the social environment. Jellinek (1960) proposes that a person becomes initiated into drinking because it is part of the social culture. Jack London, the famous writer, for instance, did not enjoy the taste of alcohol, but found that social drinking in saloons was associated with good fellowship. Bartenders, liquor salesmen, nightclub entertainers and other persons whose occupations involve a high exposure to drinking appear more susceptible to alcohol abuse. In addition, exposure to parental models who drink also seems to help initiate alcoholism. Winokur et al. (1970) found the rate of alcoholism among the parents of alcoholics to be about 40 percent. It appears that encouragement of drinking by one's social group may well be involved in starting a person on the path to alcoholism.

However, further cultural data suggest that the problem is more complicated. For instance, the Jews, Irish, Chinese, Italians, and French are all exposed to a high incidence of drinking. Yet, the Jews, Italians, and Chinese have low rates of alcohol abuse while the Irish and French have high rates (Shaw et al., 1978; Sue et al., 1979). The significant factor seems to be the extent to which drinking has become formally integrated into the culture. For the Jew, the Italian, and the Chinese, the use of alcohol is highly controlled as part of mealtime and religious rituals, and drunkenness is strongly disapproved. This does not hold true for either the Irish or the French, both of whom use alcohol in a less controlled fashion.

***Genetic Explanations.*** In addition to the psychoanalytic, psychological, and sociocultural explanations, a fourth factor in alcohol abuse may be heredity. One study is especially relevant here (Goodwin et al., 1973). It looked at men who had been adopted in in-

*In many Jewish families, drinking alcoholic beverages is a solemn part of religious* ***rituals*** *such as the Passover. When sobriety is a cultural virtue, alcohol abuse is low.*

fancy so that they were separated from their alcohol-abusing biological parents. Its findings: 18 percent of the adopted men had themselves become alcohol abusers, compared with only 5 percent of a control group, as Figure 13–1 shows. The adoptive parents were matched for socioeconomic levels and were similar in the proportion of alcohol abuse shown; hence, the results can only be interpreted as supporting a genetic hypothesis.

Additional evidence for heredity comes from animal research. One study (Rodgers & McClearn, 1962) demonstrated that some strains of mice were alcoholic while others were teetotalers. One possible way in which genetics might be involved in this different preference for alcohol is in an inheritance of a different enzyme system. Von Wartburg (1970) has found that just as the enzymes that metabolize alcohol can differ for different species, they also vary among individuals within a species. It is possible, then, that problem drinkers have different sensitivities based on different body chemistry.

***Physiological Explanations.*** Studies of possible *physiological* factors relate closely in some aspects to the genetic research, demonstrating that it is possible to selectively breed animals with high or low preference for alcohol. Further studies have attempted to differentiate such groups of animals, and several hypotheses have been formulated. One approach suggests that excessive use of alcohol damages the cortical cells, changing the metabolic pattern of brain cells so that the brain requires alcohol for continued optimal functioning (Lemere, 1956).

Physiological research has also focused on the question of why some animals seem to *avoid* the use of alcohol (Schlesinger, 1966). Research here has found that low-preference mice tend to metabolize alcohol slower, leading to speculation that an unpleasant interim product of metabolism, perhaps the substance acetaldehyde, was associated with abstinence. Such research found some support for this theory in its discovery that alcoholic mice showed greater activity of the enzyme that promotes metabolism and the elimination of alcohol. In addition, older mice from the alcoholic strain appear to show a decrease in their preference for alcohol with advancing age—a decrease that seems associated with a corresponding decrease in enzyme activity. Finally, the drug antabuse (discussed later), which is sometimes used to treat alcoholics, appears to work by slowing down the elimination of acetaldehyde (Kissin & Begleiter, 1983).

### Treatment of Alcohol Abuse

The first stage in treatment is the withdrawal of alcohol to prevent further deterioration. This drying-out or detoxification period is highly stressful, and tranquilizers are often given to help alcohol-dependent patients better tolerate the withdrawal phase. Previously, drugs such as barbiturates were used, but these are currently used less frequently because of their potential addictive danger—alcohol abusers have been known to readily substitute one addiction for another. Since health is usually impaired by malnutrition, a diet rich in vitamins and glucose is also prescribed. Once the medical aspects are taken care of, the psychological problems are ready for attention. Several different therapy approaches may be used.

***Drug Therapy.*** Chemotherapy has been extensively used in treating alcohol abuse, with 81 to 87 percent of psychiatrists in one survey reporting that they relied to some extent on drugs (Ditman, 1967). Yet, the evidence on the value of drug therapy is not convincing. Although tranquilizers are helpful in reducing the effects of withdrawal, they appear to be of no value in eliminating the drinking behavior itself (Viamontes, 1972). Lysergic acid diethylamide (LSD) received some earlier enthusiasm as a therapeutic agent, and another hallucinogenic drug, peyote, was used by Native Americans for the cure of alcohol dependence. With LSD, the argument is that it produces a transcendental experience bringing self-insight, leading to a near-religious conversion to abstinence. Studies have failed to confirm this effect, however (Abuzzahab & Anderson, 1971).

***Psychotherapy.*** A different approach to alcohol abuse is psychotherapy. Its objectives are to alter the pattern of using alcohol as a response to personal needs. A first stage is the reestablishment of a sense of worth. Next, the individual is motivated to once again seek ways to solve problems instead of drinking them away. It is important that the problem drinker clearly understand the underlying conflicts or needs, so that these issues may be dealt with directly.

A variety of needs may be involved with different persons. McClelland et al. (1972) suggest that alcohol is a means for persons to enhance their sense of social or personal power. In some women, the alcohol serves to increase their feelings of attractiveness (Wilsnack, 1973). In many persons, the alcohol is used because the person feels more able to be the kind of person he or she cannot be when sober, especially when relating with other people. Psychotherapy aims at meeting such needs by helping persons to find themselves *without* alcohol.

Some feel that psychotherapy can be quite helpful in treating alcohol abuse. However, outcome studies have usually failed to provide support for the use of conventional psychotherapy (Neuman & Tamerin, 1971). It is difficult to know why there has not been more success. One possibility may be that alcohol abuse involves such a wide spectrum of problem issues, overlearned behaviors, physiological factors, and coping deficits as to be resistant to single, more traditional approaches (Nathan, 1980).

***Alcoholics Anonymous.*** A third approach to treatment uses group support. Alcoholics Anonymous (AA) is the organization of ex-alcohol abusers who believe that the saying "Once an alcoholic, always an alcoholic" holds true unless complete abstention is maintained. It has received wide support. A nationwide survey of state hospitals showed that 88 percent relied on AA as part of their treatment program, as compared with 75 percent which used drug treatment, and 57 percent which used psychotherapy (Moore & Buchanan, 1966).

Alcoholics Anonymous claims over 8,000 worldwide groups with an estimated membership of over 300,000. The organization offers a sense of belonging and of being understood by companions while preventing the use of denial and rationalization—since all AA members have been alcohol abusers and know such defenses through personal experience. Social pressure to change is high, but much group support is available to help the alcohol abuser achieve day-to-day abstinence. As Table 13-3 indicates, the 12 steps to recovery have definite spiritual overtones.

How effective is AA? Objective data are hard to obtain. Alcoholics Anonymous (1972) reports a 60 percent success rate, while other reports suggest closer to 30 to 35 percent (Bill, 1965). Nevertheless, AA does seem to be a source for support and hope for many alcoholics who remain with the program.

***Behavior Therapy.*** A variety of aversion methods have been used to train alcohol abusers to avoid drinking (Nirenberg, 1983). Among these have been the use of electric shock, drug avoidance training, and covert avoidance training. In the first two, either shock or drugs is paired with alcohol so that alcohol becomes associated with distaste. One drug avoidance program uses Antabuse (disulfiram). A patient who drinks alcohol after taking Antabuse experiences vomiting, dizziness, headache, and cold sweat. Under controlled use, the drug conditions the person to avoid alcohol while the drug is in effect.

In covert training, the person is instructed to imagine some extremely unpleasant fantasies about alcohol. Cautela (1970) has guided alcohol abuse clients in vivid images such as the following:

> You are walking into a bar. You decide to have a glass of beer. . . . As the bartender is pouring the beer, [you feel like vomiting]. . . . As soon as your hand touches the glass, you can't hold it down any longer. . . . It goes all over . . . the glass and the beer. You can see it floating around in the beer. . . . You notice people looking at you. . . . You turn away from the beer and immediately you start to feel better. As you run out of the bar room, you start to feel better and better. (p. 87)

**TABLE 13-3**

**Twelve Steps of Alcoholics Anonymous**

1. We admitted we were powerless over alcohol—that our lives had become unmanageable.
2. Came to believe that a power greater than ourselves could restore us to sanity.
3. Made a decision to turn our will and our lives over to the care of God *as we understood Him.*
4. Made a searching and fearless moral inventory of ourselves.
5. Admitted to God, to ourselves, and to another human being the exact nature of our wrongs.
6. Were entirely ready to have God remove all these defects of character.
7. Humbly asked Him to remove our shortcomings.
8. Made a list of all persons we had harmed, and became willing to make amends to them all.
9. Made direct amends to such people wherever possible, except when to do so would injure them or others.
10. Continued to take personal inventory and when we were wrong promptly admitted it.
11. Sought through prayer and meditation to improve our conscious contact with God *as we understood Him,* praying only for knowledge of His will for us and the power to carry that out.
12. Having had a spiritual awakening as the result of these steps, we tried to carry this message to alcoholics, and to practice these principles in all our affairs.



Aversive conditioning has had mixed success. Electrical aversive conditioning seems relatively ineffective (Cannon et al., 1981). However, the evidence suggests that avoidance therapy using drugs has some value. In a major study of nearly 5,000 alcoholic persons, about 51 percent showed complete abstinence during follow-up periods of up to 10 years (Wilson, 1978). The primary problem is the tendency for patients to quit treatment too early; with Antabuse, only 1 percent of all patients will voluntarily stay on the drug. Covert training has shown less striking results, with less than 25 percent success on follow-up. Despite the drug treatment's apparent effectiveness, however, it is not considered the final answer—for even if the drinking has stopped, other issues are still unresolved. Conflict and frustrations that might be related to drinking behaviors might still be present. Therefore, aversive conditioning is generally not considered as the treatment of choice if it is used alone.

***Controlled Drinking.*** A reconceptualization of alcohol abuse has laid the foundation for another approach—controlled drinking. This method offers a contrast to AA's view that alcohol abusers differ from nonabusers in an inability to "take only one sip." The controlled drinking approach suggests that this interpretation is not only inaccurate, but has shaped treatment methods unnecessarily (Sobell & Sobell, 1978). It argues that alcohol abusers can learn social drinking while still avoiding alcohol abuse. The question, of course, is how to devise the proper training to accomplish controlled drinking. A few answers have been tried.

*Blood Alcohol Discrimination.* Lovibund and Caddy (1970) decided that problem drinkers could stop drinking at the right time if they knew how much they were drinking. In an interesting project, the researchers measured drinkers' blood alcohol levels every 15 to 20 minutes, and asked them to estimate their levels until they became reasonably accurate. The problem drinkers were then required to drink their favorite alcoholic beverage to a certain blood alcohol level (BAL), at which point they received a shock. This training taught problem drinkers to gauge their BAL with a high degree of accuracy, and furthermore, to drink only up to this level after treatment.

*Individualized Behavior Therapy.* Mark and Linda Sobell (1978) developed what they called individualized behavior therapy (IBT). This program defined both appropriate and inappropriate drinking behaviors. Appropriate behaviors cover controlled social drinking, but inappropriate behaviors represent alcohol abuse (Miller & Munoz, 1982). For example, inappropriate behaviors would include asking for a straight drink, gulping the drink, or ordering another drink within 20 minutes of a prior one. Appropriate behaviors, in contrast, include ordering a mixed drink, sipping the drink slowly, and waiting longer before reordering. Alcohol abusers were trained in an actual bar setting, where they could order and actually consume alcohol.

IBT training confronts several factors involved in alcohol abuse. First, clients receive a shock for inappropriate drinking behaviors. Second, the program also includes videotaped playbacks, so that alcohol abusers are forced to watch how they behaved when they drank too much. Third, individualized sessions are aimed at identifying the events and emotional conditions that set the stage for problem drinking. Finally, clients actually seek solutions other than drinking and are expected to carry these out.

## DRUG ABUSE

Drug use has a history nearly as old as the history of humanity. The *narcotic*[2] properties of the opium poppy were known to the Sumerian civilization dating to 7000 B.C. The records indicate that they gave it a name that is still used today, "the plant of joy." The opium derivative, morphine, was isolated in Germany in 1805, and another derivative, heroin, was produced in 1898 as a new miracle drug.

Attitudes have changed considerably regarding these drugs. At first heroin was believed to be medically safe. It was used freely in medications, thereby producing many early cases of accidental dependence. The use of morphine in the Civil War contributed another large share of drug dependence euphemistically referred to as "army disease." Patent medicines and soft drinks mixed with narcotics added to the numbers, and by 1914, when the Harrison Narcotic Act was passed, there were 175,000 addicts in the United States. Later in time, attitudes towards drug use took the opposite extreme, as seen in the warning by the FBI

2 The term *narcotic* technically refers to a class of opium-derived addictive drugs, including morphine, heroin, and codeine, used to relieve pain and induce sleep.

about marijuana, that a drug user becomes a fiend with savage caveman tendencies. His sex desires are aroused and some of the most horrible crimes result (Grinspoon, 1977, p. 17). A case was cited of Elutero G., who ". . . shot to death two women and then committed suicide by literally slicing himself to bits about the abdomen, heart, and throat, in a manner [producible only by] marijuana" (Anslinger & Tompkins, 1953, pp. 23–24).

Currently there are approximately 600,000 drug-dependent persons, most of whom are men. Of several cities with data, New York City reported nearly 13,000 drug abusers, compared to over 4,000 for Detroit; 2,000 each for Chicago, Los Angeles, and Philadelphia; and 900 for Washington, D.C. (NIDA, 1981). Drug experimentation has increased among youth, with 30 percent of high school seniors saying they used some illicit drug such as stimulants, heroin, cocaine, or hallucinogens (U.S. Dept. of Health & Human Services, 1981).

Drugs may be introduced into the body in a variety of ways, depending on the type of drug and the stage of dependency. Morphine, heroin, amphetamines, opium, the barbiturates, peyote (mescaline) or LSD may all be taken orally, either alone or with a sweet substance to disguise the unpleasant taste. As a drug user develops tolerance, however, and higher dosages are sought, hypodermic needles may be used. The most direct method is to insert the narcotic into the vein (*mainlining*), a procedure that often causes damage to the veins and surrounding skin. Inhaling or sniffing drugs such as cocaine is another method for absorbing narcotics. Opium smoking in pipes is an ancient method for taking this drug, while marijuana users inhale the smoke from cigarettes.

## Classifying Drug Abuse

Like alcohol use, drug use disorders are classified into two major categories, drug abuse and drug dependence. Some drugs may lead to either abuse or dependence, such as opium and heroin, barbiturates, amphetamines, and cannabis (marijuana). Two other categories of drugs are listed only as substance abuse drugs: cocaine and the hallucinogens (LSD, mescaline, and DMT, for instance). They are excluded from the category of substance dependence drugs, because no physical dependence has yet been found.

We should point out that drug dependence is defined if either tolerance *or* withdrawal reactions have been shown with the particular drug. Cannabis dependence is diagnosed if both tolerance and impairment of social or occupational functioning occur, even though withdrawal signs have not been conclusively demonstrated as a result of marijuana use.[3]

## Symptoms of Abuse for Some Common Drugs

Various drugs produce different effects, so that beyond the broad behavior patterns that are associated with either abuse or dependence, there is not a single, all-encompassing picture of the drug experience. Focus 13–1 suggests the range of effects. Some drugs produce a rush or a high; others have just the opposite effect, dulling the senses; still others may produce hallucinations or heightened perceptual sensitivities. Table 13–4 provides a classification of drugs according to shared characteristics, and Figure 13–1 provides an overview based on the drugs' influence as either stimulants (uppers) or depressants (downers). The following discussions look more closely at a number of drugs and characteristic effects associated with their use.

***Opium and Narcotic Derivatives.*** Opium is a dark, sticky substance prepared from the unripe pods of the opium poppy. It is usually smoked, and it gives off a pungent odor. Opium is addictive, and so are its derivatives: morphine, heroin, codeine, and Demerol.

Of the opiate derivatives, heroin is by far the leading drug used illegally in the United States. It is interesting to note that heroin was once chosen by the German-owned Bayer Company, as the catchy name for its new wonder drug, used as a cough suppressant and cure for morphine addiction (Fuqua, 1978). Heroin (H, horse, smack, or shit) is the most dangerous of drugs when obtained in the form of capsules (caps) or packages (decks). Abusers may start off sniffing it,

3 DSM-III acknowledges that the question of whether regular use of marijuana leads to tolerance is still being debated, as this chapter discusses later. At this time, DSM-III seems to be keeping the classification cannabis dependence for use when tolerance is observed or proven in the user.

## Case History 13–2:
### Confessions of an Opium Eater

Thomas DeQuincey, the renowned English author, wrote *The Confessions of an English Opium-Eater* (1924) as his first contribution to *The London Magazine.* The book was well received and was to lay the foundations of a successful career for him. Its theme centered around his confessions about his life with drugs.

DeQuincey was one of six children born of a merchant. His father died when he was seven, leaving the children in the care of four guardians. He was quite close to one sister and was deeply affected by her childhood death; he even contrived to secretly visit her corpse prior to the funeral.

DeQuincey attributed his opium addiction to his childhood unhappiness and a physical illness. A college friend suggested opium as a means of deadening the pains from a toothache, and DeQuincey continued to use opium to rid himself of the agonies from a recurring stomach condition that he acquired because of "extremities of hunger, suffered in my boyish days" (perhaps a peptic ulcer). The addiction precipitated four opium crises, but DeQuincey was able to recover his health after some 18 years of opium addiction.

Some of his experiences are worth quoting:

> Opium . . . communicates serenity and equipose to all the facilities . . . and it gives that sort of vital warmth which is approved by the judgment, and which probably always accompany a bodily constitution of primeval or antediluvian health. (pp. 171–72)
>
> . . .at the time I began to take opium daily, I could not have done otherwise. I confess. . . . I hanker too much after a state of happiness, both for myself and others; I cannot face misery . . . and am little capable of encountering present pain. . . . (p. 189)
>
> The cursed crocodile became to me the object of more horror than all the rest. I was compelled to live with him; and (as was always the case in my dreams) for centuries . . . the abominable head of the crocodile, and his leering eyes, looked out at me, multiplied into ten thousand repetitions; and I stood loathing and fascinated. So often did this hideous reptile haunt my dreams. . . . No experience was so awful to me. (p. 233)
>
> Nothing short of mortal anguish, in a physical sense, it seemed, to wean myself from opium; yet, on the other hand, death through overwhelming nervous terrors—death by brain fever or by lunacy—seemed too certainly to besiege the alternative course.
>
> I did accomplish my escape. . . . I triumphed. But infer not, reader, from this word "triumphed," a condition of joy or exultation. Think of me as one, even when four months had passed, still agitated, writhing, throbbing, palpitating, shattered. (p. 237)

then move to skin popping by injecting it into the arm or leg, and finally mainlining it by injecting it directly into the vein.

Opium and its derivatives work as depressants, dulling the cental nervous system to cause decreased fear, pain, sexual need, and hunger. With prolonged use, it also lowers ambition, intellectual efficiency, and aggression, although there is no evidence for mental deterioration. Vivid fantasies have been reported with opium, although true hallucinations do not often occur. Users can develop a tolerance for narcotics; increased need is associated with the possible danger of overdose.

Withdrawal symptoms can occur with opium dependence. These symptoms are similar to those of all drug dependence withdrawals: they include cold sweats, tremors, abdominal cramps, restlessness, retching, diarrhea, insomnia, and uncontrollable yawning. Some reactions appear to be due to the user's preconceived expectations of the difficulty of withdrawal. In fact, substance dependent persons are sometimes afraid to stop using drugs because of notions about how bad withdrawal will be . . . and would prefer to continue any other actions that will help sustain the drug habit.

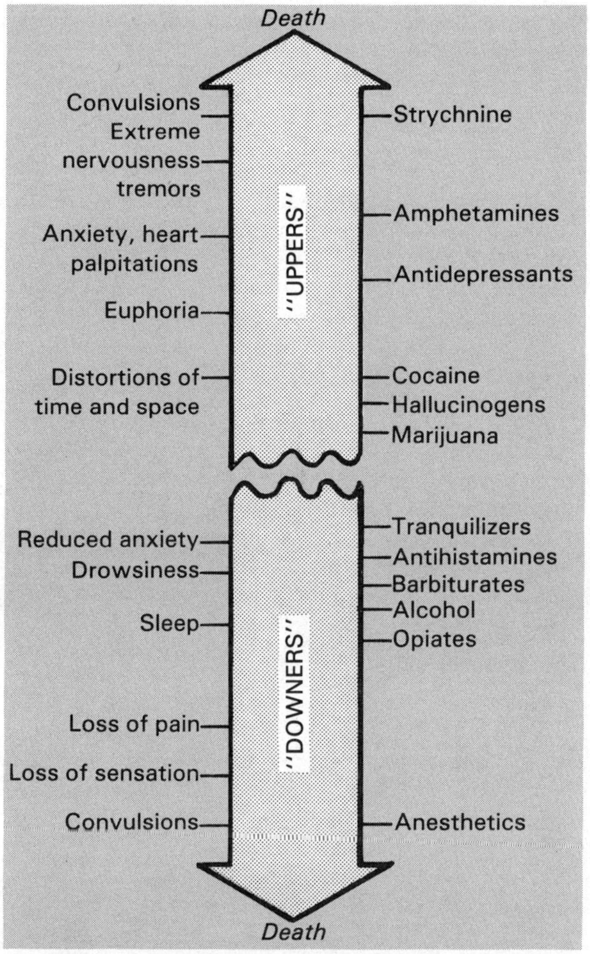


**FIGURE 13–1** "Uppers" and "downers": the continuum of drug action.

SOURCE: Redrawn from *Essentials of Abnormal Psychology by* B. Kleinmuntz, 1974, New York: Harper & Row.

***Marijuana.*** Marijuana is one of the cheapest forms of drugs. It is actually the flowers and stems of the hemp plant, which are loosely rolled into a cigarette. It is most often smoked, although it can be eaten when added to cookie batter and baked. It goes by many names, which sometimes refer to its place of origin. In a cigarette form it is called a joint; unrolled, it is grass, Acapulco gold, Mary Jane, Maui wowee, or pot. In eastern countries, the drug is called hashish, ganga or manzoul and is smoked or chewed or even consumed as a drink.

Marijuana is often used as a substitute for alcohol.

*Narcotic dependence may lead to* ***mainlining****, where the drug is introduced directly into the blood vessel with a hypodermic needle.*

Some claim that it relaxes inhibitions and increases relaxation. It often produces a mild high, heightened sensations, or pleasant passivity. The passage of time may be unusually slowed subjectively. Physiological effects often include increased heart rate, slowing of reactions, increased appetite, intense thirst, and reddening of the eyes. Marijuana is not known to have aphrodisiac qualities. The effects of marijuana are generally very difficult to predict, ranging from euphoria to anxiety or depression, depending on personality, expectations, and the dosage of THC (for tetrahydrocannabinol, the active ingredient in marijuana). Chronic use may result in sleep difficulty and lowered lung capacity (Drug Abuse Council, 1980).

Marijuana differs from the opiates in several ways. It now appears that not all users experience withdrawal symptoms on disuse of marijuana. How-

# FOCUS 13–1:
## First-hand Experiences with Substance Use

*Marijuana*

"The first thing I noticed was that I began to hear my saxophone as though it was inside my head . . . the notes came easing out of my horn like they've already been made up, greased, and stuffed into the bell, so all I had to do was blow a little and send them on their way." (Mezzrow & Wolfe, 1946, p. 72)

*Hashish*

"I felt my blood rushing through my body . . . into my eyes until I could no longer see: it beat thickly in my eyes, and so throbbed in my heart that I feared my ribs would give way." (Ludlow, 1857, p.20)

"I felt a thrill . . . a shock, throughout my entire frame, leaping to my fingers' ends, piercing my brain . . . a sense of getting something which I had not bargained for . . . [then] a reverberating peal of a grand cathedral organ . . . filled [me] . . . with a grief that was more than human." (Grinspoon, 1977, p.89)

"I hear music . . . far away, but in its very faintness there is a lure. In the soft surge and swell of the minor notes there breathes a harmony that ravishes the sense of sound. A resonant organ, with a stop of sapphire and a diapason of opal, diffuses endless octaves from star to star." (Robinson, 1946, p. 394)

*LSD*

"My body metamorphosed into a vast, dusty desert but my head sat on top and my hands were at the sides as normal . . . with sudden insight, I wanted to laugh because I now knew the meaning of self, of identity, I was me even though the me was not the same anymore with LSD." (author's experience)

*Alcohol*

"When I reach that state, the world is right again, I'm charged with confidence, and joy is mine to give . . . it's as if I am transformed, throwing off the mantle of gloom, there is no past to depress me and the future is in my control again . . . so what harm is it that I'm alcoholic?" (author's experience)

*PCP*

"After a while, the color waves seem to be less distorted, as though I were no longer seeing through water but crystal clear . . . and with the change, horrors . . . the picture changed to be writhing arms, decapitated heads trying to speak to me, bloody hands reaching out for me . . . every object standing forth sharply from the dark background . . . real and reaching for me." (author's experience)

**TABLE 13-4**

**Classification of Common Drugs According to Their Effects**

| | |
|---|---|
| *The narcotics* | Opium and its derivatives<br>Morphine<br>Heroin<br>Codeine<br>Demerol |
| *The sedatives* | Barbituates<br>Bromides<br>Chloral hydrate<br>Paraldehyde |
| *The tranquilizers* | Equanil<br>Miltown<br>Librium<br>Valium<br>Quaalude |
| *The stimulants* | Cocaine<br>Benzedrine<br>Dexedrine<br>STP |
| *The hallucinogens or psychotomimetics* | Peyote (mescaline)<br>LSD<br>Psilocybin<br>Marijuana<br>DMT<br>PCP |

ever, increased tolerance for marijuana can occur for some persons.

***Cocaine.*** This drug comes from the leaves of a coca plant and is referred to as coke, star dust, or snow. It may be taken by sniffing, swallowing, or intravenous injection.

Mild euphoria and friendly, extroverted behavior are early effects of cocaine. As a stimulant it gives some people an added lift or a sense of exhilaration. In fact, Sigmund Freud once used it on himself and his patients when he discovered its ability to lift depression and increase energy. The original Coca-Cola® was marketed in 1886 as a beverage that not only was delicious, but also served as a stimulant and cure for melancholy.[4] However, with continued cocaine abuse, the pleasant effects give way to negative ones as the abuser becomes suspicious, irritable, and develops frightening hallucinations, such as the sensation of having bugs under the skin.

Users do not develop an increased tolerance for the drug, nor are there physiological withdrawal symptoms when it is discontinued. However, a psychological craving may develop, prompting the individual to continue its use.

***Barbiturates.*** Barbiturates are used for sedation. They include phenobarbital, Nembutal, sodium amytal, and Seconal—referred to on the street as feenies, yellow jackets, blue heavens, and red devils. Before the tranquilizers were discovered, the barbiturates were the primary drugs used to help patients become calm. In fact, they are still used in general medical treatment to induce sleep. Because of this widespread acquaintance, about a million Americans have been estimated as dependent on barbiturates (Beschner & Friedman, 1979).

The barbiturates act as depressants. The individual feels relaxed, comfortable, and calm. Noticeable symptoms may include both slurred speech and unsteadiness as drowsiness increases. Tolerance levels increase until the individual has become physiologically dependent, showing withdrawal symptoms upon discontinuation. Withdrawal after prolonged intake of high dosages will produce severe epilepticlike seizures, anxiety, nausea, and tremors. There is also the danger of overdose either through deliberate increases or through accident. Newspapers are full of reports of accidental overdoses in which the patient started with the correct dose for sedation, became sleepy and confused about how much he or she took, and so took more and more pills in the effort to fall asleep. It is estimated that about 18 percent of drug-caused deaths are from barbiturates (Project DAWN, 1976–77).

***Amphetamines.*** These compounds, whose chemical structures are similar to norepinephrine (described in Chapter 4), act as central nervous system stimulants. These pep pills, bennies, cartwheels, copi-

4 Since 1903, Coca-Cola® has been flavored with coca leaves but has had none of the properties of cocaine.

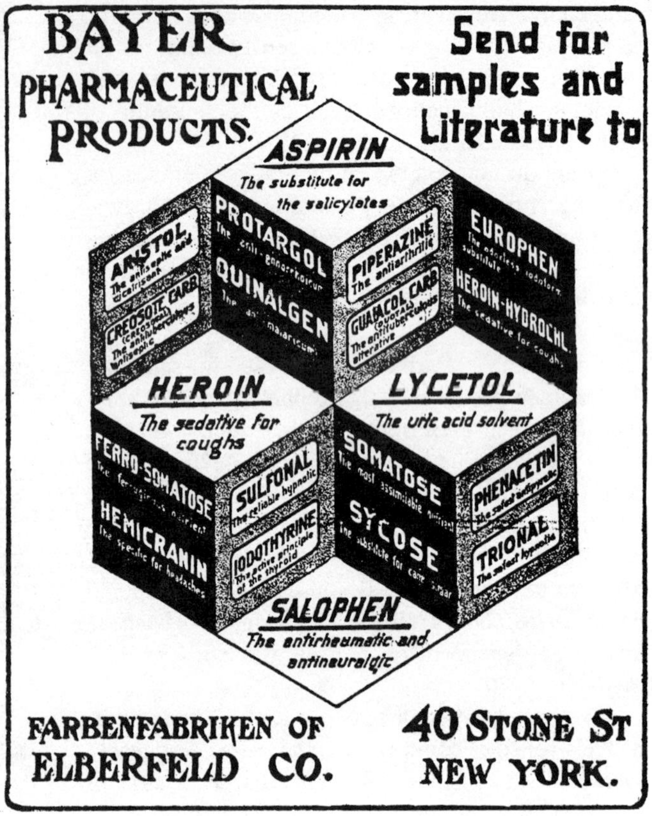


*At one time, commercial painkillers contained* ***heroin****.*

lots, or speed include Dexedrine and Benzedrine and have been used by many to remain awake during all-night study sessions or prolonged travel. Athletes have sometimes used the stimulants as an extra (and illegal) boost in competition. Amphetamines are also sometimes popular to curb appetites in weight control.

The drugs produce an increased level of alertness, elevation of mood (a rush), and a sense of well-being and confidence. The astronaut Gordon Cooper was ordered to take an amphetamine to better prepare for manual reentry when the automatic system failed (Green & Levy, 1976). Physical dependence may develop, with increased tolerance and withdrawal symptoms. Side effects involve restlessness, hostility, tension, insomnia, intense fear or panic, suicidal behavior, paranoid delusions, or hallucinations. Nausea, vomiting, diarrhea, increased blood pressure and even death are potential results. A sad circumstance in Japan was the wartime reliance on amphetamines to increase production efforts, and the release of the excess stockpile of the drug when the war ended. This led to the hospitalization of some 5,700 amphetamine abusers for psychotic symptoms by 1955; of these, nearly one-third were still hospitalized 10 years later (Imlah, 1971).

***Tranquilizers.*** Tranquilizers such as Librium and Valium are commonly used in place of barbiturates to control anxiety. When milder forms of tranquilizers were manufactured, they were believed essentially nonaddictive and were widely prescribed for minor symptoms. Thus, drugs such as Valium, Miltown, Equanil, and Librium became household items in a number of families. More recently, however, it appears that tranquilizers such as meprobamate (Miltown, Equanil) can be habit forming, and that patients may show the physical tolerance and withdrawal symptoms associated with drug dependence (Baker, 1983).

Because tranquilizers help reduce tensions, they make it easier to face conflicts. One patient (he was an expert on both) described to the author the differences between alcohol and tranquilizers as follows: "You take alcohol and your problem vanishes while you're drunk, but the morning after it not only returns, but you feel even worse than you did before! With tranquilizers, your problem is still there, but it doesn't matter to you anymore; and the next morning it isn't any bigger than it was before." Withdrawal from tranquilizers is less agonizing than with other drug addictions. However, the symptoms may include confusion, anxiety, insomnia, and convulsions in some cases.

***Lysergic Acid Diethylamide.*** Known as acid, cubes, or pearly gates, LSD is one of a group of hallucinogenic drugs (hallucination-producing) which reached great heights of popularity during the mid-20th century. It was accidentally discovered by a Swiss chemist, Albert Hoffman, who was exposed to a small quantity in a test tube and found himself subsequently undergoing a bizarre ride on his way home an hour later. Afterward, Hoffman said, "The faces of those present appeared like grotesque colored masks. . . . I lost all control of time; space and time became more and more disorganized and I was overcome with fears that I was going crazy. . . . I thought I had died. My 'ego' was suspended somewhere in space and I saw my body lying dead . . ." (Stafford, 1971).

A dose of LSD as low as a quarter-millionth of an ounce can trigger a dreamlike experience affecting the senses, judgment, memory, motor coordination, and the emotions. Perceptual distortions and visual hallucinations develop, as does *synesthesia* in some cases. Synesthesia is the responsiveness of one sense modality when another is stimulated—for example, a musical note may be experienced as a definite color, or the sound of a typewriter may be converted into a visual fireworks display. Severe emotional effects have been reported, ranging from excruciatingly pleasant feelings to terrorizing panic to a religious-like conversion.

As with marijuana and peyote, it is difficult to determine which effects are a function of the chemical properties of the drug and which are due to the expectations, suggestibility, and beliefs of the user. Negative effects do seem to occur with some frequency; for example, during an 18-month period in Los Angeles County alone, some 4,100 adverse reactions requiring professional care were noted—a dangerously high number (Ungerleider et al.,1968).

Chronic exposure to LSD may have lasting effects on the user. It may lead to extreme passivity, increased belief in magical-mystical ideas, perhaps some central nervous system alterations, and chromosomal damage (Lipton et al., 1978). In a review of studies through early 1971, Louria (1971) discovered 6 of 17 studies with evidence for chromosomal breaks involving *translocation* (a broken chromosome attaching itself to another chromosome). Translocations can lead to permanent abnormalities that may be passed on from generation to generation. Some breaks occurred even without overdoses of LSD being taken.

*Many* ***psychotomimetic*** *drugs, such as LSD, produce visual distortions in the user.*

***PCP.*** Phencyclidine, or PCP, has a number of street names, including angel dust, hog, crystal, KJ, elephant, and monkey dust. PCP was first studied medically as an anesthetic, but it was soon rejected because of serious side effects. It hit the streets and spread so rapidly during the mid-1970s as to lead to special hearings by Congress on what was called "the most devastating drug on the streets of our country."

PCP creates several possible experiences depending on dosage: buzzed, wasted, and overdosed. In the milder buzzed condition, there is a mild euphoria, alertness, and energy: "Like it would make me think quicker in class. I'd write faster, my ideas would get together." When wasted, the user felt physically slow and awkward, speeded up mentally: "The ground turned to marshmallows, like walking on sponges. . . ." When overdosed, the abuser is out of control: "I got too high . . . I froze up . . . I was crying and screaming, 'We're dying; we're gonna die' . . . [moaning]" (Feldman et al., 1979).

Users report different experiences, apparently as a result of environmental setting, expectation, and even social style. For example, the cool users of Philadelphia neighborhoods were able to control the effects of PCP, while the rowdies used PCP to become violent. The unpredictability of results actually serves as an enticement, along with the paradoxes of the experiences of being down (physically) but up (in mental speed), anesthetized but energized. Despite the belief that nothing will go wrong, three of four in one survey suffered severe ill effects involving forgetfulness, lack of coordination, and inability to comprehend (Walters, 1979).

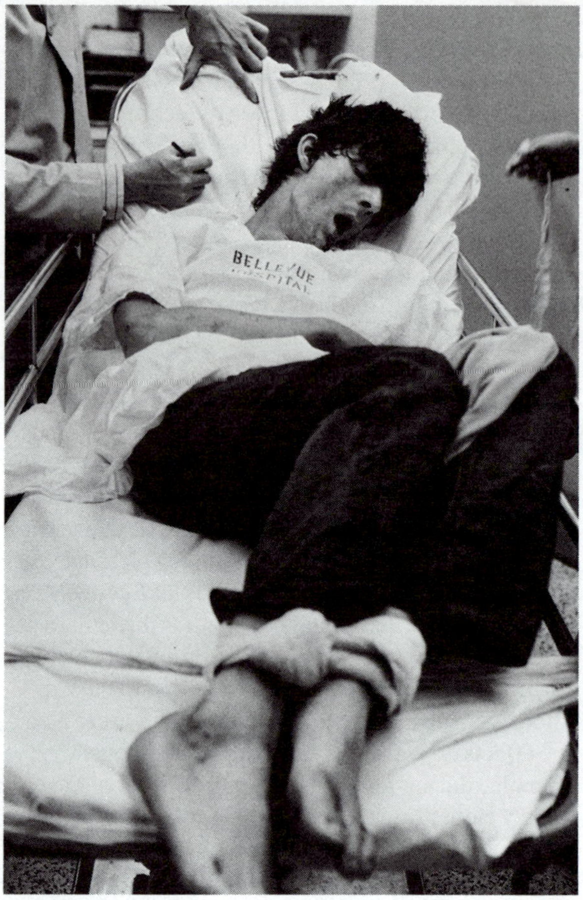


*An often serious danger of drug abuse is* ***overdosage*** *as the user becomes more dependent on drug intake.*

### Dynamics of Drug Addiction

There are actually two major routes to drug dependence: addiction without the consent or intention of the user, and addiction on a more or less voluntary basis. Physical dependence on such drugs as morphine has been known to develop unintentionally, as when the drug is used as a painkiller on battle fields or for alleviating chronic pain as in cancer. Today, *iatrogenic addiction,* or medically produced addiction, is less common for several reasons: the deliberate precautions that are taken, stronger federal control over medical practices, and the availability of nonaddicting substitutes for narcotics. Perhaps 5 percent of admissions to hospitals for drug dependence are iatrogenic addiction (Gorsuch, 1980). Physical dependence in such cases is readily broken through gradual withdrawal of the drug, and future cravings do not seem to develop in such patients, in contrast to those who have voluntarily become addicted.

The majority of known cases of drug abuse and drug dependence have occurred on a voluntary basis, and these will be the focus of our attention here. Several studies have described drug abusers as falling into several patterns: the socially deviant, the rebellious, the gang or group victim, and the neurotic or psychotic. Other explanations look to biological factors, and still others, to the drug culture itself.

***Social Deviation and Drug Abuse.*** The socially deviant pattern is the most characteristic in explaining drug dependency. This pattern involves a picture of social ineptness, insecurity, lack of assertiveness, passivity, and frequently, a continuing emotional relationship with the mother (Green, 1979).

The home environment seems to contribute heavily to the development of this pattern. The mothers are often women who have infantilized their sons while demonstrating both possessiveness and rejection. In some cases the mothers encouraged the youngsters to give up drugs while at the same time procuring more drugs for them. These parents often harbored resentment toward their offspring and attempted to dominate, overprotect, and indulge their sons. One report on physicians who had become drug dependent showed the mixed desires of these patients to remain tied to their parents while also hating their dependency (Scher, 1966). Finally, Kandel et al. (1978) discovered that adolescents perceived that lack of closeness to their fathers was predictive of their later involvement in drugs.

***Rebellion.*** The rebellious feature of some cases of substance abuse is in keeping with the antisocial aspects of narcotics use. For this group, the acting out of aggressive impulses toward society seems to be reflected in criminal acts, delinquency, and the use of narcotics (Henden, 1980). In the National Youth Polydrug Study, nearly 3,000 adolescent drug abusers in treatment centers across the nation were studied. Most were white youngsters, and about one-third of the families were white-collar workers. Of these drug abusers, 73 percent had been picked up by the police (Leukefeld & Clayton, 1979). Drug use, therefore, appears to be another phase in the overall pattern of rebelliousness. Many users come from fragmented families, which contribute to alienation, rootlessness, and striking out against society.

***Peer Influence.*** Peer influence is an important factor for many drug users (James & Andresen, 1979). A group may encourage drug use simply by making drugs available or through group enticement or even pressure. An individual may share in the use of pot, speed, or acid because it is in, for kicks, or from fear of social ostracism. The sharing of certain drugs, such as marijuana, is felt to contribute to a warm communal feeling among friends. Groups using hallucinogenic drugs have been known to develop their own cultural mores and standards in which group acceptance is based on ready acceptance and use of certain drugs; the advantages of membership include sharing of sources for obtaining drugs, sampling parties where a salesperson with different wares permits free tasting, and mutual help when one member is in trouble.

Drug users are quick to promote the virtues of the drug experience but tend to avoid serious discussion of the inherent problems. In groups using narcotics, the novice user may seek out and respond to group pressure because of an initial desire for the fraternalism and sense of belonging that membership provides. As the user becomes dependent to the point of requiring a continuous supply, he or she soon encounters the negative sanctions of the society at large. Rejected by the community, the person becomes more reliant on the group for acceptance. As this dependence on the group increases, the ability of the group to shape the user's behavior to their standards also increases.

***Maladjustment.*** Although the vast majority of drug abusers show no signs of neuroses or psychoses, a small proportion of cases of drug abuse seem to be related to an already present emotional disorder (Penk et al., 1980). In the neurotic who becomes drug dependent, the introduction to drugs appears most often to be accidental. The individual discovers that the drug helps to relieve tensions, deaden feelings, or decrease depression (Alexander & Hadaway, 1982). The drug user finds the fantasies of the drug-induced state certainly easier to face than the anxieties of life. Among psychotics, the use of drugs seems as much a result of a weakened ability to adapt to the environment as it is a desire for a state of self-gratification. For example, by using heroin, the psychotic can produce pleasure and euphoria and temporarily displace feelings of incompetence.

***Biological Factors.*** There is no firm evidence that physiological differences distinguish the drug abuser or drug dependent person from others. Some interesting theories have been pursued, however, and they deserve mention.

McAuliffe and Gordon (1980) hypothesized that some people may be prone to drug dependence. Such persons experience intense pleasure on the first contact with narcotic drugs—so much so that they keep trying to regain that experience. Another premise relates to the discovery that endorphins are produced naturally in the body. As discussed in Chapter 10, these substances are involved in our reaction to pain, as sort of a "nature's pain killer" (Simon, 1980). Drug abusers have been theorized to, therefore, be persons with deficiency in endorphin production: their lower pain tolerance leads to an increased craving for narcotics to substitute as pain-killers. Finally, Pert and Snyder (1973) have shown that specific cells in the brains of rats serve as receptor sites for opiate drugs, fitting into the cells like keys in locks. The interaction of the drug and the brain cell as they are bound together produces the drug action and experience. It is possible that the explanation for drug dependence involves this type of matching.

***Drug Use: A Product of the Drug Culture?*** In all, a complete understanding of drug use is a complex issue. One important consideration is the difference between drug use and drug abuse. Drug use may sometimes lead to drug abuse, but this is not always true. Part of the controversy over the legalization of marijuana is the inconsistent information about whether marijuana use leads to either continued dependence or dependence on other drugs. Some argue that use of marijuana does not eventually lead to experimenting with narcotics (Carr & Meyers, 1980), while others cite evidence to the contrary (Kandel, 1980).

There is little question that drug use, especially where marijuana is concerned, has increased drastically to the point that sociocultural factors must be examined. Examination of a compilation of studies suggests that by the mid-1970s, an estimated 53 percent of young persons had used marijuana, and a total of 12 million adults and youth could be counted as routine users (Weller & Halikas, 1980).

Several factors may be involved in the popularization of drugs. One factor is the basic questioning of many human institutions—the family, academic institutions, religion. At one time, these institutions provided comfortable stability and meaning, but today they are being challenged and changed. A second factor is our increased awareness of the powerful influences of political and corporate structures that give the feeling that our world cannot be readily manipulated or mastered by an individual. Instead, it exerts control over us.

These forces all contribute to dissatisfactions and a loss of security and may well provide support for the expanding drug culture. Movements toward maximizing experiences in the here-and-now, toward achieving insights into one's own self, and toward personal freedom from social restraints all relate to the changed social context, and they also help to encourage drug use. Mind-expanding hallucinogens, or drugs that promote social bonds or help individuals feel they control their own experiences, may all seem more appropriate in today's world than they have in earlier times. The drug user may feel not only that drugs are acceptable, but that he or she has a right to experiment with drugs—a right that transcends societal law. As is pointed out in Focus 13–2, however, it is still wise to carefully weigh the pros and cons before experimenting with any drug.

Finally, the American drug scene itself has been developing for some time. Advances in drugs as medication plus advertising campaigns have promoted the belief among Americans that pills can solve many physical and psychological problems. Thus, it is not surprising that the trend has given rise to drug use for its own sake.

### Treatment of Drug Dependence or Abuse

As with alcohol dependence, treatment of drug dependence must necessarily involve two phases: first, the actual physical withdrawal from the substance, and second, therapy or other treatment that will help the person stay away from drugs.

***Withdrawal and the Methadone Controversy.*** Prior to 1948, the abrupt withholding of narcotic drugs (the cold turkey method) was used to break physical dependence. This necessarily put the individual through the symptoms of withdrawal described earlier.

Since the late 40s, a controversial drug called methadone has been used as an aid to withdrawal. Methadone is an antinarcotic agent that blocks the action of heroin, morphine, or other opiate drugs. In effect, it serves as a substitute for the narcotic drugs (although it is dangerous in cases of barbiturate dependence) and has the advantage of being more readily withdrawn with less distress (Lewis & Sessler, 1980). The reduction of drug intake is conducted over a period of seven days to two weeks.

Although methadone is controversial, a number of strong arguments can be brought to bear in favor of its use. Methadone apparently has none of the harmful effects that prevent the heroin user from holding a job, and is less costly than heroin. If one argues that drug use is a social problem, not a medical one, then a person may be considered cured if he or she can return to a productive role in society—even though there may still be a physical dependence (Hall et al., 1981).

While these arguments favor the use of methadone, there have also been some criticisms about its

# FOCUS 13–2:
## Making Decisions About Drugs

Drugs seem to be a part of life within the United States today; why include them in a book about psychopathology? As this chapter discusses, drug abuse and dependence are disorders that affect a person's ability to function. Thus, even the casual drug user deserves proper information before adopting this lifestyle.

Regretfully, such information is not easy to obtain. In the medical literature before 1970, the effects of marijuana had been directly observed and reported for only 150 Western subjects (Schwartz, 1970). There has been more research since then, but without clear conclusions. This lack of sound information makes marijuana an unknown quantity in many respects; and the effects of other substances such as LSD or PCP are similarly hard to predict. This very fact makes it worthwhile for the person interested in trying drugs to ask some serious questions:

- *Why use drugs? Are they expected to relieve anxiety and help solve personal problems?* If problem-solving or insight-prompting are objectives, then the user should examine the data on the value of various drugs for this purpose. Among professionals, LSD is losing favor as a means of psychotherapeutic insight, because results have not been consistent and risks have been high. Marijuana may promote what are *felt* to be significant insights, but objective studies show that marijuana actually impairs a person's ability to make critical judgments about experiences. (Imlah, 1971)
- *Where were the drugs obtained, and under what conditions?* Dosage is extremely important for use of any drug, since too little can have no effects, but too much can be dangerous. Also important is the question of source. For example, some street-supplied LSD has been found to be composed of 10 percent LSD and 90 percent adulterants, including strychnine. PCP samples have been found to be only 60 percent pure, and amphetamines only 54 percent. (Schnoll, 1979)
- *Do the potential gains of drug experimentation balance the potential costs?* Marijuana provides a good example in answering this question. In weighing the pros and cons, this drug's positive aspects include its mild intoxicant effects and the feelings of well-being and euphoria. These arguments may seem persuasive. However, studies also report that adverse effects sometimes occur, including temporal disintegration, acute anxiety, paranoid thoughts, depression, and possibly a psychoticlike condition called marijuana or cannabis psychosis. (Thacore & Shulka, 1976)

In all, it might be claimed that drugs such as marijuana bring only potential risks—not proven ones. On the other hand, the beneficial effects of marijuana or other drugs may prove equally intangible and not always reliable. Thus, decisions to experiment with drugs should be evaluated with great care.

use. Prime among these is the fact that methadone may itself be addictive—so that even after therapy, the user is still hooked. Other drugs are being tried in the hopes that the problems of methadone can be avoided. Of these, the most promising appear to be Naltrexone and LAAM (long-acting methadone) (Renault, 1978; Senay et al., 1978). With all of these drugs, the hope is that their use will block the need for narcotics, and that these antinarcotic drugs will help the individual through the withdrawal phase. In addition to the antinarcotics, treatment programs may also use hydrotherapy, recreational and occupational therapies to make withdrawal more comfortable.

Once withdrawal has been achieved, either with or without methadone, a second phase of treatment involves dealing with the conditions associated with drug abuse. Treatments may include psychotherapy, often in a community or group setting, behavior modification, or other innovative programs.

***Psychotherapy and Therapeutic Communities.*** The aim of psychotherapy is to relieve the conditions that originally led the individual toward drugs, and at the same time to ease any depression, lowered self-esteem, or resentment that may have developed while the user was taking drugs (Appel & Kaestner, 1979). Imminent crises that could send the patient back to drugs must be anticipated: he or she must be helped to cope in other ways.

One very helpful approach in aiding former drug users to become self-sufficient is the *therapeutic community*. This approach uses all hospital persons, including the patients themselves, as therapists, at every moment, through every interaction that takes place.

The U.S. Public Health Service has maintained two hospitals for the treatment of drug addicts—one in Lexington, Kentucky and the other in Fort Worth, Texas. These two facilities are therapeutic community environments that have had a high rate of success. They require patients to accept responsibility for both their own progress and that of others.

One study compared the relative success of the two major treatment approaches today: the therapeutic community and methadone therapy. It used two measures in its comparison: first, the ability to remain heroin-free one year after treatment and second, the ability to regain social productivity either in school or employment (Bale et al., 1980). As Figure 13-2 shows, both methadone and the therapeutic community were effective, but the community approach was more effective.

***Synanon and Other Alternative Centers.*** Several alternative types of group treatment centers have surfaced throughout the country, with varying success. Some, like the well-known Synanon center in Santa Monica, California, have had at least initial success, although Synanon has come under serious ethical criticism in recent years over the degree of control it exerted over its members (Ford Foundation, 1972). The crux of Synanon's treatment approach is group meetings (the name Synanon itself comes from the mispronunciation of the word *seminar*) in which members discuss their character traits and see themselves as they are through the help of other addicts. In addition, they can work in small businesses operated by Synanon while working through their problems. Many members have gone through a cold-turkey cure, remained in residence for a period, obtained employment, participated in the critical-evaluative group meetings, and have eventually left for a self-supporting life.

***Behavior Modification.*** Behavior modification offers a very different approach to drug abuse. The treatments are similar to those discussed for alcohol abuse earlier in this chapter. Individuals with drug abuse or drug dependence have been provided with aversive training, including electric shock, chemical aversion, and covert sensitization. However, most studies on these methods looked at either single cases or small numbers, and it is difficult to draw firm conclusions about the broader use of such methods (Krasnegor, 1980).

One group of researchers (Hall et al., 1979) used operant reinforcement methods to encourage heroin addicts to remain with detoxification programs (there is normally a high dropout rate). Contingency management was used, whereby drug users were paid up to $10 each time they brought in urine specimens that were drug free, indicating that they were off morphine or barbiturates. Thus, a drug user could earn up to $56 for completing the detoxification requirements. At one point, the question of whether the drug users might

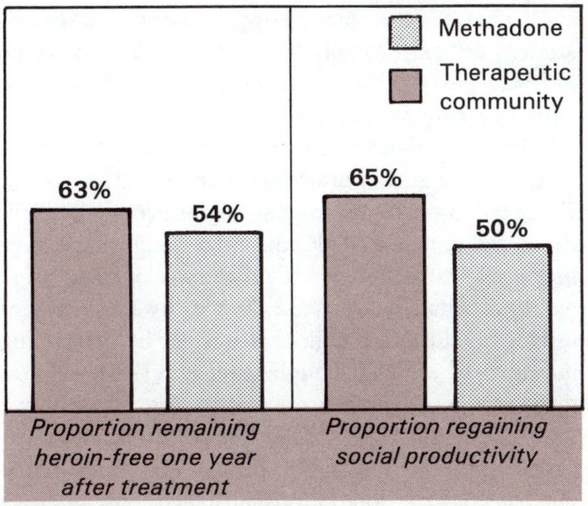


**FIGURE 13–2** Comparison of methadone and therapeutic community effectiveness.

SOURCE: Based on "Therapeutic Communities versus Methadone Maintenance" by R. Bale, W. VanStone, J. Kuldan, T. Engelsing, R. Elashoff & V. Zarcone, Jr., 1980, *Archives of General Psychiatry, 37,* pp. 179–193.

take the money and buy more heroin was raised, but this did not occur. Instead, the procedure provided an incentive which led to more drug-free days and better adherence to the detoxification efforts.

***Prognosis for Recovery.*** In general, the prognosis for a complete recovery from drug dependence is not favorable. For heroin dependence, there do not seem to be sufficient treatment programs to begin with. Thus, while we are technically capable of treating about 84,000 persons with methadone, the actual number of people addicted to heroin is closer to 300,000 to 600,000. Even where a methadone treatment is available, there is a second problem: the unwillingness of many heroin addicts to remain in treatment. About 12,000 persons leave methadone programs prematurely, and the same tendency exists within therapeutic communities (Lewis & Sessler, 1980).

For those who remain, a third issue is the fact that neither methadone nor therapeutic communities can always assure success. Despite the overall usefulness of these two programs, a number of individuals are not helped. In the Drug Abuse Reporting Program (DARP), a systematic survey was conducted of 52 federally supported treatment programs across the United States and Puerto Rico. Outcomes were coded in four categories based on whether the person was abstinent from drugs, was employed, was free from crime, and avoided relapse requiring further treatment. On the whole, the results were consistent with the Bale et al. study (1980) cited in Figure 13–2, in showing that both the methadone programs and therapeutic communities provided significant help. However, 45 percent of methadone-treated and 47 percent of therapeutic community persons showed some unfavorable outcomes, involving recidivism, continued unemployment, and criminality (Sells & Simpson, 1979). The most cautious conclusion we can draw is that treatment programs can have a positive impact on some persons who are drug abusers. However, to do so requires the willingness of the individual to stay with treatment long enough for improvements to occur—and even then, no absolute guarantees can assure success.

## EVALUATION

Substance abuse, either alcohol or drug usage, is a complex problem that raises issues about origins and treatment. For alcohol, opposing views suggest the causes to be *either* physiological or psychological or even genetic. Evidence can be brought to bear in support of each, but thus far there has not been conclusive enough information to fully confirm one explanation.

When drug dependence is examined, there is at least one clear explanation where iatrogenic addiction occurs; in this case, the use of narcotics for medical purposes has caused the patient to become drug dependent. However, for other forms of drug abuse or dependence, the origins are not nearly as evident. The influence of peer pressure, the role of emotional disturbance, and the possible contribution of physiological factors have all been examined. The fact that there has been an increase in experimentation with drugs as a life style raises the question of whether our societal norms are changing. In essence, is alcohol or drug abuse attributable to our society's adoption and approval of these behaviors?

Clearly, the search for treatment has also raised some controversy. Regarding alcohol abuse, an organization such as Alcoholics Anonymous firmly espouses that complete abstinence is the only cure. On the other hand, controlled drinking programs equally firmly claim that problem drinkers can learn to become controlled, social drinkers.

With a social problem as major as drug abuse, there are also some disagreements about treatment. Methadone has been a proven means for reducing drug dependence in many cases, yet there is public dissatisfaction due to the belief that we are simply substituting one addiction for another. And what of the use of aversive training methods for either alcohol or drug abuse? Once again, evidence supports the value of this approach; on the other hand, there are those who would claim that aversive treatment is unethical and no more than a form of punishment.

Finally, the increased introduction and use of drugs such as marijuana among youth has caused intense debate. Is marijuana conclusively damaging or are the hazards exaggerated by the conservative generation of critics? Possibly the more crucial issue is the ultimate purpose for using drugs, and whether the gains are truly worth the risks.

In all, alcohol and drug abuse represent severe social problems as they drain productivity and resources. There will probably be several origins eventually identified, rather than a single causative factor. Some have proposed that different classifications of drug users would facilitate study; for example, by frequency of usage, by clustering similar drugs, or by classifying the adverse effects. Douglass et al. (1980) suggest three groups: frequent users of differing psychoactive drugs; occasional users of illicit street drugs; and occasional users of prescription drugs. The point is that much needs to be done before substance abuse of drugs or alcohol can be better understood or treated.

## SUMMARY

The substance use disorders cover two categories: substance abuse and substance dependence. In substance abuse, the person shows pathological use of the substance and impairment of either social or occupational abilities with a duration of at least one month. In substance dependence, the symptoms of tolerance and withdrawal are found. While alcohol use may become either alcohol abuse or alcohol dependence, some drugs are subject only to drug abuse but never turn into drug dependence. This chapter describes the characteristics of a variety of drugs and their effects, as well as the various results from alcohol abuse or dependence. One outcome of alcohol abuse can be organic damage. Disorders which involve such damage are classified substance-induced organic mental disorders, but they are described in this chapter for convenience. Such alcohol-related organic disorders include alcoholic idiosyncratic intoxication, delirium tremens, alcohol amnestic disorder, and alcohol hallucinosis. The symptoms of each of these organic disorders are a result of the organic, nutritional, or physiological changes from chronic use of alcohol.

A variety of explanations have been offered to determine why persons become problem drinkers. Psychoanalytic interpretations refer to oral fixation and hostility, while other psychological explanations have examined personality traits and the tension-reducing or pleasure-inducing aspects of drinking. Sociocultural interpretations cover the role of one's peers in being initiated into drinking and in its control. Genetic explanations have received support from studies of strains of animals that appear to prefer alcohol.

Regarding the source of drug abuse, psychological interpretations have included identifying patterns of social deviancy, rebellion, peer influence, or emotional disturbances. Biological factors that have been studied include examination of endorphins, brain receptors, and the person's initial sensations of pleasure from drug stimulation. Sociocultural explanations have focused on the lack of stability of societal structures, such as religions, the family as an institution, and the school systems.

Treatment for the substance use disorders have included withdrawal from the substance where dependence has occurred. Psychotherapy can then be started to deal with alternatives to substance abuse in confronting daily conflicts. Group treatment may include innovative programs such as the therapeutic community, or patient-support groups, such as Alcoholics Anonymous or Synanon. Various forms of behavior therapy have been used, including aversive training, for both alcohol and drug abuse. For alcohol abuse, a controlled drinking program has been developed that shows promise but has created some controversy. For drug abuse, methadone treatment has shown promise but has also been the source of its own controversy.

## KEY TERMS

**Alcohol abuse**
**Alcohol amnestic disorder**
**Alcohol dependence**
**Alcohol hallucinosis**
**Alcohol idiosyncratic intoxication**
**Alcohol withdrawal delirium**
**Alcoholism**
**Chronic phase**
**Controlled drinking**
**Crucial phase**
**Delirium tremens**
**Hallucinogenic drugs**
**Iatrogenic addiction**
**Korsakoff's psychosis**
**Methadone**
**Narcotic**
**Organic mental disorder**
**Prealcoholic symptomatic phase**
**Prodromal phase**
**Substance abuse**
**Substance dependence**
**Synesthesia**
**Therapeutic community**
**Tolerance**
**Tranquilizer**
**Withdrawal**

# CHAPTER 14

## Psychosexual Disorders: Problems of Sexual Identity, Types or Levels of Sexual Arousal

- **How are the various types of sexual disorders defined?**
- **How do transsexuals, transvestites, and homosexuals differ?**
- **Does pornography lead to increased sexual perversions and sexual crimes?**
- **Is rape motivated by an uncontrolled sexual drive?**
- **How do the various sexual dysfunctions relate to the stages of the sexual response cycle?**
- **Can a normal woman be inorgasmic?**
- **Pain during intercourse is a common gynecological complaint. What might be some contributing causes?**
- **Is homosexuality a mental disorder or a way of life?**
- **George has become Christine, James is now Jan, and Robert is Bobbie or Roberta. But does this solve the transsexual's problem?**

**TABLE 14–1**

**Psychosexual Disorders**

| *Type* | *Major Characteristics* |
|---|---|
| Gender identity disorders | Conflict about one's physical and psychological identities, as in transsexualism. |
| Paraphilias | Sexual arousal only by certain unusual objects or actions, as in fetishism, masochism, and exhibitionism. |
| Psychosexual dysfunctions | Inadequacy in sexual functioning, as in orgasmic dysfunction or premature ejaculation. |
| Ego-dystonic homosexuality | Becoming sexually gratified with persons of the same sex, when such activity leads to personal distress. |

## Case History 14–1:
### A Case of Fetishism

Leo A. has been in therapy for six months following a court referral for treatment. Leo was arrested for burglary, for stealing women's undergarments off a clothesline.

Leo has had a fetish about women's panties for 11 years. While other male friends he knows buy men's magazines with centerfolds, Leo has a subscription to several women's magazines and spends his quiet hours looking at the sections on lingerie. In his sexual fantasies, he imagines himself touching and caressing a woman's panties, particularly noting odors. He will spend time shopping in the lingerie section of department stores, examining the different fabrics, colors, and sizes of panties, and has on occasion shoplifted a particularly desirable pair.

Outside of the fetish, Leo appears normal in his behaviors. He has had successful placements as an accountant, was educated in a respectable private college, drinks only socially, and is described by friends as having a "pleasing sense of humor . . . a guy you like to have at parties because he seems to provide a spark." Leo has considered marriage, but, when pressed, admits that the girls he was interested in were ones whom he had known for only a short time, and there was no reason to believe that marriage was logical. Moreover, he worried about whether he could satisfy a spouse, because of his fetish and because he has never attempted intercourse. In fact, his fantasies about his girl friends have usually been about their preferences in underwear, what they were wearing at the moment, and whether they had been washed.

Leo was an only child with parents who were highly religious and who never discussed sexual matters with their growing son. Leo once heard movements in his parents' bedroom that he now knows involved coitus, but which he could not identify at the time. Yet, he recalls becoming aroused. The next day he found his mother's underwear in the laundry and put his own on top of it. Although he does not date his fetishism to that event, he does remember it as the first time he started to notice how much smoother women's underwear were than men's. Leo says that his fetish seemed always with him; from the very first day he noticed girls, he associated his interest in them with their underwear. He reports having a few dates now and then, but seems indifferent about it. Just prior to the arrest, Leo had changed jobs and was employed as a salesman in a lingerie department, priding himself on his ability to advise customers on the various products.

Human sexuality is different from the sexual behavior of other animals. It is not controlled by instincts, nor is it limited to unfeeling or stereotyped mating behaviors. Instead, it has been partly separated from reproductive aims. This separation enriches the physical experience of sex, allowing emotional, cultural, and learning influences to broaden its various expressions (Maier, 1984). Yet, at the same time, it complicates sex. Sexuality has been accepted, condemned, or distorted in different ways over the course of history, according to the prevailing beliefs and attitudes. And within each individual, factors such as anxiety, guilt, hostility, self-images, cultural images, and conditioned responses all play a part in shaping sexuality.

As a result, a number of disorders exist that involve psychological influences on sexual attitudes and behaviors. These psychosexual disorders which are identified in Table 14–1 are the subject of this chapter. Four general types of sexual disorder are recognized in DSM-III:

- *Paraphilias*—sexual arousal by unusual objects or actions, such as pedophilia or masochism.
- *Psychosexual dysfunctions*—inadequate sexual functioning, such as inhibited orgasm or premature ejaculation.
- *Ego-dystonic homosexuality*—desire for sexual activity with same-sex partners along with personal distress.
- *Gender identity disorders*—conflict between one's physical and psychological identities, primarily transsexualism.

## PARAPHILIAS

The *paraphilias* are disorders in which a person is sexually aroused by unconventional objects or acts (Langbuin, 1983). These behaviors used to be labeled more generally as sexual deviations, but the current term is used to emphasize that the deviancy (*para*) is in the object or action by which the person is aroused (*philia*).

The sexual arousal may come from a variety of sources. Arousal from nonliving objects, as in the opening case history, is termed a *fetish;* from animals, *zoophilia;* and from prepubertal children, *pedophilia.* A person may also become aroused by certain unconventional acts, such as wearing the clothes of the other sex (*transvestism*), displaying oneself (*exhibitionism*), watching others (*voyeurism*), experiencing pain (*masochism*), or inflicting pain (*sadism*). There is no end to the variety of paraphiliac attractions, including corpses (*necrophilia*), the uttering of obscenities (*copralalia*), and lewdness on the telephone (*telephone scatologia*).

In all the paraphilias, the person is generally unable to experience successful sexual arousal with a normal adult partner. Depending on the nature, intensity, and degree of reality mixed with fantasy, the paraphilia may range from harmless to very harmful. In some cases, such as pedophilia, legal codes make the behavior a criminal action by its very nature; while in others, such as sadism, legal action may take place only if the partner was an unwilling participant and presses charges. This part of the chapter will look briefly at the various paraphilias, then discuss some of the primary approaches to treatment.

### Fetishism

*Fetishism* is a disorder in which sexual arousal derives from an object, the most common being shoes, gloves, undergarments (preferably permeated with body odor), and stockings. The object may be impersonal, or it may be associated with a particular person. The individual becomes aroused by looking at, fondling, smelling, or kissing the object. Masturbation may occur during the process, or the person may experience a spontaneous orgasm.

Fetishism appears to be more common among men than women. A fetish can involve extremely unusual objects. One case is known where the person became stimulated only by exhaust pipes "in perfect shape," shiny and undented, that softly blew out gases (Bergler, 1947); in another, a woman reached orgasm from the sight of light reflecting off eyeglasses (Allen, 1969). In still a third case, a married milkman stole 79 pairs of high-heel shoes, none in his wife's shoe size (Reinhardt, 1957).

***Dynamics of Fetishism.*** Several theories have been put forth to explain fetishism. Some studies have tried to identify personality types that might be linked to this disorder, and resultant findings suggest a reserved, nonassertive, passive-dependent type of person, with little emotionality or spontaneity (Epstein, 1960). Sexual fears and avoidance of romantic attachments also seem to be common traits. The fear of sexual failure with a real partner may be an important reason why the fetishist substitutes inanimate objects: here, there is no danger of rejection and no threat to a sense of potency, since the fetish is completely under the individual's own control (LaTorre, 1980).

Freud viewed the fetish as symbolic of more than the desired love of another person. He speculated that boys value their penises and are shocked to discover that girls do not possess them, assuming that girls have lost their penises. Fetishes become symbols of the lost penises, which have now been found. Since the penises are also representations of the mother's absent phallus, they enable gratification of incestual desires as well.

A learning theory approach suggests quite a different explanation—that conditioning causes the fetishist to associate sexuality with an object that was somehow linked to sexual fantasies or activities. In a laboratory test of this concept, Rachman (1966) first showed that a pair of black, knee-length women's boots brought no sexual arousal response among a group of three male volunteer psychologists. He then proceeded to classically condition them, by pairing the sight of these boots with colored slides of nude women. By the end of the training, the subjects showed a sexual fetish, becoming aroused by the sight of the boots alone.

***A transvestite*** *derives gratification from cross-dressing The male transvestite can dress in a deceptively alluring manner that disguises his true gender.*

## Transvestism

A second paraphilia, *transvestism,* involves sexual arousal through cross-dressing. Transvestites are almost invariably male; in fact, it has been suggested that technically, only males are transvestites, although it is conceivable that some female transvestites exist (Prince & Bentler, 1972).

There is a lack of clear information on the transvestite. At one point, the American Psychiatric Association considered the disorder for possible inclusion as a gender identity disorder[1] rather than a paraphilia. This now seems to be inappropriate, however. A survey of readers of *Transvestia,* a magazine for cross-dressers, found nearly all respondents to be exclusively heterosexual, with the rate of homosexuality being below that in the general population (Buckner, 1970). In a gender identity disorder, the person may cross-dress in public. However, the transvestite's cross-dressing tends to be accomplished privately, at home, and in secret. Some may wear a complete outfit

1 A gender identity disorder, or transsexualism, involves the belief that one's physical identity is discrepant from one's psychological identity. For instance, a male transsexual believes he is really a female trapped in a male body.

of a woman, from panties to bra to heels, a gown and wig, including makeup. The transvestite may go for a quiet stroll or attempt to pass by a friend unrecognized as a woman. In all cases, the transvestite still retains his identity as a male, does not wish to give up his masculinity, and does not cross-dress in order to engage in a homosexual encounter. Yet, the majority of transvestites report feeling like a woman when cross-dressed, as if a different personality, a feminine side, reaches fulfillment.

***Dynamics of Transvestism.*** Studies dealing with the origins of transvestism tend to identify early experiences that sound remarkably like potential contributing factors. In a survey of clinical cases, Lukianowicz (1959) identified parental rejection of the child because of his unwanted sex, the cross-dressing of children in clothes appropriate for the opposite sex, the favoring of girls in the family, a reversal of parental sex roles, and the use of cross-dressing as punishment through humiliation. Lukianowicz also found evidence for a stronger identification with and more intimate contact with a female in the family, either mother or sister. Stoller (1967) described three types of women associated with transvestites: the malicious male haters, primarily mothers, who initiated the child into cross-dressing; the symbiotes, again mothers, who are indifferent to adult males but intimately attached to their sons, whom they feminize; and the succorers, mainly wives, who are supportive of the cross-dressing of their transvestite husbands once they discover the behaviors.

### Zoophilia

A third paraphilia is *zoophilia,* or bestiality. This disorder involves the use of animals as the objects of intercourse or to sexually arouse the human through licking or rubbing. Animal copulation may be true copulation, whereby the human experiences intercourse with a dog or other animal, or it may be a version of masturbation whereby tonguing by the animal leads to an orgastic experience. The more common animals used are cows, sheep, goats, dogs and cats, although the paraphilia can develop with a broad range of animals. Where the zoophiliac is a woman, becoming pregnant by an animal is, of course, not possible since there is a species-specific element to fertilization.

Although early experimentation with animals may not be uncommon among rural or farm adolescents, the occurrence of zoophilia is considered extremely rare. It is believed that true zoophilia, namely a persistent exclusive preference for animals for sexual arousal, is more common among males than females. The zoophiliac actually prefers the animal even if human choices are available. In some cases, highly erotic reactions have been reported (for instance, at the sight of race horses, perceived as sleek, sexy, and sensuous).

***Dynamics of Zoophilia.*** A pattern of retarded social or sexual development or competency is believed related to zoophilia. Instead of maturing to develop satisfactory outlets with the opposite sex, the zoophiliac may never have developed beyond feelings of inadequacy. Animals arouse less anxiety as sexual objects: they may permit the person to have feelings of power and dominance; there is also no threat of rejection, since social skills are not required as a prelude to sex. This pattern of immature social-sexual development is common to many of the paraphilias.

### Pedophilia

*Pedophilia* involves the preference for children as a source of sexual arousal. The pedophiliac will caress the child's body, fondle the child's genitals, or induce the child to manipulate his own genitals. The pedophile may be either heterosexual or homosexual in orientation; contrary to popular opinion, the heterosexual pedophile only rarely seeks coitus, although a larger number of homosexual pedophiles seek orgasm (Langevin, 1983). The pedophile is generally a male, married, and older than most other sex offenders (about age 35).

Pedophilia is a serious criminal offense, and it arouses such unfavorable public opinion that an accused offender may sometimes be considered guilty until proven innocent. Contrary to popular belief, the pedophile does not tend to wait in a parked car and pick up a strange child on the way home from school. Instead, evidence shows that heterosexual pedophiles

**TABLE 14–2**

**Types of Pedophiles**

| | |
|---|---|
| *The aggressive type* | This type of pedophile seems motivated by sadistic and sexual needs. The primary aim is aggression, with the target happening to be children. These offenders are patrons of child prostitutes. |
| *The fixated type* | The individual is unable to develop mature interpersonal relations with male or female peers, but is comfortable only with children, whom he seeks out as companions. The sexual offense is usually with a child friend. |
| *The regressed type* | This individual has a normal adolescent and early adult adjustment; then sexual regression is precipitated by social, occupational, or marital stress. The pedophiliac activity is usually an impulsive action, with a stranger. |

SOURCE: Based on *Sex Offender,* by M. Cohen, T. Seghorn & W. Calmas, 1969, *Journal of Abnormal Psychology, 2.*

generally select a neighbor or even a relative, with about 75 percent of these sexual offenses occurring in either the pedophile's or the victim's own home (Lester, 1975).[2]

***Dynamics of Pedophilia.*** One group of researchers (Cohen et al., 1969) examined 38 male pedophiles as well as 27 convicted rapists and discovered some identifiable subtypes within each group. Three types of pedophiles—the fixated, the regressed, and the aggressive—are described in Table 14–2.

Other studies have contributed further information about the traits of pedophiles. Gebhard and Gagnon (1964) studied heterosexual pedophiles whose victims were under the age of five. Compared to other sexual offenders, they did not differ in the incidence of broken homes, sex play as children, or relationships with their parents as adults. They were often devoutly religious and less educated, and they tended to be unskilled laborers. An earlier study by Glueck (1956) suggests further information concerning homosexual pedophiles. This study found this group to be more feminine in childhood, to have less heterosexual interests and more sexual anxiety, and less feelings of adequacy. In all, except for the Cohen et al. data, pedophiles do not seem to be distinguished by unusual backgrounds.

2 *Incest,* or intercourse with one's offspring, differs from pedophilia since most incest cases are not caused by sexual desire for an immature child. Instead, most incest occurs with sexually mature offspring.

### Exhibitionism

*Exhibitionism* involves achieving sexual arousal through exhibiting one's genitals to persons of the opposite sex. The exhibitionist is almost always a male, with only a rare case among women. Stripteasing is not considered as a sexual disorder; a study of strippers found their primary motivation to be financial, and not for sexual arousal (Skipper & McCaghy, 1969).

The exhibitionist usually selects a stranger outdoors, remains a safe distance of from 6 to 60 feet away, often achieves an erection on exposure and may be particularly excited if the victim screams, shows shock, or is otherwise horrified. The exhibitionist may receive enough gratification simply by the exposure or may masturbate afterward. In the rare case, the exhibitionist will attempt to follow or make contact with the viewer-victim, but most often he will return to his car and speed away or run away on foot. One Colorado study (MacDonald, 1973) found that indecent exposures were most common on weekdays between the hours of 8 A.M. and 9 A.M. and again between 3 P.M. and 5 P.M. Exhibitionism and voyeurism, discussed next, comprise the largest number of offenses reported to police.

*An **exhibitionist** derives gratification from displaying himself. In this photo, the exhibitionist appears to be enjoying himself while others appear to be quite distraught.*

***Dynamics of Exhibitionism.*** Reviews of studies on exhibitionists (Blair & Lanyon, 1981) suggest a pattern of typical characteristics, including passivity, compulsiveness, reticence, moralism, timidity, a lack of impulse control, and heterosexual immaturity (MacDonald, 1973). In some cases, the exhibitionism seems a response to a stress and is an acting-out of conflict. It may be an expression, for instance, of ambivalence about an impending marriage, or other conflicts involving a woman. In a small number of cases, the exhibitionism is associated with a psychotic condition, such as schizophrenia (see Chapter 17).

Interestingly, exhibitionism seems to be a culture-bound disorder, most common in America and Britain, but rare in the Far East, Middle East, Africa, South America, and Hawaii (Rooth, 1973).

### Voyeurism

The Frenchman Coffignon originally used the term *voyeurism* to describe men who loiter in parks to view sexually stimulating sights. This paraphilia involves achieving sexual arousal through looking at persons who are nude, in the act of disrobing, or engaging in sexual activity. Voyeurism does not apply to sexual stimulation from pornographic magazines, burlesque shows, or erotic films, discussed in the focus on pornography. The voyeur almost exclusively prefers watching as a means of sexual release even when intercourse is available. The watching is done surreptitiously, and the voyeur persists with the "peeping" despite the risks of arrest, being bitten by watchdogs, being shot as a burglar, or even falling off a roof (all of which have occurred).

Most voyeurs are males seeking to view females; female voyeurs or homosexual male voyeurs are rare. The voyeur may patrol at night, ferreting out places for viewing and may even drill peepholes. When he comes across an exciting scene, he may fantasize that the woman is beckoning him or that he is actually involved in the lovemaking.

***Dynamics of Voyeurism.*** The voyeur seems to be stimulated by the excitement of the forbidden and the secret intrusion into unsuspecting privacy. There may be some pleasure at imagining the other person as a helpless victim, powerless to resist, who would be humiliated if she knew she were so exposed and watched. Sexual frustration does not seem to be a primary motive inasmuch as voyeurism apparently continues among those who already have sexual outlets (Oliven, 1974). Emotional immaturity and social and sexual inadequacy are common, although about one fourth of arrested voyeurs are married (Gebhard et al., 1965).

Psychoanalytic interpretation of voyeurism emphasizes the child's encounter with the *primal scene,* the child's viewing of intercourse between the parents. The voyeur is unable to overcome his fixation with this experience and he continues to need to view others, perhaps to be reassured that sexual actions are not dangerous or do not involve harming the sexual partner. It is difficult, however, to obtain conclusive support for this theory.

### Sadism and Masochism

Two paraphilias that are closely linked are sadism and masochism. *Sadism* involves sexual arousal through inflicting suffering or pain on others, while *masochism* involves sexual excitement from receiving pain. These terms have occasionally been used to refer to anyone who gains satisfaction from making others suffer or from suffering, in the same way that the term *exhibitionist* is sometimes used to describe anyone who en-

# FOCUS 14–1:

## Pornography: Does It Lead to Sex Offenses?

Spots such as the one in the picture can be found in virtually every urban area. Are such places likely to lower the moral standards of people who visit them? The U.S. Commission on Obscenity and Pornography, formed in 1970 to determine the effects of pornography on society, said "no." Their conclusion reported that there is "no reliable evidence to date that exposure to explicit sexual materials plays a significant role in the causation of delinquency or criminal sexual behavior among youths or adults" (p. 169).[3]

The Commission has not had the final say on the matter, however. There are many proponents of censorship, and they present some strong arguments. Oliven (1974, p. 464), for instance, warns that access to pornography may have "subtle erotic corruptive effects on certain unstable or borderline youngsters." Others also warn against the "hidden" effects of pornography, drawing an analogy with Bandura and Walters' research (1963) on aggression. Once children learn aggressive behaviors from watching a model, such behaviors may be released under certain circumstances even after the child has learned to inhibit them. Can pornography have similar hidden effects, so that sado-masochistic, or violent, or at the very least, sexually exploitative behaviors are learned and put "into storage" even if they're not immediately evident? Proponents of censorship believe that it can, and documentation is beginning to support this (Cunningham, 1982).

There is also strong support for the commission's recommendations. Evidence from Denmark contributed to the commission's conclusions in the first place. After this country legalized pornography, sex crimes did not increase: they may even have decreased (Kutchinsky, 1970). Other research indicates that sex offenders tend to see less erotic materials as either adults or teenagers than do normal adults (Kant & Goldstein, 1970). And finally, to counter the hidden-effects argument mentioned earlier, there is some evidence that at least soft-core pornography may have some *positive* hidden effects. Baron (1974) found that exposure of male subjects to *Playboy* and female subjects to *Playgirl* centerfolds greatly reduced the inclination of angry subjects to act aggressively. Strong sexual arousal, such as would be present in hard-core X-rated films, however, seems to increase aggression in already angry persons (Donnerstein et al., 1975).

In all, there are strong arguments on both sides: both against censorship and against pornography (Yaffé & Nelson, 1982). What do you think?

*Stores dealing in pornographic materials can be found in nearly every major city. Researchers disagree about whether* ***pornography*** *stimulates or reduces sexual crimes.*

3 While the Commission recommended unlimited adult access to pornography, it also recommended limited access for minors without parental consent.

joys public attention. However, as a clinical disorder, these terms are restricted to describing those persons who engage in the activity as a means of experiencing sexual excitement. The pain may be physical or mental and can range from humiliation to bondage, to pinching, to flagellation, to mutilation, and even to brutal rape, or torture (Langevin, 1983).

The term *sadism* takes its name from the Marquis de Sade, whose writings, such as *Justine and Juliette,* luridly describe episodes of cruel punishment of innocent young women. Masochism is named after Leopold von Sacher-Masoch, who lived about 100 years after de Sade, but who also wrote about the sexual pleasures of pain. Both authors appeared to have been involved in personal or fantasized experiences with pain and sexual gratification. Serious cases of sadism include the woman who required her husband to cut a wound open on his arm so that she could suck the blood for arousal (Krafft-Ebing, 1950), and one severe case of masochism involved a young man who would hang himself to reach an erection and orgasm (Resnick, 1972). Virtually all reported cases of accidental suicide due to sexual masochism have been men (American Psychiatric Association, 1978). Both sadistic and masochistic desires can appear in the same person, and psychoanalysts contend that sadism evolves into masochism, with masochism being sadism turned inwardly.

***Dynamics of Sadism and Masochism.*** Many speculations exist about the origins of sexual sadism or masochism. Psychoanalytic views suggest that the child misinterprets the parents sexual act as an aggressive act, which then leads the child to be similarly brutal as an adult. Sadism may also be seen as a power struggle, with the sadist using sexual violence as a

## Case History 14–2:
### A Sado-masochistic Couple

Sharon M. and Jim D. met through an ad in a ''swingers'' magazine. Sharon had placed the ad, announcing her physical characteristics and her interest in a ''male who was unafraid to dominate a willing female.'' Sharon describes herself as ''into bondage. . . . I get frantically excited when I'm lying there stretched apart by ropes, unable to get free to resist, and I know I'm helpless and I can't help myself, and I curse and I plead and I say I've changed my mind, . . . but at the same time, I'm having an orgasm.'' Jim is recently divorced and is proud of it: ''She wanted out so bad, she didn't even ask for alimony . . . so I had my fun, and it was like a free ride, and now I can do what I like.''

Jim admits to enjoying Sharon's company, but is quick to point out that he is the one that is responsible for coming up with new ideas that meet Sharon's masochistic needs: ''Sometimes I tell her that I don't feel like tying her up, or that it's going to be just sex like other people do, and once that drove her wild because she really thought I was serious.'' Neither believes that their lovemaking style is unusual: ''You'll be calling a lot of folks crazy if you consider us crazy; there's a catalog house that you can mail order from, and there's just lots of ads looking for partners.''

In spite of the apparent self-confidence in Sharon's ad, acquaintances describe her as being unassuming, inhibited, and shy. She dresses in outmoded fashions that appear to place her features in the worst light. Her sister says she had been a deeply religious child who did not have her first date until her first year out of high school and who intended to remain single because she considered sex as sinful.

Jim was expelled from school because of fighting, now works as a laborer, and has been arrested several times for assault. His personal view is that you ''have to grab for everything you can get out of life because if you don't the police will make up some law to take away what little pleasure there is left.'' Privately, Jim admits that he does not know how much longer he will stay with Sharon, but is certain ''I'll take her down a peg if she thinks she owns me.''

*The leather straps, chains, and whips on display in this shop call attention to **sadomasochistic** sexual needs.*

means of compensating for a feeling of helplessness in controlling the love of others. Masochism seems associated with a sense of shame or guilt at one's sexuality, as in Sharon's case in Case History 14–2. The masochist therefore denies him or herself the pleasure of intercourse by demanding punishment for participating in sexual encounters.

Other factors involved in sado-masochism lend themselves to behavioral interpretations, for the need to associate pain with sexual pleasure may sometimes be a conditioned response. This might happen when an initial sexual experience occurs in the presence of suffering—for example, when a young boy, already in pain, experiences sexual arousal as a hospital nurse bathes him. Finally, it is possible that in some circumstances, masochistic behavior may be self-reinforcing even without the sexual pleasure. Some pathologies, such as autism (see Chapter 20), are characterized by repetitive self-injurious behaviors, such as head banging. Some researchers (Lovaas et al., 1971) argue that such actions are in fact self-rewarding through a feedback system. If not actually rewarding, perhaps self-punishment or the actions of punishing someone else lead to a higher level of activation or general physiological arousal, permitting the more specific sexual stimulation to be heightened.

### Treatment of the Paraphilias

The paraphilias are generally amenable to therapy, depending on the severity and dynamics of each particular case. A client whose fetishism is linked to a long background of social and sexual incompetency and a deep sense of personal inadequacy, for instance, may require longer treatment than the person whose fetishism developed through a conditioning experience. The approaches of psychoanalysis and behavior therapy are both used.

***Psychoanalysis.*** Psychoanalytic therapy aims at uncovering the underlying symbolic or unconscious origins of the paraphilias. As observed, there is a recognition of sexual immaturity, and the psychoanalyst accepts that this represents a fixation at an early developmental stage, due to early gratification or early trauma. Freud reported on a case of a 47-year-old man who had been seductively overindulged by his mother during his childhood and also threatened with castration by his father. In fact, the mother often caressed her son's foot, forming the foundation for his foot fetish as an adult.

In some cases the psychoanalyst raises questions to discover any unconscious meanings to the paraphilia: does a high-heel shoe fetish represent a secret wish to be dominated (under the heel); is masochism punishment for guilty feelings about sexuality; is pedophilia a reflection of a fear of rejection by adults and hence displaced sexuality? As these meanings are identified, therapy proceeds first toward resolving the needs, conflicts or then toward encouraging the person to adopt a more mature sexual outlook. The paraphilias are considered difficult cases to treat by psychoanalysis for two reasons. First, they represent developmental problems that are viewed as having started in very early childhood and are therefore resistant to change. Second, since the symptoms are themselves pleasurable, the person may be inclined to resist therapy.

***Behavior Therapy.*** Another approach to treat paraphilias, behavior therapy, focuses on symptoms rather than causes. Kushner (1977) treated a client whose fetish for women's panties began at the age of

12 and had lasted for 21 years. Treatment consisted of a shock to the fingertips with the presentation of pictures of women's underwear, removing any pleasure associated with the garments. The fetish improved by the second treatment session and ended within 14 weeks. Levin et al. (1977) also used aversion to help a 39-year-old married man who had been convicted of molesting his 10-year-old niece. Aversive imagery was associated with pictures of young girls; as treatment progressed, his sexual attraction to girls decreased (Figure 14–1 illustrates the results).

Laws and Pawlowski (1977) treated two prisoners convicted of pedophilia. The pedophilia had gone on for 28 years in the one case and 11 years in the other.

The therapists compiled two sets of slides—one set, of adults, and the other of children. By illuminating two slide projectors at different levels, the therapists presented a child slide fully illuminated, simultaneous with the adult slide projected at very low intensity, so as not to be visible. The patients were instructed to fantasize in a sexual way to the child slide; while this was occurring, the child slide gradually faded out and the adult slide became brighter. Then the patients were asked to fantasize to the adult slide. The child slide became brighter again once the clients had become aroused, and they were instructed to covertly think, "Why am I attracted to this kid? Kids get into trouble, they're not much fun anyway."—a thought that interfered sufficiently with arousal to cause an erection to be lost. Finally, the clients were instructed to fantasize to the adult slide again, thinking, "This is much better, much more attractive." The combined effect of this treatment was to produce a shift in erotic attachment.

Another successful use of behavior therapy has combined extinction with shame aversion procedures to control exhibitionism. In one case, the client was a 36-year-old married man, the father of six girls. His exhibitionism began at age 12, when he exposed himself to his teacher. He continued to expose himself four to five times monthly for 23 years. In discussing his reaction to exposing himself to women in the hospital, he became acutely embarrassed. The therapists used this sense of shame as an aversive experience, requesting him to exhibit himself to four nurses who were instructed to react with indifference, avoid conversing, and to leave after 15 minutes. Follow-up a year later showed a continued freedom from exhibitionist behaviors (Reitz & Keil, 1977).

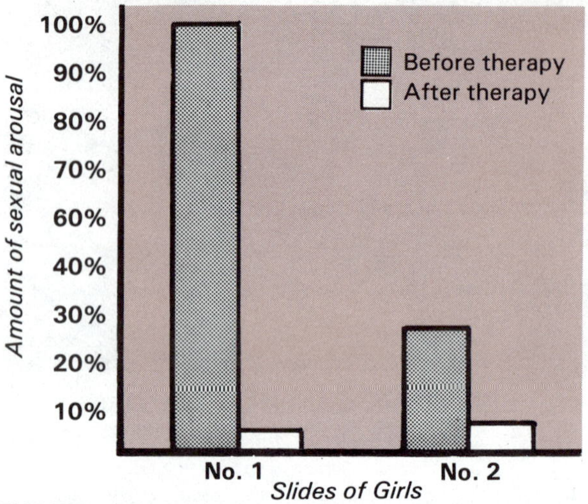


**FIGURE 14–1** Changes in sexual arousal to two slides of girls.

SOURCE: From "Variations of Covert Sensitization in the Treatment of Pedophilic Behavior: A Case Study" by S. Levin et al., 1977, *Journal of Consulting and Clincai Psychology, 45,* pp. 896–907. © 1977 the American Psych. Assn. Reprinted by permission of the author.

Another use of behavior therapy combined restraining and aversion techniques to help a college senior control sadistic sexual fantasies. The client was retrained to be responsive to normal fantasies and at the same time to find sadistic fantasies aversive. To achieve the former, he was instructed to masturbate (using sadistic fantasies if necessary) to a *Playboy* centerfold. Later, the sadistic fantasies were no longer needed and dropped out spontaneously in favor of the masturbation. The sadistic fantasies did return, however, and at this point an aversive technique was added. The client was given a highly aversive scene during a fantasy about sadism; thus, he was to imagine himself drinking a mixture of steaming hot urine with eeking fecal material, as he looked at a woman being tortured. This treatment was successful in extinguishing the fantasies (Davison, 1977).

## PSYCHOSEXUAL DYSFUNCTIONS

A second major category of psychosexual disorders are the *psychosexual dysfunctions.* In the normal human sexual response cycle, several phases are recognized. The *appetitive* phase is one of psychological desire for sexual activity. During *excitement*, the individual experiences sensations of pleasure and the corresponding physiological changes, such as erection of the penis or lubrication of the vagina. During the *plateau*, an advanced stage of excitement, high sexual tensions are maintained. The fourth phase, *orgasm*, brings sexual release, a peaking of sexual pleasure, and the corresponding ejaculatory emission or vaginal contractions. The final phase of *resolution* is a general relaxation, lowering of tension. During this period, the woman may be capable of immediate orgasmic response, while the man is incapable of stimulation.

*Dysfunctions*—inhibition or impairment in functioning—may occur in any aspect of these phases, although dysfunctions during the resolution stage have little relevance to us here. DSM-III recognizes several sexual dysfunctions as mental disorders because they are closely associated with emotional factors and also because they are sources of personal distress.

Table 14–3 presents an overview of the standard DSM-III psychiatric classification of sexual dysfunctions. It also presents the slightly different scheme developed by sex researchers Masters and Johnson of the Reproductive Biology Research Foundation. Because there is a great deal of overlap between the two classifications, we will base our discussion on the major categories derived from both: inhibited sexual excitement (erectile dysfunction), orgasmic dysfunction, premature ejaculation, vaginismus, dyspareunia, and ejaculatory incompetence (retarded ejaculation).

### Inhibited Sexual Excitement

Inhibited sexual excitement is a disorder characterized by the inability of the male to achieve an erection during sexual stimulation. It is a disorder involving inhibition of the excitement phase of the sexual response cycle. This dysfunction has also been referred to by the more descriptive term *erectile dysfunction.*

## Case History 14–3:

**Inhibited Sexual Excitement**

Dennis T. was a happily married man in every way except for a recent sexual problem. He describes his wife, Charise, in glowing adjectives and shows a deep sensitivity to her needs. Unlike some males, Dennis has always felt that marriage—especially its sexual aspects—was a two-way exchange. For these reasons, he had been very cautious about intercourse, relying on contraceptives to prevent pregnancy. They occasionally experimented with coitus interruptus, but he did not feel comfortable on the fear that some semen might still make its way into the vagina. Charise is a professional woman, who is climbing in her field, and hence they have agreed to postpone pregnancy for several years. Unlike Dennis, who had been a virgin before marriage, Charise had been sexually active during her college career.

The impotence was first noticed on an evening after a party given by Charise's office to celebrate her promotion. Dennis had been drinking more than normal; and that evening he was unable to achieve a successful erection. Charise used all of her skills, but the night ended with her accusation that he had "spoiled a perfectly good evening." Charise admits to having a high sexual drive, but dislikes reaching an orgasm by other than penile penetration.

After the first incident, Charise had an out-of-town business trip that prevented any further discussion or intercourse for a week. During this time, Dennis began to ruminate about his inadequacy and soon started to question his whole ability as not only a sexual partner, but a suitable spouse. The sexual failure became more a focus of concern, especially given Dennis' need to be a good mate and satisfy Charise's sexual demands. On Charise's return, she was particularly interested in intercourse and especially demanding. On seeing this, Dennis responded with panic and experienced the same problem. He was crushed by Charise's sarcasm and rejection. Dennis has sought treatment, convinced that he will have to offer Charise a divorce if therapy is unsuccessful.

**TABLE 14–3**

**Comparison of DSM-III and Masters and Johnson's Major Categories of Sexual Dysfunction**

| *Phase of sexual response cycle* | *DSM-III* | *Masters & Johnson* |
|---|---|---|
| Appetitive | *Inhibited sexual desire:* lack of desire for sexual activity which causes personal distress | |
| Excitement | *Inhibited sexual excitement:* inhibition of the excitement phase | *Primary and secondary erectile dysfunction* (m): difficulty achieving or sustaining erection |
| Orgasm | *Inhibited orgasm, male or female:* inhibition of orgasm after an adequate phase of sexual excitement | *Primary and secondary orgasmic* dysfunction (f): inhibition of orgasm after an adequate phase of sexual excitement |
| | *Premature ejaculation* (m): persistent early ejaculation | *Premature ejaculation* (m): equivalent to DSM-III |
| | *Functional vaginismus* (f): recurrent spasms of the vagina making penetration difficult | *Vaginismus* (f): equivalent to DSM-III |
| | *Functional dyspareunia:* recurrent genital pain associated with intercourse | *Dyspareunia:* equivalent to DSM-III |
| | | *Ejaculatory incompetence* (m): inability to ejaculate within the vagina |

SOURCES: Based on DSM-III; and *Human Sexual Inadequacy* by W. Masters and V. Johnson, 1970, Boston: Little, Brown.

The distinction is made between *primary* and *secondary* erectile dysfunction; the dysfunction is diagnosed as primary if the man has never been able to achieve an erection sufficient for either heterosexual or homosexual intercourse. The secondary diagnosis applies if he is at present unable to achieve an erection, but has in the past.

Secondary erectile dysfunction is one of the most common male sexual complaints, but fortunately it is considered to be the less severe of the two types of dysfunction. Some form of transient erectile difficulty affects about half the male population at some time in their lives (Kaplan, 1974). This may be because of fatigue or temporary daily stresses that act as distractions. However, these are considered normal, and the diagnosis of true secondary erectile dysfunction is given only when the erection failure is persistent, or the failure rate approaches 25 percent of attempts (Masters & Johnson, 1970).

Erectile difficulty clearly shows the close relationship between psychology and biology in sexual acts. An erection is the result of a physiological process, a vascular reflex that pumps blood into the penis, making it firm and erect. The reflex, however, can be inhibited by psychological factors, especially anxiety. For males suffering from erectile dysfunction, the failure can occur at different times as seen in the following quotes: "I get excited and erect during petting, but suddenly I lose it all when I'm trying to insert it"; "I met this gal with a great body and she finds me sexually attractive too, but I can't make it with her, I'm aroused and I want her but I'm impotent . . . the crazy thing is that I can stay erect and even come to a climax with my wife, but not with the other woman. . . . it's like I'm no good with the Beauty but good with the Beast."

***Dynamics of Erectile Dysfunction.*** There are a number of origins of inhibited sexual excitement, with the disorder appearing in persons ranging from the severely disturbed to those who are otherwise psychologically healthy. One pattern sometimes associated with erectile difficulty is religious training and/or ignorance that produces anxiety about sex. Several cases are reported of men with religious backgrounds which emphasized sexual taboos, and which led to misconceptions prior to marriage. When these men have married equally ignorant and frightened women, their combined anxieties and lack of sexual sensitivity or knowledge have led to increased trauma on their wedding night, as captured in the cry of one spouse, *"Do something!"* Certainly in some, but not all, circumstances, the marital or sexual partner is in a unique position to either contribute to or resolve the problem through her own attitudes or capabilities, as we'll see later in the discussion of treatments of sexual dysfunctions.

Another more severe factor may be early sexual experiences with the mother. Although this element is far more rare, Masters and Johnson relate three case histories in which the son had slept in his mother's bed far into puberty, with at least tangential evidence of seductive behaviors from the mother, such as sleeping nude beside the son.

In each of the factors discussed so far, the role of anxiety is viewed as extremely relevant. From a psychoanalytic standpoint, erectile dysfunction is seen as a defense against anxiety derived from an Oedipal conflict, unresolved incestuous desires, and displaced infantile fears. By not being able to engage in intercourse, the person avoids the guilt, anticipated castration, or anxiety. A current view is that the anxiety is itself a potent factor and may be unrelated to any defensive reactivity or early history.

In this regard, the idea of *performance anxiety* has been postulated, whereby the male becomes anxious because of a fear of not meeting the expectations of his partner. Historically, some cultures have viewed the male as the sexual macho-man who is equipped to have a sexual encounter any time, any place. Recently, the women's movement has emphasized that the woman is not simply a passive receptacle for the male; in contrast, more women now expect men to be responsive to their sexual needs. In some situations, men may feel anxiety about these demands for better performance, and this situation can be further complicated by personal experiences of erectile problems. The anxiety may spiral as the male begins to worry about a recurrence, becomes obsessed about the embarrassment, and experiences a sense of inadequacy. Such performance anxiety can easily become self-fulfilling. Added to this is the fact that a man can't disguise erectile difficulties in the same way that a woman may fake an orgasm.

Finally, in considering the possible origins of erectile difficulty, we need only to reexamine some of the quotes cited earlier to see other psychodynamic issues that may be present. For example, a man may have a fear of causing pregnancy or of deeper involvement that prevents an erection when intercourse is possible, but permits it when coitus is clearly not likely. Or the anxiety about having an extramarital affair may prevent the husband from experiencing an erection with anyone other than his wife. The impotence is sometimes an expression of marital conflict and a carry-over of the aversion which the husband feels towards his spouse. Finally, as with the other psychosexual disorders, there are organic causes for some erectile problems, such as neurological diseases. However, these organically based disorders are not classified as examples of psychosexual dysfunction.

### Primary or Situational Orgasmic Dysfunction

This disorder follows the pattern for erectile dysfunction in the recognition of *primary* orgasmic dysfunction—in which the woman has never achieved an orgasm—as opposed to the *situational* or *secondary* dysfunction, in which the woman has at some time achieved orgasm or can do so under certain conditions but not others. Just as erectile dysfunction is a male disorder, primary orgasmic dysfunction is defined by Masters and Johnson[4] as a woman's disorder, involving the lack of any orgasm through any means including intercourse, masturbation, direct clitoral stimulation, or oral-genital contact.

The woman with an orgasmic dysfunction is normal in every other way sexually. As with Marilyn in Case History 14–4, she can enjoy foreplay. She can become highly aroused, responding physiologically in releasing the normal vaginal lubrication during excite-

4 In contrast, the DSM-III classification recognizes the classification of "inhibited male orgasm" along with "inhibited female orgasm."

## Case History 14–4:
### Orgasmic Dysfunction

Marilyn B. was raised in a small-town environment in a close knit family in which caring for the needs of others was valued highly. As an adult, Marilyn never desired a career other than that of wife and mother. She met and married Cameron, a medical student. On her marriage bed, Marilyn was somewhat anxious and excited at the same time, looking forward to achieving her ideal of pleasing her husband sexually as the start of her duties as wife. Cameron was not aware of whether or not Marilyn was herself sexually gratified, only that she seemed happy.

After two years of marriage, Cameron attended some seminars on sexuality, and he began to inquire about Marilyn's experiences. At first, she offered only vague answers, emphasizing the enjoyment of coitus and the pleasure she took from being a good mate. On being pressed, she shyly acknowledged that she had never experienced anything beyond excitement. Through his readings, Cameron immediately set about helping his wife reach an orgasm, but his goal-directed concerns only made Marilyn self-conscious. She became distracted by thoughts such as "I wonder if I can climax? It's taking so long and he's so patient, but he's getting frustrated and I know he's sacrificing himself." Both became more conscious of Marilyn's state of worry. Cameron no longer seemed content reaching an orgasm alone, while Marilyn became even more anxious knowing that he was observing her reactions.

Marilyn and Cameron finally enrolled in a sexual clinic, and Cameron threw away his how-to-do-it sex manuals. Marilyn was instructed in the use of self-stimulation—not with orgasm as a goal, but only to become more aware of sensations in various parts of her own body. Cameron was gradually able to participate in this, and he received guidance in using clitoral stimulation. Throughout, Marilyn was instructed to substitute thoughts about his pleasure with selfish thoughts about her own feelings. Marilyn recently experienced her first orgasm.

ment, and she can experience the buildup of sexual tension and take pleasure in intercourse. Yet, she is incapable of moving off the plateau stage and into orgasm.

*Situational* or *secondary orgasmic dysfunction* is illustrated in a variety of cases: "I have tremendous orgasms when we have oral sex, but it's a desert and I don't feel anything when he's in me"; "I freeze when I'm touched with his hand although I know that clitoral touching is supposed to be the best orgasm; I do fine just the old-fashioned way when his penis is inserted; sometimes I try self-stimulation but again I feel like an ice cube"; "I don't understand myself. My lover and I have such a marvelous time during weekends, but I cannot make it if we try intercourse on a working night. . . . I'm not right somehow."

***Dynamics of Orgasmic Dysfunction.*** Orgasmic dysfunction may be traced to a variety of factors. In its least complex form, the cause may be inadequate sexual techniques. Male sexual partners may fail to recognize the role of clitoral stimulation in women's orgasms. Kaplan (1974) draws the conclusion, in fact, that there is only one type of orgasm, clitoral orgasm, although the experience includes sensations in and around the vagina. Orgasmic failure due to inadequate sexual skill is not considered a true case of psychosexual disorder, but does occur frequently enough to deserve comment.

More basic to explaining orgasmic dysfunction is the role of anxiety. Thus, the woman who complains that she "becomes a spectator, sitting back from a distance and watching my body, but not feeling anything" may be using this distancing as a means to avoid personal involvement—hence avoiding anxiety or guilt from experiencing pleasure.

The anxiety associated with orgasmic dysfunction may have a variety of sources. It may reflect an irrational fear of loss of control, of enjoying intercourse to the extent of becoming promiscuous, or of being hurt or even dying from the physical strain. The failure to reach orgasm may come from strongly ingrained religious beliefs about the sins of sensual pleasure, or from marital conflict that generalizes to coitus—all factors that play a parallel role in erectile difficulty in men. The role of anxiety is further illustrated by cases where situational factors are directly linked to secondary orgasmic dysfunction—as in the earlier case of the professional woman who could experience orgasms on weekends, but not during the week when she was under stress from work assignments. A traumatic experience such as rape can also lead to subsequent orgasmic dysfunction. Focus 14–2 discusses both the effect of rape on the victim and some of the motivations and conditions that seem to be associated with rape.

### Premature Ejaculation

The sexual response cycle shows a progression from desire to arousal to plateau to orgasm, but there is a great variation in the timing of orgasm. In *premature ejaculation,* the man experiences orgasm early—on seeing his partner disrobe, immediately on contact with her vagina, or after only a few thrusts of penetration, depending on the individual. In all of these cases, the common factor is an absence of voluntary control over the ejaculatory reflex.

DSM-III offers the definition that premature ejaculation "occurs before [the male] individual wishes it."[5] In addition, when the woman feels that her own sexual needs are frustrated, such premature ejaculation is judged a problem, and she may encourage her partner to seek help.

***Dynamics of Premature Ejaculation.*** There are several different explanations of premature ejaculation. According to the psychoanalytic interpretation, ejaculation is a symbolic acting out of hostility toward women—an act that defiles the woman, deprives her of pleasure, and reflects an unconscious hatred. Other experts propose that premature ejaculation represents anxiety over intercourse: early ejaculation dispenses with the need for vaginal penetration. Some propose that a generalized state of anxiety leads to a heightening of the man's overall arousal level, thus promoting premature ejaculation. Another factor may be cultural overconditioning—as when a male accepts the idea that women exist to "please men," and seeks quick gratification in the same way that prostitutes are used.

Basic to the relationship problems caused by premature ejaculation is the balance between both partners' sexual needs. When such a balance is not reached—as a result of premature ejaculation, orgasmic dysfunction, erectile inhibition, or any of the other sexual dysfunctions discussed here—it can cause frustration and anxiety for both partners. There are many opportunities for misinterpretation of the partners' motives. If the male avoids lovemaking because he sees his partner's frustration over the premature ejaculation, she may misinterpret his action as rejection. If the woman tries to solve her frustration by using frantic, thrusting movements to stimulate herself to orgasm more quickly, the result may simply be to speed her partner's orgasm even further. Each may be too upset to confide in the other, and soon the couple are caught in a vicious cycle of suppressed anger and avoidance. In this sense, one important factor in premature ejaculation and many other dysfunctions is simply the anxiety and worry that the condition itself engenders.

### Functional Dsypareunia and Vaginismus

*Functional dyspareunia* involves painful coitus and may be experienced by either male or female, although it is far more common among women. *Functional vaginismus* involves involuntary spasms of the vagina, which makes vaginal penetration difficult and can lead to pain.

In dyspareunia, the pain may occur at different stages of coitus and may vary in intensity, with pain being produced in some persons during mild or intense thrusting, and in others after intercourse. The pain of dyspareunia may be felt as immobilizing pain or as distressing physical irritation. Vaginismus, on the other hand, is directly associated with a reflexive closing of the vaginal entry on imagined, anticipated, or real attempts at vaginal penetration. If the male aggressively tries to penetrate the woman's spasmodically closed vagina, this will cause pain. The closing is so powerful

5 Masters and Johnson (1970) offer another definition, describing premature ejaculation as the situation in which the male achieves orgasm before his woman partner more than 50 percent of the time. However, factors such as the man's ability to arouse his partner, or anxiety of either partner, provide many exceptions to this definition.

# FOCUS 14–2:
## Rape

Rape is a legal offense and does not directly fit DSM-III's classification of psychosexual disorders. As a major problem, however, it relates to this text both in terms of the motivations of the rapist and the effects on the victim. We will explore several questions.

*What Is Rape?*

There are several different definitions of rape. An acceptable working definition is "the act of intercourse, involving the use of force, with a nonconsenting person" (Katz & Mazur, 1979). Rape is legally only one form of sexual assault, a category that also includes incest and molestation.

*Who Are Rape Victims?*

According to the Federal Bureau of Investigation data (1974), 1 person in every 500 has been raped. Rape victims may be either male or female. They may be from all levels of occupation and may be all appearances; the author knows of a gang rape of a crippled woman without arms or legs. Rapists, who tend to be single males from low socioeconomic levels, usually select victims similar to themselves in age; thus, Katz and Mazur conclude that "rape victims are closely related to their offenders demographically and racially, but not personally."

*Do Any Particular Conditions or Situations Seem to Be Associated with Rape?*

Rape is most frequent in big cities, during the summer months and weekend evenings. About 50 percent of rapists have been using alcohol prior to the offense (Rada, 1975); and one study reported that more rape

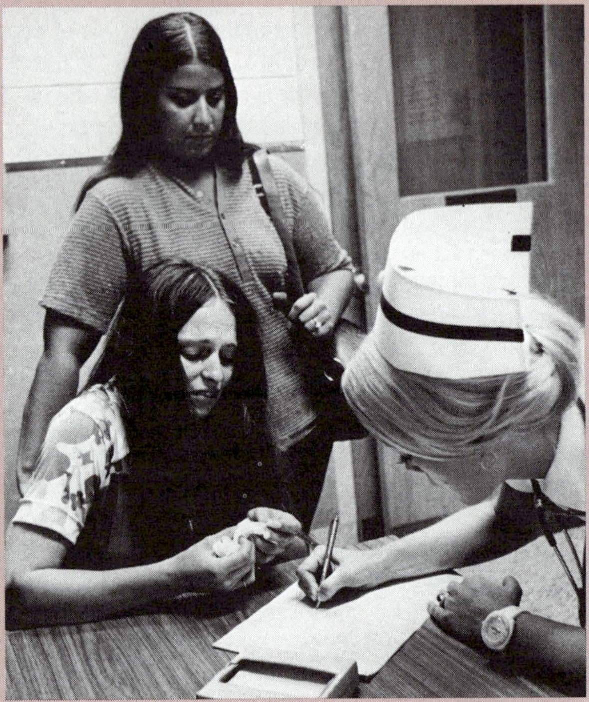

***Rape*** *has severe psychological impact. An important step is being able to report the event.*

victims were drinking prior to the assault than were rape offenders. Only a small percentage of rapes seem to be victim-precipitated, although there may be some situations in which the victim precipitates the encounter by acting provocatively (Amir, 1971).

*What Motivates the Rapist?*

There are many answers to this question. Several studies identify different types of rapists, suggesting different dynamics. A sampling includes the normally passive *sexually inadequate rapist,* who hopes the victim will yield and become enamored of him; the *aggressive rapist,* whose action is either an antisocial attack or is sadistically motivated; the *felony rapist,* who is actually initially motivated by robbery but takes advantage of an opportunity to commit rape; and the *confidence rapist,* who first attempts to seduce the woman but then forces participation, or who sets up an elaborate scheme to entrap a victim (Barbaree et al., 1979; Burgess & Holstrom, 1974). Another mode or motivation for rape is as a group action. *Gang rapes* may occur after an evening of drinking, as part of an initiation rite, or as a means of ''teaching a lesson'' to a girl.

*Is Rape a Sexual Act or an Act of Aggression?*

The answer varies according to the case. Studies have shown a range of different attitudes on the part of the rapist (Cunningham, 1982). In one study, 32 percent of victims described their attacker as hostile, but 13 percent said he was frightened (Medea & Thompson, 1974). Some rapists have been reported to be kindly and concerned, asking if an aspirin would help or even offering retribution, such as payment for cleaning soiled clothes or for damage to the front door (MacDonald, 1971).

Groth et al. (1977) concluded that it was more common for rapes to be characterized by intimidation or anger; however, those rapists who are driven by a desire to intimidate often fantasize an easy conquest and confirmation of their masculinity. Aggressive rapists who are driven by anger are releasing their rage toward women, wishing to inflict injury and humiliation, and they are dangerous.

*What Are the Effects of Rape on the Victim?*

The emotional reactions to rape are devastating: from the shock and fear during the rape (What's happening to me? . . . He's going to hurt me, stab me. . . . What can I do? I don't want to die. . . . Someone has to help me. . . . There's no one!); to the shame and embarrassment that can result from the complicated system for reporting the incident to the police and undergoing medical examination; to the protracted public exposure of a court appearance. The dread of these experiences themselves is one reason why so many rapes go unreported.

Beyond the immediate effects of rape, however, is the period of aftershock during which the person must try to regain a normal perspective on life (Resick et al., 1981). One study found that women who had been raped reported severe depression, fatigue, and tension, up to a year after the experience. Virtually all had nightmares right after the rape, and a number experienced sexual dysfunctions such as inhibited orgasm (Ellis et al., 1981).

as to prevent the consummation of many marriages, with cases involving years in duration (Kaplan, 1974). Vaginismus can be viewed as more the anticipation of pain while dyspareunia involves the actual experience of pain (which later leads to anticipation of more pain). Vaginismus clearly includes the physical activity of the closing of the vaginal entry, while dyspareunia is not as easy to localize.

Neither functional vaginismus nor functional dyspareunia is diagnosed if clear physical causes are found. For example, pain may be related to lesions, infections, or even sensitivity to chemical substances in contraceptives. A highly unusual case was reported of a woman who went into shock during her first intercourse, experienced asthma and cardiovascular collapse, with the later discovery that she had developed an allergenic sensitivity to her husband's semen (Halpern et al., 1967).

***Dynamics of Painful Coitus.*** Both dyspareunia and vaginismus are considered psychologically caused disorders. The most common premise is that the pain or reflexive contractions are responses of avoidance to coitus. Intercourse is perceived as an unwelcome activity. The initial origin of the pain may range from ingrained inhibitions about intercourse, to aversive experiences, to marital conflicts. Thus, a man or woman may have been raised to view sex as painful and not-to-be-enjoyed, or as leading to potentially harmful risks, such as infection or the pains of childbirth (for the woman). Specific experiences—for instance, an unsuccessful introduction to intercourse with an insensitive sexual partner or even the trauma of rape—may have conditioned the woman to expect pain during coitus. Finally, the pain or reflexive closing of the vagina may be motivated by an unconscious effort to frustrate and retaliate against an otherwise controlling husband.

### Ejaculatory Incompetence

*Ejaculatory incompetence,* or retarded ejaculation, is a male disorder. It involves the inability to ejaculate within the woman's vagina. Unlike erectile dysfunction, this disorder does not involve difficulty in achieving or maintaining an erection for successful penetration. It also differs from premature ejaculation. Ejaculation can occur in most cases of ejaculatory incompetence, but the male simply cannot seem to ejaculate within the woman's vagina, ejaculating on withdrawal instead.

***Dynamics of Ejaculatory Incompetence.*** The dynamics underlying this disorder are closely related to the man's anxiety, which may have several sources. Some sample cases illustrate the differing origins:

> *Religious Overtraining.* This man married a young woman of similarly restrictive religious and social background. . . . Every coital experience was potentially traumatic because, even with full erection and long continued coital connection, the husband was unable to ejaculate intravaginally. His concept of the vagina as an unclean area had been reinforced . . . whenever the urge to ejaculate arose, the mental imagery of possible vaginal contamination drove him to withdraw immediately. (Masters & Johnson, 1970, p. 118)
>
> *Concern over Rejection or Inadequacy.* The patient had left his wife and four children when he became infatuated with another woman. His ejaculatory inhibition had its onset after this woman, for whom he had sacrificed his marriage and family . . . left him for another man because she was "bored and dissatisfied" with him. [He] . . . reacted . . . with an intense agitated depression . . . he was [now] unable to ejaculate intravaginally with any partner. (Kaplan, 1974, p. 334)
>
> *Fear of Pregnancy.* A 19-year-old boy had impregnated a girl of whom he was very fond. A criminal abortion was performed . . . [and] the girl was ill for many months, almost losing her life . . . his level of guilt knew no bounds. Five years later in another community and with another girl, a marriage was established. When attempting consummation, the husband found himself completely unsuccessful in ejaculating intravaginally. . . . His was an overwhelming fear of causing pregnancy and of the possible unfortunate complications thereof. (Masters & Johnson, 1970, p. 122)
>
> *Conditioned Anxiety.* A single male . . . was surprised by the police in a local "lovers' lane" parking area while being manipulated to ejaculation by a young woman. The girl's terror and his overwhelming embarrassment and fear of public exposure left an indelible residual. . . . Since he had been on the verge of ejaculating when surprised, he thereafter was always frozen by fear of observation when a similar level of excitation developed. (Masters & Johnson, 1970, p. 124)

These dynamics are similar to those of most of the other psychosexual dysfunctions, and in general, the treatment of all of these disorders shares common aims and methods. We'll look briefly at some major approaches to treatment in the following section.

### Treatment of the Psychosexual Dysfunctions

***Psychodynamic Psychotherapy.*** Psychodynamically based therapies traditionally emphasized the need to treat sexual dysfunctions as symptoms of deeper emotional issues such as guilt, childhood-based inadequacies, or repressed sexual conflicts about parent figures. Such interpretations continue to be popular among many professional therapists, and they are generally assessed to fill in a more complete picture of the person's current attitudes, or feelings or conflicts (Cadden, 1978). In general, however, psychotherapy that focuses only on these topics has not had great success; and in fact, some contemporary therapists have noted that this approach does not produce improvement in many sexual dysfunctions (LoPiccolo, 1978). Instead, more direct techniques aiming at the dysfunction itself rather than assumed underlying conflicts have received more attention. These direct approaches include anxiety management and other behavior therapy methods, as well as the broader approaches used at sexual dysfunction clinics.

***Anxiety Management.*** Where anxiety is a primary feature, various forms of anxiety management behavior therapy methods have proven useful. Andersen (1983) provided desensitization for women experiencing primary orgasmic dysfunction, based on the premise that anxiety was preventing the women from experiencing either arousal or orgasm. The desensitization trained the women in relaxation so as to remove the tension previously associated with foreplay or coitus. The results were successful in increasing not only the women's levels of pleasure during sexual activity but also their frequency of orgasms.

Masters and Johnson use a method they call "sensate focus," which involves nonsexual, nondemanding touching first to focus on learning to experience tactile sensations as pleasurable (see Case History 14–4). This gradual exposure to viewing sensations as positive experiences is also useful in reducing sexual anxiety.

Anxiety reduction by behavior therapy has also been used with other clients where anxiety was a primary element in a dysfunction. One case in which vaginismus prevented marital consummation for one and a half years was treated through relaxation training, paired with the client's inserting graduated-size glass dilators into her vagina. The husband was also included in the therapy, which focused on attitudes as well as techniques. Eventually, he was able to first introduce the glass dilators, then ultimately engage in coitus (Cooper, 1977). Razani (1977) reduced the fears of a male who showed ejaculatory incompetence from fear of causing pregnancy. The Semans technique (which we will describe later) was combined with relaxation and desensitization to inhibit the conditioned anxiety which he had acquired from a previous girl friend, who continuously had raised apprehensions about pregnancy.

***Sex Clinics.*** Sexual dysfunction clinics, such as the Reproductive Biology Research Foundation program of Masters and Johnson, have provided broad-based treatment that includes elements of medical, educational skill, and psychological therapy (Kilmann & Mills, 1983). Some approaches towards premature ejaculation and orgasmic dysfunction will illustrate treatments that may be viewed as a type of skill training.

*The Semans Technique.* The *Semans technique* (Semans, 1956) is named after the urologist who designed it. He accepted the view that premature ejaculation was the failure to control the ejaculatory reflex. Hence, he trained patients in such inhibitory control by having the partner manually stimulate the penis until ejaculation was imminent, then desist until the sensations dissipated. Eventually, clients learned to tolerate this extravaginal stimulation "indefinitely" without reflexively ejaculating, and normal coitus was possible at this point.

*The Squeeze Technique.* The *squeeze technique* of Masters and Johnson is a variation of the Semans approach. Following initial counseling, sensate focus exercises, and celibacy, the woman manually stimulates the man's penis until orgasm is imminent; then squeezes the penis just below the rim to cause the erection to be partially lost and to prevent ejaculation. When intercourse is introduced, the woman once again interrupts imminent ejaculation by squeezing. Masters and Johnson report 98 percent success within two weeks using this treatment for premature ejaculation.

*Self-exploration.* Another technique taught in sex clinics helps women overcome primary orgasmic dysfunction by enabling them to discover that they are capable of orgasm. Much of modern sexual therapy involving inhibitions first aims at showing patients that sexual pleasure and orgasms are natural experiences (Corey et al., 1984). Many patients experiencing sexual inadequacies develop a belief that "something is wrong with my machinery" and lose confidence in their ability to experience success no matter what conditions are present. For this reason, self-stimulation with vibrators or masturbation or clitoral stimulation by a partner may be prescribed. The patient is thus given permission to discover different ways of achieving an orgasm, instead of being restricted to coitus. In addition, the recommendation may be modified such that achieving an orgasm is not an immediate goal. Instead, the woman is helped to use self-stimulation to become aware of erotic sensations. In many cases, when the expectation of an orgasm is removed, and enjoyment of the pleasuring itself becomes a goal, an orgasm will occur naturally. As later steps, clinicians will have the woman gradually approximate coitus more closely, with her partner taking on a gradually increasing role as he uses similar methods of clitoral stimulation (Annon, 1971; LoPiccolo, 1980). Shortly after this stage, the client is often able to experience orgasm through intercourse.

All of the sexual dysfunctions are likely to create not only personal anxiety, but also strained relationships with a partner. The last two disorders discussed in this chapter, ego-dystonic homosexuality and gender identity disorders, are most evident not so much in relationship problems but in the personal anguish they can create.

## EGO-DYSTONIC HOMOSEXUALITY

*Homosexuality* involves the selection of a sexual partner from one's own sex; for women, the term *lesbianism* is often used. The question of whether homosexuality involves pathology or not has aroused a great deal of controversy. Homosexual and lesbian organizations argue that homosexuality is normal and that it is society that is abnormal in its restrictive negative attitudes. Evidence to date suggests that homosexuals do not as a group appear more maladjusted than heterosexuals. One study, for instance (Thompson et al.,1971), tested 127 homosexuals, 123 male heterosexuals, 84 lesbians, and 94 heterosexual women and found no differences on personal adjustment measures (see Table 14–4). Weinberg and Williams (1974) found no differences on self-acceptance and psychosomatic symptoms, but also found homosexuals to say "yes" less often to the question "Do you feel you are a happy person?" The fact that some homosexuals experience personal adjustment conflicts is the reasoning behind the classification of *ego-dystonic homosexuality* in DSM-III's list of disorders.

### The Ego-dystonic Classification

In DSM-II, the American Psychiatric Association officially removed homosexuality from official classification as a disorder; however, one specific type of homosexuality has been returned in the DSM-III system. The current position of APA is that homosexuality per se is not pathological; but the category of ego-dystonic homosexuality is listed as a mental disorder. In *ego-dystonic homosexuality,* the person is distressed by his or her homosexual orientation and wants to gain heterosexual responsivity. The situation is diagnosed as a disorder only if the diagnostician is convinced that the distress does not result simply from a conflict with societal pressures.[6]

### Dynamics of Homosexuality

A variety of studies have aimed at identifying factors that lead to homosexuality. Bieber (1976) examined the records of over 100 homosexual male clients in psychoanalysis and concluded that these homosexuals showed a fear of heterosexuality and an aversion to fe-

6 The APA admits that this decision is a controversial one. The decision appears to be an attempt to permit recognizing that homosexuality may be experienced as an unwanted orientation by some persons who would seek therapeutic help to change.

male genitalia symbolic of castration fears. Further, he emphasized that the mothers were close-binding, intimate, and possessive towards their sons, while the fathers were remote or hostile. Another study by Evans (1969) examined members of a Los Angeles homosexual organization. Its conclusions: these persons had been frail and fearful of injury as children; had mothers who were seductive and intimate towards them, encouraging feminine attitudes and interfering with heterosexual interests; and had fathers who spent little time with their sons, and whom they viewed fearfully.

Such studies suggest that homosexuality may develop from such early role model influences or from heterosexual anxieties. In some cases, the homosexual role is accepted because of strong feelings of personal inadequacy, unattractiveness, or fears of failure or humiliation on approaching a person of the opposite sex. Psychodynamic aspects of homosexuality might involve:

- A failure to identify with the father and the masculine role for boys; or for girls, a failure to shift from the first natural love object, the mother, to one of the opposite sex.
- Feelings of inadequacy in competing with the father, followed by attempts to gain power and strength by symbolically absorbing these through intercourse with a strong male.
- An acceptance of homosexual contact as an alternative to the avoidance reaction toward women from earlier fears of castration relating to love for the mother.

In addition, biological or physiological sources of homosexuality have been examined. Kallman (1952) found 100 percent concordance for homosexuality in identical twins as compared with 15 percent for fraternal twins, but other research does not support a genetic component (Rosenthal, 1970). Suspicions about hormonal imbalance, such as possibly too little male hormone in the homosexual or too little female hormone in the lesbian, have also not been confirmed.

### Treatment of Ego-dystonic Homosexuality

***Psychoanalytic Therapy.*** Traditional psychoanalytic treatment aims toward the assumed underlying castration or Oedipal conflicts behind homosexuality, attempting to increase the homosexual's ability to achieve heterosexual gender identification. Freud (Jones, 1957, pp. 195–96) showed his compassion and insights into homosexuality in a letter he sent to a mother seeking therapy for her homosexual son:

April 9, 1937

Dear Mrs. ________:

I gather from your letter that your son is a homosexual. I am most impressed by the fact that you do not mention this term yourself in your information about him. May I question you, why do you avoid it? Homosexuality is assuredly no advantage, but it is nothing to be ashamed of, no vice, no degradation, it cannot be classified as an illness; we consider it to be a variation of the sexual function produced by a certain arrest of sexual development—Many highly respectable individuals of ancient and modern times have been homosexuals, several of the greatest men among them (Plato, Michelangelo, Leonardo da Vinci, etc.). It is a great injustice to persecute homosexuality as a crime, and cruelty, too. If you do not believe me, read the books of Havelock Ellis.

By asking me if I can help, you mean, I suppose, if I can abolish homosexuality and make normal heterosexuality take its place. The answer is, in a general way, we cannot promise to achieve it. In a certain number of cases, we succeed in developing the blighted germs of heterosexual tendencies which are present in every homosexual, in the majority of cases it is no more possible. It is a question of the quality and the age of the individual. The result of treatment cannot be predicted.

What analysis can do for your son runs in a different line. If he is unhappy, neurotic, torn by conflicts, inhibited in his social life, analysis may bring him harmony, peace of mind, full efficiency whether he remains a homosexual or gets changed. . . .

Sincerely yours with kind wishes,

Freud

Freud's letter describes the recognition that treatment may be helpful for those with ego-dystonic homosexuality who feel unhappy. Treatment goals still must be identified for individual cases. For example,

**TABLE 14–4**

**Adjustment of Homosexuals and Heterosexuals**

| | *Homosexual males* | *Heterosexual males* | *Homosexual females* | *Heterosexual females* |
|---|---|---|---|---|
| Personal adjustment* | 43 | 45 | 46 | 48 |
| Defensiveness* | 46 | 49 | 47 | 48 |
| Self-confidence* | 45 | 48 | 54 | 51 |

*High scores indicate more favorable levels. Data suggests no differences in personal adjustment; less defensiveness and self-confidence in homosexual males; and greater self-confidence in homosexual females.

SOURCE: Adapted from "Personal Adjustment of Male and Female Homosexuals and Heterosexuals" by N. Thompson, Jr., B. McCandless; & B. Strickland, 1971, *Journal of Abnormal Psychology, 78,* pp. 237–240. © 1971 by the American Psych. Assn. Adapted by permission of the author.

one person may seek a complete heterosexual orientation while another wishes only to be more comfortable as a homosexual (Shoenberg & Goldberg, 1984).

***Behavior Therapy.*** In applying behavior therapy to homosexuality, the client's goals are first analyzed to select the appropriate mode of treatment. For one individual, an increased ability to achieve heterosexual arousal may automatically produce a decline in homosexual responsiveness. Here, a sexual conditioning program aimed at increasing arousal to the opposite-sex partner may be the treatment of choice. Such programs have included a number of methods, such as providing the male client with selective reinforcement (a drink of cool juice to the thirsty client) for increases in signs of sexual arousal to slides of a nude woman, or pairing arousal from masturbation or fantasies with images of the appropriate sex partner (Annon, 1973; Quinn et al., 1970). A fading technique, similar to the pedophilia treatment discussed earlier, has been devised by Barlow et al. (1973). Here, slides of nude females are superimposed on slides of nude males for the male homosexual. The female slides are gradually faded in as the clients maintain their erection. In one case treated with this method, sexual arousal to a female slide alone was achieved in six sessions, with corollary increases in heterosexual behavior reported by the client.

In other cases, the goal of therapy may be to significantly eliminate homosexual arousal because it is suppressing an already existing heterosexuality that the client wants to be dominant. Here, an aversive therapy model may be used to lower the strength of the homosexual interest. In a typical aversion program, the homosexual is shown slides of males and females, with shock paired with the presentation of the male slides (McConaghy et al., 1981). In some cases, the aversion is obtained through the use of aversive fantasies attached to homosexual behavior, rather than shock. For example, the client is instructed to begin a fantasy about a homosexual contact, but the fantasy is guided to an anxiety-provoking conclusion: "You are about to caress, when suddenly your partner goes into a convulsion . . ." (Cautela & Wisocki, 1977).

Finally, in some instances, homosexuality is present only because of a deficiency in heterosexual skills, or because such skills are suppressed by heterosexual anxieties. In these cases, social retraining may be appropriate, along with some form of anxiety management training. In social retraining, clients are trained in appropriate social or heterosexual behaviors or assertive behaviors. Where the heterosocial or heterosexual skills are already present, but suppressed because of anxiety, therapy has focused on anxiety reduction techniques, such as relaxation training associated with heterosexual slides.

***Humanistic-existential Therapy.*** Humanistic-existential theorists tend to avoid quickly accepting the assumption that homosexuality is necessarily pathological. Instead, their views are consistent with their valuing of each person's individuality, each person's right to choice, and the contributing role of society in creating conditions that are unhealthy for people. Such therapists would not be quick to recommend that a homosexual change to a more socially conforming pattern. This choice should be an individual one based on what is most personally fulfilling or enriching.

Moreover, the focus on the homosexual may be an inaccurate and highly misleading emphasis. Instead, the humanistic-existential therapist would argue that the problem lies as much in the attitudes created by society towards homosexual preferences. This questioning of society's condemnation of homosexual behaviors has now received some support from psychologists who otherwise do not share in the humanistic-existential philosophy of treatment, such as the behaviorist Gerald Davison (see Focus 14–3). On the other hand, the humanistic-existential therapist would not categorically force a homosexual person to remain homosexual if this person were dissatisfied and wanted a heterosexual lifestyle. The point is mainly that personal freedom to choose must be present for a person to achieve a personally adjusted life, and that societal prejudices may prevent the individual from being free to see and commit to such choices.

One other psychosexual disorder remains to be discussed in this chapter. It shares with ego-dystonic homosexuality the sense of dissatisfaction with one's sexual orientation, but in this case, the distress is far more profound. We'll look more closely at transsexualism in the remaining pages of this chapter.

## Case History 14–5:
### A Case of Transsexuality

Robert H. has undergone a sex change from male to female.

> I am now one person, instead of two people. All my life, in some way or another, sometimes not knowing it clearly myself, I've been two people . . . not like the sick cases of multiple personality, but I've been psychologically a woman but physically a man. As I remember growing up, my fondest recalls were the pleasant sensations of wearing soft dresses—my mother used to dress me occasionally as a girl since she had so much wanted a girl. In fact, she always called me Bobbie, the female version of my name.
>
> Then I found out how being a boy meant a lot in school, and sissies were teased, and I was certain that I would be all-boy. So I went through a period in which I did everything, like super-macho. I often took out girls, played on the basketball team, and liked to play rough. I volunteered for the marines and drank and had the foreign ladies as well as anyone else.
>
> A change came when I was isolated in one action in combat for a couple days. I began to think. All of my secret ambitions then started to come out, things I wouldn't let myself dream about. I liked women, but more, I liked their looks, their dress, their softness, their outlook on life. . . . I knew I really was denying that I was a woman.
>
> You can't know how much pain this has brought. I'm not a homosexual or a transvestite. I'm not sick, but I had been sick about the trap I was in. It's like being in a deep well and knowing that no one is going to hear you, and you shout as loud as you can, "I don't belong here," but no one hears. It's like I'm me behind my face, looking out my eyes like looking out a window and thinking, "It's me behind here"—and then I see my beard in the mirror. I hated it. The hair on my chest was like an obscene growth that couldn't be washed off. I considered suicide, and I went into psychotherapy, but I knew that the only help would be for me to find my real body.

Robert, now Bobbie, was accepted for a sex change operation. He left his wife and moved to a different state. Bobbie wants to leave every trace of past history, including friends, behind. "It's too much trouble to explain. And when I try, I know they just think I'm mentally ill somehow."

## GENDER IDENTITY DISORDERS

More and more public attention is being given to gender identity decisions made by individuals. Such decisions, involving surgical changes of sexual characteristics (the sex change operations), reflect a commitment to a new gender identity. As in Case History 14–5, the person feels "trapped by a freak of nature in someone else's body." Although the first case of a male having his sex changed to that of a female astounded the world, enough persons have now been involved in such issues to permit study of the problem.

Gender identity disorders can be best understood in the context of a very common problem. An *identity crisis* is a common description for the normal self-doubts that face many of us during adolescence or later turning points in life. *Gender identity disorders* are crises of identity that center almost solely around one's sexual characteristics. The male questions being a male; the female is certain she should be a male. These individuals are convinced that their psychological identity is incongruent with their physical identity: indeed, they feel trapped in the wrong-sexed body.

### Symptoms and Diagnosis

Gender identity disorders may occur in both childhood and adulthood. When the disorder is identified in an adult, the term *transsexualism* is used; when recognized in a child, the term *gender identity disorder of childhood* is used. In childhood, the boy or girl has a profound urge to be of the other sex. This desire reaches beyond the simple sex role rejection sometimes seen in the sissy behaviors of some boys or the tomboy behaviors of some girls. The boy with gender identity disorder will consistently identify with feminine stereotypes, for example, taking the role of the woman in playing house.

In transsexualism as it occurs in adulthood, there is at the least a profound sense of ambivalence. The individual at first may lead a heterosexual lifestyle, and a number of transsexuals marry and have children. A homosexual orientation is more frequent, however. More males have homosexual fantasies than heterosexual fantasies, as would be consistent with their preferred identity.

More essential is the fact that the transsexual is repelled by his or her gender. In the case of the male—and the vast majority of transsexuals are men—the person loathes every reminder of his masculinity: his beard, his deeper voice, clothes, name, and genitals. He resists psychiatry or psychotherapy, because he views the problem as a physical one, not a mental one. "My *mind* is right; it is my *body* that is wrong." Tension and emotional concerns are attributed to this "cruel miscarriage of nature," not to any emotional maladjustment. The transsexual will go to great lengths to regain some semblance of what he believes to be his true identity. Costly hair removal procedures, use of hormones in the hope of obtaining changes, or wearing women's clothing (cross-dressing) are part of this effort. Where the urge to change becomes overwhelming, transsexuals may seek surgical solution, described in the discussion of treatment.

### Dynamics of Transsexualism

Despite the classification of transsexualism as a psychiatric disorder, it is not clear whether this is appropriate for all cases. At best, the topic is controversial. Some candidates for sex change have been clearly diagnosed as psychotic, and some experts consider the transsexual invariably either neurotic or psychotic (Meerloo, 1967; Buhrich, 1981). In at least one study, however, psychological testing failed to confirm any evidence of pathology in a small sample of 10 women transsexuals (Roback et al., 1979). While the controversy continues, a variety of hypotheses have been offered regarding the source or backgrounds of transsexuals.

An entirely psychological approach suggests that childhood experiences are an important factor. In some cases, the slightly feminine appearance of a boy infant may stimulate his mother to further feminize him. In these cases, the mother is believed to have herself experienced some sexual ambivalence. Having reluctantly given up her own tomboy impulses, she now encourages feminine traits in her son. In later years, the school environment begins to demand maleness,

## FOCUS 14–3:

### Focus on Homosexuality: Is It Normal? (or Is Society?)

The issue of how to view homosexuality has created much controversy. Over the years, the American Psychiatric Association has itself classified it as a "sexual deviation" (DSM-I); then removed it from that classification in DSM-II; then reinstated one form of homosexuality, ego-dystonic homosexuality, in its current DSM-III classification. The issue is far from settled, however. Today, some experts argue that the only disturbances associated with homosexuality are the result of social attitudes and cultural norms, while others argue that homosexuality is itself a symptom of maladjustment.

Gerald Davison (1976, 1978) is a leading behavior therapist who pioneered some sexual therapy methods. In attempting to convey the cultural oppression he sees as facing the homosexual, he draws the following analogy:

> Imagine for a moment that you are an anxious person and that being anxious is against the law. You must try to hide your fears from others. Your own home may be a safe place to feel anxious, but a public display of apprehension can lead to arrest or at least to social ostracism. At work one day an associate looks at you suspiciously and says, "That's funny, for a crazy moment there I thought you were anxious." "Heck no," you exclaim a bit too loudly, *"not me!"* You begin to wonder if your fellow worker will report his suspicions to your boss. If he does, your boss may inform the police or will at least change your job to one that requires less contact with customers, especially with those who have children. (p. 159)

Davison goes on to argue that therapists should shift their focus away from forcing homosexuals to change and instead work on those who too quickly label homosexuality as abnormal to "change their [own] prejudicial biases . . ." (p. 159).

In a response to Davison, Bieber (1976) first comments that there is evidence that homosexuals show pathological characteristics. He reviews research and clinical evidence and concludes "We found homosexuality to be the outcome of adverse experiences" (p. 164). Since Davison points out the effects of social attitudes about homosexuality, Bieber responds by saying: "Although societal prejudices contribute to the suffering of homosexuals, feelings of inferiority are engendered within the family (which also created the consequent homosexuality), not by society at large. Social prejudice merely reinforces what is already there. An impaired sense of masculinity . . . is induced by parents, the designers of a homosexual pattern in a child. In my view, if social pressures were entirely absent, homosexuals would still wish to change."

In fact, Bieber suggests that "When facts about therapeutic efficacy become known to them, many young homosexuals seek treatment" (p. 165). The "new myth that homosexuality is a normal variant of sexuality," he states, "is just as dangerous as prior myths that homosexuality was immoral, evil, sinful, or evidence of a degenerative disease—since the new misconception discourages homosexuals in distress from seeking help."

Davison and Bieber represent opposite views on homosexuality. Each view also reflects a form of value statement. What is your opinion of this sensitive issue?

**TABLE 14-5**

**Identification of Masculine Gender Identity**

Blanchard and Freund (1983) have developed an experimental scale for measuring the level of masculine identification among women. Women transsexuals scored the highest on items such as:

1. Between the ages of 6 and 12, did you prefer:
   —to play with boys*
   —to play with girls
2. Between the ages of 6 and 14, which did you like more, romantic stories or adventure stories?
   —liked romantic stories more
   —liked adventure stories more*
3. Between the ages of 6 and 12, did you wish you had been born a boy instead of a girl
   —often*
   —occasionally
4. Between the ages of 6 and 12, did you sometimes imagine yourself as being the courageous leader of others?
   —yes*
   —no
5. Do you think your appearance is
   —very feminine
   —quite masculine*
6. Between the ages of 13 and 16, did you put on men's underwear or clothing
   —once a month or more, for at least a year*
   —very seldom during this period
7. What qualities did you like in females to whom you were sexually attracted?
   —slightly masculine behavior
   —very feminine behavior*

SOURCE: Adapted from "Measuring Masculine Gender Identity in Females" by R. Blanchard and K. Freund, 1983, *Journal of Consulting and Clinical Psychology, 51,* pp. 205–214. © 1983 by the American Psych. Assn. Adapted by permission of the author.

thereby raising the question of dual identity: "Am I a male or a female; which is real?"

In a review of 100 cases, Pauly (1968a) found a tendency for male transsexuals to have viewed their mothers as ideal, and for the mother-son relationship to have been excessively close, while the father was ineffectual and distant. In 13 percent of the cases in this review, the transsexual was actually directly encouraged to identify with the feminine gender early in life, although the parents later changed their minds.

In contrast to the psychological hypothesis is a more physiological explanation. According to the theory of Oliven (1974), an initial factor causing transsexualism is functional damage to the steroid receptor cells in the brain. These cells govern sex hormones, and damage to these cells results in lower levels of androgen and a defect in the ability to develop masculine psychosexual differentiation. Such a physiological defect must still be reinforced by the parent in order to precipitate an overt psychological gender crisis. Oliven admits that his theory is difficult to prove. However, he speculates that one source of the receptor damage may be the use by a pregnant woman of medication, such as sedatives or tranquilizers, that blocks the male hormone.

### Treatment of Transsexualism

Transsexuals feel trapped in a paradox so basic that the disorder often defies satisfactory treatment. The two main approaches are sex surgery and psychotherapy. While surgery is the treatment of choice for the transsexual, neither solution has a high rate of success. We'll look quickly at both.

***Sex-change Surgery.*** Most transsexuals are convinced that surgery is the ultimate answer to their plight. The first transsexual operation is attributed to F. Abraham in the 1930s, but the procedure did not attract wide public attention until the sex change of Christine Jorgenson in Copenhagen in 1953. The later accounting by English writer Jan Morris (formerly James Morris) in her book *Conundrum* (1974) brought more attention as it detailed her former life as a male and her new life as a woman.

In the United States, the Gender Identity Clinic at Johns Hopkins School of Medicine and the University of Minnesota Hospital were among the first to give sanction to such surgery, and it has been estimated that over 2,500 Americans have had their sex changed by surgical means (Gagnon, 1977). In males, the surgery replaces the male organs with a vagina, that in some cases even permits achieving an orgasm. A less successful surgery for female transsexuals involves the removal of the female genitals and the substitution of

*Transexual Richard Raskin (left) before undergoing* ***sex reassignment****; (right) as Reneé Richards.*

an artificial penis of rib cartilage or plastic that has no sensation.

Because of the danger of sexual surgery being requested for neurotic or even psychotic reasons, candidates for such operations are currently required to undergo extensive presurgical observation, from six months to two years. Legal and social consequences must also be carefully considered, such as legalization of the sex change, issues of marital status, and the social considerations of how to reintegrate into a prior social structure that was based on a different sexual identity.

The surgical operation, although more widely familiar today, is still highly controversial. Pauly (1968b) reported that the ratio of postoperative satisfaction of 121 male transsexuals was about 10 to 1. However, the Gender Identity Clinic has discontinued support for sex-change surgery, based in part on a report that the follow-up results were no more helpful for those treated than for those who did not undergo the operation (Meyer & Reter, 1979).

***Psychological Approaches.*** The alternate approach to changing the body to "fit the person inside" is to try to help the individual come to terms with his or her physical gender.

This approach has many inherent difficulties. For one, transsexuals rarely want to see a psychiatrist or psychologist, believing strongly that the only solution is sex surgery. A unique case was the successful treatment of a 17-year-old male (Barlow et al., 1973). The behavior therapists first used aversive treatment and heterosexual arousal therapy, similar to those described earlier. But both of these approaches failed, and the therapists shifted to training the client in appropriate sex role behaviors. The client was taught to walk, stand, and sit in a masculine way and to maintain a social conversation on masculine topics. He was also taught to deepen his relatively high-pitched voice. Within three months, this client reported liking his now-masculine manners. He still complained of feeling socially and sexually like a girl, however, so the therapists returned to sexual arousal therapies such as reinforcement for appropriate sexual fantasies. At a one-year follow-up, the client was happy in his masculine role, reported having a steady girl friend with whom he enjoyed petting, and seemed confident in his masculine identity. This case is unique in the decision to retrain the client in gender role *behaviors* as a means of altering gender *identity,* rather than vice versa.

## EVALUATION

The psychosexual disorders represent an updated diagnostic classification. The category of psychosexual dysfunctions has been influenced by the modern clinical efforts of Masters and Johnson, particularly in the evolution of new treatment methods. Sexual dysfunction clinics have brought a new level of awareness, so that the general public can now openly discuss and seek help for sexual problems that were once sources of shame. Part of these gains have been achieved through greater openness about biological aspects of sexuality, part through changing attitudes about sharing and equality in sexual relations, and part through the development of treatment approaches that emphasize new behaviors, information, education, and normal psychology rather than solely psychiatric or emotional conflict.

A second development worthy of recognition is the clarification regarding homosexuality. In the same way that heterosexual behaviors may sometimes derive from problems of adjustment, so can homosexual behaviors involve maladjustment under certain conditions. The current DSM-III classification brings back this awareness through the inclusion of ego-dystonic homosexuality. This permits the sensible distinction between homosexuality where the individual is personally adjusted to the sex preference and lifestyle, homosexuality where distress is present but attributable to societal pressures, and homosexuality where the person feels personal distress.

Although DSM-III is improved by introducing these new elements, there are still problems in the system. Specifically, classifications of dysfunctions are unsatisfactory. Those offered by Masters and Johnson are discussed in this book since they provide a more precise system than the DSM-III system: for example, in distinguishing between primary and secondary erectile dysfunction or orgasmic dysfunction (which relates to prognosis). Additionally, although it is recognized that dysfunctions can occur in *desire,* that is, the appetitive stage of the human sexual response cycle, only inhibited desire is discussed. This ignores the category of satyriasis or nymphomania, where excess desire is present, which was previously included in DSM-II. Perhaps the two best outcomes of work in recent times on psychosexual disorders are the gains in public awareness that human sexuality and sensuality are normal, and the progress in information and attitudes regarding the sexuality of women. Once more, progress in understanding normal human characteristics has been influenced by study deriving from human pathology.

## SUMMARY

The psychosexual disorders recognize four general categories: paraphilias, psychosexual dysfunctions, ego-dystonic homosexuality, and gender identity disorders. The paraphilias involve sexual arousal from deviant objects or actions, for example, fetishism. The psychosexual dysfunctions are inadequate sexual responses, such as ejaculatory dysfunction. Ego-dystonic homosexuality is the selection of same-sex persons as sexual partners where there is experienced emotional conflict over the preference. The gender identity disorders are those in which there is conflict between a person's physical and psychological identities, such as in transsexualism. Transsexuals are those who believe that they were born in the wrong sex body.

The paraphilias derive from many origins; however, one pattern that predominates is the lack of communication in social contacts. A variety of behavior therapies have been used, typically involving first arousing sexual levels with the deviant stimulus, then fading the stimuli to substitute more acceptable objects (that is, persons of the opposite sex).

Sexual dysfunctions may have their origins in inadequate sexual techniques, performance anxiety, or fears and inhibitory attitudes. New sex clinics have been developed to offer help, including information and education, medical care, skill training, and psychological retraining.

Although homosexuality per se is no longer considered a psychiatric disorder, ego-dystonic homosexuality is included. Homosexuality may be associated with deficits in heterosexual skills, fearfulness of heterosexual contact, or failure to achieve sexual arousal when presented with opposite-sex persons. Behavior training programs have been found successful in dealing with these differing types of problems.

Various hypotheses have been offered to explain the source of transsexualism. Some evidence suggests that male transsexuals have had intimate ties to their mothers, while the father was viewed as distant. Transsexuals often request sex-change operations, but at least one clinic has discontinued such surgery since evidence does not support its success.

## KEY TERMS

**Copralalia**
**Dysfunction**
**Dyspareunia**
**Ego-dystonic homosexuality**
**Ejaculatory incompetence**
**Erectile dysfunction**
**Exhibitionism**
**Fetishism**
**Gender identity disorder of childhood**
**Gender identity disorders**
**Masochism**
**Necrophilia**
**Orgasmic dysfunction**
**Paraphilias**
**Pedophilia**
**Performance anxiety**
**Premature ejaculation**
**Psychosexual dysfunctions**
**Sadism**
**Transsexualism**
**Transvestism**
**Vaginismus**
**Voyeurism**
**Zoophilia**

# CHAPTER 15

## The Personality Disorders: Ingrained Patterns of Behaving

- **Over a century ago Pinel observed patients who appeared sane, yet who were judged as mentally disturbed. Why are persons with a personality disorder considered disturbed?**
- **Do early signs of paranoia or withdrawal predict progress in paranoid schizophrenia?**
- **In what way might cases of battered wives be associated with the personality disorders?**
- **How can a person seem so cooperative and yet be so obstructionistic?**
- **Aren't all delinquents alike?**
- **Is it possible to predict personality characteristics as early as infancy?**
- **Is criminality inherited?**
- **Are psychopaths under the influence of abnormal brain waves?**
- **How do criminal justice and psychotherapy overlap, or do they?**

**TABLE 15–1**

**Personality Disorders**

| *Type* | *Major Characteristics* |
|---|---|
| Dependent personality | The need to rely on others and the inability to take personal responsibility for life activities. |
| Passive-aggressive personality | Difficulty in expressing hostility directly, with the anger therefore appearing through passive routes, such as being obstructive by inaction or acts of omission. |
| Narcissistic personality | Being self-centered to an exaggerated degree and expecting special attention. |
| Paranoid personality | The conviction that others are trying to take advantage, leading to distrust and hypersensitivity to other's motives. |
| Schizoid personality | Seclusiveness, intense reserve, and isolation from the social environment. |
| Hystrionic or hysterical personality | The tendency towards overdramatizing life, being emotionally excitable and overreactive. |
| Antisocial personality | Persistent violation of rules, which may or may not lead to harm to others. |

# Case History 15–1:
## A Dependent Personality

Laura K. is a battered wife. Her condition was discovered only because a nurse and social worker pursued the cause of her injuries until they obtained the full history. Laura has been in emergency treatment many times, always being careful to go to different facilities, but only with the tacit approval of her husband. Laura often has not remained hospitalized when she needed to, however, because of her fear that her husband will view it as an attempt to get back at him for beating her. Her prime fear is that he will use this as an excuse to leave her, ". . . and I need him so desperately, he is my whole life, I have no direction without him, no one to tell me what to do with my life."

On deeper investigation, Laura is dominated by her husband; he tells her what to wear in the morning, when to be at home for his arrival, what meals to prepare, whom to socialize with, how to do her hair and how often, and even when to write home. She views such autocratic control positively, however, failing to see why others would pity her. In her husband's presence she is passive where her own needs are concerned, acting only when told to. She has an obvious deep emotional admiration for him, viewing him as strong, directed, and caring. In contrast, she describes herself as helpless, inadequate, "a shell without Bill."

Friends and peers describe Laura as always in need of support and help somehow, whether it be help in remembering assignments, in deciding on what classes to take, or in what topic to write about in English. Her schoolwork was average, but most of her teachers dreaded her assignment to their class, since it meant an inordinate amount of extra time with her. Her marriage seemed a perfect match in one respect: Laura seemed to have found someone to guide her life patiently and even with enjoyment; and Bill had found a totally devoted and forgiving spouse who met his needs to rule his own private kingdom.

Over a century ago, Philippe Pinel reported on patients who showed no disturbance of their rational abilities, yet whose behaviors were as maladjusted as many mentally disturbed persons. Such persons are not psychotic, nor are their disorders truly neurotic or psychophysiologic. They had to be classified differently. This group of disorders is currently recognized as the personality disorders, listed in Table 15–1.

## THE PERSONALITY DISORDERS

The personality disorders involve a wide variety of characteristics, but they share certain features in common. People with these disorders find it difficult to maintain an adjustment to life when faced with even minor stresses. The reason is a flaw in their emotional growth and development, often a failure to acquire broader skills for dealing with themselves or their surroundings. This inability is exhibited by the use of persistent behavior patterns that were devised early in life as coping mechanisms, but which have become a way of life. The behaviors may be rigid or regressive in nature, and they seem to the observer to be ingrained (Frosch, 1983).

Unlike other people who attempt to match their responses to the differing circumstances they must face, persons with personality disorders seem to rely on unchanging patterns. Thus, no matter what the circumstances, the individual may *consistently* appear to be detached, passive, uninvolved, aggressive, or unable to enjoy life. These behavioral symptoms are not dramatic enough to draw attention in the ways that neurotic behaviors do; frequently, in fact, personality disorders remain undiagnosed until the person becomes involved in a problem which focuses attention on a long history of maladjustment. And in most cases, such individuals are unaware of having a problem, but consider their behaviors as entirely normal.

There are several personality disorders listed in DSM-III. These include:

- Dependent personality
- Passive-aggressive personality
- Narcissistic personality
- Paranoid personality
- Schizoid personality
- Histrionic or hysterical personality
- Antisocial personality

This chapter briefly describes each of the personality disorders listed in Table 15–1. With the exception of the antisocial personality, only a limited discussion of dynamics is provided in this chapter, since many of the symptoms and their dynamics overlap with disorders dealt with in other chapters. However, the antisocial personality is explored more extensively at the end of this chapter.

### Dependent Personality

The identifying feature of the dependent personality disorder is the heavy reliance on others. This takes many forms. The dependent person relies on others to accept responsibility for his or her life. This means that even major decisions are deferred to another person: What job should I apply for? Where should I pick to live? He's asking me to marry him, should I? This willingness to let someone else rule one's life may seem threatening to most people. For the dependent personality, however, it is essential and reassuring. Dependent persons tend to lack self-confidence, seeing themselves as helpless, inadequate, or dumb about such matters. As soon as they find a person who is willing to be supportive and engage in making such decisions, they will then subordinate themselves, fearing that the relationship (and the support it provides) would be jeopardized if they were to make even the slightest request. As with Laura in Case History 15–1, dependent persons will often tolerate being dominated, even mentally or physically abused, in order to retain a relationship. If the abusive spouse stalks out of the house after delivering a beating, the dependent person will experience fear—but it is fear of being left alone rather than a fear of future beatings.

More women than men display this disorder. Whether or not the dependency symptoms interfere with other behaviors depends on the availability of someone to supply the needed dependency gratification; also on environmental or situational requirements. Thus, a wife with a dominant and controlling spouse can function adequately on a job, provided the job does not require independence.

### Passive-aggressive Personality

The primary trait of the passive-aggressive personality is an underlying hostility, expressed through passive behaviors rather than overt, direct aggression. In relating to a dependent personality, we would tend to initially offer reassurance and help, because such a person seems so absolutely vulnerable and in need of strong guidance. In contrast, the passive-aggressive person is frustrating to interact with because this person is obstructionistic, stubborn, intentionally inefficient, and resistant. The element of contrariness is present, but as in the case of James in Case History 15–2, the passivity of its expression is most difficult to deal with. The negativism may be so hidden as to be recognizable only after several frustrating encounters. There is a picture of superficial cooperativeness on a task, yet the task is never completed, and others may even be prevented from contributing by reason of the passive-aggressive person's inaction. Often, the negativism is recognized only after several frustrating encounters. It is actually much easier to work through an angry interaction with someone who is openly and clearly hostile.

The passive-aggressive employee may vocally support a program of action, but continuously delay action as he or she insists on having every detail clarified or every contingency discussed. Or a child may be outwardly eager to work on an assignment, but carelessly forget to bring the materials needed. When oth-

## Case History 15–2:
### Passive-aggressive Personality

James B. teaches history in a private liberal arts college in the Midwest. He has attained tenure and is respected enough in his field to have been promoted to the rank of associate professor.

Other faculty members, however, avoid asking James to serve on committees or to help in decision making. When such encounters have taken place in the past, James has always seemed to be compliant and sincerely interested, but has prevented any progress from being made. He procrastinates, always needing more time to consider the ramifications of issues. He appears endlessly noncommittal on questions and directions, yet he manages to prevent others from taking over the decision-making process. He often forgets to read the details of proposed faculty resolutions, but he is unwilling to permit a vote, expressing concern whether action may be more dangerous in the long run than the status quo. On materials he has read, and in the face of popular support for such proposals, he asks for refined and extremely clear definitions of every phrase, until concepts are carried to a level of absurdity. Yet, James vocalizes a genuine concern and support for such actions and expresses amazement and hurt when accused of obstructionism.

Where others are able to fool anger appropriately, James seems to be always in control of his feelings, never shouts or shows irritability. When given a direct and unequivocal assignment, he never refuses. But his compliance seems half-hearted and incomplete, or he is slow in completing the assignment because he overcomplies with the minutest details, or he never finishes it at all because he misinterpreted the instructions and was awaiting further directions.

Those observers who are unaware of the history of such committee encounters sometimes have difficulty in understanding the feelings of frustration and anger expressed by the committee members toward James. Such observers often feel that other faculty have been overreacting, inasmuch as James seems sincere in his interest and some of his points appear well taken.

ers are more than ready to stop talking and planning and to begin acting, the passive-aggressive person manages to find some reason to hold back.

The passive-aggressive person seems in conflict between the need to be dependent and the fear of being dominated; thus, he or she compromises by being dependent through passivity and avoiding domination through resistance. Unfortunately, such a compromise is not conducive to achievement.

### Narcissistic Personality

Mythology tells of Narcissus, a handsome Greek youth who pined away for his own reflection. The personality disorder named after him is characterized by self-idealization and self-admiration. It is self-esteem carried to the extreme.

All of the exaggerated negative associations with the word *self* are present: self-centeredness, self-aggrandizement, self-indulgent, a sense of self-importance, self-absorption, self-gratification. Self-worth is misjudged to the degree that narcissistic persons invalidly overestimate their own value, accomplishments, skills, or achievements. They may develop fantasies around the themes of unlimited but deserved wealth, or power, or ultimate recognition of their brilliance. Attention from others, in fact, is viewed as a natural right, and narcissistic persons revel in admiration and bask in being on display.

There is a shallowness to any relationship, however, inasmuch as the relating seems one way. Narcissistic persons feel entitled to special attention, favors, or getting what they want, but they lack the ability to empathize or be concerned about the needs of others. Thus, they may be annoyed that a suddenly hospitalized friend failed to remember to make theatre reservations, or enraged that others would imply even the slightest criticism—as in the stereotype of the second-rate performer who eagerly scans the theatrical reviews, then rages at the incompetence of the critics. Narcissistic persons tend to be so self-centered that they are quick to blame everyone else for their own failures. Where this defense fails, the reaction may be a temporary sense of shame, humiliation, or feeling of unworthiness—followed by a reinstatement of cool indifference and new fantasies about success.

### Paranoid Personality

A fourth personality disorder is the paranoid personality. Paranoid personalities believe others to be hostile towards them and want to take advantage of them. This disorder is a minor variation of the more severe disturbances known as the paranoid psychotic states, discussed in Chapter 17.

Paranoid personalities display traits consistent with their assumptions; they are wary, suspicious, hypersensitive, and distrustful, and they tend to ascribe evil motives to others. They may be convinced that prices are exorbitantly raised to take advantage of them; that attempts are being made to shortchange them, or that they are being given an overload of work while others are loafing. Such persons are envious and jealous of the better treatment they believe others to be receiving. At the same time, they secretly believe in their own importance: they are being short-shrifted, while others, of lesser value, are receiving better treatment.

Given these attitudes, persons with paranoid personalities are unable to maintain satisfactory relationships, but project the blame for their failures onto others. They may protect themselves from accusations by developing the skills of the quick retort or the sarcastic invective or by becoming increasingly isolated and closed to others. As such isolation increases, however, they have even less opportunity to share and test their beliefs against reality. Consequently, suspicions and misperceptions about others are left to simmer, and they brew even more false beliefs.

This downward spiral sets the paranoid personalities apart from the disorders just discussed. Whereas passive-aggressive personalities still seem interested in retaining contact with others, paranoid personalities may eventually find all encounters unsatisfying. And whereas passive-aggressive personalities create more discomfort in others, paranoid personalities appear to suffer more in their encounters with others.

### Schizoid Personality

Like the paranoid personalities, schizoid personalities alienate themselves from other people. Unlike paranoid individuals, however, schizoid behaviors are

*The* ***schizoid personality*** *finds little need for other people. Early signs may include shyness, avoidance of companions, aloofness, and emotional detachment.*

based not on active wariness but on a shy seclusiveness. Individuals with this personality disorder tend to be introverted, seclusive, and reserved. Instead of seeking out companionship, they find little need for other people and are emotionally independent. This independence is viewed as aloofness, distance, and a lack of warmth by others who attempt to relate to such persons. Schizoid persons tend to avoid both competitive and cooperative ventures and are very difficult to engage in any personal interactions.

It seems particularly difficult for schizoid persons to express normal aggressive feelings. They display few overt emotional reactions at all, in fact, responding to disturbing situations and conflicts with apparent detachment. It is likely that this mask of indifference actually covers a heightened sensitivity rather than total deficiency in feelings. The daydreams and fantasies of schizoid persons may be intense and emotional, and they are probably oversensitive to others' attitudes and actions—especially implied or overt censure. Thus, the lack of emotional reactions is actually a defense against pains of rejection, depreciation, or punishment.

Some schizoid personalities are able to make substantial contributions and are highly productive in occupations that permit isolation. Others prefer the life of the recluse or the isolated eccentric. The schizoid personality may evolve into the more serious psychotic condition known as schizophrenia (Spitzer et al., 1979). However, there is not a necessary evolution.

### Histrionic or Hysterical Personality

The histrionic or hysterical personality disorder is characterized by emotional excitability, overreactivity, and self-dramatization. This personality is seen more in women than in men. The hysterical person seems to make a theatrical performance—and a bad one—out of every situation. Emotions are stretched further than appropriate, comments are given special emphasis, and movements are provided with added sweep.

As is illustrated by Christine in Case History 15–3, the hysterical person is likely to be self-centered, often vain—an attention-seeker who is dependent on others. When frustrated, the individual may show an immaturity and react in a childish manner. The hysterical woman or man may display coy, overaffective, flamboyant mannerisms. Frequently, the hysterical person is seductive and provocative, but appears genuinely unaware of the sexual messages being conveyed and will react with surprise and fright if the signal provokes a response. The seductiveness seems more a part of the general pattern of attention seeking than of sexual interest. In fact, many believe that the underlying pattern is emotional shallowness.

Hysterical persons seem to be seeking approval through their attention-seeking or seductive behaviors. It is as if an insatiable childlike need exists to be noticed and loved—an immature need that has not developed into an ability for equal sharing or true adult warmth and affection. In fact, their love is a request to be loved as a child, not as a woman or man (Marmour, 1954).

This disorder presents an interesting comparison to the passive-aggressive personality. As in the disorder we discussed earlier, there is a powerful element of control over others. Whereas the passive-aggressive person achieves control by a passive resistant roletaking, the hysterical person seeks to maintain control by an active center-of-the-stage role. The passive-aggressive person seems to be concerned about losing control over decisions and actions and expresses an underlying hostility; the histrionic personality is afraid of losing the attentiveness of others, expressing an under-

## Case History 15–3:
### Hysterical Personality

Christine F. is a willowy, attractive woman married to a law student. She seems particularly fond of openly prompting displays of affection from her husband, coyly asking, for example, "Tell me and the world and these people just how much you need me," then after a suitable response, "Oh! Don't you all just love his romanticism?" Somehow Marlin, her husband, is able to respond to Christine's needs and is quick to give her the attention she wants. Marlin's own life is interesting and stimulating, yet Christine tends to orient all conversations around herself.

Christine thoroughly enjoys social functions and dresses handsomely. Other women see her as a flirt and coquette, finding her boring and too self-centered. In fact, both men and women who know her reflect on the onesidedness of interpersonal interactions. "No matter what we start off talking about, or whom we are listening to, when Christine arrives she somehow always manages to center the conversation on herself. . . ."

Christine seems to have several traits which are associated with attention-seeking. She dominates conversations, liberally using the pronoun *I*. Her voice emphasis is often superficially exaggerated, unfailingly startling others into attention: "What a *marvelous* experience I had!" (she saw a movie); "Oh, you can't *believe* how sad I felt!" (she was five minutes late to a dental appointment). Another characteristic of Christine seems to be a basic insensitivity to others. This shows up in her having several times insulted her hosts by loudly criticizing their close friends, by pouting when she has not obtained her way, or by looking bored when the conversation shifted to other people.

As a child, Christine was a "cute" youngster, always good for a performance in front of adults. She had an engaging manner and an endearing disposition, although she sometimes seemed too demanding and undisciplined. As she grew older, she experienced a difficult adolescence. She went through a number of relationships with various boys, and later with various men, but all were characterized as "stormy." She seemed as quick to fall in love as she was to reject the very same lover as mean, uncaring, and insensitive. For a time she was interested in psychotherapy, but as with her boyfriends, she shifted quickly from therapist to therapist. Since adolescence, her moodiness had taken the form of periods of mild depression or general body aches. However, since she met and married Marlin, she has been relatively happy and symptom free. Although she refuses to talk about him (preferring to talk about herself), on rare occasions she has enthused about how much his companionship and attention has meant.

lying need for approval. Finally, passive-aggressive persons seem to deny their own dependency, while hysterical persons seem to be seeking gratification for their dependency.

### Dynamics of Personality Disorders

The personality disorders are considered to be long-established patterns of behaviors, exhibited as early as childhood or adolescence. The psychological dynamics of some have been alluded to in the descriptions of the disorders; further elaborations for some disorders are discussed along with similar neurotic or psychotic conditions in other chapters. In this section, we'll look quickly at the broad developmental, cultural, and hereditary factors that may be associated with some personality disorders.

***Developmental Factors.*** One possible explanation for personality disorders is that they are simply prolonged symptoms from childhood behaviors. Some of the personality traits—such as the dependency behaviors and the attention-seeking actions—are, in fact, often characteristic of children. The ineptness of the dependent personality reminds one of the sincerity but inadequacy of the child who is not big enough or skilled enough to manage successfully.

Many of the apparent underlying conflicts associated with the personality disorders reflect conflicts children experience during development and socialization: for example, the conflicts over dependency, self-control, and aggression (Brim & Kagan, 1980). Additionally, some of the symptoms of personality disorders may relate to the lack of development of adult skills. The histrionic personality's inability to share the attention of others, the schizoid's poor ability to relate socially, or the dependent person's lack of any adequate coping skills all illustrate such immature or incomplete development. The psychoanalytic viewpoint would stress the importance of severe unresolved conflicts which prevent the psychological development of the person suffering from personality disorders. The nature of the disorder would be related to the period during which the conflict first occurred. Thus, there is some evidence that frustration during the oral phase of weaning may precipitate dependency strivings (Bacon, 1981).

Whether the effects of parental training are significant because of reasons claimed by psychoanalytic theorists or not, there does seem to be further evidence that early child-rearing attitudes and practices affect personality development. Kagan and Moss (1962) discovered that adult passivity (measured as emotional dependence, conformity, and passive response to frustration) was correlated with maternal protectiveness toward the child up to age three. Cameron (1963) offers the belief that sadistic treatment in infancy leads to a lack of basic trust in the individual, forming the foundation for the paranoid-type suspiciousness. It is also possible that many personality traits of long standing have been acquired and maintained because of the reward value of using such behaviors. Consistent reward of dependency by mothers was found associated with a high level of dependency behaviors in their children (Sears et al., 1957).

***Cultural Factors.*** Another explanation for personality disorders that cannot be ignored is the role of sociocultural factors. Such influences may be direct or indirect.

Direct influences on behaviors can best be seen in sociocultural determinants of sex role differences. Observing that boys are more aggressive than girls by age three, Ember (1981) suggests that this tendency is shaped by three factors: the father's modeling, the mother's permissiveness, and peer initiation. Fathers are likely to model aggression, since they have been found more likely to use physical punishment on their sons. However, since children spend more time during the day with their mothers, the father's punishment serves more as a model than a deterrent. When the sons imitate this aggressiveness, the mother's permissiveness encourages the behavior. Also, boys seem to spend more time out of the home interacting with peers, with such interactions likely to prompt conflict and aggressive behavior.

Ember sees this pattern in the reverse for girls. Fathers are more tolerant of aggression from their daughters, but typically, they are not home enough for their permissiveness to have much effect. Mothers, who may tolerate aggression in their sons, do not accept such behavior from their daughters. Hence, aggression is suppressed at home. And unlike boys, girls are likely to be kept in the household, exposed to interactions with younger siblings rather than with neighbor peers. Such interactions have been found to prompt nurturance rather than aggressive conflict.

In a review of longitudinal studies of personality from infancy to adulthood, Moss and Susman (1980) support Ember's view about sociocultural influences on sex roles, finding it to apply not only to aggression but also to passivity and dependency. What this suggests is that family and peer influence early in life could well set the stage for personality characteristics that are maintained into adulthood. Possibly behaviors such as seen in the passive-aggressive personality or the dependent personality are distorted results of such early influences.

As we mentioned earlier in Chapter 5, sociocultural factors may also have indirect influences on behavior through socialization. In addition, socioeconomic class differences may reflect differences in the type of socialization practiced. Middle-class parents, for instance, tend to rely on love-oriented disciplinary steps, such as the threat of withdrawal of affection, the use of disapproval, and the reliance on shame—and evidence suggests that this results in children developing more guilt, greater dependency, and greater conformity (Burton & Reis, 1981). On the other hand, lower-class parents tend to use punishment more and are more restrictive, with the result being greater evidence of aggressiveness in children.

***Genetic Factors.*** A third possible influence in personality disorders is genetics (Cattell, 1982; Stone, 1980). It is possible that the long-standing behaviors noted in these disorders are a function of inherited temperaments. The New York Longitudinal Study (Thomas & Chess, 1977) followed the development of more than 100 children from birth over a period of a decade, in one of the most extensive studies of temperament through childhood. The researchers discovered clear-cut differences among these children as early as infancy. Temperamental differences were observed in mood, level of activity or passivity, adaptability to minor stresses, intensity of reaction, and other similar traits. Most interesting was the finding that the group of infants who were observed early in life to be "difficult infants" turned out to comprise most of the children considered to need psychiatric help later in life. In support, Moss and Susman (1980) found study after study which pointed to the relative stability of various personality characteristics, even though changes do occur because of cultural role definitions. As an example, they refer to findings that passivity in boys persisted into adulthood, but took forms that are more socially acceptable: for instance, with passive-dependency changing to noncompetitiveness.

The study of twins is another approach to determining if genetics contributes to personality characteristics. In one study of 850 twins, the researchers concluded that personality appeared to be highly correlated among twins, with the correlation being higher for identical and lower for fraternal twins (Loehlin & Nichols, 1976). As we saw earlier in Chapter 4, identical twins share the exact same chromosomes while fraternal twins show different chromosomes; hence, if heredity influences personality, we could anticipate that the identical twins would show higher correlations. The researchers also discovered important correlations on personality test scores between identical twins on characteristics such as dominance, sociability, self-control, and socialization (see Table 15–2). We can readily see the relevance of dominance as it might relate to dependency, sociability to schizoid withdrawal, and self-control and socialization to antisocial behaviors in the various personality disorders. The similarities among twins show not only in general personality style but also in some twins' specific sharing of mannerisms, for instance, one pair of twins was said to have the "same wild look" when tense, with finger-biting and darting eyes, and another pair both rubbed their noses and rocked when tired (Farber, 1981, p. 227).

**TABLE 15–2**

**Correlations Between Twin-pairs on Different Personality Dimensions**

| | *Identical twins* | *Fraternal twins* |
|---|---|---|
| Overall personality inventory scores | .50* | .28 |
| Specific personality scores: | | |
| Dominance | .58 | .14 |
| Sociability | .60 | .40 |
| Self-control | .55 | .16 |
| Socialization | .46 | .17 |

* High correlations mean that the twins showed high similarity to one another in test scores.
SOURCE: From *Heredity, Environment, and Personality* by J. Loehlin and R. Nichols, 1976, Austin: University of Texas Press. © 1976 University of Texas Press.

Since twins raised in the same home could have similar characteristics because of a common upbringing, research on twins reared apart offers more valid information on the inheritance of personality. James Shields (1962) broadcast his interest via English television and obtained the cooperation of 44 pairs of identical twins reared apart and a similar number who had been reared together. He also studied 32 fraternal twins to complete his research. His findings showed that measures of extroversion or introversion were more similar between identical twins, even those reared apart, than between fraternal twins (see Table 15–3).

In another study, the tendency to blame others was also found to be correlated among identical twins but not among fraternal twins (Claridge et al., 1973). Both studies therefore support the premise that some personality characteristics, such as introversion and blaming, might be inherited. If we remember our previous discussion of how introversion characterizes the

**TABLE 15–3**

**Correlations Between Twin-pairs on Different Personality Dimensions for Twins Reared Apart or Together**

| | *Identical twins* | | |
|---|---|---|---|
| | *Reared apart* | *Reared together* | *Fraternal twins* |
| Extroversion-introversion (Shields) | .61* | .42 | .17 |
| Neuroticism (Shields) | .53 | .38 | .11 |
| Blaming others (Claridge et al.) | .31 | .41 | .19 |

* High correlations mean that the twins showed high similarity.

SOURCES: From *Monozygotic Twins Brought up Apart and Brought up Together* by J. Shields, 1962, London: Oxford University Press; and *Personality Differences and Biological Variations: A Study of Twins* by G. Claridge, S. Canter, & W. Hume, 1973, New York: Pergamon.

schizoid personality and the tendency to blame others characterizes the paranoid personality, then such findings offer some light on the possible background for such disorders.

### Treatment of Personality Disorders

The personality disorders are theoretically considered difficult to treat because of the belief that the symptoms reflect an ingrained lifestyle. Thus, therapists who deal with these disorders often feel pessimistic about the outcomes.

Goals for therapy vary considerably, depending on the primary symptoms of the disorder. The dependent personality for instance must achieve the level of confidence, the desire, and the skills needed to react more effectively to surroundings. In this case, the objectives of therapy may be to perceive and achieve greater rewards from action than from inaction. Passive-aggressive persons, in contrast, must come to grips with their hostility and be prevented from continuing their ambivalence. Paranoid persons need to be able to gradually build a basic trust in people and must be more willing to test out their conceptions about others. The schizoid personality may require the encouragement to deal more actively with interpersonal fears. And the hysterical personality needs to progress toward a more mature level of adjustment, through a lessening of the anxieties and demands associated with dependency.

***Resistance to Therapy.*** Most of the characteristics of these disorders are not severe enough to cause continuous suffering or life impairments. Hence, the person with a personality disorder does not feel a need for therapy.

If friends or family attempt to convince the person to seek psychotherapy, the person is likely to resist in characteristic ways. The passive-aggressive person will not directly confront the friend to find out just why he or she feels that therapy would be useful; instead, there will be another lengthy display of the very passively hostile actions that originally concerned the friend. In trying to persuade a person with a paranoid personality disorder to seek help, the likely response will be an increased wariness and withdrawal of contact by this person. For the histrionic personality, the very idea that something is wrong will trigger a dramatic denial, perhaps a light laughing-off of the very impudence of the suggestion, and a shift to other topics. For this reason, entry into psychotherapy is typically through enforced referral rather than a voluntary action.

Occasionally, however, a person with a personality disorder will be more willing to try group therapy, such as marital or couples groups. This setting tends to be perceived as less threatening: there are more people to share the spotlight, and each person has more time to adjust to sharing problems. Also, the feedback provided by peers in the group is frequently more acceptable than similar interpretations by a therapist (Gurman & Kniskern, 1978).

Of interest is the approach developed by Leeman and Mulvey (1973). In a direct way, individuals are led to understand that the treatment will be brief, that the client is to be responsible for learning more satisfying ways of managing life, that the therapist will not take on the responsibility for governing or guiding the client's daily living, and that there is an expectation that the client will show personal strengths during the course of treatment. A major goal is always how to really change and adopt new behaviors—not simply to sit and talk about what should or could be changed. This

# FOCUS 15–1:

## The Personality Disorders: Can They Be Too Obvious to Treat?

A major problem in treating the personality disorders is that people who have them rarely *think* they need treatment—and because they can function from day to day, others may not recognize the disorder.

A dramatic example of this problem is provided by Nazi Germany. A psychological analysis of the 21 top war criminals tried at Nuremberg in 1945–46—an important part of Nazi Germany's leadership—provides the following diagnoses:

| | |
|---|---|
| • *paranoid personality* | Hitler<br>Hess |
| • *schizoid personality* | Himmler<br>Kaltenbrunner |
| • *inadequate personality** | Hess<br>Rosenberg |
| • *passive-dependent personality* | von Ribbentrop<br>Frank |
| • *hypomanic personality*** | Frank |
| • *narcissistic personality* | Goering |

No evidence of gross pathology was found in 10 of these top war criminals—about half of the group. These diagnoses of the leadership of wartime Germany strongly suggest that many individuals with personality disorders may not only elude treatment, they may also inspire a following of people who believe in them.

*A number of Nazi wartime leaders have been diagnosed as suffering from personality disorders.* ***Hitler*** *may have been a paranoid personality.*

---

* A former classification referring to persons whose inadequacy is habitually impaired.

** A former classification referring to a pattern of high activity and euphoria, in a nonpsychotic person.

SOURCE: Based on *Personality Dynamics: A Biosocial Approach* by G. Gilbert, 1970, New York: Harper.

approach has seemed especially useful for working with dependent persons.

***Temperament and Therapy.*** The findings of Thomas and Chess (1977), as discussed earlier, indicated that certain temperamental traits that showed up very early in young children were associated with some personality disorders. These findings have led these researchers to suggest another approach: recommendations for preventing disorders in the first place.

As will be recalled, children identified as *difficult* even in the first few months of life were found to later comprise a large proportion of behavioral problems. These children showed early traits such as intense reactions; withdrawing in the face of new stimuli; being negative; reacting violently to frustrations; and adapting slowly to changes in the environment. Another group, seen as *slow to warm up,* were characterized by low activity levels, a tendency to withdraw from new stimuli, slowness to adapt, and low intensity of reaction.

While Thomas and Chess agree that such temperaments are likely to be stable, they also suggest that they can be modified. When parents are aware of such temperamental differences, they can help their children to adapt. With difficult children, parents must cope with the irregularity and slowness with which the children adapt to family rules. Given the negative mood and quick tantrums, impatient or punitive or inconsistent treatment by the parents will only precipitate problems. Thus, they recommend consistent treatment, painstaking handling, objective working with the children, that takes full account of the children's temperaments. For the slow-to-warm-up children, the researchers recommend that the parents permit the children to meet life at their own pace, with gentle encouragement to try new experiences.

In the school setting, similar preventative attitudes may be undertaken to avoid conflict. Children with high-activity temperaments, for instance, might be mistakenly viewed as disinterested in learning or unlikable because of their continual squirming and movement. However, the researchers caution that a more beneficial approach would be to provide a means for such children to channel their energy—rather than punishing them for a temperamental makeup they can't control. For the slow-to-warm-up pupil, they recommend repeated exposures to a learning task until the child is familiarized enough to deal with it. A firm, patient, non-laissez faire approach is seen as suitable for the difficult child who needs such an atmosphere to learn to adapt.

## ANTISOCIAL PERSONALITY

In addition to the several personality disorders just discussed, another personality disorder deserves special attention. The antisocial personality has been the focus of more research than the other disorders, in good part because it is less likely to go unnoticed. Because we have more information about the antisocial personality, we will look more closely at this disorder in the remaining pages of this chapter.

The antisocial personality involves a wide variety of characteristics, but one trait in particular is consistent: a disorder in behavior that reflects a violation of society's codes of conduct. Under the DSM-III classification system, the term *antisocial personality* is used when describing an adult, but the category called *conduct disorders* is used to describe persons under age 18 (Gelfand et al., 1982).

### Symptoms and Diagnosis

There are four different subgroups of conduct or antisocial personality disorders. As Figure 15–1 indicates, these categories vary according to two dimensions: aggressive versus unaggressive and socialized versus undersocialized. The aggressive conduct disorders involve a pattern of rule violation that is victim directed, such as violence against others, rape, vandalism, and most forms of theft, mugging, and assault. The unaggressive disorders do not tend to be directed against others and include truancy, running away from home, theft not involving confronting a victim, persistent lying, drunkenness or drug abuse. The undersocialized differ from the socialized disorders in the absence of a normal degree of attachment, affection, empathy or loyalty to others (Achenbach, 1982).

Within these four subgroups are quite distinct types of personalities. The *undersocialized aggressive* person is the callous, lone-wolf defiant assaulter; Joel in Case History 15–4 is a good example. The *socialized aggressive* person, in contrast, feels stronger ties to other people. An example might be the street fighter loyal to his "own kind" who is violent because of gang influences on his beliefs and actions. The *undersocialized unaggressive* person is the sly manipulator who is ingratiating and exploitative of others, without remorse. Finally, the *socialized unaggressive* individual is the victim of peer influence, being caught for truancy because friends talked him or her into skipping classes, participating in drug abuse because it is the "in" thing, or stealing in order to be accepted by the gang.

Perhaps the most striking of these four antisocial personalities is the undersocialized unaggressive type. In earlier classifications, this conduct disorder has gone under several names: *character disorder, psychopathic personality, constitutional psychopathic inferiority,* or *sociopath.* Many modern studies have preferred the term *sociopath.*

As an adult, this person superficially excels in social relations, is a superb mixer and the life of the party, and is charming, facile, and engaging. At the same time, however, he or she is immature, lacking loyalty, remorse, and sincerity. The con artist of fact and fiction is prototypical. Who else could convince persons to withdraw their life savings and hand it over to a complete stranger?

One example from the author's experience is John, a bright young man who might have been a successful economist. He enjoyed the respectability over short periods as a part-time lecturer at a community college and as a research economist in city planning; he also held several other jobs, including working as a seaman on a ship to the Philippines and a worker on a road gang in Alaska. Whatever he did, his goal was to do it with as little effort as possible. He freely admitted

## Case History 15–4:
### Antisocial Personality - Undersocialized Aggressive Type

Joel R. is a rapist. He is 22 years old, single, and is employed evenings as a janitor in a shopping center. In regard to his young age, his low income level, and his marital status, he is characteristic of a majority of rapists. He has been suspected of rape before but never convicted.

On this occasion, he was arrested by the sheriff based on the description of his car given by the rape victim minutes after Joel had released her in what he thought was an abandoned warehouse lot. On being confronted, Joel admitted to cruising the streets that night, offering the woman a ride, then being turned on by her perfume and impulsively taking her to the darkened lot and having intercourse with her, but with her consent, he claims.

Joel views himself as outside the law, which he believes exists to protect others and which is unfair to him. He maintains that he would not have "been attracted" to the woman had she not worn the provocative perfume or been so willing to accept a ride. His life history is full of reports of vandalism, truancy, after-school fights, poor academic performance, quarrels with authority. Although gangs did exist in his school, Joel was never interested, offering the opinion that "Gangs are for sissies who can't take care of themselves; I don't trust them and they don't trust me; I'm for me, number one, and they know that." The rape victim decided that she did not want to press charges that could mean more unwanted attention, and so Joel was released from custody. In private, and away from the police station, Joel is willing to talk about his sexual encounters. His disclosures, however, do not emphasize incidents of rape as being dominant parts of his life but seemingly occasional affairs. What seems more impressive is his pervasive alienation from social rules or custom, his almost smug flouting of the law, his concern only for his own pleasure, and his lack of anxiety or guilt about what he clearly knows to be criminal and harmful actions.

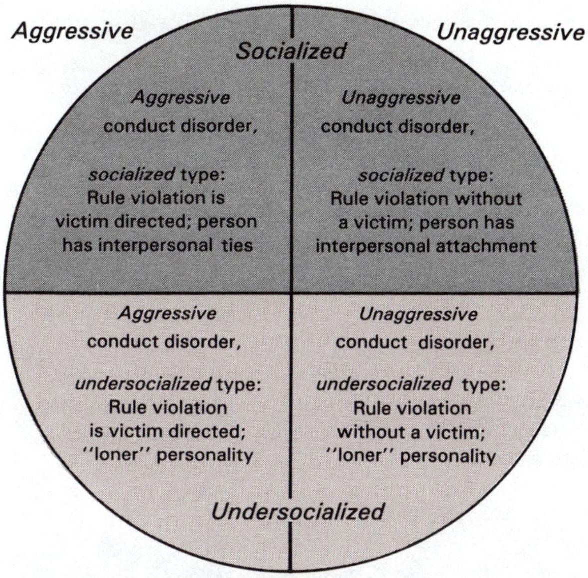


**FIGURE 15-1** The four types of antisocial personality.

that his years at college were to prove that he could "pull the wool over the instructors' eyes" and still graduate.

Besides his lack of effort, another notable trait was John's dishonesty. He was expelled from one institution for forging the dean's name on a check; and in college, most of his schoolwork was done by girl friends. He cashed many checks on nonexistent accounts. He managed to stay away from prison, however, mainly through his ability to charm his victims, who invariably felt they might be able to reform him.

John is a relatively unusual case of a sociopathic personality, inasmuch as he found it desirable to complete college and obtain a master's degree. Nevertheless, his story illustrates a pattern of unreformability that has fascinated many researchers (Cline, 1980). What factors are associated with the development of antisocial personalities? As with the other personality disorders, this disorder has been difficult to research because of the fact that persons with the disorder are often not recognized as having a mental disorder. Thus, it is difficult to obtain a research sample. One novel approach to finding several subjects with personality disorders was successful, however, as is described in Focus 15–2.

### Dynamics of the Antisocial Personality

The antisocial personality has never been fully understood or explained. A number of theories have been proposed over the years, including genetics, psychoanalytic explanations, theories based on descriptions of early risk factors, and physiological explanations.

***Genetic Theories.*** Earlier theories have suggested that an inborn defect was the cause, hence the term *constitutional inferiority.* This traced to the belief offered by Lombroso (1911) in the early part of the 20th century that there were persons who were born criminals. Such criminals were atavistic throwbacks to caveman ancestors, incapable of moral judgment or civilized self-restraint. Lombroso also held that criminal types could be recognized by their outward physical features, such as a slanting forehead, eyebrows that meet, and receding jaw (this belief was consistent with other similar theories at the time, such as phrenology, as we saw in Chapter 2) (Hartl et al., 1982).

In a more sophisticated way, the theory sometimes still finds supporters who point out the evidence of criminality in the parents of persons classed as antisocial personalities. However, we realize that such information is insufficient proof of a genetic influence. In fact, one longitudinal study of children who grew up to be antisocial showed at least some who had normal, conforming parents—a fact that had little influence on their delinquent behaviors (Robins, 1978). Similarly, in a review of available research, Cline (1980) discovered a number of examples where originally delinquent adolescents became law abiding as adults despite an early history of many offenses and arrests. If some persons are born criminal, then we would expect them to remain criminal rather than change. Even twin studies have failed to offer support for a genetic hypothesis. Farber (1981) reviewed research on twins reared apart for signs of concordance in antisocial behaviors and concluded that there is no evidence. Thus, we can generally rule out the idea that antisocial behaviors are inherited.[1]

1 The exception is the controversial link between XYY chromosone aberrations and criminality (see Chapter 4).

## FOCUS 15–2:

### Solving a Research Problem: Advertising for Antisocial Subjects

Antisocial behaviors involve manipulation of others, impulsiveness, low socialization, and poor internalization of rules. As with the other personality disorders, persons with antisocial personalities are difficult to isolate for treatment or study (unless criminal charges are brought against them) because they don't feel they need attention or help.

One psychologist used an interesting approach that worked. Widom (1977) advertised to attract research subjects. She placed ads in newspapers, not exactly calling for sociopaths, but describing the traits. Her ads ran: "Are you adventurous? Psychologist studying adventurous carefree people who've led exciting impulsive lives. If you're the kind of person who'd do almost anything for a dare . . . [*write*]"; and "Wanted charming, aggressive, carefree people who are impulsively irresponsible but are good at handling people and at looking after number one."

Except for a call or two inquiring about whether she was looking for "hookers," the ads were successful in producing volunteers for psychological testing.

*Two forms of* ***antisocial personality*** *are the aggressive socialized, such as Charles Manson, and the unaggressive socialized, such as urban gang members.*

***Psychoanalytic Theories.*** Psychoanalytic interpretations of antisocial behavior stress predictably different origins than the genetic theories. Instead, they focus on a lack of concern with ethical and moral codes, poor impulse control, and a lack of commitment to people.

According to the psychoanalytic hypothesis, the antisocial personality derives from a fixation at an early developmental stage, due to frustration and parental rejection. The fixation is characterized by the pleasure principle—the search for immediate gratification with neither concern for consequences nor the capacity for postponement. A superego could have later served as an intrinsic guide to conduct, but it never developed. In addition, the person is unable to form the meaningful relationship with parents that normally serves as a model for later relationships with people. This early lack of strong parental relations also leads to later anxiety over authority relations, which become modified into rejection of authority and perhaps even active rebellion.

There has been some support for the analytic interpretations. Examining the background of delinquents in a work called *Children Who Hate,* Redl and Wineman (1957) found the adult-child relationship to be severely damaged. Broken homes, a rapidly shifting galaxy of neglectful, cruel, and sometimes brutal parents formed a common theme in the histories of these youngsters. "Once the children were with us (in the treatment center), the parents seemed to lose interest in them almost entirely" (p. 566).

Another study showed similar findings. Robins (1978) discovered that children who became antisocial as adults tended to have had parents who were themselves antisocial, alcohol abusers, or hysterical. However, she concluded that parental actions were not of themselves the origins of antisocial behaviors, but part of a cluster of contributing factors. Similarly, others have found parents to have themselves shown antisocial behaviors, thereby modeling such actions for their children to later adopt (Lewis et al., 1983; Pfeffer et al., 1983).

***Early Risk Factors and Antisocial Personality.*** The study by Robins that we just cited has provided revealing information about early characteristics of antisocial persons. Her research actually consists of extensive longitudinal studies involving 500 white and 500 black children. The research started with these groups as children, then followed them through their 30s and 40s. Those who were diagnosed as antisocial persons as adults were the basic group whose childhood records were then reexamined. By going back into the early history of these persons, it was hoped that early conditions associated with later antisocial behaviors could be identified.

A most important finding was the fact that the antisocial diagnosis could have been made in early to middle childhood, by around age eight and often as soon as the child entered school. Most common early characteristics that seemed to predict later antisocial activities were truancy, stealing, running away from home, and sexual activity (for girls). This trend held for many, but not all, persons; for example, 59 percent of male delinquents were still law-violators after age 30, but 41 percent had become law-abiders.

Robins' data and that of others (Cline, 1980) suggest that a variety of conditions in childhood may be associated with antisocial behaviors, including maturational delay, family characteristics, and social class. Regarding maturational delay, some findings suggest that antisocial persons were physically underdeveloped when young. Family characteristics have also been noticed, such as family instability, or the presence of passive or neglectful parents. Finally, lower social class appears to be common, as evidenced by low-income housing and frequent unemployment of parents.

***Physiological Explanations.*** In addition to the genetic psychoanalytic and early risk information, a variety of theories link physiological factors to the antisocial personality. Some of these theories focus on possible brain wave abnormalities; others look at the antisocial person's autonomic response to arousal and stress.

*Brain Wave Abnormalities.* Some research has found abnormal EEG patterns in antisocial personalities, leading theorists to suggest brain abnormalities as a possible cause (Gorenstein, 1982; Harper et al., 1972). One study found EEG abnormalities in 70 percent of antisocial persons studied (Monroe & Mickle, 1967). However, these findings were no higher than for other psychiatric groups who were not considered antisocial, so the evidence is far from decisive. Perhaps the best conclusion is that abnormal EEG patterns may exist in a subset of antisocial persons, but is not a major explanation for antisocial behaviors in general.

*Low Arousal and Sensation-seeking.* Another interesting theory suggests that antisocial persons possess a lowered overall physiological arousal level. If such a deficit exists, then perhaps they feel a need to seek external stimulation through rule-breaking activities which provide for thrills to make up for this lack (Eysenck, 1970). This theory has found some support in certain test scores. For instance, antisocial persons scored higher on measures of thrill-seeking (seeking speed and danger), experience-seeking (thrills from unconventional behavior), and susceptibility to boredom than most people (Zuckerman, 1983).

*High Arousal and Self-protection.* Just the opposite theory has also been proposed, suggesting that antisocial persons are automatically more responsive, if stress responses are examined (Schacter & Latanne, 1964). The belief is that antisocial persons may be born with a highly sensitive emotional-autonomic responsivity, which they are forced to learn to deal with. They learn to adapt by becoming skilled in ignoring emotional states, so that they eventually are unable to respond to events with fear or anxiety. Inasmuch as much of socialization relies on fear of being caught and punished, the antisocial person fails to respond to societal laws.

Hare (1978) has reviewed several research studies and concluded that there is some support for this theory. He observes that antisocial persons have a pattern of a high heart rate but a low palmar sweating and interprets this to mean that such persons are adept at inhibiting the emotion of fear before it becomes too pervasive. Thus, the heart rate increases showed that arousal was occurring, but the failure of the palms to respond by sweating was seen as an index of inhibition. He concludes that the antisocial person differs from others in that "situations that have great emotional impact for most people may be of relatively little consequence to psychopathic ones" (p. 137).

It is not a simple task to organize these two disparate ideas about arousal. A sensible explanation focuses on the issue of the selection of persons to be studied. It is hard to know if those who have been studied all come from the same type of personality disorder. Even though many of the studies have examined psychopaths or sociopaths, these studies tended to use a diagnostic system prior to the more detailed breakdowns of DSM-III. Hence, it is possible that low arousal or high arousal (or family conflicts or maturational deficits or cultural influences) may account for antisocial behaviors for some types of antisocial personality disorders (such as the undersocialized nonaggressive) but not for others (such as the undersocialized aggressive).

### Treatment of the Antisocial Personality

Antisocial persons have been perceived as untreatable for so long that very little research has been devoted to their treatment. The problem is aggravated by the fact that while the symptoms are not severe in the sense of being psychotic, they are certainly not minor in nature. Such persons give the impression of being basically normal people who simply refuse responsibility and who will not learn to be different—and so they tend to be put in jail for their misdeeds. Five approaches to treatment have met with varying success: they are traditional psychotherapy, milieu therapy, behavior therapy, social-cognitive problem-solving, and family therapy.

***Psychotherapy.*** The one goal often established in treating the antisocial person is the development of a positive interpersonal relationship between therapist and client. Although this is a common goal in most psychotherapeutic settings, it is especially relevant since the antisocial individual seems to lack a basic concern for people. If a consistent, interested, accepting atmosphere can be established, the client may begin interacting on a more trusting basis (Lion, 1974).

One major task is enabling the individual to experience emotions that possibly already exist, but are not recognized or labeled correctly. Using a more active therapy style, the therapist always uses the therapy interaction as a model of life, making sure to deal with any attempts at manipulation (Pasternack, 1974). In an understanding and consistent fashion, the client is exposed to clear and firm standards of behavior. What is learned is that positive effects and interpersonal satisfactions can result if previous ways of acting are changed. The advantages of delayed gratification are experienced, as are those of cooperation with others.

***Milieu Therapy.*** A second form of therapy that has had some success is the milieu or therapeutic community approach (McCord, 1982). The Henderson Hospital community in Britain provides a good example. Patients are required to be deeply involved in all aspects, as in the therapeutic communities for drug users described in Chapter 13. Group meetings are used to arrive at democratic decisions about treatment and also about the general running of the hospital. Patients are carefully screened before admission, for evidence of potential success in school, occupation, or social areas. Therapy is generally permissive, although patients must face the implications and consequences of their actions. The approach has been quite effective. A follow-up of discharged patients after two years showed that 40 percent of over 120 subjects had been able to remain free of new court convictions or the need of further hospitalization—a rather remarkable rate (Whiteley et al., 1972).

A modified approach to milieu therapy was initiated at the Washington State Penitentiary at Walla Walla. Treatment was essentially similar to that at Henderson Hospital, except that the antisocial persons were isolated for a brief period before they were allowed to enter the therapeutic community environment. Treatment aimed at first bringing the inmates to recognize their own failures in society; only then were they guided towards accepting new norms (Hunter, 1974).

***Behavior Modification.*** A third approach to antisocial behavior is behavior therapy. Burchard (1967) offered rewards for prosocial activities and withdrawal of rewards for lying, stealing, or cheating, as a means of changing antisocial behaviors. One project at the National Training School in Washington, D.C., and another at the Robert F. Kennedy Youth Center in Morgantown, West Virginia, apply a token economy program with tokens being worth one penny. Recidivism in delinquency dropped from 76 percent to 27 percent after the program was initiated. The reward approach is consistent with findings that the antisocial person is better able to learn when reinforcement is used, but less able when punishment or threat is used.

How effective behavior modification is in the long run is open to some question; however, Jesness (1975) conducted an unusual study using two institutions for delinquents. One was redesigned on a behavior modification approach, while the other used a direct time psychotherapeutic orientation known as transactional analysis. The two treatment programs were run for two and a half years and then compared with one another. Both seemed to show results in different ways. The behavior modification program reduced aggression and showed higher improvements when outcome was measured by observer ratings of behavior. The transactional analysis group also showed reduced aggression, and greater improvements when the measure was attitude scales. Follow-up, however, showed high recidivism for both groups.

The question of what causes differences in recidivism is basic to any treatment program. Olendick and Elliott (1978) suggest that one answer may be the individual's sense of internal or external locus of control. In their behavior modification program, they found very high recidivism rates for antisocial youngsters who attributed causes to external reasons. In essence, they seemed to be saying, "What the heck, I'm not in control of my life, everything is decided by someone else." Another pair of psychologists (Snyder & White, 1979) also noted the role of self-statements in delinquent behavior. Like Olendick and Elliott, they felt that delinquents often made it more difficult to conform because of the way they talked to themselves. For example, getting up on time would be difficult with the thought "What do I care. Screw it!" They designed a therapy approach aimed toward changing these private thoughts. This treatment was found to decrease impulsive behaviors over a six-week follow-up period.

***Social-cognitive Problem-solving.*** Although not directly treating delinquents, a number of other behavioral programs have used an approach called "social-cognitive problem-solving" to reduce aggression in children or youths (Urbain & Kendall, 1980). Examples of cognitive problem-solving skills that have been found to relate to children's social adjustment include the ability to see alternative solutions to a problem (*alternative thinking*), the ability to foresee the consequences of certain decisions (*consequential thinking*), and the ability to plan a series of actions to reach specific goals in the face of obstacles (*means-ends thinking*).

Using this set of ideas, Zahavi and Asher (1978) trained preschool children in understanding the consequences of aggression and in seeking alternatives to hitting. Results indicated that aggressive children reduced their aggression following such training. In a similar approach, Camp et al. (1977) taught elementary school boys to first identify their emotions, the consequences in various situations, and alternatives. Once again aggression was reduced, but more importantly, prosocial behaviors were increased.

An interesting variation of social problem-solving emphasizes the need for persons to acquire skill in taking the perspective of others, progressing outside of the state of egocentrism. If one can appreciate the feelings or perceptions of others, then aggression might be better controlled to avoid such consequences to others. Chandler (1973) used role-playing in skits, where each youth played different characters, until he had had direct experience with all characters. The youths were young chronic delinquents. Follow-up 18 months later showed that recidivism was reduced among these trained youths.

Finally, problem-solving has been used in families to train all members in how to negotiate demands of one another. Negotiations for problem-solving may include identifying one's position more clearly, specifying where the conflict or disagreements are, developing better communications skills to convey one's feelings or position, collecting information on solutions, generating alternatives, and seeking a course of action along with its consequences. This approach has seemed useful in reducing recidivism in a number of cases of delinquency (Shure & Spivack, 1978).

***Family Therapy.*** Griest and Wells (1983) highlight the importance of considering areas of family functioning which might contribute to antisocial conduct in children.

Among these topics are psychological parental characteristics, cognitive parental characteristics, marital characteristics, and social characteristics. The parental characteristic of maladjustment has been found to be related to behavioral problems in children. We can see the connection if we look at the possible relationship between a depressed parent and the effect this may have on the child. Being depressed, the parent may have a lower tolerance for the child's activities; this, in turn, prompts a higher use of punishment even for actions that do not require correction; finally, this punishing environment precipitates antisocial actions as the child lashes back.

Among the cognitive parental characteristics is the way in which parents view their children. Parents are not always accurate judges of their children's behaviors, and have been known to see deviancy when it does not exist (Wells, 1981). If the parents perceive their children as difficult or even juvenile delinquents, this can distort communications and may even convince the children that they might just as well be delinquent since they cannot win anyway.

Regarding marital characteristics, there seems to be higher levels of deviant behaviors among families where marital problems also exist (Rickard et al., 1982). Boys of divorced parents tend to show more behavior problems than children from intact families.

Finally, the level and quality of social and community contacts a mother has available appear to relate to behavior problems in children. Mothers who live isolated lives, with few community contacts or friends, tend to have children with higher problems. Similarly, the number of negative actions shown by children is highest on those days when a mother reported lower numbers of contacts with friends, than on days when the mother talked more to her friends (Wahler, 1980).

In terms of what this all means for treatment, there is already data showing that family therapy that covers these various topics led to better improvements in children's problems (Griest et al., 1983).

## EVALUATION

The classification of *personality disorders* is one of the improved areas in the DSM-III system. Historically, this category or similar categories have been examined and reexamined to separate theory from actual findings. For example, the antisocial personality was originally assumed to reflect a character defect; such a defect meant that the persons were not amenable to treatment any more than an intellectual defect or subnormality could be changed.

Over the years, this belief was shown to really be an assumption rather than fact. Instead of inferring a defect or a missing building block, DSM-III simply says that the important components of personality disorders are the behaviors themselves from which such inferences were made. The personality disorders, therefore, represent a long-existing behavioral pattern or style of dealing with life. As such, the possibility for change through therapy is restricted only to the degree that it is difficult to alter any long-existing habit patterns.

The most promising research that will further elaborate on the early origins of personality disorders is the early risk studies and those on the interaction between temperament and environment. The early risk work is comparable to early risk studies of schizophrenics, showing that it is possible to identify antisocial persons as early as childhood. What this means is that longitudinal studies might now be designed to identify the factors contributing to later adult personality disorders. The temperament studies would include those which not only show that infants exhibit individual differences in temperaments such as mood or excitability, but also that some may have different types of reactivity to environmental stimulation. Recall the evidence that sensation-seeking or emotional inhibition might distinguish the antisocial person. In effect, it may be possible that a personality disorder is the end product of an interaction between a temperamental/physiological characteristic as it affects the person's responsiveness to the social environment and socialization efforts. Really very little is consistently known yet about this group of pathologies, with most research effort being focused on the antisocial personality.

## SUMMARY


The personality disorders involve those persons who have failed to acquire adaptive skills, and who persist in behavior or attitude patterns. These continuing patterns involve certain recognizable styles, such as dependency, passive-aggressiveness, narcissism, paranoia, withdrawal, hysteria, or antisocial behaviors. Some of these patterns may represent lack of proper development during childhood years, such that early behavioral patterns fail to be replaced by more adult ones. Socialization and cultural influences may also be a factor in influencing personality styles, but these are probably minimally important in determining actual maladjustment itself. Subcultural values and peer pressures, however, can play a more important role in a person's adopting behaviors that are maladaptive. Genetics could be involved in determining temperamental differences, which then interact with environmental events to cause a personality disorder.

Antisocial persons have been especially studied, and a variety of theories offered about the origins of their disorder. A common theory involves a belief about a failure in some area of learning. The failure may be in a lack of anxiety to prompt the need to learn, or a delayed maturation, or an impaired ability to be concerned enough about others to want to become socialized. Other theories speculate on physiological differences such as too low autonomic arousal or too high sensitivity to stress.

Treatments have been adapted to fit the particular developmental needs of the various personality disorders, ranging from individual psychotherapy, problem-solving, behavior modification, milieu community therapy, and family therapy.


## KEY TERMS

**Antisocial personality**
**Behavior modification**
**Character disorder**
**Conduct disorders**
**Constitutional inferiority**
**Dependent personality**
**Hysterical or histrionic personality**
**Milieu therapy**
**Narcissistic personality**
**Paranoid personality**
**Passive-aggressive personality**
**Personality disorders**
**Psychopath**
**Schizoid personality**
**Social-cognitive problem-solving**
**Socialized aggressive**
**Socialized unaggressive**
**Sociopath**
**Undersocialized aggressive**
**Undersocialized unaggressive**

# CHAPTER 16

## The Affective Disorders: Disturbances of Mood

- **Specifically, how can we identify a psychotic person?**
- **Some persons publicly state that they have had mystical experiences that are unique to them. How can we tell if this is a psychosis or something else?**
- **We all have ups and downs in our moods. What causes these highs and lows?**
- **Is it pathological if I am depressed and grieve for awhile because of the loss of a loved one?**
- **"My grandparent is getting on in years, and I think I'm seeing signs of depression. What should I look for?"**
- **Is there a successful therapy for mood states that go from elation to depression?**
- **What is the relative value of electroshock treatment and drug treatment for different depressions?**
- **Is it possible to learn how to be depressed?**
- **Is it possible to predict if a person is going to commit suicide?**

**TABLE 16–1**

**The Affective Disorders**

| *Type* | *Major Characteristics* |
|---|---|
| Bipolar disorder | Severe personality disturbance with extremes of sadness and euphoria in the individual's history, but not necessarily concurrently. |
| Major depression | Severe personality disturbance involving depression, without a history of euphoria. |

## Case History 16–1:
### Bipolar Disorder

Madeline K. was a 60-year-old widow who had recently lost her second husband. She was initially hospitalized at age 22, soon after her first marriage. On that occasion she showed acute manic symptoms, was treated and discharged, returned within a month with depressive features, was treated again and released. She remained essentially normal until the recent breakdown.

The records from her first hospitalization show that her husband had returned home to find her twirling around the living room bizarrely draped in her wedding gown tied with a bath towel, and wearing a lampshade. She greeted him, laughed with an ear-piercing shrillness, and invited him to stay for the exciting coming-out party she was giving. Strewn on the table were 1,000 handwritten invitations signed with a flourish and addressed to such dignitaries as the president of the United States, the justices of the Supreme Court, the board of trustees of the University of California, and the emperor of Japan. She made incessant noises, singing her own ballads, shouting mottoes which she devised, and reciting limericks.

By contrast, her most recent commitment at age 60 involved a severely depressed condition. She looked immensely weary and had not slept soundly for days. She seemed mute, but would occasionally reply if a question were repeated often enough. Through careful probing it was found that she believed herself responsible for the ''epidemics of the world.'' She felt an urge to do penance for a lifetime of sin but could not remember the exact nature of her sins. For the past three weeks she had remained indoors pondering her own evil nature, and fearful of going out and possibly infecting others through the sheer enormity of her evilness. In the hospital she typically retired to a dark corner and would sit motionless for hours. She seemed on the verge of weeping but her sorrow was never able to break loose. She was easily led from room to room, but she always resumed her previous posture and ruminating. Her recovery has been extremely slow despite repeated EST (electroshock therapy) sessions.

In this and the following chapter, some of the most severe types of mental disorders will be described. These are major disorders equivalent to the major medical illnesses and they have profound effects on the lives of the persons affected. They incapacitate the person, limiting the individual's ability to enjoy life and disrupting normal functioning.

## THE PSYCHOTIC MENTAL DISORDERS

These severe forms of mental disturbance have been called *psychoses.* Their symptoms represent the final breakdown of personality as the person fails to find even moderately effective means of dealing with stresses and conflicts. Persons with psychotic disorders share many—but not necessarily all—of several characteristics. First, there is a severe disturbance of their ability to evaluate reality: a break from reality. Also, there is often a lack of insight regarding the fact that they have a disorder. *Personality decompensation* —disorganization of personality due to excessive stress—is often present. The individual usually experiences impairment of interpersonal, intellectual, and work functioning to a degree that is severe enough to lead to hospitalization. Specific disturbances in perception, thinking, or behavior are also experienced, and these are listed in Focus 16–1.

The DSM-III classification recognizes a number of psychotic disorders: certain affective disorders, the schizophrenic disorders, the paranoid disorders, and some organic disorders (American Psychiatric Association, 1980). This classification would include the following as categories:

- The affective disorders
    - Bipolar disorder
    - Major depression
- The schizophrenic disorders
    - Disorganized type
    - Catatonic type
    - Paranoid type
- The paranoid disorders
    - Paranoia
    - Folie à deux

In this chapter, we will be discussing the affective disorders (listed in Table 16–1) as well as suicide as it relates to depression. The schizophrenic and paranoid disorders will be presented in the next chapter.

## THE AFFECTIVE DISORDERS

*Affect* is a word that refers to mood or emotions; hence the term is used to refer to those disorders in which we see a disturbance of emotions. The primary moods that seem to be involved in the affective disorders are euphoria (and its behavioral expressions) and depression. We should note now that a person who experienced the elated mood of being euphoric and who often shows an inflated self-esteem, excited activity, and grandiose plans and thoughts is described as being *manic.* On the other hand, if the person is feeling hopeless, and possibly unable to sleep, eat with any appetite, or is diminished in energy then the person may be showing the signs of *depression.*

The two major forms of affective psychotic disorders involve such mood disturbances. These are the bipolar disorder and the disorder known as major depression. The bipolar disorder derives its name from the observation that the person shows two opposite poles of emotion—the manic and the depressed. The major depression is distinguished from the bipolar disorder, which also involves depression, in that the major depression involves the depressed mood but without the manic episodes. (For this reason, it is sometimes termed unipolar depression.) Furthermore, while the bipolar disorder is always characterized by recurring mood disturbances, the major depression can be diagnosed either as a recurring condition or as a single episode in the person's life.

## BIPOLAR DISORDERS

### Symptoms of Bipolar Disorders

Kraepelin used the term *manic-depressive psychosis* to refer to the disorder characterized by recurring cycles

## FOCUS 16–1:
### Symptoms of Psychotic Disorders

Specific symptoms of the psychotic disorders may include disturbances in perceptions, thoughts, emotions, or behaviors. These symptoms suggest the presence of a psychosis, although they are not always present in all psychotic disorders:

- *Autistic thinking:* excessive preoccupation with personal fantasies, unchecked by attention to reality.
- *Delusions:* unshakeable beliefs without justification in reality. Ideas of reference refer to the belief that one is being talked about by others. Other delusions include delusions of grandeur (a belief that one is a special person) or delusions of persecution (a belief that others are out to harm the individual).
- *Disorders of emotion:* exaggerated moods, from elation to deep depression to complete lack of emotion. Emotions may be inappropriate to circumstances.
- *Disorientation:* failure to know one's own identity, or to recognize time, place, or other people.
- *Flight of ideas:* thoughts that come in rapid sequences connected only by loose associations or logic.
- *Hallucinations:* sensory experiences without the presence of actual external stimuli.
- *Motor disturbances:* motor behavior that may be uncontrollably excitable or immobile (stupor) or may imitate the movements of others.
- *Speech disturbances:* incoherence, or *echolalia* (repetition of the words of others), *neologisms* (new words), or ''word salads'' of unconnected words.

of mania and depression. The preferred name under DSM-III is *bipolar disorder* and is diagnosed when a person shows at least one episode of the euphoric state known as mania. There is frequently but not always a depressed state. Therefore, three different subtypes of bipolar disorder exist: *bipolar disorder, manic episode; bipolar disorder, depressed episode;* and *bipolar disorder, mixed.* These subtypes describe the mood which is currently dominant. In the bipolar disorder, manic episode, the person has had a prior manic condition, which is now being repeated. In the bipolar disorder, depressed episode, the person is currently experiencing a depressed mood, but has shown a manic state in the past as in Madeline's case in Case History 16–1. In the bipolar disorder, mixed, the person is showing a mixture of extreme happiness and extreme depression, with these moods alternating rapidly every few days.

These mood disturbances soon terminate, either with or without treatment (Clayton, 1981). Manic reactions run their course in a few days or weeks, while depressed reactions last longer, sometimes continuing for several months. In between periods of disturbance, the person lives an essentially normal life. These normal phases vary with the individual, some going on for decades, others coming frequently, as Figure 16–1 illustrates. Normal periods may become shorter with age.

In addition to the mood disturbances, other features also characterize the disorder (Depue et al., 1981). During the manic state, the flight of ideas interferes with normal thought processes, and during depressed phases, thought processes are retarded. Delusions are common. In the manic state, these delusions are in keeping with the general euphoria and expansiveness, including delusions of grandeur. In the depressed state, ideas of guilt, low self-esteem, and hypochondriacal beliefs abound. Hallucinations may occur in a severe disturbance. However, they are less common than in schizophrenia, with hallucinations occurring in less than 20 percent of cases of bipolar disorders.

***The Manic Episode.*** *Bipolar disorder, manic episode* is the term used to refer to those conditions of the disorder in which the manic state dominates. Manic persons are exciting to be near because their displays of spontaneity, activity, and outbursts of exuberance are infectious. These individuals are full of ideas, have multitudinous plans, possess grand visions which somehow seem vaguely in the realm of possibility when presented with the supreme confidence characteristic of the manic person.

In the manic episode, the individuals are in heightened good humor, talkative, and entertaining. They dominate their social surroundings and appear to be physically inexhaustible. They may engage in an overwhelming display of energy; for example, covering reams of paper with their impressions of life or personally knocking on the doors of every house in the vicinity of a square mile. They may go on a spending spree, turning themselves into paupers within a few hours.

Being near these persons is tiring. Their ideas are too flighty: they shift too readily, they are too circumstantial, and they cover too many irrelevant issues as they find themselves unable to deal precisely and simply with single topics. Their claims and masterful proposals are shallow and poorly supported by reality. Their motor behavior is too incessantly active, and they may be assaultive and destructive. In all, they are highly distractible, irritable, self-centered, intolerant of having their ideas or plans questioned, and boastful.

***The Depressed Episode.*** *Bipolar disorder, depressed episode* is the term used to refer to those conditions in which the depressed state dominates. Depressed patients are difficult persons to be near since they are extremely despondent, melancholic, agonizingly self-deprecating. Like a mockery of King Midas, they believe that everything that they touch will turn to dust. Their gloom pervades every thought and action, they are convinced of their utter worthlessness and their hopeless guilt. Occasionally, persons experiencing an episode of depression cannot say what they are guilty of, only that they bear the massive burden of something horribly wrong. Their past and their future are so devoid of any hope that they contemplate suicide—about 75 percent of such patients consider suicide, and nearly 15 percent actually attempt it.

During depressed episodes, persons exhibit a general slowing down of their activities. It is an effort to think out even simple problems, such as how much money they need to pay their bills. They cannot con-

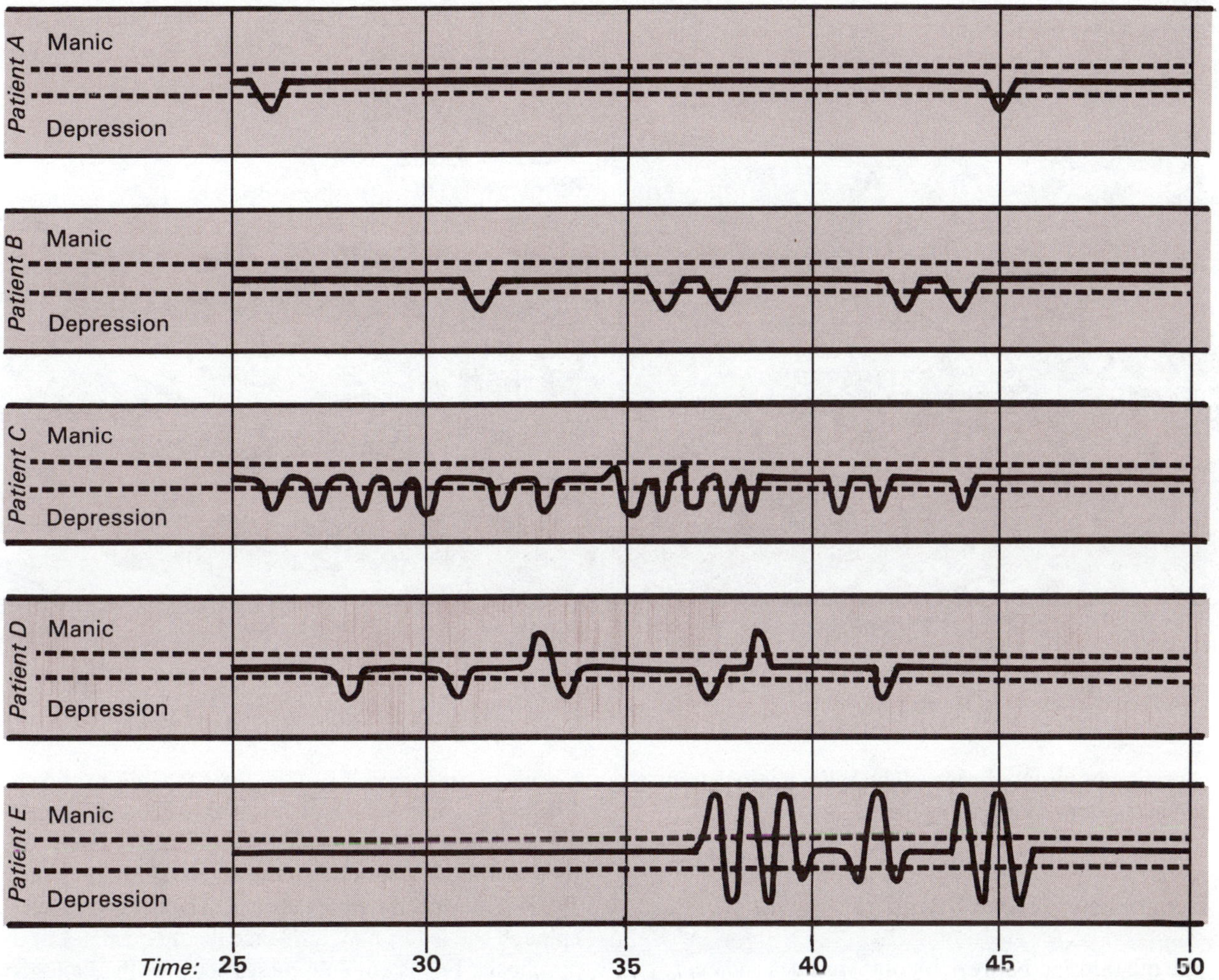


**FIGURE 16–1** Sample patterns of depressive and manic-depressive attacks among five patients. Patient A with widely interspersed depressed attacks. Patient B with depressive attacks every few years. Patient C with annual depressions but a few healthy years. Patient D with some isolated depressions, a few manic states. Patient E with alternating phases of mania and depression.

SOURCE: Adapted from *Depression and Its Treatment* by J. Pollitt, 1965, London: William Heinemann Medical Books Ltd.

centrate on little tasks such as reading a letter and complain that they cannot comprehend what the words mean anymore. They may become physically lethargic, as if oppressed by their mood. Their bodies also appear to react with a general slowing down. Gastrointestinal activity becomes retarded, leading to a loss of appetite and constipation. Persons in such a state may focus their attention on their bodies, displaying their depression through somatic delusions. They may believe, for instance, that their bowels are eaten away or their brains are disintegrating. In a combination of self-condemnation and self-aggrandizement, they may accept the delusion that they have syphilis and will infect the entire universe. Hallucinations are infrequent, but when they occur they tend to be relatively indistinct. The person may hear vague sounds or have the

THE BLUE DEVILS—!! JEALOUSY

*Throughout history, artists have attempted to depict various mental disorders. These etchings by George Cruikshank (1792-1878) show* depression *("the blues") and a pathological state of jealousy.*

sensation of visual illusions. The hallucinations transmit accusatory, derogatory messages.

## Dynamics of Bipolar Disorders

The relationship between bipolar episodes and energy and mood swings focus our attention on these characteristics. In an age when the biorhythm chart has gained some popularity in lay circles as a way of predicting energy levels, it might be tempting to think of the bipolar states as a sort of exaggerated swing of some biological pendulum.

***Physiological Factors.*** Biorhythms as popularized actually do not have any medical support regarding bipolar disorders. However, physiological factors have been studied as a possibly important part of the dynamics of bipolar disorders, including body rhythms called the *circadian rhythm.* We'll look at this connection and also at some social and psychological factors that may help to explain this psychosis.

*Chemical Substance Levels.* As was discussed in Chapter 4, a number of scientists have been looking at the ways in which changes in body chemistry might affect manic or depressed conditions (Baldessarini, 1983). One specific hypothesis is that changes in norepinephrine levels may influence the mood states of a psychosis. Focus 16–2 discusses some of the biological processes involved. To test this theory, Bunney and several colleagues (1972) at the National Institute of Mental Health systematically followed 10 patients as they passed from depression to manic states and back to depression again. Carefully measuring the levels of different body substances during these states, they discovered that norepinephrine significantly increased the day before the manic symptoms appeared, remained high during the manic phase, and then dropped to a low level during the depressed stage. Figure 16–2 shows a portion of this period, just before the onset of mania.

This evidence is persuasive, but the issue of cause and effect is still open to study. As you will remember from the discussion of scientific method in Chapter 1,

# FOCUS 16–2:
## A Physiological Theory of Depression

Although we tend to think of depression as a purely psychological state, many theorists have linked depression—both unipolar and bipolar—to physiological factors. One major explanation of depression deals with nerve transmission (Crow, 1983).

In normal persons chemicals known as *neurotransmitters* enable nerve impulses to cross synapses. A group of neurotransmitters, the *catecholamines,* may be related not only to nerve transmission but also to moods. One of these, *norepinephrine,* has been implicated in depression and has led to what has been called the *catecholamine theory of depression* (Akiskal & McKinney, 1975).

In this theory, depression is caused by depletion of norepinephrine at receptor sites in the brain. The exact mechanism whereby this relationship operates is still unclear, and there is reason to believe that the association may be more complex. One interesting piece of evidence comes from studies of bipolar disorder, where individuals alternate between depression and euphoria. Researchers have hypothesized that some type of switch mechanism operates to trigger these changes. In examining several bipolar disorder patients, they did discover biological changes in norepinephrine levels prior to the mood changes. Since some of the switches in moods occurred during sleep, it is difficult to explain the changes as due to the onset of stress.

Within a physiological explanation of depression, therapy would rely on medication to alter the condition of the human body. In fact, some medications such as the tricyclic drugs which increase the amount of norepinephrine available, do seem to lift depressions in some patients, such as those suffering from the major depression disorder.

correlational effects are impressive, and useful as first steps, but they do not necessarily prove cause and effect. Perhaps the norepinephrine changes reflect the psychotic process, rather than causing it.

Similar correlational findings have been reported between bipolar episodes and some other substances. Natural pain-relieving secretions called *endorphins* (see Chapter 4) have been found to decrease when manic states are in remission. Also, giving endorphin extracts to patients tends to reduce depressive symptoms. Electroshock therapy, which reduces depression, has been found to increase endorphin levels (Alexopoulus et al., 1983; Gerner et al., 1980). Finally, similar relationships were discovered with dopamine, in that introduction of dopamine seems to increase manic behavior in depressed persons, without necessarily helping the depression (Frazer, 1977). Although this evidence (which is also shown in Figure 16–2) is mainly correlational, with some controlled experiment designs, the accumulating documentation is impressive. It seems probable that biochemical factors will eventually be shown to have an important part in the chain of events related to bipolar symptoms.

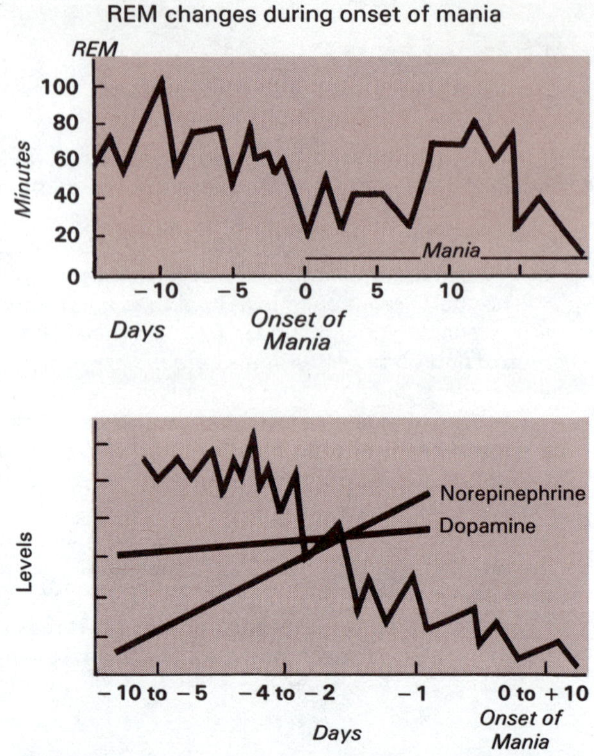


**FIGURE 16–2** The switch mechanism showing the relationship between norepinephrine, dopamine, and REM sleep changes prior to the switch from depression to mania.

SOURCE: Based in part on "The 'Switch Process' in Manic-Depressive Illness" by W. Bunney et. al., 1972, *Archives of General Psychiatry, 27,* pp. 304–309. © 1972, American Med. Assn.

*Circadian Rhythms.* Some other findings also link biophysiological factors to bipolar disorders. The *Circadian rhythm* is our sleep-wake cycle. Each animal species seems to possess a biological rhythm of activity and sleep that seems to fit physical needs to the context of one's ecological habitat. If this internal biological clock goes awry, as when we travel by jet across time zones, it causes disturbances in functioning.

Some studies now suggest that disturbed sleep patterns may be associated with bipolar depression; and one observation found sleep patterns among depressed persons to be three to six hours earlier than would be expected (Vogel et al., 1980). Furthermore, REM sleep, or dreaming, seems to be more frequent during depression (see Figure 16–2), while reduction of this sleep state seems to help the depression. Such findings have been interpreted to reflect a disturbance of the Circadian sleep rhythm as a source of depression.

***Cultural Factors.*** If biological factors seem linked to bipolar disorder, other evidence indicates that this factor does not operate alone. Cross-cultural comparisons suggest that societal factors also play a role. Reports have shown a higher incidence of this disorder in countries of the Mediterranean basin, the Fiji Islands, and in Ireland (Gold, 1951). And although the incidence of bipolar disorder is low in India, it is relatively high among Indians who have immigrated to the Fiji Islands.

There is considerable support for the idea that the expression of depressive states is influenced by culture. For example, Americans tend to experience guilt and self-punishing thoughts as a part of depression, while such thoughts are absent among some non-West- ern cultures (Marsella, 1980).

***Psychological Factors.*** Psychological factors

have been increasingly offered as the more significant contributors to the development of bipolar disorder. One significant influence, the family background, has received particular attention. We will look at this, then at two theoretical explanations of the psychodynamics involved.

*Family Background.* Studies of the early family backgrounds of bipolar patients have suggested that, in general, these persons have been born into a less stressful setting than schizophrenic patients (Arieti, 1959). The mother was willing, and in fact felt duty bound, to administer to her offspring.

In one study of hospitalized depressed women (not specifically bipolar depression), Cofer and Wittenborn (1980) found their fathers had fostered dependency. Descriptions of these women's relationships with their fathers often included statements such as "Father feared I would get into trouble" and "Father was hesitant to let me do anything on my own." Such an atmosphere of dependency encourages the child to accept the parent's standards and wishes, and discourages independence.

Later, the child is faced with greater demands by the parent, and family responsibility, rigid standards, and discipline are now stressed. The easy nonconditional atmosphere now shifts to one of conditionality and high expectations: "I'll love you if. . . ." Cofer and Wittenborn illustrated such expectations in quotes from the women they studied: "I felt I couldn't live up to father's (and mother's) expectations" and "Mother felt many things about my performance should be corrected." Thus, the child was trained early to be concerned about meeting standards and doing well, a mind-set that might well be linked to depression.

The family factors discussed earlier might cause a person to be at risk for developing bipolar disorders; a variety of psychoanalytic hypotheses have been offered to explain the kinds of influences that may precipitate the symptoms. Two common themes are that depression is a reaction to a loss and that it is aggression turned inward.

*Response to Loss.* According to one psychoanalytic interpretation, depression is an attempt to regain the acceptance of those whom the person has lost. It is a form of self-punishment—reparation for the wrongdoing which the person believes is responsible for the loss. The wrong may be a sense of not having cared enough, of not having worked hard enough, or of harboring secret feelings of resentment toward the loved one (Abraham, 1911). In this interpretation, a distinction is made between grief and depression, although both involve loss of a loved one. Grief is believed to be a conscious reaction to loss, while depression hides certain unconscious feelings (the resentment, anger, or rage).

The symptom of manic behavior may also be viewed as a reaction to loss and failure. However, instead of admitting failure, manic persons persist in an exaggerated denial. Instead of recognizing their lack of competency, they extol their own virtues. Rather than submitting to a sense of dependency they dominate and demand. A flighty, carefree attitude distracts them from the imminent threat of depression: the continuous hyperactivity presents a way to escape, avoid, cover up, ignore, deny, refuse, or use any means available to defend against their own deep inner feelings. These very methods for coping with tension and conflict become themselves pathological and futile: soon the person can run away no longer and must fall into depression.

*Anger Turned Inward.* Another common interpretation is that depression is anger that has been turned inward (Newman & Hirt, 1983). According to this view, we symbolically incorporate people we love—such as an admired parent—into ourselves. By so doing, we protect ourselves from the possibility of ever losing that person. If the loved one ever does something that disappoints us or does not live up to our ideals we may feel anger. But instead of directing the anger outward, towards the person, the anger is directed inward. This becomes the core of depression.

This process can also develop in a variety of other ways. Some analysts believe that inner-directed aggression involves real or perceived loss of a loved object whom one is ambivalent about, a person we have both positive and negative feelings towards. These negative feelings change to resentment at the desertion or loss. However, the remaining positive feelings cause guilt at the resentment, and finally the anger is transformed from being outwardly directed to being inwardly directed, thereby reducing the guilt but resulting in depression. Although many question the universal validity of these ideas as complete explanations of depression, there is some indirect evidence that the blocking of outward aggression is related to depression. Lyons (1972) found that as the open civil strife in Belfast, Ireland, created more external outlets for aggression, there was a corresponding decrease in the incidence of depression and suicides.

### Treatment of Bipolar Disorders

For any given attack, the chances of recovery are excellent since virtually all patients recover from the manic or the depressed state within approximately nine months with or without treatment. However, following *spontaneous recovery* (recovery without treatment), only 20 to 25 percent never have another episode. About 40 percent will have only two attacks, and approximately 40 to 50 percent will experience four or more episodes. Early onset of the first episode usually carries with it a better prognosis for recovery, the typical age of onset being about 30. Similarly, a better prognosis is expected for those reactions in which the manic features predominate.

The bipolar disorder is associated with several related dangers, including suicide, physical exhaustion, financial bankruptcy through manic spending sprees, or bodily injuries resulting from wild hyperactivity. Well-meaning attempts of friends who try to cheer the patient out of the depression or argue the manic into sensibility may present another danger—that of underestimating the condition. Constant supervision is needed. In some instances, patients have been known to swallow objects such as nails, hairpins, erasers, or pins in either a suicidal attempt or a manic display of fun-loving disposition. A severely depressed person may require intranasal feeding to prevent weight loss; the manic person needs to be calmed down sufficiently to accept food during a busy schedule of plans and activities. Warm baths and occupational therapy are helpful adjuncts to controlling symptoms. Additionally, several treatment approaches may be used (Davis & Maas, 1982).

***Electroshock Therapy.*** Electroshock therapy (EST) was among the first breakthroughs in the treatment of bipolar disorder. Its popularity in general psychiatric therapy is seen in one estimate that electroshock is used about 10,000 times daily in the United States (Bailine & Rau, 1981). Electroshock treatments involve sending an electrical current across the temporal area of the brain sufficient enough to cause a convulsion similar to a serious seizure. For depressives, the treatment is repeated three times per week. In an intensified format of two or three per day, it has also been used with some success to treat manic states. The course of treatment for depressive episodes is usually 8 to 10 sessions, while manic states usually involve 15 to 20 treatments.

Electroshock therapy has had qualified success. Early studies of depressed patients provided support for the use of shock therapy. For example, the Clinical Psychiatry Committee of the British Medical Council (1965) reported that about 70 percent of EST-treated patients were judged improved, as compared with about 40 percent of an untreated group. However, the treatment also carries some complications and side effects. Fractures may occur during the artificially induced convulsion and a temporary loss of memory and disorientation are often reported following treatment. Ernest Hemingway, the famous author, received two electroshock treatments and became extremely angry about the consequent memory loss, complaining, "What is the sense of ruining my head, erasing my memory, which is my capital, and putting me out of business? It was a brilliant cure but we lost the patient" (Hotchner, 1966, p. 280). One month later, Hemingway killed himself. Still, it must be said that EST has been helpful in returning depressed persons to their normal disposition and helping manic persons to become more calm and controlled. Since the discovery of drug therapy, however, EST has become less popular.

***Chemotherapy.*** Drug therapy is the modern alchemist's scientific answer to mood disturbances. The pharmacologist now has a shelfful of treatments ranging from tranquilizers to antidepressants.

Tranquilizers such as chlorpromazine have the capability of bringing the manic excitement under control within three or four days. Lithium has been prescribed for both manic and depressed episodes, with perhaps more improvement with the bipolar depres-

*Author* ***Ernest Hemingway*** *was treated with electroshock for his depression. With each temporary loss of memory, he complained that the treatment was ruining his livelihood.*

sions than the unipolar depressions discussed later in this chapter (Rosen et al., 1980). Since depressed persons tend to retain water and sodium, and lithium is similar to sodium, it has been suggested that lithium may work by readjusting the balance of body fluids. Other drugs, such as the tricyclics (including imipramine), affect the level of norepinephrine and have had some success with unipolar depressions, but less with bipolar depressions.

Overall, claims for the successful prescription of drugs range between 40 and 75 percent of cases. Lithium does seem to be the treatment of choice where drugs are used by bipolar patients, particularly where manic episodes are involved. This treatment can also reduce or prevent recurrences if lithium is taken in maintenance doses (Jefferson & Greist, 1983).

Modern decisions about the relative uses of chemotherapy versus electroshock must take into account the various effects and consequences. Drug therapy has some disadvantages, such as taking a little more time before producing its effect. And time may be crucial, particularly with the depressed symptoms. The possibility of suicide and the need for immediate intervention will often lead to the decision to use electroshock therapy instead (Scovern & Kilmann, 1980).

***Psychotherapy.*** While chemotherapy is becoming more popular as a way of terminating manic or depressed episodes, psychotherapeutic approaches aim at a more long-range goal. Since the general belief associates manic symptoms to failure, and depressed symptoms to disappointment or perceived loss, psychotherapy is directed towards stabilizing mood states through resolutions of these issues.

As an adjunct to drug therapy or to electroshock, psychotherapy sessions deal with the patient's assumed difficulty in coping. Conflicts regarding the person's felt failures and inabilities to deal with standards are considered. The person is helped to better assess his or her own strengths and to become separate from the expectations or demands of others. Humanistic therapists emphasize the desirability of working towards a richer, more individual, personal existence that represents genuine personal choices, rather than responses to the wishes of others.

## MAJOR DEPRESSION

Severe depressions can occur without the person ever experiencing the manic episode that characterizes the bipolar disorder. The person simply experiences depression and gloom. Such disorders are called *major depression* to distinguish them from the bipolar disorder. Since it is possible that an individual may experience a major depression at more than one time in life, the terms *single episode* and *recurrent* are added to make the distinction. William, in Case History 16–2, would be diagnosed as major depression, single episode.

# Case History 16–2:
## Major Depression

William D. was a successful businessman and vice president of a firm. He was 53 when he was given the responsibility of personally supervising the planning and construction of a new insurance building to house his company's offices and those of other firms. Although he was not an architect, he accepted the challenge with zest, considering the assignment an honor. He worked diligently with planners of other major structures to acquire an overall understanding of the functional characteristics of a well-designed building and the values associated with outstanding aesthetic qualities. He maintained an active social life as a means of obtaining more information, even though he often found himself tiring physically.

As time progressed, he experienced less and less real satisfaction with the structure that was growing before his eyes and through his own efforts. He found himself increasingly restless but without knowing why. Soon he started to worry about things, a number of little things that would not have bothered him at all five years earlier. His worries first centered around the row of offices that was to house his firm—he wondered if they were suitable, if they were spacious enough or too ostentatious, if someone else would have done it differently. Then be began to ruminate about his own contributions—to the firm, and to life in general. He felt that he should have been a more active and energetic vice president, closer to his employees. He questioned whether the assignment to supervise the planning of the building was really an honor and whether it was an attempt to ''kick him upstairs'' and keep him occupied while the really important decisions were being made. He felt no resentment at this, only a deep sadness at his own ineffectuality.

He became more morose daily, plunging deeper into despondency. He began to go to bed earlier and sleep later as he felt the wearisome fatigue of age as incentive dissolved. He noticed that he was constipated and speculated as to whether his intestinal tract might be calcifying, but he could not remember whether the intestines could turn into bone or not. On the urging of his wife, he went to his physician and was advised to seek psychiatric hospitalization. On reviewing his disturbing set of feelings, he readily admitted that this was the best solution. He received electroshock therapy three times a week for six weeks and was released fully recovered. He is currently eagerly anticipating his eventual retirement, has taken up fishing, and has recently acquired a summer home near the seashore.

One form of major depression often appears later in life (Campbell & Singer, 1983). *Major depression with melancholia,* once called *involutional melancholia,* seems to be associated with the climacteric, or change of life. The symptoms are essentially the same as those of major depressions occurring at other ages. They include despair and guilt (I led a wicked life of sex; I should have helped my children more than I did); frequent occurrence of hypochondriacal delusions (My bowels are stopped up . . . my liver has turned to stone . . . my brain is withered to nothing.); and nihilistic beliefs (The world is no more; all food has been contaminated and nothing tastes the same anymore).

### Major Depression versus Bipolar Symptoms

Overall, the characteristics of the person with major depression and the person experiencing the depressed episode of a bipolar disorder are the same (see Table 16–2). Symptoms include extreme sadness, loss of interest in work or recreation, insomnia, motor retardation, decreased sexual drive, inability to concentrate, low self-esteem, excessive self-blame, and loss of appetite. Psychotic aspects include delusions or hallucinations involving guilt, disease, nihilism, dying, or punishment for sins (Davis & Maas, 1983).

**TABLE 16–2**

**Depth of Depression and Frequency of Clinical Symptoms**

| | DEPTH OF DEPRESSION | | | |
|---|---|---|---|---|
| *Clinical symptoms* | *% None* | *% Mild* | *% Moderate* | *% Severe* |
| Sad face | 18 | 72 | 94 | 98 |
| Stooped posture | 6 | 32 | 70 | 87 |
| Speech slow, etc. | 25 | 53 | 72 | 75 |
| Suicidal wishes | 13 | 47 | 73 | 94 |
| Hopelessness | 14 | 58 | 85 | 86 |
| Inadequacy | 25 | 56 | 75 | 90 |
| Conscious guilt | 27 | 46 | 64 | 60 |
| Loss of interest | 14 | 56 | 83 | 92 |
| Loss of motivation | 23 | 54 | 88 | 88 |
| Fatigability | 39 | 62 | 89 | 84 |
| Loss of appetite | 17 | 33 | 61 | 88 |

SOURCE: Adapted from *Depression: Clinical, Experimental, and Theoretical Aspects* by A. T. Beck, 1967, New York: Hoeber Medical Books, p. 40. By permission of Harper & Row.

A variety of other comparisons have been made between bipolar and unipolar depression. For instance, bipolar depressives tend to show greater social isolation and withdrawal, although they seem nevertheless to be motivated towards social approval. Perhaps the depression comes on because of lack of social acceptance. Persons with bipolar depression also have been reported to rely more on denial and somatization defenses than do those with unipolar symptoms. The denial apparently is somewhat successful, since bipolar depressives also seem to have a diminished awareness of anxiety. Finally, the bipolar depressives seem to show poorer impulse control, perhaps the basic defect that also shows in the impulsive features of the manic episodes (Donnelly et al., 1980). These differences, however, are all relatively tenuous. Until they prove related to etiological differences, the only clear distinction between bipolar and major depressions is that only one includes a manic episode.

## Dynamics of Major Depression

The understanding of depressed states has attracted considerable attention in recent years, going beyond traditional psychoanalytic interpretations about inner-directed aggression. Several explanations have been offered, including the physiological ones already discussed in the section on bipolar disorders. Some of the most relevant psychological theories are the theory of learned helplessness, the cognitive explanations, and explanations that look at life events, and behavior deficits.

***Learned Helplessness.*** One intriguing psychological theory on depression is that depression is really an example of learned helplessness (Seligman, 1983). Simply stated, the premise is that we start off trying to reduce threat or anxiety in our lives. However, if we meet with environmentally imposed failures, such

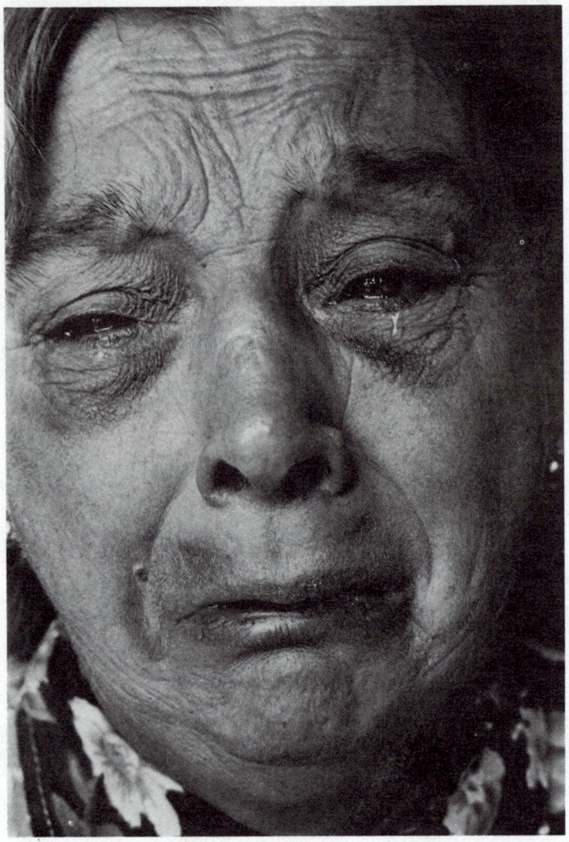

*One form of major depression that is associated with age is called* ***involutional melancholia.***

conditions can convince us that matters are out of our control and nothing we can do will really change them. As a result, we may learn to give up. This learned helplessness persists in the same way that other habits persist, even if the conditions change so as to return control to us.

Support for this theory comes from a common experiment. Here, college students are faced with circumstances which they soon learn that they are helpless to control, such as inescapable noise or unsolvable problems (Roth & Kubal, 1975). Their reactions are remarkably similar to symptoms shown by depressed patients, including weight loss and loss of appetite, motor and intellectual slowness, and social deficits.

The learned helplessness interpretation also gains some support from biochemical theories. Seligman (1983) points to evidence that animals subjected to unavoidable shock—a situation in which helplessness is quickly learned—show lower levels of brain norepinephrine (Weiss et al., 1974). This finding relates back to the association noted earlier between bipolar depression and norepinephrine depletion. Another argument relates to the fact that women appear to be more susceptible to depression than are men (Radloff & Rae, 1979). Since many women in our society seem to be trained in social roles that emphasize helplessness, this has been offered in support of the learned helplessness theory.

Some more direct support has been obtained for the learned helplessness concept in studies of depressed persons. Altman and Wittenborn (1980) questioned 88 women who had been treated for depression, finding great preoccupation with failure and helplessness and a low sense of competence. Another study of depressed college students found these students to view themselves as helpless even where they felt that other college students could succeed (Garber & Hollon, 1980).

The theory of learned helplessness is still under examination, with several theorists providing reformulations. One particularly interesting variation is the shift from an emphasis on depression as due to an uncontrollable environment to a perception of one's individual power to control the environment: "The environment may be controllable, but I am helpless to do so" (Miller & Norman, 1979). Seligman et al. (1979) extend this idea to show how learned helplessness may be related to depression along three dimensions: internal-external; stable-unstable; and global-specific. Attributing failures to internal, global, or stable and unchanging factors all contribute to a sense of helplessness and a lowered self-esteem. According to the theory, attributing lack of control to internal factors will lead to lowered self-esteem and depression, but assigning cause to external factors will not. Assigning lack of control to stable or global factors will mean experiencing helplessness and possibly depression in a variety of different situations, leading to the depression also lasting over a longer time span.

The theory of learned helplessness represents one of the more promising psychological explanations of depression, but it is still being reviewed, refined, and further studied. Another perspective is offered by the cognitive explanation.

***Cognitive Explanations.*** A second psychological formulation of depression postulates that individuals' thought processes are the cause of depression. In reviewing his therapy notes taken from depressed patients, Beck (1983) noticed that they think in distorted ways. They hold negative views in what Beck calls the *cognitive triad:* a pessimistic view of the world, a pessimistic self-concept, and a pessimistic view of the future. Thus, a successful scientist who was just elected president of a prestigious scientific group may become depressed because a negative world view causes him to devalue his achievement as superficial. Or a pessimistic self-concept may cause a devoted mother to be depressed because she believes herself to be "worthless, a bad parent, a nothing." Finally, a young student may consider suicide because of a pessimistic view of the future: "Things won't ever work out for me . . . life will never change." Since people are influenced by their thoughts, beliefs, and perceptions, the person becomes more and more depressed and self-defeating (Lewinsohn et al., 1981).

In a study of depressed women by Cofer and Wittenborn (1980), it was amazing just how many negative self-statements these women agreed to: "I feel useless," "I'm afraid I'll do the wrong thing," "I feel I cannot live up to my own expectations," "I'm not as smart as others," and "I'm not good enough to try for the top." Although Seligman would suggest that these internal thoughts are attributions of helplessness shaped by prior experiences, Beck says instead that these thoughts themselves precipitate the mood of depression. In fact, Beck and others have developed psychotherapeutic intervention programs for changing depression through changing thoughts, as we'll discuss shortly.

***Other Psychological Factors.*** In addition to the learned helplessness and cognitive theories, there are several other psychological explanations for depression. One theory sees depression as an emotional reaction to stressful life events, such as failure to reach

*President **Abraham Lincoln** suffered bouts of depression that may have been pathological.*

expected goals, or the loss of a relationship (Radloff & Rae, 1979).

Two other explanations are that depression reflects a behavioral deficit, or that it is a directly conditioned side product of anxiety. The first of these explanations relates back to the behavioral classification system presented in Focus 3–3. It explains the depressed person's loss of interest and lack of activity as a result of extinction, which has taken place because of a lack of positive rewards (Heiby, 1981; Lewinsohn, 1983). The second explanation sees a process of direct conditioning, a result of severe or prolonged anxiety. The individual is conditioned to experience anxiety; the continued tension overstresses or overloads autonomic pathways; and the excitation is channeled to other pathways such as those associated with depression (Wolpe, 1979).

### Treating Major Depression

Just as explanations for depression vary considerably, there are a range of different approaches to treatment. Most of those approaches used for the depressed episodes of the bipolar disorder also apply to the treatment of major depression, so we will present only a quick review here.

***Physiological Treatments.*** As with the bipolar disorder, electroshock therapy has proven valuable for depressed persons who represent suicide risks. Scovern and Kilmann (1980) reviewed the literature and concluded that EST was more beneficial than chemotherapy for severe depressions, particularly when time was of the essence and immediate control of the depression was desired. Among the drug treatments, one family of chemicals called the *tricyclics* is useful as antidepressants for major depression. As we have seen, the tricyclics apparently achieve their effects through action on serotonin and norepinephrine at various sites in the brain, and this in turn alters the physiological conditions that accompany depression. At one time, another group of antidepressants, the MAO (Monoamine Oxidase) inhibitors, was considered as possibly valuable for treatment of depression. These drugs act in a similar way to the tricyclics on human physiology. However, further studies have shown the MAO inhibitors to be more toxic than the tricyclics; hence, they are prescribed only if other treatment is not possible (Baker, 1983).

***Psychotherapies.*** For the person who is not so severely depressed as to be unable to interact with a psychotherapist, various psychological approaches are available.

*Psychotherapy for Guilt.* In traditional psychotherapy, including psychoanalytic approaches, the depressed person is provided with reassurance and support aimed at reestablishing a sense of self-worth as a foundation for confronting conflicts. Issues centering around early loss of important figures in life, or guilt, are approached. If there are indications of aggression-turned-inward, then the therapist will gradually attempt to draw the hostility outward. Following the theory that the release of aggression will reduce depression, a program called *Anti-Depressive Program* (ADP) has been tried. This involves deliberately provoking patients, then encouraging them to express their anger. Some initial results have been positive (Barnes, 1977).

*Humanistic-existential Therapy.* From a humanistic-existential orientation, the therapist helps the individual understand that the depressed feelings are authentic reactions to a superficial existence that has been created by others. The person may feel burdened by interpersonal events and despair of the world's demands. The therapist accepts these, but encourages the person to move beyond the despair and take full responsibility for those feelings of hopelessness. Through confronting the world of the here-and-now, the person's experiencing of others, and the person's self experience, the depressed person moves towards a more productive life, planning for the future rather than ruminating about the past. On the whole, outcome studies of traditional humanistic psychotherapies have not been very favorable regarding their success (Hollon & Beck, 1979).

*Behavior Therapy.* Differing behavioral approaches have been developed to treat depression (Kovacs, 1979). These approaches vary according to the individual. For persons whose depression relates to loss of reinforcers, programs have been introduced in which the person is gradually assigned either to return to pleasurable activities or to take on tasks which earn rewards. Rehm and his associates (1975) identified depressed women through newspaper announcements; then they used a treatment approach of guiding these subjects to make lists for themselves of activity-based goals separated into attainable steps. They also identified reinforcers which they could apply themselves as they made progress towards goals. Within six weeks, these women showed decreases in depression scores on two psychological measures of depression, reducing their negative self-references in their speech, and showing increased participation in rewarding activities.

Todd (1972) used a more cognitive approach with a 49-year-old woman, simply training her to reduce negative self-referents and to increase positive thoughts about herself through rewarding herself for each positive thought. This change alone helped her out of depression. Another cognitive approach was used to treat college students seen at a university student health service (Shaw, 1977). This therapy was based on Beck's approach to correcting the cognitive triad, discussed earlier, of distorted and negative beliefs. Within four weeks, these mildly to moderately depressed students showed significant decreases not only in their subjective feelings, but in outward signs of depression as rated by clinical staff. Finally, Rush and some colleagues (1977) added further support for the usefulness of cognitive therapy, showing it to be as effective as antidepressive drug treatment, even at one-year follow-up. However, the persons studied were patients with a less severe level of depression.

In both the bipolar disorder and major depression, we have noted that the danger exists that persons will harm themselves. In fact, suicide, a growing problem in the United States, is sometimes directly related to depressive disorders. (Recall that 94 percent of severely depressed patients in Table 16-2 had entertained suicidal wishes.) For this reason, a look at suicide is highly relevant to a discussion of depressive disorders.

## SUICIDE

It is now estimated that in the United States there is a suicide every 30 minutes, and that 10 times more people attempt suicide and may not be successful. The number of deaths by suicide has increased fourfold over the past 30 years (Paykel, 1976), amounting to a minimum of 25,000 annually. With such figures, suicide is now viewed as the "number one cause of unnecessary, premature, and stigmatizing death" in the United States and is among the leading ten ranked causes of death in Western countries (Seiden, 1974). Particularly vulnerable are minority persons and college students: suicide is the third highest cause of death for college students, with rates for blacks and American Indians being from two to five times those for whites (McIntosh, 1980).

### Dynamics of Suicide

Why should a rational human being attempt self-destruction? What must conditions be like to make death seem more attractive than life? There are many common myths and misunderstandings about suicide, as shown in Focus 16–3. Scientists have struggled for years to find answers to questions about the causes of suicide. Several overlapping explanations have been offered.

***Psychoanalytic Theories.*** Freud and the psychoanalysts have speculated that persons feel pushed to suicide because the death instinct, Thanatos, becomes overwhelming, or because aggression is turned inward. As with the explanation of depression we saw earlier, this theory may have some support: recall the finding that Belfast's suicide rates decreased as civil fighting increased, suggesting that self-aggression declined when an external target for aggression was justified instead.

Another explanation is that suicide represents an act of vengeance against others: "When I'm gone, you'll be sorry you treated me the way you did." In this, there is a strong attempt to cause guilt in others. Other reports by those who have considered suicide have included ideas about trying to regain love and affection. "I had the fantasy of the nice things my parents would be saying at my funeral," or self-punishment for past wrong-doings, "I don't deserve to go on living anymore."

***Life Stresses and Losses.*** In many cases, the attempted suicide is an attempt to escape stresses of life, "I can't face living like this anymore." The stress may be related to recent death or separation from a loved one, such as a parent. Paykel (1976) uncovered the revealing finding that most of the stresses in the lives of persons who had attempted suicide were perceived as being out of the individual's control, such as a death, a broken engagement, or being fired. All of these situations led to a sense of helplessness. Paykel also discovered that these individuals had experienced more life-stress events than other depressed persons, and that these events seemed to come to a peak level the month before the attempted suicide. It would seem that sui-

## FOCUS 16–3:
### Myths and Facts about Suicide

| *Myth* | *Fact* |
|---|---|
| People who threaten suicide do not actually commit suicide. | Facts are that 8 of every 10 successful suicides openly threatened that this was what they were going to do. |
| Suicides seriously intend to die in their attempts. | Most suicides seem to be ambivalent about dying, and are gambling with death, hoping that others will step in and help prevent it. |
| A person who attempts suicide once is forever suicidal. | Suicidal urges normally last for only a limited span of time. |
| Improvement following a depressive crisis means the suicide risk is over. | Suicides tend to occur after depressed persons have improved—about 3 months later, when they regain enough energy to act on their suicidal thoughts. |
| Suicide is more characteristic of the rich, or conversely, of the poor. | Suicide actually occurs with equal frequency among both rich and poor. |
| Suicide is inherited. | There is no proof that suicidal tendencies are inherited. |
| All suicidal persons are psychotic. | Suicidal persons are extremely unhappy, but they are not necessarily mentally ill. |

SOURCE: Adapted from *Some Facts About Suicide* by E. Shneidman and N. Farberow, 1961, Washington, D.C.: U.S. Government Printing Office.

*Marilyn Monroe, although a movie success, eventually committed suicide due to depression.*

cide represents a final solution to uncontrollable events that have piled up for the individual (Slater & Depue, 1981).

***Cultural Factors.*** Suicide rates seem to differ in a number of ways across different countries. Suicide rates are high in Denmark, Japan, Germany, Switzerland, and Sweden (about 30–45 per 100,000 persons); moderate in Canada, Belgium, Norway, and Australia; and low in England, Italy, Venezuela, Netherlands, and New Zealand (5–15 per 100,000) (Bureau of the Census, 1981). For the United States, the rate is about 26 per 100,000.

Sweden's high suicide rate has been the focus of study, and a look at this country may provide an illustration of some of the cultural dynamics of suicide. According to one view, the increased pressure towards materialism in this country has made occupational and financial success more important than ever before. Perhaps, also, the fact that there are fewer religious taboos against suicide has made this a more available solution in the face of financial or other failure.

Not only Sweden's high suicide rate, but also the way in which suicide is carried out may reflect the role of culture. One view is that the higher number of passive versus violent suicides (drug overdose versus gunshot) reflects this culture's overall pacifist values (Rudestam, 1975). Other evidence of the shaping role of culture may be drawn from the relative popularity in some countries of forms of suicide that might appear quite exotic to most Americans, for instance, self-immolation in the streets as a means of political protest, a relatively frequent occurrence during the Diem regime in Vietnam, or the rash of self-starvations of imprisoned IRA members in Ireland during the early 1980s.

### Evaluating the Risk of Suicide

Who tries suicide? Statistically speaking, persons who are most likely to try suicide are minority persons, college students, and other young persons within the age group of 15 to 24. More women *attempt* suicide than men. However, at least three times as many men succeed than women. Persons who are depressed are more likely to commit suicide, although depression is not always a predictor (Leonard, 1974). Separated or divorced persons are more vulnerable than married persons. And finally, suicide may be more common in certain professions: physicians, psychiatrists, dentists, and attorneys have high rates (Ross, 1974).

These figures represent broad statistics that tell us about suicide risk in very general terms. We have more specific information that may be helpful in predicting a person's likelihood of becoming suicidal. Such information comes from research such as "psychological autopsies" and studies of patterns of causation.

*In Japan, **suicide** can be an honorable act. Yukio Mishima committed hara-kiri to protest corruption in Japanese politics.*

***The Psychological Autopsy.*** Psychological autopsies are intensive collections of data on persons who threaten suicide or have actually killed themselves (Shneidman et al., 1970). Parents, relatives, friends, are all interviewed in extensive detail; case histories are compiled; and exhaustive study is made even of the type and content of suicide notes that the individual left behind (Gordon, 1979). It is revealing to see that the notes of actual suicide victims are recognizable for both the anguish they evidence and the general coherency of thinking and writing. Notes of suicide victims often provide explicit instructions (for example, on the funeral arrangements) or express positive feelings towards others (''I'll always love you. All I have is yours. No one ever did more for me than you. Oh please pray for me, please.'')

***Patterns of Causation.*** Although there is still mystery surrounding the causes of suicide, some patterns are emerging from psychological autopies (Farberow, 1980). First, as we've seen, life stresses play a dominant role. These include both stresses that occur at a high frequency and those that are beyond control of the individual. Among students, fear of failure was an important precursor to suicide (Paykel et al., 1975). Another pervasive factor may be loneliness or loss. The loneliness may result from the loss of a significant person in one's life or from a belief that meaningful interpersonal contact is not possible because of personal difficulties. Third, there are certain factors that, when present, seem to increase a person's imminent risk of being suicidal. A suicide ''lethality checklist'' of high-risk factors has been compiled by the Los Angeles Suicide Prevention Center to aid volunteers. Table 16–3 provides a brief version.

### Suicide Prevention

As the profile of factors associated with the risk of suicide has been put together, emphasis has been placed on crisis intervention. Since suicide threats are a kind of cry for help, and a statement of intent to commit suicide is a good predictor of a real attempt, then suicides should be offered a source of help. Suicide prevention centers, crises intervention centers, and telephone ''hot lines'' that are available 24 hours, have all been established to offer such help. These are staffed by volunteers and professionals who are trained in suicide consultation. The telephone numbers are widely publicized. The philosophy is that quick intervention can do much to help the suicidal person who has nowhere else to turn, and that offering an alternative to suicide is a major deterrent. Staff members provide understanding to the caller, offer information on sources of help, provide hope that life is not hopeless, and attempt to obtain a commitment that the caller will take some other action than immediate suicide, such as making an appointment to drop in at the center. The success of such centers is hard to evaluate: some reports suggest a reduced rate of suicide among high-risk persons, while others believe no changes have really resulted (Nielsen & Videbech, 1973). However, given that human lives are at stake, the potential of such intervention approaches must be pursued.

**TABLE 16-3**

**"Lethality Checklist" for Evaluating Suicide Risk**

"Yes" answers to the following questions indicate a higher risk of suicide:

- Does the individual communicate an intent to commit suicide? Is the person highly specific about the details of the suicide plan? (For instance, "I know how many pills it will take for my body weight; my will is folded under the telephone; I will end it at sunset looking out my window; I will be wearing . . .")
- Does the person have no family or other social support system?
- Is the person facing a concrete life stress?
- Is the individual suffering from a serious illness?
- Has the person suffered from symptoms such as insomnia, depression, or alcoholism?
- Is the individual a male?

SOURCE: Los Angeles Suicide Prevention Center

## EVALUATION

The classification of affective disorders is still not well understood in terms of causes. One problem may be in the difficulty of developing an accurate classification system. Although DSM-III relies on bipolar disorder and major depression as the two classes of the severe depressive conditions, this means that much of the prior research which has been published is hard to integrate, since older terms such as manic-depressive psychosis, and bipolar-unipolar were used in these studies. Another problem, once again possibly due to classification, is the possibility that there are differing sources of depressed behaviors even for persons suffering from the same intensity of depression. For example, moderate depressions might be traced to unresolved loss of relationship in one person, to behavior deficits and loss of reinforcement in another, to negative thoughts in still another, and to a history leading to learned helplessness in yet another. Finally, the distinction between major depression and bipolar depression based only on the absence of manic episode seem weak; especially given the building evidence that bipolar versus unipolar depression may differ in other ways, such as defenses used or response to therapies.

Accumulative research on etiology suggests that genetic and some biochemical factors seem to account to some degree for manic and depressed episodes. On the other hand, research on psychological factors is not yet consistent; what is available suggests that psychological variables are more involved in the less severe depressions. Controversies about the primary causes of mental disorders tend to occur frequently because of the complexity of human behaviors. Such differences reflect the slow progress being made in developing an accurate picture of psychopathology, its origins, and treatments. Part of this is due to the pace of development of technology that is needed to gather data more precisely. Studies of norepinephrine involve inferences from other data, since it is virtually impossible to daily monitor its levels in the brain. Part of the delayed progress is simply because humans are not laboratory animals easily subjected to a controlled environment, a controlled diet, a controlled parentage, or controlled life experiences. Finally, as mentioned earlier, it is possible that our diagnostic system is also incomplete; hence, it is possible that both cognitive and physiological explanations are correct if there is more than one type of depression. The move towards identifying a bipolar disorder and a major depression has shown great promise since these patients do seem to differ from one another in a variety of ways. However, until a complete understanding of depressions is reached, decisions about treatment—whether psychological or biological—must continue to rely on currently available information on what seems to work and on current theories and research.

## SUMMARY

The psychoses are severe forms of mental disorders, including the affective, schizophrenic, and paranoid disorders. Psychoses share the characteristics of a break from reality, lack of insight, personality decompensation, severe impairment of functioning, and disturbances in perception, thinking, or behavior.

Among the psychoses are the affective disorders, named for the important symptoms of emotional or affective states. Two major classes of affective disorders are the bipolar disorder and major depression. The bipolar disorder is characterized by recurrent emotional states, while the major depression is a severe melancholic condition that may be a single episode or recurrent, but without manic episodes. In the bipolar disorder classification, three types are recognized: bipolar disorder, manic; bipolar disorder, depressed; and bipolar disorder, mixed. These conditions are characterized by a cyclic nature; manic or depressed reactions soon terminate with time, and the person returns to a normal level of emotions only to have the pathological mood return. Manic episodes involve euphoria and hyperactivity. Depressed episodes involve despondency and lethargy.

The basic differences between the bipolar disorder and major depression are the lack of evidence of any manic episodes in the major depression, the presence of different defense mechanisms, and the differential response to different modes of therapy. Some evidence is building that the major depression type patient may show less social isolation, rely less on denial and somatization defenses, and show greater impulse control. Tricyclic medication may be more effective with major depression, while lithium seems more useful with bipolar depression. Other types of chemotherapy, electroshock, and various psychotherapies have also received attention.

A variety of hypotheses have been examined regarding the origins of the affective disorders. For the bipolar disorder, biophysiological and psychological origins seem most likely explanations. For the major depression, concepts relating to learned helplessness and cognitive processes hold much promise.

## KEY TERMS

**Affect**
**Affective disorders**
**Autistic thinking**
**Bipolar disorder**
**Circadian rhythm**
**Decompensation**
**Delusions**
**Electroshock therapy**
**Endorphins**
**Flight of ideas**
**Learned helplessness**
**Lithium**
**Major depression**
**Major depression with melancholia**
**Manic-depressive psychosis**
**Psychoses**
**REM sleep**
**Spontaneous recovery**
**Stupor**
**Tricyclics**
**Unipolar depression**

# CHAPTER 17

## The Schizophrenic and Paranoid Disorders: Disorders of Distortion

- **Mystics may sit immobile for hours, but so can catatonic schizophrenics. What is the difference?**
- **The assassin of Senator Robert F. Kennedy was diagnosed as being a paranoid schizophrenic. What does this imply?**
- **What advice should we give a person about marriage if both of that person's parents had been hospitalized for schizophrenia?**
- **In what sense can we say that parents can create a schizophrenic by their behaviors?**
- **How early in life is it possible to predict schizophrenia? What are the characteristics of high-risk children?**
- **How successful have drugs been in treating schizophrenia? Has behavior modification been of any value at all?**
- **What does the existentialist mean in claiming that schizophrenia is really a progression towards sanity?**
- **An otherwise functioning person says, "I am certain that the FBI, the Russian secret service, and the United Nations secret police are out to get me." What might you suspect about this person?**
- **How is it possible for two sisters to share the same psychotic condition?**

**TABLE 17–1**

**Schizophrenic and Paranoid Disorders**

| *Type* | *Major Characteristics* |
| --- | --- |
| | *SCHIZOPHRENIC DISORDERS* |
| Disorganized Schizophrenia | Characterized by regressive behaviors, such as giggling and gesturing, and severe disorganization |
| Catatonic Schizophrenia | Characterized by physical immobility, or violent motor outbursts |
| Paranoid Schizophrenia | Characterized by personality breakdown with delusions of persecution |
| | PARANOID DISORDERS |
| Paranoia | Characterized by systematized delusions, in the absence of emotional disturbances or deterioration of personality |
| *Folie à deux* | Characterized by two persons sharing a common delusion |

# Case History 17–1:
## A Letter to the Author

Partly because of the availability of my book, and partly because of my duties at one time as mayor of my city, I have continuously received letters, some of which are bizarre. The following excerpt from such a letter provides an illustration of symptomatic thought patterns of paranoid schizophrenia.

> For 12 years I was friends with one Mr. S., who is now a highly successful writer and physiochemist. However, one evening back in 1950 or thereabouts, Mr. S. told me that he was Lucifer and he also provided me with evidence of this, such as references. He did this just after I had been discharged from the ________ State Hospital. . . .
>
> Now in 1960 (I was told) that I would have a visitation of a supernatural nature, and in 1969, I received the divine command to send the documents. He has cost me a great deal of personal trouble, such as job loss and a divorce.
>
> Mr. S. taught me a great deal about hypnosis, so that I know that in a hypnotic trance, it could be proven that I am a real prophet. I have been sent by the God of the Old Testament and the father of Jesus, so the Moslems must be worshipping a false god.
>
> . . . the Jews believe in human sacrifice, so as I understand it, World War II, Korea, and Vietnam were military affairs where the U.S. Army was placed in insane military situations, such as doing things like trying to invade Germany via the Brenner pass in Italy. . . .
>
> I have sent thousands of documents such as this at great expense to myself . . . (and) have received a great deal of persecution and mental anguish. The life of a real prophet is not a happy one.
>
> On the matter of race, the Lord believes in a policy of love thy neighbor, so let the KKK take heed (from the author's files).

In the last chapter, we defined psychosis and identified the major psychotic disorders as the affective disorders, the schizophrenic disorders, and the paranoid disorders. We shall devote this chapter to discussion of the schizophrenic and the paranoid disorders listed in Table 17–1. Both are major psychological disorders. Schizophrenia, however, is characterized by personality determination, while the paranoid disorders are not.

## SCHIZOPHRENIA

*Schizophrenia* involves those psychotic disorders characterized by withdrawal from reality, disturbance in emotional appropriateness, and bizarre speech, thought, and motor symptoms. Delusions and hallucinations occur. Kraepelin (1925) used the term *dementia praecox* to refer to this disorder—dementia meaning progressive mental deterioration and praecox referring to the early age of onset. Bleuler (1978) disagreed that this disorder was always progression toward dementia, but proposed that it was mainly characterized by a splitting of personality. On his suggestion the new term *schizophrenia—schizin,* to divide or split, and *phren,* the mind (Greek)—has supplanted the old Kraepelinian label.

This set of disorders is one of the most severe of the major psychiatric disturbances. Research has found that almost half of mental hospital patients suffer from a schizophrenic disorder (National Institute of Mental Health, 1978). It arouses particular concern because it can begin quite early in life, mostly during the 20s, and may well continue uncured for the remainder of the patient's life. Although first-admission patients may be released within four to five months, the alarming fact is that the length of hospitalization for many persons with schizophrenic disorders is 13 years, a period equivalent to the sentence imposed for a major crime. It is indeed startling to recognize that 10 percent of patients with a schizophrenic disorder will remain permanently hospitalized as severely disturbed (Bleuler, 1978).

### The Symptoms of Schizophrenia

There are several symptoms shared by the various types of schizophrenic conditions:

***Delusions.*** At least 71 percent of persons with a schizophrenic disorder have delusions, mainly of persecution, but also of grandeur, ideas of reference, or involving sexual, religious, hypochondriacal, or nihilistic content. The very first patient interviewed by the author seemed quite normal in all ways except in his answer to why he had been sent to the hospital: "Oh, the police picked me up since I wouldn't pay the toll to use the bridge over the bay" (Why didn't you pay?) "Because I didn't *need* the bridge . . . if I wanted to I could just walk on water, I'm Jesus Christ, don't you recognize me?" Delusions more common to schizophrenia than other psychotic disorders are *thought broadcasting* (My inner thoughts are being received by the whole world), *thought insertion* (Someone is controlling my thoughts, telling me what to think), *thought withdrawal* (My mind is blank, someone is siphoning off my ideas), and delusions of being controlled (Someone is manipulating me, my movements, my wants, my thoughts).

***Hallucinations.*** Auditory hallucinations are especially common. Schizophrenic hallucinations, unlike those in psychotic depressive states, tend not to involve depression or elation. Additionally, voices heard by schizophrenics tend to "talk about" the patient (We need to do something about this maniac), while in other disorders voices are said to be "talking to" the patient (You have sinned and deserve to be flayed now) (Wing, 1978).

***Thought Disorders.*** Thought associations may become bizarre, confused, with very loose connections. The introductory Case History 17–1 illustrates such thoughts. Speech can represent this disturbance of thinking in the development of neologisms (made-up words) or word-salads—sentences of unrelated words. Schizophrenic thought disturbances have been documented in the studies cited in Focus 17–1.

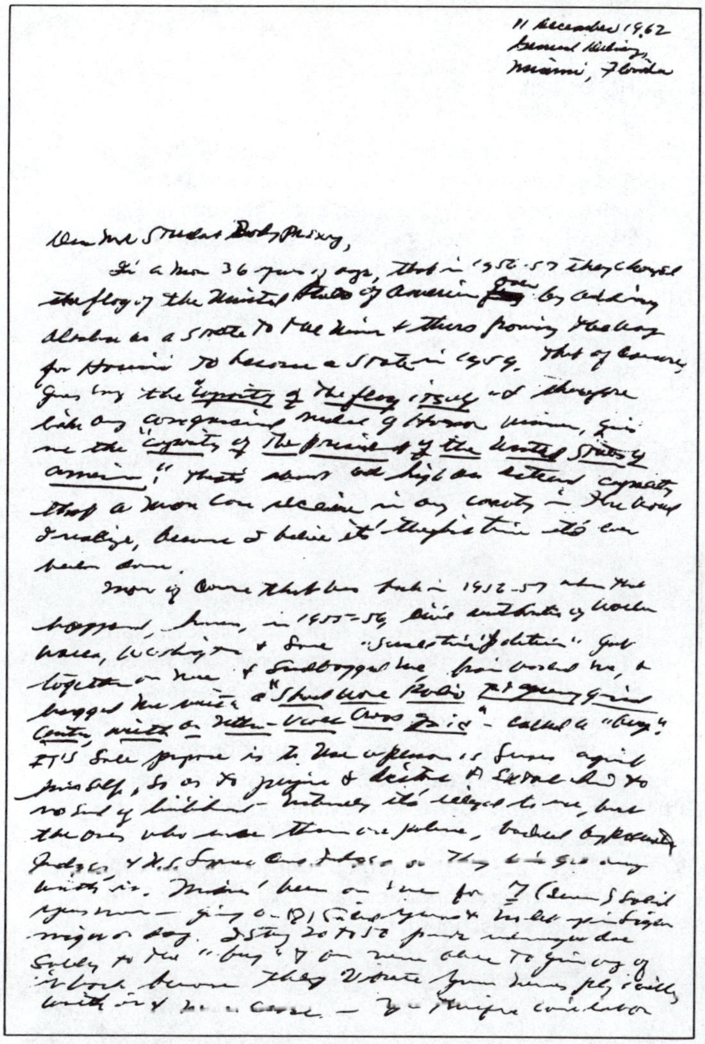

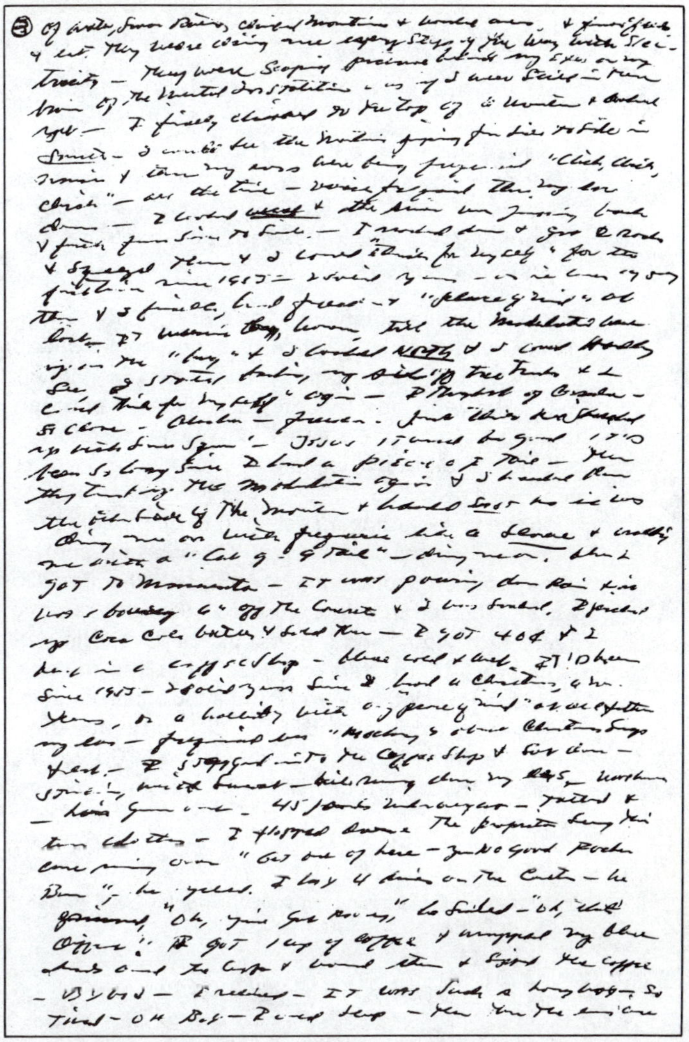

*A letter received from a mentally disturbed person illustrating delusions of **grandeur** and **persecution**. The text of the letter is as follows:*

*I'm a man 36 years of age, that in 1956–57 they changed the flag of the United States of America once by adding Alaska as a State to the Union and thus paving the way for Hawaii to become a state in 1959. That of course, gives me the "capacity of the flag itself" and therefore like any Congressional Medal of Honor winner, gives me the "capacity of the President of the United States of America," that's about as high an esteem capacity that a man can receive in any country . . . .*

*. . . in 1955–56 civil authorities . . . some "small time" politicians got together on me and sand-bagged me and brainwashed me and bugged me with a "short-wave Radio grid center, with an ultra-Violet Cross Gird" called a "bug." Its sole purpose is to use a person's senses against himself, so as to perjure and distort him to no end of humiliation . . . they vibrate your nerves physically with it and never ceases.*

*. . . I'd been there several months before they gave me "ground privileges" and once on the grounds, they started frequencing my time all the more, vibrating the back of my neck, first flicking it to the front of my face, like a "whip" or a cat of 9 tails, . . .*

# FOCUS 17–1:

## Experimental Evidence on Schizophrenia: Associational Thought

> I wish you then a good, happy, joyful, healthy, blessed and fruitful year, and many good wine-years to come, as well as a healthy and good appley-year, and sauerkraut and cabbage and squash and seed year.[1]

One notable characteristic is the presence of associational thoughts. Instead of carrying on a conversation in which thoughts are logically connected, individuals may start with one thought, associate to another, then be distracted to another, and so on. Several experimental tests have explored this tendency; two are especially revealing.

In the first, Salzinger et al. (1978) recorded monologues given by both normal persons and schizophrenic patients, preparing transcripts of the first 200 words. These transcripts were then edited to remove every fifth word, and a group of nonpsychotic persons were instructed to guess what the missing words were. Not only were the schizophrenic samples harder to predict, but the difficulty increased from the first 100 words to the second 100 words. Their ability to correctly fill in the missing word reflected the degree to which the monologue diverged from a predictable set of ideas or associations.

In the second test, Chapman and Chapman (1973) took another approach, exploring verbal associations in a vocabulary test. Consider the following problems (Rattan & Chapman, 1973):

1. *Shoot* means the same as:
   a) rifle
   b) rug
   c) sprout
2. *Scale* means the same as:
   a) pin
   b) yell
   c) climb

Two types of questions are represented. The first question includes a correct (sprout), an irrelevant (rug), and an associational (rifle) answer. The second question has only correct or irrelevant answers. On questions with associational items, persons with a schizophrenic diagnosis tested more poorly than a sample of ''dull normal'' persons; on the nonassociational questions, however, they scored as well as the control group.

In all, these research studies suggest that persons with schizophrenic disorders are very strongly influenced by inner associational experiences.

1 Quote from a greeting written to Bleuler by a patient, 1950, p.606.

***Disturbance of Emotions.*** There may be a shallowness or blunting of emotions, or emotions that are inappropriate to the circumstances. A common report is the inability to have feelings anymore, a loss of normal emotions. Or the emotions are discrepant from the circumstances at hand, such as the patient who smiled when discussing a personal tragedy.

***Disturbance of Ego Boundaries.*** The person loses a sense of personal identity or is confused about the boundaries separating the self from the rest of the world. Some refer to this as a loss of self-identity, while others refer to this as the loss of ego boundaries. An example is the patient who believed her breathing rate was tied up with cosmic forces.

***Impairment of Relationship to the Environment.*** There is often a withdrawal from contact with others and with the environment. This may be interpreted by observers as apathy, or as alienation, or as isolation, or as emotional detachment. Part of what is involved is the increasing attention by the patient to inner fantasies or associations.

***Deterioration.*** During the course of the psychosis, the schizophrenic will show behaviors that indicate a deterioration in previous ability to function. As DSM-III indicates, family and friends often observe that the person is "not the same" person that they once knew. Work competencies may be momentarily lost, social interactions become aversive, and even self-care skills may start to rapidly lose ground. The deterioration may be the result of a loss of drive, withdrawal, thought disturbances, or the presence of hallucinations.

The current view about the diagnosis of schizophrenia emphasizes that there are multiple psychological processes going on that may characterize schizophrenia. Delusions, hallucinations, thought disorders, disturbance of emotions, all reflect differing signs of such processes. Some or all of these symptoms might be present in a single case, but they are not all invariably present in all persons with schizophrenic disorders. Mark Vonnegut's writings illustrate such various symptoms, in Focus 17–2.

## The Course of Schizophrenia

The person with a schizophrenic disorder tends to go through a certain progression, although this is not always a hard-and-fast rule. During a period lasting over six months, we might be able to recognize a prodromal phase, an active phase, and a residual phase (DSM-III, 1980).

***Prodromal Phase.*** This phase involves changes in a person's behaviors that others notice. Social isolation or withdrawal is observed, or the person starts to lose interest in work or studies or other duties. Peculiar behaviors become apparent; the author had a friend whose disorder was first seen when he playfully introduced his dog to his clothes, item by item. Thought and speech begin to show signs of bizarreness, as the person may begin to adopt superstitions or become suddenly preoccupied with telepathy.

***Active Phase.*** This phase involves a full-blown psychotic disorder, with active hallucinations, loose associations, incoherence in language and disorganization of behaviors. Added to these are the special characteristics of the particular types of schizophrenic disorder, for example, the immobility of the catatonic schizophrenic disorder, the suspicion of the paranoid schizophrenic disorder, or the regressed behaviors of the disorganized schizophrenic disorder.

***Residual Phase.*** This phase sometimes follows the active phase and involves some reduction of the severity of the symptoms. Hallucinations or delusions may still be present, but the person seems less reactive to them. In fact, emotional blunting is the common feature of this phase. The residual phase is neither a recovery from nor a remission of the disorder; a spontaneous recovery is possible but considered quite rare.

## Types of Schizophrenia

The three DSM-III types of schizophrenia will be discussed in the next sections, namely:

- Schizophrenic disorder, disorganized type
- Schizophrenic disorder, catatonic type
- Schizophrenic disorder, paranoid type

# FOCUS 17–2:
## The Personal Experience of Being Schizophrenic

Mark Vonnegut experienced a schizophrenic disorder, recovered, then shared his recall in a remarkable book, *The Eden Express* (1975). The following excerpts give a first-hand flavor of what it is like to go through a schizophrenic episode and drug therapy.

On perceptual distortions

> I was completely absorbed in the sawdust floating gently to the ground . . . the incredible patterns in the bark. . . . Everything stretched infinitely in all directions. Suddenly it seemed as if everything was slowing down and I would never finish sawing the limb. . . . It seemed I had been working for hours and hours but the sun hadn't moved at all.
>
> I began wondering if I was hurting the trees and found myself apologizing. Each tree began to take on personality. I began to wonder if any of them liked me. I became completely absorbed in looking at each tree and began to notice that they were ever so slightly luminescent, shining with a soft inner light that played around the branches (p. 99).

On auditory hallucinations

> *The Voices.* Testing one, two, testing one. Checking out the circuits: ''What hath God wrought. Yip di mina di zonda za da boom di yaidi yoohoo. . . .''
>
> At first I'd had to strain to hear or understand them. They were soft and working with some pretty tricky codes. Snap-crackle-pops, the sound of the wind with blinking lights and horns for punctuation. I broke the code and somehow was able to internalize it to the point where it was just like hearing words. . . . Once you hear the voices, you realize they've always been there. It's just a matter of being tuned to them (p. 136).

On the side effects of Thorazine medication

> Thorazine has lots of unpleasant side effects. It makes you groggy, lowers your blood pressure, making you dizzy and faint when you stand up too quickly. If you go out in the sun, your skin gets red and hurts like hell. It makes muscles rigid and twitchy.
>
> The side effects were bad enough, but I liked what the drug was supposed to do even less. It's supposed to keep you calm, dull, uninterested and uninteresting. . . .
>
> What the drug is supposed to do is keep away hallucinations. What I think it does is just fog up your mind so badly you don't notice the hallucinations or much else. . . .
>
> On Thorazine everything's a bore. . . . You can read comic books and *Reader's Digest* forever. You can tolerate talking to jerks forever. Babble, babble, babble. The weather is dull, the flowers are dull, nothing's very impressive (pp. 196–97).

Although we will not discuss them, two other types of schizophrenia are also recognized. If a patient shows continuing evidence of schizophrenic symptoms but of a milder nature, then the term *schizophrenic disorder, residual type* is used. Further, if a patient shows the schizophrenic symptoms of delusions, hallucinations, or incoherence, but none of the characteristics of the disorganized, catatonic, or paranoid types then the diagnosis *schizophrenic disorder, undifferentiated type* would be used (Berner et al., 1983).

***An Alternate Classification of Schizophrenic Disorders.*** Although the label *schizophrenia* (and the disorganized, catatonic, and paranoid types) has been in common acceptance, another point of view has been acknowledged. From this viewpoint, it may be more accurate to divide the disorder into two very different groups: a reactive schizophrenia and a process schizophrenia. This distinction does not deny that the DSM-III types are valid, but calls attention to some interesting research (McNeil & Kaiji, 1978). In this research, some schizophrenic persons have been identified who share the following histories: early psychological trauma, a poor home environment, and unstable prepsychotic personality, and severe deterioration once the schizophrenic symptoms appear. These have been labeled as process schizophrenics. Other persons with a schizophrenic disorder have been identified with different histories, these being: symptoms which developed suddenly, a normal adolescence, a normal family background, and schizophrenic symptoms which tend to improve rather quickly (within a few weeks). From these differing histories, it has been hypothesized that the process schizophrenia represents the classical type—an inherited, organic disease that has an insidious onset that inexorably progresses toward deterioration. The reactive schizophrenia is hypothesized, on the other hand, as representing a disorder with an altogether different origin, as seen in its sudden onset, limited symptoms, and good response to treatment. To date, the process-reactive terminology has not been widely adopted; instead, DSM-III accepts the more traditional types.

***Schizophrenic Disorder, Disorganized Type.*** The disorganized type of schizophrenia was once called *hebephrenic schizophrenia* by Kraepelin. Today it is recognized as the form of schizophrenia showing the most disorganization of normal behavioral patterns. These types of persons are known for their childish silliness and incoherence. They show uncontrollable fits of giggling, uninhibited gestures, and grotesque grimaces. Such bizarre behavior often makes others uncomfortable because it is so unlike the controlled and meaningful actions of others, even other patients. The thoughts and activities of persons with disorganized schizophrenia appear totally without sense—as if a harlequin were deliberately mimicking madness. Speech patterns reflect the severity of the personality disturbance as the patient babbles incoherently, uses neologisms, or repeats words or meaningless phrases. As with Edna in Case History 17–2, the person often seems to be totally in a private world with private meanings. The individual may laugh hilariously for hours or smile secretly when asked a question (Tissot et al., 1980). Hallucinations do occur, typically seeming to evoke pleasant reactions; but hallucinations seem to lack any coherent theme. Systematic delusions are generally absent other than fragmented ones. One example of an incoherent delusion is recalled by Romano (1978) from his early training to illustrate what he called the "central core of madness."

> Since (the patient) would not eat, he had to be tube-fed daily. On each occasion he had to be tube-fed twice, because after the first feeding, he would vomit. After the second feeding, the food would stay down. When I asked, "Why do you vomit?" the patient answered, "Because I have no stomach." I replied, "Well, the second time I feed you the food stays down, where does it go if you have no stomach?" Almost immediately the patient answered, "It goes to the upper peninsula." I tried as best I could to trace this idea to its source, to look for related ideas through a detailed review with the patient and his family of his past and present life history, through the use of projective tests, from his infrequent spontaneous remarks, and even by pondering over fragments of occasional dreams he recounted to me; but to no avail. It remained enigmatic, strange, nonunderstandable. (p. 1)

Obscenities and feces smearing are likely symptoms. One is tempted to compare the person with a disorganized schizophrenic disorder to a very young child in temperament, poor self-control, and behavior. Regrettably this form of schizophrenia is one with an

## Case History 17–2:
### Schizophrenic Disorder, Disorganized Type

Edna K. is a 45-year-old wife of a laborer. Her illness had progressed rapidly and she was quite severely disturbed by the time she was admitted to a hospital. It was impossible to obtain a meaningful description of her condition directly from her. The following is an excerpt from her intake interview:

Dr.: I am Dr. ______. I would like to know something more about you.

Edna: You have a nasty mind. Lord, Lord! Cat's in a cradle.

Dr.: Tell me, how do you feel?

Edna: London's bell is a long, long dock. Hee! Hee! Hee! [giggles uncontrollably]

Dr.: Do you know where you are now?

Edna: D--n! S--t on you all who rip into my internals! The grugerometer will take care of you all! [shouting] I am the Queen, see my magic, I shall turn you all into smidgelings forever!

Dr.: Your husband is concerned about you. Do you know his name?

Edna: [Stands, walks to and faces the wall] Who am I, Who are we, Who are you. Who are they. [turns] I . . . I . . . I . . . I!!! [makes grotesque faces].

Edna was placed in the women's ward where she proceeded to masturbate. She always sat in a chosen spot and in a chosen way, with her feet propped under her. Occasionally, she would scream or shout obscenities; at other times she giggled to herself. She was known to attack other patients. She began to complain that her uterus was attached to a "pipeline to the Kremlin" and that she was being "internally invaded" by Communism.

Edna was placed on an EST schedule and showed some improvement after a few treatments. However, she relapsed within a week and began actively hallucinating. In lucid moments, she described her experience as including a vague sensation of being enveloped by a "cosmic cloak" of power and majesty which would suddenly burst into fragments, each dissolving or being transformed into hideous insects. She was tried on massive doses of Thorazine (chlorpromazine) and is showing gradual improvement.

early onset and one unlikely to show periods of improvements during its progress.

***Schizophrenic Disorder, Catatonic Type.*** This is possibly the most dramatic form of schizophrenia. The disturbance is exhibited primarily in motor symptoms, as individuals may show a stuporous condition, display excitement, or alternate between the two extremes. During the *catatonic stupor*, these persons seem to be in a state of physical suspension. They are usually mute, unresponsive to even uncomfortable stimulation, and immobile. They may have to be tube-fed and assisted with bladder and bowel movement. Saliva can sometimes be observed dribbling out of the mouth as the individual does not swallow. The immobility may take the form of retention of a fixed position (*catalepsy*) or the retention of any posture in which someone else places them (*waxy flexibility*), as in Case History 17-3. The phenomenon of waxy flexibility has an unbelievable quality—individuals will remain holding awkward, and what appears to be physically impossible, positions for hours. This extreme suggestibility is also noticeable in speech. These individuals may demonstrate *echolalia*, repeating everything they hear. On the other hand, the opposite may occur and the individuals may instead show an extreme *catatonic negativism* or *catatonic rigidity*. Instead of doing what they are told to do, they resist instructions (negativism); instead of being molded into a new position, they maintain a rigid, unmoving posture (rigidity). An apathetic contrariness seems to replace the suggestibility. There is some evidence that catatonics may be highly aware of their surroundings rather than inattentive during the stuporous condition. Some persons later report that they heard with extreme acuity although they had failed to show any earlier outward evidence of their alertness.

The person showing the catatonic disorder may

**TABLE 17–2**

**Characteristics Differentiating Process from Reactive Schizophrenia**

| *Process Schizophrenia* | *Reactive Schizophrenia* |
|---|---|
| Birth to the fifth year | |
| a. Early psychological trauma | a. Good psychological history |
| b. Physical illness—severe or long | b. Good physical health |
| c. Odd member of family | c. Normal member of family |
| Fifth year to adolescence | |
| a. Difficulties at school | a. Well adjusted at school |
| b. Family troubles paralleled by sudden changes in patient's behavior | b. Domestic troubles unaccompanied by behavior disruptions; patient "had what it took" |
| c. Introverted behavior trends and interests | c. Extroverted behavior trends and interests |
| d. History of breakdown of social, physical, mental functioning | d. History of adequate social, physical, mental functioning |
| e. Pathological siblings | e. Normal siblings |
| f. Overprotective or rejecting mother, "momism" | f. Normally protective, accepting mother |
| g. Rejecting father | g. Accepting father |
| Adolescence to adulthood | |
| a. Insidious, gradual onset of psychosis without pertinent stress | a. Sudden onset of psychosis; stress present and pertinent; later onset |
| b. Physical aggression | b. Verbal aggression |
| c. Poor response to treatment | c. Good response to treatment |
| d. Lengthy stay in hospital | d. Short course in hospital |

SOURCE: Adapted from "Process and Reactive Schizophrenia" by R. Kantor, J. Wallner, and C. Winder, 1953, *Journal of Consulting Psychology, 17,* p. 157.

recover from the stuporous stage and go into a *catatonic excitement.* This stage is characterized by violent aggressive and destructive outbursts. The inhibited, immobile, quiet phase is suddenly shattered by impulsive, intense, noisy, agitated movement. The stuporous person may suffer injury in limbs stiff and swollen from their long immobility or circulation cutoff from awkward postures; the excited person may suffer injury during a fit of self-destructive frenzy or an attack on the environment. Despite the seemingly severe state that must seem present when one reviews the stuporous and excitement symptoms, catatonic schizophrenia has a much better outlook for recovery than any other type of schizophrenia.

***Schizophrenic Disorder, Paranoid Type.*** *Paranoid schizophrenia* is the most common form of the schizophrenic disorders. These persons tend to be, on the average, brighter than persons with other schizophrenic disorders; however, because of their mental breakdown they are also often unable to make full use of their intellect (Magaro et al., 1981). As the term suggests, persons suffering from a paranoid schizophrenic disorder are most distinguishable for their delusions. The delusions are more often the persecutory variety with the patients believing that they are the center of a carefully devised plot. The case of Ben, in Case History 17–4, illustrates such delusions. They may believe that the communists are after them, or the FBI, or gangsters or dope peddlers, or a secret society. They might complain that the food is being slowly poisoned, or that they are being followed, talked about, or controlled by strange scientific equipment such as an "automatic electric cosmic-ray machine." The individual

## Case History 17–3:
### Schizophrenic Disorder, Catatonic Type

Manuel A. is a catatonic patient, chronically disturbed, who has been hospitalized for years. He had been a transient farm laborer, one of many who eked out a living traveling from state to state following the crops. After one particularly long, hot journey, he collapsed from what seemed to be sheer exhaustion. It was discovered that he had gradually become seclusive, staying off by himself and eating little. Most thought he was meditating as he had recently "got religious ideas." He had been seen sitting on the running board of his old car gazing off into the distance. It was from this position that he slowly fell and subsequently was taken to the hospital.

Except for some signs of fatigue and a typical transient worker's dietary deficiency, Manuel appeared physically healthy. Yet, he was unaware of his surroundings, remaining motionless, speechless, and seemingly unconscious. One evening an aide turned him on his side to straighten out the sheet, was called away to tend another patient, and forgot to return. Manuel was found the next morning, still on his side, just as he had been left the night before. His arm was turning blue from lack of circulation but he seemed to be experiencing no discomfort. Further examination confirmed that he was in the state of waxy flexibility of catatonic schizophrenia.

Manuel gradually appeared to recover. His body showed more muscle tone as he would occasionally change position. He was somewhat more responsive to others although he was echolalic, repeating phrases which others addressed to him. Within a few months he was able to communicate intelligibly. He described the onset of his illness as starting with a supernatural feeling of being flooded with omniscience. He saw "through and beyond" the surface of objects, with visions occurring one after another as if in a picture slide show. He felt as if he were transported from his earthly surroundings into a transitional space where he sometimes saw his own features, which were consecutively realistic, blurred, demoniacal, majestic, and undefinably mystical.

These experiences began to recede slowly and he soon became aware of sounds at a distance. They seemed vaguely familiar, yet unidentifiable. He tried to concentrate all his attention on them but found them elusive. Gradually, the sounds arranged themselves in order, and he found himself hearing words for the first time since his breakdown. He was still more fascinated by their quality than their meaning. However, before long he was able to regain the experiences which had so fascinated him.

might also possess delusions of grandeur, for instance, a belief of having royal ancestors. In a sense, the delusion of grandeur and the delusion of persecution go hand in hand. Being persecuted implies that one is special enough to be the center of all the attention. The corporate establishment is after you because you have the secret to a revolutionary process, someone is trying to control your thoughts because you have great hidden powers, the secret society is after you perhaps because you are possessed of dangerous knowledge. After all, the patient may think, they persecuted Jesus Christ, plotted against the mighty Caesars, and assassinated the president. It is only a short step for these patients to begin believing that they are someone really special, perhaps a prophet, a disciple, or even Jesus Christ returned. The opposite delusional development might occur, starting with the delusion of grandeur and progressing toward persecutory beliefs. In this event, the adage "Uneasy lies the head that wears the crown" applies. The individuals believe themselves to be important, and soon develop the insight that a plot is underway to dethrone them. Sirhan Sirhan, the assassin of Senator Robert F. Kennedy, was suffering from a paranoid schizophrenic disorder and preoccupied with the delusion that he was to be the savior of the Arab people. There is also evidence that he experienced spells of terror released under hypnosis.

The person with a paranoid schizophrenic disorder shows major disturbance in functioning and is unable to carry on long without treatment. Hallucinations are common in paranoid schizophrenia, often taking the form of vivid auditory hallucinations. Voices

Sirhan Sirhan, the assassin of Senator Robert Kennedy, was a paranoid schizophrenic. His notebook said Kennedy must be assassinated.

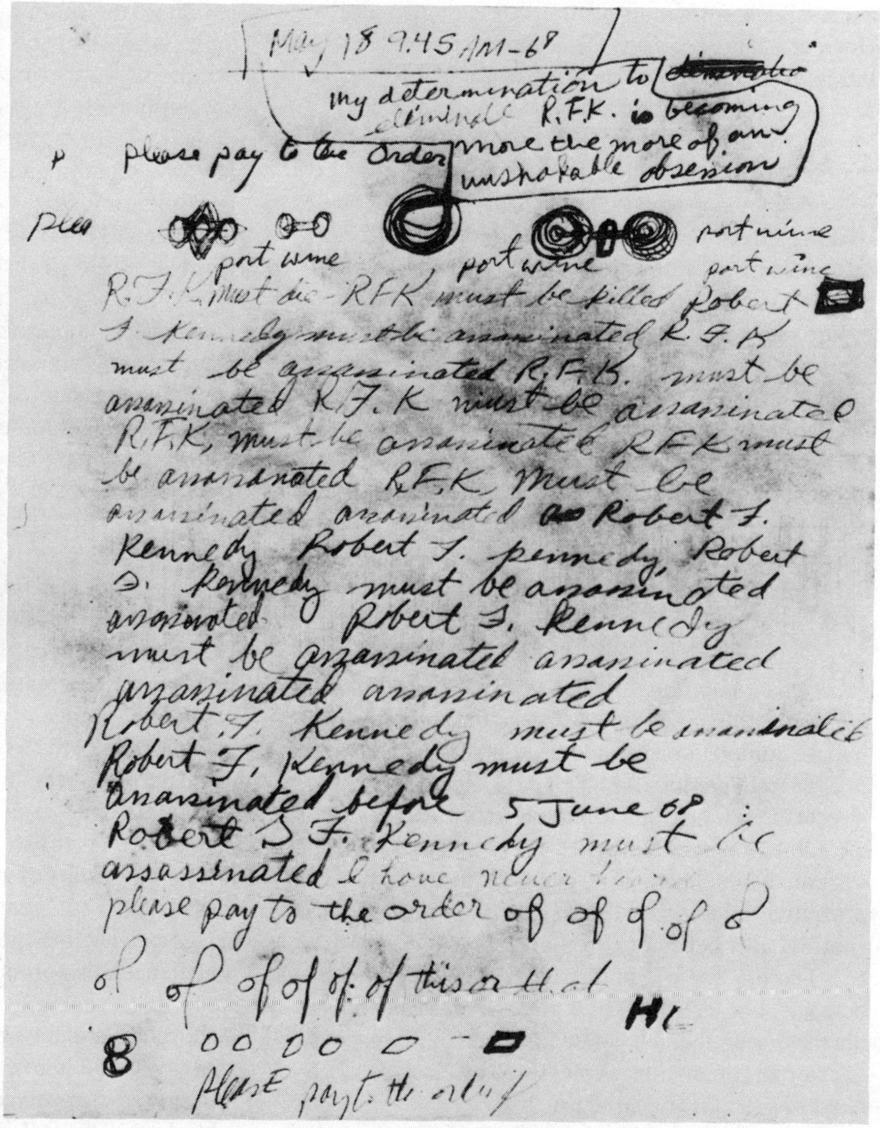


speak to the patient, commanding or cursing him. The individual may become destructive or homicidal in response to these hallucinations or delusions. In spite of these suspicious and often antagonistic attitudes, the person with a paranoid schizophrenic disorder is still more in contact with the environment than other schizophrenic types. In a way, the disorganized schizophrenic disorders *ignore* all but their own peculiar environment, the catatonic disorders *inhibit* their spontaneous reaction to the environment, and the paranoid disorders *grip* and warily inspect the environment in their delusion.

## Dynamics of Schizophrenia

Schizophrenia, under one name or another, has been recognized for more than 60 years; yet there is still no conclusive information on the cause of the illness. However, there are many clues and more scientifically sound evidence today than there was when Kraepelin first organized attention around dementia praecox.

As we saw in Part 1 of this text, both genetics and the family environment seem to be involved to a very great degree in many cases of schizophrenia. Because we have already explored these two important factors to some extent, we will look first at some physiological, cultural, existential, and psychodynamic factors before returning to a discussion of genetics and family setting.

***Physiological Factors.*** A considerable amount of research has explored possible links between physiological factors and schizophrenia. Some studies focus on the brain itself and neurological responses; others look for a relationship between toxic substances and the disorder. Others look elsewhere still, as in Focus 17–3.

*Protective Inhibition.* The theory of *protective inhibition,* by Ivan Pavlov, suggests that prolonged or intense stimulation can induce an inhibitory response in the cerebral cortex.

This view sees the catatonic stupor as a result of the inhibition spreading to the sympathetic nervous system, while catatonic excitement results from the protective inhibition's depression of normal cortical controls over behavior (Epstein & Coleman, 1970).

There is some data that lends support to this hypothesis. For instance, some persons with schizophrenia have been found to show impaired brain response to external stimulation, as measured by electroencephalograms (EEG) (Buchsbaum, 1980).

A second finding has been that attention, as measured by the ability to visually track a target, seems defective in 65 to 80 percent of schizophrenics (Gjerde, 1983). These persons also tend to display a lowered ability to attend to tasks that require ignoring irrelevant details and concentrating (Adams et al., 1981). Further studies of attention are described in Focus 17–4.

*Imbalances in the "Pleasure Center"?* Other investigations have studied the septal region of the brain. Heath and his colleagues noted abnormal EEG readings from electrodes directly implanted in the septal region of the brain of persons with psychotic symptoms. Abnormal spikes appeared when the psychotic symptoms were exacerbated, either through the use of psychomimetic drugs or through direct electrical stimulation (Heath & Guerrero-Figueroa, 1965).

The septal region has sometimes been nicknamed the "pleasure center of the brain"—after the finding that rats will continue to perform where their only reward is an electrical shock to the septal region. Meehl (1962) has proposed that persons with schizophrenia may have an imbalance between pleasure and aversive centers in the brain such that the aversive areas overcome the pleasure centers during activities involving interactions with other persons. Pleasure thereby becomes restricted to cognitive or aesthetic, that is, noninterpersonal experiences.

*Chemical Substances.* We touched on some of the theories of toxic substances or chemical imbalances in Chapter 4; such information relating to schizophrenia deserves to be briefly recalled here.

As we saw earlier, biochemical toxins such as taraxein have been considered as possible sources of schizophrenia. Such hypotheses have received support from the discovery that certain drugs, such as LSD and mescaline, can, in fact, produce psychoticlike symptoms when taken. Unfortunately, there are uncertainties in the results of such studies such that this line of theorizing is still considered inconclusive.

A related direction has been to determine whether imbalances in normal body substances might be responsible. Among such substances have been included endorphins and the neurotransmitters, norepinephrine and dopamine (Crow, 1983). To date, the neurotransmitters have received the most attention. Some researchers suggest that excess levels of these two transmitters might be involved in schizophrenia (see pp. 97–100 for our prior discussion of details) (Snyder, 1981, Berger, 1981). A rather interesting hypothesis involves yet another physiological process, the metabolism of glucose. The study of glucose metabolism has been made possible by the *positron emission transaxial tomography (PETT) scanner,* a million dollar instrument that is a version of the CAT scan (computerized axial tomography scan), which we will see mentioned for brain damage diagnosis in Chapter 18. Both instruments combine an X-ray-type method with

# Case History 17–4:
## Schizophrenic Disorder, Paranoid Type

Ben K. is a 20-year-old senior in college who was within three credits of finishing a degree in psychology when he was hospitalized. Ben had been raised in a ''schismatic'' family in which the parents were continuously arguing and blaming one another. He himself was often punished for inadequacies which were really the fault of his parents. It was as if neither parent could tolerate admitting their own basic mistakes, large or small. As an adolescent, Ben sometimes wished that he could run away and leave both his parents to their mutual miseries, but he found himself unable to do more than fantasize. He left home to attend a nearby state college and found himself still under their influence. He was always fearful of what they might do if he did not do well in his studies, if he dated someone they did not approve of, if he failed to return on weekends. He was one of many persons motivated to achieve because he was afraid of failure. He seemed congenitally unable to express anger for fear that he would prove to be unjustified in it and thereby subject to further reprimand. He enrolled as a psychology major in hopes of improving his adjustment; he found, however, that his knowledge did not automatically improve his life adjustment.

Ben acquired a temporary Christmas job in the post office. His task was to sort and place mail into boxes rented by customers. During this work, he began to feel quite worried about his midsemester examinations which had just been completed. He was certain he had done well on them but he had the same feeling of confidence before and had been disappointed. It was while he was thus ruminating that he became aware of the disappearance of a letter from a mailbox that he had filled. He did not recall seeing anyone take the letter out and was certain that he had been alert. For the next week he alternated between worrying about his grades and speculating about the missing letter. Then he was beset with an insight: the letter was top secret material, and the post office was a messenger station. He called the FBI and conveyed his message—the disappearance of the letter without his seeing anyone nearby. The FBI agent seemed unconcerned. Ben felt rebuffed and wrestled with his concern that something be done. Then he realized that the lack of concern of the FBI was a clue in itself—the federal agency was part of the plot. This development gave him a keen sense of anticipation and satisfaction until he recognized the enormity of the situation. He had given himself away by the telephone call and was now exposed to personal danger. He recalled hearing that the communists had infiltrated the FBI and now had proof of this. He wanted to immediately quit his job but was afraid that this might be too suspicious. He wanted to confide in someone but knew that no one could be trusted.

He was soon amazed at the number of clues he now became aware of which he had been ignorant of before his insight. Secret agents were posted in every corner to watch him; he could identify them because whenever he looked sharply at one, the agent would appear to be occupied with something else. Magazines with sexy pictures began to appear on the stands as a means of trapping him so that he could be arrested as a sex pervert. He soon began to take delight at uncovering their traps and frustrating their attempts. Then one morning he experienced a slight sense of grogginess on getting out of bed, a sure sign, he thought, of a secret weapon at work. He reasoned that it was some kind of ultra-ray machine turned on his soul in the midst of night while he slept. In fact, he actually began to feel parts of his brain disintegrating to dust in his head.

Ben began to hear strange voices in the air as if several people were talking at once on a telephone party line. These voices appeared loudest during the day, and particularly when he was trying to concentrate on his school work. He finally could not bear up with this last persecutory action any further and ran to the college counseling center for help. His major complaint: the spies were trying to drive him to insanity and he wanted help to overcome their efforts. Ben was referred to the state hospital for psychiatric treatment. He has a moderately good chance for recovery, but he is at this date still delusional and believes that the counseling center has also been infiltrated by his ''enemies'' and that the hospitalization is really incarceration.

# FOCUS 17–3:

## Experimental Evidence on Schizophrenia: A Hemispheric Communications Gap?

In normal functioning, there seems to be an interaction between the left and right hemispheres of the brain, so that the information being processed balances between the two hemispheres and one area does not overreact. This may not be so in some cases of schizophrenia. One hypothesis is that individuals with this disorder may not have good communication between the hemispheres of the brain (Walker & McGuire, 1982).

A study by Green (1978) tested this hypothesis. Both a schizophrenic group and a control group were required to learn a sorting task; they were given feedback about accuracy by taps on the hand. Sometimes the tap was on the hand doing the sorting, and sometimes it was on the opposite hand (to test hemispheric transfer of information). The results: the schizophrenic group did more poorly where feedback was sent to the opposite hemisphere.

Although quite tentative, Shimkunas (1978) has interpreted findings such as those of Green to mean that schizophrenics suffer in hemispheric integration. In addition, Shimkunas also postulates that differences in schizophrenic symptoms may reflect which hemisphere is affected. As the drawing shows, the two hemispheres seem to carry out different functions. Thus, if the left hemisphere is overexcited, then language, conceptual reasoning, and attentional information processing will be influenced. If the right hemisphere is overexcited, then perceptual and emotional symptoms such as hallucinations are evidenced. The failure of the hemispheres to integrate properly would explain the schizophrenic symptom of a mismatch between emotions and speech, such as inappropriate affect. It is Shimkunas' premise that the prodromal stage of schizophrenia represents the excitation of the left hemisphere, while the active stage involves the right hemisphere.

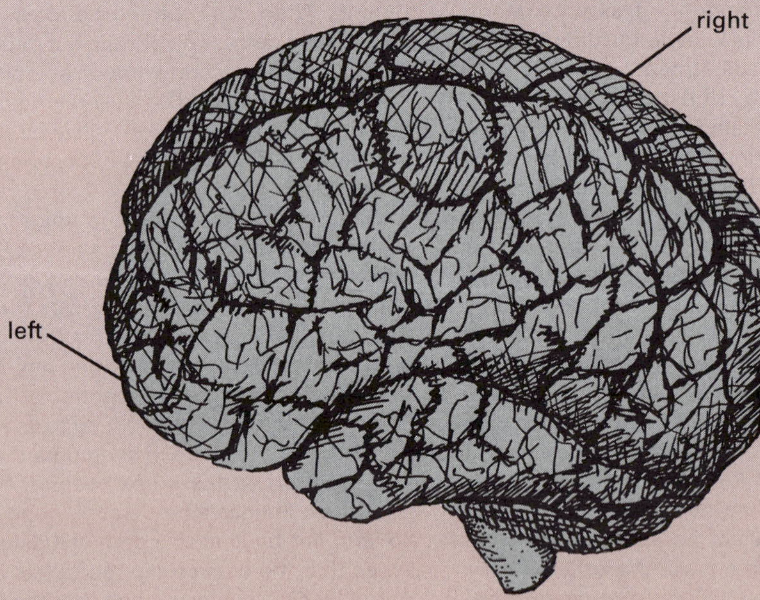

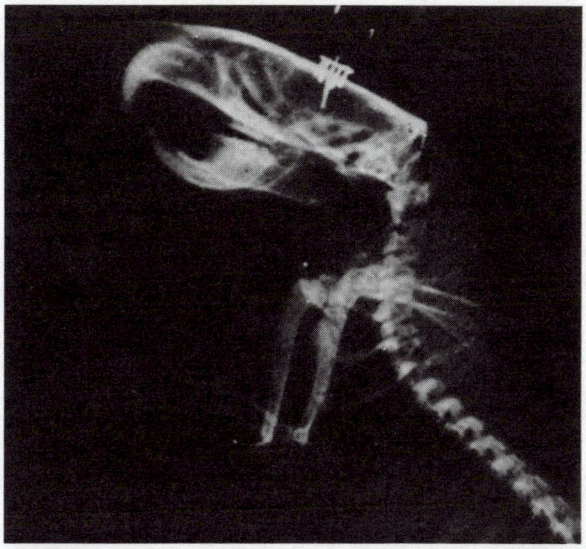

*Animal research involving electrode implants has identified the* ***septal region*** *of the brain as an important area in emotions. The x-ray photograph (left) shows the implanted electrodes in a rat brain. The animal (right) is depressing a treadle to obtain electrical stimulation of the brain; some animals will shock themselves for 24 hours without rest and as often as 5000 times an hour.*

computer technology, such that the computer re-creates cross-sectional images of the brain. In the PETT scan, a compound is either injected or inhaled and is followed through various stages in the brain (Rottenberg & Cooper, 1981; Tanaka et al., 1981). The brain depends on glucose for most of its energy. Findings are still limited, but researchers suggest that schizophrenics show less use of glucose in their frontal lobes, less use of glucose in their left cortex than their right, and also less glucose in the left side of the basal ganglion (a portion of the brain deep within the center) than the right. The first finding is consistent with long-held beliefs that the frontal lobes have some responsibility for symptoms among schizophrenics; in fact, prefrontal lobotomy—the surgical separation of the frontal lobes—is sometimes used as a treatment technique (as we will see in Chapter 22).

The finding that schizophrenics use less glucose in their left hemisphere is also consistent with other findings: for instance, the discovery that there may be an inadequate communication between hemispheres (see Focus 17–3). Finally, the discovery of the abnormal metabolism in the basal ganglion is interesting since this is a region of the brain in which dopamine activity is important, and we have seen that dopamine disturbance has been speculated as involved in schizophrenia. The PETT scan has also been the source of speculations about the association of glucose metabolism and other disorders as well. For instance, a low rate of glucose metabolism in the brain has been reported for senile dementia, a disorder associated with aging, and involving memory loss, changes in personality, and motor difficulties (which we will present in detail in Chapter 18). It has also been reported that during the manic phase of bipolar disorder, these people show a higher glucose utilization than normal persons (Dagani, 1981).

***Cultural Factors.*** Sociocultural factors have also come under investigation as possible contributors to schizophrenia. Social class has been examined as one possible variable, dating back to the classic work of Faris and Dunham (1939), which was cited in Chapter 5. This study and others showed a high incidence of

## FOCUS 17–4:

### Experimental Evidence on Schizophrenia: Distractibility

Are persons diagnosed as schizophrenic more distractible and unable to attend to information as well as others? Two experimental studies suggest some tentative answers to this question.

Oltmanns et al. (1978) tested the ability of schizophrenic persons to listen to numbers being read to them in a series and to ignore irrelevant information. The numbers were presented under either a no-distraction condition or a distraction condition (in the latter, the numbers were interspersed with irrelevant digits). The results showed schizophrenic persons to score just as well as control subjects under the no-distraction condition; however, they fared far more poorly under the distraction condition.

Asarnow and colleagues (1977) wondered whether differences in distractibility could be detected even before symptoms of schizophrenia developed. They tried to answer that question by studying high-risk children (children whose biological mothers had already been diagnosed as schizophrenic). A test of attention required the children to say if a "T" or an "F" was flashed on a screen—a rather simple test that was made more difficult by the inclusion of irrelevant additional letters as distractors. Their findings: the high-risk children's performance decreased markedly as irrelevant distractors increased.

These two studies seem to suggest that persons with schizophrenia may be less able to narrow their focus of attention than are most people (Baribeau-Braun et al., 1983). Instead, they seem more compelled to respond indiscriminately to environmental cues.

schizophrenia in those parts of the city marked by low economic status or in persons of lower social class.

Social class could contribute to the etiology of schizophrenia through any number of channels: through the communication of prescribed attitudes of ways of living and adapting; through exposure to stresses and trauma particularly associated with lower economic status; through the frustrations of limited attainment; or through the shaping of an inadequate self-concept by the low-status, low-prestige aspect of one's social class.

Since schizophrenia has been known to occur in all parts of the world, cross-cultural research is available (Draguns, 1980). Benedict (1958) did an exhaustive review of research in a number of cultures;[2] he makes several relevant conclusions. First, schizophrenia is not only a disorder of civilization but appears in primitive, nonliterate cultures as well. Second, Europeans appear to require hospitalization more than do persons in more primitive cultures, perhaps because the Western culture makes it more difficult to adjust without the protection of an institution. Primitive societies, on the other hand, may demand less complex skills and contributions, may be more tolerant of bizarre behavior, and may even condone such bizarreness in their own religio-magical rituals.

A third finding is that in primitive cultures, symptoms of schizophrenia tend to be of the more disintegrated type of the disorder. States of excitement and confusion are more common than are the systematized, intact varieties of the disorder, such as the paranoid schizophrenia we see in Western cultures (Shapiro, 1981).

***Social Pressures: the Existential View.*** Another view looks at societal factors, not just as an influence on schizophrenia, but as the source of mental disturbance. The existential psychiatrist R. D. Laing (1964) challenges the concept of schizophrenic behaviors as evidence of pathology. As we saw in the Focus on Mental Disorder: Is It a Myth? (Focus 1-5) Laing and T. S. Szasz make two essential points: first, that the activities of the "schizophrenic" may be more sane than their diagnostic label implies, and second, that our own society's attitudes must be questioned. Laing theorizes that our society forces social conformity, turns us away from our true inner values and requires adopting less meaningful pursuits—adopting a false self. When a person reaches the stage of being unable to carry on with this masquerade, then the socially required facade is dropped, distorted values are discarded, and the person withdraws from society. The individual begins a search for a more authentic identity to replace the social self which has now crumbled. The symptoms of schizophrenia reflect this regression and retreat as the person seeks a more meaningful existential reality. In this way, schizophrenia is a natural attempt at self-healing.

Laing has received support and encouragement from others such as Szasz who believe it is time to examine the assumptions promoted by our society. Laing and Szasz argue that labeling a person as mentally ill or schizophrenic is in itself damaging, since such labels precipitate many prejudices. In addition, they question whether labeling the schizophrenic as mentally ill is simply a way of sanctioning society's actions of imprisoning such persons in institutions. The psychiatrist, definitions of mental illness, and the legal system all form an implicit conspiracy that justifies incarcerating those persons who do not conform to society's behavioral norms.

***Psychodynamic Factors.*** Other views of schizophrenia offer a range of psychological explanations.

Meyer (1948) was truly committed to a psychological approach, viewing the disorder as the end result of an accumulation of faulty habits over the years. This longitudinal approach saw the patient reacting to failures in life by subterfuges such as daydreaming, brooding, withdrawal of interest. These trivial habits become more and more relied on and soon substitute for more adjustive habits. Eventually, they become extreme and turn into the symptoms of schizophrenia.

A dynamic formulation was offered by Freud (1914), who viewed hallucinations as an unsuccessful attempt by the ego to reject an unbearable wish, which returns in the form of a hallucination. Schizophrenia is understood as a withdrawal of libido from the external

2 These included cultures of Africa, American Indians, Formosa, Japan, Fiji, East India, Micronesia, China, Hawaii, as well as Blacks in Latin and South America, and displaced persons and immigrants in the United States and Canada.

world, and the alliance of the ego with the id as the ego now rejects its service to reality and alters reality.

*Anxiety and Defenses.* Anxiety also plays an important role in schizophrenia. Arieti (1955) analyzed the psychosis as "*a specific reaction to an extremely severe state of anxiety, originated in childhood, reactivated later in life.*" We can view schizophrenia as an attempt—although self-defeating—to cope with the threats of overwhelming anxiety. As a child, the person experiences a series of stresses, perhaps from traumas, or from a conflict-ridden family atmosphere. Withdrawal serves as a momentary escape from these conditions; projection enables the avoidance of threatening needs. Delusions and hallucinations also enable escaping decisions since the delusions and hallucinations now command actions.

Because these defenses are inadequate, the person experiences increasingly high levels of anxiety. Intermittent frenzied attempts may be made to fight off personality disintegration. But when all else fails, the person finally withdraws entirely into a world of hallucinatory wish-fulfillment and undemanding existence.

In addition to the several factors discussed earlier, two more explanations seem especially relevant to the development of schizophrenic conditions. These explanations focus on heredity and family setting.

**Genetic Factors.** We saw in Chapter 4 that there is considerable evidence linking genetics and schizophrenia. Readers are referred back especially to Table 4–2. To summarize briefly:

- The offspring of two schizophrenic parents are 35 to 45 times more likely to develop schizophrenia than are offspring of normal parents.
- With one schizophrenic parent, the risk of a child's becoming schizophrenic is still over 10 times that of the normal union.
- The incidence of schizophrenia in relatives of a schizophrenic person increases rapidly the closer the blood relationship. Thus, full siblings show a 10 percent, dizygotic twins show a 17 percent, and monozygotic twins show a 50 percent concordance. Monozygotic twins rate closely on a number of personality measures, as Figure 17–1 indicates. Even when they have been reared in different home environments, incidence rates for schizophrenia have still been impressive—78 percent of twins share a schizophrenic breakdown.

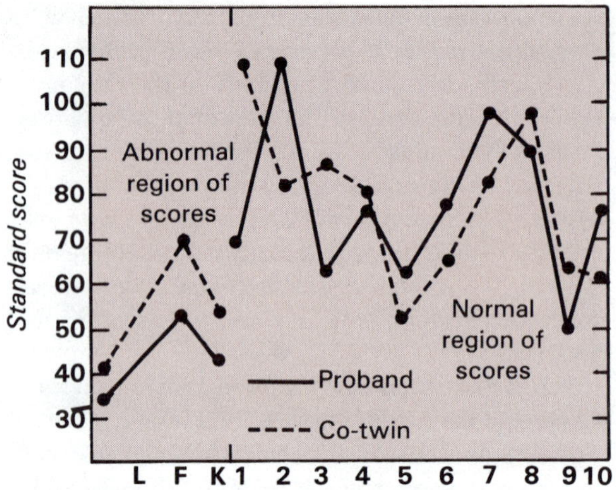


**FIGURE 17–1** Personality test profile of an identical twin pair showing the marked similarity of traits. Code: The higher the score, the greater the degree of pathology. L, F, K-Validity scales; 1-Hypochondriasis; 2-Depression; 3-Hysteria; 4-Psychopathic deviate; 5-Masculine/feminine interests; 6-Paranoia; 7-Psychasthenia; 8-Schizophrenia; 9-Social introversion.

SOURCE: Reprinted from *Roche Report—Frontiers of Hospital Psychiatry,* vol. 3, no. 6, March 15, 1966. With permission.

**Family Environment.** As important as are the genetic factors, another factor that cannot be overlooked is the family environment. Several family variables have already been noted in Chapter 5; we'll present a short review here of maternal and paternal traits, of the family unit, and of patterns of communication.

*"Schizophrenogenic" Mothers and Fathers.* The studies of mothers and fathers of schizophrenics reviewed in Chapter 5 point out the pathological environment they can create. By pathological, we do not necessarily mean that such parents are psychotic themselves, although this does occur. The pathology exists in the disturbed quality of the parents' attitudes and

actions toward their offspring, traits that are called schizophrenogenic or schizophrenia-producing.

Schizophrenogenic mothers are described as exhibiting a wide variety of seemingly contradictory traits; perhaps the most critical characteristic is the mother's inconsistency. She is aloof yet smothering; she may seem accepting and protective on the surface, yet this appears more of a reaction against her rejection; she may avoid intimacy and remain aloof, yet she seems to have an overwhelming need to be intimately involved in the child's every activity (Shapiro, 1981). When the unpredictability and inconsistency coexist, it is very difficult for the child to develop a truly satisfying relationship with the mother. As a result, the child may soon begin to actually withdraw as a self-defense against this demanding, inconsistent, interfering parent (Brody, 1981).

The fathers of schizophrenic patients have been described as detached, passive, rigid, and unable to assume the adaptive instrumental role (Lewis et al., 1981). Such men are poor models of adjustment; in fact, they are better models of maladjustment. Such a parent may be more tolerable than the mother we have just described, since he is more consistent and therefore the child knows what to expect. On the other hand, he is unable to transmit much help on the "whys and wherefores" of adaptive mechanisms, and his own demands may be so extreme as to be impossible to satisfy. The child is again left with poor reason to seek continued interpersonal contacts and little support and help in learning how to cope with life stresses.

*The Aberrant Family Unit.* If the personal traits of the individual parents are insufficient to create the conditions for pathology, their interactive influence may make up the difference. The family structure is itself often distorted (Freeman, 1981). We saw in Chapter 5 that two common patterns are the *schismatic* family, where members take opposing sides, and the *skewed* family, in which one spouse and the offspring passively accept the aberrant behavior of the more disturbed parent (Lidz, 1973).

In addition to the schismatic or skewed patterns, parents may force a child to express the maladjustment of the family. In such cases, as long as the child shows symptoms, then the rest of the family can maintain a level of pseudoadjustment. It is a common phenomenon to observe the child recover in treatment only to find the illness role has been assumed by another member of the family, or to see the hidden conflict between the parents suddenly burst into the open (Haley, 1980).

*Distorted Communications.* Of course, there are families where the conditions quite directly precipitate disorganization. Fisher and Mendell (1956) discovered families in which pathogenic perceptions and obsessions persisted over several generations. Fleck et al. (1963) considered the families of schizophrenics to be permeated by irrationality and distortions.

In some families, the distorted double-bind communication is basic to the disturbance (Lewis et al., 1981). In the *double-bind situation,* the child receives at least two conflicting messages—one statement, along with another which disqualifies it. The child is told yes and no in the same communication. The incredible complication is the fact that the child is not permitted to ask for clarification, or even acknowledge that there are confusing and interfering messages. It is like a bizarre game in which everyone agrees to behave incomprehensibly but act as if everything were entirely logical. The child soon learns to play the game extremely well; it becomes impossible to determine what the child thinks, feels, or wants—the child is well on the way towards exhibiting a "split personality."

***Children at Risk: A Diathesis-stress Theory.*** Perhaps the best way to conclude this discussion of dynamics is to examine the data on risk. A number of worldwide prospective studies involve children considered at risk for schizophrenia, mostly the offspring of schizophrenic parents (Sameroff & Zax, 1978; Schulsinger & Falloon, 1980). The long-term goal is to follow infants' development through adulthood where possible, watching for the life and biological factors connected with the development of schizophrenia.

The pioneering study is that of Mednick and Schulsinger (1978). It began in 1962 with over 200 children of schizophrenic mothers matched with over 100 children of normal parents. The children originally were as young as 10 years; by follow-up some were in their 30s. If we combine the results of the various research efforts, an approximate picture can be

**TABLE 17–3**

**High-Risk Children: A Developmental Overview of Factors Associated with Schizophrenia**

| | |
|---|---|
| *Prenatal period* | Some prenatal developmental difficulties may occur, showing in lower birth weights. |
| *Birth* | There may be problems at birth, such as obstetric complications. |
| *Infancy* | Neurological abnormalities often appear, such as smaller amplitude EEG readings, along with unusual stimulus responsivity. |
| *Preschool* | There are often signs of inattention, and either poorly controlled or overly inhibited feelings. |
| *Childhood* | Severe behavior problems may not be observed, but there may be complaints of unsocialized aggression in boys and over inhibition in girls. |
| *Adolescence* | Complaints of loneliness, lack of friends, and complaints of feeling like an outsider appear. |

SOURCES: From "Child Competency and Psychiatric Risk" by L. Fisher and J. Jones, 1980, *Journal of Nervous Mental Disorders, 168,* pp. 332–337; "Children at Risk for Schizophrenia" by D. MacCrimmon et al., 1980, *Archives of General Psychiatry, 37,* pp. 671–674; "Obstetric Factors in the Development of Schizophrenia: Complications in the Births of Preschizophrenics and in Reproduction by Schizophrenic Parents" by T. McNeil and L. Kaiji, 1978, in L. Wynne et al., *The Nature of Schizophrenia: New Approaches to Research and Treatment,* New York: Wiley.

drawn of the person likely to become schizophrenic. The various developmental characteristics that are statistically associated with high risk (they may not all appear in every case) are summarized in Table 17–3.

This composite pattern shows the interaction of several conditions, and it seems consistent with the diathesis-stress concept we saw in Chapter 4. Perhaps the schizophrenic-to-be is faced with a double developmental hazard of birth from a schizophrenic parent in a difficult delivery and rearing in an eccentric environment. Failure to cope is complicated by demands from others. If slow neurological development leads to inability to pay attention, then being pushed to attend may in turn create further inhibition. In essence, the risk of breakdown is not a simple matter of genetics or environment alone, but a dynamic transactional interaction between personal vulnerabilities and environmental pressures (Shapiro, 1981).

### Treatment of Schizophrenia

Dementia praecox was once considered disastrous, because of its early onset and its lack of response to treatment. As mentioned earlier in this chapter, the picture is still grim, although it is now known that schizophrenia can have a later onset, is responsive to treatment, and complete recoveries are possible. Modern treatment methods, especially chemotherapy, now enable half of first admissions to be discharged within four months; two thirds to be discharged within six months; and 90 percent to be discharged within one year (Wing, 1978).

Discharge, of course, is not synonymous with cure but rather control. A patient is released when symptoms are sufficiently under control that other forms of treatment such as out-patient clinics can be used. Only 25 percent of schizophrenics recover completely and permanently, although half will improve enough to return to work. Even the most optimistic statement by Bleuler (1978) still observes that "on the average, a schizophrenic once hospitalized . . . had to expect that he would spend one third of his future life in a hospital and two thirds outside" (p. 634). The prognosis for recovery has improved, however. We'll look at some of the most common approaches, past and present, in the next few pages, including psychosurgery, electroshock therapy, chemotherapy, behavior therapy, family therapy, milieu therapy, and nondirective therapy.

***Psychosurgery.*** Treatment of schizophrenia has run the gamut from the use of surgery to psychotherapy. During the decade from 1940 to 1950, psychosurgery was prescribed for schizophrenics who did not respond to other therapies. The *prefrontal lobotomy* involves cutting the nerves leading from the frontal lobe of the brain to the lower brain centers (see Chapter 22) (Heilman & Satz, 1983). For patients hospitalized for one to two years, 52 percent were found to respond well enough to be discharged in a quieter and more cooperative mood. The best results were reported for those treated within six months, with an 82 percent recovery (Freeman, 1953).

Unfortunately, this recovery does not mean a return to full functioning. Parts of the brain are irreversibly destroyed, and even then the treatment is symptomatic, not curative. The author has spoken to some persons who have undergone the surgery, and they appeared too passive to be able to return to a constructive lifestyle. Because of modern alternatives, psychosurgery has been nearly completely abandoned (Kalinowsky, 1973).

***Electroshock.*** Another approach to schizophrenia is electroshock therapy, which was described in Chapter 16. This treatment has less spectacular results with schizophrenia than was found for the affective disorders. One follow-up study over 25 years compared the course of schizophrenia before and after the advent of EST or insulin shock, a similar treatment which induces shock through administration of insulin. The results indicated that the five-year recovery rate improved from 9 percent to 22 percent after treatment was available; however, the effectiveness of shock therapy was shown to decrease with cases of more than one year's duration (Bond, 1954). Convincing figures are hard to obtain because such factors as duration of the disorder have not been controlled and because follow-up data is often lacking. Relapses are known to occur after EST, however. Catatonic stupors and disorganized schizophrenia show the poorest response to shock treatment, while catatonic excitement and paranoid schizophrenia tend to respond more favorably.

Some of the more promising findings have been those of May et al. (1976), who followed the progress of patients for three years after discharge. Those patients who had received shock treatment and chemotherapy showed the shortest hospitalization, better than patients treated by either milieu therapy or psychotherapy (both of these approaches are discussed shortly). In all, though, shock therapy is still considered basically a symptomatic treatment, reducing some of the symptoms of the disorder but not bringing about a complete cure (May et al., 1981).

***Chemotherapy.*** The tranquilizing drugs have effected the highest recovery rates in the treatment of schizophrenia, enabling reduction of the acute manifestations of the psychosis within the first three to six weeks of therapy. In fact, the NIMH Psychopharmacology Service Center has been so impressed by one group of tranquilizers known as the phenothiazines that it regarded these as antischizophrenic drugs rather than merely tranquilizers (Prien et al., 1973; May et al., 1981). There is evidence that over half of chronically disturbed schizophrenic persons can be discharged to outpatient treatment from hospitalization after massive dosages of the phenothiazines such as chlorpromazine or Thorazine (Shopsin et al., 1979).

Other drugs are also being investigated with some success. One of these is the synthetic tranquilizer haloperidol, which can have more immediate effects (Donlon et al., 1980). One major issue in any of these treatments is the possible side effects of prolonged chemotherapy. The treatment of *Dyskinesia,* the impairment of voluntary muscle control, has been described as making the "cure worse than the disease," and Mark Vonnegut's description of Thorazine (see Focus 17–2) illustrates a disturbing picture of unwanted side effects.

***Behavior Therapy.*** A different approach is offered by behavior modification techniques, which have had some success (Gomes-Schwartz, 1979). Operant conditioning procedures have been the preferred method, involving the presenting of a reinforcement whenever the patient shows the desired normal behaviors (Davis et al., 1976; Paul & Lentz, 1977).

Isaacs et al.'s (1960) work with two mute catatonic schizophrenic subjects provides a good example of one behavioral approach to the disorder. Interestingly enough, the researchers discovered that both subjects were responsive to the offer of chewing gum, which was, therefore, used as a reinforcer. A gradual teaching process was introduced, starting with the reward of gum when the subject made lip movements, then when the subject made any sound, then when the sounds were similar to the word *gum,* then when the subject spoke other words. Speech was reinstated in both subjects, taking one month for the one and ten sessions for the other. Figure 17–2 illustrates how another reinforcer, praise, was used in a similar way to eliminate psychotic speech in a subject in less than three weeks through rewarding rational speech.

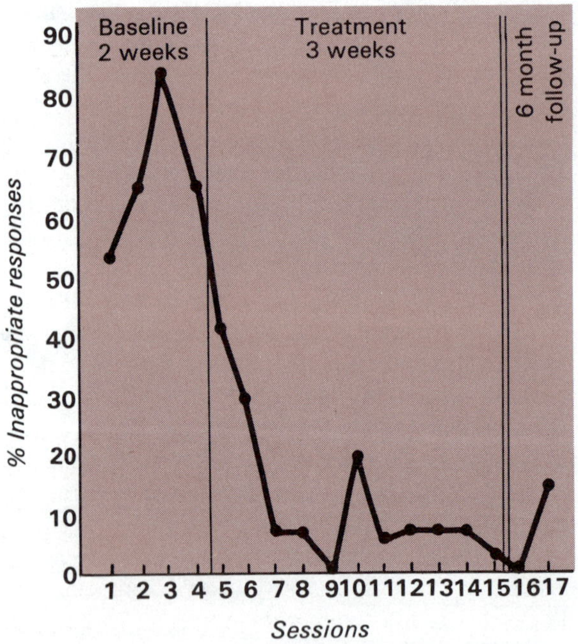


**FIGURE 17–2** The use of praise and self-instruction to eliminate psychotic speech.

SOURCE: Adapted from "Use of Covert Self-instruction for the Elimination of Psychotic Speech" by A.M. Meyers, M. Mercatoris & A. Sirota, 1976, *Journal of Consulting and Clinical Psychology, 44,* pp. 480–482.

Another case, this one treated by Ayllon and Michael (1959) involved a female patient known for episodes of extreme violence. Because of her outbursts, she had been treated with shock and undergone psychosurgery without results. During her hospitalization, she had spent 3–12 hours daily in an isolation room to control her violence. The experimenters selected a behavior pattern (sitting or lying on the floor) that was incompatible with the subject's violent behaviors and reinforced her for this response. Her violence was reduced drastically under this treatment (although when the treatment was withdrawn, the subject again behaved violently). Of course, sitting on the floor for long hours is in itself a behavior that would be considered suspect outside of the hospital. However, the important aspect of this early study is that it proved the behavioral treatment brought some improvement, even with severely disturbed persons.

*Token Economy Wards.* With contemporary acceptance of behavior modification, *token economy* wards have been used successfully to provide clients with an incentive for reacquiring normal, responsible behaviors. In many hospitals, individuals seem to be encouraged to become more and more apathetic, or to retain psychotic behaviors, since little is asked of them. The only reward comes when a person shows sick behaviors, since these bring nursing and medical attention.

The token economy is basically a type of work environment: patients may use tokens like money to purchase services, goods, or privileges, and they earn them as payment for work. "Work," in this case, refers to behaviors indicative of adjustment such as showing progress in control over symptoms, coming out of withdrawal states, and increased cooperation and communication. In the token economy virtually everything normally taken for granted must be earned, such as passes, having a private room, and even sometimes meals, towels, and bedsheets (Baker et al., 1977). Improvements have occurred to such a degree that in some cases up to 70 percent of chronic patients were able to qualify for discharge, even though these same patients had earlier been unresponsive to other therapies (Ellsworth, 1969).

***Family Therapy.*** The family therapy approach derives from the evidence that schizophrenia might at least in part be associated with distorted family interactions or family communications (Strauss et al., 1980). A major goal of family therapy is to enable the family to examine itself objectively, rather than focusing only on the patient's problems. A mother needs to truly comprehend what she is communicating when she says, "You can't possibly hold down a job . . . you're a patient, you're sick, can't you accept that?" A father needs to hear the meaning of his words, when he says, "But I do think you are important and you have rights . . . you just have no right to do everything you want, just because you want to . . . besides there's no reason to talk about it, I'll tell you when you have rights." And the patient-offspring needs help in seeing the implication of his or her thought blockage or hallucinations coming whenever family communication patterns seem to be impossible to follow.

In family therapy, communications are discussed and many questions are asked (Strauss et al., 1980). What is being said verbally? Are there hidden or nonverbal messages? Is the adolescent being asked to respond as an adult while being evaluated as a child? Are there coalitions among family members? Are there conflicts that refuse to surface and be confronted directly? Are there rewards for being ill? Finding answers to questions like these can be one step toward resolving some of the underlying issues in some cases of schizophrenia.

***Milieu Treatment.*** Another psychotherapeutic approach which has gained attention is milieu therapy. This orientation is basically the same as the milieu treatment for drugs that we saw in Chapter 13. There are no formalized distinctions between therapists and patients; instead, clients are encouraged to assume responsibility for their own therapy and that of others. Community meetings are conducted where therapists and clients play the same roles; clients are accepted as persons and are expected to participate in decisions (Moos, 1974).

Soteria House in San Jose, California is a treatment setting that combines the milieu atmosphere with the existential therapy of Laing. Soteria staff view psychotic symptoms, irrational behaviors, mystical experiences, and emotional terror as no more than extremes of basic human nature. In keeping with Laing's theory, the staff accept psychotic qualities as valid human experiences that are the patient's attempts to find meaning. Their role is to "tune into the individuals' altered states of consciousness" instead of demanding clients to conform. Nearly all clients in Soteria House are treated without medication.

The milieu aspects of this facility are seen in the lack of distinctions between staff and clients. Staff are not selected on the basis of professional titles, but on their abilities to empathize with what the schizophrenic persons are experiencing and to support this natural healing process. Results have been promising. In comparison with patients in a traditional treatment program using chemotherapy, the Soteria patients were as able to achieve employment and showed equivalent improvement in their symptoms. Further, they were able to live independent of their families within six months after discharge (Wilson, 1982).

***Client-centered Therapy.*** One more psychotherapeutic approach is worth mentioning here. An historically interesting program was directed by Carl Rogers (1967) for over five years at Mendota State Hospital. Throughout his work with humanistic approaches to therapy, Rogers consistently felt it necessary to subject his ideas to the test of empirical research. The Mendota study was meant to determine whether humanistic therapy was as applicable in helping psychotic persons as it had been for the less severely disturbed. The basic client-centered therapy orientation that we saw in Chapter 3 was used with schizophrenic patients, including the emphasis on unconditional positive regard, empathy, and the therapist's communication of genuineness. However, these methods needed to be revised to reach the uncommunicative individuals who were immersed in their psychoses. Hence, therapists tended to initiate more interactions, to guess what the patients were feeling, and to openly share more of their (the therapists') feelings and reactions to the situation.

The results were not completely successful, since clients showed greater improvement than nontreated controls on only one measure. On the other hand, despite his discouragement, Rogers felt that the more important finding was that therapy variables such as empathy and genuineness that seemed to help nonpsychotic persons were also the same ones that were valuable in helping schizophrenic clients (Rogers & Hart, 1970). Thus, those patients who received the highest levels of empathy were those who showed the greatest improvements.

### Prognostic Signs

More attention is being devoted to identifying the factors associated with a favorable prognosis for schizophrenia (Harder et al., 1981). Two kinds of approaches are especially relevant. One involves the study of factors associated with early risk among children. We discussed some of these early risk indicators in Table 17–3 and the Dynamics section of this chapter.

The second approach involves the study of factors associated with recovery or relapse in schizophrenic patients. Basically, there are a number of statistically favorable signs for recovery (Carpenter & Heinrichs, 1981; Brim & Kagan, 1980; Vaillant, 1978). These include:

- Acute onset of symptoms.
- A clear precipitating event.
- Good premorbid adjustment.
- Presence of confusion and disorientation.
- Presence of depression or history of family depression.

Readers may notice that many of these signs are also symptomatic of the reactive types of schizophrenia in the process-reactive distinction discussed earlier in this chapter. Indeed, the reactive schizophrenics have a better prognosis, both for briefer hospitalization and lower relapse rate. This may be because process schizophrenia could be a form of biologically based psychosis (Brim & Kagan, 1980).

Rating scales are now available that highlight other favorable signs for recovery, including marriage, active participation in organized clubs or athletics in early life, adequate social and occupational adjustment in the year just prior to hospitalization, absence of life event stresses, and supportive family environment (Harris, 1975; Strauss et al., 1978).

A rather thought-provoking finding was produced by a study of how family reactions can influence relapse. Patients returning to families who were anxious and critical about the person's ability to recover required more medication to prevent relapse.

It begins to appear that a person is more likely to recover from schizophrenia if coping skills and a firm adaptive foundation had been present, and if the patient can avoid slipping into a hopeless patient role but retain the social and economic skills to remain an integral part of society.

## THE PARANOID DISORDERS

A third major type of psychotic disorder, after the affective and schizophrenic disorders, are the paranoid disorders. Like schizophrenia, the paranoid disorders are characterized by thought disturbances. Thoughts typically reflect suspicion and persecutory delusions, but delusions of grandeur may also occur. There are two types of paranoid disorders. *Paranoia* is a condition involving delusions of persecution, but none of the other signs of psychosis. *Folie à deux* refers to the second type of paranoid condition in which delusions are shared by persons who have a close relationship to one another.

Although the paranoid disorders involve thought disturbances, as does schizophrenia, these disorders differ from paranoid schizophrenia in their degree of personality disorganization. The person with schizophrenia shows a gross disturbance of every aspect of personality—emotions, intellect, speech, perceptions. The individual with a paranoid diagnosis, on the other hand, is able to function adequately, experiences emotional responses appropriate to his or her beliefs, does not usually have hallucinations, but is preoccupied with beliefs which are delusional in nature. The two types of paranoid disorders share the following symptoms:

- Organized delusions of persecution and/or grandeur.
- Normal orientation and emotional reactions.

## Case History 17–5:
### Paranoia

Harold V. was a 23-year-old graduate student in psychology. He had acquired his bachelor's degree after five years of academic toil, displaying no great talent other than a tendency toward argumentativeness. On entry to graduate work, he showed a disposition toward avoiding assignments in favor of creative thinking mostly aimed at refuting accepted scientific principles. His arguments were based on possible but not probable lines of analysis, and they often twisted facts, until they fit his preconceptions. At mid-year, he was advised to reconsider his goal in education and encouraged to postpone completion of his degree until he was more certain of his choice of career. He refused to delay his education and continued in the department.

Within weeks, a highly intricate delusional system evolved of a persecutory nature. He harbored the belief that the departmental recommendation had been the first step in a plot to distract his progress. He reasoned that he was probably nearing a major scientific discovery which, if publicized, would revolutionize science and make all current scientific theories, from Darwinism to nuclear theory, obsolete. The psychology faculty were simply pawns directed to prevent him from his imminent contribution.

He felt he more clearly understood his life. He had been guided toward his undergraduate college by those who had recognized his potential genius and hoped even then to brainwash him. Magazine solicitations through the mail were attempts to direct him towards the right kind of reading. Harold believed that it was even possible that his parents were part of the scheme. He was beside himself with satisfaction when he recognized the telephone repairman coming out of the department chairman's office as the same one who had installed his telephone in his apartment—proof that his telephone wires had been tapped.

Since Harold was still enrolled in school, his draft board renewed his deferment. Harold took this event to mean that the federal government was attempting to keep him in a location where he could continue to be surveyed. In a shrewd maneuver, he decided to play the game and not reveal his newfound knowledge. Instead, he became the model student, impressing the faculty in his more controlled, seemingly attentive, and mild manner. He applied his intellect to his schoolwork and was doing relatively well. In an attempt to impress the department and to "lull them into a false sense of confidence," he joined in a group psychotherapy program. During the fourth meeting, he became excited by revelations in another member's comments, and announced in a tone of mixed anger and pride that he could no longer be treated as a fool—that he would expose the whole plot and work on his scientific discovery besides! He eventually entered more intensive individual treatment, but at this date he still retains some mild suspicions that the therapist—a psychologist—is also involved in the plot.

- Impaired judgment and thought only in areas of the delusion.
- Reliance on denial and projection as defense mechanisms.
- Suspicious and sensitive personality.
- No fragmentation, deterioration, or gross disturbance of personality.
- Hallucinations are rare, although they sometimes occur.

We will look separately at each of the two paranoid disorders.

### Paranoia

Paranoia is extremely rare. In one investigation of 5,000 successive admissions, only 3 authentic cases could be located (Pearson, 1952). The diagnosis is based on the presence of a highly systematized delu-

*A patient with a schizophrenic disorder,* ***disorganized*** *type, will show inappropriate laughter and giggling as one of the symptoms.*

*A* ***catatonic*** *stupor, exhibited by schizophrenic patients, involves bizarre postures maintained for long periods.*

sion, and the absence of any other type of mental or emotional disturbance—hallucinations, for example, are almost never present. Like Harold in Case History 17–5, the person is often average or superior in intellect and is capable of maintaining the delusion without letting it interfere with everyday functioning.

***Symptoms of Paranoia.*** Paranoia tends to begin during the 30s in rigidly organized individuals. Such persons become increasingly tense until they are living under high levels of anxiety. They soon become concerned about the motivation of others and the extent to which they can trust those around them. The delusional structure typically focuses on that part of the individual's life that is currently dissatisfying. They begin to slowly but systematically form vague suspicions. They are suddenly convinced that their suspicions have basis in fact, and everything seems to fall neatly into place.

As an example, if persons' delusions are centered around their occupations, they are certain that their work has been altered to make them look incompetent; that they are being given the worst assignment; perhaps even that their spouses are secretly laughing at their ineptness. Such notions are never completely unbelievable, and so paranoid individuals may be able to find some allies who accept their stories. However, persons with paranoia seldom confide, since they seldom trust others. In fact, they expect to be betrayed.

Despite the world of false reality in which they live, persons with paranoia are fully capable of continuing an active, outwardly normal life. However, where the delusional beliefs are concerned, these patients are adamant about what is real to them. Arguments and contradictory evidence are received with smug tolerance or scorn, but are rejected. In some chronic cases, the persecutory delusions have reached such dimensions that the patients may be tripped into a burst of hostility or accusation. It should be stressed that persons with paranoia retain contact with their social environment—in fact, their delusions keep them sensitively aware of their surroundings. Yet, they are not in full communication with others, since they are unable to share their beliefs with others.

***Types of Delusions.*** Although the delusions of the person with paranoia are typically persecutory, other forms have been identified, and these are sometimes used as a basis for categorizing paranoia. *Delusions of grandeur* may be present. These range from simple convictions that one is specially skilled or talented to the more expansive belief that one is a great spiritual, financial, or scientific genius.

Another type of delusion is the *erotic delusion,* the mistaken belief that a certain individual is in love with one. The person finds proof of love in a thousand tiny actions. A polite smile or a casual acknowledgement is interpreted as an expression of passion. Most often, the individual chosen is a public figure such as a television performer, or movie star. The patient becomes an avid follower of the lover and may even deluge this person with intimate gifts and passionate letters. Because of this, the police often become involved.

In *jealous delusions,* the person is fitfully certain that his or her loved one is unfaithful. Every effort is focused toward obtaining proof of this with the same intensity as the patient with persecutory delusions. The patient begins to time the spouse's trips to the grocers, calls home at unexpected times, and listens in on conversations with acquaintances. Any delays in return, unanswered phone calls, or suspicious words are interpreted with stark meaning.

### *Folie à Deux*

A second paranoid disorder, *folie à deux*, is a bizarre condition in which two persons close to one another develop similar delusions (Laseque & Fairet, 1877). The most common combination seems to be sister-sister, but husband-wife, and mother-child also appear with regularity. For the most part, the circumstance appears to be that one person develops a psychosis while the other has a pseudopsychosis, rather than the actual development of two psychotic conditions. Typically, a dominant psychotic person provokes delusions in a dependent, submissive individual. When the dominant person is removed, the dependent one usually recovers within a few months. *Folie à deux* appears most frequently in the form of persecutory or religious delusions. The condition may include two, three, four, or more persons with different terms being used in order to identify the numbers of people involved (thus, *folie à trois* involves three persons; *folie à quatre,* four, etc.).

One case which illustrates the bizarreness of the disorder is that of a 28-year-old woman whose psychosis eventually prompted delusions in her husband. On several occasions she confided that she was being followed, that people were doing things to her car and the apartment. Although originally dismissing such complaints, the husband later began to believe that the wiring in the apartment and car did look strange. After several weeks they were both convinced that the husband's employer was keeping them under surveillance. "Then the husband began to describe to his wife segments of worms which he picked off his skin. . . . She almost immediately accepted this and saw segments of worms on her own skin." The woman finally called the police to complain of being bugged by microphones, and this led to her hospitalization (Spensley, 1972).

Another grim case involved Patricia Nasser, the disinherited heiress to the Burns International Detective Agency fortune. Her two-year-old son, Joshua, was found on the steps of a church in 1977, and pronounced dead at a hospital, with evidence that he had been starved. Patricia and James Nassar confessed to police that they had abandoned their son on "orders from God." They also said that their five-month-old daughter, Elizabeth, had died in her crib, and that they had wrapped the body in a trash bag and dumped it out with the garbage. The couple was diagnosed as suffering from *folie à deux,* and committed to psychiatric treatment ("Insanity," 1981, January 11).

### Dynamics of Paranoid Disorders

The paranoid delusional structure seems to be the end product of overreliance on denial and projection as defenses. All self-disturbing faults such as hostility are denied, but are then projected onto others to an exaggerated extent. This action has several advantages. By blaming others, these persons are distracted from their own guilty possession of the very trait they find in others. In addition, by establishing that others are hostile, the patients permit themselves to engage in counteraggression without fear of arousing guilt feelings.

Psychoanalytic theory once stressed the belief that the basic component of paranoia was repressed homosexuality (Freud, 1914). For example, a male patient may feel guilty about homosexual leanings and defend against it through two steps: first, the denial and use of reaction formation—"I don't love him, I hate him"; then, the projection—"I don't hate him, he hates me." The erotic delusions would be found in patients who do not depend on the reaction formation defense mechanism, but proceed to the stage of "she loves me," thereby justifying their reciprocal love wishes. In grandiose delusions, the denial mechanism is more strongly actuated as patients refuse to accept their insecurity and delude themselves into believing in their own superiority.

Another factor in explaining paranoid disorders relates to family background. We know that to some degree persons develop their feelings of insecurity or unworthiness during their formative years of life (Schwartz, 1963). Parental neglect or lack of warmth provides a foundation of uncertainty. The home atmosphere itself may be one of threats, abuse, hostile criticism, or sadism, thereby encouraging the traits of seclusiveness and watchfulness. Continued negative social experiences foster further isolation, thus preventing the person from having open lines of communication with others. A person who distrusts others and who is unable to understand others' motives is forced to rely on private guesses, inadequate and unrealistic as they may be. The more a person relies on personal interpretations and the less these are validated against other people's perceptions, the more subject is the paranoid person to gross distortions. Ultimately, the paranoia progresses to such a delusional state that it is impossible to even contemplate reexamining earlier premises.

### Treatment of Paranoid Disorders

The prognosis for severe cases of paranoid disorders is extremely poor. The basic distrust, highly organized delusional system, and rationalizations are so firmly imbedded that they are not easily reached. In fact, the person may exhibit antisocial features and become involved in assassination plots or international subversive activities.

The treatment usually has two goals. The first aims to reduce the high anxiety level. The preferred procedure is to induce the person to seek help in a situation with minimal coercion, since force simply serves to exacerbate the sense of persecution. In milder cases, removal of the everyday stresses that surround the patient is helpful. If hospitalization is needed, the opportunity to recognize the helping nature of the institution will aid in decreasing the perception of the hospital as punitive.

Drugs are also used to relieve severe anxiety. Chlorpromazine is the drug of choice as it often relieves the anxiety and the attending suspiciousness and distrust. Electroshock treatment has been attempted, but only rarely is it of any value (Scovern & Kilmann, 1980). It may provide temporary relief from the delusions, perhaps through its general disruptive influence, and perhaps because it is seen as a symbolic expiation of guilt.

The second goal of treatment is the reestablishment of realistic interpersonal contact. Psychotherapist and patient meet under somewhat less wary conditions. The therapist maintains an attitude of suspended judgment, partly because it is truly difficult to separate fact from delusion, partly to prevent arousing the fear and consequent suspiciousness of the patient. By remaining somewhat detached, the therapist avoids appearing intrusive. The therapeutic condition attempts to establish a relationship of reasonable firm mutual trust such that the patient can reevaluate his perceptions and beliefs. Hopefully, the patient will eventually be able to relinquish the rigid beliefs and substitute more reality-oriented ideas. In all cases, the outcome is still viewed with caution by most psychotherapists.

## EVALUATION

Very little conclusive data exist on the etiology or treatment of schizophrenia—although evidence seems to be building that more than one type of schizophrenia exists. Hence, research on causes and therapies must be alert to possible flaws in current diagnostic systems when patients are selected for study. As mentioned at the start of this chapter, the process-reactive category has been studied with some benefits; yet, the current

DSM-III system does not directly include this potentially valuable distinction.

The search for a common cause of schizophrenia has taken several directions, some more valuable than others. In all likelihood, the greatest gains will be made from the continuation of process-reactive studies and from the children-at-risk developmental research. Certainly there is persistent enough data on genetics to support an initial contention that hereditary factors are involved as a stronger influence than once believed, although not as a sole condition. Family communications and family dynamics seem to be other candidates for consideration as contributors, whereas the actual personality traits of parents *per se* no longer seem critical. Although not well understood so far, physiological factors seem to be implicated, possibly through the involvement of dopamine, norepinephrine, or endorphins.

Therapy continues to be elusive. The discovery of the effects of the phenothiazines was a major breakthrough; however, the medication does not effect a cure. Family therapy, milieu therapy, and behavior therapy hold much promise for more complete recoveries. The most researched of the three has so far been the behavioral technique of using token economy rewards. Although controversial in terms of the concept of the ethics of controlling food, bedding, and privileges, the token economy system does seem to motivate patients to acquire normal behaviors. An interesting issue does develop, however: If a schizophrenic, who is diagnosed because of hallucinatory behaviors, learns not to show such behaviors, can we conclude that the psychosis has been cured? Does this really matter, or is the more important question whether the patient has acquired adaptive skills which permit a return (adjustment) to normal living?

Progress in understanding the origins, mechanics, or treatment of the paranoid disorders still lags. Many theories have added useful ideas, but research evidence still fails to convincingly support any particular set of ideas. The mechanics of paranoid disorders do seem to illustrate the concept of denial and projection as means of self-protection from threat. There is also likely to be a generalized anxiety associated with guilt which may derive from a variety of sources. Consider, for example, how you sometimes feel that "everyone is staring" at you when you know you're feeling embarrassed or guilty about something. Although *folie à deux* shares the common feature of the delusional beliefs with paranoia, the process is probably a different one. What is at fault is a maladaptive interpersonal relationship, with the dependent partner naively adopting the beliefs of the more dominant person. Yet, the condition which creates this unusual dependency and the attending psychosis is not known.

## SUMMARY

This chapter discussed two different types of psychotic disorders: the schizophrenic disorders, and the paranoid disorders. Schizophrenia is a psychotic condition characterized by inappropriate emotions; withdrawal; reality disturbance; bizarre speech, thought, or motor symptoms; and delusions or hallucinations. Several forms of schizophrenia have been identified, including disorganized schizophrenia, catatonic schizophrenia, and paranoid schizophrenia.

A variety of possible causes of schizophrenia have been studied, including genetic, physiological, and cultural factors. Psychological theories have examined personality dynamics, family structures, communications, or the early history of persons-at-risk. From the treatment standpoint, an important breakthrough in permitting schizophrenics to be released from continued hospitalization was the discovery of the phenothiazine drugs. Additional therapeutic approaches that seem helpful are family therapy, milieu therapy, and certain behavior therapies.

The paranoid disorders include paranoia and folie à deux, both of which are rare. Paranoid disorders are characterized by the presence of delusions, usually of persecution. Unlike the schizophrenic disorders, the paranoid disorders involve intact personalities; normal emotionality and judgment is impaired only in the area of the delusions. Paranoia is diagnosed when an individual shows a highly systematized delusional system that persists despite reality. Folie à deux is diagnosed when delusional beliefs are shared by more than one person. These disorders are believed due to denial and projection and are found difficult to treat.

## KEY TERMS

**Catalepsy**
**Catatonic excitement**
**Catatonic negativism**
**Catatonic rigidity**
**Catatonic schizophrenia**
**Catatonic stupor**
**Client-centered therapy**
**Delusions of grandeur**
**Dementia praecox**
**Disorganized schizophrenia**
**Double-bind**
**Dyskinesia**
**Echolalia**
**Erotic delusions**
***Folie à deux***
**Jealous delusions**
**Negativism**
**Neologism**
**Paranoia**
**Paranoid disorders**
**Paranoid schizophrenia**
**Prefrontal lobotomy**
**Protective inhibition theory**
**Psychosurgery**
**Schizophrenia**
**Waxy flexibility**

# CHAPTER 18

## Organic Mental Disorders: Syndromes Caused by Organic Factors

- **You are injured in an auto accident, and you now have vision problems—what could this mean?**
- **The boxer Muhammad Ali could experience side effects from his career. How might this show up in his personality?**
- **Why would a person make up a memory instead of simply admitting "I don't remember"?**
- **What is the significance of the half-hour memory to alcohol abuse?**
- **Steroids are sometimes illegally used by athletes to help their performance. Are there psychological dangers to steroid excesses?**
- **"I have a friend who hit his head, and now his personality is like a Jekyll and Hyde." Is there any cause-and-effect relationship between the two?**
- **As your parents reach old age, and possibly senility, what changes might you expect?**
- **Why should I fear a little syphilis?**
- **Is epilepsy insanity?**

**TABLE 18–1**

**The Organic Mental Disorders**

| *Type* | *Major Characteristics* |
|---|---|
| | *ORGANIC BRAIN SYNDROMES:* |
| Delirium | Organic symptoms involving confusion, difficulty in attending, or in goal-directed acts |
| Amnestic Syndrome | Organic symptoms involving loss of short-term memory |
| Delusional Syndrome | Organic symptoms involving belief in ideas that have no basis in reality |
| Hallucinosis | Organic symptoms involving sensory experiences without basis in reality |
| Affective Syndrome | Organic symptoms involving shifts in mood, such as depression or euphoria |
| Personality Syndrome | Organic symptoms involving sudden changes in a person's usually stable behavioral patterns |
| | *ORGANIC MENTAL DISORDERS:* * |
| Primary Degenerative Dementia Senile Onset | Loss of intellectual functions through a degenerative course attributed to aging, with onset after age 65 |
| Primary Degenerative Dementia Presenile Onset | Loss of intellectual functions through a degenerative process attributed to aging, with onset before age 65 |

*One other form of organic mental disorders, the substance-induced disorders, involve organic symptoms attributed to use of substances such as alcohol. These disorders are discussed in Chapter 13.

## Case History 18–1:
### Personality Change Resulting from Trauma

A classic case of trauma involving cerebral laceration was reported in 1868. The victim, Phineas P. Gage, was the young foreman of a railroad excavation crew. His disposition was such that he enjoyed the respect and favor of his men. On September 13, a premature explosion drove a tamping iron through his skull. The iron was a rod measuring three feet, seven inches long, one and one-fourth inches in diameter, and weighed thirteen and one-fourth pounds. It entered the left side of the face passing obliquely upwards and backwards to emerge at the back part of the frontal bone, as the illustration shows.

Gage was thrown onto his back by the force of the blast, convulsed a bit, then regained his speech. He was placed in an oxcart in which he rode sitting upright for a full three-quarters of a mile to his hotel room. He got out of the cart by himself and was later able to walk up a flight of stairs. He remained conscious although blood poured profusely from his skull.

Subsequently Gage, who must have been an extraordinarily strong man, recovered physically from the ordeal. However, his personality changed such that his friends felt he was "no longer Gage." Harlow (1868) reports:

> . . . His contractors, who regarded him as the most efficient and capable foreman in their employ previous to his injury considered the change in mind so marked that they could not give him his place again. The equilibrium or balance, so to speak, between his intellectual faculties and animal propensities, seem to have been destroyed. He is fitful, irreverent, indulging at times in the grossest profanity (which was not previously his custom), manifesting but little deference for his fellows, impatient of restraint or advice when it conflicts with his desires, at times pertinaciously obstinate, yet capricious and vacillating, devising many plans of future operations, which are no sooner arranged than they are abandoned in turn for others appearing more feasible. A child in his intellectual capacity and manifestations, he has the animal passions of a man. (Harlow, 1868, pp. 339–40)

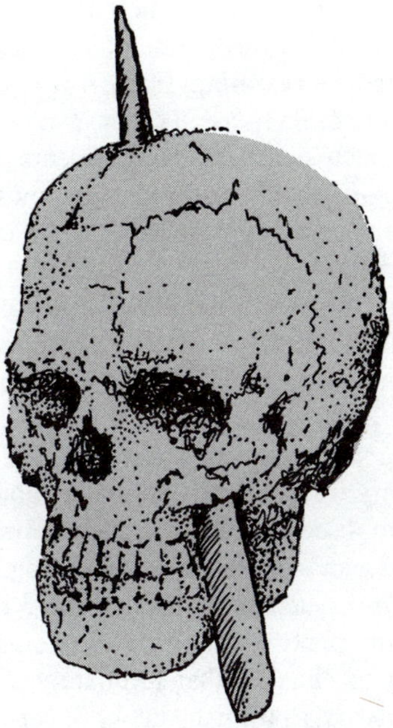

**Figure 18–1** The piercing of Phineas Gage's brain is illustrated in this drawing.

## SYMPTOMS AND CAUSES OF BRAIN DAMAGE

The case of Phineas Gage provides a rather remarkable illustration of the way in which physical damage can affect mental processes. Phineas' case involves an organic syndrome resulting from *trauma*—direct physical injury to brain tissue. Trauma can result from other factors, such as automobile accidents, constant blows from boxing, bullet or shrapnel wounds, falling objects, or even excessive pressure on an infant's head during childbirth.

The organic disorders include a number of mental dysfunctions in which *brain damage*—biochemical or structural change in the brain—is a known factor (Williams, 1979). The organic disorders discussed in this chapter have a wide range of causes besides trauma. (These disorders are listed and defined in Table 18–1.) *Infections* from diseases such as syphilis, meningitis, or encephalitis can also cause brain damage. *Metabolic aberrations,* such as prenatal vitamin deficiencies, can impair the normal internal functioning of the body, leading to changes that ultimately affect the brain. *Toxic factors,* as from the intake of carbon monoxide, sniffing glue, or exposure to lead, may also cause permanent damage. The gradual deterioration associated with *aging* involves degenerative changes not only in the body's vascular and endocrine systems but also in the central nervous system. The growth of *brain tumors* can lead to atrophy, scarring, damage to the brain tissue, or blockage of passageways for the normal flow of cerebrospinal fluid.

Because of the variety of causes, brain damage can result in a number of symptoms, ranging from mildly disturbing to very serious. These may include impairment of any or all of the following: memory, emotions, intellect, judgment, consciousness, perception, motor skills, language skills, and orientation for time, place, or person.

As Table 18–2 indicates, there is some relationship between the location of the brain damage and the symptoms that result. (Refer back to Focus 4–1: Anatomy of the Brain for a diagram that shows the locations listed in the table.) Thus, convulsive movements suggest damage to the motor area of the brain, and the appearance of visual difficulties could be traceable to occipital lobe damage (one classical symptom of this type of brain injury is the complaint of seeing double).

Some organic conditions are considered temporary, while others may take some time before the residual symptoms respond to treatment. In still other conditions, damage is irreversible, and there is no effective treatment. In general, temporary conditions are those involving delirium that results from mild concussion, poison, drug or alcohol intoxication. The longer-lasting symptoms are those developing from long-term alcohol abuse, central nervous system diseases, degeneration of the brain from senility or from tumors, congenital cranial abnormalities, or severe lead or carbon monoxide poisoning. Either temporary or permanent symptoms have been seen in brain injuries associated with boxing, as discussed in Focus 18–1.

In any case, whether conditions are temporary or permanent, organic disorders are often far more complicated than a simple physical cause-and-effect relationship. Humans are complex organisms that function, act, and react as total integrated mechanisms. Symptoms will not only be affected by the physical damage itself, but by many other factors: the premorbid personality of the person; the frustrations and stresses or conflicts with which the individual must cope; and the person's self-concept and motivational structure. Persons who have always taken pride in their intellect, for instance, will find amnesia or the reduced ability to think coherently especially stressful, and a self-reliant person may become severely depressed at being dependent on others for care.

## CLASSIFICATION OF ORGANIC DYSFUNCTIONS

There are many ways to classify the organic disorders. This chapter will follow that used by DSM-III—with a few additions—in its major divisions of *organic brain syndromes* and *organic mental disorders.* The organic brain syndromes are defined as those disorders that show certain behavioral signs or psychological symptoms without a single specific etiology. They include the following:

- Organic brain syndrome, delirium syndrome

# FOCUS 18–1:

## Boxing, Punching, and Punch-drunks

> . . . See, all the brains are in a sort of cup, and after you get hit a few times it shakes them out of that cup. When they give you smelling salts it pulls them back into the cup. It's when the brains get shook up and run together that you get punch-drunk. (Ex-boxing champion Sonny Liston, as quoted in Boyle & Ames, 1983.)

Boxing is the only "civilized" sport where the goal is to beat your opponent in the head until submission. A single directed blow can cause at the least a temporary concussion, and severe and permanent brain damage at the most. Korean boxer Duk Koo Kim died without regaining consciousness; Benny Kid Paret died in a welterweight title fight a year after he had twice received concussions in the ring; Davey Moore, former flyweight champion, was also killed in a bout which he fought while suffering from health problems.

But deaths are relatively rare in boxing. More frequent are the cumulative effects of countless head blows which are absorbed in a fighter's career. Jerry Quarry, a leading contender for the heavyweight title, had his first formal fight at the age of five in a junior Golden Gloves amateur bout. He eventually survived 300 fights. Such continuous exposure to punches increase the likelihood of brain damage. Using CAT scans, Casson reported that he found signs of brain damage in 8 professional boxers, 5 of whom were former world champions and two who were top-ranked (cited by Boyle & Ames, 1983).

As with other cases of organic brain damage, the symptoms vary with the nature and site of the damage, as we have seen in this chapter. One cluster of symptoms has been so frequent in boxing injuries that a nonscientific term was created—punch-drunk. Punch-drunk boxers show unsteady gait and slight confusion; as the brain damage worsens, hand tremors, head-nodding, and speech stammers develop; in its severe state, symptoms include personality changes, shuffling gait, mood swings, slurred speech, and memory losses.

In a special report on boxing and brain damage, *Sports Illustrated* raised questions about boxers ranging from Muhammad Ali and Jerry Quarry to the lesser-known Mark Pacheco (Boyle & Ames, 1983). Ali denies that he has any damage from his career ("they want to say I have a brain injury, that I'm crazy"), and calls attention to the neurological examination he passed at the Mayo Clinic. In contrast, the *Sports Illustrated* article reported that a re-examination of Ali's CAT scan did show abnormalities and referred to Ali's speech as having been so slurred and unintelligible in one interview that the broadcast was cancelled.

Boxing is a sport in which there is much to gain as well as much to lose. It is a brutal sport; the fan's enthusiasm rises as the level of brutality increases. A knockout is more satisfying than a knockdown, but both may mean that damage to the brain has occurred, either temporary or permanent.

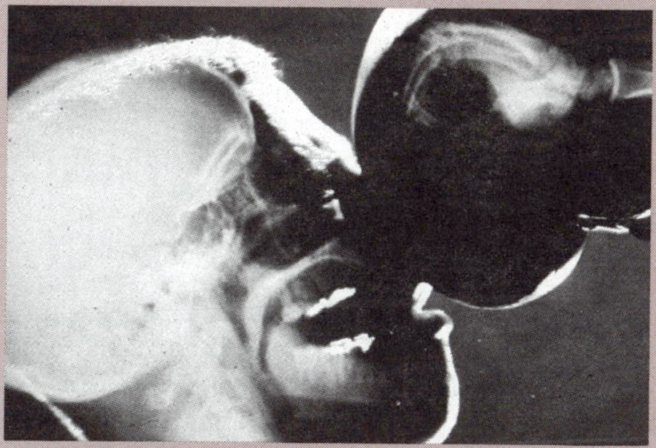

*A blow to the head, such as from boxing, can cause temporary or even permanent damage to the brain.*

**TABLE 18–2**

**Symptoms Associated with Damage to Various Parts of the Brain**

| *Frontal lobe* | *Parietal lobe* | *Temporal lobe* | *Occipital lobe* |
|---|---|---|---|
| Aphasia | Aphasia | Aphasia | Blindness in half of each eye |
| Loss of coordination | Loss of movement | Blindness in half of each eye | Aphasia |
| Convulsions | Inability to read words | Hallucinations | Inability to read words |
| Loss of memory | Convulsions | Visual size distortions | Visual hallucinations |
| Incontinence | Tactile amnesia | Convulsions | |
| Yawning | | | |
| *Cerebellum* | *Midbrain* | *Medulla* | *Motor area* |
| Loss of coordination | Eye axis deviations | Poor enunciation | Convulsions |
| Dizziness | Loss of coordination | Spasmodic eye movements | Speech defects |
| Loss of sequencing movements | Eyelid droop | Loss of coordination | Loss of fine movement |
| Spasmodic eye movements | | Vertigo | |

SOURCE: Adapted from *Psychology of Abnormal Behavior,* 2nd ed., by L. P. Thorpe, B. Katz and R. T. Lewis, 1961, New York: Ronald Press Co.

- Organic brain syndrome, amnestic syndrome
- Organic brain syndrome, delusional syndrome
- Organic brain syndrome, hallucinosis syndrome
- Organic brain syndrome, affective syndrome
- Organic brain syndrome, personality syndrome

A separate major category, the organic mental disorders, is used to describe those disorders in which a single particular etiology is actually known—for instance, alcohol or drug use or aging. Thus, the major organic mental disorders include:

- Primary degenerative dementia, senile onset
- Primary degenerative dementia, presenile onset
- Organic mental disorders, substance induced

The substance induced disorders, including alcohol intoxication and other conditions caused directly by drug abuse, have already been discussed in Chapter 13. This chapter will summarize the organic brain syndromes and the organic mental disorders arising from old age and presenile factors. In addition, although neither is officially part of the DSM-III system, both *general paresis* and *epilepsy* will be discussed briefly, for they both relate closely to the physiological etiologies discussed here.

## ORGANIC BRAIN SYNDROME: SYMPTOMS AND DIAGNOSES

### Organic Brain Syndrome, Delirium Syndrome

Organic brain syndrome, delirium syndrome, may have several causes, including infections, substance use, metabolic imbalances, blows to the head, toxic states, or some types of severe vitamin deficiencies (Plum & Posner, 1972). The major symptom is delirium—a difficulty in sustaining attention, thinking in a directed way, or engaging in goal-directed actions.

The person's attention wanders from even the

simplest activities, and this has noticeable effects in several areas of functioning. Speech may wander as the person forgets the beginning of a sentence before reaching the end. Because the individual fails to attend to what is going on, memory deficiencies also occur. New information does not register; the person may not remember what questions had been asked simply because he or she didn't listen. Long-term memory may also be defective, because the person is unable to focus enough attention on recalling the past to answer questions. Another possible symptom is a loss of orientation. Thus, the person may not know where he or she is, what date it is, or may even mistake the hospital room for a room at home.

Sleep cycle disturbances may also occur in delirium. This may be characterized either by insomnia or by just the opposite—more sleeping. Delirium states will come on rapidly, in a matter of hours; similarly, they tend to end after short duration of about a week as the causative agent is treated.

### Organic Brain Syndrome, Amnestic Syndrome

The organic brain syndrome, amnestic syndrome, may be caused by head injury, *anoxia* (deprivation of oxygen to the brain), some diseases such as encephalitis, or most commonly, alcohol abuse (Pratt, 1977).

The primary symptom of amnestic syndrome is amnesia in *short-term,* but not immediate, memory. A common two-part test illustrates this distinction (Williams, 1978). The person is presented with three objects, such as a pen, a ball, and a string. Then, after about a half hour, the subject is asked to recall the items. In the second test, the subject is asked to immediately recall several numbers as soon as they have been read off—such as "3-5-9-2-4." The amnestic person would be able to recall the digits but not remember the three objects. The half-hour time period is gauged as the amount of time it takes for immediate experience to be transferred into more permanent memory storage (Knight & Wooles, 1980). This type of memory defect, as we've seen in Chapter 8, is known as *anterograde amnesia,* the inability to take new information and retain it for more than about a half hour. A second form of amnesia that readers will remember is *retrograde amnesia,* the inability to recall events just prior to the onset of the syndrome. This form of amnesia may also be present.

Some other symptoms may also occur along with the memory defect. These may include some disorientation and possibly confabulation. Persons with amnestic syndrome characteristics will often deny having memory problems; thus, there may be a tendency to make up or confabulate stories to fill in memory gaps.

The loss of memory can have a critical impact on one's life in ways we do not often consider. Dr. Malcolm Meltzer (1983), a psychologist himself, had a heart attack. As his heart was failing, his lungs failed to carry sufficient oxygen to his brain, causing anoxia and memory impairment. In a remarkable report, he cites "recalling" that he had two children (in actuality he had one) and that he was 33 years old (when he was 44). Among his challenges was relearning how to set his alarm clock and how to change a razor blade. Thinking through problems became frustrating, since it required keeping track of several facts, and since he often forgot such details at the slightest distraction. In his words, "Soon you become reluctant to reason something out. What's the use? You decide that you can't do it, so stop thinking and accept the simplest solution" (p. 4). Memory turns out to be extremely important in many other ways as well. Dr. Meltzer found television to be work rather than pleasure, since it meant having to remember the plot in stories and which team was which in sports. Social affairs became trying, and he became more and more reticent, for instance, to ask about a person's spouse only to discover that he had attended the spouse's funeral two years earlier. Memory loss also meant an inability to take certain responsibilities, such as paying bills or making household repairs. As a consequence of these memory deficiencies, Meltzer noted his personality changing to become more passive, dependent, self-conscious, and withdrawn.

### Organic Brain Syndrome, Delusional Syndrome

The organic brain syndrome, delusional syndrome, may be caused by brain tumors, some forms of epilepsy, or drug abuse from hallucinogens or amphetamines (Williams, 1979). The major symptom is the appearance of delusions, extreme beliefs that have no basis in reality. A man once interviewed by the author was convinced that he was the assassin of President Kennedy, pleading "You have to believe me, I'm a political prisoner, since his friends would rather I suffer in a mental hospital than be executed. I killed Kennedy! I hated him so long that I finally willed him dead."

In a delusional syndrome, the person is otherwise lucid, alert, and oriented. The delusional state, however, can be extreme enough that an individual may be potentially harmful—either to others or the self. Consider, for a moment, how explosively angry you might become if you truly believed that one of your instructors was undermining your reputation and grades by spreading rumors about you to the entire faculty.

### Organic Brain Syndrome, Hallucinosis Syndrome

The organic brain syndrome, hallucinosis syndrome, may be caused by drug substances, such as the hallucinogens, and especially by alcohol abuse (Benson & Blumer, 1975). The primary symptom is the appearance of hallucinations, sensory experiences without a basis in reality. The hallucinations may appear in any sensory mode, although they tend most often to be auditory. The specific organic cause can influence which sense is affected, however, with hallucinogens tending to produce visual sensations or distortions while alcohol reactions tend to produce auditory and sometimes tactual experiences. The hallucinations may be positive or negative experiences. Further, the person may be completely aware that the hallucination is not real. The fact that this syndrome is listed as an organic disturbance makes it clear that the hallucination is the result of the alcohol or the drug acting on brain function. Hallucinations and delusional states can appear without an organic cause; in this case a different diagnosis is used, as we've seen, for example, in the schizophrenic psychoses discussed in Chapter 17.

### Organic Brain Syndrome, Affective Syndrome

The organic brain syndrome, affective syndrome, may be caused by toxic agents or by hormonal diseases such as those affecting the thyroids. Other sources may include steroids (drugs sometimes used by athletes to improve their performance), drug abuse, and, less frequently, brain injury or tumors (Salzman & Shader, 1977).

The major symptom is a disturbance in mood states, leading to either depression or euphoria. Where depression occurs, the person is sorrowful, tearful, and brooding, showing excessive bodily concerns as well as disinterest in activity. In euphoric or manic states, the person appears to be on a high, with heightened activity levels, a false sense of well-being, an impaired ability to recognize the artificiality of the euphoria, and perhaps irritability that things are not being accomplished as fast as he or she would expect.

Confirmation of this diagnosis requires laboratory or physical evidence of an organic basis, whether the organic cause is directly acting on brain function, or whether it acts via the hormonal or endocrinological function. In the event that organic factors are not proven, then the diagnostician must be alert to other possible causes and hence diagnoses, such as the affective disorders discussed in Chapter 16.

### Organic Brain Syndrome, Personality Syndrome

The organic brain syndrome, personality syndrome, is caused by structural damage to the nervous system, as through endocrine dysfunction or direct brain damage, as in Case History 18–1. Thyroid disease can be a cause, as can the incorrect use of steroids; still other causes include *concussions* (transitory loss of consciousness due to a severe blow to the head or spinal column), tumors, blood clots in the brain's vascular system, and, less frequently, temporal lobe epilepsy.

A number of primary symptoms enable a diagnosis of organic personality syndrome. Most prominent is a shift in stable behavior patterns or personality. For example, a neighbor who is usually cheerful may suddenly become hostile or seclusive. Recall the actions of Charles Whitman in the Focus on Aggression and Violence (Focus 12–1). Emotional lability (such as sudden crying or explosive, angry outbursts) is common, so that it may be hard for friends to know how to behave around such persons, for fear of "setting them off.'' Poor impulse control and lack of social judgment are also frequent. This may be seen in behaviors such as blatant shoplifting or sexual indiscretions, indications that the person has little concern for the consequences. Or instead, a person may feel an overall sense of apathy or indifference to the environment or to life, becoming withdrawn or detached from usual recreations, hobbies, or work.

## ORGANIC MENTAL DISORDERS: SYMPTOMS AND DIAGNOSES

The organic brain syndromes just discussed derive from a variety of causes. In contrast, each of the organic mental disorders is associated with a single specific cause. This section will look at the two organic degenerative disorders, senile and presenile dementia.

The primary degenerative dementias are considered to be disorders of aging (Katzman & Terry, 1983). Two of these are recognized: *primary degenerative dementia with senile onset,* and *primary degenerative dementia with presenile onset.* For convenience, we will use the shorter terms of senile dementia and presenile dementia. Both involve extreme forms of the general neurological degeneration that occurs in all of us as the human body inexorably deteriorates with age. The major symptoms of senile dementia and presenile dementia are the same, except that the term *senile dementia* has been arbitrarily used for cases in which age of onset is over 65.

### Senile Dementia

Many of the symptoms of senile dementia are commonly known, through everyday descriptions of *senility.* Cases similar to George's in Case History 18–2 are probably familiar to most readers involved with the elderly. The progression of senile dementia may be traced through several phases. The first signs are memory losses, first appearing as absent-mindedness, then a gradual fragmentation of memory for recent events, and a tendency to dwell more and more in the past (Haase, 1977). Soon the person is unable to keep track of time or of his or her own age. Irritability or touchiness may appear in this early stage, along with a lessened interest in others or the environment.

As the deterioration progresses, there is a further tendency towards being opinionated and set in ways. Behaviorally, the person neglects his or her appearance, wearing clothes in disarray, dripping food, and becoming slovenly. Physical symptoms also occur, including an overall graying, a thickening of the skin, tremors, feeble and shuffling gait, and general paucity of motion. Changes in temperament may cause the person to become querulous, agitated, and restless, perhaps weeping readily or suddenly becoming highly irritable. Waking states may become more and more interrupted by confused daydreams. Abstract thinking is impaired and life is interpreted from a concrete perspective, with words or instructions being taken literally (Kaplan, 1979). Judgment and impulse control fail. Ultimately mental functions fail, and the patient may become mute, resistant, and disoriented.

The average time between the onset of the senile dementia to eventual death is approximately five years. Some research suggests possible dysfunctioning of the body's immunity systems involved in the aging process, leading to cell deterioration in senile dementia (Cohen & Eisdorfer, 1980).

### Presenile Dementia

Presenile dementia also involves brain degeneration. In this disorder, however, the onset occurs prior to age 65. Two forms of presenile dementia are Alzheimer's disease and Pick's disease.

*Alzheimer's disease* was first described by the German neurologist, Alois Alzheimer, in 1907. The disease appears between ages 50 and 60 and afflicts about 1.5 million persons, including 5 percent of the elderly (Butler and Emr, 1982). It involves cortical atrophy and the appearance of tangled, threadlike fibers in place of normal nerve cells (Alzheimer, 1907). *Senile plaques* also appear in some cases. These are small areas in which tissues of the cortex have degenerated into granular and filamentous material (Wang, 1977). Cerebral blood flow can become restricted, leading to psychiatric symptoms (Hoyer et al., 1979).

In addition to the symptoms just described for se-

## Case History 18–2:
### Senile Dementia

George H. was an 88-year-old man placed in a Veterans hospital. As a young man, he was adventurous and fought in the Spanish-American War where he was decorated for bravery. His war experiences turned out to be the only significantly exciting part of his entire life, and he loved to relive his feats. His business was not nearly as interesting, since he became a janitor. Following his discharge, he married a high school classmate and they settled down to an uneventful marriage. Not having any children, and without any promotions, George always felt that his entire world was gray and dull—a dull job where he was mostly alone, a dull wife who gave him no children, a dull environment in a small rural town. The years passed slowly enough until his wife died; after that, time seemed to stand still.

When a neighbor found George wandering the streets, he arranged for hospitalization. At first, since other veterans were present, George felt a renewed interest on the hope that old war stories would be swapped. However, George soon discovered that the other patients talked a lot about their old memories, but were disinterested in his, and even rudely interrupted him or walked away. George's physical condition continued to deteriorate.

George's tendency to lie in bed throughout the day muttering to himself was a constant problem to the hospital staff. He resisted all recreational opportunities as well as offers of a change of scene. Several times a day he would enter a delirious state and shout for his wife. During these periods he recognized no one. He was incontinent and extremely irritable when required to use a bedpan. Although he accused the staff of secretly planning his degradation, he exhibited a total lack of concern over his own tendency to display his genitals when children were visiting the ward.

He became more and more secretive and noncommunicative and suspicious as time progressed. In his better moments, he regained some lucidity and would discuss his Spanish-American war experiences; but he progressively lost his memory for even his most favored story. In his last days, he was completely disoriented, apparently hallucinating, and agitated. He died at age 93 of a cerebral hemorrhage.

nile dementia, persons with Alzheimer's disease may also show convulsions, *aphasia* (loss or impairment of language function), or *apraxia* (inability to use objects correctly). Delusions and hallucinations occur such that the person loses touch with reality, and it is not unusual for a person to rely on confabulations to cover up for losses of memory. Within about 10 years, the person is reduced to virtually a vegetative existence.

*Pick's disease,* discovered by the Prague physician Arnold Pick in 1892, usually has its onset at about age 45, but it has been known to appear as early as age 31. Atrophy, especially of the frontal and temporal lobes, develops such that the total brain weight may be reduced from 1,340 grams to 100 grams. Speech and higher mental processes are impaired, and emotions are blunted or the person becomes irritable, suspicious, or depressed. Convulsions are rare, and delusions and hallucinations are less frequent in Pick's disease than in Alzheimer's. Persons with Pick's disease usually die within four to six years of its onset.

## GENERAL PARESIS

Although not listed as a major DSM-III disorder, general paresis deserves comment as an organically caused mental disorder. Paresis comes from *syphilis,* an infectious venereal disease believed first introduced to Europe by Christopher Columbus and his crew. Once called the "Great Pox," syphilis can result in general paresis, a disease that was initially described by a pharmacist named Haslam in 1798. Haslam was involved in the autopsy of a 42-year-old man who believed himself to be the king of Denmark, the king of

France, the master of all dead and living languages, and the peer of William the Conqueror.

Syphilis is diagnosed by the Wasserman blood test, which detects the presence of a spirochete microorganism known as *Treponema pallidum,* the cause of the disease. It may be acquired through sexual intercourse and may then be congenitally transmitted from the mother to the fetus. The disease progresses through four definable stages.

### Stages of Infection

In the first phase, within four weeks of entry, the spirochetes multiply and spread throughout the body. A sore called a *chancre,* which looks like a small pimple or open sore, appears at the point of infection. The chancre gives little discomfort; in fact, the infected person may take little notice, for it disappears by itself.

In the second phase, a dark skin rash covers the body within three to six weeks after the appearance of the chancre. The coppertoned rash may be very mild, or it may be more severe, similar to a smallpox rash. Small warts often appear on the genitals. This rash, like the chancre, soon fades, as a latency phase takes over and no overt signs are present. The individual may experience no discomfort or pain. However, spirochetes are infesting various organs during this third period, causing irreparable damage.

The latency phase may last as long as three decades before the fourth, active phase occurs. During this period, the spirochetes may increase their activity, attacking the heart, the spinal cord, or the brain. *General paresis* is the result of brain infection by the spirochetes.

## Case History 18–3:
### General Paresis

Leonard K. was a handsome man as a youth attending college in Europe. As an American, he initially found himself being coolly treated, but this only challenged him to turn on his native charm. Following graduation, he traveled the countryside in order to ''experience all the experiences there are'' before settling down. One stop was in Amsterdam where he discovered the public brothels on one notorious street of prostitutes. Not long after this experience, he noted some sores on his genitals, but soon dismissed them as a temporary infection.

Leonard is now age 55, and was referred to the hospital by his family after an episode of reckless promises, extravagant claims, and grandiose commitments. He had been usually a reserved family man, but has gradually been changing in his personality. Once a fastidious dresser, he had suddenly surprised his wife by neglecting to shave, wearing suits that had been wrinkled because he slept in them, and refusing to wash. He became more and more expansive, talkative, and occasionally violent.

By the time he was committed for treatment, he believed himself to be a state senator and spoke of his planned travels to Washington. He intended to have a new bill passed, proclaiming himself ''executive emperor''—words he had difficulty in pronouncing. He was known to stand wherever a crowd was willing to listen and loudly pronounce his views on war, religion, birth control, communism, nuclear weapons, taxes, and nearly any topic that was raised to him. His views offered solutions to world problems, solutions he was convinced were valid.

His wife described him as having become almost too mild prior to the recent outbursts. His gradual loss of memory led him to make up tales to fill in his memory gaps, tales about which he seemed unconcerned even when they were proven false. His shift to grandiosity was believed to be an attempt to compensate for his lowered self-confidence and self-esteem. He was diagnosed as suffering from general paresis following medical examinations and was placed on a treatment program consisting of 20 million units of penicillin.

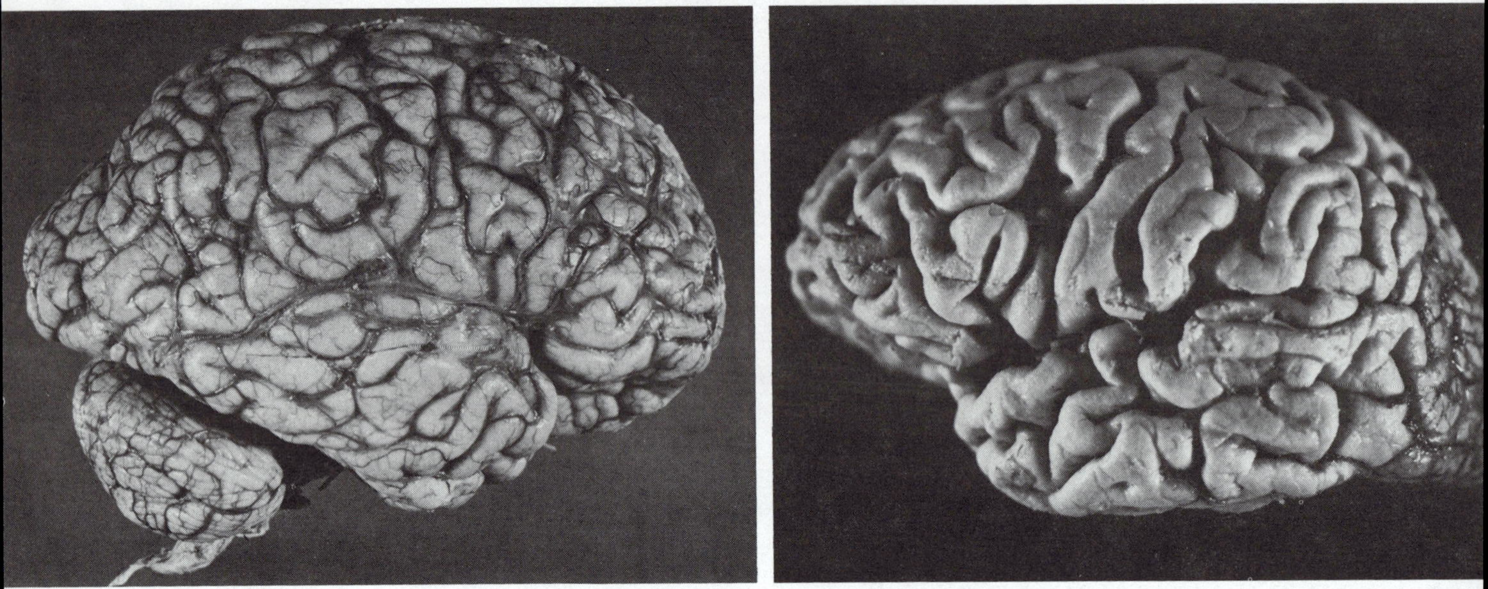

*In **Alzheimer's disorder** the brain shows atrophy (right) in contrast to the structure of a healthy brain (left).*

### Symptoms of General Paresis

General paresis appears five times more frequently in men than women (syphilis itself is twice as common in men than women). Not all syphilitic patients develop paresis. It typically appears between the ages of 35 and 50. Symptoms of general paresis are both physical and psychological.

***Physical Signs of Paresis.*** Paresis is detectable through blood and spinal fluid analysis. In addition, certain neurological signs appear. The pupils may be of different sizes, or a slowness in the pupillary reflex to light (a symptom known as the Argyll-Robertson pupil) may occur. Motor disturbances may also occur. The most important type are convulsions, although tremors of the extended fingers, tongue, or lips may appear. Handwriting disturbances are shown in very slow, irregular, and scratchy writing. Speech disorder is a very characteristic diagnostic sign. The person hesitates or slurs, saying "Meh-adis Pis'pal" instead of "Methodist Episcopal," for example. Disturbance of the spinal cord is exhibited in *locomotor ataxia,* a shuffling gait.

***Psychological Signs of Paresis.*** The psychological picture of general paresis is appalling. Progressive deterioration occurs as the spirochetes do their damage. Memory for recent events, such as the meal just eaten, is affected although the individual may recall remote events. Irritability, slovenliness, loss of judgment, and behavioral controls diminish.

As the illness progresses, either of three courses may develop: deterioration without delusions, deterioration with delusions of grandeur, or deterioration with depression and delusions. The most common of these is the slowly advancing deterioration. However, the grandiose delusional state is also common, as in the case first noted by Haslam in 1798. Persons in this state feel expansive: all is well with the world and themselves. In the depressed condition, individuals are fraught with guilt and suicidal notions. They are certain they must do penance or are convinced their brains are rotting inside their skulls. Assaultive behav-

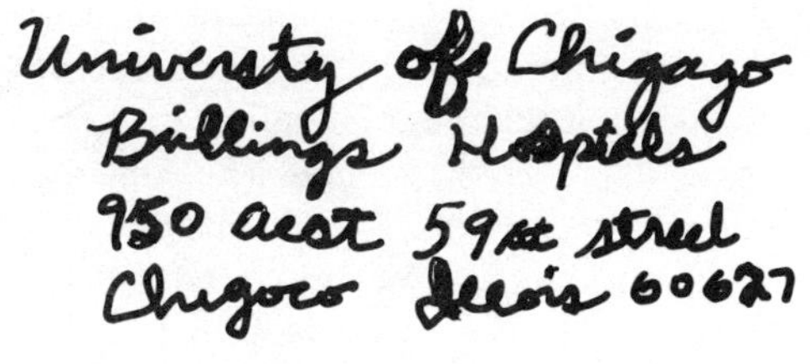

*General paresis is detectable in motor disturbances, such as in handwriting difficulties. Note the irregular, scratchy writing and retracing of misspelled words in this characteristic sample.*

ior is a frequent concomitant of the delusional states. In the final stages of the illness, the delusional symptoms diminish and the intellectual deterioration becomes the foremost feature. Sudden outbursts of destructiveness may appear, but soon the patient is bedridden, without awareness, incentive, recognition, thought, or even voluntary movement.

## TREATING ORGANIC DISORDERS

In all of the organic disorders just discussed, treatment depends on the factor that is causing the syndrome and the extent of brain damage. In discussing treatments for the organic disorders, it is, therefore, important to first talk about the diagnosis itself, and how it is made.

### Need for Diagnosis

Correct diagnosis of the organic illness, its type, location, and severity is a significant step in understanding it and in designing treatment. The diagnosis of a person's problem as involving a basic organic damage can quickly help to explain unexpected personality changes in the person, narrowing the concern from a search for an emotional cause to the search instead for the organic site involved. Certain organic diseases and damage will follow predictable courses, and therapy can be prepared with this course in mind. Finally, any treatment program and its goals need to be appropriate for the particular type of organic damage or dysfunction. The diagnosis, therefore, will determine the type of drug, surgery, or psychotherapy to be prescribed.

Two approaches to diagnosing organic damage are physical tests and psychological assessments. We'll look at each before discussing the specific treatment methods.

### Physical Tests

A variety of physical methods have been used to determine the presence of organic brain damage. We mentioned the *computerized axial tomography* (the CAT scan) in Chapter 17. As you may recall, the CAT scan combines the details obtained from X-rays with the abilities of the computer (DuBoulay & Moseley, 1977). The computer extrapolates from brain X-rays taken from different angles, mathematically reconstructing a total image of each layer of the brain. In *angiography,* an opaque substance is injected into an artery in the neck. X-rays will show all the blood vessels as the substance circulates around the brain, pointing out any irregularities (Baker, 1971). In *pneumoencephalography,* air is introduced into the cranium which outlines the various parts of the skull under X-ray (Mayo Clinic, 1983). This procedure has been useful in identifying atrophy in the brain. *Electroencephalograms,* or the recording of brain waves, are useful in diagnosing abnormal patterns considered to be associated with aging, degenerative diseases, and epilepsy (discussed later), as well as damage from blows (Struve, in press).

### Neuropsychological Assessments.

In addition to the several tests just described, a number of psychological tests are also used to assess the localization and extent of brain damage. Although no single test is adequate for this purpose, several test batteries (series of tests that together provide an accurate profile) have been useful (Goldstein & Hersen, 1984). Among the major psychological batteries are the Halstead-Reitan battery and the Luria-Nebraska Neu-

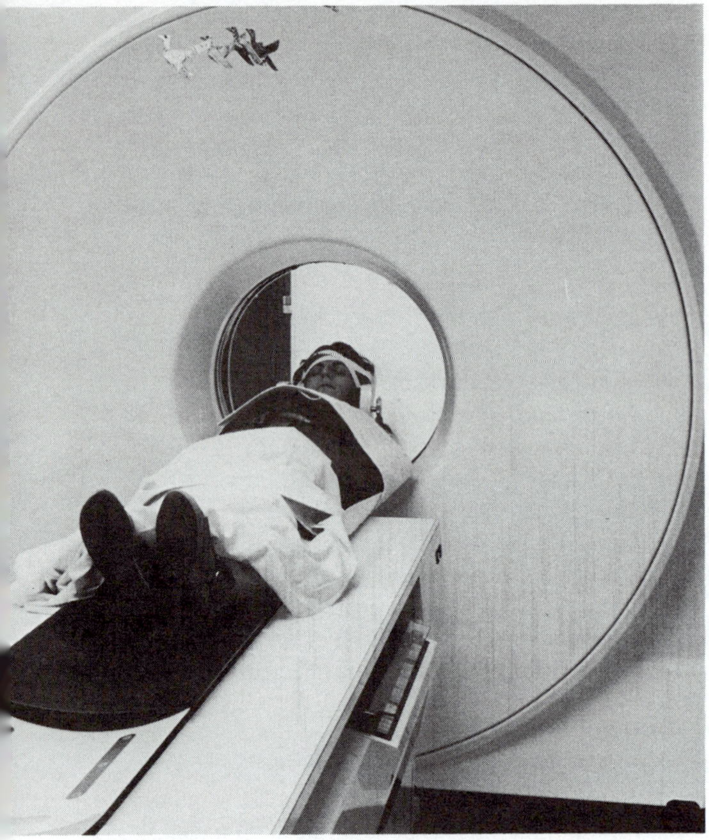

*The* ***CAT scan*** *is a computerized method for viewing the brain.*

ropsychological battery. These and other tests, such as the neuropsychological battery by Smith (1975), and the Wechsler Adult Intelligence Scale, present the patient with a range of perceptual, cognitive, and psychomotor tasks. From these performances, diagnosticians can make inferences about organic damage.

The *Halstead-Reitan battery* (Reitan & Davison, 1974; Golden et al., 1981a) is a series of tests for assessing abstraction skills, memory, motor performance, auditory perception, speech perception, and finger speed tasks. It is highly effective as a diagnostic tool—in fact, comparisons have found it as accurate as medical-neurological assessment methods (Filskov & Goldstein, 1974). One test, called the category test, assesses abstraction ability by showing figures differing in dimensions, such as size, shape, number, color, or location. The person must determine the principles by which they are grouped. The rhythm test assesses both auditory attention and discrimination by having the subject hear 30 pairs of beats from a tape recorder and then decide whether the pairs are identical or different. In still another test, the subject hears a tape of nonsense syllables and is asked to identify each from a list of four choices in print. This test measures not only attention and concentration, but also comprehension. The finger oscillation task measures the speed with which the person can push a lever with the index finger. The test involves trials with one, then the other hand as independent assessments of motor control.

The Luria-Nebraska Neuropsychological Battery (Moses et al., 1983) tests 11 areas of functioning: motor ability, rhythm functions, tactile functions, visual functions, receptive speech, expressive speech, writing functions, reading functions, arithmetical functions, memory, and intellectual processes. Some of these tasks are similar to those mentioned earlier in the Halstead-Reitan, although the actual activity is different. For example, in the rhythm segment, the subject is asked to listen to a series of "beeps" and then to indicate how many beeps there were in each group. Motor functions are tested by asking the person to enact certain instructions, such as "Touch each of your fingers in order with your thumb." Tactual functions are surveyed by having the individual decide, for example, whether he or she has been touched with the point or with the head of a pin. In tasks of visual function, the individual is asked to identify objects first from simple pictures then from more complex pictures. The receptive speech series of instructions require the person to show that he or she not only hears but can comprehend certain words or statements. In expressive speech, the person must read or express answers to questions.

### Intellectual Process Tests.

In addition to the neuropychological tests, intelligence tests such as the Wechsler Adult Intelligence Scale (Anthony et al., 1980) are also valuable in making diagnoses. Research on the Wechsler battery has demonstrated that it is valuable in identifying persons with brain damage versus those with other problems, such as psychiatric disorders. Furthermore, the battery can provide information on right brain hemisphere versus left hemisphere functioning (Golden et al., 1979).

These psychological tests are valuable in diagnosing brain damage, assessing the level of damage in specific functions, such as memory, abstract thinking, orientation, and intellectual functioning. These diagnoses of organic dysfunctions will set the direction for treatment.

## Approaches to Treatment

Depending on the cause itself and the severity of the symptoms, two broad (sometimes overlapping) approaches to treatment may be dictated. The first approach is to reverse or at least minimize the symptoms by counteracting the cause. The second approach is one of rehabilitation, in cases where damage is already irreversible or where the cause cannot be arrested. Rehabilitation involves helping persons make the best psychological and physical adjustment to their permanent disability. Helping people cope with aging is one important area of this last approach that deserves special note, so we will discuss it separately in this section.

***Treating Reversible Symptoms.*** In several organically caused disorders, the prognosis is good because symptoms can be relieved by eliminating the cause. This is often true where there is a toxic cause. Unless permanent brain damage has occurred, immediate removal of the poisonous substance can reverse the symptoms. The same is often the case where drug use is the source, for instance, of an hallucination or delusion.

Symptomatic treatment may be prescribed while the patient is recovering from the substance, or as a means for expediting recovery (Kapnick, 1978). For example, bromide poisoning, associated with overdoses of some types of sleeping pills, typically causes restlessness, a symptom that may be reduced by drugs such as paraldehyde or chloral hydrate.

Many organic syndromes are not caused by toxic substances, and these require a variety of different treatments. States of delirium caused by metabolic imbalances may be treated by correcting the metabolic or nutritional state, as in some thyroid conditions or severe vitamin deficiences. For infections, modern chemotherapy is often a direct answer. Heavy doses of penicillin, for instance, is the preferred method for treating syphilis. This antibiotic, however, is only effective when treatment occurs early in the course of the disease, before permanent damage has occurred.

Another approach that can sometimes reverse symptoms is surgery. As an example, excessive brain fluids may cause pressure on the brain, resulting in organic symptoms. Surgery can often relieve the pressure and remove the abnormality. In some cases of epilepsy, as we will see, surgery might also remove the brain segment responsible for the convulsions.

***Rehabilitation.*** In some organic disorders, the infection, toxicity, or trauma has already done its damage to brain function and has proceeded too far to be reversible. Medical treatment can still be helpful in cases where such damage has occurred, so long as the illness can be arrested and further damage avoided (Finger & Stein, 1982).

Rehabilitation medicine is a branch of medicine that aims at restoring the individual to the fullest physical, mental, social, and economic functioning possible, given the sensory, motor, or intellectual constraints that now exist (Marinelli & Orto, 1984).

In effect, this treatment enables the person to make maximum use of now-limited capabilities. If a car accident, for example, has led to paralysis and amnesia, a rehabilitation program may help the person achieve the highest level of self-care that the disability permits, even though the memory loss may be permanent. Where a personality or mood change is a function of the patient's reaction to the disability, counseling can help the patient adjust, often to the point of acceptance. In this way, emotional stability can often be restored even if other symptoms cannot be reversed (Small, 1983).

***Coping with Aging.*** For the degenerative disorders associated with aging, recovery from the deterioration is, of course, impossible. On the other hand, there is agreement that even without the presence of organic changes, aging can represent adjustment problems for the normal person (Eisenberg et al., 1984).

*Among the problems of older persons may be the sorrow of being* ***alone.***

Getting older may lead to depression or conflict if the person fears the loss of youth.

Yet for some, aging is an asset. Consider, for example, that the political leaders of most nations are well into their second half-century of life. State governors, and aspirants to the presidency, are also usually well beyond their 40s, as are most Pulitzer Prize winners or well-known writers or artists.

To a very great extent, the psychological effect of aging is influenced by the culture and environment in which a person lives (Rowles & Ohta, 1982). In those societies where wisdom is still associated with age, the elderly seem to retain both self-respect and personal optimism about life. Our own society, however, has often held less positive associations. Many persons have interpreted retirement as joblessness; aging as senility; and disability as reflecting dependency.

Preparation for old age and even the concept of death should be a crucial part of every person's planning (Kübler-Ross, 1975). The early development of a sense of self-satisfaction and esteem can carry over into the later period of lessened activity and responsibilities. Focus 18–2 provides an opportunity for you to assess your own goals, or help others assess theirs, for aging.

Throughout this chapter, we have explored several mental disorders that relate to organic causes. It is useful to talk about one more disorder, epilepsy, that, in the popular image, is often seen as a form of mental illness, retardation, or at the very least a sign of mental instability. In fact, such beliefs about epilepsy are unfounded, except in some cases of psychomotor seizures. In the last part of this chapter, we will take a closer look at epilepsy—an organic but not a mental disorder.

## EPILEPSY: AN ORGANIC BUT NOT A MENTAL DISORDER

The word *epilepsy* is derived from the Greek *epilepsia,* meaning seizure. As it is now used, the term refers to conditions involving motor or sensory convulsions that are periodic and self-limiting. The disorder has been recognized for centuries, and a number of prominent historical figures have been epileptic, including Julius Caesar, Alexander the Great, and Vincent van Gogh. The Greeks had considered it to be a divine disease, until Hippocrates refuted the belief.

The actual incidence of epilepsy in the United States today is unknown. However, it is estimated that 1 of every 100 persons may be affected (Sullivan, 1979). Most persons with convulsive disorders remain at home; only about 50,000 receive constant care in special institutions, living areas, or residential schools. Only a very small number are in psychiatric hospitals, inasmuch as the convulsive disorders are primarily neurological rather than psychiatric or psychological problems (Jerath et al., 1981).

### Symptoms and Diagnoses

Epilepsy takes many forms, depending on the area of the brain that is involved and the severity of the disturbance. The seizures may affect muscles, leading to general spasms, or they may influence perceptions. In

# FOCUS 18–2:

## Aging: Six Questions

The aging process brings with it undeniable signs of deterioration. But it is generally agreed that much of the individualistic reactions to the idea of aging are the product of psychological factors (Riley et al., 1983).

We all age. Whether you will ''grow old gracefully'' or not depends partly on the groundwork—goals, attitudes, and commitments to continued growth—that you lay now. Here are six questions that may help you set the framework for your future attitudes toward aging:

- What are your accomplishments (the things you feel best about) so far?
- What are your life goals?
- Do these life goals extend only up to retirement, or beyond?
- What fantasies do you hold about what will make it gratifying for you to look back on your life after you are retired?
- What do you wish to do with your life after you retire? Do you have specific goals for your later years?
- What do you need to do now in order to achieve a life of continuing growth?

the latter case, sensory seizures may take the form of numbness or tingling sensations (somato-sensory seizures); moving flashes of light, dark spots, stars, colors (visual seizures); or buzzing, roaring sounds (auditory seizures). The more common types of seizures are grand mal, petit mal, Jacksonian, and psychomotor. These different forms of epilepsy will each be defined in the next sections.

***Grand Mal.*** The *grand mal seizure* is the most common and also the most dramatic type of epileptic seizure. The attack is sometimes preceded by a warning called an *aura,* a sensory symptom such as the feeling that visceral pressure is gradually moving up toward the head. An aura may appear anytime from less than a second to several days before the seizure.

The grand mal seizure itself takes part in three stages: tonic, clonic, and recovery. The *tonic stage* is initiated in some by a vocal outburst, such as a cry or yell. The person's body muscles then tighten in a spasm. The trunk is rigid, the head thrown backward, the jaw tightly closed, and the hands clenched. The eyes remain open, although the person is unconscious. Respiration ceases.

Within a minute or so, the tonic stage ends and the *clonic stage* begins. This stage involves jerking movements actually due to swift alternations between contractions and relaxation of muscles, occurring as often as 15 a second. Respiration is spasmodically resumed, saliva may foam at the mouth. The clonic convulsions last for two to three minutes and are followed by *recovery,* a state of general muscular relaxation. Some individuals are amnesic but completely alert when they recover; others fall asleep. In some cases, grand mal seizures occur in a rapid series of attacks during which the individual never reaches consciousness before another convulsion begins. This condition is referred to as a *grand mal status,* or *status epilepticus.*

***Petit Mal.*** The *petit mal seizure* is the next most common form of epilepsy. Unlike the grand mal, this type of seizure is never associated with an aura, and semiconsciousness is possible. The person may be vaguely aware of others, although unable to comprehend what is being said. Such attacks are short, lasting from a second up to a minute. (However, they may occur more frequently. Up to several hundred seizures have been known to occur in a single day.)

The person shows no massive muscle convulsions during the seizure. Instead, there are only minor rhythmic movements such as scratching or trembling. The eyes are open but unseeing. The individual may simply appear to have stopped in midsentence, paused, then continued on. Confusion may be present after a sei-

## Case History 18–4:
### Petit Mal Epilepsy

Joan K. is a member of the political staff of a state senator. She first became interested in government issues through a speech she heard concerning candidates in an upcoming gubernatorial election. She enrolled in a private university with an active political science program, applied for and received a summer appointment as a political science intern in the state capitol.

Joan had been subject to petit mal seizures during childhood and continued to have them while in college. Initially, she was concerned about her ability to lead a normal life and was painfully shy, fearing that she would have a seizure in the presence of her classmates. Although the attacks were themselves not noticeable, she experienced a confusion on their termination.

In spite of the condition, she was soon more confident of her abilities and became more comfortable about her seizures. She found that others were more able to adapt to her brief attacks once they were aware of her disorder. In addition, she was actually able to help educate her peers in the facts of epilepsy, removing many inaccurate beliefs. She often worked as a babysitter once she was certain the physician had found the right combination of drugs for her. She graduated in the middle of her class with a sense of real satisfaction at her own emotional development and the progress of others in understanding epilepsy.

zure, as in the example of Joan in Case History 18–4, but it is not always present. Sometimes the person is aware only of having experienced a blank spell in which he or she did not hear what was being said for a brief period. In fact, many are able to pass through a seizure without being noticed.

Petit mal epilepsy is more common among young people than adults, and it is likely to disappear with age. This is a mixed blessing, however, for the grand mal may occasionally develop in its place.

***Jacksonian Seizure.*** The *Jacksonian seizure* is a more limited type of motor seizure than the grand mal. It consists of muscular twitches beginning on one side of the body and progressing throughout the arm or leg of the same side. The convulsions always start in the same place—for example, on the face or the hand. In some cases, the attack spreads throughout the one side, then over the entire body, occasioning the loss of consciousness. If it is restricted in focus, then it is described as a focal seizure. Such circumscribed motor seizures are usually due to tumors or other irritations to a region of the motor area in the brain.

***Psychomotor Seizure.*** A fourth type of epilepsy, the *psychomotor seizure* or *psychic equivalent,* is characterized by automatic behaviors. This type of seizure has all the same qualities of the petit mal, but it usually involves highly complex behaviors for which the person later has total amnesia (Shalev & Amir, 1983). In some cases, the individual appears to be entirely normal and attracts little attention. He or she may go on a trip during a seizure and later return to consciousness miles away without any recollection for the activities that have just taken place. In others, the seizure state leads to overtly psychotic or violent behavior. A person, for instance, could commit mass murder without any recollection for this catastrophic act. Fortunately, such activities are extremely rare. One author, Victoria Lincoln (1966), argues that the infamous Lizzie Borden murdered her parents during a psychomotor seizure. The attorneys of Jack Ruby, who shot Lee Oswald, the accused assassin of President Kennedy, pursued the defense that Ruby had been a victim of epilepsy and hence was not responsible for his actions.

### Dynamics of Epilepsy

What causes epilepsy? Convulsions can result from a variety of causes, including brain tumors, inflammation or infection of the brain, cerebral-vascular disease, trauma, withdrawal from drugs, or hypoglyce-

## Case History 18–5:
### Psychomotor Epilepsy

The following case history is taken from the book *BrainStorms* which describes different persons suffering from epilepsy (Barker, 1968).

> During an interview with him and his father I probed rather insistently . . . saying rather sharply, "Well, something must have been going on! These things don't usually come out of the blue, especially in your case."
>
> At this, the boy started to answer but stopped; his face went blank, then red, then became fixed in a frowning, frozen expression. He looked around the office as if seeking something. Then he took some paper from my desk and tore it methodically into small squares. These he proceeded to lay on the floor in lines and rough patterns, mumbling rather incoherently as he did so. Among his mumblings were a few Latin words, but mostly there emerged distinct phrases such as, "Eggplant . . . that's eggplant . . . carrots here . . . tomatoes . . . damn fool . . . tomatoes there . . . damn fool could see. . . ." He emphasized some placements with vigorous pointing and nodding. From time to time he looked contemptuously at me as if he were instructing a stubborn but idiotic pupil. Suddenly his face and manner returned to normal; he looked at me and asked, "What did you say?" (pp. 77–78)

mia (sugar deficiency in the blood) (Weiss et al., 1983). In fact, epilepsy might be more accurately labeled *the epilepsies,* since it may appear as a disease in itself, or as a side component of other disorders. Epilepsy may appear as part of a conversion disorder, but this has become increasingly rare. When the seizures are due to demonstrable organic causes, they are classified as *symptomatic epilepsy;* when there is no clear organic base, the classification used is that of *idiopathic epilepsy.*

***Epilepsy and Brain Discharges.*** Much of what we know about the causes of epilepsy comes from electroencephalograms or EEGs, the "handwriting" of the brain (Itil, 1982). EEGs show that seizures are associated with sudden electrical discharges that disturb the usual rhythmical pattern of brain activity. Recordings of the differing convulsive states are illustrated in Figure 18–2. Seizures may be experimentally triggered in normally seizure-free persons, in fact, by the presentation of a rapidly flickering light, called a *photic stimulus,* which may induce brain wave changes. "One stutterer had seizures because he blinked rapidly while trying to talk; the blinking causing light changes which, in turn, caused the convulsions" (Terzano et al., 1983).

***Epileptic Personality?*** Some theories have tried to reach further than these observable brain wave patterns in explaining epilepsy. It has sometimes been suggested that an "epileptic personality" exists, which might either predispose a person to have convulsive seizures, or reflect maladjustments that result from epilepsy. Such personality patterns are said to include the traits of rigidity, hypersensitivity, irritability, moodiness, rage over frustrations, and stubbornness.

Contrary to such theories, it is currently accepted that there is no such thing as an epileptic personality, either as a cause or an effect of epilepsy. Certainly, persons with epilepsy may sometimes exhibit one or more of the traits just described. But such traits do not appear only among epileptics, nor do they appear among all persons with epilepsy. When they do appear, they are more clearly understood simply as one possible effect of the social, psychological, and physical stresses of living with convulsions. The attempt to cope with the unpredictable seizures, as well as with the attitudes of other people and the anxieties of the disability, are all sources of stress that require considerable adjustment (Pritchard, 1983).

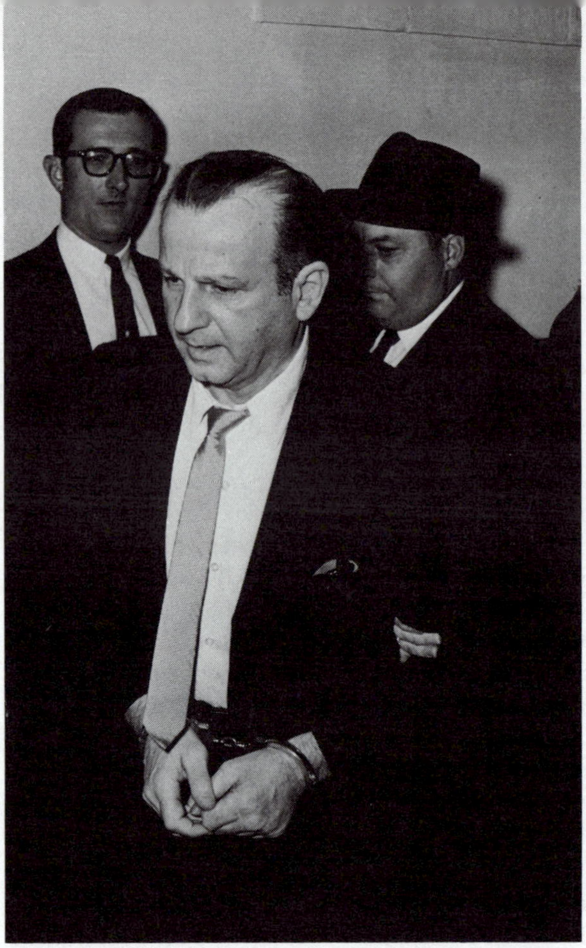

***Jack Ruby** shot Lee Oswald, the suspected assassin of John F. Kennedy. His defense attorney suggested that Ruby was having an epileptic seizure and was not responsible for his actions.*

### Treating Epilepsy

A substantial number of epileptics are able to conduct a normal life, making intellectual, social, and work adjustments that are equal to those of any nonafflicted group (Dickmen & Morgan, 1980). Moreover, there seems to be no significant relationship between the type, duration, or frequency of convulsion and the

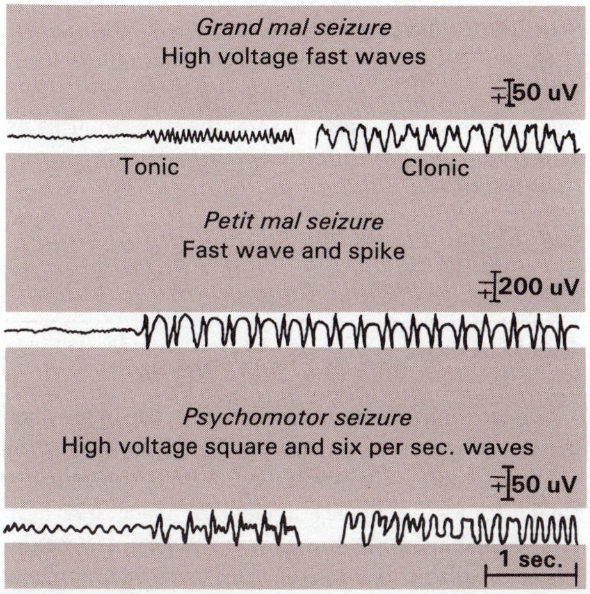


**FIGURE 18–2** Electroencephalograph brain wave patterns of different types of epilepsy; grand mal, petit mal, and psychomotor seizures.

SOURCE: Based on "Influence of Blood Sugar Level in Wave and Spike Formation in Petit Mal Epilepsy" by F.A. Gibbs, E. Gibbs & W. Lennox, 1939, *Archives of Neurology and Psychiatry, 41*, pp. 1111–1116. © 1939, American Med. Assn.

ability to adapt to everyday living. Seizures can be completely controlled in 50 to 60 percent of cases, while in another 30 percent, the number and severity of attacks can be significantly reduced. Grand mal seizures are quite responsive to treatment, so that seizures can be controlled or completely abolished in about 80 percent of cases (Kolb, 1968). Petit mal, Jacksonian, and psychomotor epilepsy are next in line in responsiveness to treatment, in that order. The prognosis is less favorable when the onset is in childhood than when the seizures have begun in adulthood.

***Medications.*** Drug therapy has proved a major contributor in controlling seizures (Masland, 1982). Bromides were once the principal form of chemotherapy. In 1912, these were replaced by phenobarbital, which is effective in treating grand mal seizures. In large doses, phenobarbital has disadvantages, however, in producing drowsiness, impaired attention and concentration, and possibly depression (Ferrari et al., 1983). In 1937, Putnam and Merritt (1938) discovered Dilantin (sodium diphenylhydantoin sodium) and inaugurated a new phase in the drug treatment of epilepsy. Dilantin can often control the seizures of grand mal and psychomotor epilepsy where phenobarbital may fail; in addition, it does not impair alertness as phenobarbital does. Dilantin may produce gastric discomfort and dizziness in some cases, however. Dilantin and phenobarbital are sometimes combined, and together they may be more effective than either drug is alone.

Petit mal convulsions tend to resist phenobarbital treatment, and they can often be brought under control with another drug, Tridione. However, this drug can aggravate other types of epilepsy, and it can have dangerous toxic effects if not properly administered (Sironi et al., 1979). Other drugs, including Phenurone and primidone, are valuable in treating psychomotor seizures.

***Surgery.*** A more drastic alternative, brain surgery, may be considered in certain severe cases of epilepsy where drug treatments aren't effective. Surgery involves excising the portion of the brain that is producing the convulsions (Brown & Feldman, 1983). Typically, it is attempted when the affected part of the brain lies mainly in one temporal lobe (the location can be detected through EEG readings).

Surgery brings both hope and risks. About two thirds of persons who undergo surgery improve to the degree that they are either free from convulsions or experience only a few isolated attacks. Dangers involve the usual hazards of such specialized operative techniques: a small percentage of patients (less than 1 percent) die postoperatively, and there is some risk of unexpected complications, such as aphasia or paralysis.

***Biofeedback.*** One other approach appears hopeful in controlling some forms of epilepsy. Operant conditioning and biofeedback have been tried, and have produced some exciting findings. Sterman (1973) has described a procedure known as *SMR training*. SMR, or sensorimotor rhythm, is seen in EEG recordings from the sensorimotor cortex of the brain. In training, a subject is instructed on how to avoid unsafe rhythms—that is, rhythms that seem associated with an attack—and is rewarded by lights and chimes when the correct SMR pattern is produced. In one instance, a 23-year-old woman received five months of training, with two 30 to 60 minute training sessions each month. Effects were positive: instead of two seizures per month, she had only one seizure every three months after training (Sterman & Friar, 1972). These findings have been replicated, although the number of persons studied still remains small (Mostofsky & Balaschak, 1977; Williams, 1982).

#### Living with Epilepsy

In all, epilepsy today represents far less disturbance of functioning than it did in the past. This is due not only to better medical treatments, but also to a greater understanding of the condition and the kinds of factors that precipitate seizures.

Prevention is an important part of living with epilepsy, for seizures can be controlled by avoiding those circumstances that aggravate the condition. We now recognize certain triggers—such as hyperventilation (deep breathing), alcohol, photic stimulation, and emotional stresses. Each of these conditions can contribute to seizures in different patients (Kogeorgos et al., 1979). For example, the flickering light patterns that occur when driving down a tree-lined lane have been known to trigger a convulsion.

Ordinarily, epileptic persons can eat the same food as any other member of the family, but in cases where attacks are related to diet, certain precautions become part of everyday meal planning. Thus, hypoglycemic persons learn to avoid going for long periods of time without food; and children are sometimes placed on ketogenic diets consisting of high fat, carbohydrate, and medium protein foods.

Families of epileptics are encouraged to involve the individual in an active and normal life. Children are able to acquire an education without difficulty, unless of course they are handicapped by other disabilities. Adults are capable of being socially useful as long as seizures are under medical control, maintaining jobs under normal working conditions, and even earning and owning a driver's license in some states (Ohio is one state where this is possible) (Fraser & Smith, 1982). In less than 5 percent of the cases of epilepsy is there any conclusive evidence of inheritance. For an epileptic marrying a nonepileptic, the chances of a convulsive child being born is estimated to be 1 in 50. However, most authorities feel that the illness itself will rarely be the sole reason involved in any advice against having offspring. In sum, then, alarming as its symptoms may be, epilepsy is not as disabling a disease as it seems.

## EVALUATION

Great technological gains have been made in the diagnosis of organic brain damage. The computerized axial tomography instrumentation permits sophisticated analyses not previously available. Along with new knowledge about the brain, psychological test batteries are available to aid in the assessment of brain function, and the field of neuropsychological assessment in psychology has reached a higher level of stature than ever before. However, despite the tendency to believe that neurology is a precise and advanced science, there is still much that we do not know about brain function. How does memory develop? Under what conditions can right and left brain interchange functions? Exactly in what ways does brain damage lead to personality alterations? How does one assess the exact contributions of brain degeneration versus psychological reactions to such degeneration? Serious attention is only now being devoted to the aging process. Historically, people are living longer and longer due to advances in nutrition, medicine, and reductions in wars or life-taking events. However, understanding the psychological phases of life has been mainly limited to infancy, childhood and adolescence, rather than adulthood and old age. Death and dying have become topics for further analysis in recent times.

Epilepsy is rather well understood as a condition related to disruptive brain discharges. It is not a psychiatric condition, nor is there a predisposing epileptic personality. As it is a medical condition, progress has been made in developing medications to keep convulsions under control. The possible usefulness of biofeedback in reducing seizures has been opened, but final judgment must await more research on more subjects.

## SUMMARY

The organic disorders are those directly attributable to biochemical or structural change in the brain. Modern techniques include both medical and psychological tests for assessing the nature of the damage which leads to symptoms. Symptoms themselves are sometimes a direct reflection of the damage, but also at times a result of the patient's reaction to the damage.

Two major classifications of organic disorders—organic brain syndromes and organic mental disorders—are recognized. These are distinguished from one another in that the organic mental disorders have a known single cause (for instance, aging, or substance abuse), while the organic brain syndromes can occur from a variety of causes (thus, delirium may be caused by infections, or substance use, or trauma). The organic brain syndromes include organic brain syndromes with delirium, with amnesia, with delusions, with hallucinations, with affective states, and with personality dysfunction. Among the organic mental disorders discussed in this chapter are senile dementia and presenile dementia, both related to aging. Although substance-induced organic symptoms are part of this classification, these were described in Chapter 13.

Two other disorders that are not classified under the DSM-III system are described in this chapter. General paresis is caused by syphilis attacking the central nervous system and results in speech slurring, motor impairment, and deterioration. Epilepsy is also discussed here, even though it is not a mental disorder. Epilepsy involves convulsions traceable to electrical discharges in the brain. Seizures may be of several types: grand mal, petit mal, Jacksonian, and psychomotor seizures. Epilepsy has now been controlled through medications, and sometimes brain surgery, enabling most epileptics to live normal and productive lives.

## KEY TERMS

**Alzheimer's disease**
**Anoxia**
**Anterograde amnesia**
**Aphasia**
**Apraxia**
**Ataxia**
**Epilepsy**
**General paresis**
**Grand mal seizures**
**Idiopathic epilepsy**
**Jacksonian seizures**
**Organic brain syndromes**
**Organic brain syndrome, affective**
**Organic brain syndrome, amnestic**
**Organic brain syndrome, delirium**
**Organic brain syndrome, delusional**
**Organic brain syndrome, hallucinosis**
**Organic brain syndrome, personality**
**Organic mental disorders**
**Petit mal seizures**
**Pick's disease**
**Presenile dementia**
**Primary degenerative dementia, presenile onset**
**Primary degenerative dementia, senile onset**
**Psychomotor seizures**
**Retrograde amnesia**
**Senile dementia**
**Senile plaques**
**Spirochetes**
***Status epilepticus***
**Syphilis**

# CHAPTER 19

## Mental Retardation: Deficiencies of Intellect

- Is being intelligent the same thing as doing well on an intelligence test?
- What contributes to the development of mental retardation?
- Why should family planning take into account the age of the parents?
- How does the iodine in salt relate to the prevention of mental retardation?
- Does diet aid in the performance of a retarded person?
- What type of mental retardation is known to be inherited?
- Can mental retardation be cured?
- What choices do parents have regarding help for a retarded child?
- Can a retarded person hope to make it in a normal environment?

**TABLE 19–1**

**Mental Retardation**

| *Type* | *Major Characteristics* |
|---|---|
| Amaurotic Familial Idiocy | Unusual sensitivity to noises, a spot on the retinal wall; related to genetics. |
| Cretinism | Stunted growth, delayed appearance of symptoms; related to endocrine disturbance. |
| Down's Syndrome | Short-stature, slanted eyes, protruding tongue; related to chromosome abnormality. |
| Hydrocephaly | Extremely enlarged upper part of the skull due to fluid in the cranium. |
| Microcephaly | Sharply receding forehead, head slopes inward to give a pointed appearance. |
| Phenylketonuria (PKU) | Normal physique, fair hair, light complexion; related to metabolic disturbance. |

# Case History 19–1:
## A Child with Down's Syndrome

Eight-year-old Jenny W. is four feet tall and full of smiles. She is the last in a family of five children and was born with Down's syndrome. Her mother had remarried later in life and became pregnant with Jenny at the age of 43. Although an amniocentesis medical examination detected the chromosomal abnormality associated with Down's syndrome, Jenny's parents wanted her despite their knowledge that she would be retarded. Jenny's father was a successful life insurance executive who had no children of his own and looked forward to the day when he could give his own child the name of his grandmother.

Jenny has the typical appearance of Down's syndrome, with a broad body, short hands and feet, a small nose, and the epicanthic eyefolds and protruding tongue. Her speech is unclear at times since she does not enunciate words well, and she walks with a slight roll and with her arms held in front. There were times during her first three years when her health was questionable, as she suffered from a heart valve defect. However, the condition seems to have stabilized and surgery has been deferred indefinitely.

Jenny is currently enrolled in a special school for the handicapped sponsored by the school district. She attends classes in the two-room school from morning to midafternoon with 15 other students, 3 of whom are characterized as Down's syndrome. Classes focus on self-help activities, such as learning to place buttons through buttonholes and to partially undress. In addition, she is learning to identify some common objects by name, to cooperate in social games, and to follow directions. Except for the difference in goals for learning, Jenny's classroom experience is similar to that of a regular classroom; there are listening tasks alternating with free play times; she is expected to share responsibilities and to put items away when finished. Meals and naps are part of the routine. Through the help of volunteers, she has been preparing for the Special Olympics, a national athletic competition for the handicapped that emphasizes participation. (The Special Olympics oath reads, "Let me win, but if I cannot win, let me be brave in the attempt.") Her enthusiasm about this event has been a focal point for her family interactions, as she has shared her hopes.

Having a child with Down's syndrome has been a mixed blessing for Jenny's parents. Despite their firm decision to permit the birth, Jenny's parents have found the years alternately disappointing and joyful. The years of infancy were difficult because of the health dangers, but in some ways more tolerable since the signs of retardation were limited to the physical characteristics and some developmental slowness. However, as Jenny has grown older, her speech, perceptual-motor coordination, memory, and physical appearance make it clear that she is retarded. Introducing Jenny to new people is always awkward, even though such occasions are frequent. The family actually discovered that visitors who ask pertinent questions such as "How did you make the decision to have her?" are more comfortable than those who try to ignore Jenny's presence or who try too hard to relate to her. The joyful times are those when Jenny's parents accept her on her own individual scale of progress, with each small gain being important because it brings her closer to her potential as a person. Jenny has always been a warm and loving person, enjoying and displaying affection—and has brought out a similar quality in her parents.

Jenny of case History 19–1 has been luckier than most people who share her deficiency. In other ways, however, her case is representative of Down's syndrome, one form of mental retardation. *Mental retardation* is the most accepted classification for a broad group of conditions with one common aspect: a significant deficit in intellectual functioning or development. The various types of mental retardations are defined in Table 19–1.

This group of conditions has gone by many names. In the Soviet Union, the term *oligophrenia* is preferred to describe confirmed cases of neurological pathology; in Great Britain, the term *amentia* is more widely accepted. In our own country, many other terms have been used synonymously—for example, feeble-mindedness, mental subnormality, mental defect, or mental deficiency. Some of these terms, however, carry connotations that *retardation* avoids. Thus, *mental retardation* has the widest acceptance among professionals, although the term *mental deficiency* has also had frequent usage.

Regardless of the terminology, mental retardation is a common condition. The President's Panel on Mental Retardation estimated that it affects 10 times more individuals than does diabetes, 20 times more than tuberculosis, 25 times more than muscular dystrophy, and 600 times more than infantile paralysis. Only the mental disorders as a group, heart disease, arthritis, and cancer affect a greater number of individuals. Estimates are that nearly 6 million persons are retarded, or about 1–3 percent of the population in any year (Mandell & Fiscus, 1981). It is predicted that 2,100 infants will be born every week who either are or will be classified as mentally retarded. In all, it is a disorder of significant proportions in our society.

## DIAGNOSING MENTAL RETARDATION

According to the official definition adopted by the American Association on Mental Deficiency (AAMD), *mental retardation* describes a condition of "subaverage general intellectual functioning existing concurrently with deficits in adaptive behavior, and manifested during the development period" (Grossman, 1977, p. 11). We can look at this diagnostic standard more closely by dividing it into two parts: intellectual functioning and other behavioral patterns.

### IQ's Place in Diagnosing Retardation

One major means for measuring intellectual abilities has been intelligence tests, such as the Stanford-Binet or Wechsler Adult Intelligence Scale, both of which measure IQ (defined in Focus 19–1). As the bell-shaped curve in Figure 19–1 shows, most people will achieve an IQ level of 100, with fewer and fewer people attaining higher or lower levels.

The IQ has served as a convenient means of identifying mental retardation, since this condition involves intellectual functioning below the level considered average for a particular age group. One problem has been to determine the cut-off point separating a person to be called retarded from a person still considered average. Traditionally, the IQ of 70 has been accepted as the level that separates retarded performance from normal performance. This is an entirely arbitrary figure. However, its establishment has provided a fairly useful frame of reference. In addition, IQ figures have been used to provide further subdivisions within the category of retardation, as we'll discuss shortly.

***Hazards of Using IQ as a Standard.*** Unfortunately, the use of the IQ yardstick involves certain hazards. Heiser and Wolman (1965, p. 840) point out that "It imputes a totally unreasonable omniscience to the intelligence test, a power which has been seldom, if ever, claimed by test constructors." More specifically, several basic problems have been noted that are inherent in intelligence tests. Among them:

- *Culture influences performance.* Immigrant families, culturally deprived youngsters, or minority groups may perform low on intelligence tests even though they may be intellectually quite competent (Wyatt, 1982). Mercer (in Soeffing, 1977) believes that using minority-based norms would lead to fewer incorrect diagnoses of minorities.
- *Different tests provide different measurements.* Tests vary in content and format, so that some may

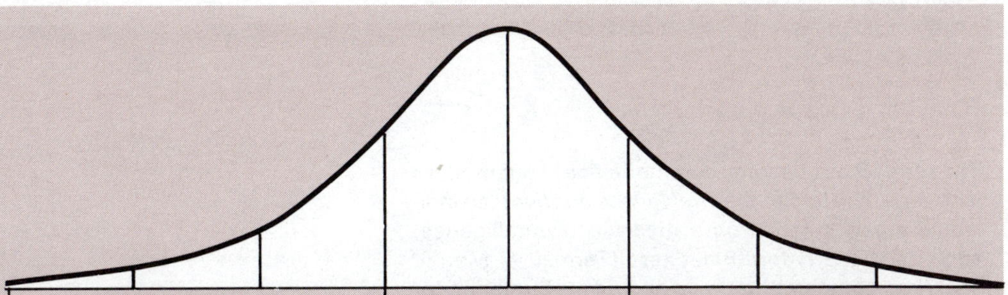

| | Below Average | | | AVERAGE | | Above Average | | |
|---|---|---|---|---|---|---|---|---|
| Percentage of scores in interval | 0.13% | 2.14% | 13.59% | 34.13% | 34.13% | 13.59% | 2.14% | 0.13% |
| Stanford Binet IQ | 52 | 68 | 84 | 100 | 116 | 132 | 148 | |
| Wechsler IQ | 55 | 70 | 85 | | 115 | 130 | 145 | |

**FIGURE 19–1** Distribution of intelligence levels.

measure verbal skills while others measure the ability to reason and solve problems. It is possible that a person would score within the retarded range on some tasks, but not on others (Suinn, 1967).

- *A person's performance may fluctuate over time.* Test performance on one day may be quite different from the same person's performance on a different day. Ideally, a test would show perfect *reliability*, meaning that results on one day would be identical with those obtained on any other day. However, most tests do show some fluctuations, so that a person may attain an IQ of 69 one day and 71 on another.

### Other Diagnostic Standards

Recognizing the limitations of IQ assessments as a sole standard for diagnosing retardation, some authorities have recommended the use of other criteria. As early as the 1940s, Doll (1941) offered an alternative definition with broader criteria, that became a model for defining retardation. He believed mental retardation involves the presence of several characteristics:

- An essentially incurable condition
- A condition that is constitutional in origin
- Intellectual subnormality
- Arrest of intellectual development
- State of social incompetence

The first two characteristics are no longer readily accepted today. Although some forms of mental retardation are incurable, other conditions are viewed as reversible, as we'll see later in this chapter. In addition, it is now recognized that mental retardation can involve intellectually subnormal performance because of environmental deprivations or severe emotional disturbance. In effect, the modern view sees mental retardation not necessarily as a fixed characteristic, but as an expression of intellectual and social inadequacy which may derive from a variety of sources (Zigler and Balla, 1983). The remaining three characteristics suggested by Doll have met with general acceptance, particularly the inclusion of the social criterion. The concept of social competence calls attention to the fact that while a person may demonstrate intellectual incompetence on IQ measures, this person may show an acceptable level of social competence in life situations (Telford & Sawrey, 1981). Social competence in its broadest sense includes an evaluation of social maturity. In children, for example, this may involve self-help, socialization, self-direction; in adults, social maturity may be exhibited in responsiveness to cultural mores, signs of responsibility and trustworthiness, and

## FOCUS 19–1:
### Measuring Intelligence by Assessing IQ

The term *IQ* has become commonplace in our modern language. It refers to the *intelligence quotient:* an individual's performance on a measure of intelligence, such as the Stanford-Binet test (Terman & Merrill, 1937) as compared to the expected performance for a normal individual at the same chronological age level.

If the child's test performance, reflecting mental age (MA), is equal to the expected performance for most children of that chronological age (CA), then it is said that the child's mental age is equal to the chronological age. This may be expressed as a quotient of the child's mental age divided by the chronological age.

Thus, if MA = CA then the quotient MA/CA = 1

If MA is greater than CA, then MA/CA = greater than 1

And if MA is less than CA, then MA/CA = less than 1

When this quotient MA/CA is multiplied by 100, the resulting figure is called the intelligence quotient. Thus where the child's mental age is equal to the chronological age (that is, where MA = CA) then the IQ would be 100.

**TABLE 19–2**

**Terms Used to Describe Mental Retardation in Relation to Measured Intelligence**

| *Range in IQ scores on tests* | *Terms used in AAMD manual (1977 revision)*[a] | *DSM-III nomenclature (1980)*[b] | *Former terms* | *Educational classification* |
|---|---|---|---|---|
| 70–84 | Borderline | Mild | Borderline | Slow learner (sometimes included in educable range) |
| 53–69 | Mild | Moderate | Moron | Educable retarded |
| 36–52 | Moderate | Severe | Imbecile | Trainable retarded |
| 20–35 | Severe | Severe | Imbecile | Trainable retarded |
| Below 20 | Profound | Severe | Idiot | Total-care group |

[a]Grossman, N., *Manual of terminology and classification in mental retardation.* Baltimore, Md.: A.A.M.D., 1977
[b]American Psychiatric Association, *Diagnostic and statistical manual of mental disorders,* 3rd. ed. Washington, D.C.: American Psychiatric Assoc., 1980.

adjustment in the community (Cartwright et al., 1981).

### Levels of Retardation

A useful means for understanding the diverse nature of mental retardation is to consider the descriptions of individuals with various levels of retardation. DSM-III as well as the American Association on Mental Deficiency offer such a classification, as shown in Table 19–2. This scheme identifies four levels of retardation: the profoundly retarded, the severely retarded, the moderately retarded, and the mildly retarded.

***Profoundly Retarded.*** Individuals who are classified as profoundly retarded have IQ performances measuring below 20 (roughly, this means that a child aged 15 would have a mental age of 3). These individuals comprise about 1 percent of all retarded persons. Usually, serious central nervous system pathology has occurred. Persons who are profoundly retarded are not responsive to any current educational or training programs; most will remain in custodial institutional care. In many cases, other handicaps are also present such as deafness, mutism, seizures, lack of motor coordinaself-support. Many adults who might be diagnosed as mentally retarded on the basis of IQ performance are managing an adequate personal, social, and vocational tion. Because poor health is characteristic, these persons generally have a short life expectancy.

***Severely Retarded.*** Persons who are considered severely retarded show IQ scores between 20 and 35. (an IQ of 35 is roughly equivalent to a mental age of 5 for a 15 year old). These persons comprise about 7 percent of all retarded persons. This group can develop limited levels of self-help skills, thus lessening their dependency on others. Many will not profit from such training opportunities, however, and will remain in institutional or residential care under close supervision and support for their entire lives. Persons in this group usually show retarded motor and speech development, as well as central nervous system pathology.

***Moderately Retarded.*** Individuals who are moderately retarded achieve IQ scores between 36 and 52 (an IQ of 52 is roughly equivalent to a mental age of about 8 for a 15 year old). This group comprises about 12 percent of all retarded persons. These individuals can achieve a semi-independent status. They are capable of acquiring self-help skills in feeding, toileting, and bathing and may be trained to achieve partial financial self-support in a special protective employment setting called a sheltered workshop. Motor and speech capabilities can be developed and improved to a level that permits employment and adequate communication. Some people in this group attain a minimal level of academic progress, possibly to the third-grade level.

***Mildly Retarded.*** This group includes individuals who achieve IQ scores between 53 and 69 (an IQ of 69 is roughly equivalent to a mental age of 10 for a 15 year old.) By far the largest group, the mildly retarded comprise about 80 percent of all retarded persons. They are capable of learning social and communication skills under specially structured and supervised classes. Many have the capacity to live a limited but independent existence. A number marry and raise families, but they frequently encounter some difficulty in managing their family matters. Although they are usually slow in their early physical development, few persons in this group exhibit observable physical disabilities as adults.

## DYNAMICS OF MENTAL RETARDATION

Before going on to describe some examples of mental retardation, we should examine its various causes. Retardation can stem from a variety of origins, including genetic, sociocultural, infections, toxic substances, trauma, metabolic defects, tumors, and psychological factors. In effect, with such diversity of both causes and (as we will see) types of retardation, it becomes clear that mental retardation is a convenient classification for persons who show intellectual and adaptive deficits in common. Beyond this commonality, there is no single cause nor single set of identifying features. We will explore some of the diverse origins of retardation in the next few pages.

### Genetic Factors

In some cases of retardation, genetic factors may be a cause. Certain conditions are transmitted directly from parent to child. For instance, a disease may be inherited via a dominant gene, as in the rare syndrome called *tuberous sclerosis*—characterized by a rash at about age four, followed by the development of tumors in the brain and other organs. Certain disorders are associated with recessive genes: *amaurotic familial idiocy* and *phenylketonuria* (PKU) are two such conditions that will be discussed later on in this chapter.

Recent advances in genetics have now made it possible to accurately count the human chromosomes, permitting breakthroughs in the understanding of some other conditions. It has now been determined that Down's syndrome is related to chromosomal abnormality, as we saw in Chapter 4 and will also discuss later in this chapter. A number of other forms of retardation have been associated with abnormal numbers of chromosomes, but unlike Down's syndrome, the extra chromosome may appear with the sex chromosome pair (normally XX for females and XY for men). A condition known as Klinefetter's Syndrome has been identified in which an XXY set appears (Jacobs & Strong, 1959), and a superfemale has been described with an XXX set of chromosomes (Jacobs et al., 1959).

### Sociocultural Factors

Sociocultural factors are a second element that significantly influences intelligence. Research has shown, for example, that an important correlation exists between a child's intellectual level and social class, the correlation being about 0.40 (where 1.00 equals perfect correlation) (Bradley & Tedesco, 1982). In addition, unskilled lower-class parents have been found to have 1.5 times as many children classified as retarded than do professional parents. This finding was the result of a massive study of 45,000 children from 36 states (McGehee & Lewis, 1942). Mental retardation is certainly not limited to the lower socioeconomic levels. However, this group does seem to have a greater proportion than it deserves. Some 10–30% of school children living in some slum areas are classified as mentally retarded, as contrasted to 1–2% in the higher socioeconomic class districts of the same cities (Mandell & Fiscus, 1981).

In explaining this striking relationship, factors such as stark poverty, paucity of stimulation, cultural barrenness, and indifference toward learning all seem to be powerful forces. With such an unfavorable early environment, children may lack even the minimal incentives to develop their intellect, to search for knowledge, to apply themselves, or to make maximal use of their native capabilities. Emotional deprivation and the lack of stimulation are powerful influences that can work against intellectual development and functioning. In some cases, a change to a more stimulating environment can lead to gains in intellectual performance. Thus, in one program in which children were brought to a daycare facility, a 16 point gain in IQ was shown by these children compared to those without the exposure (Ramey & Campbell, 1977).

A rather interesting study (Kent & Davis, 1957) demonstrated another relationship between upbringing and IQ. Here, parents' discipline was shown to relate closely to the intellectual level of the children. *Demanding* parents, who set high standards but provided stimulating opportunities for their children to learn, had offspring with an average IQ of 124. *Unconcerned* parents, who basically ignored their children as long as they kept out of trouble, had offspring with an average IQ of 97. *Overanxious* parents (who were ceaselessly apprehensive) and *normal* parents (who were placidly affectionate toward their children) had children with IQs of 107 and 110 respectively. Thus, it appears that opportunities and encouragement for intellectual achievement are effective factors in intellectual development.

### Infections

Infections of many types are a third factor that can lead to mental retardation. The infection can have its effect either before or after birth. Some diseases in a parent can affect the unborn fetus: it is now well established that the pregnant mother's infection with German measles may lead to mental defect in the fetus. The fetus is particularly susceptible during the first two to three months of pregnancy. Maternal syphilis is another acknowledged cause of fetal retardation. However, with improved prevention, detection, and treatment programs today, syphilitic conditions are rarely a cause of retardation any more.

A number of other diseases that may be contracted by children can produce permanent mental deficit. Meningitis, especially when it occurs during the first year of life, may cause severe brain damage. The extent of the damage to the brain determines the degree of the deficit. Encephalitis is a disease affecting the brain which has appeared in epidemic proportions several times in history. It has declined in this century, and only a few sporadic cases now occur. The effects are varied: about a third will recover completely, another third will die, and another third survive but with mental or physical impairment.

### Toxic Substances

Toxic agents may also contribute to retardation. Fortunately, although many poisons may be capable of causing brain damage, few such cases actually occur. Lead poisoning is one such instance. It is a rare condition in which an individual absorbs lead from some source—from chewing on lead toys or inhaling a spray paint containing lead, for instance. Paints containing lead were once commonly used for interior surfaces, and some cases of lead poisoning have resulted from children eating peeled-off pieces from old, damaged walls. Carbon monoxide, as exuded from gasoline engines, has also been known to produce brain damage.

The Thalidomide tragedy raises the possibility that drug ingestion may lead to retardation. Thalidomide is a drug that apparently had no unwarranted effects on tests with animals. It seemed to be useful for sedation, and pregnant women found it a beneficial drug. However, it was subsequently found to cause malformations in fetuses when taken within a month after conception. Although the Thalidomide infants are generally believed to have been born with physical abnormalities but normal intelligence, some cases of hydrocephaly, a physical malformation usually associated with retardation, have been reported.

### Trauma

Any physical agent or circumstance that damages the brain can lead to mental retardation, as we saw in Chapter 18. At one time, in fact, it was felt that birth injury was the major cause of cases of mental defect. However, this is no longer the case due to modern delivery methods, although some injuries do occur occasionally. When they occur, they are due to such factors as improper use of forceps, difficult and prolonged labor period, or brain damage from the lack of sufficient oxygen (*anoxia*). Anoxia can occur at later ages as well, for example, from near-drownings, attempted suicides by hanging, electrical shock, or the failure of the heart to provide oxygen-enriched blood. Similarly, extensive brain damage can also occur in adults through accidents or cerebral hemorrhaging from strokes.

The effects of radiation exposure may also be considered under the broad heading of trauma. The excessive use of X-rays during pregnancy may cause a certain malformation of the head known as microcephaly, described later in this chapter. Studies of pregnant Japanese women who had been exposed to the atomic explosion at Hiroshima in World War II indicate that a number gave birth to children who were microcephalic (Wood et al., 1967). It has also been suspected that radiation may produce chromosomal aberrations, leading to physical or mental defect. Thus, it is possible that fallout from nuclear testing will eventually have such effects on future generations born into the world (Pauling, 1962).

### Metabolism or Nutrition

Metabolic dysfunctions or deficiencies in nutrition are quite clearly factors causing mental retardation. One of the most prominently known defects is *phenylketonuria* (PKU), an abnormality in amino-acid metabolism due to a genetic error. PKU involves the inability to metabolize a certain substance because of the absence of liver enzymes needed for the process. This leads to the excessive formation of phenylpyruvic acid, which may be detected in the individual's urine. Another overt sign may be the absence of pigment, resulting in very fair skin and extremely blond hair. Fortunately, phenylketonuria can be detected during the first month of life through a simple chemical test. Early treatment by means of a special diet is of great benefit in preventing retardation (Koch, 1975).

Metabolic defects such as PKU can involve nearly every aspect of metabolic functioning. For instance, abnormalities in carbohydrate metabolism can lead to conditions such as *galactosemia,* a condition marked by cataracts, liver damage, and malnutrition. Insufficient functioning of the thyroid may produce conditions such as *cretinism,* a form of mental retardation we will cover later. Since many metabolic abnormalities are associated with genetic factors, they are sometimes placed under that classification in discussions of retardation.

### Tumors

Growths such as tumors can injure the brain directly or indirectly, by causing the cranial pressure to rise to a point causing retardation. Brain tumors are quite rare in children; therefore, this factor is of relatively less importance as a cause of retardation among the young.

One condition we cited earlier that is believed to be genetically determined is *tuberous sclerosis.* In this disease, tumors are found in nearly all the tissues of the body, including the brain, the face, the kidneys, the eyes, and even under the fingernails. The severity of the mental deficit in tumorous conditions depends on the area of the brain and amount of damage involved. In tuberous sclerosis the damage is severe, leading to profound mental retardation and, ultimately, death for most patients before they reach maturity.

### Psychological Factors

Another group of factors in mental retardation are the psychological factors. These may seem more difficult to understand than some of the more direct causes such as lead poisoning or infection. If we make the distinction between intellectual *functioning* versus intellectual *capacity,* however, we can readily see how psychological factors may be involved.

For some persons, the failure to perform intellectually may be evidence of interference from an emotional disturbance. For instance, a disorder such as infantile autism (described in the next chapter) might have occurred early enough to isolate the infant from normal intellectual and social stimulation. Another possibility is the presence of such severe psychotic symptoms that the person is unable to function up to capacity on intellectual tasks. Based on the premise that schizophrenics may be too distractible to perform intellectually on some measures (see Focus 17–1). Adams and his colleagues (1981) trained a schizophrenic man to ignore irrelevant auditory and visual distractions and psychotic thoughts and instead to attend only to relevant information. Prior to the training, this man performed poorly on parts of an intelligence test, but after the training he was able to improve to an average intellectual level.

DSM-III's multiple axis system, summarized in Figure 1–2, permits us to recognize the two different types of psychological influences on performance we just mentioned: influences early in life that deprive the person from the stimulating experiences needed for normal intellectual development; and the influences that simply prevent the person from performing up to capacity. In the former case, there is actual retardation both in functioning and in capacity; the person would therefore be described as mentally retarded (Axis I), deriving from severe psychosocial conditions (Axis IV severity of psychosocial stressors). In the latter case, the person would be described, for instance, as schizophrenic (Axis I) but functioning at a very poor level (Axis V—level of functioning).

## COMMON CLINICAL EXAMPLES OF RETARDATION

Despite the common element of intellectual deficit, different conditions of mental retardation each possess other unique clinical characteristics. We'll look at the diagnostic characteristics of several common forms of mental retardation in the discussions that follow.

***Down's syndrome**, or mongolism, is a type of mental retardation associated with chromosomal aberration. The term **mongolism** derives from the slant-eyed features of the individual.*

### Down's Syndrome

Down's syndrome, or mongolism, is a common form of mental retardation, estimated to occur in 1 per 1,500 births (Gearheart, 1980). Persons with Down's syndrome comprise between 10–20 percent of those institutionalized for mental retardation. The condition was first described in 1866 by Langdon-Down. He suggested the term *mongolism* on the premise that the facial features associated with this retardation resembled the Mongolian ethnic group. Although there is some resemblance to certain Mongolian racial features, this is superficial and the term *Down's syndrome* is preferred today.

***Physical and Mental Symptoms.*** The physical symptoms associated with Down's syndrome are quite easily recognized. The most outstanding feature is the almond-shaped, slanted eyes. The tongue in most cases shows deep fissures and tends to protrude out of the mouth, as if it is too large for the oral cavity. Since this trait is often present from birth, the tongue protrusion is frequently the first symptom to attract attention. The nose tends to be short and flat; the teeth are misshapen; the skin is milky white, dry, and rough after infancy. The hands tend to look clumsy with the fingers stubby and spread out, a foreshortened and curved little finger, and L-shaped loops instead of the normal whorl fingerprints. The short stature, protruding belly, and rudimentary genitals give an overall childlike appearance, even to adults. The voice is commonly harsh and guttural. The hair is at first soft, but later becomes dry and sparse. There is no direct relationship between the degree of physical symptoms and the degree of mental retardation.

Persons with Down's syndrome usually have poor health. About 2 percent die shortly before or during birth, and approximately 40–50 percent die within the first year of life (Richards, 1970). Infant mortality is primarily caused by heart defects, as well as diseases of the respiratory system such as pneumonia, bronchitis, and tuberculosis. Persons with Down's syndrome are also likely to have poor circulatory systems and are very sensitive to temperature extremes. The life expectancy of those who survive beyond infancy is nowhere near normal, with one estimate being 12 years (Penrose, 1961).

The degree of mental retardation associated with Down's syndrome varies considerably. Although a few persons fit the formerly used term *mongolian idiot,* many reach the moderate retardation range of functioning. As discussed earlier, persons who are moderately retarded can learn to perform simple duties, take part in ordinary family activities, and carry out household chores. Their clumsily constructed hands and poor coordination put them at a disadvantage, making it difficult to engage in tasks requiring much dexterity. The disposition of most persons with Down's syndrome, however, is often helpful in making a social adjustment. In general, they are happy and cheerful persons—affectionate and easily amused. They usually enjoy attention immensely and are good-tempered (Gibbs & Thorpe, 1983).

***Dynamics of Down's Syndrome.*** Despite its frequency, scientists aren't sure yet what causes Down's syndrome. We have learned a good bit about some correlates associated with the condition, however, and these clues point in some interesting directions that we can quickly summarize here.

Previous searches for the cause of Down's syndrome centered around the parent's age and the child's place in the birth order. One exceptional observation has associated advanced maternal age with Down's syndrome childbirths (Holvey & Talbott, 1973). The risk of giving birth to a child with Down's syndrome appears to increase with maternal age, beginning at

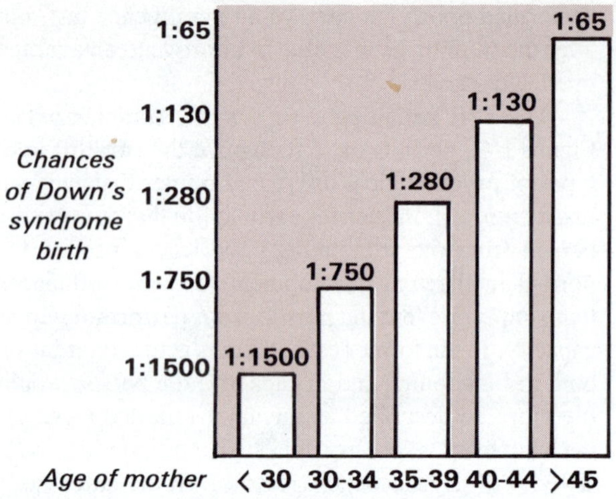


**FIGURE 19–2** Chances of a Down's syndrome birth as age of mother increases.

SOURCE: Based on data from *The Child with Down's Syndrome* by D.W. Smith and A.A. Wilson, 1973, Philadelphia: W.B. Saunders.

age 30 and rising to a peak between ages 45–49, as shown in Figure 19–2. This observation led some experts to recommend in the past that women avoid pregnancies after the age of 35, but as we'll see, prenatal detection of the syndrome is now possible so that the parents can make a decision about delivery before the child is actually born.

It has also been noted that infants with Down's syndrome are often the last born in the family. The psychological reluctance of the mother to have another child after the Down's syndrome child seems to be only part of the reason for this association. A significantly high rate of miscarriages after the Down's syndrome birth suggests a lower reproductive capacity and possibly a defective uterine environment. In addition, the physical features of the person with Down's syndrome lend some justification to the view that the poor uterine environment may lead to fetal maldevelopment. Russian studies claim that the brain shows certain signs of being underdeveloped: there is a poverty of convolutions or folds in the brain, and the cerebral hemispheres are small. Microscopic examinations have also disclosed the presence of cells that normally disappear by the sixth or seventh month of fetal life (Luria, 1963).

A fascinating clue was the discovery by Lejeune et al. (1959) that an extra chromosome is associated with

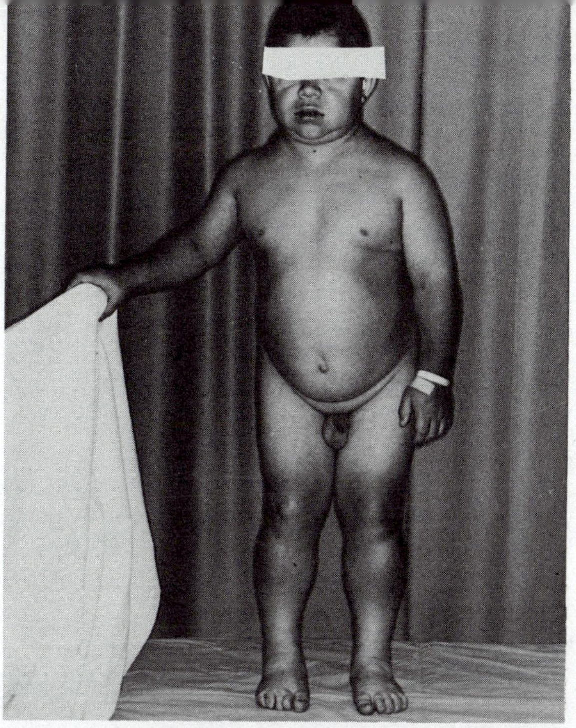

*Cretinism* *is characterized by stunted growth. The adult is short in stature, the legs may be bowed, the stomach protrudes, and the hair may be sparse. In serious cases, the tongue protrudes and motor clumsiness is evidenced.*

most cases of Down's syndrome. This abnormal chromosome, now called the Orlando chromosome, results in a *trisomy,* that is, three chromosomes instead of the normal pair. Thus, approximately 95 percent of persons with Down's syndrome possess 47 rather than the normal 46 chromosomes (Mandell & Fiscus, 1981). Although this brilliant discovery has opened new vistas in our potential understanding of the syndrome, it still does not provide a complete answer for the old question. The exact cause (or causes) of Down's syndrome is still unknown since the source of the trisomy is still not clear.

Several educated guesses have been offered, however. Hereditary factors have been considered, involving recessive genes as a possibility. However, two cases are known in which Down's syndrome females have given birth to offspring who were essentially normal in appearance, intellect, and chromosomal makeup (Forssman et al., 1961; Sawyer & Shafter, 1957). In one of these cases, the Down's syndrome woman's own father was suspected of being the father of her baby. Yet, the child produced by this mating was judged to be of superior intelligence when examined at age $11\frac{1}{2}$ years, and as an adult she enrolled in nursing training, where she made good progress.

An alternate explanation for the chromosomal abnormality is gene mutation. It has been stated confidently that the defect in development that leads to Down's syndrome takes place early in the gestation period, perhaps around the eighth week after conception (Benda, 1946). Thus, a mutation could occur at some early stage of cellular formation and growth. It has been speculated that such mutation is the result of the inadequate intrauterine environment present in older mothers. This suggestion seems to tie together a few factors, including the element of age that we mentioned earlier. It should be noted, however, that not all persons with Down's syndrome have the extra chromosome; and also that the majority of women over 35 do *not* give birth to infants with Down's syndrome. Furthermore, there has been at least one case of a child with chromosomal abnormalities and some physical symptoms of Down's syndrome, who was nevertheless intellectually normal. In this case, the chromosome count of 47 was discovered to exist in 43 percent of her cells, while the rest of her cells showed the normal 46 count (Clarke et al., 1961).

In all, then, we have many substantial clues but no firm answers. There is enough information, though, not only to provide guidelines for judging risk in a pregnancy, but also to determine whether an unborn child will be affected by Down's syndrome. A medical procedure known as *amniocentesis* is routinely used for prenatal detection of Down's syndrome. Cells shed by the fetus in the amniotic fluid are removed and studied for chromosomal abnormalities. Decisions can then be made about terminating the pregnancy (Fost, 1979).

### Cretinism

Cretinism is a form of mental retardation caused by endocrine disturbance. This was once a common type of retardation, particularly in certain parts of the world such as the Himalayas of India, the Andes and Rocky Mountains of the Americas, and the area around the Swiss Alps (Hutt & Gibby, 1979). Concentrated study of these geographic areas led to the discovery that the soils were deficient in iodine, as was the food grown in them. Cretinism has subsequently been determined to be a condition in which infants suffer from an insufficiency in iodine intake. Iodine is the major ingredient for the formation of thyroxine, a hormone secreted by the thyroid gland that is needed for proper endocrine functioning. Since this discovery, and with the mass use of iodized salt and other preventive measures, the incidence of cretinism has been drastically reduced. Today, this condition constitutes less than 5 percent of cases of mental retardation in institutions in the United States.

***Symptoms of Cretinism.*** Unlike Down's syndrome, the physical symptoms associated with cretinism usually appear sometime after birth. Infants are normal at birth, and it is not until after the sixth month of life that symptoms begin to attract attention. It is possible that this delay occurs because the infants are still carrying a sufficient prenatal supply.

An important change occurs by the second half of the first year, however. Infants become so lethargic that they fail to suck or otherwise respond. The tongue protrudes, the nose is thick and flat, the eyes are wide apart and the lids are puffy, and the lips are thick. The teeth are peg shaped and chalky, and they often decay early. The hair is scanty on both the head and eyebrows, and the skin tends to be exceedingly dry, rough, shallow, and wrinkled. These children breath with snorts and may cry with a peculiar dry leathery sound. The limbs are malformed: the legs are bowed and much too short for the body, the feet and hands are stubby and ill formed.

Persons with this condition walk with a slow, unsteady, waddling gait and show general clumsiness in motor activities. Because growth is stunted, the head appears too large for the body, the neck seems too short, the abdomen protrudes, and the genitals remain immature until some time past the age of maturity. In many respects, the person has a gnomelike or dwarfish appearance, seldom standing taller than three feet even at full growth.

Persons with cretinism are typically voracious eaters. However, they suffer from respiratory difficulties. impaired motor coordination, and a general muscular weakness. Their pulse and respiration are slow, and body temperature is two or three degrees below normal. This is reflected in a low basal metabolism which, along with laboratory tests, is helpful in diagnostic examinations.

Cretinism is most often associated with moderate retardation, although levels can range from severe to moderate depending on the extent of brain damage following iodine insufficiency. Unlike Down's syndrome, a close association exists between the severity of the physical symptoms and the severity of the mental deficit. Thus, the more marked the physical symptoms, the more severe the retardation. Persons with this condition are usually peaceful, quiet, good-tempered, and affectionate. Their dispositions are often an asset, helping them make vocational adjustments in those cases where work training is possible.

Although cretinism may be caused by inadequate amounts of iodine in the diet, it may also result from malfunctioning or maldevelopment of the thyroid, and in some cases through the pregnant mother's excessive use of antithyroid drugs. Fortunately, early and continued treatment in cases of thyroid deficiency with a synthetic form of the thyroid hormone has met with success. This is a dramatic exception to the usually pessimistic outlooks for mental retardation due to some physical disorders. In practically all cases of treatment during the early months, striking alterations of physical appearance occur, the child becomes alert and no longer apathetic, and normal intellectual functioning is achieved.

### Phenylketonuria (PKU)

Phenylketonuria is the result of another metabolic disturbance. Because of a genetic fault, the infant lacks an enzyme required to break down phenylalanine, an amino acid in protein foods. Phenylpyruvic acid is formed instead and is excreted in the urine giving off a characteristic odor. The excessive phenylalanine that remains damages the nervous system and produces mental retardation. Phenylketonuria is possibly one of the best known of the metabolic disorders, yet it is a relatively rare condition. In the United States, about 1 out of every 25,000 children is born with phenylketonuria, while approximately 1 percent of persons institutionalized for retardation are affected by this condition (Kirk & Gallagher, 1979).

Phenylketonuria was the first metabolic dysfunction to be discovered as a cause of mental retardation.

The discovery was first made in 1934 when a Norwegian mother noticed that her child had an odd musty odor, which she reported to the doctor as an additional concern besides the apparent mental retardation. The doctor, Asbjorn Folling (1934) diagnosed the case as a disorder of metabolism and reported on the details of phenylpyruvic acid in the urine, phenylalanine metabolism, and mental retardation in a total of 10 cases. Modern developments make it possible to detect PKU within the first four to seven weeks of life. A solution of ferric chloride is added to a sample of urine: the appearance of a blue-green-black color is indicative of PKU. Another simple technique is the use of a specially treated stick which is pressed against a wet diaper; again a color change, to grey-green, is a positive sign of phenylketonuria.

The physical description originally reported by Folling characterizes many but not all individuals with PKU. The generally accepted characteristics include normal physical development, dermatitis (skin rash), eczema (inflammation of the skin), and a wide spacing of the incisor teeth. Because of the endocrine disturbance, the child is fair-haired, fair-skinned, and blue-eyed, or at least of a clearly lighter complexion than the parents or siblings. Other symptoms include a stooped and flexed posture, a stiff gait, and fingering mannerisms (such as pill-rolling and finger-flicking). Abnormal electroencephalograms have also been found. A number of children with PKU may be subject to convulsions during the first decade of life; others may show behavioral peculiarities such as hyperactive behavior, decreased attention span or responsiveness to the environment, and even schizophreniclike symptoms such as catatonia.

If untreated, PKU usually leads to severe mental retardation; although moderate retardation occurs in a few cases. Early detection is crucial, for treatment before age two or three (by means of a special diet low in phenylalaline) has been known to prevent the ruinous effects of the condition. In cases where the special diet is introduced later only slight increases in intellectual functioning are produced (Bruhl et al., 1964). The length of time that the individual must stay on the diet is not known with any certainty. Estimates range from four years to the time the child is at least eight or nine years old.

### Microcephaly

*Microcephaly* describes a form of retardation associated with a small head. The small skull size causes the brain to also be extremely limited in size; and the condition typically involves severe levels of retardation. The number of microcephalic persons is not large; they comprise not more than about 1 percent of all persons institutionalized for retardation.

Microcephaly may be caused by a number of factors, including an overdose of X-rays or maternal German measles during pregnancy, certain diseases of the cerebrum, and exposure to atomic radiation. One form of microcephaly, known as true or primary microcephaly, has been attributed to the inheritance of a single recessive gene (Gearheart, 1980).

The physical characteristics of microcephaly are quite distinctive. The skull at its maximum development is less than 17 inches in circumference, as compared with the normal size of about 22 inches. The forehead and chin recede sharply, the sides of the head slope inward, and the nose appears like a beak; for those reasons, the microcephalic has sometimes been described as having a birdlike appearance or has been called a pinhead in sideshows. Because there is relatively little bone surface to be covered, the scalp may lie loosely in longitudinal furrows from front to rear. Although the person's body may be well developed, stature is typically short.

Most persons with microcephaly are severely retarded, however, there is some variation, ranging from the profoundly retarded to the moderately retarded level. The degree of mental deficit apparently does not correspond directly to the size of the head. Most persons with this form of retardation are capable of understanding what is said to them and can say a few words. Tredgold and Soddy (1963) describe persons with the true microcephaly as showing a general vivacity, a capacity for mimicry, and an alertness which makes them entertaining. In addition, these persons are usually affectionate and well behaved, adapting well to institutional life. A rare case of one exceptionally skilled microcephalic *idiot savant* has been reported by Tredgold and is discussed in Case History 19–2.

## Case History 19–2:
### A Rare Microcephalic "Idiot Savant"

J. H. Pullen was a person with *microcephaly,* a condition of mental retardation associated with a very small head size. Although retarded, Mr. Pullen also showed exceptional craftsmanship and inventiveness typical of the *idiot savant*—a person who is intellectually retarded but extremely talented in some way.

Among Pullen's productions were numerous scaled models of ships made of copper rivets, brass, iron, and wood. They were modeled complete with anchors, pulleys, engines, furnishings, and cannons. His masterpiece, however, was a 10-foot-long model of a steamship with a specially invented system of pulleys that allowed the entire upper deck to be raised for viewing below deck. Another creation was a barge carved out of ivory, ebony, and other woods and fitted with four angels and a figure of satan.

Pullen also constructed a

> monstrous human form about 13 feet high. This black-bearded, terrible-looking figure is armed with a gigantic sword and can be made to perform a variety of movements, such as opening and shutting the mouth and eyes, protruding the tongue, rotating the head, raising arms, etc., by means of an elaborate internal mechanism. It is calculated to strike terror into the heart of any juvenile beholder. (Tredgold & Soddy, 1963, p. 283)

### Hydrocephaly

*Hydrocephaly* is another form of retardation associated with a striking physical appearance. It results from an accumulation of spinal fluid within the cranium. This buildup of fluid leads to increased pressure within the cranium, resulting in damage to the brain tissue. The cerebrospinal fluid increases beyond its normal amounts, because of overproduction, or a malfunctioning in the reabsorption mechanism, or an obstruction to the normal flow and circulation of the fluid. The conditions producing hydrocephaly may occur before birth, during the first few months, or the first few years of life. These conditions include trauma, parental syphilis, tumors, or infectious diseases such as meningitis or encephalitis.

The physical symptoms of hydrocephaly (literally, "water in the head") are quite pronounced. Most evident is the extremely enlarged upper part of the skull, a result of the continuous outward pressure of the fluid. The circumference about the forehead may be as large as 30 inches or more, although the face remains normal in size; this combination produces an appearance of an inverted pyramid. The scalp is thin and the veins tend to stand out prominently. In the severest case, however, the skull may be merely a shell containing over a gallon of fluid and no more than a thin sheath of brain tissue. There appears to be no clear-cut relationship between the size of the skull and the level of retardation.

The degree of mental deficit varies from only slight impairment to profound mental retardation. Nearly all prenatal cases of hydrocephaly die before birth, and a large proportion of those afflicted after birth also fail to survive. For unknown reasons, some cases are self-arresting, and further damage to the brain ceases. These latter cases are more often seen in institutions for the retarded. Their motor coordination is impaired, and they may show weakness in their muscles. However, they are usually willing helpers and are described as obedient and affectionate.

A few approaches have been tried in treating hydrocephaly. One approach is the use of drugs in an attempt to decrease the formation of cerebrospinal fluid. The results have generally been considered helpful in momentarily alleviating the internal pressure. However, long-term effects have not been entirely satisfactory. Surgical methods have also been introduced to drain off the excess fluid into another area of the body. Tubes have been inserted with one end in the cranial cavity and the other end into the kidney or the heart itself, and a valve might be included to permit drainage out of the cranial cavity if the tubes become clogged. The mortality risk of surgery is considered high, however, and little intellectual improvement can be expected once severe brain damage has already taken place. However, successful surgical procedures have been known to lead to some improvement in the hydrocephalic's functioning.

### Amaurotic Familial Idiocy

Amaurotic familial idiocy is an inherited degenerative disease involving mental retardation as well as other physical impairments. In actuality, there are four different forms of the particular disease, differing only in terms of the age of onset and the rate at which degeneration progresses. These are *early infantile amaurotic familial idiocy, late infantile amaurotic familial idiocy, juvenile amaurotic familial idiocy,* and *late juvenile amaurotic familial idiocy.*

The best-known form is the early infantile amaurotic familial idiocy, also called *Tay-Sachs disease.* Tay-Sachs disease was first described by Tay in 1881, then neurologically studied through autopsies by Sachs in 1896. About one half of 1 percent of persons institutionalized for retardation are affected by this disorder. The condition is transmitted by a rare recessive gene. Jewish families appear to be afflicted more often than non-Jewish families; with the frequency of persons acting as carriers for the gene estimated at 1 in 40 for Jews and 1 in 380 for non-Jews (Myrianthopoulas, 1962).

Symptoms of Tay-Sachs disease normally do not develop until the second or third month of life. Once symptoms appear, they become progressively severe. The early physical signs are an unusual sensitivity to noises and listlessness; as well as an inability to sit up, keep the head erect, or turn over from a prone position. Visual acuity soon degenerates, and blindness ultimately results. If the retina is examined, a distinctive cherry-red spot can be detected. With time there is atrophy (withering away from disuse) of the muscles of the entire body and optic nerves. Hearing, however, remains acutely sensitive and the child is easily startled by unexpected or loud sounds. In some cases, seizures may occur. Intellectually, the individual quickly deteriorates from normal intelligence to the profoundly retarded level. Few children survive for longer than three years of life.

The other forms of amaurotic idiocy are similar. Late infantile amaurotic idiocy usually begins after age 3, with symptoms that are essentially the same as for the early infantile condition. The life span may extend to age 5 or 6. Juvenile amaurotic idiocy has an even later onset, between ages 6 and 8. Progress of the illness is slower and includes the additional symptoms of paralysis, personality changes, irritability, and convulsions. Individuals with this disorder live to as long as 10 to 14 years of life. The fourth form, late juvenile amaurotic idiocy, is very rare and may appear as late as ages 20–30. The symptoms are similar to those of the juvenile condition, with an even slower rate of progress. Affected persons may live to be 40 or 50 years of age.

## TREATMENT OF MENTAL RETARDATION

At one time, the belief was that mental retardation was incurable: "Once retarded, always retarded." The earlier definition by Doll, in fact, would have made it impossible to consider individuals retarded if they showed any improvement toward normal intellectual functioning. If such improvement did occur, the conclusion was drawn that an error in diagnosis had been made.

The current viewpoint, as represented by the American Association of Mental Deficiency, recognizes that changes in level of intellectual functioning are possible in retardation. The degree of possible improvement varies with different conditions, the severity of the brain damage, and the duration that elapses before treatment is initiated. A number of individuals can be returned to normal intellectual functioning with early treatment measures. Others show gains in social competency and self-care; some will profit in a more limited way from attention and emotional support; and finally, there are some persons for whom institutional custodial care is the highest level attainable (Jacobs, 1983). The treatment measures in current use fall into four categories: medical treatment, educational-training measures, residential treatment, and psychotherapeutic approaches.

## Medical Treatment

Medical treatments derive their value from the prevention of brain injury resulting from disease processes. In effect, any success is really success in the treatment of diseases—not of mental retardation per se (which is often the end product of the diseases). Early treatment of syphilis, meningitis, encephalitis, and toxic states before brain damage occurs, for instance, is imperative if retardation is to be prevented. For other conditions, prevention may involve the use of surgical techniques to remove sources of damage to the brain such as tumors and increased pressures from cerebrospinal fluid. In still other conditions, preventive treatment may consist of replacing materials of which the body is deficient. This is the case in cretinism, phenylketonuria, and other metabolic disorders. Damage can also be avoided through caution in circumstances known to be potentially dangerous, such as in the exposure to radiation or traumas connected with birth deliveries.

Medical treatment has sometimes been aimed not at prevention, but at restoration. In 1944, Zimmerman and Ross claimed that glutamic acid fed to white rats improved their ability to learn. Two years later, Albert et al. (1946) reported rises in IQ in six of eight retarded patients treated with glutamic acid. However, subsequent studies have led to the conclusion that glutamic acid therapy has little significance in restoring normal intellectual functioning to retarded persons; the changes that have occasionally occurred were attributable to factors other than the glutamic acid, and were too slight to be significant. There is still some controversy around this issue, however, and, therefore, the topic has not been completely closed (Vogel et al., 1977).

Another approach to restoring intellectual functions involves tranquilizing drugs. These have been administered in some cases in which behavior problems seem to interfere with social responsiveness and adaptability. Results to date have been very good, although individual differences tend to exist in terms of reactions to this form of chemotherapy (Menolascino & Egger, 1978).

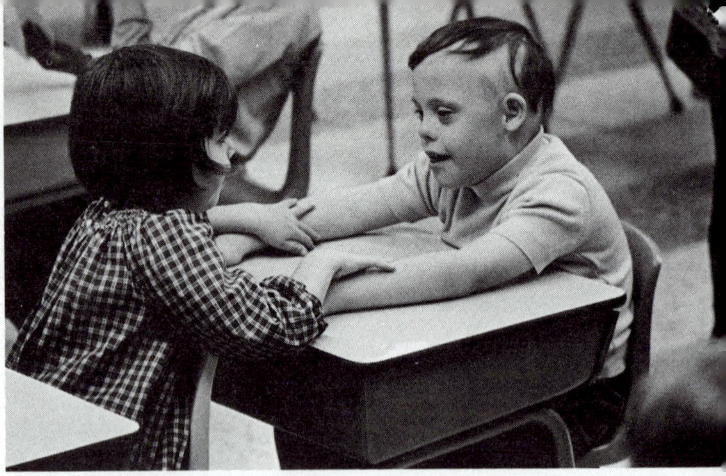

***Mainstreaming*** *involves setting up learning conditions for the retarded to attend classes with nonretarded children.*

## Educational-training Approaches

An approach to treatment that has seen a great transformation in recent years is education of retarded persons. For some time, the major approach to education was to keep retarded children out of the regular school systems and to place them in special institutions. Many parents felt that this procedure provided too limited an environment for their handicapped children, and they began to call for greater recognition of their needs. One such organization of parents, the National Association for Retarded Children (NARC), opened chapters in communities in all 50 states. Some local units backed day-school training programs on a cooperative basis, using parents as volunteers.

***Mainstreaming.*** Public pressure and awareness mounted over the years and came to fruition in court cases in the District of Columbia and the state of Pennsylvania during the 1970s. These court suits claimed that schools were unconstitutionally excluding retarded children from equal access to educational opportunities. Soon, similar suits were filed in 22 states, finally culminating in a federal mandate. The *educationally handicapped bill,* Public Law 94–142, was passed in 1975 guaranteeing every child the right to a public education, regardless of the child's handicap.

Public school districts now offer special classes and programs for mildly retarded children to encourage the development of basic skills in reading, writing, self-care, the handling of money, and the acquisition of vocational skills. The ideal goal is to *mainstream* these children—that is, to place them in the same classroom environment as children with average intellectual skills (Matson & Mulick, 1983). Even though these children may learn at a slower pace and perform at a lower level, it has been felt that the gains weigh in favor of mainstreaming and against segregated classes. While learning in the normal classroom, retarded youngsters are also able to avoid the stigma of being labeled as mentally retarded. Some of the controversy in mainstreaming is presented in Focus 19–2.

***Some Teaching Approaches.*** At the same time mainstreaming is attracting interest, studies are also focusing on ways in which teaching can be improved to provide retarded children with an equal chance for learning (Johnson et al., 1983). A few techniques have been helpful in improving children's performance. Most notable are chunking, rehearsing, and identifying cues.

*Chunking* involves grouping material into a form that is easier to remember. We all remember telephone numbers better if we listen to them in groups, such as 491-6363 rather than trying to remember them as a lengthy sequence of 4-9-1-6-3-6-3. Consider the following addition example: 3-0-3-4-8-4-4-8-2-9 and compare that sequence with chunking by area code, then by the usual grouping so that we now have (303) 484-4829. Although many normal people utilize chunking naturally, retarded persons have not learned this strategy and being trained in it does enhance their performances (MacMillan, 1972).

*Rehearsal* is another strategy that helps learning and which also is common among children, appearing spontaneously around the third grade (Frank & Rabinovitch, 1974). Rehearsal means exactly what it sounds like; the practicing or repetition of what we want to learn. Once again, retarded persons trained in using rehearsal were able to show some improvement in their performances.

Finally, incorporating steps to aid in *cue-discrimination skills,* can put the retarded child in a much better position for learning. The evidence is that retarded children take a very long time to learn reading, for example, because they are not separating the relevant from irrelevant cues (Zeaman, 1973). What is the crucial difference between "dog" and "dot?" As an example from another topic, recall those algebra word problems, such as "If one electric train is going East 55.7 miles per hour, and a cross wind is blowing from south to north at 4 miles an hour, which direction will the smoke from this train be blowing when it passes another train that is going west at 65 miles per hour?" Those persons who can quickly focus on the relevant cues, can answer such problems much more quickly. In the same vein, it has been shown that the learning of the retarded person can be speeded simply by presenting material in ways that highlight the relevant cues.

For the more severely retarded, special educational methods have been tried largely based on the lines outlined by Seguin in 1846 and elaborated on by Montessori (1912) and others. These methods are based on the stimulation of sight, hearing, touch, and muscle movements through selected activities. Children are gradually led to become observant, to develop judgment, and to learn discrimination. Personal self-care, simple skills, and basic social training are also established as limited goals that help individuals reach some degree of independence and satisfaction. Some interesting approaches use reinforcement techniques to train retarded persons (Matson, 1980; Matson et al., 1980; Suinn & Cole, 1971). Tokens which are exchangeable for cosmetics, candy, or soft drinks are given as rewards for desired responses such as self-care.

### Institutional Care

In cases of profound retardation, even limited educational goals may be beyond reach, except under closer supervision within specialized facilities. In addition, many severely retarded individuals also require medical care because of physical disabilities or illnesses. For these reasons, parents often decide on residential care for a retarded child.

Several types of residential institutions are available for such live-in services. Among these are state-supported institutions that provide training, medical, and custodial care for residents of the state for little or no cost. Also available are private profit or nonprofit operations. Some of these are national in scope with branches in different parts of the country.

The decision to institutionalize a retarded person is an extremely difficult one for relatives. Separation from the family may seem cruel, especially if the family members are already inclined to be overprotective, anxious, and guilt ridden. Sometimes, weekend visits to the institution convince the parents that the youngster will never be able to adapt to residential life, since

# FOCUS 19–2:
## Rights of the Mentally Retarded

Despite the relatively large numbers of retarded persons born annually, their rights as persons have only recently been recognized. Through a number of landmark court decisions and legislative actions during the 1970s, certain rights have now been stated:

- *The right to public education.* This basically requires that all children, regardless of handicap, have equal access to free, public education. The opportunity previously offered by some public schools as an optional program for the handicapped child is now considered a constitutional right. Additionally, the costs of education must be born in the same way as free education for nonhandicapped children is supported, and not through special assessments to the parents of the handicapped child.
- *The right to education in the least restrictive environment.* This means that those children who can participate in the regular classroom have the right to such placement. Such placement has been called *mainstreaming* and stems from a dissatisfaction with prior practices of institutionalizing retarded children as the solution to their education. The mainstreaming concept comes from evidence that some retarded children can still benefit from attending regular classes rather than specially segregated classes (Telford & Sawrey, 1981). Legislation backing mainstreaming does not require that all handicapped children be returned to the regular classroom, but only to the degree that it matches the unique needs of the child and represents the least restrictive environment to meet such needs.
- *The right to nondiscriminatory testing.* As we have noted, ethnic minority persons might not perform as well on intelligence tests which rely on nonminority norms or information. Discrimination can also exist in other ways, for instance, if the test is given verbally and the child is either not fluent in the language used or is hearing-impaired. If tests are discriminatory, then there is some risk that a normal child might be diagnosed as mentally retarded—a stigma or label that itself may place the child in jeopardy of receiving a suitable education. Consider the great impact experienced by the psychologists who permitted themselves to be diagnosed as mentally ill and treated as patients in a mental hospital (see Focus 23–1).

Although these rights are so obvious as to be self-evident, the implications have created some controversy. For instance, while no one would dispute the constitutional right to a public education, occasional complaints are raised about the perceived increased costs of separate classes or specialized programs. Similarly, complaints have been raised about the suitability of testing a child in a language different from that used in the classroom. Such issues become a mixture of views which reflect social attitudes as well as ethics and civil rights.

As an illustration, the various pros and cons of mainstreaming might be examined. Those who support mainstreaming point toward research that shows that some retarded children do equally well in the nonsegregated classroom, that mainstreaming avoids the stigma of being labeled as different, that earlier routine institutionalization was dehumanizing and damaging, and that mainstreaming might even reduce costs by reducing the need for separate facilities. Those against mainstreaming point to the increased expenditures that have followed Public Law 94-142 (the law entitling all children to a public education regardless of handicap); or express fears that classes will be slowed down to the level of the retarded student; or argue that retarded children will actually lose the individualized attention possible in special classes (Cartwright et al., 1981). The fact is that some of the anxieties about mainstreaming were due to misconception about either the legislation (that *all* handicapped children would be suddenly returned to regular classrooms) or about retardation (for instance, the belief that all retarded children show emotional problems). However, it is also true that implementing the different legislation has added costs, in the same way that extra funds are required to correct other deficiencies in human services. Just how effective the programs will ultimately be will not be known for awhile, as specialists must be trained, new approaches to educational programming must be developed, and evaluational research conducted (Mandell & Fiscus, 1981). Meanwhile, parents, educators, and taxpayers will continue to argue the pros and cons of recognizing the rights of the retarded person.

the child may appear especially upset. And even when parents are convinced that institutional care will provide a more satisfying life for their youngster, they may not be able to dispel the nagging question of whether their decision was morally right.

On the other hand, institutionalization can appear to be the best arrangement in certain cases. Severely disabling physical diseases, uncontrollable aggressive behaviors, and the parents' inability to provide even minimal supervision or care are all factors that have led to decisions to institutionalize a child. Unfortunately, the picture is further confused by the findings that although institutional life may be enriching for some, it may sometimes adversely affect a person's development and self-esteem (Telford & Sawrey, 1981).

### Psychotherapy

Psychotherapeutic approaches are another approach used in some treatment programs for retarded persons. This approach has been particularly appropriate in cases in which mental retardation is caused by emotional factors; but reports have also suggested that psychotherapy may prove beneficial even in cases where organic or hereditary factors predominate. For example, Heiser (1954) found that 12 out of 14 retarded children who had received psychotherapeutic treatment showed improvements in social and environmental behavior.

Sarason (1958) has been a leading exponent of the belief that retarded persons can profit from psychotherapy. He discusses improvements in his own patients, noting that one showed an increase in IQ from 45 to 76. In many cases, the emotional life of the retarded child has been one of parental rejection or abandonment, peer teasing and criticism, and self-dejection. Some are never fully able to grasp why they are never as capable as other children; others are struck by the impact of somehow being different from their peers. Institutionalization may be an especially trying experience.

In many ways, persons with mental handicaps face the same problems as those who are physically disabled. Social adjustment is often made difficult by other people's uncomfortable reactions to them. The individual's self-concept is often jeopardized by the jarring recognition that life's achievements may never be the same as for others (Vinter et al., 1983). Moodiness, withdrawal, and behavioral outbursts may develop in reaction to the disability. In addition, retarded persons may experience anxieties and fears as a result of their limited capacity to understand themselves and their surroundings.

Persons who have attempted to work therapeutically with the retarded have reported encouraging results although data is still impressionistic and systematic reports are still much needed (Ellis, 1982). Parental counseling also has its place in the psychotherapeutic approach. In cases where the child is to remain living at home, the parents may need aid in accepting the child's condition and in avoiding the dangers of overreacting. In cases that lead to institutionalization, parental counseling may ease the conflict over the separation.

### Prevention

Of course, an even more important step would be achieved if the conditions which lead to mental retardation could be prevented. The availability of the prenatal examination, amniocentesis, can be useful in early identification of Down's syndrome, providing a basis for decisions about possible abortion. The fact that amaurotic family idiocy has been found related to genetic defects is also important. Tests have been designed to identify parents with these faulty genes, thereby making it possible to provide genetic counseling on the advisability of having children and the risks involved. Finally, to the degree that alcohol abuse by a pregnant woman can lead to retardation in the infant educational steps are valuable regarding proper health and nutrition for prenatal care.

Prevention has also taken the direction of reaching high-risk children who might fail to develop their full intellectual potentials if left in the same environment. Project Head Start programs have offered opportunities for early stimulation for disadvantaged children prior to school enrollment, to prevent deficiencies by enriching early experiences.

Another program called the Milwaukee Project (Garber & Heber, 1977) collected data that shows the great potential benefits from such an approach. One area of Milwaukee that housed only 2.5 percent of the city's children had one-third of the educable mentally retarded in the entire city. Forty high-risk newborn infants were selected for the study, with half being assigned to a special program and half acting as controls. High-risk children were those whose mothers' IQ were less than 80. The program started at the first month of life and involved sensory stimulation and experiences to encourage language development, interpersonal skills, and problem solving. The mothers of these children were also provided training in child care methods. When the child reached the age of five, intellectual assessment was obtained to determine what, if any, effects resulted from the program. The children exposed to the early intervention program achieved an average IQ over 20 points higher than that of the control group.

## EVALUATION

In comparison with the psychiatric disorders discussed in prior chapters, mental retardation is reasonably well understood. The various forms of retardation involve deficit in intellect and skills such as self-help, social maturity, and tasks involving intellectual functioning. The problems still needing attention relate to improvements in assessment, societal attitudes, and greater sophistication in training programs. In assessment, we are highly sensitive now to misdiagnoses that can result from too heavy reliance on intelligence test performance as the sole criterion for diagnosing retardation, or the failure to take cultural-ethnic factors into account. Regarding attitudes, changes in laws will mean that retarded children will be given more opportunities to educational facilities, as part of their rights. This will place more pressure on the public to accept the presence of the retarded and also to become more understanding of the achievements possible for a retarded person.

With respect to treatment, the hope that complete restoration of intellectual potential can be obtained through drugs or vitamins has yet to be met. Psychotherapy can enable retarded persons to make fuller use of their abilities through the removal of emotional obstacles. Perhaps the most constructive approach has been the development of educational and behavioral training programs, relying on systematic stimulation and training. Too often, however, such programs are initially supported by parents and professionals, but then allowed to lose ground due to budget pressures.

## SUMMARY

Mental retardation does not fit the description of most of the mental disorders in having qualities that are directly indexes of emotional maladjustment. It is more nearly akin to the organic types of disorders in which there is a deficit in skill.

The primary deficiency in the intellectual processes is generally reflected in intellectual test performances. There are obvious problems with too heavy reliance on intelligence testing, such as the fact that factors such as culture also influence performance. For this reason, diagnoses of level of retardation will often take into account levels of self-help and social skills that are present. The accepted levels of retardation are the profoundly retarded (the most severe level), the severely retarded, the moderately retarded, and the mildly retarded.

Retardation may originate from several sources. Some forms, such as Down's syndrome, are associated with (but not necessarily explained by) chromosomal abnormality. Others are a result of damages occurring during pregnancy or after birth, such as from maternal syphilis, trauma during birth, or drug or toxic substance damage later. Faults in metabolism are implicated in phenylketonuria, while cretinism is related to thyroid deficiencies.

The major approach in treatment is really prevention. Careful guidance and the use of diagnostic methods such as amniocentesis can help decrease the number of infants born with Down's syndrome. Educational and behavioral training programs have been of enormous value in helping retarded persons to maximally develop their skills. More and more, there are programs for retaining the educably retarded in the school systems, and laws have been passed that require suitable programs.

## KEY TERMS

**Amaurotic familial idiocy**
**Amentia**
**Chunking**
**Cretinism**
**Down's syndrome**
**Endogenous**
**Exogenous**
**Hydrocephaly**
**Idiot savant**
**Intelligence quotient (IQ)**
**Microcephaly**
**Mild retardation**
**Moderate retardation**
**Phenylketonuria (PKU)**
**Profound retardation**
**Que-discrimination**
**Rehearsal**
**Severe retardation**
**Tay-Sachs disease**
**True microcephaly**

# CHAPTER 20

## Disorders of Infancy, Childhood, or Adolescence: Disturbances in Growing Up

- **If a child suffers from a pathology, what will his life as an adult be like?**
- **When should you start worrying about an infant or child being "too good"?**
- **Are too many hyperactive children put on drugs in school?**
- **Can dieting prove to be a sign of pathology?**
- **"I know a child who has a facial twitch, what should I do about it?"**
- **When should a parent start worrying about a child's bedwetting?**
- **Why is infantile autism sometimes viewed as "genius gone awry"?**
- **How effective is psychotherapy in curing childhood schizophrenia?**
- **Can one's diet really cause psychopathology through an allergy?**

**TABLE 20-1**

**Developmental Disorders**

| *Type* | *Major Characteristics* |
|---|---|
| Anxiety Disorders | Problems in which anxiety dominates, such as separation anxiety, the overanxious child, or the avoidance disorder. |
| Attentional Deficit Disorders | Inability to concentrate for long. These disorders may be with or without hyperactivity. |
| Eating Disorders | Problems of eating behavior, such as failure to eat (anorexia nervosa), eating binges (bulimina), or indiscriminate eating (pica). |
| Pervasive Developmental Disorders | Severe emotional disturbances such as infantile autism, or childhood schizophrenia. |
| Physical Disorders | Problem behaviors such as bedwetting (enuresis), nightmares (pavor nocturnus), or stuttering. |
| Stereotyped Movements | Involuntary movements such as isolated spasms (tics), spasmic complex movements, or verbalizations (Tourette's disorder). |

## Case History 20–1:
### A Hyperactive Child

Paul P. was a hyperactive child; he no longer seems so but that is getting ahead of the story. In a winter evening in 1952, fraternal twin boys were born with great excitement to a school psychologist and her husband, a physical education teacher. Particularly with this professional couple, many plans were shared between husband and wife about the educational future of their boys.

As the youngsters reached early childhood, the high activity level of the one, Paul, was something of a puzzle, but not greatly so since it was interpreted as ''he just has more steam to run off than most boys.'' At school age, however, more and more reports of wandering attention span, errors in spelling which seemed careless, and restlessness began to filter back to the teacher-parent, first politely and cautiously, then more openly. The one twin was fine, but ''Paul . . . well, he is hard to keep up with, he's not interested in classes like the other students are; in fact, he runs me ragged.''

Paul's mother's professional training alerted her to put aside her maternal protectiveness, and to consider Paul's behaviors objectively. Her conclusion was that the learning deficiency was more than simply boyish impulsivity; that there were clear signs of an attention deficit with hyperactivity. She and her husband immediately took on a broad program with the goal of encouraging Paul to sit longer and listen more carefully. This was always done through rewarding experiences, and always without frustration but with loving firmness; and always with shared happiness as goals were achieved. The father also tried to train Paul in similar skills, first via play, then games, and then sports as self-discipline evolved across the years in the context of athletics.

As Paul's self-esteem was built and his confidence flourished, his parents then described his characteristics with him, but no differently and with no more unusual reaction than a parent describing a tendency to sunburn readily. Knowing his strengths, but also knowing the care he needed in certain areas, such as in taking more pains in spelling or in controlling his excitability, Paul is now an adult. The author, as a consultant to a U.S. Olympic Team, met Paul and heard his story. No longer an impulsive restless child, Paul is now grown up . . . a disciplined, national-level competitive athlete, whose early parental training paid off in more far-reaching ways than his parents would have dreamed.

Historically, childhood disorders such as Paul's (see Case History 20–1) received relatively little notice compared to the disorders of adulthood. This was true until quite recently—a fact we may find hard to understand, given today's interest in childhood development. There are several reasons for the delay in attention to childhood disorders.

One reason is that most of the experts who were the developers of psychiatric theory and practice had little contact with children. Even Freud, the leading exponent of the importance of early experience, failed to see a single child in treatment until three years after publishing his theory on infantile sexuality in 1905.

A second important factor is that the disorders of adulthood have always been more impressive, intriguing, startling, or dramatic than the tantrums or phobias of a child. In addition, disturbed adults *demand* attention, since they are more capable of destruction or annoyance than is a child. And since society expects adults to assume an independent role, it is compelled to make special arrangements for those who are not self-sufficient. Children, on the other hand, more often remain within the family, which assumes the prime obligation for care.

One other factor has interfered with the close study of childhood disorders, and that factor is a highly important one. From the perspective of adults—who, after all, are the ones who do most of the diagnosing—childhood disorders are not always as clear-cut as most adult pathologies.

## DIAGNOSING CHILDHOOD DISORDERS: WHAT IS ABNORMAL?

Normal children frequently show behaviors that would be diagnosed as abnormal in an adult, simply by virtue of their lack of maturity. Better information on normal child development has shown certain "problem behaviors" to be normal behaviors. Eating problems, for instance, such as fussiness or finickiness, are a complaint expressed by many parents. Such poor eating is often noticed soon after a period during which the child had eaten large quantities of nearly any food placed before him. In actuality, some changes in eating habits are typical of normal development. Children eat less when they are growing at a slower rate and require less amounts of food; finickiness reflects the establishment of food preferences that are little different from adult preferential behavior except the child may rely on food coloration as the basis for preferences.

Again, aggressive behaviors, tantrums, egocentric demands, and refusals to share or to delay impulses are not difficult to understand if one takes into account the emotional and social maturational level of the child (Barret & Patton, 1983). Minor anxieties and fears seem to run an early course in many normal children, ranging from separation anxiety when the parents leave for a night out, to fears of tiny insects (Harris & Ferrari, 1983). Speech hesitations which seem like stammering or stuttering have been found to be present in about 85 percent of all children three to four years of age (Martin & Stendler, 1953).

In one long-term study of 252 randomly selected normal children, Macfarlane (Macfarlane et al., 1954) counted up the frequency of occurrence of 63 problem behaviors. Many children exhibited some of the problems at one time or another. The age of the child had a great deal to do with the type of behavior shown. For example, overt tempers and oversensitiveness increased to about age four and then declined. By age five, the persistence of tantrums, quarrelsomeness, irritability, mood swings, and negativism was suggestive of emotional disturbance (see also Wenar, 1982).

It must be noted that while the appearance of a few problems does not mean the presence of pathology, Macfarlane did find that many problems at an early age was a good predictor of problems at later ages. Regarding the appearance of childhood disorders, it is also intriguing to note that boys seem to have generally higher prevalences of psychoses, enuresis, hyperactivity, stuttering, and tics than girls (Eme, 1979).

Clearly, diagnosing childhood disorders can be more difficult than making diagnoses for adults (Gibbs, 1982). An accurate diagnostic assessment is crucial, however, for a few reasons. For one, a misdiagnosis can have a major influence on the future of the child, since early labeling as pathological can lead to a self-fulfilling prophecy. An early study by Wickman (1928) demonstrated that children's teachers tended to identify as pathological those behaviors that were disruptive, disorderly, and basically contrary to the proper conduct of a good classroom. Those behaviors that did not disturb the school routine were overlooked, even though they might be equally indicative of social or emotional problems. More so than in adult pathology, the development of insight into childhood pathology depends on an understanding of normal child development.

A second reason why early diagnosis is so important is that early treatment, for the child and sometimes for the parent, also, can be critical in either curing disorders or preventing them from developing to more disastrous proportions. While finickiness in eating is normal at some phases of development, for instance, there is also a very serious disorder called *anorexia nervosa,* which involves refusal to eat virtually anything, as we'll see later. It is vital to be able to distinguish between the two.

Fortunately, since the days of Freud, childhood disorders have become an important field of study and the need for early diagnosis is now recognized (Ollendick & Hersen, 1983). Not only professional diagnosticians, but parents and other laypersons have access to considerable information about both normal and abnormal development, from a variety of published sources. Books such as those by Carmichael (1954), Noshpitz (1979), and Knobloch and Pasamanick (1974) cannot be relied on to make a final diagnosis, but they can help parents determine whether a behavior should be cause for concern.

As a brief overview, Focus 20–1 provides a checklist for evaluating behaviors that might seem to indicate abnormality. The last point on this list—the child's ability to show progressive development—deserves further elaboration here.

Children are highly flexible and adaptable. They show a resiliency that enables them to develop and grow despite personal or environmental setbacks. They strive toward maturity in a fashion that is impressive. Immature, ineffective behaviors are quickly discarded for more mature ones as children grow. Stresses may provoke momentary retreat to regressive behaviors, but children normally return quickly to a forward developmental course. Transient events may trigger deeply felt emotions, yet these present only a temporary interference with the basic ability to enjoy life. Therefore when children consistently show behaviors that are regressive, inhibiting, fearful, ineffectual, or otherwise contrary to this progressive development, it is time for a careful evaluation.

## CLASSIFYING CHILDHOOD DISORDERS

For all the misunderstanding and confusion that have surrounded childhood disorders, these disorders are significant not only personally but statistically. The incidence of emotional disturbance among school children, severe enough to warrant special therapeutic and/or educational attention, is approximately 2 to 3 percent (Cartwright et al., 1981). Estimates suggest that this would amount to about 1 million children in the United States annually (Gearheart, 1980). Clearly, a need exists. In response, the field of child psychiatry and child clinical psychology is rapidly developing its own identity, and more appropriate diagnostic schemes are being developed. The disorders identified by DSM-III and described in this chapter are listed in Table 20–1.

### The Need for a "Different Yardstick"

Initially, the diagnostic system for classifying adult disorders was considered directly applicable to childhood disorders. In essence, all childhood problems were considered to be merely early representations of adult syndromes. This viewpoint has changed (Achenbach, 1982b). Professional workers have come to realize that the classification of childhood disorders is not a simple matter, and that a different yardstick may be needed to measure early pathology.

In the first place, traditional classifications of adult pathologies fail to identify certain disorders exhibited in children, such as *separation anxiety.* In addition, there are childhood syndromes that share some symptoms with what appear to be the adult versions of the same disorder, but which are, in fact, completely different. For example, *infantile autism* has sometimes been considered synonymous with *schizophrenia* appearing early in life. Most experts now agree that autism and adult schizophrenia are quite distinct from

# FOCUS 20–1:

## Signs of Childhood Disorders: A Preliminary Checklist

Because many of the behaviors that are abnormal in adults are normal in childhood, it may sometimes be difficult to diagnose childhood pathologies. Kessler (1966) has developed eight criteria which can be used as a checklist for determining whether symptoms are normal or whether they should be causes of concern. "Yes" answers, or a high frequency of a symptom or symptoms, may be signs that further advice should be sought.

1. Are the behaviors inappropriate for the child's age level?
2. How frequently is the symptom displayed?
3. Is regressive symptomatic behavior exhibited even under minimal stress?
4. How many symptoms are displayed?
5. To what degree does the behavior interfere with the child's normal opportunities and development?
6. Are personal feelings of suffering and concern present?
7. Does the behavior persist despite efforts to change?
8. Does the child show a general inability to relate well, to attain satisfactions from life, and to show progressive development towards maturity?

one another (although *childhood onset pervasive disorder,* sometimes called *childhood schizophrenia,* may be an early version of adult schizophrenia).

Another complicating feature is the very changeability of children. Symptoms may be highly variable depending on the child's disposition, surroundings, and level of maturity. As noted previously in the Macfarlane work, the expression of emotional conflict can take different forms as the child grows older. In a longitudinal study of 89 infants and children, Kagan and Moss (1962) discovered that the stability of observed personality traits was a function of the sex of the child, the age of the child, and the behaviors of the mother. For example, boys who showed behavioral disorganization at ages six to ten were more likely than girls to exhibit similar traits later in life. Fearfulness in girls was related to maternal restrictiveness followed by maternal hostility, while fears in boys were associated with maternal protectiveness followed by hostility and restrictiveness.

### Childhood Classification Schemes

In an attempt to provide some common frame of reference, psychopathologists have recommended a separate diagnostic classification system for childhood disorders. Unfortunately, this has not been easy to accomplish, and a proliferation of schemes has developed. Among these are one system that emphasizes psychodynamic interpretations (Group for the Advancement of Psychiatry, 1966); another based on learning theory (Kanfer & Saslaw, 1969); and still others derived from statistical factor or multivariate analysis (Achenbach, 1982b).[1] DSM-III has devoted a section to disorders "during infancy, childhood, or adolescence," listing a variety of specific diagnoses. Some of the disorders are limited to these age groups and tend not to appear in adults (for instance, separation anxiety, bedwetting, and night terrors). Others—such as attention deficit disorder, anorexia, autism, and schizophrenia—appear early in life and may persist into adulthood.

1 Still other schemes include those by Greenspan et al. (1979); Prugh (1973); Ross (1981); and Rutter et al. (1969).

This chapter will outline the mental disorders identified by DSM-III. This list is extensive; however, rather than attempting to deal with every syndrome, we will focus instead on some of the more important ones. According to DSM-III, the major categories of disturbances during infancy, childhood, or adolescence include: Attentional Deficit Disorders, with hyperactivity or without hyperactivity; Anxiety Disorders, such as separation anxiety, overanxious disorder, and avoidant disorder; Eating Disorders, such as anorexia nervosa, bulimia, pica; Stereotyped Movement Disorders, such as tics, Tourette's disorder; Physical Disorders, such as enuresis, pavor nocturnus, stuttering; and Pervasive Developmental Disorders, such as infantile autism, and childhood onset pervasive developmental disorder.

The six major categories here represent rather broad umbrellas. In the sections to follow, we will offer a brief definition of each of the disorders listed within the major groups, followed by a more intensive look at representative types.

## ATTENTIONAL DEFICIT DISORDERS

The classification of attentional deficit disorders includes two subcategories—*deficits with hyperactivity* and *deficits without hyperactivity.* Both are characterized by short attention spans and poor ability to concentrate on tasks. However, the child showing the attention disorder with hyperactivity is unable to sit still, while the child without the hyperactivity is unable to concentrate for long, but at least is able to sit without restlessness. It is possible that these two types of attention deficit disorders are actually subtypes of the same common pathology, but whether there is, in fact, a relationship is actually yet unknown. We will look more closely at the disorder with hyperactivity, since it occurs fairly frequently in our society.

### Attentional Deficit with Hyperactivity

Although we know hyperactivity is common, it is difficult to determine just *how* common it is, in part because of previous confusion over terminology and definitions (Ullman et al., 1981). Safer (1971) reported that 40 percent of children referred to child guidance clinics were there for "hyperactivity." In all likelihood, this figure is too high, however, with the reality being closer to 3 to 6 percent of elementary school children (Schwartz & Johnson, 1981).

***Symptoms of Hyperactivity.*** Two primary symptoms are associated with hyperactivity: a defect in attention and concentration; and overactive behavior. The inability to attend or to concentrate is seen in several symptoms, including short attention span; a failure to complete tasks; a tendency to make careless, impulsive errors; a failure to follow through on parents' requests; and a lack of planning or organization in activities.

In addition to these attentional symptoms are several important indexes of pathological hyperactivity. The child is apparently incapable of more than one speed of response (fast) and is also unable to show self-control by inhibiting activity on command. There is a characteristic display of high activity level in situations in which such levels are inappropriate. Finally, the activity itself is abnormal, not only in quantity but also in quality, for it is both inappropriate and nongoal-directed (Milich et al., 1982).

A more graphic description might be that a hyperactive child is like a top in perpetual motion, continuously moving in random directions, with the motion seemingly self-generating and resistant to influence.

Overactivity, of course, may describe many children on occasion, and a child may show a high activity level without being considered pathological. The difference is that the normal child is active as an appropriate response to the occasion (such as being on the playground at recess); is capable of "shifting gears" when the occasion demands; and engages in high levels of activity that are relevant to the goal at hand. ("Recess is a time to let loose. I've been sitting all day, so now I want to run.")

***An Example of Hyperactivity.*** The combination of poor concentration and hyperactivity leads to rather unfortunate consequences for the child of school age. Ross and Ross (1976) describe a day in the life of this child who acts like a disorganized tornado:

*Among the childhood disorders is* ***hyperactivity,*** *characterized by the child who seems unable to be still.*

He makes many errors in both oral and written work because he does not stop to think. He seldom follows oral directions accurately. His impulsivity is irritating to his teacher because he does not seem to care about his mistakes; his hand is often the first to be raised in answer to a question, and the answer is almost always incorrect. Teachers are seldom tolerant of this behavior and the peer group picks up the teacher's attitude and tends to make fun of the child when he impulsively blurts out a clearly incorrect answer. Sometimes the hyperactive child welcomes the attention, negative though it is, and makes a game of giving wrong answers. Once the teacher begins to doubt the child, her disbelief causes her to resent his interruptions and misbehavior, and this attitude is soon picked up by the other children in the class with the result that school becomes an intolerable experience for him. As his self-esteem continues on a downward spiral, his performance worsens and he is subjected to a barrage of deficit-amplifying-feedback that serves to exacerbate his difficulties.

***Dynamics of Hyperactivity.*** Many theories have attempted to explain the behaviors just described (Perlmutter, 1983). Initial speculation was that some form of mild brain damage was at fault, hence the former classification minimal brain dysfunction had once been used for this disorder. Indeed, short attention span and hyperactivity do occur in children with brain damage (Nichols & Chen, 1981). Although some attention deficit children may show signs of neurological damage, the current view is that brain damage is not the major factor for this disorder (Achenbach, 1982a).

Another hypothesis holds that attentional disorders with hyperactivity involves delayed maturation and physiological immaturity, with hyperactive youngsters being perhaps 18 to 24 months less mature. Genetic or constitutional factors have been explored. One pair of scientists found results suggesting that activity *level* (not hyperactivity) may well be hereditary (Werry & Sprague, 1970), while another was so impressed by the physical features of some hyperactive children that he coined the term *FLK,* or *Funny Looking Kid,* to refer to characteristic ear asymmetries, widely spaced eyes, or a wide gap between the first and second toes (Wender, 1971).

Still another explanation is that hyperactivity may be related to diet. This theory, suggested by Ben Feingold, has received dramatic attention but is yet far from conclusive (Prinz et al., 1980). A discussion of the "Feingold Diet" and some of the research that has evaluated it appears in Focus 20–2.

A broader theory is suggested by the psychoanalyst Bruno Bettelheim (1973), who posits an interaction between two causes: constitutional predisposition and child rearing. He hypothesizes that an infant's restlessness may make some mothers anxious or irritable; and that the infant may respond to the mother's impatience and tension with more activity.

In contrast to Dr. Bettelheim's idea that hyperactivity is a response to stress is the behavioral explanation that the response is instead to reward. Thus, the hyperactive infant may be one who is striving to achieve an optimal level of stimulation through activity which is socially encouraged in preschool years by those adults who respond favorably to the lively child (Wender, 1971). Physical activity tends to be encouraged in boys in our society; it is interesting, therefore, that the incidence of this disorder is far higher among boys than girls, by about 10 to 1 (American Psychiatric Association, 1978).

The mystery of attentional and hyperactivity defects continues to defy easy answers, although the search for solutions is stimulating. Part of the difficulty lies in the question of whether everyone is studying the same disorder; certainly, there has been much confusion on this matter. Those studies using the old classification *minimal brain dysfunction,* for instance, might have included different children from those relying upon the DSM-III classification (Small, 1983).

Another issue is whether attentional deficit with hyperactivity is essentially one disorder or perhaps a cluster of different subgroups. Ney (1974) postulates that there are really four types of hyperactivity—genetic, behavioral, minimal brain dysfunction, and reactive—each with different origins (heredity, social learning, brain damage, and family psychodynamics). And still another significant question is whether hyperactivity and attentional deficit are independent parallel symptoms, or whether attentional deficit might be the by-product of the hyperactivity symptoms. Finally, the difficulty of unraveling the mystery may simply reflect the complexity of the human process. It may just be too simplistic to believe that one explanation will be found. Perhaps Bettleheim's model may be more realistic—that hyperactivity is the end product of a number of causative factors interacting together.

***Treating Hyperactivity.*** Since no one yet completely understands the origins of hyperactivity, there is certainly no one panacea for this disorder. However, many mental disorders have been successfully treated on empirical grounds where theory cannot provide quick answers. Such empirical approaches have sometimes been chance discoveries, sometimes shrewd guesses based on theory, and sometimes prescriptions based on attempts to ameliorate symptoms where the cause is unknown. At this stage a number of different treatment strategies seem promising, among them the use of drugs, psychotherapy, and some innovative approaches within the classroom.

*Drugs and Hyperactivity.* Early evidence has suggested that some childhood behavior problems seem to respond to medication. On this basis, several organic

# FOCUS 20–2:
## Hyperactivity: Are You What You Eat?

What causes hyperactivity? Many attempts have sought the origins of this behavioral problem, including speculations that minimal brain damage is involved. One controversial explanation that has generated a great deal of publicity is the theory of Dr. Ben Feingold (1975; Feingold & Feingold, 1979).

Feingold is a pediatrician and specialist in allergies. His interest in the role of allergies in hyperactivity was first aroused when he treated a woman for an allergy. He put her on a special diet excluding artificial additives and salicylates (food preservatives). Not only did her allergic reactions disappear; but so did other symptoms of aggressive activity for which she had been receiving psychiatric treatment. Through experiences with other patients, Feingold became convinced not only that salicylates, food colorings, and artificial flavors were often involved in allergies, but also that they had something to do with hyperactivity. He designed a diet which has become known popularly as the Feingold diet or the Kaiser-Permanente diet. (Feingold was Chief Emeritus of the Department of Allergy at Kaiser-Permanente Medical Center.)

Feingold's hypothesis that food additives may be a cause of hyperactivity has become the center of national attention, much controversy, and also considerable research. Some early studies recorded testimonials from parents who said that using the special diet led to dramatic improvements in hyperactivity. As many as 30 to 40 percent of the families reported positive results, and one physician indicated that 76 of 100 hyperactive children in his practice improved after diet intervention (Crook, 1977; Levy et al., 1978).

Controlled studies, however, have had far less dramatic results. Conners et al. (1976) compared the effects of the diet on two groups of children—each of whom were given both a pseudo-diet and the Feingold diet at different times during the study. Although the children's teachers reported that hyperactivity decreased with the Feingold diet, such decreases were not reported by parents.

A more ambitious study was conducted by Harley et al. (1978) in which families were provided with all the food for the children—not only regular meals but also snacks. Here, researchers reported no differences in behavioral ratings between the Feingold diet and the control diet, although a number of parents noted some improvement on the Feingold diet.

Finally, Conners (1980) has followed his 1976 study with a more sophisticated design involving "challenge trials." Three different studies were conducted, each following the same basic model: those children who showed improvement on the Feingold diet were challenged by being given a cookie containing artificial additives, after which their responses were evaluated. A control group received cookies that did not have additives. In two of the challenge trials studies, the additives seemed to have no effect; in the third study, the additive-ingredient cookies did seem to bring more increases in hyperactivity.

In all, the Feingold diet remains controversial. The National Advisory Committee on Hyperkinesis and Food Additives reviewed the scientific research, including preliminary reports on the challenge studies and concluded that available evidence generally refutes Dr. Feingold's claim (Lipton & Wender, 1977). However, other reviews disagree. Harley and Matthews (1980) observed instead that the diet offers "an appealing treatment program for hyperactive children," suggesting the more cautious conclusion that a "small subgroup" of hyperactive children "may be behaviorally sensitive to certain food additives."

and pharmacological solutions have been studied.

The use of drugs to resolve the mystery of hyperactivity has led to a paradox that is a mystery in itself: a most successful and preferred treatment has turned out to be the use of stimulants such as amphetamines to calm what appears to be overstimulated behaviors. Indeed, one daily dose of Dexedrine, or three of Ritalin, can produce favorable effects in as high as 70 percent of the cases (Whalen, 1982).

Stimulants seem to improve attention span, similar to effects on nonhyperactive children (Wingartner et al., 1979). One mother reported that her hyperactive son's first response after his first pill was to take out a complex puzzle, which had always previously been a source of aggravation and frustration to him. He was able to sit for a hour, methodically and systematically showing goal-directed behavior, examining each piece. He completed the puzzle without frustration, sharing his joy with his family.

Medication has been used so extensively that many concerns have now been raised about potential dangers, lack of firm knowledge about possible side effects or dosages, and overenthusiastic reliance on medication instead of more careful diagnosis. One *Washington Post* reporter raised public concern, noting that 5 to 10 percent of school children in Omaha, Nebraska, were being given stimulants to improve their classroom performance (Maynard, 1970). Although the figures proved to be overestimates, the article has raised official awareness of the need for more careful control and study of drugs (Sroufe, 1975).

*Psychological Therapies.* Psychological therapeutic approaches have also had some success. On the whole, traditional psychotherapy has not yet achieved much success, except in helping youngsters deal with the frustrations of being hyperactive. On the premise that family interaction patterns and psychodynamics interrelate with hyperactivity, family therapy approaches have had some success, especially where short-term therapy goals are set (Weakland et al., 1974).

Behavioral therapy approaches have proven valuable in a number of ways (Fine, 1980). This approach demands that the target behavioral symptoms first be precisely defined. Thus, does not being hyperactive mean sitting, looking at the teacher, without hand movements or does it mean reducing the number of activity-play changes? Once the target is agreed on, the child is carefully involved in understanding what is desired as well as what contingent reward will be earned. Identical procedures will be earned. Identical procedures are used to help parents help their children, with the extra value of helping them change their views of hyperactivity from an emotional problem to its being viewed as a learning task (Rosenbaum et al., 1975).

A rather creative behavioral approach has aimed at training impulse control through self-regulation. The defined goal here is to think before you act. By this method, the child is guided in self-talk as a means of slowing down and planning more thoroughly (Copeland, 1981; Kendall & Braswell, 1982). Steps include self-talk involving questions about the task (O.K., what is it the teacher wanted me to do?); answers (Oh, yeh, I'm supposed to copy that picture); self-instruction (First thing is to start here, with this line); and self-reward (Hey, that's pretty good, I'm getting somewhere!). The decrease in impulsive behaviors from such self-control training is nicely illustrated in Figure 20–1. A comparable program aims at teaching the child ways to resist distractions through self-talk (Patterson & Mischel, 1975).

Also from a behavioral perspective, Ross (1981) has offered a conceptualization that relates diagnosis to treatment. As an example, he points out that attention is a construct used to refer to certain behaviors and that there are various forms of attention deficits, such as overexclusive attention (attending to one aspect of a complex stimulus environment), and overinclusive attention (attending to more aspects of the stimulus field than is required to cope effectively). In recognizing such differences, Ross designs differing treatment programs, based on discrimination learning and other learning principles. In addition, he also recognizes that the failure in attending activities may not be because of attention itself, but rather the inability to control responses. In this case, impulse control training, such as the stop, look, listen, think . . . programs, may be most helpful.

*School Intervention Studies.* Since there is some reason to believe that hyperactivity will not be outgrown as the child grows older (Eisenberg, 1979),

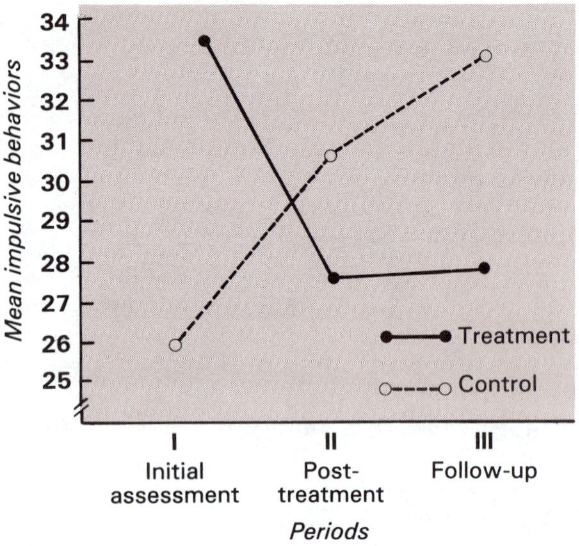


**FIGURE 20–1** Reduction of impulsive behaviors for the treatment and control group at the initial assessment, posttreatment, and follow-up periods.

SOURCE: From "A Cognitive Behavioral Treatment for Impulsivity: A Group Comparison Study" by P. Kendall and A. Finch, 1978, *Journal of Consulting and Clinical Psychology, 46,* pp. 110–118. © 1978 the American Psych. Assn. Reprinted by permission of the author.

school intervention studies have been considered in order to mainstream the child, that is, keep the child in the regular classroom. One approach is the engineered classroom, a carefully controlled class environment that stresses individual planning, flexibility, and high encouragement (Hewett et al., 1969). It is seen as a transitional classroom that prepares the child to reenter the mainstream of regular classes. The Medical College School Program (Zupnick, 1974) is a multidirected program, using a controlled classroom, behavior modification training for both teachers and parents, and group therapy to enable the parents to understand both their children's and their own problems. From children originally referred for severe behavior problems not treatable in the classroom, a number have completed the program and returned to normal classrooms. There have been no further complaints, and there have even been gains in classroom achievement.

## ANXIETY DISORDERS

A second major group of childhood disorders are the anxiety disorders. This group includes separation anxiety, overanxious disorder, and avoidant disorder. *Separation anxiety* is defined as fear associated with separation from home or family. The *overanxious disorder* is characterized by excess worry not associated with specific situations (such as parental separation). Instead, the worry is unrealistic, may be focused on events in the distant future or a preoccupation about how good past performances were. The child becomes highly self-conscious, requires much reassurance, ruminates about what is expected, and may experience stomachaches, headaches, or insomnia. The avoidant disorder might be described as a pathological shyness. Anxieties seem to be focused on strangers, including new peers in school. The fearfulness persists even after long exposure to a stranger and may show itself in the child clinging to or hiding behind the parent. The shyness and inhibition does not apply to family or other caretakers, to whom the child can show warmth and spontaneity. We will discuss separation anxiety in more detail in the next sections.

### Separation Anxiety

The anxiety felt by a child separated from parents can be a heart-rending event. The experience is quite normal in a very young child: many parents will attest to experiences where their child seemed to view being left alone for the first time as a major trauma and unforgivable experience. However, nearly all children soon adjust. When the fearfulness persists beyond reason, then the diagnosis of separation anxiety must be considered.

***Symptoms of Separation Anxiety.*** Children with separation anxiety may experience the anxiety concerns for as long as several years, with periods of recovery and periods of exacerbation. The disorder occurs with equal frequency among girls and boys. The anxiety reaches the stage of near panic and may be expressed by hysterical weeping, pleas to not be left alone, and somatic symptoms such as vomiting. At night, the child may continuously check the parents' bedroom to ensure their presence and even sleep at their doorstep.

Fears and fantasies follow themes related to separation, "I dream I wake up and I'm alone, it's dark, and I'm alone, and my mom and dad have been kidnapped, and taken far away to a strange country. . . ." There is a morbid preoccupation that illness, accident, or injury will overtake parents, or even that somehow they might become lost. Given such fearfulness, the child clings to the parent, literally staying constantly in touch. He or she may call aloud to ensure that the parent is still in the next room and will shadow the parent around the premises. At the start, such concern creates guilt or protectiveness in the parent and perhaps even an unconscious pleasure at being needed.

As the anxiety persists and the child remains demanding and unreassured, however, the parent may eventually view the child's behavior as intrusive. As the child reaches school age, he or she may now resist leaving the home since it increases the reality of separation. Outbursts of "You don't care for me . . . I can't go . . . no one really loves me" may lead the parent to relent and to postpone the inevitable.[2] The anxiety can easily become a focal point of family tension.

***Dynamics of Separation Anxiety.*** In exploring the causes of separation anxiety, it is useful to look in two directions: not only toward the child, but also to the parents. In some cases, separation anxiety seems to be a confirmation of parents' concerns. Eisenberg (1958) discovered the mothers of such children to have been apprehensively solicitous and protective during the child's infancy. They had often repeated warnings about dangers or had modeled their own fearfulness by refusing to permit babysitters in the home. Knopf (1979) sees the problem as a mutual exploitation: the child offers a somatic excuse or expresses a fear of being left; and the mother responds with speed and relief as she seizes on the child's concern and keeps the child closer to her. The origins of the mother's neurosis itself may have many sources—a difficult childbirth after years of sterility, a frustrating marital relationship with the husband, a previous health crisis, or a personal need to feel wanted and needed.

From the child's perspective, separation anxiety may represent a variety of threats. In infancy, attachment to the parent may simply have been associated with feelings of comfort, while separation was vaguely associated with the loss of physical well-being. As the child matures and becomes more perceptive, separation may represent fantasies of rejection or a threat to comfortable dependency. Allman and Jaffe (1978) suggest that separation anxiety represents a failure on the part of the child to cope with the developmental task of forming a separate identity. "Am I a person that can make it as an independent person from my parents?" In their view, a failure to resolve this identity crisis leads to the persistence of separation anxiety.

***Treating Separation Anxiety.*** The treatment of choice for separation anxiety depends on the dynamics of each particular case. In instances where both parent and child seem to be involved in a symbiotic clinging, then both persons need to be helped to cope independently (Sperling, 1979). The mother must develop insights into her own needs, the consequences of her actions on the child's development, and other sources of strength that she can develop to cope with her own life history. It is helpful for the child to appreciate the importance of being able to cautiously try out his or her own ability to be independent, while still knowing of the availability and support of the parents. Many therapists emphasize the value of graduated time away from the parent. In a behavior therapy program, Montenegro (1968) gradually increased the amount of time the child was away from the mother, using food as an anxiety inhibitor.

In some instances, excessive dependency may seem basic to the separation anxiety. Preventative steps are possible here, too, for excess dependency seems often to be fostered by the mother's inconsistency. Mothers who sometimes punish and sometimes reward dependent behavior tend to have infants with overattachment characteristics. Thus, child theorists often recommend treating the parents—teaching them to recognize when dependent behavior is appropriate and age relevant and how to maintain consistency (Schwartz & Johnson, 1981).

One other treatment approach, drug therapy, has

2 A *school phobia* differs from separation anxiety in the nature of the fear; school phobia involves the avoidance of the school itself, while separation anxiety is a fear of being away from the presence of the parent; a school phobic child will avoid school even when accompanied by the parent (Gelfand et al., 1982).

been tried with separation anxieties, with limited success (Gittelman-Klein, 1975). The major issue is the danger of using drugs for symptom control, because of potential risks to the still-maturing child—a similar question we saw earlier regarding drugs for hyperactive symptoms.

## EATING DISORDERS

A third group of childhood disorders listed in DSM-III are the eating disorders. There are three major disorders in his group. *Anorexia nervosa* involves restricted food intake; *bulimia* involves excessive food intake, and *pica* involves indiscriminative food intake. Anorexia will be discussed in detail later. Bulimia involves binge eating of high caloric foods, with the person being aware of excessive eating, but being unable to control the behavior. This disorder is most common among adolescent females, who usually are also concerned about controlling their weight, yet are unable to prevent the overeating and feel out of control (Spencer & Fremouw, 1979). Binges are followed by depressed moodiness and self-disparagement. In pica, the person is indiscriminate in what is eaten. The infant or child may eat paint chips, ceiling plaster, string, hair, cloth, marbles, pebbles, leaves, insects, or animal excrement—basically, anything. Complications can be numerous, depending on what is ingested. Fortunately, this disorder is rare.

### Anorexia Nervosa

Anorexia nervosa is a disorder that has gained considerable attention in recent years. The Grammy Award recording star, Karen Carpenter, suffered from anorexia prior to her death (Antczak, 1983). It is characterized by several symptoms, including an intense fear of gaining weight; drastic behaviors in order to prevent weight gains; a fear of being unable to retain self-control; and a distorted body image.

***Symptoms of Anorexia Nervosa.*** The word *anorexia* means literally "loss of appetite," and is a misnomer, since anorexics do not report an absence of hunger but rather a refusal to eat. Thus, it is not a defect in a need, but a maladaptive behavior problem. About one of every 150 adolescent girls are affected. The condition tends to be more common among adolescent girls, with females outnumbering males 9 to 1, although it also occurs among some adults (Sours, 1979). The individual seems preoccupied with the idea of losing weight and is convinced that she is overweight and that she will look better if she loses even more weight. She will spend hours gazing in the mirror, assessing whether enough weight has been lost, even when she already is becoming skeletal in appearance. The anorexic chooses a variety of behaviors to lose weight, particularly drastic reductions in food intake. Self-induced vomiting may occur after meals, or she may rely on laxatives to keep from gaining weight.

Interestingly, anorexics typically show model academic behavior in school, being conscientious with studies, achieving good grades, and keeping so busy with activities as to not have time for dating (Weeda-Mannak et al., 1983). As starvation continues, physiological side effects develop, such as lowered blood pressure, skin dryness, subnormal temperature, slow heart beat, and irregularity of the menstrual cycle. Other results include a lower tolerance for cold and an appearance of premature aging. The dramatic impact of seeing their offspring so undernourished will galvanize parents into trying to reverse the dieting. However, the child will resist forced feedings, hide food and pretend she has eaten it, wear bulkier clothes to mask her continued weight loss, or continue to vomit after meals. The anorexic adolescent does not believe herself to have a problem; as far as she is concerned her problem is excess weight, not starvation. Yet one estimate suggests that death from starvation occurs in 15 to 21 percent of all cases (American Psychiatric Association, 1978).

A classic case that illustrates the extreme effects of weight loss is described by Bachrach et al., (1965):

> The physical examination revealed a creature so . . . shrunken about her skeleton as to give the appearance of a poorly preserved mummy suddenly struck with the breath of life. Her pasty white skin was mottled a purple hue over her feet and stretched like so much heavy spider webbing about the bony prominences of her face. Edema-

> tous ankles and feet ballooned out grotesquely from the margins of her slippers. . . . Delicate silky threads of hair hung lifelessly from her skull. Broken gray teeth peered out between thin, white lips through which there weakly issued forth a high pitched distant voice, remarkable for its lack of pressing concern and alarm, which to the passing observer might have seemed a bit incongruous. (p. 154)

This describes the girl shown in the photographs on page 470. What explains this kind of self-destructive behavior in an otherwise conscientious, active person? A variety of factors seem to be involved which we will present next.

***Dynamics of Anorexia Nervosa.*** In addition to the model academic behaviors of the typical anorexic girl, some other personality traits seem related to the disorder. Personality characteristics often include tenseness, hyperactivity, alertness, rigidity, sensitivity, perfectionist tendencies, a lack of self-confidence, and also stubbornness (Bakwin & Bakwin, 1966). Psychoanalytic explanations call attention to the fear of sexual maturity, sex roles, or pregnancy; fear of hostile impulses expressed in oral ways; desire to maintain childlike dependency relationships; fear of the demands of social competition; or a need for self-punishment (Evans, 1982).

Kessler (1966) offers a separate explanation, listing three factors related to anorexia. First, one or both parents eat or drink too much. Second, the intake of food already has a private significance to the person, in that she may already have a past history of overeating. Third, there is a resistance to growing up and a regression rather than acceptance of the adult sexual role.

Physiological causes have also been studied, particularly focusing on the hypothalamus, since dysfunction of this organ can affect eating activities. In addition, higher levels of endorphins have been found in anorexic persons, perhaps explaining how they can ignore hunger pains (Kaye et al., 1982; Yates et al., 1983).

An intriguing hypothesis compares anorexia with compulsive runners. Some researchers, who are runners themselves, concluded that anorexics and runners have many personality traits in common, for instance, high self-expectations, tolerance of physical discomfort, denial of disability, a tendency to depression, and a suppression of anger (Yates et al., 1983). They discovered that many compulsive runners took to exercising as a reaction to a period of stress or depression, when their self-identities were threatened. In a similar way, they note that anorexia develops during a time of unrest or change, with thinness providing a self-identity, and dieting offering a sense of self-control. Compulsive runners might push themselves to further distances as their goals change; similarly, the anorexic continues to diet when one desired weight is reached; both are viewed as always moving *towards,* but never *attaining* a goal. Although this hypothesis requires much more testing, it is interesting to note that at least one other study found that families of anorexics themselves showed interests in exercise, achievement, and dieting (Crisp et al., 1980). In other words, anorexia might be seen in a person whose environment stimulates a need to achieve, and which encourages actions (such as exercising or dieting) as solutions. The families may even provide models for such solutions, including their own extremes in dietary habits (Kalucy et al., 1977). However, the results of these studies are inconclusive, as are studies of endocrine, neurotransmitters, or biochemical disturbances (Sours, 1979). Thus, despite efforts to explain anorexia through physiological or psychological studies, the fact still remains that the exact causes are not known.

***Treating Anorexia Nervosa.*** If the anorexic starvation has reached significant levels, medical care and even hospitalization is a necessary first step. The patient may be physically unable to retain food, for her stomach may automatically reject it after a certain point.

Once this initial state of physical danger is overcome, treatment can focus on the underlying motivations. Traditional psychotherapeutic treatment has emphasized dealing with the symbolic nature of the symptoms, such as the fearfulness of or the hostility to heterosexual roles it represents. The patient is helped to become more accepting of her true body image and more capable of facing the social demands of heterosexual maturity (Crisp, 1982).

Behavior therapy has had unusual success through two strategies: reducing the anorexic's fear of food and fatness and reinforcing renewed eating and weight gain (Bachrach et al., 1965). Bachrach et al. (1965) re-

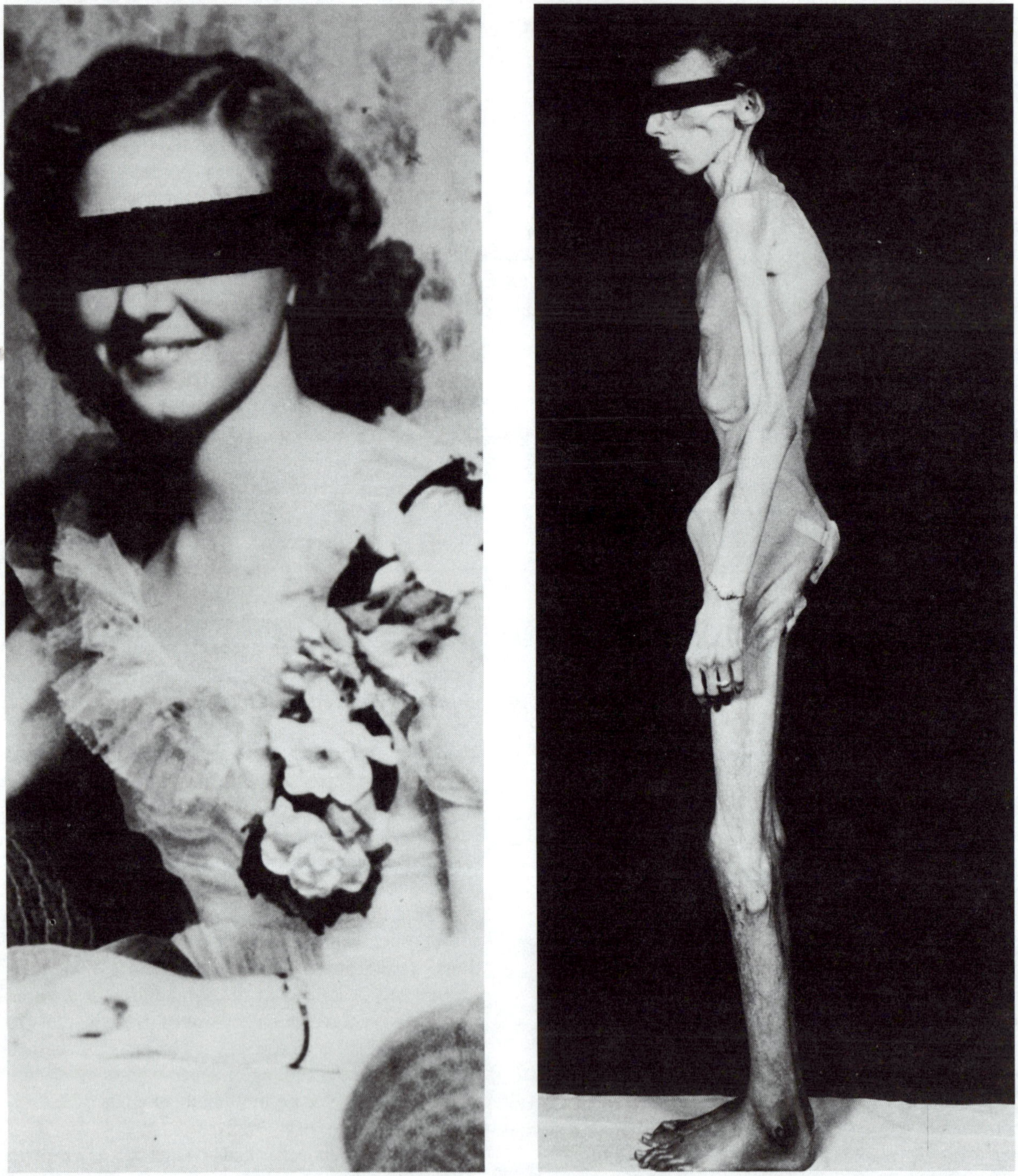

*The woman in these pictures suffered from* ***anorexia nervosa.*** *The first picture shows her at age eighteen, when she weighed 120 pounds. Nineteen years later, when she began treatment, she weighed 47 lbs. After more than a year of treatment, her weight rose to 88 pounds.*

ported on a case involving a woman who had dropped from 118 to 47 pounds (see p. 000). As treatment, they first removed the patient to a barren room and isolated her from social contact so as to increase effectiveness of rewards to be employed. Interesting discussions, social visits, music, television, and walks were made contingent upon her eating. Within less than two months, she had progressed well enough to be discharged to her home. A follow-up 16 years later (Erwin, 1977) revealed that this woman had shown a slow recidivism and had again been losing weight after the treatment termination. Thus, although the immediate life-threatening anorexic behaviors had been stopped and even reversed during treatment, a gradual return of the problem behaviors did occur. To insure maintaining the effects of treatment, programs have now added steps to train clients in self-control, to increase generalization outside the hospital, and to include family involvement in the treatment (Ollendick, 1979). Even with careful treatment, the overall prognosis is considered poor, with recovery rates being 40 to 60 percent of those treated (Schwartz & Johnson, 1981).

## STEREOTYPED MOVEMENT DISORDERS

The stereotyped movement disorders, such as tics and Tourette's disorder, are conditions involving involuntary motor movements. *Tics* differ from Tourette's disorder in that they seem to be restricted to smaller groups of muscles and may involve, for example, involuntary eye winks, facial twitches, or mild vocal tics such as a grunt. *Tourette's disorder,* on the other hand, may include complicated sounds or movements, such as barks, obscenities, repeating words of others, skipping, tongue protrusion, hopping, squatting, or throat clearing. Tourette's disorder remains a rare illness, with only about 250 cases being reported in the world.

### Transient or Chronic Tics

There are two classifications of tics: *transient* and *chronic.* Essentially, the distinction is one of degree: a tic is considered transient if it has a duration of no more than one year and chronic if it has lasted beyond one year.

***Symptoms of Tics.*** Tics are involuntary, recurring, rapid, purposeless movements. The most common are facial twitches or eye blinking. Other tics that have been shown by children also include hand twitching, head jerks, grimaces, sniffing, frowning, coughing, throat clearing, ear pulling, scratching—an almost limitless list. Nail biting, thumbsucking, head banging, or rhythmical rocking are not considered tics inasmuch as these involve voluntary coordinated, nonspasmodic movements, generally due to other causes. A tic can be voluntarily suppressed, but only temporarily and for only a few minutes or hours. After that, the spasm returns. In extreme cases, the tics occur hundreds of times during the day. They disappear during sleep and are worsened during times of stress.

It is generally believed that transient tics may begin during childhood or early adolescence, while chronic tics may begin either in childhood or after age 40, another difference between the two disorders. For tics starting in adulthood, the spasm tends to be limited to one muscle group.

***Dynamics of Tics.*** Tics may first begin through imitation of a movement seen in a parent or playmate. Kanner (1972) strongly believes that tics originated as once purposeful movements or as customary gestures that have now become habitual. He is convinced that the tic is a symptom that may directly represent a psychological conflict (head shaking may represent a negative attitude) or an indirect expression of generalized emotional strain. Kessler (1966) stresses even more heavily the symbolic nature of the tic and comments that tics usually involve conversion disorder. Involuntary eye blinking, for example, is interpreted in the same way as conversion blindness—an attempt to blot out an image that was seen. Head shaking is the expression of refusal to an unconscious wish. Facial grimaces represent a hidden insult to others.

A general picture of emotional tension may be a feature of tics, since children with tics tend to be self-conscious, sensitive, restless, and easily fatigued (Lucas, 1979). The tic may represent a compromise solution to the demands of parents and teachers to restrain too much motor activity; thus, the tic is a halfway point between being very active and not acting (Erickson, 1982). This may help explain the higher incidence of tics among Russian children, whose culture demands high regimentation and classroom control—a norm that may prevent overt expression of many behaviors. One other explanation of some cases of tics, of course, is organic. Certain illnesses, such as the spasmodic coughing or sniffing that may follow a case of encephalitis, are sometimes associated with tics.

***Treatment of Tics.*** It should be stressed that tics may be a common developmental characteristic of normal children. In one study reported by Kanner, 15 percent of the children aged two to four displayed involuntary movements, but the rate dropped to 5 percent by ages four and five. Thus, the most immediate recommendation for treatment would be to wait until sufficient time has elapsed to prove that the problem is truly a problem. Psychotherapy is aimed at reducing the stressors impinging on the child, whether they be social, emotional, or educational. Reassurance that the spasms are not evidence of organic damage may be a helpful step. Tranquilizers, such as Haloperidol, have been used to reduce reactions to stress (Barker, 1976).

With the development of behavior therapy, a variety of techniques have been useful with children and adults. Yates (1958) applied *negative practice,* having the patient deliberately practice the tic, twice a day, from several minutes to one hour. The practice intervals used did not seem to make a difference, as the client improved equally for both the short and long practice periods. The success of negative practice has received support from others working with children or adolescents with multiple tics (Lazarus, 1960; Walton, 1964).

A combination of positive and negative feedback has been tried with an adult patient who had contractions of the neck, stomach, and upper body and eye blinking tics that had been going on for 14 years. In an ingenious setup, a recorder was activated when a tic occurred. This, in turn, triggered a relay that turned on an aversive noise. On the other hand, when the patient did not show a tic, his favorite music would play instead. With this procedure, tics decreased from 166 spasms per minute to about 15 per minute (Barrett, 1962). A habit-reversal method has been used with success; this involves having the patient perform movements opposite to those involved in the tic as a means of countering the tic (Azrin et al., 1980). This procedure decreased the frequency of tics by about 95 percent after one day's practice and seemed to be continuously effective during the five months that the patients were observed.

## PHYSICAL DISORDERS

The only feature shared among the disorders in this fifth category is the fact that the major symptoms show up in physical dimensions. The category *physical disorders* is actually a classification of miscellaneous physical childhood problems and includes disorders of elimination, sleep, and speech. *Enuresis* and *encopresis* are disorders of elimination, with enuresis involving urination and encopresis involving the passage of feces. Encopresis seems related to inconsistent toilet training or family conflict where the child is the object of anger, punishment, or rejection. It is believed to spontaneously disappear (Evans, 1982).

*Pavor nocturnus,* or night terror, involves severe night experiences including panic, a hallucinatory-like reaction, followed by amnesia on awakening. There is temporary confusion, disorientation, and persistent nervous motor movements such as picking at the pillow. There is some evidence that pavor nocturnus is an evening anxiety attack occurring during non-REM sleep (Hartmann, 1973); this distinguishes it from common REM nightmares.

Stuttering is a speech disorder. It involves repetitions of sounds or unusual hesitations that disrupt the rhythmic flow of speech. In the DSM-III classification, stuttering and stammering are considered synonymous. Stuttering can begin at any age, although it is rare for an adult to suddenly be afflicted. Stuttering may be absent during singing, and is likely to spontaneously disappear in 50 to 80 percent of children, with milder cases being even more likely to recover. Stuttering is a common problem of childhood; another common difficulty about which a great deal has been written is enuresis. We will turn our attention to that disorder.

### Enuresis

The term, *enuresis,* often assumed to mean nocturnal bedwetting, but the disorder actually includes day or nighttime loss of control. *Enuresis* is accidental urination at an inappropriate time or place. Nocturnal enuresis is more common than daytime enuresis and is more common among boys than girls. There is some disagreement among clinicians about the age after which urinary accidents are considered pathological; Erickson (1982) suggests that daytime control should be achieved by age four and nighttime control by age five. Enuresis is similar to thumbsucking in that the behavior may be acceptable in early life, but is frowned upon by our society as the child grows older, is viewed as an index of immaturity or a sign of emotional problems, and leads to self-embarrassment. It also provokes family conflict and pressures.

***Dynamics of Enuresis.*** Although some enuretics may have a small bladder capacity, the primary cause of enuresis is rarely physical (Anders & Freeman, 1979). Far more common is a dimension of emotional stress—although most enuretic children do not show other symptoms of stress. Sources of the stress may include the arrival of a new sibling, separation from family, a move to new surroundings, or parental divorce. Inconsistent or rigid and punitive toilet training may lay the groundwork for enuresis.

The psychoanalytic and behaviorist views of enuresis differ sharply. Dr. Melitta Sperling (1974), a psychoanalyst, interpreted enuresis as involving repressed sexual or aggressive impulses. In some instances, she postulates, the boy fantasizes unconsciously having been castrated, and symbolically is saying, ''My penis is no good any more, it leaks'' (p. 333).

Behavioral therapists, in contrast, view enuresis as a simple learning deficit, a failure to develop cortical control over a subcortical reflex. After a review of the research literature, Anders and Freeman (1979) concluded that enuresis derives from a range of different causes, some physiological, some psychological, and some social.

***Treating Enuresis.*** If left alone, all but 2 percent of enuretic children spontaneously recover by age 14 (Doleys et al., 1982). However, because of the social impact of enuretic behaviors, treatment is usually initiated earlier.

Several approaches may be taken. Psychotherapy is widely used, aimed at relieving emotional conflicts that are sometimes believed to be basic to the problem. Little good data supports the value of brief psychotherapy, however (Werry, 1972). Drug treatment, such as the antidepressant drug Imipramine, taken in high doses, has been used with only moderate success. Relapse rates are high, and the total number of cases that are cured is low—about 30 percent (Barker, 1976).

A behavior modification technique, initially suggested by a German pediatrician in 1904, then popularized in the United States in 1938 by Mowrer and Mowrer is still considered superior to either psychotherapy or medication (Doleys, 1977). The technique is admirable for its simplicity: a bed pad is made up to act as an electrical conductor when it is wet, completing a circuit and setting off a buzzer. This is basically a classical conditioning tool. The desired response is waking up; the unconditioned stimulus is the sound of the buzzer; and the conditioned stimulus, the internal cue of bladder tension. Eventually, the buzzer conditions the child to awaken to bladder pressure, in time to get up and go to the bathroom. As a further improvement on the concept, Azrin and his colleagues (Azrin et al., 1979; Bollard & Nettelbeck, 1981) have introduced the dry-bed procedure. This involves large fluid intake before bedtime; hourly awakenings that teach the child to awaken to mild prompts; practice in going to the toilet; reward for appropriate nighttime urination; and training to be aware of differences in the wetness of the bed.

The childhood disorders discussed up to this point include a fairly broad spectrum of behaviors, ranging widely in both nature and severity. One other group of childhood disorders seems to be set apart in the same way that the adult psychoses are distinct from the other adult disorders. We will explore this last category, the pervasive developmental disorders, in the remainder of this chapter.

## Case History 20–2:
### An Autistic Child

Ken J. is the second son of two well-educated parents. Hal, his father, received his Ph.D in American history from Harvard and his writings have already achieved some recognition. Carol, his mother, received her bachelors in political science and has been an active leader in the League of Women Voters. Their first son was a bright, stimulating, and joyful child to have. Ken was born two years later, and considered a good baby who entertained himself in his crib and fussed almost not at all, especially when compared with his brother. However, thinking back, Carol remembers the almost too perfect early years; with a touch of guilt she says, "Ken was so quiet, I found I'd almost forget his needs and I could spend more time in planning my club work."

As Ken matured, however, his awareness or concern for his surroundings seemed undeveloped. Hal contrasts his two sons, "I used to bounce and throw Hal Junior in the air and he'd giggle and spit and have the laughs; Ken didn't do that, he would squirm when I picked him up, turn his head, and seemed to hate being held; I think he wanted to be alone." By preschool, there was clear concern that something was wrong. The parents first suspected mental retardation, or even brain damage because of the lack of interest and especially the slow development of speech. More serious concerns developed when Ken would go into tantrums, for apparently no good reason, with screams, screeches, and head banging. Then the head banging persisted even without tantrums, sometimes replaced by hours of rocking. Ken often seemed to be in a world of his own, marching from one room to another, ignoring the call of a nearby parent whom he would brush by.

Ken's speech development has been erratic; he sings nearly perfectly certain limericks from commercials, yet seems to have a limited vocabulary, and has forced his parents to learn the meaning of demands associated with words of Ken's own creation. "Sometimes I feel he knows more than he is willing to say, even that he is privately controlling me, and that I don't exist as a person and especially not as his father."

Five years of private psychotherapy has proved fruitless, although Hal and Carol have themselves been helped to accept the implications of the autistic diagnosis and their own feelings of guilt, sorrow, and frustration. Ken has now been transferred to a residential treatment center, with limited prognosis, but Carol can now say, "We were denying Hal Junior his right to our time as parents because we spent so much emotional energy coping with Ken. It's better for everyone this way. We love Ken and showed him, we also love Hal Junior and now we want to show him too."

## PERVASIVE DEVELOPMENTAL DISORDERS

The pervasive developmental disorders involve severe pathologies of infancy or childhood, including serious qualitative symptoms that are not normal for any age level. Although the term *psychosis* would be applicable, the current classification has carefully substituted the terminology pervasive developmental disorders in order to avoid any implication that these disorders are related to the psychoses of adulthood. The two major disorders are *infantile autism* and *childhood onset pervasive developmental disorder* (also sometimes referred to as *childhood schizophrenia*). Because of the importance of these two syndromes, both will be briefly discussed in the following section.

### Infantile Autism

In 1943, Kanner discovered in 11 children what has become an important and unusual disorder, now known as infantile autism. The symptoms are dramatic, involving extreme self-imposed isolation, communication defects, repetitive body movements, and a need to resist change and maintain the status quo. For every 10,000 children, two or three will be autistic; with boys outnumbering girls by about 3 to 1 (Russo & Newson 1982).

***Development of Autistic Symptoms.*** In the typical course of development of autism, there is a gradual evolution of some of the characteristics just

***These two autistic** boys are showing a characteristic symptom of self-stimulation.*

described. As with Ken in Case History 20–2, the early months of infancy are usually easy ones, since the infant seldom frets or makes demands for attention. Parents might notice a tendency for the infant to arch its back instead of cuddling close when picked up.

By age four months, the failure to make anticipatory movements prior to being picked up and the infant's continuous disinterest in surroundings might start to raise concern. As the child grows older, this isolation from people becomes even more noticeable as play preferences center on things and solitary play rather than peer play (Schopler & Mesibov, 1983). In a personal experience, the autistic child of a visiting friend walked several times right by without acknowledging my existence and spent the hour in various repetitive play, including eventually dunking his head in a wading pool. Although he passed near me several times, for all he noticed, I did not exist.

As the child reaches the age of speech, communication defects are clearly marked. Language is not used for the purpose of communicating; instead, sounds are used for self-stimulation. Speech that is recognizable may be stereotyped and parrotlike, with self-referents occurring in the third person. For instance, to the question, "What are you doing?", the answer may be, "She knows it's o.k." A high proportion of autistic children do not speak at all and are unresponsive to the speech of others, leading many parents to suspect their child is deaf.

Repetitive body movements often precipitate the most concern of parents. Ritualistic movements, head banging, spinning, incessant rocking, and hand-flapping are often displayed (Rutter & Schopler, 1978). Although generally isolated and unresponsive to people, autistic children still seem to have a heightened sensitivity to the environment, and may be extremely upset at minor changes in the status quo. A child may scream if greeted in the morning with "morning." instead of the usual "good morning," throw a tantrum if a different cup is on the table, or cry if a pillowcase has been changed.

Autistic children may also show remarkable memory, for example, for the exact words of a song heard years before or commercials from television. They may be fascinated by things in which others would soon lose interest such as music or a simple-moving toy; yet be annoyed by and even seemingly pained by other normal events, such as being spoken to or facing a moving object such as an egg beater.

***Dynamics of Autism.*** What causes infantile autism? No one seems to know, although many theories have been offered. Some scientists believe that autism is a case of arrested development of what might have been a super-infant. For example, Moore and Shiek (1971) argue that these fetuses are ready to be born by reason of accelerated development, are not delivered, and hence suffer damage from sensory deprivation. Rimland (1964) proposed that the infants were genetically potential geniuses "gone awry" because of damage to a part of the brain leading to a state of lowered brain arousal or alertness.

There may be some element of heredity involved in autism, although few studies are available because of the difficulty of finding enough twins. Folstein and Rutter (1978) reported concordance in 36 percent of cases where one identical twin was autistic, as compared with 0 percent concordance among fraternal twins. Other studies show the incidence of autism among relatives of autistic children to be slightly higher than the incidence among nonrelatives, but the difference is very small (Treffert, 1970).

Psychological explanations have emphasized an unsatisfactory relationship between parent and child. Zaslow and Breger (1969) suggest that a defect in social attachment develops as the parent is unable to cope with the rejecting or aloof early responses of the infant. Despert (1951) hypothesized the correlate, that the infant's aloofness is due to an initial lack of warmth from the parents; however, the evidence on this hypothesis is inconclusive. Bettelheim (1967) discusses the autistic isolation, ritualistic behaviors, and communication disorders as an expression of the child's attempt at self-protection from a threatening, powerful, disappointing world. The need to maintain the status quo also offers protection and safety.

***Treating Autism.*** As elusive as explanations for autism are, it is not surprising that the prognosis for successful treatment is also regrettably poor. Bettelheim's Orthogenic School at the University of Chicago provides milieu psychotherapy in a residential setting. Autistic children are given a 24-hour experience with adults who are not their parents, to help the children overcome their fear of the environment. This approach has been reported useful in a high percentage of cases by Bettelheim and Sanders (1979), but formal procedures for fully evaluating results have not yet been made available. Other surveys of psychotherapeutic effects have been cautious and less optimistic (Hagamen, 1980).

Another approach, drug treatment, has been attempted in a case study of identical autistic twins, using LSD. Results showed some increases in physical contacts and eye-contact, but also increases in some stereotyped behaviors (Simmons et al., 1966). However, little more has been done with drugs.

Yet another approach is offered by behavior therapy. This treatment has been actively pursued by Lovaas (1977) and it shows some promise for those behaviors that are treated (Turkington, 1982). Rather than attempting to change general traits, such as emotional isolation, Lovaas first operationalizes the traits by identifying those behaviors which, when present, would increase the learning of the desired trait. For example, Lovaas presumed that the autistic child could develop communications skills only if the child's imitative response was strengthened, since learning speech depends on hearing and imitating an adult model. Autistic children were first rewarded with food for imitating an adult's sounds; they were later rewarded for using sounds meaningfully in expressive speech (Lovaas, 1977; Koegel & Egel, 1974). Lovaas and his colleagues have also had some success in reducing self-destructive behaviors often shown by autistic children.

A different approach is based on the premise that autism involves low brain arousal. To counteract this condition, DesLauriers and Carlson (1969) have directed parents to interact with their child by using intense stimulation and direct bodily contact, rather than relying on distance receptors (such as sight and sound). Parents are urged to forcefully play with their children, using body contact to gain attention, to control any appearance of disorganized activity.

In general, the prognosis is not positive for autistic children, as about 75 percent are functioning below normal in personal or cognitive adjustment (Ornitz & Ritvo, 1976). However, in some notable cases, complete recovery has occurred by adulthood. Kanner (1973) reported that 11 of 96 persons he had seen as autistic children were functioning well in society as adults. All were employed, and 6 had completed college educations.

## Childhood Schizophrenia

While autism seems to be recognizable within the first year, childhood schizophrenia is usually preceded by several years of normal development. Childhood schizophrenia most generally appears after age five; however, some cases may develop as early as age two. Approximately three children of every 10,000 will show this disorder; with males outnumbering females by about 3 to 1 (Russo & Newsom, 1982). Childhood schizophrenia differs from the autistic disorder in several ways, as Table 20–3 indicates.

***Symptoms of Childhood Schizophrenia.*** The schizophrenic child shows profound disturbance in emotional relations with people, including social ineptitude, a lack of empathy for others, and marked withdrawal. Although the disorder does not seem associated with actual delusions or hallucinations, schizophrenic children may have morbid or bizarre fantasies which they are unable to separate from reality. Bizarre motor behavior may include body-whirling or toe-walking. One diagnostic test involves turning the head of the child; whereas a normal child

**TABLE 20–2**

**Autism versus Childhood Schizophrenia: Distinguishing Characteristics**

| *Autism* | *Childhood schizophrenia* |
|---|---|
| Good physical health. | Health problems common. |
| Typically normal EEG patterns. | Abnormal EEG patterns more likely. |
| Child stiffens when held by parent. | Child tends to mold its body to parent when held. |
| Unusual memory skills or musical talent are often noted. | Lacks unusual memory or musical skills. |
| Tends to have bright, well-educated parents. | No relationship to family IQ level. |

SOURCE: Based on *Infantile Autism* by B. Rimland, 1964, New York: Appleton-Century-Crofts.

will resist, a schizophrenic child begins to rotate the body in reaction and may continue to whirl with delight. There may also be an excessive preoccupation with objects, such as a toy, which the child will stare at but not actually use for play. Communications defects or bizarre speech can appear. Thus, the child may speak with a high-pitched voice unless instructed to speak normally, may show discontinuity between spoken words and facial or body gestures, or may fail to speak at all (a trait that is appropriately called *elective mutism*) (Asarnow, 1983).

***Dynamics of Childhood Schizophrenia.*** A number of preliminary attempts have been made to explain childhood schizophrenia. Consistent with results on adult schizophrenics, shown in Chapter 4, genetic factors may be present in childhood schizophrenia, as shown by the 88 percent concordance for identical twins, 23 percent for fraternal twins, and 8 percent for nontwin siblings (Kallman & Roth, 1956; Fish & Ritvo, 1979). Biological or physiological variables are suggested in the abnormal EEG patterns and signs of central nervous system dysfunction found by some researchers (Fish, 1978).

Severe psychological disturbance in family relations have been examined as contributing factors. For example, Bender (1974) discovered serious pathologies in about 75 percent of families with a schizophrenic child, with one or both parents either psychotic, disturbed, or somehow incompetent. Mothers of schizophrenic children, when compared with control families, were found higher in *maternal perplexity,* showing lack of spontaneity, indecisiveness and inconsistency, inappropriate control over the child or anticipation of physical needs, and inappropriateness in meeting the child's demands (Meyers & Goldfarb, 1962).

***Treating Childhood Schizophrenia.*** Various approaches to treating childhood schizophrenia have been taken, but generally there has been little success and poor prognosis.

Physiological treatments are one approach that has been extensively used for the adult schizophrenias, as readers will remember from Chapter 17. This approach has had somewhat less use for childhood schizophrenia. Bender (1953) attempted electroshock treatment, but the recovery rate seemed no better than would have occurred without treatment. Tranquilizers appear to have some promise, although their use is still considered experimental since there have been very few well-controlled studies (Campbell, 1979).

Both psychotherapy and behavior therapy have been applied with some positive results. Of interest is a study of two therapists who provided similar psychotherapy to severely disturbed boys in a clinic (Ricks et al., 1974). Therapist A's clients showed a higher rate of recovery, while Therapist B's clients were more likely to remain socially inadequate or to be released as schizophrenic.

The primary difference between the two seems to have been one of approach, to both therapy and the clients. Therapist A—nicknamed "Supershrink" by the children—was characterized by several qualities. He was responsive to feelings, yet he anchored the children in reality, helping the boys reach a sense of auton-

*One diagnostic test for* ***childhood schizophrenia*** *involves twirling the child. Afflicted children seem to delight in this, while normal children resist.*

omy. He was also firm and direct with parents, concerned with encouraging competence, and likely to use outside resources. Therapist B, in contrast, was more distant and more interested in hearing deep therapy revelations than in the boys as people.

Such a finding raises questions about whether therapists' personal characteristics may play a much more crucial role in the recovery of children than the rationale of the therapy itself. The question bears further thought, and we'll return to this issue in Chapter 21.

Obviously, a great deal still needs to be learned about the treatment for childhood schizophrenia. Part of the difficulty has been confusion over the disorder itself. One question is simply whether everyone is working on the same problem: the terminology for childhood psychotic conditions has changed frequently over the years. Some studies, for instance, have combined childhood schizophrenia with autism; one wonders how many therapists have failed to recognize a useful therapeutic procedure because of such confusion.

Whatever the reason, studies of the later lives of children with schizophrenia have thus far offered little hope. Bender's follow-up of 200 children treated by shock found only 25 percent making some social adjustment, while 89 percent were still considered schizophrenic. Another follow-up report on adults who had originally been treated as schizophrenic children showed 90 percent were still diagnosed as schizophrenic (Dahl, 1976).

There is some hope that IQ or language status at the time of initial diagnosis may be useful in predicting potential for recovery. In general, a below-average IQ at age 5 or speech development below about 33 percent of the expected level for the child's age seem to be predictors of poor recovery, while higher levels of functioning at the time of diagnosis are predictive of better recovery.

## EVALUATION

The proper identification of childhood disorders presents a unique problem. Psychiatry initially was derived from the study of abnormal *adults*. Infants, children, and adolescents show characteristics that may represent a passing developmental stage more than a permanent symptom of pathology. Indeed, as some research as shown, judgment about whether a behavior is pathological is as much influenced by the tolerance of the assessor as by the nature of the behavior itself. The criteria listed by Kessler in Focus 20–1 provide a useful general means for evaluating a child's behaviors.

An important issue is the current diagnostic classifications, which are as yet far from satisfactory. DSM-III provides one of its best classifications, if we consider the goal of describing disorders in terms which emphasize behaviors that go together *without* also including inferences about the etiology expected or theorized. However, the categories themselves still present some problems. In defining hyperactivity, for instance, the probability exists that what is considered one disorder may, in fact, be several disorders with similar symptoms. Another problem in categorization is the failure to carry through on more detailed separation between problems during infancy, childhood, and adolescence; and the lack of these developmental periods with information on pathology. Finally, etiology and treatment are not yet integrated satisfactorily. Much of this is due to the lack of conclusive data on the causes of disorders, and hence treatment plans have not been linked to etiology.

## SUMMARY

Most youngsters will show some developmental lags or quirks at some point during the process of growing up. These might once have been called problems, but many are now recognized to be common and transitory. Problems are said to exist where the behaviors are inappropriate for the child's age group, where there are frequent and multiple symptoms, where these persist across time, and where there is interference with the ability to achieve satisfactions in life.

A variety of pathologies have been identified, including attention deficit, anxiety disorders, eating disorders, movement disorders, physical disorders, and what appear to be types of psychoses: autism and childhood schizophrenia. The sources of these different disorders varies, ranging from suspected maturational delay in attention deficit, to parental influences, as in fears (Graziano et al., 1979), to conflicts over sexuality, as suspected in anorexia.

Therapy also varies with the different causation, ranging from the use of amphetamines to family therapy to residential hospitalization to behavior therapy (Phillips & Ray, 1980). It is not commonly believed that the disorders of childhood will continue into adulthood, since treatment can lead to complete recovery in most of the minor disorders, such as the anxiety, movement, or physical disorders. However, prognosis is poor for some of the others disorders, such as anorexia, autism, and childhood schizophrenia.

## KEY TERMS

**Anorexia nervosa**
**Anxiety disorders**
**Attentional deficit disorders**
**Avoidant disorder**
**Bulimia**
**Childhood schizophrenia**
**Eating disorders**
**Elective mutism**
**Encopresis**
**Enuresis**
**Hyperactivity**
**Infantile autism**
**Movement disorders**
**Overanxious disorder**
**Pavor nocturnus**
**Pervasive developmental disorders**
**Physical disorders**
**Pica**
**Separation anxiety**
**Stereotyped movement disorders**
**Tics**
**Tourette's disorder**

# PART 3

## The Therapeutic Strategies



*The three chapters in Part 3 offer a more comprehensive framework for understanding the therapies mentioned in Part 2. For convenience, we will use the headings of psychological therapies, medical therapies, and community mental health movement. The psychological and medical therapies encompass specific methods for treatment, while the community mental health movement refers to a broader set of principles and outlooks. The goal of all the therapy approaches is to help persons achieve an optimal level of adjustment from the disorders we have already discussed. In some cases, a therapy may actually also have relevance for helping normally functioning persons to further enhance their level of performance.*

*Contemporary therapies derive from either of two origins: an empirical or a theoretical. Many of the medical therapies have resulted form empirical reports: someone tries out a technique such as a drug and sees that it works. Occasionally, the discovery is actually due to serendipity, that is, pure luck. It is possible in some of the medical therapies that in fact no one can explain with any conviction why the procedure works; but this detracts in no way from the therapy's results.*

*The theoretically derived therapies, in contrast, have developed because someone organized the data about a disorder into a theory, which in turn provides a means of logically arriving at recommendations for treatment. Sometimes several different theories account for the same facts, but each theory still contributes its own set of recommendations. Some medical therapies derived from theories, but the psychological therapies are the best examples. As you shall see, the psychoanalytic, the humanistic-existential, and the behavioristic theorists all offer differing explanations and take differing approaches to treatment, each with its own successes. As has been the case throughout the text, we will offer an evaluation at the end of each chapter.*

# CHAPTER 21

## The Therapies: Psychological Therapies

- **How do the important psychological therapies work to help mental disorders?**
- **What roles have hypnosis and LSD played in therapy?**
- **What are the special strengths of psychoanalysis?**
- **Why might we claim psychoanalysis to be emotional, humanism to be experiential, and behaviorism to be behavioral?**
- **What do dreams tell you?**
- **What is biofeedback all about?**
- **If you are bothered by negative, disruptive thoughts, what programs might you undertake for better control?**
- **Is there truth to the statement that psychotherapy could make you better . . . but it could also make you worse?**
- **Of the three therapy approaches explain which one you feel is the best?**

# Case History 21–1:
## The "Working Through" Process in Psychotherapy

The psychiatrist Wolberg (1977) describes the dynamic process of therapy as follows:

> Mental health is won only after a long and painful fight . . . the patients return repetitively to old modes of living while making tentative thrusts in a new and more adaptive direction . . . shuttling back and forth, for what seems to be an interminable period. . . . This process of "working through" is usually extremely slow . . . improvement is momentary . . . the patient goes backward with an intensified resistance, retrenching with all previous defenses as the problem is investigated more deeply . . . *[but]* he will gain from this experience and take another step forward . . . (pp. 652–53).

Wolberg illustrates working through over several sessions with a young divorcee who first experiences transference towards him:

> Patient: I awoke with the feeling that I'm very much in love with you. I want you to love me very much. . . . I feel sexually attracted to you. Is it ever permissible to . . . to . . . *[blushes]*.
>
> Wolberg: You mean to have an affair? . . . I appreciate your feeling very much. It often happens that in therapy the patient falls in love with the therapist. . . .

Then there was a period where the patient, who felt little affection for people, responded with hostility to Dr. Wolberg as she began to feel again:

> Patient: I'm furious at you. I don't, didn't want to come today.
>
> Wolberg: Can you tell me why?
>
> Patient: Because you've gotten, gotten me to feel like a human being again instead of a piece of wood, and there's nothing to do about it. . . . Here you went and got me all stirred up for absolutely nothing. It's like you want to torture and hurt me.

But this woman finally was able to work through these feelings, such that she was able to have the insight at the end of the hour, "I guess I must *think* you reject me. But you really don't." Several months later, her constructive progress was shown:

> Patient: When I came to you, you were exactly what I needed at that moment. . . . I was trying to tell myself I didn't know enough about you to feel that way . . . you were probably a symbol of what I would like to have or feel for someone. . . . Then, something began to happen to me. . . . I felt that I needed you much more as a doctor than a man. . . . So I started to look around at men. I found that I was giving them a little more encouragement because I never radiated any encouragement. . . . I was very happy that I could feel that way about someone (pp. 661–663).

Wolberg's description of "working through" in Case History 21–1 provides a good starting point for discussing the psychological therapies, for it shows the importance of the client-therapist interaction in treatment. "Working through" is itself a psychoanalytic process, but the interplay portrayed in this case is basic to psychotherapy in general.

Psychotherapy may be defined as a corrective experience accomplished through the interaction between a professional therapist and one or more clients. Its aim is to restore the client to a more satisfactory and effective state of adjustment; the achievement of this aim is brought about through the establishment of certain conditions believed to be necessary for change. The methods for establishing these conditions may be called the *strategies* of psychotherapy.

There are three major strategies or orientations of psychotherapy. *Psychoanalytically* oriented therapy envisions the therapeutic relationship as a dynamic interplay between the client with maladaptive thoughts, feelings, and actions, and the therapist with treatment skills and insights. *Humanistic* therapists emphasize their own deep involvement in the clients and the clients' feelings, striving to form a relationship that will enhance the clients' own growth and adjustive potential. *Behavior* therapists systematically introduce the patient to conditions designed to unlearn maladaptive behavior and acquire more appropriate response patterns. These three psychotherapeutic orientations, their basic beliefs, and their strategies will be discussed in more detail in this chapter.

## THE THERAPY CONTRACT

The psychotherapeutic relationship has often been described as a unique relationship replicated by a very few other human interactions. Karl Menninger (1958), the chief of staff of the famed Menninger Clinic, has referred to the psychotherapeutic situation as a "contract." In this *therapeutic contract,* the therapist and client have mutually agreed to engage in every means possible to achieve the therapeutic goal of a more adaptive and satisfying life for the client. During the course of this arrangement, the client is called on to contribute equally to achieving this goal—although it is recognized that he or she may deliberately or unwittingly resist change or interfere with the treatment process, as happened in Case History 21–1. The therapist is also committed to equally applying personal skills, knowledge, and experience for the client's well-being. The therapist is not always required to obtain the client's approval for the techniques used, since the therapist is better qualified by reason of training and experience to make such decisions. However, the therapist is bound to always consider the client's overall well-being first and foremost.

The notion of a contract may make treatment appear overly impersonal. In reality, psychotherapy involves a highly personal relationship (Martin, 1983; Wolberg, 1977). This atmosphere of understanding and acceptance appears to be a primary distinguishing feature of all therapeutic approaches, whether the therapist works from a psychoanalytic, humanistic, or learning-oriented viewpoint (Truax, 1971). Recall the findings discussed in Chapter 20—there, one group of schizophrenic boys developed a great affection for their favorite therapist using the nickname "Supershrink" to acknowledge his personal qualities. As we'll see later in this chapter, the personal, empathic qualities of the therapist seem often to relate closely to the success of the treatment.

In addition to a personal concern, the therapist also brings extensive training to the therapeutic relationship. The professional qualifications of psychiatrists, clinical psychologists, psychoanalysts and social workers were all described in the Focus on Helping Professionals (see Focus 1-2). These persons who practice therapy must be either licensed or certified, depending on the state in which they practice.

Although the mutual agreement is a part of the therapeutic relationship, the interchange between therapist and client may take many different forms besides the personal, one-to-one relationship. Several popular formats are described briefly in Focus 21–1. Many of these formats are particularly compatible with one or another of the three major strategies we discuss in this chapter. For instance, group encounters are most often used as a humanistic technique; and hypnosis may be particularly helpful in some cases where psychoanalysis is used.

## FOCUS 21–1:
### Therapy Formats

*Family psychotherapy.* The family is treated as a unit instead of as individuals on the premise that personal symptoms are an expression of family interrelationship problems. When the family convenes in psychotherapy, the therapist may perceive disturbed interactions which are then subjected to discussion and change (L'Abate, 1983; Alexander & Parsons, 1982).

*Group psychotherapy.* The therapist meets with a group of clients who may share their problems and solutions with one another; try out new ways of relating to each other; work out problems related to social isolation or reality testing; and experience the emotional support of the group (Carey et al., 1984).

*Psychodrama.* On the premise that real changes occur when a person acts out private feelings, the therapist directs a "drama" involving the client as a main actor, other clients, and even a stage (Moreno, 1946). The drama usually reflects a conflict area, and the client is encouraged to spontaneously act out his or her feelings.

*Encounter groups (human relations training).* Originally a technique for helping essentially healthy people enhance social or work effectiveness, *T-groups* (training groups), *sensory awareness groups,* and *sensitivity groups* are popular formats. A common element of these groups is the emphasis on an intensive small-group experience with a focus on here-and-now issues (Anderson, 1984).

*Play therapy.* This technique allows children to express thoughts and feelings despite immaturity in speech development. The child is placed in a room with several toys selected for their capacity to encourage the expression of feelings. The play itself permits the child to work through feelings that were concealed (Axline, 1947).

*Hypnosis.* The most dramatic effect of this technique is the recall of repressed experiences—such as a traumatic event responsible for a disorder. Hypnosis may also be used to stimulate dreams, which are then evaluated in therapy. Posthypnotic suggestion has been attempted as a means of controlling undesirable behaviors, such as tics. Hypnosis is not itself curative: instead, it is a technique for obtaining effects that may be helpful in treatment (Kihlstrom, 1979).

*Among the types of therapies possible are* ***play therapy, psychodrama,*** *and* ***family therapy.***

In the remainder of this chapter, we will look more closely at the three major strategies:

- The psychoanalytic
- The humanistic-existential
- The behavioral

Each of these strategies relies on specific beliefs about people and specific techniques for solving problems. Psychoanalysis, the first strategy, will be discussed in relatively less detail than the rest because it has already been treated at length in Chapter 3.

## THE PSYCHOANALYTIC STRATEGY

In the psychoanalytic view, disorders result from self-protective defenses that impair psychological development. According to this interpretation, individuals are originally troubled by conflicts which they repress instead of recognizing clearly and dealing with directly. This repression then becomes the source of more pervasive disturbances, for it renders individuals helpless, unable to resolve problems, and susceptible to expressing unconscious conflicts through disturbing symptoms and dreams. These symptomatic byproducts of conflict all arouse anxiety, which is then covered over through the use of defense mechanisms. However, the basic conflict remains, while the defenses themselves may become severe enough to themselves become disturbing—as when compulsive actions help to distract a person from a deeper conflict (Peterfreund, 1983).

This self-protective defense system is recognized by psychoanalysts as a characteristic that appears even in therapy. The term *resistance* refers to the tendency of clients to protect themselves from the threat of facing their conflicts during psychotherapy. Analysts believe that overcoming resistance is a crucial part of the therapy process. Invariably, the conflicts have their roots in early childhood experiences. The individual often reacts to the therapist in ways characteristic of his or her early reactions to parents. This, of course, is inappropriate since the therapist's behavior is not similar to that of the client's parents. Such irrational repetition of an early emotional pattern is referred to as *transference.*

Psychoanalysis aims at a number of goals, all directly related to the basic theory underlying the approach. Among the primary goals are:

- To gradually uncover repressed material from the unconscious.
- To enable the person to become aware of resistances that impede progress in therapy.
- To experience emotionally and through insights the role of unconscious unresolved problems, in order to correct these conflicts.
- To experience and work through transference reactions so as to become able to respond to life on the basis of current realities.

A number of specific therapeutic methods have been developed to achieve such goals, and we will describe these next.

### The Methods of Analysis

Psychoanalytic techniques are directed toward the sources of pathology. *Free association* is a method developed by Freud to facilitate the recall of the repressed material. As you may recall from Chapter 3, the client is directed to say whatever passes through his or her mind without any attempt to select or censor. Freud found that this procedure enabled unconscious material to surface and thereby be identified. The *interpretation of dreams* is also used by analysts as a tool for delving into the repressed areas of the mind. Since defenses are not as strongly maintained during sleep, more information about basic conflicts is obtainable, even though it may appear in disguised forms. The *transference* situation is also useful and a necessary part of psychoanalytic treatment. Transference enables therapists to point out to clients the ways in which they have permitted their past experiences to influence their behaviors and current attitudes. These unresolved conflicts are then explored while clients attempt to develop more ways of reacting that are appropriate to their current life setting.

***Transference in Analysis.*** The use of the transference situation is so important to psychoanalysis that its development is a goal of many of psychoanalytic techniques. For example, the analytic therapist does not reveal personal information, beliefs, or attitudes, in order to be certain that any opinions that the client may later attribute to the therapist come from the client's own perceptions. The therapist maintains an attitude of interest and acceptance; thus, if the client accuses the therapist of being too demanding or too controlling, it becomes clear that these accusations are part of a transference reaction. Menninger (1958) gives an illustration of transference in a case:

> An unmarried malc laboratory technician of age 30 underwent psychoanalysis. . . . Early in the process he described his father's reserve and aloofness. . . . Ultimately, of course, it was the analyst who seemed reserved, cold and aloof. A little later, however, he recalled certain experiences with a girl cousin whose warmth . . . [made him feel] guilty, however, because of certain of his responses to her advances. . . . The analyst was not surprised, accordingly, when some months later the patient dreamed of the analyst in the form of a seductress, which evoked reproach that the analyst was expecting too much of him and encouraging him in forbidden directions. Next, it developed that there had been in his childhood a particularly stern aunt whose judgments were feared. . . . She evidently represented to him, then, what law and order, the police court and purgatory came to represent to him later. This began to appear in the transference when the analyst, who had previously been accused both of coldness and seductiveness, became a stern figure of retribution from whom the patient expected punishment and dismissal (p. 82).

***Interpretation and Insight.*** Another vehicle for therapy is *interpretation,* that is, the therapist's understanding of the meanings behind certain of the client's symptoms. Interpretations are used to stimulate insight, to decrease the power of maladaptive behavior, and to pave the way for the development of more adaptive traits.

As an example, a person who is continually late for appointments, or who seems to have nothing relevant to say during the treatment hour, may be doing so because of *resistance.* An interpretation of this to the client serves to weaken such defensive behavior. This process may proceed for quite a long time before any appreciable gain. Murray (1954), for example, followed the course of treatment of one patient and found that interpretation was followed by the decline in one form of resistance (intellectualizing) but led to the increase in another (somatic complaints). After several efforts by the therapist, the client was finally able to drop his defensiveness and come to grips with the anxiety-provoking material.

Dreams, free association, transference, and interpretation are all used to help the client achieve insight into conflicts. And this insight, according to the psychoanalytic therapist, is a corrective emotional experience that leads to personality change. One question in modern psychoanalysis is just how essential all of these specific techniques are to the therapeutic process (Masling, 1983). Focus 21–2 discusses the psychoanalytically oriented psychotherapists' answer to that question; quite another answer is provided by the humanists and existentialists, as discussed in the following section.

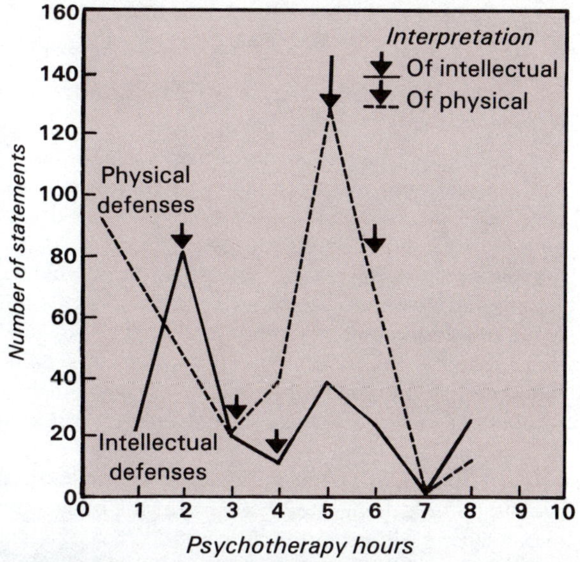


**FIGURE 21-1** The effects of interpretation in therapy on intellectual defenses and physical complaint defenses.

SOURCE: Based on "A Case Study in a Behavioral Analysis of Psychotherapy" by E. Murray, 1954, *Journal of Abnormal Social Psychology, 49,* p.305.

# FOCUS 21–2:
## Assessing Psychotherapy: Can Psychoanalysis Be Streamlined?

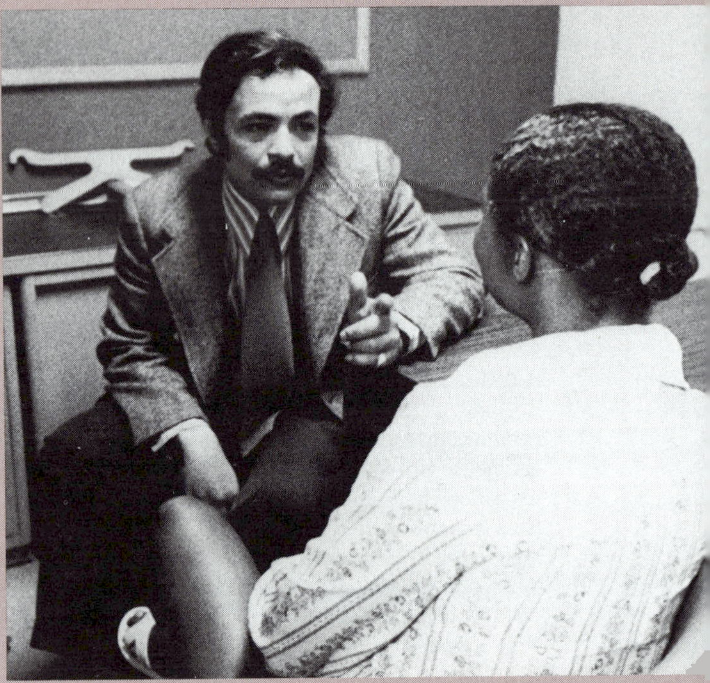

The training of a psychoanalyst is long and expensive; just as treatment by psychoanalysis is long and expensive. Psychoanalytic therapy involves years of working through conflicts repressed since early life, reaching past defenses that have been firmly established, and slowly but persistently developing newer ways of relating and adjusting. Psychoanalysis is no less expensive than modern medical treatment. Since the patient is seen for hourly treatment sessions over a course of years, the total expenditures can run into thousands of dollars.

Partly because of the difficulty inherent in such prolonged treatment, modifications of the basic psychoanalytic method have been introduced. Alexander and French (1946) have introduced a shorter-term approach which departs from standard psychoanalytic techniques without losing any of the characteristic thoroughness.

This technique, better called *psychoanalytically oriented psychotherapy,* calls on the flexible application of strategies selected to fit the particular patient's circumstances (Wolberg, 1980). Free association, for example, may be relied on if it is effective; on the other hand, it may be eliminated if it does not appear to help. The number of meetings per week is adjusted to correspond to the number required to keep the client's progress at an optimal level. Rather than listening while the client free-associates on a couch, the therapist may use ordinary face-to-face conversation or even direct confrontation with the client.

Finally, Alexander and French's approach encourages a controlled approach to transference. Whereas the traditional psychoanalytic strategy is to encourage a full transference, the psychoanalytically oriented therapist may discourage transference for some clients, if it appears feasible to do so without detracting from the treatment goals.

## THE HUMANISTIC-EXISTENTIAL STRATEGY

A second major psychological approach, *humanistic-existential* therapy, dates back to the 1940s. Its major growth as a significant treatment strategy is a more recent phenomenon, however. In some respects, this approach can truly be considered one of the triumvirate of major therapeutic strategies, along with psychoanalysis and behavior therapy.

According to the humanistic-existential view, both psychoanalysis and behavior therapy are deficient approches: psychoanalysis because it too narrowly defines the source of problems and is more pessimistic about people; and behavior therapy because it overlooks the importance of free will or freedom of choice.

The humanistic-existential perspective defines the sources of pathologies in broader terms than do either the psychoanalytic or behaviorist views. Problems may arise from feelings of alienation, the absence of meaning in life, the inability to relate to others in an open fashion, the fear of loneliness, or simply the lack of authenticity in our modern lives. The humanistic-existential approach is characterized by searching for positive growth through freedom of choice, free will, and the ability of individuals to take responsibility for their own futures.

While the two approaches—humanistic and existential—share the general perspective we have just outlined, humanism and existentialism also represent different outlooks, as Focus 21 3 describes. In the following sections, we'll look separately at samples of each approach to therapy.

### Humanistic Therapies

Although there are a number of humanistic therapies, two of the better-known approaches have been the *client-centered* approach identified with Carl Rogers and the *gestalt approach* identified with Frederick Perls.

***Client-centered Therapy.*** Client-centered therapists (Rogers, 1951; Hart & Tomlinson, 1970) disavow the view that psychopathology develops because human nature is irrational, regressively self-defensive, and destructive. According to Rogers (1957), the founder of this approach:

> I have little sympathy with the rather prevalent concept that man is basically irrational, and that his impulses, if not controlled, will lead to destruction of others and self. Man's behavior is exquisitely rational, moving with subtle and ordered complexity toward the goals his organism is endeavoring to achieve.

*The Growth Principle and Pathology.* The client-centered or Rogerian therapist sees all people as possessing both innate desire and capability toward positive self-development. We can draw the analogy of the child who is learning to walk. Despite nasty falls and numerous setbacks, children do persist in their attempts to achieve this higher level of coordination and motor skill. In a nonrepressive home environment, the child seems to seek and acquire this skill without outside guidance or instruction as if the desire to develop were inborn.

In many other ways, all people are perceived as ever moving toward self-fulfillment or *self-actualization.* More accurately, we all behave in the ways we *perceive* to be most likely to lead to this goal. It is possible to err in perceptions and select a self-damaging alternative; however, our intentions are still basically good and by no means self-destructive.

One major source of misperceptions can be the personally oriented experiences that comprise the self-concept. The self-concept, formed during childhood, becomes the core around which future experiences are evaluated. In the client-centered therapist's view of maladjustment, important experiences are distorted or denied because they are not in agreement with this basic self-concept. In support of this premise, Suinn et al. (1962) demonstrated that people tended to resist remembering information about themselves if it was not consistent with their own self-views, even when that information was favorable. For instance, a person who has a self-image of being a failure will deny being responsible for a personal success.

We may still be motivated by a search for self-actualization. However, our progress is blocked, by these distorted experiences and our own misperceptions. In effect, the maladjusted person is forced to function with incomplete and misleading information, about both the self and the environment.

## FOCUS 21–3:

### Humanistic and Existential Therapies: Common Themes and Contrasts

The humanistic and existential viewpoints share many features and are often grouped together. The outlooks and therapy approaches are distinct, however. Following is a brief summary of common and contrasting features.

*In Common*

- Each individual is unique. Therefore, there is no attempt to prescribe exact therapy techniques: to do so would be to assume that people can be reduced to formulas.
- Our uniqueness involves individualized, subjective perceptions of ourselves and the world. In therapy, therefore, it is crucial to determine how a person perceives a situation, instead of imposing the therapist's perceptions and values on the individual. Therapy emphasizes empathetic understanding.
- Life is a process of reaching for potential; the importance of growth, actualization, and fulfillment is emphasized. Therapy aims at helping persons progress toward the crucial goal of self-fulfillment.
- Rather than being controlled by external influences, humans are free agents, with the ability and the responsibility to choose their own directions. Therapy's goal is to increase individual awareness and to help individuals to take that responsibility.

*In Contrast*

- Humanism is clearly optimistic that persons have the inherent ability to make the right choices and move toward self-fulfillment. Existentialism projects a more guarded optimism. Obstacles are presented by both the external world around us and the irrational tendencies in human nature; additionally, since freedom carries demands of responsibility, it is a source of pain as well as gratification.
- Both orientations acknowledge the influence of the environment. Humanism, however, is more likely to seek to separate individuality totally from the standards of the world. To the existentialist, individuals must be viewed in the context of the world and must be helped to confront rather than ignore this environment.

*Goals of Client-centered Therapy.* Given this view of maladjustment, the major task of client-centered therapy is to establish an atmosphere conducive to greater openness to experience. The atmosphere sought is one that views the client as capable. It replaces the attitude of searching for a cure with an emphasis on growth and self-development, offering the client a setting of unconditional acceptance and encouragement. The client-centered therapist is not impressed with psychoanalytic tactics such as interpretation, since such strategies take the initiative away from the client. Instead, the goal is to become intensively involved in understanding the client, mainly through an empathy for the feelings being expressed. The therapist may repeat or restate the client's words in a struggle to ensure that there is a perfect understanding of the inner experience of the client. In all of these activities, the client-centered therapist strives to maintain a relationship free of judgment and evaluation so as not to threaten the client and prevent the self-exploration process. It is for this reason that diagnostic evaluations, as well as all attempts to discover explanations for behavior are rejected.

More than any other treatment strategy, the client-centered approach stresses the need for developing a relationship between client and therapist. In the context of a truly accepting relationship, the client will be come less fearful of self-examination; will be able to face the self as it really is; and to reorganize the self structure to include perceptions that had previously been distorted. While the client-centered theory views this relationship as crucial, studies are still searching for the factors which ensure such a relationship, as Focus 21–4 discusses. The humanistic gestalt approach, in contrast, places somewhat more emphasis on techniques.

**Gestalt Therapy.** Frederick Perls, the leader of the Gestalt movement, was originally a psychoanalyst. Perls fled Germany soon after Hitler came into power, eventually arriving in the United States, where he settled at the Esalen Center at Big Sur, California. Originally called concentration therapy, Perls later changed the name of his therapy approach to *gestalt therapy.*

*Social Restrictions and Pathology.* Like Rogers, Perls emphasizes the positive potential of all people. Humans are viewed as having the desire toward integration, wholeness, the capacity to live spontaneously, to be authentic and responsible, and to take risks in order to grow.

To an ever greater degree than Rogers, the gestalt humanist sees the origins of maladjustment in the demands of our social environment, which can constrain and control people, limiting their freedom to be themselves. Social restrictions impose a set of goals to strive towards, thereby conflicting with the more realistic personal goal of actualizing our true selves. Barriers begin to develop, along with rigid patterns of responding, and soon we lose touch with who or what we are. In turn, our own needs may influence our perception of the environment, thereby limiting our ability to see others for what they are, rather than for what we need them to be.

Awareness is a key element of gestalt therapy. This includes awareness not only of feelings, but also body sensations, and even movements and gestures. With awareness, a person is much more able to make informed decisions or to take responsible action. Awareness then becomes an essential step in therapy; in fact, Perls (1969) says, "Awareness per se—by and of itself—can be curative" (p. 16).

*Goals of Gestalt Therapy.* Gestalt therapy relies on several basic ideas. First, focusing on the here-and-now is more important than delving into the past history of events. We change through discovery; the most important types of discovery occur through experience; and the only experience is that of the present.

Second, the role of the therapist is to facilitate self-discovery, and not to force interpretations, insights, or behavioral shifts. Perls may offer his own observations in order to attract a client's attention, but the client is encouraged to personally discover the meaning or act on such awareness. Since self-discovery is related to direct experience, therapy tends to avoid indirect experiences, such as *talking about* our feelings, speculating, analyzing, tracing the origins, and so on.

A third point is that discovery is focused on awareness of *what* is happening and *how* it is happening, but not *why.* Gestalt therapists feel that asking clients "why" they are doing what they do will simply

## FOCUS 21–4:
### Assessing Psychotherapy: Client-centered Therapy

Client-centered therapy is unique in its avoidance of techniques and its emphasis on conditions such as a helping relationship and unconditional regard. How critical are these conditions to successful therapy? Halkides (1958) evaluated this question by comparing therapy sessions in terms of their conformity with such conditions. She predicted that successful cases would differ from unsuccessful ones on the following variables: (1) the therapist's empathy, (2) the therapist's unconditional positive regard, (3) the therapist's genuineness in the relationship, and (4) the therapist's ability to match the client's emotional expression. The results were intriguing. Three judges evaluated therapy interviews and supported Halkides' predictions by showing that the first three aspects of the therapy relationship were indeed associated with successful treatment.

Results such as those of Halkides stirred a great deal of enthusiasm at the time and opened the possibility that the true essence of the ideal therapist had been discovered—a person who possessed the qualities of genuineness, empathy, and warm acceptance of others. However, later data has also been reported, causing many to call for a more cautious stance (Gomes-Schwartz et al., 1978). Reviewing the literature since 1970, Parloff et al. (1978) suggest that the ''initial enthusiastic claims'' should be reduced.

Although these later authors no longer believe that the qualities of the ideal therapist have been discovered, the contribution of Rogers' thinking still remains influential. Perhaps the role of genuineness, empathy, and warmth is not so critical as to ensure that therapy will succeed or fail. However, these variables still receive acceptance as one set that can be important—along with other variables that are now also being studied.

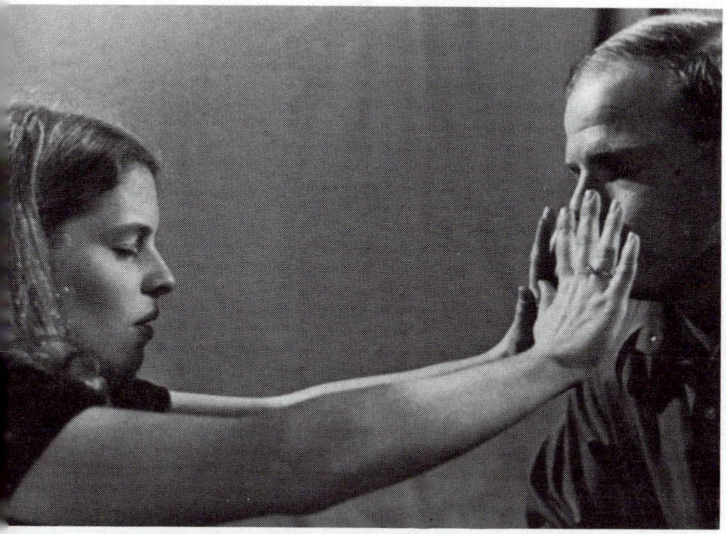

***Humanistic** therapies may involve sensory awareness experiences that emphasize attention to sensory input.*

encourage rationalization, excuses, intellectualizing—basically, avoiding the issue. For a person to accept responsibility for change, the questions must be direct: What are you needing? What are you feeling? What are you doing? What do you want to happen? The encounter groups described in Focus 21–1 discussion early in this chapter are particularly suited to this experiential orientation, as are the exercises discussed in Focus 21–5.

### Existential Therapy

Humanistic approaches such as those of Carl Rogers and Frederick Perls are similar in many respects to the existential strategies. However, existential therapy is also an entity in itself distinct from the humanist approach (Fischer & Fischer, 1983).

***Three Basic Themes.*** Existential therapy traces to philosophical views about humanity and existence discussed by philosophers such as Heidegger, Kierkegaard, Jaspers, and Sartre. In common with the humanistic approach, existential therapy does not represent a tightly systematized school of thought, but a set of attitudes and assumptions about human nature.

Several important themes were shared by the existential philosophers whose works formed the historical roots of the contemporary approach. First, there is an emphasis on the intertwining between persons and their world, rather than separation. *Being-in-the-world* conveys the thought that we are so intimately associated with the world around us that it is a distortion to try to view ourselves apart from our surroundings. To describe one is to automatically imply something about the other. In this way, the existentialist differs from the Freudian who studied the person as though the inner psyche were independent of the world, and also from the behaviorist who sometimes views behaviors as precipitated separately by external stimuli.

A second emphasis of existential philosophy is the importance of being authentic, of being genuine, of avoiding falsehood. However, by being-in-the-world we are constantly influenced to base our actions on the values of others in the world. Instead of trying to find our personal meaning in life, instead of acting on the grounds of personally developed values, we find ourselves conforming to social demands. Choice becomes lost, and along with it our freedom. To the existentialist, it is very important that persons retain "the courage to be," to choose authenticity, and to retain freedom.

Finally, the existential philosopher emphasizes the importance of existence, of being, along with the here-and-now implications. An adolescent who defiantly protests, "I didn't ask to be born in your world" is missing the point. The existentialist will reply that the relevant truth is that the adolescent has been born and *is* in the world. The worst thing that could happen is for this person to become mired in blaming the past or others, and to therefore give up personal responsibility for making current life meaningful.

***Two Existential Approaches.*** Three of the leading existential therapists are Viktor Frankl, R. D. Laing, and Rollo May. As in the humanistic approach, the very essence of existentialism is that specific techniques in therapy are not possible; instead, psychotherapy is an experiential event. We will briefly de-

## FOCUS 21–5:

### Gestalt Therapy: Some Typical Exercises

The gestalt approach to humanistic therapy has devised a number of notable techniques to accomplish its objectives. Here are three typical exercises:

*The empty chair*

If the couch is associated with psychoanalysis, then the empty chair is associated with gestalt therapy. A client is asked to shift back and forth between two chairs, with the shift requiring different roles. For example, the client may be asked to behave in ways consistent with one set of needs in one chair; and another, conflicting set of needs in the other chair. Or the client imagines that another person is in the other chair and addresses that person as he or she had always wanted to. Through such an exercise, the client is forced to examine what responses can communicate his or her feelings in a helpful manner (Greenberg & Dompierre, 1981).

*Reversals*

Another technique has clients act in ways opposite to the way they usually behave. Occasionally, fearfulness and inhibition can be traced to an unwillingness to trust in one's own resources. We might feel that "it's not within me" to be more assertive, independent, or capable of making decisions. Yet, this very belief prevents us from permitting our strengths to come to the surface. Hence, you might be told to "pretend that you're royalty and have everyone around you who *expect* you to be commanding . . . now order up a meal, and include instructions on how you want the meal cooked and served."

*I take responsibility*

Accepting personal responsibility for feelings and behaviors can reduce self-alienation, can increase active control, and can bring greater self-awareness. Where the person tends to attribute behaviors to external events, the therapist draws back instead to personal responsibility. An alcoholic insurance salesman reported, "Sure I drink, but it's only because there's so much stress around me and my business is in a slump for awhile."

The therapist suggested that the salesman repeat the sentence using the personal pronoun. Here is the result:

"Sure I drink, because I'm under stress, I'm in a slump." He was then asked to remove all reference to reasons, leading to ". . . I drink . . . I'm under stress . . . I'm in a slump." Finally, the salesman-client began to see the significance of the word "I." "*I* drink . . . I don't have to drink, no one or nothing is forcing me . . . but I drink . . . I don't need reasons to drink, and I don't need reasons to stop, as long as I'm willing to stop!"

scribe the views of Frankl and Laing in order to illustrate the nature of this experience.

As we saw in Chapter 3, Frankl (1962) formed his own ideas from personal experiences in World War II concentration camps. He concluded that spiritual meaning was the necessary key to psychological survival. To Frankl, the search for meaning in life is the prime moving force in all of us; our failure to find it produces frustration and finally abnormal behavior (1962). Meaning is discovered through the identification of values: *creative values* experienced from achievement; *experiential values* from appreciation of beauty; and *attitudinal values* experienced by confronting suffering. If we fail to seek and achieve values, then we may be subject to anxiety disorders, which represent our guilt.

*Frankl's Logotherapy.* Frankl has developed a therapy he calls *logotherapy,* from Greek words for *meaning* and *spirit.* The aim of logotherapy is to confront persons to come to grips with the meaning and purpose of their existence. This takes place in an atmosphere of sharing, dignity, and mutual concern, as the therapist reveals his or her own existence in as authentic and true a way as possible.

Despite the existentialist's deemphasis on techniques, Frankl (1975) does appear to have originated two techniques. *Dereflection* involves turning the person's focus away from their complaints and problems and shifting their attention instead to what choices they could be making if they would not be so preoccupied. *Paradoxical intention* involves requiring the person to exaggerate and repeat the primary symptoms. For example, a compulsive client might be told to actually increase the number of times the compulsive behaviors are shown, instead of trying to stop them. The purpose is to demonstrate to the client that he or she can actually control the symptoms, rather than the symptoms controlling the person.

*Laing's Search for Authenticity.* R. D. Laing (1969) takes a slightly different existential approach, emphasizing the conflict between society and the person. The so-called normal world around us is actually a place where we are all "bemused and crazed creatures, strangers to our true selves, to one another, and to the spiritual and material world" [p. 56]. Continuing pressures to conform, conflicting demands from those around us, force us to develop "divided minds"—a false self that is socially created, and a true inner self that we keep hidden. Unless we can change this, we reach maturity learning to stifle feelings, work like robots towards meaningless goals, and become conventional.

*Authenticity.* In Laing's thinking, as we saw in Chapter 1, the schizophrenic may actually be closer to sanity than most normal persons. No longer able to keep up the false self required by society, the person retreats back into the inner world, showing behaviors which are called schizophrenic, but which are actually an attempt at self-cure. Therapy becomes directed towards helping the schizophrenic to further pursue this inner exploration, rather than to try to stop the pathology. The symptomatic behaviors, such as regression, incoherence, or shouting, are encouraged rather than stifled. As the regression away from the external world progresses and the person is able to meet and confront personal meanings, authenticity replaces falsehood and the true self can emerge.

The approaches of Laing, Frankl, Rogers and Perls have gained considerable attention in the past few decades, with growing acceptance. Focus 21–6 evaluates this approach to therapy. While humanism and existentialism have become more and more influential in the field of psychology, a distinct counterpoint is provided by the third major approach to therapy, the behaviorist approach.

## THE BEHAVIORIST STRATEGY

The behaviorist view differs sharply from the two approaches just discussed. Behaviorists (Bandura, 1977; Beck, 1976; Wolpe, 1982) see psychological disorders as learned. Normal and abnormal development are similar in that the same conditions that enable any one of us to learn to speak, think, or behave normally also apply to the development of abnormal patterns of speech, thought, behavior, or emotional response.

The primary learning processes are *classical conditioning, operant conditioning,* or *modeling*. In the first process, as we saw in Chapter 3, an abnormal re-

## FOCUS 21–6:
### Assessing Psychotherapy: The Humanist-existential Approach

The humanist-existential approach has grown toward wide acceptance in recent years, with its most attractive features being also its major source of criticism. Critics point to what they feel to be the loose connection between guiding principles and actual techniques, the vagueness of what is expected in therapeutic sessions, and the difficulty of specifying desirable procedures to trainees. In their defense, humanistic-existential therapists argue that some data is available on both Rogerian and Gestalt approaches, and that the very validity of the therapies comes from their emphasis on each client's uniqueness, intangibility, and spontaneity—all of which defy systematization.

Research data provide no clear conclusions. One study of the effectiveness of a gestalt group showed that high school student subjects improved in interpersonal behaviors and openness (Gannon, 1972). However, another study (Lieberman et al., 1973) discovered that the impact of the gestalt experience may sometimes be unpredictable, depending on the characteristics of the therapy group leader. Studying 17 groups, 2 of which were gestalt in orientation, one gestalt group could be considered a failure but the other was highly successful. A significant difference was in the leaders' ways of relating. The leader–therapist of the first group was unpredictable, taunting, nonsupportive, and ridiculing. The leader of the successful group was characterized by warmth, acceptance, and genuine caring for others. Findings on the value of awareness in therapy are also conflicting, with some showing a positive relationship while others show negative ones (Gomes-Schwartz et al., 1978).

sponse is conditioned through the pairing of a neutral cue with a cue that is part of a reflex; with the result that the neutral cue soon elicits the same reflex response. In operant conditioning, maladaptive behaviors such as compulsions are acquired and reinforced by their ability to reduce anxiety. A person with symptoms of a compulsion has learned that anxiety decreases each time the ritual of activities is enacted; or a child learns that a parent acquiesces to each temper tantrum. In modeling, or vicarious learning, the individual acquires an abnormal response, such as a phobia, by seeing someone else who is frightened.

### Goals of Behavior Therapy

Unlike the psychoanalyst, the behavior therapist does not postulate that symptoms are signs of deep problems that must be dispelled through insight. The symptoms, be they phobias, tantrums, or compulsive behaviors, are present because they were learned, and they will disappear when they are unlearned. According to Eysenck (1964): "Get rid of the symptom and you have eliminated the neurosis" (p. 9).

It is possible that the individual has learned several maladaptive behaviors that may appear in the same type of situation, just as a number of adaptive responses can be learned pertaining to one situation. A child, for example, may have developed many ways for obtaining approval, each being strengthened whenever the reward of approval is achieved. In the same way, an adult may have acquired a series of pathological responses to the same event, each one showing itself as a prior response is eliminated, like an onion being peeled layer by layer. The behavior therapist works on the assumption that the client will be completely cured when the last of these learned behaviors has been unlearned and more adaptive behaviors acquired.

### Behavior Therapy Techniques

Since the behavior therapist does not require the client to develop insight, therapeutic strategies are characterized more by training than by depth analysis of feelings. The therapist may explore the client's past life situation in order to obtain clues about how the behavior was learned and what is preventing its extinction. On the other hand, the therapist may need to know only what behaviors are desired and what current events can serve as rewards or reinforcers, and nothing else about the client.

Dr. Joseph Wolpe (1958) a leading behavior therapist, has stressed: "I have no intention of devoting a great deal of time to raking up past history, because although it would be interesting and perhaps helpful, it is not necessary: 'for to overcome his (the client's) neurotic reactions it is of greater relevance to determine what stimuli do or can evoke . . . at the present time' " (p. 105).

Behavior therapists may use several procedures (Rosenbaum et al., 1983). The most common of these are counterconditioning, vicarious extinction, anxiety management training, implosive therapy and flooding, positive reinforcement, behavior rehearsal, aversion conditioning, and cognitive behavior therapy.

***Counterconditioning.*** The strategy of *counterconditioning* works by strengthening a response that is antagonistic to the unwanted, maladaptive response. Conditions are set up that permit the more desirable response to compete successfully with and replace the pathological response.

The most successful application of this procedure is called *systematic desensitization.* Wolpe (1958), who founded this methodology, advocates the use of either relaxation or assertive behavior as the means for countering the unwanted behaviors. In a typical desensitization session for phobias, the therapist first trains the client in deep muscle relaxation, has the client construct an anxiety hierarchy, then uses the relaxation response to reduce the client's sensitivity to the situation in question. The *anxiety hierarchy* is simply a ranked list of stimulus situations that evoke anxiety or fear. If the phobia is a fear of tests, then items on the anxiety hierarchy might include "Reading the first question on a final examination" or "Walking into the examination room." These items are ranked so that the therapist will know which situations bring forth the strongest feelings of anxiety or fear, and which elicit the least fear. Table 21–1 provides a few illustrations of anxiety hierarchies.

Relaxation training may involve techniques such as first tensing muscles such as the biceps, then immediately relaxing them and attending to the contrast in feelings (Jacobsen, 1938). The same technique is used

**TABLE 21-1**

**Anxiety Hierarchies of Clients in Behavior Therapy***

I. Examination or test-taking anxiety
  A. Reading an exam question and not knowing the answer.
  B. Waiting to enter the room where an exam is to be given.
  C. Studying for a forthcoming exam.
  D. Being asked by a friend about my standing in a class.
  E. Reading an assignment for a class.
  F. Discussing the content of an interesting class with a friend.

II. Phobia of flying
  A. During a flight, the plane bumps through some turbulence in the air.
  B. The plane is losing altitude prior to landing.
  C. Sitting in the airplane waiting for take-off.
  D. Sitting in the airport waiting for boarding.
  E. Seeing someone else off at the airport.
  F. Sitting in a field on a summer day watching an airplane overhead.
  G. Reading a magazine about children and model airplanes.

III. Phobia of heights
  A. Walking near the edge of a cliff and looking down.
  B. Standing on a hill looking down at a moving stream.
  C. Looking out the window from the sixth floor.
  D. Walking down a long stairway.
  E. Standing on a stool and reaching for something.
  F. Standing motionless on a bench.
  G. Standing on a stage.
  H. Standing frimly on flat ground.

*Taken from actual cases in treatment with the author.

from head to toes, permitting the individual to relax all muscles completely. Following relaxation, the session then involves pairing this new ability to relax with the anxiety provoking stimuli. At first, the subject is told to visualize the least disturbing test situation. If any anxiety or fear is aroused, the subject dismisses the scene and concentrates on relaxation, repeating this procedure until the relaxed feelings replace the anxiety responses. The client then faces gradually stronger situations on the anxiety hierarchy, proc eding on up the list until ultimately even the most feared item produces no discomfort.

If handled properly, anxieties such as test anxiety may be eliminated within a period of 5 to 15 desensitization sessions (Allen et al., 1980). Suinn has also developed a briefer procedure for treating test anxiety, with the desensitization sessions being initiated and completed within 24 hours (Suinn et al., 1970). Desensitization has proven helpful with a variety of phobias and LSD "freakouts"; and it was even used to successfully countercondition a student who complained of falling asleep while driving (Deffenbacher & Suinn, 1982; Suinn & Brittain, 1970; Suinn & Richardson, 1970).

***Vicarious Extinction or Modeling.*** Another technique for treating anxiety is *vicarious extinction* or *modeling*. It involves having the individual observe a model in situations related to the client's own anxieties (Goldfried, 1980).

Vicarious extinction has its origins in studies of vicarious acquisition of new responses, a topic we covered in Chapter 3. Albert Bandura has been highly successful in demonstrating that deviant behavior may be acquired through observing another person being rewarded for such behavior. Other researchers have also shown that vicarious acquisition of emotional responses can occur similar to classical conditioning.

Typically, an observer–subject watches as a model–performer is presented with a neutral stimulus, then apparently shocked. After the observer has witnessed the model undergoing this conditioning procedure, the observer will also display the conditioned anxiety response to the formerly neutral stimulus even though the observer had not directly experienced the shock (Rachman, 1974).

The next logical step deriving from such findings would be to extinguish emotional responses through observing a model. As we saw in Chapter 6, this approach has been used to treat children with extreme fear of dogs. By observing a sequence of scenes of models approaching dogs with no signs of fear, these phobic children soon lost their fear of dogs to the extent that many were able to freely interact with the animals.

***Anxiety Management Training.*** A third behavioral technique for reducing anxieties is *anxiety management training*. This method is designed for the "free-floating" or generalized anxiety responses not readily linked to specific anxiety stimuli, as in the generalized anxiety disorder discussed in Chapter 6. Because the client appears unable to identify the precise conditions that precipitate the tensions, desensitization is not appropriate.

Anxiety management training, developed by Suinn (1983a; Suinn & Richardson, 1970), first instructs the client in deliberately arousing the anxiety, followed by immediate application of relaxation or other coping responses to eliminate the anxiety. Fundamentally, the technique aims at helping the client to develop new means for coping with the anxiety as it develops. It differs from desensitization, which tries to prevent anxiety from occurring in the first place. Anxiety management training recognizes that sometimes anxiety does occur, and therefore trains the patient to quickly react to the anxiety through behaviors designed to immediately terminate the anxiety arousal. This technique has been successful with patients suffering from free-floating anxieties to the extent that the anxieties were not only controlled, but eventually eliminated completely (Hutchings et al., 1980; Shoemaker, 1976). Anxiety management training seems to also have success with phobias and some medical problems, such as high blood pressure (Jorgensen et al., 1981).

***Implosion and Flooding Therapies.*** Similar to anxiety management training, *implosive therapy* and *flooding*[1] both treat anxiety by having the client actually experience it. Implosive therapy or implosion aims at removing the avoidance behaviors considered to be the core of fear (Stampfl & Lewis, 1967). If a phobic person continues to avoid a feared situation, extinction will never be able to take place; in contrast, each time the person manages to avoid such situations, the fear behaviors are reinforced because they reduce the anxiety.

Implosion is influenced by psychodynamic therapy in its assumption that fundamental childhood experiences and conflicts (such as problems over sexuality, dependency, or aggression) form the foundation for later fears. To deal with these conflicts, the client is forced to confront and experience true fear by fantasizing scenes in which the worst fears come true. For example, a snake-phobic woman must imagine a huge snake crawling on her, and despite her mounting horror, it bites her (Hogan, 1968). As the fantasy evolves, the anxiety and fear is now confronted; however, since there are no actual negative consequences (no real pain is felt), the fear extinguishes.

Flooding, or response prevention, is based on the same theory that avoidance is self-reinforcing. Techniques are also very similar in forcing the client to reexperience fear. However, the psychodynamic explanations are not used, and hence the fantasy scenes are not as theatrical. Further, flooding tends to rely on real-life experiences where possible, rather than imagined scenes. For example, a technician was plagued by the compulsive need to wash his hands every time he touched a doorknob. In flooding, he was placed in a room with a washbasin, instructed to touch the doorknob, but prevented from washing. As with implosion therapy, the experience—in this case, an actual rather than a fantasized experience—provided the opportunity for the phobia to extinguish.

Research results with implosion have had variable findings, with some showing it to be superior to desensitization, a few suggesting that fears can increase if too short exposures are used, and a number finding no effects from implosion (Hekmat, 1973; McCutcheon

1 Implosion and flooding differ from anxiety management training in that the latter uses the anxiety arousal to teach the client the use of relaxation to eliminate the anxiety.

# FOCUS 21–7:
## Causing Psychotic Symptoms Through Rewards

According to the principles of reinforcement, both normal and abnormal behaviors can be strengthened if they are reinforced. Although we have many laboratory examples that demonstrate the role of rewards on normal behaviors, few examples exist where abnormal behaviors are "created" since ethical considerations prevent such studies. However, one early case has been reported. Haughton and Ayllon (1965) demonstrated that a bizarre behavior could be produced and eliminated solely through the use of reinforcement. A patient was handed a broom and rewarded by a cigarette while she held this and remained standing. Within a short time, the "holding the broom" response was so strong that she would resist any attempts by others to take it away. In order to further analyze the impact of this "compulsive" behavior on others, the experimenters asked two psychiatrists to observe and evaluate the patient through a one-way mirror. The following was the analysis by one of the psychiatrists:

> Her constant and compulsive pacing holding a broom in the manner she does could be seen as a ritualistic procedure, a magical action. When regression conquers the associative process, primitive and archaic forms of thinking control the behavior. Symbolism is a predominant mode of expression and deep seated unfulfilled desires and instinctual impulses. By magic, she controls others, cosmic powers are at her disposal and inanimate objects become living creatures.
>
> Her broom could then be:
>
> 1. A child that gives her love and she gives him in return her devotion.
> 2. A phallic symbol.
> 3. The sceptre of an omnipotent queen (pp. 97–98).

The experimenters later treated the woman by removing the rewards with the result being the total elimination of the bizarre behavior. This recovery lasted with no signs of recurrence as long as two years later.

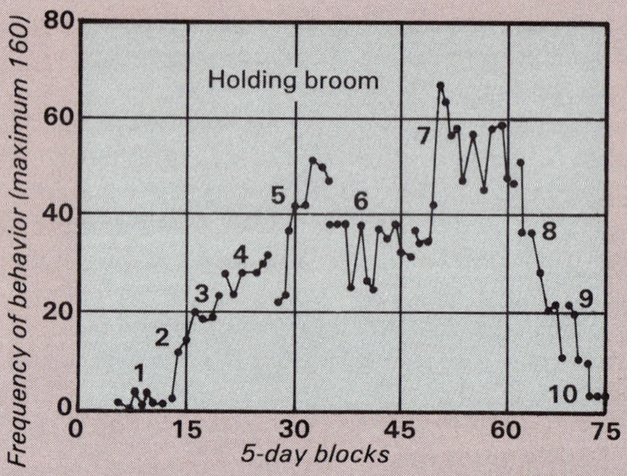


**FIGURE 21–2** Graph showing the acquisition and elimination of symptomatic behavior.

SOURCE: Based on "Production and Elimination of Symptomatic Behavior" by E. Houghton and T. Ayllen, 1965, in L.P. Ullmann and L. Krasner, *Case Studies in Behavior Modification,* New York: Holt, Rinehart & Winston.

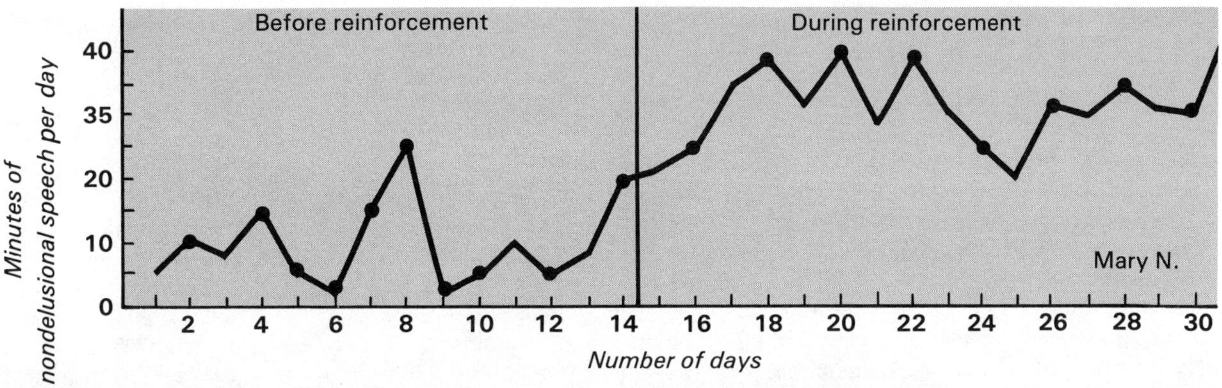


**FIGURE 21–3** Duration of nondelusional speech before and during social reinforcement.
SOURCE: Adapted from "Reducing Delusional Speech in Chronic, Paranoid, Schizophrenics" by R.P. Liberman et al., 1973, *Journal of Applied Behavior Analysis, 6,* p. 61.

& Adams, 1975). The data on flooding are more encouraging, showing its value especially with obsessive-compulsive symptoms (Marks et al., 1975).

***Positive Reinforcement.*** Different in approach from the four techniques just discussed, *positive* or *operant reinforcement* capitalizes on the principle that new responses are acquired and old responses are strengthened whenever they are followed by a reward (positive reinforcement). This point is illustrated by Focus 21–7. Children with deviant behaviors are often encouraged to develop more adaptive responses through rewards such as attention, or social approval (Ross, 1981; Sulzer-Azaroff & Mayer, 1977). Other problems that have been treated by rewarding normal instead of pathological behavior have included hysterical blindness, self-injury, violence, and hallucinatory behavior (Brady & Lind, 1961; Carr & McDowell, 1980; Foxx et al., 1980; Anderson & Alpert. 1974).

Positive reinforcement has been provided for normal speech, thereby reducing delusional speech in chronic paranoid schizophrenia. This work is interesting, inasmuch as the presence of delusions is a prime symptom in diagnosing this disorder. Liberman and his colleagues (1973) used social interaction as a positive reward and were able to help their subjects become more rational in their speech. Figure 21–3 nicely illustrates how the nondelusional behavior of one subject increased dramatically (other subjects showed similar progress).

The effectiveness of operant conditioning is striking, and some researchers have compared this approach with other nonbehavioral forms of therapy. A major study from a hospital gives us some information on the relative impact of a reinforcement program and the milieu approach (Paul & Lentz, 1977). In four and one half years of study, 90 percent of the reinforcement program patients showed improvements compared with 50 percent of the milieu patients. The study also contributed the valuable information that patients discharged from the hospital retained their improvements over time, such that 90 percent of the reinforcement group and 70 percent of the milieu group were still functioning out of the hospital after one and one half years.

Another application of operant principles is the use of biofeedback, in which people learn to control their own body functions. This technique is discussed in Focus 21–8.

***Behavior Rehearsal.*** Like operant reinforcement, *behavior rehearsal* is a technique for replacing unwanted with wanted behaviors. The new behaviors are strengthened in this case by rehearsing or practicing in a controlled therapy setting.

Frequently, people need to try out desired behaviors as a means of removing a behavior deficit or as a substitute for the maladaptive behaviors which they have acquired. For example, behavior rehearsal may be used to enable a person to practice a better response towards an aggressive spouse, an authoritarian employer, or a threatening stranger. It can be used to help a person try out new ways of interacting with others before having to actually face them.

## FOCUS 21–8:
### Biofeedback: Does It Work?

A technique that has fascinated many people is the application of operant principles through *biofeedback.* The term sounds esoteric, but biofeedback simply involves positive feedback through the use of instruments that read out bodily functions. Generally, knowing that you are right is reinforcing and helps to strengthen the responses you are learning. When used for relaxation training, for instance, the biofeedback apparatus simply translates the tenseness of muscles in the forehead into audible clicks, a reading on a dial, or a tone that changes pitch. The subject learns to discover methods to achieve relaxation (such as associating pleasant images, or thinking calming thoughts) through monitoring the feedback signals.

Since biofeedback equipment can be constructed to monitor almost any physiological process, it has been applied in treating many medical and psychosomatic problems (Blanchard & Epstein, 1977). As we saw in Chapter 9, migraine headaches are related to a change in the diameter of cranial arteries and an increase of blood flow to the brain—a physiological change that is in turn associated with a decrease in temperature of the hands. Sargent et al. (1973) used biofeedback to train subjects to increase the temperature of their hands, thus increasing peripheral blood flow, and altering the flow to the head area. Results showed a decrease in both severity and frequency of migraine headaches. Biofeedback has also been used for high blood pressure, cardiac arrhythmias, tension headaches, asthma, menstrual pain, peptic ulcers, and incontinence (Silver & Blanchard, 1978).

For a time, biofeedback training seemed to have potential as a miracle cure. However, as more studies are produced, experts are returning to more cautious positions: that the efficacy may be partly explained by a placebo effect; that less costly methods such as relaxation training may be equally powerful; and that in some areas—such as cardiac ailments—the promise of cure has not always held up. In their review of biofeedback studies, Shapiro and Surwit (1976) conclude that while tentative evidence supports biofeedback's effectiveness for some physical problems, many questions still remain. How readily can laboratory training with biofeedback instruments be transferred to real-life circumstances after patients are sent home? How thorough is the evaluation procedure for biofeedback devices now being advertised and marketed? Further evidence is needed to answer these and other questions.

*Visuo-motor behavior rehearsal* is one technique that permits persons to rehearse behaviors under conditions identical with those they must confront, yet with the security of control. Basically, the participants practice relaxation, in order to be more able to develop imagery; then they are instructed to visualize themselves involved in a realistic situation. They imagine themselves seeing and hearing the other persons; then responding with the adaptive behaviors suggested by the therapist.

One case involved a graduate student who had failed his doctoral oral examination because he clutched when faced with the examining committee. Through behavior rehearsal, he visualized being in the examining room, saw the committee members, heard a question being put to him, then verbally practiced giving answers (Suinn, 1972). As a result, the student was able to pass his examination under stressful conditions without difficulty. The visuo-motor behavior rehearsal approach has also been used by the author in his work with athletes of the U.S. National Teams and with the 1976 Winter and 1980 Summer Olympic Team members. Through this approach, National and Olympic skiers and track runners can race courses or repeat races under competitive conditions, but within the controlled environment of the treatment room (Suinn, 1980). Racing scenes are experienced so realistically that bodily movements and increase in heart rate and respiration are observable (McMahon & Hastrup, 1980; Suinn, 1983b).

***Avoidance Learning.*** *Aversive conditioning* or avoidance learning is a version of classical conditioning. By this procedure a deviant behavior that has attractive qualities for the patient is paired with a noxious event in order to give it aversive qualities instead. This technique has been used with alcoholics with variable success. For instance, the alcoholic is given a drug that produces nausea and vomiting; then the therapist offers the client an alcoholic drink just prior to the moment that the nausea sets in (Becker, 1979). Examples of this approach can be found in Chapter 13.

One particularly successful case using aversive conditioning (Raymond, 1960) involved a highly unusual symptom. The patient, a married man of 33, was referred for possible brain surgery to control his outbursts after he had attacked a perambulator (a type of baby carriage). The patient began his personal attacks on women's handbags and perambulators when he was 10 years old, averaging two or three per week. He had been brought to trial five times for incidents as follows:

> Slashed two empty prams on a railway station . . . setting them on fire.
>
> Rode his motorcycle . . . into a perambulator . . . was convicted of careless driving.
>
> Damaged a pram . . . by squirting oil.
>
> Drove his motorcycle through a muddy puddle, splashing a pram.
>
> Smearing (perambulator) with oil.

Psychoanalytic treatment convinced the patient that his attacks could be traced to symbolic sexual meanings related to two childhood incidents. This insight did little to help control the impulses. Behavior therapy was then directed at developing an aversive reaction to the attacks. The standard nausea-producing drug was used in association with the presentation of handbags and perambulators. This treatment was then replaced with confinement to a bed filled with handbags and surrounded with perambulators. Within a little over two weeks, the patient could tolerate prams and handbags no longer and was found sobbing that they be removed. He even voluntarily handed over some photographic negatives of perambulators he had secretly been carrying. He was released, brought back for one booster treatment session, and remained happily free of his symptoms when last checked some 19 months later.

***The Cognitive Behavior Therapies.*** One additional behavior therapy, *cognitive therapy,* has developed out of the recognition that our thoughts influence our emotions and actions. Unlike the other behavioral strategies just discussed, this approach sees maladaptive behaviors as precipitated by what we say to ourselves, and the ongoing thoughts we have. Cognitive treatments aim at removing disruptive cognitive patterns that underlie maladaptive behaviors.

*The Power of Negative Thinking.* Consider your own reactions to the thoughts that pass through your mind. If you awaken on a rainy morning and the first thing you say to yourself is "I'll never make it through

***Visuo-motor behavior rehearsal*** *has been used for training athletes, such as skiers, and others in adaptive skills.*

the day. Things always go wrong on rainy days. It'll be cold all day, and everyone else will stay home from classes, and I'll probably have a pop quiz on top of everything else,'' you may find your mood all day is affected by that dreary frame of reference. What is more, there may be some element of self-fulfilling prophecy, so that if there *is* a pop quiz, you do more poorly than you might have otherwise. In contrast, if you talk to yourself as follows—''It's going to be a good day regardless of the weather. I feel fine simply because my life is going well and I'm making progress with the things I want to change. If I make some mistakes today, I'll be able to overcome them''—you will probably not only feel better, but also act in a more effective manner.

Cognitive therapists are concerned with the effect of things we say to ourselves. In some cases, just the thought itself seems to have a life of its own and goes on and on without stop. In other cases, the thought may be prompted by an event. The thoughts may prevent you from taking steps to prepare for a stress, simply because they capture your attention and energy. On the other hand, the thoughts may represent a vicious cycle that imprisons you in a depressed mood.

*Cognitive Therapy Techniques.* A variety of cognitive therapy techniques have been developed to deal with such cognitive disruptors. A simple one is aimed at blocking thoughts by *thought stopping.* Thought stopping involves having the individual deliberately let negative thoughts appear, then halt them by inserting a new thought, literally the thought ''Stop!'', and perhaps even imagining a vivid stop sign (Lombardo & Turner 1979).

Where the source of the problem is the distorted meaning of a thought or an irrational belief, methods such as *rational-emotive therapy* may be useful. Developed by Albert Ellis (1962), rational-emotive therapy has individuals monitor their thoughts, then the therapist forcefully confronts them to show the irrationality of the beliefs being expressed. In the set of negative thoughts included at the start of this section, Ellis might challenge certain themes that have no foundation—such as ''Does doing well depend on one pop quiz?'' or ''Is it true that life should be exactly the way you want, must every day be predictable and controlled by your wants?''

Finally, a program called *stress inoculation training* (SIT) has been applied when cognitive interference blocks the more positive use of thoughts. The Canadian therapist, Meichenbaum (1977) instructs clients to prepare themselves to use thoughts as helping elements. For example, if you suffer from test anxiety, you might be trained in four stages of stress inoculation: preparing for a stressor, confronting the stressor, confronting feelings of being overwhelmed, and providing self-reward for coping.

The training helps you to identify which of your thoughts or feelings cause anxiety to increase, and which coping self-statements you can use to prompt a more adaptive style. For example, in preparing for the stress of the exam, you might remind yourself, ''This time I will do the best I can, using a systematic approach instead of allowing myself to get flustered'' or ''Unlike the past, I have a method for coping with the anxiety that I'm going to use so I won't panic''; during the exam itself, you may need to remind yourself, ''Just answer one question at a time, go on to the next one if you can't answer this one, don't worry about just this one, go on. . . .'' If you are feeling overwhelmed by anxious feelings during the test, then the following thoughts may help: ''Take time off for a moment, take a deep breath, slow and deep, and relax . . . calm . . . good'' or ''Don't try to eliminate the anxiety totally, just keep it manageable.'' Certainly, when the stress inoculation method is working, rewarding thoughts should also be used: ''That's great, it's helping,'' ''I am getting more under control, and when I control my ideas, my anxiety leaves.'' Using this SIT approach, Hussian and Lawrence (1978) helped introductory psychology students reduce their test anxiety, as we see in Figure 21–4.

The various behavioral techniques we've been discussing are among the most important methods used in this third major approach to psychological therapy. Their goal, unlike the two other approaches, is simply to treat symptoms; and their effectiveness, as noted in Focus 21–9 has been remarkable in some cases. The final evaluative discussion will end this chapter by looking at the three major approaches all together.

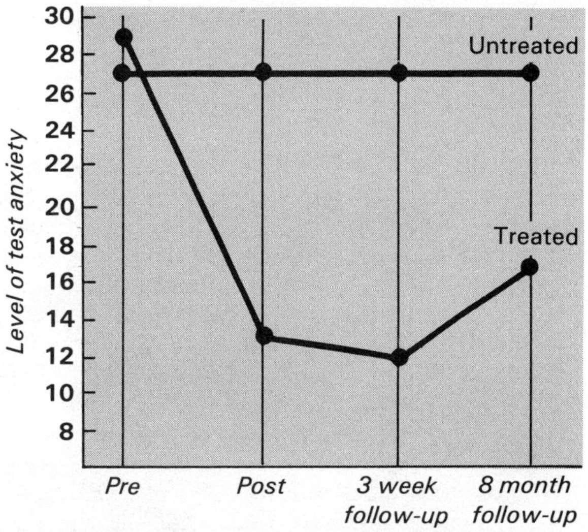


**FIGURE 21–4** The effects of stress inoculation training compared to no treatment for test anxiety.

SOURCE: Based on ''The Effects of Stress Inoculation Training Compared to No Treatment for Test Anxiety'' by Hussian & Lawrence, 1978, *Cognitive Therapy & Research, 2,* pp. 25–37.

## EVALUATION

Any evaluation of psychotherapy must inevitably examine the results of psychotherapeutic intervention, and answer the question, ''Do the clients get better?''

The best overall conclusion is ''yes'' (Shapiro & Shapiro, 1983). Through a variety of analyses of reports on psychoanalytic therapy and on other psychotherapies, Bergin and Lambert (1978) conclude that about two thirds of nonpsychotic persons in treatment will show gains. This compares very well against their estimate that only about 40 percent of these persons would have improved ''spontaneously,'' that is without any formal help. Thus, if about 65 percent is the rate with therapy and 40 percent is the rate without therapy, then psychotherapy does actively contribute to clients getting better.

A rather startling discovery, however, is the finding that psychotherapy can also potentially make people worse. Bergin (1966) showed what he first termed the *deterioration effect* as an unexpected but far-reaching finding. If therapy can harm as well as help, then it becomes crucial to find out what factors lead to such outcomes before one seeks therapy. Given the

## FOCUS 21–9:
### Assessing Psychotherapy: The Behavior Therapies

The experimenter–therapists of the behavior therapy approach have attempted to continuously evaluate their techniques. As a result, there is a relatively large amount of data available for assessing many behaviorist techniques. In nine years of private practice, Wolpe (1958) showed that nearly 90 percent of his 210 clients were either cured or much improved by behavior therapy, which lasted usually about 30 sessions for each client. These clients exhibited a variety of neuroses including anxiety, conversion disorder, depressions, and obsessive-compulsive behaviors. Lazarus (1963) also reviewed his practice, finding that 78 percent of his 408 cases had shown marked benefits. In contrast, McConaghy (1964) was able to show improvement in half of his 18 patients, some of whom were psychotic and nearly all of whom had been unsuccessfully treated by conventional psychiatric therapy. The best successes have been reported by Mowrer and Mowrer (1938), Paul (1966), and Robinson and Suinn (1969). Mowrer and Mowrer treated 30 children with bedwetting problems and was able to cure all of them with his device, which we discussed in Chapter 20. Paul selected 15 students with severe phobias about speaking in public, using counterconditioning techniques to bring improvement in 100 percent of the cases (as compared to 47 percent improvement with insight therapy; 46 percent with palcebo pill and suggestion; and 17 percent who received no treatment at all). Robinson and Suinn removed a fear of spiders in clients to the extent that all were able to approach a live four-inch spider, and some were even able to stroke its back.

complexity of studying therapy itself, this issue is a little more elusive, but some interesting information has started to show up.

First, what conditions can make therapy into a deteriorating experience? One answer to this question involves the client. Persons with low tolerance for anxiety, low motivation, and high signs of psychological deterioration were found to be more subject to getting worse with therapy (Strupp, 1980).

Another answer concerns the therapist. Two studies mentioned earlier seem to point to therapist characteristics that may lead to deterioration in their clients. Yalom and Lieberman (1971) identified seven different leadership styles among encounter groups; among them, the "aggressive stimulator" was the most damaging. This style involved impatience about attitude change, pressure to have group members reveal private aspects of themselves quickly, and an aggressive, pushy, confronting manner of relating.

Carl Rogers, in contrast, states his belief that all effective treatment requires therapists to develop a relationship that is helping in tone. Ricks' (1974) findings, mentioned earlier in this chapter and also in Chapter 20, support this: the therapist nicknamed "Supershrink" by his childhood schizophrenic clients devoted more time to the more disturbed boys and supported signs of progress toward independence; he was also firm with parents, and encouraged problem-solving. In contrast, the less successful therapist in this study, like Yalom and Lieberman's group leader, tried to have his boys move into deeply conflictual topics but without the ability to help them cope with feelings. There is some evidence that more successful therapy is the outcome if the therapist and client are similar in cognitive levels; the assumption being that such similarity permits better communication (Parloff et al., 1978).

A second question is what form of therapy is most helpful? Is one approach superior to the others? At this stage, the best answer is that each therapeutic orientation—psychoanalytic, the humanist-existential, and the behaviorist—can lay a valid claim to a fair share of positive results (Bergin & Lambert, 1978; Bergin & Suinn, 1975). When compared against one another, there is no conclusive evidence that one form is superior to another, although there is a modest trend for behavioral approaches to be more actively researched and to show somewhat better outcomes than the psychoanalytic or humanistic-existential approaches (Shapiro & Shapiro, 1982, 1983). In one study of more than 90 clients treated at the Temple University Health Sciences Center, 80 percent of both behavior therapy and analytically oriented therapy clients improved through treatment—not a bad rate for both compared to the 48 percent who received no therapy (Sloane et al., 1975).

At this point, we might suggest the following assessment of the capabilities of modern therapy:

First, it is likely that some forms of psychopathology are better helped by some types of psychotherapy and not helped and perhaps even hindered by other forms. Just as a misapplied prescription of antibiotics will lead to no improvement and perhaps even to deterioration in a physical disorder, so will misapplication of psychotherapeutic strategies lead to disappointing results.

Second, psychotherapies do have, on the whole, a positive impact (Rachman & Wilson, 1980). Conditions which facilitate improvement include certain client characteristics such as motivation, and tolerance for facing conflicts; certain therapist characteristics, such as psychological adjustment and empathy; and also certain environmental conditions (Schaffer, 1982). In an earlier chapter, for instance, we mentioned the prognostic signs for schizophrenics as including a supportive home environment. Certainly, continued growth can be enhanced by one's relationships outside therapy.

A third point to be remembered is that various strategies are designed to achieve differing goals. Desensitization emphasizes learning relaxation to replace fear and is not conducive to lengthy discussions about early childhood. Client-centered therapy encourages self-awareness and self-directedness and is not likely to offer directive guidance from the therapist. Psychoanalysis strives for extensive self-insight, self-understanding, and eventual personality reorganization, and tends not to be conducive to rapid achievement of goals. It is helpful for clients to be prepared about what to expect as the style of the therapy chosen, so as to maximally benefit.

Finally, therapeutic experiences need not be limited to persons with serious maladjustments. Being in treatment is not an admission of being "insane." The growth movement through the humanistic therapies has contributed much towards exploding this myth and demonstrating the value of therapeutic settings for human development.

## SUMMARY

This chapter focused on the various psychotherapeutic strategies developed to help people in psychological distress. The techniques have been influenced by differing theories about the cause of mental disorders, with the psychoanalytic, the humanistic-existential, and the behavioral approaches all reflecting different philosophies and viewpoints. In the psychoanalytic view, repression and resistance are said to play major roles in pathology. Hence, psychoanalytic therapy relies on techniques such as the use of transference, free-association, interpretation, and the development of insight to bring about change. In contrast, the humanistic-existential approach emphasizes the importance of self-directed growth and the opportunity for change to occur through current actions and the acceptance of responsibility. From these viewpoints, the therapy strategy has deemphasized techniques as such, and emphasized instead a therapeutic attitude or orientation. Therapy provides conditions of positive regard and support for the person to accept more personal responsibility and to seek authenticity through self-exploration. Behavioral theory draws from studies that suggest that behaviors, including pathological behaviors are learned, following certain principles of learning. Hence, the behaviorist has designed treatment methods which conform to such principles. These have included methods ranging from counterconditioning to biofeedback. In each case, training is more important than attempts to incorporate insight or depth interpretations.

While each theoretical approach has led to the development of different techniques, all have shown some success in helping individuals with their problems. At the same time, there is also evidence that the improper use of psychotherapy can also lead to a deterioration effect, where the individual becomes worse rather than better. Although therapist characteristic contributes to such deterioration, research is still at an infancy stage in identifying the specific conditions under which each of the psychotherapies is best used.

## KEY TERMS

**Anxiety hierarchy**
**Authenticity**
**Aversive training**
**Avoidance learning**
**Behavior rehearsal**
**Client-centered therapy**
**Cognitive behavior therapy**
**Counterconditioning**
**Dereflection**
**Deterioration effect**
**Encounter groups**
**Family therapy**
**Flooding**
**Free association**
**Gestalt therapy**
**Group psychotherapy**
**Human relations training**
**Hypnosis**
**Implosive therapy**
**Interpretation**
**Logotherapy**
**Modeling**
**Paradoxical intention**
**Play therapy**
**Psychodrama**
**Resistance**
**Self-actualization**
**Sensory awareness groups**
**Sensitivity groups**
**Systematic desensitization**
**Stress inoculation training**
**T-groups**
**Thought stopping**
**Transference**
**Visuo-motor behavior rehearsal**
**Vicarious extinction**

# CHAPTER 22

## The Therapies: Medical Therapies

- **Are certain drugs schizophrenia-specific?**
- **Why isn't drug therapy relied on more often?**
- **How good are mood elevating drugs for depression?**
- **Use of an electrical current for shock therapy sounds threatening and inhumane; why would we use it?**
- **Is there any justification for relying on brain surgery for mental disorders?**
- **Can an executive return to his job and be effective even after undergoing surgery to separate the frontal lobes?**
- **Why would some claim that it is a false belief that drugs work solely because of their chemical properties?**
- **How does one go about deciding whether to seek medical or psychological therapy?**
- **How effective is medical therapy for mental illness?**

## Case History 22–1:
### Electroshock and Chemotherapy

Elliot W. was a promising graduate student in theatre when he began to experience unusual thoughts. His thoughts centered around why he had to study so hard when others had it so easy. The issue grew steadily, until he became angry at his unfair lot in life. His anger became directed towards his faculty advisor (who Elliot felt was unsupportive), his wife (who he felt was forcing him to earn a living), and his landlord (who he felt could have offered Elliot an allowance and taken him in as a son).

One Friday night, Elliot stayed awake considering all the wrongs that had been done to him. He ruminated throughout the next morning, on through the night, and throughout the following day. By Sunday evening Elliot was physically exhausted, yet he was still unable to sleep. At 2 a.m. on Monday morning, he picked up his telephone, called his landlord, and began to recite a litany of curses and accusations. He then phoned his faculty advisor with a similar litany. At this point, his wife Jenny became worried and sought advice from a neighbor. When the police arrived, Elliot was aimlessly pacing around the house, shouting incoherently and wildly turning over furniture. He was taken, at his wife's urging, to a state hospital where he was admitted.

Elliot spent the next week either in restraints or heavily sedated. Electroshock treatments were begun, initially with no results. Elliot remained incoherent and failed to recognize his wife or to show any signs that he was aware of his surroundings. After nearly a month of shock treatment, Elliot became calmer, although he remained disoriented. Psychosurgery was considered inasmuch as Elliot was considered a poor prognostic case; a family history uncovered chronic schizophrenia in his mother and evidence of an emotional breakdown that led to hospitalization in a sister. However, heavy doses of Thorazine were prescribed instead, on the hope that the tranquilizer might have some effect.

Initially, the Thorazine quieted Elliot but he now seemed withdrawn and unresponsive. During all of this, Jenny continued to visit faithfully, even when Elliot seemed detached and unreachable. However, within two weeks, Elliot seemed to notice her for the first time and suddenly began weeping. With this breakthrough, his condition continued to improve slowly but consistently. He could not recall anything of the fateful weekend, but he did remember his preceding doubts and pent-up anger. Possibly because of the electroshock and possibly as a natural protective defense, Elliot also remembered nothing of his hospitalization, "It's as if I was suspended on another planet. . . . I was aware of my body and my being somewhere, but I was distant as if I was in a dream state."

After three months of further hospitalization and chemotherapy, Elliot was discharged. Instead of returning for outpatient treatment to the hospital, he immediately entered private psychotherapy with a psychoanalytically oriented therapist. Within a year, Elliot had progressed to a point of regaining his confidence and his ambition to continue his graduate training. Elliot continues in psychotherapy and speaks of his emotional crisis and hospitalization as turning points in self-discovery. He believes that he has been strengthened by the experiences and consequent therapies. Elliot is within three months of completing his master's degree in his new major of American literature and has a tentative position in a state college.

Chapter 21 discussed several psychological treatments that aim to help an individual return to a more effective, satisfactory state of adjustment. In many cases, however, such treatments may not be effective—as in Elliot's case, Case History 22-1—either because symptoms are too severe to permit a productive interaction to take place or because the disorder has an organic cause that does not seem to respond as well to psychological approaches.

The medical therapies provide a different approach to treating mental disorders. They involve techniques affecting the physical condition of the client. Historically, we've seen that many physiological treatments have been used, ranging from trephining to lobotomies. Medical therapies today are used only by practitioners with medical training. In addition, laws act as safeguards to protect the well-being of patients; for example, it is illegal to obtain many psychopharmacologic drugs without a prescription.

Included among the medical therapies are:

- Drug therapy (chemotherapy)
- Electroshock therapy
- Psychosurgery

Each of these approaches have been mentioned briefly in one or another of the earlier chapters of this text; in this chapter, we will examine them more closely and evaluate their effectiveness.

## CHEMOTHERAPY

Until approximately 1952, drug therapy was rarely used and was limited primarily to the sedatives, hypnotics, and mild stimulants. However, at about that time, the tranquilizers chlorpromazine and reserpine appeared. Such tranquilizers so revolutionized medicine that it was estimated that 3 out of every 10 prescriptions were for one of the other of these drugs. The steady decline in rate of admissions to mental hospitals since 1955 (see Figure 22-1) and the shorter length of hospitalization have been attributed in a large degree to the discovery of drugs. These drugs, which have proven so valuable in psychiatric treatment, are of two varieties: the tranquilizers and the mood changers (Lickey & Gordon, in press).

### The Tranquilizers

Tranquilizing drugs have the effect of calming a person without appreciably affecting alertness or accessibility. This distinguishes the tranquilizers from sedatives such as phenobarbital, which can produce a similar calming effect, but also make the person sleepy or sluggish. In fact, phenobarbital is often prescribed to aid a person in sleeping. Some tranquilizing drugs have been especially effective in treating psychoses such as schizophrenia; some others have been helpful in easing symptoms of less severe disorders, such as the anxiety disorders.

***Tranquilizers for Psychoses.*** Chlorpromazine was the first major tranquilizer of the phenothiazine group to be synthetically manufactured. As one sees over and over again in the development of medical treatments, serendipity was involved to a great degree in its discovery. The French scientists responsible for discovering chlorpromazine were actually trying to

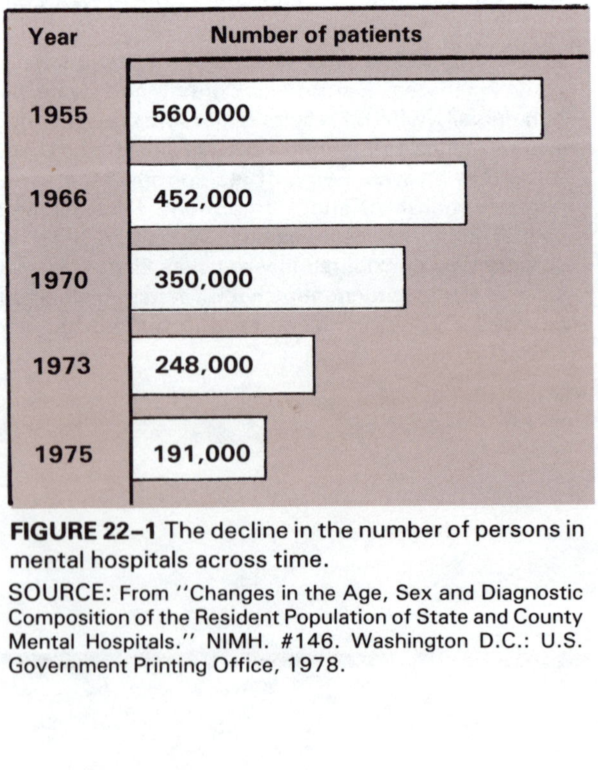


**FIGURE 22-1** The decline in the number of persons in mental hospitals across time.

SOURCE: From "Changes in the Age, Sex and Diagnostic Composition of the Resident Population of State and County Mental Hospitals." NIMH. #146. Washington D.C.: U.S. Government Printing Office, 1978.

develop a drug with strong sedative power; the tranquilizing effect of chlorpromazine occurred entirely by chance. Since then, numerous other phenothiazine derivatives have been developed, including Compazine, Stelazine, Trilafon, Sparine, and Mellaril.

Chlorpromazine has the effects of reducing anxiety, agitation, fear, restlessness, and hyperactivity without impairing thought processes. The client usually feels a sense of calm and a comfortable apathy. A patient once told the author, "Nothing really matters any more that much . . . you could tell me I'm sitting on a bomb and you can't rattle me." This drug has been particularly useful in the control of symptoms associated with schizophrenia, as we saw in Chapter 17. The impact has been so profound in permitting early release from hospitalization that Cole (1976) observed "It is remarkable that no Nobel Prize in medicine has been awarded to the discoverers." (p. 13)

An example of the effectiveness of the phenothiazines can be seen in a report of the National Institute of Mental Health (Klerman et al., 1964). A collaborative study was started in 1959 with nine hospitals across the nation. Each new schizophrenic patient was randomly assigned to one of four treatment groups involving chlorpromazine, one of two other phenothiazines, or a placebo (a pill with no therapeutic value). In order to control for bias, neither the physician nor the patient knew the true content of the medication taken. Over 300 patients were followed over a course of six weeks of treatment. The results were impressive:

- 95 percent of the phenothiazine patients improved.
- Over 75 percent of the phenothiazine patients were judged either "much improved" or "markedly Improved."
- Significant changes occurred in 17 of 21 symptoms of schizophrenia, for example, hallucinations, ideas of persecution, indifference to the environment.
- There were no noticeable differences in effectiveness among the various phenothiazines, but they were all clearly more effective than the placebo.

Such positive findings have been corroborated, and they also show that relapses decrease with continued use of medication (Shopsin et al., 1979). Just why it is so effective is still an unanswered question. We know some things about chlorpromazine's effects. It acts on several parts of the body: the hypothalamus, the reticular activating system, the limbic system, the medulla, and the autonomic nervous system, as well as affecting dopamine transmission. It is still a matter of conjecture, however, as to just why this drug is so beneficial with schizophrenia. Long-acting phenothiazines (those lasting two to four weeks) are also under study in the hopes of reducing the need for frequent medication (Groves & Mandel, 1975).

***Tranquilizers for Anxiety.*** While chlorpromazine is prescribed mainly for psychoses, other tranquilizers are helpful for minor disorders such as the anxiety disorders and psychophysiologic conditions. A typical example is meprobamate, better known under the brand name of Miltown or Equanil. Meprobamate is a drug with mild tranquilizing and muscle relaxing action.

After a period of sudden popularity in outpatient treatment, the claims for this tranquilizer have recently been more carefully considered. Of primary concern is the fact that prolonged use may be addictive, producing symptoms of withdrawal when terminated (Baker, 1983). Drowsiness, dermatitis, and even convulsions have also been reported. Librium and Valium have been prescribed as alternative anxiety agents or muscle relaxants, with very similar results to meprobamate for anxiety disorders, but less severe side effects (Greenblatt & Shader, 1974).

### The Mood Changers

Another use of chemotherapy has been to reduce both the manic and the depressed conditions in patients. Early attempts to lift depressed patients out of despondent moods tried central nervous system stimulants, including amphetamines such as Benzedrine and Dexedrine, but with minimal success. Again, serendipity stepped in. The drug iproniazid was being studied as a therapy for tuberculosis. However, it had a side effect—that of increasing physical activity and elevat-

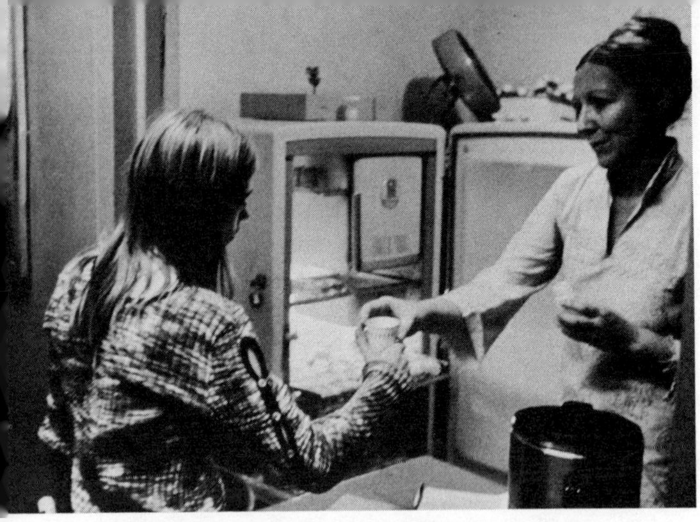

*Methadone has been used as a treatment for opiate dependence. This treatment has raised controversy since methadone itself may lead to dependency.*

ing mood—which was considered undesirable. It was discontinued for tuberculosis, but it was reintroduced six years later for depression (Kline, 1958).

Iproniazid was the first of the ''MAO-inhibitors,'' drugs which control an enzyme (Monoamine oxidase) that causes depletion of serotonin in the brain (considered at one time a possible factor in psychosis). Although there was initially great enthusiasm about the MAO-inhibitors for depression, some extremely severe and dangerous side effects, such as hypertension, have led to its reduced use. These drugs are now used as alternatives if other antidepressants fail, or instead as treatment for phobic disorders (Bassuk et al., 1983).

***Tricyclic Antidepressants.*** The tricyclic antidepressants (Tofranil and Elavil) are more desirable than the MAO-inhibitors as medications for depression. Again chance had an influence in the discovery of this group of drugs. Imipramine (Tofranil) was actually under study for use with schizophrenia before its qualities led to its application with depression. The tricyclics act to elevate mood, but vary differently from the amphetamines. Whereas the amphetamines will stimulate a kind of euphoria in normal persons, the tricyclics have no subjective effects on most people. However, when administered to depressed persons, these drugs have a pronounced ability to alter the depressed mood state.

***Lithium.*** Another drug that seems even more effective as a mood changer is lithium. It is the lightest of all alkali metals (such as sodium and potassium) found in the earth. It occurs in nature as a salt, is more abundant than lead, and can be found across the world in the ground, in minerals, in sea or fresh water, and in plants. An exciting finding is that lithium seems clearly valuable in helping manic states, but is also useful in both bipolar and unipolar depressions (Reifman & Wyatt, 1980; Rosen et al., 1980).

One important study (Prien et al., 1973) explored the preventative value of lithium in enabling bipolar or unipolar patients to avoid recurrences of depressive episodes. For the bipolar patients, only 28 percent on lithium had relapses as compared with 77 percent on a tricyclic and 77 percent on a placebo. Similar results were found for unipolar patients, in that 48 percent of lithium patients (and an equal percent of tricyclic patients) relapsed as compared to the higher 92 percent of placebo patients. Where the presenting diagnosis was not bipolar depression but bipolar disorder with both manic and depressed episodes, a second study showed that lithium was highly effective in preventing manic episodes, and to a lesser degree, also useful in preventing further depression (Stallone et al., 1973). A high school friend of the author, who had experienced a bipolar disorder, reported, ''I used to have ups and down with those other drugs, until my doctor tried lithium. I used to feel low and want to just sleep at times in my depression; and full of wild urges when I was manic . . . and those other drugs only made me feel in a fog. But now I'm in my old job in electronics, and at least I feel normal.''

### Evaluating Chemotherapy

There is little doubt that chemotherapy has had a substantial impact on psychiatric treatment. As noted earlier, the introduction of drugs on a large scale was associated with a 2 percent reduction in mental hospital residents, due to increased discharge rates (Kramer & Pollack, 1958). Some of this rise in discharge might certainly be attributed to factors other than the use of drugs, for example, the shift away from custodial care and toward community-based care (a point which we will discuss in Chapter 23). However, Brill and Patton

(1959) were able to show a decline in mental hospital census by over 4 percent in New York State hospitals, occurring after chemotherapy and before any other major changes. Moreover, unlike the history of shock therapy, this increase in discharge rate occurred without being accompanied by relapses. Gross and Reeves (1961), for example, found relapses occurring in only 13 percent of some 144 patients on chemotherapy. On the other hand, when the drug dosage was gradually reduced and replaced by a placebo (without the knowledge of either patient or physician), 58 percent of the patients showed relapses.

Despite the favorable results obtained thus far with chemotherapy, there is disagreement even among experts regarding the value and effects of drugs in psychiatry. The foremost concern is a fear of its potential side effects. This has been referred to as the efficacy versus toxicity problem—the dilemma of balancing the positive results of drugs against possible adverse side effects.

Side effects may range all the way from the minor irritation of dryness of the mouth, to jaundice, or even retinitis pigmentosa (a condition leading to blindness). Moreover, psychopharmacologists are realizing that the positive effects of the drugs themselves appear to be determined by multiple factors and not solely their chemical properties or physiological effects on the body. Individual patients, with similar diagnosis, given similar doses of the same drug, can react quite differently. For example, Wirt and Simon (1959) found that reserpine had a pathogenic rather than a therapeutic effect on some of their schizophrenic subjects. A number of factors appear to influence the effects of a drug, and some of these are outlined in Focus 22–1.

In conclusion, evidence is mounting that the proper use of drugs as a therapeutic tool is a highly complex matter. A distinct interaction exists between the class of drug and the type of mental disorder in terms of the therapeutic outcome. Generally speaking, the tranquilizers are better limited to the tension states, while the energizers or mood changers are more effective with the depressed states. Of equal importance is the interaction that appears to influence a drug's effect. The class of drug, the type of illness, the specific symptom pattern, the physical status of the patient, the attitudes of both patient and therapist toward chemotherapy, the fundamental personality pattern of the patient, and even the emotions and behaviors of persons surrounding the patient are all factors that affect a drug's impact. In a three-hospital study, with over 480 anxiety disorder patients, Rickels et al., (1971) found two causes of improvement: the medication itself and the warmth of the physician during the initial visit. Viewed in this context, chemotherapy becomes simply one small aspect of a large-scale therapeutic program.

## THE DRASTIC THERAPIES

The drug therapies are widely used for a range of disorders, and they may be made available on several levels, as an over-the-counter prescriptions as well as through direct medication at an institution. Another group of medical therapies have more restricted use. These treatments, including electroconvulsive therapy and psychosurgery (brain surgery), can be referred to as the drastic therapies.

Insulin shock, electroshock, and psychosurgery are all historically related. The three methods were all introduced within the course of a few years, starting in the early 1930s when they were heralded as psychiatric breakthroughs. The convulsive methods were developed empirically rather than devised according to a theoretical hypothesis. Dr. Manfred Sakel (1956), the discoverer of insulin shock therapy, admitted that "There is . . . no explanation sufficiently substanti ated by experiment of why the Borderline Insulin Treatment and the Classical Shock Treatment are effective. . . ." Psychosurgery, in contrast, was first attempted based on theoretical conclusions from careful consideration of known facts (Moniz, 1936).

Currently, with the availability of chemotherapy, the drastic therapies are used less as a form of psychiatric treatment. Psychosurgery is not as readily prescribed and is often limited to the extremely intractable patients who do not respond to other therapies and whose behaviors are highly detrimental to the well-being of both themselves and others. The convulsive therapies have also been curtailed in contrast to their earlier use; when prescribed, electroshock seems to be preferred more by modern psychiatrists.

## FOCUS 22–1:
### Drug Effectiveness: Influential Factors

Although drug therapy works by producing a physiological reaction in the body, its effect is nowhere near as predictable as the chemical reactions that can be produced in a laboratory. Several factors interact to influence the effect chemotherapy will have on each individual. Among them:

- *Physical state of the person.* Rate of absorption of the drug, rate of excretion, and tolerance which may have been developed are all important factors.
- *General attitude.* A person's expectation that a drug will be beneficial will enhance the therapeutic effort of that drug; this is the reason placebos and double blind studies are used in research (Fisher et al., 1962). In double-blind studies, both therapist and patient are uninformed about what drug is administered.
- *Therapist's attitude.* A therapist's sense of confidence in the therapeutic power of drugs can have as much a role in effecting recovery as the drug itself. There is even some question as to whether the therapist's belief in the drug is more influential than even the drug's own properties (Rickels et al., 1971). Once again double-blind studies are used to prevent such an experience.
- *Personality pattern of the patient.* Studies have indicated that outgoing, athletically oriented persons tend to react with anxiety and irritability when receiving doses of chlorpromazine, while introverted, intellectually oriented persons become more tranquil and indifferent to their surroundings (Janke, 1983).
- *The pathological symptoms that are exhibited.* Drug therapy appears more effective with certain symptom patterns than with others. For example, tranquilizers were found to be most effective with acute panic symptoms than symptoms involving withdrawal and periodic agitation (Katz, 1966).
- *Social circumstances.* A person who is experiencing a condition of physiological change (which drugs may produce) may become highly susceptible to social influences. Observations of LSD and marijuana use have noted that the mood or expectations of others can influence the user's experience. Furthermore, where a person does not know what to expect, the actions of others could be a determinant, for example, leading the person to feel either euphoric or angry under the same drug.

### Insulin Convulsive Therapy

Insulin therapy is one of the oldest major forms of physical treatment used in psychiatry. Sakel first experimented with insulin in 1927 in Vienna. Believing that nerve cells are weakened during illness, he hypothesized that insulin might help by blocking the release of further energy from the cell, thereby leading to energy conservation. He also felt that cases of addiction and marginal psychiatric pathologies reflected metabolic imbalances that might be corrected through the introduction of insulin.

Originally, Sakel attempted to avoid inducing convulsions; however, seizures did occur in some of his patients and, to his surprise, the seizures were followed by dramatic improvements. By 1933, the "Classical Sakel Insulin Shock Treatment" had developed with an emphasis on the curative effects of convulsion (Sakel, 1933). This method, as it is used today, involves intramuscular injection of increasing amounts of insulin until a "shock" stage, or a comatose state, is obtained.

***Phases of Treatment.*** The course of insulin shock treatment is fairly standard. The first phase is the induction phase: a period of days during which the patient receives an increasing dose each morning until a coma dose is reached.

Phase two is the repeated administration of the coma dose each day for approximately 30 to 90 treatments. Each comatose state is permitted to last for about 30 minutes to an hour. Basically, the condition is caused by hypoglycemia (reduction in sugar content) caused by the insulin; termination of the coma is therefore attained by the administration of glucose directly into the stomach. During this treatment, the patient gradually becomes weak and drowsy and perspires prior to the coma. As stupor increases, either fear or a burst of hostile activity may occasionally arise. The patient is comatose within three hours after the insulin injection. Muscular twitchings, vague motor activity, and some restless movements may occur. The patient may mutter, groan, or shriek. Severe convulsions can be controlled by the corollary use of a sedative such as phenobarbital. Once the coma is terminated, the patient is returned to the ward and permitted to resume normal hospital activities.

***Effectiveness and Risks of Insulin Shock.*** Insulin shock has been most often used to treat paranoid or catatonic schizophrenics, and patients with extreme anxiety, fear, or panic (Laqueur et al., 1962). The best results are obtained when treatment is introduced early within six months after the onset of the illness or hospitalization (Kalinowsky & Hock, 1952). When compared to the 25 to 30 percent rate of improvement of patients receiving no specific therapy, the reported 44 to 68 percent rates for insulin shock is encouraging (Staudt & Zubin, 1957). Closer examination, however, indicates that a large percentage of the patients counted as showing *immediate* improvement experience relapses within a few years. If these patients are removed from the figures, the improvement rate for insulin shock drops to between 27 to 40 percent. In further research, scientists such as Stephens and Astrup (1965) were unable to provide any support for either short- or long-term effects of insulin therapy.

Added to this are the risks of insulin shock treatments. Bruises and fractures are not uncommon results of thrashing. An irreversible coma may develop, leading to possible brain damage or even death. The mortality rate from insulin shock treatment is between 0.5 to 1 percent. Such risks are serious enough to demand careful reconsideration of the insulin technique as a therapeutic measure. Therefore, electroshock has received far greater attention in recent years.

### Electroshock Therapy

In the early 1930s, an Italian neuropsychiatrist named Ugo Cerletti became interested in the anatomical effects of convulsions on the brain. His studies involved passing an electric current through the bodies of dogs by means of electrodes attached to the mouth and rectum, then examining the brains of sacrificed animals. During a visit to Vienna, he observed Sakel's treatment techniques and speculated on the possibility of using electroshock as a substitute for insulin. He was cautioned, however, by his own fear of possible electrocution.

Subsequently, a chance visit to a slaughterhouse became a significant historical event, for it introduced Cerletti first to a modified technique whereby metallic

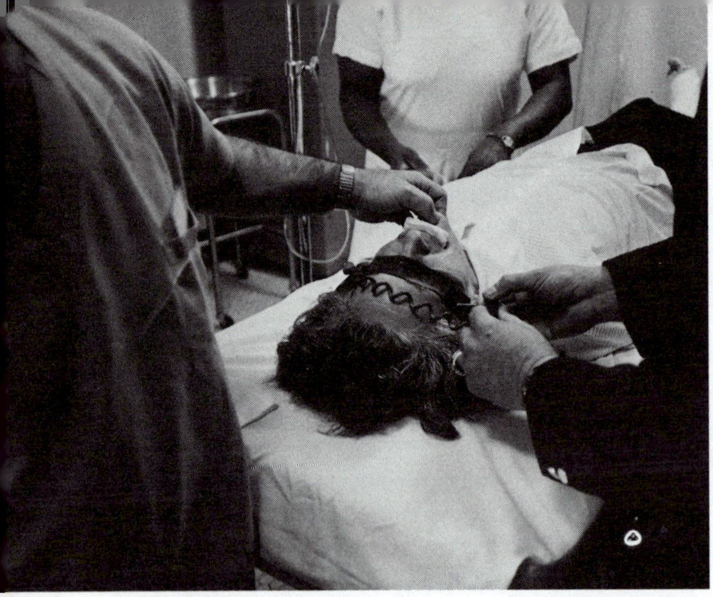

***Electroshock*** *therapy has become a useful treatment procedure for some depressions. Because of the involuntary muscle spasms caused by the current, caution is taken to prevent injury to the tongue.*

tongs could be clamped to the temples, and second, to an awareness that the electric current was not only safe but painless since the animals quickly became unconscious. Further experimentation convinced Cerletti that electricity thus controlled was harmless. Recalling that convulsive treatment was said to be psychiatrically beneficial, Cerletti selected a catatonic schizophrenic human subject, a patient referred to him by the police. The rather startling results are described in Case History 22–2.

From this promising starting point, a regular course of treatment was developed, called either electroshock or electroconvulsive therapy (EST). The EST technique today is basically unchanged from Cerletti's original method. About 110–150 volts of alternating current are administered across the temples for a period of 0.8 of a second. The usual series is about 8 to 12 treatments, administered two to three times a week (treatment for bipolar or major depressions usually requires two to four sessions, two days apart) (Fink, 1978).

The EST series often begins with premedication involving sedatives or anesthetics as a measure to prevent the patient from developing unwarranted fears. (As Focus 22–2 illustrates, dosage is extremely important: the third account, by Margaret, describes the sensation when the patient still is able to feel the shock.) As soon as the current is applied, the person loses consciousness, undergoing a convulsion that subsides within less than a minute. The person is then turned on one side and made comfortable during recovery. Upon regaining consciousness, the individual feels confused, but recovers within 30 minutes.

***Risks of EST.*** The most common complications of EST are a marked memory loss and fractures. After

## Case History 22–2:
### The First Electroshock Treatment

The first use of electroshock was an experiment, performed by Ugo Cerletti on an incoherent male schizophrenic subject who had been referred to him by the police. Cerletti (1956) describes what happened:

> As soon as the current was introduced, the patient reacted with a jolt and his body muscles stiffened; then he fell back on the bed without loss of consciousness. He started to sing abruptly at the top of his voice, then he quieted down.
>
> The electrodes were applied again . . . we observed . . . the onset of the classic epileptic convulsion. We were all breathless . . . as we watched the cadaverous cyanosis. . . . *[Finally]* he arose to sitting position and looked at us, calm and smiling, as though to inquire what we wanted of him. We asked: "What happened to you?" He answered: "I don't know. Maybe I was asleep." Thus occurred the first electrically produced convulsion in man, which I at once named "electroshock." (p. 105)

After 13 electroshock treatments, the patient was conversing rationally and discharged as functioning normally.

## FOCUS 22–2:

### Electroshock Therapy: Three Accounts

EST, like the other drastic therapies, is controversial. The treatment is severe and may have unwanted side effects; yet in certain cases it has had success. Should this form of treatment be continued? The following three accounts illustrates some points of controversy over the question, even though they do not present a single clear answer.

*Mary* (A description by an objective onlooker):

> The nurses tucked a drawsheet around Mary and stationed themselves at her feet, head, and left side. "Bite on this mouthpiece," one of them told Mary, handing her a rubber bit. The nurse at the patient's head took up two pencil-like electrodes with flat, flanged bases and smeared contact jelly on them; she and Dr. Rosen then pressed the electrodes against Mary's temples. Dr. Rosen set the dials quickly and pushed the button. At once, Mary grunted deeply, and her head jerked back. "She's totally unconscious," Dr. Rosen told me. Her eyes were clenched shut, and her face was drawn into a tight, distorted mask. Her legs rose stiffly in the air, the toes and arches of her feet curled under, and her whole body now began spasmodically thrashing about. All three nurses kept hold of her, "riding," as Dr. Rosen said, with her motions to prevent self-damage. (Hunt, 1962, p. 32)

*Margaret* (A subjective, favorable description by a patient):

> "I volunteered. I had heard about shock treatment and I had reached a state where I *was* catatonic and I couldn't move my neck. My neck was like iron, as though that burden of guilt were lead on my back. I couldn't turn my head, I was so rigid . . . I had a very brief affair with a married man and the guilt was killing me . . . (Friedberg, 1976, p. 115).
>
> But I hadn't been able to smile for months and they took me down for the first treatment and I remember them putting me on this long table and putting a rubber gag in my mouth, then shooting my arm full of sodium pentothal and that's all I remember. When I woke up I was in my bed in my room and they brought me a cup of coffee and I smiled. It was a big deal. (p. 117)
>
> I had very transient loss of memory after each treatment. For instance, I wouldn't remember that I'd been strapped to the table, when I got back each time after treatment I was more sociable than ever . . . and my neck would turn in practically all directions . . . I was interacting with all the patients; in fact I spent Christmas there. And that was one of the most heartwarming Christmases I've ever spent. Imagine, in a psychiatric ward! (p. 118)
>
> [My mother] was going through the menopause . . . and it just hit her and she went loony, and finally I persuaded her to do something about it . . . started shock treatments. I had had such good fortune with them that I figured it would be the same with her. . . . She had forgotten that she had attempted suicide, she didn't know it and she never will. . . . she became herself again, just like I did. (p. 119–20)

*Dorothy* (A subjective, unfavorable description by a patient):

> Anyway, they would stick a needle in your arm, then they would put the oxygen—it wasn't a mask, but a mouthpiece kind of thing . . . they always raised your other arm in the air . . . then *zap,* it, it, um, I mean it went from temple to temple so fast that the whole thing all at once; I really and truly thought that I had exploded and that's all I remember . . . the next time . . I remember . . . saying, "Oh, by the way, last time I wasn't quite asleep, could you wait a bit longer this time?" (Friedberg, 1976, p. 47)
>
> From shock you wake up with a splitting headache, feeling very bad all over, and not knowing what happened. Not knowing why you had a headache. And you wouldn't know where you were; you'd be lying on this bed and after a while a nurse would come in and you would think, "Where am I?" And they would sit there and say, "Your name is so-and-so" (p. 47).
>
> It gradually wore off . . . But it wasn't just the headache, it was the fact that you were so confused, and you wouldn't know anybody; everybody would just sit there and nobody would know anybody, and the nurses would sit there and go, "And this is so-and-so, and this is so-and-so" (p. 48).
>
> Now I can read a book and I can tell you everybody's middle name and what they ate and everything, but I have no idea what it's about. I read book after book and I say, "Well, that was interesting, it was good characterization," and all this kind of stuff but someone says, "What was the book about?" and I say, "Well, it was about a person who . . .:" but what was the theme of the book? I can't grasp concepts, I just can't get any conceptual material (p. 50).

a dozen or so treatments, persons invariably experience at least a brief loss of memory for the period of treatment as did Elliot in Case History 22–1. Memory loss covering longer periods are rare, occurring in only 1 of every 100 patients treated with shock (Lagones, 1983). However, even a brief amnesia can be a source of extreme anxiety for some people whose sense of well-being is dependent on their intellect, memory and alertness. The most agonizing experience reported to the author was one former client's struggle to regain his identity and orientation after each EST session: "It's like waking up everyday not knowing who you are, where you are, why you're here, or where 'here' is. Maybe an animal wouldn't care, but I couldn't stand it." This type of extreme reaction is by no means typical, however, and amnesias from treatment generally vanish completely within six months. Fractures that occur tend to be compression fractures requiring no special treatment other than the use of a bedboard to support the mattress used by the patient. Fatalities are extremely rare: estimates range from 0.05 to 0.001 percent (Fink, 1977). In a series of 30,000 ESTs given at the Philadelphia General Hospital, only three deaths and 67 fractures resulted (61 of which were of the minor compression type) (Pearson, 1963).

***Results of EST.*** Although EST has enjoyed some mild success when used with schizophrenics, its most appropriate use appears to be for depressive conditions. Its value with manic conditions has been favorable in 60 to 90 percent of cases of acute manic activity, but the more recent development of lithium seems possibly as effective or even more effective. Further studies are needed to compare the relative benefits of EST and lithium before final conclusions can be drawn (Scovern & Kilmann, 1980).

It is noteworthy that a number of the few studies comparing EST against the tricyclic antidepressant drugs tend to favor shock therapy (Avery & Winokur, 1977).

In at least one follow-up study five years after initial recovery, 66 percent of the EST-treated patients remained improved (Bond, 1954), although follow-up data is generally very hard to obtain. A variety of studies have suggested that some patient characteristics may well be associated with greater likelihood of benefitting from EST. These include symptoms of agitation with the depression, presence of guilt, delusions, and psychomotor retardation. In a major review of work on EST, Scovern and Kilmann (1980) concluded that EST was superior to chemotherapy for some depressions and provides the added advantage of reducing the time of hospitalization. Multiple monitored electroconvulsive treatment (MMECT) uses repeated seizures during each session—for example, eight seizures with three-minute intervals. One report used MMECT with two patients who had shown no improvement after four weeks of tricylic therapy, but recovered from their depression and confusion within one week of MMECT (Goldfarb & Goldfarb, 1977).

### Psychosurgery

A third drastic therapy, brain surgery, was conceived by a Portuguese neurologist Egas Moniz following his attendance at an international neurological conference in London. There, Moniz heard of two chimpanzees who first became aggressive and belligerent from an experimental neurosis when facing irresolvable problems. After their frontal lobes were severed, the chimpanzees calmed down dramatically, as if "the animal[s] had joined the 'happiness cult' . . . and had placed [their] burdens on the Lord" (Freeman, 1968, p. 52). Convinced of the value of the approach, Moniz and his colleague Almeida Lima first performed psychosurgery on a human being in 1935. The patient chosen was an elderly woman suffering from depression, anxiety, and paranoia. She had also experienced manic episodes and had contracted syphilis as a young prostitute.

Moniz reasoned that mental disturbances arise from unhealthy synapses in certain regions of the brain; after hearing the report at the conference, he narrowed the area to that of the frontal lobes. By disconnecting the neural pathways, in a way similar to the chimpanzees' surgery, Moniz expected to force new neural relationships and therefore new psychological characteristics. His first patient was cured within two months after the her prefrontal lobotomy surgery and Moniz was awarded the Nobel Prize in 1949. Unfortunately, his career was ended suddenly when one of his

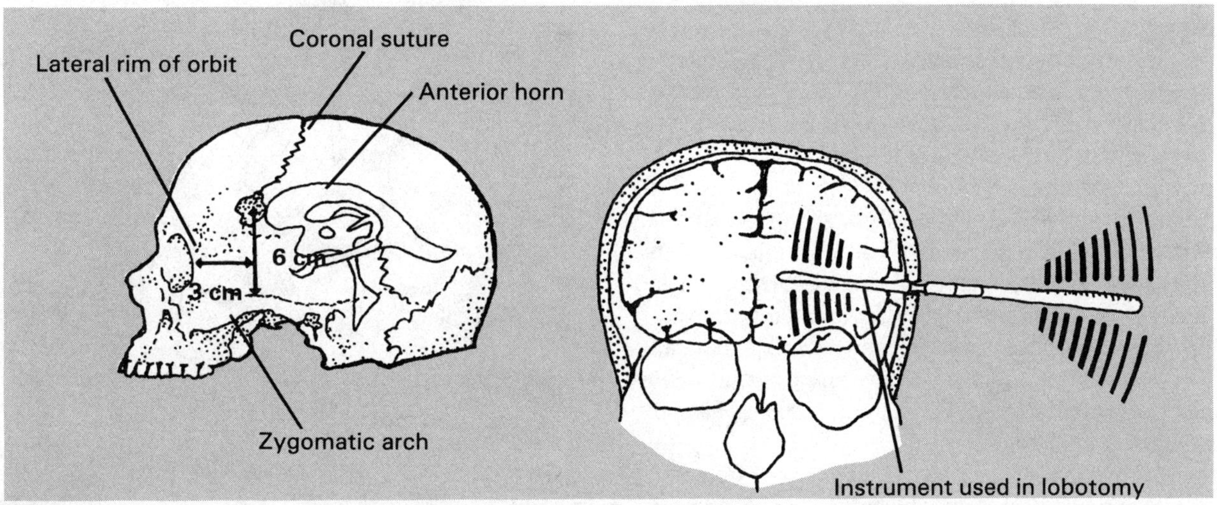


**FIGURE 22–2** Prefrontal lobotomy technique for the treatment of severe disturbances or control of intractable pain.

SOURCE: From "Prefrontal Lobotomy: Analysis and Warning" by K. Goldstein. 

lobotomized patients shot him (Scheflin & Opton, 1978).

***Surgical Methods.*** *Prefrontal lobotomy* or *leucotomy* is a surgical technique whereby a specially designed scalpel is inserted through holes drilled in the skull, severing the fibers connecting the frontal lobes with the rest of the brain (see Figure 22–2). It is currently hypothesized that the incision acts to separate conscious thoughts and ideas from disturbing emotions. This is illustrated in the fictional account of hospital life in *One Flew Over the Cuckoo's Nest* (Kesey, 1962), when a disruptive malingerer loses his rambunctiousness following surgery.

A variety of other surgical methods have now also been developed, including *topectomy, transorbital lobotomy, orbital undercutting,* various *cigulotomies,* and *capsulotomy.* Despite the uncomfortable image created by the novel, these various techniques and their results are being used all over the world, and reported at world congresses (Sweet et al., 1977). We will quickly describe each of these. *Topectomy* involves the destruction or removal of certain segments of the frontal lobe rather than total separation. *Transorbital lobotomy* is an elegant name for an inelegant procedure whereby a surgical instrument is stuck through the eye socket, thereby reaching and severing nerve tissue. Dr. Walter Freeman developed this procedure as a more efficient method for surgery, since it did not require cutting through bone and therefore could be completed more rapidly. Freeman estimated that 50 transorbital lobotomies could be done in the time it usually took for one prefrontal lobotomy. One person described Freeman's skill with this "icepick technique" (a gold-plated icepick-shaped surgical instrument was used) as follows, "He lifted up the eyelid and slid the icepick-like instrument over the eyeball. Then he would stab it suddenly . . . and move the pick from side to side to cut the brain. . . . He was proud of the fact that the [patients] *walked in* and *walked out.* None had to be carried." (Scheflin & Opton, 1978, p. 248).

A third technique, *orbital undercutting,* proceeds into the brain through holes above the eyes in the forehead. In *stereotactic surgery,* lesions are produced through implanting electrodes and sending a current through to severe neural connections. *Cingulotomy* and *capsulotomy* can be accomplished through the use of stereotactic instruments to precisely measure the location of the desired lesion and then to implant electrodes to conduct the current. Cingulotomy and capsulotomy simply refer to surgical techniques aimed at different locations.

**Risks of Psychosurgery.** The results of psychosurgery are permanent, since nerve fibers in the brain do not regenerate, and herein lies the primary risk of this treatment. In addition, research has yet failed to provide conclusive evidence to support beliefs either that lobotomy is indeed beneficial or that such techniques are completely valueless and should be banned. For these reasons, the main criterion used in prescribing psychosurgery is the presence of chronic mental disorder that has failed to respond to all other forms of treatment. Psychosurgery is considered by most authorities as a last resort procedure, relied on only when all else has failed and some form of treatment must be initiated (Teuber et al., 1977).

Perhaps more than any other medical treatment approach, psychosurgery also suffers from undesirable side effects or complications. The mortality rate ranges from 1.5 to 9 percent; and an additional 10 to 24 percent may become subject to convulsions, although this symptom is typically controllable by proper medication. Although changes in the psychological characteristics of the patient are a goal of surgery, certain unplanned changes also seem to result. Postoperative patients behave in a manner somewhat similar to brain-injured patients, showing impaired abstract ability, poorer planning, perceptual confusion and stereotyping of words when problem solving (Walsh, 1977). In some, personality changes may include transitory loss of ambition and spontaneity, lack of consideration for others, hostile outbursts, and a lowering of standards (Smith et al., 1977).

**Effects of Surgery.** Despite the dangers involved, a number of reports on the effectiveness of psychosurgery have been somewhat favorable. International conferences are able to attract many medical reports of success with various surgical techniques, with studies suggesting that results vary according to the nature of the disorder (Sweet et al., 1977). Peraita and deLerma (1977) reported their best results with obsessive-compulsives, but poor results with anxiety disorders. In a review of the literature, Flor-Henry (1977) concluded that intractable cases could be best alleviated through lesions in specific locations (orbital-frontal for the affective disorders, cingulate lesions for obsessives, and amygdaloid lesions for explosive personalities.

*A scene in an early twentieth-century mental hospital. Modern* **therapeutic techniques** *have provided hope for patients such as these.*

Scoville and Bettis (1977) kept records on 109 operations by one surgeon over 20 years, with a variety of types of patients, and rated 76 percent improved. They even reported that "Physicians, lawyers, executives, and engineers have all been able to return to their occupations, and six patients obtained higher degrees of education *after* their surgery. In fact, one patient became chairman of the board of a large insurance company."

These studies indicate some positive results, but it should be emphasized that effects as complicated as those of surgery are very difficult to evaluate. Sykes and Tredgold (1964) produced an informative report that points out the problems of lobotomy studies. Their work—an examination of 177 patients operated on from 1951 to 1960—found that 85 percent showed improvements following surgery. However, additional examination of their information shows that while this improvement included some symptoms, other symptoms remained that still required some treatment. In actuality, only 53 percent had shown improvement to the degree that either the symptoms were completely removed or no further therapy was demanded. Critics of lobotomy and other surgical approaches have often questioned the validity of counting patients as improved where this means that further treatment is still needed.

## EVALUATION

Many questions have been raised about the ethics of the drastic therapies (Valenstein, 1980). These questions, parenthetically, also apply to any therapy method, but they are especially relevant here because of the permanent change that both EST and psychosurgery can bring about.

Friedberg (1976) contends that the use of shock is an ''outrage'' against humanity and dignity and reports on interviews with 15 patients who agreed; two are quoted in Case History 22–3. Electroshock therapy has now been banned in Berkeley, California, as a result of a public vote initiated by Ted Chabasinski, a former mental patient. This ban received 60 percent of the popular vote, despite opposition by the American Psychiatric Association (Cunningham, 1983). Neville (1975) offers the most philosophically relevant arguments against psychosurgery, asking a number of pointed questions. Is it sufficient to obtain consent from a guardian or even from a patient who is mentally disordered? What rights does a person have simply as a human being—over and above being a patient who must be 'cured'? Who is to determine what behaviors must be 'controlled' in our society? Is surgery still basically an experiment?

Answers to such ethical dilemmas have been offered (Laitinen, 1977), but the issue is still clearly a dilemma. Dagi (1977) suggests the similarity in decisionmaking about surgery in general, for example, in amputations and calls for the use of great care in making a decision which is basically still a judgment. Andy (1977) calls for a collaboration between medical and legal authorities to insure individual rights. However, this physician says that ''psychosurgery is a medical and not a sociological problem'' and that in the final analysis, the decision is between the doctor and patient, with the guideline that the practice of medicine must be scientifically, morally, and ethically sensitive.

## SUMMARY

Modern medicine has progressed a long way from the trephining of skulls. The most impressive gains are clearly in the area of chemotherapy. There is strong evidence that the phenothiazines are valuable for schizophrenia, strong support for the value of lithium for manic episodes or to prevent recurring bipolar states, and good evidence for the tricyclic drugs for depressions.

Electroshock therapy has surprising support as a quick treatment for depressive episodes, and apparently to a degree better than the tricyclic drugs (although there is some disagreement). Psychosurgery has many supporters, but the evidence for support tends to lack the desirable control of careful scientific designs.

Clearly most of the medical therapies are symptomatic treatments. That is, they provide relief but do not always mean that complete recovery has occurred. Certainly relief is valuable, as the use of drugs, shock, or even psychosurgery might free the patient from incapacitating symptoms. Managing the emotional turmoil can be an important step towards controlling and eventually eliminating the source of disturbance. And in fact, attention is being directed towards ways to effectively combine therapies—such as drug treatment with psychotherapy—for more permanent results (Greenblatt, 1975).

The medical therapies will continue to form a strong base for treatment. In the United States, the primary medical therapy will probably be chemotherapy, with some retention of electroshock in hospital systems and very little psychosurgery (Asnis et al., 1978). Finally, a value of biologically oriented treatment is the possible new insights they might provide, either systematically or serendipitously, into the causes of mental disorders. If drugs which specifically affect neurotransmitters can effect improvements in symptoms, then this could be a step towards further research; and this in turn might shed light on the chain of events that precipitate some disorders.

## KEY TERMS

**Chemotherapy**
**Chlorpromazine**
**Energizers, psychic**
**Electroshock therapy**
**Imipramine**
**Insulin convulsive therapy**
**Iproniazid**
**Lobotomy**
**MAO-inhibitors**
**Monoamine oxidase (MAO)**
**Phenothiazine**
**Placebo**
**Psychosurgery**
**Reserpine**
**Tranquilizers**
**Tricyclics**

# CHAPTER 23

## The Therapies: Community Mental Health

- **What is meant by the community mental health movement? What are its fundamental principles?**
- **Why might a person prefer to be treated at home instead of in a residential psychiatric hospital?**
- **How do mobile vans and telephones fit into mental health protection?**
- **We know the steps for preventing certain physical epidemics. Can similar steps be used to prevent mental disorders?**
- **What have studies revealed about the high risk children?**
- **What did the studies of the red-tag children reveal about secondary prevention?**
- **Community psychology suggests that mental health is everyone's responsibility. What roles can nonprofessionals play in community mental health programs?**
- **President John F. Kennedy urged the development of community mental health approaches. How much progress have we made through these approaches?**
- **What criticisms of the community mental health movement have been pointed out by Ralph Nader's consumer study group?**

## Case History 23–1:
### Outpatient Help for Life Stress

Casey F. has lived a marginal existence most of his life. His father was a heavy drinker and gambler, seldom able to hold a job, and so Casey's mother was the sole supporter of her six children.

As an adult, Casey became a migrant farm worker. Drifting became a way of life, from harvest to harvest, and farm to farm. During this period, Casey seemed to experience little: he kept to himself, read little, spent little on entertainment, and made no friends. Because of injury from a fall, Casey was hospitalized. While in the hospital, Casey met another patient, a woman named Cynthia whose husband had recently died. Cynthia took an interest in Casey, gave him a ride back to her farm, and the two began to find reasons to visit each other. They were soon married.

Within a year after the wedding, Cynthia decided they would sell the farm and move to the city. The first few months after the move were a period of high spending: the couple did and saw everything, under Cynthia's dominant direction. This lifestyle was soon disturbed, however, when Cynthia delivered twin daughters. Hospital and pediatrician bills now added to the usual costs of rent, food, and transportation. In addition to his janitorial job, Casey began moonlighting with a second afternoon job.

As the months passed, life became more hectic. Cynthia began leaving the house for hours at a time, claiming the need for time off from child care. This left Casey with less time to sleep, more household chores, and the demanding responsibility of the twins. He began experiencing headaches, heart palpitations, and waves of nausea and fright; he found it hard to sleep despite his fatigue.

Eventually, Casey had to ask a fellow worker to cover for him and was forced to explain the reasons. The worker gave Casey the address of a store front close by, urging Casey to stop there. He did and was surprised to discover the staff dressed in common workers clothes and that the agency was in a low-rent building, with surplus furniture. The staff told him they were there to help solve problems, but they were willing to listen first. Reluctantly, Casey spoke of his vague fears and his physical symptoms . . . but when he was asked to describe his life situation, he quickly left. He was unwilling to return to the agency, which he soon discovered was a mental health clinic.

One day, a staff member saw Casey at the gas station, started a friendly conversation, and asked Casey to meet over dinner. Casey acquiesced, felt more at ease, and agreed to stop at the clinic on a daily basis. Discussions at the clinic covered a variety of topics: money management; the use of child-care help; and ways to protect some funds under his own name. They have made a difference. Casey is more aware of his pressures, his confusion over Cynthia's attitudes, and his own sense of helplessness and anger. His headaches have diminished, and he reports that his life seems less like a jail sentence. However, there have been recent signs that the headaches are returning as Casey has begun to talk about a possible separation or divorce.

Casey's story illustrates an innovative and highly stimulating approach to treatment, that has sometimes been called mental health's third revolution (the first being the reforms where persons with disorders were treated as human beings worthy of dignity and the second being the development of psychoanalysis as a true psychological treatment method) (Hobbs, 1964).

This third revolution, *community mental health,* is both a concept and a practice. The concept is actually a philosophy of what better treatment techniques should entail: such techniques should be applied to large groups of people; should be available to groups of people in their own environment or community; should be aimed at helping the community to develop resources for future solutions; and should be committed towards prevention and not simply treatment. As a practice, community mental health has encompassed a variety of approaches, ranging from crisis hot line telephone counseling services to the more formal community mental health centers assigned to neighborhoods. Tasks of community psychology have included coordinating community services or resource centers; training paraprofessional workers and volunteers; screening for early detection of high risk populations such as children at risk; advocacy programming to induce social systems changes; and consultation with traditional agents who contact many people as part of their jobs (for instance, police officers, teachers, clergy, community leaders, and even bartenders).

## ARGUMENTS FOR COMMUNITY-BASED CARE

The notions and practices that are basic to the community mental health movement represent a common-sense approach. A primary reason behind the movement's development was a sense of dissatisfaction with the existing facilities that provided medical and psychological therapies. One area of dissatisfaction can be found in the lack of success, and even harmfulness, of long-term hospitalization for severely disturbed persons. Consider the effects of being in a psychiatric hospital over a length of time:

- Hospitalization takes you away from persons important to you, including supportive members of your family and friends. Particularly for a child, this can be a difficult move.
- The impact of being in a hospital can be traumatic. Goffman (1961) poignantly described the dehumanizing quality of the large isolated state mental hospital, supporting other writers who found that mental institutions had shifted toward the goal of protecting *institutional* goals to the detriment of patient care (Rosenhan, 1973; Shiloh, 1971). Not infrequently, for example, a patient would be placed in a locked ward, for management purposes rather than for therapeutic purposes. Patients were threatened with restraints if they did not behave, rather than helped to reach recovery from their illness. Focus 23–1 describes the first-hand experience of some normal research subjects who committed themselves to institutions to see what hospitalization was like.

Hospitalization over long periods can cause personality changes. These effects are sometimes referred to as *institutionalism* or *institutional neurosis* (Barton, 1966). Such changes may include apathy, loss of initiative, submissiveness, a lack of interest in things not in the immediate present, and an inability to make plans for the future. In fact, patients reached a point where they even resisted discharge rather than give up their new, passive patterns of institutionalism. After a period of two years of hospital care, less than 30 percent of the patients interviewed by Wing (1962) expressed an interest or desire in returning to the community.

Hospitalization can be costly and inefficient. Small numbers of professional staff must care for the great number of patients, and this shortage is further complicated by the long time it takes to train enough therapists to alleviate the need. The traditional roles of psychiatrists or psychologists in hospital settings have been those of therapists or administrators; such activities consume a major portion of the time, especially if the therapy is conducted on a one-therapist-to-one-patient model. Meanwhile, many patients are left waiting to be seen in treatment, sitting in the hospital wards in an unproductive atmosphere.

# FOCUS 23–1:
## Hospitalization: Horror or Help?

Hospitalization has long been considered a suitable means of helping persons with mental disorders. However, many institutions have also been criticized as impersonal places that may provide medication, but not warmth or understanding. A few studies have entered mental hospitals in order to discover first-hand if the experience is helpful or harmful.

In 1968, Goldman had two colleagues admit themselves to an institution (Goldman et al., 1970). Bohr, a social psychologist, posed as an acutely depressed person; Steinberg, a clinical psychologist, acted as a chronic psychotic. Only Goldman knew they were really normal.

Two immediate changes occurred in these otherwise healthy psychologists following hospitalization. First, both experienced extreme boredom, the most meaningful events being negotiations over what menial chores they could to in exchange for privileges. The second major effect was a burning desire to escape. One man became so distraught after only one week that he planned an elaborate escape route. In a personal message to the author, Goldman (1971) revealed that the experience was so traumatic that one subject refused to discuss his reactions following hospital discharge.

A second study had similar findings. Rosenhan (1973) had eight normal persons admitted as patients. Each reported hearing voices that said ''hollow'' or ''thud.'' Once admitted, however, all behaved normally, and they attempted to convince ward personnel that they were normal. It took 7 to 52 days for these eight pseudopatients to convince the staff to discharge them; and even then, they were classified not as cured, but as ''in remission.''

These two reports raise a variety of issues. Both suggest that trained hospital staff may overlook healthy behaviors and may fail to provide helpful care. The Goldman group felt they were used as slave labor to get distasteful chores done; the Rosenhan group reported that their normal behaviors were interpreted as symptoms of disorders. A second controversy centers around the ease with which the diagnoses were made. Rosenhan argues that the diagnostic process must be faulted if a person with only one symptom (auditory hallucinations) can be labelled *schizophrenic,* as his subjects were. This point has been contested, however. Spitzer (1976) argues that hallucinations alone often do signify severe psychosis since other symptoms may temporarily not be in evidence.

A final issue concerns the hospital environment. The subjective experiences of the Goldman and Rosenhan groups certainly point out the potential harm of some institutional environments. It should be remembered, though, that not all hospitals fit this description; and data seems to argue for hospitalization in some instances, too.

## SOME INNOVATIVE SERVICES

As a response to the inadequacies, inefficiency, and problems of hospitalization, the mental health movement has developed over a period of time. In 1955 Congress established the Joint Commission on Mental Illness and Mental Health to analyze and evaluate mental health needs and to make recommendations for national mental health programs. In 1963, President John F. Kennedy delivered the first address by any head of state to Congress on the issue of mental health.

Kennedy's message urged a ''bold new approach'' and called for federally supported programs to organize, initiate, and staff a nationwide network of community mental health centers. Such centers were to provide services along new concepts, including part-time treatment rather than full-time hospitalization, emergency or crisis services, consultation, and education. Soon after, Congress approved the first funds to begin the major task. Between 1964 and 1968, some $232 million was made available. This amount is roughly equivalent to the sum required to operate the New York Department of Mental Hygiene for only five months; nevertheless it did provide the impetus needed to foster the new trends toward community care.

*A new community approach has been the* ***crisis center*** *such as this one for women.*

The basic goals of mental health centers are to improve on the organization and the delivery of services, to stimulate and mobilize resources within the community itself, and to provide effective care to all people who need it. Currently, community mental health centers are located in diverse areas, from the ghetto to the affluent community, within both small towns and large urban centers. Innovative means of meeting community mental health needs are encouraged. These include small, *mobile treatment teams* which bring treatment to people instead of requiring them to travel for therapy; *day hospitalization,* which permits a person to return home to be with family in the evenings; *night hospitalization,* which permits people to maintain jobs during the day, returning for treatment after work; *halfway houses* operated and maintained by persons who lack living resources, but no longer need hospital care; *consultation programs* to help community personnel be more effective in promoting mental health; and *telephone hotlines* to deal quickly with emergencies on a 24-hour basis for emotional problems, suicide prevention, drug reactions, or other crises (Greene & de la Cruz, 1981). Community mental health centers are attempting to tailor-make their services to fit the needs and characteristics of the communities they serve. Thus, mental health workers have been a part of the Peace Corps, VISTA, Head Start, the Job Corps, and other similar action programs.

The services just described represent several by-products of the community mental health movement; more crucial to the movement are some of the fundamental principles and outlooks on which it is based. Two foundation stones—the concept of prevention, and the idea of community-based care—are particularly important in understanding how the movement represents an alternative to institutional care. We'll look at each of these principles in the remainder of this chapter.

## PREVENTION

A basic element in the community mental health approach is its emphasis on prevention. Whereas other approaches have emphasized therapy for existing pathology, the community approach has added the idea of preventing problems from developing in the first place, where possible. The community psychology orientation offers some significant priorities. First, prevention has greater priority over treatment; second, early treatment has greater priority over treatment after the problem has progressed to a chronic stage; third, solving immediate situational stresses has greater priority over depth analysis or complete resolution of intrapsychic conflicts; and finally, confronting here-and-now problems and restoring an individual to a reasonable level of functioning have priority over curing long-standing disturbances of acquiring insight. When considering prevention itself as the main priority, the community mental health movement has borrowed some ideas from the medical field of public health in identifying levels of prevention (Bloom, 1965). The three levels in order of priority are known as primary prevention, secondary prevention, and tertiary prevention.

### Primary Prevention

*Primary prevention* refers to reducing the incidence of problems; in other words, reducing the rate of occurrence of new cases. Thus, the first priority is to prevent what is preventable. In the medical field of public health, examples of primary prevention would include the use of immunization to prevent illnesses such as diphtheria or certain types of influenza or the draining of swamps to prevent the breeding of mosquitoes which may cause malaria. In the mental health field, primary prevention would involve parent-effectiveness training to teach new parents child-rearing approaches, educational programs on drug use, the prevention of sexism in early school materials, and prenatal health programs aimed at preventing organically caused disorders that can arise out of ignorance—for instance, about Rh incompatibility, syphilis, or rubella (Dangel & Polster, 1983; MacQuiddy & Hamilton, 1983).

One major line of study involves the question of what early signs provide clues of later vulnerability to pathology (Tarter, 1983). If we know how to detect which children, for example, are at risk, then primary prevention can be carried out. Mednick and Schulsinger (1973) examined risk among children in Denmark because of the comprehensiveness of the Danish system: there, every resident's address is listed throughout life, and a National Psychiatric Register keeps up-to-date records of all psychiatric hospitalizations throughout the country. As we saw in Chapter 17, a group of *high-risk* children were selected, coming from families where the mothers had been hospitalized as schizophrenics. Another group of *low-risk* children without schizophrenic mothers were matched as a comparison group. The first findings showed that high-risk children had more birth difficulties such as longer deliveries or more abnormal placentas; showed mild association disorders when tested on a word association task; and tended to be rated as poorly adjusted although they performed adequately in school.

After five years, the authors noticed that 20 high-risk youngsters had begun to show abnormal behaviors. They were quickly matched with 20 other high-risk subjects who remained normal in order to determine what factors seemed to separate the two. The results were interesting: the abnormal youngsters' mothers had been hospitalized when their children were younger, the youngsters tended to be disciplinary problems in school, birth complications of a serious nature were more characteristic, and finally, these abnormal youngsters possessed quicker physiological reactions to auditory stress stimuli, faster recovery times, and more generalization to nonstress stimuli. Of special interest was the finding that none of the fathers of the high-risk youngsters who had remained psychologically healthy had a psychiatric history himself; on the other hand, seven fathers of the disturbed youths had now received psychiatric treatment.

As a contribution towards primary prevention, the findings of Mednick and Schulsinger suggest the importance of several prevention programs: prenatal and obstetric programs, programs focusing on socialized behavior development, and perhaps programs for aiding the remaining nonhospitalized parent to retain a positive mental health structure. Other studies attempting to identify early signs of high risk are continuing, including a follow-up on physiological hyperreactivity, social or psychological competence, and even the role of social climate in the family, educational, or work environments (Mednick & Witkin-Lanoil, 1977; Garmezy et al., 1979; Shure & Spivack, 1979; Katoff, 1984). For mental retardation, we have already described the prevention program of the Milwaukee Project where specially designed stimulation led to higher IQs among high-risk children (See Chapter 19).

### Secondary Prevention

*Secondary prevention* involves the reduction of the *prevalence* of problems—in other words, reducing the number of already existing illnesses. Community health services aim at reducing the prevalence of disorders by taking measures to shorten their duration. Such services involve making early, prompt, and effective treatment available.

Programs for the early identification of disorders fall into the secondary prevention category, and they include consultation services to family physicians, clergymen, teachers, police, and court officials (Mulvey & Reppucci, 1981). The Joint Commission on Mental Illness and Mental Health discovered that 71 percent of persons in need of psychiatric help went first to their family physician or clergy. Thus, these individuals are seen as resource persons, who could be of invaluable help in referring such patients for immediate mental health care. Some mental disorders, such as the adjustment disorders and post-traumatic stress disorders, are subject to early termination or can be arrested if early treatment is sought. Community mental health work can be aimed here at certain target populations who are particularly subject to stresses, such as prospective parents, adolescents, and migrants. Those subject to grief and bereavement reactions might also be included, primarily the elderly (Getzel & Mellar, 1984).

Cowen and Zax (1969) have spearheaded an exciting example of secondary prevention and its positive results (Cowen et al., 1975). They first divided all first-grade children in three elementary schools into two groups: red-tag and non-red-tag. Red-tag children were those who showed some level of disturbance or maladjustment. In following these children for three years, through the third grade, the red-tag children showed poorer academic achievement and were rated by teachers and peers as more maladjusted. Adjustment problems persisted into the seventh grade. For one of the three elementary schools, secondary prevention programming was developed for the red-tag children through teachers and parents. Later, aides were trained to work outside of the class with some children; these aides were women selected primarily for their interest in children, personal warmth, and outgoing dispositions. In contrast to the red-tag children without intervention programs, those receiving help showed better adjustment ratings, class grades, and reading achievement scores than control children.

### Tertiary Prevention

The third priority is to reduce the residual effects of disorders that have not been prevented, terminated, or arrested. Community mental health services should aim at services to minimize any residuals that may persist long after a disorder has ended. It is recognized that some disorders may not be reached early enough either to be prevented or to be treated early; hence, hospitalization or long-term treatment may be required. Following treatment, however, a person can be helped to overcome certain aftereffects.

Included in tertiary prevention are aftercare programs such as halfway houses or educational programs aimed at helping people deal with the return to a normal community life. Also involved may be services of a vocational nature, such as *sheltered workshops* (job settings with an accepting atmosphere). Educational programs directed at fostering a more enlightened and understanding attitude among the general public can help to remove stigmas or fears about former mental patients—an issue addressed by Chris Sizemore, of the Three Faces of Eve, in Chapter 8. Fundamentally, the objective is to help persons return to maximum economic and social productivity as quickly as possible.

## COMMUNITY-BASED CARE: SOME OUTLOOKS

The concept of prevention is one critical element in the community mental health movement. Another foundation, the idea of centering care in the community is also basic. The concept of community-based care is a focal point for many new, related outlooks (LaFollette & Pilisuk, 1981). We will discuss several of these outlooks and the services they have fostered.

### Increasing Patient Competency

Psychological disorders must be viewed not simply as maladaptive ways of life, but as immediate life problems that demand solution. Because pathology is seen as a lowered level of competency, the task of therapy is seen as increasing the patient's competency (Garmezy et al., 1979; White, 1979).

An excellent example of an attempt to reach this goal is the Project Re-Ed Program (Hobbs, 1966, 1974). Here, emotionally disturbed children were looked on in terms of their abilities rather than their deficiencies. Competence and self fulfillment objectives were stressed, rather than illness and pathology. Through this program, two institutions were organized: the Cumberland House Elementary School in Nashville, Tennessee, and the Write School in Durham, North Carolina. Goals were to be achieved through social intervention relying on a 24-hour planned schedule of desired behaviors and contingency management. The result was a success of 80 percent with increases in social maturity and social adjustment, and decreases in symptoms reported by parents.

### Increasing Outpatient Care

A second developing outlook is the view that hospitalization should not be considered as the solution for all persons. In fact, patients should be kept away from mental hospital care where feasible. Services should aim at keeping people living and functioning in their natural community environment, a goal sought for Ca-

*With the development of **medical therapies,** many patients who might have remained hospitalized have been able to return home.*

sey B. in Case History 23–1. The Kings County Hospital in Brooklyn, New York, initiated a procedure directed at providing *outpatient* care, with the patient living outside the hospital. This service involved providing immediate treatment in the hospital admitting office, with further appointments scheduled once or twice per week on an outpatient basis. Patients could arrange for more frequent visits or for crisis appointments, if necessary. This treatment approach proved to be sufficient for most patients. Of 392 who were screened over a 6-month period, only 13 percent could not be retained on an outpatient basis and had to be hospitalized. It may be tempting to dismiss such findings on the grounds that the patients probably were not so severely disturbed in the first place—yet 60 percent of the 392 patients were diagnosed as psychotic (Waltzer et al., 1963).

The Kings County Hospital approach suggests that an active outpatient treatment service can achieve goals not previously achieved by many long-term custodial programs. Similar results have been achieved elsewhere. In Denver, Colorado, 24 of the first 25 patients screened in a new program were able to remain in their homes and avoid hospitalization (Pittman et al., 1965). The Denver treatment team emphasized an active problem-solving approach, viewing psychoses

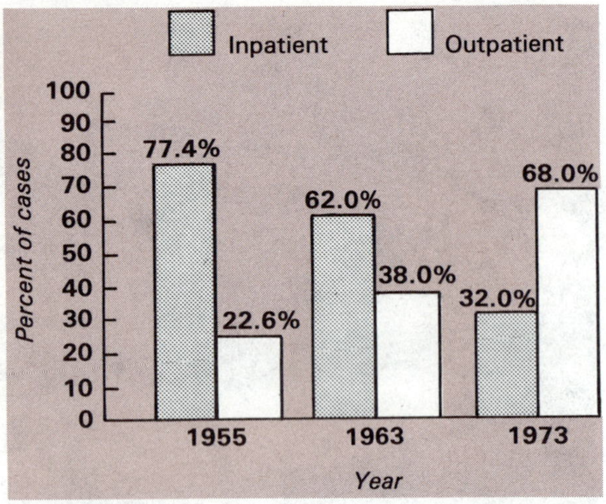


**FIGURE 23–1** Percent of psychiatric cases seen in inpatient and outpatient settings over a quarter century.
SOURCE: Adapted from "A Quarter Century of Psychiatric Care, 1950–1974: A Statistical Review" by L. Ozarin, R. Redick & C. Taube, 1976, *Hospital and Community Psychiatry, 27*, pp. 515–519.

as family crises rather than as illness. Outpatient treatment has grown tremendously in the past few decades. As Figure 23–1 shows, proportions of inpatient and outpatient treatment have nearly doubled since 1955, so that today far more persons are treated on an outpatient basis.

### Outreach Programs

A third outlook of community-based care is the idea that treatment should be mobile rather than stationary. Treatment teams should reach out into the community to provide services, rather than waiting for people to report for treatment at inconveniently located clinics.

A number of studies attest to the validity—also to the efficacy—of this idea. Pasamanick et al. (1967) were able to compare home-administered drug treatment and hospital treatment for schizophrenic persons. They found that over 77 percent of the group treated at home were able to avoid hospitalization; while the group who were hospitalized remained under hospital care for an average of 83 days. Another study sent treatment teams into the homes of psychiatric patients (Friedman et al., 1960). These teams were able to treat 60 percent of these cases without requiring hospital admissions. A third example of removing treatment from the hospital setting was a unique walk-in mental health service in San Francisco, called a psychomat. Mental health professionals made themselves available at public rooms at advertised times, and people within the community could drop in and use the service in whatever way they wished (Greening & Haigh, 1968). Other ways in which immediate help is brought to individuals are through mental health teams cruising in mobile units with radios and through crisis telephone calling centers, such as the suicide hot lines discussed in Chapter 16 (Echterling & Wylie, 1981).

### Consultation Services

Another outlook for community-based care concerns broadening of services. Mental health professionals should broaden their services to include consultation as well as direct treatment (Cooper & Hodges, 1983; Berlin, 1979); further, other community resource personnel should be sought who contribute to the mental health objectives. As mentioned previously, early identification of people who need help can often be accomplished by family physicians, clergymen, and teachers. These community members may also be able to help persons who are cautiously seeking help to make contact, by making appropriate referrals.

In some cases, professional persons such as teachers can provide adaptive skills training, given help from consultants (Morse & Ravlin, 1979). Treatment programs can be devised by traveling consultants, then implemented by select community persons. Suinn and Cole (1971) sent traveling consultation teams to work with teachers at centers for the mentally retarded. Within one morning, they were able to consult with these teachers regarding problems and design behavior modification programs tailor-made for each referral question. Telephone follow-up calls were used weekly to determine the progress of the teachers in their implementation of the programs.

### Involving Members of the Community

Finally, mental health services should be considered as a community project, involving members of the community in its planning, support, and usage. The traditional concept that treatment services are the business and sole concern of a few specialists must be discarded: this concept has divested family, friends, employers, and city officials from a responsible role in the treatment process; and it fosters the belief that disorders are a defect of the individual, rather than a response to the environment.

Although federal support gave the impetus to the community mental health movement, its survival depends on continued support from the very community served by the mental health centers. As an example, the success of a community mental health program in San Mateo, California, was at least partly the result of the participation by 23 of the 38 community psychiatrists. Each offered at least two hours of time per week to the service. Additionally, some 17 different community agencies cooperated (Chope, 1959).

Specially trained psychiatric help is not always available, however, and so paraprofessionals are playing a more and more significant role in treatment services (Carey et al., 1984). A *paraprofessional* is basically an individual without formal mental health professional training. Under the supervision of professionals, paraprofessionals have been shown effective in helping relations. Suinn (1972) has involved undergraduate students in behavior modification consultation. The paraprofessional students worked with Headstart and preschool teachers for one to two hours, assessing the nature of problems. A behavior modification program is then designed, given the facilities and resources available to the teacher in question. Precise step-by-step advice is provided, along with concrete methods for determining the progress of the program.

There are many other instances of effective use of paraprofessionals. Carkhuff and Truax (1965) have reported improvement in chronic hospitalized patients treated by paraprofessional staff. Staats et al. (1970) have taken black homemakers and minority group students and relied on them to implement a behavior modification reading program for ghetto children. Retired persons (Cowen et al., 1968), homemakers (Katkin et al., 1971), and high school students (Tefft & Kloba, 1981) have been successfully used in treatment programs, thereby opening up a potentially major source for dealing with the shortage of professional help.

## EVALUATION

The major impact of what has been called the community mental health movement has been in the development of community mental health centers stimulated by federal funds. There is no question that such centers have offered services not otherwise possible to local communities and have made the public more aware of the value of psychological services. Some innovations have developed beyond these centers, so that many communities now offer crisis hot lines, store front neighborhood centers, social action programs that take into account mental health issues, and paraprofessional and volunteer programs. Through such innovations, more than one million persons have received services that might not otherwise have been accessible (Holahan et al., 1979).

The concept of prevention has evolved to the degree that this topic is now represented in books which ordinarily would have focused only on therapy (Franks, 1974; Lichtenstein, 1980). And, as we noted earlier, a number of exciting longitudinal studies have been developed that cast light on the factors associated with early risk. As an offshoot of this, more attention is being placed on children and youth in order to prevent maladjustment early.

As community psychology expands its horizons to recognize that maladjustment is influenced by the whole social fabric, current studies are now exploring topics such as ecology and the environments and social systems and their climate. And since such topics relate to social change, many mental health professionals are recognizing the importance of social action, for example, on poverty, civil rights, sexism, legal rights for children, and unemployment (Bass et al., 1982; Hersch, 1972).

### Criticisms of the Community Mental Health Movement

Despite these advances, there are also many cogent criticisms of the community mental health field. For one, few good studies permit evaluating the actual impact of such programs on the overall mental health status of our society (Moitoza & Hersch, 1981). Has there been a decrease in the incidence or prevalence of mental illness or an increase in competency and mental health as a *direct result* of these programs? Because of the very complexity of the community environment and of programs, the topic resists carefully controlled research. Part of the problem of evaluation is simply that many mental health workers are so committed to providing service for those who need help that the value of conducting research or evaluating outcomes must take a lower priority. And for programs aimed at prevention, for example through helping children at risk, there may not even be agreement about the value of the outcomes. For example, although being a disciplinary problem in school seems associated with ratings of maladjustment later, some would argue that the disciplinary problem exists only in the eyes of the teacher-raters, and that the problem would disappear if the teachers were taught to be more tolerant. Similarly, if competency training or socialization enhances future mental health, some may argue that socialization only produces conformity to a set of standards; and who is to define what standards are desirable?

Perhaps the most visible criticism of the community movement is voiced in the book *The Madness Establishment* (Chu & Trotter, 1974)—actually a report of the findings of Ralph Nader's study group. The book articulates some concerns that have been mentioned by mental health professionals themselves. First, the number of community mental health centers actually in existence has fallen far short of the proposed federal goal (400 centers instead of 2,000). Since such goals reflect the mood of Congress and its leaders, even this progress is always subject to change. Next, the report suggests that community centers have not been valuable, if their value can be judged by the number of admissions to state mental hospitals. Hospital admissions have not decreased and may have increased since the community mental health movement has begun. Another criticism has been that the centers have not truly incorporated a community involvement. Community persons do not tend to serve on policy boards; centers are sometimes not easily accessible; and they may still be under the control of psychiatrist–directors who remain tied to traditional one-on-one therapy models. One critic accuses ''mental health professionals as a group as often [having] . . . a minimum understanding of, and little commitment to, the need for primary prevention . . . [since] most of their formal education emphasizes techniques of treatment rather than principles of prevention'' (Okin, 1977).

Finally, with the increase in ethnic minority persons in the United States, and with evidence that these minorities tend to underutilize services, a need is felt for more culturally relevant community programs (Ruiz, 1982; Sue & Moore, 1983). Beyond simply having bilingual staff members, improvements could include awareness of the attitudes of minority clients towards therapy itself, differences in ways of explaining symptoms, and differences in expectations about what constitutes useful therapy. The author recalls seeing a videotape of a Hispanic laborer being treated from a nondirective, feeling-oriented perspective, who finally exploded with, ''Feelings, feelings, feelings, I know what you want me to talk about, but all this talk is not going to help me to know what to do different in my life!'' The problem was a combination of the lack of the student-therapist's experience, complicated by the Hispanic client's expectations about the worthlessness of talk and his desire for direct guidance. The need for community health services to be tuned in to the community's perceptions as well as mental health needs is discussed in Focus 23–2.

To conclude, the criticisms cannot be overlooked. At the same time, the strengths of the community mental health orientation also cannot be ignored. Criticisms are damaging only if they do not lead to change and improvement (Mollica, 1983). Strengths are supportive only if they continue to be maintained and used. Perhaps the community movement will never reach the ideal, simply because of limits of social reality. Yet, the positive signs are there, and the philosophy of community mental health—including the concept of prevention—must remain if the approach toward mental illness and mental health is to be truly holistic.

## SUMMARY

Therapy can involve a variety of factors: a psychological approach in the psychotherapies, drugs or drastic therapies in medical treatment, or a change of orienta-

# FOCUS 23–2:

## Evaluating Minority Community Needs

One therapy problem that has captured the interest of some community mental health practitioners centers around the fact that the people in the community may view mental disorders very differently than does the therapist. Higginbotham (1979) proposes a model for developing culturally relevant programs.

A first step is to define the minority group's beliefs about the causes of deviant behavior. A symptom may be explained as being caused by a hex, for example. Thus, an Indian war veteran who felt unable to readjust to civilian life was cured of his apathy by the medicine man—who used a new blessing to terminate the warrior blessing which had initially prepared him for warfare.

Another important step is to define attitudes that may relate to symptomatic behaviors. Attitudes may include the belief that a person is responsible to the family or to the neighbors. In a case of a Hispanic depressed woman, the *cuarandera* (healing woman) attributed her depression to the accusatory beliefs of the neighbors. Therapy involved having the neighbors release their hostility by symbolically stoning the woman with balls of paper, after which forgiveness was granted and the woman's depression lifted (Widener, 1983).

A third step is to recognize the specified ways in which different cultural groups may explain disorders or life events, and what solutions are acceptable according to these explanations. Waldron and McDermott (1979) describe three cultural groups in the United States, each of which has a different outlook on life forces and solutions to personal troubles. *Culture A* is derived from a fishing and hunting society, where survival was often threatened by unpredictable forces. Beliefs in supernatural events evolved, and healing cures were sought from persons with special powers who could communicate with spirits. Within this orientation, it was relatively easy for this group to accept chemotherapy for psychopathologies; dream interpretations were also congruent with this group's orientation.

In contrast, *Culture B* is based on views that harmony within the universe is important. When dealing with mental disorders, therefore, the psychotherapist would be more effective in establishing ways to adapt to life, rather than emphasizing medical cures or self-centered goals. Finally, *Culture C* associates personal disorders with internal conflict, and important values are self-reliance, mastery of both the environment and the self, and achievement. From this orientation, psychotherapies that emphasize either self-understanding or behavioral change through one's own efforts would be more readily accepted than treatments such as drug medication, which are externally controlled.

A final step in developing culturally relevant programs is for community mental health agencies to understand their perceived function among the minority community. Knowing what is expected or needed will permit offering services that can attract community participants, permit the development of a sense of trust and eventually open the door for other services. In some communities, a center might offer initial services aimed at child rearing and financial management. In others, the access point may be youth services to enable youngsters to "learn the ways of the majority culture." In yet another community, the agency may begin with no higher aims than providing a place to rap with someone who understands street language.

In examining the traditional psychotherapy or medical therapy models, it is clear that such treatments reflect a dominant European orientation—and that this may conflict with the basic beliefs of some minority groups. An Asian may need to overcome the shame and embarrassment of seeking help about family matters from a stranger. A person from the ghetto may distrust any person from a different social class who insists on seeing people in an office rather than on the streets. So far, the community mental health movement has been useful in moving treatment from the private offices into the neighborhoods, changing from treatment during office hours only to treatment when and where needed and attempting to be more responsive to environmental constraints. The next challenge is the development of culturally sensitive approaches.

tion among the community. Returning the patient to the community, rather than isolating the person through hospitalization, is important to help the individual stay in touch with the real world. Additionally, prolonged hospitalization has been shown to worsen a patient's problems. The community mental health movement received a major thrust from Congress in the 1960s and 70s in providing local agencies for outpatient treatment and prevention.

The concept of community mental health recognizes three levels of prevention: primary, secondary, and tertiary. The first attempts to prevent that which is preventable; the second tries to cure or arrest current disorders; and the third aims at after care. Community mental health also entails a certain philosophy: that mental disorders are problems in living; that treatment should be easily available; that community members should take responsibility in the mental health of their neighbors; and that crises should be solved immediately. The community mental health has been partly successful, but still is faced with much more progress to fully realize its goals.

## KEY TERMS

- Community mental health
- High-risk children
- Institutionalism
- Institutional neurosis
- Low-risk children
- Outreach programs
- Outpatient care
- Paraprofessional
- Primary prevention
- Psychomat
- Secondary prevention
- Tertiary prevention

# GLOSSARY

**Abnormal behaviors:** Specific behaviors that characterize mental disorders. These include discomfort, lack of predictability, loss of control, and rigidity.

**Abreaction:** Treatment in which patients talk out their problems.

**Adjustment disorders:** Disorders in which maladaptive stress responses occur to stressors less severe than major catastrophes.

**Adjustment disorder with anxious mood:** Stress disorder involving the appearance of anxiety symptoms.

**Adjustment disorder with depressed mood:** Stress disorder involving the appearance of depression.

**Adjustment disorder with disturbance of conduct:** Stress disorder involving acting-out behaviors.

**Adjustment disorder with withdrawal:** Stress disorder involving withdrawal behaviors.

**Adoption studies:** Morbidity-risk studies which examine siblings who have been separated from one another.

**Adrenal glands:** Endocrine glands producing adrenaline and noradrenaline and apparently involved in stress reactions.

**Affect:** Term which refers to mood or emotions.

**Affect hunger:** A disturbance in children following maternal deprivation involving a heightened search for affection from others.

**Affectionless character:** A disturbance in children following maternal deprivation involving the lack of normal display or need for affection.

**Affective disorders:** Psychotic disorders characterized by disturbances of the emotions. Includes bipolar disorders and major depression.

**Agoraphobia:** Specific phobia involving fear of going out in public and of open spaces.

**Alcohol abuse:** Substance use disorder involving alcohol and meeting the definitions of substance abuse.

**Alcohol dependence:** Substance use disorder involving alcohol and meeting the definitions of substance dependence.

**Alcohol hallucinosis:** Organic mental disorder associated with chronic alcoholism and characterized by auditory hallucinations. In contrast to deliriums, the patient remains oriented and does not show amnesia; the cause is believed to be an underlying emotional disorder.

**Alcohol amnestic disorder (Korsakoff's psychosis):** Condition associated with chronic alcoholism and characterized by disorientation, anterograde amnesia, confabulation, and lack of insight.

**Alcoholics Anonymous:** Organization of alcholics who support one another in working toward total abstinence.

**Alcohol idiosyncratic intoxication:** Acute condition, classified as an organic mental disorder; it is associated with alcoholic intake and characterized by disorientation, emotional changes, hallucinations, and confusion. Alcohol is believed to act as a precipitating factor, releasing an unstable emotional condition or aggravating a brain dysfunction.

**Alcoholism:** Excessive use of or reliance on alcohol. The preferred current term is now *alcohol abuse* or *alcohol dependence*.

**Alcohol withdrawal delirium:** *See* Delirium tremens.

**Alzheimer's disease:** Organic disorder classified as a primary degenerative dementia, presenile type II; involves cortical atrophy and the appearance of threadlike fibers in place of normal nerve cells.

**Amaurotic familial idiocy:** A central nervous system disease resulting from a recessive gene; characterized by mental deficiency and early death. Also known as Tay-Sachs disease.

**Amentia:** Term for mental retardation.

**Amniocentesis:** Medical procedure routinely used for prenatal detection of abnormalities.

**Amphetamines:** Type of drug used as stimulants. They produce an increased level of alertness, elevation of mood, and sense of well-being and confidence.

**Amygdala:** Part of the brain whose destruction leads to elimination of rage reactions, even when the animal is mishandled.

**Anabolism:** Life-building constructive processes in Freud's theory of motivation.

**Anaclitic depression:** A disturbance in children following maternal deprivation involving mourning for the parent, followed by denial of recognition of the parent.

**Anal phase:** Freudian stage of development characterized by a shift of the erogenous zones to the anal area.

**Analytic psychology:** Theory developed by Jung in which life energy is used for cultural, creative and spiritual goals.

**Anesthesias:** Patches of insensitivity on the skin which were seen as marks of collaboration with the devil during the Middle Ages.

**Anima:** According to Jung, the feminine nature.

**Animus:** According to Jung, the masculine nature.

**Anorexia nervosa:** Eating disorder involving loss of appetite and self-starvation.

**Anoxia:** Deficiency in the supply of oxygen to the tissues.

**Anterograde amnesia:** Memory loss for events following a trauma. This condition is typical of psychogenic amnesia.

**Antisocial personality:** Disorder involving impairment of personality development and antisocial behaviors.

**Anxiety disorders:** Disorders characterized by a sense of imminent danger, increased heart rate, and other reactions to threat.

**Anxiety hierarchy:** List of situations associated with a phobia, ranked from low to high for use in behavior therapy.

**Anxiety management training:** Form of behavior therapy aimed at self-control of anxiety.

**Aphasia:** Loss or impairment of language function; caused by organic brain damage.

**Approach-avoidance conflict:** Conflict in which an attraction is paired with something which repells.

**Apraxia:** Loss or impairment of ability to perform purposeful movements; caused by organic brain damage.

**Asthma:** Illness involving muscular spasms and obstruction of air flow in the lungs.

**Attentional deficit disorders:** Disorders involving short attention span, with or without hyperactivity.

**Aura:** In reference to migraine headaches, the sensory experiences such as light flashes that precede the onset of the headache.

**Authencity:** Component of existential approach developed by Laing, which emphasized the conflict between society and the person.

**Autistic thinking:** Excessive preoccupation with personal fantasies, unchecked by attention to reality.

**Autonomic nervous system:** Part of the peripheral nervous system governing internal organs; involves the sympathetic nervous system and the parasympathetic nervous system.

**Autonomic reactions:** Type of response pattern to stress.

**Aversive conditioning:** Behavior therapy involving associating a negative consequence to an unwanted behavior.

**Avoidance learning:** *See* Aversive conditioning.

**Avoidant disorder:** Disorder characterized by low self-esteem and exceptional sensitivity to rejection, resulting in persistent shyness and avoidance of social interactions.

**Axon:** Part of the neuron that carries outgoing impulses.

**Baquet:** Device of mirrors and rods used by Mesmer.

**Barbiturates:** Depressant drugs used medically for relaxation and sleep.

**Behavioral medicine:** Field of medicine which combines aspects of medicine, psychology, nursing, and social work.

**Behaviorism:** School of psychology emphasizing the observable, nonsubjective aspects of human behavior.

**Behavior modification:** Systematic application of learning principles to the strengthening or elimination of certain behaviors.

**Behavior rehearsal:** Technique used to replace unwanted with wanted behaviors.

**Behavior therapy:** Group of psychological therapies based on the belief that maladjustment is learned and can be eliminated in accordance with the principles of learning.

**Biofeedback:** Training given to patients to allow them to control their own bodily functions, thought to be involuntary, such as blood pressure, skin temperature, and heartbeat.

**Bipolar disorder:** Affective psychotic disorder characterized by cycles of disturbance followed by improvement. In the manic condition, the patient is hyperactive; in the depressed condition, the patient is dejected and self-accusing.

**Blood alcohol discrimination:** Treatment approach for alcohol abuse in which person learns to control amount of alcohol they consume.

**Brain damage:** Biochemical or structural change in the brain.

**Briquet's syndrome.** *See* Somatization disorder

**Bulimia:** Eating disorder involving excessive eating and binging.

**Cancer:** Medical disease involving the pathological growth of cells.

**Cannabis psychosis:** Severe disorder occasionally associated with chronic marijuana abuse.

**Case study:** Scientific approach to research that examines the variables which appear to be associated in the case history of a single client.

**Castration anxiety:** Freudian premise that boys undergo an imagined fear of castration; a premise important in the Oedipal complex.

**Catabolism:** Destructive processes in Freud's theory of motivation.

**Catalepsy:** Retention of a muscularly rigid and fixed position, characteristic of catatonic schizophrenia.

**Catatonic excitement:** Stage in schizophrenic disorder, catatonic type, which is characterized by violent, aggressive, and destructive outbursts.

**Catatonic negativism:** Stage in schizophrenic disorder, catatonic type, in which the patient resists instructions.

**Catatonic rigidity:** Stage in schizophrenic disorder, catatonic type, in which the patient assumes and maintains a rigid, unmoving posture.

**Catatonic schizophrenia:** Psychotic disorder characterized by motor inhibition, along with the usual characteristics of schizophrenia.

**Catatonic stupor:** Condition of physical unresponsiveness in a catatonic schizophrenic.

**Catecholamine theory of depression:** Theory in which depression is caused by depletion of norepinephrine at receptor sites in the brain.

**Central nervous system:** Part of the nervous system involving the brain and the spinal cord.

**Cerebellum:** Part of the brain involved with coordination of muscles and maintenance of bodily equilibrium.

**Cerebral cortex:** Layer covering the cerebral hemispheres and involved in motor control and certain higher mental activities.

**Cerebral hemispheres:** Two halves of the brain, each comprising a hemisphere. Also called the cerebrum.

**Character disorder:** Older psychiatric term encompassing disorders such as the antisocial personality, alcoholism, and drug addiction. It implied a basic defect in character.

**Chemotherapy:** Use of drugs to treat illness.

**Childhood schizophrenia:** Psychotic disorder which involves profound disturbance in emotional relations and marked withdrawal in children.

**Chlorpromazine:** Tranquilizer of the phenothiazine group that has been effective in treating schizophrenia.

**Chromosomal aberration:** Abnormality in chromosomes either in structure or in number.

**Chromosome:** Elongated, microscopic substances present in human cells that contain genes.

**Chromosome studies:** Direct examination of chromosomes to determine how genetics relates to pathology.

**Chronic phase:** Final phase of alcoholism, characterized by the onset of "benders" and the loss of defense mechanisms, or justifications, for drinking.

**Chunking:** Teaching approach which involves grouping material to be memorized into a form that is easier to remember.

**Circadian cycles:** Biological clocks in living animals that govern cyclical bodily functions.

**Civil commitment:** Legal procedure for having a person either voluntarily or involuntarily admitted to a psychiatric hospital, based on potential danger to self or to others.

**Civilian catastrophic reactions:** Former category of post-traumatic stress disorder relating to civilian disasters.

**Classical conditioning:** Form of learning involving the pairing of a neutral cue with one already associated with a response.

**Claustrophobia:** Phobia involving fear of closed places.

**Client-centered therapy:** Strategy of therapy that stresses personal growth and is encouraged by the accepting attitude of the therapist.

**Cocaine:** Stimulant drug once used to deaden pain.

**Cognition:** Thought process.

**Cognitive behavior therapy:** Category of behavior therapy which identifies thoughts as producers of anxiety.

**Cognitive sets:** Type of response pattern to stress.

**Collective unconscious:** Mental storehouse believed by Jung to be a repository for memories common to all humans.

**Combat reactions:** Former category of post-traumatic stress disorder relating to civilian disasters.

**Community mental health:** Treatment philosophy of providing prevention and treatment within the locus of a community.

**Competency to stand trial:** Legal determination of whether the defendent is capable of standing trial.

**Complex:** Cluster of related emotions, memories, and residual feelings.

**Compulsive gambling:** Impulse control disorder involving the need to gamble.

**Concordance:** Cases are considered concordant if both persons studied share a common trait. Used in twin studies, where one twin is affected by a disorder, to determine the influence of genetics.

**Conditioned reflex:** A learned response made when a conditioned stimulus is presented.

**Conditioning:** Form of learning whereby a stimulus becomes associated with a response by being paired with the original stimulus eliciting the response.

**Conduct disorders:** Disorder in conduct when person is under 18 years of age.

**Confabulation:** Making up facts; a behavior that is sometimes associated with certain organic amnesias.

**Consensus:** Principle that a symptom may develop in sympathy, appearing in a part of the body separate from the disease area.

**Constitutional inferiority:** Genetic theory that suggests that an inborn defect is the cause of antisocial personality.

**Contact-comfort hypothesis:** The idea that intimate physical contact is necessary for an animal to feel secure.

**Continuous amnesia:** Memory loss of events subsequent to a specific time and lasting up to the present.

**Controlled drinking:** Refers to the goal of retraining alcoholics to drink within socially acceptable patterns.

**Controlled experiment approach:** Scientific approach to research that selectively manipulates one variable to determine its possible influence on another.

**Conversion disorder:** Disorder in which medical symptoms occur without organic cause. The symptoms do not accurately match what is known of anatomical or physiological symptoms.

**Copralalia:** Paraphilias which involve uttering obscenities.

**Coronary artery disease:** Disease of the heart involving vascular blockage and heart failure.

**Correlational approach:** Scientific approach to research that examines the relationship between two or more variables appearing in several persons to determine if the variables are related.

**Counterconditioning:** Strengthening a response that is antagonistic to or incompatible with an undesirable response.

**Creative self:** According to Adler, individuals develop their own imaginative style as they strive for superiority.

**Cretinism:** Form of mental retardation caused by malfunctioning of the thyroid glands. It involves the physical characteristics of peg-shaped teeth, rough skin, and dwarflike body.

**Criminal responsibility:** Legal determination of whether the defendant is responsible for a crime.

**Crucial phase:** Third phase of alcoholism, characterized by some attempt to regain abstinence, the loss of control over drinking, self-pity, and the inability to cover up the presence of a drinking problem.

**Cue-discrimination skills:** Teaching approach that presents material in a way that highlights the relevant cues.

**Culture:** Socially transmitted system of attitudes, ideas, values, practices, and beliefs.

**Death instinct:** Freudian motive reflecting the destructive aspect of life; also called *thanatos*.

**Decompensation:** Disorganization of personality functioning due to excessive stresses.

**Defense mechanisms:** Behaviors for coping with threats to the personality.

**Delirium tremens:** Condition associated with alochol abuse that is characterized by disorientation, hallucinations, and inability to recall the experience on recovery.

**Delusion:** Belief that is tenaciously held in the face of evidence to the contrary.

**Delusion of grandeur:** Delusion that one is one of extraordinary ability or in some other way important.

**Dementia praecox:** Early term for schizophrenia, an illness characterized by social withdrawal, thought disturbance, and emotional blunting. It was once believed to be an affliction of youth.

**Demonology:** Belief that spirits external to man are the cause of events.

**Dendrite:** Part of the neuron that carries incoming impulses.

**Denial:** Anxiety defense mechanism that involves conscious refusal to admit to a factual event.

**Deoxyribonucleic acid:** DNA; a substance which is directly involved in genetic coding and transmission.

**Dependent personality:** Persistent, mild disorder involving the inability to take personal responsibility.

**Depersonalization:** State of feeling that one's body is unreal.

**Depression:** Emotional state characterized by sadness and gloom.

**Dereflection:** Technique which involves turning the person's focus away from complaints and problems and shifting attention to the choices that should be made.

**Desensitization:** Behavior therapy involving pairing relaxation with the phobic stimulus through imagery.

**Deterioration effect:** Indication that psychotherapy can lead to a person becoming worse instead of better.

**Diathesis-stress theory:** Theory that states that a mental disorder is a result of a predisposition caused genetically, but triggered by an environmental stress.

**Discrimination learning:** The selective response to differences in stimulus characteristics.

**Disease entity theory:** Belief that mental disorders are analogous to physical diseases in that each is characterized by a typical cluster of symptoms, a common causative factor, a distinctive course, and a predictable outcome.

**Disorganized schizophrenia:** Psychotic disorder characterized by silly and inappropriate behavior and regressive features along with the usual characteristics of schizophrenia. Formerly labelled hebephrenic schizophrenia.

**Displacement:** In learning terms, the selective response to differences in stimulus characteristics.

**Dissociative disorders:** Disorders involving the sudden, transitory change in consciousness, identity, or motor behavior.

**Dizygotic twins:** Persons sharing the same intrauterine environment but having different chromosomal makeups.

**Dominant gene:** A gene whose characteristics are passed on to the offspring.

**Dopamine:** Substance found in the body which is being investigated as a possible cause of mental disorders.

**Double-bind hypothesis:** Hypothesis that an individual may communicate conflicting demands without admitting to the inconsistency.

**Down's syndrome:** Form of mental retardation associated with trisomy of chromosomes; it involves the physical characteristics of a protruding tongue, slanted eyefolds, and a stocky body.

**Downward drift hypothesis:** Idea that a mentally disturbed person ends up in a lower social class because of an inability to function.

**Dysfunction:** Impairment of normal functioning.

**Dyskenesia:** Impairment of voluntary muscle control.

**Dyspareunia:** Psychosexual dysfunction in which intercourse causes genital pain.

**Eating disorders:** Disorders involving disturbances in eating behaviors, such as anorexia nervosa, bulimia, and pica.

**Echolalia:** Repetition of the speech of others, symptomatic of some psychotic disorders.

**Ego:** Freudian term for psychological processes including reasoning, reality testing, coping behavior, and other higher mental processes.

**Ego anxiety:** Anxiety associated with a fear of aversive consequences from the environment; also called reality anxiety.

**Ego-dystonic homosexuality:** Disorder in which homosexual partner choice is disturbing to the individual.

**Ejaculatory incompetence:** Psychosexual dysfunction in which the male is unable to ejaculate intravaginally.

**Elective mutism:** Disorder involving lack of speech; frequently associated with autism.

**Electra complex:** Freudian term for a girl's repressed love for her father.

**Electroshock therapy:** Use of electrical current to bring about convulsions as a treatment method.

**Encopresis:** Physical disorder involving loss of control over fecal excretion.

**Encounter groups:** Therapy method in which an intensive small group focuses on here-and-now issues.

**Endocrine glands:** Organs within the body that secrete chemical substances necessary for metabolic functioning.

**Endorphins:** Natural substances in the brain which suppress pain and which are being studied for their possible role in psychosis.

**Enuresis:** Physical disorder of childhood involving bedwetting.

**Epidemiology:** Branch of medicine that studies the causes and distribution of epidemics.

**Epilepsy:** Brain dysfunction involving convulsions and disturbance of consciousness.

**Epinephrine:** Secretions of the adrenal glands. Also called adrenaline.

**Erectile dysfunction:** Psychosexual dysfunction involving the inhibition of sexual excitement, so that the male is unable to maintain an erection. Also known as impotence.

**Erotic delusions:** Delusion in which a person has the mistaken belief that another person is in love with them.

**Essential hypertension:** High blood pressure.

**Excitatory stimulus:** In conditioning, the stimulus which produces a certain behavior.

**Exhibitionism:** Paraphilia involving sexual arousal from displaying oneself.

**Existentialism:** Philosophical approach to psychology stressing the importance of free choice and meaning in life.

**Exorcism:** Religious rituals for casting out the demons believed to be present in possessed persons.

**Explosive disorder:** Impulse control disorder involving aggressive behaviors. Two kinds of explosive disorders have been identified: the intermittent explosive disorder, which involves a repetitive pattern of loss of control; and the isolated explosive disorder, involving a single, highly violent act.

**Factitious disorders:** Disorders involving the simulation of an illness.

**Family therapy:** Treatment of the family as a single unit instead of each member individually.

**Feral children:** Children said to have been raised by wild animals.

**Fetishism:** Paraphilia in which the individual derives sexual arousal from nonliving objects.

**Fight or flight response:** Response of body to stress in which individual is prepared to deal with danger.

**Fissure of Rolando:** Top central groove which separates the lobes of the brain.

**Fissure of Sylvius:** Lower groove which separates the lobes of the brain.

**Fixation:** Freudian term for the failure to progress beyond an early developmental phase.

**Flagellants:** Religious sect during the Middle Ages.

**Flight of ideas:** Rapid succession of ideas outside the control of the individual.

**Flooding:** Form of behavior therapy for anxiety or phobias involving continued exposure to the tensional situation.

***Folie à deux:*** Simultaneous affliction of two persons who are closely associated with the same paranoid disorder.

**Free association:** Treatment involving having patients simply verbalize their associations.

**Frontal lobe:** One of the principal lobes of the brain involved in reasoning and memory.

**Fugue:** Dissociative condition characterized by amnesia without loss of habits and skills. The patient usually leaves home and lives a different life elsewhere.

**Galactosemia:** Disease involving central nervous system pathology associated with inadequate carbohydrate metabolism.

**Ganser's syndrome:** Disorder involving the simulation of psychological symptoms.

**Gate-control theory:** Theory which states that there is a mechanism in the spinal cord that acts as a gate, controlling the neural transmission from the periphery of the skin to the spinal cord.

**Gender identity disorder:** A crisis centering on a person's sexual identity.

**Gene:** Protein molecules containing the substance DNA involved in genetic transmission.

**General adaptation syndrome:** Term referring to predictable bodily reactions to stress, involving stages of alarm, resistance, and exhaustion.

**Generalized amnesia:** Memory loss for one's complete life.

**Generalized anxiety disorder:** Disorder involving the presence of anxiety and distressed feelings of apprehension or threat of imminent danger.

**General paresis:** Organic disorder involving gradual and complete mental deterioration; caused by a syphilitic condition.

**Genital phase:** Freudian stage of development characterized by the shift to adult genital love.

**Gestalt therapy:** Humanistic therapy that emphasizes self-awareness, self-discovery, and the here-and-now.

**Grand mal seizures:** Epileptic convulsions characterized by major muscle spasms and loss of consciousness.

**Gross-stress reaction:** Former name for post-traumatic stress disorder.

**Group psychotherapy:** Treatment of several patients meeting together with one or two psychotherapists.

**Halfway houses:** Aftercare program to provide help for people in dealing with the return to normal community life.

**Hallucination:** Sensory disturbance in which a sensory experience appears but without an appropriate external stimulus.

**Hallucinogenic drugs:** Group of drugs that produces hallucinations.

**Hebephrenic symptoms:** Symptoms associated with a form of psychosis involving silliness, grimacing, and regressive behavior.

**Heterozygous:** For a given pair of chromosomes, the lack of similarity within the pair.

**Hierarchy of needs:** Scheme of needs developed by Maslow.

**High risk children:** Children whose characteristics make them probable risks for illness; high risk children for schizophrenia would be those born to families with a schizophrenic parent.

**Homeostasis:** Equilibrium of body under normal conditions.

**Homozygous:** Both chromosomes within a pair match.

**Hotlines:** Telephone services for crises calls; the telephone calls permit an immediate response to an emergency.

**Humanism:** Approach to psychology stressing the importance of human experience.

**Humanistic-existential therapy:** Major psychological approach which is characterized by searching for positive growth through freedom of choice, free will, and the ability of individuals to take responsibility for their own futures.

**Human relations training:** Use of group techniques to enhance personal development, including sensitivity groups, T-groups, and sensory-awareness experiences.

**Huntington's chorea:** Inherited form of mental disorder characterized by brain atrophy, involuntary jerky movements, distractibility, apathy, and loss of coordination.

***Hwa-byung:*** Among Koreans, an intense fear of dying.

**Hydrocephaly:** Form of mental retardation involving excessive cerebrospinal fluid in the cranium.

**Hydrotherapy:** Physical therapy involving immersion in warm water as a means of relaxing the muscles and hence calming the person.

**Hyperactivity:** Attention deficit disorder of childhood. Characterized by irrepressible motor activity, impulsive responding, and a short attention span.

**Hypnosis:** Procedure in which person is helped to develop a trancelike state, under which they are highly suggestible.

**Hypochondriasis:** Disorder involving preoccupation with and exagerated concern about physical health.

**Hysteria:** Former term for conversion disorder; a form of mental illness characterized by bodily symptoms without an organic foundation.

**Hysterical or histrionic personality:** Persistent, mild disorder involving emotional excitability and self-centeredness.

**Iatrogenic addiction:** Drug addiction due to the use of narcotics in heavy amounts for the treatment of a disease or pain.

**Id:** Freudian term for infantile psychological processes including impulses demanding immediate gratification.

**Id anxiety:** Anxiety associated with a fear of being overwhelmed by inner impulses; also known as neurotic anxiety.

**Idiopathic epilepsy:** Epileptic condition which is not clearly attributable to an organic origin.

**Idiot savant:** Person who is intellectually retarded but talented in other ways.

**Imipramine:** Antidepressant drug of the tricyclic family; it acts to elevate mood.

**Implosive therapy:** Behavior therapy using exposure to anxiety to extinguish the anxiety. Blends behavioral and psychodynamic principles.

**Impulse control disorders:** Disorders involving the inability to restrict impulsive actions.

**Impulse control training:** Training with the premise that people can learn to inhibit behaviors.

**Incidence:** Number of new cases of an illness appearing during a given period.

**Individualized behavior therapy:** Program for controlled drinking training that includes practice in controlled drinking behaviors, videotape confrontation, and help in identifying the conditions that prompt excessive drinking.

**Individual psychology:** Theory of personality developed by Adler.

**Infantile autism:** Form of mental disorder appearing early in life and classified as a psychosis. It involves bizarre movements and autistic isolation.

**Inhibitory stimulus:** In conditioning, the stimulus which inhibits a response.

**Instinct:** Pattern of behavior which is present in all animals in the same species and is unlearned.

**Institutionalism:** *See* Institutional neurosis.

**Institutional neurosis:** Effects of long-term hospitalization, such as apathy.

**Insulin convulsive therapy:** Treatment of mental illness through the use of insulin in order to produce a comatose state.

**Intelligence quotient (IQ)**: Score reflecting intellectual level, usually involving mental age divided by chronological age and multiplied by 100.

**Intermediate gene:** A gene, that is neither dominant nor recessive, but has an in-between effect.

**Interpersonal psychology:** Theory founded by Adler which differed with Freudian theory in attention to social factors and in the concepts of inferiority and creativity.

**Interpretation:** In therapy, the delineation of an association between current behavior and past events.

**Iproniazid:** The first of the MAO-inhibitor drugs.

**Irresistible impulse:** Impulse that cannot be resisted.

**Jacksonian seizures:** Epileptic convulsions characterized by circumscribed spasms beginning as muscle twitches and involving larger and larger areas of the body.

**Jealous delusions:** Delusion in which a person is fitfully certain that his or her loved one is unfaithful.

**Karyotype:** A photograph of chromosomes.

**Kleptomania:** Impulse control disorder involving the compulsion to steal without economic motives.

**Korsakoff's psychosis:** Condition associated with chronic alcoholism and characterized by disorientation, anterograde amnesia, confabulation, and lack of insight.

***La belle indifference:*** Symptom of conversion disorder involving a lack of concern or indifference by the patient about symptoms.

**Latency phase:** Freudian stage of development characterized by a temporary repression of conflict.

**Law of effect:** Principle that an organism learns those responses followed by a satisfying event and eliminates those followed by discomfort.

**Learned helplessness:** Habits of passivity and giving up as a learned result of experiences.

**Life instinct:** Freudian motive reflecting the constructive, self-preservative, aspects of life.

**Lithium:** Drug which has been successful with manic episodes and bipolar disorders.

**Living-environmental factors:** Living conditions, such as noise, pollution, heat, and overcrowding, that produce stress.

**Localized amnesia:** Memory loss for events over a set period of time.

**Locus of control:** Different persons have differing ways of attributing the reasons or causes of events; internal locus of control emphasized that a person controls such events; external locus of control emphasizes external factors as causes.

**Logotherapy:** Therapy whose aim is to confront persons with the meaning and purpose of their own existence.

**Low risk children:** Children whose characteristics do not make them high risks for illness.

**Lycanthropy:** Illness involving the belief that one is a wolf.

**Lysergic acid diethylamide (LSD)**: Drug that produces a psychotic-like condition.

**Mainstreaming:** Placing mentally retarded children in the same classroom environment as children with average intellectual skills.

**Major depression:** Psychotic condition with depressed mood as the major symptom but which lacks the manic episode that appears in bipolar disorders.

**Major depression with melancholia:** Affective psychotic disorder occurring around the climacteric and characterized by severe depression.

**Malingering:** Conscious faking or feigning of an illness for personal gain.

**Mania:** Condition involving excitability and impulsive behavior.

**Manic-depressive psychosis:** Severe disorder involving alternations between depressive and euphoric moods and including major personality disturbances. Now known as bipolar disorder.

**MAO (Monoamine oxidase) inhibitors:** Medications which seemed valuable for treatment of depression; usage has declined because of side effects.

**Marijuana:** Drug made from the flowers, stems and leaves of the hemp plant.

**Masochism:** Paraphilia in which the individual experiences sexual arousal from pain.

**Maternal perplexity:** Lack of spontaneity, indecisiveness, and inconsistency on the part of the mother.

**Maternal separation:** Separation from one's own mother.

**Medulla:** Structure in the brain which regulates reflex functions, such as breathing.

**Melancholia:** Form of mental symptoms characterized by severe depression.

**Mental disorder:** General term in the DSM-III that refers to all categories of abnormal behavior.

**Mental illness:** Term once used interchangeably with mental disorder, psychopathology, and abnormality. It is now generally limited to the description of organic illnesses.

**Mental retardation:** Deficit in intellectual capacity (typically designated as an IQ below 70) leading to impairments in academic, social, and vocational abilities.

**Mesmerism:** Originally introduced by Anton Mesmer as a means of curing illness through animal magnetism. Now known as hypnotism.

**Metabolic aberrations:** Factors, such as prenatal vitamin deficiences, which can impair the normal internal functioning of the body, leading to changes that ultimately affect the brain.

**Methadone:** A synthetic narcotic that is sometimes used to treat heroin addiction.

**Microcephaly:** Form of mental retardation involving failure of development of the cranium; an abnormally small head.

**Midbrain:** Structure in the brain which seems to control visual and auditory reflexes.

**Migraine headache:** Disorder involving severe headaches, sensory aura, and related symptoms such as nausea or sensitivity to light.

**Mild retardation:** Retardation represented by an intelligence quotient from 53 to 69. Person is capable to a degree of independent living.

**Milieu therapy:** Therapy involving the use of community personnel for therapeutic support.

**Modeling:** Method of learning by watching and imitating the behavior of someone else.

**Moderate retardation:** Retardation represented by an intelligence quotient from 36 to 52. Person is capable of a semi-independent life, self-care, and partial financial self-support.

**Mongolian idiot:** Formerly-used term for patient with Down's syndrome.

**Monoamine oxidase (MAO):** Enzyme depleting serotonin and believed to be related to depression.

**Monozygotic twins:** Persons sharing the same chromosomal makeup and the same intrauterine environment.

**Moral therapy:** Therapy based on the view that patients are simply normal persons experiencing abnormal psychological and social stresses.

**Morbidity risk studies:** If one member of a family is ill (morbid), morbidity risk studies calculate the probability of other family members developing that illness.

**Multiple personality:** Disorder involving the appearance of two or more distinct personalities.

**Münchausen's syndrome:** Disorder involving the simulation of physical symptoms.

**Narcissistic personality:** Persistent, mild disorder involving self-idealization.

**Narcotic:** Class of drugs, derived from opium, including morphine, heroin, and codeine, used to relieve pain and induce sleep.

**National character:** Certain temperamental characteristics and personality traits assumed to prevail in a particular culture.

**Necrophilia:** Paraphilia in which sexual arousal is derived from corpses.

**Negativism:** Resistance of suggestions or influence of others.

**Neo-Freudian school:** School of thought which breaks from Freudian theory in its stress on sociological factors and in its basic belief in the positive good of individuals.

**Neologism:** Newly coined word.

**Neuron:** Single cell composing the structure of nervous tissue.

**Neurosis:** Milder form of mental disturbance, without personality disorganization or loss of contact with reality.

**Neurotransmitters:** Chemicals that carry nerve impulses across the synapse from one neuron to another.

**Nociperception:** Term referring to the response of pain receptors at the tissue level.

**Norepinephrine:** Secretion of the adrenal gland. Also called nonadrenaline.

**Normal distribution curve:** Statistical representation of the distribution of characteristics among people. This frequency curve is bell-shaped, since most people fall in the middle, with fewer and fewer persons possessing either a greater or lesser amount of the trait.

**Normative approach:** Scientific approach to research that studies the presence of a variable within a large sample of a particular group of people.

**Nosology:** Classification of observations into an organized system.

**Obsessive-compulsive disorder:** Disorder characterized by repetitive thoughts (obsessiveness) or actions (compulsions) over which the person has little control.

**Occipital lobe:** One of the principal lobes of the brain involved in vision.

**Oedipus complex:** Freudian term for a boy's repressed love for his mother.

**Operant conditioning:** Method of learning involving a strengthening of a response through the presentation of a reward following the response.

**Oral phase:** Freudian state of development characterized by a focus of the erogenous zones around the oral areas.

**Organic brain syndrome:** Major DSM-III category referring to disorders associated with central nervous system; syndromes deriving from a variety of causes.

**Organic brain syndrome, affective syndrome:** Organically caused disorder characterized by disturbance in mood, such as depression or elation.

**Organic brain syndrome, amnestic syndrome:** Organically caused disorder characterized by loss of short-term memory.

**Organic brain syndrome, delirium syndrome:** Organically caused disorder characterized by delusions, that is, beliefs not based on reality.

**Organic brain syndrome, hallucinosis:** Organically caused disorder characterized by sensory experiences without basis in reality.

**Organic brain syndrome, personality syndrome:** Organically caused disorder characterized by a shift in stable behavioral patterns.

**Organic mental disorders:** Pathological behaviors attributed to brain dysfunctions.

**Orgasmic dysfunction:** Inability of a woman to achieve orgasm.

**Outpatient care:** Program in which patient lives outside the hospital, but receives immediate treatment in the hospital on an as-needed basis.

**Outreach program:** Community-based care program in which the treatment teams go out into the community to provide services.

**Overanxious disorder:** Childhood disorder involving anxiety and excess worry not associated with a specific situation.

**Pancreas:** An organ in the endocrine system that secretes insulin.

**Panic disorder:** Disorder involving recurrent anxiety attacks of extremely high intensity, overwhelming terror, or fearfulness.

**Paradoxical intention:** Behavior therapy that involves having a person repeat unwanted symptoms but in an exaggerated way.

**Paranoia:** Disorder characterized by systematized delusions and absence of other emotional or intellectual disturbance.

**Paranoid disorders:** Psychotic disorders characterized by delusional disturbance but in which the emotional reactions are appropriate to the thought content.

**Paranoid personality:** Persistent, mild disorder involving suspiciousness.

**Paranoid schizophrenia:** Subgroup of schizophrenia characterized by suspiciousness and delusions of persecution.

**Paraphilia:** Disorders involving being sexually aroused by deviant objects or acts.

**Paraprofessional:** A person who is trained to help in professional activities; may be used for hotlines or referral services under supervision.

**Parasympathetic nervous system:** Part of the autonomic nervous system often working during relaxed states, and in opposition to the sympathetic nervous system, on organs and glands.

**Parathyroid glands:** Endocrine glands whose major function is the maintenance of calcium and phosphorus balance in the blood.

**Parietal lobe:** One of the principal lobes in the brain; involved in body sensations and movement.

**Passive-aggressive personality:** Persistent mild disorder involving passivity and hostility.

**Pathogenic family pattern:** Family pattern which is pathology producing.

**Pavor nocturnus:** Physical disorder of sleep involving nightmares of an extreme nature.

**PCP:** Phencyclidine; hallucinogenic-type drug.

**Pedophilia:** Paraphilia in which sexual arousal is derived from having relations with children.

**Penetrance:** Power of genes to become expressed.

**Penis envy:** Freudian premise that girls undergo an admiration of, and repressed desire to possess, the male sexual organ.

**Pepsinogen:** Substance in the gastric glands necessary for the production of the digestive enzymes.

**Peptic ulcer:** Ulceration of the stomach.

**Performance anxiety:** Sexual dysfunction in which the male becomes anxious because of a fear of not meeting another's expectations of him.

**Peripheral nervous system:** The nervous system that acts to control many of the unconscious aspects of bodily functioning.

**Personality decompensation:** Disorganization of personality due to excessive stress.

**Personality disorders:** Disorders in which people find it difficult to adjust to life when faced with even minor stresses.

**Personification:** Concept of Sullivan's referring to stereotype perceptions.

**Pervasive developmental disorders:** Disorders involving severe psychosis, such as infantile autism or childhood schizophrenia.

**Petit mal seizures:** Epileptic convulsions characterized by brief, minor, rhythmical movements.

**Phallic phase:** Freudian stage of development characterized by interest in and manipulation of the genitals.

**Phenothiazine:** Medication that has proven especially helpful with schizophrenics. Chlorpromazine is one of the most frequently used drugs in the group.

**Phenylketonuria (PKU):** Type of mental retardation caused by the lack of an enzyme.

**Phobic disorder:** Disorder involving an excessive, irrational fear.

**Photic stimulus:** Presentation of a rapidly flickering light, which may induce brain wave changes and which precedes an epileptic seizure.

**Phrenology:** Procedure whereby diagnoses were made according to the presence and shape of bumps on the cranium.

**Physical disorders:** Disorders involving disturbances in physical activities, such as enuresis, pavor nocturnus, or stuttering.

**Physiognomy:** Procedure attempting to distinguish personality traits by the examination of topological features of the cranium.

**Pibloktoq:** Artic-based type of mental illness believed to involve hysteria.

**Pica:** Eating disorder involving indiscriminate eating.

**Pick's disease:** Organic disorder, classified as a primary degenerative dementia, presenile onset. It involves atrophy of the frontal and temporal lobes and impairment of language and intellect.

**Pituitary gland:** Endocrine gland, known as the master gland, which produces several hormones necessary to life.

**Placebo:** Any inactive medicine or treatment whose effectiveness is caused by the patient's expectation of improvement.

**Play therapy:** Therapeutic method used in treating of children that relies on play activity.

**Pleasure principle:** Freudian term for the tendency to seek immediate discharge of tension without attention to the consequences.

**Polygene:** A gene that has no effect alone, but that joins with other genes to have a cumulative effect.

**Polysymptomatic:** Having a variety of symptoms.

**Pons:** Brain structure that acts as a connecting link between the cerebellum and the cerebrum.

**Positive reinforcement:** *See* Operant conditioning.

**Possession:** Archiac belief that deviant behavior was due to the presence of an evil spirit possessing the individual. Sometimes present in contemporary supersitions among primitive peoples.

**Post-traumatic stress disorder:** Disorder involving stress responses caused by events outside the range of common experience, such as disasters.

**Prealcoholic symptomatic phase:** First phase of alcoholism characterized by the establishment of heavy drinking patterns.

**Prefrontal lobotomy:** Surgical procedure used as a treatment for psychosis.

**Premature ejaculation:** Sexual dysfunction in which a man experiences an early orgasm.

**Presenile dementia:** *See* Primary degenerative dementia, presenile onset.

**Prevalence:** Total number of existing cases of a disorder within a population group.

**Primary degenerative dementia, presenile onset:** Group of organic disorders believed to be a form of premature aging deterioration. Includes Alzheimer's disease and Pick's disease.

**Primary degenerative dementia, senile onset:** Organic disorder involving atrophy of the brain and characterized by loss of memory, emotional liability, disorientation, and moral deterioration.

**Primary prevention:** Steps to reduce the incidence of disorders, that is, to reduce the rate of new cases.

**Proband:** The individual who originally exhibited the trait being investigated in a genetic study.

**Prodromal phase:** Second phase of alcoholism characterized by spells of amnesia, secretive drinking, and dependance on alcohol.

**Profound retardation:** Retardation represented by an intelligence quotient of 20 or less. Person usually is not responsive to training, requires custodial care, and suffers from nervous system damage.

**Projection:** Defense mechanism in which a trait is initially repressed, but then attributed to others.

**Protective inhibition theory:** Theory which suggests that prolonged or intense stimulation can induce an inhibitory response in the central cortex.

**Psychoanalysis:** Theory of personality; the special treatment approach developed by Frued.

**Psychoanalytic therapy:** *See* Psychoanalysis.

**Psychodrama:** Treatment of mental illness by encouraging the client to enact different dramas of his or her life.

**Psychodynamic approach:** Complex interaction between

emotions, motivations, and behaviors underlying normal or abnormal patterns.

**Psychogenic amnesia:** Disorder involving a sudden onset of memory loss, where the person is unable to remember important personal information.

**Psychogenic fugue:** Disorder involving leaving one's customary residence or work area, taking on a new identity, with amnesia for the previous identity.

**Psychogenic pain:** Pain without organic cause.

**Psychomat:** Experimental walk-in counseling service.

**Psychomimetic drugs:** Group of drugs that produces psychoticlike behavior.

**Psychomotor seizures:** Epileptic disorder characterized by automatic behaviors.

**Psychopathic personality:** Term formerly used to describe the antisocial personality.

**Psychopathology:** Study of mental disorders or abnormal behaviors.

**Psychophysiologic disorders:** Disorders involving structural changes in the body attributed mainly to emotional disturbances. Also called psychosomatic disorders.

**Psychosexual disorders:** Disorders involving difficulties in sexual identity, arousal, functioning, or choice of partners.

**Psychosexual dysfunctions:** Disorders involving disturbance in some phase of the human sexual response cycle.

**Psychosis:** Severe form of mental disturbance involving loss of contact with reality, severe personality disorganization, sensory distortion, and lack of insight. Hospitalization is often required.

**Psychosurgery:** Medical treatment involving brain surgery, usually to remove neural pathways involving emotions.

**Psychotherapy:** Treatment of mental illness through a corrective experience resulting from the interaction between a trained therapist and a client.

**Psychotic mental disorders:** *See* Psychosis.

**Pyromania:** Impulse control disorder involving the compulsion to set fires.

**Rape:** Forced intercourse with a nonconsenting person.

**Rational-emotive therapy:** Cognitive therapy emphasizing challenging the reality of one's beliefs.

**Rationalization:** Anxiety defense mechanism that involves justifying an otherwise unacceptable impulse or action.

**Rational restructuring:** Form of cognitive behavior therapy which aims at helping person control anxiety through reevaluating the validity of thoughts.

**Reaction formation:** Defense mechanism that involves adopting impulses and actions directly opposite to those we possess.

**Reality principle:** Freudian term for the capacity to delay gratification, or to elect socially approved means for gratification.

**Recessive gene:** A gene that requires a matching similar gene for expression.

**Regression:** Return to behaviors appropriate to a previous stage of maturity.

**Rehabilitation medicine:** Branch of medicine that aims at restoring the individual to the fullest physical, mental, social, and economic functioning possible.

**Rehearsal:** Teaching strategy; it involves the practicing or repetition of what one wants to learn.

**Reinforcement:** In operant conditioning, the presentation of a reward; in classical conditional, the pairing of the neural stimulus with the stimulus normally associated with a response.

**Reinforcement-based therapy:** Therapy based on the idea that responses can be modified through the use of reinforcement.

**Repression:** Exclusion of psychological activities or contents from awareness.

**Reserpine:** Tranquilizer used to treat schizophrenia.

**Resistance:** Psychoanalytic belief that clients will attempt to protect themselves from facing personal conflicts during therapy.

**Response prevention:** Behavior therapy which aims at treating obsessive-compulsive disorders. At first the ritual is continued, but the compulsive actions are gradually limited.

**Retrograde amnesia:** Memory loss for events just prior to a trauma. This symptom is typical of some physically caused amnesias, such as those caused by concussion.

**Reversal experimental design:** Experimental technique in which a controlled experiment is reversed to test the findings.

**Sadism:** Paraphilia involving sexual arousal from inflicting pain.

**Schismatic family:** Disturbed family characterized by hostilities dividing the family into factions.

**Schizophrenia:** Psychotic disorder characterized by the blunting of emotions, social withdrawal, seclusiveness, inappropriateness of affect, autistic thinking, bizarre behavior, sensory disturbances, delusions, and disturbances of thought.

**Schizophrenogenic:** Producing the conditions leading to the development of schizophrenia.

**Secondary gain:** Additional rewards that accrue from symptoms, such as attention from others, sympathy, or relief from responsibility.

**Secondary prevention:** Steps to reduce the prevalence of problems; for example, providing services to persons considered to be under high stress.

**Selective amnesia:** Memory loss for some but not all events associated with a set period of time.

**Self-actualization:** Client-centered belief that each person is motivated toward self-growth and self-fulfillment.

**Self-concept:** Personification of one's self.

**Self-efficacy:** Concept in Bandura's theory referring to self-judgments about how well we think we can perform a given task.

**Senile dementia:** *See* Primary degeneration dementia, senile onset.

**Senile plaques:** Areas of cortical tissue degeneration; generally round and of granular and filamentous structure; involved in the aging process.

**Sensitivity groups:** Type of encounter group.

**Sensorimotor rhythm training:** Form of training in which subject is instructed on ways to avoid unsafe rhythms.

**Sensory awareness groups:** Type of encounter group.

**Separation anxiety:** Disorder involving anxiety reaction by a child due to the departure of parents.

**Septal area:** Area of brain which when stimulated produces a pleasurable emotion.

**Severe retardation:** Retardation represented by an intelligence quotient from from 20 to 35. Person is capable of limited self-help and often has nervous system damage.

***Shook yong:*** Fear of death from inversion of sex organs. Also known as *karo*.

**Skewed family:** Disturbed family characterized by one spouse going along passively with the aberrant ways of the other.

**Social-cognitive problem-solving:** Behavioral program which involves training persons to see alternative solutions to a problem.

**Socialization:** Process of acquiring the characteristics in accordance with the patterns of a society.

**Socialized aggressive personality:** Type of antisocial personality who feels strong ties to certain other people, such as a gang.

**Socialized unaggressive personality:** Type of antisocial personality who is a victim of peer influence.

**Social learning approach:** Behavior approach, developed by Bandura, which is concerned with modeling and self-efficacy.

**Society:** Organized population of a people living together and sharing a mutual sense of belonging.

**Sociopath:** Term referring to the presence of antisocial behaviors.

**Somatic nervous system:** That portion of the nervous system which is responsible for sensory-motor actions.

**Somatization disorders:** Disorders in which there is a history of medical complaints that are polysymptomatic.

**Somatoform disorders:** Disorders in which physical symptoms dominate although there is no evidence of organic causation.

**Somatopsychology:** Field that studies the psychological effects of having a physical illness or disability.

**Spontaneous recovery:** In mental disorder, this refers to the remission of symptoms without treatment.

**State anxiety:** Anxiety which is prompted by situational cues.

***Status epilepticus:*** Condition in grand mal seizures, in which the individual never reaches consciousness before another convulsion begins.

**Stereotyped movement disorders:** Disorders involving involuntary motor movements, such as tics or Tourette's disorder.

***Stigmata diaboli:*** Sign of collaboration with the devil, which was looked for during the Inquisition.

**Stratification:** Assignment of individuals to different social levels.

**Stress:** State involving apprehension, psysiological arousal, and behavioral signs of tension.

**Stress inoculation training:** Form of behavior therapy whereby persons control anxiety through plans of action, cognitive steps, and self-talk.

**Stress management:** Methods for reducing or preventing stress from becoming a problem.

**Stressor:** Events or circumstances which cause stress.

**Sublimation:** Defense mechanism that involves routing an unacceptable impulse into a socially acceptable channel.

**Substance abuse:** Category of substance use disorders characterized by pathological use, impairment of social or occupational function, and duration of at least one month.

**Substance dependence:** Category of substance use disorders characterized by tolerance or withdrawal signs.

**Substance use disorders:** Disorders involving pathological behavior changes due to taking substances that affect the central nervous system, such as alcohol or drugs.

**Suicide:** The act of taking one's own life.

**Superego:** Freudian term for psychological process involved in the setting of moral standards.

**Superego anxiety:** Anxiety associated with a fear of guilt reactions; also called moral anxiety.

**Suppression:** Defense mechanism that involves the conscious exclusion of threatening material from one's conscious thoughts.

**Sympathetic nervous system:** Part of the autonomic nervous system which becomes active during emergency states such as exertion or extreme cold.

**Symptomatic epilepsy:** Epileptic condition which is clearly attributable to an organic origin.

**Symptoms:** Characteristic signs associated with a particular disorder.

**Synapse:** Space which separates neurons.

**Syndrome:** Cluster of symptoms that disguishes a mental disorder.

**Synesthesia:** Sensory phenomenon whereby one sensory modality responds when another has been stimulated.

**Syphilis:** Infectious veneral disease caused by the spirochetes known as Treponema pallidum.

**Systematic desensitization:** Gradual exposure of a client to feared situations while relaxed.

**Tarantism:** Dance frenzy during the Middle Ages.

**Taraxein:** Toxic substance which can lead to abnormal EEG patterns and abnormal behavior.

**Tay-Sachs disease:** Form of amaurotic idiocy involving acute sensitivity to sounds, listlessness, and muscular atrophy.

**Telephone scatologia:** Paraphilia in which sexual arousal is derived from talking lewdly over the telephone.

**Temporal lobe:** One of the principle lobes of the brain that is involved in hearing.

**Tension headache:** Disorder involving dull pain; sometimes considered related to muscle tension.

**Tertiary prevention:** Steps to reduce the effects of illness following treatment; for example, the use of a halfway house and the transition back to normal living after hospital discharge.

**T-group:** Type of encounter group.

**Thalamus:** Brain structure which acts as a relay center between the cortex and sensory organs.

**Therapeutic community:** Hospital environment which emphasizes a patient's accepting responsibility for his or her recovery.

**Thought stopping:** Behavior therapy in which the client is trained in ways to prevent negative thoughts from continuing.

**Thyroid:** Glands which regulate heat and energy within the cells.

**Tics:** Disorders involving involuntary, purposeless movements.

**Token economy system:** Behavioral approach whereby persons earn tokens each time they show behaviors associated with adjustment. These tokens can then be traded for a reward.

**Tolerance:** Increasing need for higher doses of a substance to obtain the same effects of a smaller dose in the past.

**Tourette's disorder:** Disorder involving involuntary sounds or complex movements.

**Trait anxiety:** Anxiety said to be pervasive and continuing across differing situations and hence attributed to person-characteristics rather than situation-characteristics.

**Tranquilizers:** Drugs used to produce a calming effect without affecting the level of alertness.

**Transference:** In psychoanalytic theory, a process by which the patient's feelings and thoughts shift toward the therapist.

**Translocation:** Broken chromosome attaching itself to another chromosome.

**Transsexualism:** Gender identity disorder in which the patient believes that he or she was born with the body of the wrong sex.

**Transvestism:** Sexual deviancy involving dressing in the garments of the opposite sex.

**Trauma:** Medically, a severe injury or blow; psychologically, a severe stress.

**Trephining:** Primitive surgical method involving entering the skull with a crude instrument.

**Tricyclics:** Drugs which affect the level of epinephrine and which have some success with unipolar depressions. Also known as Tricyclic antidepressants.

**Trisomy:** Existence of three instead of two chromosomes in each set.

**True microcephaly:** Form of microcephaly believed to be hereditary. Also known as primary microcephaly.

**Tuberous sclerosis:** Disease involving the presence of tumors in every tissue and involving mental retardation.

**Two-factor theory:** Belief that phobias have two stages: classical conditioning which initiates the stimulus-fear linkage and avoidance-learning which strengthens and maintains the fear

**Undersocialized aggressive personality:** Type of antisocial personality who is a callous, lone-wolf, defiant assaulter.

**Undersocialized unaggressive personality:** Type of antisocial personality who is a sly manipulator of other people.

**Unipolar depression:** Descriptive term synonymous with major depression; sometimes used to distinguish major depression from bipolar depression. In DSM-III, the term major depression is used.

**Vaginismus:** Psychosexual dysfunction in which spasms of the vagina make intercourse difficult.

**Vicarious extinction:** Elimination of unwanted behaviors through the observation of a model.

**Vicarious learning:** Acquiring of new behaviors through the observation of a model.

**Visuo-motor behavior rehearsal:** Behavior therapy approach to increase adaptive behavior by imagery control.

***Vorbeigehen:*** Symptom of Ganser's syndrome exhibited when a patient gives answers to questions that just "miss the point."

**Voyeurism:** Paraphilia in which the individual becomes sexually aroused from watching others.

**Waxy flexibility:** Heightened motor responsiveness to suggestions, characteristic of catatonic schizophrenia.

**Windigo psychosis:** Form of mental disorder involving cannibalism.

**Withdrawal:** Physical distress deriving from giving up substance use; includes nausea, craving, and restlessness.

**Zeigarnik effect:** Tendency for individuals to have a better memory for unfinished tasks than for completed ones. Research suggests that this tendency is reversed when failure to complete task is perceived as threatening.

**Zoophilia:** Paraphilia involving intercourse with animals.

**Zygote:** Union of a sperm and an ovum.

# REFERENCES

## CHAPTER 1


American Psychological Association. (1980, September 9). Meeting of the APA council of representatives. Reported in *APA Monitor,* 1980, **11,** 10–11.

American Psychiatric Association. (1980). *Diagnostic and statistical manual of mental disorders* (3d ed.). Washington, DC: APA.

American Psychiatric Association, *DSM-III debate.* (1983). Washington, DC: APA.

Appel, K. (1957). Mental health and mental illness. In R. Kurtz (Ed.), *Social work yearbook.* New York: National Association of Social Workers.

Bandura, A. (1968). A social learning interpretation of psychological dysfunctions. In P. London & D. Rosenhan (Eds.), *Foundations of abnormal psychology.* New York: Holt, Rinehart & Winston.

Barron F. (1963). *Creativity and psychological health.* New York: Van Nostrand.

Beach, B. (1981). Picking between mad and bad. *Time,* **118,** p. 68.

Blashfield, R., & Draguns, J. (1976). Evaluative criteria for psychiatric classification. *Journal of Abnormal Psychology,* **85,** 140–150.

Bonnie, R. (1983). The moral basis of the insanity defense. *American Bar Association Journal,* **69,** 194–197.

Broverman, D., Broverman, I., Clarkson, F., Rosenkrants, P., & Vogel, S. (1970). Sex-role stereotypes and clinical judgments of mental health. *Journal of Consulting and Clinical Psychology,* **34,** 1.

Cattell, R. (1957). *Personality and motivation structure and measurement.* New York: World Book.

Cohen, R. & Mariano, W. (1983). *Legal guidebook in mental health.* New York: Free Press.

Durham, J. (1954). *United States,* 214 F. 2d, 862, 876 (D.C. Cir.).

Eysenck, H. (1952). *The scientific study of personality.* London: Routledge & Kegan Paul.

Freud, S. (1938). Psychopathology of everyday life. In A. Brill (Ed.), *The basic writings of Sigmund Freud.* New York: Random House.

Gest, T. (1982, July, 5). Hinckley bombshell: end of insanity pleas. *U.S. News and World Report,* p. 12–15.

Hinckley, J. (1981). Letter to Jodie Foster. *Newsweek,* **98,** p. 35.

Hinckley, J. (1982). The insanity defense and me. *Newsweek,* **100,** p. 30.

Institute for Personality Assessment and Research, University of California, Berkeley (1961). *The creative person.* Berkeley: University Extension, University of California.

Laing, R. D. (1960). *The divided self.* Chicago: Quadrangle Books.

Laing, R. D. (1972). *The obvious.* In H. Reitenbeck (Ed.), *Going crazy.* New York: Bantam.

Laing, R. D. & Esterson, A. (1964). *Sanity, madness, and the family.* London: Tavistock.

Lichtenstein, E. (1980). *Psychotherapy approaches and application.* Belmont, CA.: Wadsworth.

Mathews, J. (1981). Reagan's cease fall. *Newsweek,* **97,** 31–38.

M'Naughten, V. *The Crown of England,* 8 Eng. Rep. 718 (1843).

Morgenthau, T. (1982). A controversial verdict: Hinckley goes to the hospital. *Newsweek,* **100,** 30–31.

Nathan, P. (in press). Diagnostic and nosological issues in psychotherapy research. In Hersen, M., Michelson, L., & Bellak, A. (Eds.), *Issues in psychotherapy research.* New York: Plenum Press.

*Parsons* v. *State,* 2 So. 854, 866–867 (Ala. 1887).

Price, R. (1978). *Abnormal behavior: Perspectives in conflict.* (2nd ed.). New York: Holt, Rinehart & Winston.

Rosenhan, D. L. (1973). On being sane in insane places. *Science,* **179,** 250–258.

Sarason, I., & Ganzer, V. (1968). Concerning the medical model. *American Psychologist,* **23,** 507.

Staats, A., & Staats, C. (1963). *Complex human behavior.* New York: Holt, Rinehart, & Winston.

Szasz, T. (1965). *Psychiatric justice.* New York: Macmillan.

Terman, L., & Oden, M. (1959). *The gifted group at mid-life, Volume 5 Genetic studies of genius.* Stanford, CA: Stanford University Press.

Thigpen, C., & Cleckley, H. (1957). *The three faces of Eve.* New York: McGraw-Hill.

Thorne, F. (1953). Back to fundamentals. *Journal of Clinical Psychology,* **9,** 89.

Wittman, P. & Sheldon, W. (1948). A proposed classification of psychotic behavior reactions. *American Journal of Psychiatry,* **105,** 124.

*Wyatt* v. *Stickney,* 344 F. Supp. 373–387 (M.D. Ala. 1972).

Ziegenfuss, Jr., J. (1983). *Patients' rights and organizational models: Sociotechnical systems research on mental health programs.* Lanham, MD: University Press of America.

## CHAPTER 2


Alexander, F., & Selesnick, S. (1966). *The history of psychiatry: An evaluation of psychiatric thought and practice from prehistoric times to the present.* New York: Harper.

Bailly, J. (1784). *Rapport des comissaires chargés par le roi, de l'examen du magnetisme animal.* Paris: L'imprimerie royal.

Berkeley, G. (1709). *An essay toward a new theory of vision.* Dublin.

Celcus, A. C. De re medica III (1935). Translated by A. C. Spenser. Cambridge, MA.: Harvard University Press.

Charcot, J. (1882). Essai d'une distinction nosographique des divers états compris sous le nom d'hypnotisme. *Compt. Rend. Acad. Sc.*, **44.**

Davies, J. (1955). *Phrenology, Fad and Science.* New Haven, CT: Yale University Press.

Descartes, R. (1649). *Passions of the soul.* Amsterdam.

Deutsch, A. (1949). *The mentally ill in America.* New York: Columbia University Press.

Gomperz, T. (1901). *Greek thinkers.* Translated by L. Magnus. London.

Isensee, E. (1845). *Geschichte der Medicin, Part II,* Book 6. Berlin.

Kraepelin, E. (1883). *Lehrbuch der psychiatrie.* Germany.

Laing, R. (1964). Is schizophrenia a disease? *International Journal of Social Psychiatry,* **10,** 184.

Liébeault, A. (1866). *Du Somneil et des états analogues considérés surtout au point de vue de l'action du moral sur le physique.* Paris: Masson.

Locke, J. (1913). Essay concerning human understanding. In J. St. John (Ed.), *The philosophical works of John Locke.* London: Bell & Sons, 1913. Original work published in 1700.

Miles, L. (1835). *Phrenology, and the moral influence of phrenology.* Philadelphia: Carey, Lea & Blanchard.

Rees, T. (1957). Back to moral treatment and community care. *Journal Mental Science,* **103,** 303.

Russell, A. (1972). *Witchcraft in the Middle Ages.* New York: Cornell University Press.

Summers, M. (1928). (Trans.) of Sprenger, J., & Kraemer. H. *Malleus malificarum.* London: Rodker.

Veith, D. (1975). The far east. In J. Howells (Ed.), *World history of psychiatry.* New York: Brunner/Mazel.

Weyer, J. (1967). Delusions of Witches. In C. Goshen (Ed.), *Documentary history of psychiatry.* New York: Philosophical Library.

Zilboorg, G., & Henry, G. (1941). *A history of medical psychology.* New York: Norton.


## CHAPTER 3


Aserinsky, E., & Kleitman, N. (1953). Regularly occurring periods of eye motility and concomitant phenomena during sleep. *Science,* **118,** 273.

Atthowe, J. (1973). Token economies come of age. *Behavior Therapy,* **4**, 646–654.

Bandura, A. (1968). A social learning interpretation of psychological dysfunctions. In P. London & D. Rosenhan (Eds.), *Foundations of abnormal psychology.* New York: Holt, Rinehart & Winston.

Bandura, A. (1971). *Social learning theory.* Morristown, NJ: General Learning Press.

Bandura, A. (1977). Self-efficacy: Towards a unifying theory of behavioral change. *Psychological Review,* **84,** 191–215.

Bandura, A., Adams, N., & Beyer, J. (1977). Cognitive processes mediating behavioral change. *Journal of Personality & Social Psychology,* **35,** 125–129.

Bandura, A., Ross, D., & Ross, S. (1963). Imitation of film-mediated aggressive models. *Journal of Abnormal and Social Psychology,* **66,** 3–11.

Beck, A. (1976). *Cognitive therapy and emotional disorders.* New York: International University Press.

Bexton, W., Heron, W., & Scott, T. (1954). Effects of decreased variation in the sensory environment. *Canadian Journal of Psychology,* **8,** 70–76.

Breuer, J. & Freud, S. (1957). *Studies on hysteria.* Translated by J. Strachey. New York: Basic Books.

Cairns, R. (1961). The influence of dependency inhibition on the effectiveness of social reinforcers. *Journal of Personality,* **29,** 466.

Davitz, J. (1952). The effects of previous training on postfrustration behavior. *Journal of Abnormal and Social Psychology,* **47,** 309.

Dement, W. (1960). The effect of dream deprivation. *Science,* **131,** 1705–1707.

Dement, W. (1965). Recent studies on the biological role of rapid eye movement sleep. *American Journal of Psychiatry,* **122,** 404.

Dement, W. (1974). *Some must watch while some must sleep.* San Francisco: Freeman.

Dollard, J., Doob, L., Miller, N., Mowrer, O., & Sears, R. (1939). *Frustration and aggression.* New Haven, CT: Yale University Press.

Dollard, J. & Miller, N. (1950). Personality and psychotherapy: Analysis in terms of learning, thinking and culture. New York: McGraw-Hill.

D'Zurilla, T., & Goldfried, M. (1971). Problem solving and behavior modification. *Journal of Abnormal Psychology,* **78,** 107–126.

Ellis, A. (1962). *Reason and emotion in psychotherapy.* New York: Lyle Stuart, 1962.

Eysenck, H. (1960). *Behaviour therapy and the neuroses.* New York: Pergamon Press.

Ferster, C. (1961). Positive reinforcement and behavioral deficits of autistic children. *Child Development,* **32,** 437–454.

Fisher, S., & Greenberg, R. (1977). *The scientific credibility of Freud's theories and therapy.* New York: Basic Books.

Frankl, V. (1963). *Man's search for meaning.* New York: Washington Square Press.

Goldstein, A. (1983). *Prevention and control of aggression.* New York: Pergamon.

Hebb, D., Heath, E., & Stuart, E. (1954). Experimental deafness. *Canadian Journal of Psychology,* **8,** 152.

Jones, M. C. (1924). A laboratory study of fear: The case of Peter. *Pedagog. Ser.*, **31**, 308.

Jung, C. (1953). *Collected works.* In H. Read, M. Fordham, & G. Adler (Eds.). Princeton, NJ: Princeton University Press.

Kline, P. (1977). Cross-cultural studies of Freudian theory. In N. Warren (Ed.), *Studies in cross-cultural psychology,* Vol. 1. London: Academic Press.

Krasner, L. & Atthowe, J. (1968). Preliminary report on the application of contingent reinforcement procedures (token economy) on a "chronic" psychiatric ward. *Journal of Abnormal Psychology,* **73,** 37–43.

Lewis, D., Shanok, S., Grant, M., & Ritvo, E. (1983). Homocidally aggressive young children: Neuropsychiatric and experiential correlates. *American Journal of Psychiatry,* **140,** 148–153.

Mahoney, M. (1974). *Cognition and behavior modification.* Cambridge, MA: Ballinger.

Maslow, A. (1968). *Toward a psychology of being.* (2nd ed.) Princeton, NJ: Van Nostrand.

Masserman, J. (1943). *Behavior and neurosis.* Chicago: University of Chicago Press.

Masserman, J. (1961). *Principles of dynamic psychiatry.* Philadelphia: Saunders.

Meichenbaum, D. (1977). *Cognitive-behavior modification.* New York: Plenum Press.

Milavsky, J., Kessler, R., Stipp, H. & Rubens, W. (1983). *Television and aggression.* New York: Academic Press.

Mowrer, O. & Mowrer, W. (1938). Enuresis: A method for its study and treatment. *American Journal of Orthopsychiatry,* **8,** 436.

Pavlov, I. (1897). *Lectures on the work of the principal digestive glands.*

Pavlov, I. (1904). *Lectures on conditioned reflexes.* Moscow: Leningrad State Publishing House.

Pfeffer, C., Plutchik, R., & Mizruchi, M. (1983). Predictors of assaultiveness in latency age children. *American Journal of Psychiatry,* **140,** 31–35.

Rogers, C. (1957). The necessary and sufficient conditions for personality change. *Journal of Consulting Psychology,* **21,** 95–103.

Rogers, C. (1961). *On becoming a person.* Boston: Houghton Mifflin.

Staats, A., & Staats, C. (1963). *Complex human behavior.* New York: Holt, Rinehart & Winston.

Suinn, R. (1969). Limited sensory and social deprivation and operant control of affiliation and deferences responses. *Journal of Projective Techniques,* **33,** 535.

Sullivan, H. (1947). Conceptions of modern psychiatry. Washington, DC: William Alanson White Psychiatric Foundation.

Thorndike, E. (1905). *The elements of psychology.* New York: Seiler.

Watson, J. (1919). *Psychology from the standpoint of a behaviorist.* Philadelphia, Lippincott.

Watson, J., & Rayner, R. (1920). Conditioned emotional reactions. *Journal of Experimental Psychology,* **3,** 1–14.

Wolpe, J. (1958). *Psychotherapy by reciprocal inhibition.* Stanford, CA.: Stanford University Press.

Wolpe, J. & Rachman, S. (1960). Psychoanalytic "evidence," a critique based on Freud's case of Little Hans. *Journal of Nervous and Mental Disease,* **131,** 135–147.


## CHAPTER 4


Abrams, R., & Taylor, M. (1983). The genetics of schizophrenia: A reassessment using modern criteria. *American Journal of Psychiatry,* **140,** 171–175.

Andy, O., & Jurko, M. (1977). The human amygdala: Excitability state and aggression. In W. Sweet, S. Obrador, & J. Martin-Rodriguez (Eds.), *Neurosurgical treatment in psychiatry, pain, and epilepsy.* Baltimore: University Park Press.

Baruk, H., & Camus, L. (1949). Le principe toxique cataleptisant de la bile humaine; nouvelles études sur la catatonie biliaire expérimentale. *Presse Medicale,* **57,** 1065.

Berger, H. (1903). Experimentelle Studien zur Pathogenese acuter Psychosen. Berlin: *Klin. Wschr.* No. 30.

Berger, P. et al. (1980). B-endorphin and schizophrenia. *Archives of General Psychiatry,* **37,** 635–640.

Bunney, W., Goodwin, F., & Murphy, D. (1972). The "switch process" in manic-depressive illness. *Archives of General Psychiatry,* **27,** 312–317.

Cairns, R. (1973). Fighting and punishment from a developmental perspective. In J. Cole & D. Jensen (Eds.), *Nebraska symposium on motivation.* Vol. 20. Lincoln: University of Nebraska Press.

Cannon, W. (1963). *Wisdom of the body.* New York: Norton.

Chamove, A. (1980). Nongenetic induction of acquired levels of aggression. *Journal of Abnormal Psychology,* **89,** 469–488.

Cox, A., & Brown, M. (1977). Results of multi-target limbic surgery in the treatment of schizophrenia and aggressive states. In W. Sweet, S. Obrador, & J. Martin-Rodriguez (Eds.), *Neurosurgical treatment in psychiatry, pain, and epilepsy.* Baltimore: University Park Press.

Crow, T. (Ed.) (1983). *Disorders of neurohumoural transmission.* New York: Academic Press.

Davis, G. et al. (1979). Use of narcotic antagonists to study the role of endorphins in normal and psychiatric patients. In E. Usdin, W. Bunney, & N. Kline (Eds.), *Endorphins in mental health research.* London: MacMillan.

Davis, J. (1978). Dopamine theory of schizophrenia: A two-factor theory. In L. Wynne, R. Cromwell, & S. Matthysse (Eds.), *The nature of schizophrenia.* New York: Wiley.

DeJong, H. (1934). Presence in urine of substance which may produce catatonic symptoms. *Psychiat. et Neurol. Bl.,* **38,** 914.

Dingemanse, E., & Freud, J. (1933). Identification of catatonine. *J. Acta Brevia Neerland. Physiol. Pharmacol. Microbiol.,* **3,** 49.

Dorns, E. (1980). Variability in the Y chromosome and variability of human behavior. *Archives of General Psychiatry,* **37,** 587–594.

Freud, J., & Dingemanse, E. (1932). Über Katatonin, einen giftigen Stoff im Lipoid extrakt von Harm, Gewebsflussigkeiten und Organen. *Biochem, Zeitschr.,* **255,** 464.

Gale, A. & Edwards, J. (1983). *Vol. 1: Basic Issues Physiological correlates of human behaviour.* New York: Academic Press.

Gerner, R. Catlin, D., Gorlick, D., Hui, K. K., & Li, C. H. (1980). B-endorphin. *Archives of General Psychiatry,* **37,** 642–647.

Goddard, H. (1919). *The Kallikak family.* New York: Macmillan.

Goldner, M., & Ricketts, H. (1942). Significance of insulin inhibition by blood of schizophrenic patients. *Archives of Neurological Psychiatry,* **48,** 552.

Gottesman, I. (1963). Genetic aspects of intelligent behavior. In N. Ellis (Ed.), *The handbook of mental deficiency.* New York: McGraw-Hill.

Gottesman, I. (1978). Schizophrenia and genetics: Where are we? Are you sure? In L. Wynne, R. Cromwell, & S. Matthysse (Eds.), *The nature of schizophrenia.* New York: Wiley.

Gottesman, I., & Shields, J. (1972). *Schizophrenia and genetics: A twin study vantage point.* New York: Academic Press.

Hall, C. (1934). Emotional behavior in the rat: I. Defecation and urination as measures of individual differences in emotionality. *Journal of Comparative Psychology,* **18,** 385.

Hall, R., Gardner, E., Popkin, M., & Lecann, A. (1981). Unrecognized physical illness prompting psychiatric admission: A prospective study. *American Journal of Psychiatry,* **138,** 629–635.

Heath, R. (1955). Correlations between levels of psychological awareness and physiological activity in the central nervous system. *Psychosomatic Medicine,* **17,** 383–387.

Heath, R., Martens, S., Leach, B., Cohen, M., & Angel, C. (1957). Effect on behavior in humans with the administration of taraxein. *American Journal of Psychiatry,* **114,** 14.

Heath, R., & Mickle, W. (1960). Evaluation of seven years' experience with depth electrode studies in human patients. In E. Ramey & D. O'Doherty (Eds.), *Electrical studies on the unanesthetized brain.* New York: Paul Hoeber.

Heston, L. (1966). Psychiatric disorders in foster home reared children of schizophrenic mothers. *British Journal of Psychiatry,* **112,** 819–825.

Heston, L. (1971). Discussion: Schizophrenia—onset in infancy? *Soc. Biol.,* **18,** 114.

Hoffer, A., & Osmond, H. (1959). The adrenochrome model and schizophrenia. *Journal of Nervous and Mental Disorders,* **128,** 18–35.

Hoffer, A., & Osmond, H. (1960). *The chemical basis of clinical psychology.* Springfield, IL: C. C. Thomas.

Hoffer, A., Payza, A., Szara, S., & Axelrod, J. (1960). The presence of adrenochrome in blood. *American Journal of Psychiatry,* **116,** 32.

Hughes, J. (1975). Isolation of an endogenous compound from the brain with pharmacological properties similar to morphine. *Brain Research,* **88,** 295–308.

Kahn, M. (1951). The effect of severe defeat at various age levels on the aggressive behavior of mice. *Journal of Genetic Psychology,* **79,** 117–130.

Kallmann, F. (1946). The genetic theory of schizophrenia. *American Journal of Psychiatry,* **103,** 309–322.

Kallman, F. (1953). *Heredity in health and mental disorder.* New York: Norton.

Kety, S. (1980). The syndrome of schizophrenia: Unresolved questions and opportunities for research. *British Journal of Psychiatry,* **136,** 421–436.

Kidd, K. (1978). A genetic perspective on schizophrenia. In L. Wynne, R. Cromwell, & S. Matthysse (Eds.), *The nature of schizophrenia.* New York: Wiley.

Kringlen, E. (1978). Adult offspring of two psychotic parents, with special reference to schizophrenia. In L. Wynne, R. Cromwell, & S. Matthysse (Eds.), *The nature of schizophrenia.* New York: Wiley.

Lejeunne, J., Turpin, R., & Gautier, M. (1959). Le mongolisme, premier example d'aberration autosomique humaine. *Ann. Genetique,* **2,** 41.

Lindstrom, L., Widerlov, E., & Gunne, A. (1978). Endorphins in human cerebrospinal fluid: Clinical correlations in some psychotic states. *Acta Psychiatrica Scandinavica,* **57,** 153–164.

Manchanda, R. & Hirsch, S. (1982). (Des-Tyre) gamma-endorphin for schizophrenia. A critical review. Intern. Pharmacopsychiatry, **17,** 147–152.

Motshagen, A., & Slangen, J. (1975). Instrumental conditioning of aggressive behavior in rats. *Aggressive Behavior,* **1,** 157–163.

Olds, J. (1956). A preliminary mapping of electrical reinforcing effects in the rat brain. *Journal of Comparative Physiological Psychology,* **49,** 281.

Paul, S. (1977). Movement and madness: Towards a biological model of schizophrenia. In J. Maser & M. Seligman (Eds.), *Psychopathology: Experimental models.* San Francisco: Freeman.

Phillips, A., & Lieblich, I. (1972). Developmental and hormonal aspects of hyperemotionality produced by septal lesions in male rats. *Physiology and Behavior,* **9,** 237–242.

Rieder, H. (1957). Biological determinations of toxicity of pathologic body fluids; Examination of urinary extracts of mental patients with the help of the spider web test. *Psychiat. et Neurol. (Basel),* **134,** 387.

Robins, E., Smith, K., & Lower, I. Neuropharmacology. In *Transactions of the Josiah Macy, Jr. Foundation,* 4th Conference, 1957.

Rodgers, D., & McClearn, G. (1962). Mouse strain differences in preference for various concentrations of alcohol. *Journal of Studies on Alcohol,* **23,** 26–33.

Rosenthal, D. (Ed.) (1963). *The Genain quadruplets.* New York: Basic Books.

Rosenthal, D., Wender, P., Schulsinger, F., & Jacobsen, B. (1978). The biological and adoptive families of adopted individuals who became schizophrenic: Prevalence of mental illness and other characteristics. In L. Wynne, R. Cromwell, & S. Matthysee (Eds.), *The nature of schizophrenia.* New York: Wiley.

Schvarcz, J. (1977). Results of stimulation and destruction of the posterior hypothalamus: A long-term evaluation. In W. Sweet, S. Obrador, J. Martin-Rodriguez (Eds.), *Neurosurgical treatment in psychiatry, pain, and epilepsy.* Baltimore: University Park Press.

Scott, J. (1947). Emotional behavior of fighting mice caused by conflict between weak stimulatory and weak inhibitory training. *Journal of Comparative Physiology and Psychology,* **40,** 275.

Shields, J. (1978). Genetics. In J. Wing (Ed.), *Schizophrenia, towards a new synthesis.* London: Academy Press.

Sjögren, T. (1935). Verebungsmedizinische untersuchungen über Huntington's Chorea in einer schwedischen Bauernpopulation. *A. Mnschl. Vereb. -u. Konstitlehre,* **19,** 131.

Stuss, D. & Benson, D. (1983). Emotional concomitants of psychosurgery. In K. Heilman & P. Satz (Eds.), *Neuropsychology of human emotion.* New York: Guilford Press.

Suinn, R. (1969). The need for data on false positives among the XYY chromosomal aberrants. *Lancet,* **1,** 157.

Turkington, C. (1982). Nature wins round in studies on infants. *APA Monitor,* **13,** pp. 14, 21.

Wiener, S., Sutherland, G., Bartholomew, A., & Hudson, B. (1968). XYY males in a Melbourne prison. *Lancet,* **1,** 816.

Witt, P. (1956). *Die Wirkung von Substanzen auf den Netzbau von Spinne als biologischer Test.* Berlin: Springer.

## CHAPTER 5


Akisol, H., & McKinney, W. (1973). Depressive disorders: Toward a unified hypothesis. *Science,* **182,** 20–29.

Alanen, Y. (1968). From the mothers of schizophrenic patients to international family dynamics. In D. Rosenthal & S. Ketz (Eds.), *The transmission of schizophrenia.* London: Oxford University Press.

Albee, G. (1980). A competency model to replace the deficit model. In M. Gibbs, J. Lachenmayer, & J. Sigal (Eds.) *Community psychology: Theoretical and empirical approaches.* New York: Gardner Press.

Alers, J. (1978). *Puerto Ricans and health: Findings from New York City.* New York: Fordham University Hispanic Research Center.

Al-Issa, I. (Ed.). (1982). *Gender and psychopathology.* New York: Academic Press.

Bateson, G., Jackson, D., Haley, J., & Weakland, J. (1956). Towards a theory of schizophrenia. *Behavior Sciences,* **1,** 251–264.

Benedict, R. *The chrysanthemum and the sword.* (1946). Boston: Houghton Mifflin.

Blechman, E. (Ed.) (1983). *Behavior modification with women.* New York: Guilford.

Bowlby, J. (1944). Forty-four juvenile thieves. *International Journal of Psycho-Analysis,* **25,** 1.

Brodsky, A. & Hare-Mustin, R. (1980). *Women and psychotherapy: An assessment of research and practice.* New York: Guilford.

Broverman, D., Broverman, I., Clarkson, F., Rosenkrantz, P. & Vogel, S. (1970). Sex-role stereotypes and clinical judgments of mental health. *Journal of Consulting and Clinical Psychology,* **34,** 1.

Brown, G., Bhrolchain, M., & Harris, T. (1975). Social class and psychiatric disturbances among women in an urban population. *Sociology,* **9,** 225–254.

Brown, G., & Harris, T. (1978). *Social origins of depression.* New York: Free Press.

Chesler, P. (1972). *Women and madness.* New York: Doubleday.

Clardy, E. (1951). A study of the development and course of schizophrenic children. *Psychiatric Quarterly,* **25,** 81–90.

Collier, H. (1983). *Counseling women. A guide for therapists.* Riverside, New York: Free Press.

Cooper, B. (1978). Epidemiology. In J. Wing (Ed.), *Schizophrenia: Towards a new synthesis.* London: Academic Press.

Dohrenwend, B. (1975). Sociocultural and social-psychological facts in the genesis of mental disorders. *Journal of Health and Social Behavior,* **16,** 365–392.

Donnelly, E. (1960). The quantitative analysis of parent behavior toward psychotic children and their siblings. *Genetic Psychology Monographs,* **62,** 331.

Draguns, J. (1980). Psychological disorders of clinical severity. In H. Triandis & J. Draguns (Eds.), *Handbook of cross-cultural psychology.* Boston: Allyn & Bacon.

Dressler, W. (1978). Hypertension in St. Lucia: Social and cultural dimensions. Unpublished doctoral dissertation, University of Connecticut, Storrs.

Eichler, R., & Lirtzman, S. (1956). Religious background of patients in a mental hygiene setting. *Journal of Nervous and Mental Disorders,* **124,** 514.

Farberow, N. (1975). *Suicide in different cultures.* Baltimore: University Park Press.

Faris, R., & Dunham, H. (1939). *Mental disorders in urban areas.* Chicago: University of Chicago Press.

Favazza, A., & Oman, M. (1978). Overview: Foundations of cultural psychiatry. *American Journal of Psychiatry,* **135,** 5–11.

Fleck, S. (1976). A general systems view of families of schizophrenics. In J. Jorstad & E. Egelstad (Eds.), *Schizophrenia 75.* Oslow, Norway: Lie.

Fleck, S., Lidz, T., & Cornelison, A. (1963). Comparison of parent-child relationships of male and female schizophrenic patients. *Archives of General Psychiatry,* **8,** 1–7.

Freeman, R., & Grayson, H. (1955). Maternal attitudes in schizophrenia. *Journal of Abnormal and Social Psychology,* **50,** 45–52.

Freud, A., & Burlingham, D. (1944). *Infants without families.* New York: International University Press.

Frumkin, R., & Frumkin, M. (1957). Religion, occupation, and major mental disorders. *Journal of Human Relations,* **6,** 98–101.

Giordano, J. & Giordano, G. (1976). Ethnicity and community mental health. *Community Mental Health Review,* **1,** (3).

Goldfarb, W. (1945). Psychological privation in infancy and subsequent adjustment. *American Journal of Orthopsychiatry,* **15,** 247.

Guthrie, G., & Tanco, P. (1980). Alienation. In H. Triandis & J. Draguns (Eds.), *Handbook of cross-cultural psychology.* Vol. 6. Boston: Allyn & Bacon.

Guttentag, M., Salasin, S., & Belle, D. (1980). *The mental health of women.* New York: Academic Press.

Haley, J. (1980). *Learning borne.* New York: McGraw-Hill.

Harlow, H. (1958). The nature of love. *American Psychologist,* **13,** 673.

Harlow, H., & Suomi, S. (1974). Induced depression in monkeys. *Behavioral Biology,* **12,** 273–296.

Higginbotham, H. (1979). Culture and mental health service. In A. Marsella, R. Tharp, & T. Ciborowski (Eds.), *Perspectives of cross-cultural psychology.* New York: Academic Press.

Hill, L. (1955). *Psychotherapeutic intervention in schizophrenia.* Chicago: University of Chicago Press.

Hirsch, S., & Leff, J. (1975). *Abnormalities in parents of schizophrenics.* London: Oxford University Press.

Hollingshead, A., & Redlich, F. (1958). *Social class and mental illness.* New York: Wiley.

Horner, M. (1970). The motive to avoid success and changing aspirations of college women. In *Women on campus: 1970, a symposium.* Ann Arbor, MI: Center for the Continuing Education of Women.

Inkeles, A., Hanfmann, E., & Beier, H. (1958). Modal personality and adjustment to the Soviet socio-political system. *Human Relations,* **11,** 3.

Jaco, E. (1960). *The social epidemiology of mental disorders.* New York: Russell Sage Foundation.

Japan Ministry of Health and Welfare. (1954). Factual survey of mental hygiene. Tokyo: Ministry of Health and Welfare.

Kagan, J. (1982). *Psychological research on the human infant: An evaluative summary.* New York: William T. Grant Foundation.

Kramer, M., Rosen, B., & Willis, E. (1973). Definitions and distributions of mental disorders in a racist society. In C. Willie, M. Kramer, & B. Brown (Eds.), *Racism and mental health.* Pittsburgh: University of Pittsburgh Press.

L'Abate, L. (1983). *Family psychology: Theory, therapy and training.* Washington, DC: University Press of America.

Lamb, M. (Ed.) (1982). *Nontraditional families: Parenting and child development.* Hillsdale, NJ: Lawrence Erlbaum.

Landis, D. & Brislin, R. (1983). *Handbook of intercultural training.* New York: Pergamon.

Levine, D. (1972). A cross-national study of attitudes toward mental illness. *Journal of Abnormal Psychology,* **80,** 111.

Levine, E., & Padilla, A. (1980). *Crossing cultures in therapy: Pluralistic counseling for the Hispanic.* Monterey, CA: Brooks/Cole.

Lin, K. (1983). Hwa-Byung: A Korean culture-bound syndrome? *American Journal of Psychiatry.* **140,** 105–107.

Lin, T. (1953). A study of the incidence of mental disorder in Chinese and other cultures. *Psychiatry,* **16,** 313.

Linton, R. (1956). *Culture and mental disorders.* Springfield, IL: C. C Thomas.

Malzberg, B. (1936). *The mental health of the Negro.* Albany, NY: Research Foundation for Mental Hygiene.

Marsella, A. (1979). Cross-cultural studies of mental disorders. In A. Marsella, R. Tharp, & T. Ciborowski (Eds.), *Perspectives of cross-cultural psychology.* New York: Academic Press.

Marsella, A. (1980). Depressive experiences and disorders across cultures. In H. Triandid & J. Draguns (Eds.), *Handbook of cross-cultural psychology.* Boston: Allyn & Bacon.

Martinez, F. (1982). Clinical services for Hispanics: Management issues. In R. Becerra, M. Karno, & J. Escobar (Eds.), *Mental health and Hispanic Americans.* New York: Grune & Stratton.

Masson, H. & O'Bryne, P. (1983). *Applying family therapy.* New York: Pergamon.

Melzack, R., & Scott, T. (1957). The effects of early experience on the response to pain. *Journal of Comparative and Physiological Psychology,* **50,** 515.

Miranda, M. et al. (1976). *Psychotherapy with the Spanish speaking: Issues in research and service delivery.* Los Angeles: Spanish Speaking Mental Health Resource Center.

Mollica, R. (1983). From asylum to community: The threatened disintegration of public psychiatry. *New England Journal of Medicine* **308,** 367–373.

Murphy, H. (1959). Culture and mental disorder in Singapore. In M. Opler (Ed.), *Culture and mental health.* New York: Macmillan.

Newton, F., Olmedo, E., & Padilla, A. (1982). Hispanic Mental Health Research. Los Angeles: University of California Press.

Noyes, R., Clancy, J., Hoenk, P., & Slymen, D. (1980). The prognosis of anxiety neurosis. *Archives of General Psychiatry, 37,* 173–178.

Olson, D. (1972). Empirically unbinding the double bind: Review of research and conceptual reformations. *Family Process,* **11,** 69–94.

Papousek, H. & Papousek, M. (1983). Biological basis of social interactions: Implications of research for an understanding of behavioral deviance. *Journal of Child Psychology and Psychiatry,* **24,** 117–129.

Perlmutter, M. (Ed.) (1983). *Minnesota symposium on child psychology.* Hillsdale, NJ: Lawrence Erlbaum.

Prince, R. (1980). Variations in psychotherapeutic procedures. In H. Triandis & J. Draguns (Eds.), *Handbook of cross-cultural psychology.* Boston: Allyn & Bacon.

Radloff, L. (1975). Sex difference in depression. *Sex Roles,* **1,** 249.

Robertson, J., & Bowlby, J. (1952). Responses of young children to separation from their mothers: II. Observation of sequences of response of children aged 18–24 months during course of separation. *Courr. Cent. Int. l'Enfance,* **2,** 131.

Roskies, E., Iida-Miranda, M., & Strobel, M. (1977). Life changes as predictors of illness in immigrants. In S. Sarason & C. Speilberger (Eds.), *Stress and anxiety.* Vol. 4. Washington, DC: Hemisphere Publishing.

Rowland, J. (1964). The effects of total social isolation upon learning and social behavior of rhesus monkeys. (Doctoral dissertation, University of Wisconsin). Ann Arbor, MI: Microfilms, No. 64-9690.

Schooler, C., & Caudill, W. (1964). Symptomatology in Japanese and American schizophrenics. *Enthnology,* **3,** 172.

Seymour, G., Bernal, M., Lao, R., & Pine, C. (1982). *Report of Task Force on Minority Education and Training, Board of Ethnic Minority Affairs.* Washington, DC: American Psychological Association.

Singh, J., & Zingg, R. (1942). *Wolf child and feral man.* New York: Harper.

Sjögren, T., & Larrson, T. (1954). A methodological, psychiatric and statistical study of a large Swedish rural population. *Acta Psychiat. et. Neurol. Scand.,* Suppl. 89.

Smith, W., Burlew, A., Moseley, M., & Whitney, W. (1978). *Minority issues in mental health.* Menlo Park, CA: Addison Wesley.

Smither, R., & Rodriguez-Giegling, M. (1979). Marginality, modernity, and anxiety in Indochinese refugees. *Journal of Cross-cultural Psychology,* **10,** 469–478.

Snyder, C. (1955). Culture and sobriety: A study of drinking patterns and sociocultural factors related to sobriety among Jews. *Journal of Studies on Alcohol,* **16,** 101–117.

Sperling, M. (1974). *The major neuroses and behavior disorders in children.* New York: Jason Aronson.

Spiro, M. (1959). Cultural heritage, personal tension, and mental illness in a south sea culture. In M. Opler (Ed.), *Culture and mental health.* New York: Macmillan.

Spitz, R., & Wolf, K. (1946). Anaclitic depression. *Psychoanal. Stud. Child.,* **2,** 313–342.

Srole, L., & Fischer, A. (1980). The midtown Manhattan study vs. the 'mental paradise lost' doctrine. *Archives of General Psychiatry,* **37,** 209–221.

Strainbrook, E. (1952). Some characteristics of the psychopathology of schizophrenic behavior in Bahian society. *American Journal of Psychiatry,* **109,** 330.

Sue, S. & Chin R. (1982). Chinese American children: Psychosocial development and mental health. In G. Powell, A. Morales, and J. Yamamoto (Eds.), *The Psychosocial Development of Minority Group Children.* New York: Brunner/Mazel.

Sue, S. & Morishima, J. (1982). *The mental health of Asian Americans.* San Francisco: Jossey-Bass.

Tseng, W., & Hsu, J. (1979). Minor psychological disturbance of everyday life. In A. Marsella, R. Tharp, & T. Ciborowski (Eds.), *Perspectives of cross-cultural psychology.* New York: Academic Press.

U.S. Department of Health, Education and Welfare. (1977). *Admissions rates to state and county psychiatric hospitals by age, sex, and race.* Washington, DC: U.S. Government Printing House.

Wallace, W. (1972). Mental illness, biology, and culture. In F. Hsu (Ed.), *Psychological anthropology* (2nd ed.). Cambridge: Schenkman.

Weissman, M., & Paykel, E. (1974). *The depressed woman.* Chicago: University of Chicago Press.

Westermeyer, J. (1974). Opium smoking in Laos: A survey of 40 addicts. *American Journal of Psychiatry,* **131,** 165–170.

Williams, R. (1951). *American society, a sociological interpretation.* New York: Knopf.

Wing, J. (1978). Social influences on the course of schizophrenia. In L. Wynne, R. Cromwell, & S. Matthysse (Eds.), *The nature of schizophrenia.* New York: Wiley.

World Health Organization. (1973). *World health statistics report.* Geneva, Switzerland: WHO.

Wynne, L. (1978). From symptoms to vulnerability and beyond: An overview. In L. Wynne, R. Cromwell, & S. Matthysse (Eds.), *The nature of schizophrenia.* New York: Wiley.

Wynne, L., Singer, M., & Toohey, M. (1976). Communication of the adoptive parents of schizophrenics. In J. Jorstad & E. Ugelstad (Eds.), *Schizophrenia 75.* Oslo, Norway: Lie.

Yoshioka, T., et al. (1978). *A survey of mental health status among Asian-Americans.* Unpublished manuscript.

Zubin, J., & Spring, B. (1977). Vulnerability A new view of schizophrenia. *Journal of Abnormal Psychology,* **86,** 103–126.

## CHAPTER 6

Agras, S., Sylvester, D., & Oliveau, D. (1969). The epidemiology of common fears and phobias. *Comprehensive Psychiatry,* **10,** 151–156.

Bandura, A. (1965). Vicarious processes: A case of no-trial learning. In L. Berkowitz (Ed.), *Advances in experimental social psychology.* Vol. 2. New York: Academic Press.

Bartemeier, L., Kubie, L., Menninger, K., Romano, J., & Whitehorn. (1946). Combat exhaustion. *Journal of Nervous and Mental Disorders,* **104,** 358–389.

Barton, A. (1963). *Social organization under stress: A sociological review of disaster studies.* Washington, DC: National Academy of Sciences.

Beck, A. (1976). *Cognitive therapy and emotional disorders.* New York: International University Press.

Berzins, J. & Berzins, L. (1984). Psychotherapy. In A. Bellack & M. Hersen (Eds.), *Research methods in clinical psychology.* New York: Pergamon.

Blank, Jr., A. (1983). Stress of war: the example of Vietnam. In L. Goldberger & S. Breznitz. *Handbook of stresses: Theoretical and clinical aspects.* New York: Free Press.

Bourne, P. (1970). Psychological aspects of combat. In H. Abram (Ed.), *Psychological aspects of stress.* Springfield, IL: C. C Thomas.

Broadhurst, P., & Bignami, G. (1965). Correlative effects of psychogenetic selection: A study of the Roman high and low avoidance training. *Behaviour Research and Therapy,* **2,** 273–280.

Carey. (1977). Cited in Marks, I. Phobias and obsessions. In J. Maser & M. Seligman (Eds.), *Psychopathology: Experimental models.* San Francisco: Freeman.

Catalano, R. (1979). *Health, behavior and the community.* New York: Pergamon.

Cohen, R., & Ahearn, F. (1980). *Handbook for Mental Health Care of Disaster Victims.* Baltimore: Johns Hopkins Press.

Cole, D. (1980, May 19) Why a hostage cannot forget. *Newsweek,* 17.

Costello, C. (1982). Fears and phobias in women: A community study. *Journal of Abnormal Psychology,* **91,** 280–286.

Delprato, D. (1980). Hereditary determinants of fears and phobias: A critical review. *Behavior Therapy,* **11,** 79–103.

Egendorf, A. (1978). Psychotherapy with Vietnam veterans: Observations and suggestions. In C. Figley (Ed.), *Stress disorders among Vietnam veterans: Theory, research and treatment.* New York: Brunner/Mazel.

Ellis, A. (1962). *Reason and emotion in psychotherapy.* New York: Lyle Stuart.

Ellis, A. (1979). A note on the treatment of agoraphobics with cognitive modification versus prolonged exposure in vivo. *Behaviour Research and Therapy,* **17,** 162–164.

Fensterheim, H., & Baer, J. (1977). *Stop running scared!* New York: Rawson.

Foa, E., Jameson, J., Turner, R., & Payne, L. (1980a). Massed vs. spaced exposure sessions in the treatment of agoraphobia. *Behaviour Research and Therapy,* **18,** 333.

Foa, E., Steketee, G., & Milby, J. (1980b). Differential effects of exposure and response prevention in obsessive-compulsive washers. *Journal of Consulting and Clinical Psychology,* **48,** 71–79.

Frederick, C. (1981, April 6–10). Violence and disasters: Immediate and long-term consequences. Paper presented at Psychosocial Consequences of Violence Conference, The Hague.

Frederick, C. (1981, August 28). Disasters and mental health: The government's role. Paper presented at the Annual Meeting of the American Psychological Association, Los Angeles.

Freud, S. (1959). Analysis of a phobia in a five year old boy. In *Collected papers,* Vol. 3. New York: Basic Books. (First published in German, 1909.)

Freud, S. (1963). The sense of symptoms. In *The standard edition of the complete psychological works of Sigmund Freud.* Translated by J. Strachey. London: Hogarth.

Friedman, P., & Linn, L. (1957). Some psychiatric notes on the Andrea Dorea disaster. *American Journal of Psychiatry,* **114,** 426–432.

Gleser, G., Green, B. & Winget, C. (1981). *Prolonged psychological effects of disaster.* New York: Academic Press.

Goldfried, M. (1979). Anxiety reduction through cognitive-behavioral intervention. In P. Kendall & S. Hollon (Eds.), *Cognitive-behavioral interventions: Theory, research and procedures.* New York: Academic Press.

Goodwin, D. (1983). *Phobia: The facts.* New York: Oxford.

Hafner, R. (1983). Behaviour therapy for agoraphobic men. *Behaviour Research & Therapy,* **21,** 51–56.

Hagman, R. (1932). A study of fears of children of preschool age. *Journal of Experimental Education,* **1,** 110.

Hall, C. (1934). Emotional behavior in the rat: I. Defecation and urination as measures of individual differences in emotionality. *Journal of Comparative Psychology,* **18,** 385.

Hallam, R. (1978). Agoraphobia: A critical review of the concept. *British Journal of Psychiatry,* **133,** 314–319.

Hamilton, V. (1976). Motivation and personality in cognitive development. In V. Hamilton & M. Vernon (Eds.), *The development of cognitive processes.* London: Academic Press.

Hocking, F. (1970). Extreme environmental stress and its significance for psychopathology. *American Journal of Psychotherapy,* **24,** 4.

Hunter, E. (1976). The Vietnam POW veteran: Immediate and long-term effects. In C. Figley (Ed.), *Stress disorders among Vietnam veterans.* New York: Brunner/Mazel.

Hutchings, D., Denney, D., Basgall, J., & Houston, B. (1978). *Anxiety management and applied relaxation in reducing chronic anxiety.* Unpublished manuscript. University of Kansas, Lawrence.

Johnson, J., & Sarason, I. (1978). Life stress, depression and anxiety: Internal-external control as a moderator variable. *Journal of Psychosomatic Research,* **22,** 205–208.

Jones, E. (1957). *The life and work of Sigmund Freud,* Vol. 3. New York: Basic Books.

Kazdin, A. (1973). Covert modeling and the reduction of avoidance behavior, *Journal of Abnormal Psychology,* **81,** 87–95.

Keerdoja, E. (1980, March 17). Memories haunt Hanafi hostages. *Newsweek,* **99,** pp. 14, 16.

Lacey, J. (1976). Somatic response patterning and stress: Some revisions of activation theory. In M. Appley & R. Trumball (Eds.), *Psychological stress.* New York: McGraw-Hill.

Lader, M. (1975). *The psychophysiology of mental illness.* London: Routledge & Kegan Paul.

Lang, P. (1971). The application of psychophysiological methods to the study of psychotherapy and behavior change. In A. Bergin & S. Garfield (Eds.), *Handbook of psychotherapy and behavior change.* New York: Wiley.

Lang, P., Melamed, B., & Hart, J. (1974). Automating the desensitization procedure: A psychophysiological analysis of fear modification. In M. Kietzman (Ed.), *Experimental approaches to psychopathology.* New York: Academic Press.

Leitenberg, H., Agras, W., Butz, R., & Wincze, J. (1971). Relationship between heart rate and behavioral change during the treatment of phobia. *Journal of Abnormal Psychology* , **78,** 59.

MacQuiddy, S. & Hamilton, S. (1983). *Parent-child interaction training: A manual for parents.* Psychological Documents, **13,** 6, Ms. No. 2536.

Malick, M., Logue, J. & Frederick, C. (1983). Stress and natural disaster. In L. Goldberger & S. Breznitz (Eds), *Handbook of stress: Theoretical and clinical aspects.* New York: Free Press.

Malin, D., Radcliffe, Jr., G., & Osterman, D. (1976). Stimulus specific effect of scotophobin on mouse plasma cortecoids. *Pharmacology, Biochemistry and Behavior,* **4,** 481–482.

Marks, I. (1969). *Fears and phobias.* London: Academic Press.

Marks, I. (1970). Agoraphobia syndrome (phobic anxiety state). *Archives of General Psychiatry,* **23,** 538–553.

Marks, I. (1978). *Living with fear.* New York: McGraw-Hill.

Marks, I. (1983). Panic attacks and phobias. Letter to the Editor. *New England Journal of Medicine,* **308,** 341–342.

Marks, I., & Herst, E. (1970). The open door: A survey of agraphobics in Britain. *Social Psychiatry,* **1,** 16–24.

McLaughlin, E. (1970). Psychological reactions to the stresses of outer space. In H. Abram (Ed.), *Psychological aspects of stress.* Springfield, IL: C. C Thomas.

McPherson, F., Brougham, L., & McLaren, S. (1980). Maintenance of improvement in agoraphobic patients treated by behavioural methods—A four year follow-up. *Behaviour Research and Therapy,* **18,** 150–152.

Meichenbaum, D. (1977). *Cognitive behavior modification.* New York: Plenum.

Meyer, V., & Reich, B. (1978). Anxiety management—The marriage of physiological and cognitive variables. *Behaviour Research and Therapy,* **16,** 177–182.

Morris, R. & Kratochwill, T. (1983). *Treating children's fears and phobias.* New York: Pergamon.

Mowrer, O. (1947). On the dual nature of learning: A reinterpretation of "conditioning" and "problem-solving." *Harvard Educational Review,* **17,** 102–148.

National Institute of Mental Health (1978). *Training manual for human service workers in major disasters.* Washington, DC: U.S. Government Printing Office.

O'Connell, P. (1976, November). Trends in psychological adjustment: Observations made during successive psychiatric follow-up interviews of returned Navy-Marine Corps POWs. *Proceedings of the 3rd Annual Joint Meeting Concerning POW/MIA Matters.* San Diego, CA, p. 16.

Ost, L., & Hugdahl, K. (1981). Acquisition of phobias and anxiety response patterns in clinical patients. *Behaviour Research and Therapy,* **19,** 439–448.

Pollak, J. (1978). Relationships between psychoanalytic personality pattern, death anxiety, and self actualization. *Perceptual and Motor Skills,* **46,** 846.

Pollak, J. (1979). Obsessive-compulsive personality: A review. *Psychological Bulletin,* **86,** 225–241.

Queiroz, L., Motta, M., Madi, M., Sosai, D., & Boren, J. (1981). A functional analysis of obsessive-compulsive problems with related therapeutic procedures. *Behaviour Research Therapy,* **19,** 377–388.

Rachman, S., & deSilva, P. (1978). Abnormal and normal obsessions. *Behaviour Research and Therapy,* **16,** 223–248.

Rado, S. (1943). Pathodynamics and the treatment of traumatic war neurosis (traumatophobia). *Psychosomatic Medicine,* **63,** 362.

Reiser, J. (1980). *And I thought I was crazy!* New York: Fireside/Simon & Schuster.

Roberts, W., Penk, W., Gearing, M., Robinowitz, R., Dolan, M., & Patterson, E. (1982). Interpersonal problems of Vietnam combat veterans with symptoms of posttraumatic stress disorder. *Journal of Abnormal Psychology,* **91,** 444–450.

Rosenthal, T., & Bandura, A. (1978). Psychological modeling: Theory and practice. In S. Garfield & A. Bergin (Eds.), *Handbook of psychotherapy and behavior change: An empirical analysis.* (2nd ed.) New York: Wiley.

Ruff, G., & Korchin S. (1964). Psychological responses of the mercury astronauts to stress. In G. Grosser, N. Wechsler, & M. Greenblatt (Eds.), *The threat of impending disaster.* Cambridge: MIT Press.

Sarason, I. (1972). Experimental approaches to test anxiety: Attention and use of information. In C. Spielberger (Ed.), *Anxiety: Current trends in theory and use.* Vol. 2. New York: Academic Press.

Seligman, M. (1971). Phobias and preparedness. *Behavior Therapy,* **2,** 307–320.

Selye, H., (1979). The stress concept and some of its implications. In V. Hamilton & D. Warburton (Eds.), *Human stress and cognition.* New York: Wiley.

Shaw, B. (1982). Stress and Depression: A cognitive perspective. In R. Newfeld (Ed.), *Psychological Stress and Psychopathology.* New York: McGraw-Hill.

Shoemaker, J. (1976). *Treatments for anxiety neurosis.* Unpublished doctoral dissertation, Colorado State University, Fort Collins.

Sinnott, A., Jones, R., Scott-Fordhman, A., & Woodward, R. (1981). Augmentation of *in vivo*-exposure treatment for agoraphobia by the formation of neighbourhood self-help groups. *Behaviour Research and Therapy,* **19,** 339-348.

Smith, T. (1983). Change in irrational beliefs and the outcome of Rational-Emotive Psychotherapy. *Journal of Consulting and Clinical Psychology,* **51,** 156–157.

Spielberger, C. (1966). Theory and research on anxiety. In C. Spielberger (Ed.), *Anxiety and behavior.* New York. Academic Press.

Stern, G. (1976). *The buffalo creek disaster.* New York: Random House.

Stern, R., & Cobb, J. (1978). Phenomenology of obsessive-compulsive neurosis. *British Journal of Psychiatry,* **182,** 233–239.

Stouffer, S., Lumsdaine, A., Williams, P., Smith, M., Janis, I., Star, S., & Cottrell, L. (1949). *The American soldier: Combat and its aftermath.* Princeton, NJ: Princeton University Press.

Strange, R. (1969). Effects of combat stress on hospital ship psychiatric evacuees. In P. Bourne (Ed.), *Psychology and physiology of stress.* New York: Academic Press.

Suinn, R. (1975). Anxiety management training for general anxiety. In R. Suinn & R. Weigel (Eds.), *Innovative therapies: Critical and creative contributions.* New York: Harper & Row.

Suinn, R. (1976). Body thinking for Olympic champs. *Psychology Today,* **38.**

Suinn, R. (1977). Treatment of phobias. In G. Harris (Ed.), *The group treatment of human problems: A social learning approach.* New York: Grune & Stratton.

Suinn, R. (1983). *Manual for anxiety management training (AMT).* Fort Collins, CO: Rocky Mountain Behavioral Science Institute.

Suinn, R. (1983). The treatment of generalized anxiety disorder. In S. Turner (Ed.), *The behavioral treatment of anxiety.* New York: Plenum.

Suinn, R., & Deffenbacher, J. (1982). Behavioral self-management techniques for anxiety. In R. Karoly & F. Kanfer, *Self-management and behavior change.* New York: Pergamon.

Tasto, D., & Skjei, E. (1979). *Spare the couch.* Englewood Cliffs, NJ: Prentice-Hall.

The trauma of captivity. (1979, December 24). *Time,* **59.**

Thompson, S. (1981), Will it hurt less if I can control it? A complete answer to a simple question. *Psychological Bulletin,* **88,** 89–101.

Turner, S., Hersen, M., Bellack, A., & Wells, K. (1979). Behavioral treatment of obsessive-compulsive neurosis. *Behaviour Research and Therapy,* **17,** 95–106.

Valentine, C. (1978). The psychology of early childhood. In S. Rachman (Ed.), *Fear and courage.* San Francisco: W. H. Freeman.

Wolpe, J. (1958). *Psychotherapy by reciprocal inhibition.* Stanford, CA: Stanford University Press.

## CHAPTER 7

Abey-Wickrama, I., A'Brook, M. F., Gattoni, F. G., & Herridge, C. F. (1969). Mental hospital admissions and aircraft noise. *Lancet,* **2,** 1275–1277.

Aiello, J. R., Epstein, Y. M., & Karlin, R. A. (1975). Effects of crowding on electrodermal activity. *Sociological Symposium,* **14,** 43–57.

Bandura, A. (1977). Self-efficacy: Toward a unifying theory of behavioral change. *Psychological Review,* **84,** 191–215.

Baron, R. A., & Bell, P. A. (1976). Aggression and heat: The influence of ambient temperature, negative affect, and a cooling drink on physical aggression. *Journal of Personality and Social Psychology,* **33,** 245–255.

Baron, R. A., & Ransberger, V. M. (1978). Ambient temperature and the occurrence of collective violence: The "long hot summer" revisited. *Journal of Personality and Social Psychology,* **36,** 351–360.

Bass, B., Wyatt, G., & Powell, G. (1982). *The Afro-American Family.* New York: Grune & Stratton.

Baum, A., & Koman, S. (1976). Differential response to anticipated crowding: Psychological effects of social and spatial density. *Journal of Personality and Social Psychology,* **34,** 526–536.

Becerra, R., Karno, M., & Escobar, J. (1982). *Mental Health and Hispanic Americans.* New York: Grune & Stratton.

Briere, J., Downes, A., & Spensley, J. (1983). Summer in the city: Urban weather conditions and psychiatric emergency-room visits. *Journal of Abnormal Psychology,* **92,** 77–80.

Cohen, S., (1980). Aftereffects of stress on human performance and social behavior: A review of research and theory. *Psychological Bulletin,* **88,** 82.

Cohen, S., Glass, D. C., & Phillips, S. (1977). Environment and health. In H. E. Freeman, S. Levine, & L. G. Reeder (Eds.), *Handbook of medical sociology.* Englewood Cliffs, NJ: Prentice-Hall.

Cole, O. & Pilisuk, J. (1976). Differences in the provision of mental health service by race. *American Journal of Orthopsychiatry,* **46,** 510–525.

Donnerstein, E., & Wilson, D. W. (1976). Effects of noise and perceived control on ongoing and subsequent aggressive behavior. *Journal of Personality and Social Psychology,* **34,** 774–781.

Goldberg, L. & Breznitz, S. (1982). *Handbook of stress: Theoretical & clinical aspects.* New York: Free Press.

Goranson, R. E., & King, D. (1970). *Rioting and daily temperature: Analysis of the U.S. riots in 1967.* Unpublished manuscript, York University.

Hart, R. H. (1970). The concept of APS: Air Pollution Syndrome(s). *Journal of the South Carolina Medical Association,* **66,** 71–73.

Holmes, T., & Holmes, T., (1970). Short-term intrusions into the life style routine. *Journal of Psychosomatic Research,* **14,** 121–132.

Holmes, T., & Rahe, R. (1967). The Social Readjustment Rating Scale. *Journal of Psychosomatic Research,* **11,** 213–218.

Holroyd, K., & Lazarus, R. (1983). Stress, coping and somatic adaptation. In L. Goldberger & S. Breznitz (Eds.), *Handbook of stress: Theoretical and clinical aspects.* New York: Free Press.

Inouye, D. (1979, April 9). Minority Concerns Act of 1979. *Congressional Record, Senate,* S4192–4193.

Johnson, J., & Sarason, I. (1979). Recent developments in research on life stress. In V. Hamilton & D. Warburton (Eds.), *Human stress and cognitions.* New York: Wiley.

Joy, V. D., & Lehmann, V. (1975). *The cost of crowding: Responses and adaptations.* Unpublished manuscript, New York State Department of Mental Hygiene.

Kaminoff, R. & Proshansky, H. (1983). Environmental stress. In L. Goldberger & S. Breznitz (Eds.), *Handbook of stress: Theoretical and clinical aspects.* New York: Free Press.

Kryter, K. D. (1970). *The effects of noise on man.* New York: Academic Press.

Lang, P. (1971). The application of psychophysiological methods to the study of psychotherapy and behavior change. In A. Bergin & S. Garfield (Eds.), *Handbook of psychotherapy and behavior change.* New York: Wiley.

LaVerne, A. A. (1970). Nonspecific air pollution syndrome (NAPS): Preliminary report. *Behavioral Neuropsychiatry,* **2,** 19–21.

Lazarus, R., Coyne, J. & Folkman, S. (1982). Computers, emotions and motivation: The doctoring of Humpty Dumpty. In R. Mufeld (Ed.), *Psychological Stress and Psychopathology.* New York: McGraw-Hill.

Lieberman, M. (1983). The effects of social supports on responses to stress. In L. Goldberger & S. Breznitz (Eds.), *Handbook of stress: Theoretical and clinical aspects.* New York: Free Press.

Liljefors, I., & Rahe, R. (1970). An identical twin study of psychosocial factors in coronary heart disease in Sweden. *Psychosomatic Medicine,* **32,** 523–542.

Marx, M., Garrity, T., & Bowers, F. (1975). The influence of recent life experience on the health of college freshmen. *Journal of Psychosomatic Research,* **19,** 87–98.

Miller, S. & Selegman, M. (1982). The reformulated model of helplessness and depression: Evidence and theory. In R. Neufeld (Ed.), *Psychological Stress and Psychopathology.* New York: McGraw Hill.

Neufeld, R. (1982). On decisional processes instigated by threat: Some possible implications for stress-related research. In R. Neufeld (Ed.), *Psychological Stress and Psychopathology.* New York: McGraw Hill.

Novaco, R. (1976). Treatment of chronic anger through cognitive and relaxation controls. *Journal of Consulting and Clinical Psychology,* **44,** 481.

Pearlin, L. (1983). The social contexts of stress. In L. Goldberger & S. Breznitz (Eds.), *Handbook of stress: Theoretical and clinical aspects.* New York: Free Press.

Rahe, R., & Lind, E. (1971). Psychosocial factors and sudden cardiac death: A pilot study. *Journal of Psychosomatic Research,* **15,** 19–24.

Selye, H. (1974). *Stress without distress.* Philadelphia: Lippincott.

Selye, H. (1980). The stress concept today. In I. Kutash & L. Schlesinger (Eds.), *Handbook on stress and anxiety.* San Francisco: Jossey-Bass.

Spielberger, C. (1966). Theory and research on anxiety. In C. Spielberger (Ed.), *Anxiety and behavior.* New York: Academic Press.

Sue, S. & Morishima, J. (1982). *The mental health of Asian Americans.* San Francisco: Jossey-Bass.

Suinn, R. (1983). *Anxiety management training manual (AMT).* Fort Collins, CO: Rocky Mountain Behavioral Science Institute.

Suinn, R. (1978). *Life stresses and health visits of executive administrators.* Unpublished report, Colorado State University, Fort Collins.

Van Dyke, C., Temoshok, L., Zegars, C. & Wallerstein, R. (Eds.) (1983). *Emotions in health and illness.* New York: Grune & Stratton.

Weitzman, E., & Luce, G. (1970). Biological rhythms: Indices of pain, adrenal hormones, sleep, and sleep reversal. In NIMH, *Behavioral Sciences and Mental Health.* Washington, DC: U.S. Government Printing Office.

## CHAPTER 8

Abse, D. (1959). Hysteria. In S. Arieti (Ed.), *American handbook of psychiatry.* Vol. 1. New York: Basic Books.

Cameron, N. (1963). *Personality development and psychopathology: A dynamic approach.* Boston: Houghton Mifflin.

Cermak, L. (Ed.) (1982). *Human memory and amnesia.* Hillsdale, NJ: Lawrence Erlbaum.

Dixon, J. (1963). Depersonalization phenomena in a sample population of college students. *British Journal of Psychiatry,* **109,** 371–375.

Frederick, C. (1981, April 6–10). Violence and disasters: Immediate and long term consequences. Paper presented at Psychosocial Consequences of Violence Conference, The Hague.

Golden, C., Moses, Jr., J., Coffman, J., Miller, W. & Strider, F. (1983). *Clinical neuropsychology.* New York: Grune & Stratton.

Hale, E. (1983, April 18). Startling discoveries shed new light on enigma of multiple personality. *Chicago Tribune,* pp. 1, 5.

Hilgard, E. (1977). *Divided consciousness: Multiple controls in human thought and action.* New York: Wiley.

Hirst, W. (1982). The amnesic syndrome. Descriptions and explanations. *Psychological Bulletin,* **91,** 435–460.

Kirshner, L. (1973). Dissociative reactions: An historical review and clinical study. *Acta Psychiatrica Scandanavica,* **49,** 698–711.

Laughlin, H. (1967). *The neuroses.* Washington, DC: Butterworths.

Marx, O. (1970). Morton Prince and the dissociation of a personality. *Journal of the History of the Behavioral Sciences.*

McCurdy, H. (1941). A note on the dissociation of a personality. *Character and Personality,* **10,** 33–41.

Parkinson, S. (1982). Performance deficits in short-term memory tasks: A comparison of amnesic Korsakoff patients and the aged. In L. Cermak (Ed.), *Human memory and amnesia.* Hillsdale, NJ: Erlbaum.

Prince, M. (1908). *Dissociation of a personality.* New York: Longmans, Green.

Prince, M. (1920). Miss Beauchamp: The psychogenesis of multiple personality. *Journal of Abnormal Psychology,* **16,** 67–135.

Rosenzweig, P. (1941). Need-persistive and ego-defensive reactions to frustration as demonstrated by an experiment on repression. *Psychological Review,* **48,** 347–49.

Schneider, K. (1958). *Psychopathic personalities.* London: Cassel.

Schreiber, F. (1973). *Sybil.* Chicago: Henry Regnery.

Sizemore, C. (1982, August 25). Conversation Hour. Annual Meeting of the American Psychological Association, Washington, DC.

Sizemore, C., & Pittillo, E. (1977). *I'm Eve.* New York: Doubleday.

Taylor, W., & Martin, M. (1944). Multiple personality. *Journal of Abnormal and Social Psychology,* **39,** 281–300.

Thigpen, C., & Cleckley, H. (1957). *The three faces of Eve.* New York: McGraw-Hill.

Weckowicz, T. (1970). Depersonalization. In C. Costello (Ed.), *Symptoms of psychopathology: A handbook.* New York: Wiley.

Zeigarnik, B. (1927). Affectpsychologie untersuchurgen zur Handlungs—und Affectpsychologie Behalten erledigter und unerledigter Handlungen. *Psychologie Forschung,* **9,** 1.

## CHAPTER 9

Abse, D. W., Wilkins, M. M., VandeCastle, R. L., Buxton, W. D., Demars, J. P., Brown, R. S., & Kirschner, L. G. (1974). Personality and behavioral characteristics of lung cancer patients. *Journal of Psychosomatic Research,* **18,** 101–113.

Achterberg, A., Matthews-Simonton, S., & Simonton, O. (1977). Psychology of the exceptional cancer patient: A description of patients who outlive predicted life expectancies. *Psychotherapy: Theory, Research & Practice,* **14,** 416–422.

Adams, H., Feuerstein, M., & Fowler, J. (1980). Migraine headache: Review of parameters, etiology, and intervention. *Psychological Bulletin,* **87,** 217–237.

Alexander, F. (1950). *Psychosomatic medicine: Its principles and applications.* New York: Norton.

Andrasik, F. & Blanchard, E. (1983). Applications of biofeedback to therapy. In C. Walker (Ed.), *The handbook of clinical psychology.* Homewood, IL: Dow Jones-Irwin.

Bahnson, C. B. (1969). Psychophysiological complementarity in malignancies: Past work and future vistas. *Annals of the N.Y. Academy of Science,* **164,** 319–333.

Bahnson, C. B., & Bahnson, M. B. (1964). Cancer as an alternative to psychosis: A theoretical model of somatic and psychological regression. In D. M. Kissen & L. L. LeShan (Eds.), *Psychosomatic aspects of neoplastic disease.* London: Pitman.

Bakal, D. (1982). *The psychobiology of chronic headache.* New York: Springer.

Bastiaans, J. (1965). The place of personality traits in specific syndromes: Cause or effect. In J. Wisdon & H. Wolff (Eds.), *The role of psychosomatic disorder in adult life.* London: Pergamon.

Becker, H. (1979). Psychodynamic aspects of breast cancer. *Psychotherapy Psychosom.* **32,** 287–296.

Bild, R., & Adams, H. (1980). Modification of migraine headaches by cephalic blood volume pulse and EMG biofeedback. *Journal of Consulting and Clinical Psychology,* **48,** 51–57.

Blanchard, E., & Ahles, T. (1979). Behavioral treatment of psychophysical disorders. *Behavior Modification,* **3,** 518–549.

Blanchard, E., Theobald, D., Williamson, Silver, B., & Brown, D. (1978). Temperature biofeedback in the treatment of migraine headaches: A controlled evaluation. *Archives of General Psychiatry,* **35,** 581–588.

Bloom, L., & Cantrell, D. (1978). Anxiety management training for essential hypertension in pregnancy. *Behavior Therapy,* **9,** 377–382.

Brady, J. (1958). Ulcers in "executive" monkeys. *Scientific America,* **119,** no. 4, 95–98.

Brooks, G., & Richardson, F. (1980). Emotional skills training: A treatment program for duodenal ulcers. *Behavior Therapy,* **11,** 198–207.

Carver, C. & Glass, D. (1978). Coronary-prone behavior and interpersonal aggression. *Journal of Personality and Social Psychology,* **36,** 361–366.

Catalano, R. (1979). *Health, behavior and the community.* New York: Pergamon.

Chobanian, A., Gavras, H., Gavras, I., et al. (1978). Studies on the activity of the sympathetic nervous system in essential hypertension. *Journal of Human Stress,* **4,** 22–28.

Cobb, S., & Rose, R. (1973). Hypertension, peptic ulcer, and diabetes in air traffic controllers. *Journal of the American Medical Association,* **224,** 489–492.

Cohen, J., Syme, S., Jenkins, C., Kagan, A., & Zyzanski, S. (1979). Cultural context of Type A behavior and risk for CHD: A study of Japanese American males. *Journal of Behavioral Medicine,* **2,** 375–384.

Cullen, J. W., Fox, B. H., & Isom, R. N. (1976). *Cancer: The behavioral dimensions.* New York: Raven Press.

Daitzman, R. (in press). *Diagnosis and intervention in behavior therapy and behavioral medicine,* Vol. 1. New York: Springer.

Dalessio, D. (1972). *Headache and other head pain.* New York: Oxford University Press.

Dattore, P., Shontz, F., & Coyne, L. (1980). Premorbid personality differentiation of cancer and noncancer groups: A test of the hypothesis of cancer proneness. *Journal of Consulting and Clinical Psychology,* **48,** 388–394.

Davidson, L., Baum, A., & Collins, D. (in press). Stress and control related problems at Three Mile Island. *Journal of Applied Social Psychology.*

Dawson, A. & Simon, R. (Eds.) (1983). *Practical management of asthma.* New York: Grune & Stratton.

DeGood, D. (1975). Cognitive control factors in vascular stress response. *Psychophysiology,* **12,** 399–401.

DeLozier, J., & Gagnon, R. (1975). *National ambulatory medical care survey: 1973 summary.* U.S. May 1973–April 1974. Washington, D.C.: U.S. Government Printing Office.

Dembroski, T., Weiss, S., Shields, J., Haynes, S., & Feinleib, M. (1978). *Coronary prone behavior.* New York: Springer-Verlag.

DePiano, F. & Salzberg, H. (1979). Clinical applications of hypnosis to three psychosomatic disorders. *Psychological Bulletin,* **86,** 1223–1235.

Diamond, E. (1982). The role of anger and hostility in essential hypertension and coronary heart disease. *Psychological Bulletin,* **92,** 410–433.

Fox, B. (1978). Premorbid psychological factors as related to cancer incidence. *Behavior Modification,* **1,** 45–133.

French, T., & Alexander, F. (1941). Psychogenic factors in bronchial asthma. *Psychosomatic Medicine Monograph IV.* Washington, DC: National Research Council.

Friedman, A., vonStorch, T., & Merritt, H. (1954). Migraine and tension headaches: A clinical study of two thousand cases. *Neurology,* **4,** 773–788.

Friedman, M., & Rosenman, R. (1959). Association of specific overt behavior pattern with blood and cardiovascular findings. *Journal of the American Medical Association,* **169,** 1286.

Friedman, M. & Rosenman, R. (1974). Type A behavior and your heart. New York: Knopf.

Friedman, M., Rosenman, R., & Beyers, S. (1964). Serum lipids and conjunctival circulation after fat ingestion in men exhibiting Type-A behavior pattern. *Circulation,* **29,** 874.

Friedman, M., Rosenman, R., & Carroll, V. (1958). Changes in the serum cholesterol and blood-clotting time in men subjected to cyclic variation of occupational stress. *Circulation,* **17,** 852–861.

Friedman, M., Thoresen, C., & Gill, I. (1981). Type A behavior: Its possible role, detection, and alteration in patients with ischemic heart disease. In J. Hurst (Ed.), *Update V: The heart.* New York, McGraw-Hill.

Gantt, W. (1941). Experimental basis of neurotic behavior. *Psychosomatic Medicine Monograph 3,* No. 3 & 4. Washington, DC: National Research Council.

Gastorf, J. (1980). Time urgency of the Type A behavior pattern. *Journal of Consulting and Clinical Psychology,* **48,** 299.

Glade, P. R., Zalvidar, N. M., Mayer, L., & Cahill, L. J. (1976). The role of cellular immunity in neoplasia. *Pediatric Research,* **10,** 517–522.

Glass, D. (1977). *Behavior patterns, stress, and coronary disease.* New York: Erlbaum.

Glass, D., Krakoff, L., Contrada, R., et al. (1980). Effects of harassment and competitors upon cardiovascular and catecholominic responses in Type A and Type B individuals. *Psychophysiology,* **17,** 453–463.

Goodfriend, T. (1983). *Hypertension essentials.* New York: Grune & Stratton.

Gordon, W., Freidenbergs, I., Diller, L., Hibbard, M., Wolf, C., Levine, L., Lipkins, R., Ezrachi, O., & Lucido, D. (1980). Efficacy of psychosocial intervention with cancer patients. *Journal of Consulting and Clinical Psychology,* **48,** 743.

Graham, D. (1972). Psychosomatic medicine. In N. Greenfield & R. Steinback (Eds.), *Handbook of psychophysiology.* New York: Holt, Rinehart, & Winston.

Grace, W. & Graham, D. (1952). Relationships of specific attitudes and emotions to certain bodily diseases. *Psychosomatic Medicine,* **14,** 243–51.

Gray, C., Lyle, R., McGuire, R., & Peck, D. (1980). Electrode placement, EMG feedback, and relaxation for tension headaches. *Behaviour Research and Therapy,* **18,** 19–23.

Harrell, J. (1980). Psychological factors and hypertension: A status report. *Psychological Bulletin,* **87,** 482–501.

Harrison, R. (1975). Psychological testing in headaches: A review. *Headache,* **15,** 177–185.

Hart, K. (1980). *Stress management training for Type A individuals.* Unpublished manuscript.

Henryk-Gutt, R., & Rees, W. (1973). Psychological aspects of migraines. *Journal of Psychosomatic Research,* **17,** 141–153.

Hock, R., Rodgers, C., Reddi, C., & Kennard, D. (1978). Medicopsychological interventions in male asthmatic children: An evaluation of physiological change. *Psychosomatic Medicine,* **40,** 210–215.

Holroyd, K., & Andrasik, F. (1978). Coping and the self-control of chronic tension headache. *Journal of Consulting and Clinical Psychology,* **46,** 1036–1045.

Horne, R., & Picard, R. (1979). Psychosocial risk factors for lung cancer. *Psychosomatic Medicine,* **41,** 503–514.

Jenkins, C., Tuthill, R., Tannenbaum, S., & Kirby, C. (1979). Social stressors and excess mortality from hypertensive diseases. *Journal of Human Stress,* **5,** 29–40.

Jenkins, C., Zyzanski, S., & Rosenman, R. (1978). Coronary-prone behavior: One pattern or several? *Psychosomatic Medicine,* **40,** 25–43.

Jenkins, D. (1983). Social environment and cancer mortality in men. *New England Journal of Medicine,* **308,** 395–398.

Jessup, B. (1982). Psychophysiological factors in the treatment of the stress of pain: biofeedback. In R. Neufeld (Ed.), *Psychological Stress and Psychopathology.* New York: McGraw-Hill.

Jones, N., Kinsman, R., Dirks, J., & Dahlem, N. (1979). Psychological contributors to chronicity in asthma: Patient response styles influencing medical treatment and its outcome. *Medical Care,* **17,** 1103–1118.

King, N. (1980). The behavioral management of asthma and asthma-related problems in children: A critical review of the literature. *Journal of Behavioral Medicine,* **3,** 169.

Kinsman, R., Dirks, J., & Jones, N. (1980). Levels of psychological experience in asthma: General and illness-specific concomitants of panic-fear personality. *Journal of Clinical Psychology,* **36,** 552–561.

Kissen, D. (1969). Present status of psychosomatic cancer research. *Geriatrics,* **24,** 129–137.

Krantz, D., Baum, A., & Singer, J. (1983). *Handbook of psychology and health,* Vol. 3. Hillsdale, NJ: Erlbaum.

Lambley, P. (1976). The use of assertive training and psychodynamic insight in the treatment of migraine headaches: A case study. *Journal of Nervous and Mental Disease,* **163,** 61–64.

Leigh, H. (1983). Evaluation and management of stress in general medicine and psychosomatic approach. In L. Goldberger & S. Breznitz (Eds.), *Handbook of stress: Theoretical and clinical aspects.* New York: Free Press.

LeShan, L. (1966). An emotional life-history pattern associated with neoplastic disease. *Annals of the N. Y. Academy of Science,* **125,** 780–793.

LeShan, L., & Worthington, R. E. (1956). Some recurrent life history patterns observed in patients with malignant disease. *Journal of Nervous and Mental Disease,* **124,** 460–465.

Liddell, H. (1951). The influence of experimental neuroses on respiratory function. In H. Abramson (Ed.), *Treatment of asthma.* Baltimore: Williams & Wilkins.

Lobitz, W., & Brammell, H. (1981). Anxiety management training versus aerobic conditioning for cardiac stress management. Paper presented at the Annual Meeting of the American Psychological Association, Los Angeles.

Manuck, S., Harvey, A., Lechleiter, S., & Neal, K. (1978). Effects of coping on blood pressure responses to threat of aversive stimulation. *Psychophysiology,* **15,** 544–549.

Matthews, K. (1977). As cited in D. Glass (Ed.), *Behavior patterns, stress, and coronary disease.* Hillsdale, NJ: Erlbaum.

Matthews, K. (1982). Psychological perspectives on the Type A behavior pattern. *Psychological Bulletin,* **91,** 293–323.

McClelland, D. (1979). Inhibited power motivation and high blood pressure in men. *Journal of Abnormal Psychology,* **88,** 182–190.

Medina, J., & Diamond, S. (1977). Drug dependency in patients with chronic headaches. *Headache,* **17,** 12–14.

Meyer, K. F. (1942). The ecology of psittacosis and ornithosis. *Medicine,* **21,** 175–206.

Meyerowitz, B. (1980). Psychosocial correlates of breast cancer and its treatment. *Psychological Bulletin,* **87,** 108–131.

Mirsky, I., Futterman, P., & Kaplan, S. (1952). Blood plasma pepsinogen, II. The activity of the plasma from "normal" subjects, patients with duodenal ulcer and patients with pernicious anaemia. *Journal of Laboratory and Clinical Medicine,* **40,** 188.

Mittelmann, B., & Wolff, H. (1942). Emotions and gastroduodenal function: Experimental studies on patients with gastritis, deudenitis and peptic ulcer. *Psychosomatic Medicine,* **4,** 5.

Nemiah, J. (1971). The psychological management and treatment of patients with peptic ulcers. In J. Bostraams, H. Freyberger, & L. Levi, et al. (Eds.), *Advances in psychosomatic medicine.* Basel, Switzerland: Karger.

Olson, R. & Elliot, C. (1983). Behavioral medicine: Assessment, patient management, and treatment intervention. In C. Wallser (Ed.), *The handbook of clinical psychology.* Homewood, IL: Dow Jones-Irwin.

Parker, G., & Lipscombe, P. (1979). Parental overprotection and asthma. *Journal of Psychosomatic Research,* **23,** 295–299.

Patel, C. (1977). Biofeedback-aided relaxation and meditation in the mangement of hypertension. *Biofeedback and Self-regulation,* **2,** 1–42.

Pierloot, R. (1979). Psychogeneis of somatic disorders. *Psychotherapy and Psychosomatics,* **32,** 27–40.

Review Panel on Coronary-prone Behavior and Coronary Heart Disease (1981). Coronary-prone behavior and coronary heart disease: A critical review. *Circulation,* **63,** 1199–1215.

Rieser, M. (1975). Theoretical concepts in psychosomatic medicine. In S. Arieti (Ed.), *American handbook of psychology,* 2nd Ed., Vol. 4. New York: Basic Books.

Rosenman, R., Brand, R., Jenkins, C., Friedman, M., Straus, R., & Wurm, M. (1975). Coronary heart disease in the Western Collaborative Group Study: Final follow-up experience of 8½ years. *Journal of the American Medical Association,* **233,** 872–877.

Rosenman, R., & Friedman, M. (1961). Association of specific behavior pattern in women with blood and cardiovascular findings. *Circulation,* **24,** 1173.

Rosenman, R., & Friedman, M. (1977). Modifying Type A behavior patterns. *Journal of Psychosomatic Research,* **21,** 323–331.

Roskies, E., Kearney, H., Spevack, M., Surkis, A., Cohen, C., & Gilman, S. (1979). Generalizability and durability of treatment effects in an intervention program for coronary-prone (Type A) managers. *Journal of Behavioral Medicine,* **2,** 195–208.

Rotter, J. (1966). Generalized expectancies for internal versus external control of reinforcement. *Psychological Monograph,* **80,** No. 609.

Ruskin, A., Beard, O., & Schaffer, R. (1948). Blast hypertension: Elevated arterial pressure in the victims of the Texas City disaster. *American Journal of Medicine,* **4,** 228–236.

Sapira, J., Scheib, E., Moriarity, R., & Shapiro, A. (1971). Differences in perception between hypertensive and normotensive populations. *Psychosomatic Medicine,* **33,** 239–250.

Sargent, J., Green, E., & Walters, E. (1973). Preliminary report on the use of autogenic feedback training in the treatment of migraine and tension headaches. *Psychosomatic Medicine,* **35,** 129–135.

Sawrey, W. & Weisz, J. (1956). An experimental method of producing gastric ulcers. *Journal of Comparative and Physiological Psychology,* **49,** 269.

Scarf, M. (1980). Images that heal. *Psychology Today,* **14,** 32–46.

Schwartz, G. et al. (1979). Behavioral medicine approaches to hypertension: An integrative analysis of theory and research. *Journal of Behavioral Medicine,* **2,** 311–364.

Shapiro, A. et al. (1979). The role of stress in hypertension. *Journal of Human Stress,* **5,** 7–26.

Simonton, O., Matthews-Simonton, S., & Creighton, J. (1978). *Getting well again.* Los Angeles: Tarper.

Sklar, L., & Anisman, H. (1981). Stress and cancer. *Psychological Bulletin,* **89,** 369–406.

Stavraky, K. M., Buck, C. W., Lott, S. S., & Wanklin, J. M. (1968). Psychological factors in the outcome of human cancer. *Journal of Psychosomatic Research,* **12,** 250–259.

Stein, M. (1962). Etiology and mechanisms in the development of asthma. In J. Nodine and J. Moyer (Eds.), *Psychosomatic medicine.* Philadelphia: Lea & Febiger.

Suinn, R. (1967). Psychological reactions to physical disability. *Journal of the Association of Physical and Mental Rehabilitation,* **21,** 13.

Suinn, R. (1976). How to break the vicious cycle of stress. *Psychology Today,* **10,** 59–60.

Suinn, R. (1977). Stress management for Type A persons. In R. Williams & D. Gentry (Eds.), *Behavioral methods in medical practice.* Cambridge, MA: Ballinger.

Suinn, R. (1980). Pattern A behaviors and heart disease: Intervention approaches. In J. Ferguson & B. Taylor (Eds.), *Advances in behavioral medicine.*

Suinn, R. (1982). Intervention with Type A behaviors. *Journal of Consulting and Clinical Psychology,* **50,** 933–949.

Suinn, R., & Bloom, L. (1978). Anxiety management training for Type A persons. *Journal of Behavioral Medicine,* **1,** 25–35.

Suinn, R., & Vattano, F. (1980). *Reduction of tension headaches employing a stress management program.* Unpublished manuscript, Colorado State University, Fort Collins.

Surwit, R., Shapiro, D., & Good, I. (1978). Comparison of cardiovascular biofeedback, neuromuscular biofeedback, and meditation in the treatment of borderline essential hypertension. *Journal of Consulting and Clinical Psychology,* **46,** 252–263.

Thomas, C. B., Dusyznski, K. R., & Shaffer, J. (1979). Family attitudes reported in youth as postpredictors of cancer: Precursors study. *Psychosomatic Medicine,* **41,** 287–302.

VanEgeren, L. (1979). Social interactions, communications, and the coronary-prone behavior pattern: A psychophysiological study. *Psychosomatic Medicine,* **41,** 1–18.

Wadden, T. & Anderton, C. (1982). The clinical use of hypnosis. *Psychological Bulletin,* **91,** 215–243.

Weiner, H. (1977). *Psychobiology and human disease.* New York: Aisenier.

Weiner, H., Thaler, M., Reiser, M., & Mirsky, I. (1957). Etiology of duodenal ulcers: I. Relation of specific psychological characteristics to rate of gastric secretion (serum pepsinogen). *Psychosomatic Medicine,* **19,** 1.

Weiss, J. (1977). Ulcers. In J. Maser & M. Seligman (Eds.), *Psychopathology: Experimental models.* San Francisco: Freeman.

Williams, R. (1982, April 29). Psychological, psychophysiological and psychoneuroendocrine mechanisms linking coronary prone behavior and coronary heart disease. Paper presented at Air Force Symposium on Coronary Prone Behavior, San Antonio, Texas.

Williams, R., et. al., (1980). Type A, hostility, and coronary atherosclerosis. *Psychosomatic Medicine,* **42,** 539–549.

Wolf, S., et al. (1979). The role of stress in peptic ulcer disease. *Journal of Human Stress,* **5,** 27–37.

Wolf, S., & Wolff, H. (1943). *Human gastric function.* New York: Oxford University Press.

Wolff, H. (1963). *Cranial pain sensitive structures in headache and other head pain.* (2nd ed.) New York: Oxford University Press.

Yetiv, J. & Bianchine, S. (Eds.) (1983). *Recent advances in clinical therapeutics.* New York: Grune & Stratton.


## CHAPTER 10


Bigg, R., & Guze, S. (1972). Hysteria (Briquet's syndrome) in a psychiatric hospital: The significance of secondary depression. *American Journal of Psychiatry,* **129,** 138–142.

Bond, M., & Pearson, I. (1969). Psychological aspects of pain in women with advanced cancer of the cervix. *Journal of Psychosomatic Research,* **13,** 13–19.

Brady, J., & Lind, D. (1961). Experimental analysis of hysterical blindness. *A.M.A. Archives of General Psychiatry,* **4,** 331.

Breuer, J., & Freud, S. (1955). Studies in hysteria. In J. Strachey (Ed.), *Standard edition of the complete psychological works of Sigmund Freud.* London: Hogarth Press, (first German edition, 1895).

Engel, G. (1959). "Psychogenic" pain and the pain-prone patient. *American Journal of Medicine,* **26,** 899–918.

Fordyce, W. (1979, June). On chronic pain as behavior. Invited address, Association for Behavioral Analysis Fifth Annual Convention, Dearborn, MI.

Fordyce, W., Fowler, R. Jr., Lehmann, J., & DeLateur, B. (1968). Some implications of learning in problems of chronic pain. *Journal of Chronic Disorders,* **21,** 179–190.

Fordyce, W., Fowler, R. Jr., Lehmann, J., DeLateur, B., Sand, P., & Trieschmann, R. (1973). Operant conditioning in the treatment of chronic pain. *Archives of Physical and Medical Rehabilitation,* **54,** 399–408.

Freud, S. (1959). Fragment of an analysis of a case of hysteria. In *Collected papers,* Vol. 3. New York: Basic Books, (first published in German, 1905).

Guze, S. (1967). The diagnosis of hysteria: What are we trying to do? *American Journal of Psychiatry,* **124,** 491–498.

Guze, S., Woodruff, R. Jr., & Clayton, P. (1972). Sex, age, and the diagnosis of hysteria (Briquet's syndrome). *American Journal of Psychiatry,* **129,** 745–748.

Haskins, J. (1978). *Voodoo and hoodoo.* New York: Stein & Day.

Jones, M. (1980). Conversion reaction: Anachronism or evolutionary form: A review of the neurologic, behavioral, and psychoanalytic literature. *Psychological Bulletin,* **87,** 427–441.

Kaminsky, M. & Slavney, P. (1976). Methodology and personality in Briquet's Syndrome: A reappraisal. *American Journal of Psychiatry,* **133,** 85–87.

Kaufmann, W. (1976). *Religions in four dimensions.* New York: Readers Digest Press.

Klopfer, B. (1954). Discussion of E. Blumberg. Results of psychological testing of cancer patients. In J. Gengerelli & F. Kirkner (Eds.), *Psychological variables in human cancer.* Berkeley: University of California Press, 1954.

Kroger, W. (1977). *Clinical and experimental hypnosis* (2nd ed.). Philadelphia: Lippincott.

Liebman, R., Honig, P., & Berger, H. (1976). An integrated treatment program for psychogenic pain. *Family Process,* **15,** 397–405.

Malmo, R., Davis, J., & Barza, S. (1952). Total hysterical deafness. An experimental case study. *Journal of Personality,* **21,** 188.

Melzack, R. (1973). *The puzzle of pain.* New York: Basic Books.

Merskey, H. (1980). Psychological and psychiatric aspects of pain control. In W. Smith, H. Merskey, & S. Gross (Eds.), *Pain, meaning and management.* New York: Spectrum.

Morrison, J. (1978). Management of Briquet's syndrome (hysteria). *Western Journal of Medicine,* **128,** 482–487.

Munro, I. (1977). Briquet's syndrome or hysteria? *Lancet,* **1,** 1138–1139.

Pace, J. (1977). Psychophysiology of pain: Diagnostic and therapeutic implications. *Journal of Family Practice,* **5,** 553–557.

Pinsky, J. (1978). Chronic, intractable, benign pain: A syndrome and its treatment with intensive short-term group psychotherapy. *Journal of Human Stress,* **4,** 17–21.

Reveley, M., Woodruff, R., Robins, L., Taibleson, M., Reich, T., & Helzer, J. (1977). Evaluation of a screening interview for Briquet's syndrome (hysteria) by the study of medically ill women. *Archives of General Psychiatry,* **34,** 145–149.

Sanders, S. (1982, November). A component analysis of behavioral methods used in the treatment of chronic pain patients. Paper presented at the annual convention of the Association for the Advancement of Behavior Therapy, Los Angeles.

Satran, R., & Goldstein, M. (1973). Pain perception: Modification of threshold intolerance and cortical potentials by cutaneous stimulation. *Science,* **180,** 1201–1202.

Slavney, P., & McHugh, P. (1978). Hysteria and Briquet's syndrome. Letter to the editor. *American Journal of Psychiatry,* **135,** 750–780.

Smart, N. (1976). *The religious experience of mankind* (2nd ed.). New York: Scribner.

Stein, N. & Fruchter, H. (1983). Experiences of depression and illness behavior in patients with intractable chronic pain. *Journal of Clinical Psychology,* **39,** 31–33.

Sternback, R. (1974). *Pain patients, traits and treatment.* New York: Academic Press.

Swanson, D., Maruta, T., & Swenson, W. (1979). Results of behavior modification in the treatment of chronic pain. *Psychosomatic Medicine,* **41,** 55–61.

Szasz, T. (1968). The psychology of persistent pain: A portrait of l'homme douloureux. In A. Soulairac, J. Cahn, & J. Charpentier (Eds.), *Pain.* New York: Academic Press.

Thompson, S. (1982). Will it hurt less if I can control it? A complex answer to a simple question. *Psychological Bulletin,* **90,** 89–101.

Timmermans, G., & Sternbach, R. (1974). Factors of chronic pain: An analysis of personality and pain reaction variables. *Science,* **184,** 806–808.

Trief, P. & Yuan, H. (1983). The use of the MMPI in a chronic back pain rehabilitation program. *Journal of Clinical Psychology,* **39,** 46–53.

Urban, B. (1982). Therapeutic aspects in chronic pain: Modulation of nociperception, alleviation of suffering, and behavioral analysis. *Behavior Therapy,* **13,** 430–437.

Wernick, R., Juremko, M., & Taylor, P. (1981). Pain management in severely burned adults: stress inoculation. *Journal of Behavioral Medicine,* **3,** 103–110.

Wolpe, J. (1958). *Psychotherapy by reciprocal inhibition.* Stanford, CA: Stanford University Press.

Woodruff, R., Clayton, P., & Guze, S. (1971). Hysteria—studies of diagnosis, outcome, and prevalence. *Journal of the American Medical Association,* **215,** 425–428.

## CHAPTER 11

Asher, R. (1951). Munchausen's syndrome. *Lancet,* **260,** 339–341.

Danish Medical Association. (1983, February). *Weekly Journal.*

Ganser, S. (1898). Über einen eigenartigen hysterischen Daemmerzustand. Arch. Psychiatr. Nervenkr., **30,** 633–640.

Grinker, R., Jr. (1961). Imposture as a form of mastery. *Archives of General Psychiatry,* **5,** 449–452.

Heym, H., Sasaki, A., & Winslow, D. (1977). Cousteau diver impersonated by Munchausen patient. Letter to the editor. *Journal of the American Medical Association,* **238,** p. 1, 248.

Raff, M., Stodghill, W., & Roy, T. (1975). Fraudulent feculent fever in a female fabulist. *Southern Medical Journal,* **68,** 360–362.

Raspe, R. (1971). *The adventures of Baron Munchausen.* New York: World.

Spiro, H. (1968). Chronic factitious illness, Munchausen's syndrome. *Archives of General Psychiatry,* **18,** 569–579.

Vaisrub, S. (1978). Baron Munchausen and the abused child. *Journal of the American Medical Association,* **239,** 752.

Whitlock, F. (1967). The Ganser syndrome. *British Journal of Psychiatry,* **113,** 19–29.

## CHAPTER 12

Berkowitz, L. (1965). Some aspects of observed aggression. *Journal of Personality and Social Psychology,* **2,** 359.

Blanco, R. (1972). *Prescription for children with learning and adjustment problems.* Springfield, IL: C. C Thomas.

Bolen, D., & Boyd, W. (1968). Gambling and the gambler: A review and preliminary findings. *Archives of General Psychiatry,* **18,** 617–630.

Boyd, W., & Bolen, D. (1970). The compulsive gambler and spouse in group psychotherapy. *International Journal of Group Psychotherapy,* **20,** 77–90.

Bureau of the Census, Statistical Abstract of the United States (1980). Washington, DC: U.S. Government Printing Office.

Cady, S. (1975, February). The Gambler who must. In *Reader's Digest,* 185–188.

Cameron, M. *The booster and the snitch.* New York: Free Press, 1974.

Chamove, A. (1980). Nongenetic induction of acquired levels of aggression. *Journal of Abnormal Psychology,* **89,** 469–488.

Curtis, B. (1971). *Security control: External theft.* New York: Chain Stores.

Delgado, J. (1969). Radio-controlled behavior. *New York State Journal of Medicine,* **69,** 413–417.

Denholtz, M. (1972). "At home" aversion treatment for compulsive fire-setting behavior: Case report. In H. Rubin, et al. (Eds.), *Advances in behavior therapy: Proceedings of the 4th Conference of the Association for the Advancement of Behavior Therapy.* New York: Academic Press.

Fenichel, O. (1943). *The psychoanalytic theory of neuroses* New York: Norton.

Flynn, J., Vanegas, H., Foote, W., & Edwards, S. (1970). Neural mechanisms involved in a cat's attack on a rat. In R. Whalen, R. Thompson, M. Verzeano, & N. Weinberger (Eds.), *The neural control of behavior.* New York: Academic Press.

Freud, S. (1961). In J. Strachey (Ed.), *Complete psychological works of Sigmund Freud,* Vol. 30. London: Hogarth Press.

Gorenstein, E. (1982). Frontal lobe functions in psychopaths. *Journal of Abnormal Psychology,* **91,** 368–379.

Gorenstein, E., & Newman, J. (1980). Disinhibitory psychopathology: A new perspective and a model for research. *Psychological Review,* **87,** 301–315.

Hayes, S., Rincover, A., & Volosin, D. (1980). Variables influencing the acquisition and maintenance of aggressive behavior: Modeling versus sensory reinforcement. *Journal of Abnormal Psychology,* **89,** 254–262.

Hirsch, W. (1974). An empirical study of the pathological gambler and wife. Unpublished dissertation, California School of Professional Psychology, Los Angeles.

Kagan, J., & Moss, H. (1962). *Birth to maturity: A study in psychological development.* New York: Wiley.

Knapp, T. (1976). A functional analysis of gambling behavior. In W. Eadington (Ed.), *Gambling and society. Interdisciplinary studies on the subject of gambling.* Springfield, IL: C. C Thomas.

Kraft, T. (1970). Treatment of compulsive shoplifting by altering social contingencies. *Behaviour Research and Therapy,* **8,** 393–394.

Lindner, R. (1950). The psychodynamics of gambling. *Annals of the American Academy of Political and Social Sciences,* **268,** 93–107.

Livingston, J. (1974). Compulsive gamblers: A culture of losers. *Psychology Today,* **7,** 51–55.

Looney, D. (1983, May 30). A big loss for a gambling quarterback. *Sports Illustrated,* **50,** 30–31.

Macdonald, J. (1977). *Bombers and firesetters.* Springfield, IL: C. C Thomas.

Mahoney, M., & Mahoney, F. (1973). A residential program in behavior modification. In R. Rubin, J. Brady, & J. Henderson (Eds.), *Advances in behavior therapy,* Vol. 4. New York: Academic Press.

Martinez, T. (1976). Compulsive gambling and the conscious mood. In W. Eadington (Ed.), *Gambling and society. Interdisciplinary studies on the subject of gambling.* Springfield, IL: C. C Thomas.

Meyers, T. (1970). A contribution to the psychopathology of shoplifting. *Journal of Forensic Science,* **15,** 295–310.

Milgram, S. (1963). Behavioral study of obedience. *Journal of Abnormal and Social Psychology,* **67,** 371.

Moody, G. (1964). Churches' Council on Gambling, Annual Report.

Novaco, R. (1979). The cognitive regulation of anger and stress. In P. Kendall & S. Hollon (Eds.), *Cognitive-behavioral interventions.* New York: Academic Press.

Simmel, E., Hahn, M., & Walters, J. (Eds.) (1983). *Aggressive behavior: Genetic and neural approaches.* Hillsdale, NJ: Erlbaum.

Skinner, B. F. (1953). *Science and human behavior.* New York: Appleton-Century-Crofts.

Smith, D., King, M., & Hoebel, B. (1970). Lateral hypothalamic control of killing: Evidence for a cholinoceptive mechanism. *Science,* **167,** 900–901.

Stawar, T. (1976). Fable mod: Operantly structured fantasies as an adjunct in the modification of fire-setting behavior. *Journal of Behavior Therapy and Experimental Psychiatry,* **7,** 285–287.

Strine, G. (1971, March 30). Compulsive gamblers pursue elusive dollars forever. *Los Angeles Times,* p. 6.

Sweet, W. H., Ervin, F. R., & Mark, V. H. (1969). Focal cerebral disease temporal lobe epilepsy and violent behavior. *Transactions of the American Neurological Association,* **94,** 253–256.

Watkins, J. (1983). Treatment of disorders of impulse control. In C. Walker (Ed.), *The handbook of clinical psychology.* Homewood, IL: Dow Jones-Irwin.

Wetzel, R. (1966). Use of behavioral techniques in a case of compulsive stealing. *Journal of Consulting Psychology,* **30,** 367–374.

Wolpe, J. (1973). *The practice of behavior therapy* (2nd Ed.) New York: Pergamon.

Yarnell, H. (1940). Firesetting in children. *American Journal of Orthopsychiatry,* **10,** 727.

Zuckerman, M., Buchsbaum, M., & Murphy, D. (1980). Sensation seeking and its biological correlates. *Psychological Bulletin,* **88,** 187.

## CHAPTER 13

Abuzzahab, F. & Anderson, F. (1971). A review of LSD treatment in alcoholism. *International Pharmacopsychiatry,* **6,** 223–235.

Alcoholics Anonymous. (1972). *Profile of an AA meeting.* New York: Alcoholics Anonymous World Services.

Alexander, B., & Hadaway, P. (1982). Opiate addiction: The case for an adaptive orientation. *Psychological Bulletin,* **92,** 367–381.

Anslinger, H., & Thompkins, W. (1953). *The traffic in narcotics.* New York: Funk and Wagnalls.

Appel, P., & Kaestner, E. (1979). Interpersonal and emotional problem solving among narcotic drug abusers. *Journal of Consulting and Clinical Psychology,* **47,** 1125–1127.

Baker, C. (1983). *Physicians' Desk Reference.* Oradell, NJ: Medical Economics Co.

Bale, R., VanStone, W., Kuldau, J., Engelsing, T., Elashoff, R., & Zarcone, Jr., V. (1980). Therapeutic communities versus methadone maintenance. *Archives of General Psychiatry,* **37,** 179–193.

Beschner, G. & Friedman, A. (1979). *Youth drug abuse.* Lexington, MA: Heath.

Bill, C. (1965). The growth and effectiveness of Alcoholics Anonymous in a Southwestern city. *Quarterly Journal of Studies on Alcohol,* **26,** 279–284.

Blake, B. (1965). The application of behavior therapy to the treatment of alcoholism. *Behaviour Research and Therapy,* **3,** 75.

Braucht, G., Kirby, M., & Berry, G. (1978). Psychosocial correlates of empirical types of multiple drug abusers. *Journal of Consulting and Clinical Psychology,* **46,** 1463–1475.

Brown, R. (1980). Personality measures in gamma and delta alcoholism: A brief note. *Journal of Clinical Psychology,* **36,** 345–346.

Cahalan, D., Cisin, I., & Crossley, H. (1969). *American drinking practices.* Monogr. No. 6, New Brunswick, NJ: Rutgers Center of Alcohol Studies.

Cannon, D., Baker, T., & Wehl, C. (1981). Emetic and electrical shock alcohol aversion therapy: Six- and twelve-month follow-up. *Journal of Consulting and Clinical Psychology,* **49,** 360–368.

Carr, R. & Meyers, E. (1980). Marijuana and cocaine. In Drug Abuse Council, *The facts about "drug abuse."* New York: Free Press.

Cautela, J. (1970). The treatment of alcoholism by covert sensitization. *Psychotherapy: Theory, Research, and Practice,* **7,** 86–90.

Clark, W., & Cahalan, D. (1977). Changes in problem drinking over a four year span. In E. Pattison, M. Sobell, & L. Sobell (Eds.), *Emerging concepts of alcohol dependence.* New York: Springer.

de Quincey, T. (1924). *The confessions of an English opium-eater.* London: Macmillan.

Dickens, B., Doob, A., Warwick, O., & Winegard, W. (1982). *Report of the Committee of Enquiry into allegations concerning Drs. Linda and Mark Sobell.* Toronto, Canada: Information Center, Addiction Research Foundation.

Ditman, K. (1967). Review and evaluation of current drug therapies in alcoholism. *International Journal of Psychiatry,* **3,** 248.

Douglass, F., Khavari, K., & Farber, P. (1980). Three types of extreme drug users identified by a replicated cluster analysis. *Journal of Abnormal Psychology,* **89,** 240–249.

Drug Abuse Council. (1980). *The facts about "drug abuse."* New York: Free Press.

Ellermann, M. (1948). Social and clinical features of chronic alcoholism. *Journal of Nervous and Mental Disease,* **107,** 556.

Farber, P., Khavari, K., & Douglass, F. (1980). A factor analytic study of reasons for drinking: Empirical validations of positive and negative reinforcement dimensions. *Journal of Consulting and Clinical Psychology,* **48,** 780.

Feldman, H., Agar, M. & Beachner, G. (1979). *Angel dust.* Lexington, MA: Lexington Books.

Fenichel, O. (1945). *The psychoanalytic theory of neurosis.* New York: Norton.

Ford Foundation. (1972). *Dealing with drug abuse.* New York: Praeger.

Freud, S. (1940). *Der Witz und seine Bedeutung zum Unbewussten.* Ges. Werke. London: Imago. (First published in 1905.)

Fuqua, P. (1978). *Drug abuse: Investigation and control.* New York: McGraw-Hill.

Goodwin, D., Schulsinger, F., Hermansen, L., Guze, S., & Winokur, G. (1973). Alcohol problems in adoptees raised apart from alcoholic biological parents. *Archives of General Psychology,* **28,** 238–243.

Gorsuch, R. (1980, March). Interactive models of nonmedical drug use. In *Theories on drug abuse: Selected contemporary perspectives.* NIDA Research Monograph, **30.**

Green, H., & Levy, M. (1976). *Drug misuse . . . human abuse.* New York: Marcel Dekker.

Green, J. (1979). Overview of adolescent drug use. In G. Beschner & A. Luedman (Eds.), *Youth drug abuse.* Lexington, MA: D.C. Heath.

Grinspoon, L. (1977). *Marihuana reconsidered* (2nd ed.). Cambridge, MA: Harvard University Press.

Hall, S., Bass, A., Hargreaves, W., & Loeb, P. (1979). Contingency management and information feedback in outpatient heroin detoxification. *Behavior Therapy.* **4,** 443.

Hall, S., Loeb, P., LeVois, M., & Cooper, J. (1981). Increasing employment in ex-heroin addicts. II: methadone maintenance sample. *Behavior Therapy,* **12,** 454–460.

Hendin, H. (1980). Psychosocial theory of drug abuse: A psychodynamic approach. In D. Lettieri et al. (Eds), *Theories on drug abuse.* Washington, DC: U.S. Government Printing Office.

Honigfeld, G., & Howard, A. (1978). *Psychiatric drugs* (2nd ed.). New York: Academic Press.

Imlah, N. (1971). *Drugs in modern society.* Princeton, NJ: Auerbach Publishers.

James, J., & Andresen, E. (1979). Sea-Tac and PCP. In H. Feldman, M. Agar, & G. Beschner (Eds.), *Angel dust.* Lexington, MA: Lexington Books.

Jellinek, E. (1946). Phases in the drinking history of alcoholics. *Quarterly Journal of Studies on Alcohol,* **7,** 1.

Jellinek, E. (1960). *The disease concept of alcoholism.* New Haven, CT: Hill House Press.

Kandel, D. (1980). Developmental stages in adolescent drug involvement. In D. Lettieri et al., (Eds.), *Theories on drug abuse,* Washington, DC: U.S. Government Printing Office.

Kandel, D., Kessler, R., & Marguiles, R. (1978). Antecedents of adolescent initiation into stages of drug use: A developmental analysis. In D. Kandel (Ed.), *Longitudinal research on drug use.* Washington, DC: Hemisphere.

Keane, T., & Lisman, S. (1980). Alcohol and social anxiety in males: Behavioral, cognitive, and physiological effects. *Journal of Abnormal Psychology,* **89,** 213–233.

Kissin, B. & Begleiter, H. (Eds.). (1983). *The biology of alcoholism.* Vol. 7. New York: Athaneum.

Krasnegor, N. (1980). Analysis and modification of substance abuse: A behavioral overview. *Behavior Modification,* **4,** 35–56.

Leach, B. (1973). Does Alcoholics Anonymous really work? In P. Bourne & R. Fox (Eds.), *Alcoholism: Progress in research and treatment.* New York: Academic Press.

Lemere, F. (1953). What happens to alcoholics? *American Journal of Psychiatry,* **109,** 649.

Lemere, F. (1956). The nature and significance of brain damage from alcoholism. *American Journal of Psychiatry,* **113,** 361.

Leukefeld, C., & Clayton, R. (1979). Drug abuse and delinquency: A study of youths in treatment. In G. Beschner & A. Friedman (Eds.), *Youth drug abuse.* Lexington, MA: Heath.

Lewis, D. & Sessler, J. (1980). Heroin treatment. In Drug Abuse Council, *The facts about "drug abuse."* New York: Free Press.

Lipton, M., Mascio, A., & Killam, K. (1978). *Psychopharmacology: A generation of progress.* New York: Raven Press.

Louria, D. (1971). *Overcoming drugs, a program for action.* New York: McGraw-Hill.

Lovibond, S., & Caddy, G. (1970). Discriminated aversive control in the moderation of alcoholics' drinking behavior. *Behavior Therapy,* **1,** 437.

Lubetkin, B., Rivers, P., & Rosenberg, C. (1971). Difficulties in disulfiram therapy with alcoholics. *Quarterly Journal of Studies on Alcohol*, **32,** 168–171.

Ludlow, F. (1857). *The hasheesh eater: Being passages from the life of a Pythagorean.* New York: Harper.

McAuliffe, W. & Gordon, R. (1980). Reinforcement and the combination of effects: Summary of a theory of opiate addiction. In D. Lettieri, M. Sayers, & H. Pearson, (Eds.), *Theories on drug abuse.* Washington, DC: U.S. Government Printing Office.

Malatesta, V., Sutker, P. & Treiber, F. (1981). Sensation seeking and chronic public drunkenness. *Journal of Consulting and Clinical Psychology.*

Mardones, R., Segovia, M., & Hederra, D. (1953). Heredity of experimental alcohol preference in rats. *Quarterly Journal of Studies on Alcohol,* **14,** 1.

McClellan, A., Luborsky, L., Woody, G., & O'Brien, C. (1980). An improved diagnostic evaluational instrument for substance abuse patients. *Journal of Nervous and Mental Disease,* **168,** 26–33.

McClelland, D., Davis, W., Kalin, R., & Wanner, E. (1972). *The drinking man.* New York: Free Press.

McCollam, J., Burish, T., Maisto, S., & Sobell, M. (1980). Alcohol's effects on physiological arousal and self-reported affect and sensations. *Journal of Abnormal Behavior,* **89,** 224–233.

Menninger, K. (1938). *Man against himself.* New York: Harcourt.

Mezzrow, M., & Wolfe, B. (1946). *Really the blues.* New York.

Miller, W. & Munoz, R. (1982). *How to control your drinking.* Albuquerque, N.M.: University of New Mexico Press.

Moore, R., & Buchanan, T. (1966). State hospitals and alcoholism. A nationwide survey of treatment techniques and results. *Quarterly Journal of Studies on Alcohol,* **27,** 459.

Nathan, P. (1980). Ideal mental health services for alcoholics and problem drinkers: An exercise in pragmatics. In P. Davidson & S. Davidson (Eds.), *Behavioral medicine: Changing health lifestyles.* New York: Brunner/Mazel.

National Institute on Drug Abuse, (NIDA). (1981). *Local drug abuse: Trends, patterns and issues,* Washington, DC: U.S. Government Printing Office.

Neuman, C., & Tamerin, J. (1971). The treatment of adult alcoholics and teenage drug addicts in one hospital: A comparison and critical appraisal of factors related to outcome. *Quarterly Journal of Studies on Alcohol,* **32,** 82.

Nirenberg, T. (1983). Treatment of substance abuse. In C. Walker (Ed.), *The handbook of clinical psychology.* Homewood, IL: Dow Jones-Irwin.

O'Reilly, P. (1962). Lysergic acid and the alcoholic. *Diseases of the Nervous System,* **23,** 331.

Pattison, E., Sobell, M., & Sobell, L. (1977). *Emerging concepts of alcohol dependence.* New York: Springer.

Penk, W., Woodward, W., Robinowitz, R., & Parr, W. (1980). An MMPI comparison of polydrug and heroin abusers. *Journal of Abnormal Psychology,* **89,** 299–302.

Pert, C., & Snyder, S. (1973). Opiate receptor: Demonstration in nervous tissue. *Science,* **179,** 1011.

Powers, R., & Kutash, I. (1980). Alcohol abuse and anxiety. In I. Kutash & L. Schlesinger (Eds.), *Handbook on stress and anxiety.* San Francisco: Jossey-Bass.

Project DAWN. (1976, May–1977, April). *Drug abuse warning network: Project DAWN.*

Puskash, M., & Guereski, M. (1980). Perception of self and significant others by male and female alcoholics. *Journal of Clinical Psychology,* **36,** 571–576.

Renault, P. (1978). Treatment of heroin-dependent persons with antagonists: current status. *Bulletin of Narcotics,* **30,** 21–29.

Robinson, V. (1946). Experiments with hashish. *CIBA Symposium,* **8,** 387.

Rodgers, D., & McClearn, G. (1962). Mouse strain differences in preference for various concentrations of alcohol. *Quarterly Journal of Studies on Alcohol,* **23,** 26–33.

Scher, J. (1966). Patterns and profiles of addiction and drug abuse. *Archives of General Psychiatry,* **15,** 539.

Schlesinger, K. (1966). Genetic and biochemical correlates of alcohol preference in mice. *American Journal of Psychiatry,* **122,** 767.

Schnoll, S. (1979). Pharmacological aspects of youth drug abuse, in G. Beschner, & A. Friedman. *Youth drug abuse.* Lexington, MA: Heath.

Schultes, R. (1940). The aboriginal uses of Lophophoria Williamsii. *Cactus and Succulent Journal,* **12,** 177.

Schwarz, D. (1970). Marijuana: An attempt at perspective. In P. Blachly (Ed.), *Drug abuse, data and debate.* Springfield, IL: C. C Thomas.

Sells, S. & Simpson, D. (1979). On the effectiveness of treatment of drug abuse: evidence on the DARP research programme in the United States. *Bulletin on Narcotics,* **31,** 1–12.

Senay, E., Dorus, W., & Jhon, Y. (1978). LAAM as a maintenance drug. In A. Schecter, H. Alksne, & E. Kaufman (Eds.), *Drug abuse: Modern trends, issues and perspectives.* New York: Marcel Dekker.

Shaw, S., Cartwright, A., Spratley, T., & Harwin, J. (1978). *Responding to drinking problems.* Baltimore: University Park Press.

Sher, K. & Levenson, R. (1982). Risk for alcoholism and individual differences in the stress-response-dampening effect of alcohol. *Journal of Abnormal Psychology,* **91,** 350–367.

Silver, A. (1970). An addendum to the technique of psychotherapy with alcoholics. *Journal of Nervous and Mental Disease,* **150,** 423.

Simon, E. (1980). Opiate receptors and their implications for drug addiction. In D. Lettieri, M. Sayers, & H. Pearson. *Theories on drug abuse.* Washington, DC: U.S. Government Printing Office.

Skinner, H. & Allen, B. (1982). Alcohol dependence syndrome: Measurement and validation. *Journal of Abnormal Psychology,* **91,** 199–209.

Sobell, M. & Sobell, L. (1978). *Behavioral treatment of alcohol problems.* New York: Plenum.

Stafford, P. (1971). *Psychedelic baby reaches puberty.* New York: Praeger.

Stanton, M., Todd, T., Heard, D., Kirschner, S., Kleiman, J., Mowatt, D., Riley, P., Scott, S., & Vandeusen, J. (1978). Heroin addiction as a family phenomenon: A new conceptual model. *American Journal of Drug and Alcohol Abuse,* **5,** 125.

Steer, R., McElroy, M., & Beck, A. (1983). Correlates of self-reported and clinically assessed depression in outpatient alcoholics. *Journal of Clinical Psychology* **39,** 144–149.

Sue, S., Zane, N., & Ito, J. (1979). Alcohol drinking patterns among Asian and Caucasian Americans. *Journal of Cross-cultural Psychology,* **10,** 41–56.

Sutker, P., & Archer, R. (1979). MMPI charcteristics of opiate addicts, alcoholics and other drug abusers. In C. Newmark (Ed.), *MMPI: Current clinical and research trends.* New York: Praeger.

Tarber, R., McBride, H., Buonpane, N., & Schneider, D. (1977). Differentiation of alcoholics: Childhood history of minimal brain dysfunction, family history and drinking pattern. *Archives of General Psychiatry,* **34,** 761.

Thacore, V., & Shukla, S. (1976). Cannabis psychosis and paranoid schizophrenia. *Archives of General Psychiatry,* **33,** 383–386.

Ungerleider, J., Fisher, D., Goldsmith, S., Fuller, M., & Forgy, E. (1968). A statistical survey of adverse reactions to LSD in Los Angeles County. *American Journal of Psychiatry,* **125,** 108.

U.S. Department of Health, Education and Welfare. (1980). Alcohol, not poor diet, causes brain damage in abusers. *ADAMHA News,* **6,** 1.

U.S. Department of Health & Human Services. (1981). *Student Drug Use in America 1975–1980.* Washington, D.C.: U.S. Government Printing Office.

Von Wartburg, J. (1970). Alcohol dehydrogenase distribution in tissues of different species. In R. Popham (Ed.), *Alcohol and alcoholism.* Toronto: University of Toronto Press.

Walters, J. (1979). "Buzzin": PCP use in Philadelphia. In H. Feldman, M. Agar, & G. Beschner (Eds.), *Angel dust.* Lexington, MA: Lexington Books.

Weller, R., & Halikas, J. (1980). Objective criteria for the diagnosis of marijuana abuse. *Journal of Nervous and Mental Disease,* **168,** 98.

Wilsnack, S. (1973). Femininity by the bottle. *Addictions,* **20,** 2–19.

Wilson, G. (1978). Alcoholism and aversion therapy: Issues, ethics and evidence. In G. Marlatt & P. Nathan (Eds.) *Behavioral approaches to alcoholism.* New Brunswick, NJ: Rutgers Center of Alcohol Studies.

Winokur, G., Reich, T., Rimmer, J., & Pitts, F. (1970). Alcoholism III: Diagnosis and familial psychiatric illness in 259 probands. *Archives of General Psychiatry,* **23,** 104–111.

Zirich, J. (1981). Alcoholic subtypes and treatment effectiveness. *Journal of Consulting and Clinical Psychology,* **49,** 72–80.

## CHAPTER 14

Allen, C. (1969). *A textbook of psychosexual disorders.* New York: Oxford University Press.

American Psychiatric Association. (1978). *Diagnostic and statistical manual of mental disorders* (3rd ed.). Washington, DC: American Psychological Association.

Amir, M. (1971). *Patterns of forcible rape.* Chicago: University of Chicago Press.

Andersen, B. (1983). Primary orgasmic dysfunction: Diagnostic considerations and review of treatment. *Psychological Bulletin,* **93,** 105–136.

Annon, J. (1971, September). *The therapeutic use of masturbation in the treatment of sexual disorders.* Paper presented at the Fifth Annual Meeting of the Association for the Advancement of Behavior Therapy, Washington, DC.

Annon, J. (1973). The therapeutic use of masturbation in the treatment of sexual disorders. In R. Rubin, J. Brady, & J. Henderson (Eds.), *Advances in behavior therapy.* Vol. 4. New York: Academic Press.

Bandura, A., & Walters, R. (1963). *Social learning and personality development.* New York: Holt, Rinehart & Winston.

Barbaree H., Marshall, W., & Lanthier, R. (1979). Deviant sexual arousal in rapists. *Behaviour Research and Therapy,* **17,** 215–222.

Barlow, D., & Agras, W. (1973). Fading to increase heterosexual responsiveness in homosexuals. *Journal of Applied Behavior Analysis,* **6,** 355–366.

Barlow, D., Reynolds, E., & Agras, W. (1973). Gender identity change in a transsexual. *Archives of General Psychiatry,* **28,** 569–576.

Baron, R. (1974). The aggression-inhibiting influence of heightened sexual arousal. *Journal of Personality and Social Psychology,* **30,** 318–320.

Bergler, E. (1947). Analysis of an unusual case of fetishism. *Bulletin of the Menninger Clinic,* **2,** 67–75.

Bieber, I. (1976). A discussion of "homosexuality: The ethical challenge." *Journal of Consulting and Clinical Psychology,* **44,** 163–166.

Buckner, H. (1970). The transvestic career path. *Psychiatry,* **33,** 381–389.

Buhrich. N. (1981). Psychological adjustment in transvestism and transsexualism. *Behaviour Research and Therapy,* **19,** 407–412.

Burgess, A., & Holstrom, L. (1974). *Rape: Victims of crisis.* Bowie, MD: Brady.

Cadden, V. (1978). The psychiatrists versus Masters and Johnson. In J. LoPiccolo & L. LoPiccolo (Eds.), *Handbook of sex therapy.* New York: Plenum.

Cautela, J., & Wisocki, P. (1977). Covert sensitization for the treatment of sexual deviations. In J. Fischer & H. Gochros (Eds.), *Handbook of behavior therapy with sexual problems,* Vol. 2: *Approaches to specific problems.* New York: Pergamon.

Cohen, M., Seghorn, T., & Calmas, W. (1969). Sociometric study of the sex offender. *Journal of Abnormal Psychology,* **74,** 249–255.

Cooper, A. (1977). An innovation in the "behavioral" treatment of a case of nonconsummation due to vaginismus. In J. Fischer & H. Gochros (Eds.), *Handbook of behavior therapy with sexual problems. Vol. 2: Approaches to specific problems.* New York: Pergamon.

Corey, J., Corey, M. & Callanan, P. (1984). *Issues and ethics in the helping professions.* Monterey, CA: Brooks/Cole.

Cunningham, S. (1982, December). Violent pornography said to spur aggression. *APA Monitor,* **13.**

Davison, G. (1976). Homosexuality: The ethical challenge. *Journal of Consulting and Clinical Psychology,* **44,** 157.

Davison, G. (1977). Elimination of a sadistic fantasy by a client-controlled counterconditioning technique: A case study. In J. Fischer & H. Gocros (Eds.), *Handbook of behavior therapy with sexual problems.* Vol. 2: *Approaches to specific problems.* New York: Pergamon.

Davison, G. (1978). Not can but ought: The treatment of homosexuality. *Journal of Consulting and Clinical Psychology,* **46,** 170.

Donnerstein, E., Donnerstein, M., & Evans, R. (1975). Erotic stimuli and aggression: Facilitation or inhibition. *Journal of Personality and Social Psychology,* **21,** 237–444.

Ellis, E., Atkeson, B., & Calhoun, K. (1981). An assessment of long-term reaction to rape. *Journal of Abnormal Psychology,* **90,** 263–266.

Epstein, A. (1960). Fetishism. *Journal of Nervous and Mental Disease,* **130,** 107–119.

Evans, R. (1969). Childhood parental relationships of homosexual men. *Journal of Consulting and Clinical Psychology,* **33,** 129–135.

Federal Bureau of Investigation. (1974). *Crime in the United States.* Washington, DC: U.S. Government Printing House, Uniform Crime Reports.

Gagnon, J. (1977). *Human sexualities.* Chicago: Scott Foresman.

Gebhard, P., & Gagnon, J. (1964). Male sex offenders against very young children. *American Journal of Psychiatry,* **121,** 576–579.

Gebhard, P., Gagnon, J., Pomeroy, W., & Christenson, C. (1965). *Sex offenders: An analysis of types.* New York: Harper & Row.

Glueck, B. (1956). Psychodynamic patterns in the homosexual sex offenders. *American Journal of Psychiatry,* **112,** 584–590.

Groth, A., Burgess, A. & Holmstrom, L. (1977). Rape: Power, anger & sexuality, **134,** 1239–1243.

Halpern, B., Ky, T., & Robert, B. (1967). Clinical and immunological study of an exceptional case of reaginic type sensitization to human seminal fluid. *Immunology,* **12,** 247.

Jones, E. (1957). *The life and work of Sigmund Freud,* Vol. 3. New York: Basic Books.

Kallmann, F. (1952). Twin and sibling study of overt male homosexuality. *American Journal of Human Genetics,* **4,** 136–146.

Kant, H., & Goldstein, M. (1970). Pornography. *Psychology Today,* **4,** 58–61, 76.

Kaplan, H. (1974). *The new sex therapy.* New York: Brunner/Mazel.

Katz, S., & Mazur, M. (1979). *Understanding the rape victim: A synthesis of research findings.* New York: Wiley Interscience.

Kilmann, P. & Mills, K. (1983). *All about sex therapy.* New York: Plenum.

Krafft-Ebing, R. (1950). *Psychopathica sexualis.* New York: Pioneer Publishers.

Kushner, M. (1977). The reduction of a long-standing fetish by means of aversive conditioning. In J. Fischer & H. Gochros (Eds.), *Handbook of behavior therapy with sexual problems,* Vol. 2: *Approaches to specific problems.* New York: Pergamon.

Kutchinsky, B. (1970). Sex crimes and pornography in Copenhagen: A study of attitudes. *Technical reports of the commission on obscenity and pornography* Vol. 7. Washington, DC: U.S. Government Printing House.

Langevin, R. (1982). *Sexual strands: Understanding and treating sexual anomalies in men.* Hillcrest, NJ: Erlbaum.

LaTorre, R. (1980). Devaluation of the human love object: Heterosexual rejection as a possible antecedent to fetishism. *Journal of Abnormal Psychology,* **89,** 295–298.

Laws, D., & Pawlowski, A. (1977). An automated fading procedure to alter sexual responsiveness in pedophiles. In J. Fischer & H. Gochros (Eds.), *Handbook of behavior therapy with sexual problems,* Vol. 2: *Approaches to specific problems.* New York: Pergamon.

Lester, D. (1975). *Unusual sexual behavior: The standard deviations.* Springfield, IL: C. C Thomas.

Levin, S., Barry, S., Gambaro, S., et al. (1977). Variations of covert sensitization in the treatment of pedophilic behavior: A case study. *Journal of Consulting and Clinical Psychology,* **45,** 896–907.

LoPiccolo, J. (1978). The professionalization of sex therapy: Issues and problems. In J. LoPiccolo & L. LoPiccolo (Eds.), *Handbook of sex therapy.* New York: Plenum.

LoPiccolo, L. (1980). Low sexual desire. In S. Leiblum & L. Pervin (Eds.), *Principles and practice of sex therapy.* New York: Guilford.

Lovaas, O., Litrownick, A., & Mann, R. (1971). Response latencies to auditory stimuli in autistic children engaged in self-stimulatory behavior. *Behaviour Research and Therapy,* **9,** 39.

Lukianowicz, N. (1959). Survey of various aspects of transvestism in the light of our present knowledge. *Journal of Nervous and Mental Diseases,* **128,** 36–64.

MacDonald, J. (1971). *Rape offenders and their victims.* Springfield, IL: C. C Thomas.

MacDonald, J. (1973). *Indecent exposure.* Springfield, IL: C. C Thomas.

Maier, R. (1984). *Human sexuality in perspective.* Chicago: Nelson-Hall.

Masters, W., & Johnson, V. (1970). *Human sexual inadequacy.* Boston: Little, Brown.

McConaghy, N., Armstrong, M. & Blaszcaynski. (1981). Controlled comparison of aversive therapy and covert sensitization in compulsive homosexuality. *Behaviour Research and Therapy,* **19,** 425–434.

Medea, A., & Thompson, K. (1974). *Against rape: A survival manual for women: How to cope with rape physically and emotionally.* New York: Farrar, Straus & Giroux.

Meerlo, J. (1964). Change of sex and collaboration with the psychosis. *American Journalof Psychiatry,* **124,** 263–264.

Meyer, J., & Reter, D. (1979). Sex reassignment. *Archives of General Psychiatry,* **36,** 1010.

Morris, J. *Conundrum.* New York: Harcourt, Brace & Johanovitch, 1974.

Oliven, J. (1974). *Clinical sexuality* (3rd Ed.). Philadelphia: Lippincott.

Pauly, I. (1968a). Male psychosexual inversion. *Archives of General Psychiatry,* **13,** 172–179.

Pauly, I. (1968b). The current status of the change of sex operation. *Journal of Nervous and Mental Diseases.* **147,** 460–471.

Prince, V., & Bentler, P. (1972). Survey of 504 cases of transvestism. *Psychological Reports,* **31,** 903–917.

Quinn, J., Harbison, J., & McAllister, H. (1970). An attempt to shape human penile responses. *Behaviour Research and Therapy,* **8,** 213–216.

Rachman, S. (1966). Sexual fetishism: An experimental analogue. *Psychological Record.* **16,** 293–296.

Rada, R. Alcohol and rape. (1975). *Medical Aspects of Human Sexuality,* **9,** 48–65.

Razani, K. (1977). Ejaculatory incompetence treated by reconditioning anxiety. In J. Fischer & H. Gochros (Eds.), *Handbook of behavior therapy with sexual problems.* Vol. 2: *Approaches to specific problems.* New York: Pergamon.

Reinhardt, J. (1957). *Sex perversions and sex crimes.* Springfield, IL: C. C Thomas.

Reitz, W., & Keil, W. (1977). Behavioral treatment of an exhibitionist. In J. Fischer & H. Gochros (Eds.), *Handbook of behavior therapy with sexual problems,* Vol. 2: *Approaches to specific problems.* New York: Pergamon.

Resick, P., Calhoun, K., Atkeson, B., & Ellis, E., *Journal of Consulting and Clinical Psychology,* **49,** 705–712.

Resnick, H. (1972). Eroticized repetitive hangings. *American Journal of Psychotherapy.* **26,** 4–11.

Roback, H., McKee, E., & Webb, W. (1979). Psychopathology in female sex-change applicants and two help seeking controls. *Journal of Abnormal Psychology,* **85,** 430–432.

Rooth, G. Exhibitionism outside Europe and America. (1973). *Archives of Sexual Behavior,* **4,** 351–363.

Rosenthal, D. (1970). *Genetic theory and abnormal behavior.* New York: McGraw-Hill.

Semans, J. (1956). Premature ejaculation: A new approach. *Journal of Urology,* **49,** 353–357.

Shoenberg, R. & Goldberg, R. (Eds.) (1984). *Homosexuality and social work.* New York: Haworth Press.

Skipper, J., & McCaghy, C. (1969). Stripteasers: The anatomy and career contingencies of a deviant occupation. *Social Problems,* **17,** 391–405.

Stoller, R. (1967). Transvestite women. *American Journal of Psychiatry,* **123,** 333–339.

Thompson, N. Jr., McCandless, B., & Strickland, B. (1971). Personal adjustment of male and female homosexuals and heterosexuals. *Journal of Abnormal Psychology,* **78,** 237–240.

U.S. Commission on Obscenity and Pornography. (1970). *Report of the U.S. Commission on Obscenity and Pornography.* Washington, DC: U.S. Government Printing Office.

Weinberg, M., & Williams, C. (1974). *Male homosexuals: Their problems and adaptations.* New York: Oxford University Press.

Yaffé, M., & Nelson, E. (1982). *The influence of pornography on behaviour.* New York: Academic Press.

## CHAPTER 15

Achenbach, T. (1982). *Development psychopathology* (2nd ed.). New York: Wiley.

Bacon, M. (1981). Cross-cultural perspectives on motivations for drinking. In R. Munroe, R. Munroe, & B. Whiting (Eds). *Handbook of cross-cultural human development.* New York: Garland.

Brim, O. & Kagan, J. (1980). *Constancy and change in human development.* Boston: Boston University Press.

Burchard, J. (1967). Systematic socialization: A programmed environment for the habilitation of antisocial retardates. *Psychological Record,* **17,** 461–476.

Burton, R. & Reis, J. (1981). Internalization. In R. Munroe, R. Munroe, & B. Whiting (Eds). *Handbook of cross-cultural human development.* New York: Garland.

Cameron, N. (1963). *Personality development and psychopathology, a dynamic approach.* Boston: Houghton Mifflin.

Camp, B., Blom, G., Herbert, F., & van Doorninck. (1977). "Think Aloud": A program for developing self-control in young aggressive boys. *Journal of Abnormal Child Psychology,* **5,** 157–168.

Cattell, R. (1982). *The inheritance of personality and ability.* New York: Academic Press.

Chandler, M. (1973). Egocentrism and antisocial behavior: The assessment and training of social perspective-taking skills. *Developmental Psychology,* **9,** 326.

Claridge, G., Canter, S. & Hume, A. (1973). *Personality differences and biological variations: A study of twins.* New York: Pergamon.

Cline, H. (1980). Criminal behavior over the life span. In O. Brim & J. Kagan (Eds.) *Constancy and change in human development.* Cambridge, MA: Harvard University Press.

Ember, C. (1981). A cross-cultural perspective on sex differences. In R. Munroe, R. Munroe, & B. Whiting (Eds.), *Handbook of cross-cultural human development.* New York: Garland.

Eysenck, H. (1970). *The structure of human personality* (3rd ed.). London: Methuen.

Farber, S. (1981). *Identical twins reared apart. A reanalysis.* New York: Basic Books.

Frosch, J. (1983). *Current perspectives on personality disorders.* Washington, DC: American Psychiatric Press.

Gelfand, D., Genson, W., & Drew, C. (1982). *Understanding child behavior disorders.* New York: Holt, Rinehart & Winston.

Gilbert, G. (1970). *Personality dynamics: A biosocial approach.* New York: Harper.

Gorenstein, E. (1982). Frontal lobe functions in psychopaths. *Journal of Abnormal Psychology,* **91,** 368–379.

Griest, D., Forehand, R., Rogers, T., Breiner, J., Furey, W., & Williams, C. (1983). Effects of parent enhancement therapy on the treatment outcome and generalization of a parent training program. *Behaviour Research and Therapy.*

Griest, D., & Wells, K. (1983). Behavioral family therapy with conduct disorders in children. *Behavior Therapy,* **14,** 37–53.

Gurman, A., & Kniskern, D. (1978). Research on marital and family therapy: Progress, perspectives, and prospects. In S. Garfield & A. Bergin (Eds.), *Handbook of psychotherapy and behavior change: An empirical analysis.* New York: Wiley.

Hare, R. (1978). Electrodermal and cardiovascular correlates of psychopathy. In R. Hare & D. Schalling (Eds.), *Psychopathic behaviour: Approaches to research.* New York: Wiley.

Harper, M., Morris, M., & Bleyerveld, J. (1972). The significance of an abnormal EEG in psychopathic personalities. Australia: *New Zealand Journal of Psychiatry,* **6,** 214–224.

Hartl, E., Monnelly, E., & Elderkin, R. (1982). *Physique and delinquent behavior.* New York: Academic Press.

Hunter, W. (1974, May). Deposition in the case of *Hearn* v. *Rhay et al.* U.S. District Court, Eastern District of Washington.

Jesness, C. (1975). Comparative effectiveness of behavior modification and transactional analysis programmes for delinquents. *Journal of Consulting and Clinical Psychology,* **43,** 738–779.

Kagan, J., & Moss, H. (1962). *Birth to maturity.* New York: Wiley.

Leeman, C., & Mulvey, C. (1973). Brief psychotherapy of the dependent personality: Specific techniques. *Psychonometrics,* **25,** 36.

Lewis, D., Shanok, S., Grant, M., & Ritvo, E. (1983). Homicidally aggressive young children: Neuropsychiatric and experiential correlates. *American Journal of Psychiatry,* **140,** 140–148.

Lion, J. (1974). *Diagnosis and treatment of personality disorders.* Baltimore: Williams & Wilkins.

Loehlin, J., & Nichols, R. (1976). *Heredity, environment and personality.* Austin: University of Texas Press.

Lombroso, C. (1911). *Crime and its causes and remedies.* Boston: Little, Brown.

Marmour, J. (1954). Orality in the hysterical personality. *Journal of the American Psychoanalytic Association,* **1,** 656.

McCord, W. (1982). *The psychopath and milieu therapy.* New York: Academic Press.

Monroe, R., & Mickle, W. (1967). Alpha-chloralose activated EEG in psychiatric patients. *Journal of Nervous and Mental Disorders,* **144,** 59–68.

Moss, H. and Susman, E. (1980). Longitudinal study of personality development. In O. Brim & J. Kagan (Eds.), *Constancy and change in human development.* Cambridge, MA: Harvard University Press.

Olendick, T., & Elliott, W. (1978). Locus of control as related to effectiveness in a behavior modification program for juvenile delinquents. Unpublished manuscript, Indiana State University.

Pasternack, S. (1974). The explosive, antisocial, and passive-aggressive personalities. In J. Lion (Ed.), *Diagnosis and treatment of personality disorders.* Baltimore: Williams & Wilkins.

Pfeffer, C., Plutchik, R., Mizruchi, M. (1983). Predictors of assaultiveness in latency age children. *American Journal of Psychiatry,* **140,** 31–35.

Redl, F., & Wineman, D. (1957). *Controls from within: Techniques for the treatment of the aggressive child.* Glencoe, IL: Free Press.

Rickard, K., Forehand, R., Atkeson, B. & Lopez, C. (1982). An examination of the relationship of marital satisfaction and divorce with parent-child interactions. *Journal of Clinical and Child Psychology,* **11,** 61–65.

Robins, L. (1978). Aetiological implications in studies of childhood histories relating to antisocial personality. In R. Hare & D. Schalling (Eds.), *Psychopathic behaviour: Approaches to research.* New York: Wiley.

Schacter, S., & Latane, B. (1964). Crime, cognition and the autonomic nervous system. In H. Jones (Ed.), *Nebraska Symposium on Motivation.* Lincoln, NE: University of Nebraska Press.

Sears, R., Maccoby, E., & Levin, H. (1957). *Patterns of child rearing.* Evanston, IL: Row, Peterson.

Shields, J. (1962). *Monozygotic twins brought up apart and brought up together: An investigation into the genetic and environmental causes of variation in personality.* London: Oxford.

Shure, M., & Spivack, M. (1978). *The problem solving approach to adjustment.* San Francisco: Jossey-Bass.

Snyder, J., & White, M. (1979). The use of cognitive self-instruction in the treatment of behaviorally disturbed adolescents. *Behavior Therapy,* **10,** 227–235.

Spitzer, R., Endicott, J., & Gibbon, M. (1979). Crossing the border into borderline personality and borderline schizophrenia. *Archives of General Psychiatry,* **36,** 17–27.

Stone, M. (1980). *The borderline syndromes.* New York: McGraw-Hill.

Thomas, A., & Chess, S. (1977). *Temperament and development.* New York: Brunner/Mazel.

Thomas, A., Chess, S., & Birch, H. (1970). The origin of personality. *Scientific American,* **223,** 102.

Urbain, E., & Kendall, P. (1980). Review of social-cognitive problem-solving interventions with children. *Psychological Bulletin,* **88,** 109.

Wahler, R. (1980). The insular mother: Her problems in parent-child treatment. *Journal of Applied Behavior Analysis,* **13,** 207–219.

Wells, K. Assessment of children in outpatient settings. (1981). In M. Hersen & A. Bellack (Eds.), *Behavioral assessment: A practical handbook.* New York: Pergamon.

Whiteley, S., Briggs, D., & Turner, M. (1972). *Dealing with deviants.* London: Hogarth Press.

Widom, C. (1977). A methodology for studying non-institutionalized psychopaths. *Journal of Consulting and Clinical Psychology.*

Zahavi, S., & Asher, S. (1978). The effect of verbal instructions on preschool children's aggressive behavior. *Journal of School Psychology,* **16,** 146.

Zuckerman, M. (Ed.) (1983). Biological bases of sensation seeking, impulsivity, and anxiety. Hillsdale, NJ: Erlbaum.

## CHAPTER 16

Abraham, K. (1949). Notes on the psycho-analytical investigation and treatment of manic-depressive insanity and allied conditions. In K. Abraham, *Selected papers on psycho-analysis.* London: Hogarth Press. (Originally published in 1911.)

Akiskal, H., & McKinney, W. (1975). Overview of recent research in depression: Integration of ten conceptual models in a comprehensive clinical frame. *Archives of General Psychiatry,* **32,** 385–405.

Alexopoulus, G., Inturris, C., Lipman, R., Frances, R., Haycox, J., Dougherty, J., & Rossier, J. (1983). Plasma immunoreactive B-endorphin levels in depression. *Archives of General Psychiatry,* **40,** 181–183.

Altman, J., & Wittenborn, J. (1980). Depression-prone personality in women. *Journal of Abnormal Psychology,* **89,** 303–308.

American Psychiatric Association. (1980). *Diagnostic and statistical manual of mental disorders* (3rd ed.). Washington, DC: American Psychiatric Association.

Arieti, S. (1959). Manic-depressive psychosis. In S. Arieti (Ed.), *American handbook of psychiatry.* New York: Basic Books.

Bailine, S. & Rau, J. (1981). The decision to use ECT: A retrospective study. *Comparative Psychiatry,* **22,** 274–281.

Baker, C. (1983). *Physicians' desk reference.* Hillsdale, NJ: Medical Economics Co.

Baldessarini, R. (1983). *Biomedical aspects of depression and its treatment.* Washington, DC: American Psychiatric Press.

Barnes, M. (1977). Effects of antidepressive program on verbal behavior. *Journal of Clinical Psychology,* **33,** 545.

Beck, A. (1983). Negative cognitions. In E. Levitt, B. Lubin & J. Brooks (Eds.), *Depression: concepts, controversies, and some new facts* (2nd ed.). Hillsdale, NJ: Erlbaum.

Bunney, W., Goodwin, F., & Murphy, D. (1972). The "switch process" in manic-depressive illness: Theoretical implications. *Archives of General Psychiatry,* **27,** 312–318.

Bureau of the Census. (1981). *Statistical Abstract of the United States.* Washington, DC: U.S. Government Print. Office.

Campbell, F. & Singer, G. (1983). *Stress, drugs, and health.* New York: Pergamon.

Clayton, P. (1981). The epidemiology of bipolar affective disorder. *Comprehensive Psychiatry,* **22,** 31–43.

Clinical Psychiatry Committee. (1965). Medical Research Council, Great Britain. Clinical trial of the treatment of depressive illness. *British Medical Journal,* **2,** 881–886.

Cofer, D., & Wittenborn, J. (1980). Personality characteristics of formerly depressed women. *Journal of Abnormal Psychology,* **89,** 309–314.

Craighead, W. E. (1980). Away from a unitary model of depression. *Behavior Therapy,* **11,** 122–128.

Craw, T. (Ed.). (1983). *Disorders of (neuronoural) transmission.* New York: Academic Press.

Davis, J. & Maas, J. (1983). *The affective disorders.* Washington, DC: American Psychiatric Press.

Depue, R. Slater, J. Wolfstetter-Kausch, H., Klein, D., Goplerud, E., & Farr, D. (1981). A behavioral paradigm for identifying persons at risk for bipolar disorder: A conceptual framework and five validation studies. *Journal of Abnormal Psychology,* **90,** 381–437.

Donnelly, E., Murphy, D., & Waldman, I. (1980). Denial and somatization as characteristics of bipolar depressed group. *Journal of Clinical Psychiatry,* **36,** 159–162.

Farberow, N. (1980). *The many faces of suicide.* New York: McGraw-Hill.

Frazer, A. (1977). Biological aspects of mania and depression. In A. Frazer & A. Winokur (Eds.), *Biological bases of psychiatric disorders.* New York: Spectrum Publishers.

Garber, J., & Hollon, S. (1980). Universal versus personal helplessness in depression: Belief in uncontrollability or incompetence? *Journal of Abnormal Psychology,* **89,** 56–66.

Gerner, R., Catlin, D., Gorelick, D., Hui, K., & Li, C. (1980). B-endorphins: Intravenous infusion causes behavior change in psychiatric patients. *Archives of General Psychiatry,* **37,** 642–649.

Gold, H. (1951). Observations on cultural psychiatry during a world tour of mental hospitals. *American Journal of Psychiatry,* **108,** 462.

Gordon, R. (1979). Accident or suicide: The psychological autopsy. *Journal of Forensic Psychology,* **7,** 63–68.

Heiby, E. (1981). Depression and frequency of self-reinforcement. *Behavior Therapy,* **12,** 549–555.

Hollon, S., & Beck, A. (1979). Cognitive therapy of depression. In P. Kendall & S. Hollon (Eds.), *Cognitive-behavioral intervention.* New York: Academic Press.

Hotchner, A. (1966). *Papa Hemingway: A personal memoir.* New York: Random House.

Jefferson, J. & Greist, J. (1983). *Lithium encyclopedia for clinical practice.* Washington, DC: American Psychiatric Press.

Kovacs, M. (1979). Treatment of depressive disorders: The efficacy of behavior and cognitive therapies. *Behavior Modification,* **3,** 496–517.

Kraepelin, E. (1899). *Clinical psychiatry.* New York: Macmillan.

Leonard, C. (1974). Depression and suicidality. *Journal of Consulting and Clinical Psychology,* **42,** 98–104.

Lewinsohn, P. (1983). Defective social skills. In E. Levitt, B. Lubin, & J. Brooks (Eds.), *Depression-concepts, controversies and some new facts,* (2nd ed.). Hillsdale, NJ: Erlbaum.

Lewinsohn, P., Steinmetz, J., Larson, D., & Franklin, J. (1981). Depression-related cognitions. Antecedent or consequence? *Journal of Abnormal Psychology,* **90,** 213–219.

Lyons, H. (1972). Depressive illness and aggression in Belfast. *British Medical Journal,* **1,** 342–344.

Marsella, A. (1980). Depressive experiences and disorders across cultures. In H. Triandis & J. Draguns (Eds.), *Handbook of cross-cultural psychology.* Boston: Allyn & Bacon.

McIntosh, J. (1980). A study of suicide among United States racial minorities based on official statistics: The influence of age, sex, and other variables. *Dissertation Abstracts International,* **41,** 1135-B.

Miller, I., & Norman, W. (1979). Learned helplessness in humans: A review and attribution-theory model. *Psychological Bulletin,* **86,** 93–118.

Newman, R., & Hirt, M. (1983). The psychoanalytic theory of depression: Symptoms as a function of aggressive wishes and level of field articulation. *Journal of Abnormal Psychology,* **92,** 42–48.

Nielsen, J., & Videbech, T. (1973). Suicide frequency before and after introduction of community psychiatry in a Danish island. *British Journal of Psychiatry,* **123,** 35–39.

Paykel, E. (1976). Life stress, depression and attempted suicide. *Journal of Human Stress,* **2,** 3–12.

Paykel, E., Prusoff, B., & Myers, J. (1975). Suicide attempts and recent life events. *Archives of General Psychiatry,* **32,** 327–331.

Radloff, L., & Rae, D. (1979). Susceptibility and precipitating factors in depression: Sex differences and similarities. *Journal of Abnormal Psychology,* **88,** 174–181.

Rehm, L., Fuchs, C., Roth, D., Kornblith, S., & Romano, J. (1975). *Self-control and social skills training in the modification of depression.* Unpublished manuscript, University of Pittsburgh.

Rosen, A., Tureff, S., Daruna, J., Johnson, P., & Lyons, J. (1980). Pharmaco-therapy of schizophrenic and affective disorders: Behavioral correlates of diagnostic and demographic variables. *Journal of Abnormal Psychology,* **89,** 387–399.

Ross, M. (1974). This doctor will self destruct, *Human Behavior,* **3,** 54.

Roth, S., & Kubal, L. (1975). The effects of noncontingent reinforcement on tasks of differing importance: Facilitation and learning helplessness effects. *Journal of Personality and Social Psychology,* **32,** 680–691.

Rudestam, K. (1975). Suicide in Sweden and the U.S. In N. Farberow (Ed.), *Suicide in different cultures.* Baltimore: University Park Press.

Rush, A., Beck, A., Kovacs, M., & Hollon, S. (1977). Comparative efficacy of cognitive therapy versus pharmacotherapy in outpatient depressives. *Cognitive Therapy Research,* **1,** 17.

Scovern, A., & Kilman, P. (1980). Status of electroconvulsive therapy: Review of the outcome literature. *Psychological Bulletin,* **87,** 260–303.

Seiden, R. (1974). Suicide: Preventable death. *Public Affairs Report,* **15,** 1–5.

Seligman, M. (1983). Learned helplessness. In E. Levitt, B. Lubin, & J. Brooks (Eds.), *Depression: Concepts, controversies, and some new facts* (2nd ed.). Hillsdale, NJ: Erlbaum.

Seligman, M., Abramson, L., Semmel, A., & Baeyer, C. (1979). Depressive attributional style. *Journal of Abnormal Psychology,* **88,** 242–247.

Shaw, B. (1977). Comparison of cognitive therapy and behavior therapy in the treatment of depression. *Journal of Consulting and Clinical Psychology,* **45,** 543–551.

Shneidman, E., & Farberow, N. (1961). *Some facts about suicide.* Washington, D.C.: U.S. Government Printing House.

Shneidman, E., & Farberow, N. (1970). A psychological approach to the study of suicide notes. In E. Shneidman, N. Farberow, & R. Litman (Eds.), *The psychology of suicide.* New York: Jason Aronson.

Slater, J., & Depue, R. (1981). The contribution of environmental social support to serious suicide attempts in primary depression disorder. *Journal of Abnormal Psychology,* **90,** 275–285.

Todd, F. (1972). Coverant control of self-evaluative responses in the treatment of depression: A new use for an old priniciple. *Behavior Therapy,* **3,** 91–94.

Vogel, G., Vogel, F., McAbee, R., & Thurmond, A. (1980). Improvement of depression by REM sleep deprivation. *Archives General Psychiatry,* **37,** 247–253.

Weiss, J., Glazer, H., & Pohorecky, L. (1974). Neurotransmitters and helplessness: A chemical bridge to depression. *Psychology Today,* **8,** 58–65.

Wolpe, J. (1979). The experimental model and treatment of neurotic depression *Behaviour Research and Therapy,* **17,** 555.

## CHAPTER 17

Adams, H., Malatesta, V., Brantley, P., & Turkat, I. (1981). Modification of cognitive processes: A case study of schizophrenia. *Journal of Consulting and Clinical Psychology,* **49,** 460–464.

Arieti, S. (1955). *Interpretation of schizophrenia.* New York: Robert Brunner.

Asanarow, R., Steffy, R., & MacCrimmon, D. (1977). An attentional assessment of foster children at risk for schizophrenia. *Journal of Abnormal Psychology,* **86,** 267.

Ayllon, T., & Michael, J. (1959). The psychiatric nurse as a behavioral engineer. *Journal of Experimental Analysis of Behavior,* **2,** 323.

Baker, R., Hall, J. N., Hutchinson, K., & Bridge, G. (1977). Symptom changes in chronic schizophrenic patients on a token economy. A controlled experiment. *British Journal of Psychiatry,* **131,** 381–393.

Baribeau-Braun, J., Picton, T., & Gosselin, J. (1983). Schizophrenia: A neurophysiological evaluation of abnormal information processing. *Science,* **219,** 874–876.

Benedict, P. (1958). Sociocultural factors in schizophrenia. In L. Bellack (Ed.), *Schizophrenia: A review of the syndrome.* New York: Logos Press.

Benson, D., Stuss, D., Naeser, M., Weir, W., Kaplan, E., Levine, H. (1981). The long-term effects of prefrontal leukotomy. *Archives of Neurology and Psychology,* **38,** 165–169.

Berger, P. (1981). Biochemistry and the schizophrenias: Old concepts and new hypotheses. *Journal of Nervous and Mental Disease,* **169,** 90–99.

Berkowitz, R. (1981). The distinction between paranoid and nonparanoid forms of schizophrenia. *British Journal of Clinical Psychology,* **20,** 15–23.

Berner, P., Gabriel, E., Katschnig, H. & Kieffer, W. (1983). *Diagnostic criteria for schizophrenic and affective psychoses.* Washington, DC: American Psychiatric Press.

Bleuler, E. (1978). The long term course of schizophrenic psychoses. In L. Wynne, R. Cromwell, & S. Matthysse (Eds.), *The nature of schizophrenia.* New York: Wiley.

Bond, E. (1954). Results of psychiatric treatments with a control series. *American Journal of Psychiatry,* **110,** 561.

Brim, O., & Kagan, J. (1980). *Constancy and change in human development.* Cambridge, MA: Harvard University Press.

Brody, E. (1981). Can mother-infant interaction produce vulnerability to schizophrenia? *Journal of Nervous and Mental Disease,* **169,** 72–81.

Buchsbaum, M. (1980). Neurophysiological aspects of the schizophrenic symptom. In L. Bellak (Ed.), *Disorders of the schizophrenic syndrome.* New York: Basic Books.

Carpenter, W. & Heinrichs, D. (1981). Treatment-relevant subtypes of schizophrenia. *Journal of Nervous Mental and Disease,* **169,** 113–119.

Chapman, L., & Chapman, J. (1973). *Disordered thought in schizophrenics.* New York: Appleton-Century-Crofts.

Crow, T. (Ed.). (1983). *Disorders of neurohumoural transmission.* New York: Academic Press.

Dagani, R. (1981, November 9). Radiochemicals key to new diagnostic tool. *Chemical and Engineering News,* 30–37.

Davis, J. R., Wallace, C. J., Liberman, R. P., & Finch, B. E. (1976). The use of brief isolation to suppress delusional and hallucinatory speech. *Journal of Behavior Therapy and Experimental Psychiatry,* **7,** 269–275.

Donlon, P., Hopin, J., Tupin, J., Wicks, J., et al. (1980). Haloperidol for acute schizophrenia patients. *Archives of General Psychiatry,* **37,** 691–695.

Draguns, J. (1980). Psychological disorders of clinical severity. In H. Triandis & J. Draguns (Eds.). *Handbook of cross-cultural psychology.* Boston: Allyn & Bacon.

Ellsworth, J. R. (1969). Reinforcement therapy with chronic patients. *Hospital and Community Psychiatry,* **20,** 238–240.

Epstein, S., & Coleman, M. (1970). Drive theories of schizophrenia. *Psychosomatic Medicine,* **32,** 113–140.

Erwin, B., & Rosenbaum, G. (1979). Parietal lobe syndrome and schizophrenia: Comparison of neuropsychological deficits. *Journal of Abnormal Psychology,* **88,** 234–241.

Faris, R., & Dunham, H. (1939). *Mental disorders in urban areas.* Chicago: University of Chicago Press.

Fisher, L., & Jones, J. (1980). Child competency and psychiatric risk. *Journal of Nervous and Mental Disease,* **168,** 332–337.

Fisher, S., & Mendell, D. (1956). The communication of neurotic patterns over two and three generations. *Psychiatry,* **19,** 41.

Fleck, S., Lidz, T., & Cornelison, A. (1963). Comparison of parent-child relationships of male and female schizophrenic patients. *Archives of General Psychiatry,* **8,** 1–7.

Freeman, J. (1981). Long-term treatment of schizophrenia. *Comprehensive Psychiatry,* **22,** 94–102.

Freeman, W. (1953). Level of achievement after lobotomy. A study of one thousand cases. *American Journal of Psychiatry,* **110,** 269.

Freud, S. (1953). On narcissism: An introduction. In *Collected Papers,* Vol. 6. London: Hogarth Press. (First published in 1914.)

Gjerde, P. (1983). Attentional capacity dysfunction and arousal in schizophrenia. *Psychological Bulletin,* **93,** 57–72.

Gomes-Schwartz, B. (1979). The modification of schizophrenic behavior. *Behavior Modification,* **3,** 439–468.

Green, P. (1978). Defective interhemispheric transfer in schizophrenia. *Journal of Abnormal Psychology,* **87,** 472.

Haley, J. (1980). *Leaving home: The therapy of disturbed young people.* New York: McGraw-Hill.

Harder, D., Gift, T. Strauss, J., Ritzler, B, & Kokes, R. (1981). Life events and two-year outcome in schizophrenia. *Journal of Consulting and Clinical Psychology,* **49,** 619–627.

Harris, J. (1975). Abbreviated form of the the Phillips Rating Scale of Premorbid Adjustment in schizophrenia. *Journal of Abnormal Psychology,* **84,** 129–137.

Heath, R., & Guererro-Figueroa, R. (1965). Psychotic behavior with evoked septal dysrhythmia. *American Journal of Psychiatry,* **121,** 1080.

Heilman, D. & Satz, P. (1983). *Neuropsychology of human emotion.* New York: Guilford.

Insanity: Legitimate defense? (1981, January 11). *Coloradoan,* p. D-1.

Isaacs, W., Thomas, J., & Goldiamond, I. (1960). Application of operant conditioning to reinstate verbal behavior in psychotics. *Journal of Speech and Hearing Disorders,* **25,** 8.

Kalinowsky, L. (1973). Attempts at localization of psychological manifestations observed in various psychosurgical procedures. In L. Laitinen & K. Livingston (Eds.), *Surgical approaches in psychological training.* Lancaster: Medical & Technical Pub.

Kraepelin, E. (1925). *Dementia praecox and paraphrenia.* Edinburgh: Livingston.

Laing, R. D. (1964). Is schizophrenia a disease? *International Journal of Social Psychiatry,* **10,** 184–195.

Laseque, C., & Fairet, J. (1877). La folie à deux on folie communiquee. *Annals of Medicine and Psychology,* 5e series, T., **18,** 321.

Lewis, J., Rodnick, E., & Goldstein, M. (1981). Intrafamilial interactive behavior, parental communication deviation, and risk for schizophrenia. *Journal of Abnormal Psychology,* **90,** 448–457.

Lidz, T. (1973). *The origin and treatment of schizophrenic disorders.* New York: Basic Books.

Magaro, P., Abrams, L., & Cantrell, P. (1981). The Maine scale of paranoid and nonparanoid schizophrenia: Reliability and validity. *Journal of Consulting and Clinical Psychology,* **49,** 438–447.

May, P., Tuma, A., Dixon, W., et al. (1981) Schizophrenia: A follow up study of the results of five forms of therapy. **38,** 776–784.

May, P., Turna, A., Gale, C., et al. (1976). Schizophrenia: A follow-up of results of treatment of schizophrenia: II. Hospital stay over two to five years. *Archives of General Psychiatry,* **33,** 481–486.

McNeil, T., & Kaiji, L. (1978). Obstetric factors in the development of schizophrenia: Complications in the births of preschizophrenics and in reproduction by schizophrenic parents. In L. Wynne, R. Cromwell, & S. Matthysse (Eds.), *The nature of schizophrenia: New approaches to research and treatment.* New York: Wiley.

Mednick, S., & Schulsinger, F. (1978). Some premorbid characteristics related to breakdown in children with schizophrenic mothers. Journal of Psychiatric Research, **6,** 267–291.

Meehl, P. (1962). Schizotaxia, schizotype, schizophrenia. *American Psychologist,* **17,** 827–838.

Menn, A., & Mosher, L. (1976). The Soteria Project. An alternative to hospitalization for schizophrenics: Some clinical aspects. In J. Jorstad & E. Ugelstad (Eds.), *Schizophrenia 75.* Oslo: Lie.

Meyer, A. (1948). *The common sense psychiatry of Adolf Meyer.* A. Lief (Ed.), New York: McGraw-Hill.

Meyers, A., Mercatoris, M., & Sirota, A. (1976). Use of covert self-instruction for the elimination of psychotic speech. *Journal of Consulting and Clinical Psychology,* **44,** 480–482.

Moos, R. (1974). *Evaluating treatment environments: A social-ecological approach.* New York: Wiley.

National Institute of Mental Health. (1978). *Psychiatric services and the changing institutional scene, 1950–1985.* U.S. Department of Health, Education and Welfare, Washington, DC: U.S. Government Printing House.

Oltmanns, T., O'Hayon, J., & Neale, J. (1978). The effects of antipsychotic medication and diagnostic criteria on distractibility in schizophrenia. *Journal of Psychiatric Research,* **14,** 81–92.

Paul, G. L., & Lentz, R. J. (1977). *Psychosocial treatment of chronic mental patients: Milieu vs. social learning programs.* Cambridge, MA: Harvard University Press.

Pearson, M. (1952). *Strecker's fundamentals of psychiatry.* Philadelphia: Lippincott.

Prien, R., Caffey, E., & Klett, C. (1973). Pharmacotherapy in chronic schizophrenia. Washington, DC: Department of Medicine & Surgery, Veterans Administration.

Rattan, R., & Chapman, L. (1973). Associative intrusions in schizophrenic verbal behavior. *Journal of Abnormal Psychology,* **82,** 1969.

Rogers, C. (1967). *The therapeutic relationship and its impact: A study of psychotherapy with schizophrenics.* Madison: University of Wisconsin Press.

Rogers, C. & Hart, J. (1970). Looking back and ahead: A conversation with Carl Rogers. In J. Hart & T. Tomlinson (Eds.), *New directions in client-centered therapy.* New York: Houghton Mifflin.

Romano, J. (1978). The central core of madness. In L. Wynne, R. Cromwell, & S. Matthysse (Eds.), *The nature of schizophrenia: New approaches to research and treatment.* New York: Wiley.

Rottenberg, D., & Cooper, A. (1981). Positron emission tomography of the central nervous system. *Trends in Biochemical Sciences,* **6,** 120–122.

Salzinger, K., Portnoy, S., & Feldman, R. (1978). Communicability deficit in schizophrenics resulting from a more general deficit. In S. Schwartz (Ed.), *Language and cognition in schizophrenia.* Hillsdale, New Jersey: Erlbaum.

Salzman, L., Klein, R., & Strauss, J. (1978). Pendulum eye-tracking in remitted psychiatric patients. In L. Wynne, R. Cromwell, & S. Matthysse (Eds.), *The nature of schizophrenia: New approaches to research and treatment.* New York: Wiley.

Sameroff, A., & Zax, M. (1978). In search of schizophrenia: Young offspring of schizophrenic women. In L. Wynne, R. Cromwell, & S. Matthysse (Eds.), *The nature of schizophrenia: New approaches to research and treatment.* New York: Wiley.

Schulsinger, F., & Falloon, I. (1980). Schizophrenia in high-risk subjects: Prognostic maternal characteristics. *Journal of Abnormal Psychology,* **89,** 501–504.

Schwartz, D. (1963). A review of the "paranoid" concept. *Archives of General Psychiatry,* **8,** 349.

Scovern, A., & Kilmann, P. (1980). Status of electroconvulsive therapy: Review of the outcome literature. *Psychological Bulletin,* **87,** 260–303.

Shapiro, S. (1981). *Contemporary theories of schizophrenia.* New York: McGraw-Hill.

Shimkunas, A. (1978). Hemispheric asymmetry and schizophrenic thought disorder. In S. Schwartz (Ed.), *Language and cognition in schizophrenia.* Hillsdale, NJ: Erlbaum.

Shopsin, B., Kelin, H., Aaronson, M., & Collara, M. (1979). Compazine, chlorpromazine, and placebo in newly hospitalized, acutely schizophrenic patients. *Archives of General Psychiatry,* **36,** 657–664.

Snyder, S. (1981). Dopamine receptors, neuroleptics and schizophrenia. *American Journal of Psychiatry,* **138,** 460–464.

Spensley, J. (1972). Folie à deux with methylphenidate psychosis. *Journal of Nervous and Mental Disease,* **155,** 288–290.

Strauss, J., Bowers, M., Downey, T., Fleck, S., Jackson, S., & Levine, I. (1980). *The psychotherapy of schizophrenia.* New York: Plenum.

Strauss, J., Kokes, R., Carpenter, W., & Ritzler, B. (1978). The course of schizophrenia as a developmental process. In L. Wynne, R. Cromwell, & S. Matthysse (Eds.), *The nature of schizophrenia: New approaches to research and treatment.* New York: Wiley.

Tanaka, G. et al. (1981). Computerized tomography of the brain in schizophrenic patients: A controlled study. *Acta psychiatrica Scandinavica,* **63,** 191–197.

Tissot, R. et al. (1980). Aspects of cognitive activities in schizophrenia. *Psychol. Med.,* **10,** 657–663.

Vaillant, G. (1978). The distinction between prognosis and diagnosis in schizophrenia. In L. Wynne, R. Cromwell, & S. Matthysse (Eds.), *The nature of schizophrenia: New approaches to research and treatment.* New York: Wiley.

Vaughan, H. (1978). Toward a neurophysiology of schizophrenia. In L. Wynne, R. Cromwell, & S. Matthysse (Eds.), *The nature of schizophrenia: New approaches to research and treatment.* New York: Wiley.

Vonnegut, M. (1975). *The eden express.* New York: Bantam Books.

Walker, E., & McGuire, M. (1982). Intra- and interhemispheric information processing in schizophrenia. *Psychological Bulletin,* **92,** 701–725.

Wilson, H. (1982). *Deinstitutionalized residential care for the mentally disordered: The Soteria House approach.* New York: Grune & Stratton.

Wing, J. (1978). Social influences on the course of schizophrenia. In L. Wynne, R. Cromwell, & S. Mathysse (Eds.), *The nature of schizophrenia: New approaches to research and treatment.* New York: Wiley.

## CHAPTER 18

Alzheimer, A. (1907). Uber eine eingenartige Erkrankung der Hirnrinden. *Centralbl. Nervenheit. Psychiat.,* **18,** 177.

Anthony, W., Heston, R., & Lehman, R. (1980). An attempt to cross-validate two actuarial systems for neuropsychological test interpretation. *Journal of Consulting and Clinical Psychology,* **48,** 317–326.

Baker, H. (1971). The clinical usefulness of magnification cerebral angiography. *Radiology,* **98,** 587.

Barker, W. (1968). *Brain storms.* New York: Grove Press.

Benson, D., & Blumer, D. (1975). *Psychiatric aspects of neurological disease.* New York: Grune & Stratton.

Boyle, R. & Ames, W. (1983, April 11). Too many punches, too little concern. *Sports Illustrated,* **58,** 44–67.

Browne, T. & Feldman, T. (1983). *Epilepsy: Diagnosis and management.* Boston, MA: Little, Brown & Co.

Butler, R., & Emr, M. (1982). Alzheimer's disease: An examination. *TWA Ambassador,* **15,** 69–71.

Cohen, D., & Eisdorfer, C. (1980). Antinuclear antibodies in the cognitively impaired elderly. *Journal of Nervous and Mental Diseases,* **168,** 179–180.

Dickmen, S., & Morgan, S. (1980). Neuropsychological factors related to employability and occupational status in persons with epilepsy. *Journal of Nervous and Mental Disease,* **168,** 236–240.

Duboulay, G., & Moseley, I. (1977). *Computerized axial tomography in clinical practice.* Berlin: Springer Verlag.

Eisenberg, M., Sutkin, L. & Jansen, M. (Eds.). (1984). *Chronic illness and disability through the life span.* New York: Springer.

Ferrari, M., Barabas, G., & Matthews, W. (1983). Psychologic and behavioral disturbance among epileptic children treated with barbituate anticonvulsants. *American Journal of Psychiatry,* **140,** 112–113.

Filskov, S., & Goldstein, S. (1974). Diagnostic validity of the Halstead-Reitan neuropsychological battery. *Journal of Consulting and Clinical Psychology,* **42,** 382.

Finger, S., & Stein, D. (1982). Brain damage and recovery: Research and clinical perspectives. New York: Academic Press.

Fraser, R., & Smith, W. (1982). Adjustment to daily living. In H. Sands (Ed.), *Epilepsy* New York: Brunner/Mazel.

Golden, C., Kane, R., Sweet, J., Moses, J., Cardellino, J., Templeton, R., Vicente, P., & Graber, B. (1981), Relationship of the Halstead-Reitan neuropsychological battery to the Luria-Nebraska neuropsychological battery. *Journal of Consulting and Clinical Psychology,* **49,** 410-417.

Golden, C., Moses, J., Fishburne, F., Engum, E., Lewis, G., Wisniewski, A., Conley, F., Berg, R., & Graber, B. (1981). Cross-validation of the Luria-Nebraska neuropsychological battery for the presence, lateralization, and localization of brain damage. *Journal of Consulting and Clinical Psychology,* **49,** 491–507.

Golden, C., Purisch, A., & Hammeke, T. (1979). *The Luria-Nebraska neuropsychological battery.* Lincoln: University of Nebraska Press.

Goldstein, G. & Hersen, M. (1984). *Handbook of psychological assessment.* New York: Pergamon.

Haase, G. (1977). Diseases presenting as dementia. In C. Wells (Ed.), *Dementia.* Philadelphia: Davis.

Harlow, J. (1868). Recovery from the passage of an iron bar through the head. *Publications of the Massachusetts Medical Society,* **2,** 327.

Hoyer, S., Kruger, G., & Weinhardt, F. (1979). Brainblood flow and metabolism in relation to psychiatric status in patients with organic brain syndromes. In J. Meyer, H. Lechner, & M. Reivich (Eds.), *Cerebral vascular disease.* Amsterdam: Excerpta Medica.

Itil, T. (1982). The use of EEG in the practice of psychiatry. *Psychosomatics,* **23,** 799–813.

Jerath, B. et al. (1981). Hospitalization rates for epilepsy in the United States, 1973–1976. *Epilepsia,* **22,** 55–64.

Kaplan, O. (1979). *Psychopathology of aging* New York: Academic Press.

Kapnick, P. (1978). Organic treatment of the elderly. In M. Storandt, I. Siegler, & M. Elias (Eds.), *The clinical psychology of aging.* New York: Plenum.

Katzman, R., & Terry, R. (1983). *The neurology of aging.* Philadelphia: Davis.

Knight, R., & Wooles, I. (1980). Experimental investigation of chronic organic amnesia: A review. *Psychological Bulletin,* **88,** 753.

Kogeorgos, J., Henson, R., & Scott, D. (1979). Pattern sensitive epilepsy: A case report. *Journal of Nervous and Mental Disease,* **42,** 635–639.

Kolb, L. *Noyes' modern clinical psychiatry.* Philadelphia: Saunders, 1968.

Kübler-Ross, E. (1975). *Death: The final stage of growth.* Englewood Cliffs, NJ: Prentice-Hall.

Marinelli, R. & Orto, A. (Eds.). (1984). *The psychological and social impact of physical disability.* (2nd ed.). New York: Springer.

Marossero, F. (1975). Surgery of epilepsy, diagnostic implications of EEGs. *Journal of Neurological Science,* **19,** 84–88.

Masland, R. (1982). The nature of epilepsy. In H. Sands (Ed.), *Epilepsy.* New York: Brunner/Mazel.

Mayo Clinic, (1983). *Clinical examinations in neurology.* Philadelphia: Saunders.

Meltzer, M. (1983). Poor memory: A case report. *Journal of Clinical Psychology,* **39,** 3–10.

Moses, J., Golden, C., Ariel, R. & Gustavson, J. (1983). *Interpretation of the Luria-Nebraska Neuropsychological Battery.* New York: Grune & Stratton.

Mostofsky, D., & Belaschak, B. (1977). Psychobiological control of seizures. *Psychological Bulletin,* **84,** 723–750.

Pick, A. (1892). Uber die Beziehungen der senilen Hirnatrophic zur aphasia. *Prag. Med. Wschr.* **17,** 165.

Plum, F., & Posner, J. (1970). *Diagnoses of stupor and coma.* Philadelphia: Davis.

Pratt, R. (1977). The psychogenic loss of memory. In C. Whitty & Zangwill (Eds.), *Amnesia* (2nd ed.). London: Butterworth.

Pritchard, P. (1983). Personality and emotional complications of epilepsy. In K. Heilman & P. Satz (Eds.), *Neuropsychology of human emotion.* New York: Guilford.

Putnam, T., & Merritt, H. (1938). SDH in treatment of convulsive disorders. *Journal of the American Medical Association,* **3,** 1068.

Reitan, R., & Davison, L. (1974). *Clinical neuropsychology: Current status and applications.* New York: Winston/Wiley.

Riley, M., Hess, B., & Bondy, K. (1983). *Aging in society: Selected reviews of recent research.* New York: Academic Press.

Rowles, G., & Ohta, R. (1982). *Aging and milieu.* New York: Academic Press.

Salzman, C., & Shader, R. (1977, April). Clinical evaluation of depression in the elderly. Paper presented at Geriatric Assessment Workshop, Los Angeles.

Santos, J., & VandenBos, G. (Eds.). (1982). *Psychology and the older adult.* Washington, DC: American Psychological Association.

Shalev, R., & Amir, N. (1983). Complex partial statuts epilepticus. *Archives of Neurology,* **40,** 90–92.

Sironi, V., Franzini, A., Ravagnati, L., & Marossero, F. (1979). Interictal acute psychoses in temporal lobe epilepsy during withdrawal of anticonvulsive therapy. *Journal of Neurology, Neurosurgery, and Psychiatry,* **42,** 724–730.

Small, L. (1983). *The minimal brain dysfunctions.* New York: Free Press.

Smith, A. (1975). Neuropsychological testing in neurological disorders. In W. Friedlander (Ed.), *Advances in neurology,* Vol. 7. New York: Raven.

Sterman, M. (1973). Neurophysiological and clinical studies of sensorimotor EEG biofeedback training: Some effects on epilepsy. In L. Birk (Ed.), *Biofeedback: Behavioral medicine.* New York: Grune & Stratton.

Sterman, M., & Friar, L. (1972). Suppression of seizures in an epileptic following sensorimotor EEG feedback training. *Electroenceph. Clin. Neurophysiol.,* **33,** 89–95.

Struve, F. (in press). Clinical EEG as an assessment method in psychiatric practice. In R. Hall & F. Beresford (Eds.), *Handbook of Psychiatric Diagnostic Procedures.* New York: Spectrum.

Sullivan, M. (1979). *Living with epilepsy.* New York: Nellen.

Terzano, M., Parrino, L., Manzoni, G., Mancia, D. (1983). Seizures triggered by blinking when beginning to speak. *Archives of Neurology,* **40,** 103–106.

Wang, H. (1977). Dementia in old age. In C. Wells (Ed.), *Dementia.* Philadelphia: Davis.

Weiss, G., Feeney, D., Caveness, W., Dillon, D., Kistler, J., Mohr, H., & Rish, B. (1983). Prognostic factors for the occurrence of posttraumatic epilepsy. *Arch. Neurology,* **40,** 7–10.

Williams, D. (1982). The treatment of seizures: Special psychotherapeutic and psychological techniques. In H. Sands (Ed.), *Epilepsy.* New York: Brunner/Mazel.

Williams, M. (1978). The clinical assessment of memory. In P. Reynolds (Ed.), *Advances in psychological assessment,* Vol.4. San Francisco: Jossey-Bass.

Williams, M. (1979). *Brain damage, behavior, and the mind.* New York: Wiley.

## CHAPTER 19

Adams, H., Malatesta, V., Brantley, P., & Turkot, I. (1981). Modification of cognitive processes: A case study of schizophrenia. *Journal of Clinical Psychology,* **49,** 460–464.

Albert, K., Hock, P., & Waelsch, H. (1946). Preliminary report on the effect of glutamic acid administration in mentally retarded subjects. *Journal of Nervous and Mental Disease,* **104,** 263.

Benda, C. (1946). *Mongolism and cretinism.* New York: Grune & Stratton.

Bradley, R., & Tedesco, L. (1982). Environmental correlates of mental retardation. In J. Lachenmeyer & M. Gibbs (Eds.), *Psychopathology in childhood.* New York: Gardner Press.

Bruhl, H., Arneson, J., & Bruhl, M. (1964). Effect of low-phenylalanine diet on older phenylketonuria patients (Long-range controlled study). *American Journal of Mental Deficiency,* **69,** 225–235.

Budoff, M. (1977). The mentally retarded child in the mainstream of the public school: His relation to the school administration, his teachers, and his age-mates. In P. Mittler (Ed.), *Research to practice in mental retardation,* Vol. 2. Baltimore: University Park Press.

Cartwright, G., Cartwright, C., & Ward, M. (1981). *Educating special learners.* Belmont, CA: Wadsworth.

Clarke, C., Edwards, J., & Smallpiece, V. (1961). 21 trisomy-normal mosaicism in an intelligent child with some mongoloid characteristics. *Lancet,* **1,** 1028.

Doll, E. (1941). The essentials of an inclusive concept of mental deficiency. *American Journal of Mental Deficiency,* **46,** 214.

Ellis, N. (Ed.). (1982). *International review of research in mental retardation,* Vol. 11. New York: Academic Press.

Folling, A. (1934). Uber Ausscheidung von Phenylbrenztraubensaure in den Harn als Stoffwenchselanomalie in Verbidung mit Imbezillitat. *Hoppe Seyler A. Physiol. Chem.,* **227,** 169.

Forssman, H., Lehmann, O., & Thysell, T. (1961). Reproduction in mongolism: Chromosome studies and re-examination of a child. *American Journal of Mental Deficiency,* **65,** 495.

Fost, N. (1979). Prenatal diagnosis of Down's syndrome. *Journal of American Medical Association,* **242,** 23–26.

Frank, H., & Rabinovitch, M. (1974). Auditory short term memory: Developmental changes in rehearsal. *Child Development,* **45,** 397.

Garber, H., & Heber, F. (1977). The Milwaukee project: Indications of the effectiveness of early intervention in preventing mental retardation. In P. Mittler (Ed.), *Research to practice in mental retardation,* Vol. 1. Baltimore: University Park Press.

Gearheart, B. (1980). *Special education for the '80's.* St. Louis: Masby.

Gibbs, M., & Thorpe, J. (1983). Personality stereotype of noninstitutionalized Down syndrome children. *American Journal of Mental Deficiency,* **87,** 601–605.

Goldstein, A. (1954). A study of mongolism and non-mongoloid mental retardation in children. *Archives Pediat.,* **71,** 11.

Grossman, H. (1953). *Manual on terminology and classification in mental retardation.* Washington, DC: American Association of Mental Deficiency.

Grossman, H. (Ed.) (1977). Manual of terminology and classification in mental retardation. Baltimore, MD: American Association of Mental Deficiency Special Pub. Series, #2.

Heiser, K. (1954). Psychotherapy in a residential school for mentally retarded children. *Training School Bulletin,* **50,** 211.

Heiser, K., & Wolman, B. (1965). Mental deficiencies. In B. Wolman (Ed.), *Handbook of clinical psychology.* New York: McGraw-Hill.

Hutt, M., & Gibby, R. (1979). *The mentally retarded child.* Boston: Allyn & Bacon.

Jacobs, J. (1983). The search for help: A study of the retarded child in the community. Baltimore: University Press of America.

Jacobs, P., Baikie, A., Brown, W., MacGregor, T., MacLean, N., & Harnden, D. (1959). Evidence for the existence of a human "super female." *Lancet,* **2,** 423.

Jacobs, P., & Strong, J. (1959). A case of human intersexuality having a possible XXY sex-determining machanism. *Nature,* **183,** 302.

Johnson, R., Johnson, D., DeWeerdt, N., Lyons, V., & Zaidman, B. (1983). Integrating severely adaptively handicapped seventh-grade students into constructive relationships with nonhandicapped peers in science class. *American Journal of Mental Deficiency,* **87,** 611–618.

Kent, N., & Davis, D. (1957). Discipline in the home and intellectual development. *British Journal of Medical Psychology,* **30,** 194.

Kirk, S., & Gallagher, J. (1979). *Educating exceptional children* (3rd ed.). Boston: Houghton Mifflin.

Koch, R. (1975). *Collaborative study of children treated for phenylketonuria.* Paper presented at the Eleventh General Medicine Conference, Stateline, Nevada.

Langdon-Down, J. (1866). Observations on an ethnic classification of idiots. *London Hospital Reports,* **3,** 259.

Lejeune, J., Turpin, R., & Gautie, M. (1959). Le mongolisme, premier exemple d'aberration autosomique humaine. *Annals Genetique,* **2,** 41.

Luria, A. *The mentally retarded child.* (1963). Translated from Russian by W. Robinson. English translation edited by B. Kirman. London: Pergamon Press.

MacMillan, D. (1972). Facilitative effect on input organization as a function of verbal response to stimuli in EMR and non-retarded children. *American Journal of Mental Deficiency,* **76,** 408.

Mandell, C., & Fiscus, E., (1981). *Understanding exceptional people.* St. Paul, MN: West Publ.

Matson, J. (1980). A controlled group study of pedestrian-skill training for the mentally retarded. *Behaviour Research Therapy,* **18,** 99–106.

Matson, J. & Mulick, J. (1983). *Handbook of mental retardedness.* New York: Pergamon.

Matson, J., Ollendick, T., & Adkins, J. (1980). A comprehensive dining program for mentally retarded adults. *Behaviour Research and Therapy,* **18,** 107–112.

McGehee, W., & Lewis, W. (1942). The socio-economic status of the homes of mentally superior and retarded children and the occupational rank of their parents. *Pedagogical Seminary,* **60,** 375.

Menolascino, F., & Egger, M. (1978). *Medical dimensions in mental retardation.* Lincoln: University of Nebraska Press.

Mittler, P. (Ed.). (1977). *Research to practice in mental retardation,* Vol. 1: *Care and prevention.* Baltimore: University Park Press.

Montessori, M. (1912). *Montessori method.* Translated by A. George. New York: Stokes.

Myrianthopoulos, N. (1962). Some epidemiologic and genetic aspects of Tay-Sachs disease. In S. Aronson and B. Volk (Eds.), *Cerebral sphingolipidoses.* New York: Academic Press.

Pauling, L. (1962). Genetic effects of weapons tests. *Bulletin of the Atomic Scientists,* **18,** 15.

Penrose, L. (1961). Mongolism. *British Medical Bulletin,* **17,** 184.

Ramey, C., & Campbell, T. (1977). Prevention of developmental retardation in high-risk children. In Mittler, P. (Ed.), *Research to practice in mental retardation,* Vol. 1. *Care and prevention.* Baltimore: University Park Press.

Richards, B. (1970). *Mental abnormality: Modern trends in research.* London: Pittman.

Sarason, S. (1958). *Psychological problems in mental deficiency* (3rd ed.). New York: Harper & Row.

Sawyer, G., & Shafter, A. (1957). Reproduction in a mongoloid: A follow-up. *American Journal of Mental Deficiency,* **61,** 793.

Seguin, E. (1846). *Traitement moral, hygiène et education des idiots et des autres enfants arrières.* Paris: Ballière.

Soeffing, M. (1977). New assessment techniques for mentally retarded and culturally different: A conversation with Jane R. Mercer. In C. Drew, M. Harman, & H. Blahm (Eds.), *Mental retardation: Social and educational perspectives.* St. Louis: Mosby.

Suinn, R. (1967). The theory of cognitive style: A partial replication. *Journal of General Psychology,* **77,** 11.

Suinn, R., & Cole, C. (1971). *Development of in-service training in behavior modification through mobile educational community consultation action (MECCA) teams.* Final Report. Fort Collins: Colorado State University.

Telford, C., & Sawrey, J. (1981). *The exceptional individual* (4th ed.). Englewood Cliffs, NJ: Prentice-Hall.

Terman, L., & Merrill, M. (1937). *Measuring intelligence.* Boston: Houghton Mifflin.

Tredgold, A., & Soddy, K. (1963). *Tredgold's textbook on mental deficiency (subnormality)* (10th ed.). Baltimore: Williams & Wilkins.

Vinter, A., Mouroud, P., & Husain, O. (1983). Accuracy and stability of self-image of mentally retarded adults. *American Journal of Mental Deficiency,* **87,** 583–590.

Vogel, W., Broverman, D., Draguns, J., & Klaiber, E. (1977). The role of glutamic acid in cognitive behaviors. *Psychological Bulletin,* **65,** 367–382.

Wood, J., Johnson, K., & Omori, V. (1967). In utero exposure to the Hiroshima atomic bomb. *Pediatrics,* **39,** 385-392.

Wyatt, G. (1982). Alternatives to the use of standardized tests with Afro-American children. In B. Bass, G. Wyatt, & G. Powell (Eds.), *The Afro-American Family.* New York: Grune & Stratton.

Zeaman, D. (1973). One programmatic approach to retardation. In D. Routh (Ed.), *The experimental psychology of mental retardation.* Chicago: Aldine.

Zigler, E., & Balla, D. (1983). Mental retardation: The developmental-difference controversy. Hillsdale, NJ: Erlbaum.

Zimmerman, F., & Ross, S. (1944). Effect of glutamic acid and other amino acids on maze learning in the white rat. *Archives of Neurological Psychiatry,* **51,** 446.

## CHAPTER 20

Achenbach, T. (1982a). *Developmental psychopathology* (2nd Ed.) New York: Wiley.

Achenbach, T. (1982b). Empirical approaches to the classification of child psychopathology. In J. Lachenmeyer & M. Gibbs (Eds.), *Psychopathology in childhood.* New York: Gardner Press.

Allman, L., & Jaffe, D. (1978). *Abnormal psychology in the life cycle.* New York: Harper & Row.

American Psychiatric Association. (1978). *Diagnostic and statistical manual of mental disorders* (3rd ed.). Washington, DC: American Psychological Association.

Anders, T., & Freeman, E. (1979). Enuresis. In J. Noshpitz (Ed.), *Basic handbook of child psychiatry,* Vol. 2. New York: Basic Books.

Antczak, J. (1983, February 5). Singer Karen Carpenter dies of cardiac arrest. *The Denver Post,* E1.

Asarnow, R. (1983). Schizophrenia. In R. Tartar (Ed.), *The child at psychiatric risk.* New York: Oxford.

Azrin, N., Hontos, P., & Besalel-Azrin, V. (1979). Elimination of enuresis without a conditioning apparatus: An extension of office instruction of the child and parents. *Behavior Therapy,* **10,** 14–19.

Azrin, N., Nunn, R., & Frantz, S. (1980). Habit reversal vs. negative practice treatment of nervous tics. *Behavior Therapy,* **11,** 169–178.

Bachrach, A., Erwin, W., & Mohr, J. (1965). The control of eating behavior in an anorexic by operant conditioning techniques. In L. Ullmann & L. Krasner (Eds.), *Case studies in behavior modification.* New York: Holt, Rinehart & Winston.

Bakwin, H., & Bakwin, R. (1966). *Clinical management of behavior disorders in children.* Philadelphia: Saunders.

Barker, P. (1976). *Basic child psychiatry* (2nd ed.). Baltimore: University Park Press.

Barrett, B. (1962). Reduction in rate of multiple tics by free operant conditioning methods. *Journal of Nervous and Mental Disease,* **135,** 187–195.

Barret, E., & Patton, I. (1983). Impulsivity: Cognitive, behavioral, and psychophysiological correlates. In M. Zuckerman (Ed.), *Biological bases of sensation seeking, impulsivity, and anxiety.* New York: Academic Press.

Bender, L. (1953). Childhood schizophrenia. *Psychiatric Quarterly,* **27,** 663–681.

Bender, L. (1974). The family patterns of 100 schizophrenic children observed at Bellevue, 1935–1952. *Journal of Autism and Childhood Schizophrenia,* **4,** 279–292.

Bettelheim, B. (1967). *The empty fortress.* New York: Free Press

Bettelheim, B. (1973). Bringing up children. *Ladies Home Journal,* **90,** 28.

Bettelheim, B., & Sanders, J. (1979). Milieu therapy: The orthogenic school model. In J. Noshpitz (Ed.), *Basic handbood of child psychiatry,* Vol. 3. New York: Basic Books.

Black, M., Freeman, B., & Montgomery, J. (1975). Systematic observation of play behavior in autistic children. *Journal of Autism and Childhood Schizophrenia,* **5,** 363–371.

Bollard, J. & Nettlebeck, T. (1981). A comparison of dry-bed training and standard urine-alarm conditioning treatment of childhood bedwetting, *Behaviour Research and Therapy,* **19,** 215–226.

Campbell, M. (1979). Psychopharmacology. In J. Nosphitz (Ed.), *Basic handbook of child psychiatry.* Vol. 3. New York: Basic Books.

Carmichael, L. (1954). *Manual of child psychology.* New York: Wiley.

Cartwright, J., Cartwright, C., & Ward, M. (1981). *Educating special learners.* Belmont, CA: Wadsworth.

Conners, C. (1980). Artificial colors in the diet and disruptive behavior. In R. Knights & D. Bakker (Eds.), *Treatment of hyperactive and learning disordered children.* Baltimore: University Park Press.

Connors, C., Goyette, C., Southwick, D., Lees, J., & Andrulonis, P. (1976). Food additives and hyperkinesis: A controlled double-blind experiment. *Pediatrics,* **58,** 154.

Copeland, A. (1981). The relevance of subject variables in cognitive self-instructional programs for impulsive children. *Behavior Therapy,* **12,** 50–59.

Crisp, A. (Ed.). (1982). *Anorexia nervosa, let me be.* New York: Grune & Stratton.

Crisp, A., Hsu, L., Harding, B., & Hartshorn, J. (1980). Clinical features of anorexia nervosa: A study of a consecutive series of 102 female patients. *Journal of Psychosomatic Research,* **24,** 179–191.

Crook, W. (1977, January 12). Letter to the editor. News and Comment. *American Academy of Pediatrics.*

Dahl, V. (1976). A follow-up study of a child psychiatric clientele with special regard to the diagnosis of psychosis. Acta Psychiatrica Scandinavica, **54,** 106–112.

DesLauriers, A., & Carlson, C. (1969). *Your child is asleep: Early infantile autism, etiology, treatment, parental influences.* Homewood, IL: Dorsey.

Despert, H. (1951). Some considerations relating to the genesis of autistic behavior in children. *American Journal of Orthopsychiatry,* **21,** 335–350.

Doleys, D., Weiler, D., & Pelgram, V. (1982). Special disorders of childhood: Enuresis, encopresis and sleep disorders. In J. Lachenmeyer & M. Gibbs (Eds.), *Psychopathology in childhood.* New York: Gardner Press.

Eisenberg, L. (1958). The autistic child in adolescence. *American Journal of Psychiatry,* **112,** 607–612.

Eisenberg, L. (1979). Hyperkinetic reaction. In J. Noshpitz (Ed.), *Basic handbook of child psychiatry,* Vol. 2. New York: Basic Books.

Eme, R. (1979). Sex differences in child psychopathology: A review. *Psychological Bulletin,* **86,** 574–595.

Erickson, M. (1982). *Child psychopathology: Assessment, etiology, and treatment* (2nd ed.). Englewood Cliffs, NJ: Prentice-Hall.

Erwin, W. (1977). A 16-year follow-up of a case of severe anorexia nervosa. *Journal of Behavior Therapy and Experimental Psychiatry,* **8,** 157–160.

Evans, J. (1982). *Adolescentand pre-adolescent psychiatry.* New York: Academic Press.

Feingold, B. (1975). Hyperkinesis and learning disabilities linked to artificial food flavors and colors. *American Journal of Nursing,* **75,** 797–803.

Feingold, B., & Feingold, H. (1979). *The Feingold cookbook for hyperactive children.* New York: Random House.

Fine, M. (1980). *Intervention with hyperactive children.* New York: SP Medical.

Fish, B. (1978). Neurobiologic antecedents of schizophrenia in children. In S. Chess & A. Thomas (Eds.), *Annual progress in child psychiatry and child development.* New York: Brunner/Mazel.

Fish, B. & Ritvo, E. (1979). Psychoses of childhood. In J. Noshpitz (Ed.), *Basic handbook of child psychiatry.* Vol. 2. New York: Basic Books.

Fish, B., Shapiro, T., Halpern, F., & Wile, R. (1965). The prediction of schizophrenia in infancy III: Ten-year follow-up report of neurological and psychological development. *American Journal of Psychiatry,* **121,** 768–885.

Folstein, S., & Rutter, M. (1978). Genetic influences and infantile autism. In S. Chess & A. Thomas (Eds.), *Annual progress in child psychiatry and child development.* New York: Bruner/Mazel.

Garfinkel, P., Moldofsy, H., & Garner, D. (1977). The outcome of anorexia nervosa: Significance of clinical features, body image, and behavior modification. In R. Vegersky (Ed.), *Anorexia nervosa.* New York: Raven Press.

Gearheart, B. (1980). *Special education for the '80's.* St. Louis, MO: Mosby.

Gelfand, D., Genson, W., & Drew, C. (1982). *Understanding child behavior disorders.* New York: Holt, Rinehart & Winston.

Gibbs, M. (1982). Identification and classification of child psychopathology. In J. Lachenmeyer & M. Gibbs (Eds.), *Psychopathology in childhood.* New York: Gardner Press.

Gittelman-Klein, R. (1975). Pharmacotherapy and management of pathological separation anxiety. *International Journal of Mental Health,* **5,** 255–271.

Graziano, A., DeGiovanni, I., & Garcia, K. (1979). Behavioral treatment of children's fears: A review. *Psychological Bulletin,* **86,** 804–830.

Greenspan, S., Lourie, R., & Nover, R. (1979). A developmental approach to the classification of psychopathology in infancy and early childhood. In J. Noshpitz (Ed.), *Basic handbook of child psychiatry.* Vol. 2. New York: Basic Books.

Group for the advancement of psychiatry. (1966). Psychopathological disorders in childhood. Group for the Advancement of Psychiatry Report.

Hagamen, M. (1980). Autism and childhood schizophrenia. In J. Bemporad (Ed.), *Child development in normality and psychopathology.* New York: Bruner/Mazel.

Harley, J., & Matthews, C. (1980). Food additives and hyperactivity in children. In R. Knights & D. Bakker (Eds.), *Treatment of hyperactive and learning disordered children.* Baltimore: University Park Press.

Harley, J., Ray, R., Tomasi, L., Eichman, P., Matthews, C., Chun, R., Cleeland, C., & Traisman, E. (1978). Hyperkinesis and food additives: Testing the Feingold hypothesis. *Pediatrics,* **61,** 818.

Harris, S., & Ferrari, M. (1983). Developmental factors in child behavior therapy. *Behavior Therapy,* **14,** 54–72.

Hartmann, E. (1973). *The function of sleep.* New Haven, CT: Yale University Press.

Hewett, F., Taylor, F., & Artuso, A. (1969). The Santa Monica Project: Evaluation of an engineered classroom design with emotionally disturbed children. *Exceptional Children,* **35,** 523–529.

Kagan, J., & Moss, H. (1962). *Birth to maturity: A study in psychological development.* New York: Wiley.

Kallmann, F., & Roth, B. (1979). Genetic aspects of preadolescent schizophrenia. *American Journal of Psychiatry,* 1956, **112,** 599–609.

Kalucy, R., Crisp, A., & Harding, B. (1977). A study of 56 families with anorexia nervosa. *British Journal of Medical Psychology,* **50,** 381–395.

Kanfer, F., & Saslow, G. (1969). Behavioral diagnosis. In C. Franks (Ed.), *Behavior therapy: Appraisal and status.* New York: McGraw-Hill,

Kanner, L. (1943). Autistic disturbances of affective contact. *Nervous Child,* **2,** 217–240.

Kanner, L. (1972). *Child psychiatry* (2nd ed.). Springfield, IL: C.C Thomas.

Kanner, L. (1973). How far can autistic children go in matters of social adaptation? In L. Kanner (Ed.), *Childhood psychosis: Initial studies and insights.* Washington, DC: Winston.

Kaye, W. Pickar, D., Naber, D., & Ebert, M. (1982). Cerebrospinal fluid opioid activity in anorexia nervosa. *American Journal of Psychiatry,* **139,** 643–645.

Kendall, P., & Braswell, L. (1982). Cognitive-behavioral self-control therapy for children: A component analysis. *Journal of Counsulting and Clinical Psychology,* **50,** 672–689.

Kessler, J. (1966).*Psychopathology of childhood.* Englewood Cliffs, NJ: Prentice-Hall.

Knobloch, H., & Pasamanick, B. (1974). *Gesell and Amatruda's developmental diagnosis* (3rd. ed.). New York: Harper & Row.

Knopf, I. (1979). *Childhood psychopathology.* Englewood Cliffs, NJ: Prentice-Hall.

Koegel, R., & Egel, A. (1979). Motivating autistic children. *Journal of Abnormal Psychology,* **88,** 418–426.

Lazarus, A. (1960). Objective psychotherapy in the treatment of dysphemia. *Journal of South African Logopedic Society,* **6,** 8–10.

Levy, F., Dumbrell, S., Hobbes, G., Ryan, M., Wilton, N., & Woodhill, J. (1978). Hyperkinesis and diet: A double-blind crossover trial with a tartrazine challenge. *Medical Journal of Australia,* **1,** 61.

Lewis, M. (1979). Differential diagnosis. In J. Noshpitz (Ed.), *Basic handbook of child psychiatry.* Vol. 2. New York: Basic Books.

Lipton, M., & Wender, E. (1977, June). Statement summarizing research findings on the issue of the relationship between food-additive-free diets and hyperkinesis in children. Report presented to the Nutritition Foundation,

Lovaas, O. (1977). *The autistic child: Language development through behavior modification.* New York: Irvington.

Lovaas, O., Schreibman, L., & Koegel, R. (1974). A behavior modification approach to the treatment of autistic children. *Journal of Autism and Childhood Schizophrenia,* **4,** 111–129.

Lovibond, S., & Coote, M. (1969). Enuresis. In C. Costello (Ed.), *Symptoms of psychopathology.* New York: Wiley.

Lucas, A. (1979). Tic: Gilles de la Tourette's syndrome. In J. Noshpitz (Ed.), *Basic handbook of child psychiatry.* Vol. 2. New York: Basic Books.

Macfarlane, J., Allen, L., & Honzik, M. (1954). *A developmental study of the behavior problems of normal children between twenty-one months and fourteen years.* University of California Publications in Child Development, No. 2.

Martin, W., & Stendler, C. (1953). *Child development: The process of growing up in society.* New York: Harcourt Brace.

Maynard, R. (1970, June 29). Omaha pupils given "behavior" drugs. *Washington Post.*

Meyers, E., & Goldfarb, W (1962). Studies of perplexity in mothers of schizophrenic children. *American Journal of Psychiatry,* **118,** 902–908.

Milich, R., Loney, J. & Landau, St. (1982). Independent dimensions of hyperactivity and aggression: A validation with playroom observation data. *Journal of Abnormal Psychology,* **91,** 183–198.

Montenegro, H. (1968). Severe separation anxiety in two preschool children: Successfully treated by reciprocal inhibition. *Journal of Child Psychology and Psychiatry,* **9,** 93–103.

Moore, C., & Schiek, D. (1971). Toward a theory of early infantile autism. *Psychological Review,* **78,** 451–456.

Mowrer, O., & Mowrer, W. (1938). Enuresis: A method for its study and treatment. *American Journal of Orthopsychiatry,* **8,** 436–447.

Ney, P. (1974). Four types of hyperkinesis. *Canadian Psychiatric Association Journal,* **19,** 543–550.

Nichols, P. & Chen, T. (1981). *Minimal brain dysfunction: A prospective study.* New York: Academic Press.

Noshpitz, J. (Ed.). (1979). *Basic handbook of child psychiatry.* Vol. 1. New York: Basic Books.

Noshpitz, J. (Ed.). (1979). *Basic handbook of child psychiatry.* Vol. 2. New York: Basic Books.

Ollendick, T. (1979). Behavioral treatment of anorexia nervosa: A five year study. *Behavior Modification,* **3,** 124–135.

Ollendick, T., & Hersen, M. (1983). *Handbook of child psychopathology.* New York: Plenum.

Ornitz, E. & Ritvo, E. (1976). The syndrome of autism: A critical review. *American Journal of Psychiatry.* **133,** 60–62.

Patterson, C., & Mischel, W. (1975). Plans to resist distraction. *Developmental Psychology,* **11,** 369–378.

Perlmutter, M. (1983). *Minnesota symposium on child psychology,* Vol. 16. New York: Academic Press.

Phillips, J., & Ray, R. (1980). Behavioral approaches to childhood disorders: Review and critique. *Behavior Modification,* **4,** 3–34.

Prinz, R., Roberts, W., & Hantman, E. (1980). Dietary correlates of hyperactive behavior in children. *Journal of Consulting and Clinical Psychology,* **48,** 760.

Prugh, D. (1973). *Psychosocial disorders in childhood and adolescence: Theoretical considerations and an attempt at classification.* In Joint Commission on Mental Health of Children. The Mental Health of Children: Services, Research and Manpower. New York: Harper & Row.

Ricks, D., Thomsas, A., & Roff, M. (1974). *Life history research in psychopathology.* Vol. 3. MN: University of Minnesota Press.

Rimland, B. (1964). *Infantile autism.* New York: Appleton-Century-Crofts.

Rosenbaum, A., O'Leary, K., & Jacob, R. (1975). Behavioral intervention with hyperactive children: Group consequences as a supplement to individual contingencies. *Behavior Therapy,* **6,** 315–323.

Ross, A. (1981). *Child behavior therapy,* New York: Wiley.

Ross, D., & Ross, S. (1976). *Hyperactivity: Research, theory, and action.* New York: Wiley.

Russo, D., & Newsom, C. (1982). Psychotic disorders of childhood. In J. Lachenmeyer & M. Gibbs (eds.), *Psychopathology in childhood.* New York: Gardner Press.

Rutter, M., Greenfeld, D., & Lockyer, L. (1967). Five to fifteen year follow-up study of infantile psychosis, II: Social behavioural outcome. *British Journal of Psychiatry,* **113,** 1183–1199.

Rutter, M., et al. (1969). A triaxial classification of mental disorders in childhood. *Journal of Child Psychology and Psychiatry,* **10,** 41–61.

Rutter, M., & Schopler, E. (Eds.). (1978). *Autism: A reappraisal of concepts and treatment.* New York: Plenum.

Safer, D. (1971). Drugs for problem school children. *Journal of School Health,* **41,** 491–495.

Schopler, E., & Mesibov, G. (1983). *Autism in adolescents and adults.* New York: Plenum.

Schwartz, S., & Johnson, J. (1981). *Psychopathology of Childhood.* New York: Pergamon.

Shapiro, C. (1979). Development from one to two years: Normal coping mechanisms. In J. Noshpitz (Ed.), *Basic handbook of child psychiatry.* Vol. 1. New York: Basic Books.

Silver, L. (1979). The minimal brain dysfunction syndrome. In J. Noshpitz (Ed.), *Basic handbook of child psychiatry.* Vol. 2. New York: Basic Books.

Simmons, J., Leiken, S., Lovaas, O., Schaeffer, B., & Perloff, B. (1966). Modification of autistic behavior with LSD-25. *American Journal of Psychiatry,* **122,** 1201–1211.

Small, L. (1983). *The minimal brain dysfunctions.* New York: Free Press.

Sours, J. (1979). The primary anorexia nervosa syndrome. In J. Noshpitz (Ed.), *Basic handbook of child psychiatry.* Vol. 2. New York: Basic Books.

Spencer, J., & Fremouw, W. (1979). Binge eating as a function of restraint and weight classification. *Journal of Abnormal Psychology,* **88,** 262–267.

Sperling, L. (1979). Parent counseling and therapy. In J. Noshpitz (Ed.), *Basic handbook of child psychiatry.* Vol. 3. New York: Basic Books.

Sperling, M. (1974). *The major neuroses and behavior disorders in children.* New York: Jason Aronson.

Sroufe, L. (1975). Drug treatment of children with behavior problems. In F. Horowitz (Ed.), *Review of child development research.* Vol. 4. Chicago: University of Chicago Press.

Telford, C., & Sawrey, J. (1981). *The exceptional individual* (4th ed.). Englewood Cliffs, NJ: Prentice-Hall.

Tolstrup, K. (1975). The treatment of anorexia nervosa in childhood and adolescence. *Journal of Child Psychology and Psychiatry,* **16,** 77–78.

Treffert, D. (1970). Epidemiology of infantile autism. *Archives of General Psychiatry,* **22,** 431–438.

Turkington, C. (1982 December). For autistic, nothing succeeds like success. *APA Monitor,* p. 32.

Ullman, D., Egan, D., Fiedler, N., Jurenec, G., Pliske, R., Thompson, P., & Doherty, M. (1981). The many faces of hyperactivity: Similarities and differences in diagnostic policies. *Journal of Consulting and Clinical Psychology,* **49,** 694–704.

Walton, D. (1964). Massed practice and simultaneous reduction in drive level—Further evidence of the efficacy of this approach to the treatment of tics. In H. Eysenck (Ed.), *Experiments in behavior therapy.* London: Pergamon.

Weakland, J., Fisch, R., Watzlawick, P., & Bodin, A. (1974). Brief therapy: Focused problem solution. *Family Process,* **13,** 141–168.

Weeda-Mannak, W., et al. (1983). Towards an early recognition of anorexia nervosa. *The international journal of eating disorders,* **2.**

Weingartner, H., Rapoport, J., Buchsbaum, M., et al. (1979). Cognitive processes in normal and hyperactive children and their response to amphetamine treatment. *Journal of Abnormal Psychology,* **89,** 25–37.

Wenar, C. (1982). *Psychopathology from infancy through adolescence.* New York: Random House.

Wender, P. (1971). *Minimal brain dysfunction in children.* New York: Wiley-Interscience.

Werry, J. (1972). Psychosomatic disorders. In H. Quay & J. Werry (Eds.), *Psychopathological disorders of childhood.* New York: Wiley.

Werry, J., & Sprague, R. (1970). Methylphenidate in children: Effects of dosage. *Australian and New Zealand Journal of Psychiatry,* **8,** 9–19.

Whalen, C. (1982). Hyperactivity and psychostimulant treatment. In J. Lachenmayer & M. Gibbs (Eds.), *Psychopathology in childhood.* New York: Gardner Press.

Wickman, E. (1928). *Children's behavior and teachers' attitudes.* New York: Commonwealth Fund.

Yates, A. (1958). The application of learning theory to the treatment of tics. *Journal of Abnormal and Social Psychology,* **56,** 175-182.

Yates, A., Leehey, K., & Shisslak, C. (1983). Running—An analogue to anorexia? *New England Journal of Medicine,* **308,** 251-255.

Zaslow, R., & Breger, L. (1969). A theory and treatment of autism. In L. Breger (Ed.), *Clinical cognitive psychology.* Englewood Cliffs, NJ: Prentice-Hall.

Zupnick, S. (1974). A new approach to disturbed children: The Medical College School program. *Psychiatric Quarterly,* **48,** 76-85.

## CHAPTER 21

Alexander, F., & French, R. (1946). *Psychoanalytic therapy.* New York: Ronald.

Alexander, J. & Parsons, B. (1982). *Functional family therapy.* Monterey, CA: Brooks/Cole.

Allen, G., Elias, M., & Zlotlow, S. (1980). Behavioral interventions for alleviating test anxiety: A methodological review of current therapeutic practices. In I. Sarason (Ed.), *Test anxiety: Theory, research, and applications.* Hillsdale, NJ: Erlbaum.

Anderson, L., & Alpert, M. (1974). Operant analysis of hallucination frequency in a hospitalized schizophrenic. *Journal of Behavior Therapy and Experimental Psychiatry,* **15,** 13-18.

Anderson, S. (1984). *Counseling through group process.* New York: Springer.

Axline, V. (1974). *Play therapy.* Boston: Houghton Mifflin .

Bandura, A. (1977). *Social learning theory.* Englewood Cliffs, NJ: Prentice-Hall.

Bandura, A., Ross, D., & Ross, S. (1961). Transmission of aggression through imitation of aggressive models. *Journal of Abnormal and Social Psychology,* **63,** 575-582.

Beck, A. (1976). *Cognitive therapy and emotional disorders.* New York: International University Press.

Becker, C. (1979). Pharmacotherapy in the treatment of alcoholism. In J. Mendelson & N. Mello (Eds.), *The diagnosis and treatment of alcoholism.* New York: McGraw-Hill.

Bergin, A. (1966). Some implications of psychotherapy research for therapeutic practice. *Journal of Abnormal Psychology,* **71,** 235-246.

Bergin, A., & Lambert, M. (1978). The evaluation of therapeutic outcomes. In S. Garfield & A. Bergin (Eds.), *Handbook of psychotherapy and behavior change: An empirical analysis* (2nd ed.). New York: Wiley.

Bergin, A., & Suinn, R. (1975). Individual psychotherapy and behavior therapy. *Ann. Rev. Psychol.,* **26,** 509-556.

Blanchard, E., & Epstein, L. (1977). The clinical utility of biofeedback. In M. Hersen, R. Eisler, & P. Miller (Eds.), *Progress in behavior modification.* Vol. 4. New York: Academic Press.

Brady, J., & Lind, D. (1961). Experimental analysis of hysterical blindness. *American Medical Association Archives of General Psychiatry,* **4,** 331.

Carey, G., Carey, M. & Callanan, P. (1984). *Issues and ethics in the helping professions.* (2nd ed.) Monterey, CA: Brooks/Cole.

Carr, E., & McDowell, J. (1980). Social control of self-injurious behavior of organic etiology. *Behavior Therapy,* **11,** 402-409.

Deffenbacher, J., & Suinn, R. (1982). The self-control of anxiety. In F. Kanter & P. Karoly (Eds.), *The psychology of self-management.* New York: Pergamon.

Dies, R., & Mackenzie, K. (1983). *Advances in group psychotherapy.* New York: International University Press.

Ellis, A. (1962). *Reason and emotion in psychotherapy.* New York: Lyle Stuart.

Eysenck, H. (1964). The effects of psychotherapy. *International Journal of Psychiatry,* **1,** 99.

Fischer, C. & Fischer, W. (1983). Phenomenological-existential psychotherapy. In M. Hersen, A. Kazdin & A. Bellock (Eds.), *The clinical psychology handbook.* New York: Pergamon.

Foxx, C., Foxx, R., Jones, J., & Kieley, D. (1980). Twenty-four hour social isolation. *Behavior Modification,* **4,** 130-144.

Frankl, V. (1962). *Man's search for meaning.* Boston: Beacon Press.

Frankl, V. (1975). Paradoxical intention and dereflection. *Psychotherapy: Theory, Research and Practice,* **12,** 226.

Gannon, W. (1972). *The effects of the Gestalt oriented group approach on the interpersonal contact attitudes of selected high school students.* Doctoral dissertation, Case Western Reserve, Cleveland.

Gibb, J. (1971). The effects of human relations training. In A. Bergin & S. Garfield (Eds.), *Handbook of psychotherapy and behavior change: An empirical analysis.* New York: Wiley.

Goldfried, M. (1980). Toward the delineation of therapeutic change principles. *American Psychologist,* **35,** 991.

Gomes-Schwartz, G., Hadley, S., & Strupp, H. (1978). Individual psychotherapy and behavior therapy. In M. Rosenzweig & L. Porter (Eds.), *Annual review of psychology, 1978.* Palo Alto, CA: Annual Review.

Greenberg, L., and Dompierre, L. (1981). Specific effects of Gestalt two-chair dialogue on intrapsychic conflict in counseling, *Journal of Counseling Psychology,* **28,** 288-294.

Halkides, G. (1958). *An experimental study of four conditions necessary for therapeutic change.* Unpublished doctoral dissertation, University of Chicago.

Hart, J., & Tomlinson, T. (1970). *New directions in client-centered therapy.* New York: Houghton Mifflin.

Haughton, E., & Ayllon, T. (1965). Production and elimination of symptomatic behavior. In L. Ullman & L. Krasner (Eds.), *Case studies in behavior modification.* New York: Holt, Rinehart & Winston.

Hekmat, H. (1973). Systematic versus semantic desensitization and implosive therapy: A comparative study. *Journal of Consulting and Clinical Psychology,* **40,** 202-209.

Hogan, R. (1968). The implosive technique. *Behaviour Research and Therapy,* **6,** 423-431.

Hussian, R., & Lawrence, P. (1978). The reduction of test, state, and trial anxiety by test-specific and generalized stress inoculation training. *Cognative Therapy & Research,* **2,** 25–37.

Hutchings, D., Denney, D., Basgall, J., & Houston, B. (1980). Anxiety management and applied relaxation in reducing general anxiety. *Behaviour Research and Therapy,* **18,** 181–190.

Jacobsen, E. (1938). *Progressive relaxation.* Chicago: University of Chicago Press.

Jorgensen, R., Houston, B., & Zurawski, R. (1981). *Anxiety management training in the treatment of essential hypertension. Behaviour Research and Therapy,* **19,** 467–474.

Kihlstrom, J. (1979). Hypnosis and psychopathology: Retrospect and prospect. *Journal of Abnormal Psychology,* **88,** 459–473.

L'Abate, L. (1983). Family psychology. *Theory, therapy, and training.* Baltimore: University Press of America.

Laing, R. D. (1969). *The divided self.* New York: Pantheon.

Lambert, M., DeJullio, S., & Stein, D. (1978). Therapies and interpersonal skills: Process, outcome, methodological considerations, and recommendations for future research. *Psychological Bulletin,* **85,** 467–489.

Lazarus, A. (1963). The results of behavior therapy in 126 cases of severe neurosis. *Behaviour Research and Therapy,* **1,** 65.

Liberman, R., Teigen, J., Patterson, R., & Baker, V. (1973). Reducing delusional speech in chronic, paranoid schizophrenics. *Journal of Applied and Behavioral Analysis,* **6,** 61.

Lieberman, M., Yalom, I., & Miles, M. (1973). *Encounter groups: First facts.* New York: Basic Books.

Lombardo, T., & Turner, S. (1979). Use of thought-stopping to control obsessive ruminations in a chronic schizophrenic patient. *Behavior Modification,* **3,** 267–272.

Marks, I. (1972). Flooding (implosion) and related treatments. In W. Agras (Ed.), *Behavior modification: Prinicples and clinical applications.* Boston: Little, Brown.

Marks, I. (1976). Management of sexual disorders. In H. Leitenberg (Ed.), *Handbook of behavior modification and behavior therapy.* Englewood Cliffs, NJ: Prentice-Hall.

Marks, I., Hodgsen, R., & Rachman, S. (1975). Treatment of chronic obsessive-compulsive neurosis by in vivo exposure: A two year follow-up and issues in treatment. *British Journal of Psychiatry,* **127,** 349.

Martin, D. *Counseling and therapy skills.* Monterey, CA: Brooks/Cole, 1983.

Masling, J. (Ed.), (1983). *Empirical studies of psychoanalytic theories.* Hillsdale, NJ: Analytic Press.

McConaghy, N. (1964). A year's experience with nonverbal psychotherapy. *Medical Journal of Australia,* **1,** 831.

McCutcheon, B., & Adams, H. (1975). The physiological basis of implosive therapy. *Behaviour Research and Therapy,* **13,** 93.

McMahon, C., & Hastrup, J. (1980). The role of imagination in the disease process: Post-cartesian history. *Journal of Behavioral Medicine,* **3,** 219–221.

Meichenbaum, D. (1977). *Cognitive-behavior modification: An integrative approach.* New York: Plenum Press.

Menninger, K. (1958). *Theory of psychoanalytic technique.* New York: Basic Books.

Moreno, J. (1946). *Psychodrama.* New York: Beacon House.

Mowrer, O., & Mowrer, W. (1938). Enuresis: A method for its study and treatment. *American Journal of Orthopsychiatry,* **8,** 436–459.

Murray, E. (1954). A case study in a behavioral analysis of psychotherapy. *Journal of Abnormal and Social Psychology,* **49,** 305.

Paritzky, R., & Magoon, T. (1979). Human potential seminar outcomes as measured by the Personal Orientation Inventory and goal attainment inventories. *Journal of Counseling Psychology,* **26,** 30–36.

Parloff, M., Waskow, I., & Wolfe, B. (1978). Research on therapist variables in relation to process and outcome. In A. Bergin & S. Garfield (Eds.), *Handbook of psychotherapy and behavior change: An empirical analysis* (2nd ed.). New York: Wiley.

Paul, G., & Lentz, R. (1977). *Psychosocial treatment of chronic mental patients: Milieu versus social learning programs.* Cambridge, MA: Harvard University Press.

Paul, G. L. (1966). *Insight versus desensitization in psychotherapy.* Stanford, CA: Stanford University Press.

Perls, F. (1969). *Gestalt therapy verbatim.* Lafayette, CA: Real People Press.

Peterfreund, E. (1982). *The process of psychoanalytic therapy: Models and strategies.* Hillsdale, NJ: Analytic Press.

Rachman, S. (1974). *The meaning of fear.* Middlesex, England: Penguin.

Rachman, S., & Wilson, G. (1980). *The effects of psychological therapy* (2nd. ed.). New York: Pergamon.

Raymond, M. (1960). Case of fetishism treated by aversion therapy. In H. Eysenck (Ed.), *Behaviour therapy and the neuroses.* London: Pergamon.

Ricks, D. (1974). Supershrink: Methods of a therapist judged successful on the basis of adult outcomes of adolescent patients. In D. Ricks, M. Roff, & A. Thomas (Eds.), *Life history research in psychopathology.* Minneapolis: University of Minnesota Press.

Robinson, C., & Suinn, R. (1969). Group desensitization of a phobia in massed sessions. *Behaviour Research and Therapy,* **7,** 319.

Rogers, C. (1951). *Client-centered therapy.* Boston: Houghton Mifflin.

Rogers, C. (1957). The necessary and sufficient conditions of psychotherapeutic personality change. *Journal of Consulting Psychology,* **21,** 95.

Rosenbaum, M., Franks, C., & Jaffe, Y. (Eds.). (1983). *Perspectives on behavior therapy in the eighties.* Vol. 9. New York: Springer.

Ross, A. (1981). *Child behavior therapy.* New York: Wiley.

Samuels, S. (1977). *Enhancing self-concept in early childhood.* New York: Human Sciences.

Sargent, J., Green, E., & Walters, E. (1973). Preliminary report on the use of autogenic feedback training in the treatment of migraine and tension headaches. *Psychosomatic Medicine,* **35,** 129–135.

Schaffer, N. (1982). Multidimensional measures of therapist behavior as predictors of outcome. *Psychological Bulletin,* **92,** 670–681.

Shapiro, D., & Shapiro, D. (1982). Meta-analysis of comparative therapy outcome studies: A replication and refinement. *Psychological Bulletin,* **92,** 581–604.

Shapiro, D., & Shapiro, D. (1983). Comparative therapy outcome research: Methodological implications of meta-analysis. *Journal of Consulting and Clinical Psychology,* **51,** 54–64.

Shapiro, D., & Surwit, R. (1976). Learned control of physiological function and disease. In H. Leitenberg (Ed.), *Handbook of behavior modification and behavior therapy.* Englewood Cliffs, NJ: Prentice-Hall.

Shoemaker, J. (1976). *Treatment for anxiety neurosis.* Unpublished doctoral dissertation, Colorado State University, Fort Collins.

Silver, B., & Blanchard, E. (1978). Biofeedback and relaxation training in the treatment of psychophysiological disorders: Or are the machines really necessary? *Journal of Behavioral Medicine,* **1,** 217–240.

Sloane, R., Staples, F., Cristol, A., Horkston, N., & Whipple, K. (1975). *Short-term analytically oriented psychotherapy vs. behavior therapy.* Cambridge, MA: Harvard University Press.

Stampfl, T., & Lewis, D. (1967). Essentials of implosive therapy: A learning theory-based psychodynamic behavioral therapy. *Journal of Abnormal Psychology,* **72,** 496–503.

Strupp, H. (1980). Success and failure in time-limited psychotherapy. *Archives of General Psychiatry,* **37,** 708–716.

Suinn, R. (1972). Removing emotional obstacles to learning and performance. *Behavior Therapy,* **3,** 308.

Suinn, R. (1980). *Psychology in sports: Methods and applications.* Minneapolis: Burgess.

Suinn, R. (1983a). *Manual: Anxiety management training (AMT).* Fort Collins, CO: Rocky Mountain Behavioral Sciences Institute.

Suinn, R. (1983b). *EMG recordings of visuo-motor behavior rehearsal activities.* ABC Television.

Suinn, R., & Brittain, J. (1970). The termination of an LSD "freak-out" through the use of relaxation. *Journal of Clinical Psychology,* **26,** 127.

Suinn, R., Edie, C., & Nicoletti, J. (1970). Accelerated massed desensitization: Innovation in short-term therapy. *Behavior Therapy,* **1,** 303.

Suinn, R., Osborne, D., & Winfree, P. (1962). The self-concept and accuracy of recall of inconsistent self-related information. *Journal of Clinical Psychology,* **18,** 463.

Suinn, R., & Richardson, F. (1970). Behavior therapy of an unusual case of highway hypnosis. *Behavior Therapy and Experimental Psychiatry,* **2,** 129.

Sulzer-Azaroff, B., & Mayer, G. (1977). *Applying behavior-analysis procedures with children & youth.* New York: Holt, Rinehart & Winston.

Truax, C. (1971). Effectiveness of counselor and counselor aides: A rejoinder. *Journal of Counseling Psychology,* **18,** 365–367.

Wolberg, L. (1977). *The technique of psychotherapy* (3rd ed.), Part II. New York: Grune & Stratton.

Wolberg, L. (1980). *Handbook of short-term psychotherapy.* New York: Thieme-Stratton.

Wolpe, J. (1958). *Psychotherapy by reciprocal inhibition.* Stanford, CA: Stanford University Press.

Wolpe, J. (1982). *The practice of behavior therapy* (3rd ed.). New York: Pergamon.

Yalom, I., & Lieberman, M. (1971). A study of encounter group casualities. *Archives of General Psychiatry,* **25,** 16–30.

## CHAPTER 22

Andy, O. (1977). Decision-making in psychiatric surgery. In W. Sweet, S. Obrador, & J. Martin-Rodriguez (Eds.), *Neurosurgical treatment in psychiatry, pain, and epilepsy.* Baltimore: University Park Press.

Asnis, G., Fink, M., & Saferstein, J. (1978). ECT in metropolitan New York hospitals: A survey of practice. *American Journal of Psychiatry,* **135,** 479.

Avery, D., & Winokur, G. (1977). The efficacy of electroconvulsive therapy and antidepressants in depression. *Biological Psychiatry,* **12,** 507–523.

Baker, C. (1983). *Physicians' desk reference.* Oradell, NJ: Medical Economics.

Bond, E. (1954). Results of treatment in psychoses with a control series. *American Journal of Psychiatry,* **110,** 881.

Brill, H., & Patton, R. (1959). Analysis of population reduction in New York State Mental hospitals during the first four years of large scale therapy with psychotropic drugs. *American Journal of Psychiatry,* **116,** 495.

Cerletti, U. (1956). Electroshock therapy. In F. Marti-Ibanex, A. Sackler, M. Sackler, & R. Sackler (Eds.), *The great physiodynamic therapies in psychiatry.* New York: Hoeber.

Cole, J. (1976). Phenothiazines. In L. Simpson (Ed.), *Drug treatment of mental disorders.* New York: Raven.

Cunningham, S. (1983, January). Berkeley electroshock vote termed "an inconvenience." *APA Monitor,* **23.**

Dagi, T. (1977). Psychiatric surgery and the ethics of uncertainty. In W. Sweet, S. Obrador, & J. Martin-Rodriquez (Eds.), *Neurosurgical treatment in psychiatry, pain, and epilepsy.* Baltimore: University Park Press.

DiMascio, A. (1964). *Personality factors and variability of response to chlorpromazine.* Paper read at Eastern Psychological Association, Philadelphia.

Fink, M. (1977). Myths of "shock therapy." *American Journal of Psychiatry,* **134,** 991–996.

Fink, M. (1978). Efficacy and safety of induced seizures (EST) in men. *Comparative Psychiatry,* **19,** 1–18.

Fisher, S. et al. (1962). Drug-set interaction: The effect of expectations on drug response in out-patients. Paper read at Collegium Internationale Neuro-psychopharmacologicum, Munich.

Flor-Henry, P. (1977). Progress and problems in psychosurgery. In J. Masserman (ed.), *Current psychiatric therapies.* Vol. 17. New York: Grune & Stratton.

Freeman, W. (1968). *The psychiatrists: Personalities and pattern.* New York: Grune & Stratton.

Friedberg, J. (1976). *Shock treatment is not good for your brain.* San Francisco: Glide.

Goldfarb, C., & Goldfarb, S. (1977). Multiple monitored electroconvulsive treatment. In J. Masserman (Ed.), *Current psychiatric therapies.* Vol. 17. New York: Grune & Stratton.

Greenblatt, D., & Shader, R. (1974). *Benzodiazepines in clinical practice.* New York: Raven Press.

Greenblatt, M. (1975). *Drugs in combination with other therapies.* New York: Grune & Stratton.

Gross, M., & Reeves, W. (1961). Relapses after withdrawal of ataractic drugs: An interim report. In M. Greenblatt, D. Levinson, & G. Klerman (Eds.), *Mental patients in transition.* Springfield, IL: C. C Thomas.

Groves, J., & Mandel, M. (1975). The long acting phenothiazines. *Archives of General Psychiatry,* **32,** (7), 893–900.

Hitchcock, E., Laitinen, L., & Vaernet, K. (1972). *Psychosurgery.* Springfield, IL: C. C Thomas.

Hunt, M. M. (1962). *Mental hospital.* New York: Pyramid.

Janke, W. (Ed.). (1983). *Response variability to psychotropic drugs.* New York: Pergamon.

Kalinowsky, L., & Hoch, P. (1952). *Shock treatment, psychosurgery and other somatic treatments in psychiatry* (2nd ed.). New York: Grune & Stratton.

Katz, M. (1966). A topological approach to the problem of predicting response to treatment. In J. Wittenborn, & P. May (Eds.), *A prediction of response to pharmacotherapy.* Springfield, IL: C. C Thomas.

Kesey, K. (1962). *One flew over the cuckoo's nest.* New York: Viking.

Klerman, G., Davidson, E., & Kayce, M. (1964). Factors influencing the clinical responses to schizophrenic patients to phenothiazine drugs and to placebo. In P. Solomon & B. Glueck (Eds.), *Recent research on schizophrenia.* Washington, DC: American Psychiatric Association, 97.

Kline, N. (1958). Clinical experience with iproniazid (Marsilid). *Journal of Clinical and Experimental Psychopathology,* **19,** Suppl. 1, 72.

Kramer, M., & Pollack, E. (1958). Problems in the interpretation of trends in the population movement of the public mental hospitals. *American Journal of Public Health,* **48,** 1003.

Lagones, J. (1983). A new assault on shock therapy. *Discovery,* **4,** 54–56.

Laitinen, L. (1977). Ethical aspects of psychiatric surgery. In W. Sweet, S. Obrador, & J. Martin-Rodriguez (Eds.), *Neurosurgical treatment in psychiatry, pain, and epilepsy.* Baltimore: University Park Press.

Laqueur, H., Dussik, K., LaBurt, H., & McLaughlin, W. (1962). *Tactical and strategical considerations in the use of insulin therapy—a joint mental hospital study.* Paper read at the Second International Conference on the Biological Treatment of Mental Illness. New York: Academy of Medicine, No. 2.

Lickey, M. & Gordon, B. (in press). *Drugs for mental illness.* San Francisco: Freeman.

Moniz, E. (1936). *Tentative operatories dans le traitement de certaines psychoses.* Paris: Masson.

Neville, R. (1975). Zalmoxis or the morals of ESB and psychosurgery. In W. Gayline, J. Meister, & R. Neville (Eds.), *Operating on the mind.* New York: Basic Books.

Pearson, M. (1963). *Strecker's fundamentals of psychiatry,* 6th edition. Philadelphia: Lippincott.

Peraita, P., & deLerma, J. (1977). Frontal psychosurgery: A review of 424 cases. In W. Sweet, S. Obrador, & J. Martin-Rodriguez (Eds.), *Neurosurgical treatment in psychiatry, pain, and epilepsy.* Baltimore: University Park Press.

Prien, R., Klett, C., & Caffey, E. (1973). Lithium carbonate and imipramine in prevention of affective episodes. *Archives of General Psychiatry,* **29,** 420–425.

Reifman, A., & Wyatt, R. (1980). Lithium: A break in the rising cost of mental illness. *Archives of General Psychiatry,* **37,** 385–388.

Rickels, K., Lipman, R., Park, L., Covi, L., Uhlenhuth, E., & Mock, J. (1971). Drug, doctor warmth, and clinic setting in the symptomatic response to minor tranquilizers. *Psychopharmacologia,* **20,** 128–152.

Rosen, A., Tureff, S., Daruna, J., Johnson, P., & Lyons, J. (1980). Pharmacotherapy of schizophrenic and affective disorders: Behavioral correlates of diagnostic and demographic variables. *Journal of Abnormal Psychology,* **89,** 387–399.

Sakel, M. (1933). Neue Behandlung der Morphinsucht. *Annals of Neurological Psychiatry,* **143,** 506.

Sakel, M. (1956). The classical Sakel shock treatment. In F. Marti-Ibanex, A. Sackler, M. Sacker, & R. R. Sachler (Eds.), *The great physiodynamic therapies in psychiatry.* New York: Hoeber.

Scheflin, A. & Opton, E. (1978). *The mind manipulators.* New York: Paddington Press.

Scovern, A., & Kilmann, P. (1980). Status of electroconvulsive therapy: Review of the outcome literature. *Psychological Bulletin,* **87,** 260–303.

Scoville, W., & Bettis, D. (1977). Results of orbital undercutting today: A personal series. In W. Sweet, S. Obrador, & J. Martin-Rodriguez (Eds.), *Neurosurgical treatment in psychiatry, pain, and epilepsy.* Baltimore: University Park Press.

Shopsin, B., Klein, H., Aaronson, M., & Collara, M. (1979). Clozapine, chlorpromazine, and placebo in newly hospitalized, acutely schizophrenic patients. *Archives of General Psychiatry,* **36,** 657–664.

Smith, J., Kiloh, L., & Boots, J. (1977). Prospective evaluation of prefrontal leucotomy: Results at 30 months' follow-up. In W. Sweet, S. Obrador, & J. Martin-Rodriguez (Eds.), *Neurosurgical treatment in psychiatry, pain, and epilepsy.* Baltimore: University Park Press.

Stallone, F., Shelley, E., Mendlewicz, J., & Fieve, R. (1973). Part III. Lithium prophylaxis in manic depressive illness (double-blind study). *American Journal of Psychiatry,* **130,** 1006–1010.

Staudt, V., & Zubin, J. (1957). A biometric evaluation of the somatotherapies in schizophrenia—A critical review. *Psychological Bulletin,* **54,** 171.

Stephens, J., & Astrup, C. (1965). Treatment outcome in "process" and "non-process" schizophrenics by "A" and "B" types of therapist. *Journal of Nervous and Mental Disease,* **140,** 449.

Sweet, W., Obrador, S., & Martin-Rodriguez, J. (1977). *Neurosurgical treatment in psychiatry, pain, and epilepsy.* Baltimore: University Park Press.

Sykes, M., & Tredgold, R. (1964). Restricted orbital undercutting. A study of its effects on 350 patients over the ten years 1951–1960. *American Journal of Psychiatry,* **110,** 609.

Tueber, H., Corkin, S., & Twitchell, T. (1977). Study of cingulotomy in man: A summary. In W. Sweet, S. Obrador, & J. Martin-Rodriguez (Eds.), *Neurosurgical treatment in psychiatry, pain, and epilepsy.* Baltimore: University Park Press.

Vallenstein, E. (Ed.) (1980). *The psychosurgery debate.* San Francisco: Freeman.

Walsh, K. (1977). Neuropsychological aspects of modified leucotomy. In W. Sweet, S. Obrador, & J. Martin-Rodriguez (Eds.),

Neurosurgical treatment in psychiatry, pain, and epilepsy. Baltimore: University Park Press.

Wirt, R., & Simon, W. (1959). *Differential treatment and prognosis in schizophrenia.* Springfield, IL: C. C Thomas.

## CHAPTER 23

Achenbach, T. (1982). *Developmental psychopathology* (2nd ed.). New York: Wiley.

Alny, K., & Rabin, H. (1979). Parent training and the training of parent trainers. *Community Mental Health Journal,* **4,** 53–66.

Barton, R. (1966). *Institutional neurosis* (2nd ed.). Bristol: Wright.

Bass, B., Wyatt, G., & Powell, G. (1982). *The Afro-American family.* New York: Grune & Stratton.

Berlin, I. (1979). Mental health consultation to child-serving agencies as therapeutic intervention. In J. Noshpitz (Ed.), *Basic handbook of child psychiatry.* Vol. 3. New York: Basic Books.

Bloom, B. (1965). The "medical model" miasma theory and community mental health. *Community Mental Health Journal,* **1,** 333.

Carey, G., Carey, M. & Callanan, P. (1984). *Issues and ethics in the helping professions.* (2nd ed.). Monterey, CA: Brooks/Cole.

Carkhuff, R., & Truax, C. (1965). Lay mental health counseling. *Journal of Consulting Psychology,* **29,** 426–431.

Chope, H. (1959). Oral statements describing eight community mental health services. In *Progress and problems of community mental health service.* New York: Milbank Memorial Fund.

Chu, F., & Trotter, S. (1974). *The madness establishment: Ralph Nader's study group report on the National Institute of Mental Health.* New York: Grossman.

Cooper, S., & Hodges, W. (Eds.). (1983). *The mental health consultation field.* New York: Human Sciences.

Cowen, E., Leibowitz, E., & Leibowitz, G. (1968). Utilization of retired people as mental health aides with children. *American Journal of Orthopsychiatry,* **38,** 900–909.

Cowen, E., Lorion, R., Dorr, D., Clarfield, S., & Wilson, A. (1975). Evaluation of a preventively oriented, school-based mental health program. *Psychology in the Schools,* **12,** 161–166.

Cowen, E., & Zax, M. (1969). Early detection and prevention of emotional disorder: Conceptualizations and programming. In J. Carter (Ed.), *Research contributions from psychology to community mental health.* New York: Behavioral Publications.

Dangel, R. & Polster, R. (1983). *Parent training.* New York: Guilford.

Echterling, L., & Wylie, M. (1981). Crisis centers: A social movement perspective. *American Journal of Community Psychology,* **9,** 342–346.

Felner, R., Gitner, M., Boike, M., & Cowen, E. (1981). Parental death or divorce and the school adjustment of young children. *American Journal of Community Psychology,* **9,** 181–191.

Franks, C. (Ed.). (1984). *New developments in behavior therapy.* New York: Haworth.

Friedman, T., Rolfe, P., & Perry, S. (1960). Home treatment of psychiatric patients. *American Journal of Psychotherapy,* **116,** 807.

Garmezy, N., Masten, A., Nordstrom, L., & Ferrarese, M. (1979). The nature of competence in normal and deviate children. In M. Kent & J. Rolf (Eds.), *Primary prevention of psychopathology.* Vol. 3. *Social competence in children.* Hanover, NH: University Press of New England.

Getzel, G. & Mellar, J. (Eds.). (1984). *Gerontological social work practice with the community elderly.* New York: Haworth.

Goffman, E. (1961). *Asylums.* New York: Doubleday-Anchor.

Goldman, A., Bohr, R., & Steinberg, T. (1970). On posing as mental patients: Reminiscences and recommendations. *Professional Psychology,* **5,** 427.

Greene, L., & de la Cruz, A. (1981). Psychiatric day treatment as alternative to and transition from full-time hospitalization. *Community Mental Health Journal,* **17,** 191–202.

Greening, T., & Haigh, G. (1968). The Psychomat. *Voices,* **4,** 46.

Gruenberg, E. (1957). Application of control methods to mental illness. *American Journal of Public Health,* **47,** 944.

Guttentag, M. (1977). The prevention of sexism. In G. Albee & J. Joffe (Eds.), *Primary prevention of psychopathology.* Vol. 1. *The issues.* Hanover, NH: The University Press of New England.

Hersch, C. (1972). Social history, mental health, and community control. *American Psychologist,* **27,** 749–754.

Higginbotham, H. (1979). Culture and mental health service. In A. Marsella, R. Tharp, & T. Ciborowski (Eds.), *Perspectives of cross-cultural psychology.* New York: Academic Press.

Hobbs, N. (1964). Mental health's third revolution. *American Journal of Orthopsychiatry,* **34,** 822–833.

Hobbs, N. (1966). Helping disturbed children: Psychological and ecological strategies. *American Psychologist,* **21,** 1105.

Hobbs, N. (1974). *The futures of children.* San Francisco: Jossey-Bass.

Holahan, C., Wilcox, B., Spearly, J., & Campbell, M. (1979). The ecological perspective in community mental health. *Community Mental Health Review,* **4,** 1–7.

Katkin, S., Ginsberg, M., Rifkin, M., & Scott, J. (1971). Effectiveness of female volunteers in the treatment of outpatients. *Journal of Counseling Psychology,* **18.**

Katoff, L. (Ed.). (1984). *Primary prevention in the work place.* New York: Haworth.

LaFollette, J., & Pilisuk, M. (1981). Changing models of community mental health service. *Journal of Community Psychology,* **9,** 210–223.

Lichtenstein, E. (1980). *Psychotherapy: Approaches and applications.* Monterey, CA: Brooks/Cole.

MacQuiddy, S. & Hamilton, S. (1983). Parent-child interaction training: A manual for parents. *Psychological Documents,* **13,** 6 (Ms. No. 2536).

Mednick, S., & Schulsinger, F. (1973). A learning theory of schizophrenia: Thirteen years later. In M. Hammer, K. Saltzinger, & S. Suttone (Eds.), *Psychopathology: Contributions from the social, behavioral, and biological sciences.* New York: Wiley.

Mednick, S., & Witkin-Lanoil, G. (1977). Intervention in children at high risk for schizophrenia. In G. Albee & J. Joffe (Eds.), *Primary prevention of psychopathology.* Vol. 1. *The issues.* Hanover, NH: The University Press of New England.

Moitoza, E., & Hersel, C. (1981). Community psychology, past, present, and future: The 1965 Boston Conference participants revisited. *American Journal of Community Psychology,* **9,** 225–232.

Mollica, R. (1983). From asylum to community: The threatened disintegration of public psychiatry. *New England Journal of Medicine,* **308,** 367–373.

Moos, R. (1973). Conceptualizations of human environments. *American Psychologist,* **28,** 652–665.

Moos, R. (1974). *The social climate scales: An overview.* Palo Alto, CA: Consulting Psychologists Press.

Morse, W., & Ravlin, M. (1979). Psychoeducation in the school setting. In J. Noshpitz (Ed.), *Basic handbook of child psychiatry.* Vol. 3. New York: Basic Books.

Mulvey, E., & Reppusci, N. (1981). Police crisis intervention: An empirical investigation. *American Journal of Community Psychology,* **9,** 527–546.

Okin, R. (1977). Primary prevention of psychopathology from the perspective of a state mental health program director. In G. Albee & J. Joffe (Eds.), *Primary prevention of psychopathology.* Vol. 1. *The issues.* Hanover, NH: The University Press of New England.

Ozarin, L., Redick, R., & Taube, C. (1976). A quarter century of psychiatric care, 1950–1974: A statistical review. *Hospital and Community Psychiatry,* **27,** p. 517.

Pasamanick, B., Scarpitti, F., & Dinitz, S. (1967). *Schizophrenics in the community: An experimental study in the prevention of hospitalization.* New York: Appleton-Century-Crofts.

Phillips, J. & Ray, R. (1980). Behavioral approaches to childhood disorders: Review and critique. *Behavior Modification,* **4,** 3–34.

Pittmen, F., Langley, D., Kaplan, D., Flomenhaft, K., & DeYoung, D. (1965). *Family therapy as an alternative to psychiatric hospitalization.* Paper presented at Regional Research Conference, American Psychiatric Association, Galveston, TX.

Rosenhan, D. (1973). On being sane in insane places. *Science,* **179,** 250–258.

Ruiz, P. (1982). The Hispanic patient: Sociocultural perspectives. In R. Becerra, M. Karno, & J. Escobar (Eds.), *Mental health and Hispanic Americans.* New York: Grune & Stratton.

Shiloh, A. (1971). Sanctuary or prison. In S. Wallace (Ed.), *Total institutions.* New York: Transaction.

Shure, M., & Spivack, G. (1979). Interpersonal problem solving thinking and adjustment in the mother-child dyad. In M. Kent & J. Rolf (Eds.), *Primary prevention of psychopathology.* Vol. 3. *Social competence in children.* Hanover, NH: University Press of New England.

Spitzer, R. (1976). More on pseudoscience in science and the case for psychiatric diagnosis: A critique of D. L. Rosenhan's "On being sane in insane places" and "The contextual nature of psychiatric diagnosis." *Archives of General Psychiatry,* **33,** 459.

Staats, A., Minke, K., & Butts, P. (1970). A token-reinforcement remedial reading program administered by black therapy-technicians to problem black children. *Behavior Therapy,* **1,** 331–353.

Stuart, R. (1974). Teaching facts about drugs: Pushing or preventing. *Journal of Educational Psychology,* **66,** 189–201.

Sue, S. & Moore, T. (1983). *The pluralistic society.* New York: Human Sciences Press.

Suinn, R. (1972). *Anxiety management training.* Workshop presented at Association for the Advancement of Behavior Therapy, Sixth Annual Meeting, New York City.

Suinn, R., & Cole, C. (1971). *Developing in-service training in behavior modification through mobile educational community consultation action (MECCA) teams.* Final report. Fort Collins: Colorado State University.

Tarter, R. (Ed.). (1983). *The child at psychiatric risk.* New York: Oxford.

Tefft, B. & Kloba, J. (1981). Underachieving high school students as mental health aides with maladapting primary-grade children. *American Journal of Community Psychology,* **9,** 303–320.

Waldron, J. & McDermott, J. (1979). Transcultural considerations. In J. Noshpitz (Ed.). *Basic handbook of child psychiatry,* Vol. 3. New York: Basic Books.

Waltzer, H., Hankoff, L., Englehardt, D., & Kaufman, I. (1963). Emergency psychiatric treatment in a receiving hospital. *Mental Hospitals,* **14,** 595–600.

White, R. (1979). Competence as an aspect of personal growth. In M. Kent & J. Rolf (Eds.), *Primary prevention of psychopathology.* Vol. 3. *Social competence in children.* Hanover, NH: University Press of New England.

Widener, S. (1983, February 6). Healing from God. *Denver Post Empire,* **34,** 11–20.

Wing, J. K. (1962). Institutionalism in mental hospitals. *British Journal of Social and Clinical Psychology,* **1** (1), 38–51.

# NAME INDEX

# SUBJECT INDEX

TEXT CREDITS

P. 105. From *The Major Neuroses and Behavior Disorders in Children* by M. Sperling, 1974, New York: Jason Aronson.

P. 241. From Letter to the Editor by H. Heym, A. Sasaki & D. Winslow, 1977, *Journal of the American Medical Association, 238,* p. 1248. Copyright 1977, American Medical Assn.

P. 231. Excerpts from his case history of a chronic pain patient appears courtesy of Dr. Wilbert Fordyce.

PHOTOGRAPH CREDITS

Page 8, Ken Heyman/page 14, Wide World/page 17, Abigail Heyman — Archive Pictures/page 20, Alex Webb — Magnum/page 32, Neg. No. 283253 — Department Library Services, American Museum of Natural History/page 35, David Seymour — Magnum/page 36, Historical Pictures Service, Chicago/page 41, BBC Hulton Picture Library/page 42, Historical Pictures Service, Chicago/page 44, Jerry Cooke/page 50, The Bettman Archive/page 54, Suzanne Szasz/page 55, Abigail Heyman — Archive Pictures/page 57, Suzanne Szasz/page 58, Fred Mayer — Woodfin Camp & Assoc./page 59, The Bettman Archive/page 64, David Seymour — Magnum Photos/page 66, Jules Masserman/page 69, Albert Bandura — Stanford University/page 79, Neg. No. 2A 6259 — Department Library Services, American Museum of Natural History/page 82, John Terence Turner/page 88, UPI/page 90, Richard Suinn/page 97, Peter N. Witt, M.D. — N.C. Mental Health Research/page 106, Elliott Erwitt — Magnum/page 109, Neg. No. 232188 — (photo by D. B. MacMillan) Department Library Services, American Museum of Natural History/page 111, Arthur Sirdofsky/page 114, Culver Pictures/page 116, UPI/page 119, Charles Harbutt — Archives Pictures/page 130, Leonard Freed — Magnum/page 134, Arthur Tress — Magnum/page 136, Arthur Tress-Magnum/page 138, Colorado State University/page 145, UPI/page 147, NASA/page 148, Donald McCullin — Magnum/page 155, UPI/page 157, Bruce Davidson — Magnum/page 159, Gilles Peress — Magnum/page 162, Globe/page 164, UPI/page 180, Wide World/page 184, Globe/page 186, Bryn Campbell — Magnum/page 187, Wide World/page 195, Walter Reed Army Institute of Research, Washington, D.C./page 201, UPI/page 203, UPI/page 211, Richard Suinn/page 221, The Bettmann Archive/page 226, Jan Lukas — Photo Researchers/page 233, Marty Heitner — Taurus/page 257, Elliott Erwitt — Magnum/page 260, Eugene Richards — Magnum/page 263, Rapho-Photo Researchers/page 265 (left), UPI/page 265 (right), Stanley Milgram — New York University Film Library/page 277, Hanna W. Schreiber — Photo Researchers/page 283, Bob Combs — Rapho-Photo Researchers/page 286, The Bettmann Archive/page 287, Bob Henriques — Magnum/page 288, Leonard Freed — Magnum/page 301, Chester Higgins, Jr. — Photo Researchers/page 304, Syndication International/page 305, Jay Lurie — Black Star/page 307, Robert Eckert, Jr. — Stock, Boston/page 314, Robert Goldstein — Photo Researchers/page 325, Wide World/page 335, Leonard Freed — Magnum/page 340, Globe/page 345 (left), UPI/page 345 (right), Michael Abramson — Black Star/page 363, The Bettmann Archive/page 366 Eugene Richards — Magnum/page 371, Wide World/page 372, UPI/page 379, Richard Suinn/page 387, Wide World/page 391, James Olds — California Institute of Technology/page 402 (left), Benyas-Kaufman — Black Star/page 402 (right), Bill Bridges — Globe/page 411 (left), Wide World/page 411 (right), Howard Sochurek/page 418, Martin M. Rotker — Taurus/page 420, Martin Rotker — Taurus/page 422, Joseph Kovacs-Stock, Boston/page 426, Bill Winfrey — Black Star/page 441, Martine Franck — Magnum/page 443, Armed Forces Institute of Pathology/page 448, Bruce Roberts–Photo Researchers/page 462, Ken Karp/page 470, Naval Medical Research Institute, National Naval Medical Center, Bethesda/page 475, Constantine Manos — Magnum/page 478, Marlis Müller/page 487 (left), Burt Glinn–Magnum/page 487 (center), Adaline Starr/page 487 (right), Charles Zastrow/page 490, UPI/page 495, Mimi Forsyth — Monkmeyer/page 506, Ski Magazine/page 516, Elliott Erwitt — Magnum/page 520, Paul Fusco — Magnum/page 524, Jerry Cooke/page 532, Sybil Shelton/page 535, Pual Fusco — Magnum.

Copy editor, Sandi B. Schroeder; designer and production editor, Claudia von Hendricks; assistant editor, Kristen R. Westman; photo researchers, Lucy Tashman and Bonnie Miller; illustrators, Sally A. Ireland and Julie Zolot; cover designer, Gordon Stromberg; production manager, Pamela J. Teisler. Cover painting: Leah Ferrara, *Inner Space #3,* oil on paper, 1982.